DATE DUE

Reprints of Economic Classics

PRINCIPLES OF POLITICAL ECONOMY

PRINCIPLES

OF

POLITICAL ECONOMY

WITH

SOME OF THEIR APPLICATIONS

TO

SOCIAL PHILOSOPHY

BY

JOHN STUART MILL

EDITED WITH AN INTRODUCTION BY
SIR WILLIAM ASHLEY

[1909]

AUGUSTUS M. KELLEY • PUBLISHERS
CLIFTON 1973

First Edition 1848
(London: John W. Parker, *West Strand*, 1848)

New Edition 1909
(London: Longmans, Green & Company, 1909)

Reprinted 1961, 1965, 1969 & 1973 by
Augustus M. Kelley Publishers
REPRINTS OF ECONOMIC CLASSICS
Clifton New Jersey 07012

Library of Congress Cataloged.
The original printing of this title as follows:

Mill, John Stuart, 1806–1873.
  Principles of political economy, with some of their applications to social philosophy.   Edited with an introd. by
Sir W. J. Ashley.   New York, A. M. Kelley, bookseller,
1965.

  liii, 1013 p.   22 cm.   (Reprints of economic classics)

  Reprint of 1909 edition.
  "Bibliographical appendix": p. [981]–1004.

  1. Economics.   I. Ashley, Sir William James. 1860–1927, ed.
II. Title.

HB161.M6   1965   330   65–18329

ISBN 0-678-00073-5

Library of Congress   [3]

PRINTED IN THE UNITED STATES OF AMERICA
by SENTRY PRESS, NEW YORK, N. Y. 10013

INTRODUCTION

THE best Introduction to the *Principles of Political Economy* of John Stuart Mill is Mill's own account of his economic studies. They began at the age of thirteen; when he was approaching the end of that unique educational process, enforced by the stern will of his father, which he has described in his *Autobiography* for the amazement and pity of subsequent generations.

"It was in 1819 that he took me through a complete course of political economy. His loved and intimate friend, Ricardo, had shortly before published the book which formed so great an epoch in political economy; a book which would never have been published or written, but for the entreaty and strong encouragement of my father. . . . No didactic treatise embodying its doctrines, in a manner fit for learners, had yet appeared. My father, therefore, commenced instructing me in the science by a sort of lectures, which he delivered to me in our walks. He expounded each day a portion of the subject, and I gave him next day a written account of it, which he made me rewrite over and over again until it was clear, precise, and tolerably complete. In this manner I went through the whole extent of the science; and the written outline of it which resulted from my daily *compte rendu* served him afterwards as notes from which to write his *Elements of Political Economy*. After this I read Ricardo, giving an account daily of what I read, and discussing . . . the collateral points which offered themselves in our progress.

"On Money, as the most intricate part of the subject, he made me read in the same manner Ricardo's admirable pamphlets, written during . . . the Bullion controversy; to these succeeded Adam Smith; and . . . it was one of my father's main objects to make me apply to Smith's more superficial view of political economy the superior lights of Ricardo, and detect what was fallacious in Smith's arguments, or erroneous in any of his conclusions. Such a mode of instruction was excellently calculated to form a thinker ; but it required to be worked by a thinker, as close and vigorous as my father. The path was a thorny one, even to him, and I am sure it was so to me, notwithstanding the strong interest I took in the subject. He was often, and much beyond reason, provoked by my failures in cases where success could not have been expected ; but in the main his method was right, and it succeeded." [1]

After a year in France, during which he " passed some time in the house of M. Say, the eminent political economist, who was a friend and correspondent " of the elder Mill,[2] he went a second time over the same ground under the same guidance.

" When I returned (1821), my father was just finishing for the press his *Elements of Political Economy*, and he made me perform an exercise on the manuscript, which Mr. Bentham practised on all his own writings, making what he called ' marginal contents ' ; a short abstract of every paragraph, to enable the writer more easily to judge of, and improve, the order of the ideas, and the general character of the exposition." [3]

This was soon after reaching the age of fifteen. Four years later, in 1825, he made a systematic survey of the field for the third time. Though he was still only nineteen, he was now fully embarked upon his career as an economist, and was contributing articles on currency and commercial policy to the *Westminster Review*. Yet when, in that year, John Mill and a number of his youthful friends entered upon "the joint study of several of the branches of science" which they " wished to be masters of," it was once more the work of the elder Mill which served as the basis.

" We assembled to the number of a dozen or more. Mr. Grote lent a room of his house in Threadneedle Street. . . . We met two mornings in every week, from half-past eight till ten, at which hour most of us were called off to our daily occupations. Our first subject was Political Economy. We chose some systematic treatise as our text-book ; my father's *Elements* being our first choice. One of us read a chapter, or some smaller portion of the book. The discussion was then opened, and anyone who had an objection, or other remark to make, made

---

[1] *Autobiography*, p. 27 (Pop. ed. p. 15).
[2] *Ibid.* p. 60 (Pop. ed. p. 34).
[3] *Ibid.* p. 62 (Pop. ed. p. 36).

it. Our rule was to discuss thoroughly every point raised . . .
until all who took part were satisfied with the conclusion they
had individually arrived at ; and to follow up every topic . . .
which the chapter or the conversation suggested, never leaving
it until we had untied every knot." [1]

The figure of James Mill has been singularly obscured by the
more attractive personality of his son. It may possibly be open to
discussion how far James Mill was a trustworthy interpreter of
Ricardo. But what cannot be doubted is the extent and penetrating
character of his influence. The evidence of his son may certainly
be relied upon :

" My father's writings and conversation drew round him a
number of young men who had already imbibed, or who imbibed
from him, a greater or smaller portion of his very decided political
and philosophical opinions. The notion that Bentham was surrounded by a band of disciples who received their opinions
from his lips, is a fable. . . . The influence which Bentham
exercised was by his writings. Through them he has produced,
and is producing, effects on the condition of mankind, wider
and deeper than any which can be attributed to my father.
He is a much greater name in history. But my father exercised
a far greater personal ascendency. He *was* sought for the
vigour and instructiveness of his conversation, and did use it
largely as an instrument for the diffusion of his opinions. . . .

" It was my father's opinions which gave the distinguishing
character to the Benthamic or utilitarian propagandism of that
time. They fell singly, scattered from him, in many directions,
but they flowed from him in a continued stream principally in
three channels. One was through me, the only mind directly
formed by his instructions, and through whom considerable
influence was exercised over various young men, who became,
in their turn, propagandists. A second was through some of
the Cambridge contemporaries of Charles Austin . . . some of
the more considerable of whom afterwards sought my father's
acquaintance. . . . The third channel was that of a younger
generation of Cambridge undergraduates, contemporary . . .
with Eyton Tooke, who were . . . introduced by him to
my father. . . .

" Though none of us, probably, agreed in every respect with

[1] *Ibid.* p. 119 (Pop. ed. p. 68).

my father, his opinions, as I said before, were the principal
element which gave its colour and character to the little group
of young men who were the first propagators of what was afterwards called ' Philosophic Radicalism.' Their mode of thinking
was characterized by . . . a combination of Bentham's point
of view with that of the modern political economy, and with
the Hartleian metaphysics. Malthus's population principle
was quite as much a banner, and point of union among us,
as any opinion specially belonging to Bentham. This great
doctrine . . . we took up with ardent zeal, . . . as indicating
the sole means of realizing the improvability of human affairs
by securing full employment at high wages to the whole
labouring population through a voluntary restriction of the
increase of their numbers." [1]

What was true of James Mill's personal influence on the entire
circle of young Philosophic Radicals and over the whole range of
their beliefs, was peculiarly true of his influence on the economic
opinions of his son. The impress was deep and indelible. For
good or for ill,—and it is not the purpose of this Introduction
to interpose between the reader and the author and to assign
either praise or blame—John Mill's economics remained those
of his father down to the end of his life. His economics, that
is to say, in the sense of what he himself afterwards described as
" the theoretic principles," [2] or again as the " abstract and purely
scientific " [3] element in his writings : the whole, in fact, of the doctrine
of Distribution and Exchange in its application to competitive
conditions. After reading through the first three Books of the son's
Principles of 1848, one has but to turn to the father's *Elements*
of 1821 to realize that, though on outlying portions of the field
(like the subject of Currency) John Mill had benefited by the
discussions that had been going on during the interval, the main
conclusions, as well as the methods of reasoning, are the same
in the two treatises. How much of " the deposit " of doctrine,—
if we may borrow a theological term,—came originally from
Ricardo, how much from Malthus, from Adam Smith, from the
French Physiocrats of the eighteenth century, and from the general
movement of philosophical and political thought, is a subject on
which much has been written, but on which we cannot now enter.

---

[1] *Autobiography*, p. 101 (Pop. ed. p. 58).
[2] *Ibid.* p. 242 (Pop. ed. p. 139).
[3] *Ibid.* p. 247 (Pop. ed. p. 142).

It is sufficient for our purpose to make this one point clear : that it was through James Mill, and, as shaped by James Mill, that it chiefly reached his son.

Yet John Mill certainly thought, when he was writing his book in 1848, and still more evidently when he wrote his *Autobiography* in 1861, that there was a wide difference between himself and those whom he calls, in language curiously anticipating that of our own day, "the political economists of the old school," [1] or "the common run of political economists." [2]   And accordingly it is essential to observe that this difference consisted, not in any abandonment of the " abstract science," but in the placing of it in a new setting   In substance he kept it intact ; but he sought to surround it, so to speak, with a new environment.

To make this clear, we must return to Mill's mental history. Though eminently retentive of early impressions, he was also, in a very real sense, singularly open-minded ; and the work of his life cannot be better described than in a happy phrase of his own coinage : it was a constant effort to " build the bridges and clear the paths " which should connect new truths with his " general system of thought," [3] *i.e.* with his Benthamite and Ricardian starting point.   Of the influences, later than that of his father, which coloured his thoughts, three must be singled out for notice.   They may briefly be summed up—though each name represents much besides—as those of Coleridge, of Comte, and of his wife.

In Coleridge and in the Coleridgians—such as Maurice and Sterling, whose acquaintance he made in 1828—he recognised the English exponents of "the European reaction against the philo- sophy of the eighteenth century," [4] and its Benthamite outcome. That reaction, he came to believe, was in large measure justifiable ; and in two celebrated articles in the *London and Westminster Review* in 1838 and 1840 [5] he sought to expound Benthamism and Coleridgism as complementary bodies of truth.   He did not, indeed, extend this appreciation to Coleridge's economic utterances, and compounded for the respect he paid to his political philosophy by the vivacity with which he condemned his incursions into the more sacred field :

---

[1]. *Political Economy.*   Book iv. chap. vi. § 2.
[2] *Autobiography*, p. 246 (Pop. ed. p. 141).
[3] *Ibid.* p. 243 (Pop. ed. p. 139).
[4] *Ibid.* p. 128 (Pop. ed. p. 73).
[5] Reprinted in *Dissertations and Discussions.*   Series I.

" In political economy he writes like an arrant driveller, and it would have been well for his reputation had he never meddled with the subject. But this department of knowledge can now take care of itself." [1]

What Coleridge helped him to realise was, firstly, the historical point of view in its relation to politics, and secondly, and as a corollary, the inadequacy of *laissez faire*.

" The Germano-Coleridgian school produced . . . a philosophy of society in the only form in which it is yet possible, that of a philosophy of history." [2]

And again :

" That series of great writers and thinkers, from Herder to Michelet, by whom history . . . has been made a science of causes and effects, . . . by making the events of the past have a meaning and an intelligible place in the gradual evolution of humanity, have afforded the only means of predicting and guiding the future." [3]

Similarly, after pointing out that Coleridge was

" at issue with the *let alone* doctrine, or the theory that governments can do no better than to do nothing,"

he remarks that it was

" a doctrine generated by the manifest selfishness and incompetence of modern European governments, but of which, as a general theory, we may now be permitted to say that one-half of it is true and the other half false." [4]

It is not wonderful that the Bentham and Coleridge articles should " make a temporary alienation between Mill and his old associates and plant in their minds a painful misgiving as to his adhering to their principles," as we learn from Professor Bain, who became an intimate friend of Mill shortly afterwards.[5] As early as 1837 Mrs. Grote had been " quite persuaded that the [*London and Westminster*] *Review* would cease to be an engine of propagating sound and sane doctrines on Ethics and Politics under J. M." [6] But it is a little surprising, perhaps, that by 1841 Mill was ready to describe himself in the privacy of correspondence as having definitely withdrawn from the Benthamite school " in

[1] *Dissertations and Discussions*, I. p. 452.
[2] *Ibid.* p. 425.   [3] *Ibid.* p. 426.   [4] *Ibid.* p. 453.
[5] Alexander Bain, *John Stuart Mill, A Criticism : with personal recollections*, p. 56.   [6] *Ibid.* p. 57 *n.*

which I was brought up and in which I might almost say I was born." [1]

The letter was that in which Mill introduced himself to Comte, the first of a remarkable series which has only recently seen the light. By the time he wrote it, the influence of Coleridge had been powerfully supplemented by that of the French philosopher. Indeed, with that tendency to run into extremes which was seldom quite absent from him, Mill even declared, in addressing Comte, that it was the impression produced as far back as 1828 by the reading of a very early work by Comte which had " more than any other cause determined his definite withdrawal from the Benthamite school." In his eager enthusiasm, he probably ante-dated Comte's influence. It seems to have been the first two volumes of the *Positive Philosophy* (of which the second appeared in 1837) that first interested Mill at all deeply in Comte's views ; though, as we shall notice later, he had long been familiar with ideas akin to them in the writings of the St. Simonians.

However this may have been, it is abundantly clear that during the years 1841-3, when he was engaged in completing his great treatise on *Logic*, Mill was fascinated by Comte's general system, as set forth in the *Positive Philosophy*. In October, 1841, he wrote to Bain that he thought Comte's book, in spite of " some mistakes," was " very near the grandest work of this age." [2] In November, in the letter to Comte already quoted, he took the initiative and wrote to the French philosopher to express his " sympathy and adhesion." " I have read and re-read your *Cours* with a veritable intellectual passion," he told him.

" I had indeed already entered into a line of thought somewhat similar to your own ; but there were many things of the first importance which I had still to learn from you and I hope to show you, by and by, that I have really learnt them. There are some questions of a secondary order on which my opinions are not in accord with yours ; some day perhaps this difference will disappear ; I am not flattering myself when I believe that I have no ill-founded opinion so deeply rooted as to resist a thorough discussion,"

such as he hoped to engage Comte in. It was for this reason

---

[1] L. Lévy-Bruhl, *Lettres Inédites de John Stuart Mill à Auguste Comte* (Paris, 1899), p. 2. Writing to Comte, Mill naturally employs Comtean phraseology, and speaks of " ma sortie definitive de la section benthamiste de l'école revolutionnaire." [2] Bain, *J. S. Mill*, p. 63.

that he ventured to put himself into communication with " that one of the great minds of our time which I regard with most esteem and admiration," and believed that their correspondence might be " of immense value " for him. And in the first edition of his *Logic,* which appeared in 1843, he did not scruple to speak of Comte as " the greatest living authority on scientific methods in general." [1] Into the causes of this enthusiasm it is unnecessary to enter. Mill was tired of Benthamism : a masterly attempt to construct a philosophy of Science and of Humanity, which paid attention at the same time to historical evolution and to the achievements of modern physical and biological science (a side on which the Benthamite school had always been weak), and yet professed to be " positive," *i.e.* neither theological nor metaphysical—such an attempt had, for the time, an overmastering charm for him. The effect of his reading of Comte on his conception of the logic of the physical and biological sciences falls outside our present range. What we have now to notice are Comte's views with regard to political economy. They cannot but have shaken, at any rate for a time, Mill's confidence that what he had learnt from his father could " take care of itself."

Comte's ultimate object was, of course, the creation of " the Social Science " or " Sociology." To-day there are almost as many different conceptions of the scope of " sociology " as there are eminent sociologists ; so that it is perhaps worth while to add that Comte's ideal was a body of doctrine which should cover the life of human society in *all* its aspects. This science could be created, he held, only by the " positive " method—by the employment of the Art of Observation, in its three modes, Direct Observation or Observation proper, Experiment, and Comparison.[2] Each of these modes of Observation would necessarily assume a character appropriate to the field of enquiry. As to Observation proper : while the metaphysical school of the eighteenth century had grossly exaggerated its difficulties, on the other hand there was no utility in mere collections of disconnected facts. Some sort of provisional hypothesis or theory or anticipation was necessary, if only to give direction to our enquiries. As to Experiment : direct Experiment, as in the physical sciences, was evidently impracticable, but its place could be taken by a consideration of " pathological " states of society such as might fairly be called " indirect " Experiment.

[1] Cf. Bain, p. 72.
[2] *Cours de Philosophie Positive,* vol. iv. (1839), pp. 412 *seq.*

And as to Comparison : there was a form of this procedure, viz. the comparison of " the different consecutive conditions of humanity,"— " the historical method " in the true sense of the term,—so fruitful in sociological enquiry as to constitute the distinguishing characteristic of this particular branch of science.

To this social science of his vision Comte applied the distinction he had already applied to the preliminary sciences, between the static and the dynamic.[1] The difference between " the fundamental study of the condition of existence of society " and " the study of the laws of its continuous movement " was so clear, in his judgment, that he could foresee the ultimate division of Sociology into Social Statics and Social Dynamics. But to attach, in the formative stage of the science, any very great importance to this convenient distribution of the subject matter would, he thought, be positively dangerous, since it would tend to obscure " the indispensable and permanent combination of the two points of view."

Comte's attitude towards political economy, as it was then taught was the natural result of his views as to the proper method of creating a science of society.[2] As part of the general movement of revolutionary thought, it had had a " provisional " function, and had rendered a transitory service in discrediting the industrial policy of the *ancien régime* after that policy had become a mere hindrance to progress. It had prepared the way for a sound historical analysis by calling attention to the importance of the economic side of life. Its practical utility, however, was by this time a thing of the past : and it was now an actual obstacle to social advance. Like the rest of the revolutionary philosophy, it now tended to prolong and systematise social anarchy. It led people to regard the absence of all regulating intervention in economic affairs on the part of society as a universal dogma ; and it met all the difficulties arising out of modern industrial changes, such as " the famous and immense economic question of the effect of machinery," with " the sterile aphorism of absolute industrial liberty." And these practical consequences were but, in Comte's judgment, the consequences of its underlying scientific defects. From this sweeping condemnation Comte excepts Adam Smith, from whose example, according to him, the creators of the contemporary political economy had completely departed. But of the contemporary political economy he declares that it was fundamentally metaphysical : its creators had no real

---

[1] *Ibid.* pp. 318 *seq.*   [2] *Ibid.* pp. 264–79.

understanding of the necessity and character of scientific observation. Its "inanity" was proved by the absence in economic literature of the real tests of all truly scientific conceptions, viz. continuity and fecundity. Its sterile disputes on the meaning of terms such as *value*, and *utility*, and *production* were like the worst debates of medieval schoolmen. And the very isolation of economics from other fields of social enquiry which economists had sought to justify was its decisive condemnation.

" By the nature of the subject, in social studies the various general aspects are, quite necessarily, mutually inter-connected and inseparable in reason, so that the one aspect can only be adequately explained by the consideration of the others. It is certain that the economic and industrial analysis of society cannot be *positively* accomplished, if one leaves out all intellectual, moral and political analysis: and therefore this irrational separation furnishes an evident indication of the essentially metaphysical nature of the doctrines based upon it."

Now Mill was immensely attracted, and for the time possessed, by Comte's general conception of the Social Science or Sociology ; and in the concluding chapters of his *Logic* he took this over bodily, together with Comte's distinction between Social Statics and Social Dynamics.[1] Just as Comte rejected the " metaphysical " political philosophy of France, so Mill made clear his opinion of the inadequacy of " the interest-philosophy of the Bentham school " in its application to " the general theory of government." That philosophy, as he explained, was " founded on one comprehensive premiss : namely, that men's actions are always determined by their interests." But as this premiss was not true, what were really " the mere polemics of the day," and useful enough in that capacity, were quite erroneously " presented as the scientific treatment of a great question." And quite in the spirit of Comte he added :

" These philosophers would have applied and did apply their principles with innumerable allowances. But it is not allowances that are wanted. There is little chance of making due amends in the superstructure of a theory for the want of sufficient breadth in its foundations. It is unphilosophical to construct a science out of a few of the agencies by which the phenomena are determined, and leave the rest to the routine of practice or the sagacity of conjecture. We ought either not to pretend to scientific forms or

[1] Mill's *Logic*, book vi. chaps. 6, 10.

we ought to study all the determining agencies equally, and endeavour, as far as can be done, to include all of them within the pale of the science ; else we shall infallibly bestow a disproportionate attention upon those which our theory takes into account, while we misestimate the rest and probably underrate their importance." [1]

How, then, about political economy, which Comte had criticised in precisely the same spirit ? Mill was not at all disposed to throw overboard the Ricardian economics received from his father. In the first place, he maintained that a distinction could be drawn between the " *general* Science of Society " or "*general* Sociology " and " the separate compartments of the science, each of which asserts its conclusions only conditionally, subject to the paramount control of the laws of the general science." The ground for this contention he sets forth thus :

" Notwithstanding the universal *consensus* of the social phenomena, whereby nothing which takes place in any part of the operations of society is without its share of influence on every other part ; and notwithstanding the paramount ascendency which the general state of civilisation and social progress in any given society must hence exercise over the partial and subordinate phenomena ; it is not the less true that different species of social facts are in the main dependent, immediately and in the first resort, on different kinds of causes ; and therefore not only may with advantage, but must, be studied apart. . . .

" There is, *for example*, one large class of social phenomena of which the immediately determining causes are principally those which act through the desire of wealth ; and in which the psychological law mainly concerned is the familiar one that a greater gain is preferred to the smaller . . . A science may be thus constructed which has received the name of Political Economy." [2]

In spite of the "for example" with which political economy is introduced, it is clear that the generalisation was formulated for the sake of that one subject, subject to a qualification to be shortly mentioned.

" I would not here undertake to decide what other hypothetical or abstract sciences, similar to Political Economy, may admit of being carved out of the general body of the social science;

---

[1] *Ibid.* ii. p. 472 (ed, 3).　　　　*Ibid.* ii. pp. 480–1.

what other portions of the social phenomena are in a sufficiently close and complete dependence, in the first resort, on a particular class of causes, to make it convenient to create a preliminary science of those causes ; postponing the consideration of the causes which act through them or in concurrence with them to a later period of the enquiry." [1]

But Mill was not content with this " departmental " view, taken by itself : he proceeded to build two further " bridges " between his new and his old opinions. In an essay, written for the most part in 1830, and published in the *London and Westminster Review* in 1836,[2] Mill had laid down with the utmost stringency that the only method appropriate to political economy, *i.e.* to the Ricardian economics, was the *a priori* or deductive one. Between this and the method of Observation recommended by Comte it might have been thought that there was a sufficiently wide gulf. But Mill now proceeded to describe " the historical method,"—whereby " general " Sociology was to be built up according to Comte and himself alike,—in such terms as permitted him to designate even that a "Deductive Method," though indeed an "*Inverse* Deductive Method." Thus the evident contrast in method was softened down into the difference simply between " direct " and " inverse " deduction.[3]

The other bridge was to be a new science, or couple of sciences, still to be created. Mill explained at length in his *Logic* that there was need of what he denominated " Ethology " or a Science of Character.[4] Built upon this, there ought to be a *Political* Ethology, or " a theory of the causes which determine the type of character belonging to a people or to an age." [5] The bearing of Political Ethology on Political Economy is thus summarily indicated :

" The most imperfect part of those branches of social enquiry which have been cultivated as separate sciences is the theory of the manner in which their conclusions are affected by ethological considerations. The omission is no defect in them as abstract or hypothetical sciences, but it vitiates them in their practical application as branches of a comprehensive social science. In political economy, *for instance*, empirical laws of human nature are tacitly assumed by English thinkers, which are calculated only for Great Britain and the United States. Among other

[1] Mill's *Logic*, ii. p. 486.
[2] Reprinted in *Essays on some Unsettled Questions of Political Economy* (1844).
[3] *Logic*, ii. pp. 476–7.   [4] *Ibid.* ii. p. 441.   [5] *Ibid.* ii. p. 486.

things an intensity of competition is constantly supposed, which, as a general mercantile fact, exists in no country in the world except those two. An English political economist . . . has seldom learned that it is possible that men, in conducting the business of selling their goods over the counter, should care more about their ease or their vanity than about their pecuniary gain." [1]

In spite once more of the introductory " for instance," it is clear that it is only political economy that Mill has in his mind ; and it is primarily to remedy *its* " imperfections " that Political Ethology is to be created. Political Ethology, like Ethology itself, Mill conceived of as directly deductive in its character.

It is no part of my task to criticise either Mill or Comte : all I am seeking to do is to make clear the intellectual relations between them. And whether, in particular, a Science of National Character is possible, and, if possible, on what sort of lines it may be constructed, I " would not here undertake to decide." I go on now to the purely biographical facts,—which need the more emphasis because they have dropt altogether out of the *Autobiography*,— that Mill took this project of creating an Ethology very seriously ; that " with parental fondness he cherished this subject for a considerable time " ; [2] and that he dropt it because he could not make anything of it. [3]

It was in this mood of recoil that he began to think of composing " a special treatise on political economy, analogous to that of Adam Smith." Writing to Comte in April, 1844, he remarked that for him " this would only be the work of a few months." [4] Some particulars as to the actual period of composition are furnished by the *Autobiography*. [5]

" The *Political Economy* was far more rapidly executed than the *Logic,* or indeed than anything of importance which I had previously written. It was commenced in the autumn of 1845, and was ready for the press before the end of 1847. In this period of little more than two years there was an interval of six months during which the work was laid aside, while I was writing articles in the *Morning Chronicle* . . . urging the formation of peasant properties on the waste lands of

---

[1] *Ibid.* ii. p. 487. [2] Bain, pp. 78–9.
[3] Besides Bain's account, Mill's letters to Comte, printed by Lévy-Bruhl, pp. 260, 285, are of interest.
[4] Lévy-Bruhl, p. 308. [5] P. 235 (Pop. ed. p. 135).

Ireland. This was during the period of the Famine, the winter of 1846-47."

After what we have seen of his mental history, it is easy to anticipate that Mill would no longer be satisfied with the kind of treatment that economics had received at the hands of his father, or in subsequent years of McCulloch or Senior. The " principles " of abstract political economy, as he had inherited them, he entertained no sort of doubt about. As has been well said, within that field " Mill speaks as one expounding an established system." [1] As late as 1844 he had reprinted in the thin volume entitled *Some Unsettled Questions of Political Economy* his old essay on Method, and had expressed his complete satisfaction, within its range, with the science as it was to be found " in the writings of its best teachers." [2] But he was bound to put this science into some sort of relation with that general Social Science or Philosophy, of which he had gained, or solidified, his notion from the reading of Comte. Accordingly, he gave to his book the title: " Principles of Political Economy, *with some of their Applications to Social Philosophy.*" And he himself spoke of the work in later years in the following terms :

" It was, from the first, continually cited and referred to as an authority, because it was not a book merely of abstract science, but also of application, and treated Political Economy not as a thing by itself, but as a fragment of a greater whole ; a branch of Social Philosophy, so interlinked with all the other branches, that its conclusions, even in its own peculiar province, are only true conditionally, subject to interference and counter-action from causes not directed within its scope : while to the character of a practical guide it has no pretension, apart from other classes of considerations." [3]

It must be left to the reader to judge how far this " application " was successful,—how far, indeed, the nature of the abstract science lent itself to application. But the character of the undertaking will be rendered clearer by noticing certain of its characteristics.

Ethology, as we have seen, had receded from Mill's mind. But the thoughts which had given rise to the project have left their traces in the chapter on " Competition and Custom." [4] Here

[1] Leslie Stephen, *The English Utilitarians,* ii. 161.
[2] *Unsettled Questions,* p. 149.
[3] *Autobiography,* p. 236 (Pop. ed. p. 135).
[4] Book ii. chap. 4.

Custom is placed side by side with Competition as the other agency determining the division of produce under the rule of private property. It is pointed out not only that Competition is a comparatively modern phenomenon, so that, until recently, rents, for instance, were ruled by custom, but also that "even in the present state of intense competition" its influence is not so absolute as is often supposed : there are very often two prices in the same market. He asserts that

"political economists generally, and English political economists above others, are accustomed to lay almost exclusive stress upon the first of these agencies ; to exaggerate the effect of competition, and take into little account the other and conflicting principle. They are apt to express themselves as if they thought that competition actually does, in all cases, whatever it can be shown to be the tendency of competition to do."

The language in which he goes on to formulate an explanation and relative justification of their practice is of the utmost significance.

" This is partly intelligible, if we consider that only through the principle of competition has political economy any pretension to the character of a science. So far as rents, profits, wages, prices, are determined by competition, laws may be assigned for them. Assume competition to be their exclusive regulator, and principles of broad generality and scientific precision may be laid down, according to which they will be regulated. The political economist justly deems this his proper business : and as an abstract or hypothetical science, political economy cannot be required to do anything more."

But, as the ascription to Competition of an unlimited sway is, as a matter of fact, " a great misconception of the actual cause of human affairs."

"to escape error, we ought, in applying the conclusions of political economy to the actual affairs of life, to consider not only what will happen supposing the maximum of competition, but how far the result will be affected if competition falls short of the maximum."

After this it might perhaps be expected that Mill would himself embark on a quantitative estimate of the extent of the divergence of the " laws " of " the science " from the facts of life. But certainly no such attempt is made within the covers of his treatise—and he makes it clear that the application of his warning is to be left to the reader :

"These observations must be received as a general correction, to be applied whenever relevant, whether expressly mentioned or not, to the conclusions contained in the subsequent portions of this treatise. Our reasonings must, in general, proceed as if the known and natural effects of competition were actually produced by it."

To discuss the conception of "science" and its relation to "law" which underlies such passages; to compare it with that implied by Mill elsewhere; or to enter into the question whether a systematic ascertainment and grouping of actual facts, guided by the ordinary rules of evidence, might not deserve to be called "scientific," even if it did not result in "law"—would take us too far afield. By confining, as he did, the term "science" to the abstract argument, and by leaving the determination of its relation to actual conditions to what he himself in another connexion calls "the sagacity of conjecture," Mill undoubtedly exercised a profound influence on the subsequent character of economic writing in England.

Another result, in the *Political Economy*, of the preceding phase of Mill's social speculation, is to be found in the distinction between Statics and Dynamics which he now introduces into economics itself.[1] In the *Logic*, as we have noticed, this distinction was applied, following Comte, only to the *general* Sociology which was to be created by "the historical method." But the general Sociology being indefinitely postponed, because the Ethology which in Mill's judgment was its necessary foundation was not forthcoming, it seemed proper to employ the distinction in the "preliminary" science, and to add in the *Political Economy* itself a "theory of motion" to the "theory of equilibrium." Thus employed, however, the distinction becomes something very different from what Comte had intended. Almost the whole of Mill's Book IV on the Progress of Society consists of a highly theoretical and abstract argument as to the effect on Prices, Rents, Profits, and Wages, *within a competitive society of the present type*, of the progress of population, capital, and the arts of production, in various combinations. Much of the substance of these arguments was derived from Ricardo or his school; and the whole discussion, even when Mill takes an independent line of his own, moves within the Ricardian atmosphere. This statement of fact does not necessarily imply condemnation. It is made only to clear Mill's use of

[1] Book iv. chap. 1.

the terms "static" and "dynamic" in his *Political Economy* from the ambiguity which his own previous use of the term in relation to general Sociology might cause to cling to it. And we must except the last chapter of the Book, dealing with "the Probable Futurity of the Working Classes," which is a prophecy of the ultimate victory of Co-operation, and has little or no connexion with what goes before.

And now we come finally to what Mill himself regarded as the distinguishing characteristic of his work ; and with it we reach the third of the influences that affected the movement of his mind after his early education. I refer, of course, to the distinction which Mill drew between the laws of the Production and those of the Distribution of wealth.[1] With the formal statement in the *Principles* may be compared the passage in the *Autobiography*,[2] where Mill gives an account of the influence of Mrs. Taylor (who became his wife in April, 1851) :

" The purely scientific part of the *Political Economy* I did not learn from her ; but it was chiefly her influence that gave to the book that general tone by which it is distinguished from all previous expositions of political economy that had any pretension to being scientific. . . . This tone consisted chiefly in making the proper distinction between the laws of the Production of wealth—which are real laws of nature, dependent on the properties of objects—and the modes of its Distribution, which, subject to certain conditions, depend on human will. The common run of political economists confuse these together, under the designation of economic laws, which they deem incapable of being defeated or modified by human effort ; ascribing the same necessity to things dependent on the unchangeable conditions of our earthly existence, and to those which, being but the necessary consequences of particular social arrangements, are merely co-extensive with these : given certain institutions and customs, wages, profits, and rent will be determined by certain causes ; but this class of political economists drop the indispensable presupposition, and argue that these causes must, by an inherent necessity, against which no human means can avail, determine the shares which fall, in the division of the produce, to labourers, capitalists, and landlords.

[1] See the concluding paragraphs in the Preliminary Remarks, and book ii. chap. i. § 1.
[2] P. 246 (Pop. ed. p. 141).

The *Principles of Political Economy* yielded to none of its predecessors in aiming at the scientific appreciation of the action of these causes, under the conditions which they presuppose ; but it set the example of not treating those conditions as final. The economic generalizations which depend not on necessities of nature but on those combined with the existing arrangements of society, it deals with only as provisional, and as liable to be much altered by the progress of social improvement. I had indeed partially learnt this view of things from the thoughts awakened in me by the speculations of the St. Simonians ; but it was made a living principle pervading and animating the book by my wife's promptings."

It would be interesting, had I space, to try to distinguish the various currents of thought which converged at this time upon Mill and his wife. They were both people of warm hearts and generous sympathies ; and the one most important fact about Mill's *Principles*, besides its being the work of the son of his father, is that it was published in the great year 1848. Mill's personal friendship with Carlyle and Maurice in England, his keen interest for years in St. Simonism and all the other early phases of French " socialism," sufficiently disposed him, if he wore the old political economy at all, to wear it " with a difference." I do not propose to add one more to the numerous arguments as to the validity of the distinction between the laws of Production and the modes of Distribution. But I should like to comment on one word which was constantly in Mill's mouth in this connexion—and that is the word " provisional " ; a word which, according to his own account, he had picked up from Austin.[1] He used it twice in the letter to Comte announcing his intention to write an economic treatise :

" I know your opinion of the political economy of the day : I have a better opinion of it than you have ; but, if I write anything on the subject, it will be never losing out of sight the purely provisional character of all its concrete conclusions ; and I shall take special pains to separate the general laws of Production, which are necessarily common to all industrial societies, from the principles of the Distribution and Exchange of wealth, which necessarily presuppose a particular state of society, without implying that this state should, or even can, indefinitely continue. . . . I believe that such a treatise might have, especially in England, great provisional utility, and that

[1] *Autobiography*, p. 234 (Pop. ed. p. 134).

it will greatly help the positive spirit to make its way into political discussions." [1]

Then followed a curious interchange of letters. Comte replied politely that he was glad to learn of Mill's project, and that he did not doubt that it would be very useful, by contributing to the spread of the positive spirit.

"Although an economic analysis, properly so called, ought not, in my opinion, to be finally conceived of or undertaken apart from the general body of sociological analysis, both static and dynamic, yet I have never refused to recognise the provisional efficacy of this kind of present-day metaphysics." [2]

Mill wrote in return that he was pleased to get Comte's approbation, since he was afraid Comte might have thought his project " essentially anti-scientific ";

"and so it would really be if I did not take the greatest possible care to establish the purely provisional character of any doctrine on industrial phenomena which leaves out of sight the general movement of humanity." [3]

Comte once more replied that he thought Mill's project a happy one.

" When regarded as having the purely preliminary purpose and provisional office that are assigned to it by a general historical view, political economy loses its principal dangers and may become very useful." [4]

It is sufficiently apparent that the correspondents are at cross purposes. By " provisional " Comte means *until a positive Sociology can be created ;* Mill means *so long as the present system of private property lasts.* Until the present social system should be fundamentally changed, Mill clearly regarded the Ricardian economics as so far applicable to existing conditions as to call for no substantial revision in method or conclusions. And by this attitude,—by deferring any breach with Ricardian political economy to a time comparable in the minds of men less ardent than himself to the Greek Kalends,—he certainly strengthened its hold over many of his readers.

Since Mill's time there has been a vast amount of economic

[1] April 3, 1844. Translated from the French text in Lévy-Bruhl, p. 309.
[2] May 1, 1844. *Ibid.* p. 314. The original French should be consulted. It is impossible in a free rendering to give all the *nuances* of the original.
[3] June 6, 1844. *Ibid.* p. 322.   [4] July 22, 1844. *Ibid.* p. 338.

writing. The German Historical School has come into existence, and has reached a high point of achievement in the treatise of Gustav Schmoller. On the other hand, other bodies of theory have made their appearance, quite as abstract as the Ricardian which they reject: and here the names of Jevons and Menger stand out above the rest. An equally abstract Socialist doctrine, the creation largely of Marx, has meantime waxed and waned. But Mill's *Principles* will long continue to be read and will deserve to be read. It represents an interesting phase in the intellectual history of the nineteenth century. But its merit is more than historical. It is still one of the most stimulating books that can be put into the hands of students, if they are cautioned at the outset against regarding it as necessarily final in all its parts. On some topics there is still, in my opinion, nothing better in the English language ; on others Mill's treatment is still the best point of departure for further enquiry. Whatever its faults, few or many, it is a great treatise, conceived and executed on a lofty plane, and breathing a noble spirit. Mill—especially when we penetrate beneath the magisterial flow of his final text, as we are now enabled to do by the record in this edition of his varying moods—is a very human personality. The reader of to-day is not likely to come to him in too receptive a spirit ; and for a long time there will be much that even those who most differ from him will still be able to learn from his pages.

It remains now to describe the character of the present edition. The text is that of the seventh edition (1871), the last revised by Mill ; and it is hoped that the occasional but misleading misprints which had crept into it have now all been corrected. It has not seemed desirable to add anything in the way of editorial comment. But in the one case where Mill himself publicly abandoned an important doctrine of his *Principles*,—that of the Wages Fund —it has seemed proper to give an excerpt from his later writings in the Appendix. And the same plan has been pursued with regard to Mill's latest views on Socialism. I have also appended a series of references to the chief writers who have dealt with the main topics of Mill's treatise, especially those of a controversial nature, since his time. That I have altogether escaped the influence of personal bias in this selection I can hardly hope. If the references under any head should seem scanty or one-sided, it should be borne in mind that they are intended to include only those outstanding works whose value is generally recognised by all serious economists, and that the choice is limited in the main to the books that are easily accessible to the English-reading public.

The characteristic feature, however, of this edition is the indication in the notes of all the significant changes or additions made by Mill in the course of the six editions revised by himself. The dates of these editions, after the first in 1848, were 1849, 1852, 1857, 1862, 1865, and 1871. In every one of these Mill made noteworthy alterations. Rewriting, or the addition of whole sections or paragraphs, takes place chiefly in the earlier editions ; but even in the last, that of 1871, the "few verbal corrections" of which Mill speaks in his Preface were sufficient, in more passages than one, to give a different complexion to the argument. My attention was called to this interesting feature in the history of the *Principles* by Miss M. A. Ellis' article in the *Economic Journal* for June, 1906 ; and it seemed to me that the interest of students would be aroused by a record of the variations. Accordingly I have compared the first and the seventh edition page by page and paragraph by paragraph ; and where any striking divergence has shown itself, I have looked up the earlier editions and ascertained the date of its first appearance. This has proved an unexpectedly toilsome business, even with the assistance of the notes that Miss Ellis has been good enough to put at my disposal ; and I cannot feel quite sure that nothing has escaped my eye that ought to be noted. Mere changes of language for the sake of improving the style I have disregarded, though I have erred rather in the direction of including than of excluding every apparent indication of change of opinion or even of mood. All editorial notes are placed within square brackets ; and I have added, and marked in the same way, the dates of all Mill's own foot-notes subsequent to the first edition. As Mill's revision of the text, though considerable, was rather fragmentary, his time-references are occasionally a little bewildering : a "now" in his text may mean any time between 1848 and 1871. In every case where it seemed necessary to ascertain and to remind the reader of the time when a particular sentence was written, I have inserted the date in the text in square brackets.

Mill's punctuation is not quite so preponderatingly grammatical as punctuation has since become. As in all the books of the middle of last century, it is also largely rhetorical. The printers had already, during the course of six editions, occasionally used their discretion and dropt out a misleading comma. I have ventured to carry the process just a little further, and to strike out a few rhetorical commas that seemed to interfere with the easy understanding of the text. The Index has been prepared by Miss M. A. Ellis.

I must express my thanks to the proprietors of the *Fortnightly Review* for allowing me to make use of Mill's posthumous articles, and to Mr. Hugh Elliot for permitting me to refer to the *Letters* of Mill which he is now editing.

W. J. ASHLEY.

EDGBASTON,
  September, 1909.

PREFACE

[1848]

THE appearance of a treatise like the present, on a subject on which so many works of merit already exist, may be thought to require some explanation.

It might, perhaps, be sufficient to say, that no existing treatise on Political Economy contains the latest improvements which have been made in the theory of the subject. Many new ideas, and new applications of ideas, have been elicited by the discussions of the last few years, especially those on Currency, on Foreign Trade, and on the important topics connected more or less intimately with Colonization : and there seems reason that the field of Political Economy should be re-surveyed in its whole extent, if only for the purpose of incorporating the results of these speculations, and bringing them into harmony with the principles previously laid down by the best thinkers on the subject.

To supply, however, these deficiencies in former treatises bearing a similar title, is not the sole, or even the principal object which the author has in view. The design of the book is different from that of any treatise on Political Economy which has been produced in England since the work of Adam Smith.

The most characteristic quality of that work, and the one in which it most differs from some others which have equalled or even surpassed it as mere expositions of the general principles of the subject, is that it invariably associates the principles with their applications. This of itself implies a much wider range of ideas and of topics than are included in Political Economy, considered as a branch of abstract speculation. For practical purposes, Political Economy is inseparably intertwined with many other branches of Social Philosophy. Except on matters of mere detail, there are perhaps no practical questions, even among those which approach nearest to the character of purely economical questions, which admit of being decided on economical premises alone. And it is because Adam Smith never loses sight of this truth ; because, in his applications of Political Economy, he perpetually appeals to other and often far larger considerations than pure Political Economy affords—that he gives that well-grounded feeling of command over the principles of the subject for purposes of practice, owing to which the *Wealth of Nations,* alone among treatises on Political Economy has not only been popular with general readers, but has impressed itself strongly on the minds of men of the world and of legislators.

It appears to the present writer that a work similar in its object and general conception to that of Adam Smith, but adapted to the more extended knowledge and improved ideas of the present age, is the kind of contribution which Political Economy at present requires. The *Wealth of Nations* is in many parts obsolete, and in all, imperfect. Political Economy, properly so called, has grown up almost from infancy since the time of Adam Smith ; and the philosophy of society, from which practically that eminent thinker never separated his more peculiar theme, though still in a very early stage of its progress, has advanced many steps beyond the point at which he left it. No attempt, however, has yet been made to combine his practical mode of treating his subject with the increased knowledge since acquired of its theory, or to exhibit the economical phenomena of society in the relation in which they stand to the best social ideas of the present time, as he did, with such admirable success, in reference to the philosophy of his century.

Such is the idea which the writer of the present work has kept before him. To succeed even partially in realizing it, would be a sufficiently useful achievement, to induce him to incur willingly all the chances of failure. It is requisite, however, to add, that although his object is practical, and, as far as the nature of the subject admits, popular, he has not attempted to purchase either of those advantages by the sacrifice of strict scientific reasoning. Though he desires that his treatise should be more than a mere exposition of the abstract doctrines of Political Economy, he is also desirous that such an exposition should be found in it.[1]

---

[1] [The original Preface remained unchanged throughout the subsequent editions. But each of the later editions during the author's lifetime contained an addition peculiar to itself, either a new paragraph subjoined to the original preface or a further preface. These are reprinted in the present edition.]

[ADDITION TO THE PREFACE IN THE SECOND EDITION, 1849]

The additions and alterations in the present edition are generally of little moment ; but the increased importance which the Socialist controversy has assumed since this work was written has made it desirable to enlarge the chapter which treats of it ; the more so, as the objections therein stated to the specific schemes propounded by some Socialists have been erroneously understood as a general condemnation of all that is commonly included under that name. A full appreciation of Socialism, and of the questions which it raises, can only be advantageously attempted in a separate work.

PREFACE TO THE THIRD EDITION [JULY, 1852]

The present edition has been revised throughout, and several chapters either materially added to or entirely re-cast. Among these may be mentioned that on the " Means of abolishing Cottier Tenantry," the suggestions contained in which had reference exclusively to Ireland, and to Ireland in a condition which has been much modified by subsequent events. An addition has been made to the theory of International Values laid down in the eighteenth chapter of the Third Book.

The chapter on Property has been almost entirely re-written. I was far from intending that the statement which it contained of the objections to the best known Socialist schemes should be under-stood as a condemnation of Socialism, regarded as an ultimate result of human progress. The only objection to which any great importance will be found to be attached in the present edition is the unprepared state of mankind in general, and of the labouring classes in particular ; their extreme unfitness at present for any order of things, which would make any considerable demand on either their intellect or their virtue. It appears to me that the great end of social improvement should be to fit mankind by culti-vation for a state of society combining the greatest personal freedom with that just distribution of the fruits of labour which the present laws of property do not profess to aim at. Whether, when this state of mental and moral cultivation shall be attained, individual property in some form (though a form very remote from the present) or community of ownership in the instruments of production and a regulated division of the produce will afford the circumstances most favourable to happiness, and best calculated to bring human nature to its greatest perfection, is a question which must be left, as it safely may, to the people of that time to decide. Those of the present are not competent to decide it.

The chapter on the " Futurity of the Labouring Classes " has been enriched with the results of the experience afforded, since this work was first published, by the co-operative associations in France. That important experience shows that the time is ripe for a larger and more rapid extension of association among labourers than could have been successfully attempted before the calumniated democratic movements in Europe, which, though for the present put down by the pressure of brute force, have scattered widely the seeds of future improvement. I have endeavoured to designate more clearly the tendency of the social transformation, of which these associations are the initial step ; and at the same time to disconnect the co-operative cause from the exaggerated or altogether mistaken declamations against competition, so largely indulged in by its supporters.

[ADDITION TO THE PREFACE IN THE FOURTH EDITION, 1857]

The present edition (the fourth) has been revised throughout, and some additional explanations inserted where they appeared to be necessary. The chapters to which most has been added are those on the Influence of Credit on Prices, and on the Regulation of a Convertible Paper Currency.

[ADDITION TO THE PREFACE IN THE FIFTH EDITION, 1862]

The present fifth edition has been revised throughout, and the facts, on several subjects, brought down to a later date than in the former editions. Additional arguments and illustrations have been inserted where ·they seemed necessary, but not in general at any considerable length.

[ADDITION TO THE PREFACE IN THE SIXTH EDITION, 1865]

The present, like all previous editions, has been revised through-out, and additional explanations, or answers to new objections, have been inserted where they seemed necessary ; but not, in general, to any considerable length. The chapter in which the greatest addition has been made is that on the Rate of Interest; and for most of the new matter there introduced, as well as for many minor improvements, I am indebted to the suggestions and criticisms of my friend Professor Cairnes, one of the most scientific of living political economists.

[ADDITION TO THE PREFACE IN "THE PEOPLE'S EDITION," 1865]

The present edition is an exact transcript from the sixth, except that all extracts and most phrases in foreign languages have been translated into English, and a very small number of quotations, or parts of quotations, which appeared superfluous, have been struck out.[1] A reprint of an old controversy with the *Quarterly Review* on the condition of landed property in France, which had been subjoined as an Appendix, has been dispensed with.[2]

PREFACE TO THE SEVENTH EDITION [1871] *

The present edition, with the exception of a few verbal corrections,[3] corresponds exactly with the last Library Edition and with the People's Edition. Since the publication of these, there has been some instructive discussion on the theory of Demand and Supply, and on the influence of Strikes and Trades Unions on wages, by which additional light has been thrown on these subjects ; but the results, in the author's opinion, are not yet ripe for incorporation in a general treatise on Political Economy.† For an analogous reason, all notice of the alteration made in the Land Laws of Ireland by the recent Act, is deferred until experience shall have had time to pronounce on the operation of that well-meant attempt to deal with the greatest practical evil in the economic institutions of that country.

---

[1] [The English translations in the People's edition have similarly been substituted for the originals in this, Students', edition, but none of the quotations have been omitted.]

[2] [This example has been followed in the present, Students', edition.]

* The last in the author's lifetime; [and to the subsequent eighth and ninth Library editions].

[3] [See, however, pp. 934, 936.]

† The present state of the discussion may be learnt from a review (by the author) of Mr. Thornton's work " On Labour," in the *Fortnightly Review* of May and June, 1869, and from Mr. Thornton's reply to that review in the second edition of his very instructive book. [See Appendix O. *The Wages-Fund Doctrine.*]

CONTENTS

BOOK I

PRODUCTION

CHAPTER I. *Of the Requisites of Production*

CHAPTER II. *Of Labour as an Agent of Production*

BOOK II

DISTRIBUTION

CHAPTER I. *Of Property*

CHAPTER XVI. *Of Rent*

BOOK III

EXCHANGE

CHAPTER I. *Of Value*

CHAPTER XII. *Influence of Credit on Prices*

CHAPTER XIII. *Of an Inconvertible Paper Currency*

CHAPTER XIV. *Of Excess of Supply*

CHAPTER XIX.   Of Money, considered as an Imported
Commodity

CHAPTER XX.   Of the Foreign Exchanges

CHAPTER XXI.   Of the Distribution of the Precious Metals
through the Commercial World

BOOK IV

INFLUENCE OF THE PROGRESS OF SOCIETY ON PRODUCTION AND DISTRIBUTION

BOOK V

ON THE INFLUENCE OF GOVERNMENT

CHAPTER I. *Of the Functions of Government in General*

CHAPTER II. *Of the General Principles of Taxation*

CHAPTER III. *Of Direct Taxes*

BIBLIOGRAPHICAL APPENDIX

By the Editor

PRINCIPLES

OF

POLITICAL ECONOMY

PRELIMINARY REMARKS

In every department of human affairs, Practice long precedes Science : systematic enquiry into the modes of action of the powers of nature is the tardy product of a long course of efforts to use those powers for practical ends. The conception, accordingly, of Political Economy as a branch of science is extremely modern ; but the subject with which its enquiries are conversant has in all ages necessarily constituted one of the chief practical interests of mankind, and, in some, a most unduly engrossing one.

That subject is Wealth. Writers on Political Economy profess to teach, or to investigate, the nature of Wealth, and the laws of its production and distribution : including, directly or remotely, the operation of all the causes by which the condition of mankind, or of any society of human beings, in respect to this universal object of human desire, is made prosperous or the reverse. Not that any treatise on Political Economy can discuss or even enumerate all these causes ; but it undertakes to set forth as much as is known of the laws and principles according to which they operate.

Every one has a notion, sufficiently correct for common purposes, of what is meant by wealth. The enquiries which relate to it are in no danger of being confounded with those relating to any other of the great human interests. All know that it is one thing to be rich, another thing to be enlightened, brave, or humane ; that the questions how a nation is made wealthy, and how it is made free, or virtuous, or eminent in literature, in the fine arts, in arms, or in polity, are totally distinct enquiries. Those things, indeed, are all indirectly connected, and react upon one another. A people has sometimes become free, because it had first grown wealthy; or wealthy, because it had first become free. The creed and laws of a people act powerfully upon their economical condition; and this again, by its influence on their mental development and social relations, reacts upon their creed and laws. But though the subjects are in very close contact, they are essentially different, and have never been supposed to be otherwise.

It is no part of the design of this treatise to aim at metaphysical nicety of definition, where the ideas suggested by a term are already as determinate as practical purposes require. But, little as it might be expected that any mischievous confusion of ideas could take place on a subject so simple as the question, what is to be considered as wealth, it is matter of history, that such confusion of ideas has existed—that theorists and practical politicians have been equally and at one period universally, infected by it, and that for many generations it gave a thoroughly false direction to the policy of Europe. I refer to the set of doctrines designated, since the time of Adam Smith, by the appellation of the Mercantile System.

While this system prevailed, it was assumed, either expressly or tacitly, in the whole policy of nations, that wealth consisted solely of money; or of the precious metals, which, when not already in the state of money, are capable of being directly converted into it. According to the doctrines then prevalent, whatever tended to heap up money or bullion in a country added to its wealth. Whatever sent the precious metals out of a country impoverished it. If a country possessed no gold or silver mines, the only industry by which it could be enriched was foreign trade, being the only one which could bring in money. Any branch of trade which was supposed to send out more money than it brought in, however ample and valuable might be the returns in another shape, was looked upon as a losing trade. Exportation of goods was favoured and encouraged (even by means extremely onerous to the real resources of the country), because, the exported goods being stipulated to be paid for in money, it was hoped that the returns would actually be made in gold and silver. Importation of anything, other than the precious metals, was regarded as a loss to the nation of the whole price of the things imported; unless they were brought in to be re-exported at a profit, or unless, being the materials or instruments of some industry practised in the country itself, they gave the power of producing exportable articles at smaller cost, and thereby effecting a larger exportation. The commerce of the world was looked upon as a struggle among nations, which could draw to itself the largest share of the gold and silver in existence; and in this competition no nation could gain anything, except by making others lose as much, or, at the least, preventing them from gaining it.

It often happens that the universal belief of one age of mankind— a belief from which no one *was*, nor, without an extraordinary effort of genius and courage, *could* at that time be free—becomes to a subsequent age so palpable an absurdity, that the only difficulty then is to imagine how such a thing can ever have appeared credible. It has so happened with the doctrine that money is synonymous with wealth. The conceit seems too preposterous to be thought of as a serious opinion. It looks like one of the crude fancies of childhood, instantly corrected by a word from any grown person. But let no one feel confident that he would have escaped the delusion if he had lived at the time when it prevailed. All the associations engendered by common life, and by the ordinary course of business, concurred in promoting it. So long as those associations were the only medium through which the subject was looked at, what we now think so gross an absurdity seemed a truism. Once questioned, indeed, it was doomed; but no one was likely to think of questioning it whose mind had not become familiar with certain modes of stating and of contemplating economical phenomena, which have only found their way into the general understanding through the influence of Adam Smith and of his expositors.

In common discourse, wealth is always expressed in money. If you ask how rich a person is, you are answered that he has so many thousand pounds. All income and expenditure, all gains and losses, everything by which one becomes richer or poorer, are reckoned as the coming in or going out of so much money. It is true that in the inventory of a person's fortune are included, not only the money in his actual possession, or due to him, but all other articles of value. These, however, enter, not in their own character, but in virtue of the sums of money which they would sell for; and if they would sell for less, their owner is reputed less rich, though the things themselves are precisely the same. It is true, also, that people do not grow rich by keeping their money unused, and that they must be willing to spend in order to gain. Those who enrich themselves by commerce, do so by giving money for goods as well as goods for money ; and the first is as necessary a part of the process as the last. But a person who buys goods for purpose's of gain, does so to sell them again for money, and in the expectation of receiving more money than he laid out : to get money, therefore, seems even to the person himself the ultimate end of the whole. It often happens that he is not paid in money, but in something else ; having bought goods to a value equivalent, which are set off against those he sold. But he accepted these at a money valuation, and in the belief that they would bring in more money eventually than the price at which they were made over to him. A dealer doing a large amount of business, and turning over his capital rapidly, has but a small portion of it in ready money at any one time. But he only feels it valuable to him as it is convertible into money : he considers no transaction closed until the net result is either paid or credited in money : when he retires from business it is into money that he converts the whole, and not until then does he deem himself to have realized his gains : just as if money were the only wealth, and money's worth were only the means of attaining it. If it be now asked for what end money is desirable, unless to supply the wants or pleasures of oneself or others, the champion of the system would not be at all embarrassed by the question. True, he would say, these are the uses of wealth, and very laudable uses while confined to domestic commodities, because in that case, by exactly the amount which you expend, you enrich others of your countrymen. Spend your wealth, if you please, in whatever indulgences you have a taste for ; but your wealth is not the indulgences, it is the sum of money, or the annual money income, with which you purchase them.

While there were so many things to render the assumption which is the basis of the mercantile system plausible, there is also some small foundation in reason, though a very insufficient one for the distinction which that system so emphatically draws between money and every other kind of valuable possession. We really, and justly, look upon a person as possessing the advantages of wealth, not in proportion to the useful and agreeable things of which he is in the actual enjoyment, but to his command over the general fund of things useful and agreeable ; the power he possesses of providing for any exigency, or obtaining any object of desire. Now, money is itself that power ; while all other things, in a civilized state, seem to confer it only by their capacity of being exchanged for money. To possess any other article of wealth, is to possess that particular thing, and nothing else : if you wish for another thing instead of it, you have first to sell it, or to submit to the inconvenience and delay (if not the impossibility) of finding some one who has what you want, and is willing to barter it for what you have. But with money you are at once able to buy whatever things are for sale : and one whose fortune is in money, or in things rapidly convertible into it, seems both to himself and others to possess not any one thing, but all the things which the money places it at his option to purchase. The greatest part of the utility of wealth, beyond a very moderate quantity, is not the indulgences it procures, but the reserved power which its possessor holds in his hands of attaining purposes generally ; and this power no other kind of wealth confers so immediately or so certainly as money. It is the only form of wealth which is not merely applicable to some one use, but can be turned at once to any use. And this distinction was the more likely to make an impression upon governments, as it is one of considerable importance to them. A civilized government derives comparatively little advantage from taxes unless it can collect them in money : and if it has large or sudden payments to make, especially payments in foreign countries for wars or subsidies, either for the sake of conquering or of not being conquered (the two chief objects of national policy until a late period), scarcely any medium of payment except money will serve the purpose. All these causes conspire to make both individuals and governments, in estimating their means, attach almost exclusive importance to money, either *in esse* or *in posse*, and look upon all other things (when viewed as part of their resources) scarcely otherwise than as the remote means of obtaining that which alone, when obtained, affords the indefinite, and at the same time instantaneous, command over objects of desire, which best answers to the idea of wealth.

An absurdity, however, does not cease to be an absurdity when we have discovered what were the appearances which made it plausible ; and the Mercantile Theory could not fail to be seen in its true character when men began, even in an imperfect manner, to explore into the foundations of things, and seek their premises from elementary facts, and not from the forms and phrases of common discourse. So soon as they asked themselves what is really meant by money—what it is in its essential characters, and the precise nature of the functions it performs—they reflected that money, like other things, is only a desirable possession on account of its uses ; and that these, instead of being, as they delusively appear, indefinite, are of a strictly defined and limited description, namely, to facilitate the distribution of the produce of industry according to the convenience of those among whom it is shared. Further consideration showed that the uses of money are in no respect promoted by increasing the quantity which exists and circulates in a country ; the service which it performs being as well rendered by a small as by a large aggregate amount. Two million quarters of corn will not feed so many persons as four millions ; but two millions of pounds sterling. will carry on as much traffic, will buy and sell as many commodities, as four millions, though at lower nominal prices. Money, as money, satisfies no want ; its worth to any one, consists in its being a convenient shape in which to receive his incomings of all sorts, which incomings he afterwards, at the times which suit him best, converts into the forms in which they can be useful to him. Great as the difference would be between a country with money, and a country altogether without it, it would be only one of convenience ; a saving of time and trouble, like grinding by water power instead of by hand, or (to use Adam Smith's illustration) like the benefit derived from roads ; and to mistake money for wealth is the same sort of error as to mistake the highway which may be the easiest way of getting to your house or lands, for the house and lands themselves.[1]

Money, being the instrument of an important public and private purpose, is rightly regarded as wealth ; but everything else which serves any human purpose, and which nature does not afford gratuitously, is wealth also. To be wealthy is to have a large stock of useful articles, or the means of purchasing them. Everything forms therefore a part of wealth, which has a power of purchasing ; for which anything useful or agreeable would be given in exchange. Things for which nothing could be obtained in exchange, however useful or necessary they may be, are not wealth in the sense in which the term is used in Political Economy. Air, for example, though the most absolute of necessaries, bears no price in the market, because it can be obtained gratuitously : to accumulate a stock of it would yield no profit or advantage to any one ; and the laws of its production and distribution are the subject of a very different study from Political Economy. But though air is not wealth, mankind are much richer by obtaining it gratis, since the time

[1] [See Appendix A. *The Mercantile System.*]

and labour which would otherwise be required for supplying the most pressing of all wants, can be devoted to other purposes. It is possible to imagine circumstances in which air would be a part of wealth. If it became customary to sojourn long in places where the air does not naturally penetrate, as in diving-bells sunk in the sea, a supply of air artificially furnished would, like water conveyed into houses, bear a price : and if from any revolution in nature the atmosphere became too scanty for the consumption, or could be monopolized, air might acquire a very high marketable value. In such a case, the possession of it, beyond his own wants, would be, to its owner, wealth ; and the general wealth of mankind might at first sight appear to be increased, by what would be so great a calamity to them. The error would lie in not considering, that however rich the possessor of air might become at the expense of the rest of the community, all persons else would be poorer by all that they were compelled to pay for what they had before obtained without payment.

This leads to an important distinction in the meaning of the word wealth, as applied to the possessions of an individual, and to those of a nation, or of mankind. In the wealth of mankind, nothing is included which does not of itself answer some purpose of utility or pleasure. To an individual anything is wealth, which, though useless in itself, enables him to claim from others a part of their stock of things useful or pleasant. Take, for instance, a mortgage of a thousand pounds on a landed estate. This is wealth to the person to whom it brings in a revenue, and who could perhaps sell it in the market for the full amount of the debt. But it is not wealth to the country ; if the engagement were annulled, the country would be neither poorer nor richer. The mortgagee would have lost a thousand pounds, and the owner of the land would have gained it. Speaking nationally, the mortgage was not itself wealth, but merely gave A a claim to a portion of the wealth of B. It was wealth to A, and wealth which he could transfer to a third person ; but what he so transferred was in fact a joint ownership, to the extent of a thousand pounds, in the land of which B was nominally the sole proprietor. The position of fundholders, or owners of the public debt of a country, is similar. They are mortgagees on the general wealth of the country. The cancelling of the debt would be no destruction of wealth, but a transfer of it : a wrongful abstraction of wealth from certain members of the community, for the profit of the government, or of the tax-payers. Funded property therefore cannot be counted as part of the national wealth. This is not always borne in mind by the dealers in statistical calculations. For example, in estimates of the gross income of the country, founded on the proceeds of the income-tax, incomes derived from the funds are not always excluded: though the tax-payers are assessed on their whole nominal income, without being permitted to deduct from it the portion levied from them in taxation to form the income of the fundholder. In this calculation, therefore, one portion of the general income of the country is counted twice over, and the aggregate amount made to appear greater than it is by almost[1] thirty millions. A country, however, may include in its wealth all stock held by its citizens in the funds of foreign countries, and other debts due to them from abroad. But even this is only wealth to them by being a part ownership in wealth held by others. It forms no part of the collective wealth of the human race. It is an element in the distribution, but not in the composition, of the general wealth.

[2]Another example of a possession which is wealth to the person holding it, but not wealth to the nation, or to mankind, is slaves. It is by a strange confusion of ideas that slave property (as it is termed) is counted, at so much per head, in an estimate of the wealth, or of the capital, of the country which tolerates the existence of such property. If a human being, considered as an object possessing productive powers, is part of the national wealth when his powers are owned by another man, he cannot be less a part of it when they are owned by himself. Whatever he is worth to his master is so much property abstracted from himself, and its abstraction cannot augment the possessions of the two together, or of the country to which they both belong. In propriety of classification, however, the people of a country are not to be counted in its wealth. They are that for the sake of which its wealth exists. The term wealth is wanted to denote the desirable objects which they possess, not inclusive of, but in contradistinction to, their own persons. They are not wealth to themselves, though they are means of acquiring it.

It has been proposed to define wealth as signifying " instruments : " meaning not tools and machinery alone, but the whole accumulation possessed by individuals or communities, of means for the attainment of their ends. Thus, a field is an instrument,

---

[1] [1st ed. (1848) " about " ; 5th ed. (1862) " almost."]
[2] [Paragraph added in 6th ed. (1865).]

because it is a means to the attainment of corn. Corn is an instrument, being a means to the attainment of flour. Flour is an instrument, being a means to the attainment of bread. Bread is an instrument, as a means to the satisfaction of hunger and to the support of life. Here we at last arrive at things which are not instruments, being desired on their own account, and not as mere means to something beyond. This view of the subject is philosophically correct; or rather, this mode of expression may be usefully employed along with others, not as conveying a different view of the subject from the common one, but as giving more distinctness and reality to the common view. It departs, however, too widely from the custom of language, to be likely to obtain general acceptance, or to be of use for any other purpose than that of occasional illustration.

Wealth, then, may be defined, all useful or agreeable things which possess exchangeable value ; or, in other words, all useful or agreeable things except those which can be obtained, in the quantity desired, without labour or sacrifice. To this definition, the only objection seems to be, that it leaves in uncertainty a question which has been much debated—whether what are called immaterial products are to be considered as wealth : whether, for example, the skill of a workman, or any other natural or acquired power of body or mind, shall be called wealth, or not : a question, not of very great importance, and which, so far as requiring discussion, will be more conveniently considered in another place.* [1]

These things having been premised respecting wealth, we shall next turn our attention to the extraordinary differences in respect to it, which exist between nation and nation, and between different ages of the world ; differences both in the quantity of wealth, and in the kind of it ; as well as in the manner in which the wealth existing in the community is shared among its members.

There is, perhaps, no people or community, now existing, which subsists entirely on the spontaneous produce of vegetation. But many tribes still live exclusively, or almost exclusively, on wild animals, the produce of hunting or fishing. Their clothing is skins ; their habitations, huts rudely formed of logs or boughs of trees, and abandoned at an hour's notice. The food they use being little susceptible of storing up, they have no accumulation of it, and are often

* Infra, book i. chap. iii.
[1] [See Appendix B. *The Definition of Wealth.*]

exposed to great privations. The wealth of such a community consists solely of the skins they wear ; a few ornaments, the taste for which exists among most savages ; some rude utensils ; the weapons with which they kill their game, or fight against hostile competitors for the means of subsistence ; canoes for crossing rivers and lakes, or fishing in the sea ; and perhaps some furs or other productions of the wilderness, collected to be exchanged with civilized people for blankets, brandy, and tobacco ; of which foreign produce also there may be some unconsumed portion in store. To this scanty inventory of material wealth, ought to be added their land ; an instrument of production of which they make slender use, compared with more settled communities, but which is still the source of their subsistence, and which has a marketable value if there be any agricultural community in the neighbourhood requiring more land than it possesses. This is the state of greatest poverty in which any entire community of human beings is known to exist ; though there are much richer communities in which portions of the inhabitants are in a condition, as to subsistence and comfort, as little enviable as that of the savage.

The first great advance beyond this state consists in the domestication of the more useful animals ; giving rise to the pastoral or nomad state, in which mankind do not live on the produce of hunting, but on milk and its products, and on the annual increase of flocks and herds. This condition is not only more desirable in itself, but more conducive to further progress : and a much more considerable amount of wealth is accumulated under it. So long as the vast natural pastures of the earth are not yet so fully occupied as to be consumed more rapidly than they are spontaneously reproduced, a large and constantly increasing stock of subsistence may be collected and preserved, with little other labour than that of guarding the cattle from the attacks of wild beasts, and from the force or wiles of predatory men. Large flocks and herds, therefore, are in time possessed, by active and thrifty individuals through their own exertions, and by the heads of families and tribes through the exertions of those who are connected with them by allegiance. There thus arises, in the shepherd state, inequality of possessions ; a thing which scarcely exists in the savage state, where no one has much more than absolute necessaries, and in case of deficiency must share even those with his tribe. In the nomad state, some have an abundance of cattle, sufficient for the food of a multitude, while others have not contrived to appropriate and retain any superfluity, or perhaps any cattle at all. But subsistence has ceased to be precarious, since the more successful have no other use which they can make of their surplus than to feed the less fortunate, while every increase in the number of persons connected with them is an increase both of security and of power : and thus they are enabled to divest themselves of all labour except that of government and superintendence, and acquire dependents to fight for them in war and to serve them in peace. One of the features of this state of society is, that a part of the community, and in some degree even the whole of it, possess leisure. Only a portion of time is required for procuring food, and the remainder is not engrossed by anxious thought for the morrow, or necessary repose from muscular activity. Such a life is highly favourable to the growth of new wants, and opens a possibility of their gratification. A desire arises for better clothing. utensils, and implements, than the savage state contents itself with ; and the surplus food renders it practicable to devote to these purposes the exertions of a part of the tribe. In all or most nomad communities we find domestic manufactures of a côarse, and in some, of a fine kind. There is ample evidence that while those parts of the world which have been the cradle of modern civilization were still generally in the nomad state, considerable skill had been attained in spinning, weaving, and dyeing woollen garments, in the preparation of leather, and in what appears a still more difficult invention, that of working in metals. Even speculative science took its first beginnings from the leisure characteristic of this stage of social progress. The earliest astronomical observations are attributed, by a tradition which has much appearance of truth, to the shepherds of Chaldea.

From this state of society to the agricultural the transition is not indeed easy (for no great change in the habits of mankind is otherwise than difficult, and in general either painful or very slow), but it lies in what may be called the spontaneous course of events The growth of the population of men and cattle began in time to press upon the earth's capabilities of yielding natural pasture : and this cause doubtless produced the first tilling of the ground, just as at a later period the same cause made the superfluous hordes of the nations which had remained nomad precipitate themselves upon those which had already become agricultural ; until, these having become sufficiently powerful to repel such inroads, the invading nations, deprived of this outlet, were obliged also to become agricultural communities.

But after this great step had been completed, the subsequent

progress of mankind seems by no means to have been so rapid
(certain rare combinations of circumstances excepted) as might
perhaps have been anticipated. The quantity of human food which
the earth is capable of returning even to the most wretched system
of agriculture, so much exceeds what could be obtained in the
purely pastoral state, that a great increase of population is invariably
the result. But this additional food is only obtained by a great
additional amount of labour ; so that not only an agricultural
has much less leisure than a pastoral population, but, with the
imperfect tools and unskilful processes which are for a long time
employed (and which over the greater part of the earth have not
even yet been abandoned), agriculturists do not, unless in unusually
advantageous circumstances of climate and soil, produce so great
a surplus of food, beyond their necessary consumption, as to support any large class of labourers engaged in other departments of
industry. The surplus, too, whether small or great, is usually
torn from the producers, either by the government to which they
are subject, or by individuals, who by superior force, or by availing
themselves of religious or traditional feelings of subordination,
have established themselves as lords of the soil.

The first of these modes of appropriation, by the government,
is characteristic of the extensive monarchies which from a time
beyond historical record have occupied the plains of Asia. The government, in those countries, though varying in its qualities according
to the accidents of personal character, seldom leaves much to the
cultivators beyond mere necessaries, and often strips them so bare
even of these, that it finds itself obliged, after taking all they have,
to lend part of it back to those from whom it has been taken, in
order to provide them with seed, and enable them to support life
until another harvest. Under the régime in question, though
the bulk of the population are ill provided for, the government,
by collecting small contributions from great numbers, is enabled,
with any tolerable management, to make a show of riches quite out
of proportion to the general condition of the society ; and hence
the inveterate impression, of which Europeans have only at a late
period been disabused, concerning the great opulence of Oriental
nations. In this wealth, without reckoning the large portion which
adheres to the hands employed in collecting it, many persons of
course participate, besides the immediate household of the sovereign.
A large part is distributed among the various functionaries of
government, and among the objects of the sovereign's favour or

caprice. A part is occasionally employed in works of public utility. The tanks, wells, and canals for irrigation, without which in many tropical climates cultivation could hardly be .carried on ; the embankments which confine the rivers, the bazars for dealers, and the seraees for travellers, none of which could have been made by the scanty means in the possession of those using them, owe their existence to the liberality and enlightened self-interest of the better order of princes, or to the benevolence or ostentation of here and there a rich individual, whose fortune, if traced to its source, is always found to have been drawn immediately or remotely from the public revenue, most frequently by a direct grant of a portion of it from the sovereign.

The ruler of a society of this description, after providing largely for his own support, and that of all persons in whom he feels an interest, and after maintaining as many soldiers as he thinks needful for his security or his state, has a disposable residue, which he is glad to exchange for articles of luxury suitable to his disposition : as have also the class of persons who have been enriched by his favour, or by handling the public revenues. A demand thus arises for elaborate and costly manufactured articles, adapted to a narrow but a wealthy market. This demand is often supplied almost exclusively by the merchants of more advanced communities, but often also raises up in the country itself a class of artificers, by whom certain fabrics are carried to as high excellence as can be given by patience, quickness of perception and observation, and manual dexterity, without any considerable knowledge of the properties of objects : such as some of the cotton fabrics of India. These artificers are fed by the surplus food which has been taken by the government and its agents as their share of the produce. So literally is this the case, that in some countries the workman, instead of taking his work home, and being paid for it after it is finished, proceeds with his tools to his customer's house, and is there subsisted until the work is complete. The insecurity, however, of all possessions in this state of society, induces even the richest purchasers to give a preference to such articles as, being of an imperishable nature, and containing great value in small bulk, are adapted for being concealed or carried off. Gold and jewels, therefore, constitute a large proportion of the wealth of these nations, and many a rich Asiatic carries nearly his whole fortune on his person, or on those of the women of his harem. No one, except the monarch, thinks of investing his wealth in a manner not susceptible of removal. He indeed if he feels safe on his throne, and reasonably secure of transmitting it to his descendants, sometimes indulges a taste for durable edifices, and produces the Pyramids, or the Taj Mehal and the Mausoleum at Sekundra. The rude manufactures destined for the wants of the cultivators are worked up by village artisans, who are remunerated by land given to them rent-free to cultivate, or by fees paid to them in kind from such share of the crop as is left to the villagers by the government. This state of society, however, is not destitute of the mercantile class; composed of two divisions, grain dealers and money dealers. The grain dealers do not usually buy grain from the producers, but from the agents of government, who, receiving the revenue in kind, are glad to devolve upon others the business of conveying it to the places where the prince, his chief civil and military officers, the bulk of his troops, and the artisans who supply the wants of these various persons, are assembled. The money dealers lend to the unfortunate cultivators, when ruined by bad seasons or fiscal exactions, the means of supporting life and continuing their cultivation, and are repaid with enormous interest at the next harvest; or, on a larger scale, they lend to the government, or to those to whom it has granted a portion of the revenue, and are indemnified by assignments on the revenue collectors, or by having certain districts put into their possession, that they may pay themselves from the revenues; to enable them to do which, a great portion of the powers of government are usually made over simultaneously, to be exercised by them until either the districts are redeemed, or their receipts have liquidated the debt. Thus, the commercial operations of both these classes of dealers take place principally upon that part of the produce of the country which forms the revenue of the government. From that revenue their capital is periodically replaced with a profit, and that is also the source from which their original funds have almost always been derived. Such, in its general features, is the economical condition of most of the countries of Asia, as it has been from beyond the commencement of authentic history, and is still [1848], wherever not disturbed by foreign influences.

In the agricultural communities of ancient Europe whose early condition is best known to us, the course of things was different. These, at their origin, were mostly small town-communities, at the first plantation of which, in an unoccupied country, or in one from which the former inhabitants had been expelled, the land which was taken possession of was regularly divided, in equal or in graduated

allotments, among the families composing the community. In
some cases, instead of a town there was a confederation of towns,
occupied by people of the same reputed race, and who were supposed to have settled in the country about the same time. Each
family produced its own food and the materials of its clothing,
which were worked up within itself, usually by the women of the
family, into the coarse fabrics with which the age was contented.
Taxes there were none, as there were either no paid officers of
government, or if there were, their payment had been provided
for by a reserved portion of land, cultivated by slaves on account
of the state; and the army consisted of the body of citizens.
The whole produce of the soil, therefore, belonged, without deduction, to the family which cultivated it. So long as the progress
of events permitted this disposition of property to last, the
state of society was, for the majority of the free cultivators,
probably not an undesirable one; and under it, in some cases,
the advance of mankind in intellectual culture was extraordinarily
rapid and brilliant. This more especially happened where, along
with advantageous circumstances of race and climate, and no doubt
with many favourable accidents of which all trace is now lost, was
combined the advantage of a position on the shores of a great inland sea, the other coasts of which were already occupied by settled
communities. The knowledge which in such a position was acquired of foreign productions, and the easy access of foreign ideas
and inventions, made the chain of routine, usually so strong in a
rude people, hang loosely on these communities. To speak only
of their industrial development; they early acquired variety of
wants and desires, which stimulated them to extract from their
own soil the utmost which they knew how to make it yield; and
when their soil was sterile, or after they had reached the limit
of its capacity, they often became traders, and bought up the productions of foreign countries, to sell them in other countries with a
profit.

The duration, however, of this state of things was from the first
precarious. These little communities lived in a state of almost perpetual war. For this there were many causes. In the ruder and
purely agricultural communities a frequent cause was the mere
pressure of their increasing population upon their limited land,
aggravated as that pressure so often was by deficient harvests, in
the rude state of their agriculture, and depending as they did for
food upon a very small extent of country. On these occasions,

the community often emigrated *en masse*, or sent forth a swarm of its youth, to seek, sword in hand, for some less warlike people, who could be expelled from their land, or detained to cultivate it as slaves for the benefit of their despoilers. What the less advanced tribes did from necessity, the more prosperous did from ambition and the military spirit: and after a time the whole of these city-communities were either conquerors or conquered. In some cases, the conquering state contented itself with imposing a tribute on the vanquished : who being, in consideration of that burden, freed from the expense and trouble of their own military and naval protection, might enjoy under it a considerable share of economical prosperity, while the ascendant community obtained a surplus of wealth, available for purposes of collective luxury or magnificence. From such a surplus the Parthenon and the Propylæa were built, the sculptures of Pheidias paid for, and the festivals celebrated, for which Æschylus, Sophocles, Euripides, and Aristophanes composed their dramas. But this state of political relations, most useful, while it lasted, to the progress and ultimate interest of mankind, had not the elements of durability. A small conquering community which does not incorporate its conquests, always ends by being conquered. Universal dominion, therefore, at last rested with the people who practised this art—with the Romans ; who, whatever were their other devices, always either began or ended by taking a great part of the land to enrich their own leading citizens, and by adopting into the governing body the principal possessors of the remainder. It is unnecessary to dwell on the melancholy economical history of the Roman empire. When inequality of wealth once commences, in a community not constantly engaged in repairing by industry the injuries of fortune, its advances are gigantic ; the great masses of wealth swallow up the smaller. The Roman empire ultimately became covered with the vast landed possessions of a comparatively few families, for whose luxury, and still more for whose ostentation, the most costly products were raised, while the cultivators of the soil were slaves, or small tenants in a nearly servile condition. From this time the wealth of the empire progressively declined. In the beginning, the public revenues, and the resources of rich individuals, sufficed at least to cover Italy with splendid edifices, public and private ; but at length so dwindled under the enervating influences of mis-government, that what remained was not even sufficient to keep those edifices from decay. The strength and riches of the civilized world became inadequate to make head against the nomad population which skirted its northern frontier ; they overran the empire, and a different order of things succeeded.

In the new frame in which European society was now cast, the population of each country may be considered as composed, in unequal proportions, of two distinct nations or races, the conquerors and the conquered : the first the proprietors of the land, the latter the tillers of it. These tillers were allowed to occupy the land on conditions which, being the product of force, were always onerous, but seldom to the extent of absolute slavery. Already, in the later times of the Roman empire, predial slavery had extensively transformed itself into a kind of serfdom : the *zoloni* of the Romans were rather villeins than actual slaves ; and the incapacity and distaste of the barbarian conquerors for personally superintending industrial occupations, left no alternative but to allow to the cultivators, as an incentive to exertion, some real interest in the soil. If, for example, they were compelled to labour, three days in the week, for their superior, the produce of the remaining days was their own. If they were required to supply the provisions of various sorts, ordinarily needed for the consumption of the castle, and were often subject to requisitions in excess, yet after supplying these demands they were suffered to dispose at their will of whatever additional produce they could raise. Under this system during the Middle Ages it was not impossible, no more than in modern Russia (where, up to the recent measure of emancipation, the same system still essentially prevailed),[1] for serfs to acquire property ; and in fact, their accumulations are the primitive source of the wealth of modern Europe.

In that age of violence and disorder, the first use made by a serf of any small provision which he had been able to accumulate, was to buy his freedom and withdraw himself to some town or fortified village, which had remained undestroyed from the time of the Roman dominion ; or, without buying his freedom, to abscond thither. In that place of refuge, surrounded by others of his own class, he attempted to live, secured in some measure from the outrages and exactions of the warrior caste, by his own prowess and that of his fellows. These emancipated serfs mostly became artificers ; and lived by exchanging the produce of their industry for the surplus food and material which the soil yielded to its feudal proprietors. This gave rise to a sort of European counterpart of the economical

---

[1] [Parenthesis added in 6th ed. (1865).]

condition of Asiatic countries ; except that, in lieu of a single monarch and a fluctuating body of favourites and employés, there was
a numerous and in a considerable degree fixed class of great landholders ; exhibiting far less splendour, because individually disposing
of a much smaller surplus produce, and for a long time expending
the chief part of it in maintaining the body of retainers whom the
warlike habits of society, and the little protection afforded by government, rendered indispensable to their safety.   The greater stability,
the fixity of personal position, which this state of society afforded,
in comparison with the Asiatic polity to which it economically
corresponded, was one main reason why it was also found more
favourable to improvement.   From this time the economical
advancement of society has not been further interrupted.   Security
of person and property grew slowly, but steadily ; the arts of life
made constant progress ; plunder ceased to be the principal source
of accumulation ; and feudal Europe ripened into commercial and
manufacturing Europe.   In the latter part of the Middle Ages, the
towns of Italy and Flanders, the free cities of Germany, and some
towns of France and England, contained a large and energetic
population of artisans, and many rich burghers, whose wealth
had been acquired by manufacturing industry, or by trading in
the produce of such industry.   The Commons of England, the Tiers-
Etat of France, the bourgeoisie of the Continent generally, are the
descendants of this class.   As these were a saving class, while the
posterity of the feudal aristocracy were a squandering class, the
former by degrees substituted themselves for the latter as the owners
of a great proportion of the land.   This natural tendency was
in some cases retarded by laws contrived for the purpose of detaining
the land in the families of its existing possessors, in other cases
accelerated by political revolutions.   Gradually, though more
slowly, the immediate cultivators of the soil, in all the more civilized
countries, ceased to be in a servile or semi-servile state : though
the legal position, as well as the economical condition attained by
them, vary extremely in the different nations of Europe, and in the
great communities which have been founded beyond the Atlantic
by the descendants of Europeans.

 The world now contains several extensive regions, provided
with the various ingredients of wealth in a degree of abundance of
which former ages had not even the idea.   Without compulsory
labour, an enormous mass of food is annually extracted from
the soil, and maintains, besides the actual producers, an equal,

sometimes a greater, number of labourers occupied in producing conveniences and luxuries of innumerable kinds, or in transporting them from place to place ; also a multitude of persons employed in directing and superintending these various labours ; and over and above all these, a class more numerous than in the most luxurious ancient societies, of persons whose occupations are of a kind not directly productive, and of persons who have no occupation at all. The food thus raised supports a far larger population than had ever existed (at least in the same regions) on an equal space of ground ; and supports them with certainty, exempt from those periodically recurring famines so abundant in the early history of Europe, and in Oriental countries even now not unfrequent. Besides this great increase in the quantity of food, it has greatly improved in quality and variety ; while conveniences and luxuries, other than food, are no longer limited to a small and opulent class, but descend, in great abundance, through many widening strata in society. The collective resources of one of these communities, when it chooses to put them forth for any unexpected purpose ; its ability to maintain fleets and armies, to execute public works, either useful or ornamental, to perform national acts of beneficence like the ransom of the West India slaves ; to found colonies, to have its people taught, to do anything in short which requires expense, and to do it with no sacrifice of the necessaries or even the substantial comforts of its inhabitants, are such as the world never saw before.

But in all these particulars, characteristic of the modern industrial communities, those communities differ widely from one another. Though abounding in wealth as compared with former ages, they do so in very different degrees. Even of the countries which are justly accounted the richest, some have made a more complete use of their productive resources, and have obtained, relatively to their territorial extent, a much larger produce, than others ; nor do they differ only in amount of wealth, but also in the rapidity of its increase. The diversities in the distribution of wealth are still greater than in the production. There are great differences in the condition of the poorest class in different countries ; and in the proportional numbers and opulence of the classes which are above the poorest. The very nature and designation of the classes who originally share among them the produce of the soil, vary not a little in different places. In some, the landowners are a class in themselves, almost entirely separate from the classes engaged in industry : in others, the proprietor of the land is almost universally

its cultivator, owning the plough, and often himself holding it.
Where the proprietor himself does not cultivate, there is sometimes,
between him and the labourer, an intermediate agency, that of the
farmer who advances the subsistence of the labourers, supplies the
instruments of production, and receives, after paying a rent to the
landowner, all the produce : in other cases, the landlord, his paid
agents, and the labourers, are the only sharers.   Manufactures,
again, are sometimes carried on by scattered individuals, who own
or hire the tools or machinery they require, and employ little labour
besides that of their own family ; in other cases, by large numbers
working together in one building, with expensive and complex
machinery owned by rich manufacturers.   The same difference
exists in the operations of trade.   The wholesale operations indeed
are everywhere carried on by large capitals, where such exist ; but
the retail dealings, which collectively occupy a very great amount of
capital, are sometimes conducted in small shops, chiefly by the
personal exertions of the dealers themselves, with their families,
and perhaps an apprentice or two ; and sometimes in large establishments, of which the funds are supplied by a wealthy individual
or association, and the agency is that of numerous salaried shopmen
or shopwomen.   Besides these differences in the economical phenomena presented by different parts of what is usually called the
civilized world, all those earlier states which we previously passed
in review have continued in some part or other of the world, down to
our own time.   Hunting communities still exist in America, nomadic
in Arabia and the steppes of Northern Asia ; Oriental society
is in essentials what it has always been ; the great empire of Russia
is[1] even now, in many respects, the scarcely modified image of feudal
Europe.   Every one of the great types of human society, down to
that of the Esquimaux or Patagonians, is still extant.[2]

These remarkable differences in the state of different portions of
the human race, with regard to the production and distribution of
wealth, must, like all other phenomena, depend on causes.   And it
is not a sufficient explanation to ascribe them exclusively to the
degrees of knowledge possessed at different times and places, of the
laws of nature and the physical arts of life.   Many other causes co-
operate ; and that very progress and unequal distribution of physical

---

[1] [So since 2nd ed. (1849).   In the 1st ed. (1848) the text ran : " Russia and
Hungary are," &c.]
[2] [See Appendix C.   *The Types of Society.*]

knowledge are partly the effects, as well as partly the causes, of the state of the production and distribution of wealth.

In so far as the economical condition of nations turns upon the state of physical knowledge, it is a subject for the physical sciences, and the arts founded on them. But in so far as the causes are moral or psychological, dependent on institutions and social relations, or on the principles of human nature, their investigation belongs not to physical, but to moral and social science, and is the object of what is called Political Economy.

The production of wealth ; the extraction of the instruments of human subsistence and enjoyment from the materials of the globe, is evidently not an arbitrary thing. It has its necessary conditions. Of these, some are physical, depending on the properties of matter, and on the amount of knowledge of those properties possessed at the particular place and time. These Political Economy does not investigate, but assumes ; referring for the grounds, to physical science or common experience. Combining with these facts of outward nature other truths relating to human nature, it attempts to trace the secondary or derivative laws, by which the production of wealth is determined ; in which must lie the explanation of the diversities of riches and poverty in the present and past, and the ground of whatever increase in wealth is reserved for the future.

Unlike the laws of Production, those of Distribution are partly of human institution : since the manner in which wealth is distributed in any given society, depends on the statutes or usages therein obtaining. But though governments or nations have the power of deciding what institutions shall exist, they cannot arbitrarily determine how those institutions shall work. The conditions on which the power they possess over the distribution of wealth is dependent, and the manner in which the distribution is effected by the various modes of conduct which society may think fit to adopt, are as much a subject for scientific enquiry as any of the physical laws of nature.

The laws of Production and Distribution, and some of the practical consequences deducible from them, are the subject of the following treatise.

BOOK I

PRODUCTION

CHAPTER I

OF THE REQUISITES OF PRODUCTION

§ 1. The requisites of production are two : labour, and appropriate natural objects.

Labour is either bodily or mental ; or, to express the distinction more comprehensively, either muscular or nervous ; and it is necessary to include in the idea, not solely the exertion itself, but all feelings of a disagreeable kind, all bodily inconvenience or mental annoyance, connected with the employment of one's thoughts, or muscles, or both, in a particular occupation. Of the other requisite —appropriate natural objects—it is to be remarked, that some objects exist or grow up spontaneously, of a kind suited to the supply of human wants. There are caves and hollow trees capable of affording shelter ; fruit, roots, wild honey, and other natural products, on which human life can be supported ; but even here a considerable quantity of labour is generally required, not for the purpose of creating, but of finding and appropriating them. In all but these few and (except in the very commencement of human society) unimportant cases, the objects supplied by nature are only instrumental to human wants, after having undergone some degree of transformation by human exertion. Even the wild animals of the forest and of the sea, from which the hunting and fishing tribes derive their sustenance—though the labour of which they are the subject is chiefly that required for appropriating them—must yet, before they are used as food, be killed, divided into fragments, and subjected in almost all cases to some culinary process, which are operations requiring a certain degree of human labour. The amount of transformation which natural substances undergo before being brought into the shape in which they are directly applied to human use varies from this or a still less degree of alteration in the nature and appearance of the object, to a change so total that no trace is perceptible of the original shape and structure. There is little resemblance between a piece of a mineral substance found in the earth, and a plough, an axe, or a saw. There is less resemblance between porcelain and the decomposing granite of which it is made, or between sand mixed with sea weed, and glass. The difference is greater still between the fleece of a sheep, or a handful of cotton seeds, and a web of muslin or broad cloth; and the sheep and seeds themselves are not spontaneous growths, but results of previous labour and care. In these several cases the ultimate product is so extremely dissimilar to the substance supplied by nature, that in the custom of language nature is represented as only furnishing materials.

Nature, however, does more than supply materials; she also supplies powers. The matter of the globe is not an inert recipient of forms and properties impressed by human hands; it has active energies by which it co-operates with, and may even be used as a substitute for, labour. In the early ages people converted their corn into flour by pounding it between two stones; they next hit on a contrivance which enabled them, by turning a handle, to make one of the stones revolve upon the other; and this process, a little improved, is still the common practice of the East. The muscular exertion, however, which it required, was very severe and exhausting, insomuch that it was often selected as a punishment for slaves who had offended their masters. When the time came at which the labour and sufferings of slaves were thought worth economizing, the greater part of this bodily exertion was rendered unnecessary, by contriving that the upper stone should be made to revolve upon the lower, not by human strength, but by the force of the wind or of falling water. In this case, natural agents, the wind or the gravitation of the water, are made to do a portion of the work previously done by labour.

§ 2. Cases like this, in which a certain amount of labour has been dispensed with, its work being devolved upon some natural agent, are apt to suggest an erroneous notion of the comparative functions of labour and natural powers; as if the co-operation of those powers with human industry were limited to the cases in which they are made to perform what would otherwise be done by labour ; as if, in the case of things made (as the phrase is) by hand, nature only furnished passive materials. This is an illusion. The powers of nature are as actively operative in the one case as in the other. A workman takes a stalk of the flax or hemp plant, splits it into separate fibres, twines together several of these fibres with his fingers, aided by a simple instrument called a spindle ; having thus formed a thread, he lays many such threads side by side, and places other similar threads directly across them, so that each passes alternately over and under those which are at right angles to it ; this part of the process being facilitated by an instrument called a shuttle. He has now produced a web of cloth, either linen or sack-cloth, according to the material. He is said to have done this by hand, no natural force being supposed to have acted in concert with him. But by what force is each step of this operation rendered possible, and the web, when produced, held together ? By the tenacity, or force of cohesion, of the fibres : which is one of the forces in nature, and which we can measure exactly against other mechanical forces, and ascertain how much of any of them it suffices to neutralize or counterbalance.

If we examine any other case of what is called the action of man upon nature, we shall find in like manner that the powers of nature, or in other words the properties of matter, do all the work, when once objects are put into the right position. This one operation, of putting things into fit places for being acted upon by their own internal forces, and by those residing in other natural objects, is all that man does, or can do, with matter. He only moves one thing to or from another. He moves a seed into the ground ; and the natural forces of vegetation produce in succession a root, a stem, leaves, flowers, and fruit. He moves an axe through a tree, and it falls by the natural force of gravitation ; he moves a saw through it, in a particular manner, and the physical properties by which a softer substance gives way before a harder, make it separate into planks, which he arranges in certain positions, with nails driven through them, or adhesive matter between them, and produces a table, or a house. He moves a spark to fuel, and it ignites, and by the force generated in combustion it cooks the food, melts or softens the iron, converts into beer or sugar the malt or cane-juice, which he has previously moved to the spot. He has no other means of acting on matter than by moving it. Motion, and resistance to motion, are the only things which his muscles are constructed for. By muscular contraction he can. create a pressure on an outward object, which, if sufficiently powerful, will set it in motion, or if it be already moving, will check or modify or altogether arrest its motion, and he can do no more. But this is enough to have given all the command which mankind have acquired over natural forces immeasurably more powerful than themselves ; a command which, great as it is already, is without doubt destined to become indefinitely greater. He exerts this power either by availing himself of natural forces in existence, or by arranging objects in those mixtures and combinations by which natural forces are generated ; as when by putting a lighted match to fuel, and water into a boiler over it, he generates the expansive force of steam, a power which has been made so largely available for the attainment of human purposes.*

Labour, then, in the physical world, is always and solely employed in putting objects in motion ; the properties of matter, the laws of nature, do the rest. The skill and ingenuity of human beings are chiefly exercised in discovering movements, practicable by their powers, and capable of bringing about the effects which they desire. But, while movement is the only effect which man can immediately and directly produce by his muscles, it is not necessary that he should produce directly by them all the movements which he requires. The first and most obvious substitute is the muscular action of cattle : by degrees the powers of inanimate nature are made to aid in this too, as by making the wind, or water, things already in motion, communicate a part of their motion to the wheels, which before that invention were made to revolve by muscular force. This service is extorted from the powers of wind and water by a set of actions, consisting like the former in moving certain objects into certain positions in which they constitute what is termed a machine ; but the muscular action necessary for this is not constantly renewed but performed once for all, and there is on the whole a great economy of labour.

§ 3. Some writers have raised the question, whether nature gives more assistance to labour in one kind of industry or in another ; and have said that in some occupations labour does most, in others

* This essential and primary law of man's power over nature was, I believe, first illustrated and made prominent as a fundamental principle of Political Economy, in the first chapter of Mr. [James] Mill's *Elements*.

nature most. In this, however, there seems much confusion of
ideas. The part which nature has in any work of man, is indefinite
and incommensurable. It is impossible to decide that in any one
thing nature does more than in any other. One cannot even say
that labour does less. Less labour may be required ; but if that
which is required is absolutely indispensable, the result is just as
much the product of labour, as of nature. When two conditions
are equally necessary for producing the effect at all, it is unmeaning
to say that so much of it is produced by one and so much by the
other ; it is like attempting to decide which half of a pair of scissors
has most to do in the act of cutting ; or which of the factors, five
and six, contributes most to the production of thirty. The form
which this conceit usually assumes, is that of supposing that nature
lends more assistance to human endeavours in agriculture than in
manufactures. This notion, held by the French Economistes, and
from which Adam Smith was not free, arose from a misconception
of the nature of rent. The rent of land being a price paid for a
natural agency, and no such price being paid in manufactures, these
writers imagined that since a price was paid, it was because there
was a greater amount of service to be paid for : whereas a better
consideration of the subject would have shown that the reason
why the use of land bears a price is simply the limitation of its
quantity, and that if air, heat, electricity, chemical agencies, and the
other powers of nature employed by manufacturers, were sparingly supplied, and could, like land, be engrossed and appropriated,
a rent could be exacted for them also.

§ 4. This leads to a distinction which we shall find to be of
primary importance. Of natural powers, some are unlimited, others
limited in quantity. By an unlimited quantity is of course not meant
literally, but practically unlimited : a quantity beyond the use
which can in any, or at least in present circumstances, be made of it.
Land is, in some newly settled countries, practically unlimited in
quantity : there is more than can be used by the existing population
of the country, or by any accession likely to be made to it for generations to come. But even there, land favourably situated with
regard to markets or means of carriage is generally limited in
quantity : there is not so much of it as persons would gladly occupy
and cultivate, or otherwise turn to use. In all old countries, land
capable of cultivation, land at least of any tolerable fertility, must
be ranked among agents limited in quantity. Water, for ordinary

purposes, on the banks of rivers or lakes, may be regarded as of unlimited abundance; but if required for irrigation, it may even there be insufficient to supply all wants, while in places which depend for their consumption on cisterns or tanks, or on wells which are not copious, or are liable to fail, water takes its place among things the quantity of which is most strictly limited. Where water itself is plentiful, yet water-power, *i.e.* a fall of water applicable by its mechanical force to the service of industry, may be exceedingly limited, compared with the use which would be made of it if it were more abundant. Coal, metallic ores, and other useful substances found in the earth, are still more limited than land. They are not only strictly local but exhaustible; though, at a given place and time, they may exist in much greater abundance than would be applied to present use even if they could be obtained gratis. Fisheries, in the sea, are in most cases a gift of nature practically unlimited in amount; but the Arctic whale fisheries have long been insufficient for the demand which exists even at the very considerable price necessary to defray the cost of appropriation: and the immense extension which the Southern fisheries have in consequence assumed, is tending to exhaust them likewise. River fisheries are a natural resource of a very limited character, and would be rapidly exhausted, if allowed to be used by every one without restraint. Air, even that state of it which we term wind, may, in most situations, be obtained in a quantity sufficient for every possible use; and so likewise, on the sea coast or on large rivers, may water carriage: though the wharfage or harbour-room applicable to the service of that mode of transport is in many situations far short of what would be used if easily attainable.

It will be seen hereafter how much of the economy of society depends on the limited quantity in which some of the most important natural agents exist, and more particularly land. For the present I shall only remark, that so long as the quantity of a natural agent is practically unlimited, it cannot, unless susceptible of artificial monopoly, bear any value in the market, since no one will give anything for what can be obtained gratis. But as soon as a limitation becomes practically operative; as soon as there is not so much of the thing to be had, as would be appropriated and used if it could be obtained for asking; the ownership or use of the natural agent acquires an exchangeable value. When more water power is wanted in a particular district, than there are falls of water to supply it, persons will give an equivalent for the use of a fall of water. When there is more land wanted for cultivation than a place possesses, or than it possesses of a certain quality and certain advantages of situation, land of that quality and situation may be sold for a price, or let for an annual rent.　This subject will hereafter be discussed at length ; but it is often useful to anticipate, by a brief suggestion, principles and deductions which we have not yet reached the place for exhibiting and illustrating fully.

CHAPTER II

§ 1. THE labour which terminates in the production of an article fitted for some human use is either employed directly about the thing, or in previous operations destined to facilitate, perhaps essential to the possibility of, the subsequent ones. In making bread, for example, the labour employed about the thing itself is that of the baker; but the labour of the miller, though employed directly in the production not of bread but of flour, is equally part of the aggregate sum of labour by which the bread is produced; as is also the labour of the sower and of the reaper. Some may think that all these persons ought to be considered as employing their labour directly about the thing; the corn, the flour, and the bread being one substance in three different states. Without disputing about this question of mere language, there is still the ploughman, who prepared the ground for the seed, and whose labour never came in contact with the substance in any of its states; and the plough-maker, whose share in the result was still more remote. All these persons ultimately derive the remuneration of their labour from the bread, or its price : the plough-maker as much as the rest; for since ploughs are of no use except for tilling the soil, no one would make or use ploughs for any other reason than because the increased returns, thereby obtained from the ground, afforded a source from which an adequate equivalent could be assigned for the labour of the plough-maker. If the produce is to be used or consumed in the form of bread, it is from the bread that this equivalent must come. The bread must suffice to remunerate all these labourers, and several others; such as the carpenters and bricklayers who erected the farm-buildings; the hedgers and ditchers who made the fences necessary for the protection of the crop; the miners and smelters who extracted or prepared the iron of which the plough and other implements

were made.   These, however, and the plough-maker, do not depend
for their remuneration upon the bread made from the produce of
a single harvest, but upon that made from the produce of all the
harvests which are successively gathered until the plough, or the
buildings and fences, are worn out.   We must add yet another
kind of labour ; that of transporting the produce from the place
of its production to the place of its destined use : the labour of
carrying the corn to market, and from market to the miller's, the
flour from the miller's to the baker's, and the bread from the
baker's to the place of its final consumption.   This labour is
sometimes very considerable : flour is [1848] transported to England
from beyond the Atlantic, corn from the heart of Russia ; and in
addition to the labourers immediately employed, the waggoners
and sailors, there are also costly instruments, such as ships, in the
construction of which much labour has been expended : that labour,
however, not depending for its whole remuneration upon the bread,
but for a part only ; ships being usually, during the course of their
existence, employed in the transport of many different kinds of
commodities.

   To estimate, therefore, the labour of which any given commodity is the result is far from a simple operation.   The items
in the calculation are very numerous—as it may seem to some
persons, infinitely so ; for if, as a part of the labour employed in
making bread, we count the labour of the blacksmith who made
the plough, why not also (it may be asked) the labour of making
the tools used by the blacksmith, and the tools used in making
those tools, and so back to the origin of things ?   But after mounting
one or two steps in this ascending scale, we come into a region of
fractions too minute for calculation.   Suppose, for instance, that
the same plough will last, before being worn out, a dozen years.
Only one-twelfth of the labour of making the plough must be placed
to the account of each year's harvest.   A twelfth part of the labour
of making a plough is an appreciable quantity.   But the same
set of tools, perhaps, suffice to the plough-maker for forging a
hundred ploughs, which serve during the twelve years of their
existence to prepare the soil of as many different farms.   A twelve-
hundredth part of the labour of making his tools, is as much,
therefore, as has been expended in procuring one year's harvest
of a single farm : and when this fraction comes to be further apportioned among the various sacks of corn and loaves of bread, it is
seen at once that such quantities are not worth taking into the

account for any practical purpose connected with the commodity. It is true that, if the tool-maker had not laboured, the corn and bread never would have been produced; but they will not be sold a tenth part of a farthing dearer in consideration of his labour.

§ 2. Another of the modes in which labour is indirectly or remotely instrumental to the production of a thing requires particular notice : namely, when it is employed in producing subsistence to maintain the labourers while they are engaged in the production. This previous employment of labour is an indispensable condition to every productive operation, on any other than the very smallest scale. Except the labour of the hunter and fisher, there is scarcely any kind of labour to which the returns are immediate. Productive operations require to be continued a certain time, before their fruits are obtained. Unless the labourer, before commencing his work, possesses a store of food, or can obtain access to the stores of some one else, in sufficient quantity to maintain him until the production is completed, he can undertake no labour but such as can be carried on at odd intervals, concurrently with the pursuit of his subsistence. He cannot obtain food itself in any abundance ; for every mode of so obtaining it requires that there be already food in store. Agriculture only brings forth food after the lapse of months ; and though the labours of the agriculturist are not necessarily continuous during the whole period, they must occupy a considerable part of it. Not only is agriculture impossible without food produced in advance, but there must be a very great quantity in advance to enable any considerable community to support itself wholly by agriculture. A country like England or France is only able to carry on the agriculture of the present year, because that of past years has provided, in those countries or somewhere else, sufficient food to support their agricultural population until the next harvest. They are only enabled to produce so many other things besides food, because the food which was in store at the close of the last harvest suffices to maintain not only the agricultural labourers, but a large industrious population besides.

The labour employed in producing this stock of subsistence forms a great and important part of the past labour which has been necessary to enable present labour to be carried on. But there is a difference, requiring particular notice, between this and the other kinds of previous or preparatory labour. The miller, the reaper, the ploughman, the plough-maker, the waggoner and waggon-maker, even the sailor and ship-builder when employed, derive their remuneration from the ultimate product—the bread made from the corn on which they have severally operated, or supplied the instruments for operating. The labour that produced the food which fed all these labourers is as necessary to the ultimate result, the bread of the present harvest, as any of those other portions of labour ; but is not, like them, remunerated from it. That previous labour has received its remuneration from the previous food. In order to raise any product, there are needed labour, tools, and materials, and food to feed the labourers. But the tools and materials are of no use except for obtaining the product, or at least are to be applied to no other use, and the labour of their construction can be remunerated only from the product when obtained. The food, on the contrary, is intrinsically useful, and is applied to the direct use of feeding human beings. The labour expended in producing the food, and recompensed by it, needs not be remunerated over again from the produce of the subsequent labour which it has fed. If we suppose that the same body of labourers carried on a manufacture, and grew food to sustain themselves while doing it, they have had for their trouble the food and the manufactured article ; but if they also grew the material and made the tools, they have had nothing for that trouble but the manufactured article alone.

The claim to remuneration founded on the possession of food, available for the maintenance of labourers, is of another kind ; remuneration for abstinence, not for labour. If a person has a store of food, he has it in his power to consume it himself in idleness, or in feeding others to attend on him, or to fight for him, or to sing or dance for him. If, instead of these things, he gives it to productive labourers to support them during their work, he can, and naturally will, claim a remuneration from the produce. He will not be content with simple repayment ; if he receives merely that, he is only in the same situation as at first, and has derived no advantage from delaying to apply his savings to his own benefit or pleasure. He will look for some equivalent for this forbearance : he will expect his advance of food to come back to him with an increase, called in the language of business, a profit ; and the hope of this profit will generally have been a part of the inducement which made him accumulate a stock, by economizing in his own consumption ; or, at any rate, which made him forego the application of it, when accumulated, to his personal ease or satisfaction.

The food also which maintained other workmen while producing
the tools or materials must have been provided in advance by some
one, and he, too, must have his profit from the ultimate product;
but there is this difference, that here the ultimate product has
to supply not only the profit, but also the remuneration of the labour.
The tool-maker (say, for instance, the plough-maker) does not
indeed usually wait for his payment until the harvest is reaped;
the farmer advances it to him, and steps into his place by becoming
the owner of the plough.   Nevertheless, it is from the harvest that
the payment is to come; since the farmer would not undertake
this outlay unless he expected that the harvest would repay him,
and with a profit too on this fresh advance; that is, unless the
harvest would yield, besides the remuneration of the farm labourers
(and a profit for advancing it), a sufficient residue to remunerate
the plough-maker's labourers, give the plough-maker a profit,
and a profit to the farmer on both.

§ 3.   From these considerations it appears, that in an enumeration and classification of the kinds of industry which are intended
for the indirect or remote furtherance of other productive labour,
we need not include the labour of producing subsistence or other
necessaries of life to be consumed by productive labourers; for the
main end and purpose of this labour is the subsistence itself; and
though the possession of a store of it enables other work to be done,
this is but an incidental consequence.   The remaining modes in
which labour is indirectly instrumental to production may be
arranged under five heads.

First: Labour employed in producing materials, on which
industry is to be afterwards employed.   This is, in many cases,
a labour of mere appropriation; *extractive* industry, as it has
been aptly named by M. Dunoyer.   The labour of the miner,
for example, consists of operations for digging out of the earth
substances convertible by industry into various articles fitted
for human use.   Extractive industry, however, is not confined
to the extraction of materials.   Coal, for instance, is employed,
not only in the process of industry, but in directly warming human
beings.   When so used, it is not a material of production, but is
itself the ultimate product.   So, also, in the case of a mine of precious
stones.   These are to some small extent employed in the productive
arts, as diamonds by the glass-cutter, emery and corundum for
polishing, but their principal destination, that of ornament, is a

direct use ; though they commonly require, before being so used, some process of manufacture, which may perhaps warrant our regarding them as materials.   Metallic ores of all sorts are materials merely.

Under the head, production of materials, we must include the industry of the wood-cutter, when employed in cutting and preparing timber for building, or wood for the purposes of the carpenter's or any other art. In the forests of America, Norway, Germany, the Pyrenees and Alps, this sort of labour is largely employed on trees of spontaneous growth. In other cases, we must add to the labour of the wood-cutter that of the planter and cultivator.

Under the same head are also comprised the labours of the agriculturist in growing flax, hemp, cotton, feeding silkworms, raising food for cattle, producing bark, dye-stuffs, some oleaginous plants, and many other things only useful because required in other departments of industry. So, too, the labour of the hunter, as far as his object is furs or feathers ; of the shepherd and the cattle-breeder, in respect of wool, hides, horn, bristles, horse-hair, and the like.   The things used as materials in some process or other of manufacture are of a most miscellaneous character, drawn from almost every quarter of the animal, vegetable, and mineral kingdoms. And besides this, the finished products of many branches of industry are the materials of others. The thread produced by the spinner is applied to hardly any use except as material for the weaver. Even the product of the loom is chiefly used as material for the fabricators of articles of dress or furniture, or of further instruments of productive industry, as in the case of the sail-maker. The currier and tanner find their whole occupation in converting raw material into what may be termed prepared material. In strictness of speech, almost all food, as it comes from the hands of the agri-culturist, is nothing more than material for the occupation of the baker or the cook.

§ 4.   The second kind of indirect labour is that employed in making tools or implements for the assistance of labour. I use these terms in their most comprehensive sense, embracing all permanent instruments or helps to production, from a flint and steel for striking a light, to a steam-ship, or the most complex apparatus of manufacturing machinery. There may be some hesitation where to draw the line between implements and materials ;

and some things used in production (such as fuel) would scarcely in common language be called by either name, popular phraseology being shaped out by a different class of necessities from those of scientific exposition. To avoid a multiplication of classes and denominations answering to distinctions of no scientific importance, political economists generally include all things which are used as *immediate* means of production (the means which are not immediate will be considered presently) either in the class of implements or in that of materials. Perhaps the line is most usually and most conveniently drawn, by considering as a material every instrument of production which can only be used once, being destroyed (at least as an instrument for the purpose in hand) by a single employment. Thus fuel, once burnt, cannot be again used as fuel; what can be so used is only any portion which has remained unburnt the first time. And not only it cannot be used without being consumed, but it is only useful by being consumed; for if no part of the fuel were destroyed, no heat would be generated. A fleece, again, is destroyed as a fleece by being spun into thread; and the thread cannot be used as thread when woven into cloth. But an axe is not destroyed as an axe by cutting down a tree: it may be used afterwards to cut down a hundred or a thousand more; and though deteriorated in some small degree by each use, it does not do its work by being deteriorated, as the coal and the fleece do theirs by being destroyed; on the contrary, it is the better instrument the better it resists deterioration. There are some things, rightly classed as materials, which may be used as such a second and a third time, but not while the product to which they at first contributed remains in existence. The iron which formed a tank or a set of pipes may be melted to form a plough or a steam-engine; the stones with which a house was built may be used after it is pulled down, to build another. But this cannot be done while the original product subsists; their function as materials is suspended, until the exhaustion of the first use. Not so with the things classed as implements; they may be used repeatedly for fresh work, until the time, sometimes very distant, at which they are worn out, while the work already done by them may subsist unimpaired, and when it perishes, does so by its own laws, or by casualties of its own.*

* The able and friendly reviewer of this treatise in the Edinburgh Review (October 1848) conceives the distinction between materials and implements rather differently: proposing to consider as materials "all the things which, after having undergone the change implied in production, are themselves

The only practical difference of much importance arising from the distinction between materials and implements is one which has attracted our attention in another case. Since materials are destroyed as such by being once used, the whole of the labour required for their production, as well as the abstinence of the person who supplied the means for carrying it on, must be remunerated from the fruits of that single use. Implements, on the contrary, being susceptible of repeated employment, the whole of the products which they are instrumental in bringing into existence are a fund which can be drawn upon to remunerate the labour of their construction, and the abstinence of those by whose accumulations that labour was supported. It is enough if each product contributes a fraction, commonly an insignificant one, towards the remuneration of that labour and abstinence, or towards indemnifying the immediate producer for advancing that remuneration to the person who produced the tools.

§ 5. Thirdly : Besides materials for industry to employ itself on, and implements to aid it, provision must be made to prevent its operations from being disturbed, and its products injured, either by the destroying agencies of nature, or by the violence or rapacity of men. This gives rise to another mode in which labour, not employed directly about the product itself, is instrumental to its production ; namely, when employed for the *protection* of industry. Such is the object of all buildings for industrial purposes ; all manufactories, warehouses, docks, granaries, barns, farm-buildings devoted to cattle, or to the operations of agricultural labour. I exclude those in which the labourers live, or which are destined for their personal accommodation : these, like their food, supply actual wants, and must be counted in the remuneration of their labour. There are many modes in which labour is still more directly applied to the protection of productive operations. The herdsman has little other occupation than to protect the cattle from harm : the positive agencies concerned in the realization of the product go on nearly of themselves. I have already mentioned the labour

matter of exchange," and as implements (or instruments) " the things which are employed in producing that change, but do not themselves become part of the exchangeable result." According to these definitions, the fuel consumed in a manufactory would be considered, not as a material, but as an instrument. This use of the terms accords better than that proposed in the text with the primitive physical meaning of the word " material " ; but the distinction on which it is grounded is one almost irrelevant to political economy.

of the hedger and ditcher, of the builder of walls or dykes. To these must be added that of the soldier, the policeman, and the judge. These functionaries are not indeed employed exclusively in the protection of industry, nor does their payment constitute, to the individual producer, a part of the expenses of production. But they are paid from the taxes, which are derived from the produce of industry ; and in any tolerably governed country they render to its operations a service far more than equivalent to the cost. To society at large they are therefore part of the expenses of production ; and if the returns to production were not sufficient to maintain these labourers in addition to all the others required, production, at least in that form and manner, could not take place. Besides, if the protection which the government affords to the operations of industry were not afforded, the producers would be under a necessity of either withdrawing a large share of their time and labour from production, to employ it in defence, or of engaging armed men to defend them ; all which labour, in that case, must be directly remunerated from the produce ; and things which could not pay for this additional labour, would not be produced. Under the present arrangements, the product pays its quota towards the same protection, and, notwithstanding the waste and prodigality incident to government expenditure, obtains it of better quality at a much smaller cost.

§ 6. Fourthly : There is a very great amount of labour employed, not in bringing the product into existence, but in rendering it, when in existence, accessible to those for whose use it is intended. Many important classes of labourers find their sole employment in some function of this kind. There is first the whole class of carriers, by land or water : muleteers, waggoners, bargemen, sailors, wharfmen, coalheavers, porters, railway establishments, and the like. Next, there are the constructors of all the implements of transport ; ships, barges, carts, locomotives, &c., to which must be added roads, canals, and railways. Roads are sometimes made by the government, and opened gratuitously to the public ; but the labour of making them is not the less paid for from the produce. Each producer, in paying his quota of the taxes levied generally for the construction of roads, pays for the use of those which conduce to his convenience ; and if made with any tolerable judgment, they increase the returns to his industry by far more than an equivalent amount.

Another numerous class of labourers employed in rendering the things produced accessible to their intended consumers is the class of dealers and traders, or, as they may be termed, distributors. There would be a great waste of time and trouble, and an inconvenience often amounting to impracticability, if consumers could only obtain the articles they want by treating directly with the producers. Both producers and consumers are too much scattered, and the latter often at too great a distance from the former. To diminish this loss of time and labour, the contrivance of fairs and markets was early had recourse to, where consumers and producers might periodically meet, without any intermediate agency; and this plan answers tolerably well for many articles, especially agricultural produce, agriculturists having at some seasons a certain quantity of spare time on their hands. But even in this case, attendance is often very troublesome and inconvenient to buyers who have other occupations, and do not live in the immediate vicinity; while, for all articles the production of which requires continuous attention from the producers, these periodical markets must be held at such considerable intervals, and the wants of the consumers must either be provided for so long beforehand, or must remain so long unsupplied, that even before the resources of society admitted of the establishment of shops, the supply of these wants fell universally into the hands of itinerant dealers; the pedlar, who might appear once a month, being preferred to the fair, which only returned once or twice a year. In country districts, remote from towns or large villages, the industry of the pedlar is not yet wholly superseded. But a dealer who has a fixed abode and fixed customers is so much more to be depended on, that consumers prefer resorting to him if he is conveniently accessible; and dealers therefore find their advantage in establishing themselves in every locality where there are sufficient consumers near at hand to afford them a remuneration.

In many cases the producers and dealers are the same persons, at least as to the ownership of the funds and the control of the operations. The tailor, the shoemaker, the baker, and many other tradesmen, are the producers of the articles they deal in, so far as regards the last stage in the production. This union, however, of the functions of manufacturer and retailer is only expedient when the article can advantageously be made at or near the place convenient for retailing it, and is, besides, manufactured and sold in small parcels. When things have to be brought from a distance, the same

person cannot effectually superintend both the making and the
retailing of them ; when they are best and most cheaply made on a
large scale, a single manufactory requires so many local channels
to carry off its supply, that the retailing is most conveniently
delegated to other agency ; and even shoes and coats, when they are
to be furnished in large quantities at once, as for the supply of a regiment or of a workhouse, are usually obtained not directly from the
producers, but from intermediate dealers, who make it their business
to ascertain from what producers they can be obtained best and
cheapest.   Even when things are destined to be at last sold by retail,
convenience soon creates a class of wholesale dealers.   When products and transactions have multiplied beyond a certain point ;
when one manufactory supplies many shops, and one shop has often
to obtain goods from many different manufactories, the loss of time
and trouble both to the manufacturers and to the retailers by treating
directly with one another makes it more convenient to them to treat
with a smaller number of great dealers or merchants, who only buy
to sell again, collecting goods from the various producers and
distributing them to the retailers, to be by them further distributed
among the consumers.   Of these various elements is composed the
Distributing Class, whose agency is supplementary to that of the
Producing Class : and the produce so distributed, or its price, is
the source from which the distributors are remunerated for their
exertions, and for the abstinence which enabled them to advance
the funds needful for the business of distribution.

§ 7.   We have now completed the enumeration of the modes
in which labour employed on external nature is subservient to
production.   But there is yet another mode of employing labour,
which conduces equally, though still more remotely, to that end :
this is, labour of which the subject is human beings.   Every human
being has been brought up from infancy at the expense of much
labour to some person or persons, and if this labour, or part of it,
had not been bestowed, the child would never have attained the age
and strength which enabled him to become a labourer in his turn.
To the community at large, the labour and expense of rearing its
infant population form a part of the outlay which is a condition of
production, and which is to be replaced with increase from the
future produce of their labour.   By the individuals, this labour and
expense are usually incurred from other motives than to obtain such
ultimate return, and, for most purposes of political economy, need

not be taken into account as expenses of production. But the technical or industrial education of the community ; the labour employed in learning and in teaching the arts of production, in acquiring and communicating skill in those arts ; this labour is really, and in general solely, undergone for the sake of the greater or more valuable produce thereby attained, and in order that a remuneration, equivalent or more than equivalent, may be reaped by the learner, besides an adequate remuneration for the labour of the teacher, when a teacher has been employed.

As the labour which confers productive powers, whether of hand or of head, may be looked upon as part of the labour by which society accomplishes its productive operations, or in other words, as part of what the produce costs to society, so too may the labour employed in keeping up productive powers ; in preventing them from being destroyed or weakened by accident or disease. The labour of a physician or surgeon, when made use of by persons engaged in industry, must be regarded in the economy of society as a sacrifice incurred, to preserve from perishing by death or infirmity that portion of the productive resources of society which is fixed in the lives and bodily or mental powers of its productive members. To the individuals, indeed, this forms but a part, sometimes an imperceptible part, of the motives that induce them to submit to medical treatment : it is not principally from economical motives that persons have a limb amputated, or endeavour to be cured of a fever ; though, when they do so, there is generally sufficient inducement for it even on that score alone. This is, therefore, one of the cases of labour and outlay which, though conducive to production, yet not being incurred for that end, or for the sake of the returns arising from it, are out of the sphere of most of the general propositions which political economy has occasion to assert respecting productive labour : though, when society and not the individuals are considered, this labour and outlay must be regarded as part of the advance by which society effects its productive operations, and for which it is indemnified by the produce.

§ 8. Another kind of labour, usually classed as mental, but conducing to the ultimate product as directly, though not so immediately, as manual labour itself, is the labour of the inventors of industrial processes. I say, usually classed as mental, because in reality it is not exclusively so. All human exertion is compounded of some mental and some bodily elements. The stupidest hodman, who repeats from day to day the mechanical act of climbing a ladder, performs a function partly intellectual ; so much so, indeed, that the most intelligent dog or elephant could not, probably, be taught to do it.   The dullest human being, instructed beforehand, is capable of turning a mill ; but a horse cannot turn it without somebody to drive and watch him.   On the other hand, there is some bodily ingredient in the labour most purely mental, when it generates any, external result.   Newton could not have produced the Principia without the bodily exertion either of penmanship or of dictation ; and he must have drawn many diagrams, and written out many calculations and demonstrations, while he was preparing it in his mind.   Inventors, besides the labour of their brains, generally go through much labour with their hands, in the models which they construct and the experiments they have to make before their idea can realize itself successfully in act.   Whether mental, however, or bodily, their labour is a part of that by which the production is brought about.   The labour of Watt in contriving the steam-engine was as essential a part of production as that of the mechanics who build or the engineers who work the instrument ; and was undergone, no less than theirs, in the prospect of a remuneration from the produce.   The labour of invention is often estimated and paid on the very same plan as that of execution.   Many manufacturers of ornamental goods have inventors in their employment, who receive wages or salaries for designing patterns, exactly as others do for copying them.   All this is strictly part of the labour of production ; as the labour of the author of a book is equally a part of its production with that of the printer and binder.

In a national, or universal point of view, the labour of the savant, or speculative thinker, is as much a part of production in the very narrowest sense, as that of the inventor of a practical art ; many such inventions having been the direct consequences of theoretic discoveries, and every extension of knowledge of the powers of nature being fruitful of applications to the purposes of outward life.   The electro-magnetic telegraph was the wonderful and most unexpected consequence of the experiments of Œrsted and the mathematical investigations of Ampère : and the modern art of navigation is an unforeseen emanation from the purely speculative and apparently merely curious enquiry, by the mathematicians of Alexandria, into the properties of three curves formed by the intersection of a plane surface and a cone.   No limit can be set to the importance, even in a purely productive and material

point of view, of mere thought. Inasmuch, however, as these
material fruits, though the result, are seldom the direct purpose
of the pursuits of savants, nor is their remuneration in general derived
from the increased production which may be caused incidentally, and
mostly after a long interval, by their discoveries ; this ultimate
influence does not, for most of the purposes of political economy,
require to be taken into consideration ; and speculative thinkers
are generally classed as the producers only of the books, or other
useable or saleable articles, which directly emanate from them.
But when (as in political economy one should always be prepared
to do) we shift our point of view, and consider not individual acts,
and the motives by which they are determined, but national and
universal results, intellectual speculation must be looked upon as
a most influential part of the productive labour of society, and the
portion of its resources employed in carrying on and in remunerating
such labour as a highly productive part of its expenditure.

§ 9.   In the foregoing survey of the modes of employing labour
in furtherance of production, I have made little use of the popular
distinction of industry into agricultural, manufacturing, and commercial.   For, in truth, this division fulfils very badly the purposes
of a classification.   Many great branches of productive industry
find no place in it, or not without much straining ; for example
(not to speak of hunters or fishers) the miner, the road-maker, and
the sailor.   The limit, too, between agricultural and manufacturing
industry cannot be precisely drawn.   The miller, for instance,
and the baker—are they to be reckoned among agriculturists, or
among manufacturers ?   Their occupation is in its nature manufacturing ; the food has finally parted company with the soil before
it is handed over to them ; this, however, might be said with equal
truth of the thresher, the winnower, the makers of butter and
cheese ; operations always counted as agricultural, probably because
it is the custom for them to be performed by persons resident
on the farm, and under the same superintendence as tillage.   For
many purposes all these persons, the miller and baker inclusive,
must be placed in the same class with ploughmen and reapers.
They are all concerned in producing food, and depend for their
remuneration on the food produced ; when the one class abounds
and flourishes, the others do so too ; they form collectively the
" agricultural interest " ; they render but one service to the
community by their united labours, and are paid from one

common source. Even the tillers of the soil, again, when the produce is not food, but the materials of what are commonly termed manufactures, belong in many respects to the same division in the economy of society as manufacturers. The cotton-planter of Carolina and the wool-grower of Australia have more interests in common with the spinner and weaver than with the corn-grower. But, on the other hand, the industry which operates immediately upon the soil has, as we shall see hereafter, some properties on which many important consequences depend, and which distinguish it from all the subsequent stages of production, whether carried on by the same person or not; from the industry of the thresher and winnower, as much as from that of the cotton-spinner. When I speak, therefore, of agricultural labour, I shall generally mean this, and this exclusively, unless the contrary is either stated or implied in the context. The term manufacturing is too vague to be of much use when precision is required, and when I employ it, I wish to be understood as intending to speak popularly rather than scientifically.

CHAPTER III

§ 1. LABOUR is indispensable to production, but has not always production for its effect. There is much labour, and of a high order of usefulness, of which production is not the object. Labour has accordingly been distinguished into Productive and Unproductive. There has been not a little controversy among political economists on the question, what kinds of labour should be reputed to be unproductive ; and they have not always perceived, that there was in reality no matter of fact in dispute between them.

Many writers have been unwilling to class any labour as productive, unless its result is palpable in some material object, capable of being transferred from one person to another. There are others (among whom are Mr. M'Culloch and M. Say) who, looking upon the word unproductive as a term of disparagement, remonstrate against imposing it upon any labour which is regarded as useful —which produces a benefit or a pleasure worth the cost. The labour of officers of government, of the army and navy, of physicians, lawyers, teachers, musicians, dancers, actors, domestic servants, &c., when they really accomplish what they are paid for, and are not more numerous than is required for its performance, ought not, say these writers, to be " stigmatized " as unproductive, an expression which they appear to regard as synonymous with wasteful or worthless. But this seems to be a misunderstanding of the matter in dispute. Production not being the sole end of human existence, the term unproductive does not necessarily imply any stigma ; nor was ever intended to do so in the present case. The question is one of mere language and classification. Differences of language, however, are by no means unimportant, even when not grounded on differences of opinion ; for though either of two expressions may be consistent with the whole truth, they generally tend to fix attention upon different parts of it. We must therefore enter a little into the consideration of the various meanings which may attach to the words productive and un-productive when applied to labour.

In the first place, even in what is called the production of material objects, it must be remembered that what is produced is not the matter composing them. All the labour of all the human beings in the world could not produce one particle of matter. To weave broadcloth is but to re-arrange, in a peculiar manner, the particles of wool ; to grow corn is only to put a portion of matter called a seed, into a situation where it can draw together particles of matter from the earth and air, to form the new combination called a plant. Though we cannot create matter, we can cause it to assume pro-perties, by which, from having been useless to us, it becomes useful. What we produce, or desire to produce, is always, as M. Say rightly terms it, an utility. Labour is not creative of objects, but of utilities. Neither, again, do we consume and destroy the objects themselves ; the matter of which they were composed remains, more or less altered in form : what has really been consumed is only the qualities by which they were fitted for the purpose they have been applied to. It is, therefore, pertinently asked by M. Say and others—since, when we are said to produce objects, we only produce utility, why should not all labour which produces utility be accounted productive ? Why refuse that title to the surgeon who sets a limb, the judge or legislator who confers security, and give it to the lapidary who cuts and polishes a diamond ? Why deny it to the teacher from whom I learn an art by which I can gain my bread, and accord it to the confectioner who makes bonbons for the momentary pleasure of a sense of taste ?

It is quite true that all these kinds of labour are productive of utility ; and the question which now occupies us could not have been a question at all, if the production of utility were enough to satisfy the notion which mankind have usually formed of pro-ductive labour. Production, and productive, are of course elliptical expressions, involving the idea of a something produced ; but this something, in common apprehension, I conceive to be, not utility, but Wealth. Productive labour means labour productive of wealth. We are recalled, therefore, to the question touched upon in our first chapter, what Wealth is, and whether only material pro-ducts, or all useful products, are to be included in it.

§ 2. Now the utilities produced by labour are of three kinds. They are,

First, utilities fixed and embodied in outward objects; by labour employed in investing external material things with properties which render them serviceable to human beings. This is the common case, and requires no illustration.

Secondly, utilities fixed and embodied in human beings; the labour being in this case employed in conferring on human beings qualities which render them serviceable to themselves and others. To this class belongs the labour of all concerned in education; not only schoolmasters, tutors, and professors, but governments, so far as they aim successfully at the improvement of the people; moralists, and clergymen, as far as productive of benefit; the labour of physicians, as far as instrumental in preserving life and physical or mental efficiency; of the teachers of bodily exercises, and of the various trades, sciences, and arts, together with the labour of the learners in acquiring them; and all labour bestowed by any persons, throughout life, in improving the knowledge or cultivating the bodily or mental faculties of themselves or others.

Thirdly and lastly, utilities not fixed or embodied in any object, but consisting in a mere service rendered; a pleasure given, an inconvenience or a pain averted, during a longer or a shorter time, but without leaving a permanent acquisition in the improved qualities of any person or thing; the labour being employed in producing an utility directly, not (as in the two former cases) in fitting some other thing to afford an utility. Such, for example, is the labour of the musical performer, the actor, the public declaimer or reciter, and the showman. Some good may no doubt be produced, and much more might be produced, beyond the moment, upon the feelings and disposition, or general state of enjoyment of the spectators; or instead of good there may be harm; but neither the one nor the other is the effect intended, is the result for which the exhibitor works and the spectator pays; nothing but the immediate pleasure. Such, again, is the labour of the army and navy; they, at the best, prevent a country from being conquered, or from being injured or insulted, which is a service, but in all other respects leave the country neither improved nor deteriorated. Such, too, is the labour of the legislator, the judge, the officer of justice, and all other agents of government, in their ordinary functions, apart from any influence they may exert on the improvement of the national mind. The service which they render is to maintain peace and security; these compose the utility which they produce. It may appear to some, that carriers, and merchants or dealers, should be placed in this same class, since their labour does not add any properties to objects : but I reply that it does : it adds the property of being in the place where they are wanted, instead of being in some other place : which is a very useful property, and the utility it confers is embodied in the things themselves, which now actually are in the place where they are required for use, and in consequence of that increased utility could be sold at an increased price, proportioned to the labour expended in conferring it. This labour, therefore, does not belong to the third class, but to the first.

§ 3. We have now to consider which of these three classes of labour should be accounted productive of wealth, since that is what the term productive, when used by itself, must be understood to import. Utilities of the third class, consisting in pleasures which only exist while being enjoyed, and services which only exist while being performed, cannot be spoken of as wealth, except by an acknowledged metaphor. It is essential to the idea of wealth to be susceptible of accumulation : things which cannot, after being produced, be kept for some time before being used, are never, I think, regarded as wealth, since however much of them may be produced and enjoyed, the person benefited by them is no richer, is nowise improved in circumstances. But there is not so distinct and positive a violation of usage in considering as wealth any product which is both useful and susceptible of accumulation. The skill, and the energy and perseverance, of the artisans of a country, are reckoned part of its wealth, no less than their tools and machinery.*

* Some authorities look upon it as an essential element in the idea of wealth, that it should be capable not solely of being accumulated but of being transferred ; and inasmuch as the valuable qualities, and even the productive capacities, of a human being, cannot be detached from him and passed to some one else, they deny to these the appellation of wealth, and to the labour expended in acquiring them the name of productive labour. It seems to me, however, that the skill of an artisan (for instance) being both a desirable possession, and one of a certain durability (not to say productive even of national wealth), there is no better reason for refusing to it the title of wealth because it is attached to a man, than to a coalpit or manufactory because they are attached to a place. Besides, if the skill itself cannot be parted with to a purchaser, the use of it may ; if it cannot be sold, it can be hired ; and it may be, and is, sold outright in all countries whose laws permit that the man himself should be sold along with it. Its defect of transferability does not result from a natural but from a legal and moral obstacle.

The human being himself (as formerly observed) I do not class as wealth. He is the purpose for which wealth exists. But his acquired capacities, which exist only as means, and have been called into existence by labour, fall rightly, as it seems to me, within that designation.

According to this definition, we should regard all labour as **pro-ductive** which is employed in creating permanent utilities, whether embodied in human beings, or in any other animate or inanimate objects. This nomenclature I have, in a former publication,* recommended, as most conducive to the ends of classification ; and I am still of that opinion.

But in applying the term wealth to the industrial capacities of human beings, **there** seems always, in popular apprehension, to be a tacit reference **to material** products. The skill of an artisan is accounted wealth, **only as** being the means of acquiring wealth in a material sense ; and any qualities not tending visibly to that object are scarcely so regarded at all. A country would hardly be said to be richer, except by a metaphor, however precious a possession it might have in the genius, the virtues, or the accomplishments of its inhabitants ; unless indeed these were looked upon as market-able articles, by which it could attract the material wealth of other countries, as the Greeks of old, and several modern nations have done. While, therefore, I should prefer, were I constructing a new technical language, to make the distinction turn upon the permanence rather than upon the materiality of the product, yet when employing terms which common usage has taken complete possession of, it seems advisable so to employ them as to do the least possible violence to usage ; since any improvement in terminology obtained by straining the received meaning of a popular phrase is generally purchased beyond its value, by the obscurity arising from the conflict between new and old associations.

I shall, therefore, in this treatise, when speaking of wealth, understand by it only what is called material wealth, and by productive labour only those kinds of exertion which produce utilities embodied in material objects. But in limiting myself to this sense of the word, I mean to avail myself of the full extent of that restricted acceptation, and I shall not refuse the appellation productive, to labour which yields no material product as its direct result, provided that an increase of material products is its ultimate consequence. Thus, labour expended in the acquisition of manufacturing skill, I class as productive, not in virtue of the skill itself, but of the manu-factured products created by the skill, and to the creation of which the labour of learning the trade is essentially conducive. The labour of officers of government in affording the protection which,

---

* *Essays on some Unsettled Questions of Political Economy.* Essay III. On the words Productive and Unproductive.

afforded in some manner or other, is indispensable to the prosperity of industry, must be classed as productive even of material wealth, because without it, material wealth, in anything like its present abundance, could not exist. Such labour may be said to be productive indirectly or mediately, in opposition to the labour of the ploughman and the cotton-spinner, which are productive immediately. They are all alike in this, that they leave the community richer in material products than they found it; they increase, or tend to increase, material wealth.

§ 4. By Unproductive Labour, on the contrary, will be understood labour which does not terminate in the creation of material wealth; which, however largely or successfully practised, does not render the community, and the world at large, richer in material products, but poorer by all that is consumed by the labourers while so employed.

All labour is, in the language of political economy, unproductive, which ends in immediate enjoyment, without any increase of the accumulated stock of permanent means of enjoyment. And all labour, according to our present definition, must be classed as unproductive, which terminates in a permanent benefit, however important, provided that an increase of material products forms no part of that benefit. The labour of saving a friend's life is not productive, unless the friend is a productive labourer, and produces more than he consumes. To a religious person the saving of a soul must appear a far more important service than the saving of a life; but he will not therefore call a missionary or a clergyman productive labourers, unless they teach, as the South Sea Missionaries have in some cases done, the arts of civilization in addition to the doctrines of their religion. It is, on the contrary, evident that the greater number of missionaries or clergymen a nation maintains, the less it has to expend on other things; while the more it expends judiciously in keeping agriculturists and manufacturers at work, the more it will have for every other purpose. By the former it diminishes, *cæteris paribus*, its stock of material products; by the latter, it increases them.

Unproductive may be as useful as productive labour; it may be more useful, even in point of permanent advantage; or its use may consist only in pleasurable sensation, which when gone leaves no trace; or it may not afford even this, but may be absolute waste. In any case society or mankind grow no richer by it, but poorer. **All** material products consumed by any one while he produces nothing are so much subtracted, for the time, from the material products which society would otherwise have possessed. But though society grows no richer by unproductive labour, the individual may. An unproductive labourer may receive for his labour, from those who derive pleasure or benefit from it, a remuneration which may be to him a considerable source of wealth; but his gain is balanced by their loss; they may have received a full equivalent for their expenditure, but they are so much poorer by it. When a tailor makes a coat and sells it, there is a transfer of the price from the customer to the tailor, and a coat besides which did not previously exist; but what is gained by an actor is a mere transfer from the spectator's funds to his, leaving no article of wealth for the spectator's indemnification. Thus the community collectively gains nothing by the actor's labour; and it loses, of his receipts, all that portion which he consumes, retaining only that which he lays by. A community, however, may add to its wealth by unproductive labour, at the expense of other communities, as an individual may at the expense of other individuals. The gains of Italian opera singers, German governesses, French ballet dancers, &c., are a source of wealth, as far as they go, to their respective countries, if they return thither. The petty states of Greece, especially the ruder and more backward of those states, were nurseries of soldiers, who hired themselves to the princes and satraps of the East to carry on useless and destructive wars, and returned with their savings to pass their declining years in their own country : these were unproductive labourers, and the pay they received, together with the plunder they took, was an outlay without return to the countries which furnished it; but, though no gain to the world, it was a gain to Greece. At a later period the same country and its colonies supplied the Roman empire with another class of adventurers, who, under the name of philosophers or of rhetoricians, taught to the youth of the higher classes what were esteemed the most valuable accomplishments : these were mainly unproductive labourers, but their ample recompense was a source of wealth to their own country. In none of these cases was there any accession of wealth to the world. The services of the labourers, if useful, were obtained at a sacrifice to the world of a portion of material wealth; if useless, all that these labourers consumed was to the world waste.

. To be wasted, however, is a liability not confined to unproductive labour. Productive labour may equally be wasted, if more of it is expended than really conduces to production. If defect of skill in labourers, or of judgment in those who direct them, causes a mis-application of productive industry ; if a farmer persists in ploughing with three horses and two men, when experience has shown that two horses and one man are sufficient, the surplus labour, though em-ployed for purposes of production, is wasted. If a new process is adopted which proves no better, or not so good as those before in use, the labour expended in perfecting the invention and in carrying it into practice, though employed for a productive purpose, is wasted. Productive labour may render a nation poorer, if the wealth it pro-duces, that is, the increase it makes in the stock of useful or agreeable things, be of a kind not immediately wanted ; as when a commodity is unsaleable, because produced in a quantity beyond the present demand ; or when speculators build docks and warehouses before there is any trade. Some of the States of North America,[1] by making premature railways and canals, are thought to have made this kind of mistake ; and it was for some time doubtful whether Eng-land, in the disproportionate development of railway enterprise, had not, in some degree, followed the example. Labour sunk in expectation of a distant return, when the great exigencies or limited resources of the community require that the return be rapid, may leave the country not only poorer in the meanwhile, by all which those labourers consume, but less rich even ultimately than if immediate returns had been sought in the first instance, and enter-prises for distant profit postponed.

§ 5. The distinction of Productive and Unproductive is ap-plicable to consumption as well as to labour. All the members of the community are not labourers, but all are consumers, and consume either unproductively or productively. Whoever con-tributes nothing directly or indirectly to production, is an unpro-ductive consumer. The only productive consumers are productive labourers ; the labour of direction being of course included, as well as that of execution. But the consumption even of productive labourers is not all of it productive consumption. There is unpro-ductive consumption by productive consumers. What they consume in keeping up or improving their health, strength, and capacities of work, or in rearing other productive labourers to succeed

---

[1] [" The bankrupt states of North America " in all editions until the 7th (1871). "It remains to be shown whether England," &c., remained two lines below until the 5th ed. (1862).]

them, is productive consumption. But consumption on pleasures or luxuries, whether by the idle or by the industrious, since production is neither its object nor is any way advanced by it, must be reckoned unproductive : with a reservation perhaps of a certain quantum of enjoyment which may be classed among necessaries, since anything short of it would not be consistent with the greatest efficiency of labour. That alone is productive consumption, which goes to maintain and increase the productive powers of the community ; either those residing in its soil, in its materials, in the number and efficiency of its instruments of production, or in its people.

There are numerous products which may be said not to admit of being consumed otherwise than unproductively. The annual consumption of gold lace, pine apples, or champagne, must be reckoned unproductive, since these things give no assistance to production, nor any support to life or strength, but what would equally be given by things much less costly. Hence it might be supposed that the labour employed in producing them ought not to be regarded as productive, in the sense in which the term is understood by political economists. I grant that no labour tends to the permanent enrichment of society, which is employed in producing things for the use of unproductive consumers. The tailor who makes a coat for a man who produces nothing, is a productive labourer ; but in a few weeks or months the coat is worn out, while the wearer has not produced anything to replace it, and the community is then no richer by the labour of the tailor, than if the same sum had been paid for a stall at the opera. Nevertheless, society has been richer by the labour while the coat lasted, that is, until society, through one of its unproductive members, chose to consume the produce of the labour unproductively. The case of the gold lace or the pine apple is no further different, than that they are still further removed than the coat from the character of necessaries. These things also are wealth until they have been consumed.

§ 6. We see, however, by this, that there is a distinction, more important to the wealth of a community than even that between productive and unproductive labour; the distinction, namely, between labour for the supply of productive, and for the supply of unproductive, consumption ; between labour employed in keeping up or in adding to the productive resources of the country, and that which is employed otherwise. Of the produce of the country, a part only is destined to be consumed productively ; the remainder supplies the unproductive consumption of producers, and the entire consumption of the unproductive classes. Suppose that the proportion of the annual produce applied to the first purpose amounts to half; then one-half the productive labourers of the country are all that are employed in the operations on which the permanent wealth of the country depends. The other half are occupied from year to year and from generation to generation in producing things which are consumed and disappear without return; and whatever this half consume is as completely lost, as to any permanent effect on the national resources, as if it were consumed unproductively. Suppose that this second half of the labouring population ceased to work, and that the government or their parishes maintained them in idleness for a whole year : the first half would suffice to produce, as they had done before, their own necessaries and the necessaries of the second half, and to keep the stock of materials and implements undiminished : the unproductive classes, indeed, would be either starved or obliged to produce their own subsistence, and the whole community would be reduced during a year to bare necessaries ; but the sources of production would be unimpaired, and the next year there would not necessarily be a smaller produce than if no such interval of inactivity had occurred ; while if the case had been reversed, if the first half of the labourers had suspended their accustomed occupations, and the second half had continued theirs, the country at the end of the twelvemonth would have been entirely impoverished.

It would be a great error to regret the large proportion of the annual produce, which in an opulent country goes to supply unproductive consumption. It would be to lament that the community has so much to spare from its necessities, for its pleasures and for all higher uses. This portion of the produce is the fund from which all the wants of the community, other than that of mere living, are provided for ; the measure of its means of enjoyment, and of its power of accomplishing all purposes not productive. That so great a surplus should be available for such purposes, and that it should be applied to them, can only be a subject of congratulation. The things to be regretted, and which are not incapable of being remedied, are the prodigious inequality with which this surplus is distributed, the little worth of the objects to which the greater part of it is devoted, and the large share which falls to the lot of persons who render no equivalent service in return.[1]

[1] [See Appendix D. *Productive and Unproductive.*]

CHAPTER IV

OF CAPITAL

§ 1. It has been seen in the preceding chapters that besides the primary and universal requisites of production, labour and natural agents, there is another requisite without which no productive operations, beyond the rude and scanty beginnings of primitive industry, are possible : namely, a stock, previously accumulated, of the products of former labour. This accumulated stock of the produce of labour is termed Capital. The function of Capital in production it is of the utmost importance thoroughly to understand, since a number of the erroneous notions with which our subject is infested originate in an imperfect and confused apprehension of this point.

Capital, by persons wholly unused to reflect on the subject, is supposed to be synonymous with money. To expose this misapprehension, would be to repeat what has been said in the introductory chapter. Money is no more synonymous with capital than it is with wealth. Money cannot in itself perform any part of the office of capital, since it can afford no assistance to production. To do this, it must be exchanged for other things ; and anything, which is susceptible of being exchanged for other things, is capable of contributing to production in the same degree. What capital does for production, is to afford the shelter, protection, tools and materials which the work requires, and to feed and otherwise maintain the labourers during the process. These are the services which present labour requires from past, and from the produce of past, labour. Whatever things are destined for this use—destined to supply productive labour with these various prerequisites—are Capital.

To familiarize ourselves with the conception, let us consider what is done with the capital invested in any of the branches of business which compose the productive industry of a country. A manufacturer, for example, has one part of his capital in the form

of buildings, fitted and destined for carrying on his branch of manufacture. Another part he has in the form of machinery. A third
consists, if he be a spinner, of raw cotton, flax, or wool ; if a weaver,
of flaxen, woollen, silk, or cotton, thread ; and the like, according
to the nature of the manufacture. Food and clothing for his operatives it is not the custom of the present age that he should directly
provide ; and few capitalists, except the producers of food or
clothing, have any portion worth mentioning of their capital in
that shape. Instead of this, each capitalist has money, which he
pays to his workpeople, and so enables them to supply themselves :
he has also finished goods in his warehouses, by the sale of which he
obtains more money, to employ in the same manner, as well as to
replenish his stock of materials, to keep his buildings and machinery
in repair, and to replace them when worn out. His money and
finished goods, however, are not wholly capital, for he does not wholly
devote them to these purposes : he employs a part of the one, and
of the proceeds of the other, in supplying his personal consumption
and that of his family, or in hiring grooms and valets, or maintaining
hunters and hounds, or in educating his children, or in paying taxes,
or in charity. What then is his capital ? Precisely that part of his
possessions, whatever it be, which is to constitute his fund for
carrying on fresh production. It is of no consequence that a part,
or even the whole of it, is in a form in which it cannot directly
supply the wants of labourers.

Suppose, for instance, that the capitalist is a hardware manufacturer, and that his stock in trade, over and above his machinery,
consists at present wholly in iron goods. Iron goods cannot feed
labourers. Nevertheless, by a mere change of the destination of
these iron goods, he can cause labourers to be fed. Suppose that
with a portion of the proceeds he intended to maintain a pack of
hounds, or an establishment of servants ; and that he changes his
intention, and employs it in his business, paying it in wages to
additional workpeople. These workpeople are enabled to buy and
consume the food which would otherwise have been consumed by the
hounds or by the servants ; and thus, without the employer's having
seen or touched one particle of the food, his conduct has determined
that so much more of the food existing in the country has been
devoted to the use of productive labourers, and so much less consumed in a manner wholly unproductive. Now vary the hypothesis,
and suppose that what is thus paid in wages would otherwise have
been laid out not in feeding servants or hounds, but in buying plate

and jewels; and in order to render the effect perceptible, let us
suppose that the change takes place on a considerable scale, and
that a large sum is diverted from buying plate and jewels to employing productive labourers, whom we shall suppose to have been
previously, like the Irish peasantry [1848], only half employed
and half fed. The labourers, on receiving their increased wages,
will not lay them out in plate and jewels, but in food. There is not,
however, additional food in the country; nor any unproductive
labourers or animals, as in the former case, whose food is set free
for productive purposes. Food will therefore be imported if possible;
if not possible, the labourers will remain for a season on their short
allowance : but the consequence of this change in the demand for
commodities, occasioned by the change in the expenditure of
capitalists from unproductive to productive, is that next year more
food will be produced, and less plate and jewellery. So that again,
without having had anything to do with the food of the labourers
directly, the conversion by individuals of a portion of their property,
no matter of what sort, from an unproductive destination to a productive, has had the effect of causing more food to be appropriated
to the consumption of productive labourers. The distinction, then,
between Capital and Not-capital, does not lie in the kind of commodities, but in the mind of the capitalist—in his will to employ them
for one purpose rather than another; and all property, however
ill adapted in itself for the use of labourers, is a part of capital,
so soon as it, or the value to be received from it, is set apart for
productive reinvestment. ˙ The sum of all the values so destined
by their respective possessors, composes the capital of the country.
Whether all those values are in a shape directly applicable to productive uses, makes no difference. Their shape, whatever it may
be, is a temporary accident : but once destined for production, they
do not fail to find a way of transforming themselves into things
capable of being applied to it.

§ 2. As whatever of the produce of the country is devoted to
production is capital, so, conversely, the whole of the capital of the
country is devoted to production. This second proposition, however,
must be taken with some limitations and explanations. A˙fund may
be seeking for productive employment, and find none, adapted to
the inclinations of its possessor : it then is capital still, but unemployed capital. Or the stock may consist of unsold goods, not
susceptible of direct application to productive uses, and not, at the

moment, marketable : these, until sold, are in the condition of unemployed capital. Again, artificial or accidental circumstances may render it necessary to possess a larger stock in advance, that is, a larger capital before entering on production, than is required by the nature of things. Suppose that the government lays a tax on the production in one of its earlier stages, as for instance by taxing the material. The manufacturer has to advance the tax, before commencing the manufacture, and is therefore under a necessity of having a larger accumulated fund than is required for, or is actually employed in, the production which he carries on. He must have a larger capital, to maintain the same quantity of productive labour ; or (what is equivalent) with a given capital he maintains less labour. This mode of levying taxes, therefore, limits unnecessarily the industry of the country : a portion of the fund destined by its owners for production being diverted from its purpose, and kept in a constant state of advance to the government.

For another example : a farmer may enter on his farm at such a time of the year, that he may be required to pay one, two, or even three quarters' rent before obtaining any return from the produce. This, therefore, must be paid out of his capital. Now rent, when paid for the land itself, and not for improvements made in it by labour, is not a productive expenditure. It is not an outlay for the support of labour, or for the provision of implements or materials the produce of labour. It is the price paid for the use of an appropriated natural agent. This natural agent is indeed as indispensable (and even more so) as any implement : but the having to pay a price for it, is not. In the case of the implement (a thing produced by labour) a price of some sort is the necessary condition of its existence : but the land exists by nature. The payment for it, therefore, is not one of the expenses of production ; and the necessity of making the payment out of capital makes it requisite that there should be a greater capital, a greater antecedent accumulation of the produce of past labour, than is naturally necessary, or than is needed where land is occupied on a different system. This extra capital, though intended by its owners for production, is in reality employed unproductively, and annually replaced, not from any produce of its own, but from the produce of the labour supported by the remainder of the farmer's capital.

Finally, that large portion of the productive capital of a country which is employed in paying the wages and salaries of labourers evidently is not, all of it, strictly and indispensably necessary for production. As much of it as exceeds the actual necessaries of life and health (an excess which in the case of skilled labourers is usually considerable) is not expended in supporting labour, but in remunerating it, and the labourers could wait for this part of their remuneration until the production is completed; it needs not necessarily pre-exist as capital: and if they unfortunately had to forego it altogether, the same amount of production might take place. In order that the whole remuneration of the labourers should be advanced to them in daily or weekly payments, there must exist in advance, and be appropriated to productive use, a greater stock, or capital, than would suffice to carry on the existing extent of production: greater, by whatever amount of remuneration the labourers received, beyond what the self-interest of a prudent slave-master would assign to his slaves. In truth, it is only after an abundant capital had already been accumulated, that the practice of paying in advance any remuneration of labour beyond a bare subsistence could possibly have arisen: since whatever is so paid, is not really applied to production, but to the unproductive consumption of productive labourers, indicating a fund for production sufficiently ample to admit of habitually diverting a part of it to a mere convenience.

It will be observed that I have assumed, that the labourers are always subsisted from capital: and this is obviously the fact, though the capital needs not necessarily be furnished by a person called a capitalist. When the labourer maintains himself by funds of his own, as when a peasant-farmer or proprietor lives on the produce of his land, or an artisan works on his own account, they are still supported by capital, that is, by funds provided in advance. The peasant does not subsist this year on the produce of this year's harvest, but on that of the last. The artisan is not living on the proceeds of the work he has in hand, but on those of work previously executed and disposed of. Each is supported by a small capital of his own, which he periodically replaces from the produce of his labour. The large capitalist is, in like manner, maintained from funds provided in advance. If he personally conducts his operations, as much of his personal or household expenditure as does not exceed a fair remuneration of his labour at the market price must be considered a part of his capital, expended, like any other capital, for production: and his personal consumption, so far as it consists of necessaries, is productive consumption.

§ 3. At the risk of being tedious, I must add a few more illustrations, to bring out into a still clearer and stronger light the idea of Capital. As M. Say truly remarks, it is on the very elements of our subject that illustration is most usefully bestowed, since the greatest errors which prevail in it may be traced to the want of a thorough mastery over the elementary ideas. Nor is this surprising : a branch may be diseased and all the rest healthy, but unsoundness at the root diffuses unhealthiness through the whole tree.

Let us therefore consider whether, and in what cases, the property of those who live on the interest of what they possess, without being personally engaged in production, can. be regarded as capital. It is so called in common language, and, with reference to the individual, not improperly. All funds from which the possessor derives an income, which income he can use without sinking and dissipating the fund itself, are to him equivalent to capital. But to transfer hastily and inconsiderately to the general point of view propositions which are true of the individual has been a source of innumerable errors in political economy. In the present instance, that which is virtually capital to the individual, is or is not capital to the nation, according as the fund which by the supposition he has not dissipated, has or has not been dissipated by somebody else.

For example, let property of the value of ten thousand pounds belonging to A, be lent to B, a farmer or manufacturer, and employed profitably in B's occupation. It is as much capital as if it belonged to B. A is really a farmer or manufacturer, not personally, but in respect of his property. Capital worth ten thousand pounds is employed in production—in maintaining labourers and providing tools and materials ; which capital belongs to A, while B takes the trouble of employing it, and receives for his remuneration the difference between the profit which it yields and the interest he pays to A. This is the simplest case.

Suppose next that A's ten thousand pounds, instead of being lent to B, are lent on mortgage to C, a landed proprietor, by whom they are employed in improving the productive powers of his estate, by fencing, draining, road-making, or permanent manures. This is productive employment. The ten thousand pounds are sunk, but not dissipated. They yield a permanent return ; the land now affords an increase of produce, sufficient, in a few years, if the outlay has been judicious, to replace the amount, and in time to multiply it manifold. Here, then, is the value of ten thousand pounds, employed in increasing the produce of the country. This constitutes a capital, for which C, if he lets his land, receives the returns in the nominal form of increased rent; and the mortgage entitles A to receive from these returns, in the shape of interest, such annual sum as has been agreed on. We will now vary the circumstances, and suppose that C does not employ the loan in improving his land, but in paying off a former mortgage, or in making a provision for children. Whether the ten thousand pounds thus employed are capital or not, will depend on what is done with the amount by the ultimate receiver. If the children invest their fortunes in a productive employment, or the mortgagee on being paid off lends the amount to another land-holder to improve his land, or to a manufacturer to extend his business, it is still capital, because productively employed.

Suppose, however, that C, the borrowing landlord, is a spend-thrift, who burdens his land not to increase his fortune but to squander it, expending the amount in equipages and entertainments. In a year or two it is dissipated, and without return. A is as rich as before; he has no longer his ten thousand pounds, but he has a lien on the land, which he could still sell for that amount. C, however, is 10,000l. poorer than formerly; and nobody is richer. It may be said that those are richer who have made profit out of the money while it was being spent. No doubt if C lost it by gaming, or was cheated of it by his servants, that is a mere transfer, not a destruction, and those who have gained the amount may employ it productively. But if C has received the fair value for his expenditure in articles of subsistence or luxury, which he has consumed on himself, or by means of his servants or guests, these articles have ceased to exist, and nothing has been produced to replace them : while if the same sum had been employed in farming or manufacturing, the consumption which would have taken place would have been more than balanced at the end of the year by new products, created by the labour of those who would in that case have been the consumers. By C's prodigality, that which would have been consumed with a return, is consumed without return. C's tradesmen may have made a profit during the process ; but if the capital had been expended productively, an equivalent profit would have been made by builders, fencers, tool-makers, and the tradespeople who supply the consumption of the labouring classes ; while at the expiration of the time (to say nothing of any increase), C would have had the ten thousand pounds or its value replaced to him, which now he has not. There is, therefore, on the general result, a difference to the disadvantage of the community, of at least ten thousand pounds, being the amount of C's unproductive expenditure. To A, the difference is not material, since his income is secured to him, and while the security is good, and the market rate of interest the same, he can always sell the mortgage at its original value. To A, therefore, the lien of ten thousand pounds on C's estate, is virtually a capital of that amount; but is it so in reference to the community? It is not. A had a capital of ten thousand pounds, but this has been extinguished—dissipated and destroyed by C's prodigality. A now receives his income, not from the produce of his capital, but from some other source of income belonging to C, probably from the rent of his land, that is, from payments made to him by farmers out of the produce of *their* capital. The national capital is diminished by ten thousand pounds, and the national income by all which those ten thousand pounds, employed as capital, would have produced. The loss does not fall on the owner of the destroyed capital, since the destroyer has agreed to indemnify him for it. But his loss is only a small portion of that sustained by the community, since what was devoted to the use and consumption of the proprietor was only the interest; the capital itself was, or would have been, employed in the perpetual maintenance of an equivalent number of labourers, regularly reproducing what they consumed: and of this maintenance they are deprived without compensation.

Let us now vary the hypothesis still further, and suppose that the money is borrowed, not by a landlord, but by the State. A lends his capital to Government to carry on a war: he buys from the State what are called government securities; that is, obligations on the government to pay a certain annual income. If the government employed the money in making a railroad, this might be a productive employment, and A's property would still be used as capital; but since it is employed in war, that is, in the pay of officers and soldiers who produce nothing, and in destroying a quantity of gunpowder and bullets without return, the government is in the situation of C, the spendthrift landlord, and A's ten thousand pounds are so much national capital which once existed, but exists no longer: virtually thrown into the sea, as far as wealth or production is concerned; though for other reasons the employment of it may have been justifiable. A's subsequent income is derived, not from the produce of his own capital, but from taxes drawn from the produce of the remaining capital of the community; to whom his capital is not yielding any return, to indemnify them for the payment

it is lost and gone, and what he now possesses is a claim on the returns to other people's capital and industry. This claim he can sell, and get back the equivalent of his capital, which he may afterwards employ productively. True ; but he does not get back his own capital, or anything which it has produced ; that, and all its possible returns, are extinguished : what he gets is the capital of some other person, which that person is willing to exchange for his lien on the taxes. Another capitalist substitutes himself for A as a mortgagee of the public, and A substitutes himself for the other capitalist as the possessor of a fund employed in production, or available for it. By this exchange the productive powers of the community are neither increased nor diminished. The breach in the capital of the country was made when the government spent A's money : whereby a value of ten thousand pounds was withdrawn or withheld from productive employment, placed in the fund for unproductive consumption, and destroyed without equivalent.[1]

[1] [See Appendix E. *The Definition of Capital.*]

CHAPTER V

§ 1. If the preceding explanations have answered their purpose, they have given not only a sufficiently complete possession of the idea of Capital according to its definition, but a sufficient familiarity with it in the concrete, and amidst the obscurity with which the complication of individual circumstances surrounds it, to have prepared even the unpractised reader for certain elementary propositions or theorems respecting capital, the full comprehension of which is already a considerable step out of darkness into light.

The first of these propositions is, That industry is limited by capital. This is so obvious as to be taken for granted in many common forms of speech ; but to see a truth occasionally is one thing, to recognise it habitually, and admit no propositions inconsistent with it, is another. The axiom was until lately almost universally disregarded by legislators and political writers ; and doctrines irreconcileable with it are still very commonly professed and inculcated.

The following are common expressions implying its truth. The act of directing industry to a particular employment is described by the phrase " applying capital " to the employment. To employ industry on the land is to apply capital to the land. To employ labour in a manufacture is to invest capital in the manufacture. This implies that industry cannot be employed to any greater extent than there is capital to invest. The proposition, indeed, must be assented to as soon as it is distinctly apprehended. The expression " applying capital " is of course metaphorical : what is really applied is labour ; capital being an indispensable condition. Again, we often speak of the " productive powers of capital." This expression is not literally correct. The only productive powers are those of labour and natural agents ; or if any portion of capital can by a stretch of language be said to have a productive power of its own, it is only tools and machinery, which, like wind or water, may be said to co-operate with labour. The food of labourers and the materials of production have no productive power ; but labour cannot exert its productive power unless provided with them. There can be no more industry than is supplied with materials to work up and food to eat. Self-evident as the thing is, it is often forgotten that the people of a country are maintained and have their wants supplied, not by the produce of present labour, but of past. They consume what has been produced, not what is about to be produced. Now, of what has been produced, a part only is allotted to the support of productive labour ; and there will not and cannot be more of that labour than the portion so allotted (which is the capital of the country) can feed, and provide with the materials and instruments of production.

Yet, in disregard of a fact so evident, it long continued to be believed that laws and governments, without creating capital, could create industry. Not by making the people more laborious, or increasing the efficiency of their labour ; these are objects to which the government can, in some degree, indirectly contribute. But without any increase in the skill or energy of the labourers, and without causing any persons to labour who had previously been maintained in idleness, it was still thought that the government, without providing additional funds, could create additional employment. A government would, by prohibitory laws, put a stop to the importation of some commodity ; and when by this it had caused the commodity to be produced at home, it would plume itself upon having enriched the country with a new branch of industry, would parade in statistical tables the amount of produce yielded and labour employed in the production, and take credit for the whole of this as a gain to the country, obtained through the prohibitory law. Although this sort of political arithmetic has fallen a little into discredit in England, it still flourishes in the nations of Continental Europe. Had legislators been aware that industry is limited by capital, they would have seen that, the aggregate capital of the country not having been increased, any portion of it which they by their laws had caused to be embarked in the newly-acquired branch of industry must have been withdrawn or withheld from some other ; in which it gave, or would have given, employment to probably about the same quantity of labour which it employs in its new occupation.*

* An exception must be admitted when the industry created or upheld by the restrictive law belongs to the class of what are called domestic

§ 2. Because industry is limited by capital, we are not however to infer that it always reaches that limit. Capital may be temporarily unemployed, as in the case of unsold goods, or funds that have not yet found an investment : during this interval it does not set in motion any industry. Or there may not be as many labourers obtainable, as the capital would maintain and employ. This has been known to occur in new colonies, where capital has sometimes perished uselessly for want of labour : the Swan River settlement (now called Western Australia), in the first years after its foundation, was an instance. There are many persons maintained from existing capital, who produce nothing, or who might produce much more than they do. If the labourers were reduced to lower wages, or induced to work more hours for the same wages, or if their families, who are already maintained from capital, were employed to a greater extent than they now are in adding to the produce, a given capital would afford employment to more industry. The unproductive consumption of productive labourers, the whole of which is now supplied by capital, might cease, or be postponed until the produce came in ; and additional productive labourers might be maintained with the amount. By such means society might obtain from its existing resources a greater quantity of produce : and to such means it has been driven, when the sudden destruction of some large portion of its capital rendered the employment of the remainder with the greatest possible effect a matter of paramount consideration for the time.

When industry has not come up to the limit imposed by capital, governments may, in various ways, for example by importing additional labourers, bring it nearer to that limit : as by the importation

manufactures. These being carried on by persons already fed—by labouring families, in the intervals of other employment—no transfer of capital to the occupation is necessary to its being undertaken, beyond the value of the materials and tools, which is often inconsiderable. If, therefore, a protecting duty causes this occupation to be carried on, when it otherwise would not, there is in this case a real increase of the production of the country.

In order to render our theoretical proposition invulnerable, this peculiar case must be allowed for ; but it does not touch the practical doctrine of free trade. Domestic manufactures cannot, from the very nature of things, require protection, since the subsistence of the labourers being provided from other sources, the price of the product, however much it may be reduced, is nearly all clear gain. If, therefore, the domestic producers retire from the competition, it is never from necessity, but because the product is not worth the labour it costs, in the opinion of the best judges, those who enjoy the one and undergo the other. They prefer the sacrifice of buying their clothing to the labour of making it. They will not continue their labour unless society will give them more for it, than in their own opinion its product is worth.

of Coolies and free Negroes into the West Indies. There is another way in which governments can create additional industry. They can create capital. They may lay on taxes, and employ the amount productively. They may do what is nearly equivalent; they may lay taxes on income or expenditure, and apply the proceeds towards paying off the public debts. The fundholder, when paid off, would still desire to draw an income from his property, most of which therefore would find its way into productive employment, while a great part of it would have been drawn from the fund for unproductive expenditure, since people do not wholly pay their taxes from what they would have saved, but partly, if not chiefly, from what they would have spent. It may be added, that any increase in the productive power of capital (or, more properly speaking, of labour) by improvements in the arts of life, or otherwise, tends to increase the employment for labour; since, when there is a greater produce altogether, it is always probable that some portion of the increase will be saved and converted into capital; especially when the increased returns to productive industry hold out an additional temptation to the conversion of funds from an unproductive destination to a productive.

§ 3. While, on the one hand, industry is limited by capital, so on the other, every increase of capital gives, or is capable of giving, additional employment to industry; and this without assignable limit. I do not mean to deny that the capital, or part of it, may be so employed as not to support labourers, being fixed in machinery, buildings, improvement of land, and the like. In any large increase of capital a considerable portion will generally be thus employed, and will only co-operate with labourers, not maintain them. What I do intend to assert is, that the portion which is destined to their maintenance, may (supposing no alteration in anything else) be indefinitely increased, without creating an impossibility of finding them employment: in other words, that if there are human beings capable of work, and food to feed them, they may always be employed in producing something. This proposition requires to be somewhat dwelt upon, being one of those which it is exceedingly easy to assent to when presented in general terms, but somewhat difficult to keep fast hold of, in the crowd and confusion of the actual facts of society. It is also very much opposed to common doctrines. There is not an opinion more general among mankind than this, that the unproductive expenditure of the rich

Is necessary to the employment of the poor. Before Adam Smith, the doctrine had hardly been questioned; and even since his time, authors of the highest name and of great merit * have contended, that if consumers were to save and convert into capital more than a limited portion of their income, and were not to devote to unproductive consumption an amount of means bearing a certain ratio to the capital of the country, the extra accumulation would be merely so much waste, since there would be no market for the commodities which the capital so created would produce. I conceive this to be one of the many errors arising in political economy, from the practice of not beginning with the examination of simple cases, but rushing at once into the complexity of concrete phenomena.

Every one can see that if a benevolent government possessed all the food, and all the implements and materials, of the community, it could exact productive labour from all capable of it, to whom it allowed a share in the food, and could be in no danger of wanting a field for the employment of this productive labour, since as long as there was a single want unsaturated (which material objects could supply) of any one individual, the labour of the community could be turned to the production of something capable of satisfying that want. Now, the individual possessors of capital, when they add to it by fresh accumulations, are doing precisely the same thing which we suppose to be done by a benevolent government. As it is allowable to put any case by way of hypothesis, let us imagine the most extreme case conceivable. Suppose that every capitalist came to be of opinion that, not being more meritorious than a well-conducted labourer, he ought not to fare better; and accordingly laid by, from conscientious motives, the surplus of his profits; or suppose this abstinence not spontaneous, but imposed by law or opinion upon all capitalists, and upon landowners likewise. Unproductive expenditure is now reduced to its lowest limit: and it is asked, how is the increased capital to find employment? Who is to buy the goods which it will produce? There are no longer customers even for those which were produced before. The goods, therefore, (it is said) will remain unsold; they will perish in the warehouses; until capital is brought down to what it was originally, or rather to as much less, as the demand of the consumers has lessened. But this is seeing only one-half of the matter. In the case supposed, there would no longer be any demand for luxuries,

* For example, Mr. Malthus, Dr. Chalmers, M. de Sismondi.

on the part of capitalists and landowners. But when these classes turn their income into capital, they do not thereby annihilate their power of consumption; they do but transfer it from themselves to the labourers to whom they give employment. Now, there are two possible suppositions in regard to the labourers; either there is, or there is not, an increase of their numbers, proportional to the increase of capital. If there is, the case offers no difficulty. The production of necessaries for the new population, takes the place of the production of luxuries for a portion of the old, and supplies exactly the amount of employment which has been lost. But suppose that there is no increase of population. The whole of what was previously expended in luxuries, by capitalists and landlords, is distributed among the existing labourers, in the form of additional wages. We will assume them to be already sufficiently supplied with necessaries. What follows? That the labourers become consumers of luxuries; and the capital previously employed in the production of luxuries is still able to employ itself in the same manner: the difference being, that the luxuries are shared among the community generally, instead of being confined to a few. The increased accumulation and increased production might, rigorously speaking, continue, until every labourer had every indulgence of wealth, consistent with continuing to work; supposing that the power of their labour were physically sufficient to produce all this amount of indulgences for their whole number. Thus the limit of wealth is never deficiency of consumers, but of producers and productive power. Every addition to capital gives to labour either additional employment, or additional remuneration; enriches either the country, or the labouring class. If it finds additional hands to set to work, it increases the aggregate produce; if only the same hands, it gives them a larger share of it; and perhaps even in this case, by stimulating them to greater exertion, augments the produce itself.

§ 4. A second fundamental theorem respecting Capital relates to the source from which it is derived. It is the result of saving. The evidence of this lies abundantly in what has been already said on the subject. But the proposition needs some further illustration.

If all persons were to expend in personal indulgences all that they produce, and all the income they receive from what is produced by others, capital could not increase. All capital, with a trifling exception, was originally the result of saving. I say, with a trifling exception; because a person who labours on his own account may spend on his own account all he produces, without becoming destitute; and the provision of necessaries on which he subsists until he has reaped his harvest, or sold his commodity, though a real capital, cannot be said to have been saved, since it is all used for the supply of his own wants, and perhaps as speedily as if it had been consumed in idleness. We may imagine a number of individuals or families settled on as many separate pieces of land, each living on what their own labour produces, and consuming the whole produce. But even these must save (that is, spare from their personal consumption) as much as is necessary for seed. Some saving, therefore, there must have been, even in this simplest of all states of economical relations ; people must have produced more than they used, or used less than they produced. Still more must they do so before they can employ other labourers, or increase their production beyond what can be accomplished by the work of their own hands. All that any one employs in supporting and carrying on any other labour than his own, must have been originally brought together by saving ; somebody must have produced it and forborne to consume it. We may say, therefore, without material inaccuracy, that all capital, and especially all addition to capital, is the result of saving.

In a rude and violent state of society, it continually happens that the person who has capital is not the very person who has saved it, but some one who, being stronger, or belonging to a more powerful community, has possessed himself of it by plunder. And even in a state of things in which property was protected, the increase of capital has usually been, for a long time, mainly derived from privations which, though essentially the same with saving, are not generally called by that name, because not voluntary. The actual producers have been slaves, compelled to produce as much as force could extort from them, and to consume as little as the self-interest or the usually very slender humanity of their taskmasters would permit. This kind of compulsory saving, however, would not have caused any increase of capital, unless a part of the amount had been saved over again, voluntarily, by the master. If all that he made his slaves produce and forbear to consume, had been consumed by him on personal indulgences, he would not have increased his capital, nor been enabled to maintain an increasing number of slaves. To maintain any slaves at all, implied a previous saving ; a stock, at least of food, provided in advance. This saving may not, however, have been made by any self-imposed privation of the master ; but more probably by that of the slaves themselves while free ; the rapine or war, which deprived them of their personal liberty, having transferred also their accumulations to the conqueror.

There are other cases in which the term saving, with the associations usually belonging to it, does not exactly fit the operation by which capital is increased. If it were said for instance, that the only way to accelerate the increase of capital is by increase of saving, the idea would probably be suggested of greater abstinence, and increased privation.   But it is obvious that whatever increases the productive power of labour creates an additional fund to make savings from, and enables capital to be enlarged not only without additional privation, but concurrently with an increase of personal consumption.   Nevertheless, there is here an increase of saving, in the scientific sense.   Though there is more consumed, there is also more spared.   There is a greater excess of production over consumption.   It is consistent with correctness to call this a greater saving.   Though the term is not unobjectionable, there is no other which is not liable to as great objections.   To consume less than is produced, is saving ; and that is the process by which capital is increased ; not necessarily by consuming less, absolutely.   We must not allow ourselves to be so much the slaves of words, as to be unable to use the word saving in this sense, without being in danger of forgetting that to increase capital there is another way besides consuming less, namely, to produce more.

§ 5.   A third fundamental theorem respecting Capital, closely connected with the one last discussed, is, that although saved, and the result of saving, it is nevertheless consumed.   The word saving does not imply that what is saved is not consumed, nor even necessarily that its consumption is deferred ; but only that, if consumed immediately, it is not consumed by the person who saves it.   If merely laid by for future use, it is said to be hoarded ; and while hoarded, is not consumed at all.   But if employed as capital, it is all consumed ; though not by the capitalist.   Part is exchanged for tools or machinery, which are worn out by use; part for seed or materials, which are destroyed as such by being sown or wrought up, and destroyed altogether by the consumption of the ultimate product.   The remainder is paid in wages to productive labourers, who consume it for their daily wants ; or if they in their turn save any part, this also is not, generally speaking, hoarded, but (through savings banks, benefit clubs, or some other channel) re-employed as capital, and consumed.

The principle now stated is a strong example of the necessity of attention to the most elementary truths of our subject : for it is one of the most elementary of them all, and yet no one who has not bestowed some thought on the matter is habitually aware of it, and most are not even willing to admit it when first stated. To the vulgar, it is not at all apparent that what is saved is consumed. To them, every one who saves appears in the light of a person who hoards : they may think such conduct permissible, or even laudable, when it is to provide for a family, and the like ; but they have no conception of it as doing good to other people : saving is to them another word for keeping a thing to oneself ; while spending appears to them to be distributing it among others. The person who expends his fortune in unproductive consumption is looked upon as diffusing benefits all around ; and is an object of so much favour, that some portion of the same popularity attaches even to him who spends what does not belong to him ; who not only destroys his own capital, if he ever had any, but under pretence of borrowing, and on promise of repayment, possesses himself of capital belonging to others, and destroys that likewise.

This popular error comes from attending to a small portion only of the consequences that flow from the saving or the spending ; all the effects of either which are out of sight being out of mind. The eye follows what is saved into an imaginary strong-box, and there loses sight of it ; what is spent, it follows into the hands of tradespeople and dependents ; but without reaching the ultimate destination in either case. Saving (for productive investment), and spending, coincide very closely in the first stage of their operations. The effects of both begin with consumption ; with the destruction of a certain portion of wealth ; only the things consumed, and the persons consuming, are different. There is, in the one case, a wearing out of tools, a destruction of material, and a quantity of food and clothing supplied to labourers, which they destroy by use : in the other case, there is a consumption, that is to say, a destruction, of wines, equipages, and furniture. Thus far, the consequence to the national wealth has been much the same ; an equivalent quantity of it has been destroyed in both cases. But in the spending, this first stage is also the final stage ; that particular amount of the produce of labour has disappeared, and there is nothing left ; while, on the contrary, the saving person, during the whole time that the destruction was going on, has had labourers at work repairing it ; who are ultimately found to have replaced, with an increase, the equivalent of what has been consumed. And as this operation admits of being repeated indefinitely without any fresh act of saving, a saving once made becomes a fund to maintain a corresponding number of labourers in perpetuity, reproducing annually their own maintenance with a profit.

It is the intervention of money which obscures, to an unpractised apprehension, the true character of these phenomena. Almost all expenditure being carried on by means of money, the money comes to be looked upon as the main feature in the transaction ; and since that does not perish, but only changes hands, people overlook the destruction which takes place in the case of unproductive expenditure. The money being merely transferred, they think the wealth also has only been handed over from the spendthrift to other people. But this is simply confounding money with wealth. The wealth which has been destroyed was not the money, but the wines, equipages, and furniture which the money purchased ; and these having been destroyed without return, society collectively is poorer by the amount. It may be said, perhaps, that wines, equipages, and furniture, are not subsistence, tools, and materials, and could not in any case have been applied to the support of labour ; that they are adapted for no other than unproductive consumption, and that the detriment to the wealth of the community was when they were produced, not when they were consumed. I am willing to allow this, as far as is necessary for the argument, and the remark would be very pertinent if these expensive luxuries were drawn from an existing stock, never to be replenished. But since, on the contrary, they continue to be produced as long as there are consumers for them, and are produced in increased quantity to meet an increased demand ; the choice made by a consumer to expend five thousand a year in luxuries keeps a corresponding number of labourers employed from year to year in producing things which can be of no use to production ; their services being lost so far as regards the increase of the national wealth, and the tools, materials, and food which they annually consume being so much subtracted from the general stock of the community applicable to productive purposes. In proportion as any class is improvident or luxurious, the industry of the country takes the direction of producing luxuries for their use ; while not only the employment for productive labourers is diminished, but the subsistence and instruments which are the means of such employment do actually exist in smaller quantity.

Saving, in short, enriches, and spending impoverishes, the

community along with the individual; which is but saying in other words, that society at large is richer by what it expends in maintaining and aiding productive labour, but poorer by what it consumes in its enjoyments.*

§ 6. To return to our fundamental theorem. Everything which is produced is consumed; both what is saved and what is said to be spent; and the former quite as rapidly as the latter. All the ordinary forms of language tend to disguise this. When people talk of the ancient wealth of a country, of riches inherited

---

* It is worth while to direct attention to several circumstances which to a certain extent diminish the detriment caused to the general wealth by the prodigality of individuals, or raise up a compensation, more or less ample, as a consequence of the detriment itself. One of these is, that spendthrifts do not usually succeed in consuming all they spend. Their habitual carelessness as to expenditure causes them to be cheated and robbed on all quarters, often by persons of frugal habits. Large accumulations are continually made by the agents, stewards, and even domestic servants, of improvident persons of fortune; and they pay much higher prices for all purchases than people of careful habits, which accounts for their being popular as customers. They are, therefore, actually not able to get into their possession and destroy a quantity of wealth by any means equivalent to the fortune which they dissipate. Much of it is merely transferred to others, by whom a part may be saved. Another thing to be observed is, that the prodigality of some may reduce others to a forced economy. Suppose a sudden demand for some article of luxury, caused by the caprice of a prodigal, which not having been calculated on beforehand, there has been no increase of the usual supply. The price will rise; and may rise beyond the means or the inclinations of some of the habitual consumers, who may in consequence forego their accustomed indulgence, and save the amount. If they do not, but continue to expend as great a value as before on the commodity, the dealers in it obtain, for only the same quantity of the article, a return increased by the whole of what the spendthrift has paid; and thus the amount which he loses is transferred bodily to them, and may be added to their capital: his increased personal consumption being made up by the privations of the other purchasers, who have obtained less than usual of their accustomed gratification for the same equivalent. On the other hand, a counter-process must be going on somewhere, since the prodigal must have diminished his purchases in some other quarter to balance the augmentation in this; he has perhaps called in funds employed in sustaining productive labour, and the dealers in subsistence and in the instruments of production have had commodities left on their hands, or have received, for the usual amount of commodities, a less than usual return. But such losses of income or capital, by industrious persons except when of extraordinary amount, are generally made up by increased pinching and privation; so that the capital of the community may not be, on the whole, impaired, and the prodigal may have had his self-indulgence at the expense not of the permanent resources, but of the temporary pleasures and comforts of others. For in every case the community are poorer by what any one spends, unless others are in consequence led to curtail their spending. There are yet other and more recondite ways in which the profusion of some may bring about its compensation in the extra savings of others; but these can only be considered in that part of the Fourth Book, which treats of the limiting principle to the accumulation of capital.

from ancestors, and similar expressions, the idea suggested is that the riches so transmitted were produced long ago, at the time when they are said to have been first acquired, and that no portion of the capital of the country was produced this year, except as much as may have been this year added to the total amount. The fact is far otherwise. The greater part, in value, of the wealth now existing in England has been produced by human hands within the last twelve months. A very small proportion indeed of that large aggregate was in existence ten years ago;—of the present productive capital of the country scarcely any part, except farm-houses and manufactories, and a few ships and machines; and even these would not in most cases have survived so long, if fresh labour had not been employed within that period in putting them into repair. The land subsists, and the land is almost the only thing that subsists. Everything which is produced perishes, and most things very quickly. Most kinds of capital are not fitted by their nature to be long preserved. There are a few, and but a few productions, capable of a very prolonged existence. Westminster Abbey has lasted many centuries, with occasional repairs; some Grecian sculptures have existed above two thousand years; the Pyramids perhaps double or treble that time. But these were objects devoted to unproductive use. If we except bridges and aqueducts (to which may in some countries be added tanks and embankments), there are few instances of any edifice applied to industrial purposes which has been of great duration; such buildings do not hold out against wear and tear, nor is it good economy to construct them of the solidity necessary for permanency. Capital is kept in existence from age to age not by preservation, but by perpetual reproduction: every part of it is used and destroyed, generally very soon after it is produced, but those who consume it are employed meanwhile in producing more. The growth of capital is similar to the growth of population. Every individual who is born, dies, but in each year the number born exceeds the number who die: the population, therefore, always increases, though not one person of those composing it was alive until a very recent date.

§ 7. This perpetual consumption and reproduction of capital affords the explanation of what has so often excited wonder, the great rapidity with which countries recover from a state of devastation; the disappearance, in a short time, of all traces of the mischiefs done by earthquakes, floods, hurricanes, and the ravages of war.

An enemy lays waste a country by fire and sword, and destroys or carries away nearly all the moveable wealth existing in it : all the inhabitants are ruined, and yet, in a few years after, everything is much as it was before. This *vis medicatrix naturæ* has been a subject of sterile astonishment, or has been cited to exemplify the wonderful strength of the principle of saving, which can repair such enormous losses in so brief an interval. There is nothing at all wonderful in the matter. What the enemy have destroyed, would have been destroyed in a little time by the inhabitants themselves : the wealth which they so rapidly reproduce, would have needed to be reproduced and would have been reproduced in any case, and probably in as short a time. Nothing is changed, except that during the reproduction they have not now the advantage of consuming what had been produced previously. The possibility of a rapid repair of their disasters mainly depends on whether the country has been depopulated. If its effective population have not been extirpated at the time, and are not starved afterwards ; then, with the same skill and knowledge which they had before, with their land and its permanent improvements undestroyed, and the more durable buildings probably unimpaired, or only partially injured, they have nearly all the requisites for their former amount of production. If there is as much of food left to them, or of valuables to buy food, as enables them by any amount of privation to remain alive and in working condition, they will in a short time have raised as great a produce, and acquired collectively as great wealth and as great a capital, as before ; by the mere continuance of that ordinary amount of exertion which they are accustomed to employ in their occupations. Nor does this evince any strength in the principle of saving, in the popular sense of the term, since what takes place is not intentional abstinence, but involuntary privation.

Yet so fatal is the habit of thinking through the medium of only one set of technical phrases, and so little reason have studious men to value themselves on being exempt from the very same mental infirmities which beset the vulgar, that this simple explanation was never given (so far as I am aware) by any political economist before Dr. Chalmers ; a writer many of whose opinions I think erroneous, but who has always the merit of studying phenomena at first hand, and expressing them in a language of his own, which often uncovers aspects of the truth that the received phraseologies only tend to hide.

§ 8.   The same author carries out this train of thought to some important conclusions on another closely connected subject, that of government loans for war purposes or other unproductive expenditure.   These loans, being drawn from capital (in lieu of taxes, which would generally have been paid from income, and made up in part or altogether by increased economy) must, according to the principles we have laid down, tend to impoverish the country : yet the years in which expenditure of this sort has been on the greatest scale have often been years of great apparent prosperity : the wealth and resources of the country, instead of diminishing, have given every sign of rapid increase during the process, and of greatly expanded dimensions after its close.   This was confessedly the case with Great Britain during the last long Continental war ; and it would take some space to enumerate all the unfounded theories in political economy to which that fact gave rise, and to which it secured temporary credence ; almost all tending to exalt unproductive expenditure, at the expense of productive.   Without entering into all the causes which operated, and which commonly do operate, to prevent these extraordinary drafts on the productive resources of a country from being so much felt as it might seem reasonable to expect, we will suppose the most unfavourable case possible : that the whole amount borrowed and destroyed by the government was abstracted by the lender from a productive employment in which it had actually been invested.   The capital, therefore, of the country, is this year diminished by so much.   But unless the amount abstracted is something enormous, there is no reason in the nature of the case why next year the national capital should not be as great as ever.   The loan cannot have been taken from that portion of the capital of the country which consists of tools, machinery, and buildings.   It must have been wholly drawn from the portion employed in paying labourers : and the labourers will suffer accordingly. But if none of them are starved ; if their wages can bear such an amount of reduction, or if charity interposes between them and absolute destitution, there is no reason that their labour should produce less in the next year than in the year before.   If they produce as much as usual, having been paid less by so many millions sterling, these millions are gained by their employers.   The breach made in the capital of the country is thus instantly repaired, but repaired by the privations and often the real misery of the labouring class.   Here is ample reason why such periods, even in the most unfavourable circumstances, may easily be times of great gain to those whose prosperity usually passes, in the estimation of society, for national prosperity.*

This leads to the vexed question to which Dr. Chalmers has very particularly adverted ; whether the funds required by a government for extraordinary unproductive expenditure, are best raised by loans, the interest only being provided by taxes, or whether taxes should be at once laid on to the whole amount ; which is called in the financial vocabulary, raising the whole of the supplies within the year. Dr. Chalmers is strongly for the latter method. He says, the common notion is that in calling for the whole amount in one year, you require what is either impossible, or very inconvenient ; that the people cannot, without great hardship, pay the whole at once out of their yearly income ; and that it is much better to require of them a small payment every year in the shape of interest, than so great a sacrifice once for all. To which his answer is, that the sacrifice is made equally in either case. Whatever is spent, cannot but be drawn from yearly income. The whole and every part of the wealth produced in the country forms, or helps to form, the yearly income of somebody. The privation which it is supposed must result from taking the amount in the shape of taxes is not avoided by taking it in a loan. The suffering is not averted, but only thrown upon the labouring classes, the least able, and who

* On the other hand, it must be remembered that war abstracts from productive employment not only capital, but likewise labourers ; that the funds withdrawn from the remuneration of productive labourers are partly employed in paying the same or other individuals for unproductive labour ; and that by this portion of its effects war expenditure acts in precisely the opposite manner to that which Dr. Chalmers points out, and, so far as it goes, directly counteracts the effects described in the text. So far as labourers are taken from production, to man the army and navy, the labouring classes are *not* damaged, the capitalists are *not* benefited, and the general produce of the country *is* diminished, by war expenditure. Accordingly, Dr. Chalmers's doctrine, though true of this country, is wholly inapplicable to countries differently circumstanced ; to France, for example, during the Napoleon wars. At that period the draught on the labouring population of France, for a long series of years, was enormous, while the funds which supported the war were mostly supplied by contributions levied on the countries overrun by the French arms, a very small proportion alone consisting of French capital. In France, accordingly, the wages of labour did not fall, but rose ; the employers of labour were not benefited, but injured ; while the wealth of the country was impaired by the suspension or total loss of so vast an amount of its productive labour. In England all this was reversed. England employed comparatively few additional soldiers and sailors of her own, while she diverted hundreds of millions of capital from productive employment, to supply munitions of war and support armies for her Continental allies. Consequently, as shown in the text, her labourers suffered, her capitalists prospered, and her permanent productive resources did not fall off.

least ought, to bear it : while all the inconveniences, physical, moral, and political, produced by maintaining taxes for the perpetual payment of the interest, are incurred in pure loss. Whenever capital is withdrawn from production, or from the fund destined for production, to be lent to the State, and expended unproductively, that whole sum is withheld from the labouring classes : the loan, therefore, is in truth paid off the same year ; the whole of the sacrifice necessary for paying it off is actually made : only it is paid to the wrong persons, and therefore does not extinguish the claim ; and paid by the very worst of taxes, a tax exclusively on the labouring class. And after having, in this most painful and unjust way, gone through the whole effort necessary for extinguishing the debt, the country remains charged with it, and with the payment of its interest in perpetuity.

These views appear to me strictly just, in so far as the value absorbed in loans would otherwise have been employed in productive industry within the country. The practical state of the case, however, seldom exactly corresponds with this supposition. The loans of the less wealthy countries are made chiefly with foreign capital, which would not, perhaps, have been brought in to be invested on any less security than that of the government : while those of rich and prosperous countries are generally made, not with funds withdrawn from productive employment, but with the new accumulations constantly making from income, and often with a part of them which, if not so taken, would have migrated to colonies, or sought other investments abroad. In these cases (which will be more particularly examined hereafter *), the sum wanted may be obtained by loan without detriment to the labourers, or derangement of the national industry, and even perhaps with advantage to both, in comparison with raising the amount by taxation, since taxes, especially when heavy, are almost always partly paid at the expense of what would otherwise have been saved and added to capital. Besides, in a country which makes so great yearly additions to its wealth that a part can be taken and expended unproductively without diminishing capital, or even preventing a considerable increase, it is evident that even if the whole of what is so taken would have become capital, and obtained employment in the country, the effect on the labouring classes is far less prejudicial, and the case against the loan system much less strong, than in the case first supposed. This brief anticipation of a discussion which

* Infra. book iv. chaps. iv. v.

wilh find its proper place elsewhere appeared necessary to prevent false inferences from the premises previously laid down.

§ 9. We now pass to a fourth fundamental theorem respecting Capital, which is, perhaps, oftener overlooked or misconceived than even any of the foregoing. What supports and employs productive labour, is the capital expended in setting it to work, and not the demand of purchasers for the produce of the labour when completed. Demand for commodities is not demand for labour. The demand for commodities determines in what particular branch of production the labour and capital shall be employed ; it determines the *direction* of the labour ; but not the more or less of the labour itself, or of the maintenance or payment of the labour. These depend on the amount of the capital, or other funds directly devoted to the sustenance and remuneration of labour.

Suppose, for instance, that there is a demand for velvet ; a fund ready to be laid out in buying velvet, but no capital to establish the manufacture. It is of no consequence how great the demand may be ; unless capital is attracted into the occupation, there will be no velvet made, and consequently none bought ; unless, indeed, the desire of the intending purchaser for it is so strong, that he employs part of the price he would have paid for it in making advances to work-people, that they may employ themselves in making velvet ; that is, unless he converts part of his income into capital, and invests that capital in the manufacture. Let us now reverse the hypothesis, and suppose that there is plenty of capital ready for making velvet, but no demand. Velvet will not be made ; but there is no particular preference on the part of capital for making velvet. Manufacturers and their labourers do not produce for the pleasure of their customers, but for the supply of their own wants ; and, having still the capital and the labour which are the essentials of production, they can either produce something else which is in demand, or if there be no other demand, they themselves have one, and can produce the things which they want for their own consumption. So that the employment afforded to labour does not depend on the purchasers, but on the capital.[1] I am, of course, not taking into consideration the effects of a sudden change. If the demand ceases unexpectedly, after the commodity to supply it is already produced, this introduces a different element into the

---

[1] [This sentence replaced in the 3rd ed. (1852) the original text : " So that the capital cannot be dispensed with—the purchasers can."]

question : the capital has actually been consumed in producing something which nobody wants or uses, and it has therefore perished, and
the employment which it gave to labour is at an end, not because
there is no longer a demand, but because there is no longer a capital.
This case therefore does not test the principle.   The proper test is,
to suppose that the change is gradual and foreseen, and is attended
with no waste of capital, the manufacture being discontinued by
merely not replacing the machinery as it wears out, and not re-
investing the money as it comes in from the sale of the produce.
The capital is thus ready for a new employment, in which it will
maintain as much labour as before.   The manufacturer and his
work-people lose the benefit of the skill and knowledge which they
had acquired in the particular business, and which can only be
partially of use to them in any other ; and that is the amount of
loss to the community by the change.   But the labourers can still
work ; and the capital which previously employed them will, either
in the same hands, or by being lent to others, employ either those
labourers or an equivalent number in some other occupation.

This theorem, that to purchase produce is not to employ labour ;
that the demand for labour is constituted by the wages which precede
the production, and not by the demand which may exist for the
commodities resulting from the production ; is a proposition which
greatly needs all the illustration it can receive.   It is, to common
apprehension, a paradox ; and even among political economists
of reputation I can hardly point to any, except Mr. Ricardo and M.
Say, who have kept it constantly and steadily in view.   Almost all
others occasionally express themselves as if a person who buys commodities, the produce of labour, was an employer of labour, and
created a demand for it as really, and in the same sense, as if he
bought the labour itself directly, by the payment of wages.   It is
no wonder that political economy advances slowly, when such a
question as this still remains open at its very threshold.   [1] I apprehend, that if by demand for labour be meant the demand by which
wages are raised, or the number of labourers in employment increased,
demand for commodities does not constitute demand for labour.

---

[1] [The rest of this paragraph replaced in the 3rd ed. (1852) the original text :
" I am desirous of impressing on the reader that a demand for commodities
does not in any manner constitute a demand for labour, but only determines
into a particular channel a portion, more or less considerable, of the demand
already existing.   It determines that a part of the labour and capital of the
community shall be employed in producing certain things instead of other
things.   The demand for labour is constituted solely by the funds directly set
apart for the use of labourers."]

I conceive that a person who buys commodities and consumes them himself, does no good to the labouring classes; and that it is only by what he abstains from consuming, and expends in direct payments to labourers in exchange for labour, that he benefits the labouring classes, or adds anything to the amount of their employment.

For the better illustration of the principle, let us put the following case. A consumer may expend his income either in buying services, or commodities. He may employ part of it in hiring journeyman bricklayers to build a house, or excavators to dig artificial lakes, or labourers to make plantations and lay out pleasure grounds; or, instead of this, he may expend the same value in buying velvet and lace. The question is, whether the difference between these two modes of expending his income affects the interest of the labouring classes. It is plain that in the first of the two cases he employs labourers, who will be out of employment, or at least out of that employment, in the opposite case. But those from whom I differ say that this is of no consequence, because in buying velvet and lace he equally employs labourers, namely, those who make the velvet and lace. I contend, however, that in this last case he does not employ labourers; but merely decides in what kind of work some other person shall employ them. The consumer does not with his own funds pay to the weavers and lacemakers their day's wages. He buys the finished commodity, which has been produced by labour and capital, the labour not being paid nor the capital furnished by him, but by the manufacturer. Suppose that he had been in the habit of expending this portion of his income in hiring journeyman bricklayers, who laid out the amount of their wages in food and clothing, which were also produced by labour and capital. He, however, determines to prefer velvet, for which he thus creates an extra demand. This demand cannot be satisfied without an extra supply, nor can the supply be produced without an extra capital: where, then, is the capital to come from? There is nothing in the consumer's change of purpose which makes the capital of the country greater than it otherwise was. It appears, then, that the increased demand for velvet could not for the present be supplied, were it not that the very circumstance which gave rise to it has set at liberty a capital of the exact amount required. The very sum which the consumer now employs in buying velvet, formerly passed into the hands of journeyman bricklayers, who expended it in food and necessaries, which they now either go without, or squeeze by their competition from the shares of other labourers. The labour and capital, therefore, which formerly produced necessaries for the use of these bricklayers, are deprived of their market, and must look out for other employment ; and they find it in making velvet for the new demand. I do not mean that the very same labour and capital which produced the necessaries turn themselves to producing the velvet ; but, in some one or other of a hundred modes, they take the place of that which does. There was capital in existence to do one of two things—to make the velvet, or to produce necessaries for the journeyman bricklayers ; but not to do both. It was at the option of the consumer which of the two should happen ; and if he chooses the velvet, they go without the necessaries.

[1] For further illustration, let us suppose the same case reversed. The consumer has been accustomed to buy velvet, but resolves to discontinue that expense, and to employ the same annual sum in hiring bricklayers. If the common opinion be correct, this change in the mode of his expenditure gives no additional employment to labour, but only transfers employment from velvet-makers to bricklayers. On closer inspection, however, it will be seen that there is an increase of the total sum applied to the remuneration of labour. The velvet manufacturer, supposing him aware of the diminished demand for his commodity, diminishes the production, and sets at liberty a corresponding portion of the capital employed in the manufacture. This capital, thus withdrawn from the maintenance of velvet-makers, is not the same fund with that which the customer employs in maintaining bricklayers ; it is a second fund. There are, therefore, two funds to be employed in the maintenance and remuneration of labour, where before there was only one. There is not a transfer of employment from velvet-makers to bricklayers ; there is a new employment created for bricklayers, and a transfer of employment from velvet-makers to some other labourers, most probably those who produce the food and other things which the bricklayers consume.

In answer to this it is said, that though money laid out in buying velvet is not capital, it replaces a capital ; that though it does not create a new demand for labour, it is the necessary means of enabling the existing demand to be kept up. The funds (it may be said) of the manufacturer, while locked up in velvet, cannot be directly

---

[1] [In the 2nd ed. (1849) there was here inserted "a different mode of stating the argument." In the 3rd ed. (1852) this became the long footnote of this section ; and five new paragraphs were inserted at this point.]

applied to the maintenance of labour ; they do not begin to constitute a demand for labour until the velvet is sold, and the capital
which made it replaced from the outlay of the purchaser ; and thus,
it may be said, the velvet-maker and the velvet-buyer have not two
capitals, but only one capital between them, which by the act of
purchase the buyer transfers to the manufacturer, and if instead of
buying velvet he buys labour, he simply transfers this capital elsewhere, extinguishing as much demand for labour in one quarter as he
creates in another.

The premises of this argument are not denied. To set free
a capital which would otherwise be locked up in a form useless
for the support of labour, is, no doubt, the same thing to the
interests of labourers as the creation of a new capital. It is perfectly true that if I expend 1000*l.* in buying velvet, I enable the
manufacturer to employ 1000*l.* in the maintenance of labour,
which could not have been so employed while the velvet remained
unsold : and if it would have remained unsold for ever unless
I bought it, then by changing my purpose, and hiring bricklayers
instead, I undoubtedly create no new demand for labour : for while
I employ 1000*l.* in hiring labour on the one hand, I annihilate
for ever 1000*l.* of the velvet-maker's capital on the other. But
this is confounding the effects arising from the mere suddenness
of a change with the effects of the change itself. If when the
buyer ceased to purchase, the capital employed in making velvet
for his use necessarily perished, then his expending the same
amount in hiring bricklayers would be no creation, but merely
a transfer, of employment. The increased employment which I
contend is given to labour, would not be given unless the capital
of the velvet-maker *could* be liberated, and would not be given
until it *was* liberated. But every one knows that the capital
invested in an employment can be withdrawn from it, if sufficient
time be allowed. If the velvet-maker had previous notice, by
not receiving the usual order, he will have produced 1000*l.* less
velvet, and an equivalent portion of his capital will have been
already set free. If he had no previous notice, and the article
consequently remains on his hands, the increase of his stock will
induce him next year to suspend or diminish his production until
the surplus is carried off. When this process is complete, the
manufacturer will find himself as rich as before, with undiminished
power of employing labour in general, though a portion of his
capital will now be employed in maintaining some other kind of

it. Until this adjustment has taken place, the demand for labour
will be merely changed, not increased : but as soon as it has taken
place, the demand for labour is increased.   Where there was formerly
only one capital employed in maintaining weavers to make 1000*l.*
worth of velvet, there is now that same capital employed in making
something else, and 1000*l.* distributed among bricklayers besides.
There are now two capitals employed in remunerating two sets
of labourers ; while before, one of those capitals, that of the customer, only served as a wheel in the machinery by which the other
capital, that of the manufacturer, carried on its employment of
labour from year to year.

The proposition for which I am contending is in reality equivalent
to the following, which to some minds will appear a truism, though
to others it is a paradox : that a person does good to labourers,
not by what he consumes on himself, but solely by what he does
not so consume. If instead of laying out 100*l.* in wine or silk, I
expend it in wages, the demand for commodities is precisely equal
in both cases : in the one, it is a demand for 100*l.* worth of wine
or silk, in the other, for the same value of bread, beer, labourers'
clothing, fuel, and indulgences : but the labourers of the community have in the latter case the value of 100*l.* more of the produce
of the community distributed among them. I have consumed
that much less, and made over my consuming power to them.
If it were not so, my having consumed less would not leave more
to be consumed by others ; which is a manifest contradiction.
When less is not produced, what one person forbears to consume
is necessarily added to the share of those to whom he transfers his
power of purchase. In the case supposed I do not necessarily
consume less ultimately, since the labourers whom I pay may
build a house for me, or make something else for my future consumption. But I have at all events postponed my consumption, and
have turned over part of my share of the present produce
of the community to the labourers. If after an interval I am
indemnified, it is not from the existing produce, but from a
subsequent addition made to it. I have therefore left more of the
existing produce to be consumed by others ; and have put into the
possession of labourers the power to consume it.

[1] There cannot be a better *reductio ad absurdum* of the opposite
doctrine than that afforded by the Poor Law. If it be equally for
the benefit of the labouring classes whether I consume my means

---

[1] [This paragraph was inserted in the 6th ed. (1865).]

In the form of things purchased for my own use, or set aside a portion in the shape of wages or alms for their direct consumption, on what ground can the policy be justified of taking my money from me to support paupers ? since my unproductive expenditure would have equally benefited them, while I should have enjoyed it too. If society can both eat its cake and have it, why should it not be allowed the double indulgence ?   But common sense tells every one in his own case (though he does not see it on the larger scale), that the poor rate which he pays is really subtracted from his own consumption, and that no shifting of payment backwards and forwards will enable two persons to eat the same food.   If he had not been required to pay the rate, and had consequently laid out the amount on himself, the poor would have had as much less for their share of the total produce of the country, as he himself would have consumed more.*

* [1849] The following case, which presents the argument in a somewhat different shape, may serve for still further illustration.

Suppose that a rich individual, **A**, expends a certain amount daily in wages or alms, which, as soon as received, is expended and consumed, in the form of coarse food, by the receivers.   A dies, leaving his property to B, who discontinues this item of expenditure, and expends in lieu of it the same sum each day in delicacies for his own table.   I have chosen this supposition, in order that the two cases may be similar in all their circumstances, except that which is the subject of comparison.   In order not to obscure the essential facts of the case by exhibiting them through the hazy medium of a money transaction, let us further suppose that A, and B after him, are landlords of the estate on which both the food consumed by the recipients of A's disbursements, and the articles of luxury supplied for B's table, are produced ; and that their rent is paid to them in kind, they giving previous notice what description of produce they shall require.   The question is, whether B's expenditure gives as much employment or as much food to his poorer neighbours as A's gave.

From the case as stated, it seems to follow that while A lived, that portion of his income which he expended in wages or alms, would be drawn by him from the farm in the shape of food for labourers, and would be used as such ; while B, who came after him, would require, instead of this, an equivalent value in expensive articles of food, to be consumed in his own household : that the farmer, therefore, would, under B's régime, produce that much less, of ordinary food, and more of expensive delicacies, for each day of the year than was produced in A's time, and that there would be that amount less of food shared, throughout the year, among the labouring and poorer classes.   This is what would be conformable to the principles laid down in the text.   Those who think differently, must, on the other hand, suppose that the luxuries required by B would be produced, not instead of, but in addition to, the food previously supplied to A's labourers, and that the aggregate produce of the country would be increased in amount.   But when it is asked, how this double production would be effected—how the farmer, whose capital and labour were already fully employed, would be enabled to supply the new wants of B, without producing less of other things ; the only mode which presents itself is, that he should *first* produce the food, and then, giving that food to the

It appears, then, that a demand delayed until the work is completed, and furnishing no advances, but only reimbursing advances made by others, contributes nothing to the demand for labour ; and that what is so expended, is, in all its effects, so far as

labourers whom A formerly fed, should by means of their labour, produce the luxuries wanted by B. This, accordingly, when the objectors are hard pressed, appears to be really their meaning. But it is an obvious answer, that, on this supposition, B must wait for his luxuries till the second year, and they are wanted this year. By the original hypothesis, he consumes his luxurious dinner day by day, *pari passu* with the rations of bread and potatoes formerly served out by A to his labourers. There is not time to feed the labourers first, and supply B afterwards : he and they cannot both have their wants ministered to : he can only satisfy his own demand for commodities, by leaving as much of theirs, as was formerly supplied from that fund, unsatisfied.

It may, indeed, be rejoined by an objector, that since, on the present showing, time is the only thing wanting to render the expenditure of B consistent with as large an employment to labour as was given by A, why may we not suppose that B postpones his increased consumption of personal luxuries until they can be furnished to him by the labour of the persons whom A employed ? In that case, it may be said, he would employ and feed as much labour as his predecessors. Undoubtedly he would ; but why ? Because his income would be expended in exactly the same manner as his predecessor's ; it would be expended in wages. A reserved from his personal consumption a fund which he paid away directly to labourers ; B does the same, only instead of paying it to them himself, he leaves it in the hands of the farmer who pays it to them for him. On this supposition, B, in the first year, neither expending the amount, as far as he is personally concerned, in A's manner nor in his own, really saves that portion of his income, and lends it to the farmer. And if, in subsequent years, confining himself within the year's income, he leaves the farmer in arrears to that amount, it becomes an additional capital, with which the farmer may permanently employ and feed A's labourers. Nobody pretends that such a change as this, a change from spending an income in wages of labour to saving it for investment, deprives any labourers of employment. What is affirmed to have that effect is, the change from hiring labourers to buying commodities for personal use ; as represented by our original hypothesis.

In our illustration we have supposed no buying and selling, or use of money. But the case as we have put it, corresponds with actual fact in everything except the details of the mechanism. The whole of any country is virtually a single farm and manufactory, from which every member of the community draws his appointed share of the produce, having a certain number of counters, called pounds sterling, put into his hands, which, at his convenience, he brings back and exchanges for such goods as he prefers, up to the limit of the amount. He does not, as in our imaginary case, give notice beforehand what things he shall require ; but the dealers and producers are quite capable of finding it out by observation, and any change in the demand is promptly followed by an adaptation of the supply to it. If a consumer changes from paying away a part of his income in wages, to spending it that same day (not some subsequent and distant day) in things for his own consumption, and perseveres in this altered practice until production has had time to adapt itself to the alteration of demand, there will from that time be less food and other articles for the use of labourers, produced in the country, by exactly the value of the extra luxuries now demanded ; and the labourers, as a class, will be worse off by the precise amount.

regards the employment of the labouring class, a mere nullity ; it does not and cannot create any employment except at the expense of other employment which existed before.

But though a demand for velvet does nothing more in regard to the employment for labour and capital, than to determine so much of the employment which already existed, into that particular channel instead of any other ; still, to the producers already engaged in the velvet manufacture, and not intending to quit it, this is of the utmost importance. To them, a falling off in the demand is a real loss, and one which, even if none of their goods finally perish unsold, may mount to any height, up to that which would make them choose, as the smaller evil, to retire from the business. On the contrary, an increased demand enables them to extend their transactions—to make a profit on a larger capital, if they have it, or can borrow it ; and, turning over their capital more rapidly, they will employ their labourers more constantly, or employ a greater number than before. So that an increased demand for a commodity does really, in the particular department, often cause a greater employment to be given to labour by the same capital. The mistake lies in not perceiving that, in the cases supposed, this advantage is given to labour and capital in one department, only by being withdrawn from another ; and that, when the change has produced its natural effect of attracting into the employment additional capital proportional to the increased demand, the advantage itself ceases.

The grounds of a proposition, when well understood, usually give a tolerable indication of the limitations of it. The general principle, now stated, is that demand for commodities determines merely the direction of labour, and the kind of wealth produced, but not the quantity or efficiency of the labour, or the aggregate of wealth. But to this there are two exceptions. First, when labour is supported, but not fully occupied, a new demand for something which it can produce may stimulate the labour thus supported to increased exertions, of which the result may be an increase of wealth, to the advantage of the labourers themselves and of others. Work which can be done in the spare hours of persons subsisted from some other source, can (as before remarked) be undertaken without withdrawing capital from other occupations, beyond the amount (often very small) required to cover the expense of tools and materials, and even this will often be provided by savings made expressly for the purpose. The reason of our theorem thus failing, the theorem itself fails, and employment of this kind

may, by the springing up of a demand for the commodity, be called
into existence without depriving labour of an equivalent amount
of employment in any other quarter. The demand does not, even
in this case, operate on labour any otherwise than through the
medium of an existing capital, but it affords an inducement which
causes that capital to set in motion a greater amount of labour than
it did before.

[1] The second exception, of which I shall speak at length in a
subsequent chapter, consists in the known effect of an extension
of the market for a commodity, in rendering possible an increased
development of the division of labour, and hence a more effective
distribution of the productive forces of society. This, like the
former, is more an exception in appearance than it is in reality.
It is not the money paid by the purchaser, which remunerates
the labour ; it is the capital of the producer : the demand only
determines in what manner that capital shall be employed, and
what kind of labour it shall remunerate ; but if it determines that
the commodity shall be produced on a large scale, it enables the
same capital to produce more of the commodity, and may, by an
indirect effect in causing an increase of capital, produce an eventual
increase of the remuneration of the labourer.

The demand for commodities is a consideration of importance,
rather in the theory of exchange, than in that of production. Looking
at things in the aggregate, and permanently, the remuneration of
the producer is derived from the productive power of his own
capital. The sale of the produce for money, and the subsequent
expenditure of the money in buying other commodities, are a
mere exchange of equivalent values for mutual accommodation.
It is true that, the division of employments being one of the principal
means of increasing the productive power of labour, the power of
exchanging gives rise to a great increase of the produce ; but even
then it is production, not exchange, which remunerates labour
and capital. We cannot too strictly represent to ourselves the
operation of exchange, whether conducted by barter or through
the medium of money, as the mere mechanism by which each person
transforms the remuneration of his labour or of his capital into
the particular shape in which it is most convenient to him to possess
it ; but in no wise the source of the remuneration itself.

§ 10.   The preceding principles demonstrate the fallacy of

---

[1] [This paragraph was inserted in the 6th ed. (1865).]

many popular arguments and doctrines, which are continually
reproducing themselves in new forms. For example, it has been
contended, and by some from whom better things might have been
expected, that the argument for the income-tax, grounded on its
falling on the higher and middle classes only, and sparing the poor,
is an error ; some have gone so far as to say, an imposture ; because
in taking from the rich what they would have expended among the
poor, the tax injures the poor as much as if it had been directly
levied from them. Of this doctrine we now know what to think.
So far, indeed, as what is taken from the rich in taxes, would, if not
so taken, have been saved and converted into capital, or even expended in the maintenance and wages of servants or of any class
of unproductive labourers, to that extent the demand for labour is
no doubt diminished, and the poor injuriously affected, by the
tax on the rich ; and as these effects are almost always produced
in a greater or less degree, it is impossible so to tax the rich as
that no portion whatever of the tax can fall on the poor. But even
here the question arises, whether the government, after receiving
the amount, will not lay out as great a portion of it in the direct
purchase of labour, as the taxpayers would have done. In regard
to all that portion of the tax, which, if not paid to the government,
would have been consumed in the form of commodities (or even
expended in services if the payment has been advanced by a
capitalist), this, according to the principles we have investigated,
falls definitely on the rich, and not at all on the poor. There is
exactly the same demand for labour, so far as this portion is concerned, after the tax, as before it. The capital which hitherto
employed the labourers of the country remains, and is still capable
of employing the same number. There is the same amount of
produce paid in wages, or allotted to defray the feeding and clothing
of labourers.

If those against whom I am now contending were in the right,
it would be impossible to tax anybody except the poor. If it is
taxing the labourers, to tax what is laid out in the produce of labour,
the labouring classes pay all the taxes. The same argument, however,
equally proves, that it is impossible to tax the labourers at all ;
since the tax, being laid out either in labour or in commodities,
comes all back to them ; so that taxation has the singular property
of falling on nobody. On the same showing, it would do the labourers
no harm to take from them all they have, and distribute it among
the other members of the community. It would all be " spent

among them," which on this theory comes to the same thing. The error is produced by not looking directly at the realities of the phenomena, but attending only to the outward mechanism of paying and spending. If we look at the effects produced not on the money, which merely changes hands, but on the commodities which are used and consumed, we see that, in consequence of the income-tax, the classes who pay it do really diminish their consumption. Exactly so far as they do this, they are the persons on whom the tax falls. It is defrayed out of what they would otherwise have used and enjoyed. So far, on the other hand, as the burthen falls, not on what they would have consumed, but on what they would have saved to maintain production, or spent in maintaining or paying unproductive labourers, to that extent the tax forms a deduction from what would have been used and enjoyed by the labouring classes. But if the government, as is probably the fact, expends fully as much of the amount as the tax-payers would have done in the direct employment of labour, as in hiring sailors, soldiers, and policemen, or in paying off debt, by which last operation it even increases capital; the labouring classes not only do not lose any employment by the tax, but may possibly gain some, and the whole of the tax falls exclusively where it was intended.

All that portion of the produce of the country which any one, not a labourer,[1] actually and literally consumes for his own use, does not contribute in the smallest degree to the maintenance of labour. No one is benefited by mere consumption, except the person who consumes. And a person cannot both consume his income himself, and make it over to be consumed by others. Taking away a certain portion by taxation cannot deprive both him and them of it, but only him *or* them. To know which is the sufferer, we must understand whose consumption will have to be retrenched in consequence : this, whoever it be, is the person on whom the tax really falls.[2]

---

[1] [" Not a labourer " was inserted in the 3rd ed. (1852).]
[2] [See Appendix F. *Fundamental Propositions on Capital.*]

CHAPTER VI

§ 1. To complete our explanations on the subject of capital, it is necessary to say something of the two species into which it is usually divided. The distinction is very obvious, and though not named, has been often adverted to, in the two preceding chapters : but it is now proper to define it accurately, and to point out a few of its consequences.

Of the capital engaged in the production of any commodity, there is a part which, after being once used, exists no longer as capital : is no longer capable of rendering service to production, or at least not the same service, nor to the same sort of production. Such, for example, is the portion of capital which consists of materials. The tallow and alkali of which soap is made, once used in the manufacture, are destroyed as alkali and tallow ; and cannot be employed any further in the soap manufacture, though in their altered condition, as soap, they are capable of being used as a material or an instrument in other branches of manufacture. In the same division must be placed the portion of capital which is paid as the wages, or consumed as the subsistence, of labourers. The part of the capital of a cotton-spinner which he pays away to his work-people, once so paid, exists no longer as his capital, or as a cotton-spinner's capital : such portion of it as the workmen consume, no longer exists as capital at all : even if they save any part, it may now be more properly regarded as a fresh capital, the result of a second act of accumulation. Capital which in this manner fulfils the whole of its office in the production in which it is engaged by a single use, is called Circulating Capital. The term, which is not very appropriate, is derived from the circumstance, that this portion of capital requires to be constantly renewed by the sale of the finished product, and when renewed is perpetually parted with in buying materials and paying wages ; so that it does its work, not by being kept, but by changing hands.

Another large portion of capital, however, consists in instruments of production, of a more or less permanent character ; which produce their effect not by being parted with, but by being kept ; and the efficacy of which is not exhausted by a single use. To this class belong buildings, machinery, and all or most things known by the name of implements or tools. The durability of some of these is considerable, and their function as productive instruments is prolonged through many repetitions of the productive operation. In this class must likewise be included capital sunk (as the expression is) in permanent improvements of land. So also the capital expended once for all, in the commencement of an undertaking, to prepare the way for subsequent operations : the expense of opening a mine, for example : of cutting canals, of making roads or docks. Other examples might be added, but these are sufficient. Capital which exists in any of these durable shapes, and the return to which is spread over a period of corresponding duration, is called Fixed Capital.

Of fixed capital, some kinds require to be occasionally or periodically renewed. Such are all implements and buildings : they require, at intervals, partial renewal by means of repairs, and are at last entirely worn out, and cannot be of any further service as buildings and implements, but fall back into the class of materials. In other cases, the capital does not, unless as a consequence of some unusual accident, require entire renewal : but there is always some outlay needed, either regularly or at least occasionally, to keep it up. A dock or a canal, once made, does not require, like a machine, to be made again, unless purposely destroyed, or unless an earthquake or some similar catastrophe has filled it up : but regular and frequent outlays are necessary to keep it in repair. The cost of opening a mine needs not be incurred a second time ; but unless some one goes to the expense of keeping the mine clear of water, it is soon rendered useless. The most permanent of all kinds of fixed capital is that employed in giving increased productiveness to a natural agent, such as land. The draining of marshy or inundated tracts like the Bedford Level, the reclaiming of land from the sea, or its protection by embankments, are improvements calculated for perpetuity ; but drains and dykes require frequent repairs. The same character of perpetuity belongs to the improvement of land by subsoil draining, which adds so much to the productiveness of the clay soils ; or by permanent manures, that is, by the addition to the soil, not of the substances which enter into the composition of vegetables, and which are therefore consumed by vegetation, but of those which merely alter the relation of the soil to air and water ; as sand and lime on the heavy soils, clay and marl on the light. Even such works, however, require some, though it may be very little, occasional outlay to maintain their full effect.

These improvements, however, by the very fact of their deserving that title, produce an increase of return, which, after defraying all expenditure necessary for keeping them up, still leaves a surplus. This surplus forms the return to the capital sunk in the first instance, and that return does not, as in the case of machinery, terminate by the wearing out of the machine, but continues for ever. The land, thus increased in productiveness, bears a value in the market proportional to the increase : and hence it is usual to consider the capital which was invested, or sunk, in making the improvement, as still existing in the increased value of the land. There must be no mistake, however. The capital, like all other capital, has been consumed. It was consumed in maintaining the labourers who executed the improvement, and in the wear and tear of the tools by which they were assisted. But it was consumed productively, and has left a permanent result in the improved productiveness of an appropriated natural agent, the land. We may call the increased produce the joint result of the land and of a capital fixed in the land. But as the capital, having in reality been consumed, cannot be withdrawn, its productiveness is thenceforth indissolubly blended with that arising from the original qualities of the soil ; and the remuneration for the use of it thenceforth depends, not upon the laws which govern the returns to labour and capital, but upon those which govern the recompense for natural agents. What these are, we shall see hereafter.*

§ 2. There is a great difference between the effects of circulating and those of fixed capital, on the amount of the gross produce of the country. Circulating capital being destroyed as such, or at any rate finally lost to the owner, by a single use ; and the product resulting from that one use being the only source from which the owner can replace the capital, or obtain any remuneration for its productive employment ; the product must of course be sufficient for those purposes, or in other words, the result of a single use must be a reproduction equal to the whole amount of the circulating capital used, and a profit besides. This, however, is by no means

* Infra, book ii. chap. xvi. *On Rent.*

necessary in the case of fixed capital. Since machinery, for example, is not wholly consumed by one use, it is not necessary that it should be wholly replaced from the product of that use. The machine answers the purpose of its owner if it brings in, during each interval of time, enough to cover the expense of repairs, and the deterioration in value which the machine has sustained during the same time, with a surplus sufficient to yield the ordinary profit on the entire value of the machine.

From this it follows that all increase of fixed capital, when taking place at the expense of circulating, must be, at least temporarily, prejudicial to the interests of the labourers. This is true, not of machinery alone, but of all improvements by which capital is sunk ; that is, rendered permanently incapable of being applied to the maintenance and remuneration of labour. Suppose that a person farms his own land, with a capital of two thousand quarters of corn, employed in maintaining labourers during one year (for simplicity we omit the consideration of seed and tools), whose labour produces him annually two thousand four hundred quarters, being a profit of twenty per cent. This profit we shall suppose that he annually consumes, carrying on his operations from year to year on the original capital of two thousand quarters. Let us now suppose that by the expenditure of half his capital he effects a permanent improvement of his land, which is executed by half his labourers, and occupies them for a year, after which he will only require, for the effectual cultivation of his land, half as many labourers as before. The remainder of his capital he employs as usual. In the first year there is no difference in the condition of the labourers, except that part of them have received the same pay for an operation on the land, which they previously obtained for ploughing, sowing, and reaping. At the end of the year, however, the improver has not, as before, a capital of two thousand quarters of corn. Only one thousand quarters of his capital have been reproduced in the usual way : he has now only those thousand quarters and his improvement. He will employ, in the next and in each following year, only half the number of labourers, and will divide among them only half the former quantity of subsistence. The loss will soon be made up to them if the improved land, with the diminished quantity of labour, produces two thousand four hundred quarters as before, because so enormous an accession of gain will probably induce the improver to save a part, add it to his capital, and become a larger employer of labour. But it is conceivable that this may not be the case [1] ; for (supposing, as we may do, that the improvement will last indefinitely, without any outlay worth mentioning to keep it up) the improver will have gained largely by his improvement if the land now yields, not two thousand four hundred, but one thousand five hundred quarters ; since this will replace the one thousand quarters forming his present circulating capital, with a profit of twenty-five per cent (instead of twenty as before) on the whole capital, fixed and circulating together. The improvement, therefore, may be a very profitable one to him, and yet very injurious to the labourers.

[2] The supposition, in the terms in which it has been stated, is purely ideal ; or at most applicable only to such a case as that of the conversion of arable land into pasture, which, though formerly a frequent practice, is regarded [1849] by modern agriculturists as the reverse of an improvement.* But this does not affect the substance of the argument. Suppose that the improvement does not operate in the manner supposed—does not enable a part of the labour previously employed on the land to be dispensed with— but only enables the same labour to raise a greater produce. Suppose, too, that the greater produce, which by means of the improvement can be raised from the soil with the same labour, is all wanted, and will find purchasers. The improver will in that case require the same number of labourers as before, at the same wages. But where will he find the means of paying them ? He has no longer his original capital of two thousand quarters disposable for the purpose. One thousand of them are lost and gone—consumed in making the improvement. If he is to employ as many labourers as before, and pay them as highly, he must borrow, or obtain from some other source, a thousand quarters to supply the deficit. But these thousand quarters already maintained, or were destined to maintain,

---

[1] [So altered in 2nd ed. (1849) from the original : "this may not, and often will not, be the case."]

[2] [The first two sentences of this paragraph were inserted in the 2nd ed. (1849), and the subsequent sentences slightly changed in form.]

* [1865] The clearing away of the small farmers in the North of Scotland, within the present century, was, however, a case of it ; and Ireland, since the potato famine and the repeal of the corn laws, is another. The remarkable decrease which has lately attracted notice in the gross produce of Irish agriculture, is, to all appearance, partly attributable to the diversion of land from maintaining human labourers to feeding cattle ; and it could not have taken place without the removal of a large part of the Irish population by emigration or death. We have thus two recent instances, in which what was regarded as an agricultural improvement, has diminished the power of the country to support its population. The effect, however, of all the improvements due to modern science is to increase, or at all events, not to diminish, the gross produce.

an equivalent quantity of labour. They are not a fresh creation; their destination is only changed from one productive employment to another; and though the agriculturist has made up the deficiency in his own circulating capital, the breach in the circulating capital of the community remains unrepaired.

The argument relied on by most of those who contend that machinery can never be injurious to the labouring class, is, that by cheapening production it creates such an increased demand for the commodity, as enables, ere long, a greater number of persons than ever to find employment in producing it. This argument does not seem to me to have the weight commonly ascribed to it. The fact, though too broadly stated, is, no doubt, often true. The copyists who were thrown out of employment by the invention of printing, were doubtless soon outnumbered by the compositors and pressmen who took their place; and the number of labouring persons now occupied in the cotton manufacture is many times greater than were so occupied previously to the inventions of Hargreaves and Arkwright, which shows that, besides the enormous fixed capital now embarked in the manufacture, it also employs a far larger circulating capital than at any former time. But if this capital was drawn from other employments; if the funds which took the place of the capital sunk in costly machinery, were supplied not by any additional saving consequent on the improvements, but by drafts on the general capital of the community; what better were the labouring classes for the mere transfer? In what manner was the loss they sustained by the conversion of circulating into fixed capital made up to them by a mere shifting of part of the remainder of the circulating capital from its old employments to a new one?

All attempts to make out that the labouring classes as a collective body *cannot* suffer temporarily by the introduction of machinery, or by the sinking of capital in permanent improvements, are, I conceive, necessarily fallacious. That they would suffer in the particular department of industry to which the change applies, is generally admitted, and obvious to common sense; but it is often said, that though employment is withdrawn from labour in one department, an exactly equivalent employment is opened for it in others, because what the consumers save in the increased cheapness of one particular article enables them to augment their consumption of others, thereby increasing the demand for other kinds of labour. This is plausible, but, as was shown in the last chapter, involves a fallacy; demand for commodities being a totally different thing from demand for labour. It is true, the consumers have now additional means of buying other things ; but this will not create the other things, unless there is capital to produce them, and the improvement has not set at liberty any capital, if even it has not absorbed some from other employments. The supposed increase of production and of employment for labour in other departments therefore will not take place ; and the increased demand for commodities by some consumers, will be balanced by a cessation of demand on the part of others, namely, the labourers who were superseded by the improvement, and who will now be maintained, if at all, by sharing, either in the way of competition or of charity, in what was previously consumed by other people.

§ 3. Nevertheless, I do not believe that, as things are actually transacted, improvements in production are often, if ever, injurious, even temporarily, to the labouring classes in the aggregate. They would be so if they took place suddenly to a great amount, because much of the capital sunk must necessarily in that case be provided from funds already employed as circulating capital. But improvements are always introduced very gradually, and are seldom or never made by withdrawing circulating capital from actual production, but are made by the employment of the annual increase. There are few if any examples of a great increase of fixed capital, at a time and place where circulating capital was not rapidly increasing likewise. It is not in poor or backward countries that great and costly improvements in production are made. To sink capital in land for a permanent return—to introduce expensive machinery— are acts involving immediate sacrifice for distant objects ; and indicate, in the first place, tolerably complete security of property ; in the second, considerable activity of industrial enterprise ; and in the third, a high standard of what has been called the " effective desire of accumulation : " which three things are the elements of a society rapidly progressive in its amount of capital. Although, therefore, the labouring classes must suffer, not only if the increase of fixed capital takes place at the expense of circulating, but even if it is so large and rapid as to retard that ordinary increase to which the growth of population has habitually adapted itself ; yet, in point of fact, this is very unlikely to happen, since there is probably no country whose fixed capital increases in a ratio more than proportional to its circulating. If the whole of the railways which, during the speculative madness of 1845, obtained the sanction of

Parliament, had been constructed in the times fixed for the completion of each, this improbable contingency would, most likely, have been realized ; but this very case has afforded a striking example of the difficulties which oppose the diversion into new channels, of any considerable portion of the capital that supplies the old : difficulties generally much more than sufficient to prevent enterprises that involve the sinking of capital from extending themselves with such rapidity as to impair the sources of the existing employment for labour.

To these considerations must be added, that even if improvements did for a time decrease the aggregate produce and the circulating capital of the community, they would not the less tend in the long run to augment both. They increase the return to capital ; and of this increase the benefit must necessarily accrue either to the capitalist in greater profits, or to the customer in diminished prices ; affording, in either case, an augmented fund from which accumulation may be made, while enlarged profits also hold out an increased inducement to accumulation. In the case we before selected, in which the immediate result of the improvement was to diminish the gross produce from two thousand four hundred quarters to one thousand five hundred, yet the profit of the capitalist being now five hundred quarters instead of four hundred, the extra one hundred quarters, if regularly saved, would in a few years 'replace the one thousand quarters subtracted from his circulating capital Now the extension of business which almost certainly follows in any department in which an improvement has been made, affords a strong inducement to those engaged in it to add to their capital ; and hence, at the slow pace at which improvements are usually introduced, a great part of the capital which the improvement ultimately absorbs, is drawn from the increased profits and increased savings which it has itself called forth.

This tendency of improvements in production to cause increased accumulation, and thereby ultimately to increase the gross produce, even if temporarily diminishing it, will assume a still more decided character if it should appear that there are assignable limits both to the accumulation of capital, and to the increase of production from the land, which limits once attained, all further increase of produce must stop ; but that improvements in production, whatever may be their other effects, tend to throw one or both of these limits farther off. Now, these are truths which will appear in the clearest light in a subsequent stage of our investigation. It will be seen, that the quantity of capital which will, or even which can, be accumulated in any country and the amount of gross produce which will, or even which can, be raised, bear a proportion to the state of the arts of production there existing; and that every improvement, even if for the time it diminish the circulating capital and the gross produce, ultimately makes room for a larger amount of both, than could possibly have existed otherwise. It is this which is the conclusive answer to the objections against machinery; and the proof thence arising of the ultimate benefit to labourers of mechanical inventions, even in the existing state of society, will hereafter be seen to be conclusive.* But this does not discharge governments from the obligation of alleviating, and if possible preventing, the evils of which this source of ultimate benefit is or may be productive to an existing generation. If the sinking or fixing of capital in machinery or useful works were ever to proceed at such a pace as to impair materially the funds for the maintenance of labour, it would be incumbent on legislators to take measures for moderating its rapidity: and since improvements which do not diminish employment on the whole, almost always throw some particular class of labourers out of it, there cannot be a more legitimate object of the legislator's care than the interests of those who are thus sacrificed to the gains of their fellow-citizens and of posterity.

To return to the theoretical distinction between fixed and circulating capital. Since all wealth which is destined to be employed for reproduction comes within the designation of capital, there are parts of capital which do not agree with the definition of either species of it; for instance, the stock of finished goods which a manu facturer or dealer at any time possesses unsold in his warehouses. But this, though capital as to its destination, is not yet capital in actual exercise: it is not engaged in production, but has first to be sold or exchanged, that is, converted into an equivalent value of some other commodities; and therefore is not yet either fixed or circulating capital; but will become either one or the other, or be eventually divided between them. With the proceeds of his finished goods, a manufacturer will partly pay his work-people, partly replenish his stock of the materials of his manufacture, and partly provide new buildings and machinery, or repair the old; but how much will be devoted to one purpose, and how much to another, depends on the nature of the manufacture, and the requirements of the particular moment.

* Infra, book iv. chap. v.

It should be observed further, that the portion of capital consumed in the form of seed or material, though, unlike fixed capital, it requires to be at once replaced from the gross produce, stands yet in the same relation to the employment of labour as fixed capital does. What is expended in materials is as much withdrawn from the maintenance and remuneration of labourers, as what is fixed in machinery; and if capital now expended in wages were diverted to the providing of materials, the effect on the labourers would be as prejudicial as if it were converted into fixed capital. This, however, is a kind of change which seldom, if ever, takes place. The tendency of improvements in production is always to economize, never to increase, the expenditure of seed or material for a given produce; and the interest of the labourers has no detriment to apprehend from this source.

CHAPTER VII

ON WHAT DEPENDS THE DEGREE OF PRODUCTIVENESS
OF PRODUCTIVE AGENTS

§ 1. WE have concluded our general survey of the requisites of production. We have found that they may be reduced to three : labour, capital, and the materials and motive forces afforded by nature. Of these, labour and the raw material of the globe are primary and indispensable. Natural motive powers may be called in to the assistance of labour, and are a help, but not an essential, of production. The remaining requisite, capital, is itself the product of labour ; its instrumentality in production is therefore, in reality, that of labour in an indirect shape. It does not the less require to be specified separately. A previous application of labour to produce the capital required for consumption during the work, is no less essential than the application of labour to the work itself. Of capital, again, one, and by far the largest, portion, conduces to production only by sustaining in existence the labour which pro-duces : the remainder, namely the instruments and materials, contribute to it directly, in the same manner with natural agents, and the materials supplied by nature.

We now advance to the second great question in political economy ; on what the degree of productiveness of these agents depends. For it is evident that their productive efficacy varies greatly at various times and places. With the same population and extent of territory, some countries have a much larger amount of production than others, and the same country at one time a greater amount than itself at another. Compare England either with a similar extent of territory in Russia, or with an equal population of Russians. Compare England now with England in the Middle Ages ; Sicily, Northern Africa, or Syria at present, with the same countries at the time of their greatest prosperity, before the Roman Conquest. Some of the causes which contribute to this difference of productiveness are obvious; others not so much so.   We proceed to specify several of them.

§ 2. The most evident cause of superior productiveness is what are called natural advantages.   These are various.   Fertility of soil is one of the principal.   In this there are great varieties, from the deserts of Arabia to the alluvial plains of the Ganges, the Niger, and the Mississippi.   A favourable climate is even more important than a rich soil. There are countries capable of being inhabited, but too cold to be compatible with agriculture.   Their inhabitants cannot pass beyond the nomadic state; they must live, like the Laplanders, by the domestication of the rein-deer, if not by hunting or fishing, like the miserable Esquimaux.   There are countries where oats will ripen, but not wheat, such as the North of Scotland; others where wheat can be grown, but from excess of moisture and want of sunshine, affords but a precarious crop; as in parts of Ireland.   With each advance towards the south, or, in the European temperate region, towards the east, some new branch of agriculture becomes first possible, then advantageous; the vine, maize, silk, figs, olives, rice, dates, successively present themselves, until we come to the sugar, coffee, cotton, spices, &c., of climates which also afford, of the more common agricultural products, and with only a slight degree of cultivation, two or even three harvests in a year.   Nor is it in agriculture alone that differences of climate are important.   Their influence is felt in many other branches of production: in the durability of all work which is exposed to the air; of buildings, for example.   If the temples of Karnac and Luxor had not been injured by men, they might have subsisted in their original perfection almost for ever, for the inscriptions on some of them, though anterior to all authentic history, are fresher than is in our climate an inscription fifty years old: while at St. Petersburg, the most massive works solidly executed in granite hardly a generation ago, are already as travellers tell us, almost in a state to require reconstruction from alternate exposure to summer heat and intense frost.   The superiority of the woven fabrics of Southern Europe over those of England in the richness and clearness of many of their colours, is ascribed to the superior quality of the atmosphere, for which neither the knowledge of chemists nor the skill of dyers has been able to provide, in our hazy and damp climate, a complete equivalent.

Another part of the influence of climate consists in lessening the physical requirements of the producers.   In hot regions, mankind can exist in comfort with less perfect housing, less clothing ; fuel, that absolute necessary of life in cold climates, they can almost dispense with, except for industrial uses. They also require less aliment ; as experience had proved, long before theory had accounted for it by ascertaining that most of what we consume as food is not required for the actual nutrition of the organs, but for keeping up the animal heat, and for supplying the necessary stimulus to the vital functions, which in hot climates is almost sufficiently supplied by air and sunshine. Much, therefore, of the labour elsewhere expended to procure the mere necessaries of life, not being required, more remains disposable for its higher uses and its enjoyments ; if the character of the inhabitants does not rather induce them to use up these advantages, in over-population, or in the indulgence of repose.

Among natural advantages, besides soil and climate, must be mentioned abundance of mineral productions, in convenient situations, and capable of being worked with moderate labour. Such are the coal-fields of Great Britain, which do so much to compensate its inhabitants for the disadvantages of climate ; and the scarcely inferior resource possessed by this country and the United States, in a copious supply of an easily reduced iron ore, at no great depth below the earth's surface, and in close proximity to coal deposits available for working it. In mountain and hill districts, the abundance of natural water-power makes considerable amends for the usually inferior fertility of those regions. But perhaps a greater advantage than all these is a maritime situation, especially when accompanied with good natural harbours ; and, next to it, great navigable rivers. These advantages consist indeed wholly in saving of cost of carriage. But few who have not considered the subject, have any adequate notion how great an extent of economical advantage this comprises ; nor, without having considered the influence exercised on production by exchanges, and by what is called the division of labour, can it be fully estimated. So important is it, that it often does more than counterbalance sterility of soil, and almost every other natural inferiority ; especially in that early stage of industry in which labour and science have not yet provided artificial means of communication capable of rivalling the natural. In the ancient world, and in the Middle Ages, the most prosperous communities were not those which had the largest territory, or the most fertile soil, but rather those which had been forced by natural sterility to make the utmost use of a convenient maritime situation ;

as Athens, Tyre, Marseilles, Venice, the free cities on the Baltic, and the like.

§ 3. So much for natural advantages ; the value of which, *cæteris paribus*, is too obvious to be ever underrated. But experience testifies that natural advantages scarcely ever do for a community, no more than fortune and station do for an individual, anything like what it lies in their nature, or in their capacity, to do. Neither now nor in former ages have the nations possessing the best climate and soil been either the richest or the most powerful ; but (in so far as regards the mass of the people) generally among the poorest, though, in the midst of poverty, probably on the whole the most enjoying. Human life in those countries can be supported on so little, that the poor seldom suffer from anxiety, and in climates in which mere existence is a pleasure, the luxury which they prefer is that of repose. Energy, at the call of passion, they possess in abundance, but not that which is manifested in sustained and persevering labour : and as they seldom concern themselves enough about remote objects to establish good political institutions, the incentives to industry are further weakened by imperfect protection of its fruits. Successful production, like most other kinds of success, depends more on the qualities of the human agents, than on the circumstances in which they work : and it is difficulties, not facilities, that nourish bodily and mental energy. Accordingly the tribes of mankind who have overrun and conquered others, and compelled them to labour for their benefit, have been mostly reared amidst hardship. They have either been bred in the forests of northern climates, or the deficiency of natural hardships has been supplied, as among the Greeks and Romans, by the artificial ones of a rigid military discipline. From the time when the circumstances of modern society permitted the discontinuance of that discipline, the South has no longer produced conquering nations ; military vigour, as well as speculative thought and industrial energy, have all had their principal seats in the less favoured North.

As the second, therefore, of the causes of superior productiveness, we may rank the greater energy of labour. By this is not to be understood occasional, but regular and habitual energy. No one undergoes, without murmuring, a greater amount of occasional fatigue and hardship, or has his bodily powers, and such faculties of mind as he possesses, kept longer at their utmost stretch, than the North American Indian ; yet his indolence is proverbial, whenever he has a brief respite from the pressure of present wants. Individuals, or nations, do not differ so much in the efforts they are able and willing to make under strong immediate incentives, as in their capacity of present exertion for a distant object; and in the thoroughness of their application to work on ordinary occasions.[1] Some amount of these qualities is a necessary condition of any great improvement among mankind. To civilize a savage, he must be inspired with new wants and desires, even if not of a very elevated kind, provided that their gratification can be a motive to steady and regular bodily and mental exertion. If the negroes of Jamaica and Demerara, after their emancipation, had contented themselves, as it was predicted they would do, with the necessaries of life, and abandoned all labour beyond the little which in a tropical climate, with a thin population and abundance of the richest land, is sufficient to support existence, they would have sunk into a condition more barbarous, though less unhappy, than their previous state of slavery.

[1] [From the 4th ed. (1857) a long passage was omitted at this point. This originally ran as follows :

" In this last quality the English, and perhaps the Anglo-Americans, appear at present to surpass every other people. This efficiency of labour is connected with their whole character; with their defects, as much as with their good qualities. The majority of Englishmen and Americans have no life but in their work ; that alone stands between them and ennui. Either from original temperament, climate, or want of development, they are too deficient in senses to enjoy mere existence in repose ; and scarcely any pleasure or amusement is pleasure or amusement to them. Except, therefore, those who are alive to some of the nobler interests of humanity (a small minority in all countries), they have little to distract their attention from work, or to divide the dominion over them with the one propensity which is the passion of those who have no other, and the satisfaction of which comprises all that they imagine of success in life—the desire of growing richer, and getting on in the world. This last characteristic belongs chiefly to those who are in a condition superior to day labourers ; but the absence of any taste for amusement, or enjoyment of repose, is common to all classes. Whether from this or any other cause, the national steadiness and persistency of labour extends to the most improvident of the English working classes—those who never think of saving, or improving their condition. It has become the habit of the country ; and life in England is more governed by habit, and less by personal inclination and will, than in any other country, except perhaps China or Japan. The effect is, that where hard labour is the thing required, there are no labourers like the English ; though in natural intelligence, and even in manual dexterity, they have many superiors.

" Energy of labour, though not an unqualified good, nor one which it is desirable to nourish at the expense of other valuable attributes of human nature, is yet, in a certain measure, a necessary condition," &c.

In the 3rd ed. (1852) the characterisation had been made to apply to the English alone, and the passage began thus : " This last quality is the principal industrial excellence of the English people." ⌊After " a small minority in all countries," had been inserted " and particularly so in this ; " and for " no labourers like the English " had been substituted " no better labourers than the English."]

The motive which was most relied on for inducing them to work was their love of fine clothes and personal ornaments. No one will stand up for this taste as worthy of being cultivated, and in most societies its indulgence tends to impoverish rather than to enrich ; but in the state of mind of the negroes it might have been the only incentive that could make them voluntarily undergo systematic labour, and so acquire or maintain habits of voluntary industry which may be converted to more valuable ends. In England, it is not the desire of wealth that needs to be taught, but the use of wealth, and appreciation of the objects of desire which wealth cannot purchase, or for attaining which it is not required. Every real improvement in the character of the English, whether it consist in giving them higher aspirations, or only a juster estimate of the value of their present objects of desire, must necessarily moderate the ardour of their devotion to the pursuit of wealth. There is no need, however, that it should diminish the strenuous and business-like application to the matter in hand, which is found in the best English workmen, and is their most valuable quality.[1]

[1] [The three preceding sentences originally ran as follows : " As much as the industrial spirit required to be stimulated in their case, so much does it require to be moderated in such countries as England and the United States. There, it is not the desire of wealth . . . required. Every real improvement in the character of the English or Americans, whether it consist in giving them higher aspirations, or only more numerous and better pleasures, must necessarily moderate the all-engrossing torment of their industrialism ; must diminish, therefore, so far as it depends on that cause alone, the aggregate productiveness of their labour. There is no need, however, that it should diminish that strenuous and business-like application to the matter in hand, which is one of their most precious characteristics."

In the 3rd ed. (1852) they were modified to make the description apply to England only, and " the best English workmen ;" and in the 4th (1857) " the ardour of their devotion to the pursuit of wealth " was substituted for " the all-engrossing torment of their industrialism."

Then followed in the original the following quotation and comments, omitted in the 3rd ed. :

" ' Whoever ' (says Mr. Laing, *Notes of a Traveller*, p. 290) ' looks into the social economy of an English or Scotch manufacturing district, in which the population has become thoroughly imbued with the spirit of productiveness, will observe that it is not merely the expertness, despatch, and skill of the operative himself, that are concerned in the prodigious amount of his production in a given time, but the labourer who wheels coal to his fire, the girl who makes ready his breakfast, the whole population, in short, from the potboy who brings his beer, to the banker who keeps his employer's cash, are inspired with the same alert spirit, are in fact working to his hand with the same quickness and punctuality as he works himself. English workmen taken to the Continent always complain that they cannot get on with their work as at home, because of the slow, unpunctual, pipe-in-mouth working habits of those who have to work to their hands, and on whom their own activity and productiveness mainly depend.'

The desirable medium is one which mankind have not often known how to hit : when they labour, to do it with all their might, and especially with all their mind ; but to devote to labour, for mere pecuniary gain, fewer hours in the day, fewer days in the year, and fewer years of life.

§ 4. The third element which determines the productiveness of the labour of a community, is the skill and knowledge therein existing ; whether it be the skill and knowledge of the labourers themselves, or of those who direct their labour. No illustration is requisite to show how the efficacy of industry is promoted by the manual dexterity of those who perform mere routine processes ; by the intelligence of those engaged in operations in which the mind has a considerable part ; and by the amount of knowledge of natural powers and of the properties of objects, which is turned to the purposes of industry. That the productiveness of the labour of a people is limited by their knowledge of the arts of life, is self-evident ; and that any progress in those arts, any improved application of the objects or powers of nature to industrial uses, enables the same quantity and intensity of labour to raise a greater produce.

One principal department of these improvements consists in the invention and use of tools and machinery. The manner in which these serve to increase production and to economize labour, needs not be specially detailed in a work like the present : it will be found explained and exemplified, in a manner at once scientific and popular, in Mr. Babbage's well-known *Economy of Machinery and Manufactures.* An entire chapter of Mr. Babbage's book is composed of instances of the efficacy of machinery in " exerting forces too great for human power, and executing operations too delicate for human touch." But to find examples of work which could not be performed at all by unassisted labour, we need not go so far. Without pumps, worked by steam-engines or otherwise, the water which collects in mines could not in many situations be got rid of at all, and the mines, after being worked to a little depth,

" Foreigners are generally quite unaware that to these qualities in English industry the wealth and power which they seek to emulate are in reality owing, and not to the ' ships, colonies, and commerce ' which these qualities have called into being, and which, even if annihilated, would leave England the richest country in the world. An Englishman, of almost every class, is the most efficient of all labourers, because, to use a common phrase, his heart is in his work. But it is surely quite possible to put heart into his work without being incapable of putting it into anything else."]

must be abandoned : without ships or boats the sea could never have been crossed ; without tools of some sort, trees could not be cut down, nor rocks excavated : a plough, or at least a hoe, is necessary to any tillage of the ground. Very simple and rude instruments, however, are sufficient to render literally possible most works hitherto executed by mankind ; and subsequent inventions have chiefly served to enable the work to be performed in greater perfection, and, above all, with a greatly diminished quantity of labour : the labour thus saved becoming disposable for other employments.

The use of machinery is far from being the only mode in which the effects of knowledge in aiding production are exemplified. In agriculture and horticulture, machinery is only now [1852] beginning to show that it can do anything of importance, beyond the invention and progressive improvement of the plough and a few other simple instruments. The greatest agricultural inventions have consisted in the direct application of more judicious processes to the land itself, and to the plants growing on it : such as rotation of crops, to avoid the necessity of leaving the land uncultivated for one season in every two or three ; improved manures, to renovate its fertility when exhausted by cropping ; ploughing and draining the subsoil as well as the surface ; conversion of bogs and marshes into cultivable land ; such modes of pruning, and of training and propping up plants and trees, as experience has shown to deserve the preference ; in the case of the more expensive cultures, planting the roots or seeds further apart, and more completely pulverizing the soil in which they are placed, &c. In manufactures and commerce, some of the most important improvements consist in economizing time ; in making the return follow more speedily upon the labour and outlay. There are others of which the advantage consists in economy of material.

§ 5.   But the effects of the increased knowledge of a community in increasing its wealth, need the less illustration as they have become familiar to the most uneducated, from such conspicuous instances as railways and steam-ships. A thing not yet so well understood and recognised, is the economical value of the general diffusion of intelligence among the people. The number of persons fitted to direct and superintend any industrial enterprise, or even to execute any process which cannot be reduced almost to an affair of memory and routine, is always far short of the demand ; as is evident from the enormous difference between the salaries paid to such persons and the wages of ordinary labour. The deficiency of practical good sense, which renders the majority of the labouring class such bad calculators—which makes, for instance, their domestic economy so improvident, lax, and irregular—must disqualify them for any but a low grade of intelligent labour, and render their industry far less productive than with equal energy it otherwise might be. The importance, even in this limited aspect, of popular education, is well worthy of the attention of politicians, especially in England ; since competent observers, accustomed to employ labourers of various nations, testify that in the workman of other countries they often find great intelligence wholly apart from instruction, but that if an English labourer is anything but a hewer of wood and a drawer of water, he is indebted for it to education, which in his case is almost always self-education. Mr. Escher, of Zurich (an engineer and cotton manufacturer employing nearly two thousand working men of many different nations), in his evidence annexed to the Report of the Poor Law Commissioners, in 1840, on the training of pauper children, gives a character of English as contrasted with Continental workmen, which all persons of similar experience will, I believe, confirm.

" The Italians' quickness of perception is shown in rapidly comprehending any new descriptions of labour put into their hands, in a power of quickly comprehending the meaning of their employer, of adapting themselves to new circumstances, much beyond what any other classes have. The French workmen have the like natural characteristics, only in a somewhat lower degree. The English, Swiss, German, and Dutch workmen, we find, have all much slower natural comprehension. As workmen *only*, the preference is undoubtedly due to the English ; because, as we find them, they are all trained to special branches, on which they have had comparatively superior training, and have concentrated all their thoughts. As men of business or of general usefulness, and as men with whom an employer would best like to be surrounded, I should, however, decidedly prefer the Saxons and the Swiss, but more especially the Saxons, because they have had a very careful general education, which has extended their capacities beyond any special employment, and rendered them fit to take up, after a short preparation, any employment to which they may be called. If I have an English workman engaged in the erection of a steam-engine, he will understand that, and nothing else ; and for other circumstances or other branches of mechanics, however closely allied, he will be comparatively helpless to adapt himself to all the circumstances that may arise, to make arrangements for them, and give sound advice

or write clear statements and letters on his work in the various
related branches of mechanics."

On the connexion between mental cultivation and moral trustworthiness in the labouring class, the same witness says, " The
better educated workmen, we find, are distinguished by superior
moral habits in every respect. In the first place, they are entirely
sober ; they are discreet in their enjoyments, which are of a more
rational and refined kind ; they have a taste for much better society,
which they approach respectfully, and consequently find much
readier admittance to it ; they cultivate music ; they read ; they
enjoy the pleasures of scenery, and make parties for excursions
into the country ; they are economical, and their economy extends
beyond their own purse to the stock of their master ; they are,
consequently, honest and trustworthy."   And in answer to a question
respecting the English workmen, " Whilst in respect to the work
to which they have been specially trained they are the most skilful,
they are in conduct the most disorderly, debauched, and unruly,
and least respectable and trustworthy of any nation whatsoever
whom we have employed ; and in saying this, I express the experience of every manufacturer on the Continent to whom I have
spoken, and especially of the English manufacturers, who make
the loudest complaints.   These characteristics of depravity do not
apply to the English workmen who have received an education,
but attach to the others in the degree in which they are in want of
it.   When the uneducated English workmen are released from the
bonds of iron discipline in which they have been restrained by their
employers in England, and are treated with the urbanity and
friendly feeling which the more educated workmen on the Continent
expect and receive from their employers, they, the English workmen,
completely lose their balance : they do not understand their position,
and after a certain time become totally unmanageable and useless." *
This result of observation is borne out by experience in England
itself.   As soon as any idea of equality enters the mind of an uneducated English working man, his head is turned by it.[1]   When
he ceases to be servile, he becomes insolent.

The moral qualities of the labourers are fully as important to
the efficiency and worth of their labour, as the intellectual.   Independently of the effects of intemperance upon their bodily and

* The whole evidence of this intelligent and experienced employer of labour
is deserving of attention ; as well as much testimony on similar points by other
witnesses, contained in the same volume.

[1] [This comment was added in the 3rd ed. (1852).]

mental faculties, and of flighty, unsteady habits upon the energy and continuity of their work (points so easily understood as not to require being insisted upon), it is well worthy of meditation, how much of the aggregate effect of their labour depends on their trustworthiness. All the labour now expended in watching that they fulfil their engagement, or in verifying that they have fulfilled it, is so much withdrawn from the real business of production, to be devoted to a subsidiary function rendered needful not by the necessity of things, but by the dishonesty of men. Nor are the greatest outward precautions more than very imperfectly efficacious, where, as is now almost invariably the case with hired labourers, the slightest relaxation of vigilance is an opportunity eagerly seized for eluding performance of their contract.[1] The advantage to mankind of being able to trust one another, penetrates into every crevice and cranny of human life : the economical is perhaps the smallest part of it, yet even this is incalculable. To consider only the most obvious part of the waste of wealth occasioned to society by human improbity ; there is in all rich communities a predatory population, who live by pillaging or overreaching other people ; their numbers cannot be authentically ascertained, but on the lowest estimate, in a country like England, it is very large. The support of these persons is a direct burthen on the national industry. The police, and the whole apparatus of punishment, and of criminal and partly of civil justice, are a second burthen rendered necessary by the first. The exorbitantly-paid profession of lawyers, so far as their work is not created by defects in the law, of their own contriving, are required and supported principally by the dishonesty of mankind. As the standard of integrity in a community rises higher, all these expenses become less. But this positive saving would be far outweighed by the immense increase in the produce of all kinds of labour, and saving of time and expenditure, which would be obtained if the labourers honestly performed what they undertake ; and by the increased spirit, the feeling of power and confidence, with which works of all sorts would be planned and carried on by those who felt that all whose aid was required would do their part faithfully according to their contracts. Conjoint action is possible just in proportion as human beings can rely on each other. There are countries in Europe, of first-rate industrial

[1] [This statement took the place in the 3rd ed. (1852) of the sentence : " Nor are the greatest outward precautions comparable in efficacy to the monitor within."]

capabilities, where the most serious impediment to conducting business concerns on a large scale is the rarity of persons who are supposed fit to be trusted with the receipt and expenditure of large sums of money. There are nations whose commodities are looked shily upon by merchants, because they cannot depend on finding the quality of the article conformable to that of the sample. Such short-sighted frauds are far from unexampled in English exports. Every one has heard of " devil's dust : " and among other instances given by Mr. Babbage, is one in which a branch of export trade was for a long time actually stopped by the forgeries and frauds which had occurred in it. On the other hand, the substantial advantage derived in business transactions from proved trustworthiness, is not less remarkably exemplified in the same work. " At one of our largest towns, sales and purchases on a very extensive scale are made daily in the course of business without any of the parties ever exchanging a written document." Spread over a year's transactions, how great a return, in saving of time, trouble, and expense, is brought in to the producers and dealers of such a town from their own integrity. " The influence of established character in producing confidence operated in a very remarkable manner at the time of the exclusion of British manufactures from the Continent during the last war. One of our largest establishments had been in the habit of doing extensive business with a house in the centre of Germany ; but on the closing of the Continental ports against our manufactures, heavy penalties were inflicted on all those who contravened the Berlin and Milan decrees. The English manufacturer continued, nevertheless, to receive orders, with directions how to consign them, and appointments for the time and mode of payment, in letters, the handwriting of which was known to him, but which were never signed except by the Christian name of one of the firm, and even in some instances they were without any signature at all. These orders were executed, and in no instance was there the least irregularity in the payments." *

* Some minor instances noticed by Mr. Babbage may be cited in further illustration of the waste occasioned to society through the inability of its members to trust one another.

" The cost to the purchaser is the price he pays for any article, added to the cost of verifying the fact of its having that degree of goodness for which he contracts. In some cases the goodness of the article is evident on mere inspection ; and in those cases there is not much difference of price at different shops. The goodness of loaf sugar, for instance, can be discerned almost at a glance ; and the consequence is, that the price is so uniform, and the profit upon it so small, that no grocer is at all anxious to sell it ; whilst on the other

§ 6. Among the secondary causes which determine the productiveness of productive agents, the most important is Security. By security I mean the completeness of the protection which society affords to its members. This consists of protection *by* the government, and protection *against* the government. The latter is the more important. Where a person known to possess anything worth taking away, can expect nothing but to have it torn from him, with every circumstance of tyrannical violence, by the agents of a rapacious government, it is not likely that many will exert themselves to produce much more than necessaries. This is the acknowledged explanation of the poverty of many fertile tracts of Asia, which were once prosperous and populous. From this to the degree of security enjoyed in the best governed parts of Europe, there are numerous gradations. In many provinces of France before the Revolution, a vicious system of taxation on the land, and still more the absence of redress against the arbitrary exactions which were made under colour of the taxes, rendered it the interest of every cultivator to appear poor, and therefore to cultivate badly. The only insecurity which is altogether paralysing

hand, tea, of which it is exceedingly difficult to judge, and which can be adulterated by mixture so as to deceive the skill even of a practised eye, has a great variety of different prices, and is that article which every grocer is most anxious to sell to his customers. The difficulty and expense of verification are in some instances so great, as to justify the deviation from well-established principles. Thus, it is a general maxim that Government can purchase any article at a cheaper rate than that at which they can manufacture it themselves. But it has, nevertheless, been considered more economical to build extensive flour-mills (such as those at Deptford), and to grind their own corn, than to verify each sack of purchased flour, and to employ persons in devising methods of detecting the new modes of adulteration which might be continually resorted to." A similar want of confidence might deprive a nation, such as the United States, of a large export trade in flour.

Again: "Some years since, a mode of preparing old clover and trefoil seeds by a process called *doctoring* became so prevalent as to excite the attention of the House of Commons. It appeared in evidence before a Committee, that the old seed of the white clover was doctored by first wetting it slightly, and then drying it by the fumes of burning sulphur; and that the red clover seed had its colour improved by shaking it in a sack with a small quantity of indigo; but this being detected after a time, the *doctors* then used a preparation of logwood, fined by a little copperas, and sometimes by verdigris; thus at once improving the appearance of the old seed, and diminishing, if not destroying, its vegetative power, already enfeebled by age. Supposing no injury had resulted to good seed so prepared, it was proved that, from the improved appearance, the market price would be enhanced by this process from five to twenty-five shillings a hundred-weight. But the greatest evil arose from the circumstances of these processes rendering old and worthless seed equal in appearance to the best. One witness had tried some doctored seed, and found that not above one grain in a hundred grew, and that those which did vegetate died away afterwards; whilst about eighty or ninety per cent. of good seed usually grows.

to the active energies of producers, is that arising from the government, or from persons invested with its authority. Against all
other depredators there is a hope of defending oneself. Greece
and the Greek colonies in the ancient world, Flanders and Italy
in the Middle Ages, by no means enjoyed what any one with modern
ideas would call security : the state of society was most unsettled
and turbulent ; person and property were exposed to a thousand
dangers. But they were free countries ; they were in general
neither arbitrarily oppressed nor systematically plundered by
their governments. Against other enemies the individual energy
which their institutions called forth, enabled them to make successful
resistance : their labour, therefore, was eminently productive, and
their riches, while they remained free, were constantly on the increase.
The Roman despotism, putting an end to wars and internal conflicts
throughout the empire, relieved the subject population from much of
the former insecurity : but because it left them under the grinding
yoke of its own rapacity they became enervated and impoverished,
until they were an easy prey to barbarous but free invaders. They
would neither fight nor labour, because they were no longer suffered
to enjoy that for which they fought and laboured.

The seed so treated was sold to retail dealers in the country, who of course
endeavoured to purchase at the cheapest rate, and from them it got into the
hands of the farmers, neither of these classes being capable of distinguishing
the fraudulent from the genuine seed. Many cultivators in consequence
diminished their consumption of the articles, and others were obliged to pay a
higher price to those who had skill to distinguish the mixed seed, and who had
integrity and character to prevent them from dealing in it."

The same writer states that Irish flax, though in natural quality inferior to
none, sells, or did lately sell, in the market at a penny to twopence per pound
less than foreign or British flax ; part of the difference arising from negligence
in its preparation, but part from the cause mentioned in the evidence of Mr.
Corry, many years Secretary to the Irish Linen Board : " The owners of the
flax, who are almost always people in the lower classes of life, believe that they
can best advance their own interests by imposing on the buyers. Flax being
sold by weight, various expedients are used to increase it ; and every expedient
is injurious, particularly the damping of it ; a very common practice, which
makes the flax afterwards heat. The inside of every bundle (and the bundles
all vary in bulk) is often full of pebbles, or dirt of various kinds, to increase the
weight. In this state it is purchased and exported to Great Britain."

It was given in evidence before a Committee of the House of Commons
that the lace trade at Nottingham had greatly fallen off, from the making of
fraudulent and bad articles : that " a kind of lace called *single-press* was manufactured," (I still quote Mr. Babbage,) " which although good to the eye,
became nearly spoiled in washing by the slipping of the threads ; that not one
person in a thousand could distinguish the difference between single-press and
double-press lace ; that even workmen and manufacturers were obliged to
employ a magnifying-glass for that purpose ; and that in another similar article,
called warp-lace, such aid was essential."

Much of the security of person and property in modern nations is the effect of manners and opinion rather than of law. There are, or lately were, countries in Europe where the monarch was nominally absolute, but where, from the restraints imposed by established usage, no subject felt practically in the smallest danger of having his possessions arbitrarily seized or a contribution levied on them by the government. There must, however, be in such governments much petty plunder and other tyranny by subordinate agents, for which redress is not obtained, owing to the want of publicity which is the ordinary character of absolute governments. In England, the public are tolerably well protected, both by institutions and manners, against the agents of government; but, for the security they enjoy against other evil-doers, they are [1848] very little indebted to their institutions. The laws cannot be said to afford protection to property, when they afford it only at such a cost as renders submission to injury in general the better calculation. The security of property in England is owing (except as regards open violence) to opinion, and the fear of exposure, much more than to the direct operation of the law and the courts of justice.

Independently of all imperfection in the bulwarks which society purposely throws round what it recognises as property, there are various other modes in which defective institutions impede the employment of the productive resources of a country to the best advantage. We shall have occasion for noticing many of these in the progress of our subject. It is sufficient here to remark, that the efficiency of industry may be expected to be great, in proportion as the fruits of industry are insured to the person exerting it : and that all social arrangements are conducive to useful exertion, according as they provide that the reward of every one for his labour shall be proportioned as much as possible to the benefit which it produces. All laws or usages which favour one class or sort of persons to the disadvantage of others ; which chain up the efforts of any part of the community in pursuit of their own good, or stand between those efforts and their natural fruits—are (independently of all other grounds of condemnation) violations of the fundamental principles of economical policy ; tending to make the aggregate productive powers of the community productive in a less degree than they would otherwise be.

CHAPTER VIII

§ 1. In the enumeration of the circumstances which promote the productiveness of labour, we have left one untouched, which, because of its importance, and of the many topics of discussion which it involves, requires to be treated apart. This is co-operation, or the combined action of numbers. Of this great aid to production, a single department, known by the name of Division of Labour, has engaged a large share of the attention of political economists ; most deservedly indeed, but to the exclusion of other cases and exemplifications of the same comprehensive law. Mr. Wakefield was, I believe, the first to point out, that a part of the subject had, with injurious effect, been mistaken for the whole ; that a more fundamental principle lies beneath that of the division of labour, and comprehends it.

Co-operation, he observes,* is " of two distinct kinds : first, such co-operation as takes place when several persons help each other in the same employment ; secondly, such co-operation as takes place when several persons help each other in different employments. These may be termed Simple Co-operation and Complex Co-operation.

" The advantage of simple co-operation is illustrated by the case of two greyhounds running together, which, it is said, will kill more hares than four greyhounds running separately. In a vast number of simple operations performed by human exertion, it is quite obvious that two men working together will do more than four, or four times four men, each of whom should work alone. In the lifting of heavy weights, for example, in the felling of trees, in the sawing of timber, in the gathering of much hay or corn during a short period of fine weather, in draining a large extent of land during the short season when such a work may be properly con-

* Note to Wakefield's edition of Adam Smith, vol. i. p. 26.

ducted, in the pulling of ropes on board ship, in the rowing of large boats, in some mining operations, in the erection of a scaffolding for building, and in the breaking of stones for the repair of a road, so that the whole of the road shall always be kept in good order : in all these simple operations, and thousands more, it is absolutely necessary that many persons should work together, at the same time, in the same place, and in the same way. The savages of New Holland never help each other, even in the most simple operations ; and their condition is hardly superior, in some respects it is inferior, to that of the wild animals which they now and then catch. Let any one imagine that the labourers of England should suddenly desist from helping each other in simple employments, and he will see at once the prodigious advantages of simple co-operation. In a countless number of employments, the produce of labour is, up to a certain point, in proportion to such mutual assistance amongst the workmen. This is the first step in social improvement." The second is, when " one body of men having combined their labour to raise more food than they require, another body of men are induced to combine their labour for the purpose of producing more clothes than they require, and with those surplus clothes buying the surplus food of the other body of labourers ; while, if both bodies together have produced more food and clothes than they both require, both bodies obtain, by means of exchange, a proper capital for setting more labourers to work in their respective occupations." To simple co-operation is thus superadded what Mr. Wakefield terms Complex Co-operation. The one is the combination of several labourers to help each other in the same set of operations ; the other is the combination of several labourers to help one another by a division of operations.

There is " an important distinction between simple and complex co-operation. Of the former, one is always conscious at the time of practising it : it is obvious to the most ignorant and vulgar eye. Of the latter, but a very few of the vast numbers who practise it are in any degree conscious. The cause of this distinction is easily seen. When several men are employed in lifting the same weight, or pulling the same rope, at the same time, and in the same place, there can be no sort of doubt that they co-operate with each other ; the fact is impressed on the mind by the mere sense of sight ; but when several men, or bodies of men, are employed at different times and places, and in different pursuits, their co-operation with each other, though it may be quite as certain, is not so readily perceived

as in the other case : in order to perceive it, a complex operation
of the mind is required."

In the present state of society the breeding and feeding of sheep
is the occupation of one set of people, dressing the wool to prepare
it for the spinner is that of another, spinning it into thread of a third,
weaving the thread into broadcloth of a fourth, dyeing the cloth of a
fifth, making it into a coat of a sixth, without counting the multitude
of carriers, merchants, factors, and retailers, put in requisition at
the successive stages of this progress.   All these persons, without
knowledge of one another or previous understanding, co-operate in
the production of the ultimate result, a coat.   But these are far
from being all who co-operate in it ; for each of these persons
requires food, and many other articles of consumption, and unless
he could have relied that other people would produce these for him,
he could not have devoted his whole time to one step in the succession
of operations which produces one single commodity, a coat.   Every
person who took part in producing food or erecting houses for this
series of producers, has, however unconsciously on his part, combined his labours with theirs.   It is by a real, though unexpressed,
concert, " that the body who raise more food than they want, can
exchange with the body who raise more clothes than they want ;
and if the two bodies were separated, either by distance or disinclination—unless the two bodies should virtually form themselves
into one, for the common object of raising enough food and clothes
for the whole—they could not divide into two distinct parts the
whole operation of producing a sufficient quantity of food and
clothes."

§ 2.   The influence exercised on production by the separation
of employments, is more fundamental than, from the mode in which
the subject is usually treated, a reader might be induced to suppose.
It is not merely that when the production of different things becomes
the sole or principal occupation of different persons, a much greater
quantity of each kind of article is produced.   The truth is much
beyond this.   Without some separation of employments, very few
things would be produced at all.

Suppose a set of persons, or a number of families, all employed
precisely in the same manner ; each family settled on a piece of its
own land, on which it grows by its labour the food required for its
own sustenance, and as there are no persons to buy any surplus
produce where all are producers, each family has to produce within

itself whatever other articles it consumes. In such circumstances, if the soil was tolerably fertile, and population did not tread too closely on the heels of subsistence, there would be, no doubt, some kind of domestic manufactures ; clothing for the family might perhaps be spun and woven within it, by the labour probably of the women (a first step in the separation of employments) ; and a dwelling of some sort would be erected and kept in repair by their united labour. But beyond simple food (precarious, too, from the variations of the seasons), coarse clothing, and very imperfect lodging, it would be scarcely possible that the family should produce anything more. They would, in general, require their utmost exertions to accomplish so much. Their power even of extracting food from the soil would be kept within narrow limits by the quality of their tools, which would necessarily be of the most wretched description. To do almost anything in the way of producing for themselves articles of convenience or luxury, would require too much time, and, in many cases, their presence in a different place. Very few kinds of industry, therefore, would exist ; and that which did exist, namely the production of necessaries, would be extremely inefficient, not solely from imperfect implements, but because, when the ground and the domestic industry fed by it had been made to supply the necessaries of a single family in tolerable abundance, there would be little motive, while the numbers of the family remained the same, to make either the land or the labour produce more.

But suppose an event to occur, which would amount to a revolution in the circumstances of this little settlement. Suppose that a company of artificers, provided with tools, and with food sufficient to maintain them for a year, arrive in the country and establish themselves in the midst of the population. These new settlers occupy themselves in producing articles of use or ornament adapted to the taste of a simple people ; and before their food is exhausted they have produced these in considerable quantity, and are ready to exchange them for more food. The economical position of the landed population is now most materially altered. They have an opportunity given them of acquiring comforts and luxuries. Things which, while they depended solely on their own labour, they never could have obtained, because they could not have produced, are now accessible to them if they can succeed in producing an additional quantity of food and necessaries. They are thus incited to increase the productiveness of their industry. Among the conveniences for the first time made accessible to them, better tools are probably one : and apart from this, they have a motive to labour more assiduously, and to adopt contrivances for making their labour more effectual. By these means they will generally succeed in compelling their land to produce, not only food for themselves, but a surplus for the new comers, wherewith to buy from them the products of their industry. The new settlers constitute what is called a *market* for surplus agricultural produce : and their arrival has enriched the settlement not only by the manufactured article which they produce, but by the food which would not have been produced unless they had been there to consume it.

There is no inconsistency between this doctrine, and the proposition we before maintained, that a market for commodities does not constitute employment for labour.* The labour of the agriculturists was already provided with employment; they are not indebted to the demand of the new comers for being able to maintain themselves. What that demand does for them is, to call their labour into increased vigour and efficiency ; to stimulate them, by new motives, to new exertions. Neither do the new comers owe their maintenance and employment to the demand of the agriculturists : with a year's subsistence in store, they could have settled side by side with the former inhabitants, and produced a similar scanty stock of food and necessaries. Nevertheless we see of what supreme importance to the productiveness of the labour of producers, is the existence of other producers within reach, employed in a different kind of industry. The power of exchanging the products of one kind of labour for those of another, is a condition, but for which, there would almost always be a smaller quantity of labour altogether. When a new market is opened for any product of industry, and a greater quantity of the article is consequently produced, the increased production is not always obtained at the expense of some other product ; it is often a new creation, the result of labour which would otherwise have remained unexerted ; or of assistance rendered to labour by improvements or by modes of co-operation to which recourse would not have been had if an inducement had not been offered for raising a larger produce.

§ 3. From these considerations it appears that a country will seldom have a productive agriculture, unless it has a large town population, or the only available substitute, a large export trade in agricultural produce to supply a population elsewhere. I use

* Supra, pp. 79–90.

the phrase town population for shortness, to imply a population non-agricultural; which will generally be collected in towns or large villages, for the sake of combination of labour. The application of this truth by Mr. Wakefield to the theory of colonization has excited much attention, and is doubtless destined to excite much more. It is one of those great practical discoveries, which, once made, appears so obvious that the merit of making them seems less than it is. Mr. Wakefield was the first to point out that the mode of planting new settlements, then commonly practised—setting down a number of families side by side, each on its piece of land, all employing themselves in exactly the same manner,—though in favourable circumstances it may assure to those families a rude abundance of mere necessaries, can never be other than unfavourable to great production or rapid growth: and his system consists of arrangements for securing that every colony shall have from the first a town population bearing due proportion to its agricultural, and that the cultivators of the soil shall not be so widely scattered as to be deprived by distance of the benefit of that town population as a market for their produce. The principle on which the scheme is founded, does not depend on any theory respecting the superior productiveness of land held in large portions, and cultivated by hired labour. Supposing it true that land yields the greatest produce when divided into small properties and cultivated by peasant proprietors, a town population will be just as necessary to induce those proprietors to raise that larger produce: and if they were too far from the nearest seat of non-agricultural industry to use it as a market for disposing of their surplus, and thereby supplying their other wants, neither that surplus nor any equivalent for it would, generally speaking, be produced.

It is, above all, the deficiency of town population which limits [1848] the productiveness of the industry of a country like India. The agriculture of India is conducted entirely on the system of small holdings. There is, however, a considerable amount of combination of labour. The village institutions and customs, which are the real framework of Indian society, make provision for joint action in the cases in which it is seen to be necessary; or where they fail to do so, the government (when tolerably well administered) steps in, and by an outlay from the revenue, executes by combined labour the tanks, embankments, and works of irrigation, which are indispensable. The implements and processes of agriculture are however so wretched, that the produce of the soil, in spite of great natural fertility and a

climate highly favourable to vegetation, is miserably small : and the
land might be made to yield food in abundance for many more than
the present number of inhabitants, without departing from the
system of small holdings. But to this the stimulus is wanting,
which a large town population, connected with the rural districts
by easy and unexpensive means of communication, would afford.
That town population, again, does not grow up, because the few
wants and unaspiring spirit of the cultivators (joined until lately
with great insecurity of property, from military and fiscal rapacity)
prevent them from attempting to become consumers of town produce. In these circumstances the best chance of an early development of the productive resources of India, consists in the rapid [1]
growth of its export of agricultural produce (cotton, indigo, sugar,
coffee, &c.) to the markets of Europe. The producers of these
articles are consumers of food supplied by their fellow-agriculturists
in India ; and the market thus opened for surplus food will, if
accompanied by good government, raise up by degrees more extended
wants and desires, directed either towards European commodities,
or towards things which will require for their production in India
a larger manufacturing population.

§ 4. Thus far of the separation of employments, a form of the
combination of labour without which there cannot be the first
rudiments of industrial civilization. But when this separation is
thoroughly established ; when it has become the general practice
for each producer to supply many others with one commodity, and
to be supplied by others with most of the things which he consumes ;
reasons not less real, though less imperative, invite to a further
extension of the same principle. It is found that the productive
power of labour is increased by carrying the separation further and
further ; by breaking down more and more every process of industry
into parts, so that each labourer shall confine himself to an ever
smaller number of simple operations. And thus, in time, arise
those remarkable cases of what is called the division of labour, with
which all readers on subjects of this nature are familiar. Adam
Smith's illustration from pin-making, though so well known, is so
much to the point, that I will venture once more to transcribe it.
" The business of making a pin is divided into about eighteen distinct
operations. One man draws out the wire, another straights it, a
third cuts it, a fourth points it, a fifth grinds it at the top for receiving

[1] [" Now " was omitted before " rapid " in the 3rd ed. (1852).]

the head; to make the head requires two or three distinct operations; to put it on, is a peculiar business; to whiten the pins is another; it is even a trade by itself to put them into the paper. . . . I have seen a small manufactory where ten men only were employed, and where some of them, consequently, performed two or three distinct operations. But though they were very poor, and therefore but indifferently accommodated with the necessary machinery, they could, when they exerted themselves, make among them about twelve pounds of pins in a day. There are in a pound upwards of four thousand pins of a middling size. Those ten persons, therefore, could make among them upwards of forty-eight thousand pins in a day. Each person, therefore, making a tenth part of forty-eight thousand pins, might be considered as making four thousand eight hundred pins in a day. But if they had all wrought separately and independently, and without any of them having been educated to this peculiar business, they certainly could not each of them have made twenty, perhaps not one pin in a day."

M. Say furnishes a still stronger example of the effects of division of labour—from a not very important branch of industry certainly, the manufacture of playing cards. " It is said by those engaged in the business, that each card, that is, a piece of pasteboard of the size of the hand, before being ready for sale, does not undergo fewer than seventy operations, every one of which might be the occupation of a distinct class of workmen. And if there are not seventy classes of work-people in each card manufactory, it is because the division of labour is not carried so far as it might be ; because the same workman is charged with two, three, or four distinct operations. The influence of this distribution of employment is immense. I have seen a card manufactory where thirty workmen produced daily fifteen thousand five hundred cards, being above five hundred cards for each labourer ; and it may be presumed that if each of these workmen were obliged to perform all the operations himself, even supposing him a practised hand, he would not perhaps complete two cards in a day : and the thirty workmen, instead of fifteen thousand five hundred cards, would make only sixty." *

In watchmaking, as Mr. Babbage observes, " it was stated in evidence before a Committee of the House of Commons, that there

---

* SAY, *Cours d'Economie Politique Pratique*, vol. i. p. 340.
It is a remarkable proof of the economy of labour occasioned by this minute division of occupations, that an article, the production of which is the result of such a multitude of manual operations, can be sold for a trifling sum.

are a hundred and two distinct branches of this art, to each of which a boy may be put apprentice ; and that he only learns his master's department, and is unable, after his apprenticeship has expired, without subsequent instruction, to work at any other branch. The watch-finisher, whose business it is to put together the scattered parts, is the only one, out of the hundred and two persons, who can work in any other department than his own." *

§ 5. The causes of the increased efficiency given to labour by the division of employments are some of them too familiar to require specification ; but it is worth while to attempt a complete enumeration of them. By Adam Smith they are reduced to three. " First, the increase of dexterity in every particular workman ; secondly, the saving of the time which is commonly lost in passing from one species of work to another ; and lastly, the invention of a great number of machines which facilitate and abridge labour, and enable one man to do the work of many."

Of these, the increase of dexterity of the individual workman is the most obvious and universal. It does not follow that because a thing has been done oftener it will be done better. That depends on the intelligence of the workman, and on the degree in which his mind works along with his hands. But it will be done more easily. The organs themselves acquire greater power : the muscles employed grow stronger by frequent exercise, the sinews more pliant, and the mental powers more efficient, and less sensible of fatigue. What can be done easily has at least a better chance of being done well, and is sure to be done more expeditiously. What was at first done slowly comes to be done quickly ; what was at first done slowly with accuracy is at last done quickly with equal accuracy. This is as true of mental operations as of bodily. Even a child, after much practice, sums up a column of figures with a rapidity which resembles intuition. The act of speaking any language, of reading fluently, of playing music at sight, are cases as remarkable as they are familiar. Among bodily acts, dancing, gymnastic exercises, ease and brilliancy of execution on a musical instrument, are examples of the rapidity and facility acquired by repetition. In simpler manual operations the effect is of course still sooner produced. " The rapidity," Adam Smith observes, " with which some of the operations of certain manufactures are performed, exceeds what the human hand could, by those who had never seen them, be

* *Economy of Machinery and Manufactures*, 3rd edition, p. 201.

supposed capable of acquiring." * This skill is, naturally, attained after shorter practice, in proportion as the division of labour is more minute ; and will not be attained in the same degree at all, if the workman has a greater variety of operations to execute than allows of a sufficiently frequent repetition of each. The advantage is not confined to the greater efficiency ultimately attained, but includes also the diminished loss of time, and waste of material, in learning the art. " A certain quantity of material," says Mr. Babbage,† " will in all cases be consumed unprofitably, or spoiled, by every person who learns an art ; and as he applies himself to each new process, he will waste some of the raw material, or of the partly manufactured commodity. But if each man commit this waste in acquiring successively every process, the quantity of waste will be much greater than if each person confine his attention to one process." And in general each will be much sooner qualified to execute his one process, if he be not distracted while learning it, by the necessity of learning others.

The second advantage enumerated by Adam Smith as arising from the division of labour, is one on which I cannot help thinking that more stress is laid by him and others than it deserves. To do full justice to his opinion, I will quote his own exposition of it. " The advantage which is gained by saving the time commonly lost in passing from one sort of work to another, is much greater than we should at first view be apt to imagine it. It is impossible to pass very quickly from one kind of work to another, that is carried on in a different place, and with quite different tools. A country weaver, who cultivates a small farm, must lose a good deal of time in passing from his loom to the field, and from the field to his loom. When the two trades can be carried on in the same workhouse, the loss of time is no doubt much less. It is even in this case, however, very considerable. A man commonly saunters a little in turning his hand

---

* " In astronomical observations, the senses of the operator are rendered so acute by habit, that he can estimate differences of time to the tenth of a second ; and adjust his measuring instrument to graduations of which five thousand occupy only an inch. It is the same throughout the commonest processes of manufacture. A child who fastens on the heads of pins will repeat an operation requiring several distinct motions of the muscles one hundred times a minute for several successive hours. In a recent Manchester paper it was stated that a peculiar sort of twist or ' gimp,' which cost three shillings making when first introduced, was now manufactured for one penny ; and this not, as usually, by the invention of a new machine, but solely through the increased dexterity of the workman."—*Edinburgh Review* for **January** 1849, p. 81.

† Page 171.

from one sort of employment to another. When he first begins the
new work, he is seldom very keen and hearty ; his mind, as they say,
does not go to it, and for some time he rather trifles than applies
to good purpose. The habit of sauntering and of indolent careless
application, which is naturally, or rather necessarily acquired by
every country workman who is obliged to change his work and his
tools every half hour, and to apply his hand in twenty different ways
almost every day of his life, renders him almost always slothful
and lazy, and incapable of any vigorous application even on the
most pressing occasions." This is surely a most exaggerated description of the inefficiency of country labour, where it has any adequate
motive to exertion. Few workmen change their work and their
tools oftener than a gardener ; is he usually incapable of vigorous
application ? Many of the higher description of artisans have to
perform a great multiplicity of operations with a variety of tools.
They do not execute each of these with the rapidity with which a
factory workman performs his single operation ; but they are,
except in a merely manual sense, more skilful labourers, and in all
senses whatever more energetic.

Mr. Babbage, following in the track of Adam Smith, says,
" When the human hand, or the human head, has been for some time
occupied in any kind of work, it cannot instantly change its employment with full effect. The muscles of the limbs employed have
acquired a flexibility during their exertion, and those not in action
a stiffness during rest, which renders every change slow and unequal
in the commencement. Long habit also produces in the muscles
exercised a capacity for enduring fatigue to a much greater degree
than they could support under other circumstances. A similar
result seems to take place in any change of mental exertion ; the
attention bestowed on the new subject not being so perfect at first
as it becomes after some exercise. The employment of different
tools in the successive processes is another cause of the loss of time
in changing from one operation to another. If these tools are
simple and the change is not frequent, the loss of time is not considerable ; but in many processes of the arts, the tools are of great
delicacy, requiring accurate adjustment every time they are used ;
and in many cases, the time employed in adjusting bears a large
proportion to that employed in using the tool. The sliding-rest,
the dividing and the drilling engine are of this kind : and hence,
in manufactories of sufficient extent, it is found to be good economy
to keep one machine constantly employed in one kind of work :

one lathe, for example, having a screw motion to its sliding-rest along the whole length of its bed, is kept constantly making cylinders; another, having a motion for equalizing the velocity of the work at the point at which it passes the tool, is kept for facing surfaces ; whilst a third.is constantly employed in cutting wheels.''

I am very far from implying that these different considerations are of no weight ; but I think there are counter-considerations which are overlooked. If one kind of muscular or mental labour is different from another, for that very reason it is to some extent a rest from that other ; and if the greatest vigour is not at once obtained in the second occupation, neither could the first have been indefinitely prolonged without some relaxation of energy. It is a matter of common experience that a change of occupation will often afford relief where complete repose would otherwise be necessary, and that a person can work many more hours without fatigue at a succession of occupations, than if confined during the whole time to one. Different occupations employ different muscles, of different energies of the mind, some of which rest and are refreshed while others work. Bodily labour itself rests from mental, and conversely. The variety itself has an invigorating effect on what, for want of a more philosophical appellation, we must term the animal spirits ; so important to the efficiency of all work not mechanical, and not unimportant even to that. The comparative weight due to these considerations is different with different individuals ; some are more fitted than others for persistency in one occupation, and less fit for change ; they require longer to get the steam up (to use a metaphor now common) ; the irksomeness of setting to work lasts longer, and it requires more time to bring their faculties into full play, and therefore when this is once done, they do not like to leave off, but go on long without intermission, even to the injury of their health. Temperament has something to do with these differences. There are people whose faculties seem by nature to come slowly into action, and to accomplish little until they have been a long time employed. Others, again, get into action rapidly, but cannot, without exhaustion, continue long. In this, however, as in most other things, though natural differences are something, habit is much more. The habit of passing rapidly from one occupation to another may be acquired, like other habits, by early cultivation ; and when it is acquired, there is none of the sauntering which Adam Smith speaks of, after each change ; no want of energy and interest, but the workman comes to each part of his occupation with a freshness and a spirit which he does not retain if he persists in any one part (unless in case of unusual excitement) beyond the length of time to which he is accustomed. Women are usually (at least in their present social circumstances) of far greater versatility than men ; and the present topic is an instance among multitudes, how little the ideas and experience of women have yet counted for, in forming the opinions of mankind. There are few women who would not reject the idea that work is made vigorous by being protracted, and is inefficient for some time after changing to a new thing. Even in this case, habit, I believe, much more than nature, is the cause of the difference. The occupations of nine out of every ten men are special, those of nine out of every ten women general, embracing a multitude of details each of which requires very little time. Women are in the constant practice of passing quickly from one manual, and still more from one mental operation to another, which therefore rarely costs them either effort or loss of time, while a man's occupation generally consists in working steadily for a long time at one thing, or one very limited class of things. But the situations are sometimes reversed, and with them the characters. Women are not found less efficient than men for the uniformity of factory work, or they would not so generally be employed for it ; and a man who has cultivated the habit of turning his hand to many things, far from being the slothful and lazy person described by Adam Smith, is usually remarkably lively and active. It is true, however, that change of occupation may be too frequent even for the most versatile. Incessant variety is even more fatiguing than perpetual sameness.

The third advantage attributed by Adam Smith to the division of labour, is, to a certain extent, real. Inventions tending to save labour in a particular operation, are more likely to occur to any one in proportion as his thoughts are intensely directed to that occupation, and continually employed upon it. A person is not so likely to make practical improvements in one department of things, whose attention is very much diverted to others. But, in this, much more depends on general intelligence and habitual activity of mind, than on exclusiveness of occupation ; and if that exclusiveness is carried to a degree unfavourable to the cultivation of intelligence, there will be more lost in this kind of advantage, than gained. We may add, that whatever may be the cause of making inventions, when they are once made, the increased efficiency of labour is owing to the invention itself, and not to the division of labour.

The greatest advantage (next to the dexterity of the workmen) derived from the minute division of labour which takes place in modern manufacturing industry, is one not mentioned by Adam Smith, but to which attention has been drawn by Mr. Babbage ; the more economical distribution of labour, by classing the work-people according to their capacity. Different parts of the same series of operations require unequal degrees of skill and bodily strength ; and those who have skill enough for the most difficult, or strength enough for the hardest parts of the labour, are made much more useful by being employed solely in them ; the operations which everybody is capable of, being left to those who are fit for no others. Production is most efficient when the precise quantity of skill and strength, which is required for each part of the process, is employed in it, and no more. The operation of pin-making requires, it seems, in its different parts, such different degrees of skill, that the wages earned by the persons employed vary from fourpence half-penny a day to six shillings ; and if the workman who is paid at that highest rate had to perform the whole process, he would be working a part of his time with a waste per day equivalent to the difference between six shillings and fourpence halfpenny. Without reference to the loss sustained in quantity of work done, and supposing even that he could make a pound of pins in the same time in which ten workmen combining their labour can make ten pounds, Mr. Babbage computes that they would cost, in making, three times and three-quarters as much as they now do by means of the division of labour. In needle-making, he adds, the difference would be still greater, for in that, the scale of remuneration for different parts of the process varies from sixpence to twenty shillings a day.

To the advantage which consists in extracting the greatest possible amount of utility from skill, may be added the analogous one, of extracting the utmost possible utility from tools. " If any man," says an able writer,* " had all the tools which many different occupations require, at least three-fourths of them would constantly be idle and useless. It were clearly then better, were any society to exist where each man had all these tools, and alternately carried on each of these occupations, that the members of it should, if possible, divide them amongst them, each restricting himself to some particular employment. The advantages of the change to the whole community, and therefore to every individual in it, are

* *Statement of some New Principles on the subject of Political Economy,* by John Rae (Boston, U.S.), p. 164. [*Sociological Theory of Capital* (1905), p. 102. See infra, p. 165 n.]

great. In the first place, the various implements being in constant
employment, yield a better return for what has been laid out in
procuring them. In consequence their owners can afford to have
them of better quality and more complete construction. The result
of both events is, that a larger provision is made for the future wants
of the whole society."

§ 6. The division of labour, as all writers on the subject have
remarked, is limited by the extent of the market. If, by the separation of pin-making into ten distinct employments, forty-eight
thousand pins can be made in a day, this separation will only
be advisable if the number of accessible consumers is such as to
require, every day, something like forty-eight thousand pins. If
there is only a demand for twenty-four thousand, the division of
labour can only be advantageously carried to the extent which
will every day produce that smaller number. This, therefore, is
a further mode in which an accession of demand for a commodity
tends to increase the efficiency of the labour employed in its production. The extent of the market may be limited by several
causes : too small a population ; the population too scattered and
distant to be easily accessible; deficiency of roads and water carriage;
or, finally, the population too poor, that is, their collective labour
too little effective, to admit of their being large consumers. Indolence, want of skill, and want of combination of labour, among
those who would otherwise be buyers of a commodity, limit, therefore, the practical amount of combination of labour among its
producers. In an early stage of civilization, when the demand
of any particular locality was necessarily small, industry only
flourished among those who, by their command of the sea-coast
or of a navigable river, could have the whole world, or all that
part of it which lay on coasts or navigable rivers, as a market
for their productions. The increase of the general riches of the
world, when accompanied with freedom of commercial intercourse,
improvements in navigation, and inland communication by roads,
canals, or railways, tends to give increased productiveness to the
labour of every nation in particular, by enabling each locality to
supply with its special products so much larger a market, that a
great extension of the division of labour in their production is an
ordinary consequence.

The division of labour is also limited, in many cases, by the
nature of the employment. Agriculture, for example, is not

susceptible of so great a division of occupations as many branches of manufactures, because its different operations cannot possibly be simultaneous. One man cannot be always ploughing, another sowing, and another reaping. A workman who only practised one agricultural operation would be idle eleven months of the year. The same person may perform them all in succession, and have, in most climates, a considerable amount of unoccupied time. To execute a great agricultural improvement, it is often necessary that many labourers should work together ; but in general, except the few whose business is superintendence, they all work in the same manner. A canal or a railway embankment cannot be made without a combination of many labourers ; but they are all excavators, except the engineers and a few clerks.[1]

[1] [See Appendix G.   *Division and Combination of Labour.*]

CHAPTER IX

OF PRODUCTION ON A LARGE, AND PRODUCTION ON
A SMALL SCALE

§ 1. From the importance of combination of labour, it is an obvious conclusion, that there are many cases in which production is made much more effective by being conducted on a large scale. Whenever it is essential to the greatest efficiency of labour that many labourers should combine, even though only in the way of Simple Co-operation, the scale of the enterprise must be such as to bring many labourers together, and the capital must be large enough to maintain them. Still more needful is this when the nature of the employment allows, and the extent of the possible market encourages, a considerable division of labour. The larger the enterprise, the farther the division of labour may be carried. This is one of the principal causes of large manufactories. Even when no additional subdivision of the work would follow an enlargement of the operations, there will be good economy in enlarging them to the point at which every person to whom it is convenient to assign a special occupation, will have full employment in that occupation. This point is well illustrated by Mr. Babbage.*

" If machines be kept working through the twenty-four hours (which is evidently the only economical mode of employing them,) " it is necessary that some person shall attend to admit the workmen at the time they relieve each other ; and whether the porter or other person so employed admit one person or twenty, his rest will be equally disturbed. It will also be necessary occasionally to adjust or repair the machine ; and this can be done much better by a workman accustomed to machine-making, than by the person who uses it. Now, since the good performance and the duration of machines depend, to a very great extent, upon correcting every shake or imperfection in their parts as soon as they appear, the

* Page 214 et seqq.

prompt attention of a workman resident on the spot will considerably reduce the expenditure arising from the wear and tear of the machinery. But in the case of a single lace-frame, or a single loom, this would be too expensive a plan. Here then arises another circumstance which tends to enlarge the extent of a factory. It ought to consist of such a number of machines as shall occupy the whole time of one workman in keeping them in order : if extended beyond that number, the same principle of economy would point out the necessity of doubling or tripling the number of machines, in order to employ the whole time of two or three skilful workmen.

" When one portion of the workman's labour consists in the exertion of mere physical force, as in weaving, and in many similar arts, it will soon occur to the manufacturer, that if that part were executed by a steam-engine, the same man might, in the case of weaving, attend to two or more looms at once : and, since we already suppose that one or more operative engineers have been employed, the number of looms may be so arranged that their time shall be fully occupied in keeping the steam-engine and the looms in order.

" Pursuing the same principles, the manufactory becomes gradually so enlarged, that the expense of lighting during the night amounts to a considerable sum : and as there are already attached to the establishment persons who are up all night, and can therefore constantly attend to it, and also engineers to make and keep in repair any machinery, the addition of an apparatus for making gas to light the factory leads to a new extension, at the same time that it contributes, by diminishing the expense of lighting, and the risk of accidents from fire, to reduce the cost of manufacturing.

" Long before a factory has reached this extent, it will have been found necessary to establish an accountant's department, with clerks to pay the workmen, and to see that they arrive at their stated times ; and this department must be in communication with the agents who purchase the raw produce, and with those who sell the manufactured article." It will cost these clerks and accountants little more time and trouble to pay a large number of workmen than a small number ; to check the accounts of large transactions, than of small. If the business doubled itself, it would probably be necessary to increase, but certainly not to double, the number either of accountants, or of buying and selling agents. Every increase of business would enable the whole to be carried on with a proportionately smaller amount of labour.

As a general rule, the expenses of a business do not increase by any means proportionally to the quantity of business. Let us take as an example, a set of operations which we are accustomed to see carried on by one great establishment, that of the Post Office. Suppose that the business, let us say only of the London letter-post, instead of being centralized in a single concern, were divided among five or six competing companies. Each of these would be obliged to maintain almost as large an establishment as is now sufficient for the whole. Since each must arrange for receiving and delivering letters in all parts of the town, each must send letter-carriers into every street, and almost every alley, and this too as many times in the day as is now done by the Post Office, if the service is to be as well performed. Each must have an office for receiving letters in every neighbourhood, with all subsidiary arrangements for collecting the letters from the different offices and re-distributing them. To this must be added the much greater number of superior officers who would be required to check and control the subordinates, implying not only a greater cost in salaries for such responsible officers, but the necessity, perhaps, of being satisfied in many instances with an inferior standard of qualification, and so failing in the object.

Whether or not the advantages obtained by operating on a large scale preponderate in any particular case over the more watchful attention, and greater regard to minor gains and losses, usually found in small establishments, can be ascertained, in a state of free competition, by an unfailing test. Wherever there are large and small establishments in the same business, that one of the two which in existing circumstances carries on the production at greatest advantage will be able to undersell the other. The power of permanently underselling can only, generally speaking, be derived from increased effectiveness of labour ; and this, when obtained by a more extended division of employment, or by a classification tending to a better economy of skill, always implies a greater produce from the same labour, and not merely the same produce from less labour : it increases not the surplus only, but the gross produce of industry. If an increased quantity of the particular article is not required, and part of the labourers in consequence lose their employment, the capital which maintained and employed them is also set at liberty ; and the general produce of the country is increased by some other application of their labour.

Another of the causes of large manufactories, however, is the introduction of processes requiring expensive machinery. Expensive machinery supposes a large capital; and is not resorted to except with the intention of producing, and the hope of selling, as much of the article as comes up to the full powers of the machine. For both these reasons, wherever costly machinery is used, the large system of production is inevitable. But the power of underselling is not in this case so unerring a test as in the former, of the beneficial effect on the total production of the community. The power of underselling does not depend on the absolute increase of produce, but on its bearing an increased proportion to the expenses; which, as was shown in a former chapter,* it may do, consistently with even a diminution of the gross annual produce. By the adoption of machinery, a circulating capital, which was perpetually consumed and reproduced, has been converted into a fixed capital, requiring only a small annual expense to keep it up: and a much smaller produce will suffice for merely covering that expense, and replacing the remaining circulating capital of the producer. The machinery therefore might answer perfectly well to the manufacturer, and enable him to undersell his competitors, though the effect on the production of the country might be not an increase but a diminution. It is true, the article will be sold cheaper, and therefore, of that single article, there will probably be not a smaller, but a greater quantity sold; since the loss to the community collectively has fallen upon the work-people, and they are not the principal customers, if customers at all, of most branches of manufacture. But though that particular branch of industry may extend itself, it will be by replenishing its diminished circulating capital from that of the community generally; and if the labourers employed in that department escape loss of employment, it is because the loss will spread itself over the labouring people at large. If any of them are reduced to the condition of unproductive labourers, supported by voluntary or legal charity, the gross produce of the country is to that extent permanently diminished, until the ordinary progress of accumulation makes it up; but if the condition of the labouring classes enables them to bear a temporary reduction of wages, and the superseded labourers become absorbed in other employments, their labour is still productive, and the breach in the gross produce of the community is repaired, though not the detriment to the labourers. I have restated this exposition, which has already been made in a

* Supra, chap. vi.

former place, to impress more strongly the truth, that a mode of production does not of necessity increase the productive effect of the collective labour of a community, because it enables a particular commodity to be sold cheaper. The one consequence generally accompanies the other, but not necessarily. I will not here repeat the reasons I formerly gave, nor anticipate those which will be given more fully hereafter, for deeming the exception to be rather a case abstractedly possible, than one which is frequently realized in fact.

A considerable part of the saving of labour effected by substituting the large system of production for the small, is the saving in the labour of the capitalists themselves. If a hundred producers with small capitals carry on separately the same business, the super-intendence of each concern will probably require the whole attention of the person conducting it, sufficiently at least to hinder his time or thoughts from being disposable for anything else : while a single manufacturer possessing a capital equal to the sum of theirs, with ten or a dozen clerks, could conduct the whole of their amount of business, and have leisure too for other occupations. The small capitalist, it is true, generally combines with the business of direction some portion of the details, which the other leaves to his subordinates : the small farmer follows his own plough, the small tradesman serves in his own shop, the small weaver plies his own loom. But in this very union of functions there is, in a great proportion of cases, a want of economy. The principal in the concern is either wasting, in the routine of a business, qualities suitable for the direction of it, or he is only fit for the former, and then the latter will be ill done. I must observe, however, that I do not attach, to this saving of labour, the importance often ascribed to it. There is undoubtedly much more labour expended in the superintendence of many small capitals than in that of one large capital. For this labour however the small producers have generally a full compensation, in the feeling of being their own masters, and not servants of an employer. It may be said, that if they value this independence they will submit to pay a price for it, and to sell, at the reduced rates occasioned by the competition of the great dealer or manufacturer. But they cannot always do this and continue to gain a living. They thus gradually disappear from society. After having consumed their little capital in prolonging the unsuccessful struggle, they either sink into the condition of hired labourers, or become dependent on others for support.

§ 2. Production on a large scale is greatly promoted by the practice of forming a large capital by the combination of many small contributions ; or, in other words, by the formation of joint stock companies. The advantages of the joint stock principle are numerous and important.

In the first place, many undertakings require an amount of capital beyond the means of the richest individual or private partnership. No individual could have made a railway from London to Liverpool ; it is doubtful if any individual could even work the traffic on it, now when it is made. The government indeed could have done both ; and in countries where the practice of co-operation is only in the earlier stages of its growth, the government can alone be looked to for any of the works for which a great combination of means is requisite ; because it can obtain those means by compulsory taxation, and is already accustomed to the conduct of large operations. For reasons, however, which are tolerably well known, and of which we shall treat fully hereafter, government agency for the conduct of industrial operations is generally one of the least eligible of resources, when any other is available.

Next, there are undertakings which individuals are not absolutely incapable of performing, but which they cannot perform on the scale and with the continuity which are ever more and more required by the exigencies of a society in an advancing state. Individuals are quite capable of despatching ships from England to any or every part of the world, to carry passengers and letters ; the thing was done before joint stock companies for the purpose were heard of. But when, from the increase of population and transactions, as well as of means of payment, the public will no longer content themselves with occasional opportunities, but require the certainty that packets shall start regularly, for some places once or even twice a day, for others once a week, for others that a steam ship of great size and expensive construction shall depart on fixed days twice in each month, it is evident that to afford an assurance of keeping up with punctuality such a circle of costly operations, requires a much larger capital and a much larger staff of qualified subordinates than can be commanded by an individual capitalist. There are other cases, again, in which though the business might be perfectly well transacted with small or moderate capitals, the guarantee of a great subscribed stock is necessary or desirable as a security to the public for the fulfilment of pecuniary engagements. This is especially the case when the nature of the

business requires that numbers of persons should be willing to trust
the concern with their money : as in the business of banking, and
that of insurance : to both of which the joint stock principle is
eminently adapted. It is an instance of the folly and jobbery of
the rulers of mankind, that until a late period the joint stock principle, as a general resort, was in this country interdicted by law
to these two modes of business ; to banking altogether, and to
insurance in the department of sea risks ; in order to bestow a
lucrative monopoly on particular establishments which the government was pleased exceptionally to license, namely the Bank of
England, and two insurance companies, the London and the Royal
Exchange.

[1] Another advantage of joint stock or associated management, is
its incident of publicity. This is not an invariable, but it is a natural
consequence of the joint stock principle, and might be, as in some
important cases it already is, compulsory. In banking, insurance,
and other businesses which depend wholly on confidence, publicity
is a still more important element of success than a large subscribed
capital. A heavy loss occurring in a private bank may be kept secret ;
even though it were of such magnitude as to cause the ruin of the
concern, the banker may still carry it on for years, trying to retrieve
its position, only to fall in the end with a greater crash : but this
cannot so easily happen in the case of a joint stock company,
whose accounts are published periodically. The accounts, even if
cooked, still exercise some check ; and the suspicions of shareholders,
breaking out at the general meetings, put the public on their guard.

These are some of the advantages of joint stock over individual
management. But if we look to the other side of the question, we
shall find that individual management has also very great advantages over joint stock. The chief of these is the much keener interest
of the managers in the success of the undertaking.

The administration of a joint stock association is, in the main,
administration by hired servants. Even the committee, or board
of directors, who are supposed to superintend the management,
and who do really appoint and remove the managers, have no
pecuniary interest in the good working of the concern beyond
the shares they individually hold, which are always a very small
part of the capital of the association, and in general but a small
part of the fortunes of the directors themselves ; and the part
they take in the management usually divides their time with many

[1] [This paragraph was added in the 6th ed. (1865).]

other occupations, of as great or greater importance to their own interest; the business being the principal concern of no one except those who are hired to carry it on.   But experience shows, and proverbs, the expression of popular experience, attest, how inferior is the quality of hired servants, compared with the ministration of those personally interested in the work, and how indispensable, when hired service must be employed, is " the master's eye " to watch over it.

The successful conduct of an industrial enterprise requires two quite distinct qualifications : fidelity, and zeal.   The fidelity of the hired managers of a concern it is possible to secure.   When their work admits of being reduced to a definite set of rules, the violation of these is a matter on which conscience cannot easily blind itself, and on which responsibility may be enforced by the loss of employment.   But to carry on a great business successfully, requires a hundred things which, as they cannot be defined beforehand, it is impossible to convert into distinct and positive obligations.   First and principally, it requires that the directing mind should be incessantly occupied with the subject; should be continually laying schemes by which greater profit may be obtained, or expense saved.   This intensity of interest in the subject it is seldom to be expected that any one should feel, who is conducting a business as the hired servant and for the profit of another.   There are experiments in human affairs which are conclusive on the point.   Look at the whole class of rulers, and ministers of state.   The work they are entrusted with, is among the most interesting and exciting of all occupations ; the personal share which they themselves reap of the national benefits or misfortunes which befal the state under their rule, is far from trifling, and the rewards and punishments which they may expect from public estimation are of the plain and palpable kind which are most keenly felt and most widely appreciated.   Yet how rare a thing is it to find a statesman in whom mental indolence is not stronger than all these inducements.   How infinitesimal is the proportion who trouble themselves to form, or even to attend to, plans of public improvement, unless when it is made still more troublesome to them to remain inactive ; or who have any other real desire than that of rubbing on, so as to escape general blame.   On a smaller scale, all who have ever employed hired labour have had ample experience of the efforts made to give as little labour in exchange for the wages, as is compatible with not being turned off.   The universal neglect by domestic servants of their employer's interests, wherever these are

not protected by some fixed rule, is matter of common remark
unless where long continuance in the same service, and reciprocal good
offices, have produced either personal attachment, or some feeling of
a common interest.

Another of the disadvantages of joint stock concerns, which is
in some degree common to all concerns on a large scale, is disregard
of small gains and small savings. In the management of a great
capital and great transactions, especially when the managers have
not much interest in it of their own, small sums are apt to be counted
for next to nothing ; they never seem worth the care and trouble
which it costs to attend to them, and the credit of liberality and
openhandedness is cheaply bought by a disregard of such trifling
considerations.   But small profits and small expenses often repeated
amount to great gains and losses : and of this a large capitalist is
often a sufficiently good calculator to be practically aware ; and to
arrange his business on a *system* which, if enforced by a sufficiently
vigilant superintendence, precludes the possibility of the habitual
waste otherwise incident to a great business.   But the managers of
a joint stock concern seldom devote themselves sufficiently to the
work, to enforce unremittingly, even if introduced, through every
detail of the business, a really economical system.

From considerations of this nature, Adam Smith was led to
enunciate as a principle, that joint stock companies could never be
expected to maintain themselves without an exclusive privilege
except in branches of business which, like banking, insurance, and
some others, admit of being, in a considerable degree, reduced to
fixed rules.   This, however, is one of those over-statements of a
true principle, often met with in Adam Smith.   In his days there
were few instances of joint stock companies which had been perman
ently successful without a monopoly, except the class of cases which
he referred to ; but since his time there have been many ; and the
regular increase both of the spirit of combination and of the ability
to combine will doubtless produce many more.   Adam Smith fixed
his observation too exclusively on the superior energy and more
unremitting attention brought to a business in which the whole
stake and the whole gain belong to the persons conducting it ; and
he overlooked various countervailing considerations which go a
great way towards neutralizing even that great point of superiority

Of these one of the most important is that which relates to the
intellectual and active qualifications of the directing head.   The
stimulus of individual interest is some security for exertion, but

exertion is of little avail if the intelligence exerted is of an inferior order, which it must necessarily be in the majority of concerns carried on by the persons chiefly interested in them. Where the concern is large, and can afford a remuneration sufficient to attract a class of candidates superior to the common average, it is possible to select for the general management, and for all the skilled employ-ments of a subordinate kind, persons of a degree of acquirement and cultivated intelligence which more than compensates for their inferior interest in the result. Their greater perspicacity enables them, with even a part of their minds, to see probabilities of advan-tage which never occur to the ordinary run of men by the continued exertion of the whole of theirs ; and their superior knowledge, and habitual rectitude of perception and of judgment, guard them against blunders, the fear of which would prevent the others from hazarding their interests in any attempt out of the ordinary routine.

It must be further remarked, that it is not a necessary conse-quence of joint stock management, that the persons employed, whether in superior or in subordinate offices, should be paid wholly by fixed salaries· There are modes of connecting more or less intimately the interest of the employés with the pecuniary success of the concern. There is a long series of intermediate positions, between working wholly on one's own account, and working by the day, week, or year for an invariable payment. Even in the case of ordinary unskilled labour, there is such a thing as task-work, or working by the piece : and the superior efficiency of this is so well known, that judicious employers always resort to it when the work admits of being put out in definite portions, without the necessity of too troublesome a surveillance to guard against inferiority in the execution. In the case of the managers of joint stock companies, and of the superintending and controlling officers in many private establishments, it is a common enough practice to connect their pecuniary interest with the interest of their employers, by giving them part of their remuneration in the form of a percentage on the profits. The personal interest thus given to hired servants is not comparable in intensity to that of the owner of the capital ; but it is sufficient to be a very material stimulus to zeal and carefulness, and, when added to the advantage of superior intelligence, often raises the quality of the service much above that which the generality of masters are capable of rendering to themselves. The ulterior extensions of which this principle of remuneration is susceptible.

being of great social as well as economical importance, will be more particularly adverted to in a subsequent stage of the present inquiry.

As I have already remarked of large establishments generally, when compared with small ones, whenever competition is free its results will show whether individual or joint stock agency is best adapted to the particular case, since that which is most efficient and most economical will always in the end succeed in underselling the other.

§ 3. The possibility of substituting the large system of production for the small, depends, of course, in the first place, on the extent of the market. The large system can only be advantageous when a large amount of business is to be done : it implies, therefore, either a populous and flourishing community, or a great opening for exportation. Again, this as well as every other change in the system of production is greatly favoured by a progressive condition of capital. It is chiefly when the capital of a country is receiving a great annual increase, that there is a large amount of capital seeking for investment : and a new enterprise is much sooner and more easily entered upon by new capital, than by withdrawing capital from existing employments. The change is also much facilitated by the existence of large capitals in few hands. It is true that the same amount of capital can be raised by bringing together many small sums. But this (besides that it is not equally well suited to all branches of industry) supposes a much greater degree of commercial confidence and enterprise diffused through the community, and belongs altogether to a more advanced stage of industrial progress.

In the countries in which there are the largest markets, the widest diffusion of commercial confidence and enterprise, the greatest annual increase of capital, and the greatest number of large capitals owned by individuals, there is a tendency to substitute more and more, in one branch of industry after another, large establishments for small ones. In England, the chief type of all these characteristics, there is a perpetual growth not only of large manufacturing establishments, but also, wherever a sufficient number of purchasers are assembled, of shops and warehouses for conducting retail business on a large scale. These are almost always able to undersell the smaller tradesmen, partly, it is understood, by means of division of labour, and the economy occasioned by limiting the employment of skilled agency to cases where skill is required ; and partly, no doubt, by the saving of labour arising from the great scale of the transactions ; as it costs no more time, and not much more exertion of mind, to make a large purchase, for example, than a small one, and very much less than to make a number of small ones.

With a view merely to production, and to the greatest efficiency of labour, this change is wholly beneficial. In some cases it is attended with drawbacks, rather social than economical, the nature of which has been already hinted at. But whatever disadvantages may be supposed to attend on the change from a small to a large system of production, they are not applicable to the change from a large to a still larger. When, in any employment, the régime of independent small producers has either never been possible, or has been superseded, and the system of many work-people under one management has become fully established, from that time any further enlargement in the scale of production is generally an unqualified benefit. It is obvious, for example, how great an economy of labour would be obtained if London were supplied by a single gas or water company instead of the existing plurality. While there are even as many as two, this implies double establishments of all sorts, when one only, with a small increase, could probably perform the whole operation equally well ; double sets of machinery and works, when the whole of the gas or water required could generally be produced by one set only ; even double sets of pipes, if the companies did not prevent this needless expense by agreeing upon a division of the territory. Were there only one establishment, it could make lower charges, consistently with obtaining the rate of profit now realized. But would it do so ? Even if it did not, the community in the aggregate would still be a gainer : since the shareholders are a part of the community, and they would obtain higher profits while the consumers paid only the same. It is, however, an error to suppose that the prices are ever permanently kept down by the competition of these companies. Where competitors are so few, they always end by agreeing not to compete. They may run a race of cheapness to ruin a new candidate, but as soon as he has established his footing they come to terms with him. When, therefore, a business of real public importance can only be carried on advantageously upon so large a scale as to render the liberty of competition almost illusory, it is an unthrifty dispensation of the public resources that several costly sets of arrangements should be kept up for the purpose of rendering to the community this one service. It is much better to treat it at once as a public function ; and if it be not such as the government itself could

beneficially undertake, it should be made over entire to the company
or association which will perform it on the best terms for the public.
In the case of railways, for example, no one can desire to see the
enormous waste of capital and land (not to speak of increased nuisance) involved in the construction of a second railway to connect the
same places already united by an existing one ; while the two would
not do the work better than it could be done by one, and after a
short time would probably be amalgamated.   Only one such line
ought to be permitted, but the control over that line never ought to
be parted with by the State, unless on a temporary concession, as
in France ; and the vested right which Parliament has allowed to be
acquired by the existing companies, like all other proprietary rights
which are opposed to public utility, is morally valid only as a claim
to compensation.

§ 4.   The question between the large and the small systems
of production as applied to agriculture—between large and small
farming, the *grande* and the *petite culture*—stands, in many respects,
on different grounds from the general question between great and
small industrial establishments.   In its social aspect, and as an
element in the Distribution of Wealth, this question will occupy us
hereafter : but even as a question of production, the superiority
of the large system in agriculture is by no means so clearly established as in manufactures.

I have already remarked, that the operations of agriculture
are little susceptible of benefit from the division of labour.   There
is but little separation of employments even on the largest farm.
The same persons may not in general attend to the live stock, to the
marketing, and to the cultivation of the soil ; but much beyond that
primary and simple classification the subdivision is not carried.
The combination of labour of which agriculture is susceptible,
is chiefly that which Mr. Wakefield terms Simple Co-operation ;
several persons helping one another in the same work, at the same
time and place.   But I confess it seems to me that this able writer
attributes more importance to that kind of co-operation, in reference
to agriculture properly so called, than it deserves.   None of the
common farming operations require much of it.   There is no particular advantage in setting a great number of people to work together in
ploughing or digging or sowing the same field, or even in mowing or
reaping it unless time presses.   A single family can generally supply
all the combination of labour necessary for these purposes.   And

in the works in which an union of many efforts is really needed, there is seldom found any impracticability in obtaining it where farms are small.

The waste of productive power by subdivision of the land often amounts to a great evil, but this applies chiefly to a subdivision so minute, that the cultivators have not enough land to occupy their time. Up to that point the same principles which recommend large manufactories are applicable to agriculture. For the greatest productive efficiency, it is generally desirable (though even this proposition must be received with qualifications) that no family who have any land, should have less than they could cultivate, or than will fully employ their cattle and tools. These, however, are not the dimensions of large farms, but of what are reckoned in England very small ones. The large farmer has some advantage in the article of buildings. It does not cost so much to house a great number of cattle in one building, as to lodge them equally well in several buildings. There is also some advantage in implements. A small farmer is not so likely to possess expensive instruments. But the principal agricultural implements, even when of the best construction, are not expensive. It may not answer to a small farmer to own a threshing machine, for the small quantity of corn he has to thresh ; but there is no reason why such a machine should not in every neighbourhood be owned in common, or provided by some person to whom the others pay a consideration for its use ; especially as, when worked by steam, they are so constructed as to be moveable.* [1] The large farmer can make some saving in cost of carriage. There is nearly as much trouble in carrying a small portion of produce to market, as a much greater produce ; in bringing home a small, as a much larger quantity of manures, and articles of daily consumption. There is also the greater cheapness of buying things in large quantities. These various advantages must count for something, but it does not seem that they ought to count for very much. In England, for some generations, there has been little experience of small farms ; but in Ireland the experience has been ample, not merely under the worst but under the best

* [1852] The observations in the text may hereafter require some degree of modification from inventions such as the steam plough and the reaping machine. The effect, however, of these improvements on the relative advantages of large and small farms, will not depend on the efficiency of the instruments, but on their costliness. I see no reason to expect that this will be such as to make them inaccessible to small farmers, or combinations of small farmers.

[1] [This reference to steam threshing machines was inserted in the 5th ed. (1862) ; and " until lately " in the reference to Ireland, infra, p. 149.]

management ; and the highest Irish authorities may be cited in opposition to the opinion which on this subject commonly prevails in England. Mr. Blacker, for example, one of the most experienced agriculturists and successful improvers in the north of Ireland, whose experience was chiefly in the best cultivated, which are also the most minutely divided, parts of the country, was of opinion, that tenants holding farms not exceeding from five to eight or ten acres could live comfortably and pay as high a rent as any large farmer whatever. " I am firmly persuaded," (he says,*) " that the small farmer who holds his own plough and digs his own ground, if he follows a proper rotation of crops, and feeds his cattle in the house, can undersell the large farmer, or in other words can pay a rent which the other cannot afford ; and in this I am confirmed by the opinion of many practical men who have well considered the subject. . . The English farmer of 700 to 800 acres is a kind of man approaching to what is known by the name of a gentleman farmer. He must have his horse to ride, and his gig, and perhaps an overseer to attend to his labourers ; he certainly cannot superintend himself the labour going on in a farm of 800 acres." After a few other remarks, he adds, " Besides all these drawbacks, which the small farmer knows little about, there is the great expense of carting out the manure from the homestead to such a great distance, and again carting home the crop. A single horse will consume the produce of more land than would feed a small farmer and his wife and two children. And what is more than all, the large farmer says to his labourers, *go* to your work ; but when the small farmer has occasion to hire them, he says, *come ;* the intelligent reader will, I dare say, understand the difference."

One of the objections most urged against small farms is, that they do not and cannot maintain, proportionally to their extent, so great a number of cattle as large farms, and that this occasions such a deficiency of manure, that a soil much subdivided must always be impoverished. It will be found, however, that subdivision only produces this effect when it throws the land into the hands of cultivators so poor as not to possess the amount of live stock suitable to the size of their farms. A small farm and a badly stocked farm are not synonymous. To make the comparison fairly, we must suppose the same amount of capital which is possessed by the large farmers to be disseminated among the small ones.

* Prize Essay on *The Management of Landed Property in Ireland,* by William Blacker (1837), p. 23.

When this condition, or even any approach to it, exists, and when stall feeding is practised (and stall feeding now begins to be considered good economy even on large farms), experience, far from bearing out the assertion that small farming is unfavourable to the multiplication of cattle, conclusively establishes the very reverse. The abundance of cattle, and copious use of manure, on the small farms of Flanders, are the most striking features in that Flemish agriculture which is the admiration of all competent judges, whether in England or on the Continent.*

* " The number of beasts fed on a farm of which the whole is arable land," says the elaborate and intelligent treatise on *Flemish Husbandry*, from personal observation and the best sources, published in the Library of the Society for the Diffusion of Useful Knowledge,) " is surprising to those who are not acquainted with the mode in which the food is prepared for the cattle. A beast for every three acres of land is a common proportion, and in very small occupations, where much spade husbandry is used, the proportion is still greater. After comparing the accounts given in a variety of places and situations of the average quantity of milk which a cow gives when fed in the stall, the result is, that it greatly exceeds that of our best dairy farms, and the quantity of butter made from a given quantity of milk is also greater. It appears astonishing that the occupier of only ten or twelve acres of light arable land should be able to maintain four or five cows, but the fact is notorious in the Waes country." (pp. 59, 60.)

This subject is treated very intelligently in the work of M. Passy, *Des Systêmes de Culture et de leur Influence sur l'Economie Sociale*, one of the most impartial discussions, as between the two systems, which has yet appeared in France.

" Without doubt it is England that, on an equal surface, feeds the greatest number of animals ; Holland and some parts of Lombardy can alone vie with her in this respect : but is this a consequence of the mode of cultivation, and have not climate and local situation a share in producing it ? Of this I think there can be no doubt. In fact, whatever may have been said, wherever large and small cultivation meet in the same place, the latter, though it cannot support as many sheep, possesses, all things considered, the greatest quantity of manure-producing animals.

" In Belgium, for example, the two provinces of smallest farms are Antwerp and East Flanders, and they possess on an average for every 100 hectares (250 acres) of cultivated land, 74 horned cattle and 14 sheep. The two provinces where we find the large farms are Namur and Hainaut, and they average, for every 100 hectares of cultivated ground, only 30 horned cattle and 45 sheep. Reckoning, as is the custom, ten sheep as equal to one head of horned cattle, we find in the first case, the equivalent of 76 beasts to maintain the fecundity of the soil ; in the latter case less than 35, a difference which must be called enormous. (See the statistical documents published by the Minister of the Interior.) The abundance of animals, in the parts of Belgium which are most subdivided, is nearly as great as in England. Calculating the number in England in proportion only to the cultivated ground, there are for each 100 hectares, 65 horned cattle and nearly 260 sheep, together equal to 91 of the former, being only an excess of 15. It should besides be remembered, that in Belgium stall feeding being continued nearly the whole year, hardly any of the manure is lost, while in England grazing in the open fields diminishes considerably the quantity which can be completely utilized.

The disadvantage, when disadvantage there is, of small or rather
of peasant farming, as compared with capitalist farming, must
chiefly consist in inferiority of skill and knowledge ; but it is not
true, as a general fact, that such inferiority exists. Countries
of small farms and peasant farming, Flanders and Italy, had a good
agriculture many generations before England, and theirs is still
[1848], as a whole, probably the best agriculture in the world. The
empirical skill, which is the effect of daily and close observation,

" Again, in the Department of the Nord, the arrondissements which have the
smallest farms support the greatest quantity of animals.   While the arrondissements of Lille and Hazebrouck, besides a greater number of horses, maintain
the equivalent of 52 and 46 head of horned cattle, those of Dunkirk and Avesnes,
where the farms are larger, produce the equivalent of only 44 and 40 head.
(See the statistics of France published by the Minister of Commerce.)
   " A similar examination extended to other portions of France would yield
similar results.   In the immediate neighbourhood of towns, no doubt, the small
farmers, having no difficulty in purchasing manure, do not maintain animals :
but, as a general rule, the kind of cultivation which takes most out of the ground
must be that which is obliged to be most active in renewing its fertility.   Assuredly the small farms cannot have numerous flocks of sheep, and this is an
inconvenience ; but they support more horned cattle than the large farms.
To do so is a necessity they cannot escape from, in any country where the
demands of consumers require their existence : if they could not fulfil this
condition, they must perish.
   " The following are particulars, the exactness of which is fully attested by
the excellence of the work from which I extract them, the statistics of the
commune of Vensat (department of Puy de Dôme), lately published by Dr.
Jusseraud, mayor of the commune.   They are the more valuable, as they
throw full light on the nature of the changes which the extension of small
farming has, in that district, produced in the number and kind of animals
by whose manure the productiveness of the soil is kept up and increased.   The
commune consists of 1612 hectares, divided into 4600 *parcelles*, owned by 591
proprietors, and of this extent 1466 hectares are under cultivation.   In 1790,
seventeen farms occupied two-thirds of the whole, and twenty others the
remainder.   Since then the land has been much divided, and the subdivision
is now extreme.   What has been the effect on the quantity of cattle ?   A
considerable increase.   In 1790 there were only about 300 horned cattle, and
from 1800 to 2000 sheep ; there are now 676 of the former and only 533 of the
latter.   Thus 1300 sheep have been replaced by 376 oxen and cows, and (all
things taken into account) the quantity of manure has increased in the ratio
of 490 to 729, or more than 48 per cent, not to mention that the animals being
now stronger and better fed, yield a much **greater** contribution than formerly
to the fertilization of the ground.
   "Such is the testimony of facts on the point.   It is not true, then, that
small farming feeds fewer animals than large ; on the contrary, local circumstances being the same, it feeds a greater number : and this is only what might
have been presumed ; for, requiring more from the soil, it is obliged to take
greater pains for keeping up its productiveness.   All the other reproaches cast
upon small farming, when collated one by one with facts justly appreciated,
will be seen to be no better founded, and to have been made only because the
countries compared with one another were differently situated in respect to the
general causes of agricultural prosperity."   (pp. 116-120.)

peasant farmers often possess in an eminent degree.   The traditional knowledge, for example, of the culture of the vine, possessed by the peasantry of the countries where the best wines are produced, is extraordinary.   There is no doubt an absence of science, or at least of theory ; and to some extent a deficiency of the spirit of improvement, so far as relates to the introduction of new processes.   There is also a want of means to make experiments, which can seldom be made with advantage except by rich proprietors or capitalists. As for those systematic improvements which operate on a large tract of country at once (such as great works of draining or irrigation) or which for any other reasons do really require large numbers of workmen combining their labour, these are not in general to be expected from small farmers, or even small proprietors, though combination among them for such purposes is by no means unexampled, and will become more common as their intelligence is more developed.

Against these disadvantages is to be placed, where the tenure of land is of the requisite kind, an ardour of industry absolutely unexampled in any other condition of agriculture.   This is a subject on which the testimony of competent witnesses is unanimous. The working of the *petite culture* cannot be fairly judged where the small cultivator is merely a tenant, and not even a tenant on fixed conditions, but (as until lately in Ireland) at a nominal rent greater than can be paid, and therefore practically at a varying rent always amounting to the utmost that can be paid.   To understand the subject, it must be studied where the cultivator is the proprietor, or at least a *métayer* with a permanent tenure ; where the labour he exerts to increase the produce and value of the land avails wholly, or at least partly, to his own benefit and that of his descendants.   In another division of our subject, we shall discuss at some length the important subject of tenures of land, and I defer till then any citation of evidence on the marvellous industry of peasant proprietors. It may suffice here to appeal to the immense amount of gross produce which, even without a permanent tenure, English labourers generally obtain from their little allotments ; a produce beyond comparison greater than a large farmer extracts, or would find it his interest to extract, from the same piece of land.

And this I take to be the true reason why large cultivation is generally most advantageous as a mere investment for profit.   Land occupied by a large farmer is not, in one sense of the word, farmed so highly.   There is not nearly so much labour expended on it.   This is not on account of any economy arising from combination of labour, but because, by employing less, a greater return is obtained in proportion to the outlay. It does not answer to any one to pay others for exerting all the labour which the peasant, or even the allotment-holder, gladly undergoes when the fruits are to be wholly reaped by himself. This labour, however, is not unproductive : it all adds to the gross produce. With anything like equality of skill and knowledge, the large farmer does not obtain nearly so much from the soil as the small proprietor, or the small farmer with adequate motives to exertion : but though his returns are less, the labour is less in a still greater degree, and as whatever labour *he* employs must be paid for, it does not suit his purpose to employ more.

But although the gross produce of the land is greatest, *cæteris paribus*, under small cultivation, and although, therefore, a country is able on that system to support a larger aggregate population, it is generally assumed by English writers that what is termed the net produce, that is, the surplus after feeding the cultivators, must be smaller ; that therefore, the population disposable for all other purposes, for manufactures, for commerce and navigation, for national defence, for the promotion of knowledge, for the liberal professions, for the various functions of government, for the arts and literature, all of which are dependent on this surplus for their existence as occupations, must be less numerous ; and that the nation, therefore (waiving all question as to the condition of the actual cultivators), must be inferior in the principal elements of national power, and in many of those of general well-being. This, however, has been taken for granted much too readily. Undoubtedly the non-agricultural population will bear a less ratio to the agricultural, under small than under large cultivation. But that it will be less numerous absolutely, is by no means a consequence. If the total population, agricultural and non-agricultural, is greater, the non-agricultural portion may be more numerous in itself, and may yet be a smaller proportion of the whole. If the gross produce is larger, the net produce may be larger, and yet bear a smaller ratio to the gross produce. Yet even Mr. Wakefield sometimes appears to confound these distinct ideas. In France it is computed [1848] that two-thirds of the whole population are agricultural. In England, at most, one-third. Hence Mr. Wakefield infers, that " as in France only three people are supported by the labour of two cultivators, while in England the labour of two cultivators supports six people, English agriculture is twice as productive as French agriculture," owing to the superior efficiency of large farming through combination of labour. But in the first place, the facts themselves are overstated. The labour of two persons in England does not quite support six people, for there is not a little [1848] food imported from foreign countries, and from Ireland. In France, too, the labour of two cultivators does much more than supply the food of three persons. It provides the three persons, and occasionally foreigners, with flax, hemp, and to a certain extent with silk, oils, tobacco, and latterly sugar, which in England are wholly obtained from abroad ; nearly all the timber used in France is of home growth, nearly all which is used in England is imported ; the principal fuel of France is [1848] procured and brought to market by persons reckoned among agriculturists, in England by persons not so reckoned. I do not take into calculation hides and wool, these products being common to both countries, nor wine or brandy produced for home consumption, since England has a corresponding production of beer and spirits ; but England has [1848] no material export of either article, and a great importation of the last, while France supplies wines and spirits to the whole world. I say nothing of fruit, eggs, and such minor articles of agricultural produce, in which the export trade of France is [1865] enormous. But not to lay undue stress on these abatements, we will take the statement as it stands. Suppose that two persons, in England, do *bonâ fide* produce the food of six, while in France, for the same purpose, the labour of four is requisite. Does it follow that England must have a larger surplus for the support of a non-agricultural population ? No ; but merely that she can devote two-thirds of her whole produce to the purpose, instead of one-third. Suppose the produce to be twice as great, and the one-third will amount to as much as two-thirds. The fact might be, that owing to the greater quantity of labour employed on the French system, the same land would produce food for twelve persons which on the English system would only produce it for six : and if this were so, which would be quite consistent with the conditions of the hypothesis, then although the food for twelve was produced by the labour of eight, while the six were fed by the labour of only two, there would be the same number of hands disposable for other employment in the one country as in the other. I am not contending that the fact is so. I know that the gross produce per acre in France as a whole (though not in its most improved districts) averages much less than in England, and that, in proportion to the extent and fertility of the two countries, England has, in the sense we are now speaking of, much the largest disposable population. But the disproportion certainly is not to be measured by Mr. Wakefield's simple criterion. As well might it be said that agricultural labour in the United States, where, by a late census (1840), four families in every five appeared to be engaged in agriculture, must be still more inefficient than in France.

The inferiority of French cultivation (which, taking the country as a whole, must be allowed to be real, though much exaggerated) is probably more owing to the lower general average of industrial skill and energy in that country, than to any special cause ; and even if partly the effect of minute subdivision, it does not prove that small farming is disadvantageous, but only (what is undoubtedly the fact) that farms in France are very frequently *too* small, and, what is worse, broken up into an almost incredible number of patches or *parcelles*, most inconveniently dispersed and parted from one another.

As a question, not of gross, but of net produce, the comparative merits of the *grande* and the *petite culture*, especially when the small farmer is also the proprietor, cannot be looked upon as decided. It is a question on which good judges at present differ. The current of English opinion is [1848] in favour of large farms : on the Continent, the weight of authority seems to be on the other side. Professor Rau, of Heidelberg, the author of one of the most comprehensive and elaborate of extant treatises on political economy, and who has that large acquaintance with facts and authorities on his own subject, which generally characterises his countrymen, lays it down as a settled truth, that small or moderate-sized farms yield not only a larger gross but a larger net produce : though, he adds, it is desirable there should be some great proprietors, to lead the way in new improvements.* The most apparently impartial and discriminating judgment that I have met with is that of M. Passy, who (always speaking with reference to *net* produce) gives his verdict in favour of large farms for grain and forage ; but, for the kinds of culture which require much labour and attention, places the advantage wholly on the side of small cultivation ; including in this description, not only the vine and the olive, where a considerable amount of care and labour must be bestowed on each individual plant, but also roots, leguminous plants, and

* See pp. 352 and 353 of a French translation published at Brussels in 1839, by M. Fred. de Kemmeter, of Ghent.

those which furnish the materials of manufactures.   The small size
and consequent multiplication, of farms, according to all authorities,
are extremely favourable to the abundance of many minor products
of agriculture.*

It is evident that every labourer who extracts from the land
more than his own food, and that of any family he may have,
increases the means of supporting a non-agricultural population.
Even if his surplus is no more than enough to buy clothes, the
labourers who make the clothes are a non-agricultural population,
enabled to exist by food which he produces.   Every agricultural
family, therefore, which produces its own necessaries, adds to the
net produce of agriculture ; and so does every person born on the
land, who by employing himself on it, adds more to its gross produce than the mere food which he eats.   It is questionable whether,
even in the most subdivided districts of Europe which are cultivated
by the proprietors, the multiplication of hands on the soil has approached, or tends to approach, within a great distance of this limit.
In France, though the subdivision is confessedly too great, there is
proof positive that it is far from having reached the point at which
it would begin to diminish the power of supporting a non-agricultural
population.   This is demonstrated by the great increase of the
towns ; which have of late [1848] increased in a much greater ratio
than the population generally,† showing (unless the condition of the
town labourers is becoming rapidly deteriorated, which there is no
reason to believe) that even by the unfair and inapplicable test of
proportions, the productiveness of agriculture must be on the increase.
This, too, concurrently with the amplest evidence that in the more
improved districts of France, and in some which, until lately, were
among the unimproved, there is a considerably increased consumption
of country produce by the country population itself.

[1] Impressed with the conviction that, of all faults which can
be committed by a scientific writer on political and social subjects,
exaggeration, and assertion beyond the evidence, most require to be
guarded against, I limited myself in the early editions of this work

---

* " In the department of the Nord," says M. Passy, " a farm of 20 hectares
(50 acres) produces in calves, dairy produce, poultry, and eggs, a value of sometimes 1000 francs (£40) a year : which, deducting expenses, is an addition to the
net produce of 15 to 20 francs per hectare." *Des Systèmes de Culture*, p. 114.

† [1857] During the interval between the census of 1851 and that of 1856, the
increase of the population of Paris alone exceeded the aggregate increase of all
France : while nearly all the other large towns likewise showed an increase.

[1] [This and the following paragraph were added in the 5th ed. (1862).]

to the foregoing very moderate statements. I little knew how much stronger my language might have been without exceeding the truth, and how much the actual progress of French agriculture surpassed anything which I had at that time sufficient grounds to affirm. The investigations of that eminent authority on agricultural statistics, M. Léonce de Lavergne, undertaken by desire of the Academy of Moral and Political Sciences of the Institute of France, have led to the conclusion that since the Revolution of 1789, the total produce of French agriculture has doubled ; profits and wages having both increased in about the same, and rent in a still greater ratio. M. de Lavergne, whose impartiality is one of his greatest merits, is, moreover, so far in this instance from the suspicion of having a case to make out, that he is labouring to show, not how much French agriculture has accomplished, but how much still remains for it to do. " We have required " (he says) " no less than seventy years to bring into cultivation two million hectares " (five million English acres) " of waste land, to suppress half our fallows, double our agricultural products, increase our population by 30 per cent, our wages by 100 per cent, our rent by 150 per cent. At this rate we shall require three quarters of a century more to arrive at the point which England has already attained.",*

After this evidence, we have surely now heard the last of the incompatibility of small properties and small farms with agricultural improvement. The only question which remains open is one of degree ; the comparative rapidity of agricultural improvement under the two systems ; and it is the general opinion of those who are equally well acquainted with both, that improvement is greatest under a due admixture between them.

In the present chapter, I do not enter on the question between great and small cultivation in any other respect than as a question of production, and of the efficiency of labour. We shall return to it hereafter as affecting the distribution of the produce, and the physical and social well-being of the cultivators themselves ; in which aspects it deserves, and requires, a still more particular examination.[1]

---

* *Economie Rurale de la France depuis* 1789.   Par M. Léonce de Lavergne, Membre de l'Institut et de la Société Centrale d'Agriculture de France.   2me éd. p. 59.

[1] [See Appendix H. *Large and Small Farming.*]

CHAPTER X

§ 1. WE have now successively considered each of the agents or conditions of production, and of the means by which the efficacy of these various agents is promoted. In order to come to an end of the questions which relate exclusively to production, one more, of primary importance, remains.

Production is not a fixed, but an increasing thing. When not kept back by bad institutions, or a low state of the arts of life, the produce of industry has usually tended to increase ; stimulated not only by the desire of the producers to augment their means of consumption, but by the increasing number of the consumers. Nothing in political economy can be of more importance than to ascertain the law of this increase of production ; the conditions to which it is subject : whether it has practically any limits, and what these are. There is also no subject in political economy which is popularly less understood, or on which the errors committed are of a character to produce, and do produce, greater mischief.

We have seen that the essential requisites of production are three—labour, capital, and natural agents ; the term capital including all external and physical requisites which are products of labour, the term natural agents all those which are not. But among natural agents we need not take into account those which, existing in unlimited quantity, being incapable of appropriation, and never altering in their qualities, are always ready to lend an equal degree of assistance to production, whatever may be its extent ; as air, and the light of the sun. Being now about to consider the impediments to production, not the facilities for it, we need advert to no other natural agents than those which are liable to be deficient either in quantity or in productive power. These may be all represented by the term land. Land, in the narrowest acceptation, as the source of agricultural produce, is the chief of them ; and if we extend the term to mines and fisheries—to what is found in the earth itself, or in the waters which partly cover it, as well as to what is grown or fed on its surface, it embraces everything with which we need at present concern ourselves.

We may say, then, without a greater stretch of language than under the necessary explanation is permissible, that the requisites of production are Labour, Capital, and Land. The increase of production, therefore, depends on the properties of these elements. It is a result of the increase either of the elements themselves, or of their productiveness. The law of the increase of production must be a consequence of the laws of these elements ; the limits to the increase of production must be the limits, whatever they are, set by those laws. We proceed to consider the three elements successively, with reference to this effect ; or in other words, the law of the increase of production, viewed in respect of its dependence, first on Labour, secondly on Capital, and lastly on Land.

§ 2. The increase of labour is the increase of mankind ; of population. On this subject the discussions excited by the *Essay* of Mr. Malthus have made the truth, though by no means universally admitted, yet so fully known, that a briefer examination of the question than would otherwise have been necessary will probably on the present occasion suffice.

The power of multiplication inherent in all organic life may be regarded as infinite. There is no one species of vegetable or animal, which, if the earth were entirely abandoned to it, and to the things on which it feeds, would not in a small number of years overspread every region of the globe, of which the climate was compatible with its existence. The degree of possible rapidity is different in different orders of beings ; but in all it is sufficient, for the earth to be very speedily filled up. There are many species of vegetables of which a single plant will produce in one year the germs of a thousand ; if only two come to maturity, in fourteen years the two will have multiplied to sixteen thousand and more. It is but a moderate case of fecundity in animals to be capable of quadrupling their numbers in a single year ; if they only do as much in half a century, ten thousand will have swelled within two centuries to upwards of two millions and a half. The capacity of increase is necessarily in a geometrical progression : the numerical ratio alone is different.

To this property of organized beings, the human species forms no exception. Its power of increase is indefinite, and the actual multiplication would be extraordinarily rapid, if the power were exercised to the utmost. It never is exercised to the utmost, and yet, in the most favourable circumstances known to exist, which are those of a fertile region colonized from an industrious and civilized community, population has continued, for several generations, independently of fresh immigration, to double itself in not much more than twenty years.* That the capacity of multiplication in the human species exceeds even this, is evident if we consider how great is the ordinary number of children to a family, where the climate is good and early marriages usual ; and how small a proportion of them die before the age of maturity, in the present state of hygienic knowledge, where the locality is healthy, and the family adequately provided with the means of living. It is a very low estimate of the capacity of increase, if we only assume, that in a good sanitary condition of the people, each generation may be double the number of the generation which preceded it.

Twenty or thirty years ago, these propositions might still have required considerable enforcement and illustration ; but the evidence of them is so ample and incontestable, that they have made their way against all kinds of opposition, and may now be regarded as axiomatic : though the extreme reluctance felt to admitting them every now and then gives birth to some ephemeral theory, speedily forgotten, of a different law of increase in different circumstances, through a providential adaptation of the fecundity of the human species to the exigencies of society.† The obstacle to a just under-

* [1865] This has been disputed ; but the highest estimate I have seen of the term which population requires for doubling itself in the United States, independently of immigrants and of their progeny—that of Mr. Carey—does not exceed thirty years.

† [1852] One of these theories, that of Mr. Doubleday, may be thought to require a passing notice, because it has of late obtained some followers, and because it derives a semblance of support from the general analogies of organic life. This theory maintains that the fecundity of the human animal, and of all other living beings, is in inverse proportion to the quantity of nutriment : that an underfed population multiplies rapidly, but that all classes in comfortable circumstances are, by a physiological law, so unprolific, as seldom to keep up their numbers without being recruited from a poorer class. There is no doubt that a positive excess of nutriment, in animals as well as in fruit trees, is unfavourable to reproduction ; and it is quite possible, though by no means proved, that the physiological conditions of fecundity may exist in the greatest degree when the supply of food is somewhat stinted. But any one who might be inclined to draw from this, even if admitted, conclusions at variance with the principles of Mr. Malthus, needs only be invited to look through a volume of the Peerage, and observe the enormous families, almost universal in that

standing of the subject does not arise from these theories, but from too confused a notion of the causes which, at most times and places, keep the actual increase of mankind so far behind the capacity.

§ 3. Those causes, nevertheless, are in no way mysterious. What prevents the population of hares and rabbits from over-stocking the earth ? Not want of fecundity, but causes very different : many enemies, and insufficient subsistence ; not enough to eat, and liability to be eaten. In the human race, which is not generally subject to the latter inconvenience, the equivalents for it are war and disease. If the multiplication of mankind proceeded only like that of the other animals, from a blind instinct, it would be limited in the same manner with theirs ; the births would be as numerous as the physical constitution of the species admitted of, and the population would be kept down by deaths.* But the conduct of human creatures is more or less influenced by foresight of consequences, and by impulses superior to mere animal instincts : and they do not, therefore, propagate like swine, but

class ; or call to mind the large families of the English clergy, and generally of the middle classes of England.

[1865] It is, besides, well remarked by Mr. Carey, that, to be consistent with Mr. Doubleday's theory, the increase of the population of the United States, apart from immigration, ought to be one of the slowest on record.

[1865] Mr. Carey has a theory of his own, also grounded on a physiological truth, that the total sum of nutriment received by an organized body directs itself in largest proportion to the parts of the system which are most used ; from which he anticipates a diminution in the fecundity of human beings, not through more abundant feeding, but through the greater use of their brains incident to an advanced civilization. There is considerable plausibility in this speculation, and experience may hereafter confirm it. But the change in the human constitution which it supposes, if ever realized, will conduce to the expected effect rather by rendering physical self-restraint easier, than by dispensing with its necessity ; since the most rapid known rate of multiplication is quite compatible with a very sparing employment of the multiplying power.

* [1865] Mr. Carey expatiates on the absurdity of supposing that matter tends to assume the highest form of organization, the human, at a more rapid rate than it assumes the lower forms, which compose human food ; that human beings multiply faster than turnips and cabbages. But the limit to the increase of mankind, according to the doctrine of Mr. Malthus, does not depend on the power of increase of turnips and cabbages, but on the limited quantity of the land on which they can be grown. So long as the quantity of land is practically unlimited, which it is in the United States, and food, consequently, can be increased at the highest rate which is natural to it, mankind also may, without augmented difficulty in obtaining subsistence, increase at their highest rate. When Mr. Carey can show, not that turnips and cabbages, but that the soil itself, or the nutritive elements contained in it, tend naturally to multiply, and that too at a rate exceeding the most rapid possible increase of mankind, he will have said something to the purpose. Till then, this part at least of his argument may be considered as non-existent.

are capable, though in very unequal degrees, of being withheld by prudence, or by the social affections, from giving existence to beings born only to misery and premature death.   In proportion as mankind rise above the condition of the beasts, population is restrained by the fear of want rather than by want itself.   Even where there is no question of starvation, many are similarly acted upon by the apprehension of losing what have come to be regarded as the decencies of their situation in life.   Hitherto no other motives than these two have been found strong enough, in the generality of mankind, to counteract the tendency to increase.   It has been the practice of a great majority of the middle and the poorer classes, whenever free from external control, to marry as early, and in most countries to have as many children, as was consistent with maintaining themselves in the condition of life which they were born to, or were accustomed to consider as theirs.   Among the middle classes, in many individual instances, there is an additional restraint exercised from the desire of doing more than maintaining their circumstances—of improving them ; but such a desire is rarely found, or rarely has that effect, in the labouring classes.   If they can bring up a family as they were themselves brought up, even the prudent among them are usually satisfied.   Too often they do not think even of that, but rely on fortune, or on the resources to be found in legal or voluntary charity.

In a very backward state of society, like that of Europe in the Middle Ages, and many parts of Asia at present [1848], population is kept down by actual starvation.   The starvation does not take place in ordinary years, but in seasons of scarcity, which in those states of society are much more frequent and more extreme than Europe is now accustomed to.   In these seasons actual want, or the maladies consequent on it, carry off numbers of the population, which in a succession of favourable years again expands, to be again cruelly decimated.   In a more improved state, few, even among the poorest of the people, are limited to actual necessaries, and to a bare sufficiency of those : and the increase is kept within bounds, not by excess of deaths, but by limitation of births.   The limitation is brought about in various ways.   In some countries, it is the result of prudent or conscientious self-restraint.   There is a condition to which the labouring people are habituated ; they perceive that by having too numerous families, they must sink below that condition, or fail to transmit it to their children ; and this they do not choose to submit to.   The countries in which, so far as is known, a great degree of voluntary prudence has been longest practised on this subject, are [1848] Norway and parts of Switzerland. Concerning both, there happens to be unusually authentic information ; many facts were carefully brought together by Mr. Malthus, and much additional evidence has been obtained since his time. In both these countries the increase of population is very slow ; and what checks it, is not multitude of deaths, but fewness of births. Both the births and the deaths are remarkably few in proportion to the population ; the average duration of life is the longest in Europe ; the population contains fewer children, and a greater proportional number of persons in the vigour of life, than is known to be the case in any other part of the world. The paucity of births tends directly to prolong life, by keeping the people in comfortable circumstances ; and the same prudence is doubtless exercised in avoiding causes of disease, as in keeping clear of the principal cause of poverty. It is worthy of remark that the two countries thus honourably distinguished are countries of small landed proprietors.

There are other cases in which the prudence and forethought, which perhaps might not be exercised by the people themselves, are exercised by the state for their benefit ; marriage not being permitted until the contracting parties can show that they have the prospect of a comfortable support. Under these laws, of which I shall speak more fully hereafter, the condition of the people is reported to be good, and the illegitimate births not so numerous as might be expected. There are places, again, in which the restraining cause seems to be not so much individual prudence, as some general and perhaps even accidental habit of the country. In the rural districts of England, during the last century, the growth of population was very effectually repressed by the difficulty of obtaining a cottage to live in. It was the custom for unmarried labourers to lodge and board with their employers ; it was the custom for married labourers to have a cottage : and the rule of the English poor laws by which a parish was charged with the support of its unemployed poor, rendered landowners averse to promote marriage. About the end of the century, the great demand for men in war and manufactures made it be thought a patriotic thing to encourage population : and about the same time the growing inclination of farmers to live like rich people, favoured as it was by a long period of high prices, made them desirous of keeping inferiors at a greater distance, and, pecuniary motives arising from abuses of the poor laws being superadded, they gradually drove their labourers into cottages, which the landlords now no longer refused permission to build. In some countries an old standing custom that a girl should not marry until she had spun and woven for herself an ample *trousseau* (destined for the supply of her whole subsequent life), is said to have acted as a substantial check to population. In England, at present [1848], the influence of prudence in keeping down multiplication is seen by the diminished number of marriages in the manufacturing districts in years when trade is bad.

But whatever be the causes by which population is anywhere limited to a comparatively slow rate of increase, an acceleration of the rate very speedily follows any diminution of the motives to restraint.[1] It is but rarely that improvements in the condition of the labouring classes do anything more than give a temporary margin, speedily filled up by an increase of their numbers. The use they commonly choose to make of any advantageous change in their circumstances, is to take it out in the form which, by augmenting the population, deprives the succeeding generation of the benefit. Unless, either by their general improvement in intellectual and moral culture, or at least by raising their habitual standard of comfortable living, they can be taught to make a better use of favourable circumstances, nothing permanent can be done for them ; the most promising schemes end only in having a more numerous, but not a happier people. By their habitual standard, I mean that (when any such there is) down to which they will multiply, but not lower. Every advance they make in education, civilization, and social improvement, tends to raise this standard ; and there is no doubt that it is gradually, though slowly, rising in the more advanced countries of Western Europe. Subsistence and employment in England have never increased more rapidly than in the last forty years [1862], but every census since 1821 showed a smaller proportional increase of population than that of the period preceding ; and the produce of French agriculture and industry is increasing in a progressive ratio, while the population exhibits, in every quinquennial census, a smaller proportion of births to the population.

The subject, however, of population, in its connexion with the condition of the labouring classes, will be considered in another place : in the present we have to do with it solely as one of the

---

[1] [So from the 3rd ed. (1852). The original second clause of the sentence ran : "There is always an immense residuary power behind, ready to start into activity as soon as the pressure which restrained it is taken off."]

elements of Production : and in that character we could not dispense
with pointing out the unlimited extent of its natural powers of
increase, and the causes owing to which so small a portion of that
unlimited power is for the most part actually exercised.   After this
brief indication, we shall proceed to the other elements.[1]

[1] [See Appendix I.   *Population.*]

CHAPTER XI

§ 1. The requisites of production being labour, capital, and land, it has been seen from the preceding chapter that the impedi- ments to the increase of production do not arise from the first of these elements. On the side of labour there is no obstacle to an increase of production, indefinite in extent and of unslackening rapidity. Population has the power of increasing in an uniform and rapid geometrical ratio. If the only essential condition of produc- tion were labour, the produce might, and naturally would, increase in the same ratio ; and there would be no limit, until the numbers of mankind were brought to a stand from actual want of space.

But production has other requisites, and of these, the one which we shall next consider is Capital. There cannot be more people in any country, or in the world, than can be supported from the produce of past labour until that of present labour comes in. There will be no greater number of productive labourers in any country, or in the world, than can be supported from that portion of the produce of past labour which is spared from the enjoyments of its possessor for purposes of reproduction, and is termed Capital. We have next, therefore, to inquire into the conditions of the increase of capital : the causes by which the rapidity of its increase is determined, and the necessary limitations of that increase.

Since all capital is the product of saving, that is, of abstinence from present consumption for the sake of a future good, the increase of capital must depend upon two things—the amount of the fund from which saving can be made, and the strength of the dispositions which prompt to it.

The fund from which saving can be made, is the surplus of the produce of labour, after supplying the necessaries of life to all concerned in the production : including those employed in replacing the materials, and keeping the fixed capital in repair. More than this surplus cannot be saved under any circumstances. As much as this, though it never is saved, always might be. This surplus is the fund from which the enjoyments, as distinguished from the necessaries, of the producers are provided ; it is the fund from which all are subsisted, who are not themselves engaged in production ; and from which all additions are made to capital. It is the real net produce of the country. The phrase, net produce, is often taken in a more limited sense, to denote only the profits of the capitalist and the rent of the landlord, under the idea that nothing can be included in the net produce of capital, but what is returned to the owner of the capital after replacing his expenses. But this is too narrow an acceptation of the term. The capital of the employer forms the revenue of the labourers, and if this exceeds the necessaries of life, it gives them a surplus which they may either expend in enjoyments, or save. For every purpose for which there can be occasion to speak of the net produce of industry, this surplus ought to be in-cluded in it. When this is included, and not otherwise, the net produce of the country is the measure of its effective power ; of what it can spare for any purposes of public utility, or private indulgence ; the portion of its produce of which it can dispose at pleasure ; which can be drawn upon to attain any ends, or gratify any wishes, either of the government or of individuals ; which it can either spend for its satisfaction, or save for future advantage.

The amount of this fund, this net produce, this excess of produc-tion above the physical necessaries of the producers, is one of the elements that determine the amount of saving. The greater the produce of labour after supporting the labourers, the more there is which *can* be saved. The same thing also partly contributes to determine how much *will* be saved. A part of the motive to saving consists in the prospect of deriving an income from savings ; in the fact that capital, employed in production, is capable of not only reproducing itself but yielding an increase. The greater the profit that can be made from capital, the stronger is the motive to its accumulation. That indeed which forms the inducement to save, is not the whole of the fund which supplies the means of saving, not the whole net produce of the land, capital, and labour of the coun-try, but only a part of it, the part which forms the remuneration of the capitalist, and is called profit of stock. It will however be readily enough understood, even previously to the explanations which will be given hereafter, that when the general productiveness of labour and capital is great, the returns to the capitalist are likely to be large, and that some proportion, though not an uniform one, will commonly obtain between the two.

§ 2. But the disposition to save does not wholly depend on the external inducement to it ; on the amount of profit to be made from savings. With the same pecuniary inducement, the inclination is very different, in different persons, and in different communities. The effective desire of accumulation is of unequal strength, not only according to the varieties of individual character, but to the general state of society and civilization. Like all other moral attributes, it is one in which the human race exhibits great differences, conformably to the diversity of its circumstances and the stage of its progress.

On topics which if they were to be fully investigated would exceed the bounds that can be allotted to them in this treatise, it is satisfactory to be able to refer to other works in which the necessary developments have been presented more at length. On the subject of Population this valuable service has been rendered by the celebrated *Essay* of Mr. Malthus ; and on the point which now occupies us I can refer with equal confidence to another, though a less known work, *New Principles of Political Economy*, by Dr. Rae.* In no other book known to me is so much light thrown, both from principle and history, on the causes which determine the accumulation of capital.

All accumulation involves the sacrifice of a present, for the sake of a future good. But the expediency of such a sacrifice varies

* This treatise is an example, such as not unfrequently presents itself, how much more depends on accident, than on the qualities of a book, in determining its reception. Had it appeared at a suitable time, and been favoured by circumstances, it would have had every requisite for great success. The author, a Scotchman settled in the United States, unites much knowledge, an original vein of thought, a considerable turn for philosophic generalities, and a manner of exposition and illustration calculated to make ideas tell not only for what they are worth, but for more than they are worth, and which sometimes, I think, has that effect in the writer's own mind. The principal fault of the book is the position of antagonism in which, with the controversial spirit apt to be found in those who have new thoughts on old subjects, he has placed himself towards Adam Smith. I call this a fault, (though I think many of the criticisms just, and some of them far-seeing,) because there is much less real difference of opinion than might be supposed from Dr. Rae's animadversions ; and because what he has found vulnerable in his great predecessor is chiefly the " human *too much* " in his premises ; the portion of them that is over and above what was either required or is actually used for the establishment of his conclusions. [A re-arranged reprint of John Rae's *New Principles of Political Economy* (1834) has been edited by Professor Mixter, and published (1905) under the title *The Sociological Theory of Capital.*]

very much in different states of circumstances ; and the willingness to make it varies still more.

In weighing the future against the present, the uncertainty of all things future is a leading element ; and that uncertainty is of very different degrees.   " All circumstances " therefore, " increasing the probability of the provision we make for futurity being enjoyed by ourselves or others, tend " justly and reasonably " to give strength to the effective desire of accumulation.   Thus a healthy climate or occupation, by increasing the probability of life, has a tendency to add to this desire.   When engaged in safe occupations, and living in healthy countries, men are much more apt to be frugal, than in unhealthy or hazardous occupations, and in climates pernicious to human life.   Sailors and soldiers are prodigals.   In the West Indies, New Orleans, the East Indies, the expenditure of the inhabitants is profuse.   The same people, coming to reside in the healthy parts of Europe, and not getting into the vortex of extravagant fashion, live economically.   War and pestilence have always waste and luxury among the other evils that follow in their train.   For similar reasons, whatever gives security to the affairs of the community is favourable to the strength of this principle.   In this respect the general prevalence of law and order, and the prospect of the continuance of peace and tranquillity, have considerable influence."*   The more perfect the security, the greater will be the effective strength of the desire of accumulation.   Where property is less safe, or the vicissitudes ruinous to fortunes are more frequent and severe, fewer persons will save at all, and of those who do, many will require the inducement of a higher rate of profit on capital, to make them prefer a doubtful future to the temptation of present enjoyment.

These are considerations which affect the expediency, in the eye of reason, of consulting future interests at the expense of present. But the inclination to make the sacrifice does not solely depend upon its expediency.   The disposition to save is often far short of what reason would dictate : and at other times is liable to be in excess of it.

Deficient strength of the desire of accumulation may arise from improvidence, or from want of interest in others.   Improvidence may be connected with intellectual as well as moral causes.   Individuals and communities of a very low state of intelligence are always improvident.   A certain measure of intellectual development seems necessary to enable absent things, and especially things future,

* Rae, p. 123 [ed. Mixter, p. 57].

to act with any force on the imagination and will. The effect of want of interest in others in diminishing accumulation will be admitted, if we consider how much saving at present takes place, which has for its object the interest of others rather than of ourselves ; the education of children, their advancement in life, the future interests of other personal connexions, the power of promoting, by the bestowal of money or time, objects of public or private usefulness. If mankind were generally in the state of mind to which some approach was seen in the declining period of the Roman Empire —caring nothing for their heirs, as well as nothing for friends, the public, or any object which survived them—they would seldom deny themselves any indulgence for the sake of saving, beyond what was necessary for their own future years ; which they would place in life annuities, or in some other form which would make its existence and their lives terminate together.

§ 3.   From these various causes, intellectual and moral, there is, in different portions of the human race, a greater diversity than is usually adverted to, in the strength of the effective desire of accumulation. A backward state of general civilization is often more the effect of deficiency in this particular, than in many others which attract more attention. In the circumstances, for example, of a hunting tribe, " man may be said to be necessarily improvident, and regardless of futurity, because, in this state, the future presents nothing which can be with certainty either foreseen or governed. . . . Besides a want of the motives exciting to provide for the needs of futurity through means of the abilities of the present, there is a want of the habits of perception and action, leading to a constant connexion in the mind of those distant points, and of the series of events serving to unite them. Even, therefore, if motives be awakened capable of producing the exertion necessary to effect this connexion, there remains the task of training the mind to think and act so as to establish it."

For instance : " Upon the banks of the St. Lawrence there are several little Indian villages. They are surrounded in general by a good deal of land, from which the wood seems to have been long extirpated, and have, besides, attached to them, extensive tracts of forest. The cleared land is rarely, I may almost say never, cultivated, nor are any inroads made in the forest for such a purpose. The soil is, nevertheless, fertile, and were it not, manure lies in heaps by their houses. Were every family to enclose half an acre of ground, till it, and plant it in potatoes and maize, it would yield a sufficiency to support them one half the year. They suffer, too, every now and then, extreme want, insomuch that, joined to occasional intemperance, it is rapidly reducing their numbers. This, to us, so strange apathy proceeds not, in any great degree, from repugnance to labour ; on the contrary, they apply very diligently to it when its reward is immediate. Thus, besides their peculiar occupations of hunting and fishing, in which they are ever ready to engage, they are much employed in the navigation of the St. Lawrence, and may be seen labouring at the oar, or setting with the pole, in the large boats used for the purpose, and always furnish the greater part of the additional hands necessary to conduct rafts through some of the rapids. Nor is the obstacle aversion to agricultural labour. This is no doubt a prejudice of theirs ; but mere prejudices always yield, principles of action cannot be created. When the returns from agricultural labour are speedy and great, they are also agriculturists. Thus, some of the little islands on Lake St. Francis, near the Indian village of St. Regis, are favourable to the growth of maize, a plant yielding a return of a hundredfold, and forming, even when half ripe, a pleasant and substantial repast. Patches of the best land on these islands are therefore every year cultivated by them for this purpose. As their situation renders them inaccessible to cattle, no fence is required ; were this additional outlay necessary, I suspect they would be neglected, like the commons adjoining their village. These had apparently, at one time, been under crop. The cattle of the neighbouring settlers would now, however, destroy any crop not securely fenced, and this additional necessary outlay consequently bars their culture. It removes them to an order of instruments of slower return than that which corresponds to the strength of the effective desire of accumulation in this little society.

"It is here deserving of notice, that what instruments of this kind they do form, are completely formed. The small spots of corn they cultivate are thoroughly weeded and hoed. A little neglect in this part would indeed reduce the crop very much ; of this experience has made them perfectly aware, and they act accordingly. It is evidently not the necessary labour that is the obstacle to more extended culture, but the distant return from that labour. I am assured, indeed, that among some of the more remote tribes, the labour thus expended much exceeds that given by the whites. The same portions of ground being cropped without remission, and manure not being used, they would scarcely yield any return, were not the soil most carefully broken and pulverized, both with the hoe and the hand. In such a situation a white man would clear a fresh piece of ground. It would perhaps scarce repay his labour the first year, and he would have to look for his reward in succeeding years. On the Indian, succeeding years are too distant to make sufficient impression ; though, to obtain what labour may bring about in the course of a few months, he toils even more assiduously than the white man." *

This view of things is confirmed by the experience of the Jesuits, in their interesting efforts to civilize the Indians of Paraguay. They gained the confidence of these savages in a most extraordinary degree. They acquired influence over them sufficient to make them change their whole manner of life. They obtained their absolute submission and obedience. They established peace. They taught them all the operations of European agriculture, and many of the more difficult arts. There were everywhere to be seen, according to Charlevoix " workshops of gilders, painters, sculptors, goldsmiths, watchmakers, carpenters, joiners, dyers," &c. These occupations were not practised for the personal gain of the artificers : the produce was at the absolute disposal of the missionaries, who ruled the people by a voluntary despotism. The obstacles arising from aversion to labour were therefore very completely overcome. The real difficulty was the improvidence of the people ; their inability to think for the future : and the necessity accordingly of the most unremitting and minute superintendence on the part of their instructors. " Thus at first, if these gave up to them the care of the oxen with which they ploughed, their indolent thoughtlessness would probably leave them at evening still yoked to the implement. Worse than this, instances occurred where they cut them up for supper, thinking, when reprehended, that they sufficiently excused themselves by saying they were hungry. . . . These fathers, says Ulloa, have to visit the houses, to examine what is really wanted : for without this care, the Indians would never look after anything. They must be present, too, when animals are slaughtered, not only that the meat may be equally divided, but that nothing may be lost." " But notwithstanding all this care and superintendence," says Charlevoix, " and all the precautions which are taken to prevent any want of the necessaries of life, the missionaries are sometimes much embarrassed. It often happens that they " (the Indians) " do not reserve to themselves a sufficiency of grain, even for seed. As for

* Rae, p. 136 [ed. Mixter, p. 71].

their other provisions, were they not well looked after, they would soon be without wherewithal to support life."*

As an example intermediate, in the strength of the effective desire of accumulation, between the state of things thus depicted and that of modern Europe, the case of the Chinese deserves attention. From various circumstances in their personal habits and social condition, it might be anticipated that they would possess a degree of prudence and self-control greater than other Asiatics, but inferior to most European nations ; and the following evidence is adduced of the fact.

" Durability is one of the chief qualities, marking a high degree of the effective desire of accumulation. The testimony of travellers ascribes to the instruments formed by the Chinese a very inferior durability to similar instruments constructed by Europeans. The houses, we are told, unless of the higher ranks, are in general of unburnt bricks, of clay, or of hurdles plastered with earth ; the roofs, of reeds fastened to laths. We can scarcely conceive more unsubstantial or temporary fabrics. Their partitions are of paper, requiring to be renewed every year. A similar observation may be made concerning their implements of husbandry, and other utensils. They are almost entirely of wood, the metals entering but very sparingly into their construction ; consequently they soon wear out, and require frequent renewals. A greater degree of strength in the effective desire of accumulation would cause them to be constructed of materials requiring a greater present expenditure but being far more durable. From the same cause, much land, that in other countries would be cultivated, lies waste. All travellers take notice of large tracts of lands, chiefly swamps, which continue in a state of nature. To bring a swamp into tillage is generally a process, to complete which, requires several years. It must be previously drained, the surface long exposed to the sun, and many operations performed, before it can be made capable of bearing a crop. Though yielding, probably, a very considerable return for the labour bestowed on it, that return is not made until a long time has elapsed. The cultivation of such land implies a greater strength of the effective desire of accumulation than exists in the empire.

" The produce of the harvest is, as we have remarked, always an instrument of some order or another ; it is a provision for future want, and regulated by the same laws as those to which other means of attaining a similar end conform. It is there chiefly rice, of which

* Rae, p. 140 [ed. Mixter, p. 76].

there are two harvests, the one in June, the other in October. The period then of eight months between October and June, is that for which provision is made each year, and the different estimate they make of to-day and this day eight months will appear in the self-denial they practise now, in order to guard against want then. The amount of this self-denial would seem to be small. The father Parennin, indeed, (who seems to have been one of the most intelligent of the Jesuits and spent a long life among the Chinese of all classes,) asserts, that it is their great deficiency in forethought and frugality in this respect, which is the cause of the scarcities and famines that frequently occur."

That it is defect of providence, not defect of industry, that limits production among the Chinese, is still more obvious than in the case of the semi-agriculturized Indians. " Where the returns are quick, where the instruments formed require but little time to bring the events for which they were formed to an issue," it is well known that " the great progress which has been made in the knowledge of the arts suited to the nature of the country and the wants of its inhabitants" makes industry energetic and effective. " The warmth of the climate, the natural fertility of the country, the knowledge which the inhabitants have acquired of the arts of agriculture, and the discovery and gradual adaptation to every soil of the most useful vegetable productions, enable them very speedily to draw from almost any part of the surface, what is there esteemed an equivalent to much more than the labour bestowed in tilling and cropping it. They have commonly double, sometimes treble harvests. These when they consist of a grain so productive as rice, the usual crop, can scarce fail to yield to their skill, from almost any portion of soil that can be at once brought into culture, very ample returns. Accordingly there is no spot that labour can immediately bring under cultivation that is not made to yield to it. Hills, even mountains, are ascended and formed into terraces ; and water, in that country the great productive agent, is led to every part by drains, or carried up to it by the ingenious and simple hydraulic machines which have been in use from time immemorial among this singular people. They effect this the more easily, from the soil, even in these situations, being very deep and covered with much vegetable mould. But what yet more than this marks the readiness with which labour is forced to form the most difficult materials into instruments, where these instruments soon bring to an issue the events for which they are formed, is the frequent occurrence on many of their lakes and rivers, of structures resembling the floating gardens of the Peruvians, rafts covered with vegetable soil and cultivated. Labour in this way draws from the materials on which it acts very speedy returns. Nothing can exceed the luxuriance of vegetation when the quickening powers of a genial sun are ministered to by a rich soil and abundant moisture. It is otherwise, as we have seen, in cases where the return, though copious, is distant. European travellers are surprised at meeting these little floating farms by the side of swamps which only require draining to render them tillable. It seems to them strange that labour should not rather be bestowed on the solid earth, where its fruits might endure, than on structures that must decay and perish in a few years. The people they are among think not so much of future years as of the present time. The effective desire of accumulation is of very different strength in the one, from what it is in the other. The views of the European extend to a distant futurity, and he is surprised at the Chinese, condemned through improvidence, and want of sufficient prospective care, to incessant toil, and, as he thinks, insufferable wretchedness. The views of the Chinese are confined to narrower bounds ; he is content to live from day to day, and has learnt to conceive even a life of toil a blessing." *

When a country has carried production as far as in the existing state of knowledge it can be carried with an amount of return corresponding to the average strength of the effective desire of accumulation in that country, it has reached what is called the stationary state ; the state in which no further addition will be made to capital, unless there takes place either some improvement in the arts of production, or an increase in the strength of the desire to accumulate. In the stationary state, though capital does not on the whole increase, some persons grow richer and others poorer. Those whose degree of providence is below the usual standard, become impoverished, their capital perishes, and makes room for the savings of those whose effective desire of accumulation exceeds the average. These become the natural purchasers of the lands, manufactories, and other instruments of production owned by their less provident countrymen.

What the causes are which make the return to capital greater in one country than in another, and which, in certain circumstances, make it impossible for any additional capital to find investment unless at diminished returns, will appear clearly hereafter. In China, if that country has really attained, as it is supposed to have

* Rae, pp. 151–5 [ed. Mixter, pp. 88–92].

done, the stationary state, accumulation has stopped when the returns to capital are still [1848] as high as is indicated by a rate of interest legally twelve per cent, and practically varying (it is said) between eighteen and thirty-six. It is to be presumed therefore that no greater amount of capital than the country already possesses, can find employment at this high rate of profit, and that any lower rate does not hold out to a Chinese sufficient temptation to induce him to abstain from present enjoyment. What a contrast with Holland, where, during the most flourishing period of its history, the government was able habitually to borrow at two per cent, and private individuals, on good security, at three. Since China is not a country like Burmah or the native states of India, where an enormous interest is but an indispensable compensation for the risk incurred from the bad faith or poverty of the state, and of almost all private borrowers ; the fact, if fact it be, that the increase of capital has come to a stand while the returns to it are still so large, denotes a much less degree of the effective desire of accumulation, in other words a much lower estimate of the future relatively to the present, than that of most European nations.

§ 4. We have hitherto spoken of countries in which the average strength of the desire to accumulate is short of that which, in circumstances of any tolerable security, reason and sober calculation would approve. We have now to speak of others in which it decidedly surpasses that standard. In the more prosperous countries of Europe, there are to be found abundance of prodigals ; in some of them (and in none more than England) the ordinary degree of economy and providence among those who live by manual labour cannot be considered high : still, in a very numerous portion of the community, the professional, manufacturing, and trading classes, being those who, generally speaking, unite more of the means with more of the motives for saving than any other class, the spirit of accumulation is so strong, that the signs of rapidly increasing wealth meet every eye : and the great amount of capital seeking investment excites astonishment, whenever peculiar circumstances turning much of it into some one channel, such as railway construction or foreign speculative adventure, bring the largeness of the total amount into evidence.

There are many circumstances, which, in England, give a peculiar force to the accumulating propensity. The long exemption of the country from the ravages of war, and the far earlier period than elsewhere at which property was secure from military violence or arbitrary spoliation, have produced a long-standing and hereditary confidence in the safety of funds when trusted out of the owner's hands, which in most other countries is of much more recent origin, and less firmly established. The geographical causes which have made industry rather than war the natural source of power and importance to Great Britain, have turned an unusual proportion of the most enterprising and energetic characters into the direction of manufactures and commerce ; into supplying their wants and gratifying their ambition by producing and saving, rather than by appropriating what has been produced and saved. Much also depended on the better political institutions of this country, which by the scope they have allowed to individual freedom of action, have encouraged personal activity and self-reliance, while by the liberty they confer of association and combination, they facilitate industrial enterprise on a large scale. The same institutions in another of their aspects, give a most direct and potent stimulus to the desire of acquiring wealth. The earlier decline of feudalism having removed or much weakened invidious distinctions between the originally trading classes and those who have been accustomed to despise them ; and a polity having grown up which made wealth the real source of political influence ; its acquisition was invested with a factitious value, independent of its intrinsic utility. It became synonymous with power ; and since power with the common herd of mankind *gives* power, wealth became the chief source of personal consideration, and the measure and stamp of success in life. To get out of one rank in society into the next above it, is the great aim of English middle-class life, and the acquisition of wealth the means. And inasmuch as to be rich without industry has always hitherto constituted a step in the social scale above those who are rich by means of industry, it becomes the object of ambition to save not merely as much as will afford a large income while in business, but enough to retire from business and live in affluence on realized gains. These causes have, in England, been greatly aided by that extreme incapacity of the people for personal enjoyment, which is a characteristic of countries over which puritanism has passed. But if accumulation is, on one hand, rendered easier by the absence of a taste for pleasure, it is, on the other, made more difficult by the presence of a very real taste for expense. So strong is the association between personal consequence and the signs of wealth, that the silly desire for the appearance of a large expenditure has the force of a passion, among large classes of a nation which derives less pleasure than perhaps any other in the world from what it spends. Owing to this circumstance, the effective desire of accumulation has never reached so high a pitch in England as it did in Holland, where, there being no rich idle class to set the example of a reckless expenditure, and the mercantile classes, who possessed the substantial power on which social influence always waits, being left to establish their own scale of living and standard of propriety, their habits remained frugal and unostentatious.

In England and Holland, then, for a long time past, and now in most other countries in Europe (which are rapidly following England in the same race), the desire of accumulation does not require, to make it effective, the copious returns which it requires in Asia, but is sufficiently called into action by a rate of profit so low, that instead of slackening, accumulation seems now to proceed more rapidly than ever ; and the second requisite of increased production, increase of capital, shows no tendency to become deficient. So far as that element is concerned, production is susceptible of an increase without any assignable bounds.

The progress of accumulation would no doubt be considerably checked if the returns to capital were to be reduced still lower than at present. But why should any possible increase of capital have that effect ? This question carries the mind forward to the remaining one of the three requisites of production. The limitation to production, not consisting in any necessary limit to the increase of the other two elements, labour and capital, must turn upon the properties of the only element which is inherently, and in itself, limited in quantity. It must depend on the properties of land.

CHAPTER XII

§ 1. LAND differs from the other elements of production, labour and capital, in not being susceptible of indefinite increase. Its extent is limited, and the extent of the more productive kinds of it more limited still. It is also evident that the quantity of produce capable of being raised on any given piece of land is not indefinite. This limited quantity of land, and limited productiveness of it, are the real limits to the increase of production.

That they are the ultimate limits, must always have been clearly seen. But since the final barrier has never in any instance been reached ; since there is no country in which all the land, capable of yielding food, is so highly cultivated that a larger produce could not (even without supposing any fresh advance in agricultural knowledge) be obtained from it, and since a large portion of the earth's surface still remains entirely uncultivated ; it is commonly thought, and is very natural at first to suppose, that for the present all limitation of production or population from this source is at an indefinite distance, and that ages must elapse before any practical necessity arises for taking the limiting principle into serious consideration.

I apprehend this to be not only an error, but the most serious one, to be found in the whole field of political economy. The question is more important and fundamental than any other ; it involves the whole subject of the causes of poverty, in a rich and industrious community : and unless this one matter be thoroughly understood, it is to no purpose proceeding any further in our inquiry.

§ 2. The limitation to production from the properties of the soil, is not like the obstacle opposed by a wall, which stands immovable in one particular spot, and offers no hindrance to motion short of stopping it entirely. We may rather compare it to a highly elastic and extensible band, which is hardly ever so violently stretched that it could not possibly be stretched any more, yet the pressure of which is felt long before the final limit is reached, and felt more severely the nearer that limit is approached.

After a certain, and not very advanced, stage in the progress of agriculture,[1] it is the law of production from the land, that in any given state of agricultural skill and knowledge, by increasing the labour, the produce is not increased in an equal degree ; doubling the labour does not double the produce ; or, to express the same thing in other words, every increase of produce is obtained by a more than proportional increase in the application of labour to the land.

This general law of agricultural industry is the most important proposition in political economy. Were the law different, nearly all the phenomena of the production and distribution of wealth would be other than they are. The most fundamental errors which still prevail on our subject, result from not perceiving this law at work underneath the more superficial agencies on which attention fixes itself ; but mistaking those agencies for the ultimate causes of effects of which they may influence the form and mode, but of which it alone determines the essence.

When, for the purpose of raising an increase of produce recourse is had to inferior land, it is evident that, so far, the produce does not increase in the same proportion with the labour. The very meaning of inferior land, is land which with equal labour returns a smaller amount of produce. Land may be inferior either in fertility or in situation. The one requires a greater proportional amount of labour for growing the produce, the other for carrying it to market. If the land A yields a thousand quarters of wheat, to a given outlay in wages, manure, &c., and in order to raise another thousand recourse must be had to the land B, which is either less fertile or more distant from the market, the two thousand quarters will cost more than twice as much labour as the original thousand, and the produce of agriculture will be increased in a less ratio than the labour employed in procuring it.

Instead of cultivating the land B, it would be possible, by higher cultivation, to make the land A produce more. It might

---

[1] [From the 6th ed. (1865) was first omitted the following explanatory clause of the original : " as soon, in fact, as men have applied themselves to cultivation with any energy, and have brought to it any tolerable tools."]

be ploughed or harrowed twice instead of once, or three times instead of twice ; it might be dug instead of being ploughed ; after ploughing, it might be gone over with a hoe instead of a harrow, and the soil more completely pulverized ; it might be oftener or more thoroughly weeded ; the implements used might be of higher finish, or more elaborate construction ; a greater quantity or more expensive kinds of manure might be applied, or, when applied, they might be more carefully mixed and incorporated with the soil. These are some of the modes by which the same land may be made to yield a greater produce ; and when a greater produce must be had, some of these are among the means usually employed for obtaining it. But, that it is obtained at a more than proportional increase of expense, is evident from the fact that inferior lands are cultivated. Inferior lands, or lands at a greater distance from the market, of course yield an inferior return, and an increasing demand cannot be supplied from them unless at an augmentation of cost, and therefore of price. If the additional demand could continue to be supplied from the superior lands, by applying additional labour and capital, at no greater proportional cost, than that at which they yield the quantity first demanded of them, the owners or farmers of those lands could undersell all others, and engross the whole market. Lands of a lower degree of fertility or in a more remote situation, might indeed be cultivated by their proprietors, for the sake of subsistence or independence ; but it never could be the interest of any one to farm them for profit. That a profit can be made from them, sufficient to attract capital to such an investment, is a proof that cultivation on the more eligible lands has reached a point, beyond which any greater application of labour and capital would yield, at the best, no greater return than can be obtained at the same expense from less fertile or less favourably situated lands.

The careful cultivation of a well-farmed district of England or Scotland is a symptom and an effect of the more unfavourable terms which the land has begun to exact for any increase of its fruits. Such elaborate cultivation costs much more in proportion, and requires a higher price to render it profitable, than farming on a more superficial system ; and would not be adopted if access could be had to land of equal fertility, previously unoccupied. Where there is the choice of raising the increasing supply which society requires, from fresh land of as good quality as that already cultivated, no attempt is made to extract from land anything approaching to what it will yield on what are esteemed the best

European modes of cultivating. The land is tasked up to the point at which the greatest return is obtained in proportion to the labour employed, but no further : any additional labour is carried elsewhere. "It is long," says an intelligent traveller in the United States,* "before an English eye becomes reconciled to the lightness of the crops and the careless farming (as we should call it) which is apparent. One forgets that where land is so plentiful and labour so dear as it is here, a totally different principle must be pursued to that which prevails in populous countries, and that the consequence will of course be a want of tidiness, as it were, and finish, about everything which requires labour." Of the two causes mentioned, the plentifulness of land seems to me the true explanation, rather than the dearness of labour ; for, however dear labour may be, when food is wanted, labour will always be applied to producing it in preference to anything else. But this labour is more effective for its end by being applied to fresh soil, than if it were employed in bringing the soil already occupied into higher cultivation. Only when no soil remains to be broken up but such as either from distance or inferior quality require a considerable rise of price to render their cultivation profitable, can it become advantageous to apply the high farming of Europe to any American lands ; except, perhaps, in the immediate vicinity of towns, where saving in cost of carriage may compensate for great inferiority in the return from the soil itself. As American farming is [1848] to England, so is the ordinary English to that of Flanders, Tuscany, or the Terra di Lavoro ; where by the application of a far greater quantity of labour there is obtained a considerably larger gross produce, but on such terms as would never be advantageous to a mere speculator for profit, unless made so by much higher prices of agricultural produce.

The principle which has now been stated must be received, no doubt, with certain explanations and limitations. Even after the land is so highly cultivated that the mere application of additional labour, or of an additional amount of ordinary dressing, would yield no return proportioned to the expense, it may still happen that the application of a much greater additional labour and capital to improving the soil itself, by draining or permanent manures, would be as liberally remunerated by the produce, as any portion of the labour and capital already employed. It would sometimes be much more amply remunerated. This could not be, if

* *Letters from America*, by John Robert Godley, vol. i. p. 42. See also Lyell's *Travels in America*, vol. ii. p. 83.

capital always sought and found the most advantageous employment ;
but if the most advantageous employment has to wait longest for
its remuneration, it is only in a rather advanced stage of industrial
development that the preference will be given to it ; and even in that
advanced stage, the laws or usages connected with property in land
and the tenure of farms are often such as to prevent the disposable
capital of the country from flowing freely into the channel of agricultural improvement : and hence the increased supply, required by
increasing population, is sometimes raised at an augmenting cost by
higher cultivation, when the means of producing it without increase of
cost are known and accessible.   There can be no doubt, that if
capital were forthcoming to execute, within the next year, all known
and recognised improvements in the lands of the United Kingdom
which would pay at the existing prices, that is, which would increase
the produce in as great or a greater ratio than the expense ; the
result would be such (especially if we include Ireland in the supposition) that inferior land would not for a long time require to be
brought under tillage : probably a considerable part of the less
productive lands now cultivated, which are not particularly favoured
by situation, would go out of culture ; or (as the improvements in
question are not so much applicable to good land, but operate
rather by converting bad land into good) the contraction of cultivation might principally take place by a less high dressing and less
elaborate tilling of land generally ; a falling back to something
nearer the character of American farming ; such only of the poor
lands being altogether abandoned as were not found susceptible
of improvement.   And thus the aggregate produce of the whole
cultivated land would bear a larger proportion than before to the
labour expended on it ; and the general law of diminishing return
from land would have undergone, to that extent, a temporary
supersession.   No one, however, can suppose that even in these
circumstances, the whole produce required for the country could
be raised exclusively from the best lands, together with those
possessing advantages of situation to place them on a par with the
best.   Much would undoubtedly continue to be produced under
less advantageous conditions, and with the smaller proportional
return, than that obtained from the best soils and situations.   And
in proportion as the further increase of population required a still
greater addition to the supply, the general law would resume its
course, and the further augmentation would be obtained at a
more than proportionate expense of labour and capital.

§ 3. [1] That the produce of land increases, *cæteris paribus*, in a diminishing ratio to the increase in the labour employed, is a truth more often ignored or disregarded than actually denied. It has, however, met with a direct impugner in the well-known American political economist, Mr. H. C. Carey, who maintains that the real law of agricultural industry is the very reverse ; the produce increasing in a greater ratio than the labour, or in other words affording to labour a perpetually increasing return. To substantiate this assertion, he argues that cultivation does not begin with the better soils, and extend from them, as the demand increases, to the poorer, but begins with the poorer, and does not, till long after, extend itself to the more fertile. Settlers in a new country invariably commence on the high and thin lands ; the rich but swampy soils of the river bottoms cannot at first be brought into cultivation, by reason of their unhealthiness, and of the great and prolonged labour required for clearing and draining them. As population and wealth increase, cultivation travels down the hill sides, clearing them as it goes, and the most fertile soils, those of the low grounds, are generally (even he says universally) the latest cultivated. These propositions, with the inferences which Mr. Carey draws from them, are set forth at much length in his latest and most elaborate treatise, *Principles of Social Science ;* and he considers them as subverting the very foundation of what he calls the English political economy, with all its practical consequences, especially the doctrine of free trade.

As far as words go, Mr. Carey has a good case against several of the highest authorities in political economy, who certainly did enunciate in too universal a manner the law which they laid down, not remarking that it is not true of the first cultivation in a newly settled country. Where population is thin and capital scanty, land which requires a large outlay to render it fit for tillage must remain untilled ; though such lands, when their time has come, often yield a greater produce than those earlier cultivated, not only absolutely, but proportionally to the labour employed, even if we include that which has been expended in originally fitting them for culture. But it is not pretended that the law of diminishing return was operative from the very beginning of society : and though some

[1] [The account of Carey's argument, occupying this and the next two paragraphs, took the place in the 6th ed. (1865) of the brief paragraph referring, without mentioning any name, to the assertion that " the returns from land are greater in an advanced, than in an early, stage of cultivation—when much capital, than when little, is applied to agriculture.]

political economists may have believed it to come into operation earlier than it does, it begins quite early enough to support the conclusions they founded on it. Mr. Carey will hardly assert that in any old country—in England or France, for example—the lands left waste are, or have for centuries been, more naturally fertile than those under tillage. Judging even by his own imperfect test, that of local situation—how imperfect I need not stop to point out—is it true that in England or France at the present day the uncultivated part of the soil consists of the plains and valleys, and the cultivated, of the hills ? Every one knows, on the contrary, that it is the high lands and thin soils which are left to nature, and when the progress of population demands an increase of cultivation, the extension is from the plains to the hills. Once in a century, perhaps, a Bedford Level may be drained, or a Lake of Harlem pumped out : but these are slight and transient exceptions to the normal progress of things ; and in old countries which are at all advanced in civilization, little of this sort remains to be done.*

Mr. Carey himself unconsciously bears the strongest testimony to the reality of the law he contends against : for one of the propositions most strenuously maintained by him is, that the raw products of the soil, in an advancing community, steadily tend to rise in price. Now, the most elementary truths of political economy show that this could not happen, unless the cost of production, measured in labour, of those products, tended to rise. If the application of additional labour to the land was, as a general rule, attended with an increase in the proportional return, the price of produce, instead of rising, must necessarily fall as society advances, unless the cost of production of gold and silver fell still more : a case so rare, that there are only two periods in all history when it is known to have taken place ; the one, that which followed the opening of the Mexican and Peruvian mines ; the other, that in which we now live. At all known periods, except these two, the cost of production of the precious metals has been either stationary or rising. If, therefore, it be true that the tendency of agricultural produce is to rise in money price as wealth and population increase, there needs no other evidence that the labour required for raising

* Ireland may be alleged as an exception ; a large fraction of the entire soil of that country being still [1865] incapable of cultivation for want of drainage. But though Ireland is an old country, unfortunate social and political circumstances have kept it a poor and backward one. Neither is it at all certain that the bogs of Ireland, if drained and brought under tillage, would take their place along with Mr. Carey's fertile river bottoms, or among any but the poorer soils.

it from the soil tends to augment when a greater quantity is demanded.

I do not go so far as Mr. Carey : I do not assert that the cost of production, and consequently the price, of agricultural produce, always and necessarily rises as population increases. It tends to do so ; but the tendency may be, and sometimes is, even during long periods, held in check. The effect does not depend on a single principle, but on two antagonizing principles. There is another agency, in habitual antagonism to the law of diminishing return from land ; and to the consideration of this we shall now proceed. It is no other than the progress of civilization. I use this general and somewhat vague expression, because the things to be included are so various, that hardly any term of a more restricted signification would comprehend them all.

Of these, the most obvious is the progress of agricultural knowledge, skill, and invention. Improved processes of agriculture are of two kinds : some enable the land to yield a greater absolute produce, without an equivalent increase of labour ; others have not the power of increasing the produce, but have that of diminishing the labour and expense by which it is obtained. Among the first are to be reckoned the disuse of fallows, by means of the rotation of crops ; and the introduction of new articles of cultivation capable of entering advantageously into the rotation. The change made in British agriculture towards the close of the last century, by the introduction of turnip husbandry, is spoken of as amounting to a revolution. These improvements operate not only by enabling the land to produce a crop every year, instead of remaining idle one year in every two or three to renovate its powers, but also by direct increase of its productiveness ; since the great addition made to the number of cattle, by the increase of their food, affords more abundant manure to fertilize the corn lands. Next in order comes the introduction of new articles of food, containing a greater amount of sustenance, like the potato, or more productive species or varieties of the same plant, such as the Swedish turnip. In the same class of improvements must be placed a better knowledge of the properties of manures, and of the most effectual modes of applying them ; the introduction of new and more powerful fertilizing agents, such as guano, and the conversion to the same purpose of substances previously wasted ; inventions like subsoil-ploughing or tile draining ; improvements in the breed or feeding of labouring cattle ; augmented stock of the animals which consume and convert

into human food what would otherwise be wasted ; and the like
The other sort of improvements, those which diminish labour, but
without increasing the capacity of the land to produce, are such
as the improved construction of tools ; the introduction of new
instruments which spare manual labour, as the winnowing and
threshing machines ; a more skilful and economical application
of muscular exertion, such as the introduction, so slowly accomplished in England, of Scotch ploughing, with two horses abreast
and one man, instead of three or four horses in a team and two
men, &c. These improvements do not add to the productiveness
of the land, but they are equally calculated with the former to
counteract the tendency in the cost of production of agricultural
produce to rise with the progress of population and demand.

Analogous in effect to this second class of agricultural improvements, are improved means of communication. Good roads are
equivalent to good tools. It is of no consequence whether the
economy of labour takes place in extracting the produce from the
soil, or in conveying it to the place where it is to be consumed.
Not to say in addition, that the labour of cultivation itself is
diminished by whatever lessens the cost of bringing manure from
a distance, or facilitates the many operations of transport from
place to place which occur within the bounds of the farm. Railways
and canals are virtually a diminution of the cost of production
of all things sent to market by them ; and literally so of all those,
the appliances and aids for producing which, they serve to transmit.
By their means land can be cultivated, which could not otherwise
have remunerated the cultivators without a rise of price. Improvements in navigation have, with respect to food or materials brought
from beyond sea, a corresponding effect.

From similar considerations, it appears that many purely
mechanical improvements, which have, apparently at least, no
peculiar connexion with agriculture, nevertheless enable a given
amount of food to be obtained with a smaller expenditure of labour.
A great improvement in the process of smelting iron would tend
to cheapen agricultural implements, diminish the cost of railroads,
of waggons and carts, ships, and perhaps buildings, and many other
things to which iron is not at present applied, because it is too
costly ; and would thence diminish the cost of production of food.
The same effect would follow from an improvement in those processes of what may be termed manufacture to which the material
of food is subjected after it is separated from the ground. The

first application of wind or water power to grind corn tended to cheapen bread as much as a very important discovery in agriculture would have done ; and any great improvement in the construction of corn-mills would have, in proportion, a similar influence.   The effects of cheapening locomotion have been already considered. There are also engineering inventions which facilitate all great operations on the earth's surface.   An improvement in the art of taking levels is of importance to draining, not to mention canal and railway making.   The fens of Holland, and of some parts of England, are drained by pumps worked by the wind or by steam. Where canals of irrigation, or where tanks or embankments are necessary, mechanical skill is a great resource for cheapening production.

Those manufacturing improvements which cannot be made instrumental to facilitate, in any of its stages, the actual production of food, and therefore do not help to counteract or retard the diminution of the proportional return to labour from the soil, have, however, another effect, which is practically equivalent.   What they do not prevent, they yet, in some degree, compensate for.

The materials of manufacture being all drawn from the land, and many of them from agriculture, which supplies in particular the entire material of clothing ; the general law of production from the land, the law of diminishing return, must in the last resort be applicable to manufacturing as well as to agricultural history.   As population increases, and the power of the land to yield increased produce is strained harder and harder, any additional supply of material, as well as of food, must be obtained by a more than proportionally increasing expenditure of labour. But the cost of the material forming generally a very small portion of the entire cost of the manufacture, the agricultural labour concerned in the production of manufactured goods is but a small fraction of the whole labour worked up in the commodity.   All the rest of the labour tends constantly and strongly towards diminution, as the amount of production increases.   Manufactures are vastly more susceptible than agriculture of mechanical improvements, and contrivances for saving labour ; and it has already been seen how greatly the division of labour, and its skilful and economical distribution, depend on the extent of the market, and on the possibility of production in large masses.   In manufactures, accordingly, the causes tending to increase the productiveness of industry, preponderate greatly over the one cause which tends to diminish it : and the increase of production, called forth by the progress of society, takes place, not at an increasing, but at a continually diminishing proportional cost.   This fact has manifested itself in the progressive fall of the prices and values of almost every kind of manufactured goods during two centuries past ; a fall accelerated by the mechanical inventions of the last seventy or eighty years, and susceptible of being prolonged and extended beyond any limit which it would be safe to specify.

Now it is quite conceivable that the efficiency of agricultural labour might be undergoing, with the increase of produce, a gradual diminution ; that the price of food, in consequence, might be progressively rising, and an ever growing proportion of the population might be needed to raise food for the whole ; while yet the productive power of labour in all other branches of industry might be so rapidly augmenting, that the required amount of labour could be spared from manufactures, and nevertheless a greater produce be obtained, and the aggregate wants of the community be on the whole better supplied, than before.   The benefit might even extend to the poorest class.   The increased cheapness of clothing and lodging might make up to them for the augmented cost of their food.

There is, thus, no possible improvement in the arts of production which does not in one or another mode exercise an antagonist influence to the law of diminishing return to agricultural labour. Nor is it only industrial improvements which have this effect. Improvements in government, and almost every kind of moral and social advancement, operate in the same manner.   Suppose a country in the condition of France before the Revolution : taxation imposed almost exclusively on the industrial classes, and on such a principle as to be an actual penalty on production ; and no redress obtainable for any injury to property or person, when inflicted by people of rank, or court influence.   Was not the hurricane which swept away this system of things, even if we look no further than to its effect in augmenting the productiveness of labour, equivalent to many industrial inventions ?   The removal of a fiscal burthen on agriculture, such as tithe, has the same effect as if the labour necessary for obtaining the existing produce were suddenly reduced one-tenth.   The abolition of corn laws, or of any other restrictions which prevent commodities from being produced where the cost of their production is lowest, amounts to a vast improvement in production.   When fertile land, previously reserved as hunting ground, or for any other purpose of amusement, is set free for culture, the aggregate productiveness of agricultural industry is increased. It is well known what has been the effect in England of badly administered poor laws, and the still worse effect in Ireland of a bad system of tenancy, in rendering agricultural labour slack and ineffective. No improvements operate more directly upon the productiveness of labour, than those in the tenure of farms, and in the laws relating to landed property. The breaking up of entails, the cheapening of the transfer of property, and whatever else promotes the natural tendency of land, in a system of freedom, to pass out of hands which can make little of it into those which can make more ; the substitution of long leases for tenancy at will, and of any tolerable system of tenancy whatever for the wretched cottier system ; above all, the acquisition of a permanent interest in the soil by the cultivators of it ; all these things are as real, and some of them as great, improvements in production, as the invention of the spinning-jenny or the steam-engine.

We may say the same of improvements in education. The intelligence of the workman is a most important element in the productiveness of labour. So low, in some of the most civilized countries, is the present [1848] standard of intelligence, that there is hardly any source from which a more indefinite amount of improvement may be looked for in productive power, than by endowing with brains those who now have only hands. The carefulness, economy, and general trustworthiness of labourers are as important as their intelligence. Friendly relations, and a community of interest and feeling between labourers and employers, are eminently so : I should rather say, would be : for I know not where any such sentiment of friendly alliance now exists. Nor is it only in the labouring class that improvement of mind and character operates with beneficial effect even on industry. In the rich and idle classes, increased mental energy, more solid instruction, and stronger feelings of conscience, public spirit, or philanthropy, would qualify them to originate and promote the most valuable improvements, both in the economical resources of their country, and in its institutions and customs. To look no further than the most obvious phenomena ; the backwardness of French agriculture in the precise points in which benefit might be expected from the influence of an educated class, is partly accounted 'for by the exclusive devotion of the richer landed proprietors to town interests and town pleasures. There is scarcely any possible amelioration of human affairs which would not, among its other benefits, have a favourable operation, direct or indirect, upon the productiveness of industry. The intensity of devotion to industrial occupations would indeed in many cases be moderated by a more liberal and genial mental culture, but the labour actually bestowed on those occupations would almost always be rendered more effective.

Before pointing out the principal inferences to be drawn from the nature of the two antagonist forces by which the productiveness of agricultural industry is determined, we must observe that what we have said of agriculture is true, with little variation, of the other occupations which it represents ; of all the arts which extract materials from the globe. Mining industry, for example, usually yields an increase of produce at a more than proportional increase of expense. It does worse, for even its customary annual produce requires to be extracted by a greater and greater expenditure of labour and capital. As a mine does not reproduce the coal or ore taken from it, not only are all mines at last exhausted, but even when they as yet show no signs of exhaustion, they must be worked at a continually increasing cost ; shafts must be sunk deeper, galleries driven farther, greater power applied to keep them clear of water ; the produce must be lifted from a greater depth, or conveyed a greater distance. The law of diminishing return applies therefore to mining, in a still more unqualified sense than to agriculture : but the antagonizing agency, that of improvements in production, also applies in a still greater degree. Mining operations are more susceptible of mechanical improvements than agricultural : the first great application of the steam-engine was to mining ; and there are unlimited possibilities of improvement in the chemical processes by which the metals are extracted. There is another contingency, of no unfrequent occurrence, which avails to counterbalance the progress of all existing mines towards exhaustion : this is, the discovery of new ones, equal or superior in richness.

To resume ; all natural agents which are limited in quantity, are not only limited in their ultimate productive power, but, long before that power is stretched to the utmost, they yield to any additional demands on progressively harder terms. This law may however be suspended, or temporarily controlled, by whatever adds to the general power of mankind over nature ; and especially by any extension of their knowledge, and their consequent command, of the properties and powers of natural agents.[1]

[1] [See Appendix J. *The Law of Diminishing Return.*]

CHAPTER XIII

§ 1. FROM the preceding exposition it appears that the limit to the increase of production is two-fold ; from deficiency of capital, or of land. Production comes to a pause, either because the effective desire of accumulation is not sufficient to give rise to any further increase of capital, or because, however disposed the possessors of surplus income may be to save a portion of it, the limited land at the disposal of the community does not permit additional capital to be employed with such a return as would be an equivalent to them for their abstinence.

In countries where the principle of accumulation is as weak as it is in the various nations of Asia ; where people will neither save, nor work to obtain the means of saving, unless under the inducement of enormously high profits, nor even then if it is necessary to wait a considerable time for them ; where either productions remain scanty, or drudgery great, because there is neither capital forthcoming nor forethought sufficient for the adoption of the contrivances by which natural agents are made to do the work of human labour ; the desideratum for such a country, economically considered, is an increase of industry, and of the effective desire of accumulation. The means are, first, a better government : more complete security of property ; moderate taxes, and freedom from arbitrary exaction under the name of taxes ; a more permanent and more advantageous tenure of land, securing to the cultivator as far as possible the undivided benefits of the industry, skill, and economy he may exert. Secondly, improvement of the public intelligence : the decay of usages or superstitions which interfere with the effective employment of industry ; and the growth of mental activity, making the people alive to new objects of desire. Thirdly, the introduction of foreign arts, which raise the returns derivable from additional capital, to a rate corresponding to the low strength of the desire of accumulation :

and the importation of foreign capital, which renders the increase of production no longer exclusively dependent on the thrift or providence of the inhabitants themselves, while it places before them a stimulating example, and by instilling new ideas and breaking the chains of habit, if not by improving the actual condition of the population, tends to create in them new wants, increased ambition, and greater thought for the future.   These considerations apply more or less to all the Asiatic populations, and to the less civilized and industrious parts of Europe, as Russia, Turkey, Spain, and Ireland.

§ 2.   But there are other countries, and England is at the head of them, in which neither the spirit of industry nor the effective desire of accumulation need any encouragement ; where the people will toil hard for a small remuneration, and save much for a small profit; where, though the general thriftiness of the labouring class is much below what is desirable, the spirit of accumulation in the more prosperous part of the community requires abatement rather than increase.   In these countries there would never be any deficiency of capital, if its increase were never checked or brought to a stand by too great a diminution of its returns.   It is the tendency of the returns to a progressive diminution, which causes the increase of production to be often attended with a deterioration in the condition of the producers ; and this tendency, which would in time put an end to increase of production altogether, is a result of the necessary and inherent conditions of production from the land.

In all countries which have passed beyond a rather [1] early stage in the progress of agriculture, every increase in the demand for food, occasioned by increased population, will always, unless there is a simultaneous improvement in production, diminish the share which on a fair division would fall to each individual.   An increased production, in default of unoccupied tracts of fertile land, or of fresh improvements tending to cheapen commodities, can never be obtained but by increasing the labour in more than the same proportion.   The population must either work harder, or eat less, or obtain their usual food by sacrificing a part of their other customary comforts.   Whenever this necessity is postponed, notwithstanding an increase of population,[2] it is because the improvements which facilitate production continue progressive ; because the contrivances

[1] [In the 6th ed. (1865) " rather " replaced the original " very."]
[2] [The qualifying clause " notwithstanding . . population " was inserted in the 6th ed. (1865).]

of mankind for making their labour more effective keep up an equal struggle with nature, and extort fresh resources from her reluctant powers as fast as human necessities occupy and engross the old.

From this, results the important corollary, that the necessity of restraining population is not, as many persons believe, peculiar to a condition of great inequality of property. A greater number of people cannot, in any given state of civilization, be collectively so well provided for as a smaller. The niggardliness of nature, not the injustice of society, is the cause of the penalty attached to over-population. An unjust distribution of wealth does not even aggravate the evil, but, at most, causes it to be somewhat earlier felt. It is in vain to say, that all mouths which the increase of mankind calls into existence, bring with them hands. The new mouths require as much food as the old ones, and the hands do not produce as much. If all instruments of production were held in joint property by the whole people, and the produce divided with perfect equality among them, and if, in a society thus constituted, industry were as energetic and the produce as ample as at present, there would be enough to make all the existing population extremely comfortable; but when that population had doubled itself, as, with the existing habits of the people, under such an encouragement, it undoubtedly would in little more than twenty years, what would then be their condition ? Unless the arts of production were in the same time improved in an almost unexampled degree,[1] the inferior soils which must be resorted to, and the more laborious and scantily remunerative cultivation which must be employed on the superior soils, to procure food for so much larger a population, would, by an insuperable necessity, render every individual in the community poorer than before. If the population continued to increase at the same rate, a time would soon arrive when no one would have more than mere necessaries, and, soon after, a time when no one would have a sufficiency of those, and the further increase of population would be arrested by death.

Whether, at the present or any other time, the produce of industry proportionally to the labour employed, is increasing or diminishing, and the average condition of the people improving or deteriorating, depends upon whether population is advancing faster than improvement, or improvement than population. After a degree of density has been attained, sufficient to allow the principal

---

[1] [So from the 3rd ed. (1852). The original ran : "so unexampled a degree as to double the productive power of labour."]

benefits of combination of labour, all further increase tends in itself
to mischief, so far as regards the average condition of the people ; but
the progress of improvement has a counteracting operation, and
allows of increased numbers without any deterioration, and even
consistently with a higher average of comfort. Improvement
must here be understood in a wide sense, including not only new
industrial inventions, or an extended use of those already known,
but improvements in institutions, education, opinions, and human
affairs generally, provided they tend, as almost all improvements
do, to give new motives or new facilities to production. If the
productive powers of the country increase as rapidly as advancing
numbers call for an augmentation of produce, it is not necessary to
obtain that augmentation by the cultivation of soils more sterile than
the worst already under culture, or by applying additional labour
to the old soils at a diminished advantage ; or at all events this loss
of power is compensated by the increased efficiency with which, in
the progress of improvement, labour is employed in manufactures.
In one way or the other, the increased population is provided for,
and all are as well off as before.   But if the growth of human power
over nature is suspended or slackened, and population does not
slacken its increase ; if, with only the existing command over natural
agencies, those agencies are called upon for an increased produce ;
this greater produce will not be afforded to the increased population,
without either demanding on the average a greater effort from each,
or on the average reducing each to a smaller ration out of the aggregate produce.

    As a matter of fact, at some periods the progress of population
has been the more rapid of the two, at others that of improvement.
In England during a long interval preceding the French Revolution,
population increased slowly ; but the progress of improvement, at
least in agriculture, would seem to have been still slower, since though
nothing occurred to lower the value of the precious metals, the price
of corn rose considerably, and England, from an exporting, became
an importing country.   This evidence, however, is short of conclusive, inasmuch as the extraordinary number of abundant seasons
during the first half of the century, not continuing during the last,
was a cause of increased price in the later period, extrinsic to the
ordinary progress of society.   Whether during the same period
improvements in manufactures, or diminished cost of imported commodities, made amends for the diminished productiveness of labour
on the land, is uncertain.   But ever since the great mechanical

inventions of Watt, Arkwright, and their contemporaries, the return to labour has probably increased as fast as the population ; and would have outstripped it, if that very augmentation of return had not called forth an additional portion of the inherent power of multiplication in the human species. During the twenty or thirty years last elapsed [1857], so rapid has been the extension of improved processes of agriculture, that even the land yields a greater produce in proportion to the labour employed ; the average price of corn had become decidedly lower, even before the repeal of the corn laws had so materially lightened, for the time being, the pressure of population upon production. But though improvement may during a certain space of time keep up with, or even surpass, the actual increase of population, it assuredly never comes up to the rate of increase of which population is capable ; and nothing could have prevented a general deterioration in the condition of the human race, were it not that population has in fact been restrained. Had it been restrained still more, and the same improvements taken place, there would have been a larger dividend than there now is, for the nation or the species at large. The new ground wrung from nature by the improvements would not have been all used up in the support of mere numbers. Though the gross produce would not have been so great, there would have been a greater produce per head of the population.

§ 3. When the growth of numbers outstrips the progress of improvement, and a country is driven to obtain the means of subsistence on terms more and more unfavourable, by the inability of its land to meet additional demands except on more onerous conditions ; there are two expedients by which it may hope to mitigate that disagreeable necessity, even though no change should take place in the habits of the people with respect to their rate of increase. One of these expedients is the importation of food from abroad. The other is emigration.

The admission of cheaper food from a foreign country is equivalent to an agricultural invention by which food could be raised at a similarly diminished cost at home. It equally increases the productive power of labour. The return was before, so much food for so much labour employed in the growth of food : the return is now, a greater quantity of food, for the same labour employed in producing cottons or hardware or some other commodity, to be given in exchange for food. The one improvement, like the other, throws back the decline of the productive power of labour by a certain distance : but in the one case as in the other, it immediately resumes its course ; the tide which has receded, instantly begins to re-advance. It might seem, indeed, that when a country draws its supply of food from so wide a surface as the whole habitable globe, so little impression can be produced on that great expanse by any increase of mouths in one small corner of it, that the inhabitants of the country may double and treble their numbers, without feeling the effect in any increased tension of the springs of production, or any enhancement of the price of food throughout the world.   But in this calculation several things are overlooked.

In the first place, the foreign regions from which corn can be imported do not comprise the whole globe, but those parts of it principally which are in the immediate neighbourhood of coasts or navigable rivers.   The coast is the part of most countries which is earliest and most thickly peopled, and has seldom any food to spare. The chief source of supply, therefore, is the strip of country along the banks of some navigable river, as the Nile, the Vistula, or the Mississippi ; and of such there is not, in the productive regions of the earth, so great a multitude as to suffice during an indefinite time for a rapidly growing demand, without an increasing strain on the productive powers of the soil.   To obtain auxiliary supplies of corn from the interior in any abundance, is, in the existing state of the communications [1871], in most cases impracticable.   By improved roads, and by canals and railways, the obstacle will eventually be so reduced as not to be insuperable : but this is a slow progress ; in all the food-exporting countries except America, a very slow progress ; and one which cannot keep pace with population, unless the increase of the last is very effectually restrained.

In the next place, even if the supply were drawn from the whole instead of a small part of the surface of the exporting countries, the quantity of food would still be limited, which could be obtained from them without an increase of the proportional cost.   The countries which export food may be divided into two classes ; those in which the effective desire of accumulation is strong, and those in which it is weak.   In Australia and the United States of America, the effective desire of accumulation is strong ; capital increases fast, and the production of food might be very rapidly extended. But in such countries population also increases with extraordinary rapidity.   Their agriculture has to provide for their own expanding numbers, as well as for those of the importing countries.   They must, therefore, from the nature of the case, be rapidly driven if not to less fertile, at least what is equivalent, to remoter and less accessible lands, and to modes of cultivation like those of old countries, less productive in proportion to the labour and expense.

But the countries which have at the same time cheap food and great industrial prosperity are few, being only those in which the arts of civilized life have been transferred full-grown to a rich and uncultivated soil. Among old countries, those which are able to export food, are able only because their industry is in a very backward state; because capital, and hence population, have never increased sufficiently to make food rise to a higher price. Such countries are [1848] Russia, Poland, and the plains of the Danube. In those regions the effective desire of accumulation is weak, the arts of production most imperfect, capital scanty, and its increase, especially from domestic sources, slow. When an increased demand arose for food to be exported to other countries, it would only be very gradually that food could be produced to meet it. The capital needed could not be obtained by transfer from other employments, for such do not exist. The cottons or hardware which would be received from England in exchange for corn, the Russians and Poles do not now produce in the country : they go without them. Something might in time be expected from the increased exertions to which producers would be stimulated by the market opened for their produce ; but to such increase of exertion, the habits of countries whose agricultural population consists of serfs, or of peasants who have but just emerged from a servile condition, are the reverse of favourable, and even in this age of movement these habits do not rapidly change. If a greater outlay of capital is relied on as the source from which the produce is to be increased, the means must either be obtained by the slow process of saving, under the impulse given by new commodities and more extended intercourse (and in that case the population would most likely increase as fast), or must be brought in from foreign countries. If England is to obtain a rapidly increasing supply of corn from Russia or Poland, English capital must go there to produce it. This, however, is attended with so many difficulties, as are equivalent to great positive disadvantages. It is opposed by differences of language, differences of manners, and a thousand obstacles arising from the institutions and social relations of the country ; and after all it would inevitably so stimulate population on the spot, that nearly all the increase of food produced by its means would probably be consumed without leaving the country : so that, if it were not the almost only mode of introducing foreign arts and ideas, and giving an effectual spur to the backward civilization of those countries, little reliance could be placed on it for increasing the exports, and supplying other countries with a progressive and indefinite increase of food. But to improve the civilization of a country is a slow process, and gives time for so great an increase of population both in the country itself, and in those supplied from it, that its effect in keeping down the price of food against the increase of demand is not likely to be more decisive on the scale of all Europe, than on the smaller one of a particular nation.

The law, therefore, of diminishing return to industry, whenever population makes a more rapid progress than improvement, is not solely applicable to countries which are fed from their own soil, but in substance applies quite as much to those which are willing to draw their food from any accessible quarter that can afford it cheapest. A sudden and great cheapening of food, indeed, in whatever manner produced, would, like any other sudden improvement in the arts of life, throw the natural tendency of affairs a stage or two further back, though without altering its course.[1] There is one contingency connected with freedom of importation, which may yet produce temporary effects greater than were ever contemplated either by the bitterest enemies or the most ardent adherents of free-trade in food. Maize, or Indian corn, is a product capable of being supplied in quantity sufficient to feed the whole country, at a cost, allowing for difference of nutritive quality, cheaper even than the potato. If maize should ever substitute itself for wheat as the staple food of the poor, the productive power of labour in obtaining food would be so

---

[1] [This one sentence replaced in the 3rd ed. (1852) the following passage of the original text : " If, indeed, the release of the corn trade from restriction had produced, or should still produce, a sudden cheapening of food, this, like any other sudden improvement in the arts of life, would throw the natural tendency of affairs a stage or two further back, but without at all altering its course. There would be more for everybody in the first instance ; but this *more* would begin immediately and continue always to grow less, so long as population went on increasing, unaccompanied by other events of a countervailing tendency.

" Whether the repeal of the corn laws is likely, even temporarily, to give any considerable increase of margin for population to fill up, it would be premature as yet to attempt to decide. All the elements of the question have been thrown into temporary disorder by the consequences of bad harvests and of the potatoe failure. But as far as can be foreseen, there seems little reason to expect an importation of the customary articles of food either so great in itself, or capable of such rapid increase, as to interfere much with the operation of the general law."]

enormously increased, and the expense of maintaining a family so diminished, that it would require perhaps some generations for population, even if it started forward at an American pace, to overtake this great accession to the facilities of its support.

§ 4. Besides the importation of corn, there is another resource which can be invoked by a nation whose increasing numbers press hard, not against their capital, but against the productive capacity of their land : I mean Emigration, especially in the form of Colonization. Of this remedy the efficacy as far as it goes is real, since it consists in seeking elsewhere those unoccupied tracts of fertile land, which if they existed at home would enable the demand of an increasing population to be met without any falling off in the productiveness of labour. Accordingly, when the region to be colonized is near at hand, and the habits and tastes of the people sufficiently migratory, this remedy is completely effectual. The migration from the older parts of the American Confederation to the new territories, which is to all intents and purposes colonization, is what enables population to go on unchecked throughout the Union without having yet diminished the return to industry, or increased the difficulty of earning a subsistence. If Australia or the interior of Canada were as near to Great Britain as Wisconsin and Iowa to New York ; if the superfluous people could remove to it without crossing the sea, and were of as adventurous and restless a character, and as little addicted to staying at home, as their kinsfolk of New England, those unpeopled continents would render the same service to the United Kingdom which the old states of America derive from the new. But, these things being as they are—though a judiciously conducted emigration is a most important resource for suddenly lightening the pressure of population by a single effort—and though in such an extraordinary case as that of Ireland under the threefold operation of the potato failure, the poor law, and the general turning-out of tenantry throughout the country, spontaneous emigration may at a particular crisis remove greater multitudes than it was ever proposed to remove at once by any national scheme [1] ; it still remains to be shown by experience [2] whether a permanent stream of emigration can be kept up, sufficient to take off, as in America, all that portion of the annual increase (when proceeding at its greatest

[1] [The reference to Ireland (" and though . . . scheme ") was inserted in the 3rd ed. (1852).]
[2] [So from the 6th ed. (1865). The original ran : " There is no probability that even under the most enlightened arrangements a permanent stream, &c."]

rapidity) which, being in excess of the progress made during the same short period in the arts of life, tends to render living more difficult for every averagely-situated individual in the community.   And unless this can be done, emigration cannot, even in an economical point of view, dispense with the necessity of checks to population. Further than this we have not to speak of it in this place.   The general subject of colonization as a practical question, its importance to old countries, and the principles on which it should be conducted, will be discussed at some length in a subsequent portion of this treatise.

BOOK II

DISTRIBUTION

CHAPTER I

OF PROPERTY

§ 1. The principles which have been set forth in the first part of this treatise, are, in certain respects, strongly distinguished from those on the consideration of which we are now about to enter. The laws and conditions of the Production of wealth partake of the character of physical truths. There is nothing optional or arbitrary in them. Whatever mankind produce, must be produced in the modes, and under the conditions, imposed by the constitution of external things, and by the inherent properties of their own bodily and mental structure. Whether they like it or not, their productions will be limited by the amount of their previous accumulation, and, that being given, it will be proportional to their energy, their skill, the perfection of their machinery, and their judicious use of the advantages of combined labour. Whether they like it or not, a double quantity of labour will not raise, on the same land, a double quantity of food, unless some improvement takes place in the processes of cultivation. Whether they like it or not, the unproductive expenditure of individuals will *pro tanto* tend to impoverish the community, and only their productive expenditure will enrich it. The opinions, or the wishes, which may exist on these different matters, do not control the things themselves. We cannot, indeed, foresee to what extent the modes of production may be altered, or the productiveness of labour increased, by future extensions of our knowledge of the laws of nature, suggesting new processes of industry of which we have at present no conception. But howsoever we may succeed in making for ourselves more space within the limits set by the constitution of things, we know that there must be limits. We cannot alter the ultimate properties either of matter or mind, but can only employ those properties more or less successfully, to bring about the events in which we are interested.[1]

It is not so with the Distribution of wealth. That is a matter of human institution solely. The things once there, mankind, individually or collectively, can do with them as they like. They can place them at the disposal of whomsoever they please, and on whatever terms. Further, in the social state, in every state except total solitude, any disposal whatever of them can only take place by the consent of society,[2] or rather of those who dispose of its active force. Even what a person has produced by his individual toil, unaided by any one, he cannot keep, unless by the permission of society. Not only can society take it from him, but individuals could and would take it from him, if society only remained passive ; if it did not either interfere *en masse*, or employ and pay people for the purpose of preventing him from being disturbed in the possession. The distribution of wealth, therefore, depends on the laws and cus- toms of society. The rules by which it is determined are what the opinions and feelings of the ruling portion of the community make them, and are very different in different ages and countries ; and might be still more different, if mankind so chose.

The opinions and feelings of mankind, doubtless, are not a matter of chance. They are consequences of the fundamental laws of human nature, combined with the existing state of knowledge and experi- ence, and the existing condition of social institutions and intel- lectual and moral culture. But the laws of the generation of human opinions are not within our present subject. They are part of the general theory of human progress, a far larger and more difficult subject of inquiry than political economy. We have here to consider, not the causes, but the consequences, of the rules accord- ing to which wealth may be distributed. Those, at least, are as little arbitrary, and have as much the character of physical laws, as the laws of production. Human beings can control their own

---

[1] [So since the 3rd ed. (1852). The original ran : " But howsoever . . . things, those limits exist ; there are ultimate laws, which we did not make, which we cannot alter, and to which we can only conform."]

[2] [The concluding words of this sentence were added in the 3rd ed., and " general " was deleted before " consent."   In the next sentence the keeping of property was made to depend on " the permission " and not on " the will " of society.]

acts, but not the consequences of their acts either to themselves or to others. Society can subject the distribution of wealth to whatever rules it thinks best : but what practical results will flow from the operation of those rules must be discovered, like any other physical or mental truths, by observation and reasoning.

We proceed, then, to the consideration of the different modes of distributing the produce of land and labour, which have been adopted in practice, or may be conceived in theory. Among these, our attention is first claimed by that primary and fundamental institution, on which, unless in some exceptional and very limited cases, the economical arrangements of society have always rested, though in its secondary features it has varied, and is liable to vary. I mean, of course, the institution of individual property.

§ 2. Private property, as an institution, did not owe its origin to any of those considerations of utility, which plead for the maintenance of it when established. Enough is known of rude ages, both from history and from analogous states of society in our own time, to show that tribunals (which always precede laws) were originally established, not to determine rights, but to repress violence and terminate quarrels. With this object chiefly in view, they naturally enough gave legal effect to first occupancy, by treating as the aggressor the person who first commenced violence, by turning, or attempting to turn, another out of possession. The preservation of the peace, which was the original object of civil government, was thus attained : while by confirming, to those who already possessed it, even what was not the fruit of personal exertion, a guarantee was incidentally given to them and others that they would be protected in what was so.

In considering the institution of property as a question in social philosophy, we must leave out of consideration its actual origin in any of the existing nations of Europe. We may suppose a community unhampered by any previous possession ; a body of colonists, occupying for the first time an uninhabited country ; bringing nothing with them but what belonged to them in common, and having a clear field for the adoption of the institutions and polity which they judged most expedient ; required, therefore, to choose whether they would conduct the work of production on the principle of individual property, or on some system of common ownership and collective agency.

If private property were adopted, we must presume that it would be accompanied by none of the initial inequalities and injustices which obstruct the beneficial operation of the principle in old societies. Every full grown man or woman, we must suppose, would be secured in the unfettered use and disposal of his or her bodily and mental faculties ; and the instruments of production, the land and tools, would be divided fairly among them, so that all might start, in respect to outward appliances, on equal terms. It is possible also to conceive that in this original apportionment, compensation might be made for the injuries of nature, and the balance redressed by assigning to the less robust members of the community advantages in the distribution, sufficient to put them on a par with the rest. But the division, once made, would not again be interfered with ; individuals would be left to their own exertions and to the ordinary chances, for making an advantageous use of what was assigned to them. If individual property, on the contrary, were excluded, the plan which must be adopted would be to hold the land and all instruments of production as the joint property of the community, and to carry on the operations of industry on the common account. The direction of the labour of the community would devolve upon a magistrate or magistrates, whom we may suppose elected by the suffrages of the community, and whom we must assume to be voluntarily obeyed by them. The division of the produce would in like manner be a public act. The principle might either be that of complete equality, or of apportionment to the necessities or deserts of individuals, in whatever manner might be conformable to the ideas of justice or policy prevailing in the community.

Examples of such associations, on a small scale, are the monastic orders, the Moravians, the followers of Rapp, and others : and from the hopes[1] which they hold out of relief from the miseries and iniquities of a state of much inequality of wealth, schemes for a larger application of the same idea have reappeared and become popular at all periods of active speculation on the first principles of society. In an age like the present [1848], when a general recon-sideration of all first principles is felt to be inevitable, and when more than at any former period of history the suffering portions of the community have a voice in the discussion, it was impossible but that ideas of this nature should spread far and wide.[2] The late

---

[1] [So since the 3rd ed. (1852). In the original, " the plausible remedy."]

[2] [Here followed in the original text the following passage : " Owenism, or Socialism, in this country, and Communism on the continent, are the most prevailing forms of the doctrine. These suppose a democratic government of

revolutions in Europe have thrown up a great amount of speculation of this character, and an unusual share of attention has consequently been drawn to the various forms which these ideas have assumed : nor is this attention likely to diminish, but on the contrary, to increase more and more.

The assailants of the principle of individual property may be divided into two classes : those whose scheme implies absolute equality in the distribution of the physical means of life and enjoyment, and those who admit inequality, but grounded on some principle, or supposed principle, of justice or general expediency, and not, like so many of the existing social inequalities, dependent on accident alone. At the head of the first class, as the earliest of those belonging to the present generation, must be placed Mr. Owen and his followers. M. Louis Blanc and M. Cabet have more recently become conspicuous as apostles of similar doctrines (though the former advocates equality of distribution only as a transition to a still higher standard of justice, that all should work according to their capacity, and receive according to their wants). The characteristic name for this economical system is Communism, a word of continental origin, only of late introduced into this country. The word Socialism, which originated among the English Communists, and was assumed by them as a name to designate their own doctrine, is now [1849], on the Continent, employed in a larger sense ; not necessarily implying Communism, or the entire abolition of private property, but applied to any system which requires that the land and the instruments of production should be the property, not

the industry and funds of society, and an equal division of the fruits. In the more elaborate and refined form of the same scheme, which obtained a temporary celebrity under the name of St. Simonism, the administering authority was supposed to be a monarchy or aristocracy, not of birth but of capacity ; the remuneration of each member of the community being by salary, proportioned to the importance of the services supposed to be rendered by each to the general body."

This was replaced in the 2nd ed. (1849) by the present reference to " the late revolutions in Europe," and by the following paragraph, dividing " the assailants of the principle of individual property " into two classes. The present form, however, of the clause beginning " Nor is this attention " dates from the 3rd ed. (1852). In the 2nd it ran : " This attention is not likely to diminish ; attacks on the institution of property being, in the existing state of human intellect, a natural expression of the discontent of all those classes on whom, in whatever manner, the present constitution of society bears hardly : and it is a safe prediction that, unless the progress of the human mind can be checked, such speculations will never cease, until the laws of property are freed from whatever portion of injustice they contain, and until whatever is well grounded in the opinions and legitimate in the aims of its assailants is adopted into the framework of society."]

of individuals, but of communities or associations, or of the government. Among such systems, the two of highest intellectual pretension are those which, from the names of their real or reputed authors, have been called St. Simonism and Fourierism ; the former defunct as a system, but which during the few years of its public promulgation sowed the seeds of nearly all the Socialist tendencies which have since spread so widely in France : the second, still [1865] flourishing in the number, talent, and zeal of its adherents.

§ 3.[1] Whatever may be the merits or defects of these various schemes, they cannot be truly said to be impracticable. No reasonable person can doubt that a village community, composed of a few thousand inhabitants, cultivating in joint ownership the same extent of land which at present feeds that number of people, and producing by combined labour and the most improved processes the manufactured articles which they required, could raise an amount of productions sufficient to maintain them in comfort ; and would find the means of obtaining, and if need be, exacting, the quantity of labour necessary for this purpose, from every member of the association who was capable of work.

The objection ordinarily made to a system of community of property and equal distribution of the produce, that each person would be incessantly occupied in evading his fair share of the work, points, undoubtedly, to a real difficulty. But those who urge this objection forget to how great an extent the same difficulty exists under the system on which nine-tenths of the business of society is now conducted. The objection supposes, that honest and efficient labour is only to be had from those who are themselves individually to reap the benefit of their own exertions. But how small a part of all the labour performed in England, from the lowest-paid to the highest, is done by persons working for their own benefit. From the Irish reaper or hodman to the chief justice or the minister of state, nearly all the work of society is remunerated by day wages or fixed salaries. A factory operative has less personal interest in his work than a member of a Communist association, since he is not, like him,

[The whole of this section was rewritten in the 3rd ed. (1852), with the aid of some passages from the 2nd ed. (1849), for the reason stated in the Preface to the 3rd edition   The present first paragraph of § 4 was added, and the next paragraph modified by the omission of the assertion that the arguments of § 3 while " not applicable to St. Simonism " were, to his mind, " conclusive against Communism."   For the original text of § 3 see Appendix K.   *Mill's earlier and later writings on Socialism.*]

working for a partnership of which he is himself a member. It will no doubt be said, that though the labourers themselves have not, in most cases, a personal interest in their work, they are watched and superintended, and their labour directed, and the mental part of the labour performed, by persons who have. Even this, however, is far from being universally the fact. In all public, and many of the largest and most successful private undertakings, not only the labours of detail but the control and superintendence are entrusted to salaried officers. And though the "master's eye," when the master is vigilant and intelligent, is of proverbial value, it must be remembered that in a Socialist farm or manufactory, each labourer would be under the eye not of one master, but of the whole community. In the extreme case of obstinate perseverance in not performing the due share of work, the community would have the same resources which society now has for compelling conformity to the necessary conditions of the association. Dismissal, the only remedy at present, is no remedy when any other labourer who may be engaged does no better than his predecessor : the power of dismissal only enables an employer to obtain from his workmen the customary amount of labour, but that customary labour may be of any degree of inefficiency. Even the labourer who loses his employment by idleness or negligence, has nothing worse to suffer, in the most unfavourable case, than the discipline of a workhouse, and if the desire to avoid this be a sufficient motive in the one system, it would be sufficient in the other. I am not undervaluing the strength of the incitement given to labour when the whole or a large share of the benefit of extra exertion belongs to the labourer. But under the present system of industry this incitement, in the great majority of cases, does not exist. If Communistic labour might be less vigorous than that of a peasant proprietor, or a workman labouring on his own account, it would probably be more energetic than that of a labourer for hire, who has no personal interest in the matter at all. The neglect by the uneducated classes of labourers for hire of the duties which they engage to perform, is in the present state of society most flagrant. Now it is an admitted condition of the Communist scheme that all shall be educated : and this being supposed, the duties of the members of the association would doubtless be as diligently performed as those of the generality of salaried officers in the middle or higher classes ; who are not supposed to be necessarily unfaithful to their trust, because so long as they are not dismissed, their pay

is the same in however lax a manner their duty is fulfilled. Undoubtedly, as a general rule, remuneration by fixed salaries does
not in any class of functionaries produce the maximum of zeal :
and this is as much as can be reasonably alleged against Communistic
labour.

That even this inferiority would necessarily exist, is by no means
so certain as is assumed by those who are little used to carry
their minds beyond the state of things with which they are familiar.
Mankind are capable of a far greater amount of public spirit than
the present age is accustomed to suppose possible. History bears
witness to the success with which large bodies of human beings
may be trained to feel the public interest their own. And no soil
could be more favourable to the growth of such a feeling, than a
Communist association, since all the ambition, and the bodily
and mental activity, which are now exerted in the pursuit of separate
and self-regarding interests, would require another sphere of employment, and would naturally find it in the pursuit of the general
benefit of the community. The same cause, so often assigned in
explanation of the devotion of the Catholic priest or monk to the
interest of his order—that he has no interest apart from it—would,
under Communism, attach the citizen to the community. And
independently of the public motive, every member of the association
would be amenable to the most universal, and one of the strongest,
of personal motives, that of public opinion. The force of this
motive in deterring from any act or omission positively reproved
by the community, no one is likely to deny ; but the power also
of emulation, in exciting to the most strenuous exertions for the
sake of the approbation and admiration of others, is borne witness
to by experience in every situation in which human beings publicly
compete with one another, even if it be in things frivolous, or from
which the public derive no benefit. A contest, who can do most for
the common good, is not the kind of competition which Socialists
repudiate. To what extent, therefore, the energy of labour would
be diminished by Communism, or whether in the long run it would
be diminished at all, must be considered for the present [1852]
an undecided question.

Another of the objections to Communism is similar to that
so often urged against poor laws : that if every member of the
community were assured of subsistence for himself and any
number of children, on the sole condition of willingness to work,
prudential restraint on the multiplication of mankind would be

at an end, and population would start forward at a rate which would reduce the community, through successive stages of increasing discomfort, to actual starvation. There would certainly be much ground for this apprehension if Communism provided no motives to restraint, equivalent to those which it would take away. But Communism is precisely the state of things in which opinion might be expected to declare itself with greatest intensity against this kind of selfish intemperance. Any augmentation of numbers which diminished the comfort or increased the toil of the mass, would then cause (which now it does not) immediate and unmistakeable inconvenience to every individual in the association ; inconvenience which could not then be imputed to the avarice of employers, or the unjust privileges of the rich. In such altered circumstances opinion could not fail to reprobate, and if reprobation did not suffice, to repress by penalties of some description, this or any other culpable self-indulgence at the expense of the community. The Communistic scheme, instead of being peculiarly open to the objection drawn from danger of over-population, has the recommendation of tending in an especial degree to the prevention of that evil.

A more real difficulty is that of fairly apportioning the labour of the community among its members. There are many kinds of work, and by what standard are they to be measured one against another ? Who is to judge how much cotton spinning, or distributing goods from the stores, or bricklaying, or chimney sweeping, is equivalent to so much ploughing ? The difficulty of making the adjustment between different qualities of labour is so strongly felt by Communist writers, that they have usually thought it necessary to provide that all should work by turns at every description of useful labour : an arrangement which, by putting an end to the division of employments, would sacrifice so much of the advantage of co-operative production as greatly to diminish the productiveness of labour. Besides, even in the same kind of work, nominal equality of labour would be so great a real inequality, that the feeling of justice would revolt against its being enforced. All persons are not equally fit for all labour ; and the same quantity of labour is an unequal burthen on the weak and the strong, the hardy and the delicate, the quick and the slow, the dull and the intelligent.

But these difficulties, though real, are not necessarily insuperable. The apportionment of work to the strength and capacities of individuals, the mitigation of a general rule to provide for cases in

which it would operate harshly, are not problems to which human
intelligence, guided by a sense of justice, would be inadequate.
And the worst and most unjust arrangement which could be made
of these points, under a system aiming at equality, would be so
far short of the inequality and injustice with which labour (not to
speak of remuneration) is now apportioned, as to be scarcely worth
counting in the comparison.   We must remember too, that Communism, as a system of society, exists only in idea ; that its
difficulties, at present, are much better understood than its resources ;
and that the intellect of mankind is only beginning to contrive
the means of organizing it in detail, so as to overcome the one
and derive the greatest advantage from the other.[1]

If, therefore, the choice were to be made between Communism
with all its chances, and the present [1852] state of society with
all its sufferings and injustices ; if the institution of private property
necessarily carried with it as a consequence, that the produce of
labour should be apportioned as we now see it, almost in an inverse
ratio to the labour—the largest portions to those who have never
worked at all, the next largest to those whose work is almost nominal,
and so in a descending scale, the remuneration dwindling as the
work grows harder and more disagreeable, until the most fatiguing
and exhausting bodily labour cannot count with certainty on being
able to earn even the necessaries of life ; if this or Communism
were the alternative, all the difficulties, great or small, of Communism
would be but as dust in the balance.   But to make the comparison
applicable, we must compare Communism at its best, with the
régime of individual property, not as it is, but as it might be made.
The principle of private property has never yet had a fair trial
in any country ; and less so, perhaps, in this country than in some
others.   The social arrangements of modern Europe commenced
from a distribution of property which was the result, not of just
partition, or acquisition by industry, but of conquest and violence :
and notwithstanding what industry has been doing for many
centuries to modify the work of force, the system still retains many
and large traces of its origin.   The laws of property have never yet
conformed to the principles on which the justification of private
property rests.   They have made property of things which never
ought to be property, and absolute property where only a qualified

---

[1] [The last sentence of this paragraph (" The impossibility of foreseeing and
prescribing the exact mode in which its difficulties should be dealt with, does not
prove that it may not be the best and the ultimate form of human society ")
was omitted in the 4th ed. (1857).]

property ought to exist. They have not held the balance fairly between human beings, but have heaped impediments upon some, to give advantage to others; they have purposely fostered inequalities, and prevented all from starting fair in the race. That all should indeed start on perfectly equal terms is inconsistent with any law of private property: but if as much pains as has been taken to aggravate the inequality of chances arising from the natural working of the principle, had been taken to temper that inequality by every means not subversive of the principle itself; if the tendency of legislation had been to favour the diffusion, instead of the con-centration of wealth—to encourage the subdivision of the large masses, instead of striving to keep them together; the principle of individual property would have been found to have no necessary connexion with the physical and social evils which almost all Socialist writers assume to be inseparable from it.

Private property, in every defence made of it, is supposed to mean the guarantee to individuals of the fruits of their own labour and abstinence. The guarantee to them of the fruits of the labour and abstinence of others, transmitted to them without any merit or exertion of their own, is not of the essence of the institution, but a mere incidental consequence which, when it reaches a certain height, does not promote, but conflicts with, the ends which render private property legitimate. To judge of the final destination of the institution of property, we must suppose everything rectified which causes the institution to work in a manner opposed to that equitable principle, of proportion between remuneration and exertion, on which in every vindication of it that will bear the light it is assumed to be grounded. We must also suppose two conditions realized, without which neither Communism nor any other laws or institutions could make the condition of the mass of mankind other than degraded and miserable. One of these conditions is universal education; the other, a due limitation of the numbers of the community. With these there could be no poverty, even under the present social institutions: and these being supposed, the question of Socialism is not, as generally stated by Socialists, a question of flying to the sole refuge against the evils which now bear down humanity; but a mere question of comparative advan-tages, which futurity must determine. We are too ignorant either of what individual agency in its best form, or Socialism in its best form, can accomplish, to be qualified to decide which of the two will be the ultimate form of human society.

If a conjecture may be hazarded, the decision will probably depend mainly on one consideration, viz. which of the two systems is consistent with the greatest amount of human liberty and spontaneity. After the means of subsistence are assured, the next in strength of the personal wants of human beings is liberty ; and (unlike the physical wants, which as civilization advances become more moderate and more amenable to control) it increases instead of diminishing in intensity as the intelligence and the moral faculties are more developed. The perfection both of social arrangements and of practical morality would be, to secure to all persons complete independence and freedom of action, subject to no restriction but that of not doing injury to others : and the education which taught or the social institutions which required them to exchange the control of their own actions for any amount of comfort or affluence, or to renounce liberty for the sake of equality, would deprive them of one of the most elevated characteristics of human nature. It remains to be discovered how far the preservation of this characteristic would be found compatible with the Communistic organization of society. No doubt this, like all the other objections to the Socialist schemes, is vastly exaggerated. The members of the association need not be required to live together more than they do now, nor need they be controlled in the disposal of their individual share of the produce, and of the probably large amount of leisure which, if they limited their production to things really worth producing, they would possess. Individuals need not be chained to an occupation, or to a particular locality. The restraints of Communism would be freedom in comparison with the present condition of the majority of the human race. The generality of labourers in this and most other countries have as little choice of occupation or freedom of locomotion, are practically as dependent on fixed rules and on the will of others, as they could be on any system short of actual slavery ; to say nothing of the entire domestic subjection of one half the species, to which it is the signal honour of Owenism and most other forms of Socialism that they assign equal rights, in all respects, with those of the hitherto dominant sex. But it is not by comparison with the present bad state of society that the claims of Communism can be estimated ; nor is it sufficient that it should promise greater personal and mental freedom than is now enjoyed by those who have not enough of either to deserve the name. The question is, whether there would be any asylum left for individuality of character ; whether public opinion would not be a tyrannical yoke ; whether the absolute dependence of each on all, and surveillance of each by all, would not grind all down into a tame uniformity of thoughts, feelings, and actions. This is already one of the glaring evils of the existing state of society, notwithstanding a much greater diversity of education and pùrsuits, and a much less absolute dependence of the individual on the mass, than would exist in the Communistic régime. No society in which eccentricity is a matter of reproach can be in a wholesome state. It is yet to be ascertained whether the Communistic scheme would be consistent with that multiform development of human nature, those manifold unlikenesses, that diversity of tastes and talents, and variety of intellectual points of view, which not only form a great part of the interest of human life, but by bringing intellects into stimulating collision, and by presenting to each innumerable notions that he would not have conceived of himself, are the main-spring of mental and moral progression.

§ 4. I have thus far confined my observations to the Communistic doctrine, which forms the extreme limit of Socialism ; according to which not only the instruments of production, the land and capital, are the joint property of the community, but the produce is divided and the labour apportioned, as far as possible, equally. The objections, whether well or ill grounded, to which Socialism is liable, apply to this form of it in their greatest force. The other varieties of Socialism mainly differ from Communism in not relying solely on what M. Louis Blanc calls the point of honour of industry, but retaining more or less of the incentives to labour derived from private pecuniary interest. Thus it is already a modification of the strict theory of Communism when the principle is professed of proportioning remuneration to labour. The attempts which have been made in France to carry Socialism into practical effect, by associations of workmen manufacturing on their own account,[1] mostly began by sharing the remuneration equally, without regard to the quantity of work done by the individual : but in almost every case this plan was after a short time abandoned, and recourse was had to working by the piece. The original principle appeals tó a higher standard of justice, and is adapted to a much higher moral condition of human nature. The proportioning of remuneration to work done is really just only in so far as the

---

[1] [The words " which are now," i.e. 1852, " very numerous, and in some cases very successful " were omitted in the 4th ed. (1857).]

more or less of the work is a matter of choice : when it depends on natural difference of strength or capacity, this principle of remuneration is in itself an injustice : it is giving to those who have ; assigning most to those who are already most favoured by nature. Considered, however, as a compromise with the selfish type of character formed by the present standard of morality, and fostered by the existing social institutions, it is highly expedient ; and until education shall have been entirely regenerated, is far more likely to prove immediately successful, than an attempt at a higher ideal.

The two elaborate forms of non-communistic Socialism known as St. Simonism and Fourierism are totally free from the objections usually urged against Communism ; and though they are open to others of their own, yet by the great intellectual power which in many respects distinguishes them, and by their large and philosophic treatment of some of the fundamental problems of society and morality, they may justly be counted among the most remarkable productions of the past and present age.

The St. Simonian scheme does not contemplate an equal, but an unequal, division of the produce ; it does not propose that all should be occupied alike, but differently, according to their vocation or capacity ; the function of each being assigned, like grades in a regiment, by the choice of the directing authority, and the remuneration being by salary, proportioned to the importance, in the eyes of that authority, of the function itself, and the merits of the person who fulfils it. For the constitution of the ruling body, different plans might be adopted, consistently with the essentials of the system. It might be appointed by popular suffrage. In the idea of the original authors, the rulers were supposed to be persons of genius and virtue, who obtained the voluntary adhesion of the rest by the force of mental superiority.[1] That the scheme might in some peculiar states of society work with advantage is not improbable. There is indeed a successful experiment, of a somewhat similar kind, on record, to which I have once alluded ; that of the Jesuits in Paraguay. A race of savages, belonging to a portion of mankind more averse to consecutive exertion for a distant object than any other authentically known to us, was brought under the mental dominion of civilized and instructed men who were united among

[1] [The next sentence of the original was omitted in the 3rd ed. (1852). " Society, thus constituted, would wear as diversified a face as it does now ; would be still fuller of interest and excitement, would hold out even more abundant stimulus to individual exertion, and would nourish, it is to be feared, even more of rivalries and of animosities than at present."]

themselves by a system of community of goods. To the absolute authority of these men they reverentially submitted themselves, and were induced by them to learn the arts of civilized life, and to practise labours for the community, which no inducement that could have been offered would have prevailed on them to practise for themselves. This social system was of short duration, being prematurely destroyed by diplomatic arrangements and foreign force. That it could be brought into action at all was probably owing to the immense distance in point of knowledge and intellect which separated the few rulers from the whole body of the ruled, without any intermediate orders, either social or intellectual. In any other circumstances it would probably have been a complete failure. It supposes an absolute despotism in the heads of the association ; which would probably not be much improved if the depositaries of the despotism (contrary to the views of the authors of the system) were varied from time to time according to the result of a popular canvass. But to suppose that one or a few human beings, howsoever selected, could, by whatever machinery of subordinate agency, be qualified to adapt each person's work to his capacity, and proportion each person's remuneration to his merits—to be, in fact, the dispensers of distributive justice to every member of a community ; or that any use which they could make of this power would give general satisfaction, or would be submitted to without the aid of force—is a supposition almost too chimerical to be reasoned against. A fixed rule, like that of equality, might be acquiesced in, and so might chance, or an external necessity ; but that a handful of human beings should weigh everybody in the balance, and give more to one and less to another at their sole pleasure and judgment would not be borne, unless from persons believed to be more than men, and backed by supernatural terrors.

[1] The most skilfully combined, and with the greatest foresight of objections, of all the forms of Socialism, is that commonly known as Fourierism. This system does not contemplate the abolition of private property, nor even of inheritance ; on the contrary, it avowedly takes into consideration, as an element in the distribution of the produce, capital as well as labour. It proposes that the operations of industry should be carried on by associations of about two thousand members, combining their labour on a district of about a square league in extent, under the guidance of chiefs selected by

---

[1] [The account of Fourierism, in this and the next three paragraphs, was added in the 2nd ed. (1849).]

themselves. In the distribution, a certain minimum is first assigned for the subsistence of every member of the community, whether capable or not of labour. The remainder of the produce is shared in certain proportions, to be determined beforehand, among the three elements, Labour, Capital, and Talent. The capital of the community may be owned in unequal shares by different members, who would in that case receive, as in any other joint-stock company, proportional dividends. The claim of each person on the share of the produce apportioned to talent, is estimated by the grade or rank which the individual occupies in the several groups of labourers to which he or she belongs; these grades being in all cases conferred by the choice of his or her companions. The remuneration, when received, would not of necessity be expended or enjoyed in common; there would be separate *ménages* for all who preferred them, and no other community of living is contemplated, than that all the members of the association should reside in the same pile of buildings; for saving of labour and expense, not only in building, but in every branch of domestic economy; and in order that, the whole of the buying and selling operations of the community being performed by a single agent, the enormous portion of the produce of industry now carried off by the profits of mere distributors might be reduced to the smallest amount possible.

This system, unlike Communism, does not, in theory at least, withdraw any of the motives to exertion which exist in the present state of society. On the contrary, if the arrangement worked according to the intentions of its contrivers, it would even strengthen those motives; since each person would have much more certainty of reaping individually the fruits of increased skill or energy, bodily or mental, than under the present social arrangements can be felt by any but those who are in the most advantageous positions, or to whom the chapter of accidents is more than ordinarily favourable. The Fourierists, however, have still another resource. They believe that they have solved the great and fundamental problem of rendering labour attractive. That this is not impracticable, they contend by very strong arguments;. in particular by one which they have in common with the Owenites, viz., that scarcely any labour, however severe, undergone by human beings for the sake of subsistence, exceeds in intensity that which other human beings, whose subsistence is already provided for, are found ready and even eager to undergo for pleasure. This certainly is a most significant fact, and one from which the student in social philosophy may draw important instruction. But the argument founded on it may easily be stretched too far. If occupations full of discomfort and fatigue are freely pursued by many persons as amusements, who does not see that they are amusements exactly because they are pursued freely, and may be discontinued at pleasure ? The liberty of quitting a position often makes the whole difference between its being painful and pleasurable. Many a person remains in the same town, street, or house from January to December, without a wish or a thought tending towards removal, who, if confined to that same place by the mandate of authority, would find the imprisonment absolutely intolerable.

According to the Fourierists, scarcely any kind of useful labour is naturally and necessarily disagreeable, unless it is either regarded as dishonourable, or is immoderate in degree, or destitute of the stimulus of sympathy and emulation. Excessive toil needs not, they contend, be undergone by any one, in a society in which there would be no idle class, and no labour wasted, as so enormous an amount of labour is now wasted, in useless things ; and where full advantage would be taken of the power of association, both in increasing the efficiency of production, and in economizing consumption. The other requisites for rendering labour attractive would, they think, be found in the execution of all labour by social groups, to any number of which the same individual might simultaneously belong, at his or her own choice : their grade in each being determined by the degree of service which they were found capable of rendering, as appreciated by the suffrages of their comrades. It is inferred from the diversity of tastes and talents, that every member of the community would be attached to several groups, employing themselves in various kinds of occupation, some bodily others mental, and would be capable of occupying a high place in some one or more ; so that a real equality, or something more nearly approaching to it than might at first be supposed, would practically result : not, from the compression, but, on the contrary from the largest possible development, of the various natural superiorities residing in each individual.

Even from so brief an outline, it must be evident that this system does no violence to any of the general laws by which human action, even in the present imperfect state of moral and intellectual cultivation, is influenced ;[1] and that it would be extremely rash to

---

[1] [The remainder of the paragraph as it now stands dates from the 3rd ed. (1852). In the 2nd ed. (1849) the paragraph went on from " influenced " as

pronounce it incapable of success, or unfitted to realize a great part of the hopes founded on it by its partisans. With regard to this, as to all other varieties of Socialism, the thing to be desired, and to which they have a just claim, is opportunity of trial. They are all capable of being tried on a moderate scale, and at no risk, either personal or pecuniary, to any except those who try them. It is for experience to determine how far or how soon any one or more of the possible systems of community of property will be fitted to substitute itself for the " organization of industry " based on private ownership of

follows : " All persons would have a prospect of deriving individual advantage from every degree of labour, of abstinence, and of talent, which they individually exercised. The impediments to success would not be in the principles of the system, but in the unmanageable nature of its machinery. Before large bodies of human beings could be fit to live together in such close union, and still more, before they would be capable of adjusting, by peaceful arrangement among themselves, the relative claims of every class or kind of labour and talent, and of every individual in every class, a vast improvement in human character must be presupposed. When it is considered that each person who would have a voice in this adjustment would be a party interested in it, in every sense of the term—that each would be called on to take part by vote in fixing both the relative remuneration, and the relative estimation, of himself as compared with all other labourers, and of his own class of labour or talent as compared with all others ; the degree of disinterestedness and of freedom from vanity and irritability which would be required in such a community from every individual in it, would be such as is now only found in the élite of humanity : while if those qualities fell much short of the required standard, either the adjustment could not be made at all, or, if made by a majority, would engender jealousies and disappointments destructive of the internal harmony on which the whole working of the system avowedly depends. These, it is true, are difficulties, not impossibilities : and the Fourierists, who alone among Socialists are in a great degree alive to the true conditions of the problem which they undertake to solve, are not without ways and means of contending against these. With every advance in education and improvement, their system tends to become less impracticable, and the very attempt to make it succeed would cultivate, in those making the attempt, many of the virtues which it requires. But we have only yet considered the case of a single Fourierist community. When we remember that the communities themselves are to be the constituent units of an organised whole, (otherwise competition would rage as actively between rival communities as it now does between individual merchants or manufacturers,) and that nothing less would be requisite for the complete success of the scheme than the organisation from a single centre of the whole industry of a nation, and even of the world ; we may, without attempting to limit the ultimate capabilities of human nature, affirm, that the political economist, for a considerable time to come, will be chiefly concerned with the conditions of existence and progress belonging to a society founded on private property and individual competition ; and that, rude as is the manner in which those two principles apportion reward to exertion and to merit, they must form the basis of the principal improvements which can for the present be looked for in the economical condition of humanity."

Then began a new section : " And those improvements will be found to be far more considerable than the adherents of the various Socialist systems are willing to allow. Whatever may be the merit or demerit of their own schemes

land and capital. In the meantime we may, without attempting to limit the ultimate capabilities of human nature, affirm, that the political economist, for a considerable time to come, will be chiefly concerned with the conditions of existence and progress belonging to a society founded on private property and individual competition ; and that the object to be principally aimed at, in the present stage of human improvement, is not the subversion of the system of individual property, but the improvement of it, and the full participation of every member of the community in its benefits.[1]

of society, they have hitherto shown themselves extremely ill acquainted with the economical laws of the existing social system ; and have, in consequence, habitually assumed as necessary effects of competition, evils which are by no means inevitably attendant on it. It is from the influence of this erroneous interpretation of existing facts, that many Socialists of high principles and attainments are led to regard the competitive system as radically incompatible with the economical well-being of the mass.

" The principle of private property has never yet had a fair trial," &c., as now, supra, p. 208, and the remainder of that paragraph.

The chapter ended with the following paragraph, of which the first sentence was retained later (supra, p. 209) : " We are as yet too ignorant either of what individual agency in its best form, or Socialism in its best form, can accomplish, to be qualified to decide which of the two will be the ultimate form of human society. In the present stage of human improvement at least, it is not (I conceive) the subversion of the system of individual property that should be aimed at, but the improvement of it, and the participation of every member of the community in its benefits. Far, however, from looking upon the various classes of Socialists with any approach to disrespect, I honour the intentions of almost all who are publicly known in that character, the acquirements and talents of several, and I regard them, taken collectively, as one of the most valuable elements of human improvement now existing ; both from the impulse they give to the reconsideration and discussion of all the most important questions, and from the ideas they have contributed to many ; ideas from which the most advanced supporters of the existing order of society have still much to learn."]

[1] [See Appendix K, *Mill's earlier and later writings on Socialism*, and Appendix L, *The later history of Socialism*.]

CHAPTER II

§ 1. It is next to be considered, what is included in the idea of private property, and by what considerations the application of the principle should be bounded.

The institution of property, when limited to its essential elements, consists in the recognition, in each person, of a right to the exclusive disposal of what he or she have produced by their own exertions, or received either by gift or by fair agreement, without force or fraud, from those who produced it. The foundation of the whole is the right of producers to what they themselves have produced. It may be objected, therefore, to the institution as it now exists, that it recognises rights of property in individuals over things which they have not produced. For example (it may be said) the operatives in a manufactory create, by their labour and skill, the whole produce ; yet, instead of its belonging to them, the law gives them only their stipulated hire, and transfers the produce to some one who has merely supplied the funds, without perhaps contributing anything to the work itself, even in the form of superintendence. The answer to this is, that the labour of manufacture is only one of the conditions which must combine for the production of the commodity. The labour cannot be carried on without materials and machinery, nor without a stock of necessaries provided in advance to maintain the labourers during the production. All these things are the fruits of previous labour. If the labourers were possessed of them, they would not need to divide the produce with any one ; but while they have them not, an equivalent must be given to those who have, both for the antecedent labour, and for the abstinence by which the produce of that labour, instead of being expended on indulgences, has been reserved for this use. The capital may not have been, and in most cases was not, created by the labour and abstinence of the present possessor ; but it was created by the labour and abstinence of some former person, who may indeed have been wrongfully dispossessed of it,[1] but who, in the present age of the world, much more probably transferred his claims to the present capitalist by gift or voluntary contract : and the abstinence at least must have been continued by each successive owner, down to the present. [2] If it be said, as it may with truth, that those who have inherited the savings of others have an advantage which they may have in no way deserved, over the industrious whose predecessors have not left them anything ; I not only admit, but strenuously contend, that this unearned advantage should be curtailed, as much as is consistent with justice to those who thought fit to dispose of their savings by giving them to their descendants. But while it is true that the labourers are at a disadvantage compared with those whose predecessors have saved, it is also true that the labourers are far better off than if those predecessors had not saved. They share in the advantage, though not to an equal extent with the inheritors. The terms of co-operation between present labour and the fruits of past labour and saving, are a subject for adjustment between the two parties. Each is necessary to the other. The capitalists can do nothing without labourers, nor the labourers without capital.[3] If the labourers compete for employment, the capitalists on their part compete for labour to the full extent of the circulating capital of the country. [4] Competition is often spoken of as if it were necessarily a cause of misery and

---

[1] [This was added in the 3rd ed. (1852). The original ran : " The labour and abstinence of some former person, who, by gift or contract, transferred his claims to the present capitalist."]

[2] [This and the next two sentences were added in the 3rd ed.]

[3] [Here was omitted in the 3rd ed. the following passage of the original : " It may be said, they do not meet on an equal footing : the capitalist, as the richer, can take advantage of the labourer's necessities, and make his conditions as he pleases. He could do so, undoubtedly, if he were but one. The capitalists collectively could do so, if they were not too numerous to combine, and act as a body. But, as things are, they have no such advantage. Where combination is impossible, the terms of the contract depend on competition, that is, on the amount of capital which the collective abstinence of society has provided, compared with the number of the labourers."]

[The next two sentences, down to the word " Ireland," replaced in the 2nd ed. (1849) the following passage of the original :
" A joint administration on account of the state would not make the fund go further, or afford better terms to the labourers, unless either by enforcing, on the society collectively, greater abstinence, or by limiting more strictly the number of the labouring population. It is impossible to increase the quotient that falls to the share of each labourer, without either augmenting the dividend, or diminishing the divisor."

To the substituted passage, the words " and much . . . England " were added in the 3rd ed.]

degradation to the labouring class ; as if high wages were not precisely as much a product of competition as low wages.   The remuneration of labour is as much the result of the law of competition in the United States, as it is in Ireland, and much more completely so than in England.

The right of property includes then, the freedom of acquiring by contract.   The right of each to what he has produced implies a right to what has been produced by others, if obtained by their free consent ; since the producers must either have given it from good will, or exchanged it for what they esteemed an equivalent, and to prevent them from doing so would be to infringe their right of property in the product of their own industry.

§ 2.   Before proceeding to consider the things which the principle of individual property does not include, we must specify one more thing which it does include : and this is that a title, after a certain period, should be given by prescription.   According to the fundamental idea of property, indeed, nothing ought to be treated as such, which has been acquired by force or fraud, or appropriated in ignorance of a prior title vested in some other person ; but it is necessary to the security of rightful possessors, that they should not be molested by charges of wrongful acquisition, when by the lapse of time witnesses must have perished or been lost sight of, and the real character of the transaction can no longer be cleared up. Possession which has not been legally questioned within a moderate number of years, ought to be, as by the laws of all nations it is, a complete title.   Even when the acquisition was wrongful, the dispossession, after a generation has elapsed, of the probably *bonâ fide* possessors, by the revival of a claim which had been long dormant, would generally be a greater injustice, and almost always a greater private and public mischief, than leaving the original wrong without atonement.   It may seem hard that a claim, originally just, should be defeated by mere lapse of time ; but there is a time after which (even looking at the individual case, and without regard to the general effect on the security of possessors), the balance of hardship turns the other way.   With the injustices of men, as with the convulsions and disasters of nature, the longer they remain unrepaired, the greater become the obstacles to repairing them, arising from the aftergrowths which would have to be torn up or broken through. In no human transactions, not even in the simplest and clearest, does it follow that a thing is fit to be done now, because it was fit to be done sixty years ago. It is scarcely needful to remark, that these reasons for not disturbing acts of injustice of old date, cannot apply to unjust systems or institutions ; since a bad law or usage is not one bad act, in the remote past, but a perpetual repetition of bad acts, as long as the law or usage lasts.

Such, then, being the essentials of private property, it is now to be considered, to what extent the forms in which the institution has existed in different states of society, or still exists, are necessary consequences of its principle, or are recommended by the reasons on which it is grounded.

§ 3. Nothing is implied in property but the right of each to his (or her) own faculties, to what he can produce by them, and to whatever he can get for them in a fair market ; together with his right to give this to any other person if he chooses, and the right of that other to receive and enjoy it.

It follows, therefore, that although the right of bequest, or gift after death, forms part of the idea of private property, the right of inheritance, as distinguished from bequest, does not. That the property of persons who have made no disposition of it during their lifetime, should pass first to their children, and failing them, to the nearest relations, may be a proper arrangement or not, but is no consequence of the principle of private property. Although there belong to the decision of such questions many considerations besides those of political economy, it is not foreign to the plan of this work to suggest, for the judgment of thinkers, the view of them which most recommends itself to the writer's mind.

No presumption in favour of existing ideas on this subject is to be derived from their antiquity. In early ages, the property of a deceased person passed to his children and nearest relatives by so natural and obvious an arrangement, that no other was likely to be even thought of in competition with it. In the first place, they were usually present on the spot : they were in possession, and if they had no other title, had that, so important in an early state of society, of first occupancy. Secondly, they were already, in a manner, joint owners of his property during his life. If the property was in land, it had generally been conferred by the State on a family rather than on an individual : if it consisted of cattle or moveable goods, it had probably been acquired, and was certainly protected and defended, by the united efforts of all members of the family who were of an age to work or fight. Exclusive individual property in the modern

sense, scarcely entered into the ideas of the time ; and when the
first magistrate of the association died, he really left nothing vacant
but his own share in the division, which devolved on the member
of the family who succeeded to his authority.   To have disposed
of the property otherwise, would have been to break up a little
commonwealth, united by ideas, interest, and habits, and to cast
them adrift on the world.   These considerations, though rather felt
than reasoned about, had so great an influence on the minds of mankind, as to create the idea of an inherent right in the children to the
possessions of their ancestor ; a right which it was not competent to
himself to defeat.   Bequest, in a primitive state of society, was
seldom recognised ; a clear proof, were there no other, that property
was conceived in a manner totally different from the conception of it
in the present time.*

But the feudal family, the last historical form of patriarchal life,
has long perished, and the unit of society is not now the family or
clan, composed of all the reputed descendants of a common ancestor,
but the individual ; or at most a pair of individuals, with their
unemancipated children.   Property is now inherent in individuals,
not in families : the children when grown up do not follow the occupations or fortunes of the parent : if they participate in the parent's
pecuniary means it is at his or her pleasure, and not by a voice in the
ownership and government of the whole, but generally by the exclusive enjoyment of a part ; and in this country at least (except as far
as entails or settlements are an obstacle) it is in the power of parents
to disinherit even their children, and leave their fortune to strangers.
More distant relatives are in general almost as completely detached
from the family and its interests as if they were in no way connected
with it.   The only claim they are supposed to have on their richer
relations, is to a preference, *cæteris paribus*, in good offices, and some
aid in case of actual necessity.

So great a change in the constitution of society must make a
considerable difference in the grounds on which the disposal of property by inheritance should rest.   The reasons usually assigned
by modern writers for giving the property of a person who dies
intestate to the children, or nearest relatives, are, first, the supposition that, in so disposing of it, the law is more likely than in any other
mode to do what the proprietor would have done, if he had done
anything ; and secondly, the hardship, to those who lived with their

* [1862] See, for admirable illustrations of this and many kindred points,
Mr. Maine's profound work on *Ancient Law and its Relation to Modern Ideas.*

parents and partook in their opulence, of being cast down from the enjoyments of wealth into poverty and privation.

There is some force in both these arguments. The law ought, no doubt, to do for the children or dependents of an intestate, whatever it was the duty of the parent or protector to have done,[1] so far as this can be known by any one besides himself. Since, however, the law cannot decide on individual claims, but must proceed by general rules, it is next to be considered what these rules should be.

We may first remark, that in regard to collateral relatives, it is not, unless on grounds personal to the particular individual, the duty of any one to make a pecuniary provision for them. No one now expects it, unless there happen to be no direct heirs ; nor would it be expected even then, if the expectation were not created by the provisions of the law in case of intestacy. I see, therefore, no reason why collateral inheritance should exist at all. Mr. Bentham long ago proposed, and other high authorities have agreed in the opinion, that if there are no heirs either in the descending or in the ascending line, the property, in case of intestacy, should escheat to the State. With respect to the more remote degrees of collateral relationship, the point is not very likely to be disputed. Few will maintain that there is any good reason why the accumulations of some childless miser should on his death (as every now and then happens) go to enrich a distant relative who never saw him, who perhaps never knew himself to be related to him until there was something to be gained by it, and who had no moral claim upon him of any kind, more than the most entire stranger. But the reason of the case applies alike to all collaterals, even in the nearest degree. Collaterals have no real claims, but such as may be equally strong in the case of non-relatives ; and in the one case as in the other, where valid claims exist, the proper mode of paying regard to them is by bequest.[2]

[1] [The rest of this paragraph replaced in the 3rd ed. (1852) the following original text : " but from accident or negligence or worse causes he failed to do. Whether it would be possible, by means of a public administrator of intestate estates, to take cognizance of special claims and see justice done in detail, is a question of some difficulty into which I forbear to enter. I shall only consider what might with best reason be laid down as a general rule."]

[2] [From the 3rd ed. (1852) was omitted the following passage of the original : " If any near relatives, known to be such, were in a state of indigence, a donation. or a small pension, according to circumstances, might, in case of intestacy, be assigned to them when the State appropriated the inheritance. This would be a justice, or a generosity, which they do not experience from the present law, since that gives all to the nearest collaterals, however great may be the necessities of those more distant."]

The claims of children are of a different nature : they are real, and indefeasible.   But even of these, I venture to think that the measure usually taken is an erroneous one : what is due to children is in some respects underrated, in others, as it appears to me, exaggerated.   One of the most binding of all obligations, that of not bringing children into the world unless they can be maintained in comfort during childhood, and brought up with a likelihood of supporting themselves when of full age, is both disregarded in practice and made light of in theory in a manner disgraceful to human intelligence. On the other hand, when the parent possesses property, the claims of the children upon it seem to me to be the subject of an opposite error.   Whatever fortune a parent may have inherited, or, still more, may have acquired, I cannot admit that he owes to his children, merely because they are his children, to leave them rich, without the necessity of any exertion.   I could not admit it, even if to be so left were always, and certainly, for the good of the children themselves.   But this is in the highest degree uncertain.   It depends on individual character.   Without supposing extreme cases, it may be affirmed that in a majority of instances the good not only of society but of the individuals would be better consulted by bequeathing to them a moderate, than a large provision.   This, which is a commonplace of moralists ancient and modern, is felt to be true by many intelligent parents, and would be acted upon much more frequently, if they did not allow themselves to consider less what really is, than what will be thought by others to be, advantageous to the children.

The duties of parents to their children are those which are indissolubly attached to the fact of causing the existence of a human being.   The parent owes to society to endeavour to make the child a good and valuable member of it, and owes to the children to provide, so far as depends on him, such education, and such appliances and means, as will enable them to start with a fair chance of achieving by their own exertions a successful life.   To this every child has a claim ; and I cannot admit that, as a child, he has a claim to more. There is a case in which these obligations present themselves in their true light, without any extrinsic circumstances to disguise or confuse them : it is that of an illegitimate child.   To such a child it is generally felt that there is due from the parent, the amount of provision for his welfare which will enable him to make his life on the whole a desirable one.   I hold that to no child, merely as such, anything more is due, than what is admitted to be due to an illegitimate child :

and that no child for whom thus much has been done, has, unless on the score of previously raised expectations, any grievance, if the remainder of the parent's fortune is devoted to public uses, or to the benefit of individuals on whom in the parent's opinion it is better bestowed.

In order to give the children that fair chance of a desirable existence, to which they are entitled, it is generally necessary that they should not be brought up from childhood in habits of luxury which they will not have the means of indulging in after-life. This, again, is a duty often flagrantly violated by possessors of terminable incomes, who have little property to leave. When the children of rich parents have lived, as it is natural they should do, in habits corresponding to the scale of expenditure in which the parents indulge, it is generally the duty of the parents to make a greater provision for them, than would suffice for children otherwise brought up. I say generally, because even here there is another side to the question. It is a proposition quite capable of being maintained, that to a strong nature which has to make its way against narrow circumstances, to have known early some of the feelings and experiences of wealth, is an advantage both in the formation of character and in the happiness of life. But allowing that children have a just ground of complaint, who have been brought up to require luxuries which they are not afterwards likely to obtain, and that their claim, therefore, is good to a provision bearing some relation to the mode of their bringing up ; this, too, is a claim which is particularly liable to be stretched further than its reasons warrant. The case is exactly that of the younger children of the nobility and landed gentry, the bulk of whose fortune passes to the eldest son. The other sons, who are usually numerous, are brought up in the same habits of luxury as the future heir, and they receive as a younger brother's portion, generally what the reason of the case dictates, namely, enough to support, in the habits of life to which they are accustomed, themselves, but not a wife or children. It really is no grievance to any man, that for the means of marrying and of supporting a family, he has to depend on his own exertions.

A provision, then, such as is admitted to be reasonable in the case of illegitimate children, for younger children, wherever in short the justice of the case, and the real interests of the individuals and of society, are the only things considered, is, I conceive, all that parents owe to their children, and all, therefore, which the State owes to the children of those who die intestate. The surplus, if any, I hold that it may rightly appropriate to the general purposes of the community. I would not, however, be supposed to recommend that parents should never do more for their children than what, merely as children, they have a moral right to. In some cases it is imperative, in many laudable, and in all allowable, to do much more. For this, however, the means are afforded by the liberty of bequest. It is due, not to the children but to the parents, that they should have the power of showing marks of affection, of requiting services and sacrifices, and of bestowing their wealth according to their own preferences, or their own judgment of fitness.

§ 4. Whether the power of bequest should itself be subject to limitation, is an ulterior question of great importance. Unlike inheritance *ab intestato*, bequest is one of the attributes of property : the ownership of a thing cannot be looked upon as complete without the power of bestowing it, at death or during life, at the owner's pleasure : and all the reasons, which recommend that private property should exist, recommend *pro tanto* this extension of it. But property is only a means to an end, not itself the end. Like all other proprietary rights, and even in a greater degree than most, the power of bequest may be so exercised as to conflict with the permanent interests of the human race. It does so, when, not content with bequeathing an estate to A, the testator prescribes that on A's death it shall pass to his eldest son, and to that son's son, and so on for ever. No doubt, persons have occasionally exerted themselves more strenuously to acquire a fortune from the hope of founding a family in perpetuity ; but the mischiefs to society of such perpetuities outweigh the value of this incentive to exertion, and the incentives in the case of those who have the opportunity of making large fortunes are strong enough without it. A similar abuse of the power of bequest is committed when a person who does the meritorious act of leaving property for public uses, attempts to prescribe the details of its application in perpetuity ; when in founding a place of education (for instance) he dictates, for ever, what doctrines shall be taught. It being impossible that any one should know what doctrines will be fit to be taught after he has been dead for centuries, the law ought not to give effect to such dispositions of property, unless subject to the perpetual revision (after a certain interval has elapsed) of a fitting authority.

There are obvious limitations. But even the simplest exercise of the right of bequest, that of determining the person to whom property shall pass immediately on the death of the testator, has always been reckoned among the privileges which might be limited or varied, according to views of expediency. The limitations, hitherto, have been almost solely in favour of children. In England the right is in principle unlimited, almost the only impediment being that arising from a settlement by a former proprietor, in which case the holder for the time being cannot indeed bequeath his possessions, but only because there is nothing to bequeath, he having merely a life interest. By the Roman law, on which the civil legislation of the Continent of Europe is principally founded, bequest originally was not permitted at all, and even after it was introduced, a *legitima portio* was compulsorily reserved for each child ; and such is still the law in some of the Continental nations. By the French law since the Revolution, the parent can only dispose by will, of a portion equal to the share of one child, each of the children taking an equal portion. This entail, as it may be called, of the bulk of every one's property upon the children collectively, seems to me as little defensible in principle as an entail in favour of one child, though it does not shock so directly the idea of justice. I cannot admit that [1] parents should be compelled to leave to their children even that provision which, as children, I have contended that they have a moral claim to. Children may forfeit that claim by general unworthiness, or particular ill-conduct to the parents : they may have other resources or prospects : what has been previously done for them, in the way of education and advancement in life, may fully satisfy their moral claim ; or others may have claims superior to theirs.[2]

The extreme restriction of the power of bequest in French law was adopted as a democratic expedient, to break down the custom of primogeniture, and counteract the tendency of inherited property to collect in large masses. I agree in thinking these objects eminently desirable ; but the means used are not, I think, the most judicious. Were I framing a code of laws according to what seems to me best in itself, without regard to existing opinions and sentiments, I should prefer to restrict, not what any one might bequeath, but what any one should be permitted to acquire, by bequest or inheritance.

[1] [So since the 3rd ed. (1852). The original ran " It is questionable whether," &c.]

[2] [From the 3rd ed. was here omitted the following passage of the original : " But however the case may be as to a mere provision, I hold that justice and expediency are wholly against compelling anything beyond. That a person should be certain from childhood of succeeding to a large fortune independently of the good will and affection of any human being, is, unless under very favourable influences of other kinds, almost a fatal circumstance in his education."]

Each person should have power to dispose by will of his or her whole property ; but not to lavish it in enriching some one individual, beyond a certain maximum, which should be fixed sufficiently high to afford the means of comfortable independence. The inequalities of property which arise from unequal industry, frugality, persever-ance, talents, and to a certain extent even opportunities, are insepar-able from the principle of private property, and if we accept the principle, we must bear with these consequences of it : but I see nothing objectionable in fixing a limit to what any one may acquire by the mere favour of others, without any exercise of his faculties, and in requiring that if he desires any further accession of fortune, he shall work for it.*   I do not conceive that the degree of limitation which this would impose on the right of bequest, would be felt as a burthensome restraint by any testator who estimated a large fortune at its true value, that of the pleasures and advantages that can be purchased with it : on even the most extravagant estimate of which it must be apparent to every one, that the difference to the happiness of the possessor between a moderate independence and five times as much is insignificant when weighed against the enjoyment that might be given, and the permanent benefits diffused, by some other disposal of the four-fifths.   So long indeed.as the opinion practically prevails, that the best thing which can be done for objects of affection is to heap on them to satiety those intrinsically worthless things on which large fortunes are mostly expended, there might be little use in enacting such a law, even if it were possible to get it passed, since if there were the inclination, there would generally be the power of evading it.   The law would be unavailing unless the popular sentiment went energetically along with it ; which (judging from the tenacious adherence of public opinion in France to the law of compulsory division) it would in some states of society and govern-ment be very likely to do, however much the contrary may be the fact in England and at the present time.   If the restriction could be

* [1865] In the case of capital employed in the hands of the owner himself in carrying on any of the operations of industry, there are strong grounds for leaving to him the power of bequeathing to one person the whole of the funds actually engaged in a single enterprise.   It is well that he should be enabled to leave the enterprise under the control of whichever of his heirs he regards as best fitted to conduct it virtuously and efficiently : and the necessity (very frequent and inconvenient under the French law) would be thus obviated, of breaking up a manufacturing or commercial establishment at the death of its chief.   In like manner, it should be allowed to a proprietor who leaves to one of his successors the moral burthen of keeping up an ancestral mansion and park or pleasure-ground, to bestow along with them as much other property as is required for their sufficient maintenance.

made practically effectual, the benefit would be great. Wealth which could no longer be employed in over [1]-enriching a few, would either be devoted to objects of public usefulness, or if bestowed on individuals, would be distributed among a larger number. While those enormous fortunes which no one needs for any personal purpose but ostentation or improper power, would become much less numerous, there would be a great multiplication of persons in easy circumstances, with the advantages of leisure, and all the real enjoyments which wealth can give, except those of vanity ; a class by whom the services which a nation having leisured classes is entitled to expect from them, either by their direct exertions or by the tone they give to the feelings and tastes of the public, would be rendered in a much more beneficial manner than at present. A large portion also of the accumulations of successful industry would probably be devoted to public uses, either by direct bequests to the State, or by the endowment of institutions ; as is already done very largely in the United States, where the ideas and practice in the matter of inheritance seem to be unusually rational and beneficial.*

§ 5. The next point to be considered is, whether the reasons on which the institution of property rests are applicable to all things in which a right of exclusive ownership is at present recognised ; and if not, on what other grounds the recognition is defensible.

The essential principle of property being to assure to all persons what they have produced by their labour and accumulated by their

---

[1] [" Over " was added in the 3rd ed. (1852).]

* " Munificent bequests and donations for public purposes, whether charitable or educational, form a striking feature in the modern history of the United States, and especially of New England. Not only is it common for rich capitalists to leave by will a portion of their fortune towards the endowment of national institutions, but individuals during their lifetime make magnificent grants of money for the same objects. There is here no compulsory law for the equal partition of property among children, as in France, and on the other hand no custom of entail or primogeniture, as in England, so that the affluent feel themselves at liberty to share their wealth between their kindred and the public ; it being impossible to found a family, and parents having frequently the happiness of seeing all their children well provided for and independent long before their death. I have seen a list of bequests and donations made during the last thirty years for the benefit of religious, charitable, and literary institutions in the state of Massachusetts alone, and they amounted to no less a sum than six millions of dollars, or more than a million sterling.'—Lyell's *Travels in America*, vol. i. p. 263.

[1852] In England, whoever leaves anything beyond trifling legacies for public or beneficent objects when he has any near relatives living, does so at the risk of being declared insane by a jury after his death, or at the least, of having the property wasted in a Chancery suit to set aside the will.

abstinence, this principle cannot apply to what is not the produce of labour, the raw material of the earth. If the land derived its productive power wholly from nature, and not at all from industry, or if there were any means of discriminating what is derived from each source, it not only would not be necessary, but it would be the height of injustice, to let the gift of nature be engrossed by individuals. The use of the land in agriculture must indeed, for the time being, be of necessity exclusive ; the same person who has ploughed and sown must be permitted to reap : but the land might be occupied for one season only, as among the ancient Germans ; or might be periodically redivided as population increased : or the State might be the universal landlord, and the cultivators tenants under it, either on lease or at will.

But though land is not the produce of industry, most of its valuable qualities are so. Labour is not only requisite for using, but almost equally so for fashioning, the instrument. Considerable labour is often required at the commencement, to clear the land for cultivation. In many cases, even when cleared, its productiveness is wholly the effect of labour and art. The Bedford Level produced little or nothing until artificially drained. The bogs of Ireland, until the same thing is done to them, can produce little besides fuel. One of the barrenest soils in the world, composed of the material of the Goodwin Sands, the Pays de Waes in Flanders, has been so fertilized by industry, as to have become one of the most productive in Europe. Cultivation also requires buildings and fences, which are wholly the produce of labour. The fruits of this industry cannot be reaped in a short period. The labour and outlay are immediate, the benefit is spread over many years, perhaps over all future time. A holder will not incur this labour and outlay when strangers and not himself will be benefited by it. If he undertakes such improvements, he must have a sufficient period before him in which to profit by them : and he is in no way so sure of having always a sufficient period as when his tenure is perpetual.*

* " What endowed man with intelligence and perseverance in labour, what made him direct all his efforts towards an end useful to his race, was the sentiment of perpetuity. The lands which the streams have deposited along their course are always the most fertile, but are also those which they menace with their inundations or corrupt by marshes. Under the guarantee of perpetuity men undertook long and painful labours to give the marshes an outlet, to erect embankments against inundations, to distribute by irrigation-channels fertilizing waters over the same fields which the same waters had condemned to sterility. Under the same guarantee, man, no longer contenting himself with the annual products of the earth, distinguished among the wild vegetation the

§ 6. These are the reasons which form the justification, in an economical point of view, of property in land. It is seen, that they are only valid, in so far as the proprietor of land is its improver. Whenever, in any country, the proprietor, generally speaking, ceases to be the improver, political economy has nothing to say in defence of landed property, as there established. In no sound theory of private property was it ever contemplated that the proprietor of land should be merely a sinecurist quartered on it.

In Great Britain, the landed proprietor is not unfrequently an improver. But it cannot be said that he is generally so. And in the majority of cases he grants the liberty of cultivation [1848] on such terms, as to prevent improvements from being made by any one else. In the southern parts of the island, as there are usually no leases, permanent improvements can scarcely be made except by the landlord's capital; accordingly the South, compared with the North of England, and with the Lowlands of Scotland, is still extremely backward in agricultural improvement. The truth is, that any very general improvement of land by the landlords is hardly compatible with a law or custom of primogeniture. When the land goes wholly to the heir, it generally goes to him severed from the pecuniary resources which would enable him to improve it, the personal property being absorbed by the provision for younger children, and the land itself often heavily burthened for the same purpose. There is therefore but a small proportion of landlords who have the means of making expensive improvements, unless they do it with borrowed money, and by adding to the mortgages with which in most cases the land was already burthened when they

perennial plants, shrubs, and trees which would be useful to him, improved them by culture, changed, it may almost be said, their very nature, and multiplied their amount. There are fruits which required centuries of cultivation to bring to their present perfection, and others which have been introduced from the most remote regions. Men have opened the earth to a great depth to renew the soil, and fertilize it by the mixture of its parts and by contact with the air; they have fixed on the hillsides the soil which would have slid off, and have covered the face of the country with a vegetation everywhere abundant, and everywhere useful to the human race. Among their labours there are some of which the fruits can only be reaped at the end of ten or of twenty years; there are others by which their posterity will still benefit after several centuries. All have concurred in augmenting the productive force of nature, in giving to mankind a revenue infinitely more abundant, a revenue of which a considerable part is consumed by those who have no share in the ownership of the land, but who would not have found a maintenance but for that appropriation of the soil by which they seem, at first sight, to have been disinherited."— Sismondi, *Etude sur l'Economie Politique*, Troisième Essai, De la Richesse Territoriale.

received it. But the position of the owner of a deeply mortgaged
estate is so precarious ; economy is so unwelcome to one whose
apparent fortune greatly exceeds his real means, and the vicissitudes
of rent and price, which only trench upon the margin of his income,
are so formidable to one who can call little more than the margin his
own, that it is no wonder if few landlords find themselves in a
condition to make immediate sacrifices for the sake of future profit.
Were they ever so much inclined, those alone can prudently do it,
who have seriously studied the principles of scientific agriculture :
and great landlords have seldom seriously studied anything. They
might at least hold out inducements to the farmers to do what
they will not or cannot do themselves ; but even in granting leases,
it is in England a general complaint [1848] that they tie up their
tenants by covenants grounded on the practices of an obsolete
and exploded agriculture ; while most of them, by withholding
leases altogether, and giving the farmer no guarantee of possession
beyond a single harvest, keep the land on a footing little more
favourable to improvement than in the time of our barbarous
ancestors,

> ——— immetata quibus jugera liberas
> Fruges et Cererem ferunt,
> Nec cultura placet longior annuâ.

Landed property in England is thus very far from completely
fulfilling the conditions which render its existence economically
justifiable. But if insufficiently realized even in England, in Ireland
those conditions are [1848] not complied with at all. With individual
exceptions (some of them very honourable ones), the owners of
Irish estates do nothing for the land but drain it of its produce.
What has been epigrammatically said in the discussions on " peculiar
burthens " is literally true when applied to them, that the greatest
" burthen on land " is the landlords. Returning nothing to the
soil, they consume its whole produce, minus the potatoes strictly
necessary to keep the inhabitants from dying of famine ; and when
they have any purpose of improvement, the preparatory step
usually consists in not leaving even this pittance, but turning out
the people to beggary if not to starvation.* When landed property

---

.* [1862] I must beg the reader to bear in mind that this paragraph was
written fifteen years ago. So wonderful are the changes, both moral and
economical, taking place in our age, that, without perpetually re-writing a
work like the present, it is impossible to keep up with them. [In ed. 1865,
" eighteen years "; in ed. 1871, " more than twenty."]

has placed itself upon this footing it ceases to be defensible, and the time has come for making some new arrangement of the matter.

When the " sacredness of property " is talked of, it should always be remembered, that any such sacredness does not belong in the same degree to landed property. No man made the land. It is the original inheritance of the whole species. Its appropriation is wholly a question of general expediency. When private property in land is not expedient, it is unjust.[1] It is no hardship to any one to be excluded from what others have produced : they were not bound to produce it for his use, and he loses nothing by not sharing in what otherwise would not have existed at all. But it is some hardship to be born into the world and to find all nature's gifts previously engrossed, and no place left for the new-comer. To reconcile people to this, after they have once admitted into their minds the idea that any moral rights belong to them as human beings, it will always be necessary to convince them that the exclusive appropriation is good for mankind on the whole, themselves included. But this is what no sane human being could be persuaded of, if the relation between the landowner and the cultivator were the same everywhere as it has been in Ireland.

Landed property is felt, even by those most tenacious of its rights, to be a different thing from other property ; and where the bulk of the community have been disinherited of their share of it, and it has become the exclusive attribute of a small minority, men have generally tried to reconcile it, at least in theory, to their sense of justice, by endeavouring to attach duties to it, and erecting it into a sort of magistracy, either moral or legal. But if the state is at liberty to treat the possessors of land as public functionaries, it is only going one step further to say that it is at liberty to discard them. The claim of the landowners to the land is altogether subordinate to the general policy of the state. The principle of property gives them no right to the land, but only a right to compensation for whatever portion of their interest in the land it may be the policy of the state to deprive them of. To that, their claim is indefeasible. It is due to landowners, and to owners of any property whatever, recognised as such by the state, that they should not be dispossessed of it without receiving its pecuniary value, or an annual income equal to what they derived from it. This is due on the general

---

[1] [This, and the previous sentence replaced in the 3rd ed. (1852) the original text : " Public reasons exist for its being appropriated. But if those reasons lost their force, the thing would be unjust."]

principles on which property rests. If the land was bought with the
produce of the labour and abstinence of themselves or their ancestors,
compensation is due to them on that ground ; even if otherwise,
it is still due on the ground of prescription. Nor can it ever be
necessary for accomplishing an object by which the community
altogether will gain, that a particular portion of the community
should be immolated. When the property is of a kind to which
peculiar affections attach themselves, the compensation ought to
exceed a bare pecuniary equivalent. But, subject, to this proviso,
the state is at liberty to deal with landed property as the general
interests of the community may require, even to the extent, if it
so happen, of doing with the whole, what is done with a part whenever a bill is passed for a railroad or a new street.[1] The community has too much at stake in the proper cultivation of the land,
and in the conditions annexed to the occupancy of it, to leave
these things to the discretion of a class of persons called landlords,
when they have shown themselves unfit for the trust. The legislature, which if it pleased might convert the whole body of landlords
into fundholders or pensioners, might, *à fortiori*, commute the
average receipts of Irish landowners into a fixed rent charge, and
raise the tenants into proprietors ; supposing always[2] that the full
market value of the land was tendered to the landlords, in case they
preferred that to accepting the conditions proposed.

There will be another place for discussing the various modes of
landed property and tenure, and the advantages and inconveniences
of each ; in this chapter our concern is with the right itself, the
grounds which justify it, and (as a corollary from these) the conditions by which it should be limited. To me it seems almost an
axiom that property in land should be interpreted strictly, and that
the balance in all cases of doubt should incline against the proprietor.
The reverse is the case with property in moveables, and in all things
the product of labour : over these, the owner's power both of use
and of exclusion should be absolute, except where positive evil

---

[1] [In the 3rd ed. the following passage of the original was here omitted :
" I do not pretend that occasions can often arise on which so drastic a measure
would be fit to be taken into serious consideration. But even if this ultimate
prerogative of the state should never require to be actually exercised, it ought
nevertheless to be asserted, because the principle which permits the greater of
two things permits the less, and though to do all which the principle would
sanction should never be advisable, to do much less than all not only may be
so, but often is so in a very high degree."]
[2] [The parenthesis " (without which these acts would be nothing better
than robbery) " was omitted from the 3rd ed. (1852).]

to others would result from it : but in the case of land, no exclusive right should be permitted in any individual, which cannot be shown to be productive of positive good. To be allowed any exclusive right at all, over a portion of the common inheritance, while there are others who have no portion, is already a privilege. No quantity of moveable goods which a person can acquire by his labour, prevents others from acquiring the like by the same means ; but from the very nature of the case, whoever owns land, keeps others out of the enjoyment of it. The privilege, or monopoly, is only defensible as a necessary evil ; it becomes an injustice when carried to any point to which the compensating good does not follow it.

For instance, the exclusive right to the land for purposes of cultivation does not imply an exclusive right to it for purposes of access ; and no such right ought to be recognised, except to the extent necessary to protect the produce against damage, and the owner's privacy against invasion. The pretension of two Dukes [1848] to shut up a part of the Highlands, and exclude the rest of mankind from many square miles of mountain scenery to prevent disturbance to wild animals, is an abuse ; it exceeds the legitimate bounds of the right of landed property. When land is not intended to be cultivated, no good reason can in general be given for its being private property at all ; and if any one is permitted to call it his, he ought to know that he holds it by sufferance of the community, and on an implied condition that his ownership, since it cannot possibly do them any good, at least shall not deprive them of any, which they could have derived from the land if it had been unappropriated. Even in the case of cultivated land, a man whom, though only one among millions, the law permits to hold thousands of acres as his single share, is not entitled to think that all this is given to him to use and abuse, and deal with as if it concerned nobody but himself. The rents or profits which he can obtain from it are at his sole disposal ; but with regard to the land, in everything which he does with it, and in everything which he abstains from doing, he is morally bound, and should whenever the case admits be legally compelled, to make his interest and pleasure consistent with the public good. The species at large still retains, of its original claim to the soil of the planet which it inhabits, as much as is compatible with the purposes for which it has parted with the remainder.

§ 7. Besides property in the produce of labour, and property in land, there are other things which are or have been subjects of property, in which no proprietary rights ought to exist at all. But as the civilized world has in general made up its mind on most of these, there is no necessity for dwelling on them in this place. At the head of them, is property in human beings. It is almost superfluous to observe, that this institution can have no place in any society even pretending to be founded on justice, or on fellow-ship between human creatures. But, iniquitous as it is, yet when the state has expressly legalized it, and human beings for generations have been bought, sold, and inherited under sanction of law, it is another wrong, in abolishing the property, not to make full compen-sation. This wrong was avoided by the great measure of justice in 1833, one of the most virtuous acts, as well as the most practically beneficent, ever done collectively by a nation. Other examples of property which ought not to have been created are properties in public trusts ; such as judicial offices under the old French régime, and the heritable jurisdictions which, in countries not wholly emerged from feudality, pass with the land. Our own country affords, as cases in point, that of a commission in the army [1848], and of an advowson, or right of nomination to an ecclesiastical benefice. A property is also sometimes created in a right of taxing the public ; in a monopoly, for instance, or other exclusive privilege. These abuses prevail most in semibarbarous countries, but are not without example in the most civilized. In France there are [1848] several important trades and professions, including notaries, attorneys, brokers, appraisers, printers, and (until lately) [1] bakers and butchers, of which the numbers are limited by law. The *brevet* or privilege of one of the permitted number consequently brings a high price in the market. When such is the case, compensation probably could not with justice be refused, on the abolition of the privilege. There are other cases in which this would be more doubt-ful. The question would turn upon what, in the peculiar circum-stances, was sufficient to constitute prescription ; and whether the legal recognition which the abuse had obtained, was sufficient to constitute it an institution, or amounted only to an occasional licence. It would be absurd to claim compensation for losses caused by changes in a tariff, a thing confessedly variable from year to year ; or for monopolies like those granted to individuals by the Tudors, favours of a despotic authority, which the power that gave was competent at any time to recall.

---

[1] [Parenthesis added in 5th ed. (1862).]

So much on the institution of property, a subject of which, for the purposes of political economy, it was indispensable to treat, but on which we could not usefully confine ourselves to economical considerations. We have now to inquire on what principles and with what results the distribution of the produce of land and labour is effected, under the relations which this institution creates among the different members of the community.

CHAPTER III

§ 1. PRIVATE property being assumed as a fact, we have next to enumerate the different classes of persons to whom it gives rise ; whose concurrence, or at least whose permission, is necessary to production, and who are therefore able to stipulate for a share of the produce. We have to inquire, according to what laws the produce distributes itself among these classes, by the spontaneous action of the interests of those concerned : after which, a further question will be, what effects are or might be produced by laws, institutions, and measures of government, in superseding or modifying that spontaneous distribution.

The three requisites of production, as has been so often repeated, are labour, capital, and land : understanding by capital, the means and appliances which are the accumulated results of previous labour, and by land, the materials and instruments supplied by nature, whether contained in the interior of the earth, or constituting its surface. Since each of these elements of production may be separately appropriated, the industrial community may be considered as divided into landowners, capitalists, and productive labourers. Each of these classes, as such, obtains a share of the produce : no other person or class obtains anything except by concession from them. The remainder of the community is, in fact, supported at their expense, giving, if any equivalent, one consisting of unproductive services. These three classes, therefore, are considered in political economy as making up the whole community.

§ 2. But although these three sometimes exist as separate classes, dividing the produce among them, they do not necessarily or always so exist. The fact is so much otherwise, that there are only one or two communities in which the complete separation of these classes is the general rule. England and Scotland, with parts of Belgium and Holland, are almost the only countries in the world, where the land, capital, and labour employed in agriculture are generally the property of separate owners. The ordinary case is, that the same person owns either two of these requisites, or all three. The case in which the same person owns all three, embraces the two extremes of existing society, in respect to the independence and dignity of the labouring class. First, when the labourer himself is the proprietor. This is the commonest case in the Northern States of the American Union ; one of the commonest in France, Switzerland, the three Scandinavian kingdoms, and parts of Germany ; * and a common case in parts of Italy and in Belgium. In all these countries there are, no doubt, large landed properties, and a still greater number which, without being large, require the occasional or constant aid of hired labourers. Much, however, of the land is owned in portions too small to require any other labour than that of the peasant and his family or fully to occupy even that. The capital employed is not always that of the peasant proprietor, many of these small properties being mortgaged to obtain the means of cultivating ; but the capital is invested at the peasant's risk, and though he pays interest for it, it gives to no one any right of interference, except, perhaps, eventually to take possession of the land, if the interest ceases to be paid.

The other case in which the land, labour, and capital, belong to the same person, is the case of slave countries, in which the

---

* "The Norwegian return " (say the Commissioners of Poor Law Enquiry, to whom information was furnished from nearly every country in Europe and America by the ambassadors and consuls there) " states that at the last census in 1825, out of a population of 1,051,318 persons, there were 59,464 freeholders. As by 59,464 freeholders must be meant 59,464 heads of families, or about 300,000 individuals, the freeholders must form more than a fourth of the whole population. Mr. Macgregor states that in Denmark (by which Zealand and the adjoining islands are probably meant) out of a population of 926,110, the number of landed proprietors and farmers is 415,110, or nearly one-half. In Sleswick-Holstein, out of a population of 604,085, it is 196,017, or about one-third. The proportion of proprietors and farmers to the whole population is not given in Sweden ; but the Stockholm return estimates the average quantity of land annexed to a labourer's habitation at from one to five acres ; and though the Gottenburg return gives a lower estimate, it adds that the peasants possess much of the land. In Wurtemburg we are told that more than two-thirds of the labouring population are the proprietors of their own habitations, and that almost all own at least a garden of from three-quarters of an acre to an acre and a half." In some of these statements, proprietors and farmers are not discriminated ; but " all the returns concur in stating the number of day-labourers to be very small."—(*Preface to Foreign Communications*, p. xxxviii.) As the general *status* of the labouring people, the condition of a workman for hire is [1848] almost peculiar to Great Britain.

labourers themselves are owned by the landowner. Our West India colonies before emancipation, and the sugar colonies of the nations by whom a similar act of justice is still unperformed [1848], are examples of large establishments for agricultural and manufacturing labour (the production of sugar and rum is a combination of both) in which the land, the factories (if they may be so called), the machinery, and the degraded labourers, are all the property of a capitalist. In this case, as well as in its extreme opposite, the case of the peasant proprietor, there is no division of the produce.

§ 3.   When the three requisites are not all owned by the same person, it often happens that two of them are so. Sometimes the same person owns the capital and the land, but not the labour. The landlord makes his engagement directly with the labourer, and supplies the whole or part of the stock necessary for cultivation. This system is the usual one in those parts of Continential Europe, in which the labourers are neither serfs on the one hand, nor proprietors on the other. It was very common in France before the Revolution, and is still much practised in some parts of that country, when the land is not the property of the cultivator. It prevails generally in the level districts of Italy, except those principally pastoral, such as the Maremma of Tuscany and the Campagna of Rome. On this system the division of the produce is between two classes, the landowner and the labourer.

In other cases again, the labourer does not own the land, but owns the little stock employed on it, the landlord not being in the habit of supplying any. This system generally prevails [1848] in Ireland. It is nearly universal in India, and in most countries of the East ; whether the government retains, as it generally does, the ownership of the soil, or allows portions to become, either absolutely or in a qualified sense, the property of individuals. In India, however, things are so far better than in Ireland, that the owner of land is in the habit of making advances to the cultivators, if they cannot cultivate without them. For these advances the native landed proprietor usually demands high interest ; but the principal landowner, the government, makes them gratuitously, recovering the advance after the harvest, together with the rent. The produce is here divided as before, between the same two classes, the landowner and the labourer.

These are the principal variations in the classification of those among whom the produce of agricultural labour is distributed. In the case of manufacturing industry there never are more than two classes, the labourers and the capitalists. The original artisans in all countries were either slaves, or the women of the family. In the manufacturing establishments of the ancients, whether on a large or on a small scale, the labourers were usually the property of the capitalist. In general, if any manual labour was thought compatible with the dignity of a freeman, it was only agricultural labour. The converse system, in which the capital was owned by the labourer, was coeval with free labour, and under it the first great advances of manufacturing industry were achieved. The artisan owned the loom or the few tools he used, and worked on his own account ; or at least ended by doing so, though he usually worked for another, first as apprentice and next as journeyman, for a certain number of years, before he could be admitted a master. But the *status* of a permanent journeyman, all his life a hired labourer and nothing more, had no place in the crafts and guilds of the Middle Ages. In country villages, where a carpenter or a black-smith cannot live and support hired labourers on the returns of his business, he is even now his own workman ; and shopkeepers in similar circumstances are their own shopmen or shopwomen. But wherever the extent of the market admits of it, the distinction is now fully established between the class of capitalists, or employers of labour, and the class of labourers ; the capitalists, in general, contributing no other labour than that of direction and superin-tendence.

CHAPTER IV

§ 1. UNDER the rule of individual property, the division of the produce is the result of two determining agencies : Competition and Custom. It is important to ascertain the amount of influence which belongs to each of these causes, and in what manner the operation of one is modified by the other.

Political economists generally, and English political economists above others, have been accustomed to lay almost exclusive stress upon the first of these agencies ; to exaggerate the effect of competition, and to take into little account the other and conflicting principle. They are apt to express themselves as if they thought that competition actually does, in all cases, whatever it can be shown to be the tendency of competition to do. This is partly intelligible, if we consider that only through the principle of competition has political economy any pretension to the character of a science. So far as rents, profits, wages, prices, are determined by competition, laws may be assigned for them. Assume competition to be their exclusive regulator, and principles of broad generality and scientific precision may be laid down, according to which they will be regulated. The political economist justly deems this his proper business : and as an abstract or hypothetical science, political economy cannot be required to do, and indeed cannot do, anything more. But it would be a great misconception of the actual course of human affairs, to suppose that competition exercises in fact this unlimited sway. I am not speaking of monopolies, either natural or artificial, or of any interferences of authority with the liberty of production or exchange. Such disturbing causes have always been allowed for by political economists. I speak of cases in which there is nothing to restrain competition ; no hindrance to it either in the nature of the case or in artificial obstacles ; yet in which the result is not determined by competition, but by custom or usage ; competition either not taking place at all, or producing its effect in quite a different manner from that which is ordinarily assumed to be natural to it.

§ 2. Competition, in fact, has only become in any considerable degree the governing principle of contracts, at a comparatively modern period. The farther we look back into history, the more we see all transactions and engagements under the influence of fixed customs. The reason is evident. Custom is the most powerful protector of the weak against the strong ; their sole protector where there are no laws or government adequate to the purpose. Custom is a barrier which, even in the most oppressed condition of mankind, tyranny is forced in some degree to respect. To the industrious population, in a turbulent military community, freedom of competition is a vain phrase ; they are never in a condition to make terms for themselves by it : there is always a master who throws his sword into the scale, and the terms are such as he imposes. But though the law of the strongest decides, it is not the interest nor in general the practice of the strongest to strain that law to the utmost, and every relaxation of it has a tendency to become a custom, and every custom to become a right. Rights thus originating, and not competition in any shape, determine, in a rude state of society, the share of the produce enjoyed by those who produce it. The relations, more especially, between the landowner and the cultivator, and the payments made by the latter to the former, are, in all states of society but the most modern, determined by the usage of the country. Never until late times have the conditions of the occupancy of land been (as a general rule) an affair of competition. The occupier for the time has very commonly been considered to have a right to retain his holding, while he fulfils the customary requirements ; and has thus become, in a certain sense, a co-proprietor of the soil. Even where the holder has not acquired this fixity of tenure, the terms of occupation have often been fixed and invariable.

In India, for example, and other Asiatic communities similarly constituted, the ryots, or peasant-farmers, are not regarded as tenants at will, nor even as tenants by virtue of a lease. In most villages there are indeed some ryots on this precarious footing, consisting of those, or the descendants of those, who have settled in the place at a known and comparatively recent period : but all who are looked upon as descendants or representatives of the original inhabitants, and even many mere tenants of ancient date, are thought entitled to retain their land, as long as they pay the customary rents. What these customary rents are, or ought to be, has indeed, in most cases, become a matter of obscurity ; usurpation, tyranny, and foreign conquest having to a great degree obliterated the evidences of them. But when an old and purely Hindoo principality falls under the dominion of the British Government, or the management of its officers, and when the details of the revenue system come to be inquired into, it is usually found that though the demands of the great landholder, the State, have been swelled by fiscal rapacity until all limit is practically lost sight of, it has yet been thought necessary to have a distinct name and a separate pretext for each increase of exaction ; so that the demand has sometimes come to consist of thirty or forty different items, in addition to the nominal rent. This circuitous mode of increasing the payments assuredly would not have been resorted to, if there had been an acknowledged right in the landlord to increase the rent. Its adoption is a proof that there was once an effective limitation, a real customary rent ; and that the understood right of the ryot to the land, so long as he paid rent according to custom, was at some time or other more than nominal.* The British Government of India always simplifies the tenure by consolidating the various assessments into one, thus making the rent nominally as well as really an arbitrary thing, or at least a matter of specific agreement : but it scrupulously respects the right of the ryot to the land, though until the reforms of the present generation (reforms even now only partially carried into effect) it seldom left him much more than a bare subsistence.[1]

In modern Europe the cultivators have gradually emerged from a state of personal slavery. The barbarian conquerors of the Western Empire found that the easiest mode of managing their conquests would be to leave the occupation of the land in the hands in which they found it, and to save themselves a labour so uncongenial as the superintendence of troops of slaves, by allowing the slaves to retain in a certain degree the control of their own actions, under an obligation to furnish the lord with provisions and labour.

---

* The ancient law books of the Hindoos mention in some cases one-sixth, in others one-fourth of the produce, as a proper rent ; but there is no evidence that the rules laid down in those books were, at any period of history, really acted upon.

[1] [So since the 6th ed. (1865). The original (1848) ran : " though it seldom leaves him much more than a bare subsistence."]

A common expedient was to assign to the serf, for his exclusive use, as much land as was thought sufficient for his support, and to make him work on the other lands of his lord whenever required. By degrees these indefinite obligations were transformed into a definite one, of supplying a fixed quantity of provisions or a fixed quantity of labour : and as the lords, in time, became inclined to employ their income in the purchase of luxuries rather than in the maintenance of retainers, the payments in kind were commuted for payments in money. Each concession, at first voluntary and revocable at pleasure, gradually acquired the force of custom, and was at last recognised and enforced by the tribunals. In this manner the serfs progressively rose into a free tenantry, who held their land in perpetuity on fixed conditions. The conditions were sometimes very onerous, and the people very miserable. But their obligations were determined by the usage or law of the country, and not by competition.

Where the cultivators had never been, strictly speaking, in personal bondage, or after they had ceased to be so, the exigencies of a poor and little advanced society gave rise to another arrangement, which in some parts of Europe, even highly improved parts, has been found sufficiently advantageous to be continued to the present day. I speak of the métayer system. Under this, the land is divided, in small farms, among single families, the landlord generally supplying the stock which the agricultural system of the country is considered to require, and receiving, in lieu of rent and profit, a fixed proportion of the produce. This proportion, which is generally paid in kind, is usually, (as is implied in the words *métayer*, *mezzaiuolo*, and *medietarius*,) one-half. There are places, however, such as the rich volcanic soil of the province of Naples, where the landlord takes two-thirds, and yet the cultivator by means of an excellent agriculture contrives to live. But whether the proportion is two-thirds or one-half, it is a fixed proportion, not variable from farm to farm, or from tenant to tenant. The custom of the country is the universal rule; nobody thinks of raising or lowering rents, or of letting land on other than the customary conditions. Competition, as a regulator of rent, has no existence.

§ 3. Prices, whenever there was no monopoly, came earlier under the influence of competition, and are much more universally subject to it, than rents : but that influence is by no means, even in the present activity of mercantile competition, so absolute as is sometimes assumed. There is no proposition which meets us in the field of political economy oftener than this—that there cannot be two prices in the same market. Such undoubtedly is the natural effect of unimpeded competition ; yet every one knows that there are, almost always,[1] two prices in the same market. Not only are there in every large town, and in almost every trade, cheap shops and dear shops, but the same shop often sells the same article at different prices to different customers : and, as a general rule, each retailer adapts his scale of prices to the class of customers whom he expects. The wholesale trade, in the great articles of commerce, is really under the dominion of competition. There, the buyers as well as sellers are traders or manufacturers, and their purchases are not influenced by indolence or vulgar finery, nor depend on the smaller motives of personal convenience, but are business transactions. In the wholesale markets therefore it is true, as a general proposition, that there are not two prices at one time for the same thing : there is at each time and place a market price, which can be quoted in a price-current. But retail price, the price paid by the actual consumer, seems to feel very slowly and imperfectly the effect of competition ; and when competition does exist, it often, instead of lowering prices, merely divides the gains of the high price among a greater number of dealers. Hence it is that, of the price paid by the consumer, so large a proportion is absorbed by the gains of retailers ; and any one who inquires into the amount which reaches the hands of those who made the things he buys, will often be astonished at its smallness. When indeed the market, being that of a great city, holds out a sufficient inducement to large capitalists to engage in retail operations, it is generally found a better speculation to attract a large business by underselling others, than merely to divide the field of employment with them. This influence of competition is making itself felt more and more through the principal branches of retail trade in the large towns ; and the rapidity and cheapness of transport, by making consumers less dependent on the dealers in their immediate neighbourhood, are tending to assimilate more and more the whole country to a large town : but hitherto [1848] it is only in the great centres of business that retail transactions have been chiefly, or even much, determined, by competition. Elsewhere it rather acts, when it acts at all, as an occasional disturbing influence ; the habitual regulator is custom, modified from time to time by notions existing

[1] [Substituted in the 3rd ed. (1852) for the original " very often."]

in the minds of purchasers and sellers of some kind of equity or justice.

In many trades the terms on which business is done are a matter of positive arrangement among the trade, who use the means they always possess of making the situation of any member of the body, who departs from its fixed customs, inconvenient or disagreeable. It is well known that the bookselling trade was, until lately, one of these, and that notwithstanding the active spirit of rivalry in the trade, competition did not produce its natural effect in breaking down the trade rules.[1] All professional remuneration is regulated by custom. The fees of physicians, surgeons, and barristers, the charges of attorneys. are nearly invariable. Not certainly for want of abundant competition in those professions, but because the competition operates by diminishing each competitor's chance of fees, not by lowering the fees themselves.

Since custom stands its ground against competition to so considerable an extent, even where, from the multitude of competitors and the general energy in the pursuit of gain, the spirit of competition is strongest, we may be sure that this is much more the case where people are content with smaller gains, and estimate their pecuniary interest at a lower rate when balanced against their ease or their pleasure. I believe it will often be found, in Continental Europe, that prices and charges, of some or of all sorts, are much higher in some places than in others not far distant, without its being possible to assign any other cause than that it has always been so : the customers are used to it, and acquiesce in it. An enterprising competitor, with sufficient capital, might force down the charges, and make his fortune during the process ; but there are no enterprising competitors ; those who have capital prefer to leave it where it is, or to make less profit by it in a more quiet way

These observations must be received as a general correction to be applied whenever relevant, whether expressly mentioned or not, to the conclusions contained in the subsequent portions of this treatise. Our reasonings must, in general, proceed as if the known and natural effects of competition were actually produced by it, in all cases in which it is not restrained by some positive obstacle. Where competition, though free to exist, does not exist, or where it exists, but has its natural consequences overruled by any other agency, the conclusions will fail more or less of being applicable.

[1] [Until the 4th ed. (1857) the text ran : " the bookselling trade is one of these . . . competition does not produce " &c.]

To escape error, we ought, in applying the conclusions of political economy to the actual affairs of life, to consider not only what will happen supposing the maximum of competition, but how far the result will be affected if competition falls short of the maximum.

The states of economical relation which stand first in order to be discussed and appreciated, are those in which competition has no part, the arbiter of transactions being either brute force or established usage.   These will be the subject of the next four chapters.

CHAPTER V

OF SLAVERY

§ 1. AMONG the forms which society assumes under the influence of the institution of property, there are, as I have already
remarked, two, otherwise of a widely dissimilar character, but
resembling in this, that the ownership of the land, the labour, and
the capital, is in the same hands. One of these cases is that of
slavery, the other is that of peasant proprietors. In the one the
landowner owns the labour, in the other the labourer owns the land.
We begin with the first.

In this system all the produce belongs to the landlord. The
food and other necessaries of his labourers are part of his expenses.
The labourers possess nothing but what he thinks fit to give them,
and until he thinks fit to take it back : and they work as hard as he
chooses, or is able, to compel them. Their wretchedness is only
limited by his humanity, or his pecuniary interest. With the first
consideration we have on the present occasion nothing to do. What
the second in so detestable a constitution of society may dictate,
depends on the facilities for importing fresh slaves. If full-grown,
able-bodied slaves can be procured in sufficient numbers, and
imported at a moderate expense, self-interest will recommend working
the slaves to death, and replacing them by importation, in preference
to the slow and expensive process of breeding them. Nor are the
slave-owners generally backward in learning this lesson. It is
notorious that such was the practice in our slave colonies, while the
slave trade was legal ; and it is said to be so still in Cuba.[1]

When, as among the ancients, the slave-market could only be
supplied by captives either taken in war, or kidnapped from thinly
scattered tribes on the remote confines of the known world, it was

[1] [The original text ran on: " and in those States of the American Union
which receive a regular supply of negroes from other States." These latter words
were omitted from the 4th ed. (1857).]

generally more profitable to keep up the number by breeding, which necessitates a far better treatment of them; and for this reason, joined with several others, the condition of slaves, notwithstanding occasional enormities, was probably much less bad in the ancient world, than in the colonies of modern nations. The Helots are usually cited as the type of the most hideous form of personal slavery, but with how little truth appears from the fact that they were regularly armed (though not with the panoply of the hoplite) and formed an integral part of the military strength of the State. They were doubtless an inferior and degraded caste, but their slavery seems to have been one of the least onerous varieties of serfdom. Slavery appears in far more frightful colours among the Romans, during the period in which the Roman aristocracy was gorging itself with the plunder of a newly-conquered world. The Romans were a cruel people, and the worthless nobles sported with the lives of their myriads of slaves with the same reckless prodigality with which they squandered any other part of their ill-acquired possessions. Yet, slavery is divested of one of its worst features when it is compatible with hope : enfranchisement was easy and common : enfranchised slaves obtained at once the full rights of citizens, and instances were frequent of their acquiring not only riches, but latterly even honours. By the progress of milder legislation under the Emperors, much of the protection of law was thrown round the slave ; he became capable of possessing property ; and the evil altogether assumed a considerably gentler aspect. Until, however, slavery assumes the mitigated form of villenage, in which not only the slaves have property and legal rights, but their obligations are more or less limited by usage, and they partly labour for their own benefit ; their condition is seldom such as to produce a rapid growth either of population or of production.[1]

§ 2.   So long as slave countries are underpeopled in proportion to their cultivable land, the labour of the slaves, under any tolerable

[1] [" Or of production " was added in the 3rd ed. (1852), and the following passage of the original omitted : " This " (i.e. slow growth of population) " cannot be from physical privation, for no slave-labourers are worse fed, clothed, or lodged, than the free peasantry of Ireland.   The cause usually assigned is the great disproportion of the sexes which almost always exists where slaves are not bred but imported ; this cannot however be the sole cause, as the negro population of our West India colonies continued nearly stationary, after the slave-trade to those colonies was suppressed.   Whatever be the causes, a slave population is seldom a rapidly increasing one."   The text of the next sentence was slightly readjusted.]

management, produces much more than is sufficient for their
support; especially as the great amount of superintendence which
their labour requires, preventing the dispersion of the population,
insures some of the advantages of combined labour. Hence, in
a good soil and climate, and with reasonable care of his own interests,
the owner of many slaves has the means of being rich. The influence,
however, of such a state of society on production is perfectly well
understood. It is a truism to assert, that labour extorted by fear
of punishment is inefficient and unproductive. It is true that in
some circumstances human beings can be driven by the lash to
attempt, and even to accomplish, things which they would not
have undertaken for any payment which it could have been worth
while to an employer to offer them. And it is likely that productive
operations which require much combination of labour, the production of sugar for example, would not have taken place so soon
in the American colonies if slavery had not existed to keep masses
of labour together. There are also savage tribes so averse from
regular industry, that industrial life is scarcely able to introduce
itself among them until they are either conquered and made slaves
of, or become conquerors and make others so. But after allowing
the full value of these considerations, it remains certain that slavery
is incompatible with any high state of the arts of life, and any great
efficiency of labour. For all products which require much skill, slave
countries are usually [1] dependent on foreigners. Hopeless slavery
effectually brutifies the intellect; and intelligence in the slaves,
though often encouraged in the ancient world and in the East, is
in a more advanced state of society a source of so much danger
and an object of so much dread to the masters, that in some of the
States of America it was a highly penal offence to teach a slave
to read.[2] All processes carried on by slave labour are conducted
in the rudest and most unimproved manner. And even the animal
strength of the slave is, on an average, not half exerted. The
unproductiveness and wastefulness of the industrial system in the
Slave States is instructively displayed in the valuable writings
of Mr. Olmsted.[3] The mildest form of slavery is certainly the
condition of the serf, who is attached to the soil, supports himself
from his allotment, and works a certain number of days in the
week for his lord. Yet there is but one opinion on the extreme

[1] [" Usually " replaced " always " in the 3rd ed. (1852).]
[2] [Until the 6th ed. (1865) the reference was vague: " in some countries
it is." In the 7th ed. (1871) " is " became " was."]
[3] [This sentence was inserted in the 6th ed.]

inefficiency of serf labour.   The following passage is from Professor Jones,* whose *Essay on the Distribution of Wealth* (or rather on Rent), is a copious repertory of valuable facts on the landed tenures of different countries.

" The Russians, or rather those German writers who have observed the manners and habits of Russia, state some strong facts on this point.   Two Middlesex mowers, they say, will mow in a day as much grass as six Russian serfs, and in spite of the dearness of provisions in England and their cheapness in Russia,. the mowing a quantity of hay which would cost an English farmer half a copeck, will cost a Russian proprietor three or four copecks.†   The Prussian counsellor of state, Jacob, is considered to have proved, that in Russia, where everything is cheap, the labour of a serf is doubly as expensive as that of a labourer in England.   M. Schmalz gives a startling account of the unproductiveness of serf labour in Prussia, from his own knowledge and observation.‡   In Austria, it is distinctly stated that the labour of a serf is equal to only one-third of that of a free hired labourer.   This calculation, made in an able work on agriculture (with some extracts from which I have been favoured), is applied to the practical purpose of deciding on the number of labourers necessary to cultivate an estate of a given magnitude. So palpable, indeed, are the ill effects of labour rents on the industry of the agricultural population, that in Austria itself, where proposals of changes of any kind do not readily make their way, schemes and plans for the commutation of labour rents are as popular as in the more stirring German provinces of the North." §

What is wanting in the quality of the labour itself, is not made up by any excellence in the direction and superintendence.   As the same writer ‖ remarks, the landed proprietors " are necessarily, in their character of cultivators of their own domains, the only guides and directors of the industry of the agricultural population," since there can be no intermediate class of capitalist farmers where

* *Essay on the Distribution of Wealth and on the Sources of Taxation.*   By the Rev. Richard Jones.   Page 50.   [P. 43 of the reprint published in 1895 under the title *Peasant Rents.*]

† " Schmalz, *Economie Politique,* French translation, vol. i. p. 66."

‡ " Vol. ii. p. 107."

§ The Hungarian revolutionary government, during its brief existence, bestowed on that country one of the greatest benefits it could receive, and one which the tyranny that succeeded did not dare to take away : it freed the peasantry from what remained of the bondage of serfdom, the labour rents ; decreeing compensation to the landlords at the expense of the state, and not at that of the liberated peasants.

‖ Jones, pp. 53, 54.   [*Peasant Rents,* pp. 46, 47.]

the labourers are the property of the lord. Great landowners are everywhere an idle class, or if they labour at all, addict themselves only to the more exciting kinds of exertion ; that lion's share which superiors always reserve for themselves. " It would," as Mr. Jones observes, " be hopeless and irrational to expect, that a race of noble proprietors, fenced round with privileges and dignity, and attracted to military and political pursuits by the advantages and habits of their station, should ever become attentive cultivators as a body." Even in England, if the cultivation of every estate depended upon its proprietor, any one can judge what would be the result. There would be a few cases of great science and energy, and numerous individual instances of moderate success, but the general state of agriculture would be contemptible.

§ 3. Whether the proprietors themselves would lose by the emancipation of their slaves, is a different question from the comparative effectiveness of free and slave labour to the community. There has been much discussion of this question as an abstract thesis ; as if it could possibly admit of any universal solution. Whether slavery or free labour is most profitable to the employer, depends on the wages of the free labourer. These, again, depend on the numbers of the labouring population, compared with the capital and the land. Hired labour is generally so much more efficient than slave labour, that the employer can pay a considerably greater value in wages, than the maintenance of his slaves cost him before, and yet be a gainer by the change : but he cannot do this without limit. The decline of serfdom in Europe, and its destruction in the Western nations, were doubtless hastened by the changes which the growth of population must have made in the pecuniary interests of the master. As population pressed harder upon the land, without any improvement in agriculture, the maintenance of the serfs necessarily became more costly, and their labour less valuable. With the rate of wages such as it is in Ireland, or in England (where, in proportion to its efficiency, labour is quite as cheap as in Ireland), no one can for a moment imagine that slavery could be profitable. If the Irish peasantry were slaves, their masters would be as willing, as their landlords now [1848] are, to pay large sums merely to get rid of them. In the rich and underpeopled soil of the West India islands, there is just as little doubt that the balance of profits between free and slave labour was greatly on the side of slavery, and that the compensation granted to the slave-owners for its abolition was not more, perhaps even less,[1] than an equivalent for their loss.

More needs not be said here on a cause so completely judged and decided as that of slavery. [2] Its demerits are no longer a question requiring argument ; though the temper of mind manifested by the larger part of the influential classes in Great Britain respecting the struggle in America, shows how grievously the feelings of the present generation [1865] of Englishmen, on this subject, had fallen behind the positive acts of the generation which preceded them. That the sons of the deliverers of the West Indian Negroes should expect with complacency, and encourage by their sympathies, the establishment of a great and powerful military commonwealth, pledged by its principles and driven by its strongest interests to be the armed propagator of slavery through every region of the earth into which its power could penetrate, discloses a mental state in the leading portion of our higher and middle classes which it is melancholy to see, and will be a lasting blot in English history. Fortunately they stopped short of actually aiding, otherwise than by words, the nefarious enterprise to which they were not ashamed of wishing success ; and at the expense of the best blood of the Free States, but to their immeasurable elevation in mental and moral worth,

[1] [" In all probability less," until the 5th ed. (1862).]

[2] [The rest of the paragraph as here found was written for the 6th ed. (1865). The original (1848) ran thus : " It will be curious to see how long the other nations possessing slave colonies will be content to remain behind England in a matter of such concernment both to justice, which decidedly is not at present a fashionable virtue, and to philanthropy, which certainly is so. Europe is far more inexcusable than America in tolerating an enormity, of which she could rid herself with so much greater ease. I speak of negro-slavery, not of the servage of the Slavonic nations, who have not yet advanced beyond a state of civilization corresponding to the age of villenage in Western Europe, and can only be expected to emerge from it in the same gradual manner, however much accelerated by the salutary influence of the ideas of more advanced countries."

To this, in the 2nd ed. (1849) was added the note : " Denmark has the honour of being the first Continental nation which followed the example of England ; and the emancipation of the slaves was one of the earliest acts of the French Provisional Government. Still more recently, the progress of the American mind towards a determination to rid itself of this odious stain has been manifested by very gratifying symptoms."

In the 3rd ed. (1852) the latter part of the reference to the Slavonic nations was made to read : " who, to all appearance, will be indebted for their liberation from this great evil to the influence of the ideas of the more advanced countries, rather than to the rapidity of their own progress in improvement." In the note, " heroic and calumniated " was inserted before " French Provisional Government." In the 5th ed. (1862) the second sentence of the note was replaced by " The Dutch Government is now seriously engaged in the same beneficent enterprise."]

the curse of slavery has been cast out from the great American republic, to find its last temporary refuge in Brazil and Cuba. No European country, except Spain alone, any longer participates in the enormity. Even serfage has now ceased to have a legal existence in Europe. Denmark has the honour of being the first Continental nation which imitated England in liberating its colonial slaves; and the abolition of slavery was one of the earliest acts of the heroic and calumniated Provisional Government of France. The Dutch Government was not long behind, and its colonies and dependencies are now, I believe without exception, free from actual slavery, though forced labour for the public authorities is still [1865] a recognised institution in Java, soon, we may hope, to be exchanged for complete personal freedom.

CHAPTER VI

OF PEASANT PROPRIETORS

§ 1. IN the régime of peasant properties, as in that of slavery, the whole produce belongs to a single owner, and the distinction of rent, profits, and wages, does not exist. In all other respects, the two states of society are the extreme opposites of each other. The one is the state of greatest oppression and degradation to the labouring class. The other is that in which they are the most uncontrolled arbiters of their own lot.

The advantage, however, of small properties in land, is one of the most disputed questions in the range of political economy. On the Continent, though there are some dissentients from the prevailing opinion, the benefit of having a numerous proprietary population exists in the minds of most people in the form of an axiom. But English authorities are either unaware of the judgment of Continental agriculturists, or are content to put it aside, on the plea of their having no experience of large properties in favourable circumstances : the advantage of large properties being only felt where there are also large farms ; and as this, in arable districts, implies a greater accumulation of capital than usually exists on the Continent, the great Continental estates, except in the case of grazing farms, are mostly let out for cultivation in small portions. There is some truth in this ; but the argument admits of being retorted ; for if the Continent knows little, by experience, of cultivation on a large scale and by large capital, the generality of English writers are no better acquainted practically with peasant proprietors, and have almost always the most erroneous ideas of their social condition and mode of life. Yet the old traditions even of England are on the same side with the general opinion of the Continent. The " yeomanry " who were vaunted as the glory of England while they existed, and have been so much mourned over since they disappeared, were either small proprietors or small farmers, and if they were mostly the last, the character they bore for sturdy independence is the more noticeable. There is a part of England, unfortunately a very small part, where peasant proprietors are still [1848] common ; for such are the " statesmen " of Cumberland and Westmoreland, though they pay, I believe, generally if not universally, certain customary dues, which, being fixed, no more affect their character of proprietor, than the land-tax does. There is but one voice, among those acquainted with the country, on the admirable effects of this tenure of land in those counties. No other agricultural population in England could have furnished the originals of Wordsworth's peasantry.*

The general system, however, of English cultivation, affording no experience to render the nature and operation of peasant properties familiar, and Englishmen being in general profoundly ignorant of the agricultural economy of other countries, the very idea of peasant proprietors is strange to the English mind, and does not easily find access to it. Even the forms of language stand in the way : the familiar designation for owners of land being " landlords," a term to which " tenants " is always understood as a correlative. When, at the time of the famine, the suggestion of peasant properties as a means of Irish improvement found its way into parliamentary and newspaper discussions, there were writers of

* In Mr. Wordsworth's little descriptive work on the scenery of the Lakes, he speaks of the upper part of the dales as having been for centuries " a perfect republic of shepherds and agriculturists, proprietors, for the most part, of the lands which they occupied and cultivated. The plough of each man was confined to the maintenance of his own family, or to the occasional accommodation of his neighbour. Two or three cows furnished each family with milk and cheese. The chapel was the only edifice that presided over these dwellings, the supreme head of this pure commonwealth ; the members of which existed in the midst of a powerful empire, like an ideal society, or an organized community, whose constitution had been imposed and regulated by the mountains which protected it. Neither high-born nobleman, knight, nor esquire was here ; but many of these humble sons of the hills had a consciousness that the land which they walked over and tilled had for more than five hundred years been possessed by men of their name and blood . . . Corn was grown in these vales sufficient upon each estate to furnish bread for each family, no more. The storms and moisture of the climate induced them to sprinkle their upland property with outhouses of native stone, as places of shelter for their sheep, where in tempestuous weather, food was distributed to them. Every family spun from its own flock the wool with which it was clothed ; a weaver was here and there found among them, and the rest of their wants was supplied by the produce of the yarn, which they carded and spun in their own houses, and carried to market either under their arms or more frequently on packhorses, a small train taking their way weekly down the valley, or over the mountains, to the most commodious town."—*A Description of the Scenery of the Lakes in the North of England*, 3rd edit. pp. 50 to 53 and 63 to 65.

pretension to whom the word "proprietor" was so far from conveying any distinct idea, that they mistook the small holdings of
Irish cottier tenants for peasant properties. The subject being
so little understood, I think it important, before entering into the
theory of it, to do something towards showing how the case stands
as to matter of fact; by exhibiting, at greater length than would
otherwise be admissible, some of the testimony which exists respecting the state of cultivation, and the comfort and happiness of the
cultivators, in those countries and parts of countries, in which the
greater part of the land has neither landlord nor farmer, other than
the labourer who tills the soil.

§ 2.   I lay no stress on the condition of North America, where,
as is well known, the land, except in the former Slave States,[1] is
almost universally owned by the same person who holds the plough.
A country combining the natural fertility of America with the
knowledge and arts of modern Europe, is so peculiarly circumstanced, that scarcely anything, except insecurity of property or a
tyrannical government, could materially impair the prosperity of
the industrious classes.   I might, with Sismondi, insist more strongly
on the case of ancient Italy, especially Latium, that Campagna
which then swarmed with inhabitants in the very regions which under
a contrary régime have become uninhabitable from malaria.   But
I prefer taking the evidence of the same writer on things known
to him by personal observation.

"It is especially Switzerland," says M. de Sismondi, "which
should be traversed and studied to judge of the happiness of peasant
proprietors.   It is from Switzerland we learn that agriculture practised by the very persons who enjoy its fruits, suffices to procure
great comfort for a very numerous population ; a great independence
of character, arising from independence of position ; a great commerce of consumption, the result of the easy circumstances of all the
inhabitants, even in a country whose climate is rude, whose soil is but
moderately fertile, and where late frosts and inconstancy of seasons
often blight the hopes of the cultivator.   It is impossible to see
without admiration those timber houses of the poorest peasant, so
vast, so well closed in, so covered with carvings.   In the interior,
spacious corridors separate the different chambers of the numerous
family ; each chamber has but one bed, which is abundantly furnished

---

[1] [Substituted in the 7th ed. (1871) for "wherever free from the curse of
slavery."]

with curtains, bedclothes, and the whitest linen ; carefully kept furniture surrounds it ; the wardrobes are filled with linen ; the dairy is vast, well aired, and of exquisite cleanness ; under the same roof is a great provision of corn, salt meat, cheese and wood ; in the cow-houses are the finest and most carefully tended cattle in Europe ; the garden is planted with flowers, both men and women are cleanly and warmly clad, the women preserve with pride their ancient costume ; all carry in their faces the impress of health and strength. Let other nations boast of their opulence, Switzerland may always point with pride to her peasants." *

The same eminent writer thus expresses his opinion on peasant proprietorship in general.

" Wherever we find peasant proprietors, we also find the comfort, security, confidence in the future, and independence, which assure at once happiness and virtue. The peasant who with his children does all the work of his little inheritance, who pays no rent to any one above him, nor wages to any one below, who regulates his production by his consumption, who eats his own corn, drinks his own wine, is clothed in his own hemp and wool, cares little for the prices of the market ; for he has little to sell and little to buy, and is never ruined by revulsions of trade. Instead of fearing for the future, he sees it in the colours of hope ; for he employs every moment not required by the labours of the year, on something profitable to his children and to future generations. A few minutes' work suffices him to plant the seed·which in a hundred years will be a large tree, to dig the channel which will conduct to him a spring of fresh water, to improve by cares often repeated, but stolen from odd times, all the species of animals and vegetables which surround him. His little patrimony is a true savings bank, always ready to receive all his little gains and utilize all his moments of leisure. The ever-acting power of nature returns them a hundred-fold. The peasant has a lively sense of the happiness attached to the condition of a proprietor. Accordingly he is always eager to buy land at any price. He pays more for it than its value, more perhaps than it will bring him in ; but is he not right in estimating highly the advantage of having always an advantageous investment for his labour, without underbidding in the wages-market—of being always able to find bread, without the necessity of buying it at a scarcity price ?

" The peasant proprietor is of all cultivators the one who gets most from the soil, for he is the one who thinks most of the future, and

* _Etudes sur l'Economie Politique_, Essai III.

who has been most instructed by experience. He is also the one who employs the human powers to most advantage, because dividing his occupations among all the members of his family, he reserves some for every day of the year, so that nobody is ever out of work. Of all cultivators he is the happiest, and at the same time the land nowhere occupies, and feeds amply without becoming exhausted, so many inhabitants as where they are proprietors. Finally, of all cultivators the peasant proprietor is the one who gives most encouragement to commerce and manufactures, because he is the richest." *

This picture of unwearied assiduity, and what may be called affectionate interest in the land, is borne out in regard to the more intelligent Cantons of Switzerland by English observers. " In walking anywhere in the neighbourhood of Zurich," says Mr. Inglis, " in looking to the right or to the left, one is struck with the extraordinary industry of the inhabitants ; and if we learn that a proprietor here has a return of ten per cent. we are inclined to say, ' he deserves it.' I speak at present of country labour, though I believe that in every kind of trade also, the people of Zurich are remarkable for their assiduity ; but in the industry they show in the cultivation of their land I may safely say they are unrivalled. When I used to open my casement between four and five in the morning to look out upon the lake and the distant Alps, I saw the labourer in the fields ; and when I returned from an evening walk, long after sunset, as late, perhaps, as half-past eight, there was the labourer mowing his grass, or tying up his vines. . . It is impossible to look at a field, a garden, a hedging, scarcely even a tree, a flower, or a vegetable, without perceiving proofs of the extreme care and industry that are bestowed upon the cultivation of the soil. If, for example, a path

* And in another work (*Nouveaux Principes d'Economie Politique*, liv. iii. ch. 3,) he says : " When we traverse nearly the whole of Switzerland, and several provinces of France, Italy, and Germany, we need never ask, in looking at any piece of land, if it belongs to a peasant proprietor or to a farmer. The intelligent care, the enjoyments provided for the labourer, the adornment which the country has received from his hands, are clear indications of the former. It is true an oppressive government may destroy the comfort and brutify the intelligence which should be the result of property ; taxation may abstract the best produce of the fields, the insolence of government officers may disturb the security of the peasant, the impossibility of obtaining justice against a powerful neighbour may sow discouragement in his mind, and in the fine country which has been given back to the administration of the King of Sardinia, the proprietor, equally with the day-labourer, wears the livery of indigence." He was here speaking of Savoy, where the peasants were generally proprietors, and, according to authentic accounts, extremely miserable. But, as M. de Sismondi continues, " it is in vain to observe only one of the rules of political economy ; it cannot by itself suffice to produce good ; but at least it diminishes evil."

leads through or by the side of a field of grain, the corn is not, as in England, permitted to hang over the path, exposed to be pulled or trodden down by every passer-by ; it is everywhere bounded by a fence, stakes are placed at intervals of about a yard, and, about two or three feet from the ground, boughs of trees are passed longitudin-ally along. If you look into a field towards evening, where there are large beds of cauliflower or cabbage, you will find that every single plant has been watered. In the gardens, which around Zurich are extremely large, the most punctilious care is evinced in every production that grows. The vegetables are planted with seemingly mathematical accuracy ; not a single weed is to be seen, not a single stone. Plants are not earthed up as with us, but are planted in a small hollow, into each of which a little manure is put, and each plant is watered daily. Where seeds are sown, the earth directly above is broken into the finest powder ; every shrub, every flower is tied to a stake, and where there is wall-fruit a trellice is erected against the wall, to which the boughs are fastened, and there is not a single thing that has not its appropriate resting place." *

Of one of the remote valleys of the High Alps the same writer thus expresses himself.†

" In the whole of the Engadine the land belongs to the peasantry, who, like the inhabitants of every other place where this state of things exists, vary greatly in the extent of their possessions. . . . Generally speaking, an Engadine peasant lives entirely upon the produce of his land, with the exception of the few articles of foreign growth required in his family, such as coffee, sugar, and wine. Flax is grown, prepared, spun, and woven, without ever leaving his house. He has also his own wool, which is converted into a blue coat, with-out passing through the hands of either the dyer or the tailor. The country is incapable of greater cultivation than it has received. All has been done for it that industry and an extreme love of gain can devise. There is not a foot of waste land in the Engadine, the lowest part of which is not much lower than the top of Snowdon. Wherever grass will grow, there it is ; wherever a rock will bear a blade, verdure is seen upon it ; wherever an ear of rye will ripen, there it is to be found. Barley and oats have also their appropriate spots ; and wherever it is possible to ripen a little patch of wheat, the cultivation of it is attempted. In no country in Europe will be found

* *Switzerland, the South of France, and the Pyrenees, in* 1830. By H. D. Inglis. Vol. i. ch. 2.
† Ibid. ch. 8 and 10.

so few poor as in the Engadine. In the village of Suss, which contains about six hundred inhabitants, there is not a single individual who has not wherewithal to live comfortably, not a single individual who is indebted to others for one morsel that he eats."

Notwithstanding the general prosperity of the Swiss peasantry, this total absence of pauperism and (it may almost be said) of poverty, cannot be predicated of the whole country ; the largest and richest canton, that of Berne, being an example of the contrary ; for although, in the parts of it which are occupied by peasant pro- prietors, their industry is as remarkable and their ease and comfort as conspicuous as elsewhere, the canton is burthened with a numer- ous pauper population, through the operation of the worst regulated system of poor-law administration in Europe, except that of Eng- land before the new Poor Law.* Nor is Switzerland in some other respects a favourable example of all that peasant properties might effect. There exists a series of statistical accounts of the Swiss Cantons, drawn up mostly with great care and intelligence, containing detailed information, of tolerably recent date, respecting the condition of the land and of the people. From these, the sub- division appears to be often so minute, that it can hardly be supposed not to be excessive : and the indebtedness of the proprietors in the flourishing canton of Zurich " borders," as the writer expresses it, " on the incredible ; " † so that " only the intensest industry, frugality, temperance, and complete freedom of commerce enable them to stand their ground." Yet the general conclusion deducible from these books is that since the beginning of the century, and concurrently with the subdivision of many great estates which belonged to nobles or to the cantonal governments, there has been

* [1852] There have been considerable changes in the Poor Law adminis- tration and legislation of the Canton of Berne since the sentence in the text was written. But I am not sufficiently acquainted with the nature and opera- tion of these changes to speak more particularly of them here.

† "Eine an das unglaubliche gränzende Schuldenmasse " is the expression. (*Historisch-geographisch-statistische Gemälde der Schweiz. Erster Theil. Der Kanton Zürich.* Von Gerold Meyer von Knonau, 1834, pp. 80–81.) There are villages in Zurich, he adds, in which there is not a single property un- mortgaged. It does not, however, follow that each individual proprietor is deeply involved because the aggregate mass of encumbrances is large. In the Canton of Schaffhausen, for instance, it is stated that the landed properties are almost all mortgaged, but rarely for more than one-half their registered value (*Zwölfter Theil. Der Kanton Schaffhausen*, von Edward Im-Thurn, 1840, p. 52), and the mortgages are often for the improvement and enlargement of the estate. (*Siebenzehnter Theil. Der Kanton Thürgau*, von J. A. Pupikofer, 1837, p. 209.)

a striking and rapid improvement in almost every department of agriculture, as well as in the houses, the habits, and the food of the people. The writer of the account of Thürgau goes so far as to say, that since the subdivision of the feudal estates into peasant properties, it is not uncommon for a third or a fourth part of an estate to produce as much grain, and support as many head of cattle, as the whole estate did before.*

§ 3. One of the countries in which peasant proprietors are of oldest date, and most numerous in proportion to the population, is Norway. Of the social and economical condition of that country an interesting account has been given by Mr. Laing. His testimony in favour of small landed properties both there and elsewhere, is given with great decision. I shall quote a few passages.

" If small proprietors are not good farmers, it is not from the same cause here which we are told makes them so in Scotland—indolence and want of exertion. The extent to which irrigation is carried on in these glens and valleys shows a spirit of exertion and *co-operation* " (I request particular attention to this point), " to which the latter can show nothing similar. Hay being the principal winter support of live stock, and both it and corn, as well as potatoes, liable, from the shallow soil and powerful reflection of sunshine from the rocks, to be burnt and withered up, the greatest exertions are made to bring water from the head of each glen, along such a level as will give the command of it to each farmer at the head of his fields. This is done by leading it in wooden troughs (the half of a tree roughly scooped) from the highest perennial stream among the hills, through woods, across ravines, along the rocky, often perpendicular, sides of the glens, and from this main trough giving a lateral one to each farmer in passing the head of his farm. He distributes this supply by moveable troughs among the fields ; and at this season waters each rig successively with scoops like those used by bleachers in watering cloth, laying his trough between every two rigs. One would not believe, without seeing it, how very large an extent of land is traversed expeditiously by these artificial showers. The extent of the main troughs is very great. In one glen I walked ten miles, and found it troughed on both sides : on one, the chain is continued down the main valley for forty miles.† Those may be

---

* *Thürgau*, p. 72.
† [1852] Reichensperger (*Die Agrarfrage*) quoted by Mr. Kay (*Social Condition and Education of the People in England and Europe*,) observes, " that

bad farmers who do such things ; but they are not indolent, not
ignorant of the principle of working in concert, and keeping up
establishments for common benefit. They are undoubtedly, in
these respects, far in advance of any community of cottars in our
Highland glens. They feel as proprietors, who receive the advantage of their own exertions. The excellent state of the roads
and bridges is another proof that the country is inhabited by people
who have a common interest to keep them under repair. There
are no tolls." *

On the effects of peasant proprietorship on the Continent generally, the same writer expresses himself as follows.†

" If we listen to the large farmer, the scientific agriculturist,
the " [English] " political economist, good farming must perish
with large farms ; the very idea that good farming can exist, unless
on large farms cultivated with great capital, they hold to be absurd.

the parts of Europe where the most extensive and costly plans for watering the
meadows and lands have been carried out in the greatest perfection, are those
where the lands are very much subdivided, and are in the hands of small proprietors. He instances the plain round Valencia, several of the southern
departments of France, particularly those of Vaucluse and Bouches du Rhône,
Lombardy, Tuscany, the districts of Sienna, Lucca, and Bergamo, Piedmont,
many parts of Germany, &c., in all which parts of Europe the land is very
much subdivided among small proprietors. In all these parts great and expensive systems and plans of general irrigation have been carried out, and are
now being supported by the small proprietors themselves ; thus showing how
they are able to accomplish, by means of combination, work requiring the
expenditure of great quantities of capital." Kay, i. 126.

* Laing, *Journal of a Residence in Norway*, pp. 36, 37. [From the 3rd ed.
(1852) was omitted the following further passage from Laing, quoted in the
1st and 2nd: " It is, I am aware, a favourite and constant observation of our
agricultural writers, that these small proprietors make the worst farmers. It
may be so ; but a population may be in a wretched condition, although their
country is very well farmed ; or they may be happy, although bad cultivators.
. . . Good farming is a phrase composed of two words which have no more
application to the happiness or well-being of a people than good weaving or
good iron-founding. That the human powers should be well applied, and not
misapplied, in the production of grain, or iron, or clothing, is, no doubt, an
object of great importance ; but the happiness or well-being of a people does
not entirely depend upon it. *It has more effect on their numbers than on their
condition.* The producer of grain who is working for himself only, who is
owner of his land, and has not a third of its produce to pay as rent, can afford
to be a worse farmer by one-third, than a tenant, and is, notwithstanding, in
a preferable condition. Our agricultural writers tell us, indeed, that labourers
in agriculture are much better off as farm-servants than they would be as
small proprietors. We have only the master's word for this. Ask the servant.
The colonists told us the same thing of their slaves. If property is a good and
desirable thing, I suspect that the smallest quantity of it is good and desirable ;
and that the state of society in which it is most widely diffused is the best
constituted."]

† *Notes of a Traveller*, pp. 299 et seqq.

Draining, manuring, economical arrangement, cleaning the land, regular rotations, valuable stock and implements, all belong exclusively to large farms, worked by large capital, and by hired labour. This reads very well ; but if we raise our eyes from their books to their fields, and coolly compare what we see in the best districts farmed in large farms, with what we see in the best districts farmed in small farms, we see, and there is no blinking the fact, better crops on the ground in Flanders, East Friesland, Holstein, in short, on the whole line of the arable land of equal quality of the Continent, from the Sound to Calais, than we see on the line of British coast opposite to this line, and in the same latitudes, from the Frith of Forth all round to Dover. Minute labour on small portions of arable ground gives evidently, in equal soils and climates, a superior productiveness, where these small portions belong in property, as in Flanders, Holland, Friesland, and Ditmarsch in Holstein, to the farmer. It is not pretended by our agricultural writers, that our large farmers, even in Berwickshire, Roxburghshire, or the Lothians, approach to the garden-like cultivation, attention to manures, drainage, and clean state of the land, or in productiveness from a small space of soil not originally rich, which distinguish the small farmers of Flanders, or their system. In the best-farmed parish in Scotland or England, more land is wasted in the corners and borders of the fields of large farms, in the roads through them, unnecessarily wide because they are bad, and bad because they are wide, in neglected commons, waste spots, useless belts and clumps of sorry trees, and such unproductive areas, than would maintain the poor of the parish, if they were all laid together and cultivated. But large capital applied to farming is of course only applied to the very best of the soils of a country. It cannot touch the small unproductive spots which require more time and labour to fertilize them than is consistent with a quick return of capital. But although hired time and labour cannot be applied beneficially to such cultivation, the owner's own time and labour may. He is working for no higher terms at first from his land than a bare living. But in the course of generations fertility and value are produced ; a better living, and even very improved processes of husbandry, are attained. Furrow draining, stall feeding all summer, liquid manures, are universal in the husbandry of the small farms of Flanders, Lombardy, Switzerland. Our most improving districts under large farms are but beginning to adopt them. Dairy husbandry even, and the manufacture of the largest cheeses by the co-operation of many small farmers,* the mutual assurance of property against fire and hail-storms, by the co-operation of small farmers—the most scientific and expensive of all agricultural operations in modern times, the manufacture of beet-root sugar—the supply of the European markets with flax and hemp, by the husbandry of small farmers—the abundance of legumes, fruits, poultry, in the usual diet even of the lowest classes abroad, and the total want of such variety at the tables even of our middle classes, and this variety and abundance essentially connected with the husbandry of small farmers—all these are features in the occupation of a country by small proprietor-farmers, which must make the inquirer pause before he admits the dogma of our land doctors at home, that large farms worked by hired labour and great capital can alone bring out the greatest productiveness of the soil and furnish the greatest supply of the necessaries and conveniences of life to the inhabitants of a country."

§ 4. Among the many flourishing regions of Germany in which peasant properties prevail, I select the Palatinate, for the advantage of quoting, from an English source, the results of recent personal observation of its agriculture and its people. Mr. Howitt, a writer whose habit it is to see all English objects and English socialities *en beau*, and who, in treating of the Rhenish peasantry, certainly does not underrate the rudeness of their implements, and the inferiority of their ploughing, nevertheless shows that under the invigorating influence of the feelings of proprietorship, they make up for the imperfections of their apparatus by the intensity of their

* The manner in which the Swiss peasants combine to carry on cheese-making by their united capital deserves to be noted. "Each parish in Switzerland hires a man, generally from the district of Gruyère in the canton of Freyburg, to take care of the herd, and make the cheese. One cheeseman, one pressman or assistant, and one cowherd are considered necessary for every forty cows. The owners of the cows get credit each of them, in a book daily for the quantity of milk given by each cow. The cheeseman and his assistants milk the cows, put the milk all together, and make cheese of it, and at the end of the season each owner receives the weight of cheese proportionable to the quantity of milk his cows have delivered. By this co-operative plan, instead of the small-sized unmarketable cheeses only, which each could produce out of his three or four cows' milk, he has the same weight in large marketable cheese superior in quality, because made by people who attend to no other business. The cheeseman and his assistants are paid so much per head of the cows, in money or it. cheese, or sometimes they hire the cows, and pay the owners in money or cheese." *Notes of a Traveller*, p. 351. A similar system exists in the French Jura. See, for full details, Lavergne, *Economie Rurale de la France*, 2nd ed., pp. 139 et seqq. One of the most remarkable points in this interesting case of combination of labour is the confidence which it supposes, and which experience must justify, in the integrity of the persons employed.

application. " The peasant harrows and clears his land till it is in the nicest order, and it is admirable to see the crops which he obtains." * " The peasants † are the great and ever-present objects of country life. They are the great population of the country, because they themselves are the possessors. This country is, in fact, for the most part, in the hands of the people. It is parcelled out among the multitude. . . . . . The peasants are not, as with us, for the most part, totally cut off from property in the soil they cultivate, totally dependent on the labour afforded by others—they are themselves the proprietors. It is, perhaps, from this cause that they are probably the most industrious peasantry in the world. They labour busily, early and late, because they feel that they are labouring for themselves. . . . . . The German peasants work hard, but they have no actual want. Every man has his house, his orchard, his roadside trees, commonly so heavy with fruit, that he is obliged to prop and secure them all ways, or they would be torn to pieces. He has his corn-plot, his plot for mangel-wurzel, for hemp, and so on. He is his own master ; and he, and every member of his family, have the strongest motives to labour. You see the effect of this in that unremitting diligence which is beyond that of the whole world besides, and his economy, which is still greater. The Germans, indeed, are not so active and lively as the English. You never see them in a bustle, or as though they meant to knock off a vast deal in a little time. . . . . . They are, on the contrary, slow, but for ever doing. They plod on from day to day, and year to year—the most patient, untirable, and persevering of animals. The English peasant is so cut off from the idea of property, that he comes habitually to look upon it as a thing from which he is warned by the laws of the large proprietors, and becomes, in consequence, spiritless, purposeless. . . . . . The German bauer, on the contrary, looks on the country as made for him and his fellow-men. He feels himself a man ; he has a stake in the country, as good as that of the bulk of his neighbours ; no man can threaten him with ejection, or the workhouse, so long as he is active and economical. He walks, therefore, with a bold step ; he looks you in the face with the air of a free man, but of a respectful one."

Of their industry, the same writer thus further speaks : " There is not an hour of the year in which they do not find unceasing occupation. In the depth of winter, when the weather permits them by any

* *Rural and Domestic Life of Germany*, p. 27.
† Ibid. p. 40.

means to get out of doors, they are always finding something to do. They carry out their manure to their lands while the frost is in them. If there is not frost, they are busy cleaning ditches and felling old fruit trees, or such as do not bear well. Such of them as are too poor to lay in a sufficient stock of wood, find plenty of work in ascending into the mountainous woods, and bringing thence fuel. It would astonish the English common people to see the intense labour with which the Germans earn their firewood. In the depths of frost and snow, go into any of their hills and woods, and there you will find them hacking up stumps, cutting off branches, and gathering, by all means which the official wood-police will allow, boughs, stakes, and pieces of wood, which they convey home with the most incredible toil and patience." * After a description of their careful and laborious vineyard culture, he continues,† " In England, with its great quantity of grass lands, and its large farms, so soon as the grain is in, and the fields are shut up for hay grass, the country seems in a comparative state of rest and quiet. But here they are everywhere, and for ever, hoeing and mowing, planting and cutting, weeding and gathering. They have a succession of crops like a market-gardener. They have their carrots, poppies, hemp, flax, saintfoin, lucerne, rape, colewort, cabbage, rotabaga, black turnips, Swedish and white turnips, teazels, Jerusalem artichokes, mangel-wurzel, parsnips, kidney-beans, field beans, and peas, vetches, Indian corn, buckwheat, madder for the manufacturer, potatoes, their great crop of tobacco, millet—all, or the greater part, under the family management, in their own family allotments. They have had these things first to sow, many of them to transplant, to hoe, to weed, to clear of insects, to top ; many of them to mow and gather in successive crops. They have their water-meadows, of which kind almost all their meadows are, to flood, to mow, and reflood ; watercourses to reopen and to make anew : their early fruits to gather, to bring to market with their green crops of vegetables ; their cattle, sheep, calves, foals, most of them prisoners, and poultry to look after ; their vines, as they shoot rampantly in the summer heat, to prune, and thin out the leaves when they are too thick : and any one may imagine what a scene of incessant labour it is."

This interesting sketch, to the general truth of which any observant traveller in that highly cultivated and populous region

---

* *Rural and Domestic Life of Germany,* p. 44.
† Ibid. p. 50.

can bear witness, accords with the more elaborate delineation by a distinguished inhabitant, Professor Rau, in his little treatise *On the Agriculture of the Palatinate.** Dr. Rau bears testimony not only to the industry, but to the skill and intelligence of the peasantry ; their judicious employment of manures, and excellent rotation of crops ; the progressive improvement of their agriculture for generations past, and the spirit of further improvement which is still active. " The indefatigableness of the country people, who may be seen in activity all the day and all the year, and are never idle, because they make a good distribution of their labours, and find for every interval of time a suitable occupation, is as well known as their zeal is praiseworthy in turning to use every circumstance which presents itself, in seizing upon every useful novelty which offers, and even in searching out new and advantageous methods. One easily perceives that the peasant of this district has reflected much on his occupation : he can give reasons for his modes of proceeding, even if those reasons are not always tenable ; he is as exact an observer of proportions as it is possible to be from memory, without the aid of figures : he attends to such general signs of the times as appear to augur him either benefit or harm." †

¹ The experience of all other parts of Germany is similar. " In Saxony," says Mr. Kay, " it is a notorious fact, that during the last thirty years, and since the peasants became the proprietors of the land, there has been a rapid and continual improvement in the condition of the houses, in the manner of living, in the dress of the peasants, and particularly in the culture of the land. I have twice walked through that part of Saxony called Saxon Switzerland, in company with a German guide, and on purpose to see the state of the villages and of the farming, and I can safely challenge contradiction when I affirm that there is no farming in all Europe superior to the laboriously careful cultivation of the valleys of that part of Saxony. There, as in the cantons of Berne, Vaud, and Zurich, and in the Rhine provinces, the farms are singularly flourishing. They are kept in beautiful condition, and are always neat and well managed. The ground is cleared as if it were a garden. No hedges or brushwood encumber it. Scarcely a rush or thistle or a bit of rank grass is to be seen. The meadows are well watered every spring with liquid manure, saved from the drainings

---

* *Ueber die Landwirthschaft der Rheinpfalz, und insbesondere in der Heidelberger Gegend.* Von Dr. Karl Heinrich Rau. Heidelberg, 1830.
† Rau, pp. 15, 16.
¹ [The rest of this section was added in the 3rd ed. (1852).]

of the farm yards. The grass is so free from weeds that the Saxon meadows reminded me more of English lawns than of anything else I had seen. The peasants endeavour to outstrip one another in the quantity and quality of the produce, in the preparation of the ground, and in the general cultivation of their respective portions. All the little proprietors are eager to find out how to farm so as to produce the greatest results : they diligently seek after improvements ; they send their children to the agricultural schools in order to fit them to assist their fathers ; and each proprietor soon adopts a new improvement introduced by any of his neighbours."* If this be not overstated, it denotes a state of intelligence very different not only from that of English labourers but of English farmers.

Mr. Kay's book, published in 1850, contains a mass of evidence gathered from observation and inquiries in many different parts of Europe, together with attestations from many distinguished writers, to the beneficial effects of peasant properties. Among the testimonies which he cites respecting their effect on agriculture, I select the following.

" Reichensperger, himself an inhabitant of that part of Prussia where the land is the most subdivided, has published a long and very elaborate work to show the admirable consequences of a system of freeholds in land. He expresses a very decided opinion that not only are the *gross* products of any given number of acres held and cultivated by small or peasant proprietors greater than the gross products of an equal number of acres held by a few great proprietors, and cultivated by tenant farmers, but that the *net* products of the former, after deducting all the expenses of cultivation, are also greater than the net products of the latter. . . . He mentions one fact which seems to prove that the fertility of the land in countries where the properties are small must be rapidly increasing. He says that the price of the land which is divided into small properties in the Prussian Rhine provinces is much higher, and has been rising much more rapidly, than the price of land on the great estates. He and Professor Rau both say that this rise in the price of the small estates would have ruined the more recent purchasers, unless the productiveness of the small estates had increased in at least an equal proportion ; and *as the small proprietors have been gradually becoming more and more*

* *The Social Condition and Education of the People in England and Europe ; showing the results of the Primary Schools, and of the division of Landed Property in Foreign Countries.* By Joseph Kay, M.A., Barrister-at-Law, and late Travelling Bachelor of the University ſf Cambridge. Vol. i. pp. 138–40.

prosperous, notwithstanding the increasing prices they have paid for their land, he argues, with apparent justness, that this would seem to show that not only the gross profits of the small estates, but the net profits also have been gradually increasing, and that the net profits per acre of land, when farmed by small proprietors, are greater than the net profits per acre of land farmed by a great proprietor. He says, with seeming truth, that the increasing price of land in the small estates cannot be the mere effect of competition, or it would have diminished the profits and the prosperity of the small proprietors, and that this result has not followed the rise.

"Albrecht Thaer, another celebrated German writer on the different systems of agriculture, in one of his later works (*Grundsätze der rationellen Landwirthschaft*) expresses his decided conviction, that the *net produce* of land is greater when farmed by small proprietors than when farmed by great proprietors or their tenants. . . . This opinion of Thaer is all the more remarkable as, during the early part of his life, he was very strongly in favour of the English system of great estates and great farms."

Mr. Kay adds from his own observation, "The peasant farming of Prussia, Saxony, Holland, and Switzerland is the most perfect and economical farming I have ever witnessed in any country."*

§ 5. But the most decisive example in opposition to the English prejudice against cultivation by peasant proprietors is the case of Belgium. The soil is originally one of the worst in Europe. "The provinces," says Mr. M'Culloch,† "of West and East Flanders, and Hainault, form a far stretching plain, of which the luxuriant vegetation indicates the indefatigable care and labour bestowed upon its cultivation; for the natural soil consists almost wholly of barren sand, and its great fertility is entirely the result of very skilful management and judicious application of various manures." There exists a carefully prepared and comprehensive treatise on *Flemish Husbandry*, in the Farmer's Series of the Society for the Diffusion of Useful Knowledge. The writer observes ‡ that the Flemish agriculturists "seem to want nothing but a space to work upon : whatever be the quality or texture of the soil, in time they will make it produce something. The sands in the Campine can be compared to nothing but the sand on the sea-shore, which they probably were originally. It is highly interesting to follow

* Kay, i. 116-8.
† *Geographical Dictionary*, art. "Belgium."   ‡ Pp. 11-14.

step by step the progress of improvement. Here you see a cottage and rude cowshed erected on a spot of the most unpromising aspect. The loose white sand blown into irregular mounds is only kept together by the roots of the heath : a small spot only is levelled and surrounded by a ditch : part of this is covered with young broom, part is planted with potatoes, and perhaps a small patch of diminutive clover may show itself:" but manures, both solid and liquid, are collecting, "and this is the nucleus from which, in a few years, a little farm will spread around. . . . If there is no manure at hand, the only thing that can be sown, on pure sand, at first is broom : this grows in the most barren soils ; in three years it is fit to cut, and produces some return in faggots for the bakers and brickmakers. The leaves which have fallen have somewhat enriched the soil, and the fibres of the roots have given a slight degree of compactness. It may now be ploughed and sown with buckwheat, or even with rye without manure. By the time this is reaped, some manure may have been collected, and a regular course of cropping may begin. As soon as clover and potatoes enable the farmer to keep cows and make manure, the improvement goes on rapidly ; in a few years the soil undergoes a complete change : it becomes mellow and retentive of moisture, and enriched by the vegetable matter afforded by the decomposition of the roots of clover and other plants. . . . After the land has been gradually brought into a good state, and is cultivated in a regular manner, there appears much less difference between the soils which have been originally good, and those which have been made so by labour and industry. At least the crops in both appear more nearly alike at harvest, than is the case in soils of different qualities in other countries. This is a great proof of the excellency of the Flemish system ; for it shows that the land is in a constant state of improvement, and that the deficiency of the soil is compensated by greater attention to tillage and manuring, especially the latter."

The people who labour thus intensely on their small properties or farms, have practised for centuries those principles of rotation of crops and economy of manures, which in England are counted among modern discoveries : and even now the superiority of their agriculture, as a whole, to that of England, is admitted by competent judges. "The cultivation of a poor light soil, or a moderate soil," says the writer last quoted,* "is generally superior in Flanders to that of the most improved farms of the same kind in Britain. We

* *Flemish Husbandry*, p. 3.

surpass the Flemish farmer greatly in capital, in varied implements of tillage, in the choice and breeding of cattle and sheep," (though, according to the same authority,* they are much "before us in the feeding of their cows,") "and the British farmer is in general a man of superior education to the Flemish peasant. But in the minute attention to the qualities of the soil, in the management and application of manures of different kinds, in the judicious succession of crops, and especially in the economy of land, so that every part of it shall be in a constant state of production, we have still something to learn from the Flemings," and not from an instructed and enterprising Fleming here and there, but from the general practice.

Much of the most highly cultivated part of the country consists of peasant properties, managed by the proprietors, always either wholly or partly by spade industry.† "When the land is cultivated entirely by the spade, and no horses are kept, a cow is kept for every three acres of land, and entirely fed on artificial grasses and roots. This mode of cultivation is principally adopted in the Waes district, where properties are very small. All the labour is done by the different members of the family;" children soon beginning "to assist in various minute operations, according to their age and strength, such as weeding, hoeing, feeding the cows. If they can raise rye and wheat enough to make their bread, and potatoes, turnips, carrots and clover, for the cows, they do well; and the produce of the sale of their rape-seed, their flax, their hemp, and their butter, after deducting the expense of manure purchased, which is always considerable, gives them a very good profit. Suppose the whole extent of the land to be six acres, which is not an uncommon occupation, and which one man can manage;" then (after describing the cultivation), "if a man with his wife and three young children are considered as equal to three and a half grown up men, the family will require thirty-nine bushels of grain, forty-nine bushels of potatoes, a fat hog, and the butter and milk of one cow: an acre and a half of land will produce the grain and potatoes, and allow some corn to finish the fattening of the hog, which has the extra buttermilk: another acre in clover, carrots, and potatoes, together with the stubble turnips, will more than feed the cow; consequently two and a half acres of land is sufficient to feed this family, and the produce of the other three and a half may be sold to pay

* *Flemish Husbandry*, p. 13.
† Ibid. pp. 73 et seq.

the rent or the interest of purchase-money, wear and tear of implements, extra manure, and clothes for the family. But these acres
are the most profitable on the farm, for the hemp, flax, and colza
are included ; and by having another acre in clover and roots,
a second cow can be kept, and its produce sold. We have, therefore,
a solution of the problem, how a family can live and thrive on six
acres of moderate land." After showing by calculation that this
extent of land can be cultivated in the most perfect manner by the
family without any aid from hired labour, the writer continues,
" In a farm of *ten* acres entirely cultivated by the spade, the addition
of a man and a woman to the members of the family will render
all the operations more easy ; and with horse and cart to carry out
the manure, and bring home the produce, and occasionally draw the
harrows, *fifteen* acres may be very well cultivated. . . . Thus it
will be seen," (this is the result of some pages of details and calculations,*) "that by spade husbandry, an industrious man with a
small capital, occupying only fifteen acres of good light land, may
not only live and bring up a family, *paying a good rent*, but may
accumulate a considerable sum in the course of his life." But
the indefatigable industry by which he accomplishes this, and of
which so large a portion is expended not in the mere cultivation,
but in the improvement, for a distant return, of the soil itself—
has that industry no connexion with *not* paying rent ? Could it
exist, without presupposing either a virtually permanent tenure,
or the certain prospect, by labour and economy on hired land, of
becoming one day a landed proprietor ?

As to their mode of living, " the Flemish farmers and labourers
live much more economically than the same class in England :
they seldom eat meat, except on Sundays and in harvest : buttermilk and potatoes with brown bread is their daily food." It is on
this kind of evidence that English travellers, as they hurry through
Europe, pronounce the peasantry of every Continental country
poor and miserable, its agricultural and social system a failure,
and the English the only régime under which labourers are well
off. It is, truly enough, the only régime under which labourers,
whether well off or not, never attempt to be better. So little are
English labourers accustomed to consider it possible that a labourer
should not spend all he earns, that they habitually mistake the signs
of economy for those of poverty. Observe the true interpretation
of the phenomenon.

* *Flemish Husbandry*, p. 81.

" Accordingly *they are gradually acquiring capital*, and their great ambition is to have land of their own. They eagerly seize every opportunity of purchasing a small farm, and the price is so raised by competition, that land pays little more than two per cent interest for the purchase money. Large properties gradually disappear, and are divided into small portions, which sell at a high rate. But the wealth and industry of the population is continually increasing, being rather diffused through the masses than accumulated in individuals."

With facts like these, known and accessible, it is not a little surprising to find the case of Flanders referred to not in recommendation of peasant properties, but as a warning against them ; on no better ground than a presumptive excess of population, inferred from the distress which existed among the peasantry of Brabant and East Flanders in the disastrous year 1846–47. The evidence which I have cited from a writer conversant with the subject, and having no economical theory to support, shows that the distress, whatever may have been its severity, arose from no insufficiency in these little properties to supply abundantly, in any ordinary circumstances, the wants of all whom they have to maintain. It arose from the essential condition to which those are subject who employ land of their own in growing their own food, namely, that the vicissitudes of the seasons must be borne by themselves, and cannot, as in the case of large farmers, be shifted from them to the consumer. When we remember the season of 1846, a partial failure of all kinds of grain, and an almost total one of the potato, it is no wonder that in so unusual a calamity the produce of six acres, half of them sown with flax, hemp, or oil seeds, should fall short of a year's provision for a family. But we are not to contrast the distressed Flemish peasant with an English capitalist who farms several hundred acres of land. If the peasant were an Englishman, he would not be that capitalist, but a day labourer under a capitalist. And is there no distress, in times of dearth, among day labourers ? Was there none, that year, in countries where small proprietors and small farmers are unknown ? I am aware of no reason for believing that the distress was greater in Belgium, than corresponds to the proportional extent of the failure of crops compared with other countries.*

* [1849] As much of the distress lately complained of in Belgium, as partakes in any degree of a permanent character, appears to be almost confined to the portion of the population who carry on manufacturing labour, either by

§ 6.[1] The evidence of the beneficial operation of peasant properties in the Channel Islands is of so decisive a character, that I cannot help adding to the numerous citations already made, part of a description of the economical condition of those islands, by a writer who combines personal observation with an attentive study of the information afforded by others. Mr. William Thornton, in his *Plea for Peasant Proprietors*, a book which, by the excellence both of its materials and of its execution, deserves to be regarded as the standard work on that side of the question, speaks of the island of Guernsey in the following terms : " Not even in England is nearly so large a quantity of produce sent to market from a tract of such limited extent. This of itself might prove that the cultivators must be far removed above poverty, for being absolute owners of all the produce raised by them, they of course sell only what they do not themselves require. But the satisfactoriness of their condition is apparent to every observer. ' The happiest community,' says Mr. Hill, ' which it has ever been my lot to fall in with, is to be found in this little island of Guernsey.' ' No matter,' says Sir George Head, ' to what point the traveller may choose to bend his way, comfort everywhere prevails.' What most surprises the English visitor in his first walk or drive beyond the bounds of St. Peter's Port is the appearance of the habitations with which the landscape is thickly studded. Many of them are such as in his own country would belong to persons of middle rank ; but he is puzzled to guess what sort of people live in the other, which, though in general not large enough for farmers, are almost invariably much too good in every respect for day labourers. . . . Literally, in the whole island, with the exception of a few fishermen's huts, there is not one so mean as to be likened to the ordinary habitation of an English farm labourer. . . . ' Look,' says a late Bailiff of Guernsey, Mr. De L'Isle Brock, ' at the hovels of the English, and compare them with the cottages of our peasantry.' . . . Beggars are utterly unknown. . . . Pauperism, able-bodied pauperism at least, is

itself or in conjunction with agricultural ; and to be occasioned by a diminished demand for Belgic manufactures.

To the preceding testimonies respecting Germany, Switzerland, and Belgium, may be added the following from Niebuhr, respecting the Roman Campagna. In a letter from Tivoli, he says, " Wherever you find hereditary farmers, or small proprietors, there you also find industry and honesty. I believe that a man who would employ a large fortune in establishing small freeholds might put an end to robbery in the mountain districts."—*Life and Letters of Niebuhr*, vol. ii. p. 149.

[1] [This section was added to the 2nd ed. (1849).]

nearly as rare as mendicancy. The Savings Banks accounts also bear witness to the general abundance enjoyed by the labouring classes of Guernsey. In the year 1841, there were in England, out of a population of nearly fifteen millions, less than 700,000 depositors, or one in every twenty persons, and the average amount of the deposits was 30*l.* In Guernsey, in the same year, out of a population of 26,000, the number of depositors was 1920, and the average amount of the deposits 40*l.*" * The evidence as to Jersey and Alderney is of a similar character.

Of the efficiency and productiveness of agriculture on the small properties of the Channel Islands, Mr. Thornton produces ample evidence, the result of which he sums up as follows : " Thus it appears that in the two principal Channel Islands, the agricultural population is, in the one twice, and in the other three times, as dense as in Britain, there being in the latter country only one cultivator to twenty-two acres of cultivated land, while in Jersey there is one to eleven, and in Guernsey one to seven acres. Yet the agriculture of these islands maintains, besides cultivators, non-agricultural populations, respectively four and five times as dense as that of Britain. This difference does not arise from any superiority of soil or climate possessed by the Channel Islands, for the former is naturally rather poor, and the latter is not better than in the southern counties of England. It is owing entirely to the assiduous care of the farmers, and to the abundant use of manure."† " In the year 1837," he says in another place,‡ " the average yield of wheat in the large farms of England was only twenty-one bushels, and the highest average for any one county was no more than twenty-six bushels. The highest average since claimed for the whole of England is thirty bushels. In Jersey, where the average size of farms is only sixteen acres, the average produce of wheat per acre was stated by Inglis in 1834 to be thirty-six bushels ; but it is proved by official tables to have been forty bushels in the five years ending with 1833. In Guernsey, where farms are still smaller, four quarters per acre, according to Inglis, is considered a good, but still a very common crop." " Thirty shillings § an acre would be thought in England a very fair rent for middling land ; but in the Channel Islands, it is only very inferior land that would not let for at least 4*l.*"

§ 7.   It is from France that impressions unfavourable to peasant

* *A Plea for Peasant Proprietors.*   By William Thomas Thornton, pp. 99–104.
      † Ibid. p. 38.   ‡ Ibid. p. 9.   § Ibid. p. 32.

properties are generally drawn ; it is in France that the system is
so often asserted to have brought forth its fruit in the most wretched
possible agriculture, and to be rapidly reducing, if not to have already
reduced the peasantry, by subdivision of land, to the verge of
starvation. It is difficult to account for the general prevalence of
impressions so much the reverse of truth. The agriculture of France
was wretched and the peasantry in great indigence before the Revolution. At that time they were not, so universally as at present,
landed proprietors. There were, however, considerable districts
of France where the land, even then, was to a great extent the property of the peasantry, and among these were many of the most
conspicuous exceptions to the general bad agriculture and to the
general poverty. An authority, on this point, not to be disputed,
is Arthur Young, the inveterate enemy of small farms, the cory-
phæus of the modern English school of agriculturists ; who yet,
travelling over nearly the whole of France in 1787, 1788, and 1789,
when he finds remarkable excellence of cultivation, never hesitates
to ascribe it to peasant property. " Leaving Sauve," says he,*
" I was much struck with a large tract of land, seemingly nothing but
huge rocks ; yet most of it enclosed and planted with the most
industrious attention. Every man has an olive, a mulberry, an
almond, or a peach tree, and vines scattered among them ; so that
the whole ground is covered with the oddest mixture of these plants
and bulging rocks, that can be conceived. The inhabitants of this
village deserve encouragement for their industry ; and if I were a
French minister they should have it. They would soon turn all
the deserts around them into gardens. Such a knot of active
husbandmen, who turn their rocks into scenes of fertility, because
I suppose *their own*, would do the same by the wastes, if animated by
the same omnipotent principle." Again : † " Walk to Rossendal,"
(near Dunkirk) " where M. le Brun has an improvement on the
Dunes, which he very obligingly showed me. Between the town and
that place is a great number of neat little houses, built each with its
garden, and one or two fields enclosed, of most wretched blowing
dune sand, naturally as white as snow, but improved by industry.
The magic of *property* turns sand to gold." And again : ‡ " Going out
of Gange, I was surprised to find by far the greatest exertion in

* Arthur Young's *Travels in France*, v̥ol. i. p. 50. [In the edition of a
portion of the work by Miss Betham-Edwards, p. 53.]
† Ibid. p. 88 [ed. Betham-Edwards, p. 109].
‡ Ibid. p. 51 [ed. Betham-Edwards, p. 54].

irrigation which I had yet seen in France ; and then passed by some steep mountains, highly cultivated in terraces. Much watering at St. Lawrence. The scenery very interesting to a farmer. From Gange, to the mountain of rough ground which I crossed, the ride has been the most interesting which I have taken in France ; the efforts of industry the most vigorous ; the animation the most lively. An activity has been here, that has swept away all difficulties before it, and has clothed the very rocks with verdure. It would be a disgrace to common sense to ask the cause ; the enjoyment of property *must* have done it. Give a man the secure possession of a bleak rock, and he will turn it into a garden ; give him a nine years' lease of a garden, and he will convert it into a desert."

In his description of the country at the foot of the Western Pyrenees, he speaks no longer from surmise, but from knowledge. " Take * the road to Moneng, and come presently to a scene which was so new to me in France, that I could hardly believe my own eyes. A succession of many well-built, tight, and *comfortable* farming cottages built of stone and covered with tiles ; each having its little garden, enclosed by clipt thorn-hedges, with plenty of peach and other fruit-trees, some fine oaks scattered in the hedges, and young trees nursed up with so much care, that nothing but the foster-ing attention of the owner could effect anything like it. To every house belongs a farm, perfectly well enclosed, with grass borders mown and neatly kept around the corn-fields, with gates to pass from one enclosure to another. There are some parts of England (where small yeomen still remain) that resemble this country of Béarn ; but we have very little that is equal to what I have seen in this ride of twelve miles from Pau to Moneng. It is all in the hands of little proprietors, without the farms being so small as to occasion a vicious and miserable population. An air of neatness, warmth, and comfort breathes over the whole. It is visible in their new built houses and stables ; in their little gardens ; in their hedges ; in the courts before their doors ; even in the coops for their poultry, and the sties for their hogs. A peasant does not think of rendering his pig comfortable, if his own happiness hang by the thread of a nine years' lease. We are now in Béarn, within a few miles of the cradle of Henry IV. Do they inherit these blessings from that good prince ? The benignant genius of that good monarch seems to reign still over the country ; each peasant has *the fowl in the pot*."

* Young, vol. i. p. 56 [ed. Betham-Edwards, p. 61].

He frequently notices the excellence of the agriculture of French
Flanders, where the farms " are all small, and much in the hands of
little proprietors." *   In the Pays de Caux, also a country of small
properties, the agriculture was miserable ; of which his explanation
was that it " is a manufacturing country, and farming is but a
secondary pursuit to the cotton fabric, which spreads over the whole
of it." †   The same district is still a seat of manufactures, and a
country of small proprietors, and is now, whether we judge from the
appearance of the crops or from the official returns, one of the best
cultivated in France.   In " Flanders, Alsace, and part of Artois, as
well as on the banks of the Garonne, France possesses a husbandry
equal to our own." ‡   Those countries, and a considerable part of
Quercy, " are cultivated more like gardens than farms.   Perhaps
they are too much like gardens, from the smallness of properties." §
In those districts the admirable rotation of crops, so long practised
in Italy, but at that time generally neglected in France, was already
universal.   " The rapid succession of crops, the harvest of one being
but the signal of sowing immediately for a second," (the same fact
which strikes all observers in the valley of the Rhine) " can scarcely
be carried to greater perfection : and this is a point, perhaps, of all
others the most essential to good husbandry, when such crops are
so justly distributed as we generally find them in these provinces ;
cleaning and ameliorating ones being made the preparation for such
as foul and exhaust."

It must not, however, be supposed that Arthur Young's testimony
on the subject of peasant properties is uniformly favourable.   In
Lorraine, Champagne, and elsewhere, he finds the agriculture bad,
and the small proprietors very miserable, in consequence, as he says,
of the extreme subdivision of the land.   His opinion is thus summed
up : ‖ " Before I travelled, I conceived that small farms, in property,
were very susceptible of good cultivation ; and that the occupier of
such, having no rent to pay, might be sufficiently at his ease to work
improvements, and carry on a vigorous husbandry ; but what I
have seen in France, has greatly lessened my good opinion of them.
In Flanders, I saw excellent husbandry on properties of 30 to 100
acres ; but we seldom find here such small patches of property as
are common in other provinces.   In Alsace, and on the Garonne,
that is, on soils of such exuberant fertility as to demand no exertions,
some small properties also are well cultivated.   In Béarn, I passed

through a region of little farmers, whose appearance, neatness, ease, and happiness charmed me ; it was what property alone could, on a small scale, effect ; but these were by no means contemptibly small ; they are, as I judged by the distance from house to house, from 40 to 80 acres. Except these, and a very few other instances, I saw nothing respectable on small properties, except a most unremitting industry. Indeed, it is necessary to impress on the reader's mind, that though the husbandry I met with, in a great variety of instances on little properties, was as bad as can be well conceived, yet the industry of the possessors was so conspicuous, and so meritorious, that no commendations would be too great for it. It was sufficient to prove that property in land is, of all others, the most active instigator to severe and incessant labour. And this truth is of such force and extent, that I know no way so sure of carrying tillage to a mountain top, as by permitting the adjoining villagers to acquire it in property ; in fact, we see that in the mountains of Languedoc, &c., they have conveyed earth in baskets, on their backs, to form a soil where nature had denied it."

The experience, therefore, of this celebrated agriculturist and apostle of the *grande culture*, may be said to be, that the effect of small properties, cultivated by peasant. proprietors, is admirable when they are not *too* small : so small, namely, as not fully to occupy the time and attention of the family ; for he often complains, with great apparent reason, of the quantity of idle time which the peasantry had on their hands when the land was in very small portions, notwithstanding the ardour with which they toiled to improve their little patrimony in every way which their knowledge or ingenuity could suggest. He recommends, accordingly, that a limit of subdivision should be fixed by law ; and this is by no means an indefensible proposition in countries, if such there are, where the *morcellement*, having already gone farther than the state of capital and the nature of the staple articles of cultivation render advisable, still continues progressive. That each peasant should have a patch of land, even in full property, if it is not sufficient to support him in comfort, is a system with all the disadvantages, and scarcely any of the benefits, of small properties ; since he must either live in indigence on the produce of his land, or depend, as habitually as if he had no landed possessions, on the wages of hired labour : which, besides, if all the holdings surrounding him are of similar dimensions, he has little prospect of finding. The benefits of peasant properties are conditional on their not being too much subdivided ; that is, on their not being required to maintain too many persons, in proportion to the produce that can be raised from them by those persons. The question resolves itself, like most questions respecting the condition of the labouring classes, into one of population. Are small properties a stimulus to undue multiplication, or a check to it ?

§ 1. Before examining the influence of peasant properties on the ultimate economical interests of the labouring class, as determined by the increase of population, let us note the points respecting the moral and social influence of that territorial arrangement, which may be looked upon as established, either by the reason of the case, or by the facts and authorities cited in the preceding chapter.

The reader new to the subject must have been struck with the powerful impression made upon all the witnesses to whom I have referred, by what a Swiss statistical writer calls the " almost super-human industry " of peasant proprietors.* On this point, at least, authorities are unanimous. Those who have seen only one country of peasant properties always think the inhabitants of that country the most industrious in the world. There is as little doubt among observers, with what feature in the condition of the peasantry this pre-eminent industry is connected. It is the " magic of property " which, in the words of Arthur Young, " turns sand into gold." The idea of property does not, however, necessarily imply that there should be no rent, any more than that there should be no taxes. It merely implies that the rent should be a fixed charge, not liable to be raised against the possessor by his own improvements, or by the will of a landlord. A tenant at a quit-rent is, to all intents and purposes, a proprietor ; a copyholder is not less so than a freeholder. What is wanted is permanent possession on fixed terms. " Give a man the secure possession of a bleak rock, and he will turn it into a garden ; give him a nine years' lease of a garden, and he will convert it into a desert."

The details which have been cited, and those, still more minute, to be found in the same authorities, concerning the habitually elaborate system of cultivation, and the thousand devices of the peasant proprietor for making every superfluous hour and odd

* *Der Canton Schaffhausen* (ut supra), p. 53.

moment instrumental to some increase in the future produce and value of the land, will explain what has been said in a previous chapter * respecting the far larger gross produce which, with any-thing like parity of agricultural knowledge, is obtained from the same quality of soil on small farms, at least when they are the pro-perty of the cultivator. The treatise on *Flemish Husbandry* is especially instructive respecting the means by which untiring industry does more than outweigh inferiority of resources, im-perfection of implements, and ignorance of scientific theories. The peasant cultivation of Flanders and Italy is affirmed to produce heavier crops, in equal circumstances of soil, than the best cultivated districts of Scotland and England. It produces them, no doubt, with an amount of labour which, if paid for by an employer, would make the cost to him more than equivalent to the benefit ; but to the peasant it is not cost, it is the devotion of time which he can spare, to a favourite pursuit, if we should not rather say a ruling passion.†

[1] We have seen, too, that it is not solely by superior exertion that the Flemish cultivators succeed in obtaining these brilliant results. The same motive which gives such intensity to their industry, placed them earlier in possession of an amount of agricultural knowledge, not attained until much later in countries where agricul-ture was carried on solely by hired labour. An equally high testimony

* Supra, Book i. ch. ix. § 4.
† Read the graphic description by the historian Michelet, of the feelings of a peasant proprietor towards his land.

" If we would know the inmost thought, the passion, of the French peasant, it is very easy. Let us walk out on Sunday into the country and follow him. Behold him yonder, walking in front of us. It is two o'clock ; his wife is at vespers ; he has on his Sunday clothes ; I perceive that he is going to visit his mistress.

" What mistress ? His land.

" I do not say he goes straight to it. No, he is free to-day, and may either go or not. Does he not go every day in the week ? Accordingly, he turns aside, he goes another way, he has business elsewhere. And yet—he goes.

" It is true, he was passing close by ; it was an opportunity. He looks, but apparently he will not go in ; what for ? And yet—he enters.

" At least it is probable that he will not work ; he is in his Sunday dress : he has a clean shirt and blouse. Still, there is no harm in plucking up this weed and throwing out that stone. There is a stump, too, which is in the way ; but he has not his tools with him, ne will do it to-morrow.

" Then he folds his arms and gazes, serious and careful. He gives a long, a very long look, and seems lost in thought. At last, if he thinks himself observed, if he sees a passer-by, he moves slowly away. Thirty paces off he stops, turns round, and casts on his land a last look, sombre and profound, but to those who can see it, the look is full of passion, of heart, of devotion."—*Le Peuple*, by J. Michelet, 1re partie, ch. 1.

[1] [This paragraph was added in the 5th ed. (1862).]

is borne by M. de Lavergne * to the agricultural skill of the small proprietors in those parts of France to which the *petite culture* is really suitable. "In the rich plains of Flanders, on the banks of the Rhine, the Garonne, the Charente, the Rhone, all the practices which fertilize the land and increase the productiveness of labour are known to the very smallest cultivators, and practised by them, however considerable may be the advances which they require. In their hands, abundant manures, collected at great cost, repair and incessantly increase the fertility of the soil, in spite of the activity of cultivation. The races of cattle are superior, the crops magnificent. Tobacco, flax, colza, madder, beetroot, in some places; in others, the vine, the olive, the plum, the mulberry, only yield their abundant treasures to a population of industrious labourers. Is it not also to the *petite culture* that we are indebted for most of the garden produce obtained by dint of great outlay in the neighbourhood of Paris ? "

§ 2. Another aspect of peasant properties, in which it is essential that they should be considered, is that of an instrument of popular education. Books and schooling are absolutely necessary to education ; but not all-sufficient. The mental faculties will be most developed where they are most exercised ; and what gives more exercise to them than the having a multitude of interests, none of which can be neglected, and which can be provided for only by varied efforts of will and intelligence ? Some of the disparagers of small properties lay great stress on the cares and anxieties which beset the peasant proprietor of the Rhineland or Flanders. It is precisely those cares and anxieties which tend to make him a superior being to an English day-labourer. It is, to be sure, rather abusing the privileges of fair argument to represent the condition of a day-labourer as not an anxious one. I can conceive no circumstances in which he is free from anxiety, where there is a possibility of being out of employment ; unless he has access to a profuse dispensation of parish pay, and no shame or reluctance in demanding it.[1] The day-labourer has, in the existing state of society and

---

* *Essai sur l'Economie Rurale de l'Angleterre, de l'Ecosse, et de l'Irlande*, 3me éd. p. 127. [Cf. English translation in *Rural Economy of Great Britain and Ireland* (1855), p. 116.]

[1] [Here followed in the original text the following words, omitted in the 3rd ed, (1852) : " then indeed he may feel with the old doggrel—

Hang sorrow, cast away care,
The parish is bound to find us.

But unless so shielded, the day labourer," &c.]

population, many of the anxieties which have not an invigorating effect on the mind, and none of those which have. The position of the peasant proprietor of Continental Europe is the reverse. From the anxiety which chills and paralyses—the uncertainty of having food to eat—few persons are more exempt: it requires as rare a concurrence of circumstances as the potato failure combined with an universal bad harvest, to bring him within reach of that danger. His anxieties are the ordinary vicissitudes of more and less; his cares are that he takes his fair share of the business of life; that he is a free human being, and not perpetually a child, which seems to be the approved condition of the labouring classes according to the prevailing philanthropy. He is no longer a being of a different order from the middle classes; he has pursuits and objects like those which occupy them, and give to their intellects the greatest part of such cultivation as they receive. If there is a first principle in intellectual education, it is this—that the discipline which does good to the mind is that in which the mind is active, not that in which it is passive. The secret for developing the faculties is to give them much to do, and much inducement to do it. This detracts nothing from the importance, and even necessity, of other kinds of mental cultivation. The possession of property will not prevent the peasant from being coarse, selfish, and narrow-minded. These things depend on other influences and other kinds of instruction. But this great stimulus to one kind of mental activity in no way impedes any other means of intellectual develop-ment. On the contrary, by cultivating the habit of turning to practical use every fragment of knowledge acquired, it helps to render that schooling and reading fruitful, which without some such auxiliary influence are in too many cases like seed thrown on a rock.

§ 3. It is not on the intelligence alone that the situation of a peasant proprietor exercises an improving influence. It is no less propitious to the moral virtues of prudence, temperance, and self-control. Day-labourers, where the labouring class mainly consists of them, are usually improvident: they spend carelessly to the full extent of their means, and let the future shift for itself. This is so notorious, that many persons strongly interested in the welfare of the labouring classes, hold it as a fixed opinion that an increase of wages would do them little good, unless accompanied by at least a corresponding improvement in their tastes and habits. The tendency of peasant proprietors, and of those who hope to become proprietors, is to the contrary extreme ; to take even too much thought for the morrow. They are oftener accused of penuriousness than of prodigality. They deny themselves reasonable indulgences, and live wretchedly in order to economize. In Switzerland almost everybody saves, who has any means of saving ; the case of the Flemish farmers has been already noticed : among the French, though a pleasure-loving and reputed to be a self-indulgent people, the spirit of thrift is diffused through the rural population in a manner most gratifying as a whole, and which in individual instances errs rather on the side of excess than defect. Among those who, from the hovels in which they live, and the herbs and roots which constitute their diet, are mistaken by travellers for proofs and specimens of general indigence, there are numbers who have hoards in leathern bags, consisting of sums in five-franc pieces, which they keep by them perhaps for a whole generation, unless brought out to be expended in their most cherished gratification—the purchase of land. If there is a moral inconvenience attached to a state of society in which the peasantry have land, it is the danger of their being too careful of their pecuniary concerns ; of its making them crafty, and " calculating " in the objectionable sense. The French peasant is no simple countryman, no downright " paysan du Danube ; " both in fact and in fiction he is now " le rusé paysan." That is the stage which he has reached in the progressive development which the constitution of things has imposed on human intelligence and human emancipation. But some excess in this direction is a small and a passing evil compared with recklessness and improvidence in the labouring classes, and a cheap price to pay for the inestimable worth of the virtue of self-dependence, as the general characteristic of a people : a virtue which is one of the first conditions of excellence in the human character—the stock on which if the other virtues are not grafted, they have seldom any firm root ; a quality indispensable in the case of a labouring class, even to any tolerable degree of physical comfort ; and by which the peasantry of France, and of most European countries of peasant proprietors, are distinguished beyond any other labouring population.

§ 4. Is it likely that a state of economical relations so conducive to frugality and prudence in every other respect, should be prejudicial to it in the cardinal point of increase of population ? That it is so, is the opinion expressed by most of those English political economists who have written anything about the matter.

Mr. M'Culloch's opinion is well known. Mr. Jones affirms,* that a
" peasant population raising their own wages from the soil, and
consuming them in kind, are universally acted upon very feebly by
internal checks, or by motives disposing them to restraint. The
consequence is, that unless some external cause, quite independent
of their will, forces such peasant cultivators to slacken their rate
of increase, they will, in a limited territory, very rapidly approach
a state of want and penury, and will be stopped at last only by the
physical impossibility of procuring subsistence." He elsewhere †
speaks of such a peasantry as " exactly in the condition in which
the animal disposition to increase their numbers is checked by the
fewest of those balancing motives and desires which regulate the
increase of superior ranks or more civilized people." The " causes of
this peculiarity," Mr. Jones promised to point out in a subsequent
work, which never made its appearance. I am totally unable to conjecture from what theory of human nature, and of the motives which
influence human conduct, he would have derived them. Arthur
Young assumes the same " peculiarity," as a fact ; but, though not
much in the habit of qualifying his opinions, he does not push his
doctrine to so violent an extreme as Mr. Jones ; having, as we have
seen, himself testified to various instances in which peasant populations such as Mr. Jones speaks of, were not tending to " a state of
want and penury," and were in no danger whatever of coming into
contact with " physical impossibility of procuring subsistence."

That there should be discrepancy of experience on this matter,
is easily to be accounted for. Whether the labouring people live
by land or by wages, they have always hitherto multiplied up to the
limit set by their habitual standard of comfort. When that standard
was low, not exceeding a scanty subsistence, the size of properties,
as well as the rate of wages, has been kept down to what would
barely support life. Extremely low ideas of what is necessary for
subsistence, are perfectly compatible with peasant properties ; and
if a people have always been used to poverty, and habit has reconciled them to it, there will be over-population, and excessive subdivision of land. But this is not to the purpose. The true question is,
supposing a peasantry to possess land not insufficient but sufficient
for their comfortable support, are they more, or less, likely to fall
from this state of comfort through improvident multiplication,
than if they were living in an equally comfortable manner as hired

* *Essay on the Distribution of Wealth*, p. 146. [*Peasant Rents*, p. 132.]
† Ibid. p. 68. [*Peasant Rents*, p. 59.]

labourers ? All *à priori* considerations are in favour of their being less likely. The dependence of wages on population is a matter of speculation and discussion. That wages would fall if population were much increased is often a matter of real doubt, and always a thing which requires some exercise of the thinking faculty for its intelligent recognition. But every peasant can satisfy himself from evidence which he can fully appreciate, whether his piece of land can be made to support several families in the same comfort as it supports one. Few people like to leave to their children a worse lot in life than their own. The parent who has land to leave is perfectly able to judge whether the children can live upon it or not : but people who are supported by wages see no reason why their sons should be unable to support themselves in the same way, and trust accordingly to chance. " In even the most useful and necessary arts and manufactures," says Mr. Laing,* " the demand for labourers is not a seen, known, steady, and appreciable demand : but it is so in husbandry " under small properties. " The labour to be done, the subsistence that labour will produce out of his portion of land, are seen and known elements in a man's cal-culation upon his means of subsistence. Can his square of land, or can it not, subsist a family ? Can he marry or not ? are questions which every man can answer without delay, doubt, or speculation. It is the depending on chance, where judgment has nothing clearly set before it, that causes reckless, improvident marriages in the lower, as in the higher classes, and produces among us the evils of over-population ; and chance necessarily enters into every man's calculations, when certainty is removed altogether ; as it is, where certain subsistence is, by our distribution of property, the lot of but a small portion instead of about two-thirds of the people."

There never has been a writer more keenly sensible of the evils brought upon the labouring classes by excess of population than Sismondi, and this is one of the grounds of his earnest advocacy of peasant properties. He had ample opportunity, in more countries than one, for judging of their effect on population. Let us see his testimony. " In the countries in which cultivation by small pro-prietors still continues, population increases regularly and rapidly until it has attained its natural limits ; that is to say, inheritances continue to be divided and subdivided among several sons, as long as, by an increase of labour, each family can extract an equal in-come from a smaller portion of land. A father who possessed a

* *Notes of a Traveller*, p. 46.

vast extent of natural pasture, divides it among his sons, and they
turn it into fields and meadows ; his sons divide it among their sons,
who abolish fallows : each improvement in agricultural knowledge
admits of another step in the subdivision of property. But there
is no danger lest the proprietor should bring up his children to make
beggars of them. He knows exactly what inheritance he has to
leave them ; he knows that the law will divide it equally among
them ; he sees the limit beyond which this division would make
them descend from the rank which he has himself filled, and a just
family pride, common to the peasant and to the nobleman, makes
him abstain from summoning into life children for whom he cannot
properly provide. If more are born, at least they do not marry, or
they agree among themselves which of several brothers shall perpetuate the family. It is not found that in the Swiss Cantons the
patrimonies of the peasants are ever so divided as to reduce them
below an honourable competence ; though the habit of foreign
service, by opening to the children a career indefinite and uncal-
culable, sometimes calls forth a super-abundant population." *

There is similar testimony respecting Norway. Though there is
no law or custom of primogeniture, and no manufactures to take off
a surplus population, the subdivision of property is not carried to an
injurious extent. " The division of the land among children,"
says Mr. Laing,† " appears not, during the thousand years it has
been in operation, to have had the effect of reducing the landed
properties to the minimum size that will barely support human
existence. I have counted from five-and-twenty to forty cows
upon farms, and that in a country in which the farmer must, for at
least seven months in the year, have winter provender and houses
provided for all the cattle. It is evident that some cause or other,
operating on aggregation of landed property, counteracts the dividing effects of partition among children. That cause can be no
other than what I have long conjectured would be effective in such
a social arrangement ; viz. that in a country where land is held, not
in tenancy merely, as in Ireland, but in full ownership, its aggregation by the deaths of co-heirs, and by the marriages of the female
heirs among the body of landholders, will balance its subdivision
by the equal succession of children. The whole mass of property
will, I conceive, be found in such a state of society to consist of as
many estates of the class of 1000*l.*, as many of 100*l.*, as many of 10*l.*,
a year, at one period as another." That this should happen, supposes

---

* *Nouveaux Principes*, Book iii. ch. 3.   † *Residence in Norway*, p. 18.

diffused through society a very efficacious prudential check to population ; and it is reasonable to give part of the credit of this prudential
restraint to the peculiar adaptation of the peasant-proprietary
system for fostering it.

[1] " In some parts of Switzerland," says Mr. Kay,* " as in the
canton of Argovie for instance, a peasant never marries before he
attains the age of twenty-five years, and generally much later in life ;
and in that canton the women very seldom marry before they have
attained the age of thirty. . . . Nor do the division of land and the
cheapness of the mode of conveying it from one man to another
encourage the providence of the labourers of the rural districts only.
They act in the same manner, though perhaps in a less degree, upon
the labourers of the smaller towns. In the smaller provincial towns
it is customary for a labourer to own a small plot of ground outside
the town. This plot he cultivates in the evening as his kitchen
garden. He raises in it vegetables and fruits for the use of his
family during the winter. After his day's work is over, he and his
family repair to the garden for a short time, which they spend in
planting, sowing, weeding, or preparing for sowing or harvest,
according to the season. The desire to become possessed of one of
these gardens operates very strongly in strengthening prudential
habits and in restraining improvident marriages. Some of the
manufacturers in the canton of Argovie told me that a townsman
was seldom contented until he had bought a garden, or a garden and
house, and that the town labourers generally deferred their marriages
for some years, in order to save enough to purchase either one or
both of these luxuries."

The same writer shows by statistical evidence † that in Prussia
the average age of marriage is not only much later than in England,
but " is gradually becoming later than it was formerly," while at
the same time " fewer illegitimate children are born in Prussia than
in any other of the European countries." " Wherever I travelled,"
says Mr. Kay, ‡ " in North Germany and Switzerland, I was assured
by all that the desire to obtain land, which was felt by all the
peasants, was acting as the strongest possible check upon undue
increase of population." §

In Flanders, according to Mr. Fauche, the British Consul at

---

[1] [This and the next two paragraphs were added in the 3rd ed. (1852).]
* Vol. i. pp. 67–9.　　† Vol. i. pp. 75–9.　　‡ Ibid. p. 90.
§ The Prussian minister of statistics, in a work (*Der Volkswohlstand im
Preussischen Staate*) which I am obliged to quote at second hand from Mr. Kay,
after proving by figures the great and progressive increase of the consumption

Ostend,* " farmers' sons and those who have the means to become
farmers will delay their marriage until they get possession of a
farm." Once a farmer, the next object is to become a proprietor.
" The first thing a Dane does with his savings," says Mr. Browne,
the Consul at Copenhagen,† " is to purchase a clock, then a horse
and cow, which he hires out, and which pays a good interest. Then
his ambition is to become a petty proprietor, and this class of
persons is better off than any in Denmark. Indeed, I know of no
people in any country who have more easily within their reach all
that is really necessary for life than this class, which is very large in
comparison with that of labourers."

But the experience which most decidedly contradicts the asserted
tendency of peasant proprietorship to produce excess of population,
is the case of France. In that country the experiment is not tried
in the most favourable circumstances, a large proportion of the
properties being too small. The number of landed proprietors in
France is not exactly ascertained, but on no estimate does it fall
much short of five millions ; which, on the lowest calculation of the
number of persons of a family (and for France it ought to be a low
calculation), shows much more than half the population as either
possessing, or entitled to inherit, landed property. A majority of
the properties are so small as not to afford a subsistence to the proprietors, of whom, according to some computations, as many as
three millions are obliged to eke out their means of support either
by working for hire, or by taking additional land, generally on
metayer tenure. When the property possessed is not sufficient to
relieve the possessor from dependence on wages, the condition of a
proprietor loses much of its characteristic efficacy as a check to
over-population : and if the prediction so often made in England
had been realized, and France had become a " pauper warren," the
experiment would have proved nothing against the tendencies of
the same system of agricultural economy in other circumstances.
But what is the fact ? That the rate of increase of the French

of food and clothing per head of the population, from which he justly infers a
corresponding increase of the productiveness of agriculture, continues : " The
division of estates has, since 1831, proceeded more and more throughout the
country. There are now many more small independent proprietors than
formerly. Yet, however many complaints of pauperism are heard among the
dependent labourers, we never hear it complained that pauperism is increasing
among the peasant proprietors."—Kay, i. 262-6.

* In a communication to the Commissioners of Poor Law Enquiry, p. 640
of their Foreign Communications, Appendix F to their First Report.
† Ibid. 268.

population is the slowest in Europe. During the generation which the Revolution raised from the extreme of hopeless wretchedness to sudden abundance, a great increase of population took place. But a generation has grown up, which, having been born in improved circumstances, has not learnt to be miserable ; and upon them the spirit of thrift operates most conspicuously, in keeping the increase of population within the increase of national wealth. In a table drawn up by Professor Rau,* of the rate of annual increase of the

* The following is the table (see p. 168 of the Belgian translation of Mr. Rau's large work) :

		Per cent.			Per cent.
United States .	1820–30 .	. 2·92	Scotland . .	1821–31 .	. 1·30
Hungary (according to Rohrer)		2·40	Saxony . .	1815–30 .	. 1·15
England . .	1811–21 .	. 1·78	Baden .	1820–30 (Heunisch)	1·13
,, . .	1821–31 .	. 1·60	Bavaria . .	1814–28 .	. 1·08
Austria (Rohrer)	. . . .	. 1·30	Naples . . .	1814–24 .	. 0·83
Prussia . . .	1816–27 .	. 1·54	France . .	1817–27 (Mathieu)	0·63
,, . . .	1820–30 .	. 1·37	and more recently (Moreau de		
,, . . .	1821–31 .	. 1·27	Jonnès)		0·55
Netherlands .	1821–28 .	. 1·28			

But the number given by Moreau de Jonnès, he adds, is not entitled to implicit confidence.

The following table given by M. Quetelet (*Sur l'Homme et le Développement de ses Facultés*, vol. i. ch. 7) also on the authority of Rau, contains additional matter, and differs in some items from the preceding, probably from the author's having taken, in those cases, an average of different years :

	Per cent.		Per cent.		Per cent.
Ireland . .	. 2·45	Rhenish Prussia .	1·33	Naples . . .	. 0·83
Hungary . .	. 2·40	Austria . .	. 1·30	France . . .	. 0·63
Spain . . .	. 1·66	Bavaria . .	. 1·08	Sweden . .	. 0·58
England . .	. 1·65	Netherlands .	. 0·94	Lombardy . .	. 0·45

A very carefully prepared statement, by M. Legoyt, in the *Journal des Economistes* for May 1847, which brings up the results for France to the census of the preceding year 1846, is summed up in the following table :

	According to the census.	According to the excess of births over deaths.		According to the census.	According to the excess of births over deaths.
	per cent.	per cent.		per cent.	per cent.
Sweden . .	0·83	1·14	Wurtemburg .	0·01	1·00
Norway . .	1·36	1·30	Holland . .	0·90	1·03
Denmark . .	..	0·95	Belgium . .	..	0·76
Russia . .	..	0·61	Sardinia . .	1·08	..
Austria . .	0·85	0·90	Great Britain		
Prussia . .	1·84	1·18	(exclusive of Ireland)	} 1·95	1·00
Saxony . .	1·45	0·90			
Hanover . .	..	0·85	France . . .	0·68	0·50
Bavaria . .	..	0·71	United States .	3·27	..

populations of various countries, that of France, from 1817 to 1827, is stated at $\frac{63}{100}$ per cent, that of England during a similar decennial period being $1\frac{6}{10}$ annually, and that of the United States nearly 3. According to the official returns as analysed by M. Legóyt,* the increase of the population, which from 1801 to 1806 was at the rate of 1·28 per cent annually, averaged only 0·47 per cent from 1806 to 1831 ; from 1831 to 1836 it averaged 0·60 per cent ; from 1836 to 1841, 0·41 per cent, and from 1841 to 1846, 0·68 per cent.† ¹ At the census of 1851 the rate of annual increase shown was only 1·08 per cent in the five years, or 0·21 annually ; and at the census of 1856 only 0·71 per cent in five years, or 0·14 annually : so that, in the words of M. de Lavergne, "la population ne s'accroît presque plus en France." ‡ Even this slow increase is wholly the effect of a diminution of deaths ; the number of births not increasing at all, while the proportion of the births to the population is constantly diminishing.§ This slow growth of the numbers of the people, while

* *Journal des Economistes* for March and May 1847.

† M. Legoyt is of opinion that the population was understated in 1841, and the increase between that time and 1846 consequently overstated, and that the real increase during the whole period was something intermediate between the last two averages, or not much more than one in two hundred.

¹ [This sentence was added to the 4th ed. (1857).]

‡ *Journal des Economistes* for February 1847.—[1865] In the Journal for January 1865, M. Legoyt gives some of the numbers slightly altered, and I presume corrected. The series of percentages is 1·28, 0·31, 0·69, 0·60, 0·41, 0·68, 0·22, and 0·20. The last census in the table, that of 1861, shows a slight reaction, the percentage, independently of the newly acquired departments, being 0·32. [M. Emile Levasseur (*La Population Francaise*, 1889, vol. i. p. 315) cites a calculation of M. Loua, according to which the increase per cent for the territory which has constituted France since 1871, was for the period 1801–1821 0·56 ; 1821–1841, 0·59 ; 1841–1861, 0·36 ; 1861–1881, 0·27.]

§ The following are the numbers given by M. Legoyt :

From 1824 to 1828 } annual number	{ 981,914, being	1 in 32·30 } of the popu-
of births		lation.
,, 1829 to 1833	,,	965,444, ,,	1 in 34·00
,, 1834 to 1838	,,	972,993, ,,	1 in 34·39
,, 1839 to 1843	,,	970,617, ,,	1 in 35·27
,, 1844 and 1845	,,	983,573, ,,	1 in 35·58

In the last two years the births, according to M. Legoyt, were swelled by the effects of a considerable immigration. "This diminution of births," he observes, "while there is a constant, though not a rapid increase both of population and of marriages, can only be attributed to the progress of prudence and forethought in families. It was a foreseen consequence of our civil and social institutions, which, producing a daily increasing subdivision of fortunes, both landed and moveable, call forth in our people the instincts of conservation and of comfort."

In four departments, among which are two of the most thriving in Normandy, the deaths even then exceeded the births.—[1857] The census of 1856

capital increases much more rapidly, has caused a noticeable improvement in the condition of the labouring class. The circumstances of that portion of the class who are landed proprietors are not easily ascertained with precision, being of course extremely variable; but the mere labourers, who derived no direct benefit from the changes in landed property which took place at the Revolution, have unquestionably much improved in condition since that period.*

exhibits the remarkable fact of a positive diminution in the population of 54 out of the 86 departments. A significant comment on the pauper-warren theory. See M. de Lavergne's analysis of the returns.

* "The classes of our population which have only wages, and are therefore the most exposed to indigence, are now (1846) much better provided with the necessaries of food, lodging, and clothing than they were at the beginning of the century. This may be proved by the testimony of all persons who can remember the earlier of the two periods compared. Were there any doubts on the subject they might easily be dissipated by consulting old cultivators and workmen, as I have myself done in various localities, without meeting with a single contrary testimony; we may also appeal to the facts collected by an accurate observer, M. Villermé (*Tableau de l'État Physique et Moral des Ouvriers*, liv. ii. ch. i.)." From an intelligent work published in 1846, *Recherches sur les Causes de l'Indigence*, par A. Clément, pp. 84–5. The same writer speaks (p. 118) of: "the considerable rise which has taken place since 1789 in the wages of agricultural day-labourers;" and adds the following evidence of a higher standard of habitual requirements, even in that portion of the town population, the state of which is usually represented as most deplorable. "In the last fifteen or twenty years a considerable change has taken place in the habits of the operatives in our manufacturing towns: they now expend much more than formerly on clothing and ornament. . . . Certain classes of workpeople, such as the *canuts* of Lyons," (according to all representations, like their counterpart, our handloom weavers, the very worst paid class of artizans,) "no longer show themselves, as they did formerly, covered with filthy rags." (Page 164.)

[1862] The preceding statements were given in former editions of this work, being the best to which I had at the time access; but evidence, both of a more recent, and of a more minute and precise character, will now be found in the important work of M. Léonce de Lavergne, *Economie Rurale de la France depuis* 1789. According to that painstaking, well-informed, and most impartial enquirer, the average daily wages of a French labourer have risen, since the commencement of the Revolution, in the ratio of 19 to 30, while, owing to the more constant employment, the total earnings have increased in a still greater ratio, not short of double. The following are the words of M. de Lavergne (2nd ed. p. 57): "Arthur Young estimates at 19 sous [9½d.] the average of a day's wages, which must now be about 1 franc 50 centimes [1s. 3d.], and this increase only represents a part of the improvement. Though the rural population has remained about the same in numbers, the addition made to the population since 1789 having centred in the towns, the number of actual working days has increased, first because, the duration of life having augmented, the number of able-bodied men is greater, and next, because labour is better organized, partly through the suppression of several festival-holidays, partly by the mere effect of a more active demand. When we take into account the increased number of his working days, the annual receipts of the rural workman must have doubled. This augmentation of wages answers to at least an equal augmentation of comforts, since the prices of the chief necessaries of life have changed but little, and those of manufactured, for example of woven,

Dr. Rau testifies to a similar fact in the case of another country in which the subdivision of the land is probably excessive, the Palatinate.*

I am not aware of a single authentic instance which supports the assertion that rapid multiplication is promoted by peasant properties. Instances may undoubtedly be cited of its not being prevented by them, and one of the principal of these is Belgium ; the prospects of which, in respect to population, are at present a matter of considerable uncertainty. Belgium has the most rapidly increasing population on the Continent ; and when the circumstances of the country require, as they must soon do, that this rapidity should be checked, there will be a considerable strength of existing habit to be broken through. One of the unfavourable circumstances is the great power possessed over the minds of the people by the Catholic priesthood, whose influence is everywhere strongly exerted against restraining population. As yet, however, it must be remembered that the indefatigable industry and great agricultural skill of the people have rendered the existing rapidity of increase practically innocuous ; the great number of large estates still undivided affording by their gradual dismemberment a resource for the necessary augmentation of the gross produce ; and there are, besides, many large manufacturing towns, and mining and coal districts, which attract and employ a considerable portion of the annual increase of population.

§ 5. But even where peasant properties are accompanied by

articles, have materially diminished. The lodging of the labourers has also improved, if not in all, at least in most of our provinces."

M. de Lavergne's estimate of the average amount of a day's wages is grounded on a careful comparison, in this and in all other economical points of view, of all the different provinces of France.

* In his little book on the agriculture of the Palatinate, already cited. He says that the daily wages of labour, which during the last years of the war were unusually high, and so continued until 1817, afterwards sank to a lower money-rate, but that the prices of many commodities having fallen in a still greater proportion, the condition of the people was unequivocally improved. The food given to farm labourers by their employers has also greatly improved in quantity and quality. "It is to-day considerably better than it was about forty years ago, when the poorer class obtained less flesh-meat and puddings, and no cheese, butter, and the like " (p. 20). " Such an increase of wages " (adds the Professor), " which must be estimated not in money, but in the quantity of necessaries and conveniences which the labourer is enabled to procure, is, by universal admission, a proof that the mass of capital must have increased." It proves not only this, but also that the labouring population has not increased in an equal degree ; and that, in this instance as well as in that of France, the division of the land, even when excessive, has been compatible with a strengthening of the prudential checks to population.

an excess of numbers, this evil is not necessarily attended with the additional economical disadvantage of too great a subdivision of the land. It does not follow because landed property is minutely divided, that farms will be so. As large properties are perfectly compatible with small farms, so are small properties with farms of an adequate size ; and a subdivision of occupancy is not an inevitable consequence of even undue multiplication among peasant proprietors. As might be expected from their admirable intelligence in things relating to their occupation, the Flemish peasantry have long learnt this lesson. " The habit of not dividing properties," says Dr. Rau,* " and the opinion that this is advantageous, have been so completely preserved in Flanders, that even now, when a peasant dies leaving several children, they do not think of dividing his patrimony, though it be neither entailed nor settled in trust ; they prefer selling it entire, and sharing the proceeds, considering it as a jewel which loses its value when it is divided." That the same feeling must prevail widely even in France, is shown by the great frequency of sales of land, amounting in ten years to a fourth part of the whole soil of the country : and M. Passy, in his tract *On the Changes in the Agricultural Condition of the Department of the Eure since the year 1800,*† states other facts tending to the same conclusion. " The example," says he, " of this department attests that there does not exist, as some writers have imagined, between the distribution of property and that of cultivation, a connexion which tends invincibly to assimilate them. In no portion of it have changes of ownership had a perceptible influence on the size of holdings. While, in districts of small farming, lands belonging to the same owner are ordinarily distributed among many tenants, so neither is it uncommon, in places where the *grande culture* prevails, for the same farmer to rent the lands of several proprietors. In the plains of Vexin, in particular, many active and rich cultivators do not content themselves with a single farm ; others add to the lands of their principal holding all those in the neighbourhood which they are able to hire, and in this manner make up a total extent which in some cases reaches or exceeds two hundred hectares " (five hundred English acres). " The more the estates are

* Page 334 of the Brussels translation. He cites as an authority, Schwerz, *Landwirthschaftliche Mittheilungen,* i. 185.

† One of the many important papers which have appeared in the *Journal des Economistes,* the organ of the principal political economists of France, and doing great and increasing honour to their knowledge and ability. M. Passy's essay has been reprinted separately in a pamphlet.

dismembered, the more frequent do this sort of arrangements become : and as they conduce to the interest of all concerned, it is probable that time will confirm them."

[1] " In some places," says M. de Lavergne,[*] "in the neighbourhood of Paris, for example, where the advantages of the *grande culture* become evident, the size of farms tends to increase, several farms are thrown together into one, and farmers enlarge their holdings by renting *parcelles* from a number of different proprietors. Elsewhere farms, as well as properties of too great extent, tend to division. Cultivation spontaneously finds out the organization which suits it best." It is a striking fact, stated by the same eminent writer,[†] that the departments which have the greatest number of small *côtes foncières*, are the Nord, the Somme, the Pas de Calais, the Seine Inférieure, the Aisne, and the Oise ; all of them among the richest and best cultivated, and the first-mentioned of them the very richest and best cultivated, in France.

Undue subdivision, and excessive smallness of holdings, are undoubtedly a prevalent evil in some countries of peasant proprietors, and particularly in parts of Germany and France. The governments of Bavaria and Nassau have thought it necessary to impose a legal limit to subdivision, and the Prussian Government unsuccessfully proposed the same measure to the Estates of its Rhenish Provinces. But I do not think it will anywhere be found that the *petite culture* is the system of the peasants, and the *grande culture* that of the great landlords : on the contrary, wherever the small properties are divided among too many proprietors, I believe it to be true that the large properties also are parcelled out among too many farmers, and that the cause is the same in both cases, a backward state of capital, skill, and agricultural enterprise. There is reason to believe that the subdivision in France is not more excessive than is accounted for by this cause ; that it is diminishing, not increasing ; and that the terror expressed in some quarters, at the progress of the *morcellement*, is one of the most groundless of real or pretended panics. [‡]

[1] [This paragraph was added in the 5th ed. (1862).]
[*] *Economie Rurale de la France*, p. 455.
[†] P. 117. See, for facts of a similar tendency, pp. 141, 250, and other passages of the same important treatise : which, on the other hand, equally abounds with evidence of the mischievous effect of subdivision when too minute, or when the nature of the soil and of its products is not suitable to it.
[‡] [1852] Mr. Laing, in his latest publication, *Observations on the Social and Political State of the European People in 1848 and 1849*, a book devoted

If peasant properties have any effect in promoting subdivision beyond the degree which corresponds to the agricultural practices of the country, and which is customary on its large estates, the cause must lie in one of the salutary influences of the system ; the eminent degree in which it promotes providence on the part of those who, not being yet peasant proprietors, hope to become so. In England, where the agricultural labourer has no investment for his savings but the savings bank, and no position to which he can rise by any exercise of economy, except perhaps that of a petty shopkeeper, with its chances of bankruptcy, there is nothing at all resembling the intense spirit of thrift which takes possession of one who, from being a day labourer, can raise himself by saving to the condition of a landed proprietor. According to almost all authorities, the real cause of the *morcellement* is the higher price which can be obtained for land by selling it to the peasantry, as an investment for their small accumulations, than by disposing of it entire to some rich purchaser who has no object but to live on its income, without improving it. The hope of obtaining such an investment is the most powerful of inducements, to those who are without land, to practise the industry, frugality, and self-restraint, on which their success in this object of ambition is dependent.

As the result of this enquiry into the direct operation and indirect

to the glorification of England and the disparagement of everything elsewhere which others, or even he himself in former works, had thought worthy of praise, argues that " although the land itself is not divided and subdivided " on the death of the proprietor, " the value of the land is, and with effects almost as prejudicial to social progress. The value of each share becomes a debt or burden upon the land." Consequently the condition of the agricultural population is retrograde ; " each generation is worse off than the preceding one, although the land is neither less nor more divided, nor worse cultivated." And this he gives as the explanation of the great indebtedness of the small landed proprietors in France (pp. 97-9). If these statements were correct, they would invalidate all which Mr. Laing affirmed so positively in other writings, and repeats in this, respecting the peculiar efficacy of the possession of land in preventing over-population. But he is entirely mistaken as to the matter of fact. In the only country of which he speaks from actual residence, Norway, he does not pretend that the condition of the peasant proprietors is deteriorating. The facts already cited prove that in respect to Belgium, Germany, and Switzerland, he assertion is equally wide of the mark ; and what has been shown respecting the slow increase of population in France, demonstrates that if the condition of the French peasantry was deteriorating, it could not be from the cause supposed by Mr. Laing. The truth I believe to be that in every country without exception, in which peasant properties prevail, the condition of the people is improving, the produce of the land and even its fertility increasing, and from the larger surplus which remains after feeding the agricultural classes, the towns are augmenting both in population and in the well-being of their inhabitants.

influences of peasant properties, I conceive it to be established, that there is no necessary connexion between this form of landed property and an imperfect state of the arts of production ; that it is favourable in quite as many respects as it is unfavourable, to the most effective use of the powers of the soil ; that no other existing state of agricultural economy has so beneficial an effect on the industry, the intelligence, the frugality, and prudence of the population, nor tends on the whole so much to discourage an improvident increase of their numbers ; and that no existing state, therefore, is on the whole so favourable both to their moral and their physical welfare. Compared with the English system of cultivation by hired labour, it must be regarded as eminently beneficial to the labouring class.*   We are not on the present occasion called upon to

* French history strikingly confirms these conclusions. Three times during the course of ages the peasantry have been purchasers of land ; and these times immediately preceded the three principal eras of French agricultural prosperity.

"In the worst times," says the historian Michelet (*Le Peuple*, 1re partie, ch. 1), " the times of universal poverty, when even the rich are poor and obliged to sell, the poor are enabled to buy : no other purchaser presenting himself, the peasant in rags arrives with his piece of gold, and acquires a little bit of land. These moments of disaster in which the peasant was able to buy land at a low price, have always been followed by a sudden gush of prosperity which people could not account for. Towards 1500, for example, when France, ex-hausted by Louis XI., seemed to be completing its ruin in Italy, the noblesse who went to the wars were obliged to sell : the land, passing into new hands, suddenly began to flourish : men began to labour and to build. This happy moment, in the style of courtly historians, was called *the good Louis XII.*

" Unhappily it did not last long. Scarcely had the land recovered itself when the tax-collector fell upon it ; the wars of religion followed, and seemed to rase everything to the ground ; with horrible miseries, dreadful famines, in which mothers devoured their children. Who would believe that the country recovered from this ? Scarcely is the war ended, when from the devastated fields, and the cottages still black with the flames, comes forth the hoard of the peasant. He buys ; in ten years, France wears a new face ; in twenty or thirty, all possessions have doubled and trebled in value. This moment, again baptized by a royal name, is called *the good Henry IV.* and *the great Richelieu.*"

Of the third era it is needless again to speak : it was that of the Revolution.

Whoever would study the reverse of the picture, may compare these historic periods, characterized by the dismemberment of large and the construction of small properties, with the wide-spread national suffering which accompanied, and the permanent deterioration of the condition of the labouring classes which followed the " clearing " away of small yeomen to make room for large grazing farms, which was the grand economical event of English history during the sixteenth century. [This quotation from Michelet originally came at the end of chapter x, infra, on *Means of Abolishing Cottier Tenancy.* It was transferred to its present position in the 5th ed. (1862).]

compare it with the joint ownership of the land by associations of labourers.[1]

---

[1] [The last two sentences replaced in the 3rd ed. (1852) the concluding sentence of the original text : " Whether and in what these considerations admit of useful application to any of the social questions of our time, will be considered in a future chapter."

The position of peasant proprietors in Germany in more recent decades may be studied in Buchenberger, *Agrarwesen*, one of the volumes in Wagner's *Lehrbuch der Politischen Oekonomie* (1892), §§ 69, 70, 73 ; Blondel, *Études sur les Populations Rurales de l'Allemagne* (1897) ; and David, *Sozialismus and Landwirthschaft* (1903). As to whether *morcellement* is progressing in France, see Gide, *Économic Sociale* (1905), pp. 429 seq.]

CHAPTER VIII

§ 1. FROM the case in which the produce of land and labour belongs undividedly to the labourer, we proceed to the cases in which it is divided, but between two classes only, the labourers and the landowners : the character of capitalists merging in the one or the other, as the case may be. It is possible indeed to conceive that there might be only two classes of persons to share the produce, and that the class of capitalists might be one of them ; the character of labourer and that of landowner being united to form the other. This might occur in two ways. The labourers, though owning the land, might let it to a tenant, and work under him as hired servants. But this arrangement, even in the very rare cases which could give rise to it, would not require any particular discussion, since it would not differ in any material respect from the threefold system of labourers, capitalists, and landlords. The other case is the not uncommon one, in which a peasant proprietor owns and cultivates the land, but raises the little capital required by a mortgage upon it. Neither does this case present any important peculiarity. There is but one person, the peasant himself, who has any right or power of interference in the management. He pays a fixed annuity as interest to a capitalist, as he pays another fixed sum in taxes to the government. Without dwelling further on these cases, we pass to those which present marked features of peculiarity.

When the two parties sharing in the produce are the labourer or labourers and the landowner, it is not a very material circumstance in the case which of the two furnishes the stock, or whether, as sometimes happens, they furnish it in a determinate proportion between them. The essential difference does not lie in this, but in another circumstance, namely, whether the division of the produce between the two is regulated by custom or by competition. We will begin with the former case ; of which the metayer culture is the principal, and in Europe almost the sole, example.

The principle of the metayer system is that the labourer, or peasant, makes his engagement directly with the landowner, and pays, not a fixed rent, either in money or in kind, but a certain proportion of the produce, or rather of what remains of the produce after deducting what is considered necessary to keep up the stock. The proportion is usually, as the name imports, one-half; but in several districts in Italy it is two-thirds. Respecting the supply of stock, the custom varies from place to place; in some places the landlord furnishes the whole, in others half, in others some particular part, as for instance the cattle and seed, the labourer providing the implements.* "This connexion," says Sismondi, speaking chiefly of Tuscany,† "is often the subject of a contract, to define certain services and certain occasional payments to which the metayer binds himself; nevertheless the differences in the obligations of one such contract and another are inconsiderable; usage governs alike all these engagements, and supplies the stipulations which have not been expressed; and the landlord who attempted to depart from usage, who exacted more than his neighbour, who took for the basis of the agreement anything but the equal division of the crops, would render himself so odious, he would be so sure of not obtaining a metayer who was an honest man, that the contract of all the metayers may be considered as identical, at least in each province, and never gives rise to any competition among peasants in search of employment, or any offer to cultivate the soil on cheaper terms than one another." To the same effect Châteauvieux,‡ speaking of the metayers of Piedmont. "They consider it" (the farm) "as a patrimony, and never think of renewing the lease, but go on from

* In France before the Revolution, according to Arthur Young (i. 403), there was great local diversity in this respect. In Champagne "the landlord commonly finds half the cattle and half the seed, and the metayer, labour, implements, and taxes; but in some districts the landlord bears a share of these. In Roussillon, the landlord pays half the taxes; and in Guienne, from Auch to Fleuran, many landlords pay all. Near Augillon, on the Garonne, the metayers furnish half the cattle. At Nangis, in the Isle of France, I met with an agreement for the landlord to furnish live stock, implements, harness, and taxes; the metayer found labour and his own capitation tax: the landlord repaired the house and gates, the metayer the windows: the landlord provided seed the first year, the metayer the last; in the intervening years they supply half and half. In the Bourbonnois the landlord finds all sorts of live stock, yet the metayer sells, changes, and buys at his will; the steward keeping an account of these mutations, for the landlord has half the product of sales, and pays half the purchases." In Piedmont, he says, "the landlord commonly pays the taxes and repairs the buildings, and the tenant provides cattle, implements, and seed." (ii. 151.)

† *Etudes sur l'Economie Politique*, 6me essai: De la Condition des Cultivateurs en Toscane.

‡ *Letters from Italy.* I quote from Dr. Rigby's translation (p. 22).

generation to generation, on the same terms, without writings or registries." *

§ 2. When the partition of the produce is a matter of fixed usage, not of varying convention, political economy has no laws of distribution to investigate. It has only to consider, as in the case of peasant proprietors, the effects of the system first on the condition of the peasantry, morally and physically, and secondly, on the efficiency of the labour. In both these particulars the metayer system has the characteristic advantages of peasant properties, but has them in a less degree. The metayer has less motive to exertion than the peasant proprietor, since only half the fruits of his industry, instead of the whole, are his own. But he has a much stronger motive than a day labourer, who has no other interest in the result than not to be dismissed. If the metayer cannot be turned out except for some violation of his contract, he has a stronger motive to exertion than any tenant-farmer who has not a lease. The metayer is at least his landlord's partner, and a half-sharer in their joint gains. Where, too, the permanence of his tenure is guaranteed by custom, he acquires local attachments, and much of the feelings of a proprietor. I am supposing that this half produce is sufficient to yield him a comfortable support. Whether it is so, depends (in any given state of agriculture) on the degree of subdivision of the land ; which depends on the operation of the population principle. A multiplication of people, beyond the number that can be properly supported on the land or taken off by manufactures, is incident even to a peasant proprietary, and of course not less but rather more incident to a metayer population. The tendency, however, which we noticed in the proprietary system, to promote prudence on this point, is in no small degree common to it with the metayer system. There, also, it is a matter of easy and exact calculation whether a family can be supported or not. If it is easy to see whether the owner of the whole produce can increase the production so as to maintain a

* This virtual fixity of tenure is not however universal even in Italy ; and it is to its absence that Sismondi attributes the inferior condition of the metayers in some provinces of Naples, in Lucca, and in the Riviera of Genoa ; where the landlords obtain a larger (though still a fixed) share of the produce. In those countries the cultivation is splendid, but the people wretchedly poor. "The same misfortune would probably have befallen the people of Tuscany if public opinion did not protect the cultivator ; Jbut a proprietor would not dare to impose conditions unusual in the country, and even in changing one metayer for another he alters nothing in the terms of the engagement."—*Nouveaux Principes,* liv. iii. ch. 5.

greater number of persons equally well, it is not a less simple problem whether the owner of half the produce can do so.* There is one check which this system seems to offer, over and above those held out even by the proprietary system ; there is a landlord, who may exert a controlling power, by refusing his consent to a subdivision. I do not, however, attach great importance to this check, because the farm may be loaded with superfluous hands without being subdivided ; and because, so long as the increase of hands increases the gross produce, which is almost always the case, the landlord, who receives half the produce, is an immediate gainer, the inconvenience falling only on the labourers. The landlord is no doubt liable in the end to suffer from their poverty, by being forced to make advances to them, especially in bad seasons ; and a foresight of this ultimate inconvenience may operate beneficially on such landlords as prefer future security to present profit.

The characteristic disadvantage of the metayer system is very fairly stated by Adam Smith. After pointing out that metayers " have a plain interest that the whole produce should be as great as possible, in order that their own proportion may be so," he continues,† " it could never, however, be the interest of this species of cultivators to lay out, in the further improvement of the land, any part of the little stock which they might save from their own share of the produce, because the lord who laid out nothing was to get one-half of whatever it produced. The tithe, which is but a tenth of the produce, is found to be a very great hindrance to improvement. A tax, therefore, which amounted to one-half, must have been an

---

* M. Bastiat affirms that even in France, incontestably the least favour able example of the metayer system, its effect in repressing population is conspicuous.

" It is a well-ascertained fact that the tendency to excessive multiplication is chiefly manifested in the class who live on wages. Over these the forethought which retards marriages has little operation, because the evils which flow from excessive competition appear to them only very confusedly, and at a considerable distance. It is, therefore, the most advantageous condition of a people to be so organized as to contain no regular class of labourers for hire. In metayer countries, marriages are principally determined by the demands of cultivation ; they increase when, from whatever cause, the metairies offer vacancies injurious to production ; they diminish when the places are filled up. A fact easily ascertained, the proportion between the size of the farm and the number of hands, operates like forethought, and with greater effect. We find, accordingly, that when nothing occurs to make an opening for a superfluous population, numbers remain stationary : as is seen in our southern departments." Considérations sur le Métayage, *Journal des Economistes* for February 1846. [The description of Bastiat as " a high authority among French political economists " was omitted from the 3rd ed. (1852).]

† *Wealth of Nations*, book iii. ch. 2.

effectual ,bar to it. It might be the interest of a metayer to make
the land produce as much as could be brought out of it by means
of the stock furnished by the proprietor; but it could never be
his interest to mix any part of his own with it. In France, where
five parts out of six of the whole kingdom are said to be still occupied
by this species of cultivators, the proprietors complain that their
metayers take every opportunity of employing the master's cattle
rather in carriage than in cultivation; because in the one case they
get the whole profits to themselves, in the other they share them
with their landlord." It is indeed implied in the very nature of the
tenure that all improvements which require expenditure of capital
must be made with the capital of the landlord. This, however, is
essentially the case even in England, whenever the farmers are
tenants-at-will: or (if Arthur Young is right) even on a " nine years'
lease." If the landlord is willing to provide capital for improvements, the metayer has the strongest interest in promoting them,
since half the benefit of them will accrue to himself. As however
the perpetuity of tenure which, in the case we are discussing, he
enjoys by custom, renders his consent a necessary condition; the
spirit of routine, and dislike of innovation, characteristic of an
agricultural people when not corrected by education, are no doubt,
as the advocates of the system seem to admit, a serious hindrance to
improvement.

§ 3. The metayer system has met with no mercy from English
authorities. " There is not one word to be said in favour of the
practice," says Arthur Young,* and a " thousand arguments that
might be used against it. The hard plea of necessity can alone be
urged in its favour; the poverty of the farmers being so great,
that the landlord must stock the farm, or it could not be stocked at
all : this is a most cruel burden to a proprietor, who is thus obliged
to run much of the hazard of farming in the most dangerous of
all methods, that of trusting his property absolutely in the hands
of people who are generally ignorant, many careless, and some
undoubtedly wicked. . . . In this most miserable of all the modes of
letting land, the defrauded landlord receives a contemptible rent ;
the farmer is in the lowest state of poverty ; the land is miserably
cultivated ; and the nation suffers as severely as the parties
themselves. . . . Wherever † this system prevails, it may be taken
for granted that a useless and miserable population is found. . . .

* *Travels*, vol. i. pp. 404–5. 　　　　　　† Ibid. vol. ii. 151–3.

Wherever the country (that I saw) is poor and unwatered, in the Milanese, it is in the hands of metayers; they are almost always in debt to their landlord for seed or food, and " their condition is more wretched than that of a day labourer. . . . There * are but few districts " (in Italy) " where lands are let to the occupying tenant at a money-rent; but wherever it is found, their crops are greater; a clear proof of the imbecility of the metaying system." " Wherever it " (the metayer system) " has been adopted," says Mr. M'Culloch,† " it has put a stop to all improvement, and has reduced the cultivators to the most abject poverty." Mr. Jones ‡ shares the common opinion, and quotes Turgot and Destutt-Tracy in support of it. The impression, however, of all these writers (notwithstanding Arthur Young's occasional references to Italy) seems to be chiefly derived from France, and France before the Revolution.§ Now the situation of French metayers under the old régime by no means represents the typical form of the contract. It is essential to that form that the proprietor pays all the taxes. But in France the exemption of the noblesse from direct taxation had led the Government to throw the whole burthen of their ever-increasing fiscal exactions upon the occupiers: and it is to these exactions that Turgot ascribed the extreme wretchedness of the metayers: a wretchedness in some cases so excessive, that in Limousin and Angoumois (the provinces which he administered) they had seldom more, according to him, after deducting all burthens, than from twenty-five to thirty livres (20 to 24 shillings) per head for their whole annual consumption: " je ne dis pas en argent, mais en comptant tout ce qu'ils consomment en nature sur ce qu'ils ont récolté." ‖ When we add that they had not the virtual fixity

* *Travels*, vol. ii. 217.
† *Principles of Political Economy*, 3rd. ed. p. 471.
‡ *Essay on the Distribution of Wealth*, pp. 102–4. [*Peasant Rents*, pp. 90–92.]
§ M. de Tracy is partially an exception, inasmuch as his experience reaches lower down than the revolutionary period; but he admits (as Mr. Jones has himself stated in another place) that he is acquainted only with a limited district, of great subdivision and unfertile soil.

M. Passy is of opinion, that a French peasantry must be in indigence and the country badly cultivated on a metayer system, because the proportion of the produce claimable by the landlord is too high; it being only in more favourable climates that any land, not of the most exuberant fertility, can pay half its gross produce in rent, and leave enough to peasant farmers to enable them to grow successfully the more expensive and valuable products of agriculture. (*Systèmes de Culture*, p. 35.) This is an objection only to a particular numerical proportion, which is indeed the common one, but is not essential to the system.

‖ See the " Mémoire sur la Surcharge des Impositions qu'éprouvait la Généralité de Limoges, adressé au Conseil d'Etat en 1766," pp. 260–304 of the fourth volume of Turgot's *Works*. The occasional engagements of landlords

of tenure of the metayers of Italy ("in Limousin," says Arthur Young,* "the metayers are considered as little better than menial servants, removable at pleasure, and obliged to conform in all things to the will of the landlords,") it is evident that their case affords no argument against the metayer system in its better form. A population who could call nothing their own, who, like the Irish cottiers, could not in any contingency be worse off, had nothing to restrain them from multiplying, and subdividing the land, until stopped by actual starvation.

We shall find a very different picture, by the most accurate authorities, of the metayer cultivation of Italy. In the first place, as to subdivision. In Lombardy, according to Châteauvieux,† there are few farms which exceed fifty acres, and few which have less than ten. These farms are all occupied by metayers at half profit. They invariably display "an extent ‡ and a richness in buildings rarely known in any other country in Europe." Their plan "affords the greatest room with the least extent of building ; is best adapted to arrange and secure the crop ; and is, at the same time, the most economical, and the least exposed to accidents by fire." The courtyard "exhibits a whole so regular and commodious, and a system of such care and good order, that our dirty and ill-arranged farms can convey no adequate idea of." The same description applies to Piedmont. The rotation of crops is excellent. "I should think§ no country can bring so large a portion of its produce to market as Piedmont." Though the soil is not naturally very fertile, "the number of cities is prodigiously great." The agriculture must, therefore, be eminently favourable to the net as well as to the gross produce of the land. "Each plough works thirty-two acres in the season. . . . Nothing can be more perfect or neater than the hoeing and moulding up the maize, when in full growth, by a single plough, with a pair of oxen, without injury to a single plant, while all the weeds are effectually destroyed." So much for agricultural skill. "Nothing can be so excellent as the crop which precedes and that which follows it." The wheat "is thrashed by a cylinder, drawn by a horse, and guided by a boy, while the labourers

(as mentioned by Arthur Young) to pay a part of the taxes, were, according to Turgot, of recent origin, under the compulsion of actual necessity. "The proprietor only consents to it when he can find no metayer on other terms ; consequently, even in that case, the metayer is always reduced to what is barely sufficient to prevent him from dying of hunger" (p. 275).

* Vol. i. p. 404.

† _Letters from Italy_, translated by Rigby, p. 16.

‡ Ibid. pp. 19, 20.   § Ibid. pp. 24–31.

turn over the straw with forks. This process lasts nearly a fortnight ; it is quick and economical, and completely gets out the grain. . . . In no part of the world are the economy and the management of the land better understood than in Piedmont, and this explains the phenomenon of its great population, and immense export of provisions." All this under metayer cultivation.

Of the valley of the Arno, in its whole extent, both above and below Florence, the same writer thus speaks :*—" Forests of olive-trees covered the lower parts of the mountains, and by their foliage concealed an infinite number of small farms, which peopled these parts of the mountains ; chestnut-trees raised their heads on the higher slopes, their healthy verdure contrasting with the pale tint of the olive-trees, and spreading a brightness over this amphitheatre. The road was bordered on each side with village-houses, not more than a hundred paces from each other. . . . They are placed at a little distance from the road, and separated from it by a wall, and a terrace of some feet in extent. On the wall are commonly placed many vases of antique forms, in which flowers, aloes, and young orange-trees are growing. The house itself is completely covered with vines. . . . Before these houses we saw groups of peasant females dressed in white linen, silk corsets, and straw-hats, ornamented with flowers. . . . These houses being so near each other, it is evident that the land annexed to them must be small, and that property, in these valleys, must be very much divided ; the extent of these domains being from three to ten acres. The land lies round the houses, and is divided into fields by small canals, or rows of trees, some of which are mulberry-trees, but the greatest number poplars, the leaves of which are eaten by the cattle. Each tree supports a vine. . . . These divisions, arrayed in oblong squares, are large enough to be cultivated by a plough without wheels and a pair of oxen. There is a pair of oxen between ten or twelve of the farmers ; they employ them successively in the cultivation of all the farms. . . . Almost every farm maintains a well-looking horse, which goes in a small two-wheeled cart, neatly made, and painted red ; they serve for all the purposes of draught for the farm, and also to convey the farmer's daughters to mass and to balls. Thus, on holidays, hundreds of these little carts are seen flying in all directions, carrying the young women, decorated with flowers and ribbons."

This is not a picture of poverty ; and so far as agriculture

* Pp. 78–9.

is concerned, it effectually redeems metayer cultivation, as existing in these countries, from the reproaches of English writers; but with respect to the condition of the cultivators, Châteauvieux's testimony is, in some points, not so favourable. " It is * neither the natural fertility of the soil, nor the abundance which strikes the eye of the traveller, which constitute the well-being of its inhabitants. It is the number of individuals among whom the total produce is divided, which fixes the portion that each is enabled to enjoy. Here it is very small. I have thus far, indeed, exhibited a delightful country, well watered, fertile, and covered with a perpetual vegetation ; I have shown it divided into countless enclosures, which, like so many beds in a garden, display a thousand varying productions ; I have shown, that to all these enclosures are attached well-built houses, clothed with vines, and decorated with flowers ; but, on entering them, we find a total want of all the conveniences of life, a table more than frugal, and a general appearance of privation." Is not Châteauvieux here unconsciously contrasting the condition of the metayers with that of the farmers of other countries, when the proper standard with which to compare it is that of the agricultural day-labourers ?

Arthur Young says,† " I was assured that these metayers are (especially near Florence) much at their ease ; that on holidays they are dressed remarkably well, and not without objects of luxury, as silver, gold, and silk ; and live well, on plenty of bread, wine, and legumes. In some instances this may possibly be the case, but the general fact is contrary. It is absurd to think that metayers, upon such a farm as is cultivated by a pair of oxen, can live at their ease ; and a clear proof of their poverty is this, that the landlord, who provides half the live stock, is often obliged to lend the peasant money to procure his half. . . . The metayers, not in the vicinity of the city, are so poor that landlords even lend them corn to eat : their food is black bread, made of a mixture with vetches ; and their drink is very little wine mixed with water, and called *aquarolle ;* meat on Sundays only ; their dress very ordinary." Mr. Jones admits the superior comfort of the metayers near Florence, and attributes it partly to straw-platting, by which the women of the peasantry can earn, according to Châteauvieux,‡ from fifteen to twenty pence a day. But even this fact tells in favour of the metayer system : for in those parts of England in

which either straw-platting or lace-making is carried on by the
women and children of the labouring class, as in Bedfordshire
and Buckinghamshire, the condition of the class is not better, but
rather worse than elsewhere, the wages of agricultural labour
being depressed by a full equivalent.

In spite of Châteauvieux's statement respecting the poverty
of the metayers, his opinion, in respect to Italy at least, is given
in favour of the system. "It occupies * and constantly interests
the proprietors, which is never the case with great proprietors
who lease their estates at fixed rents. It establishes a community
of interests, and relations of kindness between the proprietors and
the metayers ; a kindness which I have often witnessed, and from
which result great advantages in the moral condition of society.
The proprietor under this system, always interested in the success
of the crop, never refuses to make an advance upon it, which the
land promises to repay with interest. It is by these advances
and by the hope thus inspired, that the rich proprietors of land
have gradually perfected the whole rural economy of Italy. It is
to them that it owes the numerous systems of irrigation which
water its soil, as also the establishment of the terrace culture on
the hills : gradual but permanent improvements, which common
peasants, for want of means, could never have effected, and which
could never have been accomplished by the farmers, nor by the
great proprietors who let their estates at fixed rents, because they are
not sufficiently interested. Thus the interested system forms of
itself that alliance between the rich proprietor, whose means provide
for the improvement of the culture, and the metayer whose care
and labour are directed, by a common interest, to make the most
of these advances."

But the testimony most favourable to the system is that of
Sismondi, which has the advantage of being specific, and from
accurate knowledge ; his information being not that of a traveller,
but of a resident proprietor, intimately acquainted with rural life.
His statements apply to Tuscany generally, and more particularly
to the Val di Nievole, in which his own property lay, and which is not
within the supposed privileged circle immediately round Florence.
It is one of the districts in which the size of farms appears to be the
smallest. The following is his description of the dwellings and
mode of life of the metayers of that district.†

---

* *Letters from Italy*, pp. 295-6.
† From his Sixth Essay, formerly referred to.

" The house, built of good walls with lime and mortar, has always at least one story, sometimes two, above the ground floor. On the ground floor are generally the kitchen, a cowhouse for two horned cattle, and the storehouse, which takes its name, *tinaia*, from the large vats (*tini*) in which the wine is put to ferment, without any pressing : it is there also that the metayer locks up his casks, his oil, and his grain. Almost always there is also a shed supported against the house, where he can work under cover to mend his tools, or chop forage for his cattle. On the first and second stories are two, three, and often four bedrooms. The largest and most airy of these is generally destined by the metayer, in the months of May and June, to the bringing up of silkworms. Great chests to contain clothes and linen, and some wooden chairs, are the chief furniture of the chambers ; but a newly-married wife always brings with her a wardrobe of walnut wood. The beds are uncurtained and unroofed, but on each of them, besides a good paillasse filled with the elastic straw of the maize plant, there are one or two mattresses of wool, or, among the poorest, of tow, a good blanket, sheets of strong hempen cloth, and on the best bed of the family a coverlet of silk padding, which is spread on festival days. The only fireplace is in the kitchen ; and there also is the great wooden table where the family dines, and the benches ; the great chest which serves at once for keeping the bread and other provisions, and for kneading ; a tolerably complete though cheap assortment of pans, dishes, and earthenware plates : one or two metal lamps, a steelyard, and at least two copper pitchers for drawing and holding water. The linen and the working clothes of the family have all been spun by the women of the house. The clothes, both of men and of women, are of the stuff called *mezza lana* when thick, *mola* when thin, and made of a coarse thread of hemp or tow, filled up with cotton or wool; it is dried by the same women by whom it is spun. It would hardly be believed what a quantity of cloth and of *mezza lana* the peasant women are able to accumulate by assiduous industry ; how many sheets there are in the store ; what a number of shirts, jackets, trowsers, petticoats, and gowns are possessed by every member of the family. By way of example I add in a note the inventory of the peasant family best known to me : it is neither one of the richest nor of the poorest, and lives happily by its industry on half the produce of less than ten *arpents* of land.* The young women had a marriage portion of fifty crowns,

* Inventory of the *trousseau* of Jane, daughter of Valente Papini, on her

twenty paid down, and the rest by instalments of two every year. The Tuscan crown is worth six francs [4s. 10d.]. The commonest marriage portion of a peasant girl in the other parts of Tuscany, where the metairies are larger, is 100 crowns, 600 francs."

Is this poverty, or consistent with poverty ? When a common, M. de Sismondi even says *the* common, marriage portion of a metayer's daughter is 24l. English money, equivalent to at least 50l. in Italy and in that rank of life ; when one whose dowry is only half that amount, has the wardrobe described, which is represented by Sismondi as a fair average ; the class must be fully comparable, in general condition, to a large proportion even of capitalist farmers in other countries ; and incomparably above the day-labourers of any country, except a new colony, or the United States. Very little can be inferred, against such evidence, from a traveller's impression of the poor quality of their food. Its unexpensive character may be rather the effect of economy than of necessity. Costly feeding is not the favourite luxury of a southern people ; their diet in all classes is principally vegetable, and no peasantry on the Continent has the superstition of the English labourer respecting white bread. But the nourishment of the Tuscan peasant, according to Sismondi, "is wholesome and various : its basis is an excellent wheaten bread, brown, but pure from bran and from all mixture. In the bad season they take but two meals a day : at ten in the morning they eat their pollenta, at the beginning of the night their soup, and after it bread with a relish of some sort (*companatico*). In summer they have three meals, at eight, at one, and in the evening ; but the fire is lighted only once a day, for dinner, which consists of soup, and a dish of salt meat or dried fish, or haricots, or greens, which are eaten with bread. Salt meat enters in a very small quantity into this diet, for it is reckoned that forty pounds of salt pork per head suffice amply for a year's provision ; twice a week a small piece of it is put into the soup. On Sundays they have always on

marriage with Giovacchino Landi, the 29th of April 1835, at Porta Vecchia, near Pescia :
   " 28 shifts, 7 best dresses (of particular fabrics of silk), 7 dresses of printed cotton, 2 winter working dresses (*mezza lana*), 3 summer working dresses and petticoats (*mola*), 3 white petticoats, 5 aprons of printed linen, 1 of black silk, 1 of black merino, 9 coloured working aprons (*mola*), 4 white, 8 coloured, and 3 silk, handkerchiefs, 2 embroidered veils and one of tulle, 3 towels, 14 pairs of stockings, 2 hats (one of felt, the other of fine straw) ; 2 cameos set in gold, 2 golden earrings, 1 chaplet with two Roman silver crowns, 1 coral necklace with its cross of gold. . . . All the richer married women of the class have, besides, the *veste di seta*, the great holiday dress, which they only wear four or five times in their lives."

the table a dish of fresh meat, but a piece which weighs only a pound
or a pound and a half suffices for the whole family, however numerous
it may be. It must not be forgotten that the Tuscan peasants
generally produce olive oil for their own consumption : they use
it not only for lamps, but as seasoning to all the vegetables prepared
for the table, which it renders both more savoury and more nutritive.
At breakfast their food is bread, and sometimes cheese and fruit ;
at supper, bread and salad. Their drink is composed of the inferior
wine of the country, the *vinella* or *piquette* made by fermenting in
water the pressed skins of the grapes. They always, however, reserve
a little of their best wine for the day when they thresh their corn, and
for some festivals which are kept in families. About fifty bottles
of vinella per annum and five sacks of wheat (about 1000 pounds
of bread) are considered as the supply necessary for a full grown
man."

The remarks of Sismondi on the moral influences of this state
of society are not less worthy of attention. The rights and obligations of the metayer being fixed by usage, and all taxes and rates
being paid by the proprietor, " the metayer has the advantages
of landed property without the burthen of defending it. It is the
landlord to whom, with the land, belong all its disputes: the tenant
lives in peace with all his neighbours ; between him and them
there is no motive for rivalry or distrust, he preserves a good understanding with them, as well as with his landlord, with the tax-
collector, and with the church : he sells little, and buys little ; he
touches little money, but he seldom has any to pay. The gentle and
kindly character of the Tuscans is often spoken of, but without
sufficiently remarking the cause which has contributed most to
keep up that gentleness ; the tenure, by which the entire class
of farmers, more than three-fourths of the population, are kept
free from almost every occasion for quarrel." The fixity of tenure
which the metayer, so long as he fulfils his own obligations, possesses
by usage, though not by law, gives him the local attachments,
and almost the strong sense of personal interest, characteristic
of a proprietor. " The metayer lives on his metairie as on his
inheritance, loving it with affection, labouring incessantly to improve
it, confiding in the future, and making sure that his land will be
tilled after him by his children and his children's children. In fact
the majority of metayers live from generation to generation on
the same farm ; they know it in its details with a minuteness
which the feeling of property can alone give. The plots terrassed

up, one above the other, are often not above four feet wide ; but there is not one of them, the qualities of which the metayer has not studied. This one is dry, the other is cold and damp : here the soil is deep, there it is a mere crust which hardly covers the rock ; wheat thrives best on one, rye on another : here it would be labour wasted to sow Indian corn, elsewhere the soil is unfit for beans and lupins, further off flax will grow admirably, the edge of this brook will be suited for hemp. In this way one learns with surprise from the metayer, that in a space of ten arpents, the soil, the aspect, and the inclination of the ground present greater variety than a rich farmer is generally able to distinguish in a farm of five hundred acres. For the latter knows that he is only a temporary occupant ; and moreover, that he must conduct his operations by general rules, and neglect details. But the experienced metayer has had his intelligence so awakened by interest and affection, as to be the best of observers ; and with the whole future before him, he thinks not of himself alone, but of his children and grandchildren. Therefore, when he plants an olive, a tree which lasts for centuries, and excavates at the bottom of the hollow in which he plants it a channel to let out the water by which it would be injured, he studies all the strata of the earth which he has to dig out." *

§ 4. I do not offer these quotations as evidence of the intrinsic excellence of the metayer system ; but they surely suffice to prove that neither " land miserably cultivated " nor a people in " the most abject poverty " have any necessary connexion with it, and that the unmeasured vituperation lavished upon the system by English writers is grounded on an extremely narrow view of the subject.

---

* Of the intelligence of this interesting people, M. de Sismondi speaks in the most favourable terms. Few of them can read ; but there is often one member of the family destined for the priesthood, who reads to them on winter evenings. Their language differs little from the purest Italian. The taste for improvisation in verse is general. " The peasants of the Vale of Nievole frequent the theatre in summer on festival days, from nine to eleven at night : their admission costs them little more than five French sous [2½d.]. Their favourite author is Alfieri ; the whole history of the Atridæ is familiar to these people who cannot read, and who seek from that austere poet a relaxation from their rude labours." Unlike most rustics, they find pleasure in the beauty of their country. " In the hills of the vale of Nievole there is in front of every house a threshing-ground, seldom of more than 25 or 30 square fathoms ; it is often the only level space in the whole farm ; it is at the same time a terrace which commands the plains and the valley, and looks out upon a delightful country. Scarcely ever have I stood still to admire it, without the metayer's coming out to enjoy my admiration, and point out with his finger the beauties which he thought might have escaped my notice."

I look upon the rural economy of Italy as simply so much additional evidence in favour of small occupations with permanent tenure. It is an example of what can be accomplished by those two elements, even under the disadvantage of the peculiar nature of the metayer contract, in which the motives to exertion on the part of the tenant are only half as strong as if he farmed the land on the same footing of perpetuity at a money-rent, either fixed, or varying according to some rule which would leave to the tenant the whole benefit of his own exertions. The metayer tenure is not one which we should be anxious to introduce where the exigencies of society had not naturally given birth to it ; but neither ought we to be eager to abolish it on a mere *à priori* view of its disadvantages. If the system in Tuscany works as well in practice as it is represented to do, with every appearance of minute knowledge, by so competent an authority as Sismondi ; if the mode of living of the people, and the size of farms, have for ages maintained and still maintain themselves * such as they are said to be by him, it were to be regretted that a state of rural well-being so much beyond what is realized in most European countries, should be put to hazard by an attempt to introduce, under the guise of agricultural improvement, a system of money-rents and capitalist farmers. Even where the metayers are poor, and the subdivision great, it is not to be assumed, as of course, that the change would be for the better. The enlargement of farms, and the introduction of what are called agricultural improvements, usually diminish the number of labourers employed on the land ; and unless the growth of capital in trade and manufactures affords an opening for the displaced population, or unless there are reclaimable wastes on which they can be located, competition will so reduce wages, that they will probably be worse off as day-labourers than they were as metayers.

Mr. Jones very properly objects against the French Economists of the last century, that in pursuing their favourite object of introducing money-rents, they turned their minds solely to putting farmers in the place of metayers, instead of transforming the existing metayers into farmers ; which, as he justly remarks, can scarcely

---

* " We never, says Sismondi, " find a family of metayers proposing to their landlord to divide the metairie, unless the work is really more than they can do, and they feel assured of retaining the same enjoyments on a smaller piece of ground. We never find several sons áll marrying, and forming as many new families : only one marries and undertakes the charge of the household : none of the others marry unless the first is childless, or unless some one of them has the offer of a new metairie." *New Principles of Political Economy*, book iii. ch. 5.

be effected, unless, to enable the metayers to save and become owners of stock, the proprietors submit for a considerable time to a diminution of income, instead of expecting an increase of it, which has generally been their immediate motive for making the attempt. If this transformation were effected, and no other change made in the metayer's condition ; if, preserving all the other rights which usage insures to him, he merely got rid of the landlord's claim to half the produce, paying in lieu of it a moderate fixed rent ; he would be so far in a better position than at present, as the whole, instead of only half the fruits of any improvement he made, would now belong to himself ; but even so, the benefit would not be without alloy ; for a metayer, though not himself a capitalist, has a capitalist for his partner, and has the use, in Italy at least, of a considerable capital, as is proved by the excellence of the farm buildings : and it is not probable that the landowners would any longer consent to peril their moveable property on the hazards of agricultural enter-prise, when assured of a fixed money income without it. Thus would the question stand, even if the change left undisturbed the metayer's virtual fixity of tenure, and converted him, in fact, into a peasant proprietor at a quitrent. But if we suppose him converted into a mere tenant, displaceable at the landlord's will, and liable to have his rent raised by competition to any amount which any unfor-tunate being in search of subsistence can be found to offer or promise for it ; he would lose all the features in his condition which preserve it from being deteriorated ; he would be cast down from his present position of a kind of half proprietor of the land, and would sink into a cottier tenant.

CHAPTER IX

OF COTTIERS

§ 1. By the general appellation of cottier tenure I shall designate all cases without exception in which the labourer makes his contract for land without the intervention of a capitalist farmer, and in which the conditions of the contract, especially the amount of rent, are determined not by custom but by competition. The principal European example of this tenure is Ireland, and it is from that country that the term cottier is derived.* By far the greater part of the agricultural population of Ireland might until very lately have been said to be [1] cottier-tenants; except so far as the Ulster tenant-right constituted an exception. There was, indeed, a numerous class of labourers who (we may presume through the refusal either of proprietors or of tenants in possession to permit any further subdivision) had been unable to obtain even the smallest patch of land as permanent tenants. But, from the deficiency of capital, the custom of paying wages in land was so universal, that even those who worked as casual labourers for the cottiers or for such large farmers as were found in the country, were usually paid not in money, but by permission to cultivate for the season a piece of ground which was generally delivered to them by the farmer ready manured, and was known by the name of conacre. For this they agreed to pay a money rent, often of several pounds an acre, but no money actually passed, the debt being worked out in labour, at a money valuation.

The produce, on the cottier system, being divided into two

---

* In its original acceptation, the word " cottier " designated a class of sub-tenants, who rent a cottage and an acre or two of land from the small farmers. But the usage of writers has long since stretched the term to include those small farmers themselves, and generally all peasant farmers whose rents are determined by competition.

[1] [" May be said to be " in 1st ed. (1848): altered as above in 5th ed. (1862). Similarly the account of the labourers in the following sentences was changed from the present to the past tense.]

portions, rent, and the remuneration of the labourer ; the one is evidently determined by the other. The labourer has whatever the landlord does not take : the condition of the labourer depends on the amount of rent. But rent, being regulated by competition, depends upon the relation between the demand for land, and the supply of it. The demand for land depends on the number of competitors, and the competitors are the whole rural population. The effect, therefore, of this tenure, is to bring the principle of population to act directly on the land, and not, as in England, on capital. Rent, in this state of things, depends on the proportion between population and land. As the land is a fixed quantity, while population has an unlimited power of increase ; unless something checks that increase, the competition for land soon forces up rent to the highest point consistent with keeping the population alive. The effects, therefore, of cottier tenure depend on the extent to which the capacity of population to increase is controlled, either by custom, by individual prudence, or by starvation and disease.

It would be an exaggeration to affirm that cottier tenancy is absolutely incompatible with a prosperous condition of the labouring class. If we could suppose it to exist among a people to whom a high standard of comfort was habitual ; whose requirements were such, that they would not offer a higher rent for land than would leave them an ample subsistence, and whose moderate increase of numbers left no unemployed population to force up rents by competition, save when the increasing produce of the land from increase of skill would enable a higher rent to be paid without inconvenience; the cultivating class might be as well remunerated, might have as large a share of the necessaries and comforts of life, on this system of tenure as on any other. They would not, however, while their rents were arbitrary, enjoy any of the peculiar advantages which metayers on the Tuscan system derive from their connexion with the land. They would neither have the use of a capital belonging to their landlords, nor would the want of this be made up by the intense motives to bodily and mental exertion which act upon the peasant who has a permanent tenure. On the contrary, any increased value given to the land by the exertions of the tenant, would have no effect but to raise the rent against himself, either the next year, or at farthest when his lease expired. The landlords might have justice or good sense enough not to avail themselves of the advantage which competition would give them ; and different landlords would do so in different degrees. But it is never safe to expect that a class or body of men will act in opposition to their immediate pecuniary interest; and even a doubt on the subject would be almost as fatal as a certainty, for when a person is considering whether or not to undergo a present exertion or sacrifice for a comparatively remote future, the scale is turned by a very small probability that the fruits of the exertion or of the sacrifice will be taken away from him. The only safeguard against these uncertainties would be the growth of a custom, insuring a permanence of tenure in the same occupant, without liability to any other increase of rent than might happen to be sanctioned by the general sentiments of the community. The Ulster tenant-right is such a custom. The very considerable sums which outgoing tenants obtain from their successors, for the goodwill of their farms,* in the first place actually limit the competition for land to persons who have such sums to offer : while the same fact also proves that full advantage is not taken by the landlord of even that more limited competition, since the landlord's rent does not amount to the whole of what the incoming tenant not only offers but actually pays. He does so in the full confidence that the rent will not be raised ; and for this he has the guarantee of a custom, not recognised by law, but deriving its binding force from another sanction, perfectly well understood in Ireland.† Without one or other of these supports, a custom limiting the rent of land is not likely to grow up in any progressive community. If wealth and population were stationary, rent also would generally be stationary, and after remaining a long time unaltered, would probably come to be considered unalterable. But all progress in wealth and population tends to a rise of rents. Under a metayer system there is an established mode in which the owner of land is sure of participating in the increased produce drawn from it. But on the

* " It is not uncommon for a tenant without a lease to sell the bare privilege of occupancy or possession of his farm, without any visible sign of improvement having been made by him, at from ten to sixteen, up to twenty and even forty years' purchase of the rent."—(*Digest of Evidence taken by Lord Devon's Commission*, Introductory Chapter.) The compiler adds, " the comparative tranquillity of that district " (Ulster) " may perhaps be mainly attributable to this fact."

† " It is in the great majority of cases not a reimbursement for outlay incurred, or improvements effected on the land, but a mere life insurance or purchase of immunity from outrage."—(*Digest, ut supra.*) " The present tenant-right of Ulster " (the writer judiciously remarks) " is an embryo *copyhold*." " Even there, if the tenant-right be disregarded, and a tenant be ejected without having received the price of his goodwill, outrages are generally the consequence."—(Ch. viii.) " The disorganised state of Tipperary, and the agrarian combination throughout Ireland, are but a methodized war to obtain the Ulster tenant-right."

cottier system he can only do so by a readjustment of the contract, while that readjustment, in a progressive community, would almost always be to his advantage. His interest, therefore, is decidedly opposed to the growth of any custom commuting rent into a fixed demand.

§ 2. Where the amount of rent is not limited, either by law or custom, a cottier system has the disadvantages of the worst metayer system, with scarcely any of the advantages by which, in the best forms of that tenure, they are compensated. It is scarcely possible that cottier agriculture should be other than miserable. There is not the same necessity that the condition of the cultivators should be so. Since by a sufficient restraint on population competition for land could be kept down, and extreme poverty prevented ; habits of prudence and a high standard of comfort, once established, would have a fair chance of maintaining themselves : though even in these favourable circumstances the motives to prudence would be considerably weaker than in the case of metayers, protected by custom (like those of Tuscany) from being deprived of their farms : since a metayer family, thus protected, could not be impoverished by any other improvident multiplication than their own, but a cottier family, however prudent and self-restraining, may have the rent raised against it by the consequences of the multiplication of other families. Any protection to the cottiers against this evil could only be derived from a salutary sentiment of duty or dignity, pervading the class. From this source, however, they might derive considerable protection. If the habitual standard of requirement among the class were high, a young man might not choose to offer a rent which would leave him in a worse condition than the preceding tenant ; or it might be the general custom, as it actually is in some countries, not to marry until a farm is vacant.

But it is not where a high standard of comfort has rooted itself in the habits of the labouring class, that we are ever called upon to consider the effects of a cottier system. That system is found only where the habitual requirements of the rural labourers are the lowest possible ; where as long as they are not actually starving, they will multiply : and population is only checked by the diseases, and the shortness of life, consequent on insufficiency of merely physical necessaries. This was [1] the state of the largest portion of the Irish peasantry. When a people have sunk into this state,

---

[1] [" Is unhappily " until the 5th ed. (1862).]

and still more when they have been in it from time immemorial, the cottier system is an almost insuperable obstacle to their emerging from it.   When the habits of the people are such that their increase is never checked but by the impossibility of obtaining a bare support, and when this support can only be obtained from land, all stipulations and agreements respecting amount of rent are merely nominal ; the competition for land makes the tenants undertake to pay more than it is possible they should pay, and when they have paid all they can, more almost always remains due.

"As it may fairly be said of the Irish peasantry," said Mr. Revans, the Secretary to the Irish Poor Law Enquiry Commission,* " that every family which has not sufficient land to yield its food has one or more of its members supported by begging, it will easily be conceived that every endeavour is made by the peasantry to obtain small holdings, and that they are not influenced in their biddings by the fertility of the land, or by their ability to pay the rent, but solely by the offer which is most likely to gain them possession. The rents which they promise, they are almost invariably incapable of paying ; and consequently they become indebted to those under whom they hold, almost as soon as they take possession.   They give up, in the shape of rent, the whole produce of the land with the exception of a sufficiency of potatoes for a subsistence ; but as this is rarely equal to the promised rent, they constantly have against them an increasing balance.   In some cases, the largest quantity of produce which their holdings ever yielded, or which, under their system of tillage, they could in the most favourable seasons be made to yield, would not be equal to the rent bid ; consequently, if the peasant fulfilled his engagement with his landlord, which he is rarely able to accomplish, he would till the ground for nothing, and give his landlord a premium for being allowed to till it.   On the sea coast, fishermen, and in the northern counties those who have looms, frequently pay more in rent than the market value of the whole produce of the land they hold.   It might be supposed that they would be better without land under such circumstances.   But fishing might fail during a week or two, and so might the demand for the produce of the loom, when, did they not possess the land upon which their food is grown, they might starve.   The full amount of the rent bid, however, is rarely paid.   The peasant remains

* *Evils of the State of Ireland, their Causes and their Remedy.*   Page 10. A pamphlet containing, among other things, an excellent digest and selection of evidence from the mass collected by the Commission presided over by Archbishop Whately.

constantly in debt to his landlord ; his miserable possessions—the wretched clothing of himself and of his family, the two or three stools, and the few pieces of crockery, which his wretched hovel contains, would not, if sold, liquidate the standing and generally accumulating debt. The peasantry are mostly a year in arrear, and their excuse for not paying more is destitution. Should the produce of the holding, in any year, be more than usually abundant, or should the peasant by any accident become possessed of any property, his comforts cannot be increased ; he cannot indulge in better food, nor in a greater quantity of it. His furniture cannot be increased, neither can his wife or children be better clothed. The acquisition must go to the person under whom he holds. The accidental addition will enable him to reduce his arrear of rent, and thus to defer ejectment. But this must be the bound of his expectation."

As an extreme instance of the intensity of competition for land, and of the monstrous height to which it occasionally forced up the nominal rent ; we may cite from the evidence taken by Lord Devon's Commission,* a fact attested by Mr. Hurly, Clerk of the Crown for Kerry : " I have known a tenant bid for a farm that I was perfectly well acquainted with, worth 50*l.* a year : I saw the competition get up to such an extent, that he was declared the tenant at 450*l.*"

§ 3. In such a condition, what can a tenant gain by any amount of industry or prudence, and what lose by any recklessness ? If the landlord at any time exerted his full legal rights, the cottier would not be able even to live. If by extra exertion he doubled the produce of his bit of land, or if he prudently abstained from producing mouths to eat it up, his only gain would be to have more left to pay to his landlord ; while, if he had twenty children, they would still be fed first, and the landlord could only take what was left. Almost alone amongst mankind the cottier is in this condition, that he can scarcely be either better or worse off by any act of his own. If he were industrious or prudent, nobody but his landlord would gain ; if he is lazy or intemperate, it is at his landlord's expense. A situation more devoid of motives to either labour or self-command, imagination itself cannot conceive. The inducements of free human beings are taken away, and those of a slave not substituted. He has nothing to hope, and nothing to fear, except being dispossessed of his holding, and against this he protects himself by the *ultima ratio* of a defensive civil war. Rockism and Whiteboyism were [1] the determination of

* *Evidence,* p. 851.   [1] [' Are ' until the 5th ed. (1862).]

a people who had nothing that could be called theirs but a daily meal of the lowest description of food, not to submit to being deprived of that for other people's convenience.

Is it not, then, a bitter satire on the mode in which opinions are formed on the most important problems of human nature and life, to find public instructors of the greatest pretension, imputing the backwardness of Irish industry, and the want of energy of the Irish people in improving their condition, to a peculiar indolence and *insouciance* in the Celtic race ? Of all vulgar modes of escaping from the consideration of the effect of social and moral influences on the human mind, the most vulgar is that of attributing the diversities of conduct and character to inherent natural differences. What race would not be indolent and insouciant when things are so arranged, that they derive no advantage from forethought or exertion ? If such are the arrangements in the midst of which they live and work, what wonder if the listlessness and indifference so engendered are not shaken off the first moment an opportunity offers when exertion would really be of use ? It is very natural that a pleasure-loving and sensitively organized people like the Irish, should be less addicted to steady routine labour than the English, because life has more excitements for them independent of it ; but they are not less fitted for it than their Celtic brethren the French, nor less so than the Tuscans, or the ancient Greeks. An excitable organization is precisely that in which, by adequate inducements, it is easiest to kindle a spirit of animated exertion. It speaks nothing against the capacities of industry in human beings, that they will not exert themselves without motive. No labourers work harder, in England or America, than the Irish ; but not under a cottier system.

§ 4. The multitudes who till the soil of India, are in a condition sufficiently analogous to the cottier system, and at the same time sufficiently different from it, to render the comparison of the two a source of some instruction. In most parts of India there are, and perhaps have always been, only two contracting parties, the landlord and the peasant : the landlord being generally the sovereign, except where he has, by a special instrument, conceded his rights to an individual, who becomes his representative. The payments, however, of the peasants, or ryots as they are termed, have seldom if ever been regulated, as in Ireland, by competition. Though the customs locally obtaining were infinitely various, and though practically no custom could be maintained against the sovereign's will, there was always a rule of some sort common to a neighbourhood ; the collector did not make his separate bargain with the peasant, but assessed each according to the rule adopted for the rest. The idea was thus kept up of a right of property in the tenant, or, at all events, of a right to permanent possession ; and the anomaly arose of a fixity of tenure in the peasant-farmer, co-existing with an arbitrary power of increasing the rent.

When the Mogul government substituted itself throughout the greater part of India for the Hindoo rulers, it proceeded on a different principle. A minute survey was made of the land, and upon that survey an assessment was founded, fixing the specific payment due to the government from each field. If this assessment had never been exceeded, the ryots would have been in the comparatively advantageous position of peasant-proprietors, subject to a heavy, but a fixed quit-rent. The absence, however, of any real protection against illegal extortions, rendered this improvement in their condition rather nominal than real ; and, except during the occasional accident of a humane and vigorous local administrator, the exactions had no practical limit but the inability of the ryot to pay more.

It was to this state of things that the English rulers of India succeeded ; and they were, at an early period, struck with the importance of putting an end to this arbitrary character of the land-revenue, and imposing a fixed limit to the government demand. They did not attempt to go back to the Mogul valuation. It has been in general the very rational practice of the English Government in India to pay little regard to what was laid down as the theory of the native institutions, but to inquire into the rights which existed and were respected in practice, and to protect and enlarge those. For a long time, however, it blundered grievously about matters of fact, and grossly misunderstood the usages and rights which it found existing. Its mistakes arose from the inability of ordinary minds to imagine a state of social relations fundamentally different from those with which they are practically familiar. England being accustomed to great estates and great landlords, the English rulers took it for granted that India must possess the like ; and looking round for some set of people who might be taken for the objects of their search, they pitched upon a sort of tax-gatherers called zemindars. " The zemindar," says the philosophical historian of India,* " had some of the attributes which belong to a landowner ; he collected the rents of a particular district, he governed the cultivators of that

* Mill's *History of British India*, book vi. ch. 8.

district, lived in comparative splendour, and his son succeeded him when he died. The zemindars, therefore, it was inferred without delay, were the proprietors of the soil, the landed nobility and gentry of India. It was not considered that the zemindars, though they collected the rents, did not keep them; but paid them all away with a small deduction to the government. It was not considered that if they governed the ryots, and in many respects exercised over them despotic power, they did not govern them as tenants of theirs, holding their lands either at will or by contract under them. The possession of the ryot was an hereditary possession; from which it was unlawful for the zemindar to displace him; for every farthing which the zemindar drew from the ryot, he was bound to account; and it was only by fraud, if, out of all that he collected, he retained an *ana* more than the small proportion which, as pay for collection, he was permitted to receive."

" There was an opportunity in India," continues the historian, " to which the history of the world presents not a parallel. Next after the sovereign, the immediate cultivators had, by far, the greatest portion of interest in the soil. For the rights (such as they were) of the zemindars, a complete compensation might have easily been made. The generous resolution was adopted, of sacrificing to the improvement of the country, the proprietary rights of the sovereign. The motives to improvement which property gives, and of which the power was so justly appreciated, might have been bestowed upon those upon whom they would have operated with a force incomparably greater than that with which they could operate upon any other class of men : they might have been bestowed upon those from whom alone, in every country, the principal improvements in agriculture must be derived, the immediate cultivators of the soil. And a measure worthy to be ranked among the noblest that ever were taken for the improvement of any country, might have helped to compensate the people of India for the miseries of that misgovernment which they had so long endured. But the legislators were English aristocrats ; and aristocratical prejudices prevailed."

The measure proved a total failure, as to the main effects which its well-meaning promoters expected from it. Unaccustomed to estimate the mode in which the operation of any given institution is modified even by such variety of circumstances as exists within a single kingdom, they flattered themselves that they had created, throughout the Bengal provinces, English landlords, and it proved that they had only created Irish ones. The new landed aristocracy disappointed every expectation built upon them. They did nothing for the improvement of their estates, but everything for their own ruin. The same pains not being taken, as had been taken in Ireland, to enable landlords to defy the consequences of their improvidence, nearly the whole land of Bengal had to be sequestrated and sold, for debts or arrears of revenue, and in one generation most of the ancient zemindars had ceased to exist. Other families, mostly the descendants of Calcutta money dealers, or of native officials who had enriched themselves under the British government, now occupy their place ; and live as useless drones on the soil which has been given up to them. Whatever the government has sacrificed of its pecuniary claims, for the creation of such a class, has at the best been wasted.[1]

In the parts of India into which the British rule has been more recently introduced, the blunder has been avoided of endowing a useless body of great landlords with gifts from the public revenue. In most parts of the Madras and in part of the Bombay Presidency, the rent is paid directly to the government by the immediate cultivator. In the North-Western Provinces, the government makes its engagement with the village community collectively, determining the share to be paid by each individual, but holding them jointly responsible for each other's default. But in the greater part of India, the immediate cultivators have not obtained a perpetuity of tenure at a fixed rent. The government manages the land on the principle on which a good Irish landlord manages his estate : not putting it up to competition, not asking the cultivators

[1] [In the original text there next came the following passages : " But in this ill judged measure there was one redeeming point, to which may probably be ascribed all the progress which the Bengal provinces have since made in production and in amount of revenue. The ryots were reduced, indeed, to the rank of tenants of the zemindar ; but tenants with fixity of tenure. The rents were left to the zemindars to fix at their discretion ; but once fixed, were never more to be altered. This is now the law and practice of landed tenure, in the most flourishing part of the British Indian dominions.

" In the parts of India into which the British rule has been more recently introduced, the blunder has been avoided of endowing a useless body of great landlords with gifts from the public revenue ; but along with the evil, the good also has been left undone. The government has done less for the ryots than it has required to be done for them by the landlords of its creation."

These were omitted (as incorrect—see note of 1871, infra, p. 328) in the 3rd ed. (1852). In that edition was added the reference to Madras and Bombay, with the statement that " the rent on each class of land is fixed in perpetuity." This incorrect statement was struck out of the 4th ed. (1857), and the reference to the North-Western Provinces added.]

what they will promise to pay, but determining for itself what they can afford to pay, and defining its demand accordingly. In many districts a portion of the cultivators are considered as tenants of the rest, the government making its demand from those only (often a numerous body) who are looked upon as the successors of the original settlers or conquerors of the village. Sometimes the rent is fixed only for one year, sometimes for three or five ; but the uniform tendency of present policy is towards long leases, extending, in the northern provinces of India, to a term of thirty years. This arrangement has not existed for a sufficient time to have shown by experience, how far the motives to improvement which the long lease creates in the minds of the cultivators, fall short of the influence of a perpetual settlement.*   But the two plans, of annual settlements and of short leases, are irrevocably condemned. They can only be said to have succeeded, in comparison with the unlimited oppression which existed before. They are approved by nobody, and were never looked upon in any other light than as temporary arrangements, to be abandoned when a more complete knowledge of the capabilities of the country should afford data for something more permanent.[1]

* [1871] Since this was written, the resolution has been adopted by the Indian government of converting the long leases of the northern provinces into perpetual tenures at fixed rents.
[1] [See Appendix M.   *Indian Tenures.*]

CHAPTER X

§ 1. WHEN the first edition of this work was written and published,[1] the question, what is to be done with a cottier population, was to the English Government the most urgent of practical questions. The majority of a population of eight millions, having long grovelled in helpless inertness and abject poverty under the cottier system, reduced by its operation to mere food of the cheapest description, and to an incapacity of either doing or willing anything for the improvement of their lot, had at last, by the failure of that lowest quality of food, been plunged into a state in which the alternative seemed to be either death, or to be permanently supported by other people, or a radical change in the economical arrangements under which it had hitherto been their misfortune to live. Such an emergency had compelled attention to the subject from the legislature and from the nation, but it could hardly be said with much result; for, the evil having originated in a system of land tenancy which withdrew from the people every motive to industry or thrift except the fear of starvation, the remedy provided by Parliament was to take away even that, by conferring on them a legal claim to eleemosynary support : while, towards correcting the cause of the mischief, nothing was done, beyond vain complaints, though at the price to the national treasury of ten millions sterling for the delay.

" It is needless," (I observed) " to expend any argument in proving that the very foundation of the economical evils of Ireland is the cottier system ; that while peasant rents fixed by competition are the practice of the country, to expect industry, useful activity, any restraint on population but death, or any the smallest diminution of poverty, is to look for figs on thistles and grapes on thorns. If

[1] [These words were added in the 3rd ed. (1852), and the following sentences changed from the present to the past tense.]

our practical statesmen are not ripe for the recognition of this fact ; or if while they acknowledge it in theory, they have not a sufficient feeling of its reality, to be capable of founding upon it any course of conduct ; there is still another, and a purely physical consideration, from which they will find it impossible to escape. If the one crop on which the people have hitherto supported themselves continues to be precarious, either some new and great impulse must be given to agricultural skill and industry, or the soil of Ireland can no longer feed anything like its present population. The whole produce of the western half of the island, leaving nothing for rent, will not now keep permanently in existence the whole of its people : and they will necessarily remain an annual charge on the taxation of the empire, until they are reduced either by emigration or by starvation to a number corresponding with the low state of their industry, or unless the means are found of making that industry much more productive."

[1] Since these words were written, events unforeseen by any one have saved the English rulers of Ireland from the embarrassments which would have been the just penalty of their indifference and want of foresight. Ireland, under cottier agriculture, could no longer supply food to its population : Parliament, by way of remedy, applied a stimulus to population, but none at all to production ; the help, however, which had not been provided for the people of Ireland by political wisdom, came from an unexpected source. Self-supporting emigration—the Wakefield system, brought into effect on the voluntary principle and on a gigantic scale (the expenses of those who followed being paid from the earnings of those who went before) has, for the present, reduced the population down to the number for which the existing agricultural system can find employment and support. The census of 1851, compared with that of 1841, showed in round numbers a diminution of population of a million and a half. The subsequent census (of 1861) shows a further diminution of about half a million. The Irish having thus found the way to that flourishing continent which for generations will be capable of supporting in undiminished comfort the increase of the population of the whole world ; the peasantry of Ireland having learnt to fix their eyes on a terrestrial paradise beyond the ocean, as a sure refuge both from the oppression of the Saxon and from the tyranny of nature ; there can be little doubt that however

[1] [This and the next two paragraphs date from the 3rd ed. (1852), and take the place of the whole of the original § 2.]

much the employment for agricultural labour may hereafter be diminished by the general introduction throughout Ireland of English farming—or even if, like the county of Sutherland, all Ireland should be turned into a grazing farm—the superseded people would migrate to America with the same rapidity, and as free of cost to the nation, as the million of Irish who went thither during the three years previous to 1851. Those who think that the land of a country exists for the sake of a few thousand landowners, and that as long as rents are paid, society and government have fulfilled their function, may see in this consummation a happy end to Irish difficulties.

But this is not a time, nor is the human mind now in a condition, in which such insolent pretensions can be maintained. The land of Ireland, the land of every country, belongs to the people of that country. The individuals called landowners have no right, in morality and justice, to anything but the rent, or compensation for its saleable value. With regard to the land itself, the paramount consideration is, by what mode of appropriation and of cultivation it can be made most useful to the collective body of its inhabitants. To the owners of the rent it may be very convenient that the bulk of the inhabitants, despairing of justice in the country where they and their ancestors have lived and suffered, should seek on another continent that property in land which is denied to them at home. But the legislature of the empire ought to regard with other eyes the forced expatriation of millions of people. When the inhabitants of a country quit the country *en masse* because its Government will not make it a place fit for them to live in, the Government is judged and condemned. There is no necessity for depriving the landlords of one farthing of the pecuniary value of their legal rights ; but justice requires that the actual cultivators should be enabled to become in Ireland what they will become in America—proprietors of the soil which they cultivate.

Good policy requires it no less. Those who, knowing neither Ireland nor any foreign country, take as their sole standard of social and economical excellence English practice, propose as the single remedy for Irish wretchedness, the transformation of the cottiers into hired labourers. But this is rather a scheme for the improvement of Irish agriculture, than of the condition of the Irish people. The status of a day-labourer has no charm for infusing forethought, frugality, or self-restraint, into a people devoid of them. If the Irish peasantry could be universally changed into receivers of wages, the old habits and mental characteristics of the people remaining, we should merely see four or five millions of people living as day-labourers in the same wretched manner in which as cottiers they lived before ; equally passive in the absence of every comfort, equally reckless in multiplication, and even, perhaps, equally listless at their work ; since they could not be dismissed in a body, and if they could, dismissal would now be simply remanding them to the poor-rate. Far other would be the effect of making them peasant proprietors. A people who in industry and providence have everything to learn—who are confessedly among the most backward of European populations in the industrial virtues—require for their regeneration the most powerful incitements by which those virtues can be stimulated : and there is no stimulus as yet comparable to property in land. A permanent interest in the soil to those who till it, is almost a guarantee for the most unwearied laboriousness : against over-population, though not infallible, it is the best preservative yet known, and where it failed, any other plan would probably fail much more egregiously ; the evil would be beyond the reach of merely economic remedies.

The case of Ireland is similar in its requirements to that of India. In India, though great errors have from time to time been committed, no one ever proposed, under the name of agricultural improvement, to eject the ryots or peasant farmers from their possession ; the improvement that has been looked for, has been through making their tenure more secure to them, and the sole difference of opinion is between those who contend for perpetuity, and those who think that long leases will suffice. The same question exists as to Ireland : and it would be idle to deny that long leases, under such landlords as are sometimes to be found, do effect wonders, even in Ireland. But then they must be leases at a low rent. Long leases are in no way to be relied on for getting rid of cottierism. During the existence of cottier tenancy, leases have always been long ; twenty-one years and three lives concurrent, was a usual term. But the rent being fixed by competition, at a higher amount than could be paid, so that the tenant neither had, nor could by any exertion acquire, a beneficial interest in the land, the advantage of a lease was nearly nominal. In India, the government, where it has not imprudently made over its proprietary rights to the zemindars,[1] is able to prevent this evil, because, being itself the landlord, it can fix the rent according to its own judgment ; but under individual

[1] [This clause was inserted in the 3rd ed. (1852).]

landlords, while rents are fixed by competition, and the competitors
are a peasantry struggling for subsistence, nominal rents are inevitable, unless the population is so thin, that the competition
itself is only nominal. The majority of landlords will grasp at
immediate money and immediate power; and so long as they
find cottiers eager to offer them everything, it is useless to rely
on them for tempering the vicious practice by a considerate
self-denial.

A perpetuity is a stronger stimulus to improvement than a
long lease : not only because the longest lease, before coming to
an end, passes through all the varieties of short leases down to no
lease at all ; but for more fundamental reasons. It is very shallow,
even in pure economics, to take no account of the influence of
imagination : there is a virtue in " for ever " beyond the longest
term of years ; even if the term is long enough to include children,
and all whom a person individually cares for, yet until he has
reached that high degree of mental cultivation at which the public
good (which also includes perpetuity) acquires a paramount ascendancy over his feelings and desires, he will not exert himself with
the same ardour to increase the value of an estate, his interest in
which diminishes in value every year. Besides, while perpetual
tenure is the general rule of landed property, as it is in all the countries
of Europe, a tenure for a limited period, however long, is sure to be
regarded as a something of inferior consideration and dignity, and
inspires less of ardour to obtain it, and of attachment to it when
obtained. But where a country is under cottier tenure, the question
of perpetuity is quite secondary to the more important point, a
limitation of the rent. Rent paid by a capitalist who farms for
profit, and not for bread, may safely be abandoned to competition ;
rent paid by labourers cannot, unless the labourers were in a state of
civilization and improvement which labourers have nowhere yet
reached, and cannot easily reach under such a tenure. Peasant
rents ought never to be arbitrary, never at the discretion of the
landlord : either by custom or law, it is imperatively necessary that
they should be fixed ; and where no mutually advantageous custom,
such as the metayer system of Tuscany, has established itself,
reason and experience recommend that they should be fixed by
authority : thus changing the rent into a quit-rent, and the farmer
into a peasant proprietor.

For carrying this change into effect on a sufficiently large scale
to accomplish the complete abolition of cottier tenancy, the mode

which most obviously suggests itself is the direct one of doing the thing outright by Act of Parliament; making the whole land of Ireland the property of the tenants, subject to the rents now really paid (not the nominal rent), as a fixed rent charge.   This, under the name of "fixity of tenure," was one of the demands of the Repeal Association during the most successful period of their agitation; and was better expressed by Mr. Conner, its earliest, most enthusiastic, and most indefatigable apostle,* by the words, "a valuation and a perpetuity."   In such a measure there would not have been any injustice, provided the landlords were compensated for the present value of the chances of increase which they were prospectively required to forego.   The rupture of existing social relations would hardly have been more violent than that effected by the ministers Stein and Hardenberg when, by a series of edicts, in the early part of the present century, they revolutionized the state of landed property in the Prussian monarchy, and left their names to posterity among the greatest benefactors of their country.   To enlightened foreigners writing on Ireland, Von Raumer and Gustave de Beaumont, a remedy of this sort seemed so exactly and obviously what the disease required, that they had some difficulty in comprehending how it was that the thing was not yet done.

This, however, would have been, in the first place, a complete expropriation of the higher classes of Ireland : which, if there is any truth in the principles we have laid down, would be perfectly warrantable, but only if it were the sole means of effecting a great public good.   In the second place, that there should be none but peasant proprietors, is in itself far from desirable.   Large farms, cultivated by large capital, and owned by persons of the best education which the country can give, persons qualified by instruction to appreciate scientific discoveries, and able to bear the delay and risk of costly experiments, are an important part of a good agricultural system.   Many such landlords there are even in Ireland ; and it would be a public misfortune to drive them from their posts. A large proportion also of the present holdings are probably still too small to try the proprietary system under the greatest advantages; nor are the tenants always the persons one would desire to select as the first occupants of peasant-properties.   There are numbers of them on whom it would have a more beneficial effect to give

* Author of numerous pamphlets, entitled *True Political Economy of Ireland, Letter to the Earl of Devon, Two Letters on the Rackrent Oppression of Ireland,* and others.   Mr. Conner has been an agitator on the subject since 1832.

them the hope of acquiring a landed property by industry and frugality, than the property itself in immediate possession.[1]

There are, however, much milder measures, not open to similar objections, and which, if pushed to the utmost extent of which they are susceptible, would realize in no inconsiderable degree the object sought. One of them would be, to enact that whoever reclaims waste land becomes the owner of it, at a fixed quit-rent equal to a moderate interest on its mere value as waste. It would of course be a necessary part of this measure, to make compulsory on landlords the surrender of waste lands (not of an ornamental character) whenever required for reclamation. Another expedient, and one in which individuals could co-operate, would be to buy as much as possible of the land offered for sale, and sell it again in small portions as peasant-properties. A Society for this purpose

[Here was dropt out, from the 3rd ed. (1852) the following section of the original text:

" § 5. Some persons who desire to avoid the term fixity of tenure, but who cannot be satisfied without some measure co-extensive with the whole country, have proposed the universal adoption of ' tenant-right.' Under this equivocal phrase, two things are confounded. What it commonly stands for in Irish discussion, is the Ulster practice, which is in fact, fixity of tenure. It supposes a customary, though not a legal, limitation of the rent; without which the tenant evidently could not acquire a beneficial and saleable interest. Its existence is highly salutary, and is one principal cause of the superiority of Ulster in efficiency of cultivation, and in the comfort of the people, notwithstanding a minuter sub-division of holdings than in the other provinces. But to convert this customary limitation of rent into a legal one, and to make it universal, would be to establish a fixity of tenure by law, the objections to which have already been stated.

" The same appellation (tenant right) has of late years been applied, more particularly in England, to something altogether different, and falling as much short of the exigency, as the enforcement of the Ulster custom would exceed it. This English tenant right, with which a high agricultural authority has connected his name by endeavouring to obtain for it legislative sanction, amounts to no more than this, that on the expiration of a lease, the landlord should make compensation to the tenant for ' unexhausted improvements.' This is certainly very desirable, but provides only for the case of capitalist farmers, and of improvements made by outlay of money; of the worth and cost of which, an experienced land agent or a jury of farmers could accurately judge. The improvements to be looked for from peasant cultivators are the result not of money but of their labour, applied at such various times and in such minute portions as to be incapable of judicial appreciation. For such labour, compensation could not be given on any principle but that of paying to the tenant the whole difference between the value of the property when he received it, and when he gave it up: which would as effectually annihilate the right of property of the landlord as if the rent had been fixed in perpetuity, while it would not offer the same inducements to the cultivator, who improves from affection and passion as much as from calculation, and to whom his own land is a widely different thing from the most liberal possible pecuniary compensation for it."]

was at one time projected (though the attempt to establish it
proved unsuccessful) on the principles, so far as applicable, ot
the Freehold Land Societies, which have been so successfully
established in England, not primarily for agricultural, but for
electoral purposes.[1]

This is a mode in which private capital may be employed in
renovating the social and agricultural economy of Ireland, not
only without sacrifice but with considerable profit to its owners.
The remarkable success of the Waste Land Improvement Society,
which proceeded on a plan far less advantageous to the tenant,
is an instance of what an Irish peasantry can be stimulated to do,

[1] [Little more than this remained in the 3rd ed. (1852)—modified to its
present shape in the 5th (1862)—of the argument in favour of measures of
reclamation of waste land which occupied five pages in the original edition.
It opened thus: " There is no need to extend them to all the population, or all
the land.   It is enough if there be land available, on which to locate so great
a portion of the population, that the remaining area of the country shall not
be required to maintain greater numbers than are compatible with large
farming and hired labour.   For this purpose there is an obvious resource in
the waste lands ; which are happily so extensive, and a large proportion of
them so improvable, as to afford a means by which, without making the present
tenants proprietors, nearly the whole surplus population might be converted
into peasant proprietors elsewhere.''

After this argument came the following account of the English experiments
associated with the name of Feargus O'Connor : " There are yet other means,
by which not a little could be done in the dissemination of peasant proprietors
over even the existing area of cultivation.   There is at the present time an
experiment in progress, in more than one part of England, for the creation of
peasant proprietors.   The project is of Chartist origin, and its first colony is
now in full operation near Rickmansworth, in Hertfordshire.   The plan is as
follows :—Funds were raised by subscription, and vested in a joint-stock
company.   With part of these funds an estate of several hundred acres was
bought.   This estate was divided into portions of two, three, and four acres, on
each of which a house was erected by the Association.   These holdings were
let to select labourers, to whom also such sums were advanced as were thought
to amount to a sufficient capital for cultivation by spade labour.   An annual
payment, affording to the Company an interest of five per ɔent. on their outlay,
was laid on the several holdings as a fixed quit-rent, never in any circumstances to be raised.   The tenants are thus proprietors from the first, and their
redemption of the quit-rent, by saving from the produce of their labour, is
desired and calculated upon.

" The originator of this experiment appears to have successfully repelled
(before a tribunal by no means prepossessed in his favour, a Committee of the
House of Commons) the imputations which were lavished upon his project,
and upon his mode of executing it.   Should its issue ultimately be unfavourable,
the cause of failure will be in the details of management, not in the principle.
These well-conceived arrangements afford a mode in which private capital may
co-operate in renovating &c.''   In the first edition it was said that " at present
there seems no reason to believe '' the issue would be unfavourable ; and in
the second the reference was inserted to the parliamentary enquiry.   For the
subsequent history of the National Land Company, see L. Jebb, *Small Holdings,*
(1907), p. 121.]'

by a sufficient assurance that what they do will be for their own advantage. It is not even indispensable to adopt perpetuity as the rule ; long leases at moderate rents, like those of the Waste Land Society, would suffice, if a prospect were held out to the farmers of being allowed to purchase their farms with the capital which they might acquire, as the Society's tenants were so rapidly acquiring under the influence of its beneficent system.* When the lands were sold, the funds of the association would be liberated, and it might recommence operations in some other quarter.

§ 2.[1] Thus far I had written in 1856. Since that time the great crisis of Irish industry has made further progress, and it is necessary to consider how its present state affects the opinions, on prospects or on practical measures, expressed in the previous part of this chapter.

* [1857] Though this society, during the years succeeding the famine, was forced to wind up its affairs, the memory of what it accomplished ought to be preserved. The following is an extract in the *Proceedings* of Lord Devon's Commission (page 84) from the report made to the society in 1845, by their intelligent manager, Colonel Robinson :—

"Two hundred and forty-five tenants, many of whom were a few years since in a state bordering on pauperism, the occupiers of small holdings of from ten to twenty plantation acres each, have, by their own free labour, with the society's aid, improved their farms to the value of 4396l. ; 605l. having been added during the last year, being at the rate of 17l. 18s. per tenant for the whole term, and 2l. 9s. for the past year ; the benefit of which improvements each tenant will enjoy during the unexpired term of a thirty-one years' lease.

"These 245 tenants and their families have, by spade industry, reclaimed and brought into cultivation 1032 plantation acres of land, previously unproductive mountain waste, upon which they grew, last year, crops valued by competent practical persons at 3896l., being in the proportion of 15l. 18s. each tenant ; and their live stock, consisting of cattle, horses, sheep, and pigs, now actually upon the estates, is valued, according to the present prices of the neighbouring markets, at 4162l., of which 1304l. has been added since February 1844, being at the rate of 16l. 19s. for the whole period, and 5l. 6s. for the last year ; during which time their stock has thus increased in value a sum equal to their present annual rent ; and by the statistical tables and returns referred to in previous reports, it is proved that the tenants, in general, improve their little farms, and increase their cultivation and crops, in nearly direct proportion to the number of available working persons of both sexes of which their families consist."

There cannot be a stronger testimony to the superior amount of gross, and even of net produce, raised by small farming under any tolerable system of landed tenure ; and it is worthy of attention that the industry and zeal were greatest among the smaller holders ; Colonel Robinson noticing, as exceptions to the remarkable and rapid progress of improvement, some tenants who were " occupants of larger farms than twenty acres, a class too often deficient in the enduring industry indispensable for the successful prosecution of mountain improvements."

[1] [A brief section, beginning thus, was added in the 5th ed. (1862). This was omitted, and the present § 2 added in the 6th ed. (1865).]

The principal change in the situation consists in the great diminution, holding out a hope of the entire extinction, of cottier tenure.
The enormous decrease in the number of small holdings, and increase
in those of a medium size, attested by the statistical returns, sufficiently proves the general fact, and all testimonies show that the
tendency still continues.* It is probable that the repeal of the
corn laws, necessitating a change in the exports of Ireland from the
products of tillage to those of pasturage, would of itself have sufficed
to bring about this revolution in tenure. A grazing farm can only be

* There is, however, a partial counter-current, of which I have not seen any
public notice. " A class of men, not very numerous, but sufficiently so to do
much mischief, have, through the Landed Estates Court, got into possession of
land in Ireland, who, of all classes, are least likely to recognise the duties of a
landlord's position. These are small traders in towns, who by dint of sheer
parsimony, frequently combined with money-lending at usurious rates, have
succeeded, in the course of a long life, in scraping together as much money as
will enable them to buy fifty or a hundred acres of land. These people never
think of turning farmers, but, proud of their position as landlords, proceed to
turn it to the utmost account. An instance of this kind came under my notice
lately. The tenants on the property were, at the time of the purchase, some
twelve years ago, in a tolerably comfortable state. Within that period their
rent has been raised three several times ; and it is now, as I am informed by
the priest of the district, nearly double its amount at the commencement of the
present proprietor's reign. The result is that the people, who were formerly in
tolerable comfort, are now reduced to poverty : two of them have left the
property and squatted near an adjacent turf bog, where they exist trusting for
support to occasional jobs. If this man is not shot, he will injure himself
through the deterioration of his property, but meantime he has been getting
eight or ten per cent on his purchase-money. This is by no means a rare case.
The scandal which such occurrences cause, casts its reflection on transactions
of a wholly different and perfectly legitimate kind, where the removal of the
tenants is simply an act of mercy for all parties.
"The anxiety of landlords to get rid of cottiers is also to some extent neu-
tralized by the anxiety of middlemen to get them. About one-fourth of the
whole land of Ireland is held under long leases ; the rent received, when the
lease is of long standing, being generally greatly under the real value of the
land. It rarely happens that the land thus held is cultivated by the owner of
the lease : instead of this, he sublets it at a rackrent to small men, and lives
on the excess of the rent which he receives over that which he pays. Some of
these leases are always running out ; and as they draw towards their close, the
middleman has no other interest in the land than, at any cost of permanent
deterioration, to get the utmost out of it during the unexpired period of the
term. For this purpose the small cottier tenants precisely answer his turn.
Middlemen in this position are as anxious to obtain cottiers as tenants, as the
landlords are to be rid of them ; and the result is a transfer of this sort of tenant
from one class of estates to the other. The movement is of limited dimensions,
but it does exist, and so far as it exists, neutralizes the general tendency.
Perhaps it may be thought that this system will reproduce itself ; that the
same motives which led to the existence of middlemen will perpetuate the
class ; but there is no danger of this. Landowners are now perfectly alive to
the ruinous consequences of this system, however convenient for a time ; and a
clause against sub-letting is now becoming a matter of course in every lease."—
(*Private Communication from Professor Cairnes.*)

managed by a capitalist farmer, or by the landlord. But a change involving so great a displacement of the population˖has been immensely facilitated and made more rapid by the vast emigration, as well as by that greatest boon ever conferred on Ireland by any Government, the Encumbered Estates Act; the best provisions of which have since, through the Landed Estates Court, been permanently incorporated into the social system of the country. The greatest part of the soil of Ireland, there is reason to believe, is now farmed either by the landlords, or by small capitalist farmers. That these farmers are improving in circumstances, and accumulating capital, there is considerable evidence, in particular the great increase of deposits in the banks of which they are the principal customers. So far as that class is concerned, the chief thing still wanted is security of tenure, or assurance of compensation for improvements. The means of supplying these wants are now engaging the attention of the most competent minds; Judge Longfield's address, in the autumn of 1864, and the sensation created by it, are an era in the subject, and a point has now been reached when we may confidently expect that within a very few years something effectual will be done.

But what, meanwhile, is the condition of the displaced cottiers, so far as they have not emigrated; and of the whole class who subsist by agricultural labour, without the occupation of any land ? As yet, their state is one of great poverty, with but slight prospect of improvement. Money wages, indeed, have risen much above the wretched level of a generation ago : but the cost of subsistence has also risen so much above the old potato standard, that the real improvement is not equal to the nominal ; and according to the best information to which I have access, there is little appearance of an improved standard of living among the class. The population, in fact, reduced though it be, is still far beyond what the country can support as a mere grazing district of England. It may not, perhaps, be strictly true that, if the present number of inhabitants are to be maintained at home, it can only be either on the old vicious system of cottierism, or as small proprietors growing their own food. The lands which will remain under tillage would, no doubt, if sufficient security for outlay were given, admit of a more extensive employment of labourers by the small capitalist farmers ; and this, in the opinion of some competent judges, might enable the country to support the present number of its population in actual existence. But no one will pretend that this resource is sufficient to maintain them in any condition in which it is fit that the great body of the peasantry of a country should exist. Accordingly the emigration, which for a time had fallen off, has, under the additional stimulus of bad seasons, revived in all its strength. It is calculated that within the year 1864 not less than 100,000 emigrants left the Irish shores. As far as regards the emigrants themselves and their posterity, or the general interests of the human race, it would be folly to regret this result. The children of the immigrant Irish receive the education of Americans, and enter, more rapidly and completely than would have been possible in the country of their descent, into the benefits of a higher state of civilization. In twenty or thirty years they are not mentally distinguishable from other Americans. The loss, and the disgrace, are England's : and it is the English people and government whom it chiefly concerns to ask themselves, how far it will be to their honour and advantage to retain the mere soil of Ireland, but to lose its inhabitants. With the present feelings of the Irish people, and the direction which their hope of improving their condition seems to be permanently taking, England, it is probable, has only the choice between the depopulation of Ireland, and the conversion of a part of the labouring population into peasant proprietors. The truly insular ignorance of her public men respecting a form of agricultural economy which predominates in nearly every other civilized country, makes it only too probable that she will choose the worse side of the alternative. Yet there are germs of a tendency to the formation of peasant proprietors on Irish soil, which require only the aid of a friendly legislator to foster them ; as is shown in the following extract from a private communication by my eminent and valued friend, Professor Cairnes :—

" On the sale, some eight or ten years ago, of the Thomond, Portarlington, and Kingston estates, in the Encumbered Estates Court, it was observed that a considerable number of occupying tenants purchased the fee of their farms. I have not been able to obtain any information as to what followed that proceeding— whether the purchasers continued to farm their small properties, or under the mania of landlordism tried to escape from their former mode of life. But there are other facts which have a bearing on this question. In those parts of the country where tenant-right prevails, the prices given for the goodwill of a farm are enormous. The following figures, taken from the schedule of an estate in the neighbourhood of Newry, now passing through the Landed Estates Court, will give an idea, but a very inadequate one, of the prices which this mere customary right generally fetches.

" Statement showing the prices at which the tenant-right of certain farms near Newry was sold :—

	Acres.			Rent.				Purchase-money of tenant-right.
Lot 1	23	..	..	£74	..	..	..	£ 33
2	24	..	..	77	..	..	..	240
3	13	..	..	39	..	..	..	110
4	14	..	..	34	..	..	..	85
5	10	..	..	33	..	..	..	172
6	5	..	..	13	..	..	..	75
7	8	..	..	26	..	..	..	130
8	11	..	..	33	..	..	..	130
9	2	..	..	5	..	..	..	5
	110			£334				£980

" The prices here represent on the whole about three years purchase of the rental : but this, as I have said, gives but an inadequate idea of that which is frequently, indeed of that which is ordinarily, paid. The right, being purely customary, will vary in value with the confidence generally reposed in the good faith of the landlord. In the present instance, circumstances have come to light in the course of the proceedings connected with the sale of the estate, which give reason to believe that the confidence in this case was not high ; consequently, the rates above given may be taken as considerably under those which ordinarily prevail. Cases, as I am informed on the highest authority, have in other parts of the country come to light, also in the Landed Estates Court, in which the price given for the tenant-right was equal to that of the whole fee of the land. It is a remarkable fact that people should be found to give, say twenty or twenty-five years' purchase, for land which is still subject to a good round rent. Why, it will be asked, do they not purchase land out and out for the same, or a slightly larger, sum ? The answer to this question I believe is to be found in the state of our land laws. The cost of transferring land in small portions is, relatively to the purchase money, very considerable, even in the Landed Estates Court ; while the goodwill of a farm may be transferred without any cost at all. The cheapest conveyance that could be drawn in that Court, where the utmost economy, consistent with the present mode of remunerating legal services, is strictly enforced, would, irrespective of stamp duties, cost 10l.—a very sensible addition to the purchase of a small peasant estate : a conveyance to transfer a thousand acres might not cost more, and would probably not cost much more. But, in truth, the mere cost of conveyance represents but the least part of the obstacles which exist to obtaining land in small portions. A far more serious impediment is the complicated state of the ownership of land, which renders it frequently impracticable to subdivide a property into such portions as would bring the land within the reach of small bidders. The remedy for this state of things, however, lies in measures of a more radical sort than I fear it is at all probable that any House of Commons we are soon likely to see would even with patience consider. A registry of titles may succeed in reducing this complex condition of ownership to its simplest expression; but where real complication exists, the difficulty is not to be got rid of by mere simplicity of form; and a registry of titles—while the powers of disposition at present enjoyed by landowners remain undiminished, while every settler and testator has an almost unbounded licence to multiply interests in land, as pride, the passion for dictation, or mere whim may suggest—will, in my opinion, fail to reach the root of the evil. The effect of these circumstances is to place an immense premium upon large dealings in land—indeed in most cases practically to preclude all other than large dealings; and while this is the state of the law, the experiment of peasant proprietorship, it is plain, cannot be fairly tried. The facts, however, which I have stated, show, I think, conclusively, that there is no obstacle in the disposition of the people to the introduction of this system."

I have concluded a discussion, which has occupied a space almost disproportioned to the dimensions of this work; and I here close the examination of those simpler forms of social economy in which the produce of the land either belongs undividedly to one class, or is shared only between two classes. We now proceed to the hypothesis of a threefold division of the produce, among labourers, landlords, and capitalists; and in order to connect the coming discussions as closely as possible with those which have now for some time occupied us, I shall commence with the subject of Wages.[1]

---

[1] [See Appendix N. *Irish Agrarian Development.*]

CHAPTER XI

§ 1. UNDER the head of Wages are to be considered, first, the causes which determine or influence the wages of labour generally, and secondly, the differences that exist between the wages of different employments. It is convenient to keep these two classes of considerations separate; and in discussing the law of wages, to proceed in the first instance as if there were no other kind of labour than common unskilled labour of the average degree of hardness and disagreeableness.

Wages, like other things, may be regulated either by competition or by custom. In this country there are few kinds of labour of which the remuneration would not be lower than it is, if the employer took the full advantage of competition. Competition, however, must be regarded, in the present state of society, as the principal regulator of wages, and custom or individual character only as a modifying circumstance, and that in a comparatively slight degree.[1]

Wages, then, depend mainly upon the demand and supply of labour; or, as it is often expressed, on the proportion between population and capital. By population is here meant the number only of the labouring class, or rather of those who work for hire; and by capital only circulating capital, and not even the whole of that, but the part which is expended in the direct purchase of labour. To this, however, must be added all funds which, without

[1] [The present text of this paragraph dates from the 3rd ed. (1852). The original text ran, after the word "custom": "but the last is not a common case. A custom on the subject, even if established, could not easily maintain itself unaltered in any other than a stationary state of society. An increase or a falling off in the demand for labour, an increase or diminution of the labouring population, could hardly fail to engender a competition which would break down any custom respecting wages, by giving either to one side or to the other a strong direct interest in infringing it. We may at all events speak of the wages of labour as determined, in ordinary circumstances, by competition."]

forming a part of capital, are paid in exchange for labour, such as the wages of soldiers, domestic servants, and all other unproductive labourers. There is unfortunately no mode of expressing by one familiar term, the aggregate of what has been called the wages-fund of a country : and as the wages of productive labour form nearly the whole of that fund, it is usual to overlook the smaller and less important part, and to say that wages depend on population and capital. It will be convenient to employ this expression, remembering, however, to consider it as elliptical, and not as a literal statement of the entire truth.

With these limitations of the terms, wages not only depend upon the relative amount of capital and population, but cannot, under the rule of competition,[1] be affected by anything else. Wages (meaning, of course, the general rate) cannot rise, but by an increase of the aggregate funds employed in hiring labourers, or a diminution in the number of the competitors for hire ; nor fall, except either by a diminution of the funds devoted to paying labour, or by an increase in the number of labourers to be paid.[2]

§ 2.   There are, however, some facts in apparent contradiction to this doctrine, which it is incumbent on us to consider and explain.

For instance, it is a common saying that wages are high when trade is good. The demand for labour in any particular employment is more pressing, and higher wages are paid, when there is a brisk demand for the commodity produced ; and the contrary when there is what is called a stagnation : then workpeople are dismissed, and those who are retained must submit to a reduction of wages : though in these cases there is neither more nor less capital than before. This is true ; and is one of those complications in the concrete phenomena, which obscure and disguise the operation of general causes : but it is not really inconsistent with the principles laid down. Capital which the owner does not employ in purchasing labour, but keeps idle in his hands, is the same thing to the labourers, for the time being, as if it did not exist. All capital is, from the variations of trade, occasionally in this state. A manufacturer, finding a slack demand for his commodity, forbears to employ labourers in increasing a stock which he finds it difficult to dispose of ; or if he goes on until all his capital is locked up in unsold goods, then at least he must of necessity pause until he can get paid for

---

[1] [The qualification inserted in 3rd ed. (1852).]
[2] [See Appendix O. *The Wages Fund Doctrine.*]

some of them. But no one expects either of these states to be permanent; if he did, he would at the first opportunity remove his capital to some other occupation, in which it would still continue to employ labour. The capital remains unemployed for a time, during which the labour market is overstocked, and wages fall. Afterwards the demand revives, and perhaps becomes unusually brisk, enabling the manufacturer to sell his commodity even faster than he can produce it: his whole capital is then brought into complete efficiency, and if he is able, he borrows capital in addition, which would otherwise have gone into some other employment. At such times wages, in his particular occupation, rise. If we suppose, what in strictness is not absolutely impossible, that one of these fits of briskness or of stagnation should affect all occupations at the same time, wages altogether might undergo a rise or a fall. These, however, are but temporary fluctuations: the capital now lying idle will next year be in active employment, that which is this year unable to keep up with the demand will in its turn be locked up in crowded warehouses; and wages in these several departments will ebb and flow accordingly: but nothing can permanently alter general wages, except an increase or a diminution of capital itself (always meaning by the term, the funds of all sorts devoted to the payment of labour) compared with the quantity of labour offering itself to be hired.

Again, it is another common notion that high prices make high wages; because the producers and dealers, being better off, can afford to pay more to their labourers. I have already said that a brisk demand, which causes temporary high prices, causes also temporary high wages. But high prices, in themselves, can only raise wages if the dealers, receiving more, are induced to save more, and make an addition to their capital, or at least to their purchases of labour. This is indeed likely enough to be the case; and if the high prices came direct from heaven, or even from abroad, the labouring class might be benefited, not by the high prices themselves, but by the increase of capital occasioned by them. The same effect, however, is often attributed to a high price which is the result of restrictive laws, or which is in some way or other to be paid by the remaining members of the community; they having no greater means than before to pay it with. High prices of this sort, if they benefit one class of labourers, can only do so at the expense of others; since if the dealers by receiving high prices are enabled to make greater savings, or otherwise increase their purchases of labour, all other people by paying those high prices have their means of saving, or of purchasing labour, reduced in an equal degree ; and it is a matter of accident whether the one alteration or the other will have the greatest effect on the labour market. Wages will probably be temporarily higher in the employment in which prices have risen, and somewhat lower in other employments : in which case, while the first half of the phenomenon excites notice, the other is generally overlooked, or if observed, is not ascribed to the cause which really produced it. Nor will the partial rise of wages last long : for though the dealers in that one employment gain more, it does not follow that there is room to employ a greater amount of savings in their own business : their increasing capital will probably flow over into other employments, and there counterbalance the diminution previously made in the demand for labour by the diminished savings of other classes.

Another opinion often maintained is, that wages (meaning of course money wages) vary with the price of food ; rising when it rises, and falling when it falls. This opinion is, I conceive, only partially true ; and in so far as true, in no way affects the dependence of wages on the proportion between capital and labour : since the price of food, when it affects wages at all, affects them through that law. Dear or cheap food, caused by variety of seasons, does not affect wages (unless they are artificially adjusted to it by law or charity) : or rather, it has some tendency to affect them in the contrary way to that supposed ; since in times of scarcity people generally compete more violently for employment, and lower the labour market against themselves. But dearness or cheapness of food, when of a permanent character, and capable of being calculated on beforehand, may affect wages. In the first place, if the labourers have, as is often the case, no more than enough to keep them in working condition, and enable them barely to support the ordinary number of children, it follows that if food grows permanently dearer without a rise of wages, a greater number of the children will prematurely die ; and thus wages will be ultimately higher, but only because the number of people will be smaller, than if food had remained cheap. But, secondly, even though wages were high enough to admit of food's becoming more costly without depriving the labourers and their families of necessaries ; though they could bear, physically speaking, to be worse off, perhaps they would not consent to be so. They might have habits of comfort which were to them as necessaries, and sooner than forego which, they would put an additional restraint on their power of multiplication; so that wages would rise, not by increase of deaths but by diminution of births. In these cases, then, wages do adapt themselves to the price of food, though after an interval of almost a generation. Mr. Ricardo considers these two cases to comprehend all cases. He assumes that there is everywhere a minimum rate of wages : either the lowest with which it is physically possible to keep up the population, or the lowest with which the people will choose to do so. To this minimum he assumes that the general rate of wages always tends ; that they can never be lower, beyond the length of time required for a diminished rate of increase to make itself felt and can never long continue higher. This assumption contains sufficient truth to render it admissible for the purposes of abstract science ; and the conclusion which Mr. Ricardo draws from it, namely, that wages in the long run rise and fall with the permanent price of food, is, like almost all his conclusions, true hypothetically, that is, granting the suppositions from which he sets out. But in the application to practice, it is necessary to consider that the minimum of which he speaks, especially when it is not a physical, but what may be termed a moral minimum, is itself liable to vary. If wages were previously so high that they could bear reduction, to which the obstacle was a high standard of comfort habitual among the labourers, a rise in the price of food, or any other disadvantageous change in their circumstances, may operate in two ways : it may correct itself by a rise of wages brought about through a gradual effect on the prudential check to population ; or it may permanently lower the standard of living of the class, in case their previous habits in respect of population prove stronger than their previous habits in respect of comfort. In that case the injury done to them will be permanent, and their deteriorated condition will become a new minimum, tending to perpetuate itself as the more ample minimum did before. It is to be feared that of the two modes in which the cause may operate, the last is the most frequent, or at all events sufficiently so to render all propositions ascribing a self-repairing quality to the calamities which befall the labouring classes practically of no validity. There is considerable evidence that the circumstances of the agricultural labourers in England have more than once in our history sustained great permanent deterioration, from causes which operated by diminishing the demand for labour, and which, if population had exercised its power of self-adjustment in obedience to the previous standard of comfort, could only have had a temporary effect : but unhappily the poverty in which the class was plunged during a long series of years brought that previous standard into disuse ; and the next generation, growing up without having possessed those pristine comforts, multiplied in turn without any attempt to retrieve them.*

The converse case occurs when, by improvements in agriculture, the repeal of corn laws, or other such causes, the necessaries of the labourers are cheapened, and they are enabled, with the same wages, to command greater comforts than before. Wages will not fall immediately ; it is even possible that they may rise ; but they will fall at last, so as to leave the labourers no better off than before, unless during this interval of prosperity the standard of comfort, regarded as indispensable by the class, is permanently raised. Unfortunately this salutary effect is by no means to be counted upon : it is a much more difficult thing to raise, than to lower, the scale of living which the labourer will consider as more indispensable than marrying and having a family. If they content themselves with enjoying the greater comfort while it lasts, but do not learn to require it, they will people down to their old scale of living. If from poverty their children had previously been insufficiently fed or improperly nursed, a greater number will now be reared, and the competition of these, when they grow up, will depress wages, probably in full proportion to the greater cheapness of food. If the effect is not produced in this mode, it will be produced by earlier and more numerous marriages, or by an increased number of births to a marriage. According to all experience, a great increase invariably takes place in the number of marriages, in seasons of cheap food and full employment. I cannot, therefore, agree in the importance so often attached to the repeal of the corn laws, considered merely as a labourers' question, or to any of the schemes, of which some one or other is at all times in vogue, for making the labourers a very little better off. Things which only affect them a very little make no permanent impression upon their habits and requirements, and they soon slide back into their former state. To produce permanent advantage, the temporary cause operating upon them must be sufficient to make a great change in their condition—a change such as will be felt for many years, notwithstanding any stimulus which it may

---

* See the historical sketch of the condition of the English peasantry, prepared from the best authorities, by Mr. William Thornton, in his work entitled *Over-Population and its Remedy :* a work honourably distinguished from most others which have been published in the present generation, by its rational treatment of questions affecting the economical condition of the labouring classes.

give during one generation to the increase of people. When, indeed, the improvement is of this signal character, and a generation grows up which has always been used to an improved scale of comfort, the habits of this new generation in respect to population become formed upon a higher minimum, and the improvement in their condition becomes permanent. Of cases in point, the most remarkable is France after the Revolution. The majority of the population being suddenly raised from misery, to independence and comparative comfort; the immediate effect was that population, notwithstanding the destructive wars of the period, started forward with unexampled rapidity, partly because improved circumstances enabled many children to be reared who would otherwise have died, and partly from increase of births. The succeeding generation, however, grew up with habits considerably altered ; and though the country was never before in so prosperous a state, the annual number of births is now nearly stationary,* and the increase of population extremely slow.†

§ 3. Wages depend, then, on the proportion between the number of the labouring population, and the capital or other funds devoted to the purchase of labour ; we will say, for shortness, the capital. If wages are higher at one time or place than at another, if the subsistence and comfort of the class of hired labourers are more ample, it is for no other reason than because capital bears a greater proportion to population. It is not the absolute amount of accumulation

* Supra, pp. 293–5.
† A similar, though not an equal, improvement in the standard of living took place among the labourers of England during the remarkable fifty years from 1715 to 1765, which were distinguished by such an extraordinary succession of fine harvests (the years of decided deficiency not exceeding five in all that period) that the average price of wheat during those years was much lower than during the previous half century. Mr. Malthus computes that on the average of sixty years preceding 1720, the labourer could purchase with a day's earnings only two-thirds of a peck of wheat, while from 1720 to 1750 he could purchase a whole peck. The average price of wheat, according to the Eton tables, for fifty years ending with 1715, was 41s. 7¾d. per quarter, and for the last twenty-three of these, 45s. 8d., while for the fifty years following, it was no more than 34s. 11d. So considerable an improvement in the condition of the labouring class, though arising from the accidents of seasons, yet continuing for more than a generation, had time to work a change in the habitual requirements of the labouring class ; and this period is always noted as the date of " a marked improvement of the quality of the food consumed, and a decided elevation in the standard of their comforts and conveniences."—(Malthus, *Principles of Political Economy*, p. 225.) For the character of the period, see Mr. Tooke's excellent *History of Prices*, vol. i. pp. 38 to 61, and for the prices of corn, the Appendix to that work.

or of production, that is of importance to the labouring class; it is not the amount even of the funds destined for distribution among the labourers : it is the proportion between those funds and the numbers among whom they are shared. The condition of the class can be bettered in no other way than by altering that proportion to their advantage : and every scheme for their benefit, which does not proceed on this as its foundation, is, for all permanent purposes, a delusion.

In countries like North America and the Australian colonies, where the knowledge and arts of civilized life, and a high effective desire of accumulation, co-exist with a boundless extent of unoccupied land, the growth of capital easily keeps pace with the utmost possible increase of population, and is chiefly retarded by the impracticability of obtaining labourers enough. All, therefore, who can possibly be born can find employment without overstocking the market : every labouring family enjoys in abundance the necessaries, many of the comforts, and some of the luxuries of life ; and, unless in case of individual misconduct, or actual inability to work, poverty does not, and dependence need not, exist. A similar advantage, though in a less degree, is occasionally enjoyed by some special class of labourers in old countries, from an extraordinarily rapid growth, not of capital generally, but of the capital employed in a particular occupation. So gigantic has been the progress of the cotton manufacture since the inventions of Watt and Arkwright, that the capital engaged in it has probably quadrupled in the time which population requires for doubling. While, therefore, it has attracted from other employments nearly all the hands which geographical circumstances and the habits or inclinations of the people rendered available ; and while the demand it created for infant labour has enlisted the immediate pecuniary interest of the operatives in favour of promoting, instead of restraining, the increase of population ; nevertheless wages in the great seats of the manufacture are generally so high, that the collective earnings of a family amount, on an average of years, to a very satisfactory sum ; and there is, as yet, no sign of permanent decrease, while the effect has also been felt in raising the general standard of agricultural wages in the counties adjoining.

But those circumstances of a country, or of an occupation, in which population can with impunity increase at its utmost rate, are rare, and transitory. Very few are the countries presenting the needful union of conditions. Either the industrial arts are backward and stationary, and capital therefore increases slowly ; or, the effective desire of accumulation being low, the increase soon reaches its limit ; or, even though both these elements are at their highest known degree, the increase of capital is checked, because there is not fresh land to be resorted to, of as good quality as that already occupied. Though capital should for a time double itself simultaneously with population, if all this capital and population are to find employment on the same land, they cannot without an unexampled succession of agricultural inventions continue doubling the produce ; therefore, if wages do not fall, profits must ; and when profits fall, increase of capital is slackened. Besides, even if wages did not fall, the price of food (as will be shown more fully hereafter) would in these circumstances necessarily rise ; which is equivalent to a fall of wages.

Except, therefore, in the very peculiar cases which I have just noticed, of which the only one of any practical importance is that of a new colony, or a country in circumstances equivalent to it ; it is impossible that population should increase at its utmost rate without lowering wages. Nor will the fall be stopped at any point, short of that which either by its physical or its moral operation, checks the increase of population. In no old country, therefore, does population increase at anything like its utmost rate ; in most at a very moderate rate : in some countries, not at all. These facts are only to be accounted for in two ways. Either the whole number of births which nature admits of, and which happen in some circumstances, do not take place ; or if they do, a large proportion of those who are born, die. The retardation of increase results either from mortality or prudence ; from Mr. Malthus's positive, or from his preventive check : and one or the other of these must and does exist, and very powerfully too, in all old societies. Wherever population is not kept down by the prudence either of individuals or of the state, it is kept down by starvation or disease.

Mr. Malthus has taken great pains to ascertain, for almost every country in the world, which of these checks it is that operates ; and the evidence which he collected on the subject, in his *Essay on Population*, may even now be read with advantage. Throughout Asia, and formerly in most European countries in which the labouring classes were not in personal bondage, there is, or was, no restrainer of population but death. The mortality was not always the result of poverty : much of it proceeded from unskilful and careless management of children, from uncleanly and otherwise unhealthy habits

of life among the adult population, and from the almost periodical
occurrence of destructive epidemics. Throughout Europe these
causes of shortened life have much diminished, but they have not
ceased to exist. Until a period not very remote,[1] hardly any of
our large towns kept up its population, independently of the stream
always flowing into them from the rural districts : this was still
true of Liverpool until very recently ; and even in London the
mortality is larger, and the average duration of life shorter, than in
rural districts where there is much greater poverty. In Ireland,
epidemic fevers, and deaths from the exhaustion of the constitution
by insufficient nutriment, have always accompanied even the most
moderate deficiency of the potato crop. Nevertheless, it cannot
now be said that in any part of Europe, population is principally
kept down by disease, still less by starvation, either in a direct or
in an indirect form. The agency by which it is limited is chiefly
preventive, not (in the language of Mr. Malthus) positive. But the
preventive remedy seldom, I believe, consists in the unaided operation of prudential motives on a class wholly or mainly composed of
labourers for hire, and looking forward to no other lot. In England,
for example, I much doubt if the generality of agricultural labourers
practise any prudential restraint whatever. They generally marry
as early, and have as many children to a marriage, as they would
or could do if they were settlers in the United States. During the
generation which preceded the enactment of the present Poor Law,
they received the most direct encouragement to this sort of
improvidence : being not only assured of support, on easy terms,
whenever out of employment, but, even when in employment, very
commonly receiving from the parish a weekly allowance proportioned
to their number of children ; and the married with large families
being always, from a short-sighted economy, employed in preference
to the unmarried ; which last premium on population still exists.
Under such prompting, the rural labourers acquired habits of recklessness, which are so congenial to the uncultivated mind that, in
whatever manner produced, they in general long survive their
immediate causes. There are so many new elements at work in
society, even in those deeper strata which are inaccessible to the
mere movements on the surface, that it is hazardous to affirm anything positive on the mental state or practical impulses of classes
and bodies of men, when the same assertion may be true to-day, and
may require great modification in a few years' time. It does, how-

[1] [The original text of 1848 is practically unchanged in this paragraph.]

ever, seem, that if the rate of increase of population depended solely on the agricultural labourers, it would, as far as dependent on births, and unless repressed by deaths, be as rapid in the southern counties of England as in America. The restraining principle lies in the very great proportion of the population composed of the middle classes and the skilled artizans, who in this country almost equal in number the common labourers, and on whom prudential motives do, in a considerable degree, operate.

§ 4. Where a labouring class who have no property but their daily wages, and no hope of acquiring it, refrain from over-rapid multiplication, the cause, I believe, has always hitherto been, either actual legal restraint, or a custom of some sort which, without intention on their part, insensibly moulds their conduct, or affords immediate inducements not to marry. It is not generally known in how many countries of Europe direct legal obstacles are opposed to improvident marriages. The communications made to the original Poor Law Commission by our foreign ministers and consuls in different parts of Europe, contain a considerable amount of information on this subject. Mr. Senior, in his preface to those communications,* says that in the countries which recognise a legal right to relief, " marriage on the part of persons in the actual receipt of relief appears to be everywhere prohibited, and the marriage of those who are not likely to possess the means of independent support is allowed by very few. Thus we are told that in Norway no one can marry without ' showing to the satisfaction of the clergyman, that he is permanently settled in such a manner as to offer a fair prospect that he can maintain a family.'

" In Mecklenburg, that ' marriages are delayed by conscription in the twenty-second year, and military service for six years ; besides, the parties must have a dwelling, without which a clergyman is not permitted to marry them. The men marry at from twenty-five to thirty, the women not much earlier, as both must first gain by service enough to establish themselves.'

" In Saxony, that ' a man may not marry before he is twenty-one years old, if liable to serve in the army. In Dresden, professionists (by which word artizans are probably meant) may not marry until they become masters in their trade.'

" In Wurtemburg, that ' no man is allowed to marry till his

* Forming an Appendix (F) to the *General Report* of the Commissioners, and also published by authority as a separate volume.

twenty-fifth year, on account of his military duties, unless permission be especially obtained or purchased : at that age he must also obtain permission, which is granted on proving that he and his wife would have together sufficient to maintain a family or to establish themselves ; in large towns, say from 800 to 1000 florins (from 66*l.* 13*s.* 4*d.* to 84*l.* 3*s.* 4*d.*) ; in smaller, from 400 to 500 florins ; in villages, 200 florins (16*l.* 13*s.* 4*d.*) ' " *

The minister at Munich says, " the great cause why the number of the poor is kept so low in this country arises from the prevention by law of marriages in cases in which it cannot be proved that the parties have reasonable means of subsistence ; and this regulation is in all places and at all times strictly adhered to. The effect of a constant and firm observance of this rule has, it is true, a considerable influence in keeping down the population of Bavaria, which is at present low for the extent of country, but it has a most salutary effect in averting extreme poverty and consequent misery." †

At Lubeck, " marriages among the poor are delayed by the necessity a man is under, first, of previously proving that he is in regular employ, work, or profession, that will enable him to maintain a wife : and secondly, of becoming a burgher, and equipping himself in the uniform of the burgher guard, which together may cost him nearly 4*l.*" ‡   At Frankfort, " the government prescribes no age for marrying, but the permission to marry is only granted on proving a livelihood." §

The allusion, in some of these statements, to military duties, points out an indirect obstacle to marriage, interposed by the laws of some countries in which there is no direct legal restraint. In Prussia, for instance, the institutions which compel every able-bodied man to serve for several years in the army, at the time of life at which imprudent marriages are most likely to take place, are probably a full equivalent, in effect on population, for the legal restrictions of the smaller German states.

[1] " So strongly," says Mr. Kay, " do the people of Switzerland understand from experience the expediency of their sons and daughters postponing the time of their marriages, that the councils of state of four or five of the most democratic of the cantons, elected, be it remembered, by universal suffrage, have passed laws by which all young persons who marry before they have proved to the

---

* Preface, p. xxxix.
† Preface, p. xxxiii., or p. 554 of the Appendix itself.
‡ Appendix, p. 419.   § Ibid. p. 567.
[1] [This paragraph was added in the 3rd ed. (1852).]

magistrate of their district that they are able to support a family, are
rendered liable to a heavy fine. In Lucerne, Argovie, Unterwalden,
and, I believe, St. Gall, Schweitz, and Uri, laws of this character
have been in force for many years." *

§ 5. Where there is no general law restrictive of marriage,
there are often customs equivalent to it. When the guilds or trade
corporations of the Middle Ages were in vigour, their bye-laws or
regulations were conceived with a very vigilant eye to the advantage
which the trade derived from limiting competition : and they made
it very effectually the interest of artizans not to marry until after
passing through the two stages of apprentice and journeyman, and
attaining the rank of master.† In Norway, where the labour is

* Kay, op. cit. i. 68.
† " In general," says Sismondi, " the number of masters in each corporation
was fixed, and no one but a master could keep a shop, or buy and sell on his own
account. Each master could only train a certain number of apprentices, whom
he instructed in his trade ; in some corporations he was only allowed one.
Each master could also employ only a limited number of workmen, who were
called companions, or journeymen ; and in the trades in which he could only
take one apprentice, he was only allowed to have one, or at most two, journeymen. No one was allowed to buy, sell, or work at a trade, unless he was either
an apprentice, a journeyman, or a master ; no one could become a journeyman
without having served a given number of years as an apprentice, nor a master,
unless he had served the same number of years as a journeyman, and unless he
had also executed what was called his *chef d' œuvre* (*masterpiece*), a piece of work
appointed in his trade, and which was to be judged of by the corporation. It is
seen that this organization threw entirely into the hands of the masters the
recruiting of the trade. They alone could take apprentices ; but they were
not compelled to take any ; accordingly they required to be paid, often at a
very high rate, for the favour ; and a young man could not enter into a trade if
he had not, at starting, the sum required to be paid for his apprenticeship, and
the means necessary for his support during that apprenticeship ; since for four,
five, or seven years, all his work belonged to his master. His dependence on the
master during that time was complete ; for the master's will, or even caprice,
could close the door of a lucrative profession upon him. After the apprentice
became a journeyman he had a little more freedom ; he could engage with any
master he chose, or pass from one to another ; and as the condition of a journeyman was only accessible through apprenticeship, he now began to profit by the
monopoly from which he had previously suffered, and was almost ure of getting
well paid for a work which no one else was allowed to perform. He depended,
however, on the corporation for becoming a master, and did not, therefore,
regard himself as being yet assured of his lot, or as having a permanent position.
In general he did not marry until he had passed as a master.
" It is certain both in fact and in theory that the existence of trade corporations hindered, and could not but hinder, the birth of a superabundant population. By the statutes of almost all the guilds, a man could not pass as a master
before the age of twenty-five : but if he had no capital of his own, if he had not
made sufficient savings, he continued to work as a journeyman much longer ;
some, perhaps the majority of artisans, remained journeymen all their lives.
There was, however, scarcely an instance of their marrying before they were

chiefly agricultural, it is [1848] forbidden by law to engage a farm-servant for less than a year ; which was the general English practice until the poor-laws destroyed it, by enabling the farmer to cast his labourers on parish pay whenever he did not immediately require their labour. In consequence of this custom, and of its enforcement by law, the whole of the rather limited class of agricultural labourers in Norway have an engagement for a year at least, which, if the parties are content with one another, naturally becomes a permanent engagement : hence it is known in every neighbourhood whether there is, or is likely to be, a vacancy, and unless there is, a young man does not marry, knowing that he could not obtain employment. The custom still [1848] exists in Cumberland and Westmoreland, except that the term is half a year instead of a year ; and seems to be still attended with the same consequences. The farm-servants " are lodged and boarded in their masters' houses, which they seldom leave until, through the death of some relation or neighbour, they succeed to the ownership or lease of a cottage farm. What is called surplus labour does not here exist." *   I have mentioned in another chapter the check to population in England during the last century, from the difficulty of obtaining a separate dwelling place.† Other customs restrictive of population might be specified : in some parts of Italy it is the practice, according to Sismondi, among the poor, as it is well known to be in the higher ranks, that all but one of the sons remain unmarried.   But such family arrangements are not likely to exist among day-labourers. They are the resource of small proprietors and metayers, for preventing too minute a subdivision of the land.

In England generally there is now scarcely a relic of these indirect checks to population ; except that in parishes owned by one or a very small number of landowners, the increase of resident labourers is still occasionally obstructed, by preventing cottages from being built, or by pulling down those which exist ; thus restraining the population liable to become locally chargeable, without any material effect on population generally, the work required in those parishes being performed by labourers settled elsewhere. The surrounding districts always feel themselves much aggrieved by this practice, against which they cannot defend themselves by similar means,

received as masters : had they been so imprudent as to desire it, no father would have given his daughter to a man without a position."—*Nouveaux Principes*, book iv. ch. 10.   See also Adam Smith, book i. ch. 10, part 2.
    * See Thornton on *Over-Population*, page 18, and the authorities there cited.
    † Supra, p. 201.

since a single acre of land owned by any one who does not enter into the combination, enables him to defeat the attempt, very profitably to himself, by covering that acre with cottages. To meet these complaints an Act has within the last few years been passed by Parliament, by which the poor-rate is made a charge not on the parish, but on the whole union.[1] This enactment, in other respects very beneficial, removes the small remnant of what was once a check to population : the value of which, however, from the narrow limits of its operation, had become very trifling.

§ 6. In the case, therefore, of the common agricultural labourer, the checks to population may almost be considered as non-existent. If the growth of the towns, and of the capital there employed, by which the factory operatives are maintained at their present average rate of wages notwithstanding their rapid increase, did not also absorb a great part of the annual addition to the rural population, there seems no reason in the present habits of the people why they should not fall into as miserable a condition as the Irish previous to 1846 ; and if the market for our manufactures should, I do not say fall off, but even cease to expand at the rapid rate of the last fifty years, there is no certainty that this fate may not be reserved for us.[2] Without carrying our anticipations forward to such a calamity, which the great and growing intelligence of the factory population would, it may be hoped, avert, by an adaptation of their habits to their circumstances ; the existing condition of the labourers of some of the most exclusively agricultural counties, Wiltshire, Somersetshire, Dorsetshire, Bedfordshire, Buckinghamshire, is sufficiently painful to contemplate. The labourers of these counties, with large families, and eight or perhaps nine shillings [3] for their weekly wages when in full employment, have for some time been one of the stock objects of popular compassion : it is time that they had the benefit also of some application of common sense.

Unhappily, sentimentality rather than common sense usually presides over the discussion of these subjects ; and while there is a growing sensitiveness to the hardships of the poor, and a ready

[1] [The proposal was mentioned in the 1st ed. (1848) ; the Act was referred to in the 7th ed. (1871). For the Union Chargeability Act of 1865 and previous and subsequent legislation, see *Majority Report* of the Poor Law Commission (1909), Part iv. ch. 4.]

[2] [The words here following in the original text : " Especially considering how much the Irish themselves contribute to it, by migrating to this country and underbidding its native inhabitants," were omitted from the 5th ed. (1862).]

[3] [So ed. 5 (1862). In 1st ed. (1848) " seven or perhaps eight."]

disposition to admit claims in them upon the good offices of other people, there is an all but universal unwillingness to face the real difficulty of their position, or advert at all to the conditions which nature has made indispensable to the improvement of their physical lot. Discussions on the condition of the labourers, lamentations over its wretchedness, denunciations of all who are supposed to be indifferent to it, projects of one kind or another for improving it, were in no country and in no time of the world so rife as in the present generation ; but there is a tacit agreement to ignore totally the law of wages, or to dismiss it in a parenthesis, with such terms as "hard-hearted Malthusianism," as if it were not a thousand times more hard-hearted to tell human beings that they may, than that they may not, call into existence swarms of creatures who are sure to be miserable, and most likely to be depraved; and forgetting that the conduct, which it is reckoned so cruel to disapprove, is a degrading slavery to a brute instinct in one of the persons concerned, and most commonly, in the other, helpless submission to a revolting abuse of power.[1]

So long as mankind remained in a semi-barbarous state, with the indolence and the few wants of a savage, it probably was not desir-able that population should be restrained ; the pressure of physical want may have been a necessary stimulus, in that state of the human mind, to the exertion of labour and ingenuity required for accom-plishing that greatest of all past changes in human modes of existence, by which industrial life attained predominance over the hunting, the pastoral, and the military or predatory state. Want, in that age of the world, had its uses, as even slavery had ; and there may be corners of the earth where those uses are not yet superseded, though they might easily be so were a helping hand held out by more civilized communities. But in Europe the time, if it ever existed, is long past, when a life of privation had the smallest tendency to make men either better workmen or more civilized beings. It is, on the contrary, evident, that if the agricul-tural labourers were better off, they would both work more efficiently, and be better citizens. I ask, then, is it true, or not, that if their numbers were fewer they would obtain higher wages ? This is the question, and no other : and it is idle to divert attention from it, by

[1] [From the 3rd ed. (1852) was here omitted a paragraph of the original text criticising " the conduct, during ten important years, of a large portion of the Tory party " with regard to " an enactment " (the Poor Law Reform of 1834) " most salutary in principle, in which their own party had concurred, but of which their rivals were almost accidentally the nominal authors."]

attacking any incidental position of Malthus or some other writer, and pretending that to refute that, is to disprove the principle of population. Some, for instance, have achieved an easy victory over a passing remark of Mr. Malthus, hazarded chiefly by way of illustration, that the increase of food may perhaps be assumed to take place in an arithmetical ratio, while population increases in a geometrical : when every candid reader knows that Mr. Malthus laid no stress on this unlucky attempt to give numerical precision to things which do not admit of it, and every person capable of reasoning must see that it is wholly superfluous to his argument. Others have attached immense importance to a correction which more recent political economists have made in the mere language of the earlier followers of Mr. Malthus. Several writers had said that it is the tendency of population to *increase faster* than the means of subsistence. The assertion was true in the sense in which they meant it, namely, that population would in most circumstances increase faster than the means of subsistence, if it were not checked either by mortality or by prudence. But inasmuch as these checks act with unequal force at different times and places, it was possible to interpret the language of these writers as if they had meant that population is usually gaining ground upon subsistence, and the poverty of the people becoming greater. Under this interpretation of their meaning, it was urged that the reverse is the truth : that as civilization advances, the prudential check tends to become stronger, and population to slacken its rate of increase, relatively to subsistence ; and that it is an error to maintain that population, in any improving community, tends to increase faster than, or even so fast as, subsistence. The word tendency is here used in a totally different sense from that of the writers who affirmed the proposition : but waiving the verbal question, is it not allowed on both sides, that in old countries, population presses too closely upon the means of subsistence ? And though its pressure diminishes, the more the ideas and habits of the poorest class of labourers can be improved, to which it is to be hoped that there is always some tendency in a progressive country, yet since that tendency has hitherto been, and still is, extremely faint, and (to descend to particulars) has not yet extended to giving to the Wiltshire labourers higher wages than eight shillings a week, the only thing which it is necessary to consider is, whether that is a sufficient and suitable provision for a labourer ? for if not, population does, as an existing fact, bear too great a proportion to the wages-fund ;

and whether it pressed still harder or not quite so hard at some former period, is practically of no moment, except that, if the ratio is an improving one, there is the better hope that by proper aids and encouragements it may be made to improve more and faster.

It is not, however, against reason, that the argument on this subject has to struggle ; but against a feeling of dislike, which will only reconcile itself to the unwelcome truth, when every device is exhausted by which the recognition of that truth can be evaded. It is necessary, therefore, to enter into a detailed examination of these devices, and to force every position which is taken up by the enemies of the population principle in their determination to find some refuge for the labourers, some plausible means of improving their condition, without requiring the exercise, either enforced or voluntary, of any self-restraint, or any greater control than at present over the animal power of multiplication.   This will be the object of the next chapter.[1]

[1] [See Appendix P.   *The Movement of Population.*]

CHAPTER XII

§ 1. THE simplest expedient which can be imagined for keeping
the wages of labour up to the desirable point, would be to fix them
by law : and this is virtually the object aimed at in a variety of
plans which have at different times been, or still are, current, for
remodelling the relation between labourers and employers. No
one probably ever suggested that wages should be absolutely fixed ;
since the interests of all concerned often require that they should
be variable ; but some have proposed to fix a minimum of wages,
leaving the variations above that point to be adjusted by competition.
Another plan which has found many advocates among the leaders of
the operatives, is that councils should be formed, which in England
have been called local boards of trade, in France " conseus de
prud'hommes," and other names ; consisting of delegates from the
workpeople and from the employers, who, meeting in conference,
should agree upon a rate of wages, and promulgate it from authority,
to be binding generally on employers and workmen ; the ground
of decision being, not the state of the labour-market, but natural
equity ; to provide that the workmen shall have *reasonable* wages
and the capitalist reasonable profits.

Others again (but these are rather philanthropists interesting
themselves for the labouring classes, than the labouring people
themselves) are shy of admitting the interference of authority in
contracts for labour : they fear that if law intervened, it would
intervene rashly and ignorantly ; they are convinced that two parties,
with opposite interests, attempting to adjust those interests by
negotiation through their representatives on principles of equity,
when no rule could be laid down to determine what was equitable,
would merely exasperate their differences instead of healing them ;
but what it is useless to attempt by the legal sanction, these persons
desire to compass by the moral. Every employer, they think,
ought to give *sufficient* wages ; and if he does it not willingly, should

be compelled to it by general opinion ; the test of sufficient wages being their own feelings, or what they suppose to be those of the public. This is, I think, a fair representation of a considerable body of existing opinion on the subject.

I desire to confine my remarks to the principle involved in all these suggestions, without taking into account practical difficulties, serious as these must at once be seen to be. I shall suppose that by one or other of these contrivances, wages could be kept above the point to which they would be brought by competition. This is as much as to say, above the highest rate which can be afforded by the existing capital consistently with employing all the labourers. For it is a mistake to suppose that competition merely keeps down wages. It is equally the means by which they are kept up. When there are any labourers unemployed, these, unless maintained by charity, become competitors for hire, and wages fall ; but when all who were out of work have found employment, wages will not, under the freest system of competition, fall lower. There are strange notions afloat concerning the nature of competition. Some people seem to imagine that its effect is something indefinite ; that the competition of sellers may lower prices, and the competition of labourers may lower wages, down to zero, or some unassignable minimum. Nothing can be more unfounded. Goods can only be lowered in price by competition to the point which calls forth buyers sufficient to take them off ; and wages can only be lowered by competition until room is made to admit all the labourers to a share in the distribution of the wages-fund. If they fell below this point, a portion of capital would remain unemployed for want of labourers ; a counter-competition would commence on the side of capitalists, and wages would rise.

Since, therefore, the rate of wages which results from competition distributes the whole existing wages-fund among the whole labouring population ; if law or opinion succeeds in fixing wages above this rate, some labourers are kept out of employment ; and as it is not the intention of the philanthropists that these should starve, they must be provided for by a forced increase of the wages-fund ; by a compulsory saving. It is nothing to fix a minimum of wages, unless there be a provision that work, or wages at least, be found for all who apply for it. This, accordingly, is always part of the scheme ; and is consistent with the ideas of more people than would approve of either a legal or a moral minimum of wages. Popular sentiment looks upon it as the duty of the rich, or of the state, to find employment for all the poor. If the moral influence of opinion does not induce the rich to spare from their consumption enough to set all the poor to work at "reasonable wages," it is supposed to be incumbent on the state to lay on taxes for the purpose, either by local rates or votes of public money. The proportion between labour and the wages-fund would thus be modified to the advantage of the labourers, not by restriction of population, but by an increase of capital.

§ 2. If this claim on society could be limited to the existing generation; if nothing more were necessary than a compulsory accumulation, sufficient to provide permanent employment at ample wages for the existing numbers of the people ; such a proposition would have no more strenuous supporter than myself. Society mainly consists of those who live by bodily labour ; and if society, that is, if the labourers, lend their physical force to protect individuals in the enjoyment of superfluities, they are entitled to do so and have always done so, with the reservation of a power to tax those superfluities for purposes of public utility; among which purposes the subsistence of the people is the foremost. Since no one is responsible for having been born, no pecuniary sacrifice is too great to be made by those who have more than enough, for the purpose of securing enough to all persons already in existence.

But it is another thing altogether, when those who have produced and accumulated are called upon to abstain from consuming until they have given food and clothing, not only to all who now exist, but to all whom these or their descendants may think fit to call into existence. Such an obligation, acknowledged and acted upon, would suspend all checks, both positive and preventive ; there would be nothing to hinder population from starting forward at its rapidest rate ; and as the natural increase of capital would, at the best, not be more rapid than before, taxation, to make up the growing deficiency, must advance with the same gigantic strides. The attempt would of course be made to exact labour in exchange for support. But experience has shown the sort of work to be expected from recipients of public charity. When the pay is not given for the sake of the work, but the work found for the sake of the pay, inefficiency is a matter of certainty : to extract real work from day-labourers without the power of dismissal, is only practicable by the power of the lash. It is conceivable,[1] doubtless, that this objection might be

---

[1] [This and the two following sentences were inserted in the 2nd ed. (1849), and allowed to remain in subsequent editions.]

got over. The fund raised by taxation might be spread over the labour market generally, as seems to be intended by the supporters of the *droit au travail* in France ; without giving to any unemployed labourer a right to demand support in a particular place or from a particular functionary. The power of dismissal as regards individual labourers would then remain ; the government only undertaking to create additional employment when there was a deficiency, and reserving, like other employers, the choice of its own workpeople. But let them work ever so efficiently, the increasing population could not, as we have so often shown, increase the produce proportionally : the surplus, after all were fed, would bear a less and less proportion to the whole produce, and to the population : and the increase of people going on in a constant ratio, while the increase of produce went on in a diminishing ratio, the surplus would in time be wholly absorbed ; taxation for the support of the poor would engross the whole income of the country ; the payers and the receivers would be melted down into one mass. The check to population, either by death or prudence, could not then be staved off any longer, but must come into operation suddenly and at once ; everything which places mankind above a nest of ants or a colony of beavers, having perished in the interval.

These consequences have been so often and so clearly pointed out by authors of reputation, in writings known and accessible, that ignorance of them on the part of educated persons is no longer pardonable. It is doubly discreditable in any person setting up for a public teacher, to ignore these considerations ; to dismiss them silently, and discuss or declaim on wages and poor-laws, not as if these arguments could be refuted, but as if they did not exist.

Every one has a right to live. We will suppose this granted. But no one has a right to bring creatures into life, to be supported by other people. Whoever means to stand upon the first of these rights must renounce all pretension to the last. If a man cannot support even himself unless others help him, those others are entitled to say that they do not also undertake the support of any offspring which it is physically possible for him to summon into the world. Yet there are abundance of writers and public speakers, including many of most ostentatious pretensions to high feeling, whose views of life are so truly brutish, that they see hardship in preventing paupers from breeding hereditary paupers in the workhouse itself. Posterity will one day ask, with astonishment, what sort of people it could be among whom such preachers could find proselytes.

It would be possible for the state to guarantee employment at ample wages to all who are born. But if it does this, it is bound in self-protection, and for the sake of every purpose for which government exists, to provide that no person shall be born without its consent. If the ordinary and spontaneous motives to self-restraint are removed, others must be substituted. Restrictions on marriage, at least equivalent to those existing [1848] in some of the German states, or severe penalties on those who have children when unable to support them, would then be indispensable. Society can feed the necessitous, if it takes their multiplication under its control : or (if destitute of all moral feeling for the wretched offspring) it can leave the last to their discretion, abandoning the first to their own care. But it cannot with impunity take the feeding upon itself, and leave the multiplying free.

To give profusely to the people, whether under the name of charity or of employment, without placing them under such influences that prudential motives shall act powerfully upon them, is to lavish the means of benefiting mankind, without attaining the object. Leave the people in a situation in which their condition manifestly depends upon their numbers, and the greatest permanent benefit may be derived from any sacrifice made to improve the physical well-being of the present generation, and raise, by that means, the habits of their children. But remove the regulation of their wages from their own control ; guarantee to them a certain payment, either by law, or by the feeling of the community ; and no amount of comfort that you can give them will make either them or their descendants look to their own self-restraint as the proper means of preserving them in that state. You will only make them indignantly claim the continuance of your guarantee to themselves and their full complement of possible posterity.

On these grounds some writers have altogether condemned the English poor-law, and any system of relief to the able-bodied, at least when uncombined with systematic legal precautions against over-population. The famous Act of the 43rd of Elizabeth undertook, on the part of the public, to provide work and wages for all the destitute able-bodied : and there is little doubt that if the intent of that Act had been fully carried out, and no means had been adopted by the administrators of relief to neutralize its natural tendencies, the poor-rate would by this time have absorbed the whole net produce of the land and labour of the country. It is not at all surprising, therefore, that Mr. Malthus and others should at first have concluded against all poor laws whatever. It required much experience, and careful examination of different modes of poor-law management, to give assurance that the admission of an absolute right to be supported at the cost of other people, could exist in law and in fact, without fatally relaxing the springs of industry and the restraints of prudence. This, however, was fully substantiated by the investigations of the original Poor Law Commissioners. Hostile as they are unjustly accused of being to the principle of legal relief, they are the first who fully proved the compatibility of any Poor Law, in which a right to relief was recognised, with the permanent interests of the labouring class and of posterity. By a collection of facts, experimentally ascertained in parishes scattered throughout England, it was shown that the guarantee of support could be freed from its injurious effects upon the minds and habits of the people, if the relief, though ample in respect to necessaries, was accompanied with conditions which they disliked, consisting of some restraints on their freedom, and the privation of some indulgences. Under this proviso, it may be regarded as irrevocably established, that the fate of no member of the community needs be abandoned to chance ; that society can and therefore ought to insure every individual belonging to it against the extreme of want ; that the condition even of those who are unable to find their own support, needs not be one of physical suffering, or the dread of it, but only of restricted indulgence, and enforced rigidity of discipline. This is surely something gained for humanity, important in itself, and still more so as a step to something beyond ; and humanity has no worse enemies than those who lend themselves, either knowingly or unintentionally, to bring odium on this law, or on the principles in which it originated.

§ 3. Next to the attempts to regulate wages, and provide artificially that all who are willing to work shall receive an adequate price for their labour, we have to consider another class of popular remedies, which do not profess to interfere with freedom of contract ; which leave wages to be fixed by the competition of the market, but, when they are considered insufficient, endeavour by some subsidiary resource to make up to the labourers for the insufficiency. Of this nature was the expedient resorted to by parish authorities during thirty or forty years previous to 1834, generally known as the Allowance System. This was first introduced when, through a succession of bad seasons, and conseq ent high prices of food, the

wages of labour had become inadequate to afford to the families of
the agricultural labourers the amount of support to which they had
been accustomed. Sentiments of humanity, joined with the idea
then inculcated in high quarters, that people ought not to be allowed
to suffer for having enriched their country with a multitude of
inhabitants, induced the magistrates of the rural districts to commence giving parish relief to persons already in private employment :
and when the practice had once been sanctioned, the immediate
interest of the farmers, whom it enabled to throw part of the support
of their labourers upon the other inhabitants of the parish, led to a
great and rapid extension of it. The principle of this scheme being
avowedly that of adapting the means of every family to its necessities,
it was a natural consequence that more should be given to the
married than to the single, and to those who had large families
than to those who had not : in fact, an allowance was usually
granted for every child. So direct and positive an encouragement
to population is not, however, inseparable from the scheme : the
allowance in aid of wages might be a fixed thing, given to all labourers
alike, and as this is the least objectionable form which the system
can assume, we will give it the benefit of the supposition

It is obvious that this is merely another mode of fixing a minimum
of wages ; no otherwise differing from the direct mode, than in
allowing the employer to buy the labour at its market price, the
difference being made up to the labourer from a public fund. The
one kind of guarantee is open to all the objections which have been
urged against the other. It promises to the labourers that they shall
all have a certain amount of wages, however numerous they may be
and removes, therefore, alike the positive and the prudential obstacles
to an unlimited increase. But besides the objections common to all
attempts to regulate wages without regulating population, the
allowance system has a peculiar absurdity of its own. This is,
that it inevitably takes from wages with one hand what it adds to
them with the other. There is a rate of wages, either the lowest on
which the people can, or the lowest on which they will consent, to
live. We will suppose this to be seven shillings a week. Shocked
at the wretchedness of this pittance, the parish authorities humanely
make it up to ten. But the labourers are accustomed to seven, and
though they would gladly have more, will live on that (as the fact
proves) rather than restrain the instinct of multiplication. Their
habits will not be altered for the better by giving them parish pay.
Receiving three shillings from the parish, they will be as well off

as before though they should increase sufficiently to bring down
wages to four shillings. They will accordingly people down to that
point; or perhaps, without waiting for an increase of numbers,
there are unemployed labourers enough in the workhouse to produce
the effect at once. It is well known that the allowance system did
practically operate in the mode described, and that under its influence
wages sank to a lower rate than had been known in England before.
During the last century, under a rather rigid administration of the
poor laws, population increased slowly, and agricultural wages were
considerably above the starvation point. Under the allowance
system the people increased so fast, and wages sank so low, that with
wages and allowance together, families were worse off than they
had been before with wages alone. When the labourer depends
solely on wages, there is a virtual minimum. If wages fall below the
lowest rate which will enable the population to be kept up, depopulation at least restores them to that lowest rate. But if the deficiency
is to be made up by a forced contribution from all who have anything
to give, wages may fall below starvation point; they may fall
almost to zero. This deplorable system, worse than any other
form of poor-law abuse yet invented, inasmuch as it pauperizes not
merely the unemployed part of the population but the whole, received
a severe check from the Poor Law of 1834 : I wish it could be said
that there are no signs of its revival.[1]

§ 4. But while this is generally condemned, there is another
mode of relief in aid of wages, which is still highly popular; a mode
greatly preferable, morally and socially, to parish allowance, but
tending, it is to be feared, to a very similar economical result : I
mean the much-boasted Allotment System. This, too, is a contrivance to compensate the labourer for the insufficiency of his
wages, by giving him something else as a supplement to them : but
instead of having them made up from the poor-rate, he is enabled
to make them up for himself, by renting a small piece of ground,
which he cultivates like a garden by spade labour, raising potatoes
and other vegetables for home consumption, with perhaps some
additional quantity for sale. If he hires the ground ready manured,
he sometimes pays for it at as high a rate as eight pounds an acre :
but getting his own labour and that of his family for nothing, he

[1] [The present text dates only from the 7th ed. (1871). Until then it had
read : " This deplorable system . . . has been abolished, and of this one abuse
at least it may be said that nobody professes to wish for its revival."]

is able to gain several pounds by it even at so high a rent.* The patrons of the system make it a great point that the allotment shall be in aid of wages, and not a substitute for them ; that it shall not be such as a labourer can live on, but only sufficient to occupy the spare hours and days of a man in tolerably regular agricultural employment, with assistance from his wife and children. They usually limit the extent of a single allotment to a quarter, or something between a quarter and half an acre. If it exceeds this, without being enough to occupy him entirely, it will make him, they say, a bad and uncertain workman for hire : if it is sufficient to take him entirely out of the class of hired labourers, and to become his sole means of subsistence, it will make him an Irish cottier : for which assertion, at the enormous rents usually demanded, there is some foundation. But in their precautions against cottierism, these well-meaning persons do not perceive, that if the system they patronize is not a cottier system, it is, in essentials, neither more nor less than a system of conacre.

There is no doubt a material difference between eking out insufficient wages by a fund raised by taxation, and doing the same thing by means which make a clear addition to the gross produce of the country. There is also a difference between helping a labourer by means of his own industry, and subsidizing him in a mode which tends to make him careless and idle. On both these points, allotments have an unquestionable advantage over parish allowances. But in their effect on wages and population, I see no reason why the two plans should substantially differ. All subsidies in aid of wages enable the labourer to do with less remuneration, and therefore ultimately bring down the price of labour by the full amount, unless a change be wrought in the ideas and requirements of the labouring class ; an alteration in the relative value which they set upon the gratification of their instincts, and upon the increase of their comforts and the comforts of those connected with them. That any such change in their character should be produced by the allotment system, appears to me a thing not to be expected. The possession of land, we are sometimes told, renders the labourer provident. Property in land does so ; or what is equivalent to property, occupation on fixed terms and on a permanent tenure. But mere hiring from year to year was never found to have any such effect. Did possession of land render the

* See the Evidence on the subject of Allotments, collected by the Com missioners of Poor Law Enquiry.

Irishman provident ?   Testimonies, it is true, abound, and I do
not seek to discredit them, of the beneficial change produced in the
conduct and condition of labourers, by receiving allotments.   Such
an effect is to be expected while those who hold them are a small
number ; a privileged class, having a status above the common level,
which they are unwilling to lose.   They are also, no doubt, almost
always, originally a select class, composed of the most favourable
specimens of the labouring people : which, however, is attended
with the inconvenience that the persons to whom the system
facilitates marrying and having children, are precisely those who
would otherwise be the most likely to practise prudential restraint.
As affecting the general condition of the labouring class, the scheme,
as it seems to me, must be either nugatory or mischievous.   If
only a few labourers have allotments, they are naturally those who
could do best without them, and no good is done to the class : while,
if the system were general, and every or almost every labourer had
an allotment, I believe the effect would be much the same as when
every or almost every labourer had an allowance in aid of wages.   I
think there can be no doubt that if, at the end of the last century,
the Allotment instead of the Allowance system had been generally
adopted in England, it would equally have broken down the practical
restraints on population which at that time did really exist ; population would have started forward exactly as in fact it did ; and in
twenty years, wages plus the allotment would have been, as wages
plus the allowance actually were, no more than equal to the former
wages without any allotment.   The only difference in favour of
allotments would have been, that they make the people grow their
own poor-rates.

I am at the same time quite ready to allow, that in some circumstances, the possession of land at a fair rent, even without ownership,
by the generality of labourers for hire, operates as a cause not of low,
but of high wages.   This, however, is when their land renders them,
to the extent of actual necessaries, independent of the market for
labour.   There is the greatest difference between the position of
people who live by wages, with land as an extra resource, and of
people who can, in case of necessity, subsist entirely on their land,
and only work for hire to add to their comforts.   Wages are likely
to be high where none are compelled by necessity to sell their labour.
" People who have at home some kind of property to apply their
labour to, will not sell their labour for wages that do not afford them
a better diet than potatoes and maize, although in saving for

themselves, they may live very much on potatoes and maize. We are often surprised in travelling on the Continent, to hear of a rate of day's wages very high, considering the abundance and cheapness of food. It is want of the necessity or the inclination to take work, that makes day-labour scarce, and, considering the price of provisions, dear, in many parts of the Continent, where property in land is widely diffused among the people."* There are parts of the Continent, where, even of the inhabitants of the towns, scarcely one seems to be exclusively dependent on his ostensible employment; and nothing else can explain the high price they put on their services, and the carelessness they evince as to whether they are employed at all. But the effect would be far different if their land or other resources gave them only a fraction of a subsistence, leaving them under an undiminished necessity of selling their labour for wages in an overstocked market. Their land would then merely enable them to exist on smaller wages, and to carry their multiplication so much the further before reaching the point below which they either could not, or would not descend.

To the view I have taken of the effect of allotments, I see no argument which can be opposed, but that employed by Mr. Thornton,† with whom on this subject I am at issue. His defence of allotments is grounded on the general doctrine, that it is only the very poor who multiply without regard to consequences, and that if the condition of the existing generation could be greatly improved, which he thinks might be done by the allotment system, their successors would grow up with an increased standard of requirements, and would not have families until they could keep them in as much comfort as that in which they had been brought up themselves. I agree in as much of this argument as goes to prove that a sudden and very great improvement in the condition of the poor has always, through its effect on their habits of life, a chance of becoming permanent. What happened at the time of the French Revolution is an example. But I cannot think that the addition of a quarter or even half an acre to every labourer's cottage, and that too at a rack rent, would (after the fall of wages which would be necessary to absorb the already existing mass of pauper labour) make so great a difference in the comforts of the family for a generation to come, as to raise up from childhood a labouring population with a really higher permanent standard of requirements and habits. So small a portion

* Laing's *Notes of a Traveller*, p. 456.
† See Thornton on *Over-Population*, ch. viii.

of land could only be made a permanent benefit, by holding out encouragement to acquire by industry and saving, the means of buying it outright : a permission which, if extensively made use of, would be a kind of education in forethought and frugality to the entire class, the effects of which might not cease with the occasion. The benefit would however arise, not from what was given them, but from what they were stimulated to acquire.

No remedies for low wages have the smallest chance of being efficacious, which do not operate on and through the minds and habits of the people. While these are unaffected, any contrivance, even if successful, for temporarily improving the condition of the very poor, would but let slip the reins by which population was previously curbed ; and could only, therefore, continue to produce its effect, if, by the whip and spur of taxation, capital were compelled to follow at an equally accelerated pace. But this process could not possibly continue for long together, and whenever it stopped, it would leave the country with an increased number of the poorest class, and a diminished proportion of all except the poorest, or, if it continued long enough, with none at all. For " to this complexion must come at last " all social arrangements, which remove the natural checks to population without substituting any others.

CHAPTER XIII

§ 1. By what means, then, is poverty to be contended against ?
How is the evil of low wages to be remedied ? If the expedients
usually recommended for the purpose are not adapted to it, can no
others be thought of ? Is the problem incapable of solution ?
Can political economy do nothing, but only object to everything,
and demonstrate that nothing can be done ?

If this were so, political economy might have a needful, but
would have a melancholy, and a thankless task. If the bulk of
the human race are always to remain as at present, slaves to toil
in which they *have* no interest, and therefore *feel* no interest—
drudging from early morning till late at night for bare necessaries,
and with all the intellectual and moral deficiencies which that
implies—without resources either in mind or feelings—untaught, for
they cannot be better taught than fed ; selfish, for all their thoughts
are acquired for themselves ; without interests or sentiments as
citizens and members of society, and with a sense of injustice
rankling in their minds, equally for what they have not, and for
what others have ; I know not what there is which should make a
person with any capacity of reason, concern himself about the
destinies of the human race. There would be no wisdom for any
one but in extracting from life, with Epicurean indifference, as
much personal satisfaction to himself and those with whom he
sympathises, as it can yield without injury to any one, and letting
the unmeaning bustle of so-called civilized existence roll by unheeded.
But there is no ground for such a view of human affairs. Poverty,
like most social evils, exists because men follow their brute instincts
without due consideration. But society is possible, precisely because
man is not necessarily a brute. Civilization in every one of its
aspects is a struggle against the animal instincts. Over some even
of the strongest of them, it has shown itself capable of acquiring

abundant control. It has artificialized large portions of mankind
to such an extent, that of many of their most natural inclinations
they have scarcely a vestige or a remembrance left. If it has not
brought the instinct of population under as much restraint as is
needful, we must remember that it has never seriously tried. What
efforts it has made, have mostly been in the contrary direction.
Religion, morality, and statesmanship have vied with one another in
incitements to marriage, and to the multiplication of the species,
so it be but in wedlock. Religion has not even yet discontinued
its encouragements. The Roman Catholic clergy (of any other
clergy it is unnecessary to speak, since no other have any considerable
influence over the poorer classes) everywhere think it their duty to
promote marriage, in order to prevent fornication. There is still
in many minds a strong religious prejudice against the true doctrine.
The rich, provided the consequences do not touch themselves, think
it impugns the wisdom of Providence to suppose that misery can
result from the operation of a natural propensity : the poor think
that " God never sends mouths but he sends meat." No one would
guess from the language of either, that man had any voice or choice
in the matter. So complete is the confusion of ideas on the whole
subject ; owing in a great degree to the mystery in which it is
shrouded by a spurious delicacy, which prefers that right and
wrong should be mismeasured and confounded on one of the subjects
most momentous to human welfare, rather than that the subject
should be freely spoken of and discussed. People are little aware
of the cost to mankind of this scrupulosity of speech. The diseases
of society can, no more than corporal maladies, be prevented or
cured without being spoken about in plain language. All experience
shows that the mass of mankind never judge of moral questions for
themselves, never see anything to be right or wrong until they have
been frequently told it ; and who tells them that they have any duties
in the matter in question, while they keep within matrimonial
limits ? Who meets with the smallest condemnation, or rather,
who does not meet with sympathy and benevolence, for any
amount of evil which he may have brought upon himself and those
dependent on him, by this species of incontinence ? While a man
who is intemperate in drink, is discountenanced and despised by
all who profess to be moral people,[1] it is one of the chief grounds

---

[1] [The remainder of this sentence appeared first in the 3rd ed. (1852). In
the 1st and 2nd ed. (1848, 1849), the text ran : " Is it not to this hour the
favourite recommendation for any parochial office bestowed by popular election

made use of in appeals to the benevolent, that the applicant has a large family and is unable to maintain them.*

One cannot wonder that silence on this great department of human duty should produce unconsciousness of moral obligations, when it produces oblivion of physical facts. That it is possible to delay marriage, and to live in abstinence while unmarried, most people are willing to allow ; but when persons are once married, the idea, in this country, never seems to enter any one's mind that having or not having a family, or the number of which it shall consist, is amenable to their own control. One would imagine that children were rained down upon married people, direct from heaven, without their being art or part in the matter ; that it was really, as the common phrases have it, God's will, and not their own, which decided the numbers of their offspring. Let us see what is a Continental philosopher's opinion on this point ; a man among the most benevolent of his time, and the happiness of whose married life has been celebrated.

"When dangerous prejudices," says Sismondi,† "have not become accredited, when a morality contrary to our true duties towards others, and especially towards those to whom we have given life, is not inculcated in the name of the most sacred authority ; no prudent man contracts matrimony before he is in a condition which gives him an assured means of living, and no married man has a greater number of children than he can properly bring up. The head of a family thinks, with reason, that his children may be contented with the condition in which he himself has lived ; and his desire will be that the rising generation should represent exactly the departing one : that one son and one daughter arrived at the marriageable age should replace his own father and mother ; that the children of his children should in their turn replace himself and his wife ; that his daughter should find in another family the precise equivalent of the lot which will be given in his own family to the daughter of another, and that the income which sufficed for the parents will suffice for the children." In a country increasing in

to have a large family and to be unable to maintain them ? Do not the candidates placard their intemperence upon walls, and publish it through the town in circulars ? " Cf. Dickens, *The Election for Beadle* in *Sketches by Boz,* " Our Parish," ch. iv.]

* Little improvement can be expected in morality until the producing large families is regarded with the same feelings as drunkenness or any other physical excess. But while the aristocracy and clergy are foremost to set the example of this kind of incontinence, what can be expected of the poor ?

† *Nouveaux Principes*, liv. vii. ch. 5.

wealth, some increase of numbers would be admissible, but that is a question of detail, not of principle. " Whenever this family has been formed, justice and humanity require that he should impose on himself the same restraint which is submitted to by the unmarried. When we consider how small, in every country, is the number of natural children, we must admit that this restraint is on the whole sufficiently effectual. In a country where population has no room to increase, or in which its progress must be so slow as to be hardly perceptible, when there are no places vacant for new establishments, a father who has eight children must expect, either that six of them will die in childhood, or that three men and three women among his cotemporaries, and in the next generation three of his sons and three of his daughters, will remain unmarried on his account."

§ 2. Those who think it hopeless that the labouring classes should be induced to practise a sufficient degree of prudence in regard to the increase of their families, because they have hitherto stopt short of that point, show an inability to estimate the ordinary principles of human action. Nothing more would probably be necessary to secure that result, than an opinion generally diffused that it was desirable. As a moral principle, such an opinion has never yet existed in any country : it is curious that it does not so exist in countries in which, from the spontaneous operation of individual forethought, population is, comparatively speaking, efficiently repressed. What is practised as prudence is still not recognised as duty ; the talkers and writers are mostly on the other side, even in France, where a sentimental horror of Malthus is almost as rife as in this country. Many causes may be assigned, besides the modern date of the doctrine, for its not having yet gained possession of the general mind. Its truth has, in some respects, been its detriment. One may be permitted to doubt whether, except among the poor themselves (for whose prejudices on this subject there is no difficulty in accounting) there has ever yet been, in any class of society, a sincere and earnest desire that wages should be high. There has been plenty of desire to keep down the poor-rate ; but, that done, people have been very willing that the working classes should be ill off. Nearly all who are not labourers themselves, are employers of labour, and are not sorry to get the commodity cheap. It is a fact, that even Boards of Guardians, who are supposed to be official apostles of anti-population doctrines, will seldom hear patiently of anything which they are pleased to designate as

Malthusianism. Boards of Guardians in rural districts, principally consist of farmers, and farmers, it is well known, in general dislike even allotments, as making the labourers " too independent." From the gentry, who are in less immediate contact and collision of interest with the labourers, better things might be expected, and the gentry of England are usually charitable. But charitable people have human infirmities, and would, very often, be secretly not a little dissatisfied if no one needed their charity : it is from them one oftenest hears the base doctrine, that God has decreed there shall always be poor. When one adds to this, that nearly every person who has had in him any active spring of exertion for a social object, has had some favourite reform to effect which he thought the admission of this great principle would throw into the shade ; has had corn laws to repeal, or taxation to reduce, or small notes to issue, or the charter to carry, or the church to revive or abolish, or the aristocracy to pull down, and looked upon every one as an enemy who thought anything important except his object ; it is scarcely wonderful that since the population doctrine was first promulgated, nine-tenths of the talk has always been against it, and the remaining tenth only audible at intervals ; and that it has not yet penetrated far among those who might be expected to be the least willing recipients of it, the labourers themselves.

But let us try to imagine what would happen if the idea became general among the labouring class, that the competition of too great numbers was the special cause of their poverty ; so that every labourer looked (with Sismondi) upon every other who had more than the number of children which the circumstances of society allowed to each, as doing him a wrong—as filling up the place which he was entitled to share. Any one who supposes that this state of opinion would not have a great effect on conduct, must be profoundly ignorant of human nature ; can never have considered how large a portion of the motives which induce the generality of men to take care even of their own interest, is derived from regard for opinion—from the expectation of being disliked or despised for not doing it. In the particular case in question, it is not too much to say that over-indulgence is as much caused by the stimulus of opinion as by the mere animal propensity ; since opinion universally, and especially among the most uneducated classes, has connected ideas of spirit and power with the strength of the instinct, and of inferiority with its moderation or absence ; a perversion of senti-ment caused by its being the means, and the stamp, of a dominion exercised over other human beings. The effect would be great of merely removing this factitious stimulus ; and when once opinion shall have turned itself into an adverse direction, a revolution will soon take place in this department of human conduct. We are often told that the most thorough perception of the dependence of wages on population will not influence the conduct of a labouring man, because it is not the children he himself can have that will produce any effect in generally depressing the labour market. True : and it is also true, that one soldier's running away will not lose the battle ; accordingly it is not that consideration which keeps each soldier in his rank : it is the disgrace which naturally and inevitably attends on conduct by any one individual, which if pursued by a majority everybody can see would be fatal. Men are seldom found to brave the general opinion of their class, unless supported either by some principle higher than regard for opinion, or by some strong body of opinion elsewhere.

It must be borne in mind also, that the opinion here in question, as soon as it attained any prevalence, would have powerful auxiliaries in the great majority of women. It is seldom by the choice of the wife that families are too numerous ; on her devolves (along with all the physical suffering and at least a full share of the privations) the whole of the intolerable domestic drudgery resulting from the excess. To be relieved from it would be hailed as a blessing by multitudes of women who now never venture to urge such a claim, but who would urge it, if supported by the moral feelings of the community. Among the barbarisms which law and morals have not yet ceased to sanction, the most disgusting surely is, that any human being should be permitted to consider himself as having a *right* to the person of another.

If the opinion were once generally established among the labouring class that their welfare required a due regulation of the numbers of families, the respectable and well-conducted of the body would conform to the prescription, and only those would exempt themselves from it, who were in the habit of making light of social obligations generally; and there would be then an evident justification for converting the moral obligation against bringing children into the world who are a burthen to the community, into a legal one ; just as in many other cases of the progress of opinion, the law ends by enforcing against recalcitrant minorities obligations which to be useful must be general, and which, from a sense of their utility, a large majority have voluntarily consented to take upon themselves.

There would be no need, however, of legal sanctions, if women were admitted, as on all other grounds they have the clearest title to be, to the same rights of citizenship with men. Let them cease to be confined by custom to one physical function as their means of living and their source of influence, and they would have for the first time an equal voice with men in what concerns that function : and of all the improvements in reserve for mankind which it is now possible to foresee, none might be expected to be so fertile as this in almost every kind of moral and social benefit.[1]

It remains to consider what chance there is that opinions and feelings, grounded on the law of the dependence of wages on population, will arise among the labouring classes ; and by what means such opinions and feelings can be called forth. Before considering the grounds of hope on this subject, a hope which many persons, no doubt, will be ready, without consideration, to pronounce chimerical, I will remark, that unless a satisfactory answer can be made to these two questions, the industrial system prevailing in this country, and regarded by many writers as the *ne plus ultra* of civilization—the dependence of the whole labouring class of the community on the wages of hired labour, is irrevocably condemned. The question we are considering is, whether, of this state of things, over-population and a degraded condition of the labouring class are the inevitable consequence. If a prudent regulation of population be not reconcilable with the system of hired labour, the system is a nuisance, and the grand object of economical statesmanship should be (by whatever arrangements of property, and alterations in the modes of applying industry), to bring the labouring people under the influence of stronger and more obvious inducements to this kind of prudence, than the relation of workmen and employers can afford.

But there exists no such incompatibility. The causes of poverty are not so obvious at first sight to a population of hired labourers, as they are to one of proprietors, or as they would be to a socialist community. They are, however, in no way mysterious. The dependence of wages on the number of the competitors for employment, is so far from hard of comprehension, or unintelligible to the labouring classes, that by great bodies of them it is already recognised and habitually acted on. It is familiar to all Trade Unions : every successful combination to keep up wages owes its

---

[1] [The two last sentences were added in the 3rd ed. (1852).]

success to contrivances for restricting the number of the competitors
all skilled trades are anxious to keep down their own numbers, an
many impose, or endeavour to impose, as a condition upon employer
that they shall not take more than a prescribed number of apprer
tices.   There is, of course, a great difference between limiting the
numbers by excluding other people, and doing the same thing by
restraint imposed on themselves : but the one as much as the othe
shows a clear perception of the relation between their numbers an
their remuneration.   The principle is understood in its applicatio:
to any one employment, but not to the general mass of employmen
For this there are several reasons : first, the operation of causes i
more easily and distinctly seen in the more circumscribed field
secondly, skilled artizans are a more intelligent class than ordinar
manual labourers :   and the habit of concert, and of passing i
review their general condition as a trade, keeps up a better under
standing of their collective interests :   thirdly and lastly, they ar
the most provident, because they are the best off, and have the mos
to preserve.   What, however, is clearly perceived and admitted i
particular instances, it cannot be hopeless to see understood an
acknowledged as a general truth.   Its recognition, at least i
theory, seems a thing which must necessarily and immediately com
to pass, when the minds of the labouring classes become capable o
taking any rational view of their own aggregate condition.   Of thi
the great majority of them have until now been incapable, eithe:
from the uncultivated state of their intelligence, or from poverty
which leaving them neither the fear of worse, nor the smallest hop
of better, makes them careless of the consequences of their actions
and without thought for the future.

§ 3.   For the purpose therefore of altering the habits of th
labouring people, there is need of a twofold action, directec
simultaneously upon their intelligence and their poverty.   A
effective national education of the children of the labouring class, i
the first thing needful ; and, coincidently with this, a system o
measures which shall (as the Revolution did in France) extinguis
extreme poverty for one whole generation.
     This is not the place for discussing, even in the most genera
manner, either the principles or the machinery of national education
But it is to be hoped that opinion on the subject is advancing, anc
that an education of mere words would not now be deemed sufficient
slow as our progress is toward providing anything better even fo

the classes to whom society professes to give the very best education it can devise. Without entering into disputable points, it may be asserted without scruple, that the aim of all intellectual training for the mass of the people should be to cultivate common sense ; to qualify them for forming a sound practical judgment of the circumstances by which they are surrounded. Whatever, in the intellectual department, can be superadded to this, is chiefly ornamental ; while this is the indispensable groundwork on which education must rest. Let this object be acknowledged and kept in view as the thing to be first aimed at, and there will be little difficulty in deciding either what to teach, or in what manner to teach it.

An education directed to diffuse good sense among the people, with such knowledge as would qualify them to judge of the tendencies of their actions, would be certain, even without any direct inculcation, to raise up a public opinion by which intemperance and improvidence of every kind would be held discreditable, and the improvidence which overstocks the labour market would be severely condemned, as an offence against the common weal. But though the sufficiency of such a state of opinion, supposing it formed, to keep the increase of population within proper limits, cannot, I think, be doubted ; yet, for the formation of the opinion, it would not do to trust to education alone. Education is not compatible with extreme poverty. It is impossible effectually to teach an indigent population. And it is difficult to make those feel the value of comfort who have never enjoyed it, or those appreciate the wretchedness of a precarious subsistence, who have been made reckless by always living from hand to mouth. Individuals often struggle upwards into a condition of ease ; but the utmost that can be expected from a whole people is to maintain themselves in it ; and improvement in the habits and requirements of the mass of unskilled day-labourers will be difficult and tardy, unless means can be contrived of raising the entire body to a state of tolerable comfort, and maintaining them in it until a new generation grows up.

Towards effecting this object there are two resources available, without wrong to any one, without any of the liabilities of mischief attendant on voluntary or legal charity, and not only without weakening, but on the contrary strengthening, every incentive to industry, and every motive to forethought.

§ 4. The first is a great national measure of colonization. I mean, a grant of public money, sufficient to remove at once, and establish in the colonies, a considerable fraction of the youthful agricultural population.   By giving the preference, as Mr. Wakefield proposes, to young couples, or when these cannot be obtained, to families with children nearly grown up, the expenditure would be made to go the farthest possible towards accomplishing the end, while the colonies would be supplied with the greatest amount of what is there in deficiency and here in superfluity, present and prospective labour.   It has been shown by others, and the grounds of the opinion will be exhibited in a subsequent part of the present work, that colonization on an adequate scale might be so conducted as to cost the country nothing, or nothing that would not be certainly repaid ; and that the funds required, even by way of advance, would not be drawn from the capital employed in maintaining labour, but from that surplus which cannot find employment at such profit as constitutes an adequate remuneration for the abstinence of the possessor, and which is therefore sent abroad for investment, or wasted at home in reckless speculations. That portion of the income of the country which is habitually ineffective for any purpose of benefit to the labouring class, would bear any draught which it could be necessary to make on it for the amount of emigration which is here in view.

[1] The second resource would be, to devote all common land, hereafter brought into cultivation, to raising a class of small proprietors.   It has long enough been the practice to take these lands from public use for the mere purpose of adding to the domains of the rich.   It is time that what is left of them should be retained as an estate sacred to the benefit of the poor.   The machine for administering it already exists, having been created by the General Inclosure Act.   What I would propose (though,

<hr>

[1] [The following sentences of the original text were omitted in the 3rd ed. (1852) from the beginning of this paragraph : " To the case of Ireland, in her present crisis of transition, colonization, as the exclusive remedy, is, I conceive, unsuitable.   The Irish are nearly the worst adapted people in Europe for settlers in the wilderness : nor should the founders of nations, destined perhaps to be the most powerful in the world, be drawn principally from the least civilized and least improved inhabitants of old countries.   It is most fortunate therefore that the unoccupied lands of Ireland herself afford a resource so nearly adequate to the emergency, as reduces emigration to a rank merely subsidiary.   In England and Scotland, with a population much less excessive, and better adapted to a settler's life, colonization must be the chief resource for easing the labour market, and improving the condition of the existing generation of labourers so materially as to raise the permanent standard of habits in the generation following.   But England too has waste lands, though less extensive than those of Ireland : and the second resource, &c."]

I confess, with small hope of its being soon adopted) is, that in all future cases in which common land is permitted to be enclosed, such portion should first be sold or assigned as is sufficient to compensate the owners of manorial or common rights, and that the remainder should be divided into sections of five acres or thereabouts, to be conferred in absolute property on individuals of the labouring class who would reclaim and bring them into cultivation by their own labour. The preference should be given to such labourers, and there are many of them, as had saved enough to maintain them until their first crop was got in, or whose character was such as to induce some responsible person to advance to them the requisite amount on their personal security. The tools, the manure, and in some cases the subsistence also might be supplied by the parish, or by the state; interest for the advance, at the rate yielded by the public funds, being laid on as a perpetual quit-rent, with power to the peasant to redeem it at any time for a moderate number of years' purchase. These little landed estates might, if it were thought necessary, be made indivisible by law; though, if the plan worked in the manner designed, I should not apprehend any objectionable degree of subdivision. In case of intestacy, and in default of amicable arrangement among the heirs, they might be bought by government at their value, and regranted to some other labourer who would give security for the price. The desire to possess one of these small properties would probably become, as on the Continent, an inducement to prudence and economy pervading the whole labouring population; and that great desideratum among a people of hired labourers would be provided, an intermediate class between them and their employers; affording them the double advantage, of an object for their hopes, and, as there would be good reason to anticipate, an example for their imitation.

It would, however, be of little avail that either or both of these measures of relief should be adopted, unless on such a scale as would enable the whole body of hired labourers remaining on the soil to obtain not merely employment, but a large addition to the present wages—such an addition as would enable them to live and bring up their children in a degree of comfort and independence to which they have hitherto been strangers. When the object is to raise the permanent condition of a people, small means do not merely produce small effects, they produce no effect at all. Unless comfort can be made as habitual to a whole generation as indigence is now,

nothing is accomplished ; and feeble half-measures do but fritter
away resources, far better reserved until the improvement of public
opinion and of education shall raise up politicians who will not think
that merely because a scheme promises much, the part of
statesmanship is to have nothing to do with it.

[1] I have left the preceding paragraphs as they were written, since
they remain true in principle, though it is no longer urgent to apply
these specific recommendations to the present state of this country.
The extraordinary cheapening of the means of transport, which is
one of the great scientific achievements of the age, and the
knowledge which nearly all classes of the people have now acquired, or
are in the way of acquiring, of the condition of the labour market in
remote parts of the world, have opened up a spontaneous emigration
from these islands to the new countries beyond the ocean, which
does not tend to diminish, but to increase ; and which, without any
national measure of systematic colonization, may prove sufficient
to effect a material rise of wages in Great Britain, as it has already
done in Ireland, and to maintain that rise unimpaired for one or
more generations. Emigration, instead of an occasional vent, is
becoming a steady outlet for superfluous numbers ; and this new
fact in modern history, together with the flush of prosperity
occasioned by free trade, have granted to this overcrowded country a
temporary breathing-time, capable of being employed in accomplishing those moral and intellectual improvements in all classes of the
people, the very poorest included, which would render improbable
any relapse into the over-peopled state. Whether this golden
opportunity will be properly used, depends on the wisdom of our
councils ; and whatever depends on that, is always in a high degree
precarious. The grounds of hope are, that there has been no time
in our history when mental progress has depended so little on governments, and so much on the general disposition of the people ; none
in which the spirit of improvement has extended to so many branches
of human affairs at once, nor in which all kinds of suggestions tending to the public good in every department, from the humblest
physical to the highest moral or intellectual, were heard with so
little prejudice, and had so good a chance of becoming known and
being fairly considered.

[1] [Added in the 6th ed. (1865).

CHAPTER XIV

OF THE DIFFERENCES OF WAGES IN DIFFERENT
EMPLOYMENTS

§ 1. In treating of wages, we have hitherto confined ourselves to the causes which operate on them generally, and *en masse ;* the laws which govern the remuneration of ordinary or average labour : without reference to the existence of different kinds of work which are habitually paid at different rates, depending in some degree on different laws. We will now take into consideration these differences, and examine in what manner they affect or are affected by the conclusions already established.

A well-known and very popular chapter of Adam Smith* contains the best exposition yet given of this portion of the subject. I cannot indeed think his treatment so complete and exhaustive as it has sometimes been considered ; but, as far as it goes, his analysis is tolerably successful.

The differences, he says, arise partly from the policy of Europe, which nowhere leaves things at perfect liberty, and partly " from certain circumstances in the employments themselves, which either really, or at least in the imaginations of men, make up for a small pecuniary gain in some, and counterbalance a great one in others." These circumstances he considers to be : " First, the agreeableness or disagreeableness of the employments themselves ; secondly, the easiness and cheapness, or the difficulty and expense of learning them ; thirdly, the constancy or inconstancy of employment in them ; fourthly, the small or great trust which must be reposed in those who exercise them ; and fifthly, the probability or improbability of success in them."

Several of these points he has very copiously illustrated : though his examples are sometimes drawn from a state of facts now no longer existing. " The wages of labour vary with the ease or

* *Wealth of Nations,* book i. ch. 10.

hardship, the cleanliness or dirtiness, the honourableness or dishonour-ableness of the employment. Thus, in most places, take the year round, a journeyman tailor earns less than a journeyman weaver. His work is much easier." Things have much altered, as to a weaver's remuneration, since Adam Smith's time ; and the artizan whose work was more difficult than that of a tailor, can never, I think, have been the common weaver. "A journeyman weaver earns less than a journeyman smith. His work is not always easier, but it is much cleanlier." A more probable explanation is, that it requires less bodily strength. "A journeyman blacksmith, though an artificer, seldom earns so much in twelve hours as a collier, who is only a labourer, does in eight. His work is not quite so dirty, is less dangerous, and is carried on in daylight, and above ground. Honour makes a great part of the reward of all honourable professions. In point of pecuniary gain, all things considered," their recompense is, in his opinion, below the average. "Disgrace has the contrary effect. The trade of a butcher is a brutal and an odious business, but it is in most places more profitable than the greater part of common trades. The most detestable of all employments, that of public executioner, is, in proportion to the quantity of work done, better paid than any common trade whatever."

One of the causes which make handloom weavers cling [1848] to their occupation in spite of the scanty remuneration which it now yields, is said to be a peculiar attractiveness arising from the freedom of action which it allows to the workman. "He can play or idle," says a recent authority.* "as feeling or inclination lead him ; rise early or late, apply himself assiduously or carelessly, as he pleases, and work up at any time, by increased exertion, hours previously sacrificed to indulgence or recreation. There is scarcely another condition of any portion of our working population thus free from external control. The factory operative is not only mulcted of his wages for absence, but, if of frequent occurrence, discharged altogether from his employment. The bricklayer, the carpenter, the painter, the joiner, the stonemason, the outdoor labourer, have each their appointed daily hours of labour, a disregard of which would lead to the same result." Accordingly, "the weaver will stand by his loom while it will enable him to exist, however miserably ; and many, induced temporarily to quit it, have returned to it again, when work was to be had."

"Employment is much more constant," continues Adam

* Mr. Muggeridge's *Report* to the Handloom Weavers Inquiry Commission.

Smith, " in some trades than in others.   In the greater part of manufactures, a journeyman may be pretty sure of employment almost
every day in the year that he is able to work " (the interruptions
of business arising from overstocked markets or from a suspension
of demand, or from a commercial crisis, must be excepted).   " A
mason or bricklayer, on the contrary, can work neither in hard
frost nor in foul weather, and his employment at all other times
depends upon the occasional calls of his customers.   He is liable,
in consequence, to be frequently without any.   What he earns,
therefore, while he is employed, must not only maintain him while
he is idle, but make him some compensation for those anxious and
desponding moments which the thought of so precarious a situation
must sometimes occasion.   When the computed earnings of the
greater part of manufacturers, accordingly, are nearly upon a level
with the day wages of common labourers, those of masons and
bricklayers are generally from one-half more to double those wages.
No species of skilled labour, however, seems more easy to learn than
that of masons and bricklayers.   The high wages of those workmen,
therefore, are not so much the recompense of their skill, as the
compensation for the inconstancy of their employment.

" When the inconstancy of the employment is combined with the
hardship, disagreeableness, and dirtiness of the work, it sometimes
raises the wages of the most common labour above those of the
most skilled artificers.   A collier working by the piece is supposed,
at Newcastle, to earn commonly about double, and in many parts
of Scotland about three times, the wages of common labour.   His
high wages arise altogether from the hardship, disagreeableness,
and dirtiness of his work.   His employment may, upon most
occasions, be as constant as he pleases.   The coal-heavers in London
exercise a trade which in hardship, dirtiness, and disagreeableness,
almost equals that of colliers ; and from the unavoidable irregularity
in the arrival of coal-ships, the employment of the greater part of
them is necessarily very inconstant.   If colliers, therefore, commonly
earn double and triple the wages of common labour, it ought not
to seem unreasonable that coal-heavers should sometimes earn
four or five times those wages.   In the inquiry made into their
condition a few years ago, it was found that at the rate at which
they were then paid, they could earn about four times the wages of
common labour in London.   How extravagant soever these earnings
may appear, if they were more than sufficient to compensate all the
disagreeable circumstances of the business, there would soon be so

great a number of competitors as, in a trade which has no exclusive privilege, would quickly reduce them to a lower rate."

These inequalities of remuneration, which are supposed to compensate for the disagreeable circumstances of particular employments, would, under certain conditions, be natural consequences of perfectly free competition : and as between employments of about the same grade, and filled by nearly the same description of people, they are, no doubt, for the most part, realized in practice. But it ıs altogether a false view of the state of facts, to present this as the relation which generally exists between agreeable and disagreeable employments. The really exhausting and the really repulsive labours, instead of being better paid than others, are almost invariably paid the worst of all, because performed by those who have no choice. It would be otherwise in a favourable state of the general labour market. If the labourers in the aggregate, instead of exceeding, fell short of the amount of employment, work which was generally disliked would not be undertaken, except for more than ordinary wages. But when the supply of labour so far exceeds the demand that to find employment at all is an uncertainty, and to be offered it on any terms a favour, the case is totally the reverse. Desirable labourers, those whom every one is anxious to have, can still exercise a choice. The undesirable must take what they can get. The more revolting the occupation, the more certain it is to receive the minimum of remuneration, because it devolves on the most helpless and degraded, on those who from squalid poverty, or from want of skill and education, are rejected from all other employments. Partly from this cause, and partly from the natural and artificial monopolies which will be spoken of presently, the inequalities of wages are generally in an opposite direction to the equitable principle of compensation erroneously represented by Adam Smith as the general law of the remuneration of labour. The hardships and the earnings, instead of being directly proportional, as in any just arrangements of society they would be, are generally in an inverse ratio to one another.[1]

[1] [This paragraph was inserted in the 3rd ed. (1852). At the same time the following paragraph disappeared from the preceding page : " There is no difficulty in understanding the operative principle in all these cases. If, with complete freedom of competition, labour of different degrees of desireableness were paid alike, competitors would crowd into the more attractive employments, and desert the less eligible, thus lowering wages in the first, and raising them in the second, until there would be such a difference of reward as to balance in common estimation the difference of eligibility. Under the unobstructed influence of competition, wages tend to adjust themselves in such a manner

One of the points best illustrated by Adam Smith is the influence exercised on the remuneration of an employment by the uncertainty of success in it. If the chances are great of total failure, the reward in case of success must be sufficient to make up, in the general estimation, for those adverse chances. But, owing to another principle of human nature, if the reward comes in the shape of a few great prizes, it usually attracts competitors in such numbers, that the average remuneration may be reduced not only to zero, but even to a negative quantity. The success of lotteries proves that this is possible: since the aggregate body of adventurers in lotteries necessarily lose, otherwise the undertakers could not gain. The case of certain professions is considered by Adam Smith to be similar. " The probability that any particular person shall ever be qualified for the employment to which he is educated, is very different in different occupations. In the greater part of mechanic trades, success is almost certain, but very uncertain in the liberal professions. Put your son apprentice to a shoemaker, there is little doubt of his learning to make a pair of shoes ; but send him to study the law, it is at least twenty to one if ever he makes such proficiency as will enable him to live by the business. In a perfectly fair lottery those who draw the prizes ought to gain all that is lost by those who draw the blanks. In a profession where twenty fail for one that succeeds, that one ought to gain all that should have been gained by the unsuccessful twenty. The counsellor-at-law, who, perhaps, at near forty years of age, begins to make something by his profession, ought to receive the retribution, not only of his own so tedious and expensive education, but of that of more than twenty others who are never likely to make anything by it. How extravagant soever the fees of counsellors-at-law may sometimes appear, their real retribution is never equal to this. Compute, in any particular place, what is likely to be annually gained, and what is likely to be annually spent, by all the different workmen in any common trade, such at that of shoemakers or weavers, and you will find that the former sum will generally exceed the latter. But make the same computation with regard to all the counsellors and students of law, in all the different inns of court, and you will find that their annual gains bear but a small proportion to their annual expense, even though you rate the former as high, and the latter as low, as can well be done."

that the situation and prospects of the labourers in all employments shall be, in the general estimation, as nearly as possible on a par.'']

Whether this is true in our own day, when the gains of the few
are incomparably greater than in the time of Adam Smith, but also
the unsuccessful aspirants much more numerous, those who have
the appropriate information must decide. It does not, however,
seem to be sufficiently considered by Adam Smith, that the prizes
which he speaks of comprise not the fees of counsel only, but the
places of emolument and honour to which their profession gives
access, together with the coveted distinction of a conspicuous
position in the public eye.

Even where there are no great prizes, the mere love of excitement
is sometimes enough to cause an adventurous employment to be
overstocked. This is apparent " in the readiness of the common
people to enlist as soldiers, or to go to sea. . . . The dangers and
hair-breadth escapes of a life of adventures, instead of disheartening
young people, seem frequently to recommend a trade to them.
A tender mother, among the inferior ranks of people, is often
afraid to send her son to school at a seaport town, lest the sight of
the ships and the conversation and adventures of the sailors should
entice him to go to sea. The distant prospect of hazards from
which we can hope to extricate ourselves by courage and address,
is not disagreeable to us, and does not raise the wages of labour in
any employment. It is otherwise with those in which courage and
address can be of no avail. In trades which are known to be very
unwholesome, the wages of labour are always remarkably high.
Unwholesomeness is a species of disagreeableness, and its effect upon
the wages of labour are to be ranked under that general head."

§ 2. The preceding are cases in which inequality of remuneration
is necessary to produce equality of attractiveness, and are examples
of the equalizing effect of free competition. The following are
cases of real inequality, and arise from a different principle. " The
wages of labour vary according to the small or great trust which
must be reposed in the workmen. The wages of goldsmiths and
jewellers are everywhere superior to those of many other workmen,
not only of equal, but of much superior ingenuity ; on account of
the precious materials with which they are intrusted. We trust our
health to the physician, our fortune and sometimes our life and
reputation to the lawyer and attorney. Such confidence could
not safely be reposed in people of a very mean or low condition.
Their reward must be such, therefore, as may give them that rank in
society which so important a trust requires."

The superiority of reward is not here the consequence of com-petition, but of its absence : not a compensation for disadvantages inherent in the employment, but an extra advantage ; a kind of monopoly price, the effect not of a legal, but of what has been termed a natural monopoly. If all labourers were trustworthy, it would not be necessary to give extra pay to working goldsmiths on account of the trust. The degree of integrity required being supposed to be uncommon, those who can make it appear that they possess it are able to take advantage of the peculiarity, and obtain higher pay in proportion to its rarity. This opens a class of considerations which Adam Smith, and most other political economists, have taken into far too little account, and from inattention to which, he has given a most imperfect exposition of the wide difference between the remuneration of common labour and that of skilled employments.

Some employments require a much longer time to learn, and a much more expensive course of instruction than others ; and to this extent there is, as explained by Adam Smith, an inherent reason for their being more highly remunerated. If an artizan must work several years at learning his trade before he can earn anything, and several years more before becoming sufficiently skilful for its finer operations, he must have a prospect of at last earning enough to pay the wages of all this past labour, with compensation for the delay of payment, and an indemnity for the expenses of his education. His wages, consequently, must yield, over and above the ordinary amount, an annuity sufficient to repay these sums, with the common rate of profit, within the number of years he can expect to live and to be in working condition. This, which is necessary to place the skilled employments, all circumstances taken together, on the same level of advantage with the unskilled, is the smallest difference which can exist for any length of time between the two remunerations, since otherwise no one would learn the skilled employments. And this amount of difference is all which Adam Smith's principles account for. When the disparity is greater, he seems to think that it must be explained by apprentice laws, and the rules of corporations which restrict admission into many of the skilled employments. But, independently of these or any other artificial monopolies, there is a natural monopoly in favour of skilled labourers against the unskilled, which makes the difference of reward exceed, sometimes in a manifold proportion, what is sufficient merely to equalize their advantages. If unskilled labourers had it in their power to compete with skilled, by merely taking the trouble of learning the

trade, the difference of wages might not exceed what would compensate them for that trouble, at the ordinary rate at which labour
is remunerated. But the fact that a course of instruction is required,
of even a low degree of costliness, or that the labourer must be
maintained for a considerable time from other sources, suffices
everywhere to exclude the great body of the labouring people
from the possibility of any such competition. Until lately,[1] all
employments which required even the humble education of reading
and writing, could be recruited only from a select class, the majority
having had no opportunity of acquiring those attainments. All
such improvements, accordingly, were immensely overpaid, as
measured by the ordinary remuneration of labour. Since reading
and writing have been brought within the reach of a multitude,
the monopoly price of the lower grade of educated employments
has greatly fallen, the competition for them having increased in
an almost incredible degree. There is still, however, a much
greater disparity than can be accounted for on the principle of
competition. A clerk from whom nothing is required but the
mechanical labour of copying, gains more than an equivalent for
his mere exertion if he receives the wages of a bricklayer's labourer.
His work is not a tenth part as hard, it is quite as easy to learn,
and his condition is less precarious, a clerk's place being generally
a place for life. The higher rate of his remuneration, therefore,
must be partly ascribed to monopoly, the small degree of education
required being not even yet so generally diffused as to call forth
the natural number of competitors ; and partly to the remaining
influence of an ancient custom, which requires that clerks should
maintain the dress and appearance of a more highly paid class.
In some manual employments, requiring a nicety of hand which
can only be acquired by long practice, it is difficult to obtain at any
cost workmen in sufficient numbers, who are capable of the most
delicate kind of work ; and the wages paid to them are only limited
by the price which purchasers are willing to give for the commodity
they produce. This is the case with some working watchmakers,
and with the makers of some astronomical and optical instruments.
If workmen competent to such employments were ten times as
numerous as they are, there would be purchasers for all which they
could make, not indeed at the present prices, but at those lower
prices which would be the natural consequence of lower wages.
Similar considerations apply in a still greater degree to employments

[1] [Writing in 1848.]

which it is attempted to confine to persons of a certain social rank, such as what are called the liberal professions ; into which a person of what is considered too low a class of society is not easily admitted, and if admitted, does not easily succeed.

So complete, indeed, has hitherto been the separation, so strongly marked the line of demarcation, between the different grades of labourers, as to be almost equivalent to an hereditary distinction of caste ; each employment being chiefly recruited from the children of those already employed in it, or in employments of the same rank with it in social estimation, or from the children of persons who, if originally of a lower rank, have succeeded in raising themselves by their exertions. The liberal professions are mostly supplied by the sons of either the professional, or the idle classes : the more highly skilled manual employments are filled up from the sons of skilled artizans, or the class of tradesmen who rank with them : the lower classes of skilled employments are in a similar case ; and unskilled labourers, with occasional exceptions, remain from father to son in their pristine condition. Consequently the wages of each class have hitherto been regulated by the increase of its own population, rather than of the general population of the country. If the professions are overstocked, it is because the class of society from which they have always mainly been supplied, has greatly increased in number, and because most of that class have numerous families, and bring up some at least of their sons to professions. If the wages of artizans remain so much higher than those of common labourers, it is because artizans are a more prudent class, and do not marry so early or so inconsiderately. The changes, however, now so rapidly taking place in usages and ideas, are undermining all these distinctions ; the habits or disabilities which chained people to their hereditary condition are fast wearing away, and every class is exposed to increased and increasing competition from at least the class immediately below it. The general relaxation of conventional barriers, and the increased facilities of education which already are, and will be in a much greater degree, brought within the reach of all, tend to produce, among many excellent effects, one which is the reverse ; they tend to bring down the wages of skilled labour. The inequality of remuneration between the skilled and the unskilled is, without doubt, very much greater than is justifiable ; but it is desirable that this should be corrected by raising the unskilled, not by lowering the skilled. If, however, the other changes taking place in society are not accompanied by a

strengthening of the checks to population on the part of labourers
generally, there will be a tendency to bring the lower grades of
skilled labourers under the influence of a rate of increase regulated
by a lower standard of living than their own, and thus to deteriorate
their condition without raising that of the general mass ; the stimulus
given to the multiplication of the lowest class being sufficient to fill
up without difficulty the additional space gained by them from those
immediately above.

§ 3. A modifying circumstance still remains to be noticed,
which interferes to some extent with the operation of the principles
thus far brought to view. While it is true, as a general rule, that
the earnings of skilled labour, and especially of any labour which
requires school education, are at a monopoly rate, from the impossibility, to the mass of the people, of obtaining that education ;
it is also true that the policy of nations, or the bounty of individuals,
formerly did much to counteract the effect of this limitation of
competition, by offering eleemosynary instruction to a much larger
class of persons than could have obtained the same advantages by
paying their price. Adam Smith has pointed out the operation of
this cause in keeping down the remuneration of scholarly or bookish
occupations generally, and in particular of clergymen, literary men,
and schoolmasters, or other teachers of youth. I cannot better set
forth this part of the subject than in his words.

" It has been considered as of so much importance that a proper
number of young people should be educated for certain professions,
that sometimes the public, and sometimes the piety of private
founders, have established many pensions, scholarships, exhibitions,
bursaries, &c. for this purpose, which draw many more people into
those trades than could otherwise pretend to follow them. In all
Christian countries, I believe, the education of the greater part of
churchmen is paid for in this manner. Very few of them are
educated altogether at their own expense. The long, tedious, and
expensive education, therefore, of those who are, will not always
procure them a suitable reward, the Church being crowded with
people who, in order to get employment, are willing to accept of a
much smaller recompense than what such an education would
otherwise have entitled them to : and in this manner the competition of the poor takes away the reward of the rich. It would be
indecent, no doubt, to compare either a curate or a chaplain with
a journeyman in any common trade. The pay of a curate or a

chaplain, however, may very properly be considered as of the same nature with the wages of a journeyman. They are, all three, paid for their work according to the contract which they may happen to make with their respective superiors. Till after the middle of the fourteenth century, five marks, containing as much silver as ten pounds of our present money, was in England the usual pay of a curate or a stipendiary parish priest, as we find it regulated by the decrees of several different national councils. At the same period fourpence a day, containing the same quantity of silver as a shilling of our present money, was declared to be the pay of a master-mason, and threepence a day, equal to ninepence of our present money, that of a journeyman mason.* The wages of both these labourers, therefore, supposing them to have been constantly employed, were much superior to those of the curate. The wages of the master-mason, supposing him to have been without employment one-third of the year, would have fully equalled them. By the 12th of Queen Anne, c. 12, it is declared, ' That whereas for want of sufficient maintenance and encouragement to curates, the cures have in several places been meanly supplied, the bishop is therefore empowered to appoint by writing under his hand and seal a sufficient certain stipend or allowance, not exceeding fifty, and not less than twenty pounds a year.' Forty pounds a year is reckoned at present very good pay for a curate, and notwithstanding this act of parliament, there are many curacies under twenty pounds a year. This last sum does not exceed what is frequently earned by common labourers in many country parishes. Whenever the law has attempted to regulate the wages of workmen, it has always been rather to lower them than to raise them. But the law has upon many occasions attempted to raise the wages of curates, and for the dignity of the Church, to oblige the rectors of parishes to give them more than the wretched maintenance which they themselves might be willing to accept of. And in both cases the law seems to have been equally ineffectual, and has never been either able to raise the wages of curates or to sink those of labourers to the degree that was intended, because it has never been able to hinder either the one from being willing to accept of less than the legal allowance, on account of the indigence of their situation and the multitude of their competitors ; or the other from receiving more, on account of the contrary competition of those who expected to derive either profit or pleasure from employing them."

* See the Statute of Labourers, 25 Edw. III.

" In professions in which there are no benefices, such as law (?)
and physic, if an equal proportion of people were educated at the
public expense, the competition would soon be so great as to sink
very much their pecuniary reward. It might then not be worth
any man's while to educate his son to either of those professions at
his own expense. They would be entirely abandoned to such as
had been educated by those public charities ; whose numbers and
necessities would oblige them in general to content themselves with
a very miserable recompense.

" That unprosperous race of men, commonly called men of
letters, are pretty much in the situation which lawyers and physicians
probably would be in upon the foregoing supposition. In every
part of Europe, the greater part of them have been educated for the
Church, but have been hindered by different reasons from entering
into holy orders. They have generally, therefore, been educated
at the public expense, and their numbers are everywhere so
great as to reduce the price of their labour to a very paltry
recompense.

" Before the invention of the art of printing, the only employment by which a man of letters could make anything by his talents,
was that of a public or private teacher, or by communicating to
other people the curious and useful knowledge which he had acquired
himself : and this is still surely a more honourable, a more useful,
and in general even a more profitable employment than that other
of writing for a bookseller, to which the art of printing has given
occasion. The time and study, the genius, knowledge, and application requisite to qualify an eminent teacher of the sciences, are at
least equal to what is necessary for the greatest practitioners in
law and physic. But the usual reward of the eminent teacher
bears no proportion to that of the lawyer or physician ; because the
trade of the one is crowded with indigent people who have been
brought up to it at the public expense, whereas those of the other
two are encumbered with very few who have not been educated at
their own. The usual recompense, however, of public and private
teachers, small as it may appear, would undoubtedly be less than
it is, if the competition of those yet more indigent men of letters who
write for bread was not taken out of the market. Before the invention of the art of printing, a scholar and a beggar seem to have
been terms very nearly synonymous. The different governors of
the universities before that time appear to have often granted
licences to their scholars to beg."

§ 4.   The demand for literary labour has so greatly increased since Adam Smith wrote, while the provisions for eleemosynary education have nowhere been much added to, and in the countries which have undergone revolutions have been much diminished, that little effect in keeping down the recompense of literary labour can now be ascribed to the influence of those institutions.   But an effect nearly equivalent is now produced by a cause somewhat similar— the competition of persons who, by analogy with other arts, may be called amateurs.   Literary occupation is one of those pursuits in which success may be attained by persons the greater part of whose time is taken up by other employments ; and the education necessary for it is the common education of all cultivated persons. The inducements to it, independently of money, in the present state of the world, to all who have either vanity to gratify, or personal or public objects to promote, are strong.   These motives now attract into this career a great and increasing number of persons who do not need its pecuniary fruits, and who would equally resort to it if it afforded no remuneration at all.   In our own country (to cite known examples), the most influential, and on the whole most eminent philosophical writer of recent times (Bentham), the greatest political economist (Ricardo), the most ephemerally celebrated, and the really greatest poets (Byron and Shelley), and the most successful writer of prose fiction (Scott), were none of them authors by profession ; and only two of the five, Scott and Byron, could have supported themselves by the works which they wrote.   Nearly all the higher departments of authorship are, to a great extent, similarly filled.   In consequence, although the highest pecuniary prizes of successful authorship are incomparably greater than at any former period, yet on any rational calculation of the chances, in the existing competition, scarcely any writer can hope to gain a living by books, and to do so by magazines and reviews becomes [1848] daily more difficult.   It is only the more troublesome and disagreeable kinds of literary labour, and those which confer no personal celebrity, such as most of those connected with newspapers, or with the smaller periodicals, on which an educated person can now rely for subsistence. Of these, the remuneration is, on the whole, decidedly high ; because, though exposed to the competition of what used to be called " poor scholars " (persons who have received a learned education from some public or private charity), they are exempt from that of amateurs, those who have other means of support being seldom candidates for such employments.   Whether these considerations are not connected with something radically amiss in the idea of authorship as a profession, and whether any social arrangement under which the teachers of mankind consist of persons giving out doctrines for bread, is suited to be, or can possibly be, a permanent thing—would be a subject well worthy of the attention of thinkers.

The clerical, like the literary profession, is frequently adopted by persons of independent means, either from religious zeal, or for the sake of the honour or usefulness which may belong to it, or for a chance of the high prizes which it holds out: and it is now principally for this reason that the salaries of curates are so low ; those salaries, though considerably raised by the influence of public opinion, being still generally insufficient as the sole means of support for one who has to maintain the externals expected from a clergyman of the established church.

When an occupation is carried on chiefly by persons who derive the main portion of their subsistence from other sources, its remuneration may be lower almost to any extent than the wages of equally severe labour in other employments. The principal example of the kind is domestic manufactures. When spinning and knitting were carried on in every cottage, by families deriving their principal support from agriculture, the price at which their produce was sold (which constituted the remuneration of the labour) was often so low, that there would have been required great perfection of machinery to undersell it. The amount of the remuneration in such a case depends chiefly upon whether the quantity of the commodity, produced by this description of labour, suffices to supply the whole of the demand. If it does not, and there is consequently a necessity for some labourers who devote themselves entirely to the employment, the price of the article must be sufficient to pay those labourers at the ordinary rate, and to reward therefore very handsomely the domestic producers. But if the demand is so limited that the domestic manufacture can do more than satisfy it, the price is naturally kept down to the lowest rate at which peasant families think it worth while to continue the production. It is, no doubt, because the Swiss artizans do not depend for the whole of their subsistence upon their looms, that Zurich is able to maintain a competition in the European market with English capital, and English fuel and machinery.* Thus far, as to the remuneration of

* Four-fifths of the manufacturers of the Canton of Zurich are small farmers, generally proprietors of their farms. The cotton manufacture occupies either wholly or partially 23,000 people, nearly a tenth part of the popu-

the subsidiary employment; but the effect to the labourers of having this additional resource, is almost certain to be (unless peculiar counteracting causes intervene) a proportional diminution of the wages of their main occupation. The habits of the people (as has already been so often remarked) everywhere require some particular scale of living, and no more, as the condition without which they will not bring up a family. Whether the income which maintains them in this condition comes from one source or from two, makes no difference : if there is a second source of income, they require less from the first ; and multiply (at least this has always hitherto been the case) to a point which leaves them no more from both employments, than they would probably have had from either if it had been their sole occupation.

For the same reason it is found that, *cœteris paribus*, those trades are generally the worst paid, in which the wife and children of the artizan aid in the work. The income which the habits of the class demand, and down to which they are almost sure to multiply, is made up, in those trades, by the earnings of the whole family, while in others the same income must be attained by the labour of the man alone. It is even probable that their collective earnings will amount to a smaller sum than those of the man alone in other trades ; because the prudential restraint on marriage is unusually weak when the only consequence immediately felt is an improvement of circumstances, the joint earnings of the two going further in their domestic economy after marriage than before. Such accordingly is the fact, in the case of handloom weavers. In most kinds of weaving, women can and do earn as much as men, and children are employed at a very early age ; but the aggregate earnings of a family are lower than in almost any other kind of industry, and the marriages earlier. It is noticeable also that there are certain branches of handloom weaving in which wages are much above the rate common in the trade, and that these are the branches in which neither women nor young persons are employed. These facts were authenticated by the inquiries of the Handloom Weavers Commission, which made its report in 1841. [1] No argument can be hence derived for the exclusion of women from the liberty of competing in the labour market : since, even when no more is earned

lation, and they consume a greater quantity of cotton per inhabitant than either France or England. See the *Statistical Account of Zurich* formerly cited, pp. 105, 108, 110.

[1] [The first and third of the following sentences were added in the 3rd ed. (1852) ; the second was inserted in the 6th ed. (1865).]

by the labour of a man and a woman than would have been earned
by the man alone, the advantage to the woman of not depending on
a master for subsistence may be more than an equivalent.   It cannot,
however, be considered desirable as a *permanent* element in the
condition of a labouring class, that the mother of the family (the case
of a single woman is totally different) should be under the necessity
of working for subsistence, at least elsewhere than in their place of
abode.   In the case of children, who are necessarily dependent, the
influence of their competition in depressing the labour market is an
important element in the question of limiting their labour, in order
to provide better for their education.

§ 5.   It deserves consideration, why the wages of women are
generally lower, and very much lower, than those of men.   They
are not universally so.   Where men and women work at the same
employment, if it be one for which they are equally fitted in point
of physical power, they are not always unequally paid.[1]   Women,
in factories, sometimes [2] earn as much as men ; and so they do in
handloom weaving, which, being paid by the piece, brings their
efficiency to a sure test.   When the efficiency is equal, but the pay
unequal, the only explanation that can be given is custom ; grounded
either in a prejudice, or in the present constitution of society,
which, making almost every woman, socially speaking, an appendage
of some man, enables men to take systematically the lion's share of
whatever belongs to both.[3]   But the principal question relates to
the peculiar employments of women.   The remuneration of these
is always, I believe, greatly below that of employments of equal
skill and equal disagreeableness, carried on by men.   In some of
these cases the explanation is evidently that already given : as in
the case of domestic servants, whose wages, speaking generally,
are not determined by competition, but are greatly in excess of the
market value of the labour, and in this excess, as in almost all things
which are regulated by custom, the male sex obtains by far the
largest share.   In the occupations in which employers take full

---

[1] [So from the 3rd ed. (1852).   The original text ran : " it does not appear
that they are in general unequally paid."]

[2] ["Sometimes " added in the 3rd ed.]

[3] [Here the following passage was omitted from the 3rd ed. : " When an
employment (as is the case with many trades) is divided into several parts, of
some of which men alone are considered capable, while women or children are
employed in the others, it is natural that those who cannot be dispensed with,
should be able to make better terms for themselves than those who can."]

advantage of competition, the low wages of women as compared with the ordinary earnings of men are a proof that the employments are overstocked : that although so much smaller a number of women, than of men, support themselves by wages, the occupations which law and usage make accessible to them are comparatively so few, that the field of their employment is still more overcrowded. It must be observed, that as matters now stand, a sufficient degree of overcrowding may depress the wages of women to a much lower minimum than those of men. The wages, at least of single women, must be equal to their support, but need not be more than equal to it ; the minimum, in their case, is the pittance absolutely requisite for the sustenance of one human being. Now the lowest point to which the most superabundant competition can permanently depress the wages of a man is always somewhat more than this. Where the wife of a labouring man does not by general custom contribute to his earnings, the man's wages must be at least sufficient to support himself, a wife, and a number of children adequate to keep up the population, since if it were less the population would not be kept up. And even if the wife earns something, their joint wages must be sufficient not only to support themselves, but (at least for some years) their children also. The *ne plus ultra* of low wages, therefore (except during some transitory crisis, or in some decaying employment), can hardly occur in any occupation which the person employed has to live by, except the occupations of women.

§ 6. Thus far, we have, throughout this discussion, proceeded on the supposition that competition is free, so far as regards human interference ; being limited only by natural causes, or by the unintended effect of general social circumstances. But law or custom may interfere to limit competition. If apprentice laws, or the regulations of corporate bodies, make the access to a particular employment slow, costly, or difficult, the wages of that employment may be kept much above their natural proportion to the wages of common labour. They might be so kept without any assignable limit, were it not that wages which exceed the usual rate require corresponding prices, and that there is a limit to the price at which even a restricted number of producers can dispose of all they produce. In most civilized countries, the restrictions of this kind which once existed have been either abolished or very much relaxed, and will, no doubt, soon disappear entirely. In some trades, however, and to some extent, the combinations of workmen produce a similar effect. Those combinations always fail to uphold wages at an artificial rate, unless they also limit the number of competitors. But they do occasionally succeed in accomplishing this. In several trades the workmen have been able to make it almost impracticable for strangers to obtain admission either as journeymen or as apprentices, except in limited numbers, and under such restrictions as they choose to impose. It was given in evidence to the Handloom Weavers Commission, that this is one of the hardships which aggravate the grievous condition of that depressed class. Their own employment is overstocked and almost ruined ; but there are many other trades which it would not be difficult for them to learn : to this, however, the combinations of workmen in those other trades are said to interpose an obstacle hitherto insurmountable.

Notwithstanding, however, the cruel manner in which the exclusive principle of these combinations operates in a case of this peculiar nature, the question, whether they are on the whole more useful or mischievous, requires to be decided on an enlarged consideration of consequences, among which such a fact as this is not one of the most important items. Putting aside the atrocities sometimes committed by workmen in the way of personal outrage or intimidation, which cannot be too rigidly repressed ; if the present state of the general habits of the people were to remain for ever unimproved, these partial combinations, in so far as they do succeed in keeping up the wages of any trade by limiting its numbers, might be looked upon as simply intrenching around a particular spot against the inroads of over-population, and making the wages of the class depend upon their own rate of increase, instead of depending on that of a more reckless and improvident class than themselves. What at first sight seems the injustice of excluding the more numerous body from sharing the gains of a comparatively few, disappears when we consider that by being admitted they would not be made better off, for more than a short time ; the only permanent effect which their admission would produce, would be to lower the others to their own level. To what extent the force of this consideration is annulled when a tendency commences towards diminished over-crowding in the labouring classes generally, and what grounds of a different nature there may be for regarding the existence of trade combinations as rather to be desired than deprecated, will be considered in a subsequent chapter of this work with the subject of Combination Laws.[1]

§ 7. To conclude this subject, I must repeat an observation already made, that there are kinds of labour of which the wages are fixed by custom, and not by competition. Such are the fees or

---

[1] [The present text of this paragraph dates from the 5th ed. (1862). In the original of 1848 it ran, after the words " this peculiar nature " : " I find it impossible to wish, in the present state of the general habits of the people, that no such combinations existed. Acts of atrocity are sometimes committed by them, in the way . . . repressed : and even their legitimate liberty of refusing to work unless their own terms are conceded to them, they not unfrequently exercise in an injudicious, unenlightened manner, ultimately very injurious to themselves. But in so far as they do succeed in keeping up the wages of any trade by limiting its numbers, I look upon them as simply intrenching . . . themselves. And I should rejoice if by trade regulations, or even by trades unions, the employments thus specially protected could be multiplied to a much greater extent than experience has shown to be practicable. What at first sight seems the injustice . . . level. If indeed the general mass of the people were so improved in their standard of living, as not to press closer against the means of employment than those trades do ; if, in other words, there were no greater degree of overcrowding outside the barrier, than within it—there would be no need of a barrier, and if it had any effects at all, they must be bad ones ; but in that case the barrier would fall of itself, since there would no longer be any motive for keeping it up. On similar grounds, if there were no other escape from that fatal immigration of Irish, which has done and is doing so much to degrade the condition of our agricultural, and some classes of our town population, I should see no injustice, and the greatest possible expediency, in checking that destructive inroad by prohibitive laws. But there is a better mode of putting an end to this mischief, namely, by improving the condition of the Irish themselves ; and England owes as atonement to Ireland for past injuries, which she ought to suffer almost any inconvenience rather than fail to make good, by using her power in as determined a manner for the elevation of that unfortunate people, as she used it through so many dreary centuries for their abasement and oppression."
In the 3rd ed. (1852) this was replaced by the following (which appeared also in the 4th (1857)) : " their existence, it is probable, has, in time past, produced more good than evil. Putting aside the atrocities sometimes committed by them, in the way . . . themselves. The time, however, is past when the friends of human improvement can look with complacency on the attempts of small sections of the community, whether belonging to the labouring or any other class, to organize a separate class interest in antagonism to the general body of labourers, and to protect that interest by shutting out, even if only by a moral compulsion, all competitors from their more highly paid department. The mass of the people are no longer to be thrown out of the account, as too hopelessly brutal to be capable of benefiting themselves by any opening made for them, and sure only, if admitted into competition, to lower others to their own level. The aim of all efforts should now be, not to keep up the monopoly of separate knots of labourers against the rest, but to raise the moral state and social condition of the whole body ; and of this it is an indispensable part that no one should be excluded from the superior advantages of any skilled employment, who has intelligence enough to learn it, and honesty enough to be entrusted with it."]

charges of professional persons : of physicians, surgeons, barristers, and even attorneys. These, as a general rule, do not vary, and though competition operates upon those classes as much as upon any others, it is by dividing the business, not, in general, by diminishing the rate at which it is paid. The cause of this, perhaps, has been the prevalence of an opinion that such persons are more trustworthy if paid highly in proportion to the work they perform ; insomuch that if a lawyer or a physician offered his services at less than the ordinary rate, instead of gaining more practice, he would probably lose that which he already had. For analogous reasons it is usual to pay greatly beyond the market price of their labour all persons in whom the employer wishes to place peculiar trust, or from whom he requires something besides their mere services. For example, most persons who can afford it pay to their domestic servants higher wages than would purchase in the market the labour of persons fully as competent to the work required. They do this, not merely from ostentation, but also from more reasonable motives : either because they desire that those they employ should serve them cheerfully, and be anxious to remain in their service ; or because they do not like to drive a hard bargain with people whom they are in constant intercourse with ; or because they dislike to have near their persons, and continually in their sight, people with the appearance and habits which are the usual accompaniments of a mean remuneration. Similar feelings operate in the minds of persons in business, with respect to their clerks, and other employés. Liberality, generosity, and the credit of the employer, are motives which, to whatever extent they operate, preclude taking the utmost advantage of competition : and doubtless such motives might, and even now do, operate on employers of labour in all the great departments of industry ; and most desirable is it that they should. But they can never raise the average wages of labour beyond the ratio of population to capital. By giving more to each person employed, they limit the power of giving employment to numbers ; and however excellent their moral effect, they do little good economically, unless the pauperism of those who are shut out leads indirectly to a readjustment by means of an increased restraint on population.

CHAPTER XV

§ 1.   HAVING treated of the labourer's share of the produce, we next proceed to the share of the capitalist; the profits of capital or stock; the gains of the person who advances the expenses of production—who, from funds in his possession, pays the wages of the labourers, or supports them during the work; who supplies the requisite buildings, materials, and tools or machinery; and to whom, by the usual terms of the contract, the produce belongs, to be disposed of at his pleasure.   After indemnifying him for his outlay, there commonly remains a surplus, which is his profit; the net income from his capital : the amount which he can afford to spend in necessaries or pleasures, or from which by further saving he can add to his wealth.

As the wages of the labourer are the remuneration of labour, so the profits of the capitalist are properly, according to Mr. Senior's well-chosen expression, the remuneration of abstinence.   They are what he gains by forbearing to consume his capital for his own uses, and allowing it to be consumed by productive labourers for their uses.   For this forbearance he requires a recompense.   Very often in personal enjoyment he would be a gainer by squandering his capital, the capital amounting to more than the sum of the profits which it will yield during the years he can expect to live.   But while he retains it undiminished, he has always the power of con-suming it if he wishes or needs ; he can bestow it upon others at his death ; and in the meantime he derives from it an income, which he can without impoverishment apply to the satisfaction of his own wants or inclinations.

Of the gains, however, which the possession of a capital enables a person to make, a part only is properly an equivalent for the use of the capital itself ; namely, as much as a solvent person would be willing to pay for the loan of it.   This, which as everybody knows is called interest, is all that a person is enabled to get by merely abstaining from the immediate consumption of his capital, and allowing it to be used for productive purposes by others. The remuneration which is obtained in any country for mere abstinence, is measured by the current rate of interest on the best security : such security as precludes any appreciable chance of losing the principal. What a person expects to gain, who superintends the employment of his own capital, is always more, and generally much more, than this. The rate of profit greatly exceeds the rate of interest. The surplus is partly compensation for risk. By lending his capital, on unexceptionable security, he runs little or no risk. But if he embarks in business on his own account, he always exposes his capital to some, and in many cases to very great, danger of partial or total loss. For this danger he must be compensated, otherwise he will not incur it. He must likewise be remunerated for the devotion of his time and labour. The control of the operations of industry usually belongs to the person who supplies the whole or the greatest part of the funds by which they are carried on, and who, according to the ordinary arrangement, is either alone interested, or is the person most interested (at least directly), in the result. To exercise this control with efficiency, if the concern is large and complicated, requires great assiduity, and often, no ordinary skill. This assiduity and skill must be remunerated.

The gross profits from capital, the gains returned to those who supply the funds for production, must suffice for these three purposes. They must afford a sufficient equivalent for abstinence, indemnity for risk, and remuneration for the labour and skill required for superintendence. These different compensations may be either paid to the same, or to different persons. The capital, or some part of it, may be borrowed : may belong to some one who does not undertake the risks or the trouble of business. In that case, the lender or owner is the person who practises the abstinence ; and is remunerated for it by the interest paid to him, while the difference between the interest and the gross profits remunerates the exertions and risks of the undertaker.* Sometimes, again, the capital, or a part of it, is supplied by what is called a sleeping partner ; who shares the risks of the employment, but not the trouble, and who, in consideration of those risks, receives not a mere interest,

---

* It is to be regretted that this word, in this sense, is not familiar to an English ear. French political economists enjoy a great advantage in being able to speak currently of *les profits de l'entrepreneur*.

but a stipulated share of the gross profits. Sometimes the capital is supplied and the risk incurred by one person, and the business carried on exclusively in his name, while the trouble of management is made over to another, who is engaged for that purpose at a fixed salary. Management, however, by hired servants, who have no interest in the result but that of preserving their salaries, is proverbially inefficient, unless they act under the inspecting eye, if not the controlling hand, of the person chiefly interested : and prudence almost always recommends giving to a manager not thus controlled a remuneration partly dependent on the profits ; which virtually reduces the case to that of a sleeping partner. Or finally, the same person may own the capital, and conduct the business ; adding, if he will and can, to the management of his own capital, that of as much more as the owners may be willing to trust him with. But under any or all of these arrangements, the same three things require their remuneration, and must obtain it from the gross profit : abstinence, risk, exertion. And the three parts into which profit may be considered as resolving itself, may be described respectively as interest, insurance and wages of superintendence.

§ 2. The lowest rate of profit which can permanently exist, is that which is barely adequate, at the given place and time, to afford an equivalent for the abstinence, risk, and exertion implied in the employment of capital. From the gross profit has first to be deducted as much as will form a fund sufficient on the average to cover all losses incident to the employment. Next it must afford such an equivalent to the owner of the capital for forbearing to consume it, as is then and there a sufficient motive to him to persist in his abstinence. How much will be required to form this equivalent depends on the comparative value placed, in the given society, upon the present and the future : (in the words formerly used) on the strength of the effective desire of accumulation. Further, after covering all losses, and remunerating the owner for forbearing to consume,[1] there must be something left to recompense the labour and skill of the person who devotes his time to the business. This recompense too must be sufficient to enable at least the owners of the larger capitals to receive for their trouble, or to pay to some manager for his, what to them or him will be a sufficient inducement for undergoing it. If the surplus is no more than this, none but

---

[1] [So from the 3rd ed. (1852). The original text had " for his self-denial."]

large masses of capital will be employed productively ; and if it did not even amount to this, capital would be withdrawn from production, and unproductively consumed, until, by an indirect consequence of its diminished amount, to be explained hereafter, the rate of profit was raised.

Such, then, is the minimum of profits : but that minimum is exceedingly variable, and at some times and places extremely low ; on account of the great variableness of two out of its three elements. That the rate of necessary remuneration for abstinence, or in other words the effective desire of accumulation, differs widely in different states of society and civilization, has been seen in a former chapter. There is a still wider difference in the element which consists in compensation for risk.   I am not now speaking of the differences in point of risk between different employments of capital in the same society, but of the very different degrees of security of property in different states of society.   Where, as in many of the governments of Asia, property is in perpetual danger of spoliation from a tyrannical government, or from its rapacious and ill-controlled officers ; where to possess or to be suspected of possessing wealth, is to be a mark not only for plunder, but perhaps for personal ill-treatment to extort the disclosure and surrender of hidden valuables ; or where, as in the European Middle Ages, the weakness of the government, even when not itself inclined to oppress, leaves its subjects exposed without protection or redress to active spoliation, or audacious withholding of just rights, by any powerful individual ; the rate of profit which persons of average dispositions will require, to make them forego the immediate enjoyment of what they happen to possess, for the purpose of exposing it and themselves to these perils, must be something very considerable.   And these contingencies affect those who live on the mere interest of their capital, in common with those who personally engage in production.   In a generally secure state of society, the risks which may be attendant on the nature of particular employments seldom fall on the person who lends his capital, if he lends on good security ; but in a state of society like that of many parts of Asia, no security (except perhaps the actual pledge of gold or jewels) is good : and the mere possession of a hoard, when known or suspected, exposes it and the possessor to risks, for which scarcely any profit he could expect to obtain would be an equivalent ; so that there would be still less accumulation than there is, if a state of insecurity did not also multiply the occasions on which the possession of a treasure may be the means of saving life or averting serious calamities. Those who lend under these wretched governments, do it at the utmost peril of never being paid. In most of the native states of India, the lowest terms on which any one will lend money, even to the government, are such, that if the interest is paid only for a few years, and the principal not at all, the lender is tolerably well indemnified. If the accumulation of principal and compound interest is ultimately compromised at a few shillings in the pound, he has generally made an advantageous bargain.

§ 3. The remuneration of capital in different employments, much more than [1] the remuneration of labour, varies according to the circumstances which render one employment more attractive, or more repulsive, than another. The profits, for example, of retail trade, in proportion to the capital employed, exceed those of whole-sale dealers or manufacturers, for this reason among others, that there is less consideration attached to the employment. The greatest, however, of these differences, is that caused by difference of risk. The profits of a gunpowder manufacturer must be considerably greater than the average, to make up for the peculiar risks to which he and his property are constantly exposed. When, however, as in the case of marine adventure, the peculiar risks are capable of being, and commonly are, commuted for a fixed payment, the premium of insurance takes its regular place among the charges of production, and the compensation which the owner of the ship or cargo receives for that payment, does not appear in the estimate of his profits, but is included in the replacement of his capital.

The portion, too, of the gross profit, which forms the remuneration for the labour and skill of the dealer or producer, is very different in different employments. This is the explanation always given of the extraordinary rate of apothecaries' profit; the greatest part, as Adam Smith observes, being frequently no more than the reasonable wages of professional attendance; for which, until a late alteration of the law, the apothecary could not demand any remuneration, except in the prices of his drugs. Some occupations require a considerable amount of scientific or technical education, and can [1848] only be carried on by persons who combine with that education a considerable capital. Such is the business of an engineer, both in the original sense of the term, a machine-maker,

[1] [" Much more than " replaced in the 3rd ed.(1852) the " like " of the original text. Cf. supra, book ii. ch. xiv. § 1.]

and in its popular or derivative sense, an undertaker of public works. These are always the most profitable employments. There are cases, again, in which a considerable amount of labour and skill is required to conduct a business necessarily of limited extent. In such cases, a higher than common rate of profit is necessary to yield only the common rate of remuneration. " In a small seaport town," says Adam Smith, " a little grocer will make forty or fifty per cent upon a stock of a single hundred pounds, while a considerable wholesale merchant in the same place will scarce make eight or ten per cent upon a stock of ten thousand. The trade of the grocer may be necessary for the conveniency of the inhabitants, and the narrowness of the market may not admit the employment of a larger capital in the business. The man, however, must not only live by his trade, but live by it suitably to the qualifications which it requires. Besides possessing a little capital, he must be able to read, write, and account and must be a tolerable judge, too, of perhaps fifty or sixty different sorts of goods, their prices, qualities, and the markets where they are to be had cheapest. Thirty or forty pounds a year cannot be considered as too great a recompense for the labour of a person so accomplished. Deduct this from the seemingly great profits of his capital, and little more will remain, perhaps, than the ordinary profits of stock. The greater part of the apparent profit is, in this case, too, real wages."

All the natural monopolies (meaning thereby those which are created by circumstances, and not by law) which produce or aggravate the disparities in the remuneration of different kinds of labour, operate similarly between different employments of capital. If a business can only be advantageously carried on by a large capital, this in most countries limits so narrowly the class of persons who can enter into the employment, that they are enabled to keep their rate of profit above the general level. A trade may also, from the nature of the case, be confined to so few hands, that profits may admit of being kept up by a combination among the dealers. It is well known that even among so numerous a body as the London booksellers, this sort of combination long continued to exist.[1] I have already mentioned the case of the gas and water companies.

§ 4. After due allowance is made for these various causes

[1] [So from the 4th ed. (1857). In earlier editions : " this sort of combination exists ; though individual interest is often too strong for its rules ; nor, indeed, does the combination itself include the whole trade."

of inequality, namely, differences in the risk or agreeableness of different employments, and natural or artificial monopolies; the rate of profit on capital in all employments tends to an equality Such is the proposition usually laid down by political economists, and under proper explanations it is true.

That portion of profit which is properly interest, and which forms the remuneration for abstinence, is strictly the same, at the same time and place, whatever be the employment. The rate of interest, on equally good security, does not vary according to the destination of the principal, though it does vary from time to time very much according to the circumstances of the market. There is no employment in which, in the present state of industry, competition is so active and incessant as in the lending and borrowing of money. All persons in business are occasionally, and most of them constantly, borrowers : while all persons not in business, who possess monied property, are lenders. Between these two great bodies there is a numerous, keen, and intelligent class of middlemen, composed of bankers, stockbrokers, discount brokers, and others, alive to the slightest breath of probable gain. The smallest circumstance, or the most transient impression on the public mind, which tends to an increase or diminution of the demand for loans either at the time or prospectively, operates immediately on the rate of interest : and circumstances in the general state of trade, really tending to cause this difference of demand, are continually occurring, sometimes to such an extent, that the rate of interest on the best mercantile bills has been known to vary in little more than a year (even without the occurrence of the great derangement called a commercial crisis) from four, or less, to eight or nine per cent. But, at the same time and place, the rate of interest is the same, to all who can give equally good security. The market rate of interest is at all times a known and definite thing.

It is far otherwise with gross profit; which, though (as will presently be seen) it does not vary much from employment to employment, varies very greatly from individual to individual, and can scarcely be in any two cases the same. It depends on the knowledge, talents, economy, and energy of the capitalist himself, or of the agents whom he employs ; on the accidents of personal connexion ; and even on chance. Hardly any two dealers in the same trade, even if their commodities are equally good and equally cheap, carry on their business at the same expense, or turn over their capital in the same time. That equal capitals give equal profits, as a general maxim of trade, would be as false as that equal age or size gives equal bodily strength, or that equal reading or experience gives equal knowledge. The effect depends as much upon twenty other things, as upon the single cause specified.

But though profits thus vary, the parity, on the whole, of different modes of employing capital (in the absence of any natural or artificial monopoly) is, in a certain and a very important sense, maintained. On an average (whatever may be the occasional fluctuations) the various employments of capital are on such a footing as to hold out, not equal profits, but equal expectations [1] of profit, to persons of average abilities and advantages. By equal, I mean after making compensation for any inferiority in the agreeableness or safety of an employment. If the case were not so ; if there were, evidently, and to common experience, more favourable chances of pecuniary success in one business than in others, more persons would engage their capital in the business, or would bring up their sons to it ; which in fact always happens when a business, like that of an engineer at present [1848], or like any newly established and prosperous manufacture, is seen to be a growing and thriving one. If, on the contrary, a business is not considered thriving ; if the chances of profit in it are thought to be inferior to those in other employments ; capital gradually leaves it, or at least new capital is not attracted to it ; and by this change in the distribution of capital between the less profitable and the more profitable employments, a sort of balance is restored. The expectations of profit, therefore, in different employments, cannot long continue very different : they tend to a common average, though they are generally oscillating from one side to the other side of the medium.

This equalizing process, commonly described as the transfer of capital from one employment to another, is not necessarily the onerous, slow, and almost impracticable operation which it is very often represented to be. In the first place, it does not always imply the actual removal of capital already embarked in an employment. In a rapidly progressive state of capital, the adjustment often takes place by means of the new accumulations of each year, which direct themselves in preference towards the more thriving trades. Even when a real transfer of capital is necessary, it is by no means implied that any of those who are engaged in the unprofitable employment relinquish business and

---

[1] [Altered from " chances " as late as the 5th ed. (1862).]

break up their establishments. The numerous and multifarious channels of credit, through which, in commercial nations, unemployed capital diffuses itself over the field of employment, flowing over in greater abundance to the lower levels, are the means by which the equalization is accomplished. The process consists in a limitation by one class of dealers or producers, and an extension by the other, of that portion of their business which is carried on with borrowed capital. There is scarcely any dealer or producer on a considerable scale, who confines his business to what can be carried on by his own funds. When trade is good, he not only uses to the utmost his own capital, but employs, in addition, much of the credit which that capital obtains for him. When, either from over-supply or from some slackening in the demand for his commodity, he finds that it sells more slowly or obtains a lower price, he contracts his operations, and does not apply to bankers or other money dealers for a renewal of their advances to the same extent as before. A business which is increasing holds out, on the contrary, a prospect of profitable employment for a larger amount of this floating capital than previously, and those engaged in it become applicants to the money dealers for larger advances, which, from their improving circumstances, they have no difficulty in obtaining. A different distribution of floating capital between two employments has as much effect in restoring their profits to an equilibrium, as if the owners of an equal amount of capital were to abandon the one trade and carry their capital into the other. This easy, and as it were spontaneous, method of accommodating production to demand, is quite sufficient to correct any inequalities arising from the fluctuations of trade, or other causes of ordinary occurrence. In the case of an altogether declining trade, in which it is necessary that the production should be, not occasionally varied, but greatly and permanently diminished, or perhaps stopped altogether, the process of extricating the capital is, no doubt, tardy and difficult, and almost always attended with considerable loss ; much of the capital fixed in machinery, buildings, permanent works, &c. being either not applicable to any other purpose, or only applicable after expensive alterations ; and time being seldom given for effecting the change in the mode in which it would be effected with least loss, namely, by not replacing the fixed capital as it wears out. There is besides, in totally changing the destination of a capital, so great a sacrifice of established connexion, and of acquired skill and experience, that people are always very slow in resolving upon it, and hardly ever do so until long after a change of fortune has become hopeless. These, however, are distinctly exceptional cases, and even in these the equalization is at last effected. It may also happen that the return to equilibrium is considerably protracted, when, before one inequality has been corrected, another cause of inequality arises ; which is said to have been continually the case, during a long series of years, with the production of cotton in the Southern States of North America ; the commodity having been upheld at what was virtually a monopoly price, because the increase of demand, from successive improvements in the manufacture, went on with a rapidity so much beyond expectation that for many years the supply never completely over-took it. But it is not often that a succession of disturbing causes, all acting in the same direction, are known to follow one another with hardly any interval. Where there is no monopoly, the profits of a trade are likely to range sometimes above and sometimes below the general level, but tending always to return to it ; like the oscillations of the pendulum.

In general, then, although profits are very different to different individuals, and to the same individual in different years, there cannot be much diversity at the same time and place in the average profits of different employments, (other than the standing differences necessary to compensate for difference of attractiveness,) except for short periods, or when some great permanent revulsion has overtaken a particular trade. If any popular impression exists that some trades are more profitable than others, independently of monopoly, or of such rare accidents as have been noticed in regard to the cotton trade, the impression is in all probability fallacious, since if it were shared by those who have greatest means of knowledge and motives to accurate examination, there would take place such an influx of capital as would soon lower the profits to the common level. It is true that, to persons with the same amount of original means, there is more chance of making a large fortune in some employments than in others. But it would be found that in those same employ-ments, bankruptcies also are more frequent, and that the chance of greater success is balanced by a greater probability of complete failure. Very often it is more than balanced : for, as was remarked in another case, the chance of great prizes operates with a greater degree of strength than arithmetic will warrant, in attracting competitors ; and I doubt not that the average gains, in a trade in which large fortunes may be made, are lower than in those in which gains are slow, though comparatively sure, and in which nothing is to be ultimately hoped for beyond a competency. The timber trade of Canada is [1848] one example of an employment of capital partaking so much of the nature of a lottery, as to make it an accredited opinion that, taking the adventurers in the aggregate, there is more money lost by the trade than gained by it; in other words, that the average rate of profit is less than nothing. In such points as this, much depends on the characters of nations, according as they partake more or less of the adventurous, or, as it is called when the intention is to blame it, the gambling spirit. This spirit is much stronger in the United States than in Great Britain; and in Great Britain than in any country of the Continent. In some Continental countries the tendency is so much the reverse, that safe and quiet employments probably yield a less average profit to the capital engaged in them, than those which offer greater gains at the price of greater hazards.

It must not however be forgotten, that even in the countries of most active competition, custom also has a considerable share in determining the profits of trade. There is sometimes an idea afloat as to what the profit of an employment should be, which though not adhered to by all the dealers, nor perhaps rigidly by any, still exercises a certain influence over their operations. There has been in England a kind of notion, how widely prevailing I know not, that fifty per cent is a proper and suitable rate of profit in retail transactions: understand, not fifty per cent on the whole capital, but an advance of fifty per cent on the wholesale prices; from which have to be defrayed bad debts, shop rent, the pay of clerks, shopmen, and agents of all descriptions, in short all the expenses of the retail business. If this custom were universal, and strictly adhered to, competition indeed would still operate, but the consumer would not derive any benefit from it, at least as to price; the way in which it would diminish the advantages of those engaged in the retail trade, would be by a greater subdivision of the business. In some parts of the Continent the standard is as high as a hundred per cent. The increase of competition however, in England at least, is rapidly tending to break down customs of this description. In the majority of trades (at least in the great emporia of trade), there are now numerous dealers whose motto is, " small gains and frequent "—a great business at low prices, rather than high prices and few transactions; and by turning over their capital more rapidly, and adding to it by borrowed capital when needed, the dealers often obtain individually higher profits; though they necessarily lower the profits of those among their competitors who do not adopt the same principle. [1] Nevertheless, competition, as remarked * in a previous chapter, has, as yet, but a limited dominion over retail prices; and consequently the share of the whole produce of land and labour which is absorbed in the remuneration of mere distributors, continues exorbitant; and there is no function in the economy of society which supports a number of persons so disproportioned to the amount of work to be performed.

§ 5. The preceding remarks have, I hope, sufficiently elucidated what is meant by the common phrase, "the ordinary rate of profit;" and the sense in which, and the limitations under which, this ordinary rate has a real existence. It now remains to consider, what causes determine its amount.

[2] To popular apprehension it seems as if the profits of business depended upon prices. A producer or dealer seems to obtain his profits by selling his commodity for more than it cost him. Profit altogether, people are apt to think, is a consequence of purchase and sale. It is only (they suppose) because there are purchasers for a commodity, that the producer of it is able to make any profit. Demand—customers—a market for the commodity, are the cause of the gains of capitalists. It is by the sale of their goods, that they replace their capital, and add to its amount.

This, however, is looking only at the outside surface of the economical machinery of society. In no case, we find, is the mere money which passes from one person to another, the fundamental matter in any economical phenomenon. If we look more narrowly into the operations of the producer, we shall perceive that the money he obtains for his commodity is not the cause of his having a profit, but only the mode in which his profit is paid to him.

The cause of profit is, that labour produces more than is required for its support. The reason why agricultural capital yields a profit, is because human beings can grow more food than is necessary to feed them while it is being grown, including the time occupied in constructing the tools, and making all other needful preparations : from which it is a consequence, that if a capitalist undertakes to feed the labourers on condition of receiving the produce, he has

---

[1] [The rest of this paragraph was added in the 3rd ed. (1852).]
* Vide supra, book ii. ch. iv. § 3.
[2] [The remainder of this section was added in the 4th ed. (1857).]

some of it remaining for himself after replacing his advances. To vary the form of the theorem : the reason why capital yields a profit, is because food, clothing, materials, and tools, last longer than the time which was required to produce them ; so that if a capitalist supplies a party of labourers with these things, on condition of receiving all they produce, they will, in addition to reproducing their own necessaries and instruments, have a portion of their time remaining, to work for the capitalist. We thus see that profit arises, not from the incident of exchange, but from the productive power of labour ; and the general profit of the country is always what the productive power of labour makes it, whether any exchange takes place or not. If there were no division of employments, there would be no buying or selling, but there would still be profit. If the labourers of the country collectively produce twenty per cent more than their wages, profits will be twenty per cent, whatever prices may or may not be. The accidents of price may for a time make one set of producers get more than the twenty per cent, and another less, the one commodity being rated above its natural value in relation to other commodities, and the other below, until prices have again adjusted themselves ; but there will always be just twenty per cent divided among them all.

I proceed, in expansion of the considerations thus briefly indicated, to exhibit more minutely the mode in which the rate of profit is determined.

§ 6. I assume, throughout, the state of things, which, where the labourers and capitalists are separate classes, prevails, with few exceptions, universally ; namely, that the capitalist advances the whole expenses, including the entire remuneration of the labourer. That he should do so, is not a matter of inherent necessity ; the labourer might wait until the production is complete, for all that part of his wages which exceeds mere necessaries ; and even for the whole, if he has funds in hand, sufficient for his temporary support. But in the latter case, the labourer is to that extent really a capitalist, investing capital in the concern, by supplying a portion of the funds necessary for carrying it on ; and even in the former case he may be looked upon in the same light, since, contributing his labour at less than the market price, he may be regarded as lending the difference to his employer, and receiving it back with interest (on whatever principle computed) from the proceeds of the enterprise.

The capitalist, then, may be assumed to make all the advances, and receive all the produce. His profit consists of the excess of the produce above the advances ; his *rate* of profit is the ratio which that excess bears to the amount advanced. But what do the advances consist of ?

It is, for the present, necessary to suppose, that the capitalist does not pay any rent ; has not to purchase the use of any appropriated natural agent. This indeed is scarcely ever the exact truth. The agricultural capitalist, except when he is the owner of the soil he cultivates, always, or almost always, pays rent : and even in manufactures, (not to mention ground-rent,) the materials of the manufacture have generally paid rent, in some stage of their production. The nature of rent, however, we have not yet taken into consideration ; and it will hereafter appear, that no practical error, on the question we are now examining, is produced by disregarding it.

If, then, leaving rent out of the question, we inquire in what it is that the advances of the capitalist, for purposes of production, consist, we shall find that they consist of wages of labour.

A large portion of the expenditure of every capitalist consists in the direct payment of wages. What does not consist of this, is composed of materials and implements, including buildings. But materials and implements are produced by labour ; and as our supposed capitalist is not meant to represent a single employment, but to be a type of the productive industry of the whole country, we may suppose that he makes his own tools, and raises his own materials. He does this by means of previous advances, which, again, consist wholly of wages. If we suppose him to buy the materials and tools instead of producing them, the case is not altered : he then repays to a previous producer the wages which that previous producer has paid. It is true, he repays it to him with a profit ; and if he had produced the things himself, he himself must have had that profit, on this part of his outlay, as well as on every other part. The fact, however, remains, that in the whole process of production, beginning with the materials and tools, and ending with the finished product, all the advances have consisted of nothing but wages ; except that certain of the capitalists concerned have, for the sake of general convenience, had their share of profit paid to them before the operation was completed. Whatever, of the ultimate product, is not profit, is repayment of wages.

§ 7. It thus appears that the two elements on which, and which alone, the gains of the capitalists depend, are, first, the magnitude of the produce, in other words, the productive power of labour ; and secondly, the proportion of that produce obtained by the labourers themselves ; the ratio which the remuneration of the labourers bears to the amount they produce. These two things form the data for determining the gross amount divided as profit among all the capitalists of the country ; but the *rate* of profit, the percentage on the capital, depends only on the second of the.two elements, the labourer's proportional share, and not on the amount to be shared. If the produce of labour were doubled, and the labourers obtained the same proportional share as before, that is, if their remuneration was also doubled, the capitalists, it is true, would gain twice as much ; but as they would also have had to advance twice as much, the rate of their profit would be only the same as before.

We thus arrive at the conclusion of Ricardo and others, that the rate of profits depends on wages ; rising as wages fall, and falling as wages rise. In adopting, however, this doctrine, I must insist upon making a most necessary alteration in its wording. Instead of saying that profits depend on wages, let us say (what Ricardo really meant) that they depend on the *cost of labour*.

Wages, and the cost of labour ; what labour brings in to the labourer, and what it costs to the capitalist ; are ideas quite distinct, and which it is of the utmost importance to keep so. For this purpose it is essential not to designate them, as is almost always done, by the same name. Wages, in public discussions, both oral and printed, being looked upon from the point of view of the payers, much oftener than from that of the receivers, nothing is more common than to say that wages are high or low, meaning only that the cost of labour is high or low. The reverse of this would be oftener the truth : the cost of labour is frequently at its highest where wages are lowest. This may arise from two causes. In the first place, the labour, though cheap, may be inefficient. In no European country are wages so low as they are (or at least were [1]) in Ireland : the remuneration of an agricultural labourer in the west of Ireland not being more than half the wages of even the lowest-paid Englishman, the Dorsetshire labourer. But if, from inferior skill and industry, two days' labour of an Irishman accomplished no more work than an English labourer performed in one, the Irishman's labour cost as much as the Englishman's, though it brought in so much less to himself. The capitalist's profit is determined by the former of these

[1] [Added in the 4th ed. (1857).]

two things, not by the latter. That a difference to this extent really existed in the efficiency of the labour, is proved not only by abundant testimony, but by the fact, that notwithstanding the lowness of wages, profits of capital are not understood to have been higher in Ireland than in England.

The other cause which renders wages, and the cost of labour, no real criteria of one another, is the varying costliness of the articles which the labourer consumes. If these are cheap, wages, in the sense which is of importance to the labourer, may be high, and yet the cost of labour may be low; if dear, the labourer may be wretchedly off, though his labour may cost much to the capitalist. This last is the condition of a country over-peopled in relation to its land; in which, food being dear, the poorness of the labourer's real reward does not prevent labour from costing much to the purchaser, and low wages and low profits co-exist. The opposite case is exemplified in the United States of America. The labourer there enjoys a greater abundance of comforts than in any other country of the world, except some of the newest colonies; but owing to the cheap price at which these comforts can be obtained (combined with the great efficiency of the labour), the cost of labour to the capitalist is at least not higher, nor the rate of profit lower, than in Europe.[1]

The cost of labour, then, is, in the language of mathematics, a function of three variables : the efficiency of labour; the wages of labour (meaning thereby the real reward of the labourer) ; and the greater or less cost at which the articles composing that real reward can be produced or procured. It is plain that the cost of labour to the capitalist must be influenced by each of these three circumstances, and by no others. These, therefore, are also the circumstances which determine the rate of profit; and it cannot be in any way affected except through one or other of them. If labour generally became more efficient, without being more highly rewarded; if, without its becoming less efficient, its remuneration fell, no increase taking place in the cost of the articles composing that remuneration ; or if those articles became less costly, without the labourer's obtaining more of them ; in any one of these three cases, profits would rise. If, on the contrary, labour became less efficient (as it might

[1] [So from the 6th ed. (1865). The earlier editions ran : " the cost of labour to the capitalist is considerably lower than in Europe. It must be so, since the rate of profit is higher ; as indicated by the rate of interest, which is six per cent at New York when it is three or three and a quarter per cent in London."]

do from diminished bodily vigour in the people, destruction of fixed capital, or deteriorated education) ; or if the labourer obtained a higher remuneration, without any increased cheapness in the things composing it ; or if, without his obtaining more, that which he did obtain became more costly ; profits, in all these cases, would suffer a diminution. And there is no other combination of circumstances, in which the general rate of profit of a country, in all employments indifferently, can either fall or rise.

The evidence of these propositions can only be stated generally, though, it is hoped, conclusively, in this stage of our subject. It will come out in greater fulness and force when, having taken into consideration the theory of Value and Price, we shall be enabled to exhibit the law of profits in the concrete—in the complex entanglement of circumstances in which it actually works. This can only be done in the ensuing Book. One topic still remains to be discussed in the present one, so far as it admits of being treated independently of considerations of Value ; the subject of Rent; to which we now proceed.[1]

[1] [See Appendix Q. *Profits.*]

CHAPTER XVI

§ 1. THE requisites of production being labour, capital, and natural agents; the only person, besides the labourer and the capitalist, whose consent is necessary to production, and who can claim a share of the produce as the price of that consent, is the person who, by the arrangements of society, possesses exclusive power over some natural agent. The land is the principal of the natural agents which are capable of being appropriated, and the consideration paid for its use is called rent. Landed proprietors are the only class, of any numbers or importance, who have a claim to a share in the distribution of the produce, through their ownership of something which neither they nor any one else have produced. If there be any other cases of a similar nature, they will be easily understood, when the nature and laws of rent are comprehended.

It is at once evident, that rent is the effect of a monopoly; though the monopoly is a natural one, which may be regulated, which may even be held as a trust for the community generally, but which cannot be prevented from existing. The reason why landowners are able to require rent for their land, is that it is a commodity which many want, and which no one can obtain but from them. If all the land of the country belonged to one person, he could fix the rent at his pleasure. The whole people would be dependent on his will for the necessaries of life, and he might make what conditions he chose. This is the actual state of things in those Oriental kingdoms in which the land is considered the property of the state. Rent is then confounded with taxation, and the despot may exact the utmost which the unfortunate cultivators have to give. Indeed, the exclusive possessor of the land of a country could not well be other than despot of it. The effect would be much the same if the land belonged to so few people, that they could, and did, act together as one man, and fix the rent by agreement among themselves. This case, however, is nowhere known to exist: and the only remaining supposition is that of free competition ; the landowners being supposed to be, as in fact they are, too numerous to combine.

§ 2. A thing which is limited in quantity, even though its possessors do not act in concert, is still a monopolized article. But even when monopolized, a thing which is the gift of nature, and requires no labour or outlay as the condition of its existence, will, if there be competition among the holders of it, command a price, only if it exists in less quantity than the demand. If the whole land of a country were required for cultivation, all of it might yield a rent. But in no country of any extent do the wants of the population require that all the land, which is capable of cultivation, should be cultivated. The food and other agricultural produce which the people need, and which they are willing and able to pay for at a price which remunerates the grower, may always be obtained without cultivating all the land ; sometimes without cultivating more than a small part of it ; the lands most easily cultivated being preferred in a very early stage of society ; [1] the most fertile, or those in the most convenient situations, in a more advanced state. There is always, therefore, some land which cannot, in existing circumstances, pay any rent ; and no land ever pays rent, unless, in point of fertility or situation, it belongs to those superior kinds which exist in less quantity than the demand—which cannot be made to yield all the produce required for the community, unless on terms still less advantageous than the resort to less favoured soils.

There is land, such as the deserts of Arabia, which will yield nothing to any amount of labour ; and there is land, like some of our hard sandy heaths, which would produce something, but, in the present state of the soil, not enough to defray the expenses of production. Such lands, unless by some application of chemistry to agriculture still remaining to be invented, cannot be cultivated for profit, unless some one actually creates a soil, by spreading new ingredients over the surface, or mixing them with the existing materials. If ingredients fitted for this purpose exist in the subsoil, or close at hand, the improvement even of the most unpromising spots may answer as a speculation : but if those ingredients are costly, and must be brought from a distance, it will seldom answer to do this for the sake of profit, though the " magic of property " will sometimes effect it. Land which cannot possibly yield a profit, is sometimes cultivated at a loss, the cultivators having their wants

[1] [This clause was inserted in the 6th ed. (1865).]

partially supplied from other sources ; as in the case of paupers, and some monasteries or charitable institutions, among which may be reckoned the Poor Colonies of Belgium. The worst land which can de cultivated as a means of subsistence, is that which will just replace the seed, and the food of the labourers employed on it, together with what Dr. Chalmers calls their secondaries ; that is, the labourers required for supplying them with tools, and with the remaining necessaries of life. Whether any given land is capable of doing more than this, is not a question of political economy, but of physical fact. The supposition leaves nothing for profits, nor anything for the labourers except necessaries : the land, therefore, can only be cultivated by the labourers themselves, or else at a pecuniary loss : and à fortiori, cannot in any contingency afford a rent. The worse land which can be cultivated as an investment for capital, is that which, after replacing the seed, not only feeds the agricultural labourers and their secondaries, but affords them the current rate of wages, which may extend to much more than mere necessaries ; and leaves for those who have advanced the wages of these two classes of labourers, a surplus equal to the profit they could have expected from any other employment of their capital. Whether any given land can do more than this, is not merely a physical question, but depends partly on the market value of agricultural produce. What the land can do for the labourers and for the capitalist, beyond feeding all whom it directly or indirectly employs, of course depends upon what the remainder of the produce can be sold for. The higher the market value of produce, the lower are the soils to which cultivation can descend, consistently with affording to the capital employed the ordinary rate of profit.

As, however, differences of fertility slide into one another by insensible gradations ; and differences of accessibility, that is, of distance from markets, do the same ; and since there is land so barren that it could not pay for its cultivation at any price ; it is evident that, whatever the price may be, there must in any extensive region be some land which at that price will just pay the wages of the cultivators, and yield to the capital employed the ordinary profit, and no more. Until, therefore, the price rises higher, or until some improvement raises that particular land to a higher place in the scale of fertility, it cannot pay any rent. It is evident, however, that the community needs the produce of this quality of land ; since if the lands more fertile or better situated than it, could have sufficed to supply the wants of society, the price would not have risen so high as to render its cultivation profitable. This land, therefore, will be cultivated ; and we may lay it down as a principle, that so long as any of the land of a country which is fit for cultivation, and not withheld from it by legal or other factitious obstacles, is not cultivated, the worst land in actual cultivation (in point of fertility and situation together) pays no rent.

§ 3. If, then, of the land in cultivation, the part which yields least return to the labour and capital employed on it gives only the ordinary profit of capital, without leaving anything for rent ; a standard is afforded for estimating the amount of rent which will be yielded by all other land. Any land yields just as much more than the ordinary profits of stock, as it yields more than what is returned by the worst land in cultivation. The surplus is what the farmer can afford to pay as rent to the landlord ; and since, if he did not so pay it, he would receive more than the ordinary rate of profit, the competition of other capitalists, that competition which equalizes the profits of different capitals, will enable the landlord to appropriate it. The rent, therefore, which any land will yield, is the excess of its produce beyond what would be returned to the same capital if employed on the worst land in cultivation. This is not, and never was pretended to be, the limit of metayer rents, or of cottier rents ; but it is the limit of farmers' rents. No land rented to a capitalist farmer will permanently yield more than this ; and when it yields less, it is because the landlord foregoes a part of what, if he chose, he could obtain.

This is the theory of rent, first propounded at the end of the last century by Dr. Anderson, and which, neglected at the time, was almost simultaneously rediscovered, twenty years later, by Sir Edward West, Mr. Malthus, and Mr. Ricardo. It is one of the cardinal doctrines of political economy ; and until it was understood, no consistent explanation could be given of many of the more complicated industrial phenomena. The evidence of its truth will be manifested with a great increase of clearness, when we come to trace the laws of the phenomena of Value and Price. Until that is done, it is not possible to free the doctrine from every difficulty which may present itself, nor perhaps to convey, to those previously unacquainted with the subject, more than a general apprehension of the reasoning by which the theorem is arrived at. Some, however, of the objections commonly made to it, admit of a complete answer even in the present stage of our inquiries.

It has been denied that there can be any land in cultivation which pays no rent; because landlords (it is contended) would not allow their lands to be occupied without payment. Those who lay any stress on this as an objection, must think that land of the quality which can but just pay for its cultivation, lies together in large masses, detached from any land of better quality. If an estate consisted wholly of this land, or of this and still worse, it is likely enough that the owner would not give the use of it for nothing; he would probably (if a rich man) prefer keeping it for other purposes, as for exercise, or ornament, or perhaps as a game preserve. No farmer could afford to offer him anything for it, for purposes of culture; though something would probably be obtained for the use of its natural pasture, or other spontaneous produce. Even such land, however, would not necessarily remain uncultivated. It might be farmed by the proprietor; no unfrequent case even in England. Portions of it might be granted as temporary allotments to labouring families, either from philanthropic motives, or to save the poor-rate; or occupation might be allowed to squatters, free of rent, in the hope that their labour might give it value at some future period. Both these cases are of quite ordinary occurrence. So that even if an estate were wholly composed of the worst land capable of profitable cultivation, it would not necessarily lie uncultivated because it could pay no rent. Inferior land, however, does not usually occupy, without interruption, many square miles of ground; it is dispersed here and there, with patches of better land intermixed, and the same person who rents the better land, obtains along with it the inferior soils which alternate with it. He pays a rent, nominally for the whole farm, but calculated on the produce of those parts alone (however small a portion of the whole) which are capable of returning more than the common rate of profit. It is thus scientifically true, that the remaining parts pay no rent.

§ 4. Let us, however, suppose that there were a validity in this objection, which can by no means be conceded to it; that when the demand of the community had forced up food to such a price as would remunerate the expense of producing it from a certain quality of soil, it happened nevertheless that all the soil of that quality was withheld from cultivation, by the obstinacy of the owners in demanding a rent for it, not nominal, nor trifling, but sufficiently onerous to be a material item in the calculations of a farmer. What would then happen? Merely that the increase of produce, which the wants of society required, would for the time be obtained wholly (as it always is partially), not by an extension of cultivation, but by an increased application of labour and capital to land already cultivated.

Now we have already seen that this increased application of capital, other things being unaltered, is always attended with a smaller proportional return. We are not to suppose some new agricultural invention made precisely at this juncture ; nor a sudden extension of agricultural skill and knowledge, bringing into more general practice, just then, inventions already in partial use. We are to suppose no change, except a demand for more corn, and a consequent rise of its price. The rise of price enables measures to be taken for increasing the produce, which could not have been taken with profit at the previous price. The farmer uses more expensive manures ; or manures land which he formerly left to nature ; or procures lime or marl from a distance, as a dressing for the soil ; or pulverizes or weeds it more thoroughly ; or drains, irrigates, or subsoils portions of it, which at former prices would not have paid the cost of the operation ; and so forth. These things, or some of them, are done, when, more food being wanted, cultivation has no means of expanding itself upon new lands. And when the impulse is given to extract an increased amount of produce from the soil, the farmer or improver will only consider whether the outlay he makes for the purpose will be returned to him with the ordinary profit, and not whether any surplus will remain for rent. Even, therefore, if it were the fact, that there is never any *land* taken into cultivation, for which rent, and that too of an amount worth taking into consideration, was not paid ; it would be true, nevertheless, that there is always some *agricultural capital* which pays no rent, because it returns nothing beyond the ordinary rate of profit : this capital being the portion of capital last applied —that to which the last addition to the produce was due : or (to express the essentials of the case in one phrase), that which is applied in the least favourable circumstances. But the same amount of demand, and the same price, which enable this least productive portion of capital barely to replace itself with the ordinary profit, enable every other portion to yield a surplus proportioned to the advantage it possesses. And this surplus it is, which competition enables the landlord to appropriate. The rent of all land is measured by the excess of the return to the whole capital employed on it, above what is necessary to replace the capital with the ordinary rate of profit, or in other words, above what the same capital would yield if it were all employed in as disadvantageous circumstances as the least productive portion of it ; whether that least productive portion of capital is rendered so by being employed on the worst soil, or by being expended in extorting more produce from land which already yielded as much as it could be made to part with on easier terms.

It is not pretended that the facts of any concrete case conform with absolute precision to this or any other scientific principle. We must never forget that the truths of political economy are truths only in the rough : they have the certainty, but not the precision, of exact science.[1] It is not, for example, strictly true that a farmer will cultivate no land, and apply no capital, which returns less than the ordinary profit. He will expect the ordinary profit on the bulk of his capital. But when he has cast in his lot with his farm, and bartered his skill and exertions, once for all, against what the farm will yield to him, he will probably be willing to expend capital on it (for an immediate return) in any manner which will afford him a surplus profit, however small, beyond the value of the risk, and the interest which he must pay for the capital if borrowed, or can get for it elsewhere if it is his own. But a new farmer, entering on the land, would make his calculations differently, and would not commence unless he could expect the full rate of ordinary profit on all the capital which he intended embarking in the enterprise. Again, prices may range higher or lower during the currency of a lease, than was expected when the contract was made, and the land, therefore, may be over or under-rented : and even when the lease expires, the landlord may be unwilling to grant a necessary diminution of rent, and the farmer, rather than relinquish his occupation, or seek a farm elsewhere when all are occupied, may consent to go on paying too high a rent. Irregularities like these we must always expect ; it is impossible in political economy to obtain general theorems embracing the complication of circumstances which may affect the result in an individual case. When, too,[2] the farmer class, having but little capital, cultivate for subsistence rather than for profit, and do not think of quitting their farm while they are able to live by it, their rents approximate to the character of cottier rents, and may be forced up by competition (if the number of competitors exceeds the number of farms) beyond

---

[1] [This explanatory phrase was added in the 6th ed. (1865).]
[2] [This sentence was inserted in the 3rd ed. (1852).]

the amount which will leave to the farmer the ordinary rate of profit. The laws which we are enabled to lay down respecting rents, profits, wages, prices, are only true in so far as the persons concerned are free from the influence of any other motives than those arising from the general circumstances of the case, and are guided, as to those, by the ordinary mercantile estimate of profit and loss. Applying this twofold supposition to the case of farmers and land-lords, it will be true that the farmer requires the ordinary rate of profit on the whole of his capital ; that whatever it returns to him beyond this he is obliged to pay to the landlord, but will not consent to pay more ; that there is a portion of capital applied to agriculture in such circumstances of productiveness as to yield only the ordinary profits ; and that the difference between the produce of this, and of any other capital of similar amount, is the measure of the tribute which that other capital can and will pay, under the name of rent, to the landlord. This constitutes a law of rent, as near the truth as such a law can possibly be : though of course modified or disturbed in individual cases, by pending contracts, individual miscalculations, the influence of habit, and even the particular feelings and dispositions of the persons concerned.

§ 5. A remark is often made, which must not here be omitted, though, I think, more importance has been attached to it than it merits. Under the name of rent, many payments are commonly included which are not a remuneration for the original powers of the land itself, but for capital expended on it. The additional rent which land yields in consequence of this outlay of capital, should, in the opinion of some writers, be regarded as profit, not rent. But before this can be admitted, a distinction must be made. The annual payment by a tenant almost always includes a consideration for the use of the buildings on the farm ; not only barns, stables, and other outhouses, but a house to live in, not to speak of fences and the like. The landlord will ask, and the tenant give, for these, whatever is considered sufficient to yield the ordinary profit, or rather (risk and trouble being here out of the question) the ordinary interest, on the value of the buildings : that is, not on what it has cost to erect them, but on what it would now cost to erect others as good : the tenant being bound, in addition, to leave them in as good repair as he found them, for otherwise a much larger payment than simple interest would of course be required from him. These buildings are as distinct a thing from the farm as the stock or the

timber on it ; and what is paid for them can no more be called rent
of land, than a payment for cattle would be, if it were the custom
that the landlord should stock the farm for the tenant. The buildings,
like the cattle, are not land, but capital, regularly consumed and
reproduced ; and all payments made in consideration for them are
properly interest.

But with regard to capital actually sunk in improvements, and
not requiring periodical renewal, but spent once for all in giving
the land a permanent increase of productiveness, it appears to me
that the return made to such capital loses altogether the character of
profits, and is governed by the principles of rent. It is true that a
landlord will not expend capital in improving his estate, unless he
expects from the improvement an increase of income surpassing the
interest of his outlay. Prospectively, this increase of income may be
regarded as profit ; but when the expense has been incurred, and
the improvement made, the rent of the improved land is governed
by the same rules as that of the unimproved. Equally fertile land
commands an equal rent, whether its fertility is natural or acquired ;
and I cannot think that the incomes of those who own the Bedford
Level or the Lincolnshire Wolds ought to be called profit and not
rent because those lands would have been worth next to nothing
unless capital had been expended on them. The owners are not
capitalists, but landlords ; they have parted with their capital ;
it is consumed, destroyed ; and neither is, nor is to be, returned to
them, like the capital of a farmer or manufacturer, from what it
produces. In lieu of it they now have land of a certain richness,
which yields the same rent, and by the operation of the same causes,
as if it had possessed f om the beginning the degree of fertility which
has been artificially given to it.

Some writers, in particular Mr. H. C. Carey, take away, still
more completely than I have attempted to do, the distinction
between these two sources of rent, by rejecting one of them altogether,
and considering all rent as the effect of capital expended. In
proof of this, Mr. Carey contends that the whole pecuniary value of
all the land in any country, in England for instance, or in the
United States, does not amount to anything approaching to the
sum which has been laid out, or which it would even now be necessary
to lay out, in order to bring the country to its present condition
from a state of primæval forest. This startling statement has been
seized on by M. Bastiat [1] and others, as a means of making out a

---

[1] [The reference to Bastiat was inserted in the 3rd ed. (1852). The

stronger case than could otherwise be made in defence of property in land. Mr. Carey's proposition, in its most obvious meaning, is equivalent to saying, that if there were suddenly added to the lands of England an unreclaimed territory of equal natural fertility, it would not be worth the while of the inhabitants of England to reclaim it : because the profits of the operation would not be equal to the ordinary interest on the capital expended. To which assertion, if any answer could be supposed to be required, it would suffice to remark, that land not of equal but of greatly inferior quality to that previously cultivated, is continually reclaimed in England, at an expense which the subsequently accruing rent is sufficient to replace completely in a small number of years. The doctrine, moreover, is totally opposed to Mr. Carey's own economical opinions. No one maintains more strenuously than Mr. Carey the undoubted truth, that as society advances in population, wealth, and combination of labour, land constantly rises in value and price. This, however, could not possibly be true, if the present value of land were less than the expense of clearing it and making it fit for cultivation ; for it must have been worth this immediately after it was cleared ; and according to Mr. Carey it has been rising in value ever since.

When, however, Mr. Carey asserts that the whole land of any country is not now worth the capital which has been expended on it, he does not mean that each particular estate is worth less than what has been laid out in improving it, and that, to the proprietors, the improvement of the land has been, in the final result, a miscalculation. He means, not that the land of Great Britain would not now sell for what has been laid out upon it, but that it would not sell for that amount plus the expense of making all the roads, canals, and railways. This is probably true, but is no more to the purpose, and no more important in political economy, than if the statement had been, that it would not sell for the sums laid out on it plus the national debt, or plus the cost of the French Revolutionary war, or any other expense incurred for a real or imaginary public advantage. The roads, railways, and canals were not constructed to give value to land : on the contrary, their natural effect was to lower its value, by rendering other and rival lands accessible : and the landlords of the southern counties actually petitioned Parliament against the turnpike roads on this very account.

remainder of this paragraph, together with the following paragraph, took their present form finally in the 6th ed. (1865).]

The tendency of improved communications is to lower existing rents, by trenching on the monopoly of the land nearest to the places where large numbers of consumers are assembled. Roads and canals are not intended to raise the value of the land which already supplies the markets, but (among other purposes) to cheapen the supply, by letting in the produce of other and more distant lands;· and the more effectually this purpose is attained, the lower rent will be. If we could imagine that the railways and canals of the United States, instead of only cheapening communication, did their business so effectually as to annihilate cost of carriage altogether, and enable the produce of Michigan to reach the market of New York as quickly and as cheaply as the produce of Long Island— the whole value of all the land of the United States (except such as lies convenient for building) would be annihilated ; or rather, the best would only sell for the expense of clearing, and the government tax of a dollar and a quarter per acre ; since land in Michigan, equal to the best in the United States, may be had in unlimited abundance by that amount of outlay. But it is strange that Mr. Carey should think this fact inconsistent with the Ricardo theory of rent. Admitting all that he asserts, it is still true that as long as there is land which yields no rent, the land which does yield rent, does so in consequence of some advantage which it enjoys, in fertility or vicinity to markets, over the other ; and the measure of its advantage is also the measure of its rent. And the cause of its yielding rent is that it possesses a natural monopoly ; the quantity of land, as favourably circumstanced as itself, not being sufficient to supply the market. These propositions constitute the theory of rent laid down by Ricardo ; and if they are true, I cannot see that it signifies much whether the rent which the land yields at the present time, is greater or less than the interest of the capital which has been laid out to raise its value, together with the interest of the capital which has been laid out to lower its value.

Mr. Carey's objection, however, has somewhat more of ingenuity than the arguments commonly met with against the theory of rent ; a theorem which may be called the *pons asinorum* of political economy, for there are, I am inclined to think, few persons who have refused their assent to it except from not having thoroughly understood it. The loose and inaccurate way in which it is often apprehended by those who affect to refute it, is very remarkable. Many, for instance, have imputed absurdity to Mr. Ricardo's theory, because it is absurd to say that the *cultivation* of inferior land is the cause of rent on the superior.   Mr. Ricardo does not say that it is the cultivation of inferior land, but the *necessity of cultivating* it, from the insufficiency of the superior land to feed a growing population : between which and the proposition imputed to him there is no less a difference than that between demand and supply. Others again allege as an objection against Ricardo, that if all land were of equal fertility, it might still yield a rent.   But Ricardo says precisely the same.   He says that if all lands were equally fertile, those which are nearer to their market than others, and are therefore less burthened with cost of carriage, would yield a rent equivalent to the advantage ;   and that the land yielding no rent would then be, not the least fertile, but the least advantageously situated, which the wants of the community required to be brought into cultivation.   It is also distinctly a portion of Ricardo's doctrine, that even apart from differences of situation, the land of a country supposed to be of uniform fertility would, all of it, on a certain supposition, pay rent : namely, if the demand of the community required that it should all be cultivated, and cultivated beyond the point at which a further application of capital begins to be attended with a smaller proportional return.   It would be impossible to show that, except by forcible exaction, the whole land of a country can yield a rent on any other supposition.[1]

§ 6.   After this view of the nature and causes of rent, let us turn back to the subject of profits, and bring up for reconsideration one of the propositions laid down in the last chapter.   We there stated, that the advances of the capitalist, or in other words, the expenses of production, consist solely in wages of labour ;   that whatever portion of the outlay is not wages, is previous profit, and whatever is not previous profit, is wages.   Rent, however, being an element which it is impossible to resolve into either profits or wages, we were obliged, for the moment, to assume that the capitalist is not required to pay rent—to give an equivalent for the use of an appropriated natural agent :   and I undertook to show in the proper place, that this is an allowable supposition, and that rent does not really form any part of the expenses of production, or of the advances of the capitalist.   The grounds on which this assertion was made are now apparent.   It is true that all tenant farmers, and many

[1] [So from the 5th ed. (1862).   Until then the concluding sentence of the paragraph had been : " It would be difficult to show that the whole land of the country can yield a rent on any other supposition."]

other classes of producers, pay rent. But we have now seen, that
whoever cultivates land, paying a rent for it, gets in return for his
rent an instrument of superior power to other instruments of the
same kind for which no rent is paid. The superiority of the instrument is in exact proportion to the rent paid for it. If a few persons
had steam-engines of superior power to all others in existence, but
limited by physical laws to a number short of the demand, the rent
which a manufacturer would be willing to pay for one of these
steam-engines could not be looked upon as an addition to his outlay,
because by the use of it he would save in his other expenses the
equivalent of what it cost him : without it he could not do the
same quantity of work, unless at an additional expense equal to
the rent. The same thing is true of land. The real expenses of
production are those incurred on the worst land, or by the capital
employed in the least favourable circumstances. This land or
capital pays, as we have seen, no rent ; but the expenses to which
it is subject cause all other land or agricultural capital to be subjected to an equivalent expense in the form of rent. Whoever
does pay rent gets back its full value in extra advantages, and the
rent which he pays does not place him in a worse position than, but
only in the same position as, his fellow-producer who pays no rent,
but whose instrument is one of inferior efficiency.

We have now completed the exposition of the laws which regulate
the distribution of the produce of land, labour, and capital, as far
as it is possible to discuss those laws independently of the instrumentality by which in a civilized society the distribution is effected ;
the machinery of Exchange and Price. The more complete elucidation and final confirmation of the laws which we have laid down,
and the deduction of their most important consequences, must be
preceded by an explanation of the nature and working of that
machinery—a subject so extensive and complicated as to require a
separate Book.[1]

[1] [See Appendix R. *Rent.*]

BOOK III

EXCHANGE

CHAPTER I

OF VALUE

§ 1. THE subject on which we are now about to enter fills so important and conspicuous a position in political economy, that in the apprehension of some thinkers its boundaries confound themselves with those of the science itself. One eminent writer has proposed as a name for Political Economy, " Catallactics," or the science of exchanges : by others it has been called the Science of Values. If these denominations had appeared to me logically correct, I must have placed the discussion of the elementary laws of value at the commencement of our inquiry, instead of postponing it to the Third Part ; and the possibility of so long deferring it is alone a sufficient proof that this view of the nature of Political Economy is too confined. It is true that in the preceding Books we have not escaped the necessity of anticipating some small portion of the theory of Value, especially as to the value of labour and of land. It is nevertheless evident, that of the two great departments of Political Economy, the production of wealth and its distribution, the consideration of Value has to do with the latter alone ; and with that, only so far as competition, and not usage or custom, is the distributing agency. The conditions and laws of Production would be the same as they are, if the arrangements of society did not depend on Exchange, or did not admit of it. Even in the present system of industrial life, in which employments are minutely subdivided, and all concerned in production depend for their remuneration on the price of a particular commodity, exchange is not the fundamental law of the distribution of the produce, no more than roads and carriages are the essential laws of motion, but merely a part of the machinery for effecting it. To confound these ideas seems to me not only a logical, but a practical blunder. It is a case of the error too common in political economy, of not distinguishing between necessities arising from the nature of things, and those created by social arrangements: an error which appears to me to be at all times producing two opposite mischiefs; on the one hand, causing political economists to class the merely temporary truths of their subject among its permanent and universal laws; and on the other, leading many persons to mistake the permanent laws of Production (such as those on which the necessity is grounded of restraining population) for temporary accidents arising from the existing constitution of society—which those who would frame a new system of social arrangements are at liberty to disregard.

In a state of society, however, in which the industrial system is entirely founded on purchase and sale, each individual, for the most part, living not on things in the production of which he himself bears a part, but on things obtained by a double exchange, a sale followed by a purchase—the question of Value is fundamental. Almost every speculation respecting the economical interests of a society thus constituted implies some theory of Value: the smallest error on that subject infects with corresponding error all our other conclusions; and anything vague or misty in our conception of it creates confusion and uncertainty in everything else. Happily, there is nothing in the laws of value which remains [1848] for the present or any future writer to clear up; the theory of the subject is complete: the only difficulty to be overcome is that of so stating it as to solve by anticipation the chief perplexities which occur in applying it: and to do this, some minuteness of exposition, and considerable demands on the patience of the reader, are unavoidable. He will be amply repaid however (if a stranger to these inquiries), by the ease and rapidity with which a thorough understanding of this subject will enable him to fathom most of the remaining questions of political economy.

§ 2. We must begin by settling our phraseology. Adam Smith, in a passage often quoted, has touched upon the most obvious ambiguity of the word value; which, in one of its senses, signifies usefulness, in another, power of purchasing; in his own language, value in use and value in exchange. But (as Mr. De Quincey has remarked) in illustrating this double meaning Adam Smith has himself fallen into another ambiguity. Things (he says) which have the greatest value in use have often little or no value in exchange ; which is true, since that which can be obtained without labour or sacrifice will command no price, however useful or needful it may be. But he proceeds to add, that things which have the greatest value in exchange, as a diamond for example, may have little or no value in use. This is employing the word use, not in the sense in which political economy is concerned with it, but in that other sense in which use is opposed to pleasure. Political economy has nothing to do with the comparative estimation of different uses in the judgment of a philosopher or of a moralist. The use of a thing, in political economy, means its capacity to satisfy a desire or serve a purpose. Diamonds have this capacity in a high degree, and unless they had it, would not bear any price. Value in use, or as Mr. De Quincey calls it, *teleologic* value, is the extreme limit of value in exchange. The exchange value of a thing may fall short, to any amount, of its value in use ; but that it can ever exceed the value in use implies a contradiction ; it supposes that persons will give, to possess a thing, more than the utmost value which they themselves put upon it as a means of gratifying their inclinations.

The word Value, when used without adjunct, always means, in political economy, value in exchange ; or as it has been called by Adam Smith and his successors, exchangeable value, a phrase which no amount of authority that can be quoted for it can make other than bad English. Mr. De Quincey substitutes the term Exchange Value, which is unexceptionable.

Exchange value requires to be distinguished from Price. The words Value and Price were used as synonymous by the early political economists, and are not always discriminated even by Ricardo. But the most accurate modern writers, to avoid the wasteful expenditure of two good scientific terms on a single idea, have employed Price to express the value of a thing in relation to money ; the quantity of money for which it will exchange. By the price of a thing, therefore, we shall henceforth understand its value in money ; by the value, or exchange value of a thing, its general power of purchasing ; the command which its possession gives over purchaseable commodities in general.

§ 3. But here a fresh demand for explanation presents itself. What is meant by command over commodities in general ? The same thing exchanges for a great quantity of some commodities, and for a very small quantity of others. A suit of clothes exchanges for a great quantity of bread, and for a very small quantity of precious stones. The value of a thing in exchange for some commodities may be rising, for others falling. A coat may exchange for less bread this year than last, if the harvest has been bad, but for more glass or iron, if a tax has been taken off those commodities, or an improvement made in their manufacture. Has the value of the coat, under these circumstances, fallen or risen ? It is impossible to say : all that can be said is, that it has fallen in relation to one thing, and risen in respect to another. But there is another case, in which no one would have any hesitation in saying what sort of change had taken place in the value of the coat : namely, if the cause in which the disturbance of exchange values originated was something directly affecting the coat itself, and not the bread or the glass. Suppose, for example, that an invention had been made in machinery by which broadcloth could be woven at half the former cost. The effect of this would be to lower the value of a coat, and if lowered by this cause, it would be lowered not in relation to bread only or to glass only, but to all purchaseable things, except such as happened to be affected at the very time by a similar depressing cause. We should therefore say that there had been a fall in the exchange value or general purchasing power of a coat. The idea of general exchange value originates in the fact, that there really are causes which tend to alter the value of a thing in exchange for things generally, that is, for all things which are not themselves acted upon by causes of similar tendency.

In considering exchange value scientifically, it is expedient to obstract from it all causes except those which originate in the very commodity under consideration. Those which originate in the commodities with which we compare it, affect its value in relation to those commodities ; but those which originate in itself affect its value in relation to all commodities. In order the more completely to confine our attention to these last, it is convenient to assume that all commodities but the one in question remain invariable in their relative values. When we are considering the causes which raise or lower the value of corn, we suppose that woollens, silks, cutlery, sugar, timber, &c., while varying in their power of purchasing corn, remain constant in the proportions in which they exchange for one another. On this assumption, any one of them may be taken as a representative of all the rest ; since in whatever manner corn varies in value with respect to any one commodity, it varies in the same manner and degree with respect to every other ; and the upward or downward movement of its value estimated in some one thing is all that need be considered. Its money value, therefore, or price, will represent as well as anything else its general exchange value, or purchasing power ; and from an obvious convenience will often be employed by us in that representative character ; with the pro- viso that money itself do not vary in its general purchasing power, but that the prices of all things, other than that which we happen to be considering, remain unaltered.

§ 4. The distinction between Value and Price, as we have now defined them, is so obvious, as scarcely to seem in need of any illustration. But in political economy the greatest errors arise from overlooking the most obvious truths. Simple as this dis- tinction is, it has consequences with which a reader unacquainted with the subject would do well to begin early by making himself thoroughly familiar. The following is one of the principal. There is such a thing as a general rise of prices. All commodities may rise in their money price. But there cannot be a general rise of values. It is a contradiction in terms. A can only rise in value by exchanging for a greater quantity of B and C ; in which case these must exchange for a smaller quantity of A. All things cannot rise relatively to one another. If one-half of the commodities in the market rise in exchange value, the very terms imply a fall of the other half ; and reciprocally, the fall implies a rise. Things which are exchanged for one another can no more all fall, or all rise, than a dozen runners can each outrun all the rest, or a hundred trees all overtop one another. Simple as this truth is, we shall presently see that it is lost sight of in some of the most accredited doctrines both of theorists and of what are called practical men. And as a first specimen we may instance the great importance attached in the imagination of most people to a rise or fall of general prices. Because when the price of any one commodity rises, the circumstance usually indicates a rise of its value, people have an indistinct feeling when all prices rise, as if all things simultaneously had risen in value, and all the possessors had become enriched. That the money prices of all things should rise or fall, provided they all rise or fall equally, is in itself, and apart from existing contracts, of no consequence. It affects nobody's wages, profits, or rent. Every one gets more money in the one case and less in the other ; but of all that is to be bought with money they get neither more nor less than before. It makes no other difference than that of using more or fewer counters to reckon by. The only thing which in this case is really altered in value is money ; and the only persons who either gain or lose are the holders of money, or those who have to receive or to pay fixed sums of it. There is a difference to annuitants and to creditors the one way, and to those who are burthened with annuities, or with debts, the contrary way. There is a disturbance, in short, of fixed money contracts ; and this is an evil, whether it takes place in the debtor's favour or in the creditor's. But as to future transactions there is no difference to any one. Let it therefore be remembered (and occasions will often arise for calling it to mind) that a general rise or a general fall of values is a contradiction ; and that a general rise or a general fall of prices is merely tantamount to an alteration in the value of money, and is a matter of complete indifference, save in so far as it affects existing contracts for receiving and paying fixed pecuniary amounts, [1] and (it must be added) as it affects the interests of the producers of money.

§ 5. Before commencing the inquiry into the laws of value and price, I have one further observation to make. I must give warning, once for all, that the cases I contemplate are those in which values and prices are determined by competition alone. In so far only as they are thus determined can they be reduced to any assignable law. The buyers must be supposed as studious to buy cheap, as the sellers to sell dear. The values and prices, therefore, to which our conclusions apply, are mercantile values and prices ; such prices as are quoted in price-currents ; prices in the wholesale markets, in which buying as well as selling is a matter of business ; in which the buyers take pains to know, and generally do know, the lowest price at which an article of a given quality can be obtained ; and in which, therefore, the axiom is true, that there cannot be for the same article, of the same quality, two prices in the same market. Our propositions will be true in a much more qualified sense of retail prices ; the prices paid in shops for articles of personal con- sumption. For such things there often are not merely two, but many prices, in different shops, or even in the same shop ; habit and accident having as much to do in the matter as general causes. Purchases for private use, even by people in business, are not

---

[1] [The remaining words of the sentence were added in the 6th ed. (1865).]

always made on business principles : the feelings which come into play in the operation of getting, and in that of spending their income, are often extremely different. Either from indolence, or carelessness, or because people think it fine to pay and ask no questions, three-fourths of those who can afford it give much higher prices than necessary for the things they consume ; while the poor often do the same from ignorance and defect of judgment, want of time for searching and making inquiry, and not unfrequently from coercion, open or disguised. For these reasons, retail prices do not follow with all the regularity which might be expected the action of the causes which determine wholesale prices. The influence of those causes is ultimately felt in the retail markets, and is the real source of such variations in retail prices as are of a general and permanent character. But there is no regular or exact correspondence. Shoes of equally good quality are sold in different shops at prices which differ considerably ; and the price of leather may fall without causing the richer class of buyers to pay less for shoes. Nevertheless, shoes do sometimes fall in price ; and when they do, the cause is always some such general circumstance as the cheapening of leather : and when leather is cheapened, even if no difference shows itself in shops frequented by rich people, the artizan and the labourer generally get their shoes cheaper, and there is a visible diminution in the contract prices at which shoes are delivered for the supply of a workhouse or of a regiment. In all reasoning about prices, the proviso must be understood, " supposing all parties to take care of their own interest." Inattention to these distinctions has led to improper applications of the abstract principles of political economy, and still oftener to an undue discrediting of those principles, through their being compared with a different sort of facts from those which they contemplate, or which can fairly be expected to accord with them.

CHAPTER II

§ 1. THAT a thing may have any value in exchange, two conditions are necessary. It must be of some use ; that is (as already explained), it must conduce to some purpose, satisfy some desire. No one will pay a price, or part with anything which serves some of his purposes, to obtain a thing which serves none of them. But, secondly, the thing must not only have some utility, there must also be some difficulty in its attainment. " Any article whatever," says Mr. De Quincey,* " to obtain that artificial sort of value which is meant by exchange value, must begin by offering itself as a means to some desirable purpose ; and secondly, even though possessing incontestably this preliminary advantage, it will never ascend to an exchange value in cases where it can be obtained gratuitously and without effort ; of which last terms both are necessary as limitations. For often it will happen that some desirable object may be obtained gratuitously ; stoop, and you gather it at your feet ; but still, because the continued iteration of this stooping exacts a laborious effort, very soon it is found that to gather for yourself virtually is not gratuitous. In the vast forests of the Canadas, at intervals, wild strawberries may be gratuitously gathered by shiploads : yet such is the exhaustion of a stooping posture, and of a labour so monotonous, that everybody is soon glad to resign the service into mercenary hands."

As was pointed out in the last chapter, the utility of a thing in the estimation of the purchaser is the extreme limit of its exchange value : higher the value cannot ascend ; peculiar circumstances are required to raise it so high. This topic is happily illustrated by Mr. De Quincey. " Walk into almost any possible shop, buy the

---

* *Logic of Political Economy*, p. 13.

first article you see ; what will determine its price ? In the ninety-nine cases out of a hundred, simply the element D—difficulty of attainment. The other element U, or intrinsic utility, will be perfectly inoperative. Let the thing (measured by its uses) be, for your purposes, worth ten guineas, so that you would rather give ten guineas than lose it ; yet, if the difficulty of producing it be only worth one guinea, one guinea is the price which it will bear. But still not the less, though U is inoperative, can U be supposed absent ? By no possibility ; for, if it *had* been absent, assuredly you would not have bought the article even at the lowest price. U acts upon *you*, though it does not act upon the price. On the other hand, in the hundredth case, we will suppose the circumstances reversed : you are on Lake Superior in a steam-boat, making your way to an unsettled region 800 miles a-head of civilization, and consciously with no chance at all of purchasing any luxury whatsoever, little luxury or big luxury, for the space of ten years to come. One fellow-passenger, whom you will part with before sunset, has a powerful musical snuff-box ; knowing by experience the power of such a toy over your own feelings, the magic with which at times it lulls your agitations of mind, you are vehemently desirous to pur-chase it. In the hour of leaving London you had forgot to do so ; here is a final chance. But the owner, aware of your situation not less than yourself, is determined to operate by a strain pushed to the very uttermost upon U, upon the intrinsic worth of the article in your individual estimate for your individual purposes. He will not hear of D as any controlling power or mitigating agency in the case ; and finally, although at six guineas a-piece in London or Paris you might have loaded a waggon with such boxes, you pay sixty rather than lose it when the last knell of the clock has sounded, which summons you to buy now or to forfeit for ever. Here, as before, only one element is operative ; before it was D, now it is U. But after all, D was not absent, though inoperative. The inertness of D allowed U to put forth its total effect. The practical com-pression of D being withdrawn, U springs up like water in a pump when released from the pressure of air. Yet still that D was present to your thoughts, though the price was otherwise regulated, is evident ; both because U and D must coexist in order to found any case of exchange value whatever, and because undeniably you take into very particular consideration this D, the extreme difficulty of attainment (which here is the greatest possible, viz. an impossibility) before you consent to have the price racked up to U. The special

D has vanished ; but it is replaced in your thoughts by an un-limited D. Undoubtedly you have submitted to U in extremity as the regulating force of the price ; but it was under a sense of D's latent presence. Yet D is so far from exerting any positive force, that the retirement of D from all agency whatever on the price— this it is which creates as it were a perfect vacuum, and through that vacuum U rushes up to its highest and ultimate gradation."

This case, in which the value is wholly regulated by the necessities or desires of the purchaser, is the case of strict and absolute monopoly; in which, the article desired being only obtainable from one person, he can exact any equivalent, short of the point at which no pur-chaser could be found. But it is not a necessary consequence, even of complete monopoly, that the value should be forced up to this ultimate limit ; as will be seen when we have considered the law of value in so far as depending on the other element, difficulty of attainment.

§ 2. The difficulty of attainment which determines value is not always the same kind of difficulty. It sometimes consists in an absolute limitation of the supply. There are things of which it is physically impossible to increase the quantity beyond certain narrow limits. Such are those wines which can be grown only in peculiar circumstances of soil, climate, and exposure. Such also are ancient sculptures ; pictures by old masters ; rare books or coins, or other articles of antiquarian curiosity. Among such may also be reckoned houses and building-ground in a town of definite extent (such as Venice, or any fortified town where fortifications are necessary to security) ; the most desirable sites in any town whatever ; houses and parks peculiarly favoured by natural beauty, in places where that advantage is uncommon. Potentially, all land whatever is a commodity of this class ; and might be practically so in countries fully occupied and cultivated.

But there is another category (embracing the majority of all things that are bought and sold), in which the obstacle to attain-ment consists only in the labour and expense requisite to produce the commodity. Without a certain labour and expense it cannot be had : but when any one is willing to incur these, there needs be no limit to the multiplication of the product. If there were labourers enough and machinery enough, cottons, woollens, or linens might be produced by thousands of yards for every single yard now manu-factured. There would be a point, no doubt, where further increase would be stopped by the incapacity of the earth to afford more of the material. But there is no need, for any purpose of political economy, to contemplate a time when this ideal limit could become a practical one.

There is a third case, intermediate between the two preceding, and rather more complex, which I shall at present merely indicate, but the importance of which in political economy is extremely great. There are commodities which can be multiplied to an indefinite extent by labour and expenditure, but not by a fixed amount of labour and expenditure. Only a limited quantity can be produced at a given cost: if more is wanted, it must be produced at a greater cost. To this class, as has been often repeated, agricultural produce belongs; and generally all the rude produce of the earth; and this peculiarity is a source of very important consequences; one of which is the necessity of a limit to population; and another, the payment of rent.

§ 3. These being the three classes, in one or other of which all things that are bought and sold must take their place, we shall consider them in their order. And first, of things absolutely limited in quantity, such as ancient sculptures or pictures.

Of such things it is commonly said, that their value depends upon their scarcity: but the expression is not sufficiently definite to serve our purpose. Others say, with somewhat greater precision, that the value depends on the demand and the supply. But even this statement requires much explanation, to make it a clear exponent of the relation between the value of a thing, and the causes of which that value is an effect.

The supply of a commodity is an intelligible expression : it means the quantity offered for sale ; the quantity that is to be had, at a given time and place, by those who wish to purchase it. But what is meant by the demand ? Not the mere desire for the commodity. A beggar may desire a diamond ; but his desire, however great, will have no influence on the price. Writers have therefore given a more limited sense to demand, and have defined it, the wish to possess, combined with the power of purchasing. To distinguish demand in this technical sense, from the demand which is synonymous with desire, they call the former *effectual* demand.* After this

* Adam Smith, who introduced the expression "effectual demand," employed it to denote the demand of those who are willing and able to give for the commodity what he calls its natural price, that is the price which will

explanation, it is usually supposed that there remains no further difficulty, and that the value depends upon the ratio between the effectual demand, as thus defined, and the supply.

These phrases, however, fail to satisfy any one who requires clear ideas, and a perfectly precise expression of them. Some confusion must always attach to a phrase so inappropriate as that of a *ratio* between two things not of the same denomination. What ratio can there be between a quantity and a desire, or even a desire combined with a power ? A ratio between demand and supply is only intelligible if by demand we mean the quantity demanded, and if the ratio intended is that between the quantity demanded and the quantity supplied. But again, the quantity demanded is not a fixed quantity, even at the same time and place ; it varies according to the value ; if the thing is cheap, there is usually a demand for more of it than when it is dear. The demand, therefore, partly depends on the value. But it was before laid down that the value depends on the demand. From this contradiction how shall we extricate ourselves ? How solve the paradox, of two things, each depending upon the other ?

Though the solution of these difficulties is obvious enough, the difficulties themselves are not fanciful ; and I bring them forward thus prominently, because I am certain that they obscurely haunt every inquirer into the subject who has not openly faced and distinctly realized them. Undoubtedly the true solution must have been frequently given, though I cannot call to mind any one who had given it before myself, except the eminently clear thinker and skilful expositor, J. B. Say. I should have imagined, however, that it must be familiar to all political economists, if the writings of several did not give evidence of some want of clearness on the point, and if the instance of Mr. De Quincey did not prove that the complete non-recognition and implied denial of it are compatible with great intellectual ingenuity, and close intimacy with the subject matter.

§ 4. Meaning, by the word demand, the quantity demanded, and remembering that this is not a fixed quantity, but in general varies according to the value, let us suppose that the demand at some particular time exceeds the supply, that is, there are persons ready to buy, at the market value, a greater quantity than is offered for sale.

enable it to be permanently produced and brought to market.—See his chapter on Natural and Market Price (book i. ch. 7).

Competition takes place on the side of the buyers, and the value rises : but how much ? In the ratio (some may suppose) of the deficiency : if the demand exceeds the supply by one-third, the value rises one-third. By no means : for when the value has risen one-third, the demand may still exceed the supply ; there may, even at that higher value, be a greater quantity wanted than is to be had ; and the competition of buyers may still continue. If the article is a necessary of life, which, rather than resign, people are willing to pay for at any price, a deficiency of one-third may raise the price to double, triple, or quadruple.* Or, on the contrary, the competition may cease before the value has risen in even the proportion of the deficiency. A rise, short of one-third, may place the article beyond the means, or beyond the inclinations, of purchasers to the full amount. At what point, then, will the rise be arrested ? At the point, whatever it be, which equalizes the demand and the supply : at the price which cuts off the extra third from the demand, or brings forward additional sellers sufficient to supply it. When, in either of these ways, or by a combination of both, the demand becomes equal and no more than equal to the supply, the rise of value will stop.

The converse case is equally simple. Instead of a demand beyond the supply, let us suppose a supply exceeding the demand. The competition will now be on the side of the sellers : the extra quantity can only find a market by calling forth an additional demand equal to itself. This is accomplished by means of cheapness ; the value falls, and brings the article within the reach of more numerous customers, or induces those who were already consumers to make increased purchases. The fall of value required to re-establish equality is different in different cases. The kinds of things in which it is commonly greatest are at the two extremities of the scale ; absolute necessaries, or those peculiar luxuries, the taste for which is confined to a small class. In the case of food, as those who have already enough do not require more on account of its cheapness, but rather expend in other things what they save in food, the increased consumption occasioned by cheapness carries off, as experience

---

* " The price of corn in this country has risen from 100 to 200 per cent and upwards, when the utmost computed deficiency of the crops has not been more than between one-sixth and one-third below an average, and when that deficiency has been relieved by foreign supplies. If there should be a deficiency of the crops amounting to one-third, without any surplus from a former year, and without any chance of relief by importation, the price might rise five, six, or even tenfold."—Tooke's *History of Prices*, vol. i. pp. 13–5.

shows, only a small part of the extra supply caused by an abundant harvest; * and the fall is practically arrested only when the farmers withdraw their corn, and hold it back in hopes of a higher price; or by the operations of speculators who buy corn when it is cheap, and store it up to be brought out when more urgently wanted. Whether the demand and supply are equalized by an increased demand, the result of cheapness, or by withdrawing a part of the supply, equalized they are in either case.

Thus we see that the idea of a *ratio*, as between demand and supply, is out of place, and has no concern in the matter: the proper mathematical analogy is that of an *equation*. Demand and supply, the quantity demanded and the quantity supplied, will be made equal. If unequal at any moment, competition equalizes them, and the manner in which this is done is by an adjustment of the value. If the demand increases, the value rises; if the demand diminishes, the value falls: again, if the supply falls off, the value rises; and falls if the supply is increased. The rise or the fall continues until the demand and supply are again equal to one another: and the value which a commodity will bring in any market is no other than the value which, in that market, gives a demand just sufficient to carry off the existing or expected supply.

This, then, is the Law of Value, with respect to all commodities not susceptible of being multiplied at pleasure. Such commodities, no doubt, are exceptions. There is another law for that much larger class of things, which admit of indefinite multiplication. But it is not the less necessary to conceive distinctly and grasp firmly the theory of this exceptional case. In the first place, it will be found to be of great assistance in rendering the more common case intelligible. And in the next place, the principle of the exception stretches wider, and embraces more cases, than might at first be supposed.

§ 5.   There are but few commodities which are naturally and necessarily limited in supply. But any commodity whatever may be artificially so. Any commodity may be the subject of a monopoly: like tea, in this country, up to 1834; tobacco in France, opium in British India, at present [1848]. The price of a monopolized commodity is commonly supposed to be arbitrary; depending on the will of the monopolist, and limited only (as in Mr. De Quincey's

---

* See Tooke, and the *Report* of the Agricultural Committee of 1821.

case of the musical box in the wilds of America) by the buyer's extreme estimate of its worth to himself. This is in one sense true, but forms no exception, nevertheless, to the dependence of the value on supply and demand. The monopolist can fix the value as high as he pleases, short of what the consumer either could not or would not pay; but he can only do so by limiting the supply. The Dutch East India Company obtained a monopoly price for the produce of the Spice Islands, but to do so they were obliged, in good seasons, to destroy a portion of the crop. Had they persisted in selling all that they produced, they must have forced a market by reducing the price, so low, perhaps, that they would have received for the larger quantity a less total return than for the smaller : at least they showed that such was their opinion by destroying the surplus. Even on Lake Superior, Mr. De Quincey's huckster could not have sold his box for sixty guineas, if he had possessed two musical boxes and desired to sell them both. Supposing the cost price of each to be six guineas, he would have taken seventy for the two in preference to sixty for one ; that is, although his monopoly was the closest possible, he would have sold the boxes at thirty-five guineas each, notwithstanding that sixty was not beyond the buyer's estimate of the article for his purposes. Monopoly value, therefore, does not depend on any peculiar principle, but is a mere variety of the ordinary case of demand and supply.

Again, though there are few commodities which are at all times and for ever unsusceptible of increase of supply, any commodity whatever may be temporarily so ; and with some commodities this is habitually the case. Agricultural produce, for example, cannot be increased in quantity before the next harvest; the quantity of corn already existing in the world is all that can be had for sometimes a year to come. During that interval corn is practically assimilated to things of which the quantity cannot be increased. In the case of most commodities, it requires a certain time to increase their quantity; and if the demand increases, then, until a corresponding supply can be brought forward, that is, until the supply can accommodate itself to the demand, the value will so rise as to accommodate the demand to the supply.

There is another case, the exact converse of this. There are some articles of which the supply may be indefinitely increased, but cannot be rapidly diminished. There are things so durable that the quantity in existence is at all times very great in comparison with the annual produce. Gold, and the more durable metals, are things of this sort; and also houses. The supp rofits such things might be at once diminished by destroying tled be but to do this could only be the interest of the possessor if h ge for a monopoly of the article, and could repay himself for the destru of a part by the increased value of the remainder.   The value, t·eater fore, of such things may continue fcr a long time so low, either or its excess of supply or falling off in the demand, as to put a comphour stop to further production; the diminution of supply by wearinof out being so slow a process, that a long time is requisite, even under a total suspension of production, to restore the original value. During that interval the value will be regulated solely by supply and demand, and will rise very gradually as the existing stock wears out, until there is again a remunerating value, and production resumes its course.

Finally, there are commodities of which, though capable of being increased or diminished to a great, and even an unlimited extent, the value never depends upon anything but demand and supply.   This is the case, in particular, with the commodity Labour; of the value of which we have treated copiously in the preceding Book: and there are many cases besides, in which we shall find it necessary to call in this principle to solve difficult questions of exchange value. This will be particularly exemplified when we treat of International Values; that is, of the terms of interchange between things produced in different countries, or, to speak more generally, in distant places. But into these questions we cannot enter, until we shall have examined the case of commodities which can be increased in quantity indefinitely and at pleasure; and shall have determined by what law, other than that of Demand and Supply, the permanent or average values of such commodities are regulated.   This we shall do in the next chapter.

CHAPTER III

OF COST OF PRODUCTION, IN ITS RELATION TO VALUE

§ 1. WHEN the production of a commodity is the effect of labour and expenditure, whether the commodity is susceptible of unlimited multiplication or not, there is a minimum value which is the essential condition of its being permanently produced. The value at any particular time is the result of supply and demand; and is always that which is necessary to create a market for the existing supply. But unless that value is sufficient to repay the Cost of Production, and to afford, besides, the ordinary expectation of profit, the commodity will not continue to be produced. Capitalists will not go on permanently producing at a loss. They will not even go on producing at a profit less than they can live on. Persons whose capital is already embarked, and cannot be easily extricated, will persevere for a considerable time without profit, and have been known to persevere even at a loss, in hope of better times. But they will not do so indefinitely, or when there is nothing to indicate that times are likely to improve. No new capital will be invested in an employment, unless there be an expectation not only of some profit, but of a profit as great (regard being had to the degree of eligibility of the employment in other respects) as can be hoped for in any other occupation at that time and place. When such profit is evidently not to be had, if people do not actually withdraw their capital, they at least abstain from replacing it when consumed. The cost of production, together with the ordinary profit, may therefore be called the *necessary* price, or value, of all things made by labour and capital. Nobody willingly produces in the prospect of loss. Whoever does so, does it under a miscalculation, which he corrects as fast as he is able.

When a commodity is not only made by labour and capital, but can be made by them in indefinite quantity, this Necessary Value, the minimum with which the producers will be content, is also, if competition is free and active, the maximum which they can expect. If the value of a commodity is such that it repays the cost of production not only with the customary, but with a higher rate of profit, capital rushes to share in this extra gain, and by increasing the supply of the article, reduces its value. This is not a mere supposition or surmise, but a fact familiar to those conversant with commercial operations.   Whenever a new line of business presents itself, offering a hope of unusual profits, and whenever any established trade or manufacture is believed to be yielding a greater profit than customary, there is sure to be in a short time so large a production or importation of the commodity, as not only destroys the extra profit, but generally goes beyond the mark, and sinks the value as much too low as it had before been raised too high ; until the over-supply is corrected by a total or partial suspension of further production. As already intimated,* these variations in the quantity produced do not presuppose or require that any person should change his employment. Those whose business is thriving, increase their produce by availing themselves more largely of their credit, while those who are not making the ordinary profit, restrict their operations, and (in manufacturing phrase) work short time. In this mode is surely and speedily effected the equalization, not of profits perhaps, but of the expectations of profit, in different occupations.

As a general rule, then, things tend to exchange for one another at such values as will enable each producer to be repaid the cost of production with the ordinary profit ; in other words, such as will give to all producers the same rate of profit on their outlay. But in order that the profit may be equal where the outlay, that is, the cost of production, is equal, things must on the average exchange for one another in the ratio of their cost of production : things of which the cost of production is the same, must be of the same value. For only thus will an equal outlay yield an equal return. If a farmer with a capital equal to 1000 quarters of corn, can produce 1200 quarters, yielding him a profit of 20 per cent ; whatever else can be produced in the same time by a capital of 1000 quarters must be worth, that is, must exchange for, 1200 quarters, otherwise the producer would gain either more or less than 20 per cent.

Adam Smith and Ricardo have called that value of a thing which is proportional to its cost of production, its Natural Value

* Supra, p. 412.

(or its Natural Price). They meant by this, the point about which the value oscillates, and to which it always tends to return ; the centre value, towards which, as Adam Smith expresses it, the market value of a thing is constantly gravitating ; and any deviation from which is but a temporary irregularity, which, the moment it exists, sets forces in motion tending to correct it. On an average of years sufficient to enable the oscillations on one side of the central line to be compensated by those on the other, the market value agrees with the natural value ; but it very seldom coincides exactly with it at any particular time. The sea everywhere tends to a level ; but it never is at an exact level ; its surface is always ruffled by waves, and often agitated by storms. It is enough that no point, at least in the open sea, is permanently higher than another. Each place is alternately elevated and depressed ; but the ocean preserves its level.

§ 2. The latent influence by which the values of things are made to conform in the long run to the cost of production is the variation that would otherwise take place in the supply of the commodity. The supply would be increased if the thing continued to sell above the ratio of its cost of production, and would be diminished if it fell below that ratio. But we must not therefore suppose it to be necessary that the supply should *actually* be either diminished or increased. Suppose that the cost of production of a thing is cheapened by some mechanical invention, or increased by a tax. The value of the thing would in a little time, if not immediately, fall in the one case, and rise in the other ; and it would do so, because, if it did not, the supply would in the one case be increased, until the price fell, in the other diminished, until it rose. For this reason, and from the erroneous notion that value depends on the *proportion* between the demand and the supply, many persons suppose that this proportion must be altered whenever there is any change in the value of the commodity ; that the value cannot fall through a diminution of the cost of production, unless the supply is permanently increased ; nor rise, unless the supply is permanently diminished. But this is not the fact : there is no need that there should be any actual alteration of supply ; and when there is, the alteration, if permanent, is not the cause, but the consequence of the alteration in value. If, indeed, the supply *could* not be increased, no diminution in the cost of production would lower the value : but there is by no means any necessity that it *should*. The mere possibility often suffices ; the dealers are aware of what would happen, and their mutual competition makes them anticipate the result by lowering the price. Whether there will be a greater permanent supply of the commodity after its production has been cheapened, depends on quite another question, namely, on whether a greater quantity is wanted at the reduced value. Most commonly a greater quantity is wanted, but not necessarily. " A man," says Mr. De Quincey,* " buys an article of instant applicability to his own purposes the more readily and the more largely as it happens to be cheaper. Silk handkerchiefs having fallen to half-price, he will buy, perhaps, in threefold quantity ; but he does not buy more steam-engines because the price is lowered. His demand for steam-engines is almost always predetermined by the circumstances of his situation. So far as he considers the cost at all, it is much more the cost of working this engine than the cost upon its purchase. But there are many articles for which the market is absolutely and merely limited by a pre-existing *system*, to which those articles are attached as subordinate parts or members. How could we force the dials or faces of timepieces by artificial cheapness to sell more plentifully than the inner works or movements of such timepieces ? Could the sale of wine-vaults be increased without increasing the sale of wine ? Or the tools of shipwrights find an enlarged market whilst shipbuilding was stationary ? . . . . Offer to a town of 3000 inhabitants a stock of hearses, no cheapness will tempt that town into buying more than one. Offer a stock of yachts, the chief cost lies in manning, victualling, repairing ; no diminution upon the mere price to a purchaser will tempt into the market any man whose habits and propensities had not already disposed him to such a purchase. So of professional costume for bishops, lawyers, students at Oxford." Nobody doubts, however, that the price and value of all these things would be eventually lowered by any diminution of their cost of production ; and lowered through the apprehension entertained of new competitors, and an increased supply ; though the great hazard to which a new competitor would expose himself, in an article not susceptible of any considerable extension of its market, would enable the established dealers to maintain their original prices much longer than they could do in an article offering more encouragement to competition.

Again, reverse the case, and suppose the cost of production

---

* *Logic of Political Economy*, pp. 230–1.

increased, as for example by laying a tax on the commodity. The value would rise; and that, probably, immediately. Would the supply be diminished? Only if the increase of value diminished the demand. Whether this effect followed, would soon appear, and if it did, the value would recede somewhat, from excess of supply, until the production was reduced, and would then rise again. There are many articles for which it requires a very considerable rise of price materially to reduce the demand; in particular, articles of necessity, such as the habitual food of the people in England, wheaten bread: of which there is probably almost as much consumed, at the present cost price, as there would be with the present population at a price considerably lower. Yet it is especially in such things that dearness or high price is popularly confounded with scarcity. Food may be dear from scarcity, as after a bad harvest; but the dearness (for example) which is the effect of taxation, or of corn laws, has nothing whatever to do with insufficient supply: such causes do not much diminish the quantity of food in a country: it is other things rather than food that are diminished in quantity by them, since, those who pay more for food not having so much to expend otherwise, the production of other things contracts itself to the limits of a smaller demand.

It is, therefore, strictly correct to say, that the value of things which can be increased in quantity at pleasure, does not depend (except accidentally, and during the time necessary for production to adjust itself,) upon demand and supply; on the contrary, demand and supply depend upon it. There is a demand for a certain quantity of the commodity at its natural or cost value, and to that the supply in the long run endeavours to conform. When at any time it fails of so conforming, it is either from miscalculation, or from a change in some of the elements of the problem: either in the natural value, that is, in the cost of production; or in the demand, from an alteration in public taste or in the number or wealth of the consumers. These causes of disturbance are very liable to occur, and when any one of them does occur, the market value of the article ceases to agree with the natural value. The real law of demand and supply, the equation between them, still holds good: if a value different from the natural value be necessary to make the demand equal to the supply, the market value will deviate from the natural value; but only for a time; for the permanent tendency of supply is to conform itself to the demand which is found by experience to exist for the commodity when selling at its natural value. If the supply is either more or less than this, it is so accidentally, and affords either more or less than the ordinary rate of profit; which, under free and active competition, cannot long continue to be the case.

To recapitulate : demand and supply govern the value of all things which cannot be indefinitely increased ; except that even for them, when produced by industry, there is a minimum value, determined by the cost of production. But in all things which admit of indefinite multiplication, demand and supply only determine the perturbations of value, during a period which cannot exceed the length of time necessary for altering the supply. While thus ruling the oscillations of value, they themselves obey a superior force, which makes value gravitate towards Cost of Production, and which would settle it and keep it there, if fresh disturbing influences were not continually arising to make it again deviate. To pursue the same strain of metaphor, demand and supply always rush to an equilibrium, but the condition of *stable* equilibrium is when things exchange for each other according to their cost of production, or, in the expression we have used, when things are at their Natural Value.

CHAPTER IV

§ 1. THE component elements of Cost of Production have been set forth in the First Part of this enquiry.* The principal of them, and so much the principal as to be nearly the sole, we found to be Labour. What the production of a thing costs to its producer, or its series of producers, is the labour expended in producing it If we consider as the producer the capitalist who makes the advances, the word Labour may be replaced by the word Wages : what the produce costs to him, is the wages which he has had to pay. At the first glance indeed this seems to be only a part of his outlay, since he has not only paid wages to labourers, bu has likewise provided them with tools, materials, and perhaps buildings. These tools, materials, and buildings, however, were produced by labour and capital ; and their value, like that of the article to the production of which they are subservient, depends on cost of production, which again is resolvable into labour. The cost of production of broad-cloth does not wholly consist in the wages of weavers ; which alone are directly paid by the cloth manufacturer. It consists also of the wages of spinners and woolcombers, and, it may be added of shepherds, all of which the clothier has paid for in the price of yarn. It consists too of the wages of builders and brickmakers, which he has reimbursed in the contract price of erecting his factory. It partly consists of the wages of machine-makers, iron-founders, and miners. And to these must be added the wages of the carriers who transported any of the means and appliances of the production to the place where they were to be used, and the product itself to the place where it is to be sold.

The value of commodities, therefore, depends principally (we shall present¹ʸ see ːether it depends solely) on the quantity of

* Supra, pp. 29–31.

labour required for their production ; including in the idea of production, that of conveyance to the market. "In estimating," says Ricardo,* " the exchangeable value of stockings, for example, we shall find that their value, comparatively with other things, depends on the total quantity of labour necessary to manufacture them and bring them to market. First, there is the labour necessary to cultivate the land on which the raw cotton is grown ; secondly, the labour of conveying the cotton to the country where the stockings are to be manufactured, which includes a portion of the labour bestowed in building the ship in which it is conveyed, and which is charged in the freight of the goods ; thirdly, the labour of the spinner and weaver ; fourthly, a portion of the labour of the engineer, smith, and carpenter, who erected the buildings and machinery by the help of which they are made ; fifthly, the labour of the retail dealer and of many others, whom it is unnecessary further to particularize. The aggregate sum of these various kinds of labour determines the quantity of other things for which these stockings will exchange, while the same consideration of the various quantities of labour which have been bestowed on those other things, will equally govern the portion of them which will be given for the stockings.

" To convince ourselves that this is the real foundation of exchangeable value, let us suppose any improvement to be made in the means of abridging labour in any one of the various processes through which the raw cotton must pass before the manufactured stockings come to the market to be exchanged for other things ; and observe the effects which will follow. If fewer men were required to cultivate the raw cotton, or if fewer sailors were employed in navigating, or shipwrights in constructing, the ship in which it was conveyed to us ; if fewer hands were employed in raising the buildings and machinery, or if these, when raised, were rendered more efficient ; the stockings would inevitably fall in value, and command less of other things. They would fall, because a less quantity of labour was necessary to their production, and would therefore exchange for a smaller quantity of those things in which no such abridgement of labour had been made.

" Economy in the use of labour never fails to reduce the relative value of a commodity, whether the saving be in the labour necessary to the manufacture of the commodity itself, or in that necessary to

* *Principles of Political Economy and Taxation,* ch. i. sect. 3.

the formation of the capital, by the aid of which it is produced. In either case the price of stockings would fall, whether there were fewer men employed as bleachers, spinners, and weavers, persons immediately necessary to their manufacture : or as sailors, carriers, engineers, and smiths, persons more indirectly concerned. In the one case, the whole saving of labour would fall on the stockings, because that portion of labour was wholly confined to the stockings ; in the other, a portion only would fall on the stockings, the remainder being applied to all those other commodities, to the production of which the buildings, machinery, and carriage, were subservient."

§ 2. It will have been observed that Ricardo expresses himself as if the *quantity* of labour which it costs to produce a commodity and bring it to market, were the only thing on which its value depended. But since the cost of production to the capitalist is not labour but wages, and since wages may be either greater or less, the quantity of labour being the same ; it would seem that the value of the product cannot be determined solely by the quantity of labour, but by the quantity together with the remuneration ; and that values must partly depend on wages.

In order to decide this point, it must be considered, that value is a relative term : that the value of a commodity is not a name for an inherent and substantive quality of the thing itself, but means the quantity of other things which can be obtained in exchange for it. The value of one thing must always be understood relatively to some other thing, or to things in general. Now the relation of one thing to another cannot be altered by any cause which affects them both alike. A rise or fall of general wages is a fact which affects all commodities in the same manner, and therefore affords no reason why they should exchange for each other in one rather than in another proportion. To suppose that high wages make high values, is to suppose that there can be such a thing as general high values. But this is a contradiction in terms : the high value of some things is synonymous with the low value of others. The mistake arises from not attending to values, but only to prices. Though there is no such thing as a general rise of values, there is such a thing as a general rise of prices. As soon as we form distinctly the idea of values, we see that high or low wages can have nothing to do with them ; but that high wages make high prices, is a popular and widely-spread opinion. The whole amount of error involved in this proposition can only be seen thoroughly

when we come to the theory of money ; at present we need only say
that, if it be true, there can be no such thing as a real rise of wages;
for if wages could not rise without a proportional rise of the price
of everything, they could not, for any substantial purpose, rise at all.
This surely is a sufficient *reductio ad absurdum*, and shows the
amazing folly of the propositions which may and do become, and
long remain, accredited doctrines of popular political economy.
It must be remembered too that general high prices, even supposing
them to exist, can be of no use to a producer or dealer, considered
as such ; for if they increase his money returns, they increase in the
same degree all his expenses.   There is no mode in which capitalists
can compensate themselves for a high cost of labour, through any
action on values or prices.   It cannot be prevented from taking its
effect on low profits.   If the labourers really get more, that is, get
the produce of more labour, a smaller percentage must remain for
profit.   From this Law of Distribution, resting as it does on a law
of arithmetic, there is no escape.   The mechanism of Exchange and
Price may hide it from us, but is quite powerless to alter it.

§ 3.   Although, however, *general* wages, whether high or low,
do not affect values, yet if wages are higher in one employment than
another, or if they rise and fall permanently in one employment
without doing so in others, these inequalities do really operate upon
values.   The causes which make wages vary from one employment
to another, have been considered in a former chapter.   When the
wages of an employment permanently exceed the average rate, the
value of the thing produced will, in the same degree, exceed the
standard determined by mere quantity of labour.   Things, for
example, which are made by skilled labour, exchange for the produce
of a much greater quantity of unskilled labour ; for no reason but
because the labour is more highly paid.   If, through the extension of
education, the labourers competent to skilled employments were so
increased in number as to diminish the difference between their
wages and those of common labour, all things produced by labour
of the superior kind would fall in value, compared with things
produced by common labour, and these might be said therefore
to rise in value.   We have before remarked that the difficulty of
passing from one class of employments to a class greatly superior,
has hitherto caused the wages of all those classes of labourers who
are separated from one another by any very marked barrier, to
depend more than might be supposed upon the increase of the

population of each class considered separately; and that the inequalities in the remuneration of labour are much greater than
could exist if the competition of the labouring people generally
could be brought practically to bear on each particular employment.
It follows from this that wages in different employments do not rise
or fall simultaneously, but are, for short and sometimes even for
long periods, nearly independent of one another. All such disparities
evidently alter the *relative* costs of production of different commodities, and will therefore be completely represented in their
natural or average value.

It thus appears that the maxim laid down by some of the best
political economists, that wages do not enter into value, is expressed
with greater latitude than the truth warrants, or than accords with
their own meaning. Wages do enter into value. The relative
wages of the labour necessary for producing different commodities,
affect their value just as much as the relative *quantities* of labour.
It is true, the absolute wages paid have no effect upon values; but
neither has the absolute quantity of labour. If that were to vary
simultaneously and equally in all commodities, values would not
be affected. If, for instance, the general efficiency of all labour
were increased, so that all things without exception could be produced in the same quantity as before with a smaller amount of
labour, no trace of this general diminution of cost of production
would show itself in the values of commodities. Any change
which might take place in them would only represent the unequal
degrees in which the improvement affected different things; and
would consist in cheapening those in which the saving of labour had
been the greatest, while those in which there had been some, but
a less saving of labour, would actually rise in value. In strictness,
therefore, wages of labour have as much to do with value as quantity
of labour: and neither Ricardo nor any one else has denied the
fact. In considering, however, the causes of *variations* in value,
quantity of labour is the thing of chief importance; for when that
varies, it is generally in one or a few commodities at a time, but the
variations of wages (except passing fluctuations) are usually general,
and have no considerable effect on value.

§ 4. Thus far of labour, or wages, as an element in cost of
production. But in our analysis, in the First Book, of the requisites
of production, we found that there is another necessary element in
it besides labour. There is also capital; and this being the result

of abstinence, the produce, or its value, must be sufficient to remunerate, not only all the labour required, but the abstinence of
all the persons by whom the remuneration of the different classes
of labourers was advanced.   The return for abstinence is Profit.
And profit, we have also seen, is not exclusively the surplus remaining to the capitalist after he has been compensated for his outlay,
but forms, in most cases, no unimportant part of the outlay itself.
The flax-spinner, part of whose expenses consists of the purchase
of flax and of machinery, has had to pay, in their price, not only the
wages of the labour by which the flax was grown and the machinery
made, but the profits of the grower, the flax-dresser, the miner, the
iron-founder, and the machine-maker.   All these profits, together
with those of the spinner himself, were again advanced by the
weaver, in the price of his material, linen yarn : and along with
them the profits of a fresh set of machine-makers, and of the miners
and iron-workers who supplied them with their metallic material.
All these advances form part of the cost of production of linen.
Profits, therefore, as well as wages, enter into the cost of production
which determines the value of the produce.

Value, however, being purely relative, cannot depend upon
absolute profit, no more than upon absolute wages, but upon
relative profits only.   High general profits cannot, any more than
high general wages, be a cause of high values, because high general
values are an absurdity and a contradiction.   In so far as profits
enter into the cost of production of all things, they cannot affect the
value of any.   It is only by entering in a greater degree into the
cost of production of some things than of others, that they can have
any influence on value.

For example, we have seen that there are causes which necessitate
a permanently higher rate of profit in certain employments than in
others.   There must be a compensation for superior risk, trouble,
and disagreeableness.   This can only be obtained by selling the
commodity at a value above that which is due to the quantity of
labour necessary for its production.   If gunpowder exchanged for
other things in no higher ratio than that of the labour required from
first to last for producing it, no one would set up a powder-mill.
Butchers are certainly a more prosperous class than bakers, and do
not seem to be exposed to greater risks, since it is not remarked that
they are oftener bankrupts.   They seem, therefore, to obtain higher
profits, which can only arise from the more limited competition
caused by the unpleasantness, and to a certain degree, the

unpopularity, of their trade. But this higher profit implies that they sell their commodity at a higher value than that due to their labour and outlay. All inequalities of profit which are necessary and permanent, are represented in the relative values of the commodities.

§ 5. Profits, however, may enter more largely into the conditions of production of one commodity than of another, even though there be no difference in the *rate* of profit between the two employments. The one commodity may be called upon to yield profit during a longer period of time than the other. The example by which this case is usually illustrated is that of wine. Suppose a quantity of wine, and a quantity of cloth, made by equal amounts of labour, and that labour paid at the same rate. The cloth does not improve by keeping ; the wine does. Suppose that, to attain the desired quality, the wine requires to be kept five years. The producer or dealer will not keep it, unless at the end of five years he can sell it for as much more than the cloth as amounts to five years' profit, accumulated at compound interest. The wine and the cloth were made by the same original outlay. Here then is a case in which the natural values, relatively to one another, of two commodities, do not conform to their cost of production alone, but to their cost of production *plus* something else. Unless, indeed, for the sake of generality in the expression, we include the profit which the wine-merchant foregoes during the five years, in the cost of production of the wine : looking upon it as a kind of additional outlay, over and above his other advances, for which outlay he must be indemnified at last.

All commodities made by machinery are assimilated, at least approximately, to the wine in the preceding example. In comparison with things made wholly by immediate labour, profits enter more largely into their cost of production. Suppose two commodities, A and B, each requiring a year for its production, by means of a capital which we will on this occasion denote by money, and suppose to be 1000*l*. A is made wholly by immediate labour, the whole 1000*l*. being expended directly in wages. B is made by means of labour which costs 500*l*. and a machine which cost 500*l*., and the machine is worn out by one year's use. The two commodities will be exactly of the same value ; which, if computed in money, and if profits are 20 per cent per annum, will be 1200*l*. But of this 1200*l*., in the case of A, only 200*l*., or one-sixth, is profit :

while in the case of B there is not only the 200*l.*, but as much of 500*l.* (the price of the machine) as consisted of the profits of the machine-maker ; which, if we suppose the machine also to have taken a year for its production, is again one-sixth. So that in the case of A only one-sixth of the entire return is profit, whilst in B the element of profit comprises not only a sixth of the whole, but an additional sixth of a large part.

The greater the proportion of the whole capital which consists of machinery, or buildings, or material, or anything else which must be provided before the immediate labour can commence, the more largely will profits enter into the cost of production. It is equally true, though not so obvious at first sight, that greater durability in the portion of capital which consists of machinery or buildings, has precisely the same effect as a greater amount of it. As we just supposed one extreme case, of a machine entirely worn out by a year's use, let us now suppose the opposite and still more extreme case of a machine which lasts for ever, and requires no repairs. In this case, which is as well suited for the purpose of illustration as if it were a possible one, it will be unnecessary that the manufacturer should ever be repaid the 500*l.* which he gave for the machine, since he has always the machine itself, worth 500*l.* ; but he must be paid, as before, a profit on it. The commodity B, therefore, which in the case previously supposed was sold for 1200*l.* of which sum 1000*l.* were to replace the capital and 200*l.* were profit, can now be sold for 700*l.*, being 500*l* to replace wages, and 200*l.* profit on the entire capital. Profit, therefore, enters into the value of B in the ratio of 200*l.* out of 700*l.*, being two-sevenths of the whole, or $28\frac{4}{7}$ per cent, while in the case of A, as before, it enters only in the ratio of one-sixth, or $16\frac{2}{3}$ per cent. The case is of course purely ideal, since no machinery or other fixed capital lasts for ever ; but the more durable it is, the nearer it approaches to this ideal case, and the more largely does profit enter into the return. If, for instance, a machine worth 500*l.* loses one-fifth of its value by each year's use, 100*l.* must be added to the return to make up this loss, and the price of the commodity will be 800*l.* Profit therefore will enter into it in the ratio of 200*l.* to 800*l.*, or one-fourth, which is still a much higher proportion than one-sixth, or 200*l.* in 1200*l.*, as in case A.

From the unequal proportion in which, in different employments, profits enter into the advances of the capitalist, and therefore into the returns required by him, two consequences follow in regard to value. One is, that commodities do not exchange in the ratio simply of the quantities of labour required to produce them ; not even if we allow for the unequal rates at which different kinds of labour are permanently remunerated. We have already illustrated this by the example of wine : we shall now further exemplify it by the case of commodities made by machinery. Suppose, as before, an article A made by a thousand pounds' worth of immediate labour. But instead of B, made by 500*l.* worth of immediate labour and a machine worth 500*l.*, let us suppose C, made by 500*l.* worth of immediate labour with the aid of a machine which has been produced by another 500*l.* worth of immediate labour : the machine requiring a year for making, and worn out by a year's use ; profits being as before 20 per cent. A and C are made by equal quantities of labour, paid at the same rate : A costs 1000*l.* worth of direct labour ; C, only 500*l.* worth, which however is made up to 1000*l.* by the labour expended in the construction of the machine. If labour, or its remuneration, were the sole ingredient of cost of production, these two things would exchange for one another. But will they do so ? Certainly not. The machine having been made in a year by an outlay of 500*l.*, and profits being 20 per cent, the natural price of the machine is 600*l.* : making an additional 100*l.* which must be advanced, over and above his other expenses, by the manufacturer of C, and repaid to him with a profit of 20 per cent. While, therefore, the commodity A is sold for 1200*l.*, C cannot be permanently sold for less than 1320*l.*

A second consequence is, that every rise or fall of general profits will have an effect on values. Not indeed by raising or lowering them generally, (which, as we have so often said, is a contradiction and an impossibility) : but by altering the proportion in which the values of things are affected by the unequal lengths of time for which profit is due. When two things, though made by equal labour, are of unequal value because the one is called upon to yield profit for a greater number of years or months than the other ; this difference of value will be greater when profits are greater, and less when they are less. The wine which has to yield five years' profit more than the cloth, will surpass it in value much more if profits are 40 per cent, than if they are only 20. The commodities A and C, which, though made by equal quantities of labour, were sold for 1200*l.* and 1320*l.*, a difference of 10 per cent, would, if profits had been only half as much, have been sold for 1100*l.* and 1155*l.*, a difference of only 5 per cent.

It follows from this, that even a general rise of wages, when it involves a real increase in the cost of labour, does in some degree influence values. It does not affect them in the manner vulgarly supposed, by raising them universally. But an increase in the cost of labour lowers profits; and therefore lowers in natural value the things into which profits enter in a greater proportion than the average, and raises those into which they enter in a less proportion than the average. All commodities in the production of which machinery bears a large part, especially if the machinery is very durable, are lowered in their relative value when profits fall; or, what is equivalent, other things are raised in value relatively to them. This truth is sometimes expressed in a phraseology more plausible than sound, by saying that a rise of wages raises the value of things made by labour, in comparison with those made by machinery. But things made by machinery, just as much as any other things, are made by labour, namely, the labour which made the machinery itself : the only difference being that profits enter somewhat more largely into the production of things for which machinery is used, though the principal item of the outlay is still labour. It is better, therefore, to associate the effect with fall of profits than with rise of wages ; especially as this last expression is extremely ambiguous, suggesting the idea of an increase of the labourer's real remuneration, rather than of what is alone to the purpose here, namely, the cost of labour to its employer.

§ 6. Besides the natural and necessary elements in cost of production—labour and profits—there are others which are artificial and casual, as for instance a tax. The tax on malt is as much a part of the cost of production of that article as the wages of the labourers. The expenses which the law imposes, as well as those which the nature of things imposes, must be reimbursed with the ordinary profit from the value of the produce, or the things will not continue to be produced. But the influence of taxation on value is subject to the same conditions as the influence of wages and of profits. It is not general taxation, but differential taxation, that produces the effect. If all productions were taxed so as to take an equal percentage from all profits, relative values would be in no way disturbed. If only a few commodities were taxed, their value would rise : and if only a few were left untaxed, their value would fall. If half were taxed and the remainder untaxed, the first half would rise and the last would fall relatively to each other.

This would be necessary in order to equalize the expectation of profit in all employments, without which the taxed employments would ultimately, if not immediately, be abandoned. But general taxation, when equally imposed, and not disturbing the relations of different productions to one another, cannot produce any effect on values.

We have thus far supposed that all the means and appliances which enter into the cost of production of commodities, are things whose own value depends on their cost of production. Some of them, however, may belong to the class of things which cannot be increased *ad libitum* in quantity, and which therefore, if the demand goes beyond a certain amount, command a scarcity value. The materials of many of the ornamental articles manufactured in Italy are the substances called rosso, giallo, and verde antico, which, whether truly or falsely I know not, are asserted to be solely derived from the destruction of ancient columns and other ornamental structures ; the quarries from which the stone was originally cut being exhausted, or their locality forgotten.* A material of such a nature, if in much demand, must be at a scarcity value ; and this value enters into the cost of production, and consequently into the value, of the finished article. The time seems to be approaching when the more valuable furs will come under the influence of a scarcity value of the material. Hitherto the diminishing number of the animals which produce them, in the wildernesses of Siberia, and on the coasts of the Esquimaux Sea, has operated on the value only through the greater labour which has become necessary for securing any given quantity of the article, since, without doubt, by employing labour enough, it might still be obtained in much greater abundance for some time longer.

But the case in which scarcity value chiefly operates in adding to cost of production, is the case of natural agents. These, when unappropriated, and to be had for the taking, do not enter into cost of production, save to the extent of the labour which may be necessary to fit them for use. Even when appropriated, they do not (as we have already seen) bear a value from the mere fact of the appropriation, but only from scarcity, that is, from limitation of supply. But it is equally certain that they often do bear a scarcity value. Suppose a fall of water, in a place where there are more mills wanted than there is water-power to supply them ; the use of the fall of

---

* [1862] Some of these quarries, I believe, have been rediscovered, and are again worked.

water will have a scarcity value, sufficient either to bring the demand down to the supply, or to pay for the creation of an artificial power, by steam or otherwise, equal in efficiency to the water-power.

A natural agent being a possession in perpetuity, and being only serviceable by the products resulting from its continued employment, the ordinary mode of deriving benefit from its ownership is by an annual equivalent, paid by the person who uses it, from the proceeds of its use. This equivalent always might be, and generally is, termed rent. The question, therefore, respecting the influence which the appropriation of natural agents produces on values, is often stated in this form : Does Rent enter into Cost of Production ? and the answer of the best political economists is in the negative. The temptation is strong to the adoption of these sweeping expressions, even by those who are aware of the restrictions with which they must be taken ; for there is no denying that they stamp a general principle more firmly on the mind, than if it were hedged round in theory with all its practical limitations. But they also puzzle and mislead, and create an impression unfavourable to political economy, as if it disregarded the evidence of facts. No one can deny that rent sometimes enters into cost of production. If I buy or rent a piece of ground, and build a cloth manufactory on it, the ground-rent forms legitimately a part of my expenses of production, which must be repaid by the product. And since all factories are built on ground, and most of them in places where ground is peculiarly valuable, the rent paid for it must, on the average, be compensated in the values of all things made in factories. In what sense it is true that rent does not enter into the cost of production or affect the value of agricultural produce, will be shown in the succeeding chapter.

CHAPTER V

§ 1. WE have investigated the laws which determine the value of two classes of commodities : the small class which, being limited to a definite quantity, have their value entirely determined by demand and supply, save that their cost of production (if they have any) constitutes a minimum below which they cannot permanently fall ; and the large class, which can be multiplied *ad libitum* by labour and capital, and of which the cost of production fixes the maximum as well as the minimum at which they can permanently exchange. But there is still a third kind of commodities to be considered : those which have, not one, but several costs of production : which can always be increased in quantity by labour and capital, but not by the same amount of labour and capital ; of which so much may ɒe produced at a given cost, but a further quantity not without a greater cost. These commodities form an intermediate class, partaking of the character of both the others. The principal of them is agricultural produce. We have already made abundant reference to the fundamentaı truth, that in agriculture, the state of the art being given, doubling the labour does not double the produce ; that if an increased quantity of produce ıs required, the additional supply is obtained at a greater cost than the first. Where a hundred quarters of corn are all that is at present required from the lands of a given village, if the growth of population made it necessary to raise a hundred more, either by breaking up worse land now uncultivated, or ɒy a more elaborate cultivation of the land already under the plough, the additionaı ʌundred, or some part of them at least, might cost double or treble as much per quarter as the former supply.

If the first hundred quarters were all raised at the same expense (only the ɒest land being cultivated) ; and if that expense would be remunerated with the ordinary profit by a price of 20s. the quarter ;

the natural price of wheat, so long as no more than that quantity was required, would be 20s. ; and it could only rise above, or fall below that price, from vicissitudes of seasons, or other casual variations in supply.   But if the population of the district advanced, a time would arrive when more than a hundred quarters would be necessary to feed it.   We must suppose that there is no access to any foreign supply   By the hypothesis, no more than a hundred quarters can be produced in the district, unless by either bringing worse land into cultivation, or altering the system of culture to a more expensive one.   Neither of these things will be done without a rise in price.   This rise of price will gradually be brought about by the increasing demand.   So long as the price has risen, but not risen enough to repay with the ordinary profit the cost of producing an additional quantity, the increased value of the limited supply partakes of the nature of a scarcity value.   Suppose that it will not answer to cultivate the second best land, or land of the second degree of remoteness, for a less return than 25s. the quarter ; and that this price is also necessary to remunerate the expensive operations by which an increased produce might be raised from land of the first quality.   If so, the price will rise, through the increased demand, until it reaches 25s.   That will now be the natural price ; being the price without which the quantity, for which society has a demand at that price, will not be produced.   At that price, however, society can go on for some time longer ; could go on perhaps for ever, if population did not increase.   The price, having attained that point, will not again permanently recede (though it may fall tem-porarily from accidental abundance) ; nor will it advance further, so long as society can obtain the supply it requires without a second increase of the cost of production.

I have made use of Price in this reasoning, as a convenient symbol of Value, from the greater familiarity of the idea ; and I shall continue to do so as far as may appear to be necessary.

In the case supposed, different portions of the supply of corn have different costs of production.   Though the 20, or 50, or 150 quarters additional have been produced at a cost proportional to 25s., the original hundred quarters per annum are still produced at a cost only proportional to 20s.   This is self-evident, if the original and the additional supply are produced on different qualities of land.   It is equally true if they are produced on the same land. Suppose that land of the best quality, which produced 100 quarters at 20s., has been made to produce 150 by an expensive process, which it would not answer to undertake without a price of 25s. The cost which requires 25s. is incurred for the sake of 50 quarters alone : the first hundred might have continued for ever to be produced at the original cost, and with the benefit, on that quantity, of the whole rise of price caused by the increased demand : no one, therefore, will incur the additional expense for the sake of the additional fifty, unless they alone will pay for the whole of it. The fifty, therefore, will be produced at their natural price, proportioned to the cost of their production ; while the other hundred will now bring in 5s. a quarter more than their natural price—than the price corresponding to, and sufficing to remunerate, their lower cost of production.

If the production of any, even the smallest, portion of the supply, requires as a necessary condition a certain price, that price will be obtained for all the rest. We are not able to buy one loaf cheaper than another because the corn from which it was made, being grown on a richer soil, has cost less to the grower. The value, therefore, of an article (meaning its natural, which is the same with its average value) is determined by the cost of that portion of the supply which is produced and brought to market at the greatest expense. This is the Law of Value of the third of the three classes into which all commodities are divided.

§ 2. If the portion of produce raised in the most unfavourable circumstances obtains a value proportioned to its cost of production ; all the portions raised in more favourable circumstances, selling as they must do at the same value, obtain a value more than proportioned to their cost of production. Their value is not, correctly speaking, a scarcity value, for it is determined by the circumstances of the production of the commodity, and not by the degree of dearness necessary for keeping down the demand to the level of a limited supply. The owners, however, of those portions of the produce enjoy a privilege ; they obtain a value which yields them more than the ordinary profit. If this advantage depends upon any special exemption, such as being free from a tax, or upon any personal advantages, physical or mental, or any peculiar process only known to themselves, or upon the possession of a greater capital than other people, or upon various other things which might be enumerated, they retain it to themselves as an extra gain, over and above the general profits of capital, of the nature, in some sort, of a monopoly profit. But when, as in the case which we are more particularly considering, the advantage depends on the possession of a natural agent of peculiar quality, as for instance of more fertile land than that which determines the general value of the commodity ; and when this natural agent is not owned by themselves ; the person who does own it, is able to exact from them, in the form of rent, the whole extra gain derived from its use. We are thus brought by another road to the Law of Rent, investigated in the concluding chapter of the Second Book. Rent, we again see, is the difference between the unequal returns to different parts of the capital employed on the soil. Whatever surplus any portion of agricultural capital produces, beyond what is produced by the same amount of capital on the worst soil, or under the most expensive mode of cultivation, which the existing demands of society compel a recourse to ; that surplus will naturally be paid as rent from that capital, to the owner of the land on which it is employed.

It was long thought by political economists, among the rest even by Adam Smith, that the produce of land is always at a monopoly value, because (they said) in addition to the ordinary rate of profit, it always yields something further for rent. This we now see to be erroneous. A thing cannot be at a monopoly value, when its supply can be increased to an indefinite extent if we are only willing to incur the cost. If no more corn than the existing quantity is grown, it is because the value has not risen high enough to remunerate any one for growing it. Any land (not reserved for other uses, or for pleasure) which at the existing price, and by the existing processes, will yield the ordinary profit, is tolerably certain, unless some artificial hindrance intervenes, to be cultivated, although nothing may be left for rent. As long as there is any land fit for cultivation, which at the existing price cannot be profitably cultivated at all, there must be some land a little better, which will yield the ordinary profit, but allow nothing for rent : and that land, if within the boundary of a farm, will be cultivated by the farmer ; if not so, probably by the proprietor, or by some other person on sufferance. Some such land at least, under cultivation, there can scarcely fail to be.

Rent, therefore, forms no part of the cost of production which determines the value of agricultural produce. Circumstances no doubt may be conceived in which it might do so, and very largely too. We can imagine a country so fully peopled, and with all its cultivable soil so completely occupied, that to produce any additional quantity would require more labour than the produce would feed :

and if we suppose this to be the condition of the whole world, or of a country debarred from foreign supply, then, if population continued increasing, both the land and its produce would really rise to a monopoly or scarcity price. But this state of things never can have really existed anywhere, unless possibly in some small island cut off from the rest of the world; nor is there any danger whatever that it should exist. It certainly exists in no known region at present. Monopoly, we have seen, can take effect on value, only through limitation of supply. In all countries of any extent there is more cultivable land than is yet cultivated; and while there is any such surplus, it is the same thing, so far as that quality of land is concerned, as if there were an infinite quantity. What is practically limited in supply is only the better qualities; and even for those, so much rent cannot be demanded as would bring in the competition of the lands not yet in cultivation; the rent of a piece of land must be somewhat less than the whole excess of its productiveness over that of the best land which it is not yet profitable to cultivate; that is, it must be about equal to the excess above the worst land which it is profitable to cultivate. The land or the capital most unfavourably circumstanced among those actually employed, pays no rent; and that land or capital determines the cost of production which regulates the value of the whole produce. Thus rent is, as we have already seen, no cause of value, but the price of the privilege which the inequality of the returns to different portions of agricultural produce confers on all except the least favoured portions.

Rent, in short, merely equalizes the profits of different farming capitals, by enabling the landlord to appropriate all extra gains occasioned by superiority of natural advantages. If all landlords were unanimously to forego their rent, they would but transfer it to the farmers, without benefiting the consumer; for the existing price of corn would still be an indispensable condition of the production of part of the existing supply, and if a part obtained that price the whole would obtain it. Rent, therefore, unless artificially increased by restrictive laws, is no burthen on the consumer: it does not raise the price of corn, and is no otherwise a detriment to the public, than inasmuch as if the state had retained it, or imposed an equivalent in the shape of a land-tax, it would then have been a fund applicable to general instead of private advantage.

§ 3. Agricultural productions are not the only commodities

which have several different costs of production at once, and which in consequence of that difference, and in proportion to it, afford a rent. Mines are also an instance. Almost all kinds of raw material extracted from the interior of the earth—metal, coals, precious stones, &c., are obtained from mines differing considerably in fertility, that is, yielding very different quantities of the product to the same quantity of labour and capital. This being the case, it is an obvious question, why are not the most fertile mines so worked as to supply the whole market ? No such question can arise as to land ; it being self-evident, that the most fertile lands could not possibly be made to supply the whole demand of a fully-peopled country ; and even of what they do yield, a part is extorted from them by a labour and outlay as great as that required to grow the same amount on worse land. But it is not so with mines ; at least, not universally. There are, perhaps, cases in which it is impossible to extract from a particular vein, in a given time, more than a certain quantity of ore, because there is only a limited surface of the vein exposed, on which more than a certain number of labourers cannot be simultaneously employed. But this is not true of all mines. In collieries, for example, some other cause of limitation must be sought for. In some instances the owners limit the quantity raised, in order not too rapidly to exhaust the mine : in others there are said to be combinations of owners, to keep up a monopoly price by limiting the production. Whatever be the causes, it is a fact that mines of different degrees of richness are in operation, and since the value of the produce must be proportional to the cost of production at the worst mine (fertility and situation taken together), it is more than proportional to that of the best. All mines superior in produce to the worst actually worked, will yield, therefore, a rent equal to the excess. They may yield more ; and the worst mine may itself yield a rent. Mines being comparatively few, their qualities do not graduate gently into one another, as the qualities of land do ; and the demand may be such as to keep the value of the produce considerably above the cost of production at the worst mine now worked, without being sufficient to bring into operation a still worse. During the interval, the produce is really at a scarcity value.

Fisheries are another example. Fisheries in the open sea are not appropriated, but fisheries in lakes or rivers almost always are so, and likewise oyster-beds or other particular fishing grounds on coasts. We may take salmon fisheries as an example of the whole class. Some rivers are far more productive in salmon than others.

None, however, without being exhausted, can supply more than a very limited demand. The demand of a country like England can only be supplied by taking salmon from many different rivers of unequal productiveness, and the value must be sufficient to repay the cost of obtaining the fish from the least productive of these. All others, therefore, will if appropriated afford a rent equal to the value of their superiority. Much higher than this it cannot be, if there are salmon rivers accessible which from distance or inferior productiveness have not yet contributed to supply the market. If there are not, the value, doubtless, may rise to a scarcity rate, and the worst fisheries in use may then yield a considerable rent.

Both in the case of mines and of fisheries, the natural order of events is liable to be interrupted by the opening of a new mine, or a new fishery, of superior quality to some of those already in use. The first effect of such an incident is an increase of the supply ; which of course lowers the value to call forth an increased demand. This reduced value may be no longer sufficient to remunerate the worst of the existing mines or fisheries, and these may consequently be abandoned. If the superior mines or fisheries, with the addition of the one newly opened, produce as much of the commodity as is required at the lower value corresponding to their lower cost of production, the fall of value will be permanent, and there will be a corresponding fall in the rents of those mines or fisheries which are not abandoned. In this case, when things have permanently adjusted themselves, the result will be, that the scale of qualities which supply the market will have been cut short at the lower end, while a new insertion will have been made in the scale at some point higher up ; and the worst mine or fishery in use—the one which regulates the rents of the superior qualities and the value of the commodity—will be a mine or fishery of better quality than that by which they were previously regulated.

Land is used for other purposes than agriculture, especially for residence ; and when so used, yields a rent, determined by principles similar to those already laid down. The ground rent of a building, and the rent of a garden or park attached to it, will not be less than the rent which the same land would afford in agriculture : but may be greater than this to an indefinite amount ; the surplus being either in consideration of beauty or of convenience, the convenience often consisting in superior facilities for pecuniary gain. Sites of remarkable beauty are generally limited in supply, and therefore, if in great demand, are at a scarcity value. Sites superior

only in convenience are governed as to their value by the ordinary
principles of rent. The ground rent of a house in a small village is
but little higher than the rent of a similar patch of ground in the
open fields : but that of a shop in Cheapside will exceed these, by
the whole amount at which people estimate the superior facilities
of money-making in the more crowded place. The rents of wharfage,
dock and harbour room, water-power, and many other privileges
may be analysed on similar principles.

§ 4. Cases of extra profit analogous to rent, are more frequent
in the transactions of industry than is sometimes supposed. Take
the case, for example, of a patent, or exclusive privilege for the use
of a process by which cost of production is lessened. If the value of
the product continues to be regulated by what it costs to those who
are obliged to persist in the old process, the patentee will make an
extra profit equal to the advantage which his process possesses over
theirs. This extra profit is essentially similar to rent, and sometimes even assumes the form of it ; the patentee allowing to other
producers the use of his privilege, in consideration of an annual
payment. So long as he, and those whom he associates in the
privilege, do not produce enough to supply the whole market, so
long the original cost of production, being the necessary condition of
producing a part, will regulate the value of the whole ; and the
patentee will be enabled to keep up his rent to a full equivalent for
the advantage which his process gives him. In the commencement
indeed he will probably forego a part of this advantage for the sake
of underselling others : the increased supply which he brings forward
will lower the value, and make the trade a bad one for those who do
not share in the privilege : many of whom therefore will gradually
retire, or restrict their operations, or enter into arrangements with
the patentee : as his supply increases theirs will diminish, the value
meanwhile continuing slightly depressed. But if he stops short in
his operations before the market is wholly supplied by the new process,
things will again adjust themselves to what was the natural value
before the invention was made, and the benefit of the improvement
will accrue solely to the patentee.

The extra gains which any producer or dealer obtains through
superior talents for business, or superior business arrangements,
are very much of a similar kind. If all his competitors had the
same advantages, and used them, the benefit would be transferred
to their customers, through the diminished value of the article :

he only retains it for himself because he is able to bring his commodity to market at a lower cost, while its value is determined by a higher. All advantages, in fact, which one competitor has over another, whether natural or acquired, whether personal or the result of social arrangements, bring the commodity, so far, into the Third Class, and assimilate the possessor of the advantage to a receiver of rent. Wages and profits represent the universal elements in production, while rent may be taken to represent the differential and peculiar : any difference in favour of certain producers, or in favour of production in certain circumstances, being the source of a gain, which, though not called rent unless paid periodically by one person to another, is governed by laws entirely the same with it. The price paid for a differential advantage in producing a commodity cannot enter into the general cost of production of the commodity.

A commodity may no doubt, in some contingencies, yield a rent even under the most disadvantageous circumstances of its production : but only when it is, for the time, in the condition of those commodities which are absolutely limited in supply, and is therefore selling at a scarcity value ; which never is, nor has been, nor can be, a permanent condition of any of the great rent-yielding commodities : unless through their approaching exhaustion, if they are mineral products (coal for example), or through an increase of population, continuing after a further increase of production becomes impossible : a contingency, which the almost inevitable progress of human culture and improvement in the long interval which has first to elapse, forbids us to consider as probable.

CHAPTER VI

§ 1. WE have now attained a favourable point for looking back, and taking a simultaneous view of the space which we have traversed since the commencement of the present Book. The following are the principles of the theory of Value, so far as we have yet ascertained them.

I. Value is a relative term. The value of a thing means the quantity of some other thing, or of things in general, which it exchanges for. The values of all things can never, therefore, rise or fall simultaneously. There is no such thing as a general rise or a general fall of values. Every rise of value supposes a fall, and every fall a rise.

II. The temporary or Market Value of a thing depends on the demand and supply ; rising as the demand rises, and falling as the supply rises. The demand, however, varies with the value, being generally greater when the thing is cheap than when it is dear ; and the value always adjusts itself in such a manner that the demand is equal to the supply.

III. Besides their temporary value, things have also a permanent, or, as it may be called, a Natural Value, to which the market value, after every variation, always tends to return ; and the oscillations compensate for one another, so that, on the average, commodities exchange at about their natural value.

IV. The natural value of some things is a scarcity value ; but most things naturally exchange for one another in the ratio of their cost of production, or at what may be termed their Cost Value.

V. The things which are naturally and permanently at a scarcity value are those of which the supply cannot be increased at all, or not sufficiently to satisfy the whole of the demand which would exist for them at their cost value.

VI. A monopoly value means a scarcity value. Monopoly

cannot give a value to anything except through a limitation of the supply.

VII. Every commodity of which the supply can be indefinitely increased by labour and capital, exchanges for other things proportionally to the cost necessary for producing and bringing to market the most costly portion of the supply required. The natural value is synonymous with the Cost Value ; and the cost value of a thing means the cost value of the most costly portion of it.

VIII. Cost of Production consists of several elements, some of which are constant and universal, others occasional. The universal elements of cost of production are, the wages of the labour, and the profits of the capital. The occasional elements are taxes, and any extra cost occasioned by a scarcity value of some of the requisites.

IX. Rent is not an element in the cost of production of the commodity which yields it ; except in the cases (rather conceivable than actually existing) in which it results from, and represents, a scarcity value. But when land capable of yielding rent in agriculture is applied to some other purpose, the rent which it would have yielded is an element in the cost of production of the commodity which it is employed to produce.

X. Omitting the occasional elements ; things which admit of indefinite increase, naturally and permanently exchange for each other according to the comparative amount of wages which must be paid for producing them, and the comparative amount of profits which must be obtained by the capitalists who pay those wages.

XI. The *comparative* amount of wages does not depend on what wages are in themselves. High wages do not make high values, nor low wages low values. The comparative amount of wages depends partly on the comparative quantities of labour required, and partly on the comparative rates of its remuneration.

XII. So, the comparative rate of profits does not depend on what profits are in themselves ; nor do high or low profits make high or low values. It depends partly on the comparative lengths of time during which the capital is employed, and partly on the comparative rate of profits in different employments.

XIII. If two things are made by the same quantity of labour, and that labour paid at the same rate, and if the wages of the labourer have to be advanced for the same space of time, and the nature of the employment does not require that there be a permanent

difference in their rate of profit; then, whether wages and profits
be high or low, and whether the quantity of labour expended be
much or little, these two things will, on the average, exchange for
one another.

XIV. If one of two things commands, on the average, a greater
value than the other, the cause must be that it requires for its
production either a greater quantity of labour, or a kind of labour
permanently paid at a higher rate; or that the capital, or part of
the capital, which supports that labour, must be advanced for a
longer period; or lastly, that the production is attended with some
circumstance which requires to be compensated by a permanently
higher rate of profit.

XV. Of these elements, the quantity of labour required for the
production is the most important: the effect of the others is smaller,
though none of them are insignificant.

XVI. The lower profits are, the less important become the
minor elements of cost of production, and the less do commodities
deviate from a value proportioned to the quantity and quality
of the labour required for their production.

XVII. But every fall of profits lowers, in some degree, the
cost value of things made with much or durable machinery, and
raises that of things made by hand; and every rise of profits does
the reverse.

§ 2. Such is the general theory of Exchange Value. It is
necessary, however, to remark that this theory contemplates a
system of production carried on by capitalists for profit, and not
by labourers for subsistence. In proportion as we admit this
last supposition—and in most countries we must admit it, at least
in respect of agricultural produce, to a very great extent—such
of the preceding theorems as relate to the dependence of value on
cost of production will require modification. Those theorems are all
grounded on the supposition that the producer's object and aim is
to derive a profit from his capital. This granted, it follows that he
must sell his commodity at the price which will afford the ordinary
rate of profit, that is to say, it must exchange for other commodities
at its cost value. But the peasant proprietor, the metayer, and
even the peasant-farmer or allotment-holder—the labourer, under
whatever name, producing on his own account—is seeking, not an
investment for his little capital, but an advantageous employment
for his time and labour. His disbursements, beyond his own

maintenance and that of his family, are so small, that nearly the whole proceeds of the sale of the produce are wages of labour. When he and his family have been fed from the produce of the farm (and perhaps clothed with materials grown thereon, and manufactured in the family) he may, in respect of the supplementary remuneration derived from the sale of the surplus produce, be compared to those labourers who, deriving their subsistence from an independent source, can afford to sell their labour at any price which is to their minds worth the exertion. A peasant, who supports himself and his family with one portion of his produce, will often ·sell the remainder very much below what would be its cost value to the capitalist.

There is, however, even in this case, a minimum, or inferior limit, of value. The produce which he carries to market, must bring in to him the value of all necessaries which he is compelled to purchase ; and it must enable him to pay his rent. Rent, under peasant cultivation, is not governed by the principles set forth in the chapters immediately preceding, but is either determined by custom, as in the case of metayers, or, if fixed by competition, depends on the ratio of population to land. Rent, therefore, in this case, is an element of cost of production. The peasant must work until he has cleared his rent and the price of all purchased necessaries. After this, he will go on working only if he can sell the produce for such a price as will overcome his aversion to labour.

The minimum just mentioned is what the peasant must obtain in exchange for the whole of his surplus produce. But inasmuch as this surplus is not a fixed quantity, but may be either greater or less according to the degree of his industry, a minimum value for the whole of it does not give any minimum value for a definite quantity of the commodity. In this state of things, therefore, it can hardly be said that the value depends at all on cost of production. It depends entirely on demand and supply, that is, on the proportion between the quantity of surplus food which the peasants choose to produce, and the numbers of the non-agricultural, or rather of the non-peasant population. If the buying class were numerous and the growing class lazy, food might be permanently at a scarcity price. I am not aware that this case has anywhere a real existence. If the growing class is energetic and industrious, and the buyers few, food will be extremely cheap. This also is a rare case, though some parts of France perhaps approximate to it. The common cases are, either that, as in Ireland until lately, the peasant class is indolent and the buyers few, or the peasants industrious and the town population numerous and opulent, as in Belgium, the north of Italy, and parts of Germany. The price of the produce will adjust itself to these varieties of circumstances unless modified, as in many cases it is, by the competition of producers who are not peasants, or by the prices of foreign markets.

§ 3. Another anomalous case is that of slave-grown produce : which presents, however, by no means the same degree of complication. The slave-owner is a capitalist, and his inducement to production consists in a profit on his capital. This profit must amount to the ordinary rate. In respect to his expenses, he is in the same position as if his slaves were free labourers working with their present efficiency, and were hired with wages equal to their present cost. If the cost is less, in proportion to the work done, than the wages of free labour would be, so much the greater are his profits : but if all other producers in the country possess the same advantage, the values of commodities will not be at all affected by it. The only case in which they can be affected, is when the privilege of cheap labour is confined to particular branches of production, free labourers at proportionally higher wages being employed in the remainder. In this case, as in all cases of permanent inequality between the wages of different employments, prices and values receive the impress of the inequality. Slave-grown will exchange for non-slave-grown commodities in a less ratio than that of the quantity of labour required for their production ; the value of the former will be less, of the latter greater, than if slavery did not exist.

The further adaptation of the theory of value to the varieties of existing or possible industrial systems may be left with great advantage to the intelligent reader. It is well said by Montesquieu, " Il ne faut pas toujours tellement épuiser un sujet, qu'on ne laisse rien à faire au lecteur. Il ne s'agit pas de faire lire, mais de faire penser." *

* *Esprit des Lois*, liv. xi. *ad finem.* [See Appendix S. *The Theory of Value.*]

CHAPTER VII

OF MONEY

§ 1. HAVING proceeded thus far in ascertaining the general laws of Value, without introducing the idea of Money (except occasionally for illustration,) it is time that we should now superadd that idea, and consider in what manner the principles of the mutual interchange of commodities are affected by the use of what is termed a Medium of Exchange.

In order to understand the manifold functions of a Circulating Medium, there is no better way than to consider what are the principal inconveniences which we should experience if we had not such a medium. The first and most obvious would be the want of a common measure for values of different sorts. If a tailor had only coats, and wanted to buy bread or a horse, it would be very troublesome to ascertain how much bread he ought to obtain for a coat, or how many coats he should give for a horse. The calculation must be recommenced on different data, every time he bartered his coats for a different kind of article ; and there could be no current price, or regular quotations of value. Whereas now each thing has a current price in money, and he gets over all difficulties by reckoning his coat at 4*l*. or 5*l*., and a four-pound loaf at 6*d*. or 7*d*. As it is much easier to compare different lengths by expressing them in a common language of feet and inches, so it is much easier to compare values by means of a common language of pounds, shillings, and pence. In no other way can values be arranged one above another in a scale ; in no other can a person conveniently calculate the sum of his possessions ; and it is easier to ascertain and remember the relations of many things to one thing, than their innumerable cross relations with one another. This advantage of having a common language in which values may be expressed, is, even by itself, so important, that some such mode of expressing and computing them would probably be used even if a pound or a shilling did not express any real thing, but a mere unit of calculation. It is said that there are African tribes in which this somewhat artificial contrivance actually prevails. They calculate the value of things in a sort of money of account, called macutes. They say one thing is worth ten macutes, another fifteen, another twenty.* There is no real thing called a macute : it is a conventional unit, for the more convenient comparison of things with one another.

This advantage, however, forms but an inconsiderable part of the economical benefits derived from the use of money. The inconveniences of barter are so great, that without some more commodious means of effecting exchanges, the division of employments could hardly have been carried to any considerable extent. A tailor, who had nothing but coats, might starve before he could find any person having bread to sell who wanted a coat : besides, he would not want as much bread at a time as would be worth a coat, and the coat could not be divided. Every person, therefore, would at all times hasten to dispose of his commodity in exchange for anything which, though it might not be fitted to his own immediate wants, was in great and general demand, and easily divisible, so that he might be sure of being able to purchase with it whatever was offered for sale. The primary necessaries of life possess these properties in a high degree. Bread is extremely divisible, and an object of universal desire. Still, this is not the sort of thing required : for, of food, unless in expectation of a scarcity, no one wishes to possess more at once, than is wanted for immediate consumption ; so that a person is never sure of finding an immediate purchaser for articles of food ; and unless soon disposed of, most of them perish. The thing which people would select to keep by them for making purchases, must be one which, besides being divisible and generally desired, does not deteriorate by keeping. This reduces the choice to a small number of articles.

§ 2. By a tacit concurrence, almost all nations, at a very early period, fixed upon certain metals, and especially gold and silver, to serve this purpose. No other substances unite the necessary qualities in so great a degree, with so many subordinate advantages. Next to food and clothing, and in some climates even before clothing, the strongest inclination in a rude state of society is for personal ornament, and for the kind of distinction which is obtained by rarity or costliness in such ornaments. After the immediate

* Montesquieu, *Esprit des Lois*, liv. xxii. ch. 8.

necessities of life were satisfied, every one was eager to accumulate as great a store as possible of things at once costly and ornamental; which were chiefly gold, silver, and jewels. These were the things which it most pleased every one to possess, and which there was most certainty of finding others willing to receive in exchange for any kind of produce. They were among the most imperishable of all substances. They were also portable, and containing great value in small bulk, were easily hid; a consideration of much importance in an age of insecurity. Jewels are inferior to gold and silver in the quality of divisibility; and are of very various qualities, not to be accurately discriminated without great trouble. Gold and silver are eminently divisible, and when pure, always of the same quality; and their purity may be ascertained and certified by a public authority.

Accordingly, though furs have been employed as money in some countries, cattle in others, in Chinese Tartary cubes of tea closely pressed together, the shells called cowries on the coast of Western Africa, and in Abyssinia at this day blocks of rock salt; though even of metals, the less costly have sometimes been chosen, as iron in Lacedæmon from an ascetic policy, copper in the early Roman republic from the poverty of the people; gold and silver have been generally preferred by nations which were able to obtain them, either by industry, commerce, or conquest. To the qualities which originally recommended them, another came to be added, the importance of which only unfolded itself by degrees. Of all commodities they are among the least influenced by any of the causes which produce fluctuations of value. No commodity is quite free from such fluctuations. Gold and silver have sustained, since the beginning of history, one great permanent alteration of value, from the discovery of the American mines; and some temporary variations, such as that which, in the last great war,[1] was produced by the absorption of the metals in hoards, and in the military chests of the immense armies constantly in the field. In the present age the opening of new sources of supply, so abundant as the Ural mountains, California, and Australia,[2] may be the commencement of another period of decline, on the limits of which it would be useless at present to speculate. But on the whole, no commodities are so little exposed to causes of variation. They fluctuate less than almost any other things in their cost of production. And from

[1] [*I.e.* the Napoleonic war.]

[2] [So from the 3rd ed. (1852). In the 1st ed. (1848): "so abundant as the mines of the Ural mountains and of Siberia." In the 2nd ed. (1849): "to which may now be added California."]

their durability, the total quantity in existence is at all times so great in proportion to the annual supply, that the effect on value even of a change in the cost of production is not sudden : a very long time being required to diminish materially the quantity in existence, and even to increase it very greatly not being a rapid process. Gold and silver, therefore, are more fit than any other commodity to be the subject of engagements for receiving or paying a given quantity at some distant period. If the engagement were made in corn, a failure of crops might increase the burthen of the payment in one year to fourfold what was intended, or an exuberant harvest sink it in another to one-fourth. If stipulated in cloth, some manufacturing invention might permanently reduce the payment to a tenth of its original value. Such things have occurred even in the case of payments stipulated in gold and silver ; but the great fall of their value after the discovery of America, is, as yet,[1] the only authenticated instance ; and in this case the change was extremely gradual, being spread over a period of many years.

When gold and silver had become virtually a medium of exchange, by becoming the things for which people generally sold, and with which they generally bought, whatever they had to sell or to buy ; the contrivance of coining obviously suggested itself. By this process the metal was divided into convenient portions, of any degree of smallness, and bearing a recognised proportion to one another ; and the trouble was saved of weighing and assaying at every change of possessors, an inconvenience which on the occasion of small purchases would soon have become insupportable. Governments found it their interest to take the operation into their own hands, and to interdict all coining by private persons ; indeed, their guarantee was often the only one which would have been relied on, a reliance however which very often it ill deserved ; profligate governments having until a very modern period seldom scrupled, for the sake of robbing their creditors, to confer on all other debtors a licence to rob theirs, by the shallow and impudent artifice of lowering the standard ; that least covert of all modes of knavery, which consists in calling a shilling a pound, that a debt of one hundred pounds may be cancelled by the payment of a hundred shillings. It would have been as simple a plan, and would have answered the purpose as well, to have enacted that " a hundred " should always be interpreted to mean five, which would have effected the same reduction in all pecuniary contracts, and would

----

[1] [" As yet " added in 2nd ed. (1849).]

not have been at all more shameless. Such strokes of policy have not
wholly ceased to be recommended, but they have ceased to be
practised ; except occasionally through the medium of paper
money, in which case the character of the transaction, from the
greater obscurity of the subject, is a little less barefaced.

§ 3. Money, when its use has grown habitual, is the medium
through which the incomes of the different members of the community are distributed to them, and the measure by which they
estimate their possessions. As it is always by means of money that
people provide for their different necessities, there grows up in their
minds a powerful association leading them to regard money as wealth
in ڞ more peculiar sense than any other article ; and even those who
pass their lives in the production of the most useful objects, acquire
the habit of regarding those objects as chiefly important by their
capacity of being exchanged for money. A person who parts with
money to obtain commodities, unless he intends to sell them, appears
to the imagination to be making a worse bargain than a person who
parts with commodities to get money ; the one seems to be spending
his means, the other adding to them. Illusions which, though now in
some measure dispelled, were long powerful enough to overmaster the
mind of every politician, both speculative and practical, in Europe.
It must be evident, however, that the mere introduction of a
particular mode of exchanging things for one another by first
exchanging a thing for money, and then exchanging the money
for something else, makes no difference in the essential character
of transactions. It is not with money that things are really purchased. Nobody's income (except that of the gold or silver miner)
is derived from the precious metals. The pounds or shillings which
a person receives weekly or yearly, are not what constitutes his
income ; they are a sort of tickets or orders which he can present
for payment at any shop he pleases, and which entitle him to
receive a certain value of any commodity that he makes choice of.
The farmer pays his labourers and his landlord in these tickets,
as the most convenient plan for himself and them ; but their
real income is their share of his corn, cattle, and hay, and it makes
no essential difference whether he distributes it to them directly,
or sells it for them and gives them the price ; but as they would have
to sell it for money if he did not, and as he is a seller at any rate,
it best suits the purposes of all, that he should sell their share along
with his own, and leave the labourers more leisure for work and the

landlord for being idle. The capitalists, except those who are
producers of the precious metals, derive no part of their income from
those metals, since they only get them by buying them with their
own produce : while all other persons have their incomes paid to
them by the capitalists, or by those who have received payment from
the capitalists ; and as the capitalists have nothing, from the first,
except their produce, it is that and nothing else which supplies all
incomes furnished by them. There cannot, in short, be intrinsically
a more insignificant thing, in the economy of society, than money ;
except in the character of a contrivance for sparing time and labour.
It is a machine for doing quickly and commodiously, what would be
done, though less quickly and commodiously, without it : and like
many other kinds of machinery, it only exerts a distinct and
independent influence of its own when it gets out of order.

The introduction of money does not interfere with the operation
of any of the Laws of Value laid down in the preceding chapters.
The reasons which make the temporary or market value of things
depend on the demand and supply, and their average and permanent
values upon their cost of production, are as applicable to a money
system as to a system of barter. Things which by barter would
exchange for one another, will, if sold for money, sell for an equal
amount of it, and so will exchange for one another still, though
the process of exchanging them will consist of two operations
instead of only one. The relations of commodities to one another
remain unaltered by money : the only new relation introduced is
their relation to money itself ; how much or how little money they
will exchange for ; in other words, how the Exchange Value of money
itself is determined. And this is not a question of any difficulty,
when the illusion is dispelled, which caused money to be looked
upon as a peculiar thing, not governed by the same laws as other
things. Money is a commodity, and its value is determined like
that of other commodities, temporarily by demand and supply,
permanently and on the average by cost of production. The
illustration of these principles, considered in their application to
money, must be given in some detail, on account of the confusion
which, in minds not scientifically instructed on the subject, envelopes
the whole matter ; partly from a lingering remnant of the misleading associations, and partly from the mass of vapoury and
baseless speculation with which this, more than any other topic
of political economy, has in latter times become surrounded. I
shall therefore treat of the Value of Money in a chapter apart.

CHAPTER VIII

§ 1. IT is unfortunate that in the very outset of the subject we have to clear from our path a formidable ambiguity of language. The Value of Money is to appearance an expression as precise, as free from possibility of misunderstanding, as any in science. The value of a thing is what it will exchange for : the value of money is what money will exchange for ; the purchasing power of money. If prices are low, money will buy much of other things, and is of high value ; if prices are high, it will buy little of other things, and is of low value. The value of money is inversely as general prices : falling as they rise, and rising as they fall.

But unhappily the same phrase is also employed, in the current language of commerce, in a very different sense. Money, which is so commonly understood as the synonym of wealth, is more especially the term in use to denote it when it is the subject of borrowing. When one person lends to another, as well as when he pays wages or rent to another, what he transfers is not the mere money, but a right to a certain value of the produce of the country, to be selected at pleasure ; the lender having first bought this right by giving for it a portion of his capital. What he really lends is so much capital ; money is the mere instrument of transfer. But the capital usually passes from the lender to the receiver through the means either of money, or of an order to receive money, and at any rate it is in money that the capital is computed and estimated. Hence, borrowing capital is universally called borrowing money ; the loan market is called the money market : those who have their capital disposable for investment on loan are called the monied class : and the equivalent given for the use of capital, or in other words, interest, is not only called the interest of money, but, by a grosser perversion of terms, the value of money. This misapplication of language, assisted by some fallacious appearances which we shall notice and clear up hereafter,* has created a general notion among persons in business, that the Value of Money, meaning the rate of interest, has an intimate connexion with the Value of Money in its proper sense, the value or purchasing power of the circulating medium. We shall return to this subject before long : at present it is enough to say, that by Value I shall always mean Exchange Value, and by money the medium of exchange, not the capital which is passed from hand to hand through that medium.

§ 2. The value or purchasing power of money depends, in the first instance, on demand and supply. But demand and supply, in relation to money, present themselves in a somewhat different shape from the demand and supply of other things.

The supply of a commodity means the quantity offered for sale. But it is not usual to speak of offering money for sale. People are not usually said to buy or sell money. This, however, is merely an accident of language. In point of fact, money is bought and sold like other things, whenever other things are bought and sold *for* money. Whoever sells corn, or tallow, or cotton, buys money. Whoever buys bread, or wine, or clothes, sells money to the dealer in those articles. The money with which people are offering to buy is money offered for sale. The supply of money, then, is the quantity of it which people are wanting to lay out ; that is, all the money they have in their possession, except what they are hoarding, or at least keeping by them as a reserve for future contingencies. The supply of money, in short, is all the money in *circulation* at the time.

The demand for money, again, consists of all the goods offered for sale. Every seller of goods is a buyer of money, and the goods he brings with him constitute his demand. The demand for money differs from the demand for other things in this, that it is limited only by the means of the purchaser. The demand for other things is for so much and no more ; but there is always a demand for as much money as can be got. Persons may indeed refuse to sell, and withdraw their goods from the market, if they cannot get for them what they consider a sufficient price. But this is only when they think that the price will rise, and that they shall get more money by waiting. If they thought the low price likely to be permanent, they would take what they could get. It is always a *sine quâ non* with a dealer to dispose of his goods.

* Infra, chap. xxiii.

As the whole of the goods in the market compose the demand for money, so the whole of the money constitutes the demand for goods. The money and the goods are seeking each other for the purpose of being exchanged. They are reciprocally supply and demand to one another. It is indifferent whether, in characterizing the phenomena, we speak of the demand and supply of goods, or the supply and the demand of money. They are equivalent expressions.

We shall proceed to illustrate this proposition more fully. And in doing this, the reader will remark a great difference between the class of questions which now occupy us, and those which we previously had under discussion respecting Values. In considering Value, we were only concerned with causes which acted upon particular commodities apart from the rest. Causes which affect all commodities alike do not act upon values. But in considering the relation between goods and money, it is with the causes that operate upon all goods whatever that we are specially concerned. We are comparing goods of all sorts on one side, with money on the other side, as things to be exchanged against each other.

Suppose, everything else being the same, that there is an increase in the quantity of money, say by the arrival of a foreigner in a place, with a treasure of gold and silver. When he commences expending it (for this question it matters not whether productively or unproductively), he adds to the supply of money, and, by the same act, to the demand for goods. Doubtless he adds, in the first instance, to the demand only for certain kinds of goods, namely, those which he selects for purchase ; he will immediately raise the price of those, and so far as he is individually concerned, of those only. If he spends his funds in giving entertainments, he will raise the prices of food and wine. If he expends them in establishing a manufactory, he will raise the prices of labour and materials. But at the higher prices, more money will pass into the hands of the sellers of these different articles ; and they, whether labourers or dealers, having more money to lay out, will create an increased demand for all the things which they are accustomed to purchase : these accordingly will rise in price, and so on until the rise has reached everything. I say everything, though it is of course possible that the influx of money might take place through the medium of some new class of consumers, or in such a manner as to alter the proportions of different classes of consumers to one another, so that a greater share of the national income than before would thenceforth be expended in some articles, and a smaller in others; exactly as if a change had taken place in the tastes and wants of the community. If this were the case, then until production had accommodated itself to this change in the comparative demand for different things, there would be a real alteration in values, and some things would rise in price more than others, while some perhaps would not rise at all. These effects, however, would evidently proceed, not from the mere increase of money, but from accessory circumstances attending it. We are now only called upon to consider what would be the effect of an increase of money, considered by itself. Supposing the money in the hands of individuals to be increased, the wants and inclinations of the community collectively in respect to consumption remaining exactly the same ; the increase of demand would reach all things equally, and there would be an universal rise of prices. We might suppose, with Hume, that some morning, every person in the nation should wake and find a gold coin in his pocket : this example, however, would involve an alteration of the proportions in the demand for different commodities ; the luxuries of the poor would, in the first instance, be raised in price in a much greater degree than other things. Let us rather suppose, therefore, that to every pound, or shilling, or penny, in the possession of any one, another pound, shilling, or penny, were suddenly added. There would be an increased money demand, and consequently an increased money value, or price, for things of all sorts. This increased value would do no good to any one ; would make no difference, except that of having to reckon pounds, shillings, and pence, in higher numbers. It would be an increase of values only as estimated in money, a thing only wanted to buy other things with ; and would not enable any one to buy more of them than before. Prices would have risen in a certain ratio, and the value of money would have fallen in the same ratio.

It is to be remarked that this ratio would be precisely that in which the quantity of money had been increased. If the whole money in circulation was doubled, prices would be doubled. If it was only increased one-fourth, prices would rise one-fourth. There would be one-fourth more money, all of which would be used to purchase goods of some description. When there had been time for the increased supply of money to reach all markets, or (according to the conventional metaphor) to permeate all the channels of circulation, all prices would have risen one-fourth. But the general rise of price is independent of this diffusing and equalizing process. Even if some prices were raised more, and others less, the average rise would be one-fourth. This is a necessary consequence of the fact that a fourth more money would have been given for only the same quantity of goods. *General* prices, therefore, would in any case be a fourth higher.

The very same effect would be produced on prices if we suppose the goods diminished, instead of the money increased : and the contrary effect if the goods were increased or the money diminished. If there were less money in the hands of the community, and the same amount of goods to be sold, less money altogether would be given for them, and they would be sold at lower prices ; lower, too, in the precise ratio in which the money was diminished. So that the value of money, other things being the same, varies inversely as its quantity ; every increase of quantity lowering the value, and every diminution raising it, in a ratio exactly equivalent.

This, it must be observed, is a property peculiar to money. We did not find it to be true of commodities generally, that every diminution of supply raised the value exactly in proportion to the deficiency, or that every increase lowered it in the precise ratio of the excess. Some things are usually affected in a greater ratio than that of the excess or deficiency, others usually in a less : because, in ordinary cases of demand, the desire, being for the thing itself, may be stronger or weaker : and the amount of what people are willing to expend on it, being in any case a limited quantity, may be affected in very unequal degrees by difficulty or facility of attainment. But in the case of money, which is desired as the means of universal purchase, the demand consists of everything which people have to sell ; and the only limit to what they are willing to give is the limit set by their having nothing more to offer. The whole of the goods being in any case exchanged for the whole of the money which comes into the market to be laid out, they will sell for less or more of it, exactly according as less or more is brought.

§ 3. From what precedes, it might for a moment be supposed that all the goods on sale in a country, at any one time, are exchanged for all the money existing and in circulation at that same time : or, in other words, that there is always in circulation in a country a quantity of money equal in value to the whole of the goods then and there on sale. But this would be a complete misapprehension. The money laid out is equal in value to the goods it purchases ; but the quantity of money laid out is not the same thing with the quantity in circulation.   As the money passes from hand to hand, the same piece of money is laid out many times, before all the things on sale at one time are purchased and finally removed from the market : and each pound or dollar must be counted for as many pounds or dollars, as the number of times it changes hands in order to effect this object.   The greater part of the goods must also be counted more than once, not only because most things pass through the hands of several sets of manufacturers and dealers before they assume the form in which they are finally consumed, but because in times of speculation (and all times are so, more or less) the same goods are often bought repeatedly, to be resold for a profit, before they are bought for the purpose of consumption at all.

If we assume the quantity of goods on sale, and the number of times those goods are resold, to be fixed quantities, the value of money will depend upon its quantity, together with the average number of times that each piece changes hands in the process. The whole of the goods sold (counting each resale of the same goods as so much added to the goods) have been exchanged for the whole of the money, multiplied by the number of purchases made on the average by each piece.   Consequently, the amount of goods and of transactions being the same, the value of money is inversely as its quantity multiplied by what is called the rapidity of circulation. And the quantity of money in circulation is equal to the money value of all the goods sold, divided by the number which expresses the rapidity of circulation.

The phrase, rapidity of circulation, requires some comment. It must not be understood to mean the number of purchases made by each piece of money in a given time.   Time is not the thing to be considered.   The state of society may be such that each piece of money hardly performs more than one purchase in a year : but if this arises from the small number of transactions—from the small amount of business done, the want of activity in traffic, or because what traffic there is, mostly takes place by barter—it constitutes no reason why prices should be lower, or the value of money higher.   The essential point is, not how often the same money changes hands in a given time, but how often it changes hands in order to perform a given amount of traffic.   We must compare the number of purchases made by the money in a given time, not with the time itself, but with the goods sold in that same time.   If each piece of money changes hands on an average ten times while goods are sold to the value of a million sterling, it is evident that the money required to circulate those goods is 100,000*l.* And conversely, if the money in circulation is 100,000*l.*, and each piece changes hands by the purchase of goods ten times in a month, the sales of goods for money which take place every month must amount on the average to 1,000,000*l.*

Rapidity of circulation being a phrase so ill adapted to express the only thing which it is of any importance to express by it, and having a tendency to confuse the subject by suggesting a meaning extremely different from the one intended, it would be a good thing if the phrase could be got rid of, and another substituted, more directly significant of the idea meant to be conveyed. Some such expression as " the efficiency of money," though not unexceptionable, would do better ; as it would point attention to the quantity of work done, without suggesting the idea of estimating it by time. Until an appropriate term can be devised, we must be content, when ambiguity is to be apprehended, to express the idea by the circumlocution which alone conveys it adequately, namely, the average number of purchases made by each piece in order to effect a given pecuniary amount of transactions.

§ 4. The proposition which we have laid down respecting the dependence of general prices upon the quantity of money in circulation, must be understood as applying only to a state of things in which money, that is, gold or silver, is the exclusive instrument of exchange, and actually passes from hand to hand at every purchase, credit in any of its shapes being unknown. When credit comes into play as a means of purchasing, distinct from money in hand, we shall hereafter find that the connexion between prices and the amount of the circulating medium is much less direct and intimate, and that such connexion as does exist no longer admits of so simple a mode of expression. But on a subject so full of complexity as that of currency and prices, it is necessary to lay the foundation of our theory in a thorough understanding of the most simple cases, which we shall always find lying as a groundwork or substratum under those which arise in practice. That an increase of the quantity of money raises prices, and a diminution lowers them, is the most elementary proposition in the theory of currency, and without it we should have no key to any of the others. In any state of things, however, except the simple and primitive one which we have supposed, the proposition is only true other things being the same : and what those other things are, which must be the same, we are not yet ready to pronounce.   We can, however, point out, even now, one or two of the cautions with which the principle must be guarded in attempting to make use of it for the practical explanation of phenomena ; cautions the more indispensable, as the doctrine, though a scientific truth, has of late years been the foundation of a greater mass of false theory, and erroneous interpretation of facts, than any other proposition relating to interchange.   From the time of the resumption of cash payments by the Act of 1819, and especially since the commercial crisis of 1825, the favourite explanation of every rise or fall of prices has been the "currency ; " and like most popular theories, the doctrine has been applied with little regard to the conditions necessary for making it correct.

For example, it is habitually assumed that whenever there is a greater amount of money in the country, or in existence, a rise of prices must necessarily follow.   But this is by no means an inevitable consequence.   In no commodity is it the quantity in existence, but the quantity offered for sale, that determines the value.   Whatever may be the quantity of money in the country, only that part of it will affect prices which goes into the market of commodities, and is there actually exchanged against goods.   Whatever increases the amount of this portion of the money in the country, tends to raise prices.   But money hoarded does not act on prices.   Money kept in reserve by individuals to meet contingencies which do not occur, does not act on prices.   The money in the coffers of the Bank, or retained as a reserve by private bankers, does not act on prices until drawn out, nor even then unless drawn out to be expended in commodities.

It frequently happens that money, to a considerable amount, is brought into the country, is there actually invested [1] as capital, and again flows out, without having ever once acted upon the markets of commodities, but only upon the market of securities, or, as it is commonly though improperly called, the money market. Let us return to the case already put for illustration, that of a foreigner landing in the country with a treasure.   We supposed him to employ his treasure in the purchase of goods for his own use, or in setting up a manufactory and employing labourers ; and in either case he would, *cæteris paribus*, raise prices.   But instead of doing either of these things, he might very probably prefer to invest his fortune at interest ; which we shall suppose him to do in the most obvious way, by becoming a competitor for a portion of

[1] ["Invested" substituted for "employed" in 3rd ed. (1852).]

the stock, exchequer bills, railway debentures, mercantile bills, mortgages, &c., which are at all times in the hands of the public. By doing this he would raise the prices of those different securities, or in other words would lower the rate of interest; and since this would disturb the relation previously existing between the rate of interest on capital in the country itself, and that in foreign countries, it would probably induce some of those who had floating capital seeking employment, to send it abroad for foreign investment rather than buy securities at home at the advanced price. As much money might thus go out as had previously come in, while the prices of commodities would have shown no trace of its temporary presence. This is a case highly deserving of attention : and it is a fact now beginning to be recognised, that the passage of the precious metals from country to country is determined much more than was formerly supposed by the state of the loan market in different countries, and much less by the state of prices.

Another point must be adverted to, in order to avoid serious error in the interpretation of mercantile phenomena. If there be, at any time, an increase in the number of money transactions, a thing continually liable to happen from differences in the activity of speculation, and even in the time of year (since certain kinds of business are transacted only at particular seasons) ; an increase of the currency which is only proportional to this increase of trans- actions, and is of no longer duration, has no tendency to raise prices. At the quarterly periods when the public dividends are paid at the Bank, a sudden increase takes place of the money in the hands of the public ; an increase estimated at from a fifth to two- fifths of the whole issues of the Bank of England. Yet this never has any effect on prices ; and in a very few weeks, the currency has again shrunk into its usual dimensions, by a mere reduction in the demands of the public (after so copious a supply of ready money) for accommodation from the Bank in the way of discount or loan. In like manner the currency of the agricultural districts fluctuates in amount at different seasons of the year. It is always lowest in August : " it rises generally towards Christmas, and obtains its greatest elevation about Lady-day, when the farmer commonly lays in his stock, and has to pay his rent and summer taxes," and when he therefore makes his principal applications to country bankers for loans. " Those variations occur with the same regularity as the season, and with just as little disturbance of the markets as the quarterly fluctuations of the notes of the Bank of England.

As soon as the extra payments have been completed, the superfluous" currency, which is estimated at half a million, "as certainly and immediately is reabsorbed and disappears." *

If extra currency were not forthcoming to make these extra payments, one of three things must happen. Either the payments must be made without money, by a resort to some of those contrivances by which its use is dispensed with ; or there must be an increase in the rapidity of circulation, the same sum of money being made to perform more payments ; or, if neither of these things took place, money to make the extra payments must be withdrawn from the market for commodities, and prices, consequently, must fall. An increase of the circulating medium, conformable in extent and duration to the temporary stress of business, does not raise prices, but merely prevents this fall.

The sequel of our investigation will point out many other qualifications with which the proposition must be received, that the value of the circulating medium depends on the demand and supply, and is in the inverse ratio of the quantity ; [1] qualifications which, under a complex system of credit like that existing in England, render the proposition an extremely incorrect expression of the fact.

---

* Fullarton, *Regulation of Currencies*, 2nd edit. pp. 87-9.

[1] [The rest of the sentence was added in the 4th ed. (1857), and the proposition described as " a totally incorrect expression of the fact."   In the 5th ed. (1862) " extremely " was substituted for " totally."]

CHAPTER IX

§ 1. BUT money, no more than commodities in general, has its value definitely determined by demand and supply. The ultimate regulator of its value is Cost of Production.

We are supposing, of course, that things are left to themselves. Governments have not always left things to themselves. They have undertaken to prevent the quantity of money from adjusting itself according to spontaneous laws, and have endeavoured to regulate it at their pleasure; generally with a view of keeping a greater quantity of money in the country, than would otherwise have remained there. It was, until lately, the policy of all governments to interdict the exportation and the melting of money; while, by encouraging the exportation and impeding the importation of other things, they endeavoured to have a stream of money constantly flowing in. By this course they gratified two prejudices; they drew, or thought that they drew, more money into the country, which they believed to be tantamount to more wealth; and they gave, or thought that they gave, to all producers and dealers, high prices, which, though no real advantage, people are always inclined to suppose to be one.

In this attempt to regulate the value of money artificially by means of the supply, governments have never succeeded in the degree, or even in the manner, which they intended. Their prohibitions against exporting or melting the coin have never been effectual. A commodity of such small bulk in proportion to its value is so easily smuggled, and still more easily melted, that it has been impossible by the most stringent measures to prevent these operations. All the risk which it was in the power of governments to attach to them, was outweighed by a very moderate profit.* In

---

* The effect of the prohibition cannot, however, have been so entirely insignificant as it has been supposed to be by writers on the subject. The

the more indirect mode of aiming at the same purpose, by throwing difficulties in the way of making the returns for exported goods in any other commodity than money, they have not been quite so unsuccessful. They have not, indeed, succeeded in making money flow continuously into the country ; but they have to a certain extent been able to keep it at a higher than its natural level ; and have, thus far, removed the value of money from exclusive dependence on the causes which fix the value of things not artificially interfered with.

We are, however, to suppose a state, not of artificial regulation, but of freedom. In that state, and assuming no charge to be made for coinage, the value of money will conform to the value of the bullion of which it is made. A pound weight of gold or silver in coin, and the same weight in an ingot, will precisely exchange for one another. On the supposition of freedom, the metal cannot be worth more in the state of bullion than of coin ; for as it can be melted without any loss of time, and with hardly any expense, this would of course be done until the quantity in circulation was so much diminished as to equalize its value with that of the same weight in bullion. It may be thought however that the coin, though it cannot be of less, may be, and being a manufactured article will naturally be, of greater value than the bullion contained in it, on the same principle on which linen cloth is of more value than an equal weight of linen yarn. This would be true, were it not that Government, in this country, and in some others, coins money gratis for anyone who furnishes the metal. The labour and expense of coinage, when not charged to the possessor, do not raise the value of the article. If Government opened an office where, on delivery of a given weight of yarn, it returned the same weight of cloth to any one who asked for it, cloth would be worth no more in the market than the yarn it contained. As soon as coin is worth a fraction more than the value of the bullion, it becomes the interest of the holders of bullion to send it to be coined. If Government, however, throws the expense of coinage, as is reasonable, upon the holder, by making a charge to cover the expense (which is done by giving back rather less in coin than has been received in bullion, and is called levying a seignorage), the coin will rise,

facts adduced by Mr. Fullarton, in the note to page 7 of his work on the *Regulation of Currencies*, shows that it required a greater percentage of difference in value between coin and bullion than has commonly been imagined, to bring the coin to the melting-pot.

to the extent of the seignorage, above the value of the bullion. If the Mint kept back one per cent to pay the expense of coinage, it would be against the interest of the holders of bullion to have it coined, until the coin was more valuable than the bullion by at least that fraction. The coin, therefore, would be kept one per cent higher in value, which could only be by keeping it one per cent less in quantity, than if its coinage were gratuitous.

The Government might attempt to obtain a profit by the transaction, and might lay on a seignorage calculated for that purpose ; but whatever they took for coinage beyond its expenses, would be so much profit on private coining. Coining, though not so easy an operation as melting, is far from a difficult one, and, when the coin produced is of full weight and standard fineness, is very difficult to detect. If, therefore, a profit could be made by coining good money, it would certainly be done : and the attempt to make seignorage a source of revenue would be defeated. Any attempt to keep the value of the coin at an artificial elevation, not by a seignorage, but by refusing to coin, would be frustrated in the same manner.*

§ 2. The value of money, then, conforms, permanently, and, in a state of freedom, almost immediately, to the value of the metal of which it is made ; with the addition, or not, of the expenses of coinage, according as those expenses are borne by the individual or by the state. This simplifies extremely the question which we have here to consider : since gold and silver bullion are commodities like any others, and their value depends, like that of other things, on their cost of production.

To the majority of civilized countries, gold and silver are foreign products : and the circumstances which govern the values of foreign products, present some questions which we are not yet ready to examine. For the present, therefore, we must suppose the country which is the subject of our inquiries, to be supplied with gold and

---

* In England, though there is no seignorage on gold coin, (the Mint returning in coin the same weight of pure metal which it receives in bullion,) there is a delay of a few weeks after the bullion is deposited, before the coin can be obtained, occasioning a loss of interest, which, to the holder, is equivalent to a trifling seignorage. From this cause, the value of coin is in general slightly above that of the bullion it contains. An ounce of gold, according to the quantity of metal in a sovereign, should be worth $3l.$ $17s.$ $10\frac{1}{2}d.$; but it was usually quoted at $3l.$ $17s.$ $6d.$, until the Bank Charter Act of 1844 made it imperative on the Bank to give its notes for all bullion offered to it at the rate of $3l.$ $17s.$ $9d.$

silver by its own mines, reserving for future consideration how far
our conclusions require modification to adapt them to the more
usual case.

Of the three classes into which commodities are divided—
those absolutely limited in supply, those which may be had in
unlimited quantity at a given cost of production, and those which
may be had in unlimited quantity, but at an increasing cost of
production—the precious metals, being the produce of mines,
belong to the third class. Their natural value, therefore, is in the
long run proportional to their cost of production in the most unfavourable existing circumstances, that is, at the worst mine which
it is necessary to work in order to obtain the required supply. A
pound weight of gold will, in the gold-producing countries, ultimately tend to exchange for as much of every other commodity as
is produced at a cost equal to its own ; meaning by its own cost the
cost in labour and expense, at the least productive sources of supply
which the then existing demand makes it necessary to work. The
average value of gold is made to conform to its natural value in
the same manner as the values of other things are made to conform to their natural value. Suppose that it were selling above its
natural value ; that is, above the value which is an equivalent for
the labour and expense of mining, and for the risks attending a
branch of industry in which nine out of ten experiments have
usually been failures. A part of the mass of floating capital which
is on the look out for investment, would take the direction of mining
enterprise ; the supply would thus be increased, and the value
would fall. If, on the contrary, it were selling below its natural
value, miners would not be obtaining the ordinary profit ; they
would slacken their works ; if the depreciation was great, some of
the inferior mines would perhaps stop working altogether : and a
falling off in the annual supply, preventing the annual wear and
tear from being completely compensated, would by degrees reduce
the quantity, and restore the value.

When examined more closely, the following are the details of
the process. If gold is above its natural or cost value—the coin,
as we have seen, conforming in its value to the bullion—money
will be of high value. and the prices of all things, labour included,
will be low. These low prices will lower the expenses of all producers ;
but as their returns will also be lowered, no advantage will be
obtained by any producer, except the producer of gold : whose
returns from his mine, not depending on price, will be the same as

before, and his expenses being less, he will obtain extra profits, and will be stimulated to increase his production. *E converso* if the metal is below its natural value : since this is as much as to say that prices are high, and the money expenses of all producers unusually great : for this, however, all other producers will be compensated by increased money returns : the miner alone will extract from his mine no more metal than before, while his expenses will be greater : his profits therefore being diminished or annihilated, he will diminish his production, if not abandon his employment.

In this manner it is that the value of money is made to conform to the cost of production of the metal of which it is made. It may be well, however, to repeat (what has been said before) that the adjustment takes a long time to effect, in the case of a commodity so generally desired and at the same time so durable as the precious metals. Being so largely used not only as money but for plate and ornament, there is at all times a very large quantity of these metals in existence : while they are so slowly worn out, that a comparatively small annual production is sufficient to keep up the supply, and to make any addition to it which may be required by the increase of goods to be circulated, or by the increased demand for gold and silver articles by wealthy consumers. Even if this small annual supply were stopt entirely, it would require many years to reduce the quantity so much as to make any very material difference in prices. The quantity may be increased much more rapidly than it can be diminished ; but the increase must be very great before it can make itself much felt over such a mass of the precious metals as exists in the whole commercial world. And hence the effects of all changes in the conditions of production of the precious metals are at first, and continue to be for many years, questions of quantity only, with little reference to cost of production. [1] More especially is this the case when, as at the present time, many new sources of supply have been simultaneously opened, most of them practicable by labour alone, without any capital in advance beyond a pickaxe and a week's food ; and when the operations are as yet wholly experimental, the comparative permanent productiveness of the different sources being entirely unascertained.

§ 3. Since, however, the value of money really conforms, like that of other things, though more slowly, to its cost of production,

[1] [The final sentence of this paragraph was added in the 3rd ed. (1852).]

some political economists have objected altogether to the statement
that the value of money depends on its quantity combined with
the rapidity of circulation ; which, they think, is assuming a law for
money that does not exist for any other commodity, when the truth
is that it is governed by the very same laws. To this we may
answer, in the first place, that the statement in question assumes no
peculiar law. It is simply the law of demand and supply, which is
acknowledged to be applicable to all commodities, and which, in
the case of money as of most other things, is controlled, but not set
aside, by the law of cost of production, since cost of production
would have no effect on value if it could have none on supply. But,
secondly, there really is, in one respect, a closer connexion between
the value of money and its quantity, than between the values of
other things and their quantity. The value of other things conforms to the changes in the cost of production, without requiring,
as a condition, that there should be any actual alteration of the
supply : the potential alteration is sufficient ; and if there even be
an actual alteration, it is but a temporary one, except in so far as
the altered value may make a difference in the demand, and so
require an increase or diminution of supply, as a consequence,
not a cause, of the alteration in value. Now this is also true of
gold and silver, considered as articles of expenditure for ornament
and luxury ; but it is not true of money. If the permanent cost
of production of gold were reduced one-fourth, it might happen
that there would not be more of it bought for plate, gilding, or
jewellery, than before ; and if so, though the value would fall, the
quantity extracted from the mines for these purposes would be no
greater than previously. Not so with the portion used as money ;
that portion could not fall in value one-fourth, unless actually
increased one-fourth ; for, at prices one-fourth higher, one-fourth
more money would be required to make the accustomed purchases ;
and if this were not forthcoming, some of the commodities would be
without purchasers, and prices could not be kept up. Alterations,
therefore, in the cost of production of the precious metals, do not
act upon the value of money except just in proportion as they
increase or diminish its quantity ; which cannot be said of any
other commodity. It would therefore, I conceive, be an error,
both scientifically and practically, to discard the proposition
which asserts a connexion between the value of money and its
quantity.

It is evident, however, that the cost of production, in the long run, regulates the quantity; and that every country (temporary fluctuations excepted) will possess, and have in circulation, just that quantity of money which will perform all the exchanges required of it, consistently with maintaining a value conformable to its cost of production. The prices of things will, on the average, be such that money will exchange for its own cost in all other goods : and, precisely because the quantity cannot be prevented from affecting the value, the quantity itself will (by a sort of self-acting machinery) be kept at the amount consistent with that standard of prices—at the amount necessary for performing, at those prices, all the business required of it.

" The quantity wanted will depend partly on the cost of producing gold, and partly on the rapidity of its circulation. The rapidity of circulation being given, it would depend on the cost of production : and the cost of production being given, the quantity of money would depend on the rapidity of its circulation." * After what has been already said, I hope that neither of these propositions stands in need of any further illustration.

Money, then, like commodities in general, having a value dependent on, and proportional to, its cost of production ; the theory of money is, by the admission of this principle, stript of a great part of the mystery which apparently surrounded it. We must not forget, however, that this doctrine only applies to the places in which the precious metals are actually produced ; and that we have yet to enquire whether the law of the dependence of value on cost of production applies to the exchange of things produced at distant places. But however this may be, our propositions with respect to value will require no other alteration, where money is an imported commodity, than that of substituting for the cost of its production the cost of obtaining it in the country. Every foreign commodity is bought by giving for it some domestic production ; and the labour and capital which a foreign commodity costs to us is the labour and capital expended in producing the quantity of our own goods which we give in exchange for it. What this quantity depends upon,—what determines the proportions of interchange between the productions of one country and those of another,—is indeed a question of somewhat greater complexity than those we

---

* From some printed, but not published, Lectures of Mr. Senior : in which the great differences in the business done by money, as well as in the rapidity of its circulation in different states of society and civilization, are interestingly illustrated.

have hitherto considered.   But this at least is indisputable, that
within the country itself the value of imported commodities is
determined by the value, and consequently by the cost of production,
of the equivalent given for them ; and money, where it is an imported
commodity, is subject to the same law.[1]

---

[1] [See Appendix T.   *The Value of Money.*]

CHAPTER X

§ 1. THOUGH the qualities necessary to fit any commodity for being used as money are rarely united in any considerable perfection, there are two commodities which possess them in an eminent, and nearly an equal degree ; the two precious metals, as they are called ; gold and silver. Some nations have accordingly attempted to compose their circulating medium of these two metals indiscriminately.

There is an obvious convenience in making use of the more costly metal for larger payments and the cheaper one for smaller : and the only question relates to the mode in which this can best be done. The mode most frequently adopted has been to establish between the two metals a fixed proportion ; to decide, for example, that a gold coin called a sovereign should be equivalent to twenty of the silver coins called shillings : both the one and the other being called, in the ordinary money of account of the country, by the same denomination, a pound : and it being left free to every one who has a pound to pay, either to pay it in the one metal or in the other.

At the time when the valuation of the two metals relatively to each other, say twenty shillings to the sovereign, or twenty-one shillings to the guinea, was first made, the proportion probably corresponded, as nearly as it could be made to do, with the ordinary relative values of the two metals grounded on their cost of production : and if those natural or cost values always continued to bear the same ratio to one another, the arrangement would be unobjectionable. This, however, is far from being the fact. Gold and silver, though the least variable in value of all commodities, are not invariable, and do not always vary simultaneously. Silver, for example, was lowered in permanent value more than gold, by the discovery of the American mines ; and those small variations of value which take place occasionally do not affect both metals alike.

Suppose such a variation to take place : the value of the two metals relatively to one another no longer agreeing with their rated proportion, one or other of them will now be rated below its bullion value, and there will be a profit to be made by melting it.

Suppose, for example, that gold rises in value relatively to silver, so that the quantity of gold in a sovereign is now worth more than the quantity of silver in twenty shillings. Two consequences will ensue. No debtor will any longer find it his interest to pay in gold. He will always pay in silver, because twenty shillings are a legal tender for a debt of one pound, and he can procure silver convertible into twenty shillings for less gold than that contained in a sovereign. The other consequence will be, that unless a sovereign can be sold for more than twenty shillings, all the sovereigns will be melted, since as bullion they will purchase a greater number of shillings than they exchange for as coin. The converse of all this would happen if silver, instead of gold, were the metal which had risen in comparative value. A sovereign would not now be worth so much as twenty shillings, and whoever had a pound to pay would prefer paying it by a sovereign ; while the silver coins would be collected for the purpose of being melted, and sold as bullion for gold at their real value, that is, above the legal valuation. The money of the community, therefore, would never really consist of both metals, but of the one only which, at the particular time, best suited the interest of debtors ; and the standard of the currency would be constantly liable to change from the one metal to the other, at a loss, on each change, of the expense of coinage on the metal which fell out of use.

It appears, therefore, that the value of money is liable to more frequent fluctuations when both metals are a legal tender at a fixed valuation, than when the exclusive standard of the currency is either gold or silver. Instead of being only affected by variations in the cost of production of one metal it is subject to derangement from those of two. The particular kind of variation to which a currency is rendered more liable by having two legal standards, is a fall of value, or what is commonly called a depreciation ; since practically that one of the two metals will always be the standard, of which the real has fallen below the rated value. If the tendency of the metals be to rise in value, all payments will be made in the one which has risen least ; and if to fall, then in that which has fallen most.

§ 2. The plan of a double standard is still occasionally brought forward by here and there a writer or orator as a great improvement in currency. It is probable that, with most of its adherents, its chief merit is its tendency to a sort of depreciation, there being at all times abundance of supporters for any mode, either open or covert, of lowering the standard. Some, however, are influenced by an exaggerated estimate of an advantage which to a certain extent is real, that of being able to have recourse, for replenishing the circulation, to the united stock of gold and silver in the commercial world, instead of being confined to one of them, which, from acci-dental absorption, may not be obtainable with sufficient rapidity. The advantage without the disadvantages of a double standard, seems to be best obtained by those nations with whom one only of the two metals is a legal tender, but the other also is coined, and allowed to pass for whatever value the market assigns to it.[1]

When this plan is adopted, it is naturally the more costly metal which is left to be bought and sold as an article of commerce. But nations which, like England, adopt the more costly of the two as their standard, resort to a different expedient for retaining them both in circulation, namely, to make silver a legal tender, but only for small payments. In England, no one can be compelled to receive silver in payment for a larger amount than forty shillings. With this regulation there is necessarily combined another, namely, that silver coin should be rated, in comparison with gold, somewhat above its intrinsic value ; that there should not be, in twenty shillings, as much silver as is worth a sovereign : for if there were, a very slight turn of the market in its favour would make it worth more than a sovereign, and it would be profitable to melt the silver coin. The over-valuation of the silver coin creates an inducement to buy silver and send it to the Mint to be coined, since it is given back at a higher value than properly belongs to it : this, however, has been guarded

---

[1] [The following passage, which occurred in the original ed. (1848) at this point, was omitted in the 3rd ed. (1852) :

" This is the case in France. Silver alone is (I believe) a legal tender, and all sums are expressed and accounts kept in francs, a silver coin. Gold is also coined, for convenience, but does not pass at a fixed valuation : the twenty francs marked on a napoleon are merely nominal, napoleons being never to be bought for that sum, but always bearing a small premium, or agio as it is called ; though, as the agio is very trifling, (the bullion value differing very little from twenty francs), it is seldom possible to pass a napoleon for more than that sum in ordinary retail transactions. Silver, then, is the real money of the country, and gold coin only a merchandise ; but, though not a legal tender, it answers all the real purposes of one, since no creditor is at all likely to refuse receiving it at the market price, in payment of his debt."]

against, by limiting the quantity of the silver coinage, which is not left, like that of gold, to the discretion of individuals, but is determined by the government, and restricted to the amount supposed to be required for small payments.   The only precaution necessary is, not to put so high a valuation upon the silver, as to hold out a strong temptation to private coining.[1]

[1] [See Appendix U.   *Bimetallism.*]

CHAPTER XI

§ 1. The functions of credit have been a subject of as much misunderstanding and as much confusion of ideas, as any single topic in Political Economy. This is not owing to any peculiar difficulty in the theory of the subject, but to the complex nature of some of the mercantile phenomena arising from the forms in which credit clothes itself ; by which attention is diverted from the properties of credit in general, to the peculiarities of its particular forms.

As a specimen of the confused notions entertained respecting the nature of credit, we may advert to the exaggerated language so often used respecting its national importance. Credit has a great, but not, as many people seem to suppose, a magical power ; it cannot make something out of nothing. How often is an extension of credit talked of as equivalent to a creation of capital, or as if credit actually were capital. It seems strange that there should be any need to point out, that credit being only permission to use the capital of another person, the means of production cannot be increased by it, but only transferred. If the borrower's means of production and of employing labour are increased by the credit given him, the lender's are as much diminished. The same sum cannot be used as capital both by the owner and also by the person to whom it is lent : it cannot supply its entire value in wages, tools, and materials, to two sets of labourers at once. It is true that the capital which A has borrowed from B, and makes use of in his business, still forms part of the wealth of B for other purposes : he can enter into arrangements in reliance on it, and can borrow, when needful, an equivalent sum on the security of it ; so that to a superficial eye it might seem as if both B and A had the use of it at once. But the smallest consideration will show that when B has parted with his capital to A, the use of it as capital rests with A alone, and that B has no other service from it than in so far as his ultimate claim upon it serves him to obtain the use of another capital from a third person C.   All capital (not his own) of which any person has really the use, is, and must be, so much subtracted from the capital of some one else.*

§ 2.   But though credit is but a transfer of capital from hand to hand, it is generally, and naturally, a transfer to hands more competent to employ the capital efficiently in production.   If there were no such thing as credit, or if, from general insecurity and want of confidence, it were scantily practised, many persons who possess more or less of capital, but who, from their occupations, or for want of the necessary skill and knowledge, cannot personally superintend its employment, would derive no benefit from it : their funds would either lie idle, or would be, perhaps, wasted and annihilated in unskilful attempts to make them yield a profit.   All this capital is now lent at interest, and made available for production.   Capital thus circumstanced forms a large portion of the productive resources of any commercial country ; and is naturally attracted to those producers or traders who, being in the greatest business, have the means of employing it to most advantage ; because such are both the most desirous to obtain it, and able to give the best security. Although, therefore, the productive funds of the country are not increased by credit, they are called into a more complete state of productive activity.   As the confidence on which credit is grounded

---

* [1865] To make the proposition in the text strictly true, a corrective, though a very slight one, requires to be made.   The circulating medium existing in a country at a given time, is partly employed in purchases for productive, and partly for unproductive consumption.   According as a larger proportion of it is employed in the one way or in the other, the real capital of the country is greater or less.   If, then, an addition were made to the circulating medium in the hands of unproductive consumers exclusively, a larger portion of the existing stock of commodities would be bought for unproductive consumption, and a smaller for a productive, which state of things, while it lasted, would be equivalent to a diminution of capital ; and on the contrary, if the addition made be to the portion of the circulating medium which is in the hands of producers, and destined for their business, a greater portion of the commodities in the country will for the present be employed as capital, and a less portion unproductively.   Now an effect of this latter character naturally attends some extensions of credit, especially when taking place in the form of bank notes, or other instruments of exchange.   The additional bank notes are, in ordinary course, first issued to producers or dealers, to be employed as capital ; and though the stock of commodities in the country is no greater than before, yet as a greater share of that stock now comes by purchase into the hands of producers and dealers, to that extent what would have been unproductively consumed is applied to production, and there is a real increase of capital.   The effect ceases, and a counter-process takes place, when the additional credit is stopped, and the notes called in.

extends itself, means are developed by which even the smallest portions of capital, the sums which each person keeps by him to meet contingencies, are made available for productive uses. The principal instruments for this purpose are banks of deposit. Where these do not exist, a prudent person must keep a sufficient sum unemployed in his own possession, to meet every demand which he has even a slight reason for thinking himself liable to. When the practice, however, has grown up of keeping this reserve not in his own custody but with a banker, many small sums, previously lying idle, becoming aggregated in the banker's hands ; and the banker, being taught by experience what proportion of the amount is likely to be wanted in a given time, and knowing that if one depositor happens to require more than the average, another will require less, is able to lend the remainder, that is, the far greater part, to producers and dealers : thereby adding the amount, not indeed to the capital in existence, but to that in employment, and making a corresponding addition to the aggregate production of the community.

While credit is thus indispensable for rendering the whole capital of the country productive, it is also a means by which the industrial talent of the country is turned to better account for purposes of production. Many a person who has either no capital of his own, or very little, but who has qualifications for business which are known and appreciated by some possessors of capital, is enabled to obtain either advances in money, or more frequently goods on credit, by which his industrial capacities are made instrumental to the increase of the public wealth ; and this benefit will be reaped far more largely, whenever, through better laws and better education, the community shall have made such progress in integrity, that personal character can be accepted as a sufficient guarantee not only against dishonestly appropriating, but against dishonestly risking, what belongs to another.

Such are, in the most general point of view, the uses of credit to the productive resources of the world. But these considerations only apply to the credit given to the industrious classes—to producers and dealers. Credit given by dealers to unproductive consumers is never an addition, but always a detriment, to the sources of public wealth. It makes over in temporary use, not the capital of the unproductive classes to the productive, but that of the productive to the unproductive. If A, a dealer, supplies goods to B, a landowner or annuitant, to be paid for at the end of five years, as much of the capital of A as is equal to the value of these goods

remains for five years unproductive. During such a period, if payment had been made at once, the sum might have been several times
expended and replaced, and goods to the amount might have been
several times produced, consumed, and reproduced: consequently
B's withholding 100*l.* for five years, even if he pays at last, has cost
to the labouring classes of the community during that period an
absolute loss of probably several times that amount.   A, individually, is compensated, by putting a higher price upon his goods,
which is ultimately paid by B : but there is no compensation
made to the labouring classes, the chief sufferers by every
diversion of capital, whether permanently or temporarily, to
unproductive uses.   The country has had 100*l.* less of capital
during those five years, B having taken that amount from A's
capital, and spent it unproductively, in anticipation of his own
means, and having only after five years set apart a sum from his
income and converted it into capital for the purpose of indemnifying A.

§ 3.   Thus far of the general function of Credit in production.
It is not a productive power in itself, though, without it, the productive powers already existing could not be brought into complete
employment.   But a more intricate portion of the theory of Credit
is its influence on prices ; the chief cause of most of the mercantile
phenomena which perplex observers.   In a state of commerce in
which much credit is habitually given, general prices at any moment
depend much more upon the state of credit than upon the quantity of
money.   For credit, though it is not productive power, is purchasing
power ; and a person who, having credit, avails himself of it in the
purchase of goods, creates just as much demand for the goods, and
tends quite as much to raise their price, as if he made an equal
amount of purchases with ready money.

The credit which we are now called upon to consider, as a distinct
purchasing power, independent of money, is of course not credit in
its simplest form, that of money lent by one person to another, and
paid directly into his hands ; for when the borrower expends this in
purchases, he makes the purchases with money, not credit, and
exerts no purchasing power over and above that conferred by the
money.   The forms of credit which create purchasing power are
those in which no money passes at the time, and very often none
passes at all, the transaction being included with a mass of other
transactions in an account, and nothing paid but a balance.   This

takes place in a variety of ways, which we shall proceed to examine, beginning, as is our custom, with the simplest.

First : Suppose A and B to be two dealers, who have transactions with each other both as buyers and as sellers. A buys from B on credit. B does the like with respect to A. At the end of the year, the sum of A's debts to B is set against the sum of B's debts to A, and it is ascertained to which side a balance is due. This balance, which may be less than the amount of many of the transactions singly, and is necessarily less than the sum of the transactions, is all that is paid in money ; and perhaps even this is not paid, but carried over in an account current to the next year. A single payment of a hundred pounds may in this manner suffice to liquidate a long series of transactions, some of them to the value of thousands.

But secondly : The debts of A to B may be paid without the intervention of money, even though there be no reciprocal debts of B to A. A may satisfy B by making over to him a debt due to himself from a third person, C. This is conveniently done by means of a written instrument, called a bill of exchange, which is, in fact, a transferable order by a creditor upon his debtor, and when accepted by the debtor, that is, authenticated by his signature, becomes an acknowledgment of debt.

§ 4. Bills of exchange were first introduced to save the expense and risk of transporting the precious metals from place to place. " Let it be supposed," says Mr. Henry Thornton,* " that there are in London ten manufacturers who sell their article to ten shopkeepers in York, by whom it is retailed ; and that there are in York ten manufacturers of another commodity, who sell it 'o ten shopkeepers in London. There would be no occasion for the ten shopkeepers in London to send yearly to York guineas for the payment of the York manufacturers, and for the ten York shopkeepers to send yearly as many guineas to London. It would only be necessary for the York manufacturers to receive from each of the shopkeepers at their own door the money in question, giving in return letters which should acknowledge the receipt of it ; and which should also direct the money, lying ready in the hands of their debtors in London, to be paid to the London manufacturers, so as to cancel the debt in London

---

* *Enquiry into the Nature and Effects of the Paper Credit of Great Britain,* p. 24. This work, published in 1802, is even now [1848] the clearest exposition that I am acquainted with, in the English language, of the modes in which credit is given and taken in a mercantile community.

in the same manner as that at York. The expense and the risk of all transmission of money would thus be saved. Letters ordering the transfer of the debt are termed, in the language of the present day, bills of exchange. They are bills by which the debt of one person is exchanged for the debt of another ; and the debt, perhaps, which is due in one place, for the debt due in another."

Bills of exchange having been found convenient as means of paying debts at distant places without the expense of transporting the precious metals, their use was afterwards greatly extended from another motive. It is usual in every trade to give a certain length of credit for goods bought : three months, six months, a year, even two years, according to the convenience or custom of the particular trade. A dealer who has sold goods, for which he is to be paid in six months, but who desires to receive payment sooner, draws a bill on his debtor payable in six months, and gets the bill discounted by a banker or other money-lender, that is, transfers the bill to him, receiving the amount, minus interest for the time it has still to run. It has become one of the chief functions of bills of exchange to serve as a means by which a debt due from one person can thus be made available for obtaining credit from another. The convenience of the expedient has led to the frequent creation of bills of exchange not grounded on any debt previously due to the drawer of the bill by the person on whom it is drawn. These are called *accommodation* bills ; and sometimes, with a tinge of disapprobation, *fictitious* bills. Their nature is so clearly stated, and with such judicious remarks, by the author whom I have just quoted, that I shall transcribe the entire passage.*

" A, being in want of 100*l.*, requests B to accept a note or bill drawn at two months, which B, therefore, on the face of it, is bound to pay ; it is understood, however, that A will take care either to discharge the bill himself, or to furnish B with the means of paying it. A obtains ready money for the bill on the joint credit of the two parties. A fulfils his promise of paying it when due, and thus concludes the transaction. This service rendered by B to A is, however, not unlikely to be requited, at a more or less distant period, by a similar acceptance of a bill on A, drawn and discounted for B's convenience.

" Let us now compare such a bill with a real bill. Let us consider in what points they differ, or seem to differ ; and in what they agree.

" They agree, inasmuch as each is a discountable article ; each

* Pp. 29–33.

has also been created for the purpose of being discounted ; and each is, perhaps, discounted in fact. Each, therefore, serves equally to supply means of speculation to the merchant. So far, moreover, as bills and notes constitute what is called the circulating medium, or paper currency of the country, and prevent the use of guineas, the fictitious and the real bill are upon an equality ; and if the price of commodities be raised in proportion to the quantity of paper currency, the one contributes to that rise exactly in the same manner as the other.

" Before we come to the points in which they differ, let us advert to one point in which they are commonly supposed to be unlike ; but in which they cannot be said always or necessarily to differ.

" Real notes (it is sometimes said) represent actual property. There are actual goods in existence, which are the counterpart to every real note. Notes which are not drawn in consequence of a sale of goods, are a species of false wealth, by which a nation is deceived. These supply only an imaginary capital ; the others indicate one that is real.

" In answer to this statement it may be observed, first, that the notes given in consequence of a real sale of goods cannot be considered as on that account *certainly* representing any actual property. Suppose that A sells 100*l.* worth of goods to B at six months' credit, and takes a bill at six months for it; and that B, within a month after, sells the same goods, at a like credit, to C, taking a like bill ; and again, that C, after another month, sells them to D, taking a like bill, and so on. There may then, at the end of six months, be six bills of 100*l.* each, existing at the same time ; and every one of these may possibly have been discounted. Of all these bills, then, only one represents any actual property.

" In order to justify the supposition that a real bill (as it is called) represents actual property, there ought to be some power in the bill-holder to prevent the property which the bill represents, from being turned to other purposes than that of paying the bill in question. No such power exists ; neither the man who holds the real bill, nor the man who discounts it, has any property in the specific goods for which it was given : he as much trusts to the general ability to pay of the giver of the bill, as the holder of any fictitious bill does. The fictitious bill may, in many cases, be a bill given by a person having a large and known capital, a part of which the fictitious bill may be said in that case to represent. The supposition that real bills represent property, and that fictitious bills do not, seems, therefore, to be one by which more than justice is done to one of these species of bills, and something less than justice to the other.

" We come next to some points in which they differ.

" First, the fictitious note, or note of accommodation, is liable to the objection that it professes to be what it is not. This objection, however, lies only against those fictitious bills which are passed as real. In many cases it is sufficiently obvious what they áre. Secondly, the fictitious bill is, in general, less likely to be punctually paid than the real one. There is a general presumption, that the dealer in fictitious bills is a man who is a more adventurous speculator than he who carefully abstains from them. It follows, thirdly, that fictitious bills, besides being less safe, are less subject to limitation as to their quantity. The extent of a man's actual sales forms some limit to the amount of his real notes ; and as it is highly desirable in commerce that credit should be dealt out to all persons in some sort of regular and due proportion, the measure of a man's actual sales, certified by the appearance of his bills drawn in virtue of those sales, is some rule in the case, though a very imperfect one in many respects.

" A fictitious bill, or bill of accommodation, is evidently in substance the same as any common promissory note ; and even better in this respect, that there is but one security to the promissory note, whereas in the case of the bill of accommodation, there are two. So much jealousy subsists lest traders should push their means of raising money too far, that paper, the same in its general nature with that which is given, being the only paper which can be given, by men out of business, is deemed somewhat discreditable when coming from a merchant. And because such paper, when in the merchant's hand, necessarily imitates the paper which passes on the occasion of a sale of goods, the epithet fictitious has been cast upon it ; an epithet which has seemed to countenance the confused and mistaken notion, that there is something altogether false and delusive in the nature of a certain part both of the paper and of the apparent wealth of the country."

A bill of exchange, when merely discounted, and kept in the portfolio of the discounter until it falls due, does not perform the functions or supply the place of money, but is itself bought and sold for money. It is no more currency than the public funds, or any other securities. But when a bill drawn upon one person is paid to another (or even to the same person) in discharge of a debt or a pecuniary claim, it does something for which, if the bill did not exist, money would be required : it performs the functions of currency. This is a use to which bills of exchange are often applied. "They not only," continues Mr. Thornton,* "spare the use of ready money; they also occupy its place in many cases. Let us imagine a farmer in the country to discharge a debt of 10*l.* to his neighbouring grocer, by giving him a bill for that sum, drawn on his cornfactor in London for grain sold in the metropolis ; and the grocer to transmit the bill, he having previously indorsed it, to a neighbouring sugar-baker, in discharge of a like debt ; and the sugar-baker to send it, when again indorsed, to a West India merchant in an outport, and the West India merchant to deliver it to his country banker, who also indorses it, and sends it into further circulation. The bill in this case will have effected five payments, exactly as if it were a 10*l.* note payable to a bearer on demand. A multitude of bills pass between trader and trader in the country, in the manner which has been described ; and they evidently form, in the strictest sense, a part of the circulating medium of the kingdom."

Many bills, both domestic and foreign, are at last presented for payment quite covered with indorsements, each of which represents either a fresh discounting, or a pecuniary transaction in which the bill has performed the functions of money. Within the present generation,[1] the circulating medium of Lancashire, for sums above five pounds, was almost entirely composed of such bills.

§ 5. A third form in which credit is employed as a substitute for currency, is that of promissory notes. A bill drawn upon any one and accepted by him, and a note of hand by him promising to pay the same sum, are, as far as he is concerned, exactly equivalent, except that the former commonly bears interest and the latter generally does not ; and that the former is commonly payable only after a certain lapse of time, and the latter payable at sight. But it is chiefly in the latter form that it has become, in commercial countries, an express occupation to issue such substitutes for money. Dealers in money (as lenders by profession are improperly called) desire, like other dealers, to stretch their operations beyond what can be carried on by their own means : they wish' to lend, not their capital merely, but their credit, and not only such portion of their

* P. 40.
[1] [So from the 4th ed. (1857). The original (1848) ran : " Up to twenty years ago."]

credit as consists of funds actually deposited with them, but their power of obtaining credit from the public generally, so far as they think they can safely employ it. This is done in a very convenient manner by lending their own promissory notes payable to bearer on demand : the borrower being willing to accept these as so much money, because the credit of the lender makes other people willingly receive them on the same footing, in purchases or other payments. These notes, therefore, perform all the functions of currency, and render an equivalent amount of money which was previously in circulation, unnecessary. As, however, being payable on demand, they may be at any time returned on the issuer, and money demanded for them, he must, on pain of bankruptcy, keep by him as much money. as will enable him to meet any claims of that sort which can be expected to occur within the time necessary for providing himself with more : and prudence also requires that he should not attempt to issue notes beyond the amount which experience shows can remain in circulation without being presented for payment.

The convenience of this mode of (as it were) coining credit, having once been discovered, governments have availed themselves of the same expedient, and have issued their own promissory notes in payment of their expenses ; a resource the more useful, because it is the only mode in which they are able to borrow money without paying interest, their promises to pay on demand being, in the estimation of the holders, equivalent to money in hand. The practical differences between such government notes and the issues of private bankers, and the further diversities of which this class of substitutes for money are susceptible, will be considered presently.

§ 6. A fourth mode of making credit answer the purposes of money, by which, when carried far enough, money may be very completely superseded, consists in making payments by cheques. The custom of keeping the spare cash reserved for immediate use or against contingent demands, in the hands of a banker, and making all payments, except small ones, by orders on bankers, is in this country spreading to a continually larger portion of the public. If the person making the payment, and the person receiving it, keep their money with the same banker, the payment takes place without any intervention of money, by the mere transfer of its amount in the banker's books from the credit of the payer to that of the receiver. If all persons in London kept their cash at the same banker's, and made all their payments by means of cheques, no money would be required or used for any transactions beginning and terminating in London. This ideal limit is almost attained in fact, so far as regards transactions between dealers. It is chiefly in the retail transactions between dealers and consumers, and in the payment of wages, that money or bank notes now pass, and then only when the amounts are small. In London, even shop-keepers of any amount of capital or extent of business have generally an account with a banker ; which, besides the safety and convenience of the practice, is to their advantage in another respect, by giving them an understood claim to have their bills discounted in cases when they could not otherwise expect it. As for the merchants and larger dealers, they habitually make all payments in the course of their business by cheques. They do not, however, all deal with the same banker, and when A gives a cheque to B, B usually pays it not into the same but into some other bank. But the convenience of business has given birth to an arrangement which makes all the banking houses of the City of London, for certain purposes, virtually one establishment. A banker does not send the cheques which are paid into his banking house, to the banks on which they are drawn, and demand money for them. There is a building called the Clearing-house, to which every City banker sends, each afternoon, all the cheques on other bankers which he has received during the day, and they are there exchanged for the cheques on him which have come into the hands of other bankers, the balances only being paid in money ; [1] or even these not in money, but in cheques on the Bank of England. By this contrivance, all the business transactions of the City of London during that day, amount-ing often to millions of pounds, and a vast amount besides of country transactions, represented by bills which country bankers have drawn upon their London correspondents, are [1848] liquidated by payments not exceeding on the average 200,000*l.**

By means of the various instruments of credit which have now

[1] [The concluding clause of this sentence was added in the 4th ed. (1857).]
* According to Mr. Tooke (*Inquiry into the Currency Principle*, p. 27) the adjustments of the Clearing-house " in the year 1839 amounted to 954,401,600*l.*, making an average amount of payments of upwards of 3,000,000*l.* of bills of exchange and cheques daily effected through the medium of little more than 200,000*l.* of bank notes."—[1862] At present a very much greater amount of transactions is daily liquidated, without bank notes at all, cheques on the Bank of England supplying their place.

been explained, the immense business of a country like Great
Britain is transacted with an amount of the precious metals sur-
prisingly small ; many times smaller, in proportion to the pecuniary
value of the commodities bought and sold, than is found necessary
in France, or any other country in which, the habit and the disposition to give credit not being so generally diffused, these " economizing expedients," as they have been called, are not practised to
the same extent.   What becomes of the money thus superseded
in its functions, and by what process it is made to disappear from
circulation, are questions the discussion of which must be for a
short time postponed.

CHAPTER XII

§ 1. HAVING now formed a general idea of the modes in which credit is made available as a substitute for money, we have to consider in what manner the use of these substitutes affects the value of money, or, what is equivalent, the prices of commodities. It is hardly necessary to say that the permanent value of money— the natural and average prices of commodities—are not in question here. These are determined by the cost of producing or of obtaining the precious metals. An ounce of gold or silver will in the long run exchange for as much of every other commodity, as can be produced or imported at the same cost with itself. And an order, or note of hand, or bill payable at sight, for an ounce of gold, while the credit of the giver is unimpaired, is worth neither more nor less than the gold itself.

It is not, however, with ultimate or average, but with immediate and temporary prices, that we are now concerned. These, as we have seen, may deviate very widely from the standard of cost of production. Among other causes of fluctuation, one we have found to be the quantity of money in circulation. Other things being the same, an increase of the money in circulation raises prices, a diminution lowers them. If more money is thrown into circulation than the quantity which can circulate at a value conformable to its cost of production, the value of money, so long as the excess lasts, will remain below the standard of cost of production, and general prices will be sustained above the natural rate.

But we have now found that there are other things, such as bank notes, bills of exchange, and cheques, which circulate as money, and perform all the functions of it : and the question arises, Do these various substitutes operate on prices in the same manner as money itself ? Does an increase in the quantity of transferable paper tend to raise prices, in the same manner and degree as an increase in the quantity of money ? There has been no small amount of discussion on this point among writers of currency, without any result so conclusive as to have yet obtained general assent.

I apprehend that bank notes, bills, or cheques, as such, do not act on prices at all. What does act on prices is Credit, in whatever shape given, and whether it gives rise to any transferable instruments capable of passing into circulation or not.

I proceed to explain and substantiate this opinion.

§ 2. Money acts upon prices in no other way than by being tendered in exchange for commodities. The demand which influences the prices of commodities consists of the money offered for them. But the money offered is not the same thing with the money possessed. It is sometimes less, sometimes very much more. In the long run indeed, the money which people lay out will be neither more nor less than the money which they have to lay out : but this is far from being the case at any given time. Sometimes they keep money by them for fear of an emergency, or in expectation of a more advantageous opportunity for expending it. In that case the money is said not to be in circulation : in plainer language, it is not offered, nor about to be offered, for commodities. Money not in circulation has no effect on prices. The converse, however, is a much commoner case ; people make purchases with money not in their possession. An article, for instance, which is paid for by a cheque on a banker, is bought with money which not only is not in the payer's possession, but generally not even in the banker's, having been lent by him (all but the usual reserve) to other persons. We just now made the imaginary supposition that all persons dealt with a bank, and all with the same bank, payments being universally made by cheques. In this ideal case, there would be no money anywhere except in the hands of the banker : who might then safely part with all of it, by selling it as bullion, or lending it, to be sent out of the country in exchange for goods or foreign securities. But though there would then be no money in possession, or ultimately perhaps even in existence, money would be offered, and commodities bought with it, just as at present. People would continue to reckon their incomes and their capitals in money, and to make their usual purchases with orders for the receipt of a thing which would have literally ceased to exist. There would be in all this nothing to complain of, so long as the money, in disappearing, left an equivalent value in other things, applicable when required to the reimbursement of those to whom the money originally belonged.

In the case however of payment by cheques, the purchases are at any rate made, though not with money in the buyer's possession, yet with money to which he has a right. But he may make purchases with money which he only expects to have, or even only pretends to expect. He may obtain goods in return for his acceptances payable at a future time; or on his note of hand; or on a simple book credit, that is, on a mere promise to pay. All these purchases have exactly the same effect on price, as if they were made with ready money. The amount of purchasing power which a person can exercise is composed of all the money in his possession or due to him, and of all his credit. For exercising the whole of this power he finds a sufficient motive only under peculiar circumstances; but he always possesses it; and the portion of it which he at any time does exercise, is the measure of the effect which he produces on price.

Suppose that, in the expectation that some commodity will rise in price, he determines, not only to invest in it all his ready money, but to take up on credit, from the producers or importers, as much of it as their opinion of his resources will enable him to obtain. Every one must see that by thus acting he produces a greater effect on price, than if he limited his purchases to the money he has actually in hand. He creates a demand for the article to the full amount of his money and credit taken together, and raises the price proportionally to both. And this effect is produced, though none of the written instruments called substitutes for currency may be called into existence; though the transaction may give rise to no bill of exchange, nor to the issue of a single bank note. The buyer, instead of taking a mere book credit, might have given a bill for the amount; or might have paid for the goods with bank notes borrowed for that purpose from a banker, thus making the purchase not on his own credit with the seller, but on the banker's credit with the seller, and his own with the banker. Had he done so, he would have produced as great an effect on price as by a simple purchase to the same amount on a book credit, but no greater effect. The credit itself, not the form and mode in which it is given, is the operating cause.

§ 3. The inclination of the mercantile public to increase their demand for commodities by making use of all or much of their credit as a purchasing power, depends on their expectation of profit. When there is a general impression that the price of some commodity is likely to rise, from an extra demand, a short crop, obstruction to importation, or any other cause, there is a disposition among dealers to increase their stocks, in order to profit by the expected rise. This disposition tends in itself to produce the effect which it looks forward to, a rise of price : and if the rise is considerable and progressive, other speculators are attracted, who, so long as the price has not begun to fall, are willing to believe that it will continue rising. These, by further purchases, produce a further advance : and thus a rise of price for which there were originally some rational grounds, is often heightened by merely speculative purchases, until it greatly exceeds what the original grounds will justify. After a time this begins to be perceived ; the price ceases to rise, and the holders, thinking it time to realize their gains, are anxious to sell. Then the price begins to decline : the holders rush into the market to avoid a still greater loss, and, few being willing to buy in a falling market, the price falls much more suddenly than it rose. Those who have bought at a higher price than reasonable calculation justified, and who have been overtaken by the revulsion before they had realized, are losers in proportion to the greatness of the fall, and to the quantity of the commodity which they hold, or have bound themselves to pay for.

Now all these effects might take place in a community to which credit was unknown : the prices of some commodities might rise from speculation, to an extravagant height, and then fall rapidly back. But if there were no such thing as credit, this could hardly happen with respect to commodities generally. If all purchases were made with ready money, the payment of increased prices for some articles would draw an unusual proportion of the money of the community into the markets for those articles, and must therefore draw it away from some other class of commodities, and thus lower their prices. The vacuum might, it is true, be partly filled up by increased rapidity of circulation ; and in this manner the money of the community is virtually increased in a time of speculative activity, because people keep little of it by them, but hasten to lay it out in some tempting adventure as soon as possible after they receive it. This resource, however, is limited : on the whole, people cannot, while the quantity of money remains the same, lay out much more of it in some things, without laying out less in others. But what they cannot do by ready money, they can do by an extension of credit.

When people go into the market and purchase with money which they hope to receive hereafter, they are drawing upon an unlimited, not a limited fund. Speculation thus supported, may be going on in any number of commodities, without disturbing the regular course of business in others. It might even be going on in all commodities at once. We could imagine that in an epidemic fit of the passion of gambling, all dealers, instead of giving only their accustomed orders to the manufacturers or growers of their commodity, commenced buying up all of it which they could procure, as far as their capital and credit would go. All prices would rise enormously, even if there were no increase of money, and no paper credit, but a mere extension of purchases on book credits. After a time those who had bought would wish to sell, and prices would collapse.

This is the ideal extreme case of what is called a commercial crisis. There is said to be a commercial crisis, when a great number of merchants and traders at once, either have, or apprehend that they shall have, a difficulty in meeting their engagements. The most usual cause of this general embarrassment is the recoil of prices after they have been raised by a spirit of speculation, intense in degree, and extending to many commodities. Some accident which excites expectations of rising prices, such as the opening of a new foreign market, or simultaneous indications of a short supply of several great articles of commerce, sets speculation at work in several leading departments at once. The prices rise, and the holders realize, or appear to have the power of realizing, great gains. In certain states of the public mind, such examples of rapid increase of fortune call forth numerous imitators, and speculation not only goes much beyond what is justified by the original grounds for expecting rise of price, but extends itself to articles in which there never was any such ground : these, however, rise like the rest as soon as speculation sets in. At periods of this kind a great extension of credit takes place. Not only do all whom the contagion reaches employ their credit much more freely than usual ; but they really have more credit, because they seem to be making unusual gains, and because a generally reckless and adventurous feeling prevails, which disposes people to give as well as take credit more largely than at other times, and give it to persons not entitled to it. In this manner, in the celebrated speculative year 1825, and at various other periods during the present century, the prices of many of the principal articles of commerce rose greatly, without any fall in others, so that general prices might, without incorrectness, be said to have risen.

When, after such a rise, the reaction comes, and prices begin to fall, though at first perhaps only through the desire of the holders to realize, speculative purchases cease : but were this all, prices would only fall to the level from which they rose, or to that which is justified by the state of the consumption and of the supply. They fall, however, much lower ; for as, when prices were rising, and everybody apparently making a fortune, it was easy to obtain almost any amount of credit, so now, when everybody seems to be losing, and many fail entirely, it is with difficulty that firms of known solidity can obtain even the credit to which they are accustomed, and which it is the greatest inconvenience to them to be without ; because all dealers have engagements to fulfil, and nobody feeling sure that the portion of his means which he has entrusted to others will be available in time, no one likes to part with ready money, or to postpone his claim to it. To these rational considerations there is superadded, in extreme cases, a panic as unreasoning as the previous over-confidence ; money is borrowed for short periods at almost any rate of interest, and sales of goods for immediate payment are made at almost any sacrifice. Thus general prices, during a commercial revulsion, fall as much below the usual level as during the previous period of speculation they have risen above it : the fall, as well as the rise, originating not in anything affecting money, but in the state of credit ; an unusually extended employment of credit during the earlier period, followed by a great diminution, never amounting, however, to an entire cessation of it, in the later.

It is not, however, universally true that the contraction of credit, characteristic of a commercial crisis, must have been preceded by an extraordinary and irrational extension of it. There are other causes ; and one of the more recent crises, that of 1847, is an instance, having been preceded by no particular extension of credit, and by no speculations ; except those in railway shares, which, though in many cases extravagant enough, yet being carried on mostly with that portion of means which the speculators could afford to lose, were not calculated to produce the wide-spread ruin which arises from vicissitudes of price in the commodities in which men habitually deal, and in which the bulk of their capital is invested. The crisis of 1847 belonged to another class of mercantile phenomena. There occasionally happens a concurrence of circumstances tending to withdraw from the loan market a considerable portion of the capital which usually supplies it. These circumstances, in the present case, were great foreign payments, (occasioned by a high price of cotton and an unprecedented importation of food,) together with the continual demands on the circulating capital of the country by railway calls and the loan transactions of railway companies, for the purpose of being converted into fixed capital and made unavailable for future lending. These various demands fell principally, as such demands always do, on the loan market. A great, though not the greatest, part of the imported food was actually paid for by the proceeds of a government loan. The extra payments which purchasers of corn and cotton, and railway shareholders, found themselves obliged to make, were either made with their own spare cash, or with money raised for the occasion. On the first supposition, they were made by withdrawing deposits from bankers, and thus cutting off a part of the streams which fed the loan market; on the second supposition, they were made by actual drafts on the loan market, either by the sale of securities, or by taking up money at interest. This combination of a fresh demand for loans, with a curtailment of the capital disposable for them, raised the rate of interest, and made it impossible to borrow except on the very best security. Some firms, therefore, which by an improvident and unmercantile mode of conducting business had allowed their capital to become either temporarily or permanently unavailable, became unable to command that perpetual renewal of credit which had previously enabled them to struggle on. These firms stopped payment: their failure involved more or less deeply many other firms which had trusted them; and, as usual in such cases, the general distrust, commonly called a panic, began to set in, and might have produced a destruction of credit equal to that of 1825, had not circumstances, which may almost be called accidental, given to a very simple measure of the government (the suspension of the Bank Charter Act of 1844) a fortunate power of allaying panic, to which, when considered in itself, it had no sort of claim.*

§ 4. The general operation of credit upon prices being such as we have described, it is evident that if any particular mode or form of credit is calculated to have a greater operation on prices than

---

* [1865] The commercial difficulties, not however amounting to a commercial crisis, of 1864, had essentially the same origin. Heavy payments for cotton imported at high prices, and large investments in banking and other joint stock projects, combined with the loan operations of foreign governments, made such large drafts upon the loan market as to raise the rate of discount on mercantile bills as high as nine per cent.

others, it can only be by giving greater facility, or greater encouragement, to the multiplication of credit transactions generally. If
bank notes, for instance, or bills, have a greater effect on prices
than book credits, it is not by any difference in the transactions
themselves, which are essentially the same, whether taking place
in the one way or in the other : it must be that there are likely to be
more of them. If credit is likely to be more extensively used as a
purchasing power when bank notes or bills are the instruments used,
than when the credit is given by mere entries in an account, to that
extent and no more there is ground for ascribing to the former
a greater power over the markets than belongs to the latter.

Now it appears that there is some such distinction. As far as
respects the particular transactions, it makes no difference in the
effect on price whether A buys goods of B on simple credit, or gives a
bill for them, or pays for them with bank notes lent to him by a
banker C. The difference is in a subsequent stage. If A has bought
the goods on a book credit, there is no obvious or convenient mode
by which B can make A's debt to him a means of extending his own
credit. Whatever credit he has, will be due to the general opinion
entertained of his solvency ; he cannot specifically pledge A's debt
to a third person, as a security for money lent or goods bought.
But if A has given him a bill for the amount, he can get this
discounted, which is the same thing as borrowing money on the joint
credit of A and himself : or he may pay away the bill in exchange
for goods, which is obtaining goods on the same joint credit. In
either case, here is a second credit transaction, grounded on the first,
and which would not have taken place if the first had been transacted
without the intervention of a bill. Nor need the transactions end
here. The bill may be again discounted, or again paid away for
goods, several times before it is itself presented for payment. Nor
would it be correct to say that these successive holders, if they had
not had the bill, might have attained their purpose by purchasing
goods on their own credit with the dealers. They may not all of
them be persons of credit, or they may already have stretched their
credit as far as it will go. And at all events, either money or goods
are more readily obtained on the credit of two persons than of one.
Nobody will pretend that it is as easy a thing for a merchant to
borrow a thousand pounds on his own credit, as to get a bill discounted to the same amount, when the drawee is of known solvency.

If we now suppose that A, instead of giving a bill, obtains a
loan of bank notes from a banker C, and with them pays B for his

goods, we shall find the difference to be still greater. B is now independent even of a discounter : A's bill would have been taken in payment only by those who were acquainted with his reputation for solvency, but a banker is a person who has credit with the public generally, and whose notes are taken in payment by every one, at least in his own neighbourhood : insomuch that, by a custom which has grown into law, payment in bank notes is a complete acquittance to the payer, whereas, if he has paid by a bill, he still remains liable to the debt, if the person on whom the bill is drawn fails to pay it when due. B therefore can expend the whole of the bank notes without at all involving his own credit ; and whatever power he had before of obtaining goods on book credit, remains to him unimpaired, in addition to the purchasing power he derives from the possession of the notes. The same remark applies to every person in succession, into whose hands the notes may come. It is only A, the first holder, (who used his credit to obtain the notes as a loan from the issuer,) who can possibly find the credit he possesses in other quarters abated by it ; and even in his case that result is not probable ; for though, in reason, and if all his circumstances were known, every draft already made upon his credit ought to diminish by so much his power of obtaining more, yet in practice the reverse more frequently happens, and his having been trusted by one person is supposed to be evidence that he may safely be trusted by others also.

It appears, therefore, that bank notes are a more powerful instrument for raising prices than bills, and bills than book credits. It does not, indeed, follow that credit *will* be more used because it *can* be. When the state of trade holds out no particular temptation to make large purchases on credit, dealers will use only a small portion of the credit power, and it will depend only on convenience whether the portion which they use will be taken in one form or in another. It is not until the circumstances of the markets, and the state of the mercantile mind, render many persons desirous of stretching their credit to an unusual extent, that the distinctive properties of the different forms of credit display themselves. Credit already stretched to the utmost in the form of book debts, would be susceptible of a great additional extension by means of bills, and of a still greater by means of bank notes. The first, because each dealer, in addition to his own credit, would be enabled to create a further purchasing pqwer out of the credit which he had himself given to others : the second, because the banker's credit with the

public at large, coined into notes, as bullion is coined into pieces of
money to make it portable and divisible, is so much purchasing
power superadded, in the hands of every successive holder, to that
which he may derive from his own credit. To state the matter
otherwise ; one single exertion of the credit-power in the form of
book credit is only the foundation of a single purchase : but if a
bill is drawn, that same portion of credit may serve for as many
purchases as the number of times the bill changes hands : while
every bank note issued renders the credit of the banker a purchasing power to that amount in the hands of all the successive
holders, without impairing any power they may possess of effecting
purchases on their own credit. Credit, in short, has exactly the
same purchasing power with money ; and as money tells upon
prices not simply in proportion to its amount, but to its amount
multiplied by the number of times it changes hands, so also does
credit ; and credit transferable from hand to hand is in that proportion more potent than credit which only performs one purchase.

§ 5.   All this purchasing power, however, is operative upon
prices only according to the proportion of it which is used ; and
the effect, therefore, is only felt in a state of circumstances calculated to lead to an unusually extended use of credit.   In such a state
of circumstances, that is, in speculative times, it cannot, I think, be
denied, that prices are likely to rise higher if the speculative purchases are made with bank notes, than when they are made with bills,
and when made by bills than when made by book credits.   This,
however, is of far less practical importance than might at first be
imagined ; because, in point of fact, speculative purchases are not,
in the great majority of cases, made either with bank notes or with
bills, but are made almost exclusively on book credits.   " Applications to the Bank for extended discount," says the highest authority
on such subjects,* (and the same thing must be true of applications
to other banks) " occur rarely if ever in the origin or progress of
extensive speculations in commodities.   These are entered into, for
the most part if not entirely, in the first instance, on credit, for the
length of term usual in the several trades ; thus entailing on the
parties no immediate necessity for borrowing so much as may be
wanted for the purpose beyond their own available capital.   This
applies particularly to speculative purchases of commodities on the
spot, with a view to resale.   But these generally form the smaller

* Tooke, *History of Prices*, vol. iv. pp. 125–6.

proportion of engagements on credit. By far the largest of those entered into on the prospect of a rise of prices, are such as have in view importations from abroad. The same remark, too, is applicable to the export of commodities, when a large proportion is on the credit of the shippers or their consignees. As long as circumstances hold out the prospect of a favourable result, the credit of the parties is generally sustained. If some of them wish to realize, there are others with capital and credit ready to replace them ; and if the events fully justify the grounds on which the speculative transactions were entered into (thus admitting of sales for consumption in time to replace the capital embarked) there is no unusual demand for borrowed capital to sustain them. It is only when by the vicissitudes of political events, or of the seasons, or other adventitious circumstances, the forthcoming supplies are found to exceed the computed rate of consumption, and a fall of prices ensues, that an increased demand for capital takes place ; the market rate of interest then rises, and increased applications are made to the Bank of England for discount." So that the multiplication of bank notes and other transferable paper does not, for the most part, accompany and facilitate the speculation ; but comes into play chiefly when the tide is turning, and difficulties begin to be felt.

Of the extraordinary height to which speculative transactions can be carried upon mere book credits, without the smallest addition to what is commonly called the currency, very few persons are at all aware. " The power of purchase," says Mr. Tooke,* " by persons having capital and credit, is much beyond anything that those who are unacquainted practically with speculative markets have any idea of. . . . A person having the reputation of capital enough for his regular business, and enjoying good credit in his trade, if he takes a sanguine view of the prospect of a rise of price of the article in which he deals, and is favoured by circumstances in the outset and progress of his speculation, may effect purchases to an extent perfectly enormous, compared with his capital." Mr. Tooke confirms this statement by some remarkable instances, exemplifying the immense purchasing power which may be exercised, and rise of price which may be produced, by credit not represented by either bank notes or bills of exchange.

" Amongst the earlier speculators for an advance in the price of tea, in consequence of our dispute with China in 1839, were several

* _Inquiry into the Currency Principle_, pp. 79 and 136–8,

retail grocers and tea-dealers. There was a general disposition among the trade to get in stock : that is, to lay in at once a quantity which would meet the probable demand from their customers for several months to come. Some, however, among them, more sanguine and adventurous than the rest, availed themselves of their credit with the importers and wholesale dealers, for purchasing quantities much beyond the estimated demand in their own business. As the purchases were made in the first instance ostensibly, and perhaps really, for the legitimate purposes and within the limits of their regular business, the parties were enabled to buy without the condition of any deposit ; whereas speculators, known to be such, are required to pay 2*l.* per chest, to cover any probable difference of price which might arise before the expiration of the prompt, which, for this article, is three months. Without, therefore, the outlay of a single farthing of actual capital or currency in any shape, they made purchases to a considerable extent ; and with the profit realized on the resale of a part of these purchases, they were enabled to pay the deposit on further quantities when required, as was the case when the extent of the purchases attracted attention.   In this way, the speculation went on at advancing prices (100 per cent and upwards) till nearly the expiration of the prompt ; and if at that time circumstances had been such as to justify the apprehension which at one time prevailed, that all future supplies would be cut off, the prices might have still further advanced, and at any rate not have retrograded.   In this case, the speculators might have realized, if not all the profit they had anticipated, a very handsome sum, upon which they might have been enabled to extend their business greatly, or to retire from it altogether, with a reputation for great sagacity in thus making their fortune.   But instead of this favourable result, it so happened that two or three cargoes of tea which had been transhipped were admitted, contrary to expectation, to entry on their arrival here, and it was found that further indirect shipments were in progress.   Thus the supply was increased beyond the calculation of the speculators : and, at the same time, the consumption had been diminished by the high price.   There was, consequently, a violent reaction on the market ; the speculators were unable to sell without such a sacrifice as disabled them from fulfilling their engagements, and several of them consequently failed.   Among these, one was mentioned, who having a capital not exceeding 1200*l.* which was locked up in his business, had contrived to buy 4000 chests, value above 80,000*l.*, the loss upon which was about 16,000*l.*

"The other example which I have to give, is that of the operation on the corn market between 1838 and 1842. There was an instance of a person who, when he entered on his extensive speculations, was, as it appeared by the subsequent examination of his affairs, possessed of a capital not exceeding 5000*l*., but being successful in the outset, and favoured by circumstances in the progress of his operations, he contrived to make purchases to such an extent, that when he stopped payment his engagements were found to amount to between 500,000*l*. and 600,000*l*. Other instances might be cited of parties without any capital at all, who, by dint of mere credit, were enabled, while the aspect of the market favoured their views, to make purchases to a very great extent.

" And be it observed, that these speculations, involving enormous purchases on little or no capital, were carried on in 1839 and 1840, when the money market was in its most contracted state ; or when, according to modern phraseology, there was the greatest scarcity of money."

But though the great instrument of speculative purchases is book credits, it cannot be contested that in speculative periods an increase does take place in the quantity both of bills of exchange and of bank notes. This increase, indeed, so far as bank notes are concerned, hardly ever takes place in the earliest stage of the speculations : advances from bankers (as Mr. Tooke observes) not being applied for in order to purchase, but in order to hold on without selling when the usual term of credit has expired, and the high price which was calculated on has not arrived. But the tea speculators mentioned by Mr. Tooke could not have carried their speculations beyond the three months which are the usual term of credit in their trade, unless they had been able to obtain advances from bankers, which, if the expectation of a rise of price had still continued, they probably could have done.

Since, then, credit in the form of bank notes is a more potent instrument for raising prices than book credits, an unrestrained power of resorting to this instrument may contribute to prolong and heighten the speculative rise of prices, and hence to aggravate the subsequent recoil. But in what degree ? and what importance ought we to ascribe to this possibility ? It may help us to form some judgment on this point, if we consider the proportion which the utmost increase of bank notes in a period of speculation, bears, I do not say to the whole mass of credit in the country, but to the bills of exchange alone. The average amount of bills in existence at any one time is supposed greatly to exceed [1848] a hundred millions sterling.* The bank note circulation of Great Britain and Ireland seldom exceeds forty millions, and the increase in speculative periods at most two or three. And even this, as we have seen, hardly ever comes into play until that advanced period of the speculation at which the tide shows signs of turning, and the dealers generally are rather thinking of the means of fulfilling their existing engagements, than meditating an extension of them : while the quantity of bills in existence is largely increased from the very commencement of the speculations.

§ 6. It is well known that, of late years, an artificial limitation of the issue of bank notes has been regarded by many political economists, and by a great portion of the public, as an expedient of supreme efficacy for preventing, and when it cannot prevent, for moderating, the fever of speculation ; and this opinion received the recognition and sanction of the legislature by the Currency Act of 1844. At the point, however, which our inquiries have reached, though we have conceded to bank notes a greater power over prices than is possessed by bills or book credits, we have not

* The most approved estimate is that of Mr. Leatham, grounded on the official returns of bill stamps issued.   The following are the results :—

Year.	Bills created in Great Britain and Ireland, founded on returns of Bill Stamps issued from the Stamp Office.	Average amount in circulation at one time in each year.
1832	£356,153,409	£89,038,352
1833	383,659,585	95,914,896
1834	379,155,052	94,788,763
1835	405,403,051	101,350,762
1836	485,943,473	121,485,868
1837	455,084,445	113,771,111
1838	465,504,041	116,376,010
1839	528,493,842	132,123,460

" Mr. Leatham," says Mr. Tooke, " gives the process by which, upon the data furnished by the returns of stamps, he arrives at these results ; and I am disposed to think that they are as near an approximation to the truth as the nature of the materials admits of arriving at."—*Inquiry into the Currency Principle*, p. 26.—[1862] Mr. Newmarch (Appendix No. 39 to *Report of the Committee on the Bank Acts* in 1857, and *History of Prices*, vol. vi. p. 587) shows grounds for the opinion that the total bill circulation in 1857 was not much less than 180 millions sterling and that it sometimes rises to 200 millions.

found reason to think that this superior efficacy has much share in producing the rise of prices which accompanies a period of speculation, nor consequently that any restraint applied to this one instrument can be efficacious to the degree which is often supposed, in moderating either that rise, or the recoil which follows it. We shall be still less inclined to think so, when we consider that there is a fourth form of credit transactions, by cheques on bankers, and transfers in a banker's books, which is exactly parallel in every respect to bank notes, giving equal facilities to an extension of credit, and capable of acting on prices quite as powerfully. In the words of Mr. Fullarton,* " there is not a single object at present attained through the agency of Bank of England notes, which might not be as effectually accomplished by each individual keeping an account with the bank, and transacting all his payments of five pounds and upwards by cheque." A bank, instead of lending its notes to a merchant or dealer, might open an account with him, and credit the account with the sum it had agreed to advance : on an understanding that he should not draw out that sum in any other mode than by drawing cheques against it in favour of those to whom he had occasion to make payments. These cheques might possibly even pass from hand to hand like bank notes; more commonly, however, the receiver would pay them into the hands of his own banker, and when he wanted the money, would draw a fresh cheque against it : and hence an objector may urge that as the original cheque would very soon be presented for payment, when it must be paid either in notes or in coin, notes or coin to an equal amount must be provided as the ultimate means of liquidation. It is not so, however. The person to whom the cheque is transferred may perhaps deal with the same banker, and the cheque may return to the very bank on which it was drawn : this is very often the case in country districts ; if so, no payment will be called for, but a simple transfer in the banker's books will settle the transaction. If the cheque is paid into a different bank, it will not be presented for payment, but liquidated by set-off against other cheques ; and in a state of circumstances favourable to a general extension of banking credits, a banker who has granted more credit, and has therefore more cheques drawn on him, will also have more cheques on other bankers paid to him, and will only have to provide notes or cash for the payment of balances ; for which purpose the ordinary

* *On the Regulation of Currencies*, p. 41.

reserve of prudent bankers, one-third of their liabilities, will abundantly suffice. Now, if he had granted the extension of credit by
means of an issue of his own notes, he must equally have retained,
in coin or Bank of England notes, the usual reserve : so that he
can, as Mr. Fullarton says, give every facility of credit by what
may be termed a cheque circulation, which he could give by a note
circulation.

This extension of credit by entries in a banker's books, has all
that superior efficiency in acting on prices, which we ascribed to
an extension by means of bank notes. As a bank note of 20l.,
paid to any one, gives him 20l. of purchasing power based on credit,
over and above whatever credit he had of his own, so does a cheque
paid to him do the same : for, although he may make no purchase
with the cheque itself, he deposits it with his banker, and can draw
against it. As this act of drawing a cheque against another which
has been exchanged and cancelled, can be repeated as often as a
purchase with a bank note, it effects the same increase of purchasing
power. The original loan, or credit, given by the banker to his
customer, is potentially multiplied as a means of purchase, in the
hands of the successive persons to whom portions of the credit are
paid away, just as the purchasing power of a bank note is multiplied
by the number of persons through whose hands it passes before it
is returned to the issuer.

These considerations abate very much from the importance of
any effect which can be produced in allaying the vicissitudes of
commerce, by so superficial a contrivance as the one so much relied
on of late, the restriction of the issue of bank notes by an artificial
rule. An examination of all the consequences of that restriction,
and an estimate of the reasons for and against it, must be deferred
until we have treated of the foreign exchanges, and the international
movements of bullion. At present we are only concerned with
the general theory of prices, of which the different influence of
different kinds of credit is an essential part.

§ 7.[1]   There has been a great amount of discussion and argument
on the question whether several of these forms of credit, and in
particular whether bank notes, ought to be considered as money.
The question is so purely verbal as to be scarcely worth raising,
and one would have some difficulty in comprehending why so much

---

[1] [This section was added in the 4th ed. (1857).]

importance is attached to it, if there were not some authorities who, still adhering to the doctrine of the infancy of society and of political economy, that the quantity of money compared with that of commodities, determines general prices, think it important to prove that bank notes and no other forms of credit are money, in order to support the inference that bank notes and no other forms of credit influence prices. It is obvious, however, that prices do not depend on money, but on purchases. Money left with a banker, and not drawn against, or drawn against for other purposes than buying commodities, has no effect on prices, any more than credit which is not used. Credit which is used to purchase commodities affects prices in the same manner as money. Money and credit are thus exactly on a par, in their effect on prices ; and whether we choose to class bank notes with the one or the other, is in this respect entirely immaterial.

Since, however, this question of nomenclature has been raised, it seems desirable that it should be answered. The reason given for considering bank notes as money, is, that by law and usage they have the property, in common with metallic money, of finally closing the transactions in which they are employed ; while no other mode of paying one debt by transferring another has that privilege. The first remark which here suggests itself is, that on this showing, the notes at least of private banks are not money ; for a creditor cannot be forced to accept them in payment of a debt. They certainly close the transaction if he does accept them ; but so, on the same supposition, would a bale of cloth, or a pipe of wine ; which are not for that reason regarded as money. It seems to be an essential part of the idea of money that it be legal tender. An inconvertible paper which is legal tender is universally admitted to be money ; in the French language the phrase *papier-monnaie* actually *means* inconvertibility, convertible notes being merely *billets à porteur*. It is only in the case of Bank of England notes under the law of convertibility, that any difficulty arises ; those notes not being a legal tender from the Bank itself, though a legal tender from all other persons. Bank of England notes undoubtedly do close transactions, so far as respects the buyer. When he has once paid in Bank of England notes, he can in no case be required to pay over again. But I confess I cannot see how the transaction can be deemed complete, as regards the seller, when he will only be found to have received the price of his commodity provided the Bank keeps its promise to pay. An instrument which would be deprived of all value by the insolvency of a corporation, cannot be money in any sense in which money is opposed to credit. It either is not money, or it is money and credit too. It may be most suitably described as coined credit. The other forms of credit may be distinguished from it as credit in ingots.

§ 8. Some high authorities have claimed for bank notes, as compared with other modes of credit, a greater distinction in respect to influence on price, than we have seen reason to allow; a difference, not in degree, but in kind. They ground this distinction on the fact that all bills and cheques, as well as all book-debts, are from the first intended to be, and actually are, ultimately liquidated either in coin or in notes. The bank notes in circulation, jointly with the coin, are therefore, according to these authorities, the basis on which all the other expedients of credit rest; and in proportion to the basis will be the superstructure; insomuch that the quantity of bank notes determines that of all the other forms of credit. If bank notes are multiplied, there will, they seem to think, be more bills, more payments by cheque, and, I presume, more book credits; and by regulating and limiting the issue of bank notes, they think that all other forms of credit are, by an indirect consequence, brought under a similar limitation. I believe I have stated the opinion of these authorities correctly, though I have nowhere seen the grounds of it set forth with such distinctness as to make me feel quite certain that I understand them. It may be true that, according as there are more or fewer bank notes, there is also in general (though not invariably), more or less of other descriptions of credit; for the same state of affairs which leads to an increase of credit in one shape, leads to an increase of it in other shapes. But I see no reason for believing that the one is the cause of the other.[1] If indeed we begin by assuming, as I suspect is tacitly done, that prices are regulated by coin and bank notes, the proposition maintained will certainly follow; for, according as prices are higher or lower, the same purchases will give rise to bills, cheques, and book credits of a larger or a smaller amount. But the premise in this reasoning is the very proposition to be proved. Setting this assumption aside, I know not how the conclusion can be substantiated. The credit given to any one by

[1] [This and the preceding sentence replaced in the 4th ed. (1857) the following sentence of the original text : " I can see no reason for the doctrine, that according as there are more or fewer bank notes, there will be more or less of other descriptions of credit."]

those with whom he deals, does not depend on the quantity of bank notes or coin in circulation at the time, but on their opinion of his solvency : if any consideration of a more general character enters into their calculation, it is only in a time of pressure on the loan market, when they are not certain of being themselves able to obtain the credit on which they have been accustomed to rely ; and even then, what they look to is the general state of the loan market, and not (preconceived theory apart) the amount of bank notes. So far as to the willingness to *give* credit. And the willingness of a dealer to *use* his credit depends on his expectations of gain, that is, on his opinion of the probable future price of his commodity; an opinion grounded either on the rise or fall already going on, or on his prospective judgment respecting the supply and the rate of consumption. When a dealer extends his purchases beyond his immediate means of payment, engaging to pay at a specified time, he does so in the expectation either that the transaction will have terminated favourably before that time arrives, or that he shall then be in possession of sufficient funds from the proceeds of his other transactions. The fulfilment of these expectations depends upon prices, but not especially upon the amount of bank notes. He may; doubtless, also ask himself, in case he should be disappointed in these expectations, to what quarter he can look for a temporary advance, to enable him, at the worst, to keep his engagements. But in the first place, this prospective reflection on the somewhat more or less of difficulty which he may have in tiding over his embarrassments, seems too slender an inducement to be much of a restraint in a period supposed to be one of rash adventure, and upon persons so confident of success as to involve themselves beyond their certain means of extrication. And further, I apprehend that their confidence of being helped out in the event of ill-fortune, will mainly depend on their opinion of their own individual credit, with, perhaps, some consideration, not of the quantity of the currency, but of the general state of the loan market. They are aware that, in case of a commercial crisis, they shall have difficulty in obtaining advances. But if they thought it likely that a commercial crisis would occur before they had realized, they would not speculate. If no great contraction of general credit occurs, they will feel no doubt of obtaining any advances which they absolutely require, provided the state of their own affairs at the time affords in the estimation of lenders a sufficient prospect that those advances will be repaid.

CHAPTER XIII

§ 1. AFTER experience had shown that pieces of paper, of no intrinsic value, by merely bearing upon them the written profession of being equivalent to a certain number of francs, dollars, or pounds, could be made to circulate as such, and to produce all the benefit to the issuers which could have been produced by the coins which they purported to represent; governments began to think that it would be a happy device if they could appropriate to themselves this benefit, free from the condition to which individuals issuing such paper substitutes for money were subject, of giving, when required, for the sign, the thing signified. They determined to try whether they could not emancipate themselves from this unpleasant obligation, and make a piece of paper issued by them pass for a pound, by merely calling it a pound, and consenting to receive it in payment of the taxes. And such is the influence of almost all established governments, that they have generally succeeded in attaining this object: I believe I might say they have always succeeded for a time, and the power has only been lost to them after they had compromised it by the most flagrant abuse.

In the case supposed, the functions of money are performed by a thing which derives its power for performing them solely from convention; but convention is quite sufficient to confer the power; since nothing more is needful to make a person accept anything as money, and even at any arbitrary value, than the persuasion that it will be taken from him on the same terms by others. The only question is, what determines the value of such a currency; since it cannot be, as in the case of gold and silver (or paper exchangeable for them at pleasure), the cost of production.

We have seen, however, that even in the case of a metallic currency, the immediate agency in determining its value is its quantity. If the quantity, instead of depending on the ordinary mercantile motives of profit and loss, could be arbitrarily fixed by authority, the value would depend on the fiat of that authority, not on cost of production. The quantity of a paper currency not convertible into the metals at the option of the holder, can be arbitrarily fixed; especially if the issuer is the sovereign power of the state. The value, therefore, of such a currency is entirely arbitrary

Suppose that, in a country of which the currency is wholly metallic, a paper currency is suddenly issued, to the amount of half the metallic circulation; not by a banking establishment, or in the form of loans, but by the government, in payment of salaries and purchase of commodities. The currency being suddenly increased by one-half, all prices will rise, and among the rest, the prices of all things made of gold and silver. An ounce of manufactured gold will become more valuable than an ounce of gold coin, by more than that customary difference which compensates for the value of the workmanship; and it will be profitable to melt the coin for the purpose of being manufactured, until as much has been taken from the currency by the subtraction of gold, as had been added to it by the issue of paper. Then prices will relapse to what they were at first, and there will be nothing changed except that a paper currency has been substituted for half of the metallic currency which existed before. Suppose, now, a second emission of paper; the same series of effects will be renewed; and so on, until the whole of the metallic money has disappeared: that is, if paper be issued of as low a denomination as the lowest coin; if not, as much will remain as convenience requires for the smaller payments. The addition made to the quantity of gold and silver disposable for ornamental purposes, will somewhat reduce, for a time, the value of the article; and as long as this is the case, even though paper has been issued to the original amount of the metallic circulation, as much coin will remain in circulation along with it, as will keep the value of the currency down to the reduced value of the metallic material; but the value having fallen below the cost of production, a stoppage or diminution of the supply from the mines will enable the surplus to be carried off by the ordinary agents of destruction, after which, the metals and the currency will recover their natural value. We are here supposing, as we have supposed throughout, that the country has mines of its own, and no commercial intercourse with other countries; for, in a country having foreign trade, the coin which is rendered superfluous by an issue of paper is carried off by a much prompter method.

Up to this point, the effects of a paper currency are substantially the same, whether it is convertible into specie or not. It is when the metals have been completely superseded and driven from circulation, that the difference between convertible and inconvertible paper begins to be operative. When the gold or silver has all gone from circulation, and an equal quantity of paper has taken its place, suppose that a still further issue is superadded. The same series of phenomena recommences : prices rise, among the rest the prices of gold and silver articles, and it becomes an object as before to procure coin in order to convert it into bullion. There is no longer any coin in circulation ; but if the paper currency is convertible, coin may still be obtained from the issuers, in exchange for notes. All additional notes, therefore, which are attempted to be forced into circulation after the metals have been completely superseded, will return upon the issuers in exchange for coin ; and they will not be able to maintain in circulation such a quantity of convertible paper as to sink its value below the metal which it represents. It is not so, however, with an inconvertible currency. To the increase of that (if permitted by law) there is no check. The issuers may add to it indefinitely, lowering its value and raising prices in proportion ; they may, in other words, depreciate the currency without limit.

Such a power, in whomsoever vested, is an intolerable evil. All variations in the value of the circulating medium are mischievous : they disturb existing contracts and expectations, and the liability to such changes renders every pecuniary engagement of long date entirely precarious. The person who buys for himself, or gives to another, an annuity of 100*l.*, does not know whether it will be equivalent to 200*l.* or to 50*l.* a few years hence. Great as this evil would be if it depended only on accident, it is still greater when placed at the arbitrary disposal of an individual or a body of individuals ; who may have any kind or degree of interest to be served by an artificial fluctuation in fortunes ; and who have at any rate a strong interest in issuing as much as possible, each issue being in itself a source of profit. Not to add, that the issuers may have, and in the case of a government paper, always have, a direct interest in lowering the value of the currency, because it is the medium in which their own debts are computed.

§ 2. In order that the value of the currency may be secure from being altered by design, and may be as little as possible liable to fluctuation from accident, the articles least liable of all known commodities to vary in their value, the precious metals, have been made in all civilized countries the standard of value for the circulating medium ; and no paper currency ought to exist of which the value cannot be made to conform to theirs. Nor has this fundamental maxim ever been entirely lost sight of, even by the governments which have most abused the power of creating inconvertible paper. If they have not (as they generally have) professed an intention of paying in specie at some indefinite future time, they have at least, by giving to their paper issues the names of their coins, made a virtual, though generally a false, profession of intending to keep them at a value corresponding to that of the coins. This is not impracticable, even with an inconvertible paper. There is not indeed the self-acting check which convertibility brings with it. But there is a clear and unequivocal indication by which to judge whether the currency is depreciated, and to what extent. That indication is, the price of the precious metals. When holders of paper cannot demand coin to be converted into bullion, and when there is none left in circulation, bullion rises and falls in price like other things ; and if it is above the Mint price, if an ounce of gold, which would be coined into the equivalent of $3l.$ $17s.$ $10\frac{1}{2}d.$, is sold for $4l.$ or $5l.$ in paper, the value of the currency has just sunk that much below what the value of a metallic currency would be. If, therefore, the issue of inconvertible paper were subjected to strict rules, one rule being that whenever bullion rose above the Mint price, the issues should be contracted until the market price of bullion and the Mint price were again in accordance, such a currency would not be subject to any of the evils usually deemed inherent in an inconvertible paper.

But also such a system of currency would have no advantages sufficient to recommend it to adoption. An inconvertible currency, regulated by the price of bullion, would conform exactly, in all its variations, to a convertible one ; and the only advantage gained would be that of exemption from the necessity of keeping any reserve of the precious metals ; which is not a very important consideration, especially as a government, so long as its good faith is not suspected, needs not keep so large a reserve as private issuers, being not so liable to great and sudden demands, since there never can be any real doubt of its solvency. Against this small advantage is to be set, in the first place, the possibility of fraudulent tampering with the price of bullion for the sake of acting on the currency ; in the manner of the fictitious sales of corn, to influence the averages, so much and so justly complained of while the corn laws were in force. But a still stronger consideration is the importance of adhering to a simple principle, intelligible to the most untaught capacity. Everybody can understand convertibility ; every one sees that what can be at any moment exchanged for five pounds is worth five pounds. Regulation by the price of bullion is a more complex idea, and does not recommend itself through the same familiar associations. There would be nothing like the same confidence, by the public generally, in an inconvertible currency so regulated, as in a convertible one : and the most instructed person might reasonably doubt whether such a rule would be as likely to be inflexibly adhered to. The grounds of the rule not being so well understood by the public, opinion would probably not enforce it with as much rigidity, and, in any circumstances of difficulty, would be likely to turn against it ; while to the government itself a suspension of convertibility would appear a much stronger and more extreme measure, than a relaxation of what might possibly be considered a somewhat artificial rule. There is therefore a great preponderance of reasons in favour of a convertible, in preference to even the best regulated inconvertible currency. The temptation to over-issue, in certain financial emergencies, is so strong, that nothing is admissible which can tend, in however slight a degree, to weaken the barriers that restrain it.

§ 3. Although no doctrine in political economy rests on more obvious grounds than the mischief of a paper currency not maintained at the same value with a metallic, either by convertibility, or by some principle of limitation equivalent to it ; and although, accordingly, this doctrine has, though not till after the discussions of many years, been tolerably effectually drummed into the public mind ; yet dissentients are still numerous, and projectors every now and then start up, with plans for curing all the economical evils of society by means of an unlimited issue of inconvertible paper. There is, in truth, a great charm in the idea. To be able to pay off the national debt, defray the expenses of government without taxation, and in fine, to make the fortunes of the whole community, is a brilliant prospect, when once a man is capable of believing that printing a few characters on bits of paper will do it. The philosopher's stone could not be expected to do more.

As these projects, however often slain, always resuscitate, it is not superfluous to examine one or two of the fallacies by which the schemers impose upon themselves. One of the commonest is, that a paper currency cannot be issued in excess so long as every note issued *represents* property, or has a *foundation* of actual property to rest on. These phrases, of representing and resting, seldom convey any distinct or well-defined idea : when they do, their meaning is no more than this—that the issuers of the paper must *have* property, either of their own, or entrusted to them, to the value of all the notes they issue : though for what purpose does not very clearly appear ; for if the property cannot be claimed in exchange for the notes, it is difficult to divine in what manner its mere existence can serve to uphold their value. I presume, however, it is intended as a guarantee that the holders would be finally reimbursed, in case any untoward event should cause the whole concern to be wound up. On this theory there have been many schemes for " coining the whole land of the country into money " and the like.

In so far as this notion has any connexion at all with reason, it seems to originate in confounding two entirely distinct evils, to which a paper currency is liable. One is, the insolvency of the issuers ; which, if the paper is grounded on their credit—if it makes any promise of payment in cash, either on demand or at any future time—of course deprives the paper of any value which it derives from the promise. To this evil paper credit is equally liable, however moderately used ; and against it a proviso that all issues should be " founded on property," as for instance that notes should only be issued on the security of some valuable thing expressly pledged for their redemption, would really be efficacious as a precaution. But the theory takes no account of another evil, which is incident to the notes of the most solvent firm, company, or government ; that of being depreciated in value from being issued in excessive quantity. The assignats, during the French Revolution, were an example of a currency grounded on these principles. The assignats " represented " an immense amount of highly valuable property, namely the lands of the crown, the church, the monasteries, and the emigrants ; amounting possibly to half the territory of France. They were, in fact, orders or assignments on this mass of land. The revolutionary government had the idea of " coining " these lands into money ; but, to do them justice, they did not originally contemplate the immense multiplication of issues to which they were eventually driven by the failure of all other financial resources. They imagined that the assignats would come rapidly back to the issuers in exchange for la nd, and that they should be

able to reissue them continually until the lands were all disposed
of, without having at any time more than a very moderate quantity
in circulation. Their hope was frustrated : the land did not sell
so quickly as they expected ; buyers were not inclined to invest
their money in possessions which were likely to be resumed without
compensation if the Revolution succumbed : the bits of paper
which represented land, becoming prodigiously multiplied, could
no more keep up their value than the land itself would have done
if it had all been brought to market at once : and the result was that
it at last required an assignat of six hundred francs to pay for a
pound of butter.[1]

The example of the assignats has been said not to be conclusive,
because an assignat only represented land in general, but not a
definite quantity of land. To have prevented their depreciation,
the proper course, it is affirmed, would have been to have made a
valuation of all the confiscated property at its metallic value, and
to have issued assignats up to, but not beyond, that limit ; giving
to the holders a right to demand any piece of land, at its registered
valuation, in exchange for assignats to the same amount. There
can be no question about the superiority of this plan over the one
actually adopted. Had this course been followed, the assignats could
never have been depreciated to the inordinate degree they were ;
for—as they would have retained all their purchasing power in
relation to land, however much they might have fallen in respect
to other things—before they had lost very much of their market
value, they would probably have been brought in to be exchanged
for land. It must be remembered, however, that their not being
depreciated would pre-suppose that no greater number of them
continued in circulation than would have circulated if they had
been convertible into cash. However convenient, therefore, in a
time of revolution, this currency convertible into land on demand
might have been, as a contrivance for selling rapidly a great quantity
of land with the least possible sacrifice ; it is difficult to see what
advantage it would have, as the permanent system of a country,
over a currency convertible into coin : while it is not at all difficult
to see what would be its disadvantages ; since land is far more
variable in value than gold and silver ; and besides, land, to most
persons, being rather an encumbrance than a desirable possession,
except to be converted into money, people would submit to a

---

[1] [Until the 6th ed. (1865) the paragraph ended with " five hundred francs
to pay for a cup of coffee."]

much greater depreciation before demanding land, than they will before demanding gold or silver.* [1]

* Among the schemes of currency to which, strange to say, intelligent writers have been found to give their sanction, one is as follows : that the state should receive, in pledge or mortgage, any kind or amount of property, such as land, stock, &c., and should advance to the owners inconvertible paper money to the estimated value. Such a currency would not even have the recommendations of the imaginary assignats supposed in the text ; since those into whose hands the notes were paid by the persons who received them, could not return them to the government, and demand in exchange land or stock which was only pledged, not alienated. There would be no reflux of such assignats as these, and their depreciation would be indefinite.

[1] [In the 2nd ed. (1849) was inserted the following section, which did not disappear till the 5th ed. (1862) :

"§ 4. One of the most transparent of the fallacies by which the principle of the convertibility of paper money has been assailed, is that which pervades a recent work by Mr. John Gray, *Lectures on the Nature and Use of Money :* the author of the most ingenious, and least exceptionable plan of an inconvertible currency which I have happened to meet with. This writer has seized several of the leading doctrines of political economy with no ordinary grasp, and among others, the important one, that commodities are the real market for commodities, and that Production is essentially the cause and measure of Demand. But this proposition, true in a state of barter, he affirms to be false under a monetary system regulated by the precious metals, because if the aggregate of goods is increased faster than the aggregate of money, prices must fall, and all producers must be losers ; now neither gold nor silver, nor any other valuable thing, 'can by any possibility be increased *ad libitum*, as fast as all other valuable things put together : ' a limit, therefore, is arbitrarily set to the amount of production which can take place without loss to the producers : and on this foundation Mr. Gray accuses the existing system of rendering the produce of this country less by at least one hundred million pounds annually, than it would be under a currency which admitted of expansion in exact proportion to the increase of commodities.

"But, in the first place, what hinders gold, or any other commodity whatever, from being 'increased as fast as all other valuable things put together ? ' If the produce of the world, in all commodities taken together, should come to be doubled, what is to prevent the annual produce of gold from being doubled likewise ? for that is all that would be necessary, and not (as might be inferred from Mr. Gray's language) that it should be doubled as many times over as there are other 'valuable things' to compare it with. Unless it can be proved that the production of bullion cannot be increased by the application of increased labour and capital, it is evident that the stimulus of an increased value of the commodity will have the same effect in extending the mining operations, as it is admitted to have in all other branches of production.

"But, secondly, even if the currency could not be increased at all, and if every addition to the aggregate produce of the country must necessarily be accompanied by a proportional diminution of general prices ; it is incomprehensible how any person who has attended to the subject can fail to see that a fall of price, thus produced, is no loss to producers : they receive less money ; but the smaller amount goes exactly as far, in all expenditure, whether productive or personal, as the larger quantity did before. The only difference would be in the increased burthen of fixed money payments ; and of that (coming, as it would, very gradually) a very small portion would fall on the productive classes, who have rarely any debts of old standing, and who would

§ 4.   Another of the fallacies from which the advocates of an inconvertible currency derive support, is the notion that an increase of the currency quickens industry.   This idea was set afloat by Hume, in his *Essay* on *Money*, and has had many devoted adherents since ;   witness the Birmingham currency school, of whom Mr. Attwood was at one time the most conspicuous representative. Mr. Attwood maintained that a rise of prices, produced by an increase of paper currency, stimulates every producer to his utmost exertions, and brings all the capital and labour of the country into complete employment ;   and that this has invariably happened in all periods of rising prices, when the rise was on a sufficiently great scale.   I presume, however, that the inducement which, according to Mr. Attwood, excited this unusual ardour in all persons engaged in production, must have been the expectation of getting more commodities generally, more real wealth, in exchange for the produce of their labour, and not merely more pieces of paper.   This expectation, however, must have been, by the very terms of the supposition, disappointed, since, all prices being supposed to rise equally, no one was really better paid for his goods than before.   Those who agree with Mr. Attwood could only succeed in winning people on to these unwonted exertions by a prolongation of what would in fact be a delusion ;   contriving matters so, that by a progressive rise of money prices, every producer shall always seem to be in the very act of obtaining an increased remuneration which he never, in reality, does obtain.   It is unnecessary to advert to any other of the objections to this plan than that of its total impracticability. It calculates on finding the whole world persisting for ever in the belief that more pieces of paper are more riches, and never discovering that, with all their paper, they cannot buy more of anything than they could before.   No such mistake was made during any of the periods of high prices, on the experience of which this school lays so much stress.   At the periods which Mr. Attwood mistook for times of prosperity, and which were simply (as all periods of high prices, under a convertible currency, must be) times of speculation, the speculators did not think they were growing rich because the high prices would last, but because they would not last, and because whoever contrived to realize while they did last, would find himself, after the recoil, in possession of a greater number of pounds sterling, without their having become of less value.   If, at

suffer almost solely in the increased onerousness of their contribution to the taxes which pay the interest of the National Debt."]

the close of the speculation, an issue of paper had been made, sufficient to keep prices up to the point which they attained when at the highest, no one would have been more disappointed than the speculators ; since the gain which they thought to have reaped by realizing in time (at the expense of their competitors, who bought when they sold, and had to sell after the revulsion) would have faded away in their hands, and instead of it they would have got nothing except a few more paper tickets to count by.

Hume's version of the doctrine differed in a slight degree from Mr. Attwood's. He thought that all commodities would not rise in price simultaneously, and that some persons therefore would obtain a real gain, by getting more money for what they had to sell, while the things which they wished to buy might not yet have risen. And those who would reap this gain would always be (he seems to think) the first comers. It seems obvious, however, that for every person who thus gains more than usual, there is necessarily some other person who gains less. The loser, if things took place as Hume supposes, would be the seller of the commodities which are slowest to rise ; who, by the supposition, parts with his goods at the old prices, to purchasers who have already benefited by the new. This seller has obtained for his commodity only the accustomed quantity of money, while there are already some things of which that money will no longer purchase as much as before. If, therefore, he knows what is going on, he will raise his price, and then the buyer will not have the gain, which is supposed to stimulate his industry. But if, on the contrary, the seller does not know the state of the case, and only discovers it when he finds, in laying his money out, that it does not go so far, he then obtains less than the ordinary remuneration for his labour and capital ; and if the other dealer's industry is encouraged, it should seem that his must, from the opposite cause, be impaired.

§ 5. There is no way in which a general and permanent rise of prices, or in other words, depreciation of money, can benefit anybody, except at the expense of somebody else. The substitution of paper for metallic currency is a national gain : any further increase of paper beyond this is but a form of robbery.

An issue of notes is a manifest gain to the issuers, who, until the notes are returned for payment, ontain the use of them as if they were a real capital : and so long as the notes are no permanent addition to the currency, out merely supersede gold or silver to the same amount, the gain of the issuer is a loss to no one ; it is obtained by saving to the community the expense of the more costly material. But if there is no gold or silver to be superseded —if the notes are added to the currency, instead of being substituted for the metallic part of it—all holders of currency lose, by the depreciation of its value, the exact equivalent of what the issuer gains. A tax is virtually levied on them for his benefit. It will be objected by some, that gains are also made by the producers and dealers who, by means of the increased issue, are accommodated with loans. Theirs, however, is not an additional gain, but a portion of that which is reaped by the issuer at the expense of all possessors of money. The profits arising from the contribution levied upon the public, he does not keep to himself, but divides with his customers.

But besides the benefit reaped by the issuers, or by others through them, at the expense of the public generally, there is another unjust gain obtained by a larger class, namely by those who are under fixed pecuniary obligations. All such persons are freed, by a depreciation of the currency, from a portion of the burthen of their debts or other engagements : in other words, part of the property of their creditors is gratuitously transferred to them. On a superficial view it may be imagined that this is an advantage to industry ; since the productive classes are great borrowers, and generally owe larger debts to the unproductive (if we include among the latter all persons not actually in business) than the unproductive classes owe to them ; especially if the national debt be included. It is only thus that a general rise of prices can be a source of benefit to producers and dealers ; by diminishing the pressure of their fixed burthens. And this might be accounted an advantage, if integrity and good faith were of no importance to the world, and to industry and commerce in particular. Not many, however, have been found to say that the currency ought to be depreciated on the simple ground of its being desirable to rob the national creditor and private creditors of a part of what is in their bond. The schemes which have tended that way have almost always had some appearance of special and circumstantial justification, such as the necessity of compensating for a prior injustice committed in the contrary direction.

§ 6. Thus in England, for many years subsequent to 1819, it was pertinaciously contended, that a large portion of the national debt and a multitude of private debts still in existence, were contracted between 1797 and 1819, when the Bank of England was exempted from giving cash for its notes ; and that it is grossly unjust to borrowers (that is, in the case of the national debt, to all tax-payers) that they should be paying interest on the same nominal sums in a currency of full value, which were borrowed in a depreciated one.[1] The depreciation, according to the views and objects of the particular writer, was represented to have averaged thirty, fifty, or even more than fifty per cent : and the conclusion was, that either we ought to return to this depreciated currency, or to strike off from the national debt, and from mortgages or other private debts of old standing, a percentage corresponding to the estimated amount of the depreciation.

To this doctrine, the following was the answer usually made. Granting that, by returning to cash payments without lowering the standard, an injustice was done to debtors, in holding them liable for the same amount of a currency enhanced in value, which they had borrowed while it was depreciated ; it is now too late to make reparation for this injury. The debtors and creditors of to-day are not the debtors and creditors of 1819 : the lapse of years has entirely altered the pecuniary relations of the community ; and it being impossible now to ascertain the particular persons who were either benefited or injured, to attempt to retrace our steps would not be redressing a wrong, but superadding a second act of wide-spread injustice to the one already committed. This argument is certainly conclusive on the practical question ; but it places the honest conclusion on too narrow and too low a ground. It concedes that the measure of 1819, called Peel's Bill, by which cash payments were resumed at the original standard of 3l. 17s. 10½d., was really the injustice it was said to be. This is an admission wholly opposed to the truth. Parliament had no alternative ; it was absolutely bound to adhere to the acknowledged standard ; as may be shown on three distinct grounds, two of fact, and one of principle.

The reasons of fact are these. In the first place, it is not true that the debts, private or public, incurred during the Bank restriction, were contracted in a currency of lower value than that in which the interest is now paid. It is indeed true that the suspension of the obligation to pay in specie did put it in the power of the Bank to depreciate the currency. It is true also that the Bank really exercised

[1] [Until the 5th ed. (1862) the text ran : " from 1819 to the present time, it has been . . . contended," and " the answer " was spoken of in the present tense.]

that power, though to a far less extent than is often pretended ;
since the difference between the market price of gold and the Mint
valuation, during the greater part of the interval, was very trifling,
and when it was greatest, during the last five years of the war,
did not much exceed thirty per cent.   To the extent of that
difference, the currency was depreciated, that is, its value was
below that of the standard to which it professed to adhere.   But the
state of Europe at that time was such—there was so unusual an
absorption of the precious metals, by hoarding, and in the military
chests of the vast armies which then desolated the Continent,
that the value of the standard itself was very considerably raised :
and the best authorities, among whom it is sufficient to name Mr.
Tooke, have, after an elaborate investigation, satisfied themselves
that the difference between paper and bullion was not greater
than the enhancement in value of gold itself, and that the paper,
though depreciated relatively to the then value of gold, did not
sink below the ordinary value, at other times, either of gold or of
a convertible paper.   If this be true (and the evidences of the
fact are conclusively stated in Mr. Tooke's *History of Prices*) the
foundation of the whole case against the fundholder and other
creditors on the ground of depreciation is subverted.

    But, secondly, even if the currency had really been lowered
in value at each period of the Bank restriction, in the same degree
in which it was depreciated in relation to its standard, we must
remember that a part only of the national debt, or of other permanent
engagements, was incurred during the Bank restriction.   A large
part had been contracted before 1797 ; a still larger during the early
years of the restriction, when the difference between paper and gold
was yet small.   To the holders of the former part, an injury was
done, by paying the interest for twenty-two years in a depreciated
currency : those of the second, suffered an injury during the years
in which the interest was paid in a currency more depreciated than
that in which the loans were contracted.   To have resumed cash
payments at a lower standard would have been to perpetuate the
injury to these two classes of creditors, in order to avoid giving an
undue benefit to a third class, who had lent their money during the
few years of greatest depreciation.   As it is, there was an underpay-
ment to one set of persons, and an overpayment to another.   The
late Mr. Mushet took the trouble to make an arithmetical comparison
between the two amounts.   He ascertained, by calculation, that if
an account had been made out in 1819, of what the fundholders had

gained and lost by the variation of the paper currency from its standard, they would have been found as a body to have been losers ; so that if any compensation was due on the ground of depreciation, it would not be from the fundholders collectively, but to them.

Thus it is with the facts of the case. But these reasons of fact are not the strongest. There is a reason of principle, still more powerful. Suppose that, not a part of the debt merely, but the whole, had been contracted in a depreciated currency, depreciated not only in comparison with its standard, but with its own value before and after ; and that we were now paying the interest on this debt in a currency fifty or even a hundred per cent more valuable than that in which it was contracted. What difference would this make in the obligation of paying it, if the condition that it should be so paid was part of the original compact ? Now this is not only truth, but less than the truth. The compact stipulated better terms for the fundholder than he has received. During the whole continuance of the Bank restriction, there was a parliamentary pledge, by which the legislature was as much bound as any legislature is capable of binding itself, that cash payments should be resumed on the original footing, at farthest in six months after the conclusion of a general peace. This was therefore an actual condition of every loan ; and the terms of the loan were more favourable in consideration of it. Without some such stipulation, the Government could not have expected to borrow, unless on the terms on which loans are made to the native princes of India. If it had been understood and avowed that, after borrowing the money, the standard at which it was commuted might be permanently lowered, to any extent which to the " collective wisdom " of a legislature of borrowers might seem fit—who can say what rate of interest would have been a sufficient inducement to persons of common sense to risk their savings in such an adventure ? However much the fundholders had gained by the resumption of cash payments, the terms of the contract insured their giving ample value for it. They gave value for more than they received ; since cash payments were not resumed in six months, but in as many years, after the peace. So that waiving all our arguments except the last, and conceding all the facts asserted on the other side of the question, the fundholders, instead of being unduly benefited, are the injured party ; and would have a claim to compensation, if such claims were not very properly barred by the impossibility of adjudication, and by the salutary general maxim of law and policy, " quod interest reipublicæ ut sit finis litium."

CHAPTER XIV

OF EXCESS OF SUPPLY

§ 1. AFTER the elementary exposition of the theory of money contained in the last few chapters, we shall return to a question in the general theory of Value, which could not be satisfactorily discussed until the nature and operations of Money were in some measure understood, because the errors against which we have to contend mainly originate in a misunderstanding of those operations.

We have seen that the value of everything gravitates towards a certain medium point (which has been called the Natural Value), namely, that at which it exchanges for every other thing in the ratio of their cost of production. We have seen, too, that the actual or market value coincides, or nearly so, with the natural value only on an average of years ; and is continually either rising above, or falling below it, from alterations in the demand, or casual fluctuations in the supply : but that these variations correct themselves, through the tendency of the supply to accommodate itself to the demand which exists for the commodity at its natural value. A general convergence thus results from the balance of opposite divergences. Dearth, or scarcity, on the one hand, and over-supply, or in mercantile language, glut, on the other, are incident to all commodities. In the first case, the commodity affords to the producers or sellers, while the deficiency lasts, an unusually high rate of profit : in the second, the supply being in excess of that for which a demand exists at such a value as will afford the ordinary profit, the sellers must be content with less, and must, in extreme cases, submit to a loss.

Because this phenomenon of over-supply, and consequent inconvenience or loss to the producer or dealer, may exist in the case of any one commodity whatever, many persons, including some distinguished political economists, have thought that it may exist with regard to all commodities ; that there may be a general overproduction of wealth ; a supply of commodities in the aggregate, surpassing the demand ; and a consequent depressed condition of all classes of producers. Against this doctrine, of which Mr. Malthus and Dr. Chalmers in this country, and M. de Sismondi on the Continent, were the chief apostles, I have already contended in the First Book ; * but it was not possible, in that stage of our inquiry, to enter into a complete examination of an error (as I conceive) essentially grounded on a misunderstanding of the phenomena of Value and Price.

The doctrine appears to me to involve so much inconsistency in its very conception, that I feel considerable difficulty in giving any statement of it which shall be at once clear, and satisfactory to its supporters. They agree in maintaining that there may be, and sometimes is, an excess of productions in general beyond the demand for them ; that when this happens, purchasers cannot be found at prices which will repay the cost of production with a profit ; that there ensues a general depression of prices or values (they are· seldom accurate in discriminating between the two), so that producers, the more they produce, find themselves the poorer, instead of richer ; and Dr. Chalmers accordingly inculcates on capitalists the practice of a moral restraint in reference to the pursuit of gain ; while Sismondi deprecates machinery, and the various inventions which increase productive power. They both maintain that accumulation of capital may proceed too fast, not merely for the moral, but for the material, interests of those who produce and accumulate ; and they enjoin the rich to guard against this evil by an ample unproductive consumption.

§ 2. When these writers speak of the supply of commodities as outrunning the demand, it is not clear which of the two elements of demand they have in view—the desire to possess, or the means of purchase ; whether their meaning is that there are, in such cases, more consumable products in existence than the public desires to consume, or merely more than it is able to pay for. In this uncertainty, it is necessary to examine both suppositions.

First, let us suppose that the quantity of commodities produced is not greater than the community would be glad to consume : is it, in that case, possible that there should be a deficiency of demand for all commodities for want of the means of payment ? Those who think so cannot have considered what it is which constitutes the means of payment for commodities. It is simply commodities.

* Supra, pp. 66–8.

Each person's means of paying for the productions of other people consists of those which he himself possesses. All sellers are inevitably and *ex vi termini* buyers. Could we suddenly double the productive powers of the country, we should double the supply of commodities in every market ; but we should, by the same stroke, double the purchasing power. Everybody would bring a double demand as well as supply : everybody would be able to buy twice as much, because every one would have twice as much to offer in exchange. It is probable, indeed, that there would now be a superfluity of certain things. Although the community would willingly double its aggregate consumption, it may already have as much as it desires of some commodities, and it may prefer to do more than double its consumption of others, or to exercise its increased purchasing power on some new thing. If so, the supply will adapt itself accordingly, and the values of things will continue to conform to their cost of production. At any rate, it is a sheer absurdity that all things should fall in value, and that all producers should, in consequence, be insufficiently remunerated. If values remain the same, what becomes of prices is immaterial, since the remuneration of producers does not depend on how much money, but on how much of consumable articles, they obtain for their goods. Besides, money is a commodity ; and if all commodities are supposed to be doubled in quantity, we must suppose money to be doubled too, and then prices would no more fall than values would.

§ 3. A general over-supply, or excess of all commodities above the demand, so far as demand consists in means of payment, is thus shown to be an impossibility. But it may perhaps be supposed that it is not the ability to purchase, but the desire to possess, that falls short, and that the general produce of industry may be greater than the community desires to consume—the part, at least, of the community which has an equivalent to give. It is evident enough that produce makes a market for produce, and that there is wealth in the country with which to purchase all the wealth in the country ; but those who have the means may not have the wants, and those who have the wants may be without the means. A portion, therefore, of the commodities produced may be unable to find a market from the absence of means in those who have the desire to consume, and the want of desire in those who have the means.

This is much the most plausible form of the doctrine, and does not, like that which we first examined, involve a contradiction. There may easily be a greater quantity of any particular commodity than is desired by those who have the ability to purchase, and it is abstractedly conceivable that this might be the case with all commodities. The error is in not perceiving that though all who have an equivalent to give *might* be fully provided with every consumable article which they desire, the fact that they go on adding to the production proves that this is not *actually* the case. Assume the most favourable hypothesis for the purpose, that of a limited community, every member of which possesses as much of necessaries and of all known luxuries as he desires : and since it is not conceivable that persons whose wants were completely satisfied would labour and economize to obtain what they did not desire, suppose that a foreigner arrives and produces an additional quantity of something of which there was already enough. Here, it will be said, is over-production : true, I reply ; over-production of that particular article : the community wanted no more of that, but it wanted something. The old inhabitants, indeed, wanted nothing ; but did not the foreigner himself want something ? When he produced the superfluous article, was he labouring without a motive ? He has produced, but the wrong thing instead of the right. He wanted, perhaps, food, and has produced watches, with which everybody was sufficiently supplied. The new comer brought with him into the country a demand for commodities, equal to all that he could produce by his industry, and it was his business to see that the supply he brought should be suitable to that demand. If he could not produce something capable of exciting a new want or desire in the community, for the satisfaction of which some one would grow more food and give it to him in exchange, he had the alternative of growing food for himself ; either on fresh land, if there was any unoccupied, or as a tenant, or partner, or servant, of some former occupier, willing to be partially relieved from labour. He has produced a thing not wanted instead of what was wanted ; and he himself, perhaps, is not the kind of producer who is wanted ; but there is no over-production ; production is not excessive, but merely ill assorted. We saw before, that whoever brings additional commodities to the market, brings an additional power of purchase ; we now see that he brings also an additional desire to consume ; since if he had not that desire, he would not have troubled himself to produce. Neither of the elements of demand, therefore, can be wanting, when there is an additional supply ; though it is perfectly possible that the demand may be for one thing, and the supply may unfortunately consist of another.

Driven to his last retreat, an opponent may perhaps allege that there are persons who produce and accumulate from mere habit; not because they have any object in growing richer, or desire to add in any respect to their consumption, but from *vis inertiæ*. They continue producing because the machine is ready mounted, and save and re-invest their savings because they have nothing on which they care to expend them. I grant that this is possible, and in some few instances probably happens ; but these do not in the smallest degree affect our conclusion. For, what do these persons do with their savings ? They invest them productively ; that is, expend them in employing labour. In other words, having a purchasing power belonging to them, more than they know what to do with, they make over the surplus of it for the general benefit of the labouring class. Now, will that class also not know what to do with it ? Are we to suppose that they too have their wants perfectly satisfied, and go on labouring from mere habit ? Until this is the case ; until the work-ing classes have also reached the point of satiety—there will be no want of demand for the produce of capital, however rapidly it may accumulate ; since, if there is nothing else for it to do, it can always find employment in producing the necessaries or luxuries of the labouring class. And when they too had no further desire for necessaries or luxuries, they would take the benefit of any further increase of wages by diminishing their work ; so that the over-production which then for the first time would be possible in idea, could not even then take place in fact, for want of labourers. Thus, in whatever manner the question is looked at, even though we go to the extreme verge of possibility to invent a supposition favourable to it, the theory of general over-production implies an absurdity.

§ 4. What then is it by which men who have reflected much on economical phenomena, and have even contributed to throw new light upon them by original speculations, have been led to embrace so irrational a doctrine ? I conceive them to have been deceived by a mistaken interpretation of certain mercantile facts. They imagined that the possibility of a general over-supply of commodities was proved by experience. They believed that they saw this phenomenon in certain conditions of the markets, the true explana-tion of which is totally different.

I have already described the state of the markets for commodities which accompanies what is termed a commercial crisis. At such times there is really an excess of all commodities above the money demand : in other words, there is an under-supply of money. From the sudden annihilation of a great mass of credit, every one dislikes to part with ready money, and many are anxious to procure it at any sacrifice. Almost everybody therefore is a seller, and there are scarcely any buyers ; so that there may really be, though only while the crisis lasts, an extreme depression of general prices, from what may be indiscriminately called a glut of commodities or a dearth of money. But it is a great error to suppose, with Sismondi, that a commercial crisis is the effect of a general excess of production. It is simply the consequence of an excess of speculative purchases. It is not a gradual advent of low prices, but a sudden recoil from prices extravagantly high : its immediate cause is a contraction of credit, and the remedy is, not a diminution of supply, but the restoration of confidence. It is also evident that this temporary derangement of markets is an evil only because it is temporary. The fall being solely of money prices, if prices did not rise again no dealer would lose, since the smaller price would be worth as much to him as the larger price was before. In no manner does this phenomenon answer to the description which these celebrated economists have given of the evil of over-production. The permanent decline in the circumstances of producers, for want of markets, which those writers contemplate, is a conception to which the nature of a commercial crisis gives no support.

The other phenomenon from which the notion of a general excess of wealth and superfluity of accumulation seems to derive countenance, is one of a more permanent nature, namely, the fall of profits and interest which naturally takes place with the progress of population and production. The cause of this decline of profit is the increased cost of maintaining labour, which results from an increase of population and of the demand for food, outstripping the advance of agricultural improvement. This important feature in the economical progress of nations will receive full consideration and discussion in the succeeding Book.* It is obviously a totally different thing from a want of market for commodities, though often confounded with it in the complaints of the producing and trading classes. The true interpretation of the modern or present state of industrial economy is that there is hardly any amount of business which may

* Infra, book iv. chap. 4.

not be done, if people will be content to do it on small profits ; and this all active and intelligent persons in business perfectly well know : but even those who comply with the necessities of their time, grumble at what they comply with, and wish that there were less capital, or, as they express it, less competition, in order that there might be greater profits. Low profits, however, are a different thing from deficiency of demand ; and the production and accumulation which merely reduce profits, cannot be called excess of supply or of production. What the phenomenon really is, and its effects and necessary limits, will be seen when we treat of that express subject.

I know not of any economical facts, except the two I have specified, which can have given occasion to the opinion that a general over-production of commodities ever presented itself in actual experience. I am convinced that there is no fact in commercial affairs which, in order to its explanation, stands in need of that chimerical supposition.

The point is fundamental ; any difference of opinion on it involves radically different conceptions of Political Economy, especially in its practical aspect. On the one view, we have only to consider how a sufficient production may be combined with the best possible distribution ; but, on the other, there is a third thing to be considered —how a market can be created for produce, or how production can be limited to the capabilities of the market. Besides, a theory so essentially self-contradictory cannot intrude itself without carrying confusion into the very heart of the subject, and making it impossible even to conceive with any distinctness many of the more complicated economical workings of society. This error has been, I conceive, fatal to the systems, as systems, of the three distinguished economists to whom I before referred, Malthus, Chalmers, and Sismondi ; all of whom have admirably conceived and explained several of the elementary theorems of political economy, but this fatal misconception has spread itself like a veil between them and the more difficult portions of the subject, not suffering one ray of light to penetrate. Still more is this same confused idea constantly crossing and bewildering the speculations of minds inferior to theirs. It is but justice to two eminent names to call attention to the fact, that the merit of having placed this most important point in its true light belongs principally, on the Continent, to the judicious J. B. Say, and in this country to Mr. [James] Mill ; who (besides the conclusive exposition which he gave of the subject in his *Elements of Political*

Economy) had set forth the correct doctrine with great force and clearness in an early pamphlet, called forth by a temporary controversy, and entitled *Commerce Defended;* the first of his writings which attained any celebrity, and which he prized more as having been his first introduction to the friendship of David Ricardo, the most valued and most intimate friendship of his life.

CHAPTER XV

OF A MEASURE OF VALUE

§ 1. THERE has been much discussion among political economists respecting a Measure of Value. An importance has been
attached to the subject greater than it deserved, and what has
been written respecting it has contributed not a little to the reproach
of logomachy, which is brought, with much exaggeration, but not
altogether without ground, against the speculations of political
economists. It is necessary, however, to touch upon the subject, if
only to show how little there is to be said on it.

A Measure of Value, in the ordinary sense of the word measure,
would mean something by comparison with which we may ascertain what is the value of any other thing. When we consider farther,
that value itself is relative, and that two things are necessary to
constitute it, independently of the third thing which is to measure it ;
we may define a Measure of Value to be something, by comparing
with which any two other things, we may infer their value in relation
to one another.

In this sense, any commodity will serve as a measure of value at
a given time and place ; since we can always infer the proportion in
which things exchange for one another, when we know the proportion in which each exchanges for any third thing. To serve as a
convenient measure of value is one of the functions of the commodity
selected as a medium of exchange. It is in that commodity that the
values of all other things are habitually estimated. We say that one
thing is worth 2l., another 3l. ; and it is then known, without express
statement, that one is worth two-thirds of the other, or that the
things exchange for one another in the proportion of 2 to 3. Money
is a complete measure of their value.

But the desideratum sought by political economists is not a
measure of the value of things at the same time and place, but a
measure of the value of the same thing at different times and places :

something by comparison with which it may be known whether any given thing is of greater or less value now than a century ago, or in this country than in America or China. And for this also, money, or any other commodity, will serve quite as well as at the same time and place, provided we can obtain the same data ; provided we are able to compare with the measure not one commodity only, but the two or more which are necessary to the idea of value. If wheat is now [1852] 40s. the quarter, and a fat sheep the same, and if in the time of Henry the Second wheat was 20s., and a sheep 10s., we know that a quarter of wheat was then worth two sheep, and is now only worth one, and that the value therefore of a sheep, estimated in wheat, is twice as great as it was then ; quite independently of the value of money at the two periods, either in relation to those two articles (in respect to both of which we suppose it to have fallen), or to other commodities in respect to which we need not make any supposition.

What seems to be desired, however, by writers on the subject, is some means of ascertaining the value of a commodity by merely comparing it with the measure, without referring it specially to any other given commodity. They would wish to be able, from the mere fact that wheat is now 40s. the quarter, and was formerly 20s., to decide whether wheat has varied in its value, and in what degree, without selecting a second commodity, such as a sheep, to compare it with ; because they are desirous of knowing, not how much wheat has varied in value relatively to sheep, but how much it has varied relatively to things in general.

The first obstacle arises from the necessary indefiniteness of the idea of general exchange value—value in relation not to some one commodity, but to commodities at large. Even if we knew exactly how much a quarter of wheat would have purchased, at the earlier period, of every marketable article considered separately, and that it will now purchase more of some things and less of others, we should often find it impossible to say whether it had risen or fallen in relation to things in general. How much more impossible, when we only know how it has varied in relation to the measure. To enable the money price of a thing at two different periods to measure the quantity of things in general which it will exchange for, the same sum of money must correspond at both periods to the same quantity of things in general, that is, money must always have the same exchange value, the same general purchasing power. Now, not only is this not true of money, or of any other commodity, but we

cannot even suppose any state of circumstances in which it would
be true.

§ 2. A measure of exchange value, therefore, being impossible,
writers have formed a notion of something, under the name of a
measure of value, which would be more properly termed a measure of
cost of production. They have imagined a commodity invariably
produced by the same quantity of labour ; to which supposition it
is necessary to add, that the fixed capital employed in the production
must bear always the same proportion to the wages of the immediate
labour, and must be always of the same durability : in short, the
same capital must be advanced for the same length of time, so that
the element of value which consists of profits, as well as that which
consists of wages, may be unchangeable. We should then have a
commodity always produced under one and the same combination
of all the circumstances which affect permanent value. Such a
commodity would be by no means constant in its exchange value ;
for (even without reckoning the temporary fluctuations arising from
supply and demand) its exchange value would be altered by every
change in the circumstances of production of the things against
which it was exchanged. But if there existed such a commodity,
we should derive this advantage from it, that whenever any other
thing varied permanently in relation to it, we should know that the
cause of variation was not in it, but in the other thing. It would
thus be suited to serve as a measure, not indeed of the value of other
things, but of their cost of production. If a commodity acquired a
greater permanent purchasing power in relation to the invariable
commodity, its cost of production must have become greater ; and
in the contrary case, less. This measure of cost is what political
economists have generally meant by a measure of value.

But a measure of cost, though perfectly conceivable, can no
more exist in fact, than a measure of exchange value. There is no
commodity which is invariable in its cost of production. Gold and
silver are the least variable, but even these are liable to changes in
their cost of production, from the exhaustion of old sources of supply,
the discovery of new, and improvements in the mode of working.
If we attempt to ascertain the changes in the cost of production of
any commodity from the changes in its money price, the conclusion
will require to be corrected by the best allowance we can make for the
intermediate changes in the cost of the production of money itself.

Adam Smith fancied that there were two commodities peculiarly fitted to serve as a measure of value : corn, and labour. Of corn, he said that although its value fluctuates much from year to year, it does not vary greatly from century to century. This we now know to be an error : corn tends to rise in cost of production with every increase of population, and to fall with every improvement in agriculture, either in the country itself, or in any foreign country from which it draws a portion of its supplies. The supposed constancy of the cost of the production of corn depends on the maintenance of a complete equipoise between these antagonizing forces, an equipoise which, if ever realized, can only be accidental. With respect to labour as a measure of value, the language of Adam Smith is not uniform. He sometimes speaks of it as a good measure only for short periods, saying that the value of labour (or wages) does not vary much from year to year, though it does from generation to generation. On other occasions he speaks as if labour were intrinsically the most proper measure of value, on the ground that one day's ordinary muscular exertion of one man, may be looked upon as always, to him, the same amount of effort or sacrifice. But this proposition, whether in itself admissible or not, discards the idea of exchange value altogether, substituting a totally different idea, more analogous to value in use. If a day's labour will purchase in America twice as much of ordinary consumable articles as in England, it seems a vain subtlety to insist on saying that labour is of the same value in both countries, and that it is the value of the other things which is different. Labour, in this case, may be correctly said to be twice as valuable, both in the market and to the labourer himself, in America as in England.

If the object were to obtain an approximate measure by which to estimate value in use, perhaps nothing better could be chosen than one day's subsistence of an average man, reckoned in the ordinary food consumed by the class of unskilled labourers. If in any country a pound of maize flour will support a labouring man for a day, a thing might be deemed more or less valuable in proportion to the number of pounds of maize flour it exchanged for. If one thing, either by itself or by what it would purchase, could maintain a labouring man for a day, and another could maintain him for a week, there would be some reason in saying that the one was worth, for ordinary human uses, seven times as much as the other. But this would not measure the worth of the thing to its possessor for his own purposes, which might be greater to any amount, though it could not be less, than the worth of the food which the thing would purchase.

The idea of a Measure of Value must not be confounded with the idea of the regulator, or determining principle, of value.   When it is said by Ricardo and others, that the value of a thing is regulated by quantity of labour, they do not mean the quantity of labour for which the thing will exchange, but the quantity required for producing it.   This, they mean to affirm, determines its value ; causes it to be of the value it is, and of no other.   But when Adam Smith and Malthus say that labour is a measure of value, they do not mean the labour by which the thing was or can be made, but the quantity of labour which it will exchange for, or purchase ; in other words, the value of the thing estimated in labour.   And they do not mean that this *regulates* the general exchange value of the thing, or has any effect in determining what that value shall be, but only ascertains what it is, and whether and how much it varies from time to time and from place to place.   To confound these two ideas would be much the same thing as to overlook the distinction between the thermometer and the fire.

CHAPTER XVI

§ 1. THE general laws of value, in all the more important cases of the interchange of commodities in the same country, have now been investigated. We examined, first, the case of monopoly, in which the value is determined by either a natural or an artificial limitation of quantity, that is, by demand and supply ; secondly, the case of free competition, when the article can be produced in indefinite quantity at the same cost ; in which case the permanent value is determined by the cost of production, and only the fluctuations by supply and demand ; thirdly, a mixed case, that of the articles which can be produced in indefinite quantity, but not at the same cost ; in which case the permanent value is determined by the greatest cost which it is necessary to incur in order to obtain the required supply. And lastly, we have found that money itself is a commodity of the third class ; that its value, in a state of freedom, is governed by the same laws as the values of other commodities of its class ; and that prices, therefore, follow the same laws as values.

From this it appears that demand and supply govern the fluctuations of values and prices in all cases, and the permanent values and prices of all things of which the supply is determined by any agency other than that of free competition : but that, under the régime of competition, things are, on the average, exchanged for each other at such values, and sold at such prices, as afford equal expectation of advantage to all classes of producers ; which can only be when things exchange for one another in the ratio of their cost of production.

It is now, however, necessary to take notice of certain cases, to which, from their peculiar nature, this law of exchange value is inapplicable.

It sometimes happens that two different commodities have what may be termed a joint cost of production. They are both products of the same operation, or set of operations, and the outlay is incurred for the sake of both together, not part for one and part for the other. The same outlay would have to be incurred for either of the two, if the other were not wanted or used at all. There are not a few instances of commodities thus associated in their production : for example, coke and coal-gas are both produced from the same material, and by the same operation. In a more partial sense, mutton and wool are an example : beef, hides, and tallow : calves and dairy produce : chickens and eggs. Cost of production can have nothing to do with deciding the value of the associated commodities relatively to each other. It only decides their joint value. The gas and the coke together have to repay the expenses of their production, with the ordinary profit. To do this, a given quantity of gas, together with the coke which is the residuum of its manufacture, must exchange for other things in the ratio of their joint cost of production. But how much of the remuneration of the producer shall be derived from the coke, and how much from the gas, remains to be decided. Cost of production does not determine their prices, but the sum of their prices. A principle is wanting to apportion the expenses of production between the two.

Since cost of production here fails us, we must revert to a law of value anterior to cost of production, and more fundamental, the law of demand and supply. The law is, that the demand for a commodity varies with its value, and that the value adjusts itself so that the demand shall be equal to the supply. This supplies the principle of repartition which we are in quest of.

Suppose that a certain quantity of gas is produced and sold at a certain price, and that the residuum of coke is offered at a price which, together with that of the gas, repays the expenses with the ordinary rate of profit. Suppose, too, that at the price put upon the gas and coke respectively, the whole of the gas finds an easy market, without either surplus or deficiency, but that purchasers cannot be found for all the coke corresponding to it. The coke will be offered at a lower price in order to force a market. But this lower price, together with the price of the gas, will not be remunerating : the manufacture, as a whole, will not pay its expenses with the ordinary profit, and will not, on these terms, continue to be carried on. The gas, therefore, must be sold at a higher price, to make up for the deficiency on the coke. The demand consequently contracting, the production will be somewhat reduced ; and prices will become stationary when, by the joint effect of the rise of gas and the fall of coke, so much less of the first is sold, and so much more of the second, that there is now a market for all the coke which results from the existing extent of the gas manufacture.

Or suppose the reverse case ; that more coke is wanted at the present prices, than can be supplied by the operations required by the existing demand for gas. Coke, being now in deficiency, will rise in price. The whole operation will yield more than the usual rate of profit, and additional capital will be attracted to the manufacture. The unsatisfied demand for coke will be supplied ; but this cannot be done without increasing the supply of gas too ; and as the existing demand was fully supplied already, an increased quantity can only find a market by lowering the price. The result will be that the two together will yield the return required by their joint cost of production, but that more of this return than before will be furnished by the coke, and less by the gas. Equilibrium will be attained when the demand for each article fits so well with the demand for the other, that the quantity required of each is exactly as much as is generated in producing the quantity required of the other. If there is any surplus or deficiency on either side ; if there is a demand for coke, and not a demand for all the gas produced along with it, or *vice versâ ;* the values and prices of the two things will so readjust themselves that both shall find a market.

When, therefore, two or more commodities have a joint cost of production, their natural values relatively to each other are those which will create a demand for each, in the ratio of the quantities in which they are sent forth by the productive process. This theorem is not in itself of any great importance : but the illustration it affords of the law of demand, and of the mode in which, when cost of production fails to be applicable, the other principle steps in to supply the vacancy, is worthy of particular attention, as we shall find in the next chapter but one that something very similar takes place in cases of much greater moment.

§ 2. Another case of value which merits attention, is that of the different kinds of agricultural produce. This is rather a more complex question than the last, and requires that attention should be paid to a greater number of influencing circumstances.

The case would present nothing peculiar, if different agricultural products were either grown indiscriminately and with equal advantage on the same soils, or wholly on different soils. The difficulty

arises from two things : first, that most soils are fitter for one kind
of produce than another, without being absolutely unfit for any ;
and secondly, the rotation of crops.

For simplicity we will confine our supposition to two kinds of
agricultural produce ; for instance, wheat and oats. If all soils
were equally adapted for wheat and for oats, both would be
grown indiscriminately on all soils, and their relative cost of production, being the same everywhere, would govern their relative value
If the same labour which grows three quarters of wheat on any given
soil, would always grow on that soil five quarters of oats, the three
and the five quarters would be of the same value. If, again, wheat
and oats could not be grown on the same soil at all, the value of each
would be determined by its peculiar cost of production on the least
favourable of the soils adapted for it which the existing demand
required a recourse to. The fact, however, is that both wheat and
oats can be grown on almost any soil which is capable of producing
either : but some soils, such as the stiff clays, are better adapted for
wheat, while others (the light sandy soils) are more suitable for oats.
There might be some soils which would yield, to the same quantity
of labour, only four quarters of oats to three of wheat ; others
perhaps less than three of wheat to five quarters of oats. Among
these diversities, what determines the relative value of the two
things ?

It is evident that each grain will be cultivated in preference
on the soils which are better adapted for it than for the other ; and
if the demand is supplied from these alone, the values of the two
grains will have no reference to one another. But when the demand
for both is such as to require that each should be grown not only on
the soils peculiarly fitted for it, but on the medium soils which,
without being specifically adapted to either, are about equally suited
for both, the cost of production on those medium soils will determine
the relative value of the two grains ; while the rent of the soils
specifically adapted to each will be regulated by their productive
power, considered with reference to that one alone to which they are
peculiarly applicable. Thus far the question presents no difficulty
to any one to whom the general principles of value are familiar.

It may happen, however, that the demand for one of the two,
as for example wheat, may so outstrip the demand for the other, as
not only to occupy the soils specially suited for wheat, but to engross
entirely those equally suitable to both, and even encroach upon those
which are better adapted to oats. To create an inducement for this

unequal apportionment of the cultivation, wheat must be relatively dearer, and oats cheaper, than according to the cost of their production on the medium land.   Their relative value must be in proportion to the cost on that quality of land, whatever it may be, on which the comparative demand for the two grains requires that both of them should be grown.   If, from the state of the demand, the two cultivations meet on land more favourable to one than to the other, that one will be cheaper and the other dearer, in relation to each other and to things in general, than if the proportional demand were as we at first supposed.

Here, then, we obtain a fresh illustration, in a somewhat different manner, of the operation of demand, not as an occasional disturber of value, but as a permanent regulator of it, conjoined with, or supplementary to, cost of production.

The case of rotation of crops does not require separate analysis, being a case of joint cost of production, like that of gas and coke. If it were the practice to grow white and green crops on all lands in alternate years, the one being necessary as much for the sake of the other as for its own sake ; the farmer would derive his remuneration for two years' expenses from one white and one green crop, and the prices of the two would so adjust themselves as to create a demand which would carry off an equal breadth of white and of green crops.

There would be little difficulty in finding other anomalous cases of value, which it might be a useful exercise to resolve : but it is neither desirable nor possible, in a work like the present, to enter more into details than is necessary for the elucidation of principles. I now therefore proceed to the only part of the general theory of exchange which has not yet been touched upon, that of International Exchanges, or, to speak more generally, exchanges between distant places.

CHAPTER XVII

§ 1. THE causes which occasion a commodity to be brought from a distance, instead of being produced, as convenience would seem to dictate, as near as possible to the market where it is to be sold for consumption, are usually conceived in a rather superficial manner. Some things it is physically impossible to produce, except in particular circumstances of heat, soil, water, or atmosphere. But there are many things which, though they could be produced at home without difficulty, and in any quantity, are yet imported from a distance. The explanation which would be popularly given of this would be, that it is cheaper to import than to produce them : and this is the true reason. But this reason itself requires that a reason be given for it. Of two things produced in the same place, if one is cheaper than the other, the reason is that it can be produced with less labour and capital, or, in a word, at less cost. Is this also the reason as between things produced in different places ? Are things never imported but from places where they can be produced with less labour (or less of the other element of cost, time) than in the place to which they are brought ? Does the law, that permanent value is proportioned to cost of production, hold good between commodities produced in distant places, as it does between those produced in adjacent places ?

We shall find that it does not. A thing may sometimes be sold cheapest, by being produced in some other place than that at which it can be produced with the smallest amount of labour and abstinence. England might import corn from Poland and pay for it in cloth, even though England had a decided advantage over Poland in the production of both the one and the other. England might send cottons to Portugal in exchange for wine, although Portugal might be able to produce cottons with a less amount of labour and capital than England could.

This could not happen between adjacent places. If the north bank of the Thames possessed an advantage over the south bank in the production of shoes, no shoes would be produced on the south side ; the shoemakers would remove themselves and their capitals to the north bank, or would have established themselves there originally ; for being competitors in the same market with those on the north side, they could not compensate themselves for their disadvantage at the expense of the consumer : the amount of it would fall entirely on their profits ; and they would not long content themselves with a smaller profit, when, by simply crossing a river, they could increase it. But between distant places, and especially between different countries, profits may continue different ; because persons do not usually remove themselves or their capitals to a distant place without a very strong motive. If capital removed to remote parts of the world as readily, and for as small an inducement, as it moves to another quarter of the same town ; if people would transport their manufactories to America or China whenever they could save a small percentage in their expenses by it ; profits would be alike (or equivalent) all over the world, and all things would be produced in the places where the same labour and capital would produce them in greatest quantity and of best quality. A tendency may, even now, be observed towards such a state of things ; capital is becoming more and more cosmopolitan ; there is so much greater similarity of manners and institutions than formerly, and so much less alienation of feeling, among the more civilized countries, that both population and capital now move from one of those countries to another on much less temptation than heretofore. But there are still extraordinary differences, both of wages and of profits, between different parts of the world. It needs but a small motive to transplant capital, or even persons, from Warwickshire to Yorkshire ; but a much greater to make them remove to India, the colonies, or Ireland. To France, Germany, or Switzerland, capital moves perhaps almost as readily as to the colonies ; the differences of language and government being scarcely so great a hindrance as climate and distance. To countries still barbarous, or, like Russia or Turkey, only beginning to be civilized, capital will not migrate, unless under the inducement of a very great extra profit.

Between all distant places therefore in some degree, but especially between different countries (whether under the same supreme government or not), there may exist great inequalities in the return to labour and capital, without causing them to move from one place to the other in such quantity as to level those inequalities. The capital belonging to a country will, to a great extent, remain in the country, even if there be no mode of employing it in which it would not be more productive elsewhere. Yet even a country thus circumstanced might, and probably would, carry on trade with other countries. It would export articles of some sort, even to places which could make them with less labour than itself ; because those countries, supposing them to have an advantage over it in all productions, would have a greater advantage in some things than in others, and would find it their interest to import the articles in which their advantage was smallest, that they might employ more of their labour and capital on those in which it was greatest.

§ 2. As I have said elsewhere* after Ricardo (the thinker who has done most towards clearing up this subject)† "it is not a difference in the *absolute* cost of production, which determines the interchange, but a difference in the *comparative* cost. It may be to our advantage to procure iron from Sweden in exchange for cottons, even although the mines of England as well as her manufactories should be more productive than those of Sweden ; for if we have an advantage of one-half in cottons, and only an advantage of a quarter in iron, and could sell our cottons to Sweden at the price which Sweden must pay for them if she produced them herself, we should obtain our iron with an advantage of one-half as well as our cottons. We may often, by trading with foreigners, obtain their commodities at a smaller expense of labour and capital than they cost to the foreigners themselves. The bargain is still advantageous to the foreigner, because the commodity which he receives in exchange, though it has cost us less, would have cost him more."

To illustrate the cases in which interchange of commodities will not, and those in which it will, take place between two countries, Mr. [James] Mill, in his *Elements of Political Economy*,‡ makes the supposition that Poland has an advantage over England in the production both of cloth and of corn. He first supposed the advantage

---

* *Essays on some Unsettled Questions of Political Economy*, Essay I.

† [1862] I at one time believed Mr. Ricardo to have been the sole author of the doctrine now universally received by political economists, on the nature and measure of the benefit which a country derives from foreign trade. But Colonel Torrens, by the republication of one of his early writings, *The Economists Refuted*, has established at least a joint claim with Mr. Ricardo to the origination of the doctrine, and an exclusive one to its earliest publication.

‡ Third ed. p. 120.

to be of equal amount in both commodities; the cloth and the corn, each of which required 100 days' labour in Poland, requiring each 150 days' labour in England. "It would follow, that the cloth of 150 days' labour in England, if sent to Poland, would be equal to the cloth of 100 days' labour in Poland; if exchanged for corn, therefore, it would exchange for the corn of only 100 days' labour. But the corn of 100 days' labour in Poland was supposed to be the same quantity with that of 150 days' labour in England. With 150 days' labour in cloth, therefore, England would only get as much corn in Poland, as she could raise with 150 days' labour at home; and she would, in importing it, have the cost of carriage besides. In these circumstances no exchange would take place." In this case the comparative cost of the two articles in England and in Poland were supposed to be the same, though the absolute costs were different; on which supposition we see that there would be no labour saved to either country by confining its industry to one of the two productions and importing the other.

It is otherwise when the comparative, and not merely the absolute costs of the two articles are different in the two countries. "If," continues the same author, "while the cloth produced with 100 days' labour in Poland was produced with 150 days' labour in England, the corn which was produced in Poland with 100 days' labour could not be produced in England with less than 200 days' labour; an adequate motive to exchange would immediately arise. With a quantity of cloth which England produced with 150 days' labour, she would be able to purchase as much corn in Poland as was there produced with 100 days' labour; but the quantity which was there produced with 100 days' labour, would be as great as the quantity produced in England with 200 days' labour." By importing corn, therefore, from Poland, and paying for it with cloth, England would obtain for 150 days' labour what would otherwise cost her 200; being a saving of 50 days' labour on each repetition of the transaction: and not merely a saving to England, but a saving absolutely: for it is not obtained at the expense of Poland, who, with corn that costs her 100 days' labour, has purchased cloth which, if produced at home, would have cost her the same. Poland, therefore, on this supposition, loses nothing; but also she derives no advantage from the trade, the imported cloth costing her as much as if it were made at home. To enable Poland to gain anything by the interchange, something must be abated from the gain of England: the corn produced in Poland by 100 days' labour must be able to purchase from

England more cloth than Poland could produce by that amount of labour ; more therefore than England could produce by 150 days' labour, England thus obtaining the corn which would have cost her 200 days, at a cost exceeding 150, though short of 200. England therefore no longer gains the whole of the labour which is saved to the two jointly by trading with one another.

§ 3. From this exposition we perceive in what consists the benefit of international exchange, or, in other words, foreign commerce. Setting aside its enabling countries to obtain commodities which they could not themselves produce at all ; its advantage consists in a more efficient employment of the productive forces of the world. If two countries which trade together attempted, as far as was physically possible, to produce for themselves what they now import from one another, the labour and capital of the two countries would not be so productive, the two together would not obtain from their industry so great a quantity of commodities, as when each employs itself in producing, both for itself and for the other, the things in which its labour is relatively most efficient. The addition thus made to the produce of the two combined, constitutes the advantage of the trade. It is possible that one of the two countries may be altogether inferior to the other in productive capacities, and that its labour and capital could be employed to greatest advantage by being removed bodily to the other. The labour and capital which have been sunk in rendering Holland habitable, would have produced a much greater return if transported to America or Ireland. The produce of the whole world would be greater, or the labour less, than it is, if everything were produced where there is the greatest absolute facility for its production. But nations do not, at least in modern times, emigrate *en masse ;* and while the labour and capital of a country remain in the country, they are most beneficially employed in producing, for foreign markets as well as for its own, the things in which it lies under the least disadvantage, if there be none in which it possesses an advantage

§ 4. Before proceeding further, let us contrast this view of the benefits of international commerce with other theories which have prevailed, and which to a certain extent still prevail, on the same subject.

According to the doctrine now stated, the only direct advantage of foreign commerce consists in the imports. A country obtains things which it either could not have produced at all, or which it must have produced at a greater expense of capital and labour than the cost of the things which it exports to pay for them. It thus obtains a more ample supply of the commodities it wants, for the same labour and capital; or the same supply, for less labour and capital, leaving the surplus disposable to produce other things. The vulgar theory disregards this benefit, and deems the advantage of commerce to reside in the exports : as if not what a country obtains, but what it parts with, by its foreign trade, was supposed to constitute the gain to it. An extended market for its produce—an abundant consumption for its goods—a vent for its surplus—are the phrases by which it has been customary to designate the uses and recommendations of commerce with foreign countries. This notion is intelligible, when we consider that the authors and leaders of opinion on mercantile questions have always hitherto been the selling class. It is in truth a surviving relic of the Mercantile Theory, according to which, money being the only wealth, selling, or, in other words, exchanging goods for money, was (to countries without mines of their own) the only way of growing rich—and importation of goods, that is to say, parting with money, was so much subtracted from the benefit.

The notion that money alone is wealth has been long defunct, but it has left many of its progeny behind it ; and even its destroyer Adam Smith, retained some opinions which it is impossible to trace to any other origin. Adam Smith's theory of the benefit of foreign trade was that it afforded an outlet for the surplus produce of a country, and enabled a portion of the capital of the country to replace itself with a profit. These expressions suggest ideas inconsistent with a clear conception of the phenomena. The expression, surplus produce, seems to imply that a country is under some kind of necessity of producing the corn or cloth which it exports ; so that the portion which it does not itself consume, if not wanted and consumed elsewhere, would either be produced in sheer waste, or, if it were not produced, the corresponding portion of capital would remain idle, and the mass of productions in the country would be diminished by so much. Either of these suppositions would be entirely erroneous. The country produces an exportable article in excess of its own wants from no inherent necessity, but as the cheapest mode of supplying itself with other things. If prevented from exporting this surplus, it would cease to produce it, and would no longer import anything, being unable to give an equivalent ; but the labour and capital which had been employed in producing with a view to

exportation, would find employment in producing those desirable objects which were previously brought from abroad : or, if
some of them could not be produced, in producing substitutes for
them.   These articles would of course be produced at a greater cost
than that of the things with which they had previously been purchased from foreign countries.   But the value and price of the
articles would rise in proportion ; and the capital would just as
much be replaced, with the ordinary profit from the returns, as it
was when employed in producing for the foreign market.   The only
losers (after the temporary inconvenience of the change) would be
the consumers of the heretofore imported articles ; who would be
obliged either to do without them, consuming in lieu of them something which they did not like as well, or to pay a higher price for them
than before.

There is much misconception in the common notion of what
commerce does for a country.   When commerce is spoken of as
a source of national wealth, the imagination fixes itself upon the large
fortunes acquired by merchants, rather than upon the saving of
price to consumers.   But the gains of merchants, when they enjoy
no exclusive privilege, are no greater than the profits obtained by the
employment of capital in the country itself.   If it be said that the
capital now employed in foreign trade could not find employment
in supplying the home market, I might reply, that this is the fallacy
of general over-production, discussed in a former chapter : but the
thing is in this particular case too evident to require an appeal to
any general theory.   We not only see that the capital of the merchant
would find employment, but we see what employment.   There would
be employment created equal to that which would be taken away.
Exportation ceasing, importation to an equal value would cease also,
and all that part of the income of the country which had been expended in imported commodities, would be ready to expend itself
on the same things produced at home, or on others instead of them.
Commerce is virtually a mode of cheapening production ; and in all
such cases the consumer is the person ultimately benefited ; the
dealer, in the end, is sure to get his profit, whether the buyer obtains
much or little for his money.   This is said without prejudice to the
effect (already touched upon, and to be hereafter fully discussed)
which the cheapening of commodities may have in raising profits ;
in the case when the commodity cheapened, being one of those
consumed by labourers, enters into the cost of labour, by which the
rate of profits is determined.

§ 5. Such, then, is the direct economical advantage of foreign trade. But there are, besides, indirect effects, which must be counted as benefits of a high order. One is, the tendency of every extension of the market to improve the processes of production. A country which produces for a larger market than its own, can introduce a more extended division of labour, can make greater use of machinery, and is more likely to make inventions and improvements in the processes of production. Whatever causes a greater quantity of anything to be produced in the same place, tends to the general increase of the productive powers of the world.* There is another consideration, principally applicable to an early stage of industrial advancement. A people may be in a quiescent, indolent, unculti-vated state, with all their tastes either fully satisfied or entirely undeveloped, and they may fail to put forth the whole of their pro-ductive energies for want of any sufficient object of desire. The opening of a foreign trade, by making them acquainted with new objects, or tempting them by the easier acquisition of things which they had not previously thought attainable, sometimes works a sort of industrial revolution in a country whose resources were previously undeveloped for want of energy and ambition in the people : inducing those who were satisfied with scanty comforts and little work, to work harder for the gratification of their new tastes, and even to save, and accumulate capital, for the still more complete satisfaction of those tastes at a future time.

But the economical advantages of commerce are surpassed in importance by those of its effects which are intellectual and moral. It is hardly possible to overrate the value, in the present low state of human improvement, of placing human beings in contact with persons dissimilar to themselves, and with modes of thought and action unlike those with which they are familiar. Commerce is now what war once was, the principal source of this contact. Com-mercial adventurers from more advanced countries have generally been the first civilizers of barbarians. And commerce is the purpose of the far greater part of the communication which takes place between civilized nations. Such communication has always been, and is peculiarly in the present age, one of the primary sources of progress. To human beings, who, as hitherto educated, can scarcely cultivate even a good quality without running it into a fault, it is indispensable to be perpetually comparing their own notions and

* Vide supra, book i. chap. ix. § 1.

customs with the experience and example of persons in different circumstances from themselves : and there is no nation which does not need to borrow from others, not merely particular arts or practices, but essential points of character in which its own type is inferior.   Finally, commerce first taught nations to see with good will the wealth and prosperity of one another.   Before, the patriot, unless sufficiently advanced in culture to feel the world his country, wished all countries weak, poor, and ill-governed, but his own : he now sees in their wealth and progress a direct source of wealth and progress to his own country.   It is commerce which is rapidly rendering war obsolete, by strengthening and multiplying the personal interests which are in natural opposition to it.   And it may be said without exaggeration that the great extent and rapid increase of international trade, in being the principal guarantee of the peace of the world, is the great permanent security for the uninterrupted progress of the ideas, the institutions, and the character of the human race.

CHAPTER XVIII

§ 1. THE values of commodities produced at the same place, or in places sufficiently adjacent for capital to move freely between them—let us say, for simplicity, of commodities produced in the same country—depend (temporary fluctuations apart) upon their cost of production. But the value of a commodity brought from a distant place, especially from a foreign country, does not depend on its cost of production in the place from whence it comes. On what, then, does it depend? The value of a thing in any place depends on the cost of its acquisition in that place; which, in the case of an imported article, means the cost of production of the thing which is exported to pay for it.

Since all trade is in reality barter, money being a mere instrument for exchanging things against one another, we will, for simplicity, begin by supposing the international trade to be in form, what it always is in reality, an actual trucking of one commodity against another. As far as we have hitherto proceeded, we have found all the laws of interchange to be essentially the same, whether money is used or not; money never governing, but always obeying, those general laws.

If, then, England imports wine from Spain, giving for every pipe of wine a bale of cloth, the exchange value of a pipe of wine in England will not depend upon what the production of the wine may have cost in Spain, but upon what the production of the cloth has cost in England. Though the wine may have cost in Spain the equivalent of only ten days' labour, yet, if the cloth costs in England twenty days' labour, the wine, when brought to England, will exchange for the produce of twenty days' English labour, *plus* the cost of carriage; including the usual profit on the importer's capital, during the time it is locked up, and withheld from other employment.

The value, then, in any country, of a foreign commodity, depends on the quantity of home produce which must be given to the foreign country in exchange for it. In other words, the values of foreign commodities depend on the terms of international exchange. What, then, do these depend upon ? What is it which, in the case supposed, causes a pipe of wine from Spain to be exchanged with England for exactly that quantity of cloth ? We have seen that it is not their cost of production. If the cloth and the wine were both made in Spain, they would exchange at their cost of production in Spain ; if they were both made in England, they would exchange at their cost of production in England : but all the cloth being made in England, and all the wine in Spain, they are in circumstances to which we have already determined that the law of cost of production is not applicable. We must accordingly, as we have done before in a similar embarrassment, fall back upon an antecedent law, that of supply and demand : and in this we shall again find the solution of our difficulty.

I have discussed this question in a separate Essay, already once referred to ; and a quotation of part of the exposition then given will be the best introduction to my present view of the subject. I must give notice that we are now in the region of the most complicated questions which political economy affords ; that the subject is one which cannot possibly be made elementary ; and that a more continuous effort of attention than has yet been required will be necessary to follow the series of deductions. The thread, however, which we are about to take in hand, is in itself very simple and manageable ; the only difficulty is in following it through the windings and entanglements of complex international transactions.

§ 2. " When the trade is established between the two countries, the two commodities will exchange for each other at the same rate of interchange in both countries—bating the cost of carriage, of which, for the present, it will be more convenient to omit the consideration. Supposing, therefore, for the sake of argument, that the carriage of the commodities from one country to the other could be effected without labour and without cost, no sooner would the trade be opened than the value of the two commodities, estimated in each other, would come to a level in both countries.

" Suppose that 10 yards of broadcloth cost in England as much labour as 15 yards of linen, and in Germany as much as 20." In common with most of my predecessors, I find it advisable, in these intricate investigations, to give distinctness and fixity to the conception by numerical examples. These examples must sometimes, as in the present case, be purely supposititious. I should have preferred real ones ; but all that is essential is, that the numbers should be such as admit of being easily followed through the subsequent combinations into which they enter.

This supposition then being made, it would be the interest of England to import linen from Germany, and of Germany to import cloth from England. " When each country produced both commodities for itself, 10 yards of cloth exchanged for 15 yards of linen in England, and for 20 in Germany. They will now exchange for the same number of yards of linen in both. For what number ? If for 15 yards, England will be just as she was, and Germany will gain all. If for 20 yards, Germany will be as before, and England will derive the whole of the benefit. If for any number intermediate between 15 and 20, the advantage will be shared between the two countries. If, for example, 10 yards of cloth exchange for 18 of linen, England will gain an advantage of 3 yards on every 15, Germany will save 2 out of every 20. The problem is, what are the causes which determine the proportion in which the cloth of England and the linen of Germany will exchange for each other.

" As exchange value, in this case as in every other, is proverbially fluctuating, it does not matter what we suppose it to be when we begin : we shall soon see whether there be any fixed point above which it oscillates, which it has a tendency always to approach to, and to remain at. Let us suppose, then, that by the effect of what Adam Smith calls the higgling of the market, 10 yards of cloth in both countries exchange for 17 yards of linen.

" The demand for a commodity, that is, the quantity of it which can find a purchaser, varies, as we have before remarked, according to the price. In Germany the price of 10 yards of cloth is now 17 yards of linen, or whatever quantity of money is equivalent in Germany to 17 yards of linen. Now, that being the price, there is some particular number of yards of cloth, which will be in demand, or will find purchasers, at that price. There is some given quantity of cloth, more than which could not be disposed of at that price ; less than which, at that price, would not fully satisfy the demand. Let us suppose this quantity to be 1000 times 10 yards.

" Let us now turn our attention to England. There, the price of 17 yards of linen is 10 yards of cloth, or whatever quantity of money is equivalent in England to 10 yards of cloth.   There is some particular number of yards of linen which, at that price, will exactly satisfy the demand, and no more.   Let us suppose that this number is 1000 times 17 yards.

"As 17 yards of linen are to 10 yards of cloth, so are 1000 times 17 yards to 1000 times 10 yards.   At the existing exchange value, the linen which England requires will exactly pay for the quantity of cloth which, on the same terms of interchange, Germany requires.   The demand on each side is precisely sufficient to carry off the supply on the other.   The conditions required by the principle of demand and supply are fulfilled, and the two commodities will continue to be interchanged, as we supposed them to be, in the ratio of 17 yards of linen for 10 yards of cloth.

" But our suppositions might have been different.   Suppose that, at the assumed rate of interchange, England has been disposed to consume no greater quantity of linen than 800 times 17 yards : it is evident that, at the rate supposed, this would not have sufficed to pay for the 1000 times 10 yards of cloth which we have supposed Germany to require at the assumed value.   Germany would be able to procure no more than 800 times 10 yards at that price.   To procure the remaining 200, which she would have no means of doing but by bidding higher for them, she would offer more than 17 yards of linen in exchange for 10 yards of cloth : let us suppose her to offer 18.   At this price, perhaps, England would be inclined to purchase a greater quantity of linen.   She would consume, possibly, at that price, 900 times 18 yards.   On the other hand, cloth having risen in price, the demand of Germany for it would probably have diminished.   If, instead of 1000 times 10 yards, she is now contented with 900 times 10 yards, these will exactly pay for the 900 times 18 yards of linen which England is willing to take at the altered price : the demand on each side will again exactly suffice to take off the corresponding supply ; and 10 yards for 18 will be the rate at which, in both countries, cloth will exchange for linen.

" The converse of all this would have happened, if, instead of 800 times 17 yards, we had supposed that England, at the rate of 10 for 17, would have taken 1200 times 17 yards of linen.   In this case, it is England whose demand is not fully supplied ; it is England who, by bidding for more linen, will alter the rate of interchange to her own disadvantage ; and 10 yards of cloth will fall, in both countries, below the value of 17 yards of linen. By this fall of cloth, or, what is the same thing, this rise of linen, the demand of Germany for cloth will increase, and the demand of England for linen will diminish, till the rate of interchange has so adjusted itself that the cloth and the linen will exactly pay for one another ; and when once this point is attained, values will remain without further alteration.

" It may be considered, therefore, as established, that when two countries trade together in two commodities, the exchange value of these commodities relatively to each other will adjust itself to the inclinations and circumstances of the consumers on both sides, in such manner that the quantities required by each country, of the articles which it imports from its neighbour, shall be exactly sufficient to pay for one another. As the inclinations and circumstances of consumers cannot be reduced to any rule, so neither can the proportions in which the two commodities will be interchanged. We know that the limits, within which the variation is confined, are the ratio between their costs of production in the one country, and the ratio between their costs of production in the other. Ten yards of cloth cannot exchange for more than 20 yards of linen, nor for less than 15. But they may exchange for any inter-mediate number. The ratios, therefore, in which the advantage of the trade may be divided between the two nations are various. The circumstances on which the proportionate share of each country more remotely depends, admit only of a very general indication.

" It is even possible to conceive an extreme case, in which the whole of the advantage resulting from the interchange would be reaped by one party, the other country gaining nothing at all. There is no absurdity in the hypothesis that, of some given commodity, a certain quantity is all that is wanted at any price ; and that, when that quantity is obtained, no fall in the exchange value would induce other consumers to come forward, or those who are already supplied to take more. Let us suppose that this is the case in Germany with cloth. Before her trade with England commenced, when 10 yards of cloth cost her as much labour as 20 yards of linen, she nevertheless consumed as much cloth as she wanted under any circumstances, and, if she could obtain it at the rate of 10 yards of cloth for 15 of linen, she would not consume more. Let this fixed quantity be 1000 times 10 yards. At the rate, however, of 10 for 20, England would want more linen than

would be equivalent to this quantity of cloth. She would, consequently, offer a higher value for linen ; or, what is the same thing,
she would offer her cloth at a cheaper rate. But, as by no lowering
of the value could she prevail on Germany to take a greater quantity
of cloth, there would be no limit to the rise of linen or fall of cloth,
until the demand of England for linen was reduced by the rise of
its value, to the quantity which 1000 times 10 yards of cloth would
purchase. It might be, that to produce this diminution of the
demand a less fall would not suffice than that which would make
10 yards of cloth exchange for 15 of linen. Germany would
then gain the whole of the advantage, and England would be
exactly as she was before the trade commenced. It would be for
the interest, however, of Germany herself to keep her linen a little
below the value at which it could be produced in England, in order
to keep herself from being supplanted by the home producer.
England, therefore, would always benefit in some degree by the
existence of the trade, though it might be a very trifling one."
   In this statement, I conceive, is contained the first elementary
principle of International Values.   I have, as is indispensable in such
abstract and hypothetical cases, supposed the circumstances to be
much less complex than they really are : in the first place, by sup-
pressing the cost of carriage ; next, by supposing that there are only
two countries trading together ; and lastly, that they trade only in
two commodities.   To render the exposition of the principle complete
it is necessary to restore the various circumstances thus temporarily
left out to simplify the argument.   Those who are accustomed to
any kind of scientific investigation will probably see, without formal
proof, that the introduction of these circumstances cannot alter the
theory of the subject.   Trade among any number of countries, and
in any number of commodities, must take place on the same essential
principles as trade between two countries and in two commodities.
Introducing a greater number of agents precisely similar cannot
change the law of their action, no more than putting additional
weights into the two scales of a balance alters the law of gravitation.
It alters nothing but the numerical results.   For more complete
satisfaction, however, we will enter into the complex cases with
the same particularity with which we have stated the simpler
one.

   § 3.   First, let us introduce the element of cost of carriage.
The chief difference will then be, that the cloth and the linen will

no longer exchange for each other at precisely the same rate in both countries. Linen, having to be carried to England, will be dearer there by its cost of carriage; and cloth will be dearer in Germany by the cost of carrying it from England. Linen, estimated in cloth, will be dearer in England than in Germany, by the cost of carriage of both articles: and so will cloth in Germany, estimated in linen. Suppose that the cost of carriage of each is equivalent to one yard of linen; and suppose that, if they could have been carried without cost, the terms of interchange would have been 10 yards of cloth for 17 of linen. It may seem at first that each country will pay its own cost of carriage; that is, the carriage of the article it imports; that in Germany 10 yards of cloth will exchange for 18 of linen, namely, the original 17, and 1 to cover the cost of carriage of the cloth; while in England, 10 yards of cloth will only purchase 16 of linen, 1 yard being deducted for the cost of carriage of the linen. This, however, cannot be affirmed with certainty; it will only be true, if the linen which the English consumers would take at the price of 10 for 16, exactly pays for the cloth which the German consumers would take at 10 for 18. The values, whatever they are, must establish this equilibrium. No absolute rule, therefore, can be laid down for the division of the cost, no more than for the division of the advantage: and it does not follow that in whatever ratio the one is divided, the other will be divided in the same. It is impossible to say, if the cost of carriage could be annihilated, whether the producing or the importing country would be most benefited. This would depend on the play of international demand.

Cost of carriage has one effect more. But for it, every commodity would (if trade be supposed free) be either regularly imported or regularly exported. A country would make nothing for itself which it did not also make for other countries. But in consequence of cost of carriage there are many things, especially bulky articles, which every, or almost every, country produces within itself. After exporting the things in which it can employ itself most advantageously, and importing those in which it is under the greatest disadvantage, there are many lying between, of which the relative cost of production in that and in other countries differs so little, that the cost of carriage would absorb more than the whole saving in cost of production which would be obtained by importing one and exporting another. This is the case with numerous commodities of common consumption; including the coarser qualities of many articles of food and manufacture, of which the finer kinds are the subject of extensive international traffic.

§ 4. Let us now introduce a greater number of commodities than the two we have hitherto supposed. Let cloth and linen, however, be still the articles of which the comparative cost of production in England and in Germany differs the most; so that, if they were confined to two commodities, these would be the two which it would be most their interest to exchange. We will now again omit cost of carriage, which, having been shown not to affect the essentials of the question, does but embarrass unnecessarily the statement of it. Let us suppose, then, that the demand of England for linen is either so much greater than that of Germany for cloth, or so much more extensible by cheapness, that if England had no commodity but cloth which Germany would take, the demand of England would force up the terms of interchange to 10 yards of cloth for only 16 of linen, so that England would gain only the difference between 15 and 16, Germany the difference between 16 and 20. But let us now suppose that England has also another commodity, say iron, which is in demand in Germany, and that the quantity of iron which is of equal value in England with 10 yards of cloth, (let us call this quantity a hundredweight) will, if produced in Germany, cost as much labour as 18 yards of linen, so that if offered by England for 17 it will undersell the German producer. In these circumstances, linen will not be forced up to the rate of 16 yards for 10 of cloth, but will stop, suppose at 17 ; for although, at that rate of interchange, Germany will not take enough cloth to pay for all the linen required by England, she will take iron for the remainder, and it is the same thing to England whether she gives a hundredweight of iron or 10 yards of cloth, both being made at the same cost. If we now superadd coals or cottons on the side of England, and wine, or corn, or timber, on the side of Germany, it will make no difference in the principle. The exports of each country must exactly pay for the imports ; meaning now the aggregate exports and imports, not those of particular commodities taken singly. The produce of fifty days' English labour, whether in cloth, coals, iron, or any other exports, will exchange for the produce of forty, or fifty, or sixty days' German labour, in linen, wine, corn, or timber, according to the international demand. There is some proportion at which the demand of the two countries for each other's products will exactly correspond : so that the things supplied by England to Germany will be completely paid for, and no more, by those supplied by Germany to England. This accordingly will be the ratio in which the produce of English and the produce of German labour will exchange for one another.

If, therefore, it be asked what country draws to itself the greatest share of the advantage of any trade it carries on, the answer is, the country for whose productions there is in other countries the greatest demand, and a demand the most susceptible of increase from additional cheapness. In so far as the productions of any country possess this property, the country obtains all foreign commodities at less cost. It gets its imports cheaper, the greater the intensity of the demand in foreign countries for its exports. It also gets its imports cheaper, the less the extent and intensity of its own demand for them. The market is cheapest to those whose demand is small. A country which desires few foreign productions, and only a limited quantity of them, while its own commodities are in great request in foreign countries, will obtain its limited imports at extremely small cost, that is, in exchange for the produce of a very small quantity of its labour and capital.

Lastly, having introduced more than the original two commodities into the hypothesis, let us also introduce more than the original two countries. After the demand of England for the linen of Germany has raised the rate of interchange to 10 yards of cloth for 16 of linen, suppose a trade opened between England and some other country which also exports linen. And let us suppose that, if England had no trade but with the third country, the play of international demand would enable her to obtain from it, for 10 yards of cloth or its equivalent, 17 yards of linen. She evidently would not go on buying linen from Germany at the former rate: Germany would be undersold, and must consent to give 17 yards, like the other country. In this case, the circumstances of production and of demand in the third country are supposed to be in themselves more advantageous to England than the circumstances of Germany; but this supposition is not necessary: we might suppose that if the trade with Germany did not exist, England would be obliged to give to the other country the same advantageous terms which she gives to Germany; 10 yards of cloth for 16, or even less than 16, of linen. Even so, the opening of the third country makes a great difference in favour of England. There is now a double market for English export, while the demand of England for linen is only what it was before. This necessarily obtains for England more advantageous terms of interchange. The two countries, requiring much more of her produce than was required by either alone, must, in order to obtain it, force an increased demand for their exports, by offering them at a lower value.

It deserves notice, that this effect in favour of England from the opening of another market for her exports, will equally be produced even though the country from which the demand comes should have nothing to sell which England is willing to take. Suppose that the third country, though requiring cloth or iron from England, produces no linen, nor any other article which is in demand there. She however produces exportable articles, or she would have no means of paying for imports : her exports, though not suitable to the English consumer, can find a market somewhere. As we are only supposing three countries, we must assume her to find this market in Germany, and to pay for what she imports from England by orders on her German customers. Germany, therefore, besides having to pay for her own imports, now owes a debt to England on account of the third country, and the means for both purposes must be derived from her exportable produce. She must therefore tender that produce to England on terms sufficiently favourable to force a demand equivalent to this double debt. Everything will take place precisely as if the third country had bought German produce with her own goods, and offered that produce to England in exchange for hers. There is an increased demand for English goods, for which German goods have to furnish the payment ; and this can only be done by forcing an increased demand for them in England, that is, by lowering their value. Thus an increase of demand for a country's exports in any foreign country enables her to obtain more cheaply even those imports which she procures from other quarters. And conversely, an increase of her own demand for any foreign commodity compels her, *cæteris paribus*, to pay dearer for all foreign commodities.

The law which we have now illustrated, may be appropriately named, the Equation of International Demand. It may be concisely stated as follows. The produce of a country exchanges for the produce of other countries, at such values as are required in order that the whole of her exports may exactly pay for the whole of her imports. This law of International Values is but an extension of the more general law of Value, which we called the Equation of Supply and Demand.* We have seen that the value of a commodity always so adjusts itself as to bring the demand to the exact level of the supply.

---

* Supra, book iii. chap. ii. § 4.

But all trade, either between nations or individuals, is an interchange of commodities, in which the things that they respectively have to sell constitute also their means of purchase : the supply brought by the one constitutes his demand for what is brought by the other. So that supply and demand are but another expression for reciprocal demand : and to say that value will adjust itself so as to equalize demand with supply, is in fact to say that it will adjust itself so as to equalize the demand on one side with the demand on the other.

§ 5. To trace the consequences of this law of International Values through their wide ramifications, would occupy more space than can be here devoted to such a purpose.[1] But there is one of its applications which I will notice, as being in itself not unimportant, as bearing on the question which will occupy us in the next chapter, and especially as conducing to the more full and clear understanding of the law itself.

We have seen that the value at which a country purchases a foreign commodity does not conform to the cost of production in the country from which the commodity comes. Suppose now a change in that cost of production ; an improvement, for example, in the process of manufacture. Will the benefit of the improvement be fully participated in by other countries ? Will the commodity be sold as much cheaper to foreigners, as it is produced cheaper at home ? This question, and the considerations which must be entered into in order to resolve it, are well adapted to try the worth of the theory.

Let us first suppose, that the improvement is of a nature to create a new branch of export : to make foreigners resort to the country for a commodity which they had previously produced at home. On this supposition, the foreign demand for the productions of the country is increased ; which necessarily alters the international values to its advantage, and to the disadvantage of foreign countries, who, therefore, though they participate in the benefit of the new product, must purchase that benefit by paying for all the other

[1] [Here was omitted in the 3rd ed. (1852) the following passage of the original : " Several of those consequences were indicated in the Essay already quoted ; and others have been pointed out in the writings of Colonel Torrens, who appears to me substantially correct in his general view of the subject, and who has supported it with great closeness and consecutiveness of reasoning, though his conclusions are occasionally pushed much beyond what appear to me the proper limits of the principle on which they are grounded."]

productions of the country at a dearer rate than before. How much dearer, will depend on the degree necessary for re-establishing, under these new conditions, the Equation of International Demand. These consequences follow in a very obvious manner from the law of international values, and I shall not occupy space in illustrating them, but shall pass to the more frequent case, of an improvement which does not create a new article of export, but lowers the cost of production of something which the country already exported.

It being advantageous, in discussions of this complicated nature, to employ definite numerical amounts, we shall return to our original example. Ten yards of cloth, if produced in Germany, would require the same amount of labour and capital as twenty yards of linen ; but by the play of international demand, they can be obtained from England for seventeen. Suppose now, that by a mechanical improvement made in Germany, and not capable of being transferred to England, the same quantity of labour and capital which produced twenty yards of linen, is enabled to produce thirty. Linen falls one-third in value in the German market, as compared with other commodities produced in Germany. Will it also fall one-third as compared with English cloth, thus giving to England, in common with Germany, the full benefit of the improvement ? Or (ought we not rather to say), since the cost to England of obtaining linen was not regulated by the cost to Germany of producing it, and since England, accordingly, did not get the entire benefit even of the twenty yards which Germany could have given for ten yards of cloth, but only obtained seventeen—why should she now obtain more, merely because this theoretical limit is removed ten degrees further off ?

It is evident that, in the outset, the improvement will lower the value of linen in Germany, in relation to all other commodities in the German market, including, among the rest, even the imported commodity, cloth. If 10 yards of cloth previously exchanged for 17 yards of linen, they will now exchange for half as much more, or $25\frac{1}{2}$ yards. But whether they will continue to do so will depend on the effect which this increased cheapness of linen produces on the international demand. The demand for linen in England could scarcely fail to be increased. But it might be increased either in proportion to the cheapness, or in a greater proportion than the cheapness, or in a less proportion.

If the demand was increased in the same proportion with the cheapness, England would take as many times $25\frac{1}{2}$ yards of linen, as the number of times 17 yards which she took previously. She would expend in linen exactly as much of cloth, or of the equivalents of cloth, as much in short of the collective income of her people, as she did before. Germany, on her part, would probably require, at that rate of interchange, the same quantity of cloth as before, because it would in reality cost her exactly as much ; 25½ yards of linen being now of the same value in her market as 17 yards were before. In this case, therefore, 10 yards of cloth for 25½ of linen is the rate of interchange which under these new conditions would restore the equation of international demand ; and England would obtain linen one-third cheaper than before, being the same advantage as was obtained by Germany.

It might happen, however, that this great cheapening of linen would increase the demand for it in England in a greater ratio than the increase of cheapness ; and that, if she before wanted 1000 times 17 yards, she would now require more than 1000 times 25½ yards to satisfy her demand. If so, the equation of international demand cannot establish itself at that rate of interchange ; to pay for the linen England must offer cloth on more advantageous terms ; say, for example, 10 yards for 21 of linen ; so that England will not have the full benefit of the improvement in the production of linen, while Germany, in addition to that benefit, will also pay less for cloth. But again, it is possible that England might not desire to increase her consumption of linen in even so great a proportion as that of the increased cheapness ; she might not desire so great a quantity as 1000 times 25½ yards : and in that case Germany must force a demand by offering more than 25½ yards of linen for 10 of cloth ; linen will be cheapened in England in a still greater degree than in Germany ; while Germany will obtain cloth on more unfavourable terms ; and at a higher exchange value than before.

After what has already been said, it is not necessary to particularize the manner in which these results might be modified by introducing into the hypothesis other countries and other commodities. There is a further circumstance by which they may also be modified. In the case supposed the consumers of Germany have had a part of their incomes set at liberty by the increased cheapness of linen, which they may indeed expend in increasing their consumption of that article, but which they may likewise expend in other articles, and among others, in cloth or other imported commodities. This would be an additional element in the international demand, and would modify more or less the terms of interchange.

Of the three possible varieties in the influence of cheapness on demand, which is the more probable—that the demand would be increased more than the cheapness, as much as the cheapness, or less than the cheapness ?   This depends on the nature of the particular commodity, and on the tastes of purchasers.   When the commodity is one in general request, and the fall of its price brings it within reach of a much larger class of incomes than before, the demand is often increased in a greater ratio than the fall of price, and a larger sum of money is on the whole expended in the article.   Such was the case with coffee, when its price was lowered by successive reductions of taxation ; and such would probably be the case with sugar, wine, and a large class of commodities which, though not necessaries, are largely consumed, and in which many consumers indulge when the articles are cheap and economize when they are dear.   But it more frequently happens that when a commodity falls in price, less money is spent in it than before : a greater quantity is consumed, but not so great a value.   The consumer who saves money by the cheapness of the article, will be likely to expend part of the saving in increasing his consumption of other things : and unless the low price attracts a large class of new purchasers who were either not customers of the article at all, or only in small quantity and occasionally, a less aggregate sum will be expended on it.   Speaking generally, therefore, the third of our three cases is the most probable : and an improvement in an exportable article is likely to be as beneficial (if not more beneficial) to foreign countries, as to the country where the article is produced.

§ 6.[1] Thus far had the theory of international values been carried in the first and second editions of this work.   But intelligent criticisms (chiefly those of my friend Mr. William Thornton), and subsequent further investigation, have shown that the doctrine stated in the preceding pages, though correct as far as it goes, is not yet the complete theory of the subject matter.

It has been shown that the exports and imports between the two countries (or, if we suppose more than two, between each country and the world) must in the aggregate pay for each other, and must therefore be exchanged for one another at such values as will be compatible with the equation of international demand.   That this, however, does not furnish the complete law of the phenomenon, appears from the following consideration : that several different

---

[1] [§§ 6-8 were inserted in the 3rd ed. (1852).]

rates of international value may all equally fulfil the conditions of this law.

The supposition was, that England could produce 10 yards of cloth with the same labour as 15 of linen, and Germany with the same labour as 20 of linen ; that a trade was opened between the two countries ; that England thenceforth confined her production to cloth, and Germany to linen ; and, that if 10 yards of cloth should thenceforth exchange for 17 of linen, England and Germany would exactly supply each other's demand : that, for instance, if England wanted at that price 17,000 yards of linen, Germany would want exactly the 10,000 yards of cloth, which, at that price, England would be required to give for the linen.   Under these suppositions it appeared, that 10 cloth for 17 linen would be, in point of fact, the international values.

But it is quite possible that some other rate, such as 10 cloth for 18 linen, might also fulfil the conditions of the equation of international demand.   Suppose that, at this last rate, England would want more linen than at the rate of 10 for 17, but not in the ratio of the cheapness ; that she would not want the 18,000 which she could now buy with 10,000 yards of cloth, but would be content with 17,500, for which she would pay (at the new rate of 10 for 18) 9722 yards of cloth.   Germany, again, having to pay dearer for cloth than when it could be bought at 10 for 17, would probably reduce her consumption to an amount below 10,000 yards, perhaps to the very same number, 9722.   Under these conditions the Equation of International Demand would still exist.   Thus, the rate of 10 for 17, and that of 10 for 18, would equally satisfy the Equation of Demand : and many other rates of interchange might satisfy it in like manner.   It is conceivable that the conditions might be equally satisfied by every numerical rate which could be supposed.   There is still therefore a portion of indeterminateness in the rate at which the international values would adjust themselves ; showing that the whole of the influencing circumstances cannot yet have been taken into account.

§ 7. It will be found that, to supply this deficiency, we must take into consideration not only, as we have already done, the quantities demanded in each country of the imported commodities ; but also the extent of the means of supplying that demand which are set at liberty in each country by the change in the direction of its industry.

To illustrate this point it will be necessary to choose more convenient numbers than those which we have hitherto employed. Let it be supposed that in England 100 yards of cloth, previously to the trade, exchanged for 100 of linen, but that in Germany 100 of cloth exchanged for 200 of linen. When the trade was opened, England would supply cloth to Germany, Germany linen to England, at an exchange value which would depend partly on the element already discussed, viz. the comparative degree in which, in the two countries, increased cheapness operates in increasing the demand ; and partly on some other element not yet taken into account. In order to isolate this unknown element, it will be necessary to make some definite and invariable supposition in regard to the known element. Let us therefore assume, that the influence of cheapness on demand conforms to some simple law, common to both countries and to both commodities. As the simplest and most convenient, let us suppose that in both countries any given increase of cheapness produces an exactly proportional increase of consumption ; or, in other words, that the value expended in the commodity, the cost incurred for the sake of obtaining it, is always the same, whether that cost affords a greater or a smaller quantity of the commodity.

Let us now suppose that England, previously to the trade, required a million of yards of linen, which were worth, at the English cost of production, a million yards of cloth. By turning all the labour and capital with which that linen was produced to the production of cloth, she would produce for exportation a million yards of cloth. Suppose that this is the exact quantity which Germany is accustomed to consume. England can dispose of all this cloth in Germany at the German price ; she must consent indeed to take a little less until she has driven the German producer from the market, but as soon as this is effected, she can sell her million of cloth for two millions of linen ; being the quantity that the German clothiers are enabled to make by transferring their whole labour and capital from cloth to linen. Thus England would gain the whole benefit of the trade, and Germany nothing. This would be perfectly consistent with the equation of international demand : since England (according to the hypothesis in the preceding paragraph) now requires two millions of linen (being able to get them at the same cost at which she previously obtained only one), while, the prices in Germany not being altered, Germany requires as before exactly a million of cloth, and can obtain it by employing the labour and capital set at liberty from the production of cloth, in producing the two millions of linen required by England.

Thus far we have supposed that the additional cloth which England could make, by transferring to cloth the whole of the capital previously employed in making linen, was exactly sufficient to supply the whole of Germany's existing demand. But suppose next that it is more than sufficient. Suppose that while England could make with her liberated capital a million yards of cloth for exportation, the cloth which Germany had heretofore required was 800,000 yards only, equivalent at the German cost of production to 1,600,000 yards of linen. England therefore could not dispose of a whole million of cloth in Germany at the German prices. Yet she wants, whether cheap or dear (by our supposition), as much linen as can be bought for a million of cloth : and since this can only be obtained from Germany, or by the more expensive process of production at home, the holders of the million of cloth will be forced by each other's competition to offer it to Germany on any terms (short of the English cost of production) which will induce Germany to take the whole. What these terms would be, the supposition we have made enables us exactly to define. The 800,000 yards of cloth which Germany consumed, cost her the equivalent of 1,600,000 linen, and that invariable cost is what she is willing to expend in cloth, whether the quantity it obtains for her be more or less. England therefore, to induce Germany to take a million of cloth, must offer it for 1,600,000 of linen. The international values will thus be 100 cloth for 160 linen, intermediate between the ratio of the costs of production in England, and that of the costs of production in Germany : and the two countries will divide the benefit of the trade, England gaining in the aggregate 600,000 yards of linen, and Germany being richer by 200,000 additional yards of cloth.

Let us now stretch the last supposition still farther, and suppose that the cloth previously consumed by Germany, was not only less than the million yards which England is enabled to furnish by discontinuing her production of linen, but less in the full proportion of England's advantage in the production, that is, that Germany only required half a million. In this case, by ceasing altogether to produce cloth, Germany can add a million, but a million only, to her production of linen; and this million, being the equivalent of what the half million previously cost her, is all that she can be induced by any degree of cheapness to expend in cloth. England will be forced by her own competition to give a whole million of cloth for this million of linen, just as she was forced in the preceding case to give it for 1,600,000. But England could have produced at the same cost a million yards of linen for herself. England therefore derives, in this case, no advantage from the international trade. Germany gains the whole ; obtaining a million of cloth instead of half a million, at what the half million previously cost her. Germany, in short, is, in this third case, exactly in the same situation as England was in the first case ; which may easily be verified by reversing the figures.

As the general result of the three cases, it may be laid down as a theorem, that under the supposition we have made of a demand exactly in proportion to the cheapness, the law of international values will be as follows :—

The whole of the cloth which England can make with the capital previously devoted to linen, will exchange for the whole of the linen which Germany can make with the capital previously devoted to cloth.

Or, still more generally,

The whole of the commodities which the two countries can respectively make for exportation, with the labour and capital thrown out of employment by importation, will exchange against one another.

This law, and the three different possibilities arising from it in respect to the division of the advantage, may be conveniently generalized by means of algebraical symbols, as follows :—

Let the quantity of cloth which England can make with the labour and capital withdrawn from the production of linen, be $= n$.

Let the cloth previously required by Germany (at the German cost of production) be $= m$.

Then n of cloth will always exchange for exactly $2m$ of linen.

Consequently if $n = m$, the whole advantage will be on the side of England.

If $n = 2m$, the whole advantage will be on the side of Germany.

If n be greater than m, but less than $2m$, the two countries will share the advantage ; England getting $2m$ of linen where she before got only n ; Germany getting n of cloth where she before got only m.

It is almost superfluous to observe that the figure 2 stands where it does only because it is the figure which expresses the advantage of Germany over England in linen as estimated in cloth, and (what is the same thing) of England over Germany in cloth as estimated in linen. If we had supposed that in Germany, before the trade, 100 of cloth exchanged for 1000 instead of 200 of linen, then n (after the trade commenced) would have exchanged for $10m$ instead of $2m$. If instead of 1000 or 200 we had supposed only 150, n would have exchanged for only $\frac{3}{2}m$. If (in fine) the cost value of cloth (as estimated in linen) in Germany exceeds the cost value similarly estimated in England, in the ratio of p to q, then will n, after the opening of the trade, exchange for $\frac{p}{q}$ m.*

§ 8. We have now arrived at what seems a law of International Values of great simplicity and generality. But we have done so by setting out from a purely arbitrary hypothesis respecting the relation between demand and cheapness. We have assumed their relation to be fixed, though it is essentially variable. We have supposed that every increase of cheapness produces an exactly proportional extension of demand; in other words, that the same invariable value is laid out in a commodity whether it be cheap or dear; and the

---

* It may be asked, why we have supposed the number n to have as its extreme limits, m and $2m$ (or $\frac{p}{q}m$) ? why may not n be less than m, or greater than $2m$; and if so, what will be the result ?

This we shall now examine; and, when we do so, it will appear that n is always, practically speaking, confined within these limits.

Suppose, for example, that n is less than m; or, reverting to our former figures, that the million yards of cloth, which England can make, will not satisfy the whole of Germany's pre-existing demand; that demand being (let us suppose) for 1,200,000 yards. It would then, at first sight, appear that England would supply Germany with cloth up to the extent of a million; that Germany would continue to supply herself with the remaining 200,000 by home production: that this portion of the supply would regulate the price of the whole; that England therefore would be able permanently to sell her million of cloth at the German cost of production (viz. for two millions of linen) and would gain the whole advantage of the trade, Germany being no better off than before.

That such, however, would not be the practical result, will soon be evident. The residuary demand of Germany for 200,000 yards of cloth furnishes a resource to England for purposes of foreign trade of which it is still her interest to avail herself; and though she has no more labour and capital which she can withdraw from linen for the production of this extra quantity of cloth, there must be some other commodities in which Germany has a relative advantage over her (though perhaps not so great as in linen): these she will now import, instead of producing, and the labour and capital formerly employed in producing them will be transferred to cloth, until the required amount is made up. If this transfer just makes up the 200,000, and no more, this augmented n will now be equal to m; England will sell the whole 1,200,000 at the German values : and will still gain the whole advantage of the trade. But if the transfer makes up more than the 200,000, England will have more cloth than 1,200,000 yards to offer; n will become greater than m, and England must part with enough of the advantage to induce Germany to take the surplus. Thus the case, which seemed at first sight to be beyond the limits, is transformed practically into a case either coinciding with one of the limits or between them. And so with every other case which can be supposed

law which we have investigated holds good only on this hypothesis, or some other practically equivalent to it. Let us now, therefore, combine the two variable elements of the question, the variations of each of which we have considered separately. Let us suppose the relation between demand and cheapness to vary, and to become such as would prevent the rule of interchange laid down in the last theorem from satisfying the conditions of the Equation of International Demand. Let it be supposed, for instance, that the demand of England for linen is exactly proportional to the cheapness, but that of Germany for cloth, not proportional. To revert to the second of our three cases, the case in which England by discontinuing the production of linen could produce for exportation a million yards of cloth, and Germany by ceasing to produce cloth could produce an additional 1,600,000 yards of linen. If the one of these quantities exactly exchanged for the other, the demand of England would on our present supposition be exactly satisfied, for she requires all the linen which can be got for a million yards of cloth : but Germany perhaps, though she required 800,000 cloth at a cost equivalent to 1,600,000 linen, yet when she can get a million of cloth at the same cost, may not require the whole million ; or may require more than a million. First, let her not require so much ; but only as much as she can now buy for 1,500,000 linen. England will still offer a million for these 1,500,000 ; but even this may not induce Germany to take so much as a million ; and if England continues to expend exactly the same aggregate cost on linen whatever be the price, she will have to submit to take for her million of cloth any quantity of linen (not less than a million) which may be requisite to induce Germany to take a million of cloth. Suppose this to be 1,400,000 yards. England has now reaped from the trade a gain not of 600,000 but only of 400,000 yards ; while Germany, besides having obtained an extra 200,000 yards of cloth, has obtained it with only seven-eighths of the labour and capital which she previously expended in supplying herself with cloth, and may expend the remainder in increasing her own consumption of linen, or of any other commodity.

Suppose on the contrary that Germany, at the rate of a million cloth for 1,600,000 linen, requires more than a million yards of cloth. England having only a million which she can give without trenching upon the quantity she previously reserved for herself, Germany must bid for the extra cloth at a higher rate than 160 for 100, until she reaches a rate (say 170 for 100) which will either bring down her own demand for cloth to the limit of a million, or else

tempt England to part with some of the cloth she previously
consumed at home.

Let us next suppose that the proportionality of demand to
cheapness, instead of holding good in one country but not in the other,
does not hold good in either country, and that the deviation is of the
same kind in both ; that, for instance, neither of the two increases
its demand in a degree equivalent to the increase of cheapness.
On this supposition, at the rate of one million cloth for 1,600,000
linen, England will not want so much as 1,600,000 linen, nor Germany
so much as a million cloth : and if they fall short of that amount in
exactly the same degree : if England only wants linen to the amount
of nine-tenths of 1,600,000 (1,440,000), and Germany only nine
hundred thousand of cloth, the interchange will continue to take
place at the same rate. And so if England wants a tenth more than
1,600,000, and Germany a tenth more than a million. This coinci-
dence (which, it is to be observed, supposes demand to extend
cheapness in a corresponding, but not in an equal degree *) evidently
could not exist unless by mere accident : and, in any other case, the
equation of international demand would require a different adjustment of international values.

The only general law, then, which can be laid down, is this.
The values at which a country exchanges its produce with foreign
countries depend on two things : first, on the amount and extensibility of their demand for its commodities, compared with its demand for theirs ; and secondly, on the capital which it has to spare
from the production of domestic commodities for its own consumption. The more the foreign demand for its commodities exceeds its
demand for foreign commodities, and the less capital it can spare
to produce for foreign markets, compared with what foreigners
spare to produce for its markets, the more favourable to it will be
the terms of interchange : that is, the more it will obtain of foreign
commodities in return for a given quantity of its own.

But these two influencing circumstances are in reality reducible
to one : for the capital which a country has to spare from the
production of domestic commodities for its own use is in proportion
to its own demand for foreign commodities : whatever proportion
of its collective income it expends in purchases from abroad, that

* The increase of demand from 800,000 to 900,000, and that from a million
to 1,440,000, are neither equal in themselves, nor bear an equal proportion to
the increase of cheapness. Germany's demand for cloth has increased one-
eighth, while the cheapness is increased one-fourth. England's demand for
linen is increased 44 per cent, while the cheapness is increased 60 per cent.

same proportion of its capital is left without a home market for its productions. The new element, therefore, which for the sake of scientific correctness we have introduced into the theory of international values, does not seem to make any very material difference in the practical result. It still appears, that the countries which carry on their foreign trade on the most advantageous terms, are those whose commodities are most in demand by foreign countries, and which have themselves the least demand for foreign commodities. From which, among other consequences, it follows, that the richest countries, *cæteris paribus*, gain the least by a given amount of foreign commerce : since, having a greater demand for commodities generally, they are likely to have a greater demand for foreign commodities, and thus modify the terms of interchange to their own disadvantage. Their aggregate gains by foreign trade, doubtless, are generally greater than those of poorer countries, since they carry on a greater amount of such trade, and gain the benefit of cheapness on a larger consumption : but their gain is less on each individual article consumed.

§ 9. We now pass to another essential part of the theory of the subject. There are two senses in which a country obtains commodities cheaper by foreign trade ; in the sense of Value, and in the sense of Cost. It gets them cheaper in the first sense, by their falling in value relatively to other things : the same quantity of them exchanging, in the country, for a smaller quantity than before of the other produce of the country. To revert to our original figures ; in England, all consumers of linen obtained, after the trade was opened, 17 or some greater number of yards for the same quantity of all other things for which they before obtained only 15. The degree of cheapness, in this sense of the term, depends on the laws of International Demand, so copiously illustrated in the preceding sections. But in the other sense, that of Cost, a country gets a commodity cheaper when it obtains a greater quantity of the commodity with the same expenditure of labour and capital. In this sense of the term, cheapness in a great measure depends upon a cause of a different nature : a country gets its imports cheaper, in proportion to the general productiveness of its domestic industry ; to the general efficiency of its labour. The labour of one country may be, as a whole, much more efficient than that of another ; all or most of the commodities capable of being produced in both may be produced in one at less absolute cost than in the other ; which, as we have seen, will not necessarily prevent the two countries from exchanging commodities. The things which the more favoured country will import from others, are of course those in which it is least superior ; but by importing them it acquires, even in those commodities, the same advantage which it possesses in the articles it gives in exchange for them. Thus the countries which obtain their own productions at least cost, also get their imports at least cost.

This will be made still more obvious if we suppose two competing countries. England sends cloth to Germany, and gives 10 yards of it for 17 yards of linen, or for something else which in Germany is the equivalent of those 17 yards. Another country, as for example France, does the same. The one giving 10 yards of cloth for a certain quantity of German commodities, so must the other : if, therefore, in England, these 10 yards are produced by only half as much labour as that by which they are produced in France, the linen or other commodities of Germany will cost to England only half the amount of labour which they will cost to France. England would thus obtain her imports at less cost than France, in the ratio of the greater efficiency of her labour in the production of cloth : which might be taken, in the case supposed, as an approximate estimate of the efficiency of her labour generally ; since France, as well as England, by selecting cloth as her article of export, would have shown that with her also it was the commodity in which labour was relatively the most efficient. It follows, therefore, that every country gets its imports at less cost, in proportion to the general efficiency of its labour.

This proposition was first clearly seen and expounded by Mr. Senior,* but only as applicable to the importation of the precious metals. I think it important to point out that the proposition holds equally true of all other imported commodities ; and further, that it is only a portion of the truth. For, in the case supposed, the cost to England of the linen which she pays for with ten yards of cloth, does not depend solely upon the cost to herself of ten yards of cloth, but partly also upon how many yards of linen she obtains in exchange for them. What her imports cost to her is a function of two variables ; the quantity of her own commodities which she gives for them, and the cost of those commodities. Of these, the last alone depends on the efficiency of her labour : the first depends on the law of international values ; that is, on the intensity and extensibility

* *Three Lectures on the Cost of Obtaining Money.*

of the foreign demand for her commodities, compared with her demand for foreign commodities.

In the case just now supposed, of a competition between England and France, the state of international values affected both competitors alike, since they were supposed to trade with the same country, and to export and import the same commodities. The difference, therefore, in what their imports cost them, depended solely on the other cause, the unequal efficiency of their labour. They gave the same quantities ; the difference could only be in the cost of production. But if England traded to Germany with cloth, and France with iron, the comparative demand in Germany for those two commodities would bear a share in determining the comparative cost, in labour and capital, with which England and France would obtain German products. If iron were more in demand in Germany than cloth, France would recover, through that channel, part of her disadvantage ; if less, her disadvantage would be increased. The efficiency, therefore, of a country's labour, is not the only thing which determines even the *cost* at which that country obtains imported commodities—while it has no share whatever in determining either their exchange *value*, or, as we shall presently see, their *price*.[1]

[1] [See Appendix V. *International Values.*]

CHAPTER XIX

ON MONEY, CONSIDERED AS AN IMPORTED COMMODITY

§ 1. THE degree of progress which we have now made in the theory of Foreign Trade, puts it in our power to supply what was previously deficient in our view of the theory of Money ; and this, when completed, will in its turn enable us to conclude the subject of Foreign Trade.

Money, or the material of which it is composed, is, in Great Britain, and in most other countries, a foreign commodity. Its value and distribution must therefore be regulated, not by the law of value which obtains in adjacent places, but by that which is applicable to imported commodities—the law of International Values.

In the discussion into which we are now about to enter, I shall use the terms Money and the Precious Metals indiscriminately. This may be done without leading to any error ; it having been shown that the value of money, when it consists of the precious metals, or of a paper currency convertible into them on demand, is entirely governed by the value of the metals themselves : from which it never permanently differs, except by the expense of coinage when this is paid by the individual and not by the state.

Money is brought into a country in two different ways. It is imported (chiefly in the form of bullion) like any other merchandize, as being an advantageous article of commerce. It is also imported in its other character of a medium of exchange, to pay some debt due to the country, either for goods exported or on any other account. There are other ways in which it may be introduced casually ; these are the two in which it is received in the ordinary course of business and which determine its value. The existence of these two distinct modes in which money flows into a country, while other commodities are habitually introduced only in the first of these modes, occasions somewhat more of complexity and obscurity than exists in the case of other commodities, and for this reason only is any special and minute exposition necessary.

§ 2.   In so far as the precious metals are imported in the ordinary way of commerce, their value must depend on the same causes, and conform to the same laws, as the value of any other foreign production.   It is in this mode chiefly that gold and silver diffuse themselves from the mining countries into all other parts of the commercial world.   They are the staple commodities of those countries, or at least are among their great articles of regular export; and are shipped on speculation, in the same manner as other exportable commodities.   The quantity, therefore, which a country (say England) will give of its own produce, for a certain quantity of bullion, will depend, if we suppose only two countries and two commodities, upon the demand in England for bullion, compared with the demand in the mining country (which we will call Brazil) for what England has to give.   They must exchange in such proportions as will leave no unsatisfied demand on either side, to alter values by its competition.   The bullion required by England must exactly pay for the cottons or other English commodities required by Brazil.   If, however, we substitute for this simplicity the degree of complication which really exists, the equation of international demand must be established not between the bullion wanted in England and the cottons or broadcloth wanted in Brazil, but between the whole of the imports of England and the whole of her exports.   The demand in foreign countries for English products must be brought into equilibrium with the demand in England for the products of foreign countries; and all foreign commodities, bullion among the rest, must be exchanged against English products in such proportions as will, by the effect they produce on the demand, establish this equilibrium.

There is nothing in the peculiar nature or uses of the precious metals which should make them an exception to the general principles of demand.   So far as they are wanted for purposes of luxury or the arts, the demand increases with the cheapness, in the same irregular way as the demand for any other commodity. So far as they are required for money, the demand increases with the cheapness in a perfectly regular way, the quantity needed being always in inverse proportion to the value.   This is the only real difference, in respect to demand, between money and other things ; and for the present purpose it is a difference altogether immaterial.

Money, then, if imported solely as a merchandize, will, like other imported commodities, be of lowest value in the countries for whose exports there is the greatest foreign demand, and which have themselves the least demand for foreign commodities. To these two circumstances it is however necessary to add two others, which produce their effect through cost of carriage. The cost of obtaining bullion is compounded of two elements ; the goods given to purchase it, and the expense of transport : of which last, the bullion countries will bear a part, (though an uncertain part,) in the adjustment of international values. The expense of transport is partly that of carrying the goods to the bullion countries, and partly that of bringing back the bullion : both these items are influenced by the distance from the mines ; and the former is also much affected by the bulkiness of the goods. Countries whose exportable produce consists of the finer manufactures, obtain bullion, as well as all other foreign articles, *cæteris paribus*, at less expense than countries which export nothing but bulky raw produce.

To be quite accurate, therefore, we must say—The countries whose exportable productions are most in demand abroad, and contain greatest value in smallest bulk, which are nearest to the mines, and which have least demand for foreign productions, are those in which money will be of lowest value, or, in other words, in which prices will habitually range the highest. If we are speaking not of the value of money, but of its cost, (that is, the quantity of the country's labour which must be expended to obtain it,) we must add to these four conditions of cheapness a fifth condition, namely, " whose productive industry is the most efficient." This last, however, does not at all affect the value of money, estimated in commodities : it affects the general abundance and facility with which all things, money and commodities together, can be obtained.

Although, therefore, Mr. Senior is right in pointing out the great efficiency of English labour as the chief cause why the precious metals are obtained at less *cost* by England than by most other countries, I cannot admit that it at all accounts for their being of less *value ;* for their going less far in the purchase of commodities. This, in so far as it is a fact, and not an illusion, must be occasioned by the great demand in foreign countries for the staple commodities of England, and the generally unbulky character of those commodities, compared with the corn, wine, timber, sugar, wool, hides,

tallow, hemp, flax, tobacco, raw cotton, &c., which form the exports
of other commercial countries.   These two causes will account for
a somewhat higher range of general prices in England than elsewhere,
notwithstanding the counteracting influence of her own great demand
for foreign commodities.   I am, however, strongly of opinion that
the high prices of commodities, and low purchasing power of money
in England, are more apparent than real.   Food, indeed, is somewhat dearer ; and food composes so large a portion of the expenditure
when the income is small and the family large, that to such families
England is a dear country.   Services, also, of most descriptions,
are dearer than in the other countries of Europe, from the less
costly mode of living of the poorer classes on the Continent.   But
manufactured commodities (except most of those in which good
taste is required) are, decidedly cheaper ; or would be so if buyers
would be content with the same quality of material and of workmanship.   What is called the dearness of living in England is
mainly an affair not of necessity but of foolish custom ; it being
thought imperative by all classes in England above the condition
of a day-labourer that the things they consume should either be
of the same quality with those used by much richer people, or at
least should be as nearly as possible undistinguishable from them
in outward appearance.

§ 3.   From the preceding considerations, it appears that those
are greatly in error who contend [1] that the value of money, in
countries where it is an imported commodity, must be entirely
regulated by its value in the countries which produce it ; and
cannot be raised or lowered in any permanent manner unless some
change has taken place in the cost of production at the mines.   On
the contrary, any circumstance which disturbs the equation of
international demand with respect to a particular country, not only
may, but must, affect the value of money in that country—its value
at the mines remaining the same.   The opening of a new branch
of export trade from England ; an increase in the foreign demand
for English products, either by the natural course of events, or by
the abrogation of duties ; a check to the demand in England for
foreign commodities, by the laying on of import duties in England
or of export duties elsewhere ; these and all other events of similar
tendency, would make the imports of England (bullion and other

----

[1] [In the 1st and 2nd editions here followed : " (as has been done in the
controversies called forth by the recent publications of Colonel Torrens)."]

things taken together) no longer an equivalent for the exports ; and the countries which take her exports would be obliged to offer their commodities, and bullion among the rest, on cheaper terms, in order to re-establish the equation of demand : and thus England would obtain money cheaper, and would acquire a generally higher range of prices. Incidents the reverse of these would produce effects the reverse—would reduce prices ; or, in other words, raise the value of the precious metals. It must be observed, however, that money would be thus raised in value only with respect to home commodities : in relation to all imported articles it would remain as before, since their values would be affected in the same way and in the same degree with its own. A country which, from any of the causes mentioned, gets money cheaper, obtains all its other imports cheaper likewise.

It is by no means necessary that the increased demand for English commodities, which enables England to supply herself with bullion at a cheaper rate, should be a demand in the mining countries. England might export nothing whatever to those countries, and yet might be the country which obtained bullion from them on the lowest terms, provided there were a sufficient intensity of demand in other foreign countries for English goods, which would be paid for circuitously with gold and silver from the mining countries. The whole of its exports are what a country exchanges against the whole of its imports, and not its exports and imports to and from any one country ; and the general foreign demand for its productions will determine what equivalent it must give for imported goods, in order to establish an equilibrium between its sales and purchases generally ; without regard to the maintenance of a similar equilibrium between it and any country singly.

CHAPTER XX

§ 1. WE have thus far considered the precious metals as a commodity, imported like other commodities in the common course of trade, and have examined what are the circumstances which would in that case determine their value. But those metals are also imported in another character, that which belongs to them as a medium of exchange ; not as an article of commerce, to be sold for money, but as themselves money, to pay a debt, or effect a transfer of property. It remains to consider whether the liability of gold and silver to be transported from country to country for such purposes, in any way modifies the conclusions we have already arrived at, or places those metals under a different law of value from that to which, in common with all other imported commodities, they would be subject if international trade were an affair of direct barter.

Money is sent from one country to another for various purposes : such as the payment of tributes or subsidies ; remittances of revenue to or from dependencies, or of rents or other incomes to their absent owners ; emigration of capital, or transmission of it for foreign investment. The most usual purpose, however, is that of payment for goods. To show in what circumstances money actually passes from country to country for this or any of the other purposes mentioned, it is necessary briefly to state the nature of the mechanism by which international trade is carried on, when it takes place not by barter but through the medium of money.

§ 2. In practice, the exports and imports of a country not only are not exchanged directly against each other, but often do not even pass through the same hands. Each is separately bought and paid for with money. We have seen, however, that, even in the same country, money does not actually pass from hand to hand each time that purchases are made with it, and still less does this happen between different countries. The habitual mode of paying and receiving payment for commodities, between country and country, is by bills of exchange.

A merchant in England, A, has exported English commodities, consigning them to his correspondent B in France. Another merchant in France, C, has exported French commodities, suppose of equivalent value, to a merchant D in England. It is evidently unnecessary that B in France should send money to A in England, and that D in England should send an equal sum of money to C in France. The one debt may be applied to the payment of the other, and the double cost and risk of carriage be thus saved. A draws a bill on B for the amount which B owes to him : D, having an equal amount to pay in France, buys this bill from A, and sends it to C, who, at the expiration of the number of days which the bill has to run, presents it to B for payment. Thus the debt due from France to England, and the debt due from England to France, are both paid without sending an ounce of gold or silver from one country to the other.

In this statement, however, it is supposed, that the sum of the debts due from France to England, and the sum of those due from England to France, are equal; that each country has exactly the same number of ounces of gold or silver to pay and to receive. This implies (if we exclude for the present any other international payments than those occurring in the course of commerce), that the exports and imports exactly pay for one another, or, in other words, that the equation of international demand is established. When such is the fact, the international transactions are liquidated without the passage of any money from one country to the other. But if there is a greater sum due from England to France, than is due from France to England, or *vice versâ*, the debts cannot be simply written off against one another. After the one has been applied, as far as it will go, towards covering the other, the balance must be transmitted in the precious metals. In point of fact, the merchant who has the amount to pay, will even then pay for it by a bill. When a person has a remittance to make to a foreign country, he does not himself search for some one who has money to receive from that country, and ask him for a bill of exchange. In this, as in other branches of business, there is a class of middlemen or brokers, who bring buyers and sellers together, or stand between them, buying bills from those who have money to receive, and selling bills to those who have money to pay. When a customer comes to a broker for a bill on Paris or Amsterdam, the broker sells to him, perhaps the bill he may himself have bought that morning from a merchant, perhaps a bill on his own correspondent in the foreign city : and to enable his correspondent to pay, when due, all the bills he has granted, he remits to him all those which he has bought and has not resold. In this manner these brokers take upon themselves the whole settlement of the pecuniary transactions between distant places, being remunerated by a small commission or percentage on the amount of each bill which they either sell or buy. Now, if the brokers find that they are asked for bills on the one part, to a greater amount than bills are offered to them on the other, they do not on this account refuse to give them : but since, in that case, they have no means of enabling the correspondents on whom their bills are drawn, to pay them when due, except by transmitting part of the amount in gold or silver, they require from those to whom they sell bills an additional price, sufficient to cover the freight and insurance of the gold and silver, with a profit sufficient to compensate them for their trouble and for the temporary occupation of a portion of their capital. This premium (as it is called) the buyers are willing to pay, because they must otherwise go to the expense of remitting the precious metals themselves, and it is done cheaper by those who make doing it a part of their especial business. But though only some of those who have a debt to pay would have actually to remit money, all will be obliged, by each other's competition, to pay the premium ; and the brokers are for the same reason obliged to pay it to those whose bills they buy. The reverse of all this happens if, on the comparison of exports and imports, the country, instead of having a balance to pay, has a balance to receive. The brokers find more bills offered to them than are sufficient to cover those which they are required to grant. Bills on foreign countries consequently fall to a discount ; and the competition among the brokers, which is exceedingly active, prevents them from retaining this discount as a profit for themselves, and obliges them to give the benefit of it to those who buy the bills for purposes of remittance.

Let us suppose that all countries had the same currency, as in the progress of political improvement they one day will have : and, as the most familiar to the reader, though not the best, let us suppose this currency to be the English. When England had the same number of pounds sterling to pay to France, which France had to pay to her, one set of merchants in England would want bills, and another set would have bills to dispose of, for the very same number of pounds sterling ; and consequently a bill on France for 100*l.* would sell for exactly 100*l.*, or, in the phraseology of merchants, the exchange would be at par. As France also, on this supposition, would have an equal number of pounds sterling to pay and to receive, bills on England would be at par in France, whenever bills on France were at par in England.

If, however, England had a larger sum to pay to France than to receive from her, there would be persons requiring bills on France for a greater number of pounds sterling than there were bills drawn by persons to whom money was due. A bill on France for 100*l.* would then sell for more than 100*l.*, and bills would be said to be at a premium. The premium, however, could not exceed the cost and risk of making the remittance in gold, together with a trifling profit ; because if it did, the debtor would send the gold itself, in preference to buying the bill.

If, on the contrary, England had more money to receive from France than to pay, there would be bills offered for a greater number of pounds than were wanted for remittance, and the price of bills would fall below par : a bill for a 100*l.* might be bought for somewhat less than 100*l.*, and bills would be said to be at a discount.

When England has more to pay than to receive, France has more to receive than to pay, and *vice versâ*. When, therefore, in England, bills on France bear a premium, then, in France, bills on England are at a discount : and when bills on France are at a discount in England, bills on England are at a premium in France. If they are at par in either country, they are so, as we have already seen, in both.

Thus do matters stand between countries, or places, which have the same currency. So much of barbarism, however, still remains in the transactions of the most civilized nations, that almost all independent countries choose to assert their nationality by having, to their own inconvenience and that of their neighbours, a peculiar currency of their own. To our present purpose this makes no other difference, than that instead of speaking of *equal* sums of money, we have to speak of *equivalent* sums. By equivalent sums, when both currencies are composed of the same metal, are meant sums which contain exactly the same quantity of the metal, in weight and fineness ; but when, as in the case of France and England, the metals are different, what is meant is that the quantity of gold in the one sum, and the quantity of silver in the other, are of the same value in the general market of the world : there being no material difference between one place and another in the relative value of these metals.   Suppose 25 francs to be (as within a trifling fraction it is) the equivalent of a pound sterling.   The debts and credits of the two countries would be equal, when the one owed as many times 25 francs, as the other owed pounds.   When this was the case, a bill on France for 2500 francs would be worth in England 100*l.*, and a bill on England for 100*l.* would be worth in France 2500 francs.   The exchange is then said to be at par : and 25 francs (in reality 25 francs and a trifle more) * is called the par of exchange with France.   When England owed to France more than the equivalent of what France owed to her, a bill for 2500 francs would be at a premium, that is, would be worth more than 100*l.*   When France owed to England more than the equivalent of what England owed to France, a bill for 2500 francs would be worth less than 100*l.*, or would be at a discount.

When bills on foreign countries are at a premium, it is customary to say that the exchanges are against the country, or unfavourable to .it.   In order to understand these phrases, we must take notice of what " the exchange," in the language of merchants, really means.   It means the power which the money of the country has of purchasing the money of other countries.   Supposing 25 francs to be the exact par of exchange, then when it requires more than 100*l.* to buy a bill for 2500 francs, 100*l.* of English money are worth less than their real equivalent of French money : and this is called an exchange unfavourable to England.   The only persons in England, however, to whom it is really unfavourable are those who have money to pay in France ; for they come into the bill market as buyers, and have to pay a premium : but to those who have money to receive in France, the same state of things is favourable ; for they come as sellers, and receive the premium.   The premium, however, indicates that a balance is due by England, which might have to be eventually liquidated in the precious metals : and since, according to the old theory, the benefit of a trade consisted in bringing money into the country, this prejudice introduced the practice of calling the exchange favourable when it indicated a

* [1862] Written before the change in the relative value of the two metals produced by the gold discoveries. The par of exchange between gold and silver currencies is now variable, and no one can foresee at what point it will ultimately rest.

balance to receive, and unfavourable when it indicated one to pay : and the phrases in turn tended to maintain the prejudice.

§ 3. It might be supposed at first sight that when the exchange is unfavourable, or, in other words, when bills are at a premium, the premium must always amount to a full equivalent for the cost of transmitting money : since, as there is really a balance to pay, and as the full cost must therefore be incurred by some of those who have remittances to make, their competition will compel all to submit to an equivalent sacrifice. And such would certainly be the case, if it were always necessary that whatever is destined to be paid should be paid immediately. The expectation of great and immediate foreign payments sometimes produces a most start-ling effect on the exchanges.* But a small excess of imports above exports, or any other small amount of debt to be paid to foreign countries, does not usually affect the exchanges to the full extent of the cost and risk of transporting bullion. The length of credit allowed generally permits, on the part of some of the debtors, a postponement of payment, and in the mean time the balance may turn the other way, and restore the equality of debts and credits without any actual transmission of the metals. And this is the more likely to happen, as there is a self-adjusting power in the variations of the exchange itself. Bills are at a premium because a greater money value has been imported than exported. But the premium is itself an extra profit to those who export. Besides the price they obtain for their goods, they draw for the amount and gain the premium. It is, on the other hand, a diminution of profit to those who import. Besides the price of the goods, they have to pay a premium for remittance. So that what is called an un-favourable exchange is an encouragement to export, and a discourage-ment to import. And if the balance due is of small amount, and

* On the news of Bonaparte's landing from Elba, the price of bills advanced in one day as much as ten per cent. Of course this premium was not a mere equivalent for cost of carriage, since the freight of such an article as gold, even with the addition of war insurance, could never have amounted to so much. This great price was an equivalent not for the difficulty of sending gold, but for the anticipated difficulty of procuring it to send ; the expectation being that there would be such immense remittances to the Continent in subsidies and for the support of armies, as would press hard on the stock of bullion in the country (which was then entirely denuded of specie), and this, too, in a shorter time than would allow of its being replenished. Accordingly the price of bullion rose likewise, with the same suddenness. It is hardly necessary to say that this took place during the Bank restriction. In a convertible state of the currency, no such thing could have occurred until the Bank stopped payment.

is the consequence of some merely casual disturbance in the ordinary course of trade, it is soon liquidated in commodities, and the account adjusted by means of bills, without the transmission of any bullion. Not so, however, when the excess of imports above exports, which has made the exchange unfavourable, arises from a permanent cause. In that case, what disturbed the equilibrium must have been the state of prices, and it can only be restored by acting on prices. It is impossible that prices should be such as to invite to an excess of imports, and yet that the exports should be kept permanently up to the imports by the extra profit on exportation derived from the premium on bills; for if the exports were kept up to the imports, bills would not be at a premium, and the extra profit would not exist. It is through the prices of commodities that the correction must be administered.

Disturbances, therefore, of the equilibrium of imports and exports, and consequent disturbances of the exchange, may be considered as of two classes; the one casual or accidental, which, if not on too large a scale, correct themselves through the premium on bills, without any transmission of the precious metals; the other arising from the general state of prices, which cannot be corrected without the subtraction of actual money from the circulation of one of the countries, or an annihilation of credit equivalent to it; since the mere transmission of bullion (as distinguished from money), not having any effect on prices, is of no avail to abate the cause from which the disturbance proceeded.

It remains to observe, that the exchanges do not depend on the balance of debts and credits with each country separately, but with all countries taken together. England may owe a balance of payments to France; but it does not follow that the exchange with France will be against England, and that bills on France will be at a premium; because a balance may be due to England from Holland or Hamburg, and she may pay her debts to France with bills on those places; which is technically called arbitration of exchange. There is some little additional expense, partly commission and partly loss of interest, in settling debts in this circuitous manner, and to the extent of that small difference the exchange with one country may vary apart from that with others; but in the main, the exchanges with all foreign countries vary together, according as the country has a balance to receive or to pay on the general result of its foreign transactions.

CHAPTER XXI

§ 1. HAVING now examined the mechanism by which the
commercial transactions between nations are actually conducted,
we have next to inquire whether this mode of conducting them
makes any difference in the conclusions respecting international
values, which we previously arrived at on the hypothesis of barter.
The nearest analogy would lead us to presume the negative.
We did not find that the intervention of money and its substitutes
made any difference in the law of value as applied to adjacent
places. Things which would have been equal in value if the mode
of exchange had been by barter, are worth equal sums of money.
The introduction of money is a mere addition of one more commodity, of which the value is regulated by the same laws as that
of all other commodities. We shall not be surprised, therefore, if
we find that international values also are determined by the same
causes under a money and bill system, as they would be under a
system of barter; and that money has little to do in the matter,
except to furnish a convenient mode of comparing values.

All interchange is, in substance and effect, barter: whoever
sells commodities for money, and with that money buys other goods,
really buys those goods with his own commodities. And so of
nations: their trade is a mere exchange of exports for imports;
and whether money is employed or not, things are only in their
permanent state when the exports and imports exactly pay for each
other. When this is the case, equal sums of money are due from
each country to the other, the debts are settled by bills, and there
is no balance to be paid in the precious metals. The trade is in
a state like that which is called in mechanics a condition of stable
equilibrium.

But the process by which things are brought back to this state when they happen to deviate from it, is, at least outwardly, not the same in a barter system and in a money system. Under the first, the country which wants more imports than its exports will pay for, must offer its exports at a cheaper rate, as the sole means of creating a demand for them sufficient to re-establish the equilibrium. When money is used, the country seems to do a thing totally different. She takes the additional imports at the same price as before, and as she exports no equivalent, the balance of payments turns against her ; the exchange becomes unfavourable, and the difference has to be paid in money. This is in appearance a very distinct operation from the former. Let us see if it differs in its essence, or only in its mechanism.

Let the country which has the balance to pay be England, and the country which receives it, France. By this transmission of the precious metals, the quantity of the currency is diminished in England, and increased in France. This I am at liberty to assume. As we shall see hereafter, it would be a very erroneous assumption if made in regard to *all* payments of international balances. A balance which has only to be paid once, such as the payment made for an extra importation of corn in a season of dearth, may be paid from hoards, or from the reserves of bankers, without acting on the circulation. But we are now supposing that there is an excess of imports over exports, arising from the fact that the equation of international demand is not yet established : that there is at the ordinary prices a permanent demand in England for more French goods than the English goods required in France at the ordinary prices will pay for. When this is the case, if a change were not made in the prices, there would be a perpetually renewed balance to be paid in money. The imports require to be permanently diminished, or the exports to be increased ; which can only be accomplished through prices ; and hence, even if the balances are at first paid from hoards, or by the exportation of bullion, they will reach the circulation at last, for until they do, nothing can stop the drain.

When, therefore, the state of prices is such that the equation of international demand cannot establish itself, the country requiring more imports than can be paid for by the exports ; it is a sign that the country has more of the precious metals or their substitutes in circulation, than can permanently circulate, and must necessarily part with some of them before the balance can be restored. The currency is accordingly contracted : prices fall, and, among the rest, the prices of exportable articles ; for which, accordingly, there arises, in foreign countries, a greater demand : while imported commodities have possibly risen in price, from the influx of money into foreign countries, and at all events have not participated in the general fall. But until the increased cheapness of English goods induces foreign countries to take a greater pecuniary value, or until the increased dearness (positive or comparative) of foreign goods makes England take a less pecuniary value, the exports of England will be no nearer to paying for the imports than before, and the stream of the precious metals which had begun to flow out of England, will still flow on. This efflux will continue, until the fall of prices in England brings within reach of the foreign market some commodity which England did not previously send thither ; or until the reduced prices of the things which she did send, has forced a demand abroad for a sufficient quantity to pay for the imports, aided, perhaps, by a reduction of the English demand for foreign goods, through their enhanced price, either positive or comparative.

Now this is the very process which took place on our original supposition of barter. Not only, therefore, does the trade between nations tend to the same equilibrium between exports and imports, whether money is employed or not, but the means by which this equilibrium is established are essentially the same. The country whose exports are not sufficient to pay for her imports, offers them on cheaper terms, until she succeeds in forcing the necessary demand : in other words, the Equation of International Demand, under a money system as well as under a barter system, is the law of international trade. Every country exports and imports the very same things, and in the very same quantity, under the one system as under the other. In a barter system, the trade gravitates to the point at which the sum of the imports exactly exchanges for the sum of the exports: in a money system, it gravitates to the point at which the sum of the imports and the sum of the exports exchange for the same quantity of money. And since things which are equal to the same thing are equal to one another, the exports and imports which are equal in money price, would, if money were not used, precisely exchange for one another.*

* The subjoined extract from the separate Essay previously referred to, will give some assistance in following the course of the phenomena. It is adapted to the imaginary case used for illustration throughout that Essay, the case of a trade between England and Germany in cloth and linen.

" We may, at first, make whatever supposition we will with respect to the value of money. Let us suppose, therefore, that before the opening of the trade, the price of cloth is the same in both countries, namely six shillings per yard.

§ 2. It thus appears that the law of international values, and, consequently, the division of the advantages of trade among the nations which carry it on, are the same, on the supposition of money, as they would be in a state of barter. In international, as in ordinary domestic interchanges, money is to commerce only what oil is to machinery, or railways to locomotion—a contrivance to diminish friction. In order still further to test these conclusions, let us proceed to re-examine, on the supposition of money, a question which we have already investigated on the hypothesis of barter,

As ten yards of cloth were supposed to exchange in England for 15 yards of linen, in Germany for 20, we must suppose that linen is sold in England at four shillings per yard, in Germany at three. Cost of carriage and importer's profit are left, as before, out of consideration.

" In this state of prices, cloth, it is evident, cannot yet be exported from England into Germany: but linen can be imported from Germany into England. It will be so ; and, in the first instance, the linen will be paid for in money.

" The efflux of money from England, and its influx into Germany, will raise money prices in the latter country and lower them in the former. Linen will rise in Germany above three shillings per yard, and cloth above six shillings. Linen in England, being imported from Germany, will (since cost of carriage is not reckoned) sink to the same price as in that country, while cloth will fall below six shillings. As soon as the price of cloth is lower in England than in Germany, it will begin to be exported, and the price of cloth in Germany will fall to what it is in England. As long as the cloth exported does not suffice to pay for the linen imported, money will continue to flow from England into Germany, and prices generally will continue to fall in England and rise in Germany. By the fall, however, of cloth in England, cloth will fall in Germany also, and the demand for it will increase. By the rise of linen in Germany, linen must rise in England also, and the demand for it will diminish. As cloth fell in price and linen rose, there would be some particular price of both articles at which the cloth exported and the linen imported would exactly pay for each other. At this point prices would remain, because money would then cease to move out of England into Germany. What this point might be, would entirely depend upon the circumstances and inclinations of the purchasers on both sides. If the fall of cloth did not much increase the demand for it in Germany, and the rise of linen did not diminish very rapidly the demand for it in England, much money must pass before the equilibrium is restored ; cloth would fall very much, and linen would rise, until England, perhaps, had to pay nearly as much for it as when she produced it for herself. But if, on the contrary, the fall of cloth caused a very rapid increase of the demand for it in Germany, and the rise of linen in Germany reduced very rapidly the demand in England from what it was under the influence of the first cheapness produced by the opening of the trade; the cloth would very soon suffice to pay for the linen, little money would pass between the two countries, and England would derive a large portion of the benefit of the trade. We have thus arrived at precisely the same conclusion, in supposing the employment of money, which we found to hold under the supposition of barter.

" In what shape the benefit accrues to the two nations from the trade is clear enough. Germany, before the commencement of the trade, paid six shillings per yard for broadcloth : she now obtains it at a lower price. This, however, is not the whole of her advantage. As the money prices of all her

namely, to what extent the benefit of an improvement in the production of an exportable article is participated in by the countries importing it.

The improvement may either consist in the cheapening of some article which was already a staple production of the country, or in the establishment of some new branch of industry, or of some process rendering an article exportable which had not till then been exported at all. It will be convenient to begin with the case of a new export, as being somewhat the simpler of the two.

The first effect is that the article falls in price, and a demand

other commodities have risen, the money-incomes of all her producers have increased. This is no advantage to them in buying from each other, because the price of what they buy has risen in the same ratio with their means of paying for it ; but it is an advantage to them in buying anything which has not risen, and, still more, anything which has fallen. They, therefore, benefit as consumers of cloth, not merely to the extent to which cloth has fallen, but also to the extent to which other prices have risen. Suppose that this is one-tenth. The same proportion of their money incomes as before will suffice to supply their other wants ; and the remainder, being increased one-tenth in amount, will enable them to purchase one-tenth more cloth than before, even though cloth had not fallen : but it has fallen ; so that they are doubly gainers. They purchase the same quantity with less money, and have more to expend upon their other wants.

" In England, on the contrary, general money-prices have fallen. Linen, however, has fallen more than the rest, having been lowered in price by importation from a country where it was cheaper ; whereas the others have fallen only from the consequent efflux of money. Notwithstanding, therefore, the general fall of money-prices, the English producers will be exactly as they were in all other respects, while they will gain as purchasers of linen.

" The greater the efflux of money required to restore the equilibrium, the greater will be the gain of Germany, both by the fall of cloth and by the rise of her general prices. The less the efflux of money requisite, the greater will be the gain of England ; because the price of linen will continue lower, and her general prices will not be reduced so much. It must not, however, be imagined that high money-prices are a good, and low money-prices an evil, in themselves. But the higher the general money-prices in any country, the greater will be that country's means of purchasing those commodities which, being imported from abroad, are independent of the causes which keep prices high at home."

In practice, the cloth and the linen would not, as here supposed, be at the same price in England and in Germany : each would be dearer in money-price in the country which imported than in that which produced it, by the amount of the cost of carriage, together with the ordinary profit on the importer's capital for the average length of time which elapsed before the commodity could be disposed of. But it does not follow that each country pays the cost of carriage of the commodity it imports ; for the addition of this item to the price may operate as a greater check to demand on one side than on the other ; and the equation of international demand, and consequent equilibrium of payments, may not be maintained. Money would then flow out of one country into the other, until, in the manner already illustrated, the equilibrium was restored : and, when this was effected, one country would be paying more than its own cost of carriage, and the other less.

arises for it abroad. This new exportation disturbs the balance, turns the exchanges, money flows into the country (which we shall suppose to be England), and continues to flow until prices rise. This higher range of prices will somewhat check the demand in foreign countries for the new article of export; and will diminish the demand which existed abroad for the other things which England was in the habit of exporting. The exports will thus be diminished; while at the same time the English public, having more money, will have a greater power of purchasing foreign commodities. If they make use of this increased power of purchase, there will be an increase of imports: and by this, and the check to exportation, the equilibrium of imports and exports will be restored. The result to foreign countries will be, that they have to pay dearer than before for their other imports, and obtain the new commodity cheaper than before, but not so much cheaper as England herself does. I say this, being well aware that the article would be actually at the very same price (cost of carriage excepted) in England and in other countries. The cheapness, however, of the article is not measured solely by the money-price, but by that price compared with the money incomes of the consumers. The price is the same to the English and to the foreign consumers; but the former pay that price from money incomes which have been increased by the new distribution of the precious metals; while the latter have had their money incomes probably diminished by the same cause. The trade, therefore, has not imparted to the foreign consumer the whole, but only a portion, of the benefit which the English consumer has derived from the improvement; while England has also benefited in the prices of foreign commodities. Thus, then, any industrial improvement which leads to the opening of a new branch of export trade, benefits a country not only by the cheapness of the article in which the improvement has taken place, but by a general cheapening of all imported products.

Let us now change the hypothesis, and suppose that the improvement, instead of creating a new export from England, cheapens an existing one. When we examined this case on the supposition of barter, it appeared to us that the foreign consumers might either obtain the same benefit from the improvement as England herself, or a less benefit, or even a greater benefit, according to the degree in which the consumption of the cheapened article is calculated to extend itself as the article diminishes in price. The same conclusions will be found true on the supposition of money.

Let the commodity in which there is an improvement be cloth. The first effect of the improvement is that its price falls, and there is an increased demand for it in the foreign market. But this demand is of uncertain amount. Suppose the foreign consumers to increase their purchases in the exact ratio of the cheapness, or, in other words, to lay out in cloth the same sum of money as before; the same aggregate payment as before will be due from foreign countries to England; the equilibrium of exports and imports will remain undisturbed, and foreigners will obtain the full advantage of the increased cheapness of cloth. But if the foreign demand for cloth is of such a character as to increase in a greater ratio than the cheapness, a larger sum than formerly will be due to England for cloth, and when paid will raise English prices, the price of cloth included; this rise, however, will affect only the foreign purchaser, English incomes being raised in a corresponding proportion; and the foreign consumer will thus derive a less advantage than England from the improvement. If, on the contrary, the cheapening of cloth does not extend the foreign demand for it in a proportional degree, a less sum of debts than before will be due to England for cloth, while there will be the usual sum of debts due from England to foreign countries; the balance of trade will turn against England, money will be exported, prices (that of cloth included) will fall, and cloth will eventually be cheapened to the foreign purchaser in a still greater ratio than the improvement has cheapened it to England. These are the very conclusions which we deduced on the hypothesis of barter.

The result of the preceding discussion cannot be better summed up than in the words of Ricardo.* " Gold and silver having been chosen for the general medium of circulation, they are, by the competition of commerce, distributed in such proportions amongst the different countries of the world as to accommodate themselves to the natural traffic which would take place if no such metals existed, and the trade between countries were purely a trade of barter." Of this principle, so fertile in consequences, previous to which the theory of foreign trade was an unintelligible chaos, Mr. Ricardo, though he did not pursue it into its ramifications, was the real originator. No writer who preceded him appears to have had a glimpse of it : and few are those who even since his time have had an adequate conception of its scientific value.

* *Principles of Political Economy and Taxation*, 3rd ed. p. 143.

§ 3. It is now necessary to inquire, in what manner this law of the distribution of the precious metals by means of the exchanges, affects the exchange value of money itself ; and how it tallies with the law by which we found that the value of money is regulated when imported as a mere article of merchandize. For there is here a semblance of contradiction, which has, I think, contributed more than anything else to make some distinguished political economists resist the evidence of the preceding doctrines. Money, they justly think, is no exception to the general laws of value ; it is a commodity like any other, and its average or natural value must depend on the cost of producing, or at least of obtaining it. That its distribution through the world, therefore, and its different value in different places, should be liable to be altered, not by causes affecting itself, but by a hundred causes unconnected with it; by everything which affects the trade in other commodities, so as to derange the equilibrium of exports and imports ; appears to these thinkers a doctrine altogether inadmissible.

But the supposed anomaly exists only in semblance. The causes which bring money into or carry it out of a country through the exchanges to restore the equilibrium of trade, and which thereby raise its value in some countries and lower it in others, are the very same causes on which the local value of money would depend if it were never imported except as a merchandize, and never except directly from the mines. When the value of money in a country is permanently lowered by an influx of it through the balance of trade, the cause, if it is not diminished cost of production, must be one of those causes which compel a new adjustment, more favourable to the country, of the equation of international demand : namely, either an increased demand abroad for her commodities, or a diminished demand on her part for those of foreign countries. Now an increased foreign demand for the commodities of a country, or a diminished demand in the country for imported commodities, are the very causes which, on the general principles of trade, enable a country to purchase all imports, and consequently the precious metals, at a lower value. There is therefore no contradiction, but the most perfect accordance in the results of the two different modes in which the precious metals may be obtained. When money flows from country to country in consequence of changes in the international demand for commodities, and by so doing alters its own local value, it merely realizes, by a more rapid process, the effect which would otherwise take place more slowly, by an alteration in the relative breadth of the streams by which the precious metals flow into different regions of the earth from the mining countries. As, therefore, we before saw that the use of money as a medium of exchange does not in the least alter the law on which the values of other things, either in the same country or internationally, depend, so neither does it alter the law of the value of the precious metal itself : and there is in the whole doctrine of international values, as now laid down, a unity and harmony which is a strong collateral presumption of truth.

§ 4. Before closing this discussion, it is fitting to point out in what manner and degree the preceding conclusions are affected by the existence of international payments not originating in commerce, and for which no equivalent in either money or commodities is expected or received ; such as a tribute, or remittances of rent to absentee landlords, or of interest to foreign creditors, or a government expenditure abroad, such as England incurs in the management of some of her colonial dependencies.

To begin with the case of barter. The supposed annual remittances being made in commodities, and being exports for which there is to be no return, it is no longer requisite that the imports and exports should pay for one another : on the contrary, there must be an annual excess of exports over imports, equal to the value of the remittance. If, before the country became liable to the annual payment, foreign commerce was in its natural state of equilibrium, it will now be necessary for the purpose of effecting the remittance, that foreign countries should be induced to take a greater quantity of exports than before : which can only be done by offering those exports on cheaper terms, or, in other words, by paying dearer for foreign commodities. The international values will so adjust themselves that either by greater exports, or smaller imports, or both, the requisite excess on the side of exports will be brought about ; and this excess will become the permanent state. The result is that a country which makes regular payments to foreign countries, besides losing what it pays, loses also something more, by the less advantageous terms on which it is forced to exchange its productions for foreign commodities.

The same results follow on the supposition of money. Commerce being supposed to be in a state of equilibrium when the obligatory remittances begin, the first remittance is necessarily made in money. This lowers prices in the remitting country, and raises them in the

receiving.   The natural effect is that more commodities are exported
than before, and fewer imported, and that, on the score of commerce
alone, a balance of money will be constantly due from the receiving
to the paying country.   When the debt thus annually due to the
tributary country becomes equal to the annual tribute or other
regular payment due from it, no further transmission of money takes
place ; the equilibrium of exports and imports will no longer exist,
but that of payments will ; the exchange will be at par, the two
debts will be set off against one another, and the tribute or remittance will be virtually paid in goods.   The result to the interest
of the two countries will be as already pointed out : the paying
country will give a higher price for all that it buys from the receiving
country, while the latter, besides receiving the tribute, obtains the
exportable produce of the tributary country at a lower price.

CHAPTER XXII

§ 1. IN our inquiry into the laws of international trade, we
commenced with the principles which determine international
exchanges and international values on the hypothesis of barter. We
next showed that the introduction of money as a medium of exchange
makes no difference in the laws of exchanges and of values between
country and country, no more than between individual and individual : since the precious metals, under the influence of those
same laws, distribute themselves in such proportions among the
different countries of the world, as to allow the very same exchanges
to go on, and at the same values, as would be the case under a
system of barter. We lastly considered how the value of money
itself is affected, by those alterations in the state of trade which
arises from alterations either in the demand and supply of commodities, or in their cost of production. It remains to consider the
alterations in the state of trade which originate not in commodities
but in money.

Gold and silver may vary like other things, though they are not
so likely to vary as other things, in their cost of production. The
demand for them in foreign countries may also vary. It may
increase, by augmented employment of the metals for purposes of
art and ornament, or because the increase of production and of
transactions has created a greater amount of business to be done by
the circulating medium. It may diminish, for the opposite reasons ;
or from the extension of the economizing expedients by which the
use of metallic money is partially dispensed with. These changes
act upon the trade between other countries and the mining countries,
and upon the value of the precious metals, according to the general
laws of the value of imported commodities : which have been set
forth in the previous chapters with sufficient fulness.

What I propose to examine in the present chapter, is not those circumstances affecting money, which alter the permanent conditions of its value ; but the effects produced on international trade by casual or temporary variations in the value of money, which have no connexion with any causes affecting its permanent value.   This is a subject of importance, on account of its bearing upon the practical problem which has excited so much discussion for sixty years past, the regulation of the currency.

§ 2.   Let us suppose in any country a circulating medium purely metallic, and a sudden casual increase made to it ; for example, by bringing into circulation hoards of treasure, which had been concealed in a previous period of foreign invasion or internal disorder. The natural effect would be a rise of prices.   This would check exports, and encourage imports ; the imports would exceed the exports, the exchanges would become unfavourable, and the newly acquired stock of money would diffuse itself over all countries with which the supposed country carried on trade, and from them, progressively, through all parts of the commercial world.   The money which thus overflowed would spread itself to an equal depth over all commercial countries.   For it would go on flowing until the exports and imports again balanced one another : and this (as no change is supposed in the permanent circumstances of international demand) could only be, when the money had diffused itself so equally that prices had risen in the same ratio in all countries, so that the alteration of price would be for all practical purposes ineffective, and the exports and imports, though at a higher money valuation, would be exactly the same as they were originally.   This diminished value of money throughout the world (at least, if the diminution was considerable) would cause a suspension, or at least a diminution, of the annual supply from the mines : since the metal would no longer command a value equivalent to its highest cost of production.   The annual waste would, therefore, not be fully made up, and the usual causes of destruction would gradually reduce the aggregate quantity of the precious metals to its former amount ; after which their production would recommence on its former scale. The discovery of the treasure would thus produce only temporary effects ; namely, a brief disturbance of international trade until the treasure had disseminated itself through the world, and then a temporary depression in the value of the metal, below that which corresponds to the cost of producing or of obtaining it ; which depression would gradually be corrected, by a temporarily diminished production in the producing countries, and importation in the importing countries.

The same effects which would thus arise from the discovery of a treasure, accompany the process by which bank notes, or any of the other substitutes for money, take the place of the precious metals. Suppose that England possessed a currency wholly metallic of twenty millions sterling, and that suddenly twenty millions of bank notes were sent into circulation. If these were issued by bankers, they would be employed in loans, or in the purchase of securities, and would therefore create a sudden fall in the rate of interest, which would probably send a great part of the twenty millions of gold out of the country as capital to seek a higher rate of interest elsewhere, before there had been time for any action on prices. But we will suppose that the notes are not issued by bankers or money-lenders of any kind, but by manufacturers, in the payment of wages and purchase of materials, or by the government in its ordinary expenses, so that the whole amount would be rapidly carried into the markets for commodities. The following would be the natural order of consequences. All prices would rise greatly. Exportation would almost cease ; importation would be prodigiously stimulated. A great balance of payments would become due, the exchanges would turn against England, to the full extent of the cost of exporting money ; and the surplus coin would pour itself rapidly forth, over the various countries of the world, in the order of their proximity, geographically and commercially, to England. The efflux would continue until the currencies of all countries had come to a level ; by which I do not mean, until money became of the same value everywhere, but until the differences were only those which existed before, and which corresponded to permanent differences in the cost of obtaining it. When the rise of prices had extended itself in an equal degree to all countries, exports and imports would everywhere revert to what they were at first, would balance one another, and the exchanges would return to par. If such a sum of money as twenty millions, when spread over the whole surface of the commercial world, were sufficient to raise the general level in a perceptible degree, the effect would be of no long duration. No alteration having occurred in the general conditions under which the metals were procured, either in the world at large or in any part of it, the reduced value would no longer be remunerating and the supply from the mines would cease partially or wholly, until the twenty millions were absorbed ; * after which absorption, the currencies of all countries would be, in quantity and in value, nearly at their original level. I say nearly, for in strict accuracy there would be a slight difference. A somewhat smaller annual supply of the precious metals would now be required, there being in the world twenty millions less of metallic money undergoing waste. The equilibrium of payments, consequently, between the mining countries and the rest of the world, would thenceforth require that the mining countries should either export rather more of something else, or import rather less of foreign commodities ; which implies a somewhat lower range of prices than previously in the mining countries, and a somewhat higher in all others ; a scantier currency in the former, and rather fuller currencies in the latter. This effect, which would be too trifling to require notice except for the illustration of a principle, is the only permanent change which would be produced on international trade, or on the value or quantity of the currency of any country.

Effects of another kind, however, will have been produced. Twenty millions, which formerly existed in the unproductive form of metallic money, have been converted into what is, or is capable of becoming, productive capital. This gain is at first made by England at the expense of other countries, who have taken her superfluity of this costly and unproductive article off her hands, giving for it an equivalent value in other commodities. By degrees the loss is made up to those countries by diminished influx from the mines, and finally the world has gained a virtual addition of twenty millions to its productive resources. Adam Smith's illustration, though so well known, deserves for its extreme aptness to be once more repeated. He compares the substitution of paper in the room of the precious metals, to the construction of a highway through the air, by which the ground now occupied by roads would become available for agriculture. As in that case a portion of the soil, so in this a part of the accumulated wealth of the country, would be relieved from a function in which it was only employed in rendering other soils and capitals productive, and would itself become applicable to production ; the office it previously fulfilled being equally well discharged by a medium which costs nothing.

* [1862] I am here supposing a state of things in which gold and silver mining are a permanent branch of industry, carried on under known conditions ; and not the present state of uncertainty, in which gold-gathering is a game of chance, prosecuted (for the present) in the spirit of an adventure, not in that of a regular industrial pursuit.

The value saved to the community by thus dispensing with metallic money, is a clear gain to those who provide the substitute. They have the use of twenty millions of circulating medium which have cost them only the expense of an engraver's plate. If they employ this accession to their fortunes as productive capital, the produce of the country is increased, and the community benefited, as much as by any other capital of equal amount. Whether it is so employed or not, depends, in some degree, upon the mode of issuing it. If issued by the government, and employed in paying off debt, it would probably become productive capital. The government, however, may prefer employing this extraordinary resource in its ordinary expenses ; may squander it uselessly, or make it a mere temporary substitute for taxation to an equivalent amount ; in which last case the amount is saved by the taxpayers at large, who either add it to their capital or spend it as income. When paper currency is supplied, as in our own country, by bankers and banking companies, the amount is almost wholly turned into productive capital : for the issuers, being at all times liable to be called upon to refund the value, are under the strongest inducements not to squander it, and the only cases in which it is not forthcoming are cases of fraud or mismanagement. A banker's profession being that of a money-lender, his issue of notes is a simple extension of his ordinary occupation. He lends the amount to farmers, manufacturers, or dealers, who employ it in their several businesses. So employed, it yields, like any other capital, wages of labour and profits of stock. The profit is shared between the banker, who receives interest, and a succession of borrowers, mostly for short periods, who after paying the interest, gain a profit in addition, or a convenience equivalent to profit. The capital itself in the long run becomes entirely wages, and when replaced by the sale of the produce, becomes wages again ; thus affording a perpetual fund, of the value of twenty millions, for the maintenance of productive labour, and increasing the annual produce of the country by all that can be produced through the means of a capital of that value. To this gain must be added a further saving to the country, of the annual supply of the precious metals necessary for repairing the wear and tear, and other waste, of a metallic currency.

The substitution, therefore, of paper for the precious metals, should always be carried as far as is consistent with safety ; no greater amount of metallic currency being retained than is necessary to maintain, both in fact and in public belief, the convertibility of the paper. A country with the extensive commercial relations of

England is liable to be suddenly called upon for large foreign payments, sometimes in loans, or other investments of capital abroad,
sometimes as the price of some unusual importation of goods, the
most frequent case being that of large importations of food consequent on a bad harvest. To meet such demands it is necessary that
there should be, either in circulation or in the coffers of the banks,
coin or bullion to a very considerable amount, and that this, when
drawn out by any emergency, should be allowed to return after the
emergency is past. But since gold wanted for exportation is almost
invariably drawn from the reserves of the banks, and is never likely
to be taken directly from the circulation while the banks remain
solvent, the only advantage which can be obtained from retaining
partially a metallic currency for daily purposes is that the banks
may occasionally replenish their reserves from it.

§ 3. When metallic money had been entirely superseded and
expelled from circulation, by the substitution of an equal amount of
bank notes, any attempt to keep a still further quantity of paper
in circulation must, if the notes are convertible, be a complete failure.
The new issue would again set in motion the same train of consequences by which the gold coin had already been expelled. The
metals would, as before, be required for exportation, and would be for
that purpose demanded from the banks, to the full extent of the
superfluous notes ; which thus could not possibly be retained in
circulation. If, indeed, the notes were inconvertible, there would
be no such obstacle to the increase of their quantity. An inconvertible paper acts in the same way as a convertible, while there remains
any coin for it to supersede : the difference begins to manifest itself
when all the coin is driven from circulation (except what may be
retained for the convenience of small change), and the issues still
go on increasing. When the paper begins to exceed in quantity
the metallic currency which it superseded, prices of course rise ;
things which were worth 5*l.* in metallic money, become worth 6*l.*
in inconvertible paper, or more, as the case may be. But this rise of
price will not, as in the cases before examined, stimulate import,
and discourage export. The imports and exports are determined
by the metallic prices of things, not by the paper prices : and it is
only when the paper is exchangeable at pleasure for the metals that
paper prices and metallic prices must correspond.

Let us suppose that England is the country which has the depreciated paper. Suppose that some English production could be

bought, while the currency was still metallic, for 5*l*., and sold in France for 5*l*. 10*s*., the difference covering the expense and risk, and affording a profit to the merchant. On account of the depreciation this commodity will now cost in England 6*l*., and cannot be sold in France for more than 5*l*. 10*s*., and yet it will be exported as before. Why ? Because the 5*l*. 10*s*., which the exporter can get for it in France, is not depreciated paper, but gold or silver: and since in England bullion has risen, in the same proportion with other things—if the merchant brings the gold or silver to England, he can sell his 5*l*. 10*s*. for 6*l*. 12*s*., and obtain as before 10 per cent for profit and expenses.

It thus appears, that a depreciation of the currency does not affect the foreign trade of the country : this is carried on precisely as if the currency maintained its value. But though the trade is not affected, the exchanges are. When the imports and exports are in equilibrium, the exchange, in a metallic currency, would be at par ; a bill on France for the equivalent of five sovereigns, would be worth five sovereigns. But five sovereigns, or the quantity of gold contained in them, having come to be worth in England 6*l*., it follows that a bill on France for 5*l*. will be worth 6*l*. When, therefore, the *real* exchange is at par, there will be a *nominal* exchange against the country, of as much per cent as the amount of the depreciation. If the currency is depreciated 10, 15, or 20 per cent, then in whatever way the real exchange, arising from the variations of international debts and credits, may vary, the quoted exchange will always differ 10, 15, or 20 per cent from it. However high this nominal premium may be, it has no tendency to send gold out of the country, for the purpose of drawing a bill against it and profiting by the premium ; because the gold so sent must be procured, not from the banks and at par, as in the case of a convertible currency, but in the market at an advance of price equal to the premium. In such cases, instead of saying that the exchange is unfavourable, it would be a more correct representation to say that the par has altered, since there is now required a larger quantity of English currency to be equivalent to the same quantity of foreign. The exchanges, however, continue to be computed according to the metallic par. The quoted exchanges, therefore, when there is a depreciated currency, are compounded of two elements or factors ; the real exchange, which follows the variations of international payments, and the nominal exchange, which varies with the depreciation of the currency, but which, while there is any depreciation at all, must always be unfavourable. Since the amount of depreciation is exactly measured by the degree in which the market price of bullion exceeds the Mint valuation, we have a sure criterion to determine what portion of the quoted exchange, being referable to depreciation, may be struck off as nominal ; the result so corrected expressing the real exchange.

The same disturbance of the exchanges and of international trade, which is produced by an increased issue of convertible bank notes, is in like manner produced by those extensions of credit, which, as was so fully shown in a preceding chapter, have the same effect on prices as an increase of the currency. Whenever circumstances have given such an impulse to the spirit of speculation as to occasion a great increase of purchases on credit, money prices rise, just as much as they would have risen if each person who so buys on credit had bought with money. All the effects, therefore, must be similar. As a consequence of high prices, exportation is checked and importation stimulated ; though in fact the increase of importation seldom waits for the rise of prices which is the consequence of speculation, inasmuch as some of the great articles of import are usually among the things in which speculative overtrading first shows itself. There is, therefore, in such periods, usually a great excess of imports over exports ; and when the time comes at which these must be paid for, the exchanges become unfavourable, and gold flows out of the country. In what precise manner this efflux of gold takes effect on prices, depends on circumstances of which we shall presently speak more fully ; but that its effect is to make them recoil downwards, is certain and evident. The recoil, once begun, generally becomes a total rout, and the unusual extension of credit is rapidly exchanged for an unusual contraction of it. Accordingly, when credit has been imprudently stretched, and the speculative spirit carried to excess, the turn of the exchanges, and consequent pressure on the banks to obtain gold for exportation, are generally the proximate cause of the catastrophe. But these phenomena, though a conspicuous accompaniment, are no essential part of the collapse of credit called a commercial crisis ; which, as we formerly showed,* might happen to as great an extent, and is quite as likely to happen, in a country, if any such there were, altogether destitute of foreign trade.

* Supra, pp. 525–7.

CHAPTER XXIII

§ 1. THE present seems the most proper place for discussing the circumstances which determine the rate of interest. The interest of loans, being really a question of exchange value, falls naturally into the present division of our subject : and the two topics of Currency and Loans, though in themselves distinct, are so intimately blended in the phenomena of what is called the money market, that it is impossible to understand the one without the other, and in many minds the two subjects are mixed up in the most inextricable confusion.

In the preceding Book * we defined the relation in which interest stands to profit. We found that the gross profit of capital might be distinguished into three parts, which are respectively the remuneration for risk, for trouble, and for the capital itself, and may be termed insurance, wages of superintendence, and interest. After making compensation for risk, that is, after covering the average losses to which capital is exposed either by the general circumstances of society or by the hazards of the particular employment, there remains a surplus, which partly goes to repay the owner of the capital for his abstinence, and partly the employer of it for his time and trouble. How much goes to the one and how much to the other, is shown by the amount of the remuneration which, when the two functions are separated, the owner of capital can obtain from the employer for its use. This is evidently a question of demand and supply. Nor have demand and supply any different meaning or effect in this case from what they have in all others. The rate of interest will be such as to equalize the demand for loans with the supply of them. It will be such, that exactly as much as some people are desirous to borrow at that rate, others shall be willing

---

* Supra, book ii. ch. xv. § 1.

to lend. If there is more offered than demanded, interest will fall; if more is demanded than offered, it will rise; and, in both cases, to the point at which the equation of supply and demand is re-established.

Both the demand and supply of loans fluctuate more incessantly than any other demand or supply whatsoever. The fluctuations in other things depend on a limited number of influencing circumstances; but the desire to borrow, and the willingness to lend, are more or less influenced by every circumstance which affects the state or prospects of industry or commerce, either generally or in any of their branches. The rate of interest, therefore, on good security, which alone we have here to consider (for interest in which considerations of risk bear a part may swell to any amount) is seldom, in the great centres of money transactions, precisely the same for two days together; as is shown by the never-ceasing variations in the quoted prices of the funds and other negotiable securities. Nevertheless, there must be, as in other cases of value, some rate which (in the language of Adam Smith and Ricardo) may be called the natural rate; some rate about which the market rate oscillates, and to which it always tends to return. This rate partly depends on the amount of accumulation going on in the hands of persons who cannot themselves attend to the employment of their savings, and partly on the comparative taste existing in the community for the active pursuits of industry, or for the leisure, ease, and independence of an annuitant.

§ 2. To exclude casual fluctuations, we will suppose commerce to be in a quiescent condition, no employment being unusually prosperous, and none particularly distressed. In these circumstances, the more thriving producers and traders have their capital fully employed, and many are able to transact business to a considerably greater extent than they have capital for. These are naturally borrowers: and the amount which they desire to borrow, and can obtain credit for, constitutes the demand for loans on account of productive employment. To these must be added the loans required by Government, and by landowners, or other unproductive consumers who have good security to give. This constitutes the mass of loans for which there is an habitual demand.

Now it is conceivable that there might exist, in the hands of persons disinclined or disqualified for engaging personally in business, a mass of capital equal to, and even exceeding, this demand. In that case there would be an habitual excess of competition on the part of lenders, and the rate of interest would bear a low proportion to the rate of profit. Interest would be forced down to the point which would either tempt borrowers to take a greater amount of loans than they had a reasonable expectation of being able to employ in their business, or would so discourage a portion of the lenders, as to make them either forbear to accumulate, or endeavour to increase their income by engaging in business on their own account, and incurring the risks, if not the labours, of industrial employment.

On the other hand, the capital owned by persons who prefer lending it at interest, or whose avocations prevent them from personally superintending its employment, may be short of the habitual demand for loans. It may be in great part absorbed by the investments afforded by the public debt and by mortgages, and the remainder may not be sufficient to supply the wants of commerce. If so, the rate of interest will be raised so high as in some way to re-establish the equilibrium. When there is only a small difference between interest and profit, many borrowers may no longer be willing to increase their responsibilities and involve their credit for so small a remuneration : or some who would otherwise have engaged in business, may prefer leisure, and become lenders instead of borrowers, or others, under the inducement of high interest and easy investment for their capital, may retire from business earlier, and with smaller fortunes, than they otherwise would have done. Or, lastly, there is another process by which, in England and other commercial countries, a large portion of the requisite supply of loans is obtained. Instead of its being afforded by persons not in business, the affording it may itself become a business. A portion of the capital employed in trade may be supplied by a class of professional money lenders. These money lenders, however, must have more than a mere interest ; they must have the ordinary rate of profit on their capital, risk and all other circumstances being allowed for. But it can never answer to any one who borrows for the purposes of his business, to pay a full profit for capital from which he will only derive a full profit : and money-lending, as an employment, for the regular supply of trade, cannot, therefore, be carried on except by persons who, in addition to their own capital, can lend their credit, or, in other words, the capital of other people : that is, bankers, and persons (such as bill-brokers) who are virtually bankers, since they receive money in deposit. A bank which lends its notes, lends capital which it borrows from the community, and for which it pays no interest. A bank of deposit lends capital which it collects from the community in small parcels; sometimes without paying any interest, as is the case with the London private bankers; and if, like the Scotch, the joint stock, and most of the country banks, it does pay interest, it still pays much less than it receives; for the depositors, who in any other way could mostly obtain for such small balances no interest worth taking any trouble for, are glad to receive even a little. Having this subsidiary resource, bankers are enabled to obtain, by lending at interest, the ordinary rate of profit on their own capital. In any other manner, money-lending could not be carried on as a regular mode of business, except upon terms on which none would consent to borrow but persons either counting on extraordinary profits, or in urgent need : unproductive consumers who have exceeded their means, or merchants in fear of bankruptcy. The disposable capital deposited in banks ; that represented by bank notes ; the capital of bankers themselves, and that which their credit, in any way in which they use it, enables them to dispose of ; these, together with the funds belonging to those who, either from necessity or preference, live upon the interest of their property, constitute the general loan fund of the country : and the amount of this aggregate fund, when set against the habitual demands of producers and dealers, and those of the Government and of unproductive consumers, determines the permanent or average rate of interest ; which must always be such as to adjust these two amounts to one another.* But while the whole of this mass of lent capital takes effect upon the *permanent* rate of interest, the *fluctuations* depend almost entirely upon the portion which is in the hands of bankers ; for it is that portion almost exclusively which, being lent for short times only, is continually in the market seeking an investment. The capital of those who live on the interest of their own fortunes, has generally sought and found some fixed investment, such as the public funds, mortgages, or the

---

* I do not include in the general loan fund of the country the capitals, large as they sometimes are, which are habitually employed in speculatively buying and selling the public funds and other securities. It is true that all who buy securities add, for the time, to the general amount of money on loan, and lower *pro tanto* the rate of interest. But as the persons I speak of buy only to sell again at a higher price, they are alternately in the position of lenders and of borrowers : their operations raise the rate of interest at one time, exactly as much as they lower it at another. Like all persons who buy and sell on speculation, their function is to equalize, not to raise or lower, the value of the commodity. When they speculate prudently, they temper the fluctuations of price ; when imprudently, they often aggravate them.

bonds of public companies, which investment, except under peculiar temptations or necessities, is not changed.

§ 3. Fluctuations in the rate of interest arise from variations either in the demand for loans, or in the supply. The supply is liable to variation, though less so than the demand. The willingness to lend is greater than usual at the commencement of a period of speculation, and much less than usual during the revulsion which follows. In speculative times, money-lenders as well as other people are inclined to extend their business by stretching their credit; they lend more than usual (just as other classes of dealers and producers employ more than usual) of capital which does not belong to them. Accordingly, these are the times when the rate of interest is low; though for this too (as we shall hereafter see) there are other causes. During the revulsion, on the contrary, interest always rises inordinately, because, while there is a most pressing need on the part of many persons to borrow, there is a general disinclination to lend. This disinclination, when at its extreme point, is called a panic. It occurs when a succession of unexpected failures has created in the mercantile, and sometimes also in the non-mercantile public, a general distrust in each other's solvency; disposing every one not only to refuse fresh credit, except on very onerous terms, but to call in, if possible, all credit which he has already given. Deposits are withdrawn from banks; notes are returned on the issuers in exchange for specie; bankers raise their rate of discount, and withhold their customary advances; merchants refuse to renew mercantile bills. At such times the most calamitous consequences were formerly experienced from the attempt of the law to prevent more than a certain limited rate of interest from being given or taken. Persons who could not borrow at five per cent, had to pay, not six or seven, but ten or fifteen per cent, to compensate the lender for risking the penalties of the law : or had to sell securities or goods for ready money at a still greater sacrifice.

In the intervals between commercial crises, there is usually a tendency in the rate of interest to a progressive decline, from the gradual process of accumulation : which process, in the great commercial countries, is sufficiently rapid to account for the almost periodical recurrence of these fits of speculation; since, when a few years have elapsed without a crisis, and no new and tempting channel for investment has been opened in the meantime, there is always found to have occurred in those few years so large an increase of capital seeking investment, as to have lowered considerably the rate of interest, whether indicated by the prices of securities or by the rate of discount on bills ; and this diminution of interest tempts the possessor to incur hazards in hopes of a more considerable return.

[1] The rate of interest is, at times, affected more or less permanently by circumstances, though not of frequent, yet of occasional occurrence, which tend to alter the proportion between the class of interest-receiving and that of profit-receiving capitalists. Two causes of this description, operating in contrary ways, have manifested themselves of late years, and are now producing considerable effects in England. One is the gold discoveries. The masses of the precious metals which are constantly arriving from the gold countries, are, it may safely be said, wholly added to the funds that supply the loan market. So great an additional capital, not divided between the two classes of capitalists, but aggregated bodily to the capital of the interest-receiving class, disturbs the pre-existing ratio between the two, and tends to depress interest relatively to profit. Another circumstance of still more recent date, but tending to the contrary effect, is the legalization of joint-stock associations with limited liability. The shareholders in these associations, now so rapidly multiplying, are drawn almost exclusively from the lending class ; from those who either left their disposable funds in deposit, to be lent out by bankers, or invested them in public or private securities, and received the interest. To the extent of their shares in any of these companies (with the single exception of banking companies) they have become traders on their own capital ; they have ceased to be lenders, and have even, in most cases, passed over to the class of borrowers. Their subscriptions have been abstracted from the funds which feed the loan market, and they themselves have become competitors for a share of the remainder of those funds : of all which the natural effect is a rise of interest. And it would not be surprising if, for a considerable time to come, the ordinary rate of interest in England should bear a higher proportion to the common rate of mercantile profit, than it has borne at any time since the influx of new gold set in.*

[1] [This paragraph and the accompanying note were added in the 6th ed. (1865).]

* [1865] To the cause of augmentation in the rate of interest, mentioned in the text, must be added another, forcibly insisted on by the author of an able article in the *Edinburgh Review* for January, 1865 ; the increased and increasing willingness to send capital abroad for investment. Owing to the vastly augmented

The demand for loans varies much more largely than the supply, and embraces longer cycles of years in its aberrations. A time of war, for example, is a period of unusual drafts on the loan market. The Government, at such times, generally incurs new loans, and as these usually succeed each other rapidly as long as the war lasts, the general rate of interest is kept higher in war than in peace, without reference to the rate of profit, and productive industry is stinted of its usual supplies. During part of the last war with France, the Government could not borrow under six per cent, and of course all other borrowers had to pay at least as much. Nor does the influence of these loans altogether cease when the Government ceases to contract others ; for those already contracted continue to afford an investment for a greatly increased amount of the disposable capital of the country, which if the national debt were paid off, would be added to the mass of capital seeking investment, and (independently of temporary disturbance) could not but, to some extent, permanently lower the rate of interest.

The same effect on interest which is produced by Government loans for war expenditure, is produced by the sudden opening of any new and generally attractive mode of permanent investment. The only instance of the kind in recent history on a scale comparable to that of the war loans, is the absorption of capital in the construction of railways. This capital must have been principally drawn from the deposits in banks, or from savings which would have gone into deposit, and which were destined to be ultimately employed in buying securities from persons who would have employed the purchase money in discounts or other loans at interest : in either case, it was a draft on the general loan fund. It is, in fact, evident, that unless savings were made expressly to be employed in railway adventure, the amount thus employed must have been derived either from the actual capital of persons in business, or from capital which would have been lent to persons in business. In the first case, the subtraction, by crippling their means, obliges them to be larger borrowers ; in the second, it leaves less for them to borrow ; in either case it equally tends to raise the rate of interest.

facilities of access to foreign countries, and the abundant information incessantly received from them, foreign investments have ceased to inspire the terror that belongs to the unknown ; capital flows, without misgiving, to any place which affords an expectation of high profit ; and the loan market of the whole commercial world is rapidly becoming one. The rate of interest, therefore, in the part of the world out of which capital most freely flows, cannot any longer remain so much inferior to the rate elsewhere, as it has hitherto been.

§ 4.[1]   I have, thus far, considered loans, and the rate of interest, as a matter which concerns capital in general, in direct opposition to the popular notion, according to which it only concerns money. In loans, as in all other money transactions, I have regarded the money which passes, only as the medium, and commodities as the thing really transferred—the real subject of the transaction.   And this is, in the main, correct : because the purpose for which, in the ordinary course of affairs, money is borrowed, is to acquire a purchasing power over commodities.   In an industrious and commercial country, the ulterior intention commonly is, to employ the commodities as capital : but even in the case of loans for unproductive consumption, as those of spendthrifts, or of the Government, the amount borrowed is taken from a previous accumulation, which would otherwise have been lent to carry on productive industry ; it is, therefore, so much subtracted from what may correctly be called the amount of loanable capital.

There is, however, a not unfrequent case, in which the purpose of the borrower is different from what I have here supposed.   He may borrow money, neither to employ it as capital nor to spend it unproductively, but to pay a previous debt.   In this case, what he wants is not purchasing power, but legal tender, or something which a creditor will accept as equivalent to it.   His need is specifically for money, not for commodities or capital.   It is the demand arising from this cause, which produces almost all the great and sudden variations of the rate of interest.   Such a demand forms one of the earliest features of a commercial crisis.   At such a period, many persons in business, who have contracted engagements, have been prevented by a change of circumstances from obtaining in time the means on which they calculated for fulfilling them.   These means they must obtain at any sacrifice, or submit to bankruptcy ; and what they must have is money.   Other capital, however much of it they may possess, cannot answer the purpose unless money can first be obtained for it ; while, on the contrary, without any increase of the capital of the country, a mere increase of circulating instruments of credit (be they of as little worth for any other purpose as the box of one pound notes discovered in the vaults of the Bank of England during the panic of 1825) will effectually serve their turn if only they are allowed to make use of it.   An increased issue of notes, in the form of loans, is all that is required to satisfy the

[1] [The first three paragraphs of this section were added in the 6th ed. (1865).]

demand, and put an end to the accompanying panic. But although, in this case, it is not capital, or purchasing power, that the borrower needs, but money as money, it is not only money that is transferred to him. The money carries its purchasing power with it wherever it goes ; and money thrown into the loan market really does, through its purchasing power, turn over an increased portion of the capital of the country into the direction of loans. Though money alone was wanted, capital passes ; and it may still be said with truth that it is by an addition to loanable capital that the rise of the rate of interest is met and corrected.

Independently of this, however, there is a real relation, which it is indispensable to recognise, between loans and money. Loanable capital is all of it in the form of money. Capital destined directly for production exists in many forms ; but capital destined for lending exists normally in that form alone. Owing to this circumstance, we should naturally expect that among the causes which affect more or less the rate of interest, would be found not only causes which act through capital, but some causes which act, directly at least, only through money.

[1] The rate of interest bears no necessary relation to the quantity or value of the money in circulation. The permanent amount of the circulating medium, whether great or small, affects only prices ; not the rate of interest. A depreciation of the currency, when it has become an accomplished fact, affects the rate of interest in no manner whatever. It diminishes indeed the power of money to buy commodities, but not the power of money to buy money. I, a hundred pounds will buy a perpetual annuity of four pounds a year, a depreciation which makes the hundred pounds worth only half as much as before, has precisely the same effect on the four pounds, and cannot therefore alter the relation between the two. The greater or smaller number of counters which must be used to express a given amount of real wealth, makes no difference in the position or interests of lenders or borrowers, and therefore makes no difference in the demand and supply of loans. There is the same amount of real capital lent and borrowed ; and if the capital in the hands of lenders is represented by a greater number of pounds sterling, the same greater number of pounds sterling will, in consequence of the rise of prices, be now required for the purposes to which the borrowers intend to apply them.

[1] [The text of this and the next seven paragraphs is an expansion in the 6th ed. (1865) of two paragraphs of the earlier editions.]

But though the greater or less quantity of money makes in itself no difference in the rate of interest, a change from a less quantity to a greater, or from a greater to a less, may and does make a difference in it.

Suppose money to be in process of depreciation by means of an inconvertible currency, issued by a government in payment of its expenses. This fact will in no way diminish the demand for real capital on loan ; but it will diminish the real capital loanable, because, this existing only in the form of money, the increase of quantity depreciates it. Estimated in capital, the amount offered is less, while the amount required is the same as before. Estimated in currency, the amount offered is only the same as before, while the amount required, owing to the rise of prices, is greater. Either way, the rate of interest must rise. So that in this case increase of currency really affects the rate of interest, but in the contrary way to that which is generally supposed ; by raising, not by lowering it.

The reverse will happen as the effect of calling in, or diminishing in quantity, a depreciated currency. The money in the hands of lenders, in common with all other money, will be enhanced in value, that is, there will be a greater amount of real capital seeking borrowers ; while the real capital wanted by borrowers will be only the same as before, and the money amount less : the rate of interest, therefore, will tend to fall.

We thus see that depreciation, merely as such, while in process of taking place, tends to raise the rate of interest : and the expectation of further depreciation adds to this effect ; because lenders who expect that their interest will be paid, and the principal perhaps redeemed, in a less valuable currency than they lent, of course require a rate of interest sufficient to cover this contingent loss.

But this effect is more than counteracted by a contrary one, when the additional money is thrown into circulation not by purchases but by loans. In England, and in most other commercial countries, the paper currency in common use, being a currency provided by bankers, is all issued in the way of loans, except the part employed in the purchase of gold and silver. The same operation, therefore, which adds to the currency also adds to the loans : the whole inciease of currency in the first instance swells the loan market. Considered as an addition to loans it tends to lower interest, more than in its character of depreciation it tends to raise it ; for the former effect depends on the ratio which the new money bears to the money lent, while the latter depends on its ratio to all the money in circulation. An increase, therefore, of currency issued by banks, tends, while the process continues, to bring down or to keep down the rate of interest. A similar effect is produced by the increase of money arising from the gold discoveries; almost the whole of which, as already noticed, is, when brought to Europe, added to the deposits in banks, and consequently to the amount of loans; and when drawn out and invested in securities, liberates an equivalent amount of other loanable capital. The newly-arrived gold can only get itself invested, in any given state of business, by lowering the rate of interest; and as long as the influx continues, it cannot fail to keep interest lower than, all other circumstances being supposed the same, would otherwise have been the case.

As the introduction of additional gold and silver, which goes into the loan market, tends to keep down the rate of interest, so any considerable abstraction of them from the country invariably raises it; even when occurring in the course of trade, as in paying for the extra importations caused by a bad harvest, or for the high-priced cotton which, under the influence of the American civil war, was imported from so many parts of the world. The money required for these payments is taken in the first instance from the deposits in the hands of bankers, and to that extent starves the fund that supplies the loan market.

The rate of interest, then, depends essentially and permanently on the comparative amount of real capital offered and demanded in the way of loan; but is subject to temporary disturbances of various sorts from increase and diminution of the circulating medium; which derangements are somewhat intricate, and sometimes in direct opposition to first appearances. All these distinctions are veiled over and confounded, by the unfortunate misapplication of language which designates the rate of interest by a phrase (" the value of money ") which properly expresses the purchasing power of the circulating medium. The public, even mercantile, habitually fancies that ease in the money market, that is, facility of borrowing at low interest, is proportional to the quantity of money in circulation. Not only, therefore, are bank notes supposed to produce effects as currency, which they only produce as loans, but attention is habitually diverted from effects similar in kind and much greater in degree, when produced by an action on loans which does not happen to be accompanied by any action on the currency.

For example, in considering the effect produced by the proceedings of banks in encouraging the excesses of speculation, an immense effect is usually attributed to their issues of notes, but until of late hardly any attention was paid to the management of their deposits ; though nothing is more certain than that their imprudent extensions of credit take place more frequently by means of their deposits than of their issues. " There is no doubt," says Mr. Tooke,* " that banks, whether private or joint stock, may, if imprudently conducted, minister to an undue extension of credit for the purpose of speculations, whether in commodities, or in over-trading in exports or imports, or in building or mining operations, and that they have so ministered not unfrequently, and in some cases to an extent ruinous to themselves, and without ultimate benefit to the parties to whose views their resources were made subservient." But, " supposing all the deposits received by a banker to be in coin, is he not, just as much as the issuing banker, exposed to the importunity of customers, whom it may be impolitic to refuse, for loans or discounts, or to be tempted by a high interest ? and may he not be induced to encroach so much upon his deposits as to leave him, under not improbable circumstances, unable to meet the demands of his depositors ? In what respect, indeed, would the case of a banker in a perfectly metallic circulation differ from that of a London banker at the present day ? He is not a creator of money, he cannot avail himself of his privilege as an issuer in aid of his other business, and yet there have been lamentable instances of London bankers issuing money in excess."

In the discussions, too, which have been for so many years carried on respecting the operations of the Bank of England, and the effects produced by those operations on the state of credit, though for nearly half a century there never has been a commercial crisis which the Bank has not been strenuously accused either of producing or of aggravating, it has been almost universally assumed that the influence of its acts was felt only through the amount of its notes in circulation, and that if it could be prevented from exercising any discretion as to that one feature in its position, it would no longer have any power liable to abuse.   This at least is an error which, after the experience of the year 1847, we may hope has been committed for the last time.   During that year the hands of the bank were absolutely tied, in its character of a bank of issue ; but through its

* *Inquiry into the Currency Principle*, ch. xiv.

operations as a bank of deposit it exercised as great an influence, or apparent influence, on the rate of interest and the state of credit, as at any former period ; it was exposed to as vehement accusations of abusing that influence ; and a crisis occurred, such as few that preceded it had equalled, and none perhaps surpassed, in intensity.

§ 5. Before quitting the general subject of this chapter, I will make the obvious remark, that the rate of interest determines the value and price of all those saleable articles which are desired and bought, not for themselves, but for the income which they are capable of yielding. The public funds, shares in joint-stock companies, and all descriptions of securities, are at a high price in proportion as the rate of interest is low. They are sold at the price which will give the market rate of interest on the purchase money, with allowance for all differences in the risk incurred, or in any circumstance of convenience. Exchequer bills, for example, usually sell at a higher price than consols, proportionally to the interest which they yield ; because, though the security is the same, yet the former being annually paid off at par unless renewed by the holder, the purchaser (unless obliged to sell in a moment of general emergency), is in no danger of losing anything by the resale, except the premium he may have paid.

The price of land, mines, and all other fixed sources of income, depends in like manner on the rate of interest. Land usually sells at a higher price, in proportion to the income afforded by it, than the public funds, not only because it is thought, even in this country, to be somewhat more secure, but because ideas of power and dignity are associated with its possession. But these differences are constant, or nearly so ; and in the variations of price, land follows, *cæteris paribus*, the permanent (though of course not the daily) variations of the rate of interest. When interest is low, land will naturally be dear ; when interest is high, land will be cheap. The last long war presented a striking exception to this rule, since the price of land as well as the rate of interest was then remarkably high. For this, however, there was a special cause. The continuance of a very high average price of corn for many years had raised the rent of land even more than in proportion to the rise of interest and fall of the selling price of fixed incomes. Had it not been for this accident, chiefly dependent on the seasons, land must have sustained as great a depreciation in value as the public funds : which it probably would do, were a similar war to break out hereafter ; to the signal disappointment of those landlords and farmers who, generalizing from the casual circumstances of a remarkable period, so long persuaded themselves that a state of war was peculiarly advantageous, and a state of peace disadvantageous, to what they chose to call the interests of agriculture.

CHAPTER XXIV

§ 1. THE frequent recurrence during the last half century of the painful series of phenomena called a commercial crisis, has directed much of the attention both of economists and of practical politicians to the contriving of expedients for averting, or, at the least, mitigating its evils. And the habit which grew up during the era of the Bank restriction, of ascribing all alterations of high and low prices to the issues of banks, has caused inquirers in general to fix their hopes of success in moderating those vicissitudes upon schemes for the regulation of bank notes. A scheme of this nature, after having obtained the sanction of high authorities, so far established itself in the public mind, as to be, with general approbation, converted into a law, at the renewal of the Charter of the Bank of England in 1844 : and the regulation is still in force, though with a great abatement of its popularity, and with its *prestige* impaired by three [1] temporary suspensions, on the responsibility of the executive, the earliest little more than three years after its enactment. It is proper that the merits of this plan for the regulation of a convertible bank note currency should be here considered. Before touching upon the practical provisions of Sir Robert Peel's Act of 1844, I shall briefly state the nature, and examine the grounds, of the theory on which it is founded.

It is believed by many, that banks of issue universally, or the Bank of England in particular, have a power of throwing their notes into circulation, and thereby raising prices, arbitrarily ; that this power is only limited by the degree of moderation with which they think fit to exercise it ; that when they increase their issues beyond the usual amount, the rise of prices, thus produced, generates a spirit of speculation in commodities, which carries prices still higher,

---

[1] [So from the 7th ed. (1871). In the original (1848) : " a temporary suspension " &c. ; in the 5th ed. (1862) : " two temporary suspensions."]

and ultimately causes a reaction and recoil, amounting in extreme cases to a commercial crisis : and that every such crisis which has occurred in this country within mercantile memory, has been either or ginally produced by this cause, or greatly aggravated by it.   To this extreme length the currency theory has not been carried by the eminent political economists who have given to a more moderate form of the same theory the sanction of their names.   But I have not overstated the extravagance of the popular version ; which is a remarkable instance to what lengths a favourite theory will hurry, not the closet students whose competency in such questions is often treated with so much contempt, but men of the world and of business, who pique themselves on the practical knowledge which they have at least had ample opportunities of acquiring.   Not only has this fixed idea of the currency as the prime agent in the fluctuations of price made them shut their eyes to the multitude of circumstances which, by influencing the expectation of suppiy, are the true causes of almost all speculations, and of almost all fluctuations of price ; but in order to bring about the chronologicaı agreement required by their theory between the variations of bank issues and those of prices, they have played such fantastic tricks with facts and dates as would be thought incredible, if an eminent practicaı authority had not taken the trouble of meeting them, on the ground of mere history, with an elaborate exposure.   I refer, as all conversant with the subject must be aware, to Mr. Tooke's *History of Prices*.   The result of Mr. Tooke's investigations was thus stated by himself, in his examination before the Commons' Committee on the Bank Charter question in 1832 ; and the evidences of it stand recorded in his book : " In point of fact, and historically, as far as my researches have gone, in every signal instance of a rise or fall of prices, the rise or fall has preceded, and therefore could not be the effect of, an enlargement or contraction of the bank circulation."

The extravagance of the currency theorists, in attributing almost every rise or fall of prices to an enlargement or contraction of the issues of bank notes, has raised up, by reaction, a theory the extreme opposite of the former, of which, in scientific discussion, the most prominent representatives are Mr. Tooke and Mr. Fullarton.   This counter-theory denies to bank notes, so long as their convertibility is maintained, any power whatever of raising prices, and to banks any power of increasing their circulation, except as a consequence of, and in proportion to, an increase of the business to be done.   This last statement is supported by the unanimous assurances of all the country bankers who have been examined before successive Parliamentary Committees on the subject. They all bear testimony that (in the words of Mr. Fullarton *) " the amount of their issues is exclusively regulated by the extent of local dealings and expenditure in their respective districts, fluctuating with the fluctuations of production and price, and that they neither can increase their issues beyond the limits which the range of such dealings and expenditure prescribes, without the certainty of having their notes immediately returned to them, nor diminish them, but at an almost equal certainty of the vacancy being filled up from some other source." From these premises it is argued by Mr. Tooke and Mr. Fullarton that bank issues, since they cannot be increased in amount unless there be an increased demand, cannot possibly raise prices ; cannot encourage speculation, nor occasion a commercial crisis ; and that the attempt to guard against that evil by an artificial management of the issue of notes is of no effect for the intended purpose, and liable to produce other consequences extremely calamitous.

§ 2.   As much of this doctrine as rests upon testimony, and not upon inference, appears to me incontrovertible. I give complete credence to the assertion of the country bankers very clearly and correctly condensed into a small compass in the sentence just quoted from Mr. Fullarton. I am convinced that they cannot possibly increase their issue of notes in any other circumstances than those which are there stated. I believe, also, that the theory, grounded by Mr. Fullarton upon this fact, contains a large portion of truth, and is far nearer to being the expression of the whole truth than any form whatever of the currency theory.

There are two states of the markets : one which may be termed the quiescent state, the other the expectant, or speculative, state. The first is that in which there is nothing tending to engender in any considerable portion of the mercantile public a desire to extend their operations. The producers produce and the dealers purchase only their usual stocks, having no expectation of a more than usually rapid vent for them. Each person transacts his ordinary amount of business, and no more ; or increases it only in correspondence with the increase of his capital or connexion, or with the gradual growth of the demand for his commodity, occasioned by the public prosperity.

* *Regulation of Currencies* p. 85.

Not meditating any unusual extension of their own operations, producers and dealers do not need more than the usual accommodation from bankers and other money lenders ; and as it is only by extending their loans that bankers increase their issues, none but a momentary augmentation of issues is in these circumstances possible.   If at a certain time of the year a portion of the public have larger payments to make than at other times, or if an individual, under some peculiar exigency, requires an extra advance, they may apply for more bank notes, and obtain them ; but the notes will no more remain in circulation than the extra quantity of Bank of England notes which are issued once in every three months in payment of the dividends.   The person to whom, after being borrowed, the notes are paid away, has no extra payments to make, and no peculiar exigency, and he keeps them by him unused, or sends them into deposit, or repays with them a previous advance made to him by some banker : in any case he does not buy commodities with them, since by the supposition there is nothing to induce him to lay in a larger stock of commodities than before.   [1]Even if we suppose, as we may do, that bankers create an artificial increase of the demand for loans by offering them below the market rate of interest, the notes they issue will not remain in circulation ; for when the borrower, having completed the transaction for which he availed himself of them, has paid them away, the creditor or dealer who receives them, having no demand for the immediate use of an extra quantity of notes, sends them into deposit.   In this case, therefore, there can be no addition, at the discretion of bankers, to the general circulating medium : any increase of their issues either comes back to them, or remains idle in the hands of the public, and no rise takes place in prices.

But there is another state of the markets, strikingly contrasted with the preceding, and to this state it is not so obvious that the theory of Mr. Tooke and Mr. Fullarton is applicable ; namely, when an impression prevails, whether well founded or groundless, that the supply of one or more great articles of commerce is likely to fall short of the ordinary consumption.   In such circumstances all persons connected with those commodities desire to extend their operations.   The producers or importers desire to produce or import a larger quantity, speculators desire to lay in a stock in order to profit by the expected rise of price, and holders of the commodity desire

---

[1] [Sentence inserted in 5th ed. (1862).]

additional advances to enable them to continue holding. All these classes are disposed to make a more than ordinary use of their credit, and to this desire it is not denied that bankers very often unduly administer. Effects of the same kind may be produced by anything which, exciting more than usual hopes of profit, gives increased briskness to business : for example, a sudden foreign demand for commodities on a large scale, or the expectation of it ; such as occurred on the opening of Spanish America to English trade, and has occurred on various occasions in the trade with the United States. Such occurrences produce a tendency to a rise of price in exportable articles, and generate speculations, sometimes of a reasonable, and (as long as a large proportion of men in business prefer excitement to safety) frequently of an irrational or immoderate character. In such cases there is a desire in the mercantile classes, or in some portion of them, to employ their credit, in a more than usual degree, as a power of purchasing. This is a state of business which, when pushed to an extreme length, brings on the revulsion called a commercial crisis ; and it is a known fact that such periods of speculation hardly ever pass off without having been attended, during some part of their progress, by a considerable increase of bank notes.

To this, however, it is replied by Mr. Tooke and Mr. Fullarton, that the increase of the circulation always follows instead of preceding the rise of prices, and is not its cause, but its effect. That in the first place, the speculative purchases by which prices are raised, are not effected by bank notes but by cheques, or still more commonly on a simple book credit : and secondly, even if they were made with bank notes borrowed for that express purpose from bankers, the notes, after being used for that purpose, would, if not wanted for current transactions, be returned into deposit by the persons receiving them. In this I fully concur, and I regard it as proved, both scientifically and historically, that during the ascending period of speculation, and as long as it is confined to transactions between dealers, the issues of bank notes are seldom materially increased, nor contribute anything to the speculative rise of prices. It seems to me, however, that this can no longer be affirmed when speculation has proceeded so far as to reach the producers. Speculative orders given by merchants to manufacturers induce them to extend their operations, and to become applicants to bankers for increased advances, which, if made in notes, are not paid away to persons who return them into deposit, but are partially expended in paying wages, and pass into the various channels of retail trade, where they become directly effective in producing a further rise of prices. I cannot but think that this employment of bank notes must have been powerfully operative on prices at the time when notes of one and two pounds' value were permitted by law. Admitting, however, that the prohibition of notes below five pounds has now rendered this part of their operation comparatively insignificant by greatly limiting their applicability to the payment of wages, there is another form of their instrumentality which comes into play in the latter stages of speculation, and which forms the principal argument of the more moderate supporters of the currency theory. Though advances by bankers are seldom demanded for the purpose of buying on speculation, they are largely demanded by unsuccessful speculators for the purpose of holding on ; and the competition of these speculators for a share of the loanable capital makes even those who have not speculated more dependent than before on bankers for the advances they require. Between the ascending period of speculation and the revulsion, there is an interval extending to weeks and sometimes months, of struggling against a fall. The tide having shown signs of turning, the speculative holders are unwilling to sell in a falling market, and in the meantime they require funds to enable them to fulfil even their ordinary engagements. It is this stage that is ordinarily marked by a considerable increase in the amount of the bank-note circulation. That such an increase does usually take place is denied by no one. And I think it must be admitted that this increase tends to prolong the duration of the speculations ; that it enables the speculative prices to be kept up for some time after they would otherwise have collapsed ; and therefore prolongs and increases the drain of the precious metals for exportation, which is the leading feature of this stage in the progress of a commercial crisis : the continuance of which drain at last endangering the power of the banks to fulfil their engagement of paying their notes on demand, they are compelled to contract their credit more suddenly and severely than would have been necessary if they had been prevented from propping up speculation by increased advances, after the time when the recoil had become inevitable.

§ 3. To prevent this retardation of the recoil, and ultimate aggravation of its severity, is the object of the scheme for regulating the currency, of which Lord Overstone, Mr. Norman, and Colonel

Torrens, were the first promulgators, and which has, in a slightly modified form, been enacted into law.*

According to the scheme in its original purity, the issue of promissory notes for circulation was to be confined to one body. In the form adopted by Parliament, all existing issuers were permitted to retain this privilege, but none were to be hereafter admitted to it, even in the place of those who might discontinue their issues : and, for all except the Bank of England, a maximum of issues was prescribed, on a scale intentionally low. To the Bank of England no maximum was fixed for the aggregate amount of its notes, but only for the portion issued on securities, or, in other words, on loan. These were never to exceed a certain limit, fixed in the first instance at fourteen millions.† All issues beyond that amount must be in exchange for bullion; of which the Bank is bound to purchase, at a trifle below the Mint valuation, any quantity which is offered to it, giving its notes in exchange. In regard, therefore, to any issue of notes beyond the limit of fourteen millions, the Bank is purely passive, having no function but the compulsory one of giving its notes for gold at 3*l.* 17*s.* 9*d.*, and gold for its notes at

* [1857] I think myself justified in affirming that the mitigation of commercial revulsions is the real, and only serious, purpose of the Act of 1844. I am quite aware that its supporters insist (especially since 1847) on its supreme efficacy in "maintaining the convertibility of the Bank note." But I must be excused for not attaching any serious importance to this one among its alleged merits. The convertibility of the Bank note was maintained, and would have continued to be maintained, at whatever cost, under the old system. As was well said by Lord Overstone in his evidence, the Bank can always, by a sufficiently violent action on credit, save itself at the expense of the mercantile public. That the Act of 1844 mitigates the violence of that process, is a sufficient claim to prefer in its behalf. Besides, if we suppose such a degree of mismanagement on the part of the Bank, as, were it not for the Act, would endanger the continuance or convertibility, the same (or a less) degree of mismanagement, practised under the Act, would suffice to produce a suspension of payments by the Banking Department ; an event which the compulsory separation of the two departments brings much nearer to possibility than it was before, and which, involving as it would the probable stoppage of every private banking establishment in London, and perhaps also the non-payment of the dividends to the national creditor, would be a far greater immediate calamity than a brief interruption of the convertibility of the note ; insomuch that, to enable the Bank to resume payment of its deposits, no Government would hesitate a moment to suspend payment of the notes, if suspension of the Act of 1844 proved insufficient.

† A conditional increase of this maximum is permitted, but only when by arrangement with any country bank the issues of that bank are discontinued, and Bank of England notes substituted ; and even then the increase is limited to two-thirds of the amount of the country notes to be thereby superseded. Under this provision the amount of notes which the Bank of England is now [1871] at liberty to issue against securities, is about fifteen millions.

3*l.* 17*s.* 10½*d.*, whenever and by whomsoever it is called upon to do so.

The object for which this mechanism is intended is that the bank-note currency may vary in its amount at the exact times, and in the exact degree, in which a purely metallic currency would vary. And the precious metals being the commodity that has hitherto approached nearest to that invariability, in all the circumstances influencing value, which fits a commodity for being adopted as a medium of exchange, it seems to be thought that the excellence of the Act of 1844 is fully made out, if under its operation the issues conform in all their variations of quantity, and therefore, as is inferred, of value, to the variations which would take place in a currency wholly metallic.

[1] Now, all reasonable opponents of the Act, in common with its supporters, acknowledge as an essential requisite of any substitute for the precious metals, that it should conform exactly in its permanent value to a metallic standard. And they say, that so long as it is convertible into specie on demand, it does and must so conform. But when the value of a metallic or of any other currency is spoken of, there are two points to be considered ; the permanent or average value, and the fluctuations. It is to the permanent value of a metallic currency that the value of a paper currency ought to conform. But there is no obvious reason why it should be required to conform to the fluctuations too. The only object of its conforming at all is steadiness of value ; and with respect to fluctuations the sole thing desirable is that they should be the smallest possible. Now the fluctuations in the value of the currency are determined, not by its quantity, whether it consist of gold or of paper, but by the expansions and contractions of credit. To discover, therefore, what currency will conform the most nearly to the permanent value of the precious metals, we must find under what currency the variations in credit are least frequent and least extreme. Now, whether this object is best attained by a metallic currency (and therefore by a paper currency exactly conforming in quantity to it) is precisely the question to be decided. If it should prove that a paper currency which follows all the fluctuations in quantity of a metallic, leads to more violent revulsions of credit than one which is not held to this rigid conformity, it will follow that the currency which agrees most exactly in quantity with a metallic currency is not that which adheres closest to its value ; that is

[1] [Paragraph inserted in 4th ed. (1857).]

to say, its permanent value, with which alone agreement is desirable.

Whether this is really the case or not we will now inquire. And first, let us consider whether the Act effects the practical object chiefly relied on in its defence by the more sober of its advocates, that of arresting speculative extensions of credit at an earlier period, with a less drain of gold, and consequently by a milder and more gradual process. I think it must be admitted that to a certain degree it is successful in this object.

I am aware of what may be urged, and reasonably urged, in opposition to this opinion. It may be said, that when the time arrives at which the banks are pressed for increased advances to enable speculators to fulfil their engagements, a limitation of the issue of notes will not prevent the banks, if otherwise willing, from making these advances; that they have still their deposits as a source from which loans may be made beyond the point which is consistent with prudence as bankers; and that even if they refused to do so, the only effect would be that the deposits themselves would be drawn out to supply the wants of the depositors; which would be just as much an addition to the bank notes and coin in the hands of the public, as if the notes themselves were increased. This is true, and is a sufficient answer to those who think that the advances of banks to prop up failing speculations are objectionable chiefly as an increase of the currency. But the mode in which they are really objectionable, is as an extension of credit. [1] If, instead of increasing their discounts, the banks allow their deposits to be drawn out, there is the same increase of currency (for a short time at least), but there is not an increase of loans, at the time when there ought to be a diminution. If they do increase their discounts, not by means of notes, but at the expense of the deposits alone, their deposits (properly so called) are definite and exhaustible, while notes may be increased to any amount, or, after being returned, may be reissued without limit. It is true that a bank, if willing to add indefinitely to its liabilities, has the power of making its nominal deposits as

---

[1] [The present text of the remainder of this paragraph dates only from the 6th ed. (1865). The original simply ran : " If, instead of lending their notes, the banks allow the demand of their customers for disposable capital to act on the deposits, there is the same increase of currency, (for a short time at least,) but there is not an increase of loans. The rate of interest, therefore, is not prevented from rising at the first moment when the difficulties consequent on excess of speculation begin to be felt. Speculative holders," &c. No change was made in this before 1865, except the insertion of the words " On the contrary . . . interest " before the last sentence in the 4th ed. (1857).]

unlimited a fund as its issues could be ; it has only to make its advances in a book credit, which is creating deposits out of its own liabilities, the money for which it has made itself responsible becoming a deposit in its hands, to be drawn against by cheques ; and the cheques when drawn may be liquidated (either at the same bank or at the clearing house) without the aid of notes, by a mere transfer of credit from one account to another. I apprehend it is chiefly in this way that undue extensions of credit, in periods of speculation, are commonly made. But the banks are not likely to persist in this course when the tide begins to turn. It is not when their deposits have already begun to flow out, that they are likely to create deposit accounts which represent, instead of funds placed in their hands, fresh liabilities of their own. But experience proves that extension of credit, when in the form of notes, goes on long after the recoil from over-speculation has commenced. When this mode of resisting the revulsion is made impossible, and deposits and book credits are left as the only sources from which undue advances can be made, the rate of interest is not so often, or so long, prevented from rising, after the difficulties consequent on excess of speculation begin to be felt. On the contrary, the necessity which the banks feel of diminishing their advances to maintain their solvency, when they find their deposits flowing out, and cannot supply the vacant place by their own notes, accelerates the rise of the rate of interest. Speculative holders are therefore obliged to submit earlier to that loss by resale, which could not have been prevented from coming on them at last : the recoil of prices and collapse of general credit take place sooner.

To appreciate the effects which this acceleration of the crisis has in mitigating its intensity, let us advert more particularly to the nature and effects of that leading feature in the period just preceding the collapse, the drain of gold. A rise of prices produced by a speculative extension of credit, even when bank notes have not been the instrument, is not the less effectual (if it lasts long enough) in turning the exchanges : and when the exchanges have turned from this cause, they can only be turned back, and the drain of gold stopped, either by a fall of prices or by a rise of the rate of interest. A fall of prices will stop it by removing the cause which produced it, and by rendering goods a more advantageous remittance than gold, even for paying debts already due. A rise of the rate of interest, and consequent fall of the prices of securities, will accomplish the purpose still more rapidly, by inducing foreigners, instead of taking away the gold which is due to them, to leave it for investment within the country, and even send gold into the country to take advantage of the increased rate of interest. Of this last mode of stopping a drain of gold, the year 1847 afforded signal examples. But until one of these two things takes place—until either prices fall, or the rate of interest rises—nothing can possibly arrest, or even moderate, the efflux of gold. Now, neither will prices fall nor interest rise, so long as the unduly expanded credit is upheld by the continued advances of bankers. It is well known that when a drain of gold has set in, even if bank notes have not increased in quantity, it is upon them that the contraction first falls, the gold wanted for exportation being always obtained from the Bank of England in exchange for its notes. But under the system which preceded 1844, the Bank of England, being subjected, in common with other banks, to the importunities for fresh advances which are characteristic of such a time, could, and often did, immediately re-issue the notes which had been returned to it in exchange for bullion. It is a great error, certainly, to suppose that the mischief of this re-issue chiefly consisted in preventing a contraction of the currency. It was, however, quite as mischievous as it has ever been supposed to be. As long as it lasted, the efflux of gold could not cease, since neither would prices fall nor interest rise while these advances continued. Prices, having risen without any increase of bank notes, could well have fallen without a diminution of them ; but having risen in consequence of an extension of credit, they could not fall without a contraction of it. As long, therefore, as the Bank of England and the other banks persevered in this course, so long gold continued to flow out, until so little was left that the Bank of England, being in danger of suspension of payments, was compelled at last to contract its discounts so greatly and suddenly as to produce a much more extreme variation in the rate of interest, inflict much greater loss and distress on individuals, and destroy a much greater amount of the ordinary credit of the country, than any real necessity required.

I acknowledge (and the experience of 1847 has proved to those who overlooked it before) that the mischief now described may be wrought, and in large measure, by the Bank of England, through its deposits alone. It may continue or even increase its discounts and advances, when it ought to contract them ; with the ultimate effect of making the contraction much more severe and sudden than necessary. I cannot but think, however, that banks which commit this error with their deposits, would commit it still more if they were at liberty to make increased loans with their issues as well as their depósits. I am compelled to think that the being restricted from increasing their issues, is a real impediment to their making those advances which arrest the tide at its turn, and make it rush like a torrent afterwards[1]: and when the Act is blamed for interposing obstacles at a time when not obstacles but facilities are needed, it must in justice receive credit for interposing them when they are an acknowledged benefit. In this particular, therefore, I think it cannot be denied, that the new system is a real improvement upon the old.

§ 4. But however this may be, it seems to me certain that these advantages, whatever value may be put on them, are purchased by still greater disadvantages.

In the first place, a large extension of credit by bankers, though most hurtful when, credit being already in an inflated state, it can only serve to retard and aggravate the collapse, is most salutary when the collapse has come, and when credit instead of being in excess is in distressing deficiency, and increased advances by bankers, instead of being an addition to the ordinary amount of floating credit, serve to replace a mass of other credit which has been suddenly destroyed. Antecedently to 1844, if the Bank of England occasionally aggravated the severity of a commercial revulsion by rendering the collapse of credit more tardy and hence more violent than necessary, it in return rendered invaluable services during the revulsion itself, by coming forward with advances to support solvent firms, at a time when all other paper and almost all mercantile credit

---

[1] [From the 6th ed. (1865) disappeared the following lines and the accompanying footnote, which had remained sin⌐ ⌐ 1848 :

" If the restrictions of the Act of 1844 were no obstacle to the advances of banks in the interval preceding the crisis, why were they found an insuperable obstacle during the crisis ? an obstacle which nothing less could overcome than a suspension of the law, through the assumption by the Government of a temporary dictatorship ? Evidently they were an obstacle."

Footnote.—" It would not be to the purpose to say, by way of objection, that the obstacle may be evaded by granting the increased advance in book credits, to be drawn against by cheques, without the aid of bank notes.   This is indeed possible, as Mr. Fullarton has remarked, and as I have myself said in a former chapter.   But this substitute for bank note currency certainly has not yet been organised; and the law having clearly manifested its intention that, in the case supposed, increased credits should not be granted, it is yet a problem whether the law would not reach what might be regarded as an evasion of its prohibitions, or whether deference to the law would not produce (as it has hitherto done), on the part of banking establishments, conformity to its spirit and purpose, as well as to its mere letter."]

had become comparatively valueless. This service was eminently conspicuous in the crisis of 1825-6, the severest probably ever experienced; during which the Bank increased what is called its circulation by many millions, in advances to those mercantile firms of whose ultimate solvency it felt no doubt; advances which if it had been obliged to withhold, the severity of the crisis would have been still greater than it was. If the Bank, it is justly remarked by Mr. Fullarton,* complies with such applications, "it must comply with them by an issue of notes, for notes constitute the only instrumentality through which the Bank is in the practice of lending its credit. But those notes are not intended to circulate, nor do they circulate. There is no more demand for circulation than there was before. On the contrary, the rapid decline of prices which the case in supposition presumes, would necessarily contract the demand for circulation. The notes would either be returned to the Bank of England as fast as they were issued, in the shape of deposits, or would be locked up in the drawers of the private London bankers, or distributed by them to their correspondents in the country, or intercepted by other capitalists, who, during the fervour of the previous excitement, had contracted liabilities which they might be imperfectly prepared on the sudden to encounter. In such emergencies, every man connected with business, who has been trading on other means than his own, is placed on the defensive, and his whole object is to make himself as strong as possible, an object which cannot be more effectually answered than by keeping by him as large a reserve as possible in paper which the law has made a legal tender. The notes themselves never find their way into the produce market; and if they at all contribute to retard" (or, as I should rather say, to moderate) "the fall of prices, it is not by promoting in the slightest degree the effective demand for commodities, not by enabling consumers to buy more largely for consumption, and so giving briskness to commerce, but by a process exactly the reverse, by enabling the holders of commodities to hold on, by obstructing traffic and repressing consumption."

The opportune relief thus afforded to credit, during the excessive contraction which succeeds to an undue expansion, is consistent with the principle of the new system; for an extraordinary contraction of credit, and fall of prices, inevitably draw gold into the country, and the principle of the system is that the bank-note currency shall be permitted, and even compelled, to enlarge itself, in all cases in

* P. 106.

which a metallic currency would do the same. But, what the
principle of the law would encourage, its provisions in this instance
preclude, by not suffering the increased issues to take place until
the gold has actually arrived : which is never until the worst part
of the crisis has passed, and almost all the losses and failures attendant on it are consummated. The machinery of the system withholds,
until for many purposes it comes too late, the very medicine which
the theory of the system prescribes as the appropriate remedy.*
   This function of banks in filling up the gap made in mercantile
credit by the consequences of undue speculation and its revulsion, is
so entirely indispensable, that if the Act of 1844 continues unrepealed,
there can be no difficulty in foreseeing that its provisions must be
suspended, as they were in 1847, in every period of great commercial
difficulty, as soon as the crisis has really and completely set in.†
Were this all, there would be no absolute inconsistency in maintaining the restriction as a means of preventing a crisis, and relaxing it
for the purpose of relieving one. But there is another objection,
of a still more radical and comprehensive character, to the new
system.
   Professing, in theory, to require that a paper currency shall vary
in its amount in exact conformity to the variations of a metallic
currency, it provides, in fact, that in every case of an efflux of gold,
a corresponding diminution shall take place in the quantity of bank
notes ; in other words, that every exportation of the precious metals
shall be virtually drawn from the circulation ; it being assumed
that this would be the case if the currency were wholly metallic.
This theory, and these practical arrangements, are adapted to the
case in which the drain of gold originates in a rise of prices produced
by an undue expansion of currency or credit ; but they are adapted
to no case beside.
   When the efflux of gold is the last stage of a series of effects
arising from an increase of the currency, or from an expansion of
credit tantamount in its effect on prices to an increase of currency,

* [1857] True, the Bank is not precluded from making increased advances
from its deposits, which are likely to be of unusually large amount, since, at
these periods, every one leaves his money in deposit in order to have it within
call. But, that the deposits are not always sufficient was conclusively proved
in 1847, when the Bank stretched to the very utmost the means of relieving
commerce which its deposits afforded, without allaying the panic, which however ceased at once when the Government decided on suspending the Act.
   † [1862] This prediction was verified on the very next occurrence of a
commercial crisis, in 1857 ; when Government were again under the necessity
of suspending, on their own responsibility, the provisions of the Act.

it is in that case a fair assumption that in a purely metallic system the gold exported would be drawn from the currency itself; because such a drain, being in its nature unlimited, will necessarily continue as long as currency and credit are undiminished. But an exportation of the precious metals often arises from no causes affecting currency or credit, but simply from an unusual extension of foreign payments, arising either from the state of the markets for commodities, or from some circumstance not commercial. In this class of causes, four, of powerful operation, are included, of each of which the last fifty years of English history afford repeated instances. The first is that of an extraordinary foreign expenditure by government, either political or military; as in the revolutionary war, and, as long as it lasted, during the Crimean war. The second is the case of a large exportation of capital for foreign investment; such as the loans and mining operations which partly contributed to the crisis of 1825, and the American speculations which were the principal cause of the crisis of 1839. The third is a failure of crops in the countries which supply the raw material of important manufactures; such as the cotton failure in America, which compelled England, in 1847, to incur unusual liabilities for the purchase of that commodity at an advanced price. The fourth is a bad harvest, and a great consequent importation of food; of which the years 1846 and 1847 presented an example surpassing all antecedent experience.

In none of these cases, if the currency were metallic, would the gold or silver exported for the purposes in question be necessarily, or even probably, drawn wholly [1] from the circulation. It would be drawn from the hoards, which under a metallic currency always exist to a very large amount; in uncivilized countries, in the hands of all who can afford it; in civilized countries chiefly in the form of bankers' reserves. Mr. Tooke, in his *Inquiry into the Currency Principle*, bears testimony to this fact; but it is to Mr. Fullarton that the public are indebted for the clearest and most satisfactory elucidation of it. As I am not aware that this part of the theory of currency has been set forth by any other writer with anything like the same degree of completeness, I shall quote somewhat largely from this able production.

" No person who has ever resided in an Asiatic country, where hoarding is carried on to a far larger extent in proportion to the existing stock of wealth, and where the practice has become much more deeply engrafted in the habits of the people, by traditionary

---

[1] [" Wholly " inserted in 4th ed. (1857).]

apprehensions of insecurity and the difficulty of finding safe and remunerative investments, than in any European community—no person who has had personal experience of this state of society, can be at a loss to recollect innumerable instances of large metallic treasures extracted in times of pecuniary difficulty from the coffers of individuals by the temptation of a high rate of interest, and brought in aid of the public necessities, nor, on the other hand, of the facility with which those treasures have been absorbed again, when the inducements which had drawn them into light were no longer in operation. In countries more advanced in civilization and wealth than the Asiatic principalities, and where no man is in fear of attracting the cupidity of power by an external display of riches, but where the interchange of commodities is still almost universally conducted through the medium of a metallic circulation, as is the case with most of the commercial countries on the Continent of Europe, the motives for amassing the precious metals may be less powerful than in the majority of Asiatic principalities ; but the ability to accumulate being more widely extended, the absolute quantity amassed will be found probably to bear a considerably larger proportion to the population.* In those states which lie exposed to hostile invasion, or whose social condition is unsettled and menacing, the motive indeed must still be very strong ; and in a nation carrying on an extensive commerce, both foreign and internal, without any considerable aid from any of the banking substitutes for money, the reserves of gold and silver indispensably required to secure the regularity of payments, must of themselves engross a share of the circulating coin which it would not be easy to estimate.

" In this country, where the banking system has been carried to an extent and perfection unknown in any other part of Europe, and may be said to have entirely superseded the use of coin, except for retail dealings and the purposes of foreign commerce, the incentives to private hoarding exist no longer, and the hoards have all been transferred to the banks, or rather, I should say, to the Bank of England. But in France, where the bank-note circulation is still comparatively limited, the quantity of gold and silver coin in existence I find now currently estimated, on what are described as

---

* It is known, from unquestionable facts, that the hoards of money at all times existing in the hands of the French peasantry, often from a remote date, surpass any amount which could have been imagined possible ; and even in so poor a country as Ireland, it has of late been ascertained that the small farmers sometimes possess hoards quite disproportioned to their visible means of subsistence.

the latest authorities, at the enormous sum of 120 millions sterling; nor is the estimate at all at variance with the reasonable probabilities of the case. Of this vast treasure there is every reason to presume that a very large proportion, probably by much the greater part, is absorbed in the hoards. If you present for payment a bill for a thousand francs to a French banker, he brings you the silver in a sealed bag from his strong room. And not the banker only, but every merchant and trader, according to his means, is under the necessity of keeping by him a stock of cash sufficient not only for his ordinary disbursements, but to meet any unexpected demands. That the quantity of specie accumulated in these innumerable depôts, not in France only, but all over the Continent, where banking institutions are still either entirely wanting or very imperfectly organized, is not merely immense in itself, but admits of being largely drawn upon, and transferred even in vast masses from one country to another, with very little, if any, effect on prices, or other material derangements, we have had some remarkable proofs : " among others, " the signal success which attended the simultaneous efforts of some of the principal European powers (Russia, Austria, Prussia, Sweden, and Denmark) to replenish their treasuries, and to replace with coin a considerable portion of the depreciated paper which the necessities of the war had forced upon them, and this at the very time when the available stock of the precious metals over the world had been reduced by the exertions of England to recover her metallic currency. . . . There can be no doubt that these combined operations were on a scale of very extraordinary magnitude, that they were accomplished without any sensible injury to commerce or public prosperity, or any other effect than some temporary derangement of the exchanges, and that the private hoards of treasure accumulated throughout Europe during the war must have been the principal source from which all this gold and silver was collected. And no person, I think, can fairly contemplate the vast superflux of metallic wealth thus proved to be at all times in existence, and, though in a dormant and inert state, always ready to spring into activity on the first indication of a sufficiently intense demand, without feeling themselves compelled to admit the possibility of the mines being even shut up for years together, and the production of the metals altogether suspended, while there might be scarcely a perceptible alteration in the exchangeable value of the metal." *

* *Regulation of Currencies*, pp. 71–4.

Applying this to the currency doctrine and its advocates, "one might imagine," says Mr. Fullarton,* "that they supposed the gold which is drained off for exportation from a country using a currency exclusively metallic, to be collected by driblets at the fairs and markets, or from the tills of the grocers and mercers. They never even allude to the existence of such a thing as a great hoard of the metals, though upon the action of the hoards depends the whole economy of international payments between specie-circulating communities, while any operation of the money collected in hoards upon prices must, even according to the currency hypothesis, be wholly impossible. We know from experience what enormous payments in gold and silver specie-circulating countries are capable, at times, of making, without the least disturbance of their internal prosperity ; and whence is it supposed that these payments come, but from their hoards ? Let us think how the money market of a country transacting all its exchanges through the medium of the precious metals only, would be likely to be affected by the necessity of making a foreign payment of several millions. Of course the necessity could only be satisfied by a transmission of capital; and would not the competition for the possession of capital for transmission which the occasion would call forth, necessarily raise the market rate of interest.? If the payment was to be made by the government, would not the government, in all probability, have to open a new loan on terms more than usually favourable to the lender ? " If made by merchants, would it not be drawn either from the deposits in banks, or from the reserves which merchants keep by them in default of banks, or would it not oblige them to obtain the necessary amount of specie by going into the money market as borrowers ? " And would not all this inevitably act upon the hoards, and draw forth into activity a portion of the gold and silver which the money-dealers had been accumulating, and some of them with the express view of watching such opportunities for turning their treasures to advantage ? . . .

" To come to the present time [1844], the balance of payments with nearly all Europe has for about four years past been in favour of this country, and gold has been pouring in till the influx amounts to the unheard-of sum of about fourteen millions sterling. Yet, in all this time, has any one heard a complaint of any serious suffering inflicted on the people of the Continent ? Have prices there been

* *Regulation of Currencies*, pp. 139–42.

greatly depressed beyond their range in this country? Have wages fallen, or have merchants been extensively ruined by the universal depreciation of their stock? There has occurred nothing of the kind. The tenor of commercial and monetary affairs has been everywhere even and tranquil; and in France more particularly, an improving revenue and extended commerce bear testimony to the continued progress of internal prosperity. It may be doubted, indeed, if this great efflux of gold has withdrawn, from that portion of the metallic wealth of the nation which really circulates, a single napoleon. And it has been equally obvious, from the undisturbed state of credit, that not only has the supply of specie indispensable for the conduct of business in the retail market been all the while uninterrupted, but that the hoards have continued to furnish every facility requisite for the regularity of mercantile payments. It is of the very essence of the metallic system, that the hoards, in all cases of probable occurrence, should be equal to both objects; that they should, in the first place, supply the bullion demanded for exportation, and in the next place, should keep up the home circulation to its legitimate complement. Every man trading under that system, who, in the course of his business, may have frequent occasion to remit large sums in specie to foreign countries, must either keep by him a sufficient treasure of his own or must have the means of borrowing enough from his neighbours, not only to make up when wanted the amount of his remittances, but to enable him, moreover, to carry on his ordinary transactions at home without interruption."

In a country in which credit is carried to so great an extent as in England, one great reserve, in a single establishment, the Bank of England, supplies the place, as far as the precious metals are concerned, of the multitudinous reserves of other countries. The theoretical principle, therefore, of the currency doctrine would require, that all those drains of the metal which, if the currency were purely metallic, would be taken from the hoards, should be allowed to operate freely upon the reserve in the coffers of the Bank of England, without any attempt to stop it either by a diminution of the currency or by a contraction of credit. Nor to this would there be any well-grounded objection, unless the drain were so great as to threaten the exhaustion of the reserve, and a consequent stoppage of payments; a danger against which it is possible to take adequate precautions, because in the cases which we are considering, the drain is for foreign payments of definite amount, and stops of

itself as soon as these are effected.   And in all systems it is admitted
that the habitual reserve of the Bank should exceed the utmost
amount to which experience warrants the belief that such a drain
may extend ; which extreme limit Mr. Fullarton affirms to be seven
millions, but Mr. Tooke recommends an average reserve of ten, and
in his last publication, of twelve millions.   [1] Under these circumstances, the habitual reserve, which would never be employed in
discounts, but kept to be paid out exclusively in exchange for
cheques or bank notes, would be sufficient for a crisis of this description ; which therefore would pass off without having its difficulties
increased by a contraction either of credit or of the circulation.
But this, the most advantageous *dénouement* that the case admits of,
and not only consistent with but required by the professed principle
of the system, the panegyrists of the system claim for it as a great
merit that it prevents.   They boast, that on the first appearance
of a drain for exportation—whatever may be its cause, and whether,
under a metallic currency, it would involve a contraction of credit
or not—the Bank is at once obliged to curtail its advances.   And
this, be it remembered, when there has been no speculative rise
of prices which it is indispensable to correct, no unusual extension
of credit requiring contraction ; but the demand for gold is solely
occasioned by foreign payments on account of government, or large
corn importations consequent on a bad harvest.

[2] Even supposing that the reserve is insufficient to meet the
foreign payments, and that the means wherewith to make them have
to be taken from the loanable capital of the country, the consequence
of which is a rise of the rate of interest ; in such circumstances some
pressure on the money market is unavoidable, but that pressure is
much increased in severity by the separation of the Banking from
the Issue Department.   The case is generally stated as if the Act only
operated in one way, namely, by preventing the Bank, when it has

---

[1] [The rest of this paragraph replaced in the 6th ed. (1865) the following
passage of the original text :
" The machinery, however, of the new system insists upon bringing about
by force, what its principle not only does not require, but positively condemns.
Every drain for exportation, whatever may be its cause, and whether under a
metallic currency it would affect the circulation or not, is now compulsorily
drawn from that source alone.   The bank-note circulation, and the discounts
or other advances of the Bank, must be diminished by an amount equal to that
of the metal exported, though it be to the full extent of seven or ten millions.
And this, be it remembered," &c.]
[2] [From this point to the end of the section the text was largely rewritten
in the 4th ed. (1857), and the note added in the 5th (1862).]

parted with (say) three millions of bullion in exchange for three millions of its notes, from again lending those notes, in discounts or other advances. But the Act really does much more than this. It is well known, that the first operation of a drain is always on the Banking Department. The bank deposits constitute the bulk of the unemployed and disposable capital of the country ; and capital wanted for foreign payments is almost always obtained mainly by drawing out deposits. Supposing three millions to be the amount wanted, three millions of notes are drawn from the Banking Department (either directly or through the private bankers, who keep the bulk of their reserves with the Bank of England), and the three millions of notes, thus obtained, are presented at the Issue Department, and exchanged against gold for exportation. Thus a drain upon the country at large of only three millions is a drain upon the Bank virtually of six millions. The deposits have lost three millions, and the reserve of the Issue Department has lost an equal amount. As the two departments, so long as the Act remains in operation, cannot even in the utmost extremity help one another, each must take its separate precautions for its own safety. Whatever measures, therefore, on the part of the Bank, would have been required under the old system by a drain of six millions, are now rendered necessary by a drain only of three. The Issue Department protects itself in the manner prescribed by the Act, by not re-issuing the three millions of notes which have been returned to it. But the Banking Department must take measures to replenish its reserve, which has been reduced by three millions. Its liabilities having also decreased three millions, by the loss of that amount of deposits, the reserve, on the ordinary banking principle of a third of the liabilities, will bear a reduction of one million. But the other two millions it must procure by letting that amount of advances run out, and not renewing them. Not only must it raise its rate of interest, but it must effect, by whatever means, a diminution of two millions in the total amount of its discounts : or it must sell securities to an equal amount. This violent action on the money market for the purpose of replenishing the Banking reserve, is wholly occasioned by the Act of 1844. If the restrictions of that Act did not exist, the Bank, instead of contracting its discounts, would simply transfer two millions, either in gold or in notes, from the Issue to the Banking Department ; not in order to lend them to the public, but to secure the solvency of the Banking Department in the event of further unexpected demands by the depositors. And unless the drain continued, and reached so great an amount as to seem likely to exceed the whole of the gold in the reserves of both departments, the Bank would be under no necessity, while the pressure lasted, of withholding from commerce its accustomed amount of accommodation, at a rate of interest corresponding to the increased demand.*

I am aware it will be said that by allowing drains of this character to operate freely upon the Bank reserve until they cease of themselves, a contraction of the currency and of credit would not be prevented, but only postponed ; since if a limitation of issues were not resorted to for the purpose of checking the drain in its commencement, the same or a still greater limitation must take place afterwards, in order, by acting on prices, to bring back this large quantity of gold, for the indispensable purpose of replenishing the Bank reserve.   But in this argument several things are overlooked.   In the first place, the gold might be brought back, not by a fall of prices, but by the much more rapid and convenient medium of a rise of the rate of interest, involving no fall of any prices except the price of securities.   Either English securities would be bought on account of foreigners, or foreign securities held in England would be sent abroad for sale, both which operations took place largely during the mercantile difficulties of 1847, and not only checked the efflux of gold, but turned the tide and brought the metal back.   It was not, therefore, brought back by a contraction of the currency, though

* [1862] This, which I have called " the double action of drains," has been strangely understood as if I had asserted that the Bank is compelled to part with six millions' worth of property by a drain of three millions.   Such an assertion would be too absurd to require any refutation.   Drains have a double action, not upon the pecuniary position of the Bank itself, but upon the measures it is forced to take in order to stop the drain.   Though the Bank itself is no poorer, its two reserves, the reserve in the banking department and the reserve in the issue department, have each been reduced three millions by a drain of only three.   And as the separation of the departments renders it necessary that each of them separately should be kept as strong as the two together need be if they could help one another, the Bank's action on the money market must be as violent on a drain of three millions, as would have been required on the old system for one of six.   The reserve in the banking department being less than it otherwise would be by the entire amount of the bullion in the issue department, and the whole amount of the drain falling in the first instance on that diminished reserve, the pressure of the whole drain on the half reserve is as much felt, and requires as strong measures to·stop it, as a pressure of twice the amount on the entire reserve.   As I have said elsewhere,* " it is as if a man having to lift a weight were restricted from using both hands to do it, and were only allowed to use one hand at a time : in which case it would be necessary that each of his hands should be as strong as the two together."

* Evidence before the Committee of the House of Commons on the Bank Acts, in 1857.

In this case it certainly was so by a contraction of loans. But even this is not always indispensable. For in the second place, it is not necessary that the gold should return with the same suddenness with which it went out. A great portion would probably return in the ordinary way of commerce, in payment for exported commodities. The extra gains made by dealers and producers in foreign countries through the extra payments they receive from this country, are very likely to be partly expended in increased purchases of English commodities, either for consumption or on speculation, though the effect may not manifest itself with sufficient rapidity to enable the transmission of gold to be dispensed with in the first instance. These extra purchases would turn the balance of payments in favour of the country, and gradually restore a portion of the exported gold; and the remainder would probably be brought back, without any considerable rise of the rate of interest in England, by the fall of it in foreign countries, occasioned by the addition of some millions of gold to the loanable capital of those countries. Indeed, in the state of things consequent on the gold discoveries, when the enormous quantity of gold annually produced in Australia, and much of that from California, is distributed to other countries through England, and a month seldom passes without a large arrival, the Bank reserves can replenish themselves without any re-importation of the gold previously carried off by a drain. All that is needful is an inter-mission, and a very brief intermission is sufficient, of the exportation.

For these reasons it appears to me, that notwithstanding the beneficial operation of the Act of 1844 in the first stages of one kind of commercial crisis (that produced by over-speculation), it on the whole materially aggravates the severity of commercial revulsions. And not only are contractions of credit made more severe by the Act, they are also made greatly more frequent. "Suppose," says Mr. George Walker, in a clear, impartial, and conclusive series of papers in the *Aberdeen Herald*, forming one of the best existing discussions of the present question—"suppose that, of eighteen millions of gold, ten are in the Issue Department and eight are in the Banking Depart-ment. The result is the same as under a metallic currency with only eight millions in reserve, instead of eighteen. . . . . . The effect of the Bank Act is, that the proceedings of the Bank under a drain are not determined by the amount of gold within its vaults, but are, or ought to be, determined by the portion of it belonging to the Banking Department. With the whole of the gold at its disposal, it may find it unnecessary to interfere with credit, or force down prices, if a drain leave a fair reserve behind.   With only the banking reserve at its disposal, it must, from the narrow margin it has to operate on, meet all drains by counteractives more or less strong, to the injury of the commercial world ; and if it fail to do so, as it may fail, the consequence is destruction.   Hence the extraordinary and frequent variations of the rate of interest under the Bank Act.   Since 1847, when the eyes of the Bank were opened to its true position, it has felt it necessary, as a precautionary measure, that every variation in the reserve should be accompanied by an alteration in the rate of interest."   To make the Act innocuous, therefore, it would be necessary that the Bank, in addition to the whole of the gold in the Issue Department, should retain as great a reserve in gold or notes in the Banking Department alone, as would suffice under the old system for the security both of the issues and of the deposits.

§ 5.   There remain two questions respecting a bank-note currency, which have also been a subject of considerable discussion of late years : whether the privilege of providing it should be confined to a single establishment, such as the Bank of England, or a plurality of issuers should be allowed ; and in the latter case, whether any peculiar precautions are requisite or advisable, to protect the holders of notes against losses occasioned by the insolvency of the issuers.
     The course of the preceding speculations has led us to attach so much less of peculiar importance to bank notes, as compared with other forms of credit, than accords with the notions generally current, that questions respecting the regulation of so very small a part of the general mass of credit cannot appear to us of such momentous import as they are sometimes considered.   Bank notes, however, have so far a real peculiarity, that they are the only form of credit sufficiently convenient for all the purposes of circulation to be able entirely to supersede the use of metallic money for internal purposes.   Though the extension of the use of cheques has a tendency more and more to diminish the number of bank notes, as it would that of the sovereigns or other coins which would take their place if they were abolished ; there is sure, for a long time to come, to be a considerable supply of them, wherever the necessary degree of commercial confidence exists, and their free use is permitted.   The exclusive privilege, therefore, of issuing them, if reserved to the Government or to some one body, is a source of great pecuniary gain.   That this gain should be obtained for the nation at large is both practicable and desirable : and if the management of a bank-note currency

ought to be so completely mechanical, so entirely a thing of fixed rule, as it is made by the Act of 1844, there seems no reason why this mechanism should be worked for the profit of any private issuer, rather than for the public treasury. If, however, a plan be preferred which leaves the variations in the amount of issues in any degree whatever to the discretion of the issuers, it is not desirable that to the ever-growing attributions of the Government so delicate a function should be superadded ; and that the attention of the heads of the state should be diverted from larger objects, by their being besieged with the applications, and made a mark for all the attacks, which are never spared to those deemed to be responsible for any acts, however minute, connected with the regulation of the currency. It would be better that treasury notes, exchangeable for gold on demand, should be issued to a fixed amount, not exceeding the minimum of a bank-note currency ; the remainder of the notes which may be required being left to be supplied either by one or by a number of private banking establishments. Or an establishment like the Bank of England might supply the whole country, on condition of lending fifteen or twenty millions of its notes to the government without interest ; which would give the same pecuniary advantage to the state as if it issued that number of its own notes.

The reason ordinarily alleged in condemnation of the system of plurality of issuers which existed in England before the Act of 1844, and under certain limitations still subsists, is that the competition of these different issuers induces them to increase the amount of their notes to an injurious extent. But we have seen that the power which bankers have of augmenting their issues, and the degree of mischief which they can produce by it, are quite trifling compared with the current over-estimate. As remarked by Mr. Fullarton,* the extraordinary increase of banking competition occasioned by the establishment of the joint-stock banks, a competition often of the most reckless kind, has proved utterly powerless to enlarge the aggregate mass of the bank-note circulation ; that aggregate circulation having, on the contrary, actually decreased. In the absence of any special case for an exception to freedom of industry, the general rule ought to prevail. It appears desirable, however, to maintain one great establishment like the Bank of England, distinguished from other banks of issue in this, that it alone is required to pay in gold, the others being at liberty to pay their notes with notes of the central establishment. The object of this is that there may be one body

* Pp. 89–92.

responsible for maintaining a reserve of the precious metals sufficient
to meet any drain that can reasonably be expected to take place.
By disseminating this responsibility among a number of banks,
it is prevented from operating efficaciously upon any : or if it be still
enforced against one, the reserves of the metals retained by all the
others are capital kept idle in pure waste, which may be dispensed
with by allowing them at their option to pay in Bank of England
notes.

§ 6.   The question remains whether, in case of a plurality of
issuers, any peculiar precautions are needed to protect the holders
of notes from the consequences of failure of payment.   Before
1826, the insolvency of banks of issue was a frequent and very serious
evil, often spreading distress through a whole neighbourhood, and
at one blow depriving provident industry of the results of long and
painful saving.   This was one of the chief reasons which induced
Parliament, in that year, to prohibit the issue of bank notes of a
denomination below five pounds, that the labouring classes at least
might be as little as possible exposed to participate in this suffering.
As an additional safeguard, it has been suggested to give the holders
of notes a priority over other creditors, or to require bankers to
deposit stock or other public securities as a pledge for the whole
amount of their issues.   The insecurity of the former bank-note
currency of England was partly the work of the law, which, in order
to give a qualified monopoly of banking business to the Bank of
England, had actually made the formation of safe banking establishments a punishable offence, by prohibiting the existence of any
banks, in town or country, whether of issue or deposit, with a
number of partners exceeding six.   This truly characteristic specimen
of the old system of monopoly and restriction was done away with
in 1826, both as to issues and deposits, everywhere but in a district
of sixty-five miles radius round London, and in 1833 in that district
also, as far as relates to deposits. [1] It was hoped that the numerous

----

[1] [The remainder of this paragraph replaced in the 4th ed. (1857) the
following sentences of the original (1848) text :
   " The numerous joint-stock banks since established have, by furnishing
a more trustworthy currency, made it almost impossible for any private
banker to maintain his circulation, unless his capital and character inspire the
most complete confidence.   And although there has been in some instances
very gross mismanagement by joint-stock banks (less, however, in the department of issues than in that of deposits) the failure of these banks is extremely
rare, and the cases still rarer in which loss has ultimately been sustained by
any one except the shareholders.   The banking system of England is now

joint-stock banks since established would have furnished a more trustworthy currency, and that under their influence the banking system of England would have been almost as secure to the public as that of Scotland (where banking was 'always free) has been for two centuries past. But the almost incredible instances of reckless and fraudulent mismanagement which these institutions have of late afforded (though in some of the most notorious cases the delinquent establishments have not been banks of issue), have shown only too clearly that, south of the Tweed at least, the joint-stock principle applied to banking is not the adequate safeguard it was so confidently supposed to be : and it is difficult now to resist the conviction, that if plurality of issuers is allowed to exist, some kind of special security in favour of the holders of notes should be exacted as an imperative condition.[1]

almost as secure to the public, as that of Scotland (where banking was always free) has been for two centuries past ; and the legislature might without any bad consequences, at least of this kind, revoke its interdict (which was never extended to Scotland) against one and two pound notes. I cannot, therefore, think it at all necessary, or that it would be anything but vexatious meddling, to enforce any kind of special security in favour of the holders of notes. The true protection to creditors of all kinds is a good law of insolvency (a part of the law at present shamefully deficient), and, in the case of joint-stock companies at least, complete publicity of their accounts : the publicity now very properly given to their issues being a very small portion of what a state has a right to require in return for their being allowed to constitute themselves, and be recognised by the law, as a collective body."]

[1] [See Appendix W. *The Regulation of Currency.*]

CHAPTER XXV

§ 1. IN the phraseology of the Mercantile System, the language and doctrines of which are still the basis of what may be called the political economy of the selling classes, as distinguished from the buyers or consumers, there is no word of more frequent recurrence or more perilous import than the word *underselling*. To undersell other countries—not to be undersold by other countries—were spoken of, and are still very often spoken of, almost as if they were the sole purposes for which production and commodities exist. The feelings of rival tradesmen, prevailing among nations, overruled for centuries all sense of the general community of advantage which commercial countries derive from the prosperity of one another : and that commercial spirit, which is now one of the strongest obstacles to wars, was during a certain period of European history their principal cause.

Even in the more enlightened view now attainable of the nature and consequences of international commerce, some, though a comparatively small, space must still be made for the fact of commercial rivality. Nations may, like individual dealers, be competitors, with opposite interests, in the markets of some commodities, while in others they are in the more fortunate relation of reciprocal customers. The benefit of commerce does not consist, as it was once thought to do, in the commodities sold ; but, since the commodities sold are the means of obtaining those which are bought, a nation would be cut off from the real advantage of commerce, the imports, if it could not induce other nations to take any of its commodities in exchange ; and in proportion as the competition of other countries compels it to offer its commodities on cheaper terms, on pain of not selling them at all, the imports which it obtains by its foreign trade are procured at greater cost.

These points have been adequately, though incidentally, illustrated in some of the preceding chapters. But the great space which the topic has filled, and continues to fill, in economical speculations, and in the practical anxieties both of politicians and of dealers and manufacturers, makes it desirable, before quitting the subject of international exchange, to subjoin a few observations on the things which do, and on those which do not, enable countries to undersell one another.

One country can only undersell another in a given market, to the extent of entirely expelling her from it, on two conditions. In the first place, she must have a greater advantage than the second country in the production of the article exported by both ; meaning by a greater advantage (as has been already so fully explained) not absolutely, but in comparison with other commodities ; and in the second place, such must be her relation with the customer country in respect to the demand for each other's products, and such the consequent state of international values, as to give away to the customer country more than the whole advantage possessed by the rival country ; otherwise the rival will still be able to hold her ground in the market.

Let us revert to the imaginary hypothesis of a trade between England and Germany in cloth and linen : England being capable of producing 10 yards of cloth at the same cost with 15 yards of linen, Germany at the same cost with 20, and the two commodities being exchanged between the two countries (cost of carriage apart) at some intermediate rate, say 10 for 17. Germany could not be permanently undersold in the English market, and expelled from it, unless by a country which offered not merely more than 17, but more than 20 yards of linen for 10 of cloth. Short of that, the competition would only oblige Germany to pay dearer for cloth, but would not disable her from exporting linen. The country, therefore, which could undersell Germany, must, in the first place, be able to produce linen at less cost, compared with cloth, than Germany herself ; and in the next place, must have such a demand for cloth, or other English commodities, as would compel her, even when she became sole occupant of the market, to give a greater advantage to England than Germany could give by resigning the whole of hers ; to give, for example, 21 yards for 10. For if not—if, for example, the equation of international demand, after Germany was excluded, gave a ratio of 18 for 10, Germany could again enter into the competition ; Germany would be now the underselling nation ; and there would be a point, perhaps 19 for 10, at which both countries would be able to maintain their ground, and to sell in England enough linen to pay for the cloth, or other English commodities, for which, on these newly-adjusted terms of interchange, they had a demand. In like manner, England, as an exporter of cloth, could only be driven from the German market by some rival whose superior advantages in the production of cloth enabled her, and the intensity of whose demand for German produce compelled her, to offer 10 yards of cloth, not merely for less than 17 yards of linen, but for less than 15. In that case, England could no longer carry on the trade without loss ; but in any case short of this, she would merely be obliged to give to Germany more cloth for less linen than she had previously given.

It thus appears that the alarm of being permanently undersold may be taken much too easily ; may be taken when the thing really to be anticipated is not the loss of the trade, but the minor inconvenience of carrying it on at a diminished advantage ; an inconvenience chiefly falling on the consumers of foreign commodities, and not on the producers or sellers of the exported article. It is no sufficient ground of apprehension to the English producers to find that some other country can sell cloth in foreign markets, at some particular time, a trifle cheaper than they can themselves afford to do in the existing state of prices in England. Suppose them to be temporarily undersold, and their exports diminished ; the imports will exceed the exports, there will be a new distribution of the precious metals, prices will fall, and as all the money expenses of the English producers will be diminished, they will be able (if the case falls short of that stated in the preceding paragraph) again to compete with their rivals. The loss which England will incur, will not fall upon the exporters, but upon those who consume imported commodities ; who, with money incomes reduced in amount, will have to pay the same or even an increased price for all things produced in foreign countries.

§ 2. Such, I conceive, is the true theory, or rationale, of underselling. It will be observed that it takes no account of some things which we hear spoken of, oftener perhaps than any others, in the character of causes exposing a country to be undersold.

According to the preceding doctrine, a country cannot be undersold in any commodity, unless the rival country has a stronger inducement than itself for devoting its labour and capital to the production of the commodity; arising from the fact that by doing so it occasions a greater saving of labour and capital, to be shared between itself and its customers—a greater increase of the aggregate produce of the world. The underselling, therefore, though a loss to the under-sold country, is an advantage to the world at large ; the substituted commerce being one which economizes more of the labour and capital of mankind, and adds more to their collective wealth, than the commerce superseded by it. The advantage, of course, con-sists in being able to produce the commodity of better quality, or with less labour (compared with other things) ; or perhaps not with less labour, but in less time ; with a less prolonged detention of the capital employed. This may arise from greater natural advantages (such as soil, climate, richness of mines) ; superior capability, either natural or acquired, in the labourers ; better division of labour, and better tools, or machinery. But there is no place left in this theory for the case of lower wages. This, however, in the theories commonly current, is a favourite cause of underselling. We continually hear of the disadvantage under which the British pro-ducer labours, both in foreign markets and even in his own, through the lower wages paid by his foreign rivals. These lower wages, we are told, enable, or are always on the point of enabling them to sell at lower prices, and to dislodge the English manufacturer from all markets in which he is not artificially protected.

Before examining this opinion on grounds of principle, it is worth while to bestow a moment's consideration upon it as a ques-tion of fact. Is it true, that the wages of manufacturing labour are lower in foreign countries than in England, in any sense in which low wages are an advantage to the capitalist ? The artisan of Ghent or Lyons may earn less wages in a day, but does he not do less work ? Degrees of efficiency considered, does his labour cost less to his employer ? Though wages may be lower on the Continent, is not the Cost of Labour, which is the real element in the competition, very nearly the same ? That it is so seems the opinion of competent judges, and is confirmed by the very little difference in the rate of profit between England and the Continental countries. But if so, the opinion is absurd that English producers can be undersold by their Continental rivals from this cause. It is only in America that the supposition is *primâ facie* admissible. In America, wages are much higher than in England, if we mean by wages the daily earn-ings of a labourer : but the productive power of American labour is so great—its efficiency, combined with the favourable circumstances in which it is exerted, makes it worth so much tc the purchaser, that the Cost of Labour is lower in America than in England ; as is indicated by the fact that the general rate of profits and of interest is higher.[1]

§ 3.   But is it true that low wages, even in the sense of low Cost of Labour, enable a country to sell cheaper in the foreign market ?   I mean, of course, low wages which are common to the whole productive industry of the country.

If wages, in any of the departments of industry which supply exports, are kept, artificially, or by some accidental cause, below the general rate of wages in the country, this is a real advantage in the foreign market.   It lessens the *comparative* cost of production of those articles, in relation to others ; and has the same effect as if their production required so much less labour.   Take, for instance, the case of the United States in respect to certain commodities, prior to the civil war.[2]   Tobacco and cotton, two great articles of export, were produced by slave labour, while food and manufactures generally were produced by free labourers, either working on their own account or paid by wages.   In spite of the inferior efficiency of slave labour, there can be no reasonable doubt that in a country where the wages of free labour were so high, the work executed by slaves was a better bargain to the capitalist.   To whatever extent it was so, this smaller cost of labour, being not general, but limited to those employments, was just as much a cause of cheapness in the products, both in the home and in the foreign market, as if they had been made by a less quantity of labour.   If, when the slaves in the Southern States were emancipated, their wages rose to the general level of the earnings of free labour in America, that country might have been obliged to erase some of the slave-grown articles from the catalogue of its exports, and would certainly be unable to sell any of them in the foreign market at the accustomed price. Accordingly, American cotton is now habitually at a much higher price than before the war.   Its previous cheapness was partly an artificial cheapness, which may be compared to that produced by a bounty on production or on exportation : or, considering the

---

[1] [Until the 6th ed. (1865) the concluding clause ran : " as is proved by the fact that the general rate of profits and of interest is very much higher."]

[2] [The concluding clause of this sentence was added in the 7th ed. (1871) ; the following sentences changed from the present to the past tense ; and the sentence about the price of American cotton was inserted.]

means by which it was obtained, an apter comparison would be with the cheapness of stolen goods.

An advantage of a similar economical, though of a very different moral character, is that possessed by domestic manufactures ; fabrics produced in the leisure hours of families partially occupied in other pursuits, who, not depending for subsistence on the produce of the manufacture, can afford to sell it at any price, however low, for which they think it worth while to take the trouble of producing. In an account of the Canton of Zurich, to which I have had occasion to refer on another subject, it is observed,* " The workman of Zurich is to-day a manufacturer, to-morrow again an agriculturist, and changes his occupations with the seasons, in a continual round. Manufacturing industry and tillage advance hand in hand, in inseparable alliance, and in this union of the two occupations the secret may be found, why the simple and unlearned Swiss manufacturer can always go on competing, and increasing in prosperity, in the face of those extensive establishments fitted out with great economic, and (what is still more important) intellectual, resources. Even in those parts of the Canton where manufactures have extended themselves the most widely, only one-seventh of all the families belong to manufactures alone ; four-sevenths combine that employment with agriculture. The advantage of this domestic or family manufacture consists chiefly in the fact, that it is compatible with all other avocations, or rather that it may in part be regarded as only a supplementary employment. In winter, in the dwellings of the operatives, the whole family employ themselves in it : but as soon as spring appears, those on whom the early field labours devolve abandon the in-door work ; many a shuttle stands still ; by degrees as the field-work increases, one member of the family follows another, till at last, at the harvest, and during the so-called ' great works,' all hands seize the implements of husbandry ; but in unfavourable weather, and in all otherwise vacant hours, the work in the cottage is resumed, and when the ungenial season again recurs, the people return in the same gradual order to their home occupation, until they have all resumed it."

In the case of these domestic manufactures, the comparative cost of production, on which the interchange between countries depends, is much lower than in proportion to the quantity of labour employed. The workpeople, looking to the earnings of their loom

* *Historisch-geographisch-statistisches Gemälde der Schweiz.* Erstes Heft, 1834, p. 105.

for a part only, if for any part, of their actual maintenance, can afford to work for a less remuneration than the lowest rate of wages which can permanently exist in the employments by which the labourer has to support the whole expense of the family. Working, as they do, not for an employer but for themselves, they may be said to carry on the manufacture at no cost at all, except the small expense of a loom and of the material ; and the limit of possible cheapness is not the necessity of living by their trade but that of earning enough by the work to make that social employment of their leisure hours not disagreeable.

§ 4.   These two cases, of slave labour and of domestic manu-factures, exemplify the conditions under which low wages enable a country to sell its commodities cheaper in foreign markets, and consequently to undersell its rivals, or to avoid being undersold by them.   But no such advantage is conferred by low wages when common to all branches of industry.   General low wages never caused any country to undersell its rivals, nor did general high wages ever hinder it from doing so.

To demonstrate this, we must return to an elementary principle which was discussed in a former chapter.*   General low wages do not cause low prices, nor high wages high prices, within the country itself.   General prices are not raised by a rise of wages, any more than they would be raised by an increase of the quantity of labour required in all production.   Expenses which affect all commodities equally, have no influence on prices.   If the maker of broadcloth or cutlery, and nobody else, had to pay higher wages, the price of his commodity would rise, just as it would if he had to employ more labour ; because otherwise he would gain less profit than other producers, and nobody would engage in the employment.   But if everybody has to pay higher wages, or everybody to employ more labour, the loss must be submitted to ; as it affects everybody alike, no one can hope to get rid of it by a change of employment, each therefore resigns himself to a diminution of profits, and prices remain as they were.   In like manner, general low wages, or a general increase in the productiveness of labour, does not make prices low, but profits high.   If wages fall, (meaning here by wages the cost of labour,) why, on that account, should the producer lower his price ? He will be forced, it may be said, by the competition of other capitalists who will crowd into his employment.   But other capitalists

* Supra, book iii. ch. iv.

are also paying lower wages, and by entering into competition with him they would gain nothing but what they are gaining already. The rate then at which labour is paid, as well as the quantity of it which is employed, affects neither the value nor the price of the commodity produced, except in so far as it is peculiar to that commodity, and not common to commodities generally.

Since low wages are not a cause of low prices in the country itself, so neither do they cause it to offer its commodities in foreign markets at a lower price. It is quite true that if the cost of labour is lower in America than in England, America could sell her cottons to Cuba at a lower price than England, and still gain as high a profit as the English manufacturer. But it is not with the profit of the English manufacturer that the American cotton spinner will make his comparison ; it is with the profits of other American capitalists. These enjoy, in common with himself, the benefit of a low cost of labour, and have accordingly a high rate of profit. This high profit the cotton spinner must also have : he will not content himself with the English profit. It is true he may go on for a time at that lower rate, rather than change his employment ; and a trade may be carried on, sometimes for a long period, at a much lower profit than that for which it would have been originally engaged in. Countries which have a low cost of labour, and high profits, do not for that reason undersell others, but they do oppose a more obstinate resistance to being undersold, because the producers can often submit to a diminution of profit without being unable to live, and even to thrive, by their business. But this is all which their advantage does for them : and in this resistance they will not long persevere, when a change of times which may give them equal profits with the rest of their countrymen has become manifestly hopeless.

§ 5. There is a class of trading and exporting communities, on which a few words of explanation seem to be required. These are hardly to be looked upon as countries, carrying on an exchange of commodities with other countries, but more properly as outlying agricultural or manufacturing establishments belonging to a larger community. Our West India colonies, for example, cannot be regarded as countries, with a productive capital of their own. If Manchester, instead of being where it is, were on a rock in the North Sea, (its present industry nevertheless continuing,) it would still be but a town of England, not a country trading with England ; it would be merely, as now, a place where England finds it convenient to carry on her cotton manufacture. The West Indies, in like manner, are the place where England finds it convenient to carry on the production of sugar, coffee, and a few other tropical commodities. All the capital employed is English capital; almost all the industry is carried on for English uses; there is little production of anything except the staple commodities, and these are sent to England, not to be exchanged for things exported to the colony and consumed by its inhabitants, but to be sold in England for the benefit of the proprietors there. The trade with the West Indies is therefore hardly to be considered as external trade, but more resembles the traffic between town and country, and is amenable to the principles of the home trade. The rate of profit in the colonies will be regulated by English profits; the expectation of profit must be about the same as in England, with the addition of compensation for the disadvantages attending the more distant and hazardous employment; and after allowance is made for those disadvantages, the value and price of West India produce in the English market must be regulated, (or rather must have been regulated formerly,) like that of any English commodity, by the cost of production. For the last twelve or fifteen years [1] this principle has been in abeyance : the price was first kept up beyond the ratio of the cost of production by deficient supplies, which could not, owing to the deficiency of labour, be increased; and more recently the admission of foreign competition has introduced another element, and some of [2] the West India Islands are undersold, not so much because wages are higher than in Cuba and Brazil, as because they are higher than in England : for were they not so, Jamaica could sell her sugars at Cuban prices, and still obtain, though not a Cuban, an English rate of profit.

It is worth while also to notice another class of small, but in this case mostly independent communities, which have supported and enriched themselves almost without any productions of their own, (except ships and marine equipments,) by a mere carrying trade, and commerce of *entrepôt ;* by buying the produce of one country, to sell it at a profit in another. Such were Venice and the Hanse Towns. The case of these communities is very simple. They made themselves and their capital the instruments, not of production, but of accomplishing exchanges between the productions of other countries. These exchanges are attended with an advantage to those countries

[1] [So since 6th ed. (1865) ; replacing " ten or twelve " in 1st ed. (1848).]
[2] [" Some of " inserted in 5th ed. (1862).]

—an increase of the aggregate returns to industry—part of which went to indemnify the agents for the necessary expenses of transport, and another part to remunerate the use of their capital and mercantile skill.   The countries themselves had not capital disposable for the operation.   When the Venetians became the agents of the general commerce of Southern Europe, they had scarcely any competitors : the thing would not have been done at all without them, and there was really no limit to their profits except the limit to what the ignorant feudal nobility could and would give for the unknown luxuries then first presented to their sight.   At a later period competition arose, and the profit of this operation, like that of others, became amenable to natural laws.   The carrying trade was taken up by Holland, a country with productions of its own and a large accumulated capital.   The other nations of Europe also had now capital to spare, and were capable of conducting their foreign trade for themselves : but Holland, having, from a variety of circumstances, a lower rate of profit at home, could afford to carry for other countries at a smaller advance on the original cost of the goods, than would have been required by their own capitalists ; and Holland, therefore, engrossed the greatest part of the carrying trade of all those countries which did not keep it to themselves by Navigation Laws, constructed, like those of England, for that express purpose.

CHAPTER XXVI

§ 1. WE have now completed, as far as is compatible with our purposes and limits, the exposition of the machinery through which the produce of a country is apportioned among the different classes of its inhabitants ; which is no other than the machinery of Exchange, and has for the exponents of its operation the laws of Value and of Price. We shall now avail ourselves of the light thus acquired, to cast a retrospective glance at the subject of Distribution. The division of the produce among the three classes, Labourers, Capitalists, and Landlords, when considered without any reference to Exchange, appeared to depend on certain general laws. It is fit that we should now consider whether these same laws still operate, when the distribution takes place through the complex mechanism of exchange and money ; or whether the properties of the mechanism interfere with and modify the presiding principles.

The primary division of the produce of human exertion and frugality is, as we have seen, into three shares, wages, profits, and rent ; and these shares are portioned out to the persons entitled to them, in the form of money, and by a process of exchange ; or rather, the capitalist, with whom in the usual arrangements of society the produce remains, pays in money, to the other two sharers, the market value of their labour and land. If we examine, on what the pecuniary value of labour, and the pecuniary value of the use of land, depend, we shall find that it is on the very same causes by which we found that wages and rent would be regulated if there were no money and no exchange of commodities.

It is evident, in the first place, that the law of Wages is not affected by the existence or non-existence of Exchange or Money. Wages depend on the ratio between population and capital ; and would do so if all the capital in the world were the property of one association, or if the capitalists among whom it is shared maintained each an establishment for the production of every article consumed in the community, exchange of commodities having no existence. As the ratio between capital and population, in all old countries, depends on the strength of the checks by which the too rapid increase of population is restrained, it may be said, popularly speaking, that wages depend on the checks to population ; that when the check is not death, by starvation or disease, wages depend on the prudence of the labouring people ; and that wages in any country are habitually at the lowest rate to which in that country the labourer will suffer them to be depressed rather than put a restraint upon multiplication.

What is here meant, however, by wages, is the labourer's real scale of comfort ; the quantity he obtains of the things which nature or habit has made necessary or agreeable to him: wages in the sense in which they are of importance to the receiver. In the sense in which they are of importance to the payer, they do not depend exclusively on such simple principles. Wages in the first sense, the wages on which the labourer's comfort depends, we will call real wages, or wages in kind. Wages in the second sense, we may be permitted to call, for the present, money wages ; assuming, as it is allowable to do, that money remains for the time an invariable standard, no alteration taking place in the conditions under which the circulating medium itself is produced or obtained. If money itself undergoes no variation in cost, the money price of labour is an exact measure of the Cost of Labour, and may be made use of as a convenient symbol to express it.

The money wages of labour are a compound result of two elements: first, real wages, or wages in kind, or, in other words, the quantity which the labourer obtains of the ordinary articles of consumption ; and secondly, the money prices of those articles. In all old countries —all countries in which the increase of population is in any degree checked by the difficulty of obtaining subsistence—the habitual money price of labour is that which will just enable the labourers, one with another, to purchase the commodities without which they either cannot or will not keep up the population at its customary rate of increase.[1] Their standard of comfort being given, (and by the standard of comfort in a labouring class, is meant that, rather than forego which, they will abstain from multiplication,) money wages depend on the money price, and therefore on the cost of

[1] [So since 3rd ed. (1852). The original text ran: "the commodities without which they will not consent to continue the race."]

production, of the various articles which the labourers habitually consume : because if their wages cannot procure them a given quantity of these, their increase will slacken, and their wages rise. Of these articles, food and other agricultural produce are so much the principal, as to leave little influence to anything else.

It is at this point that we are enabled to invoke the aid of the principles which have been laid down in this Third Part. The cost of production of food and agricultural produce has been analyzed in a preceding chapter. It depends on the productiveness of the least fertile land, or of the least productively employed portion of capital, which the necessities of society have as yet put in requisition for agricultural purposes. The cost of production of the food grown in these least advantageous circumstances, determines, as we have seen, the exchange value and money price of the whole. In any given state, therefore, of the labourers' habits, their money wages depend on the productiveness of the least fertile land, or least productive agricultural capital ; on the point which cultivation has reached in its downward progress—in its encroachments on the barren lands, and its gradually increased strain upon the powers of the more fertile. Now, the force which urges cultivation in this downward course is the increase of people ; while the counter-force which checks the descent, is the improvement of agricultural science and practice, enabling the same soil to yield to the same labour more ample returns. The costliness of the most costly part of the produce of cultivation is an exact expression of the state, at any given moment, of the race which population and agricultural skill are always running against each other.

§ 2. It is well said by Dr. Chalmers, that many of the most important lessons in political economy are to be learnt at the extreme margin of cultivation, the last point which the culture of the soil has reached in its contest with the spontaneous agencies of nature. The degree of productiveness of this extreme margin is an index to the existing state of the distribution of the produce among the three classes, of labourers, capitalists, and landlords.

When the demand of an increasing population for more food cannot be satisfied without extending cultivation to less fertile land, or incurring additional outlay, with a less proportional return, on land already in cultivation, it is a necessary condition of this increase of agricultural produce that the value and price of that produce must first rise. But as soon as the price has risen sufficiently to give to the additional outlay of capital the ordinary profit, the rise will not go on still further for the purpose of enabling the new land, or the new expenditure on old land, to yield rent as well as profit. The land or capital last put in requisition, and occupying what Dr. Chalmers calls the margin of cultivation, will yield, and continue to yield, no rent. But if this yields no rent, the rent afforded by all other land or agricultural capital will be exactly so much as it produces more than this. The price of food will always on the average be such, that the worst land, and the least productive instalment of the capital employed on the better lands, shall just replace the expenses with the ordinary profit. If the least favoured land and capital just do thus much, all other land and capital will yield an extra profit, equal to the proceeds of the extra produce due to their superior productiveness; and this extra profit becomes, by competition, the prize of the landlords. Exchange, and money, therefore, make no difference in the law of rent: it is the same as we originally found it. Rent is the extra return made to agricultural capital when employed with peculiar advantages; the exact equivalent of what those advantages enable the producers to economize in the cost of production : the value and price of the produce being regulated by the cost of production to those producers who have no advantages; by the return to that portion of agricultural capital, the circumstances of which are the least favourable.

§ 3. Wages and Rent being thus regulated by the same principles, when paid in money, as they would be if apportioned in kind, it follows that Profits are so likewise. For the surplus, after replacing wages and paying rent, constitutes Profits.

We found in the last chapter of the Second Book, that the advances of the capitalist, when analyzed to their ultimate elements, consist either in the purchase or maintenance of labour, or in the profits of former capitalists; and that therefore profits, in the last resort, depend upon the Cost of Labour, falling as that rises, and rising as it falls. Let us endeavour to trace more minutely the operation of this law.

There are two modes in which the Cost of Labour, which is correctly represented (money being supposed invariable) by the money wages of the labourer, may be increased. The labourer may obtain greater comforts ; wages in kind—real wages—may rise. Or the progress of population may force down cultivation to inferior soils, and more costly processes ; thus raising the cost of production, the

value, and the price, of the chief articles of the labourer's consumption. On either of these suppositions, the rate of profit will fall.

If the labourer obtains more abundant commodities, only by
reason of their greater cheapness ; if he obtains a greater quantity,
but not on the whole a greater cost ; real wages will be increased, but
not money wages, and there will be nothing to affect the rate of
profit. But if he obtains a greater quantity of commodities of
which the cost of production is not lowered, he obtains a greater
cost ; his money wages are higher. The expense of these increased
money wages falls wholly on the capitalist. There are no conceivable
means by which he can shake it off. It may be said—it is, not
unfrequently, said—that he will get rid of it by raising his price.
But this opinion we have already, and more than once, fully refuted.*

The doctrine, indeed, that a rise of wages causes an equivalent
rise of prices, is, as we formerly observed, self-contradictory : for
if it did so, it would not be a rise of wages ; the labourer would get
no more of any commodity than he had before, let his money wages
rise ever so much ; a rise of real wages would be an impossibility.
This being equally contrary to reason and to fact, it is evident that
a rise of money wages does not raise prices ; that high wages are not
a cause of high prices. A rise of general wages falls on profits.
There is no possible alternative.

Having disposed of the case in which the increase of money
wages, and of the Cost of Labour, arises from the labourer's obtaining
more ample wages in kind, let us now suppose it to arise from the
increased cost of production of the things which he consumes ;
owing to an increase of population, unaccompanied by an equivalent
increase of agricultural skill. The augmented supply required by
the population would not be obtained, unless the price of food rose
sufficiently to remunerate the farmer for the increased cost of
production. The farmer, however, in this case sustains a twofold
disadvantage. He has to carry on his cultivation under less favourable conditions of productiveness than before. For this, as it is a
disadvantage belonging to him only as a farmer, and not shared by
other employers, he will, on the general principles of value, be
compensated by a rise of the price of his commodity : indeed, until
this rise has taken place, he will not bring to market the required
increase of produce. But this very rise of price involves him in
another necessity, for which he is not compensated. As the real

* Supra, book iii. ch. iv. § 2, and ch. xxv. § 4.

wages of labour are by supposition unaltered, he must pay higher money wages to his labourers. This necessity, being common to him with all other capitalists, forms no ground for a rise of price. The price will rise, until it has placed him in as good a situation in respect of profits, as other employers of labour : it will rise so as to indemnify him for the increased labour which he must now employ in order to produce a given quantity of food : but the increased wages of that labour are a burthen common to all, and for which no one can be indemnified. It will be paid wholly from profits.

Thus we see that increased wages, when common to all descriptions of productive labourers, and when really representing a greater Cost of Labour, are always and necessarily at the expense of profits. And by reversing the cases, we should find in like manner that diminished wages, when representing a really diminished Cost of Labour, are equivalent to a rise of profits. But the opposition of pecuniary interest thus indicated between the class of capitalists and that of labourers, is to a great extent only apparent. Real wages are a very different thing from the Cost of Labour, and are generally highest at the times and places where, from the easy terms on which the land yields all the produce as yet required from it, the value and price of food being low, the cost of labour to the employer, notwithstanding its ample remuneration, is comparatively cheap, and the rate of profit consequently high.[1] We thus obtain a full confirmation of our original theorem that Profits depend on the Cost of Labour : or, to express the meaning with still greater accuracy, the rate of profit and the cost of labour vary inversely as one another, and are joint effects of the same agencies or causes.

But does not this proposition require to be slightly modified, by making allowance for that portion (though comparatively small) of the expenses of the capitalist, which does not consist in wages paid by himself or reimbursed to previous capitalists, but in the profits of those previous capitalists ? Suppose, for example, an invention in the manufacture of leather, the advantage of which should consist in rendering it unnecessary that the hides should remain for so great a length of time in the tan-pit. Shoemakers, saddlers, and other workers in leather, would save a part of that portion of the cost of their material which consists of the tanner's profits during the time his capital is locked up ; and this saving, it may be said, is a source from which they might derive an increase

---

[1] The words " as at present in the United States " were omitted at this point from the 6th ed. (1865).]

of profit, though wages and the Cost of Labour remained exactly the same. In the case here supposed, however, the consumer alone would benefit, since the prices of shoes, harness, and all other articles into which leather enters, would fall, until the profits of the producers were reduced to the general level. To obviate this objection, let us suppose that a similar saving of expense takes place in all departments of production at once. In that case, since values and prices would not be affected, profits would probably be raised ; but if we look more closely into the case we shall find, that it is because the cost of labour would be lowered. In this, as in any other case of increase in the general productiveness of labour, if the labourer obtained only the same real wages, profits would be raised : but the same real wages would imply a smaller Cost of Labour ; the cost of production of all things having been, by the supposition, diminished. If, on the other hand, the real wages of labour rose proportionally, and the Cost of Labour to the employer remained the same, the advances of the capitalist would bear the same ratio to his returns as before, and the rate of profit would be unaltered. The reader who may wish for a more minute examination of this point, will find it in the volume of separate Essays to which reference has before been made.* The question is too intricate in comparison with its importance, to be further entered into in a work like the present ; and I will merely say, that it seems to result from the considerations adduced in the Essay, that there is nothing in the case in question to affect the integrity of the theory which affirms an exact correspondence, in an inverse direction, between the rate of profit and the Cost of Labour.

* Essay IV. on *Profits and Interest.*

BOOK IV

INFLUENCE OF THE PROGRESS OF SOCIETY ON PRODUCTION AND DISTRIBUTION

CHAPTER I

GENERAL CHARACTERISTICS OF A PROGRESSIVE STATE OF WEALTH

§ 1. The three preceding Parts include as detailed a view as our limits permit, of what, by a happy generalization of a mathematical phrase, has been called the Statics of the subject. We have surveyed the field of economical facts, and have examined how they stand related to one another as causes and effects; what circumstances determine the amount of production, of employment for labour, of capital and population; what laws regulate rent, profits, and wages; under what conditions and in what proportions commodities are interchanged between individuals and between countries. We have thus obtained a collective view of the economical phenomena of society, considered as existing simultaneously. We have ascertained, to a certain extent, the principles of their interdependence; and when the state of some of the elements is known, we should now be able to infer, in a general way, the contemporaneous state of most of the others. All this, however, has only put us in possession of the economical laws of a stationary and unchanging society. We have still to consider the economical condition of mankind as liable to change, and indeed (in the more advanced portions of the race, and in all regions to which their influence reaches) as at all times undergoing progressive changes. We have to consider what these changes are, what are their laws, and what their ultimate tendencies; thereby adding a theory of motion to our theory of equilibrium—the Dynamics of political economy to the Statics.

In this inquiry, it is natural to commence by tracing the operation of known and acknowledged agencies. Whatever may be the other changes which the economy of society is destined to undergo, there is one actually in progress, concerning which there can be no dispute. In the leading countries of the world, and in all others as they come within the influence of those leading countries, there is at least one progressive movement which continues with little interruption from year to year and from generation to generation ; a progress in wealth ; an advancement of what is called material prosperity. All the nations which we are accustomed to call civilized, increase gradually in production and in population : and there is no reason to doubt, that not only these nations will for some time continue so to increase, but that most of the other nations of the world, including some not yet founded, will successively enter upon the same career. It will, therefore, be our first object to examine the nature and consequences of this progressive change ; the elements which constitute it, and the effects it produces on the various economical facts of which we have been tracing the laws, and especially on wages, profits, rents, values, and prices.

§ 2. Of the features which characterize this progressive economical movement of civilized nations, that which first excites attention, through its intimate connexion with the phenomena of Production, is the perpetual, and so far as human foresight can extend, the unlimited, growth of man's power over nature. Our knowledge of the properties and laws of physical objects shows no sign of approaching its ultimate boundaries : it is advancing more rapidly, and in a greater number of directions at once, than in any previous age or generation, and affording such frequent glimpses of unexplored fields beyond, as to justify the belief that our acquaintance with nature is still almost in its infancy. This increasing physical knowledge is now, too, more rapidly than at any former period, converted, by practical ingenuity, into physical power. The most marvellous of modern inventions, one which realizes the imaginary feats of the magician, not metaphorically but literally— the electro-magnetic telegraph—sprang into existence but a few years after the establishment of the scientific theory which it realizes and exemplifies. Lastly, the manual part of these great scientific operations is now never wanting to the intellectual : there is no difficulty in finding or forming, in a sufficient number of the working hands of the community, the skill requisite for executing the most delicate processes of the application of science to practical uses. From this union of conditions, it is impossible not to look forward to a vast multiplication and long succession of contrivances for economizing labour and increasing its produce ; and to an ever wider diffusion of the use and benefit of those contrivances.

Another change, which has always hitherto characterized, and will assuredly continue to characterize, the progress of civilized society, is a continual increase of the security of person and property. The people of every country in Europe, the most backward as well as the most advanced, are, in each generation, better protected against the violence and rapacity of one another, both by a more efficient judicature and police for the suppression of private crime, and by the decay and destruction of those mischievous privileges which enabled certain classes of the community to prey with impunity upon the rest. They are also, in every generation, better protected, either by institutions or by manners and opinion, against arbitrary exercise of the power of government. Even in semi-barbarous Russia, acts of spoliation directed against individuals, who have not made themselves politically obnoxious, are not supposed to be now so frequent as much to affect any person's feelings of security. Taxation, in all European countries, grows less arbitrary and oppressive, both in itself and in the manner of levying it. Wars, and the destruction they cause, are now usually [1] confined, in almost every country, to those distant and outlying possessions at which it comes into contact with savages. Even the vicissitudes of fortune which arise from inevitable natural calamities, are more and more softened to those on whom they fall, by the continual extension of the salutary practice of insurance.

Of this increased security, one of the most unfailing effects is a great increase both of production and of accumulation. Industry and frugality cannot exist where there is not a preponderant probability that those who labour and spare will be permitted to enjoy. And the nearer this probability approaches to certainty, the more do industry and frugality become pervading qualities in a people. Experience has shown that a large proportion of the results of labour and abstinence may be taken away by fixed taxation, without impairing, and sometimes even with the effect of stimulating, the qualities from which a great production and an abundant capital take their rise. But those qualities are not proof

[1] [" Usually " inserted in 4th ed. (1857).]

against a high degree of uncertainty. The Government may carry off a part; but there must be assurance that it will not interfere, nor suffer any one to interfere, with the remainder.

One of the changes which most infallibly attend the progress of modern society, is an improvement in the business capacities of the general mass of mankind. I do not mean that the practical sagacity of an individual human being is greater than formerly. I am inclined to believe that economical progress has hitherto had even a contrary effect. A person of good natural endowments, in a rude state of society, can do a great number of things tolerably well, has a greater power of adapting means to ends, is more capable of extricating himself and others from an unforeseen embarrassment, than ninety-nine in a hundred of those who have known only what is called the civilized form of life. How far these points of inferiority of faculties are compensated, and by what means they might be compensated still more completely, to the civilized man as an individual being, is a question belonging to a different inquiry from the present. But to civilized human beings collectively considered, the compensation is ample. What is lost in the separate efficiency of each, is far more than made up by the greater capacity of united action. In proportion as they put off the qualities of the savage, they become amenable to discipline; capable of adhering to plans concerted beforehand, and about which they may not have been consulted; of subordinating their individual caprice to a preconceived determination, and performing severally the parts allotted to them in a combined undertaking. Works of all sorts, impracticable to the savage or the half-civilized, are daily accomplished by civilized nations, not by any greatness of faculties in the actual agents, but through the fact that each is able to rely with certainty on the others for the portion of the work which they respectively undertake. The peculiar characteristic, in short, of civilized beings, is the capacity of co-operation; and this, like other faculties, tends to improve by practice, and becomes capable of assuming a constantly wider sphere of action.

Accordingly there is no more certain incident of the progressive change taking place in society, than the continual growth of the principle and practice of co-operation. Associations of individuals voluntarily combining their small contributions now perform works, both of an industrial and of many other characters, which no one person or small number of persons are rich enough to accomplish, or for the performance of which the few persons capable of accomplishing them were formerly enabled to exact the most inordinate remuneration. As wealth increases and business capacity improves, we may look forward to a great extension of establishments, both for industrial and other purposes, formed by the collective contributions of large numbers ; establishments like those called by the technical name of joint-stock companies, or the associations less formally constituted, which are so numerous in England, to raise funds for public or philanthropic objects, [1]or, lastly, those associations of workpeople either for production, or to buy goods for their common consumption, which are now specially known by the name of co-operative societies.

The progress which is to be expected in the physical sciences and arts, combined with the greater security of property, and greater freedom in disposing of it, which are obvious features in the civilization of modern nations, and with the more extensive and more skilful employment of the joint-stock principle, afford space and scope for an indefinite increase of capital and production, and for the increase of population which is its ordinary accompaniment. That the growth of population will overpass the increase of production, there is not much reason to apprehend ; and that it should even keep pace with it, is inconsistent with the supposition of any real improvement in the poorest classes of the people. It is, however, quite possible that there might be a great progress in industrial improvement, and in the signs of what is commonly called national prosperity ; a great increase of aggregate wealth, and even, in some respects, a better distribution of it ; that not only the rich might grow richer, but many of the poor might grow rich, that the intermediate classes might become more numerous and powerful, and the means of enjoyable existence be more and more largely diffused, while yet the great class at the base of the whole might increase in numbers only, and not in comfort nor in cultivation. We must, therefore, in considering the effects of the progress of industry, admit as a supposition, however greatly we deprecate as a fact, an increase of population as long-continued, as indefinite, and possibly even as rapid, as the increase of production and accumulation.

With these preliminary observations on the causes of change at work in a society which is in a state of economical progress, I proceed to a more detailed examination of the changes themselves.

---

[1] [The remaining words of the sentence were added in the 6th ed. (1865).]

CHAPTER II

§ 1. THE changes which the progress of industry causes or presupposes in the circumstances of production, are necessarily attended with changes in the values of commodities.

The permanent values of all things which are neither under a natural nor under an artificial monopoly, depend, as we have seen, on their cost of production. But the increasing power which mankind are constantly acquiring over nature, increases more and more the efficiency of human exertion, or, in other words, diminishes cost of production. All inventions by which a greater quantity of any commodity can be produced with the same labour or the same quantity with less labour, or which abridge the process, so that the capital employed needs not be advanced for so long a time, lessen the cost of production of the commodity. As, however, value is relative ; if inventions and improvements in production were made in all commodities, and all in the same degree, there would be no alteration in values. Things would continue to exchange for each other at the same rates as before ; and mankind would obtain a greater quantity of all things in return for their labour and abstinence, without having that greater abundance measured and declared (as it is when it affects only one thing) by the diminished exchange value of the commodity.

As for prices, in these circumstances they would be affected or not, according as the improvements in production did or did not extend to the precious metals. If the materials of money were an exception to the general diminution of cost of production, the values of all other things would fall in relation to money, that is, there would be a fall of general prices throughout the world. But if money, like other things, and in the same degree as other things, were obtained in greater abundance and cheapness, prices would be no more affected than values would : and there would be no visible sign in the state of the markets, of any of the changes which had taken place ; except that there would be (if people continued to labour as much as before) a greater quantity of all sorts of commodities, circulated at the same prices by a greater quantity of money.

Improvements in production are not the only circumstance accompanying the progress of industry which tends to diminish the cost of producing, or at least of obtaining, commodities. Another circumstance is the increase of intercourse between different parts of the world. As commerce extends, and the ignorant attempts to restrain it by tariffs become obsolete, commodities tend more and more to be produced in the places in which their production can be carried on at the least expense of labour and capital to mankind. As civilization spreads, and security of person and property becomes established, in parts of the world which have not hitherto had that advantage, the productive capabilities of those places are called into fuller activity, for the benefit both of their own inhabitants and of foreigners. The ignorance and misgovernment in which many of the regions most favoured by nature are still grovelling, afford work, probably, for many generations before those countries will be raised even to the present level of the most civilized parts of Europe. Much will also depend on the increasing migration of labour and capital to unoccupied parts of the earth, of which the soil, climate, and situation are found, by the ample means of exploration now possessed, to promise not only a large return to industry, but great facilities of producing commodities suited to the markets of old countries. Much as the collective industry of the earth is likely to be increased in efficiency by the extension of science and of the industrial arts, a still more active source of increased cheapness of production will be found, probably, for some time to come, in the gradually unfolding consequences of Free Trade, and in the increasing scale on which Emigration and Colonization will be carried on.

From the causes now enumerated, unless counteracted by others, the progress of things enables a country to obtain at less and less of real cost, not only its own productions but those of foreign countries. Indeed, whatever diminishes the cost of its own productions, when of an exportable character, enables it, as we have already seen, to obtain its imports at less real cost.

§ 2. But is it the fact, that these tendencies are not counteracted ? Has the progress of wealth and industry no effect in regard to cost of production, but to diminish it ? Are no causes of an opposite character brought into operation by the same progress, sufficient in some cases not only to neutralize, but to overcome the former, and convert the descending movement of cost of production into an ascending movement ? We are already aware that there are such causes, and that, in the case of the most important classes of commodities, food and materials, there is a tendency diametrically opposite to that of which we have been speaking. The cost of production of these commodities tends to increase.

This is not a property inherent in the commodities themselves. If population were stationary, and the produce of the earth never needed to be augmented in quantity, there would be no cause for greater cost of production. Mankind would, on the contrary, have the full benefit of all improvements in agriculture, or in the arts subsidiary to it, and there would be no difference, in this respect, between the products of agriculture and those of manufactures.[1] The only products of industry which, if population did not increase, would be liable to a real increase of cost of production, are those which, depending on a material which is not renewed, are either wholly or partially exhaustible ; such as coal, and most if not all metals ; for even iron, the most abundant as well as most useful of metallic products, which forms an ingredient of most minerals and of almost all rocks, is susceptible of exhaustion so far as regards its richest and most tractable ores.

When, however, population increases, as it has never yet failed to do when the increase of industry and of the means of subsistence made room for it, the demand for most of the productions of the earth, and particularly for food, increases in a corresponding proportion. And then comes into effect that fundamental law of production from the soil, on which we have so frequently had occasion to expatiate ; the law, that increased labour, in any given state of agricultural skill, is attended with a less than proportional increase of produce. The cost of production of the fruits of the earth increases, *cæteris paribus*, with every increase of the demand.

No tendency of a like kind exists with respect to manufactured articles. The tendency is in the contrary direction. The larger

---

[1] [The following passage of the original (1848) text was omitted in the 5th ed. (1862) : " The former, indeed, so far as present foresight can extend, does not seem to be susceptible to improved processes to so great a degree as some branches of manufacture ; but inventions may be in reserve for the future which may invert this relation."]

the scale on which manufacturing operations are carried on, the more cheaply they can in general be performed. Mr. Senior has gone the length of enunciating as an inherent law of manufacturing industry, that in it increased production takes place at a smaller cost, while in agricultural industry increased production takes place at a greater cost. I cannot think, however, that even in manufactures, increased cheapness follows increased production by anything amounting to a law. It is a probable and usual, but not a necessary consequence.

As manufactures, however, depend for their materials either upon agriculture, or mining, or the spontaneous produce of the earth, manufacturing industry is subject, in respect of one of its essentials, to the same law as agriculture. But the crude material generally forms so small a portion of the total cost, that any tendency which may exist to a progressive increase in that single item, is much over-balanced by the diminution continually taking place in all the other elements; to which diminution it is impossible at present to assign any limit.

The tendency, then, being to a perpetual increase of the productive power of labour in manufactures, while in agriculture and mining there is a conflict between two tendencies, the one towards an increase of productive power, the other towards a diminution of it, the cost of production being lessened by every improvement in the processes, and augmented by every addition to population; it follows that the exchange values of manufactured articles, compared with the products of agriculture and of mines, have, as population and industry advance, a certain and decided tendency to fall. Money being a product of mines, it may also be laid down as a rule, that manufactured articles tend, as society advances, to fall in money price. The industrial history of modern nations, especially during the last hundred years, fully bears out this assertion.

§ 3. Whether agricultural produce increases in absolute as well as comparative cost of production, depends on the conflict of the two antagonist agencies, increase of population, and improvement in agricultural skill. In some, perhaps in most, states of society, (looking at the whole surface of the earth,) both agricultural skill and population are either stationary, or increase very slowly, and the cost of production of food, therefore, is nearly stationary. In a society which is advancing in wealth, population generally increases faster than agricultural skill, and food consequently tends to become more costly ; but there are times when a strong impulse sets in towards agricultural improvement. Such an impulse has shown itself in Great Britain during the last twenty or thirty [1] years. In England and Scotland agricultural skill has of late increased considerably faster than population, insomuch that food and other agricultural produce, notwithstanding the increase of people, can be grown at less cost than they were thirty years ago [2] : and the abolition of the Corn Laws has given an additional stimulus to the spirit of improvement. In some other countries, and particularly in France, the improvement of agriculture gains ground still more decidedly upon population, because though agriculture, except in a few provinces, advances slowly, population advances still more slowly, and even with increasing slowness ; its growth being kept down, not by poverty, which is diminishing, but by prudence.

Which of the two conflicting agencies is gaining upon the other at any particular time, might be conjectured with tolerable accuracy from the money price of agricultural produce (supposing bullion not to vary materially in value), provided a sufficient number of years could be taken, to form an average independent of the fluctuations of seasons. This, however, is hardly practicable, since Mr. Tooke has shown that even so long a period as half a century may include a much greater proportion of abundant and a smaller of deficient seasons than is properly due to it. A mere average, therefore, might lead to conclusions only the more misleading, for their deceptive semblance of accuracy. There would be less danger of error in taking the average of only a small number of years, and correcting it by a conjectural allowance for the character of the seasons, than in trusting to a longer average without any such correction. It is hardly necessary to add, that in founding conclusions on quoted prices, allowance must also be made as far as possible for any changes in the general exchange value of the precious metals.* [3]

§ 4. Thus far, of the effect of the progress of society on the permanent or average values and prices of commodities. It re-

---

[1] [The " fifteen or twenty " of the 1st ed. (1848) was replaced in the 6th ed. (1865) by " twenty or twenty-five," and in the 7th (1871) by " twenty or thirty."]

[2] [Written in 1848.]

* [1852] A still better criterion, perhaps, than that suggested in the text would be the increase or diminution of the amount of the labourer's wages estimated in agricultural produce.

[3] [See Appendix X. *Prices in the 19th Century.*]

mains to be considered in what manner the same progress affects their fluctuations. Concerning the answer to this question there can be no doubt. It tends in a very high degree to diminish them.

In poor and backward societies, as in the East, and in Europe during the Middle Ages, extraordinary differences in the price of the same commodity might exist in places not very distant from each other, because the want of roads and canals, the imperfection of marine navigation, and the insecurity of communications generally, prevented things from being transported from the places where they were cheap to those where they were dear. The things most liable to fluctuations in value, those directly influenced by the seasons, and especially food, were seldom carried to any great distances. Each locality depended, as a general rule, on its own produce and that of its immediate neighbourhood. In most years, accordingly, there was, in some part or other of any large country, a real dearth. Almost every season must be unpropitious to some among the many soils and climates to be found in an extensive tract of country ; but as the same season is also in general more than ordinarily favourable to others, it is only occasionally that the aggregate produce of the whole country is deficient, and even then in a less degree than that of many separate portions ; while a deficiency at all considerable, extending to the whole world, is a thing almost unknown. In modern times, therefore, there is only dearth, where there formerly would have been famine, and sufficiency everywhere when anciently there would have been scarcity in some places and superfluity in others.

The same change has taken place with respect to all other articles of commerce. The safety and cheapness of communications, which enable a deficiency in one place to be supplied from the surplus of another, at a moderate or even a small advance on the ordinary price, render the fluctuations of prices much less extreme than formerly. This effect is much promoted by the existence of large capitals, belonging to what are called speculative merchants, whose business it is to buy goods in order to resell them at a profit.

These dealers naturally buying things when they are cheapest, and storing them up to be brought again into the market when the price has become unusually high ; the tendency of their operations is to equalize price, or at least to moderate its inequalities. The prices of things are neither so much depressed at one time, nor so much raised at another, as they would be if speculative dealers did not exist.

Speculators, therefore, have a highly useful office in the economy of society ; and (contrary to common opinion) the most useful portion of the class are those who speculate in commodities affected by the vicissitudes of seasons. If there were no corn-dealers, not only would the price of corn be liable to variations much more extreme than at present, but in a deficient season the necessary supplies might not be forthcoming at all. Unless there were speculators in corn, or unless, in default of dealers, the farmers became speculators, the price in a season of abundance would fall without any limit or check, except the wasteful consumption that would invariably follow. That any part of the surplus of one year remains to supply the deficiency of another, is owing either to farmers who withhold corn from the market, or to dealers who buy it when at the cheapest and lay it up in store.

§ 5.   Among persons who have not much considered the subject, there is a notion that the gains of speculators are often made by causing an artificial scarcity ; that they create a high price by their own purchases, and then profit by it. This may easily be shown to be fallacious. If a corn-dealer makes purchases on speculation, and produces a rise, when there is neither at the time nor afterwards any cause for a rise of price except his own proceedings ; he no doubt appears to grow richer as long as his purchases continue, because he is a holder of an article which is quoted at a higher and higher price : but this apparent gain only seems within his reach so long as he does not attempt to realize it. If he has bought, for instance, a million of quarters, and by withholding them from the market, has raised the price ten shillings a quarter ; just so much as the price has been raised by withdrawing a million quarters, will it be lowered by bringing them back, and the best that he can hope is that he will lose nothing except interest and his expenses. If by a gradual and cautious sale he is able to realize, on some portion of his stores, a part of the increased price, so also he will undoubtedly have had to pay a part of that price on some portion of his purchases. He runs considerable risk of incurring a still greater loss ; for the temporary high price is very likely to have tempted others, who had no share in causing it, and who might otherwise not have found their way to his market at all, to bring their corn there, and intercept a part of the advantage. So that instead of profiting by a scarcity caused by himself, he is by no means unlikely, after buying in an average market, to be forced to sell in a superabundant one.

As an individual speculator cannot gain by a rise of price solely of his own creating, so neither can a number of speculators gain collectively by a rise which their operations have artificially produced. Some among a number of speculators may gain, by superior judgment or good fortune [1] in selecting the time for realizing, but they make this gain at the expense, not of the consumer, but of the other speculators who are less judicious. They, in fact, convert to their own benefit the high price produced by the speculations of the others, leaving to these the loss resulting from the recoil. It is not to be denied, therefore, that speculators may enrich themselves by other people's loss. But it is by the losses of other speculators. As much must have been lost by one set of dealers as is gained by another set.

When a speculation in a commodity proves profitable to the speculators as a body, it is because, in the interval between their buying and reselling, the price rises from some cause independent of them, their only connexion with it consisting in having foreseen it. In this case, their purchases make the price begin to rise sooner than it otherwise would do, thus spreading the privation of the consumers over a longer period, but mitigating it at the time of its greatest height : evidently to the general advantage. In this, however, it is assumed that they have not overrated the rise which they looked forward to. For it often happens that speculative purchases are made in the expectation of some increase of demand, or deficiency of supply, which after all does not occur, or not to the extent which the speculator expected. In that case the speculation, instead of moderating fluctuation, has caused a fluctuation of price which otherwise would not have happened, or aggravated one which would. But in that case, the speculation is a losing one, to the speculators collectively, however much some individuals may gain by it. All that part of the rise of price by which it exceeds what there are independent grounds for, cannot give to the speculators as a body any benefit, since the price is as much depressed by their sales as it was raised by their purchases ; and while they gain nothing by it, they lose, not only their trouble and expenses, but almost always much more, through the effects incident to the artificial rise of price, in checking consumption, and bringing forward supplies from unforeseen quarters. The operations, therefore, of speculative dealers, are useful to the public whenever profitable to themselves ; and though they are sometimes injurious to the public, by heightening the fluctuations which their more usual office is to alleviate, yet

[1] [" Or good fortune " added in 3rd ed. (1852).]

whenever this happens the speculators are the greatest losers. The interest, in short, of the speculators as a body, coincides with the interest of the public ; and as they can only fail to serve the public interest in proportion as they miss their own, the best way to promote the one is to leave them to pursue the other in perfect freedom.

I do not deny that speculators may aggravate a *local* scarcity. In collecting corn from the villages to supply the towns, they make the dearth penetrate into nooks and corners which might otherwise have escaped from bearing their share of it. To buy and resell in the same place, tends to alleviate scarcity ; to buy in one place and resell in another, may increase it in the former of the two places, but relieves it in the latter, where the price is higher, and which, there-fore, by the very supposition, is likely to be suffering more. And these sufferings always fall hardest on the poorest consumers, since the rich, by outbidding, can obtain their accustomed supply undiminished if they choose. To no persons, therefore, are the operations of corn-dealers on the whole so beneficial as to the poor. Accidentally and exceptionally, the poor may suffer from them : it might sometimes be more advantageous to the rural poor to have corn cheap in winter, when they are entirely dependent on it, even if the consequence were a dearth in spring, when they can perhaps obtain partial substitutes. But there are no substitutes, procurable at that season, which serve in any great degree to replace bread-corn as the chief article of food : if there were, its price would fall in the spring, instead of continuing, as it always does, to rise till the approach of harvest.

There is an opposition of immediate interest, at the moment of sale, between the dealer in corn and the consumer, as there always is between the seller and the buyer : and a time of dearth being that in which the speculator makes his largest profits, he is an object of dislike and jealousy at that time, to those who are suffering while he is gaining. It is an error, however, to suppose that the corn-dealer's business affords him any extraordinary profit : he makes his gains not constantly, but at particular times, and they must therefore occasionally be great, but the chances of profit in a business in which there is so much competition, cannot on the whole be greater than in other employments. A year of scarcity, in which great gains are made by corn-dealers, rarely comes to an end without a recoil which places many of them in the list of bankrupts. There have been few more promising seasons for corn-dealers than the

year 1847, and seldom was there a greater break-up among the
speculators than in the autumn of that year. The chances of
failure, in this most precarious trade, are a set-off against great
occasional profits. If the corn-dealer were to sell his stores, during
a dearth, at a lower price than that which the competition of the
consumers assigns to him, he would make a sacrifice, to charity or
philanthropy, of the fair profits of his employment, which may be
quite as reasonably required from any other person of equal means.
His business being a useful one, it is the interest of the public that
the ordinary motives should exist for carrying it on, and that neither
law nor opinion should prevent an operation beneficial to the
public from being attended with as much private advantage as is
compatible with full and free competition.

It appears, then, that the fluctuations of values and prices
arising from variations of supply, or from alterations in real (as
distinguished from speculative) demand, may be expected to
become more moderate as society advances. With regard to those
which arise from miscalculation, and especially from the alternations
of undue expansion and excessive contraction of credit, which
occupy so conspicuous a place among commercial phenomena, the
same thing cannot be affirmed with equal confidence. Such vicissitudes, beginning with irrational speculation and ending with a
commercial crisis, have not hitherto become either less frequent or
less violent with the growth of capital and extension of industry.
Rather they may be said to have become more so : in consequence,
as is often said, of increased competition ; but, as I prefer to say,
of a low rate of profits and interest, which makes capitalists dissatisfied with the ordinary course of safe mercantile gains.[1] The
connexion of this low rate of profit with the advance of population
and accumulation, is one of the points to be illustrated in the
ensuing chapters.

[1] [See Appendix Y. *Commercial Cycles.*]

CHAPTER III

INFLUENCE OF THE PROGRESS OF INDUSTRY AND POPULATION, ON
RENTS, PROFITS, AND WAGES

§ 1. CONTINUING the inquiry into the nature of the economical
changes taking place in a society which is in a state of industrial
progress, we shall next consider what is the effect of that progress
on the distribution of the produce among the various classes who
share in it. We may confine our attention to the system of distribution which is the most complex, and which virtually includes
all others—that in which the produce of manufactures is shared
between two classes, labourers and capitalists, and the produce of
agriculture among three, labourers, capitalists, and landlords.
The characteristic features of what is commonly meant by industrial progress resolve themselves mainly into three, increase of
capital, increase of population, and improvements in production ;
understanding the last expression in its widest sense, to include the
process of procuring commodities from a distance, as well as that of
producing them. The other changes which take place are chiefly
consequences of these ; as, for example, the tendency to a progressive
increase of the cost of production of food ; arising from an increased
demand, which may be occasioned either by increased population, or
by an increase of capital and wages, enabling the poorer classes to
increase their consumption. It will be convenient to set out by
considering each of the three causes, as operating separately ; after
which we can suppose them combined in any manner we think fit.
Let us first suppose that population increases, capital and the
arts of production remaining stationary. One of the effects of this
change of circumstances is sufficiently obvious : wages will fall ;
the labouring class will be reduced to an inferior condition. The
state of the capitalist, on the contrary, will be improved. With
the same capital, he can purchase more labour, and obtain more
produce. His rate of profit is increased. The dependence of the

rate of profits on the cost of labour is here verified ; for the labourer obtaining a diminished quantity of commodities, and no alteration being supposed in the circumstances of their production, the diminished quantity represents a diminished cost. The labourer obtains not only a smaller real reward, but the product of a smaller quantity of labour. The first circumstance is the important one to himself, the last to his employer.

Nothing has occurred, thus far, to affect in any way the value of any commodity ; and no reason, therefore, has yet shown itself, why rent should be either raised or lowered. But if we look forward another stage in the series of effects, we may see our way to such a consequence. The labourers have increased in numbers : their condition is reduced in the same proportion ; the increased numbers divide among them only the produce of the same amount of labour as before. But they may economize in their other comforts, and not in their food : each may consume as much food, and of as costly a quality as previously ; or they may submit to a reduction, but not in proportion to the increase of numbers. On this supposition, notwithstanding the diminution of real wages, the increased population will require an increased quantity of food. But since industrial skill and knowledge are supposed to be stationary, more food can only be obtained by resorting to worse land, or to methods of cultivation which are less productive in proportion to the outlay. Capital for this extension of agriculture will not be wanting ; for though, by hypothesis, no addition takes place to the capital in existence, a sufficient amount can be spared from the industry which previously supplied the other and less pressing wants which the labourers have been obliged to curtail. The additional supply of food, therefore, will be produced, but produced at a greater cost ; and the exchange value of agricultural produce must rise. It may be objected, that profits having risen, the extra cost of producing food can be defrayed from profits, without any increase of price. It could, undoubtedly, but it will not ; because, if it did, the agriculturist would be placed in an inferior position to other capitalists. The increase of profits, being the effect of diminished wages, is common to all employers of labour. The increased expenses arising from the necessity of a more costly cultivation, affect the agriculturist alone. For this peculiar burthen he must be peculiarly compensated, whether the general rate of profit be high or low. He will not submit indefinitely to a deduction from his profits to which other capitalists are not subject. He will not extend his cultivation by laying out fresh capital, unless for a return sufficient to yield him as high a profit as could be obtained by the same capital in other investments. The value, therefore, of his commodity will rise, and rise in proportion to the increased cost. The farmer will thus be indemnified for the burthen which is peculiar to himself, and will also enjoy the augmented rate of profit which is common to all capitalists.

It follows, from principles with which we are already familiar, that in these circumstances rent will rise. Any land can afford to pay, and under free competition will pay, a rent equal to the excess of its produce above the return to an equal capital on the worst land, or under the least favourable conditions. Whenever, therefore, agriculture is driven to descend to worse land, or more onerous processes, rent rises. Its rise will be twofold, for, in the first place, rent in kind, or corn rent, will rise ; and in the second, since the value of agricultural produce has also risen, rent, estimated in manufactured or foreign commodities (which is represented, *cæteris paribus*, by money rent) will rise still more.

The steps of the process (if, after what has been formerly said, it is necessary to retrace them) are as follows. Corn rises in price, to repay with the ordinary profit the capital required for producing additional corn on worse land or by more costly processes. So far as regards this additional corn, the increased price is but an equivalent for the additional expense ; but the rise, extending to all corn, affords on all, except the last produced, an extra profit. If the farmer was accustomed to produce 100 quarters of wheat at 40*s.*, and 120 quarters are now required, of which the last twenty cannot be produced under 45*s.*, he obtains the extra five shillings on the entire 120 quarters, and not on the last twenty alone. He has thus an extra 25*l.* beyond the ordinary profits, and this, in a state of free competition, he will not be able to retain. He cannot however be compelled to give it up to the consumer, since a less price than 45*s.* would be inconsistent with the production of the last twenty quarters. The price, then, will remain at 45*s.*, and the 25*l.* will be transferred by competition not to the consumer but to the landlord. A rise of rents is therefore inevitably consequent on an increased demand for agricultural produce, when unaccompanied by increased facilities for its production. A truth which, after this final illustration, we may henceforth take for granted.

The new element now introduced—an increased demand for food —besides occasioning an increase of rent, still further disturbs the distribution of the produce between capitalists and labourers.   The increase of population will have diminished the reward of labour : and if its cost is diminished as greatly as its real remuneration, profits will be increased by the full amount.   If, however, the increase of population leads to an increased production of food, which cannot be supplied but at an enhanced cost of production, the cost of labour will not be so much diminished as the real reward of it, and profits, therefore, will not be so much raised.   It is even possible that they might not be raised at all.   The labourers may previously have been so well provided for, that the whole of what they now lose may be struck off from their other indulgences, and they may not, either by necessity or choice, undergo any reduction in the quantity or quality of their food.   To produce the food for the increased number may be attended with such an increase of expense, that wages, though reduced in quantity, may represent as great a cost, may be the product of as much labour, as before, and the capitalist may not be at all benefited.   On this supposition the loss to the labourer is partly absorbed in the additional labour required for producing the last instalment of agricultural produce ;   and the remainder is gained by the landlord, the only sharer who always benefits by an increase of population.

§ 2.   Let us now reverse our hypothesis, and instead of supposing capital stationary and population advancing, let us suppose capital advancing and population stationary ;   the facilities of production, both natural and acquired, being, as before, unaltered. The real wages of labour, instead of falling, will now rise ;   and since the cost of production of the things consumed by the labourer is not diminished, this rise of wages implies an equivalent increase of the cost of labour, and diminution of profits.   To state the same deduction in other terms ;   the labourers not being more numerous, and the productive power of their labour being only the same as before, there is no increase of the produce ;   the increase of wages, therefore, must be at the charge of the capitalist.   It is not impossible that the cost of labour might be increased in even a greater ratio than its real remuneration.   The improved condition of the labourers may increase the demand for food.   The labourers may have been so ill off before, as not to have food enough ;   and may now consume more :   or they may choose to expend their increased means partly or wholly in a more costly quality of food, requiring more labour and more land ;   wheat, for example, instead of oats, or potatoes.   This extension of agriculture implies, as usual, a greater cost of production and a higher price, so that besides the increase of the cost of labour arising from the increase of its reward, there will be a further increase (and an additional fall of profits) from the increased costliness of the commodities of which that reward consists. The same causes will produce a rise of rent. What the capitalists lose, above what the labourers gain, is partly transferred to the landlord, and partly swallowed up in the cost of growing food on worse land or by a less productive process.

§ 3. Having disposed of the two simple cases, an increasing population and stationary capital, and an increasing capital and stationary population, we are prepared to take into consideration the mixed case, in which the two elements of expansion are combined, both population and capital increasing. If either element increases faster than the other, the case is so far assimilated with one or other of the two preceding : we shall suppose them, therefore, to increase with equal rapidity ; the test of equality being, that each labourer obtains the same commodities as before, and the same quantity of those commodities. Let us examine what will be the effect, on rent and profits, of this double progress.

Population having increased, without any falling off in the labourer's condition, there is of course a demand for more food. The arts of production being supposed stationary, this food must be produced at an increased cost. To compensate for this greater cost of the additional food, the price of agricultural produce must rise. The rise extending over the whole amount of food produced, though the increased expenses only apply to a part, there is a greatly increased extra profit, which, by competition, is transferred to the landlord. Rent will rise, both in quantity of produce and in cost ; while wages, being supposed to be the same in quantity, will be greater in cost. The labourer obtaining the same amount of necessaries, money wages have risen ; and as the rise is common to all branches of production, the capitalist cannot indemnify himself by changing his employment, and the loss must be borne by profits.

It appears, then, that the tendency of an increase of capital and population is to add to rent at the expense of profits : though rent does not gain all that profits lose, a part being absorbed in increased expenses of production, that is, in hiring or feeding a greater number of labourers to obtain a given amount of agricultural produce. By profits, must of course be understood the *rate* of profit; for a lower rate of profit on a larger capital may yield a larger gross profit, considered absolutely, though a smaller in proportion to the entire produce.

This tendency of profits to fall, is from time to time counteracted by improvements in production : whether arising from increase of knowledge, or from an increased use of the knowledge already possessed.   This is the third of the three elements, the effects of which on the distribution of the produce we undertook to investigate ; and the investigation will be facilitated by supposing, as in the case of the other two elements, that it operates, in the first instance, alone.

§ 4.   Let us then suppose capital and population stationary, and a sudden improvement made in the arts of production ; by the invention of more efficient machines, or less costly processes, or by obtaining access to cheaper commodities through foreign trade.

The improvement may either be in some of the necessaries or indulgences which enter into the habitual consumption of the labouring class ; or it may be applicable only to luxuries consumed exclusively by richer people.   Very few, however, of the great industrial improvements are altogether of this last description. Agricultural improvements, except such as specially relate to some of the rarer and more peculiar products, act directly upon the principal objects of the labourer's expenditure.   The steam-engine, and every other invention which affords a manageable power, are applicable to all things, and of course to those consumed by the labourer.   Even the power-loom and the spinning-jenny, though applied to the most delicate fabrics, are available no less for the coarse cottons and woollens worn by the labouring class.   All improvements in locomotion cheapen the transport of necessaries as well as of luxuries.   Seldom is a new branch of trade opened, without, either directly or in some indirect way, causing some of the articles which the mass of the people consume to be either produced or imported at smaller cost.   It may safely be affirmed, therefore, that improvements in production generally tend to cheapen the commodities on which the wages of the labouring class are expended.

In so far as the commodities affected by an improvement are those which the labourers generally do not consume, the improvement has no effect in altering the distribution of the produce.   Those particular commodities, indeed, are cheapened ; being produced at less cost, they fall in value and in price, and all who consume them, whether landlords, capitalists, or skilled and privileged labourers, obtain increased means of enjoyment. The rate of profits, however, is not raised. There is a larger gross profit, reckoned in quantity of commodities. But the capital also, if estimated in those commodities, has risen in value. The profit is the same percentage on the capital that it was before. The capitalists are not benefited as capitalists, but as consumers. The landlords and the privileged classes of labourers, if they are consumers of the same commodities, share the same benefit.

The case is different with improvements which diminish the cost of production of the necessaries of life, or of commodities which enter habitually into the consumption of the great mass of labourers. The play of the different forces being here rather complex, it is necessary to analyse it with some minuteness.

As formerly observed,* there are two kinds of agricultural improvements. Some consist in a mere saving of labour, and enable a given quantity of food to be produced at less cost, but not on a smaller surface of land than before. Others enable a given extent of land to yield not only the same produce with less labour, but a greater produce ; so that, if no greater produce is required, a part of the land already under culture may be dispensed with. As the part rejected will be the least productive portion, the market will thenceforth be regulated by a better description of land than what was previously the worst under cultivation.

To place the effect of the improvement in a clear light, we must suppose it to take place suddenly, so as to leave no time, during its introduction, for any increase of capital or of population. Its first effect will be a fall of the value and price of agricultural produce. This is a necessary consequence of either kind of improvement, but especially of the last.

An improvement of the first kind, not increasing the produce, does not dispense with any portion of the land ; the margin of cultivation (as Dr. Chalmers terms it) remains where it was ; agriculture does not recede, either in extent of cultivated land, or in elaborateness of method : and the price continues to be regulated by the same land, and by the same capital, as before. But since that land or capital, and all other land or capital which produces food, now yields its produce at smaller cost, the price of food will fall proportionally. If onetenth of the expense of production has been saved, the price of produce will fall one-tenth.

* Supra, pp. 183–4.

But suppose the improvement to be of the second kind; enabling the land to produce, not only the same corn with one-tenth less labour, but a tenth more corn with the same labour.   Here the effect is still more decided.   Cultivation can now be contracted, and the market supplied from a smaller quantity of land.   Even if this smaller surface of land were of the same average quality as the larger surface, the price would fall one-tenth, because the same produce would be obtained with a tenth less labour.   But since the portion of land abandoned will be the least fertile portion, the price of produce will thenceforth be regulated by a better quality of land than before.   In addition, therefore, to the original diminution of one-tenth in the cost of production, there will be a further diminution, corresponding with the recession of the " margin " of agriculture to land of greater fertility.   There will thus be a twofold fall of price.

Let us now examine the effect of the improvements, thus suddenly made, on the division of the produce ; and in the first place, on rent. By the former of the two kinds of improvement, rent would be diminished.   By the second, it would be diminished still more.

Suppose that the demand for food requires the cultivation of three qualities of land, yielding, on an equal surface, and at an equal expense, 100, 80, and 60 bushels of wheat.   The price of wheat will, on the average, be just sufficient to enable the third quality to be cultivated with the ordinary profit.   The first quality therefore will yield forty and the second twenty bushels of extra profit, constituting the rent of the landlord.   And first, let an improvement be made, which, without enabling more corn to be grown, enables the same corn to be grown with one-fourth less labour.   The price of wheat will fall one-fourth, and 80 bushels will be sold for the price for which 60 were sold before.   But the produce of the land which produces 60 bushels is still required, and the expenses being as much reduced as the price, that land can still be cultivated with the ordinary profit.   The first and second qualities will therefore continue to yield a surplus of 40 and 20 bushels, and corn rent will remain the same as before.   But corn having fallen in price one-fourth, the same corn rent is equivalent to a fourth less of money and of all other commodities.   So far, therefore, as the landlord expends his income in manufactured or foreign products, he is one-fourth worse off than before.   His income as landlord is reduced to three-quarters of its amount : it is only as a consumer of corn that he is as well off.

If the improvement is of the other kind, rent will fall in a still greater ratio. Suppose that the amount of produce which the market requires, can be grown not only with a fourth less labour, but on a fourth less land. If all the land already in cultivation continued to be cultivated, it would yield a produce much larger than necessary. Land, equivalent to a fourth of the produce, must now be abandoned; and as the third quality yielded exactly one-fourth, (being 60 out of 240,) that quality will go out of cultivation. The 240 bushels can now be grown on land of the first and second qualities only; being, on the first, 100 bushels plus one-third, or $133\frac{1}{3}$ bushels; on the second, 80 bushels plus one-third, or $106\frac{2}{3}$ bushels; together 240. The second quality of land, instead of the third, is now the lowest, and regulates the price. Instead of 60, it is sufficient if $106\frac{2}{3}$ bushels repay the capital with the ordinary profit. The price of wheat will consequently fall, not in the ratio of 60 to 80, as in the other case, but in the ratio of 60 to $106\frac{2}{3}$. Even this gives an insufficient idea of the degree in which rent will be affected. The whole produce of the second quality of land will now be required to repay the expenses of production. That land, being the worst in cultivation, will pay no rent. And the first quality will only yield the difference between $133\frac{1}{3}$ bushels and $106\frac{2}{3}$, being $26\frac{2}{3}$ bushels instead of 40. The landlords collectively will have lost $33\frac{1}{3}$ out of 60 bushels in corn rent alone, while the value and price of what is left will have been diminished in the ratio of 60 to $106\frac{2}{3}$.

It thus appears, that the interest of the landlord is decidedly hostile to the sudden and general introduction of agricultural improvements. This assertion has been called a paradox, and made a ground for accusing its first promulgator, Ricardo, of great intellectual perverseness, to say nothing worse. I cannot discern in what the paradox consists; and the obliquity of vision seems to me to be on the side of his assailants. The opinion is only made to appear absurd by stating it unfairly. If the assertion were that a landlord is injured by the improvement of his estate, it would certainly be indefensible; but what is asserted is, that he is injured by the improvement of the estates of other people, although his own is included. Nobody doubts that he would gain greatly by the improvement if he could keep it to himself, and unite the two benefits, an increased produce from his land, and a price as high as before. But if the increase of produce took place simultaneously on all lands, the price would not be as high as before; and there is nothing unreasonable in supposing that the landlords would be, not benefited, but injured. It is admitted that whatever permanently reduces the price of produce diminishes rent : and it is quite in accordance with common notions to suppose that if, by the increased productiveness of land, less land were required for cultivation, its value, like that of other articles for which the demand had diminished, would fall.

I am quite willing to admit that rents have not really been lowered by the progress of agricultural improvement ; but why ? Because improvement has never in reality been sudden, but always slow ; at no time much outstripping, and often falling far short of, the growth of capital and population, which tends as much to raise rent, as the other to lower it, and which is enabled, as we shall presently see, to raise it much higher, by means of the additional margin afforded by improvements in agriculture. First, however, we must examine in what manner the sudden cheapening of agricultural produce would affect profits and wages.

In the beginning, money wages would probably remain the same as before, and the labourers would have the full benefit of the cheapness. They would be enabled to increase their consumption either of food or of other articles, and would receive the same cost, and a greater quantity. So far, profits would be unaffected. But the permanent remuneration of the labourers essentially depends on what we have called their habitual standard ; the extent of the requirements which, as a class, they insist on satisfying before they choose to have children. If their tastes and requirements receive a durable impress from the sudden improvement in their condition, the benefit to the class will be permanent. But the same cause which enables them to purchase greater comforts and indulgences with the same wages, would enable them to purchase the same amount of comforts and indulgences with lower wages ; and a greater population may now exist, without reducing the labourers below the condition to which they are accustomed. Hitherto this and no other has been the use which the labourers have commonly made of any increase of their means of living ; they have treated it simply as convertible into food for a greater number of children. It is probable, therefore, that population would be stimulated, and that after the lapse of a generation the real wages of labour would be no higher than before the improvement : the reduction being partly brought about by a fall of money wages, and partly through the price of food, the cost of which, from the demand occasioned by the increase of population, would be increased. To the extent to which money wages fell, profits would rise ; the capitalist obtaining a greater quantity of equally efficient labour by the same outlay of capital. We thus see that a diminution of the cost of living, whether arising from agricultural improvements or from the importation of foreign produce, if the habits and requirements of the labourers are not raised, usually lowers money wages and rent, and raises the general rate of profit.

What is true of improvements which cheapen the production of food, is true also of the substitution of a cheaper for a more costly variety of it. The same land yields to the same labour a much greater quantity of human nutriment in the form of maize or potatoes, than in the form of wheat. If the labourers were to give up bread, and feed only on those cheaper products, taking as their compensation, not a greater quantity of other consumable commodities, but earlier marriages and larger families, the cost of labour would be much diminished, and if labour continued equally efficient, profits would rise ; while rent would be much lowered, since food for the whole population could be raised on half or a third part of the land now sown with corn. At the same time, it being evident that land too barren to be cultivated for wheat might be made in case of necessity to yield potatoes sufficient to support the little labour necessary for producing them, cultivation might ultimately descend lower, and rent eventually rise higher, on a potato or maize system, than on a corn system ; because the land would be capable of feeding a much larger population before reaching the limit of its powers.

If the improvement, which we suppose to take place, is not in the production of food, but of some manufactured article·consumed by the labouring class, the effect on wages and profits will at first be the same ; but the effect on rent very different. It will not be lowered ; it will even, if the ultimate effect of the improvement is an increase of population, be raised : in which last case profits will be lowered. The reasons are too evident to require statement.

§ 5. We have considered, on the one hand, the manner in which the distribution of the produce into rent, profits, and wages, is affected by the ordinary increase of population and capital, and on the other, how it is affected by improvements in production, and more especially in agriculture. We have found that the former cause lowers profits ; and raises rent and the cost of labour : while the tendency of agricultural improvements is to diminish rent ; and all improvements which cheapen any article of the labourer's consumption, tend to diminish the cost of labour and to raise profits. The tendency of each cause in its separate state being thus ascertained, it is easy to determine the tendency of the actual course of things, in which the two movements are going on simultaneously, capital and population increasing with tolerable steadiness, while improvements in agriculture are made from time to time, and the knowledge and practice of improved methods become diffused gradually through the community.

The habits and requirements of the labouring classes being given (which determine their real wages), rents, profits, and money wages at any given time, are the result of the composition of these rival forces. If during any period agricultural improvement advances faster than population, rent and money wages during that period will tend downward, and profits upward. If population advances more rapidly than agricultural improvement, either the labourers will submit to a reduction in the quantity or quality of their food, or if not, rent and money wages will progressively rise, and profits will fall.

Agricultural skill and knowledge are of slow growth, and still slower diffusion. Inventions and discoveries, too, occur only occasionally, while the increase of population and capital are con-tinuous agencies. It therefore seldom happens that improvement even during a short time, has so much the start of population and capital as actually to lower rent, or raise the rate of profits. There are many countries in which the growth of population and capital is not rapid, but in these agricultural improvement is less active still. Population almost everywhere treads close on the heels of agricultural improvement, and effaces its effects as fast as they are produced.

The reason why agricultural improvement seldom lowers rent, is that it seldom cheapens food, but only prevents it from growing dearer ; and seldom, if ever, throws land out of cultivation, but only enables worse and worse land to be taken in for the supply of an increasing demand. What is sometimes called the natural state of a country which is but half cultivated, namely, that the land is highly productive, and food obtained in great abundance by little labour, is only true of unoccupied countries colonized by a civilized people. In the United States the worst land in cultivation is of a high quality (except sometimes in the immediate vicinity of markets or means of conveyance, where a bad quality is compensated by a good situation) [1] ; and even if no further improvements were made in

---

[1] [Parenthesis added in 2nd ed. (1849).]

agriculture or locomotion, cultivation would have many steps yet to descend, before the increase of population and capital would be brought to a stand ; but in Europe five hundred years ago, though so thinly peopled in comparison to the present population, it is probable that the worst land under the plough was, from the rude state of agriculture, quite as unproductive as the worst land now cultivated ; and that cultivation had approached as near to the ultimate limit of profitable tillage, in those times as in the present. What the agricultural improvements since made have really done is, by increasing the capacity of production of land in general, to enable tillage to extend downwards to a much worse natural quality of land than the worst which at that time would have admitted of cultivation by a capitalist for profit ; thus rendering a much greater increase of capital and population possible, and removing always a little and a little further off the barrier which restrains them ; population meanwhile always pressing so hard against the barrier, that there is never any visible margin left for it to seize, every inch of ground made vacant for it by improvement being at once filled up by its advancing columns. Agricultural improvement may thus be considered to be not so much a counterforce conflicting with increase of population, as a partial relaxation of the bonds which confine that increase.

The effects produced on the division of the produce by an increase of production, under the joint influence of increase of population and capital and improvements of agriculture, are very different from those deduced from the hypothetical cases previously discussed. In particular, the effect on rent is most materially different. We remarked that—while a great agricultural improvement made suddenly and universally would in the first instance inevitably lower rent—such improvements enable rent, in the progress of society, to rise gradually to a much higher limit than it could otherwise attain, since they enable a much lower quality of land to be ultimately cultivated. But in the case we are now supposing, which nearly corresponds to the usual course of things, this ultimate effect becomes the immediate effect. Suppose cultivation to have reached, or almost reached, the utmost limit permitted by the state of the industrial arts, and rent, therefore, to have attained nearly the highest point to which it can be carried by the progress of population and capital, with the existing amount of skill and knowledge. If a great agricultural improvement were suddenly introduced, it might throw back rent for a considerable space, leaving it to regain its lost ground by the progress of population and capital, and afterwards to go on further. But, taking place, as such improvement always does, very gradually, it causes no retrograde movement of either rent or cultivation ; it merely enables the one to go on rising, and the other extending, long after they must otherwise have stopped. It would do this even without the necessity of resorting to a worse quality of land ; simply by enabling the lands already in cultivation to yield a greater produce, with no increase of the proportional cost. If, by improvements of agriculture, all the lands in cultivation could be made, even with double labour and capital, to yield a double produce, (supposing that in the meantime population increased so as to require this double quantity) all rents would be doubled.

To illustrate the point, let us revert to the numerical example in a former page. Three qualities of land yield respectively 100, 80, and 60 bushels to the same outlay on the same extent of surface. If No. 1 could be made to yield 200, No. 2, 160, and No. 3, 120 bushels, at only double the expense, and therefore without any increase of the cost of production, and if the population, having doubled, required all this increased quantity, the rent of No. 1 would be 80 bushels instead of 40, and of No. 2, 40 instead of 20, while the price and value per bushel would be the same as before : so that corn rent and money rent would both be doubled. I need not point out the difference between this result, and what we have shown would take place if there were an improvement in production without the accompaniment of an increased demand for food.

Agricultural improvement, then, is always ultimately, and in the manner in which it generally takes place also immediately, beneficial to the landlord. We may add, that when it takes place in that manner, it is beneficial to no one else. When the demand for produce fully keeps pace with the increased capacity of production, food is not cheapened ; the labourers are not, even temporarily, benefited ; the cost of labour is not diminished, nor profits raised. There is a greater aggregate production, a greater produce divided among the labourers, and a larger gross profit ; but the wages being shared among a larger population, and the profits spread over a larger capital, no labourer is better off, nor does any capitalist derive from the same amount of capital a larger income.

The result of this long investigation may be summed up as follows. The economical progress of a society constituted of landlords, capitalists, and labourers, tends to the progressive enrichment of the landlord class ; [1] while the cost of the labourer's subsistence tends on the whole to increase,[2] and profits to fall. Agricultural improvements are a counteracting force to the two last effects ; but the first, though a case is conceivable in which it would be temporarily checked, is ultimately in a high degree promoted by those improvements ; and the increase of population tends to transfer all the benefits derived from agricultural improvement to the landlords alone. What other consequences, in addition to these, or in modification of them, arise from the industrial progress of a society thus constituted, I shall endeavour to show in the succeeding chapter.

[1] [See Appendix Z. *Rents in the* 19*th Century.*]
[2] [See Appendix AA. *Wages in the* 19*th Century.*]

CHAPTER IV

§ 1. The tendency of profits to fall as society advances, which has been brought to notice in the preceding chapter, was early recognized by writers on industry and commerce; but the laws which govern profits not being then understood, the phenomenon was ascribed to a wrong cause. Adam Smith considered profits to be determined by what he called the competition of capital; and concluded that when capital increased, this competition must likewise increase, and profits must fall. It is not quite certain what sort of competition Adam Smith had here in view. His words in the chapter on Profits of Stock * are, " When the stocks of many rich merchants are turned into the same trade, their mutual competition naturally tends to lower its profits; and when there is a like increase of stock in all the different trades carried on in the same society, the same competition must produce the same effect in them all." This passage would lead us to infer that, in Adam Smith's opinion, the manner in which the competition of capital lowers profits is by lowering prices; that being usually the mode in which an increased investment of capital in any particular trade, lowers the profits of that trade. But if this was his meaning, he overlooked the circumstance, that the fall of price, which if confined to one commodity really does lower the profits of the producer, ceases to have that effect as soon as it extends to all commodities; because, when all things have fallen, nothing has really fallen, except nominally; and even computed in money, the expenses of every producer have diminished as much as his returns. Unless indeed labour be the one commodity which has not fallen in money price, when all other things have : if so, what has really taken place is a rise of wages; and it is that, and not the fall of prices, which has lowered

---

* *Wealth of Nations*, book i. ch. 9.

the profits of capital.   There is another thing which escaped the notice of Adam Smith ; that the supposed universal fall of prices, through increased competition of capitals, is a thing which cannot take place.   Prices are not determined by the competition of the sellers only, but also by that of the buyers ; by demand as well as supply.   The demand which affects money prices consists of all the money in the hands of the community, destined to be laid out in commodities ; and as long as the proportion of this to the commodities is not diminished, there is no fall of general prices.   Now, howsoever capital may increase, and give rise to an increased production of commodities, a full share of the capital will be drawn to the business of producing or importing money, and the quantity of money will be augmented in an equal ratio with the quantity of commodities.   For if this were not the case, and if money, therefore, were, as the theory supposes, perpetually acquiring increased purchasing power, those who produced or imported it would obtain constantly increasing profits ; and this could not happen without attracting labour and capital to that occupation from other employments.   If a general fall of prices, and increased value of money, were really to occur, it could only be as a consequence of increased cost of production, from the gradual exhaustion of the mines.

It is not tenable, therefore, in theory, that the increase of capital produces, or tends to produce, a general decline of money prices. Neither is it true, that any general decline of prices, as capital increased, has manifested itself in fact.   The only things observed to fall in price with the progress of society, are those in which there have been improvements in production, greater than have taken place in the production of the precious metals ; as for example, all spun and woven fabrics.   Other things, again, instead of falling, have risen in price, because their cost of production, compared with that of gold and silver, has increased.   Among these are all kinds of food, comparison being made with a much earlier period of history.   The doctrine, therefore, that competition of capital lowers profits by lowering prices, is incorrect in fact, as well as unsound in principle.

But it is not certain that Adam Smith really held that doctrine ; for his language on the subject is wavering and unsteady, denoting the absence of a definite and well-digested opinion.   Occasionally he seems to think that the mode in which the competition of capital lowers profits, is by raising wages.   And when speaking of the rate of profit in new colonies, he seems on the very verge of grasping the complete theory of the subject. "As the colony increases, the profits of stock gradually diminish. When the most fertile and best situated lands have been all occupied, less profit can be made by the cultivators of what is inferior both in soil and situation." Had Adam Smith meditated longer on the subject, and systematized his view of it by harmonizing with each other the various glimpses which he caught of it from different points, he would have perceived that this last is the true cause of the fall of profits usually consequent upon increase of capital.

§ 2. Mr. Wakefield, in his Commentary on Adam Smith, and his important writings on Colonization, takes a much clearer view of the subject, and arrives, through a substantially correct series of deductions, at practical conclusions which appear to me just and important ; but he is not equally happy in incorporating his valuable speculations with the results of previous thought, and reconciling them with other truths. Some of the theories of Dr. Chalmers, in his chapter " On the Increase and Limits of Capital," and the two chapters which follow it, coincide in their tendency and spirit with those of Mr. Wakefield ; but Dr. Chalmers' ideas, though delivered, as is his custom, with a most attractive semblance of clearness, are really on this subject much more confused than even those of Adam Smith, and more decidedly infected with the often refuted notion that the competition of capital lowers general prices ; the subject of Money apparently not having been included among the parts of political economy which this acute and vigorous writer had carefully studied.

Mr. Wakefield's explanation of the fall of profits is briefly this. Production is limited not solely by the quantity of capital and of labour, but also by the extent of the " field of employment." The field of employment for capital is twofold ; the land of the country, and the capacity of foreign markets to take its manufactured commodities. On a limited extent of land, only a limited quantity of capital can find employment at a profit. As the quantity of capital approaches this limit, profit falls ; when the limit is attained, profit is annihilated ; and can only be restored through an extension of the field of employment, either by the acquisition of fertile land, or by opening new markets in foreign countries, from which food and materials can be purchased with the products of domestic capital. These propositions are, in my opinion, substantially true ; and, even to the phraseology in which they are expressed, considered as adapted to popular and practical rather than scientific uses, I have nothing to object. The error which seems to me imputable to Mr. Wakefield is that of supposing his doctrines to be in contradiction to the principles of the best school of preceding political economists, instead of being, as they really are, corollaries from those principles ; though corollaries which, perhaps, would not always have been admitted by those political economists themselves.

The most scientific treatment of the subject which I have met with is in an essay on the effects of Machinery, published in the *Westminster Review* for January 1826, by Mr. William Ellis : * which was doubtless unknown to Mr. Wakefield, but which had preceded him, though by a different path, in several of his leading conclusions. This essay excited little notice, partly from being published anonymously in a periodical, and partly because it was much in advance of the state of political economy at the time. In Mr. Ellis's view of the subject, the questions and difficulties raised by Mr. Wakefield's speculations and by those of Dr. Chalmers, find a solution consistent with the principles of political economy laid down in the present treatise.

§ 3. There is at every time and place some particular rate of profit, which is the lowest that will induce the people of that country and time to accumulate savings, and to employ those savings productively. This minimum rate of profit varies according to circumstances. It depends on two elements. One is, the strength of the effective desire of accumulation ; the comparative estimate, made by the people of that place and era, of future interests when weighed against present. This element chiefly affects the inclination to save. The other element, which affects not so much the willingness to save as the disposition to employ savings productively, is the degree of security of capital engaged in industrial operations. A state of general insecurity no doubt affects also the disposition to save. A hoard may be a source of additional danger to its reputed possessor. But as it may also be a powerful means of averting dangers, the effects in this respect may perhaps be looked upon as balanced. But in employing any funds which a person may possess as capital on his own account, or in lending it to others to be so employed, there is always some additional risk, over and

* [1862] Now so much better known through his apostolic exertions, by pen, purse, and person, for the improvement of popular education, and especially for the introduction into it of the elements of practical political economy.

above that incurred by keeping it idle in his own custody. This extra risk is great in proportion as the general state of society is insecure : it may be equivalent to twenty, thirty, or fifty per cent, or to no more than one or two ; something, however, it must always be : and for this, the expectation of profit must be sufficient to compensate.

There would be adequate motives for a certain amount of saving, even if capital yielded no profit. There would be an inducement to lay by in good times a provision for bad ; to reserve something for sickness and infirmity, or as a means of leisure and independence in the latter part of life, or a help to children in the outset of it. Savings, however, which have only these ends in view, have not much tendency to increase the amount of capital permanently in existence. These motives only prompt persons to save at one period of life what they purpose to consume at another, or what will be consumed by their children before they can completely provide for themselves. The savings by which an addition is made to the national capital usually emanate from the desire of persons to improve what is termed their condition in life, or to make a provision for children or others, independent of their exertions. Now, to the strength of these inclinations it makes a very material difference how much of the desired object can be effected by a given amount and duration of self-denial ; which again depends on the rate of profit. And there is in every country some rate of profit, below which persons in general will not find sufficient motive to save for the mere purpose of growing richer, or of leaving others better off than themselves. Any accumulation, therefore, by which the general capital is increased, requires as its necessary condition a certain rate of profit ; a rate which an average person will deem to be an equivalent for abstinence, with the addition of a sufficient insurance against risk. There are always some persons in whom the effective desire of accumulation is above the average, and to whom less than this rate of profit is a sufficient inducement to save ; but these merely step into the place of others whose taste for expense and indulgence is beyond the average, and who, instead of saving, perhaps even dissipate what they have received.

I have already observed that this minimum rate of profit, less than which is not consistent with the further increase of capital, is lower in some states of society than in others ; and I may add, that the kind of social progress characteristic of our present civilization tends to diminish it. In the first place, one of the acknowledged effects of that progress is an increase of general security.   Destruction by wars, and spoliation by private or public violence, are less and less to be apprehended ; and the improvements which may be looked for in education and in the administration of justice, or, in their default, increased regard for opinion, afford a growing protection against fraud and reckless mismanagement.   The risks attending the investment of savings in productive employment require, therefore, a smaller rate of profit to compensate for them than was required a century ago, and will hereafter require less than at present.   In the second place, it is also one of the consequences of civilization that mankind become less the slaves of the moment, and more habituated to carry their desires and purposes forward into a distant future.   This increase of providence is a natural result of the increased assurance with which futurity can be looked forward to ; and is, besides, favoured by most of the influences which an industrial life exercises over the passions and inclinations of human nature.   In proportion as life has fewer vicissitudes, as habits become more fixed, and great prizes are less and less to be hoped for by any other means than long perseverance, mankind become more willing to sacrifice present indulgence for future objects.   This increased capacity of forethought and self-control may assuredly find other things to exercise itself upon than increase of riches, and some considerations connected with this topic will shortly be touched upon. The present kind of social progress, however, decidedly tends, though not perhaps to increase the desire of accumulation, yet to weaken the obstacles to it, and to diminish the amount of profit which people absolutely require as an inducement to save and accumulate.   For these two reasons, diminution of risk and increase of providence, a profit or interest of three or four per cent is as sufficient a motive to the increase of capital in England at the present day, as thirty or forty per cent in the Burmese Empire, or in England at the time of King John.   In Holland during the last century a return of two per cent on government security, was consistent with an undiminished, if not with an increasing, capital. But though the minimum rate of profit is thus liable to vary, and though to specify exactly what it is would at any given time be impossible, such a minimum always exists ; and whether it be high or low, when once it is reached, no further increase of capital can for the present take place.   The country has then attained what is known to political economists under the name of the stationary state.

§ 4. We now arrive at the fundamental proposition which this chapter is intended to inculcate. When a country has long possessed a large production, and a large net income to make savings from, and when, therefore, the means have long existed of making a great annual addition to capital; (the country not having, like America [1848], a large reserve of fertile land still unused ;) it is one of the characteristics of such a country, that the rate of profit is habitually within, as it were, a hand's breadth of the minimum, and the country therefore on the very verge of the stationary state. By this I do not mean that this state is likely, in any of the great countries of Europe, to be soon actually reached, or that capital does not still yield a profit considerably greater than what is barely sufficient to induce the people of those countries to save and accumulate. My meaning is, that it would require but a short time to reduce profits to the minimum, if capital continued to increase at its present rate, and no circumstances having a tendency to raise the rate of profit occurred in the meantime. The expansion of capital would soon reach its ultimate boundary, if the boundary itself did not continually open and leave more space.

In England, the ordinary rate of interest on government securities, in which the risk is next to nothing, may be estimated [1848] at a little more than three per cent : in all other investments, therefore, the interest or profit calculated upon (exclusively of what is properly a remuneration for talent or exertion) must be as much more than this amount as is equivalent to the degree of risk to which the capital is thought to be exposed. Let us suppose that in England even so small a net profit as one per cent, exclusive of insurance against risk, would constitute a sufficient inducement to save, but that less than this would not be a sufficient inducement. I now say, that the mere continuance of the present annual increase of capital, if no circumstance occurred to counteract its effect, would suffice in a small number of years to reduce the rate of net profit to one per cent.

To fulfil the conditions of the hypothesis, we must suppose an entire cessation of the exportation of capital for foreign investment. No more capital sent abroad for railways or loans ; no more emigrants taking capital with them, to the colonies, or to other countries ; no fresh advances made, or credits given, by bankers or merchants to their foreign correspondents. We must also assume that there are no fresh loans for unproductive expenditure, by the government, or on mortgage, or otherwise ; and none of the waste of capital which now takes place by the failure of undertakings which people are tempted to engage in by the hope of a better income than can be obtained in safe paths at the present habitually low rate of profit. We must suppose the entire savings of the community to be annually invested in really productive employment within the country itself ; and no new channels opened by industrial inventions, or by a more extensive substitution of the best known processes for inferior ones.

Few persons would hesitate to say, that there would be great difficulty in finding remunerative employment every year for so much new capital, and most would conclude that there would be what used to be termed a general glut ; that commodities would be produced, and remain unsold, or be sold only at a loss. But the full examination which we have already given to this question,* has shown that this is not the mode in which the inconvenience would be experienced. The difficulty would not consist in any want of a market. If the new capital were duly shared among many varieties of employment, it would raise up a demand for its own produce, and there would be no cause why any part of that produce should remain longer on hand than formerly. What would really be, not merely difficult, but impossible, would be to employ this capital without submitting to a rapid reduction of the rate of profit.

As capital increased, population either would also increase, or it would not. If it did not, wages would rise, and a greater capital would be distributed in wages among the same number of labourers. There being no more labour than before, and no improvements to render the labour more efficient, there would not be any increase of the produce ; and as the capital, however largely increased, would only obtain the same gross return, the whole savings of each year would be exactly so much subtracted from the profits of the next and of every following year. It is hardly necessary to say that in such circumstances profits would very soon fall to the point at which further increase of capital would cease. An augmentation of capital, much more rapid than that of population, must soon reach its extreme limit, unless accompanied by increased efficiency of labour (through inventions and discoveries, or improved mental and physical education), or unless some of the idle people, or of the unproductive labourers, became productive.

If population did increase with the increase of capital and in

* Book iii. ch. 14.

proportion to it, the fall of profits would still be inevitable. Increased population implies increased demand for agricultural produce. In the absence of industrial improvements, this demand can only be supplied at an increased cost of production, either by cultivating worse land, or by a more elaborate and costly cultivation of the land already under tillage. The cost of the labourer's subsistence is therefore increased ; and unless the labourer submits to a deterioration of his condition, profits must fall. In an old country like England, if, in addition to supposing all improvement in domestic agriculture suspended, we suppose that there is no increased production in foreign countries for the English market, the fall of profits would be very rapid. If both these avenues to an increased supply of food were closed, and population continued to increase, as it is said to do, at the rate of a thousand a day, all waste land which admits of cultivation in the existing state of knowledge would soon be cultivated, and the cost of production and price of food would be so increased, that, if the labourers received the increased money wages necessary to compensate for their increased expenses, profits would very soon reach the minimum. The fall of profits would be retarded if money wages did not rise, or rose in a less degree ; but the margin which can be gained by a deterioration of the labourers' condition is a very narrow one : in general they *cannot* bear much reduction ; when they can, they have also a higher standard of necessary requirements, and *will* not. On the whole, therefore, we may assume that in such a country as England, if the present annual amount of savings were to continue, without any of the counteracting circumstances which now keep in check the natural influence of those savings in reducing profit, the rate of profit would speedily attain the minimum, and all further accumulation of capital would for the present cease.

§ 5. What, then, are these counteracting circumstances, which, in the existing state of things, maintain a tolerably equal struggle against the downward tendency of profits, and prevent the great annual savings which take place in this country from depressing the rate of profit much nearer to that lowest point to which it is always tending, and which, left to itself, it would so promptly attain ? The resisting agencies are of several kinds.

First among them, we may notice one which is so simple and so conspicuous, that some political economists, especially M. de Sismondi and Dr. Chalmers, have attended to it almost to the exclusion of all others. This is, the waste of capital in periods of over-trading and rash speculation, and in the commercial revulsions by which such times are always followed. It is true that a great part of what is lost at such periods is not destroyed, but merely transferred, like a gambler's losses, to more successful speculators. But even of these mere transfers, a large portion is always to foreigners, by the hasty purchase of unusual quantities of foreign goods at advanced prices. And much also is absolutely wasted. Mines are opened, railways or bridges made, and many other works of uncertain profit commenced, and in these enterprises much capital is sunk which yields either no return, or none adequate to the outlay. Factories are built and machinery erected beyond what the market requires, or can keep in employment. Even if they are kept in employment, the capital is no less sunk; it has been converted from circulating into fixed capital, and has ceased to have any influence on wages or profits. Besides this, there is a great unproductive consumption of capital, during the stagnation which follows a period of general over-trading. Establishments are shut up, or kept working without any profit, hands are discharged, and numbers of persons in all ranks, being deprived of their income, and thrown for support on their savings, find themselves, after the crisis has passed away, in a condition of more or less impoverishment. Such are the effects of a commercial revulsion : and that such revulsions are almost periodical, is a consequence of the very tendency of profits which we are considering. By the time a few years have passed over without a crisis, so much additional capital has been accumulated, that it is no longer possible to invest it at the accustomed profit : all public securities rise to a high price, the rate of interest on the best mercantile security falls very low, and the complaint is general among persons in business that no money is to be made. Does not this demonstrate how speedily profit would be at the minimum, and the stationary condition of capital would be attained, if these accumulations went on without any counteracting principle ? But the diminished scale of all safe gains inclines persons to give a ready ear to any projects which hold out, though at the risk of loss, the hope of a higher rate of profit ; and speculations ensue, which, with the subsequent revulsions, destroy, or transfer to foreigners, a considerable amount of capital, produce a temporary rise of interest and profit, make room for fresh accumulations, and the same round is recommenced.

This, doubtless, is one considerable cause which arrests profits in their descent to the minimum, by sweeping away from time to time a part of the accumulated mass by which they are forced down. But this is not, as might be inferred from the language of some writers, the principal cause. If it were, the capital of the country would not increase ; but in England it does increase greatly and rapidly. This is shown by the increasing productiveness of almost all taxes, by the continual growth of all the signs of national wealth, and by the rapid increase of population, while the condition of the labourers is certainly not declining, but on the whole improving.[1] These things prove that each commercial revulsion, however disastrous, is very far from destroying all the capital which has been added to the accumulations of the country since the last revulsion preceding it, and that, invariably, room is either found or made for the profitable employment of a perpetually increasing capital, consistently with not forcing down profits to a lower rate.

§ 6. This brings us to the second of the counter-agencies, namely, improvements in production. These evidently have the effect of extending what Mr. Wakefield terms the field of employment, that is, they enable a greater amount of capital to be accumulated and employed without depressing the rate of profit : provided always that they do not raise, to a proportional extent, the habits and requirements of the labourer. If the labouring class gain the full advantage of the increased cheapness, in other words, if money wages do not fall, profits are not raised, nor their fall retarded. But if the labourers people up to the improvement in their condition, and so relapse to their previous state, profits will rise. All inventions which cheapen any of the things consumed by the labourers, unless their requirements are raised in an equivalent degree, in time lower money wages : and by doing so, enable a greater capital to be accumulated and employed, before profits fall back to what they were previously.

Improvements which only affect things consumed exclusively by the richer classes, do not operate precisely in the same manner. The cheapening of lace or velvet has no effect in diminishing the cost of labour ; and no mode can be pointed out in which it can raise the rate of profit, so as to make room for a larger capital before the minimum is attained. It, however, produces an effect which is virtually equivalent ; it lowers, or tends to lower, the minimum

---

[1] [So since the 6th ed. (1865). The original (1848) ran : " the condition of the labourers certainly is not on the whole declining."]

itself.   In the first place, increased cheapness of articles of consumption promotes the inclination to save, by affording to all consumers
a surplus which they may lay by, consistently with their accustomed
manner of living ; and unless they were previously suffering actual
hardships, it will require little self-denial to save some part at least
of this surplus.   In the next place, whatever enables people to live
equally well on a smaller income, inclines them to lay by capital for
a lower rate of profit.   If people can live on an independence of 500*l.*
a year in the same manner as they formerly could on one of 1000*l.*,
some persons will be induced to save in hopes of the one, who
would have been deterred by the more remote prospect of the other.
All improvements, therefore, in the production of almost any commodity, tend in some degree to widen the interval which has to be
passed before arriving at the stationary state : but this effect
belongs in a much greater degree to the improvements which affect
the articles consumed by the labourer, since these conduce to it in
two ways ; they induce people to accumulate for a lower profit,
and they also raise the rate of profit itself.

§ 7.   Equivalent in effect to improvements in production,
is the acquisition of any new power of obtaining cheap commodities
from foreign countries.   If necessaries are cheapened, whether
they are so by improvements at home or importation from abroad,
is exactly the same thing to wages and profits.   Unless the labourer
obtains, and by an improvement of his habitual standard, keeps,
the whole benefit, the cost of labour is lowered, and the rate of profit
raised.   As long as food can continue to be imported for an increasing
population without any diminution of cheapness, so long the
declension of profits through the increase of population and capital
is arrested, and accumulation may go on without making the rate
of profit draw nearer to the minimum.   And on this ground it is
believed by some, that the repeal of the corn laws has opened
to this country a long era of rapid increase of capital with an
undiminished rate of profit.

Before inquiring whether this expectation is reasonable, one
remark must be made, which is much at variance with commonly
received notions.   Foreign trade does not necessarily increase the
field of employment for capital.   It is not the mere opening of a
market for a country's productions, that tends to raise the rate
of profits.   If nothing were obtained in exchange for those productions but the luxuries of the rich, the expenses of no capitalist

would be diminished ; profits would not be at all raised, nor room made for the accumulation of more capital without submitting to a reduction of profits : and if the attainment of the stationary state were at all retarded, it would only be because the diminished cost at which a certain degree of luxury could be enjoyed, might induce people, in that prospect, to make fresh savings for a lower profit than they formerly were willing to do. When foreign trade makes room for more capital at the same profit, it is by enabling the necessaries of life, or the habitual articles of the labourer's consumption, to be obtained at smaller cost. It may do this in two ways ; by the importation either of those commodities themselves, or of the means and appliances for producing them. Cheap iron has, in a certain measure, the same effect on profits and the cost of labour as cheap corn, because cheap iron makes cheap tools for agriculture and cheap machinery for clothing. But a foreign trade which neither directly, nor by any indirect consequence, increases the cheapness of anything consumed by the labourers, does not, any more than an invention or discovery in the like case, tend to raise profits or retard their fall ; it merely substitutes the production of goods for foreign markets in the room of the home production of luxuries, leaving the employment for capital neither greater nor less than before. It is true, that there is scarcely any export trade which, in a country that already imports necessaries or materials, comes within these conditions : for every increase of exports enables the country to obtain all its imports on cheaper terms than before.

A country which, as is now the case with England,[1] admits food of all kinds, and all necessaries and the materials of necessaries, to be freely imported from all parts of the world, no longer depends on the fertility of her own soil to keep up her rate of profits, but on the soil of the whole world. It remains to consider how far this resource can be counted upon, for making head during a very long period against the tendency of profits to decline as capital increases.

It must, of course, be supposed that with the increase of capital, population also increases ; for if it did not, the consequent rise of wages would bring down profits, in spite of any cheapness of food. Suppose then that the population of Great Britain goes on increasing at its present rate, and demands every year a supply of imported food considerably beyond that of the year preceding. This annual increase in the food demanded from the exporting countries can

---

[1] [So from the 5th ed. (1862). In the 1st ed. (1848) the parenthesis had been : " (which is now very nearly, and will soon be entirely, our own case)."]

only be obtained either by great improvements in their agriculture, or by the application of a great additional capital to the growth of food. The former is likely to be a very slow process, from the rudeness and ignorance of the agricultural classes in the food-exporting countries of Europe, while the British colonies and the United States are already in possession of most of the improvements yet made, so far as suitable to their circumstances. There remains as a resource, the extension of cultivation. And on this it is to be remarked, that the capital by which any such extension can take place, is mostly still to be created. In Poland, Russia, Hungary, Spain, the increase of capital is extremely slow. In America it is rapid, but not more rapid than the population. The principal fund at present available for supplying this country with a yearly increasing importation of food, is that portion of the annual savings of America which has heretofore been applied to increasing the manufacturing establishments of the United States, and which free trade in corn may possibly divert from that purpose to growing food for our market. This limited source of supply, unless great improvements take place in agriculture, cannot be expected to keep pace with the growing demand of so rapidly increasing a population as that of Great Britain ; and if our population and capital continue to increase with their present rapidity, the only mode in which food can continue to be supplied cheaply to the one, is by sending the other abroad to produce it.[1]

§ 8.   This brings us to the last of the counter-forces which check the downward tendency of profits, in a country whose capital increases faster than that of its neighbours and whose profits are therefore nearer to the minimum. This is, the perpetual overflow of capital into colonies or foreign countries, to seek higher profits than can be obtained at home. I believe this to have been for many years one of the principal causes by which the decline of profits in England has been arrested. It has a twofold operation. In the first place, it does what a fire, or an inundation, or a commercial crisis would have done : it carries off a part of the increase of capital from which the reduction of profits proceeds. Secondly, the capital so carried off is not lost, but is chiefly employed either in founding colonies, which become large exporters of cheap agricultural produce, or in extending and perhaps improving the agriculture of older

[1] [See Appendix BB. *The Importation of Food.*]

communities. It is to the emigration of English capital, that we have chiefly to look for keeping up a supply of cheap food and cheap materials of clothing, proportional to the increase of our population ; thus enabling an increasing capital to find employment in the country, without reduction of profit, in producing manufactured articles with which to pay for this supply of raw produce. Thus, the exportation of capital is an agent of great efficacy in extending the field of employment for that which remains : and it may be said truly that, up to a certain point, the more capital we send away, the more we shall possess and be able to retain at home.

In countries which are further advanced in industry and population, and have therefore a lower rate of profit, than others, there is always, long before the actual minimum is reached, a practical minimum, viz., when profits have fallen so much below what they are elsewhere, that, were they to fall lower, all further accumulations would go abroad. In the present state of the industry of the world, when there is occasion, in any rich and improving country, to take the minimum of profits at all into consideration for practical purposes, it is only this practical minimum that needs be considered. As long as there are old countries where capital increases very rapidly, and new countries where profit is still high, profits in the old countries will not sink to the rate which would put a stop to accumulation ; the fall is stopped at the point which sends capital abroad. It is only, however, by improvements in production, and even in the production of things consumed by labourers, that the capital of a country like England is prevented from speedily reaching that degree of lowness of profit, which would cause all further savings to be sent to find employment in the colonies, or in foreign countries.[1]

[1] [See Appendix CC. *The Tendency of Profits to a Minimum.*]

CHAPTER V

§ 1. THE theory of the effect of accumulation on profits, laid down in the preceding chapter, materially alters many of the practical conclusions which might otherwise be supposed to follow from the general principles of Political Economy, and which were, indeed, long admitted as true by the highest authorities on the subject.

It must greatly abate, or rather, altogether destroy, in countries where profits are low, the immense importance which used to be attached by political economists to the effects which an event or a measure of government might have in adding to or subtracting from the capital of the country. We have now seen that the lowness of profits is a proof that the spirit of accumulation is so active, and that the increase of capital has proceeded at so rapid a rate, as to outstrip the two counter-agencies, improvements in production, and increased supply of cheap necessaries from abroad : and that unless a considerable portion of the annual increase of capital were either periodically destroyed, or exported for foreign investment, the country would speedily attain the point at which further accumulation would cease, or at least spontaneously slacken, so as no longer to overpass the march of invention in the arts which produce the necessaries of life. In such a state of things as this, a sudden addition to the capital of the country, unaccompanied by any increase of productive power, would be but of transitory duration ; since, by depressing profits and interest, it would either diminish by a corresponding amount the savings which would be made from income in the year or two following, or it would cause an equivalent amount to be sent abroad, or to be wasted in rash speculations. Neither, on the other hand, would a sudden abstraction of capital, unless of inordinate amount, have any real effect in impoverishing the country. After a few months or years, there would exist in the country just as much capital as if none had been taken away. The abstraction, by raising profits and interest, would give a fresh stimulus to the accumulative principle, which would speedily fill up the vacuum. Probably, indeed, the only effect that would ensue, would be that for some time afterwards less capital would be exported, and less thrown away in hazardous speculation.

In the first place, then, this view of things greatly weakens, in a wealthy and industrious country, the force of the economical argument against the expenditure of public money for really valuable, even though industriously unproductive, purposes. If for any great object of justice or philanthropic policy, such as the industrial regeneration of Ireland, or a comprehensive measure of colonization or of public education, it were proposed to raise a large sum by way of loan, politicians need not demur to the abstraction of so much capital, as tending to dry up the permanent sources of the country's wealth, and diminish the fund which supplies the subsistence of the labouring population. The utmost expense which could be requisite for any of these purposes, would not in all probability deprive one labourer of employment, or diminish the next year's production by one ell of cloth or one bushel of grain. In poor countries, the capital of the country requires the legislator's sedulous care; he is bound to be most cautious of encroaching upon it, and should favour to the utmost its accumulation at home, and its introduction from abroad. But in rich, populous, and highly cultivated countries, it is not capital which is the deficient element, but fertile land; and what the legislator should desire and promote, is not a greater aggregate saving, but a greater return to savings, either by improved cultivation, or by access to the produce of more fertile lands in other parts of the globe. In such countries, the government may take any moderate portion of the capital of the country and expend it as revenue, without affecting the national wealth: the whole being either drawn from that portion of the annual savings which would otherwise be sent abroad, or being subtracted from the unproductive expenditure of individuals for the next year or two, since every million spent makes room for another million to be saved before reaching the overflowing point. When the object in view is worth the sacrifice of such an amount of the expenditure that furnishes the daily enjoyments of the people, the only well-grounded economical objection against taking the necessary funds directly from capital, consists of the inconveniences attending the process of raising a revenue by taxation, to pay the interest of a debt.

The same considerations enable us to throw aside as unworthy of regard, one of the common arguments against emigration as a means of relief for the labouring class. Emigration, it is said, can do no good to the labourers, if, in order to defray the cost, as much must be taken away from the capital of the country as from its population. That anything like this proportion could require to be abstracted from capital for the purpose even of the most extensive colonization, few, I should think, would now assert: but even on that untenable supposition, it is an error to suppose that no benefit would be conferred on the labouring class. If one-tenth of the labouring people of England were transferred to the colonies, and along with them one-tenth of the circulating capital of the country, either wages, or profits, or both, would be greatly benefited by the diminished pressure of capital and population upon the fertility of the land. There would be a reduced demand for food: the inferior arable lands would be thrown out of cultivation, and would become pasture; the superior would be cultivated less highly, but with a greater proportional return; food would be lowered in price, and though money wages would not rise, every labourer would be considerably improved in circumstances, an improvement which, if no increased stimulus to population and fall of wages ensued, would be permanent; while if there did, profits would rise, and accumulation start forward so as to repair the loss of capital. The landlords alone would sustain some loss of income; and even they, only if colonization went to the length of actually diminishing capital and population, but not if it merely carried off the annual increase.

§ 2. From the same principles we are now able to arrive at a final conclusion respecting the effects which machinery, and generally the sinking of capital for a productive purpose, produce upon the immediate and ultimate interests of the labouring class. The characteristic property of this class of industrial improvements is the conversion of circulating capital into fixed: and it was shown in the first Book,* that in a country where capital accumulates slowly, the introduction of machinery, permanent improvements of land, and the like, might be, for the time, extremely injurious; since the capital so employed might be directly taken from the wages fund, the subsistence of the people and the employment for labour curtailed, and the gross annual produce of the country actually diminished. But in a country of great annual savings and low

* Supra, p. 94.

profits, no such effects need be apprehended. Since even the emigration of capital, or its unproductive expenditure, or its absolute waste, do not in such a country, if confined within any moderate bounds, at all diminish the aggregate amount of the wages fund— still less can the mere conversion of a like sum into fixed capital, which continues to be productive, have that effect. It merely draws off at one orifice what was already flowing out at another ; or if not, the greater vacant space left in the reservoir does but cause a greater quantity to flow in. Accordingly, in spite of the mis- chievous derangements of the money-market which were at one time occasioned by the sinking of great sums in railways, I was never able to agree with those who apprehended mischief, from this source, to the productive resources of the country.[1] Not on the absurd ground (which to any one acquainted with the elements of the subject needs no confutation) that railway expenditure is a mere transfer of capital from hand to hand, by which nothing is lost or destroyed. This is true of what is spent in the purchase of the land ; a portion too of what is paid to parliamentary agents, counsel, engineers, and surveyors is saved by those who receive it, and becomes capital again : but what is laid out in the *bonâ fide* con- struction of the railway itself is lost and gone ; when once expended, it is incapable of ever being paid in wages or applied to the mainte- nance of labourers again ; as a matter of account, the result is that so much food and clothing and tools have been consumed, and the country has got a railway instead. But what I would urge is, that sums so applied are mostly a mere appropriation of the annual over- flowing which would otherwise have gone abroad, or been thrown away unprofitably, leaving neither a railway nor any other tangible result. The railway gambling of 1844 and 1845 probably saved the country from a depression of profits and interest, and a rise of all public and private securities, which would have engendered still wilder speculations, and when the effects came afterwards to be complicated by the scarcity of food, would have ended in a still more formidable crisis than was experienced in the years immediately following. In the poorer countries of Europe, the rage for railway construction might have had worse consequences than in England, were it not that in those countries such enterprises are in a great measure carried on by foreign capital. The railway operations of

[1] [The present form of this sentence dates from the 6th ed. (1865). The original [1848] text ran : " the great sums in process of being sunk," and " I cannot agree."]

the various nations of the world may be looked upon as a sort of competition for the overflowing capital of the countries where profit is low and capital abundant, as England and Holland.   The English railway speculations are a struggle to keep our annual increase of capital at home ; those of foreign countries are an effort to obtain it.*

It already appears from these considerations, that the conversion of circulating capital into fixed, whether by railways, or manufactories, or ships, or machinery, or canals, or mines, or works of drainage and irrigation, is not likely, in any rich country, to diminish the gross produce or the amount of employment for labour.   How much then is the case strengthened, when we consider that these transformations of capital are of the nature of improvements in production, which, instead of ultimately diminishing circulating capital, are the necessary conditions of its increase, since they alone enable a country to possess a constantly augmenting capital without reducing profits to the rate which would cause accumulation to stop.   There is hardly any increase of fixed capital which does not enable the country to contain eventually a larger circulating capital than it otherwise could possess and employ within its own limits ; for there is hardly any creation of fixed capital which, when it proves successful, does not cheapen the articles on which wages are habitually expended.   All capital sunk in the permanent improvement of land lessens the cost of food and materials ; almost all improvements in machinery cheapen the labourer's clothing or lodging, or the tools with which these are made ; improvements in locomotion, such as railways, cheapen to the consumer all things which are brought from a distance.   All these improvements make the labourers better off with the same money wages, better off if they do not increase their rate of multiplication.   But if they do, and wages consequently fall, at least profits rise, and, while accumulation receives an immediate stimulus, room is made for a greater amount of capital before a sufficient motive arises for sending it abroad.   Even the improvements which do not cheapen the things consumed by the labourer, and which, therefore, do not raise profits nor retain capital in the country, nevertheless, as we have seen, by lowering the minimum of profit for which people will ultimately

---

* [1852] It is hardly needful to point out how fully the remarks in the text have been verified by subsequent facts.   The capital of the country, far from having been in any degree impaired by the large amount sunk in railway construction, was soon again overflowing.

consent to save, leave an ampler margin than previously for eventual accumulation, before arriving at the stationary state.

We may conclude, then, that improvements in production, and emigration of capital to the more fertile soils and unworked mines of the uninhabited or thinly peopled parts of the globe, do not, as appears to a superficial view, diminish the gross produce and the demand for labour at home; but, on the contrary, are what we have chiefly to depend on for increasing both, and are even the necessary conditions of any great or prolonged augmentation of either. Nor is it any exaggeration to say, that within certain, and not very narrow, limits, the more capital a country like England expends in these two ways, the more she will have left.

CHAPTER VI

§ 1. THE preceding chapters comprise the general theory of the economical progress of society, in the sense in which those terms are commonly understood ; the progress of capital, of population, and of the productive arts. But in contemplating any progressive movement, not in its nature unlimited, the mind is not satisfied with merely tracing the laws of the movement ; it cannot but ask the further question, to what goal ? Towards what ultimate point is society tending by its industrial progress ? When the progress ceases, in what condition are we to expect that it will leave mankind ?

It must always have been seen, more or less distinctly, by political economists, that the increase of wealth is not boundless : that at the end of what they term the progressive state lies the stationary state, that all progress in wealth is but a postponement of this, and that each step in advance is an approach to it. We have now been led to recognise that this ultimate goal is at all times near enough to be fully in view ; that we are always on the verge of it, and that if we have not reached it long ago, it is because the goal itself flies before us. The richest and most prosperous countries would very soon attain the stationary state, if no further improvements were made in the productive arts, and if there were a suspension of the overflow of capital from those countries into the uncultivated or ill-cultivated regions of the earth.

This impossibility of ultimately avoiding the stationary state— this irresistible necessity that the stream of human industry should finally spread itself out into an apparently stagnant sea—must have been, to the political economists of the last two generations, an unpleasing and discouraging prospect ; for the tone and tendency of their speculations goes completely to identify all that is economically desirable with the progressive state, and with that alone.

With Mr. M'Culloch, for example, prosperity does not mean a large production and a good distribution of wealth, but a rapid increase of it; his test of prosperity is high profits; and as the tendency of that very increase of wealth, which he calls prosperity, is towards low profits, economical progress, according to him, must tend to the extinction of prosperity. Adam Smith always assumes that the condition of the mass of the people, though it may not be positively distressed, must be pinched and stinted in a stationary condition of wealth, and can only be satisfactory in a progressive state. The doctrine that, to however distant a time incessant struggling may put off our doom, the progress of society must " end in shallows and in miseries," far from being, as many people still believe, a wicked invention of Mr. Malthus, was either expressly or tacitly affirmed by his most distinguished predecessors, and can only be successfully combated on his principles. Before attention had been directed to the principle of population as the active force in determining the remuneration of labour, the increase of mankind was virtually treated as a constant quantity; it was, at all events, assumed that in the natural and normal state of human affairs population must constantly increase, from which it followed that a constant increase of the means of support was essential to the physical comfort of the mass of mankind. The publication of Mr. Malthus' *Essay* is the era from which better views of this subject must be dated; and notwithstanding the acknowledged errors of his first edition, few writers have done more than himself, in the subsequent editions, to promote these juster and more hopeful anticipations.

Even in a progressive state of capital, in old countries, a conscientious or prudential restraint on population is indispensable, to prevent the increase of numbers from outstripping the increase of capital, and the condition of the classes who are at the bottom of society from being deteriorated. Where there is not, in the people, or in some very large proportion of them, a resolute resistance to this deterioration—a determination to preserve an established standard of comfort—the condition of the poorest class sinks, even in a progressive state, to the lowest point which they will consent to endure. The same determination would be equally effectual to keep up their condition in the stationary state, and would be quite as likely to exist. Indeed, even now, the countries in which the greatest prudence is manifested in the regulating of population are often those in which capital increases least rapidly. Where there is an indefinite prospect of employment for increased numbers, there is apt to appear less necessity for prudential restraint. If it were evident that a new hand could not obtain employment but by displacing, or succeeding to, one already employed, the combined influences of prudence and public opinion might in some measure be relied on for restricting the coming generation within the numbers necessary for replacing the present.

§ 2. I cannot, therefore, regard the stationary state of capital and wealth with the unaffected aversion so generally manifested towards it by political economists of the old school. I am inclined to believe that it would be, on the whole, a very considerable improvement on our present condition. I confess I am not charmed with the ideal of life held out by those who think that the normal state of human beings is that of struggling to get on ; that the trampling, crushing, elbowing, and treading on each other's heels, which form the existing type of social life, are the most desirable lot of human kind, or anything but the disagreeable symptoms of one of the phases of industrial progress. It may be a necessary stage in the progress of civilization, and those European nations which have hitherto been so fortunate as to be preserved from it, may have it yet to undergo. It is an incident of growth, not a mark of decline, for it is not necessarily destructive of the higher aspirations and the heroic virtues ; as America, in her great civil war, has proved to the world, both by her conduct as a people and by numerous splendid individual examples, and as England, it is to be hoped, would also prove, on an equally trying and exciting occasion.[1] But it is not a kind of social perfection which philanthropists to come will feel any very eager desire to assist in realizing. Most fitting, indeed, is it, that while riches are power, and to grow as rich as possible the universal object of ambition, the path to its attainment should be open to all, without favour or partiality. But the best state for human nature is that

---

[1] [This and the preceding sentence replaced in the 6th ed. (1865) the following passage of the original [1848] text : " The northern and middle states of America are a specimen of this stage of civilization in very favourable circumstances ; having, apparently, got rid of all social injustices and inequalities that affect persons of Caucasian race and of the male sex, while the proportion of population to capital and land is such as to ensure abundance to every able-bodied member of the community who does not forfeit it by misconduct. They have the six points of Chartism, and they have no poverty : and all that these advantages seem to have done for them is that the life of the whole of one sex is devoted to dollar-hunting, and of the other to breeding dollar-hunters." Into this, however, had been inserted since the 2nd ed. (1849), after " done for them," the parenthesis " (notwithstanding some incipient signs of a better tendency)."]

in which, while no one is poor, no one desires to be richer, nor has any reason to fear being thrust back by the efforts of others to push themselves forward.

That the energies of mankind should be kept in employment by the struggle for riches, as they were formerly by the struggle of war, until the better minds succeed in educating the others into better things, is undoubtedly more desirable than that they should rust and stagnate. While minds are coarse they require coarse stimuli, and let them have them. In the mean time, those who do not accept the present very early stage of human improvement as its ultimate type, may be excused for being comparatively indifferent to the kind of economical progress which excites the congratulations of ordinary politicians ; the mere increase of production and accumulation. For the safety of national independence it is essential that a country should not fall much behind its neighbours in these things. But in themselves they are of little importance, so long as either the increase of population or anything else prevents the mass of the people from reaping any part of the benefit of them. I know not why it should be matter of congratulation that persons who are already richer than any one needs to be, should have doubled their means of consuming things which give little or no pleasure except as representative of wealth ; or that numbers of individuals should pass over, every year, from the middle classes into a richer class, or from the class of the occupied rich to that of the unoccupied. It is only in the backward countries of the world that increased production is still an important object : in those most advanced, what is economically needed is a better distribution, of which one indispensable means is a stricter restraint on population. Levelling institutions, either of a just or of an unjust kind, cannot alone accomplish it ; they may lower the heights of society, but they cannot, of themselves, permanently [1] raise the depths.

On the other hand, we may suppose this better distribution of property attained, by the joint effect of the prudence and frugality of individuals, and of a system of legislation favouring equality of fortunes, so far as is consistent with the just claim of the individual to the fruits, whether great or small, of his or her own industry. We may suppose, for instance (according to the suggestion thrown out in a former chapter [*]), a limitation of the sum which any one person

---

[1] [" Permanently " inserted in 2nd ed. (1849) ; " of themselves " in 3rd (1852).]

[*] Supra, pp. 227-9.

may acquire by gift or inheritance to the amount sufficient to constitute a moderate independence. Under this twofold influence society would exhibit these leading features : a well-paid and affluent body of labourers ; no enormous fortunes, except what were earned and accumulated during a single lifetime ; but a much larger body of persons than at present, not only exempt from the coarser toils, but with sufficient leisure, both physical and mental, from mechanical details, to cultivate freely the graces of life, and afford examples of them to the classes less favourably circumstanced for their growth. This condition of society, so greatly preferable to the present, is not only perfectly compatible with the stationary state, but, it would seem, more naturally allied with that state than with any other.

There is room in the world, no doubt, and even in old countries, for a great increase of population, supposing the arts of life to go on improving, and capital to increase. But even if innocuous, I confess I see very little reason for desiring it. The density of population necessary to enable mankind to obtain, in the greatest degree, all the advantages both of co-operation and of social intercourse, has, in all the most populous countries, been attained. A population may be too crowded, though all be amply supplied with food and raiment. It is not good for man to be kept perforce at all times in the presence of his species. A world from which solitude is extirpated is a very poor ideal. Solitude, in the sense of being often alone, is essential to any depth of meditation or of character ; and solitude in the presence of natural beauty and grandeur, is the cradle of thoughts and aspirations which are not only good for the individual, but which society could ill do without. Nor is there much satisfaction in contemplating the world with nothing left to the spontaneous activity of nature ; with every rood of land brought into cultivation, which is capable of growing food for human beings ; every flowery waste or natural pasture ploughed up, all quadrupeds or birds which are not domesticated for man's use exterminated as his rivals for food, every hedgerow or superfluous tree rooted out, and scarcely a place left where a wild shrub or flower could grow without being eradicated as a weed in the name of improved agriculture. If the earth must lose that great portion of its pleasantness which it owes to things that the unlimited increase of wealth and population would extirpate from it, for the mere purpose of enabling it to support a larger, but not a better or a happier population, I sincerely hope, for the sake of posterity, that they will be content to be stationary, long before necessity compels them to it.

It is scarcely necessary to remark that a stationary condition of capital and population implies no stationary state of human improvement. There would be as much scope as ever for all kinds of mental culture, and moral and social progress ; as much room for improving the Art of Living, and much more likelihood of its being improved, when minds ceased to be engrossed by the art of getting on. Even the industrial arts might be as earnestly and as successfully cultivated, with this sole difference, that instead of serving no purpose but the increase of wealth, industrial improvements would produce their legitimate effect, that of abridging labour. Hitherto [1848] it is questionable if all the mechanical inventions yet made have lightened the day's toil of any human being. They have enabled a greater population to live the same life of drudgery and imprisonment, and an increased number of manufacturers and others to make fortunes. They have increased the comforts of the middle classes. But they have not yet begun to effect those great changes in human destiny, which it is in their nature and in their futurity to accomplish. Only when, in addition to just institutions, the increase of mankind shall be under the deliberate guidance of judicious foresight, can the conquests made from the powers of nature by the intellect and energy of scientific discoverers become the common property of the species, and the means of improving and elevating the universal lot.

CHAPTER VII

ON THE PROBABLE FUTURITY OF THE LABOURING CLASSES

§ 1. The observations in the preceding chapter had for their principal object to deprecate a false ideal of human society. Their applicability to the practical purposes of present times consists in moderating the inordinate importance attached to the mere increase of production, and fixing attention upon improved distribution, and a large remuneration of labour, as the two desiderata. Whether the aggregate produce increases absolutely or not, is a thing in which, after a certain amount has been obtained, neither the legislator nor the philanthropist need feel any strong interest : but, that it should increase relatively to the number of those who share in it, is of the utmost possible importance ; and this, (whether the wealth of mankind be stationary, or increasing at the most rapid rate ever known in an old country,) must depend on the opinions and habits of the most numerous class, the class of manual labourers.

[1] When I speak, either in this place or elsewhere, of " the labouring classes," or of labourers as a " class," I use those phrases in compliance with custom, and as descriptive of an existing, but by no means a necessary or permanent, state of social relations. I do not recognise as either just or salutary, a state of society in which there is any " class " which is not labouring ; any human beings, exempt

[1] [This paragraph replaced in the 3rd ed. (1852) the following paragraph of the original (1848) text :

" The economic condition of that class, and along with it of all society, depends therefore essentially on its moral and intellectual, and that again on its social, condition. In the details of political economy, general views of society and politics are out of place ; but in the more comprehensive inquiries it is impossible to exclude them ; since the various leading departments of human life do not develop themselves separately, but each depends on all, or is profoundly modified by them. To obtain any light on the great economic question of the future, which gives the chief interest to the phenomena of the present—the physical condition of the labouring classes—we must consider it, not separately, but in conjunction with all other points of their condition."]

from bearing their share of the necessary labours of human life, except those unable to labour, or who have fairly earned rest by previous toil. So long, however, as the great social evil exists of a non-labouring class, labourers also constitute a class, and may be spoken of, though only provisionally, in that character.

Considered in its moral and social aspect, the state of the labouring people has latterly been a subject of much more speculation and discussion than formerly ; and the opinion that it is not now what it ought to be, has become very general. The suggestions which have been promulgated, and the controversies which have been excited, on detached points rather than on the foundations of the subject, have put in evidence the existence of two conflicting theories, respecting the social position desirable for manual labourers. The one may be called the theory of dependence and protection, the other that of self-dependence.

According to the former theory, the lot of the poor, in all things which affect them collectively, should be regulated *for* them, not *by* them. They should not be required or encouraged to think for themselves, or give to their own reflection or forecast an influential voice in the determination of their destiny. It is supposed to be the duty of the higher classes to think for them, and to take the responsibility of their lot, as the commander and officers of an army take that of the soldiers composing it. This function, it is contended, the higher classes should prepare themselves to perform conscientiously, and their whole demeanour should impress the poor with a reliance on it, in order that, while yielding passive and active obedience to the rules prescribed for them, they may resign themselves in all other respects to a trustful *insouciance*, and repose under the shadow of their protectors. The relation between rich and poor, according to this theory (a theory also applied to the relation between men and women) [1] should be only partly authoritative ; it should be amiable, moral, and sentimental : affectionate tutelage on the one side, respectful and grateful deference on the other. The rich should be *in loco parentis* to the poor, guiding and restraining them like children. Of spontaneous action on their part there should be no need. They should be called on for nothing but to do their day's work, and to be moral and religious. Their morality and religion should be provided for them by their superiors, who should see them properly taught it, and should do all that is necessary

---

[1] [Parenthesis inserted in 3rd ed. (1852).]

to ensure their being, in return for labour and attachment, properly fed, clothed, housed, spiritually edified, and innocently amused.

This is the ideal of the future, in the minds of those whose dissatisfaction with the Present assumes the form of affection and regret towards the Past.[1] Like other ideals, it exercises an unconscious influence on the opinions and sentiments of numbers who never consciously guide themselves by any ideal. It has also this in common with other ideals, that it has never been historically realised. It makes its appeal to our imaginative sympathies in the character of a restoration of the good times of our forefathers. But no times can be pointed out in which the higher classes of this or any other country performed a part even distantly resembling the one assigned to them in this theory. It is an idealization, grounded on the conduct and character of here and there an individual. All privileged and powerful classes, as such, have used their power in the interest of their own selfishness, and have indulged their self-importance in despising, and not in lovingly caring for, those who were, in their estimation, degraded, by being under the necessity of working for their benefit. I do not affirm that what has always been must always be, or that human improvement has no tendency to correct the intensely selfish feelings engendered by power ; but though the evil may be lessened, it cannot be eradicated, until the power itself is withdrawn. This, at least, seems to me undeniable, that long before the superior classes could be sufficiently improved to govern in the tutelary manner supposed, the inferior classes would be too much improved to be so governed.

I am quite sensible of all that is seductive in the picture of society which this theory presents. Though the facts of it have no prototype in the past, the feelings have. In them lies all that there is of reality in the conception. As the idea is essentially repulsive of a society only held together by the relations and feelings arising out of pecuniary interests, so there is something naturally attractive in a form of society abounding in strong personal attachments and disinterested self-devotion. Of such feelings it must be admitted that the relation of protector and protected has hitherto been the richest source. The strongest attachments of human beings in general, are towards the things or the persons that stand between them and some dreaded evil. Hence, in an age of lawless violence and insecurity, and general hardness and roughness of

---

[1] [Carlyle's *Past and Present* appeared in 1843.]

manners, in which life is beset with dangers and sufferings at every step, to those who have neither a commanding position of their own, nor a claim on the protection of some one who has—a generous giving of protection, and a grateful receiving of it, are the strongest ties which connect human beings ; the feelings arising from that relation are their warmest feelings ; all the enthusiasm and tenderness of the most sensitive natures gather round it ; loyalty on the one part and chivalry on the other are principles exalted into passions. I do not· desire to depreciate these qualities.[1]   The error lies in not perceiving, that these virtues and sentiments, like the clanship and the hospitality of the wandering Arab, belong emphatically to a rude and imperfect state of the social union ; and that the feelings between protector and protected, whether between kings and subjects, rich and poor, or men and women,[2] can no longer have this beautiful and endearing character where there are no longer any serious dangers from which to protect.   What is there in the present state of society to make it natural that human beings, of ordinary strength and courage, should glow with the warmest gratitude and devotion in return for protection ?   The laws protect them, wherever the laws do not criminally fail in their duty.[3]   To be under the power of some one, instead of being as formerly the sole condition of safety, is now, speaking generally, the only situation which exposes to grievous wrong.   The so-called protectors are now the only persons against whom, in any ordinary circumstances, protection is needed.   The brutality and tyranny with which every police report is filled, are those of husbands to wives, of parents to children.   That the law does not prevent these atrocities, that it is only now making a first timid attempt to repress and punish them, is no matter of necessity, but the deep disgrace of those by whom the laws are made and administered.   No man or woman who either possesses or is able to earn an independent livelihood,

---

[1] [In the 3rd ed. (1852) " qualities " replaced " virtues," and the next sentence was omitted : " That the most beautiful developments of feeling and character often grow out of the most painful, and in many respects the most hardening and corrupting, circumstances of our condition, is now, and probably will long be, one of the chief stumbling-blocks both in the theory and in the practice of morals and education."]

[2] [" Whether . . . women " inserted in 3rd ed.]

[3] [So since the 3rd ed.   The original text ran : " The laws protect them : where laws do not reach, manners and opinion shield them."   The reference to police reports and atrocities later in the paragraph was introduced in the 3rd ed., and " the protection of the law " was expanded into the protection which the law " ought to give."]

requires any other protection than that which the law could and ought to give. This being the case, it argues great ignorance of human nature to continue taking for granted that relations founded on protection must always subsist, and not to see that the assumption of the part of protector, and of the power which belongs to it, without any of the necessities which justify it, must engender feelings opposite to loyalty.

Of the working men, at least in the more advanced countries of Europe, it may be pronounced certain, that the patriarchal or paternal system of government is one to which they will not again be subject. That question was decided, when they were taught to read, and allowed access to newspapers and political tracts ; when dissenting preachers were suffered to go among them, and appeal to their faculties and feelings in opposition to the creeds professed and countenanced by their superiors ; when they were brought together in numbers, to work socially under the same roof ; when railways enabled them to shift from place to place, and change their patrons and employers as easily as their coats ; when they were encouraged to seek a share in the government, by means of the electoral franchise.[1] The working classes have taken their interests into their own hands, and are perpetually showing that they think the interests of their employers not identical with their own, but opposite to them. Some among the higher classes flatter themselves that these tendencies may be counteracted by moral and religious education : but they have let the time go by for giving an education which can serve their purpose. The principles of the Reformation have reached as low down in society as reading and writing, and the poor will not much longer accept morals and religion of other people's prescribing. I speak more particularly of this country, especially the town population, and the districts of the most scientific agriculture or the highest wages, Scotland and the north of England. Among the more inert and less modernized agricultural population of the southern counties, it might be possible for the gentry to retain, for some time longer, something of the ancient deference and submission of the poor, by bribing them with high wages and constant employment ; by insuring them support, and never requiring them to do anything which they do not like. But these are two conditions which never have been combined, and never can be, for long together. A guarantee of subsistence can only be practically kept up, when

---

[1] [The last clause inserted in 3rd ed. (1852).]

work is enforced and superfluous multiplication restrained by at least a moral compulsion. It is then, that the would-be revivers of old times which they do not understand, would feel practically in how hopeless a task they were engaged. The whole fabric of patriarchal or seignorial influence, attempted to be raised on the foundation of caressing the poor, would be shattered against the necessity of enforcing a stringent Poor-law.

§ 2. It is on a far other basis that the well-being and well-doing of the labouring people must henceforth rest. The poor have come out of leading-strings, and cannot any longer be governed or treated like children. To their own qualities must now be commended the care of their destiny. Modern nations will have to learn the lesson, that the well-being of a people must exist by means of the justice and self-government, the δικαιοσύνη and σωφροσύνη, of the individual citizens. The theory of dependence attempts to dispense with the necessity of these qualities in the dependent classes. But now, when even in position they are becoming less and less dependent, and their minds less and less acquiescent in the degree of dependence which remains, the virtues of independence are those which they stand in need of. Whatever advice, exhortation, or guidance is held out to the labouring classes, must henceforth be tendered to them as equals, and accepted by them with their eyes open. The prospect of the future depends on the degree in which they can be made rational beings.

There is no reason to believe that prospect other than hopeful. The progress indeed has hitherto been, and still is, slow. But there is a spontaneous education going on in the minds of the multitude, which may be greatly accelerated and improved by artificial aids. The instruction obtained from newspapers and political tracts may not be the most solid kind of instruction, but it is an immense improvement upon none at all. [1] What it does for a people has been admirably exemplified during the cotton crisis, in the case of the Lancashire spinners and weavers, who have acted with the consistent good sense and forbearance so justly applauded, simply because, being readers of newspapers, they understood the causes of the calamity which had befallen them, and knew that it was in no way imputable either to their employers or to the Government. It is not certain that their conduct would have been as rational and

---

[1] [This and the following sentence were inserted in the 6th ed. (1865).]

exemplary, if the distress had preceded the salutary measure of
fiscal emancipation which gave existence to the penny press. The
institutions for lectures and discussion, the collective deliberations
on questions of common interest, the trade unions, the political
agitation, all serve to awaken public spirit, to diffuse variety of
ideas among the mass, and to excite thought and reflection in the
more intelligent. Although the too early attainment of political
franchises by the least educated class might retard, instead of
promoting, their improvement, there can be little doubt that it has
been greatly stimulated by the attempt to acquire them.[1] In the
meantime, the working classes are now part of the public ; in all
discussions on matters of general interest they, or a portion of them,
are now partakers ; all who use the press as an instrument may, if it
so happens, have them for an audience ; the avenues of instruction
through which the middle classes acquire such ideas as they have,
are accessible to, at least, the operatives in the towns. With these
resources, it cannot be doubted that they will increase in intelligence,
even by their own unaided efforts ; while there is reason to hope
that great improvements both in the quality and quantity of school
education will be effected by the exertions either of government or
of individuals, and that the progress of the mass of the people in
mental cultivation, and in the virtues which are dependent on it,
will take place more rapidly, and with fewer intermittences and
aberrations, than if left to itself.

From this increase of intelligence, several effects may be confidently anticipated. First : that they will become even less
willing than at present to be led and governed, and directed into
the way they should go, by the mere authority and *prestige* of
superiors. If they have not now, still less will they have hereafter,
any deferential awe, or religious principle of obedience, holding
them in mental subjection to a class above them. The theory of
dependence and protection will be more and more intolerable to
them, and they will require that their conduct and condition shall
be essentially self-governed. It is, at the same time, quite possible

---

[1] [Here was omitted from the 2nd ed. (1849) the following passage of the
1st (1848) : " It is of little importance that some of them may, at a certain
stage of their progress, adopt mistaken opinions. Communists are already
numerous, and are likely to increase in number ; but nothing tends more to
the mental development of the working classes than that all the questions
which Communism raises should be largely and freely discussed by them ;
nothing could be more instructive than that some should actually form communities, and try practically what it is to live without the institution of
property."]

that they may demand, in many cases, the intervention of the legislature in their affairs, and the regulation by law of various things which concern them, often under very mistaken ideas of their interest. Still, it is their own will, their own ideas and suggestions, to which they will demand that effect should be given, and not rules laid down for them by other people. It is quite consistent with this, that they should feel respect for superiority of intellect and knowledge, and defer much to the opinions, on any subject, of those whom they think well acquainted with it. Such deference is deeply grounded in human nature ; but they will judge for themselves of the persons who are and are not entitled to it.

§ 3. It appears to me impossible but that the increase of intelligence, of education, and of the love of independence among the working classes, must be attended with the corresponding growth of the good sense which manifests itself in provident habits of conduct, and that population, therefore, will bear a gradually diminishing ratio to capital and employment. This most desirable result would be much accelerated by another change, which lies in the direct line of the best tendencies of the time ; the opening of industrial occupations freely to both sexes. The same reasons which make it no longer necessary that the poor should depend on the rich, make it equally unnecessary that women should depend on men ; and the least which justice requires is that law and custom should not enforce dependence (when the correlative protection has become superfluous) by ordaining that a woman, who does not happen to have a provision by inheritance, shall have scarcely any means open to her of gaining a livelihood, except as a wife and mother. Let women who prefer that occupation, adopt it ; but that there should be no option, no other *carrière* possible for the great majority of women, except in the humbler departments of life, is a flagrant social injustice.[1] The ideas and institutions by

---

[1] [The original (1848) text ran : " that there should be no other *carrière* possible . . . is one of those social injustices which call loudest for remedy. Among the salutary consequences of correcting it, one of the most probable would be a great diminution," &c.

In the 2nd ed. (1849) the following sentence was inserted after " remedy " : " The ramifications of this subject are far too numerous and intricate to be pursued here. The social and political equality of the sexes is not a question of economical detail, but one of principle, so intimately connected with all the more vital points of human improvement, that none of them can be thoroughly discussed independently of it. But for this very reason it cannot be disposed of by way of parenthesis, in a treatise devoted to other subjects.

which the accident of sex is made the groundwork of an inequality
of legal rights, and a forced dissimilarity of social functions, must
ere long be recognised as the greatest hindrance to moral, social, and
even intellectual improvement. On the present occasion I shall
only indicate, among the probable consequences of the industrial and
social independence of women, a great diminution of the evil of
over population It is by devoting one-half of the human species
to that exclusive function, by making it fill the entire life of one
sex and interweave itself with almost all the objects of the other,
that the animal instinct in question is nursed into the disproportionate preponderance which it has hitherto exercised in human
life.

§ 4. The political consequences of the increasing power and
importance of the operative classes, and of the growing ascendancy
of numbers, which, even in England and under the present institutions, is rapidly giving to the will of the majority at least a negative
voice in the acts of government, are too wide a subject to be discussed
in this place. But, confining ourselves to economical considerations,
and notwithstanding the effect which improved intelligence in the
working classes, together with just laws, may have in altering the
distribution of the produce to their advantage, I cannot think that
they will be permanently contented with the condition of labouring
for wages as their ultimate state.[1] They may be willing to pass

It is sufficient for the immediate purpose, to point out, among the probable
consequences of the industrial and social independence of women, a great
diminution," &c.

This was replaced in the 3rd ed. (1852) by the present text, and a note
attached : " It is truly disgraceful that in a woman's reign not one step has
been made by law towards removing even the smallest portion of the existing
injustice to women. The brutal part of the populace can still maltreat, not to
say kill, their wives, with the next thing to impunity ; and as to civil and
social *status*, in framing a new reform bill for the extension of the elective
franchise, the opportunity was not taken for so small a recognition of something like equality of rights, as would have been made by admitting to the
suffrage women of the same class and the same householding and tax-paying
qualifications as the men who already possess it."

Further comments were added to the note in the 4th ed. (1857) : " Mr.
Fitzroy's Act for the Better Protection of Women and Children against Assaults,
is a well-meant though inadequate attempt to wipe off the former reproach.
The second is more flagrant than ever, *another* Reform Bill having been since
presented, largely extending the franchise among many classes of men, but
leaving all women in their existing state of political as well as social servitude."

The whole note disappeared in the 5th ed. (1862).]

[1] [At this point was omitted from the 3rd ed. (1852) the following passage
of the original (1848) text : " To work at the bidding and for the profit of

through the class of servants in their way to that of employers ; but not to remain in it all their lives. To begin as hired labourers, then after a few years to work on their own account, and finally employ others, is the normal condition of labourers in a new country, rapidly increasing in wealth and population, like America or Australia. [1] But in an old and fully peopled country, those who begin life as labourers for hire, as a general rule, continue such to the end, unless they sink into the still lower grade of recipients of public charity. In the present stage of human progress, when ideas of equality are daily spreading more widely among the poorer classes, and can no longer be checked by anything short of the entire suppression of printed discussion and even of freedom of speech, it is not to be expected that the division of the human race into two hereditary classes, employers and employed, can be permanently maintained. The relation is nearly as unsatisfactory to the payer of wages as to the receiver. If the rich regard the poor, as by a kind of natural law, their servants and dependents, the rich in their turn are regarded as a mere prey and pasture for the poor ; the subject of demands and expectations wholly indefinite, increasing in extent with every concession made to them. [2] The total absence of regard for justice or fairness in the relations between the two, is as marked on the side of the employed as on that of the employers. We look in vain among the working classes in general for the just pride which will choose to give good work for good wages ; for the most part, their sole endeavour is to receive as much, and return as little in the shape of service, as possible. It will sooner or later become insupportable to the employing classes, to live in close and hourly contact with persons whose interests and feelings are in hostility to them. Capitalists are almost as much interested as labourers in

another, without any interest in the work—the price of their labour being adjusted by hostile competition, one side demanding as much and the other paying as little as possible—is not, even wheñ wages are high, a satisfactory state to human beings of educated intelligence, who have ceased to think themselves naturally inferior to those whom they serve."]

[1] [The rest of the paragraph, with the exception of the two sentences indicated in the next note, replaced in the 3rd ed. (1852) the following single sentence of the original text : " But something else is required when wealth increases slowly, or has reached the stationary state, when positions, instead of being more mobile, would tend to be much more permanent than at present, and the condition of any portion of mankind could only be desirable, if made desirable from the first."]

[2] [This and the following sentence are an expansion in the 4th ed. (1857) of the clause in the 3rd : " while the return given in the shape of service is sought to be reduced to the lowest minimum."]

placing the operations of industry on such a footing, that those who labour for them may feel the same interest in the work, which is felt by those who labour on their own account.

The opinion expressed in a former part of this treatise respecting small landed properties and peasant proprietors, may have made the reader anticipate that a wide diffusion of property in land is the resource on which I rely for exempting at least the agricultural labourers from exclusive dependence on labour for hire. Such, however, is not my opinion. I indeed deem that form of agricultural economy to be most groundlessly cried down, and to be greatly preferable, in its aggregate effects on human happiness, to hired labour in any form in which it exists at present; because the prudential check to population acts more directly, and is shown by experience to be more efficacious; and because, in point of security, of independence, of exercise of any other than the animal faculties, the state of a peasant proprietor is far superior to that of an agricultural labourer in this or in any other old country. Where the former system already exists, and works on the whole satisfactorily, I should regret, in the present state of human intelligence, to see it abolished in order to make way for the other, under a pedantic notion of agricultural improvement as a thing necessarily the same in every diversity of circumstances. In a backward state of industrial improvement, as in Ireland, I should urge its introduction, in preference to an exclusive system of hired labour; as a more powerful instrument for raising a population from semi-savage listlessness and recklessness, to persevering industry and prudent calculation.

But a people who have once adopted the large system of production, either in manufactures or in agriculture, are not likely to recede from it; and when population is kept in due proportion to the means of support, it is not desirable that they should. Labour is unquestionably more productive on the system of large industrial enterprises; the produce, if not greater absolutely, is greater in proportion to the labour employed: the same number of persons can be supported equally well with less toil and greater leisure; which will be wholly an advantage, as soon as civilization and improvement have so far advanced, that what is a benefit to the whole shall be a benefit to each individual composing it.[1] And in the moral aspect of

---

[1] [The remainder of this paragraph (subjected subsequently to verbal alterations) replaced in the 3rd ed. (1852) the following original (1848) text:
" The problem is, to obtain the efficiency and economy of production on a large

the question, which is still more important than the economical, something better should be aimed at as the goal of industrial improvement, than to disperse mankind over the earth in single families, each ruled internally, as families now are, by a patriarchal despot, and having scarcely any community of interest, or necessary mental communion, with other human beings. The domination of the head of the family over the other members, in this state of things, is absolute ; while the effect on his own mind tends towards concentration of all interests in the family, considered as an expansion of self, and absorption of all passions in that of exclusive possession, of all cares in those of preservation and acquisition. As a step out of the merely animal state into the human, out of reckless abandonment to brute instincts into prudential foresight and self-government, this moral condition may be seen without displeasure. But if public spirit, generous sentiments, or true justice and equality are desired, association, not isolation, of interests, is the school in which these excellences are nurtured. The aim of improvement should be not solely to place human beings in a condition in which they will be able to do without one another, but to enable them to work with or for one another in relations not involving dependence. Hitherto there has been no alternative for those who lived by their labour, but that of labouring either each for himself alone, or for a master. But the civilizing and improving influences of association, and the efficiency and economy of production on a large scale, may be obtained without dividing the producers into two parties with hostile interests and feelings, the many who do the work being mere servants under the command of the one who supplies the funds, and having no interest of their own in the enterprise except to earn their wages with as little labour as possible. The speculations and discussions of the last fifty years, and the events of the last thirty,[1] are abundantly conclusive on this point. If the improvement which even triumphant military despotism has only retarded, not stopped, shall continue its course,[2] there can be little doubt that the *status* of hired labourers will gradually tend to confine itself to the

scale, without dividing the producers into two parties with hostile interests, employers and employed, the many who do the work being mere servants under the command of the one who supplies the funds, and having no interest of their own in the enterprise, except to fulfil their contract and earn their wages.'']

[1] [3rd ed. (1852), '' five ''; 4th (1857), '' ten ''; 6th (1865), '' twenty ''; 7th (1871), '' thirty.'']

[2] [So since 5th ed. (1862). In the 3rd and 4th, '' Unless the military despotism now triumphant on the Continent should succeed in its nefarious attempts to throw back the human mind.'']

description of workpeople whose low moral qualities render them unfit for anything more independent: and that the relation of masters and workpeople will be gradually superseded by partnership, in one of two forms : in some cases, association of the labourers with the capitalist ; in others, and perhaps finally in all,[1] association of labourers among themselves.

[2] § 5. The first of these forms of association has long been practised, not indeed as a rule, but as an exception. In several departments of industry there are already cases in which every one who contributes to the work, either by labour or by pecuniary resources, has a partner's interest in it, proportional to the value of his contribution. It is already a common practice to remunerate those in whom peculiar trust is reposed, by means of a percentage on the profits : and cases exist in which the principle is, with excellent success, carried down to the class of mere manual labourers. In the American ships trading to China, it has long been the

[1] [In 3rd ed. : " temporarily and in some cases . . ., in other cases and finally in all." In 5th ed. (1862) : " perhaps finally in all." In 6th ed. (1865), " temporarily " omitted.]

[2] [The following passage, inserted at this point in the 2nd ed. (1849) disappeared from the 3rd (1852).

" § 5. It is this feeling, of the nature of the problem " (see supra, p. 761, n. 1), " almost as much as despair of the improvement of the condition of the labouring masses by other means, which has caused so great a multiplication of projects for the ' organization of industry ' by the extension and development of the co-operative or joint stock principle : some of the more conspicuous of which have been described and characterized in an early chapter of this work. It is most desirable that all these schemes should have opportunity and encouragement to test their capabilities by actual experiment. There are, in almost all of them, many features, in themselves well worth submitting to that test ; while, on the other hand, the exaggerated expectations entertained by large and growing multitudes in all the principal nations of the world, concerning what it is possible, in the present state of human improvement, to effect by such means, have no chance of being corrected except by a fair trial in practice. The French Revolution of February 1848, at first seemed to have opened a fair field for the trial of such experiments, on a perfectly safe scale, and with every advantage that could be derived from the countenance of a government which sincerely desired their success. It is much to be regretted that these prospects have been frustrated, and that the reaction of the middle class against anti-property doctrines has engendered for the present an unreasoning and undiscriminating antipathy to all ideas, however harmless or however just, which have the smallest savour of Socialism. This is a disposition of mind, of which the influential classes, both in France and elsewhere, will find it necessary to divest themselves. Socialism has now become irrevocably one of the leading elements in European politics. The questions raised by it will not be set at rest by merely refusing to listen to it ; but only by a more and more complete realization of the ends which Socialism aims at, not neglecting its means so far as they can be employed with advantage."]

custom for every sailor to have an interest in the profits of the voyage; and to this has been ascribed the general good conduct of those seamen, and the extreme rarity of any collision between them and the government or people of the country. An instance in England, not so well known as it deserves to be, is that of the Cornish miners. " In Cornwall the mines are worked strictly on the system of joint adventure ; gangs of miners contracting with the agent, who represents the owner of the mine, to execute a certain portion of a vein and fit the ore for market, at the price of so much in the pound of the sum for which the ore is sold. These contracts are put up at certain regular periods, generally every two months, and taken by a voluntary partnership of men accustomed to the mine. This system has its disadvantages, in consequence of the uncertainty and irregularity of the earnings, and consequent necessity of living for long periods on credit ; but it has advantages which more than counterbalance these drawbacks. It produces a degree of intelligence, independence, and moral elevation, which raise the condition and character of the Cornish miner far above that of the generality of the labouring class. We are told by Dr. Barham, that ' they are not only, as a class, intelligent for labourers, but men of considerable knowledge.' Also, that ' they have a character of independence, something American, the system by which the contracts are let giving the takers entire freedom to make arrangements among themselves ; so that each man feels, as a partner in his little firm, that he meets his employers on nearly equal terms.' . . . With this basis of intelligence and independence in their character, we are not surprised when we hear that ' a very great number of miners are now located on possessions of their own, leased for three lives or ninety-nine years, on which they have built houses ; ' or that ' 281,541*l*. are deposited in savings banks in Cornwall, of which two-thirds are estimated to belong to miners.' " *

Mr. Babbage, who also gives an account of this system, observes that the payment to the crews of whaling ships is governed by a similar principle ; and that " the profits arising from fishing with nets on the south coasts of England are thus divided : one-half the produce belongs to the owner of the boat and net ; the other half is divided in equal portions between the persons using it, who are also bound to assist in repairing the net when required." Mr.

* This passage is from the Prize Essay on the *Causes and Remedies of National Distress*, by Mr. Samuel Laing. The extracts which it includes are from the Appendix to the *Report of the Children's Employment Commission.*

Babbage has the great merit of having pointed out the practicability, and the advantage, of extending the principle to manufacturing industry generally.* [1]

* *Economy of Machinery and Manufactures,* 3rd edition, ch. 26.
[1] [The long quotation from Babbage, which appeared in the 1st and 2nd eds. (1848, 1849), disappeared from the 3rd (1852) : " I venture to quote the principal part of his observations on the subject.

' The general principles on which the proposed system is founded, are—1st. That a considerable part of the wages received by each person employed, should depend on the profits made by the establishment ; and 2nd. That every person connected with it should derive more advantage from applying any improvement he might discover, to the factory in which he is employed, than he could by any other course.

' It would be difficult to prevail on the large capitalist to enter upon any system, which would change the division of the profits arising from the employment of his capital in setting skill and labour in action ; any alteration, therefore, must be expected rather from the small capitalist, or from the higher class of workmen, who combine the two characters ; and to these latter classes, whose welfare will be first affected, the change is most important. I shall therefore first point out the course to be pursued in making the experiment ; and then, taking a particular branch of trade as an illustration, I shall examine the merits and defects of the proposed system as applied to it.

' Let us suppose, in some large manufacturing town, ten or twelve of the most intelligent and skilful workmen to unite, whose characters for sobriety and steadiness are good, and are well known among their class. Such persons will each possess some small portion of capital ; and let them join with one or two others who have raised themselves into the class of small master-manufacturers, and therefore possess rather a larger portion of capital. Let these persons, after well considering the subject, agree to establish a manufactory of fire-irons and fenders ; and let us suppose that each of the ten workmen can command forty pounds, and each of the small capitalists possesses two hundred pounds : thus they have a capital of 800*l.* with which to commence business, and for the sake of simplifying, let us further suppose the labour of each of these twelve persons to be worth two pounds a week. One portion of their capital will be expended in procuring the tools necessary for their trade, which we shall take at 400*l.*, and this must be considered as their fixed capital. The remaining 400*l.* must be employed as circulating capital, in purchasing the iron with which their articles are made, in paying the rent of their workshops, and in supporting themselves and their families until some portion of it is replaced by the sale of the goods produced.

' Now the first question to be settled is, what proportion of the profit should be allowed for the use of capital, and what for skill and labour ? It does not seem possible to decide this question by any abstract reasoning : if the capital supplied by each partner is equal, all difficulty will be removed ; if otherwise, the proportion must be left to find its level, and will be discovered by experience ; and it is probable that it will not fluctuate much. Suppose it to be agreed that the capital of 800*l.* shall receive the wages of one workman. At the end of each week, every workman is to receive one pound as wages, and one pound is to be divided amongst the owners of the capital. After a few weeks the returns will begin to come in ; and they will soon become nearly uniform. Accurate accounts should be kept of every expense and of all the sales ; and at the end of each week the profit should be divided. A certain portion should be laid aside as a reserved fund, another portion for repair of the tools, and the remainder being divided into thirteen parts, one of these parts would be divided amongst

¹ Some attention has been excited by an experiment of this nature, commenced above thirty years ago by a Paris tradesman,

the capitalists and one belong to each workman. Thus each man would, in ordinary circumstances, make up his usual wages of two pounds weekly. If the factory went on prosperously, the wages of the men would increase ; if the sales fell off, they would be diminished. It is important that every person employed in the establishment, whatever might be the amount paid for his services, whether he act as labourer or porter, or as the clerk who keeps the accounts, or as book-keeper employed for a few hours once a week to superintend them, should receive one-half of what his service is worth in fixed salary, the other part varying with the success of the undertaking.

' The result of such arrangements in a factory would be,

' 1.   That every person engaged in it would have a direct interest in its prosperity ; since the effect of any success, or falling off, would almost immediately produce a corresponding change in his own weekly receipts.

' 2.   Every person concerned in the factory would have an immediate interest in preventing any waste or mismanagement in all the departments.

' 3.   The talents of all connected with it would be strongly directed to improvement in every department.

' 4.   None but workmen of high character and qualifications could obtain admission into such establishments, because when any additional hands were required, it would be the common interest of all to admit only the most respectable and skilful, and it would be far less easy to impose upon a dozen workmen than upon the single proprietor of a factory.

' 5.   When any circumstance produced a glut in the market, more skill would be directed to diminishing the cost of production ; and a portion of the time of the men might then be occupied in repairing and improving their tools, for which a reserved fund would pay, thus checking present, and at the same time facilitating future, production.

' 6.   Another advantage, of no small importance, would be the total removal of all real or imaginary causes for combinations.   The workmen and the capitalist would so shade into each other—would so evidently have a common interest, and their difficulties and distresses would be mutually so well understood, that instead of combining to oppress one another, the only combination which could exist would be a most powerful union between both parties to overcome their common difficulties.

' One of the difficulties attending such a system is, that capitalists would at first fear to embark in it, imagining that the workmen would receive too large a share of the profits : and it is quite true that the workmen would have a larger share than at present : but at the same time, it is presumed the effect of the whole system would be, that the total profits of the establishment being much increased, the smaller proportion allowed to capital under this system would yet be greater in actual amount, than that which results to it from the larger share in the system now existing.

' A difficulty would occur also in discharging workmen who behaved ill, or who were not competent to their work ; this would arise from their having a certain interest in the reserved fund, and perhaps from their possessing a certain portion of the capital employed ; but without entering into detail, it may be observed, that such cases might be determined on by meetings of the whole establishment ; and that if the policy of the laws favoured such establishments, it would scarcely be more difficult to enforce just regulations than it now is to enforce some which are unjust, by means of combinations either amongst the masters or the men.' ']

¹ [In the original ed. (1849) this paragraph began thus : " In this imaginary

a house-painter, M. Leclaire,* and described by him in a pamphlet published in the year 1842. M. Leclaire, according to his statement, employs on an average two hundred workmen, whom he pays in the usual manner, by fixed wages or salaries. He assigns to himself, besides interest for his capital, a fixed allowance for his labour and responsibility as manager. At the end of the year, the surplus profits are divided among the body, himself included, in the proportion of their salaries.† The reasons by which M. Leclaire was led to adopt this system are highly instructive. Finding the conduct of his workmen unsatisfactory, he first tried the effect of giving higher wages, and by this he managed to obtain a body of excellent workmen, who would not quit his service for any other. " Having thus succeeded " (I quote from an abstract of the pamphlet in *Chambers' Journal*,‡) " in producing some sort of stability in the arrangement of his establishment, M. Leclaire expected, he says, to enjoy greater peace of mind. In this, however, he was disappointed. So long as he was able to superintend everything himself, from the general concerns of his business down to its minutest details, he did enjoy a certain satisfaction ; but from the moment that, owing to the increase of his business, he found that he could be nothing more than the centre from which orders were issued, and to which reports were brought in, his former anxiety and discomfort returned upon him." He speaks lightly of the other sources of anxiety to which a tradesman is subject, but describes as an incessant cause of vexation the losses arising from the misconduct of workmen. An employer " will find workmen whose indifference to his interest is such that they do not perform two-thirds of the amount of work which they are capable of ; hence the continual fretting of masters,

<hr />

case " described by Babbage, see supra, p. 766, n. 1, " it is supposed that each labourer brings some small portion of capital into the concern : but the principle is equally applicable to the ordinary case in which the whole capital belongs to an individual capitalist. An application of it to such a case is actually in progress by a Paris tradesman," &c. The present text, but with " about ten years ago," dates from the 3rd ed. (1852). The 4th, 5th, and 6th eds. (1857, 1862, 1865) have " about sixteen years ago " ; the 7th (1871) " above thirty."]

   * His establishment is 11, Rue Saint Georges.

   † [1849] It appears, however, that the workmen whom M. Leclaire had admitted to this participation of profits, were only a portion (rather less than half) of the whole number whom he employed. This is explained by another part of his system. M. Leclaire pays the full market rate of wages to all his workmen. The share of profit assigned to them is, therefore, a clear addition to the ordinary gains of their class, which he very laudably uses as an instrument of improvement, by making it the reward of desert, or the recompense for peculiar trust.

   ‡ For September 27, 1845.

who, seeing their interests neglected, believe themselves entitled to suppose that workmen are constantly conspiring to ruin those from whom they derive their livelihood. If the journeyman were sure of constant employment, his position would in some respects be more enviable than that of the master, because he is assured of a certain amount of day's wages, which he will get whether he works much or little. He runs no risk, and has no other motive to stimulate him to do his best than his own sense of duty. The master, on the other hand, depends greatly on chance for his returns : his position is one of continual irritation and anxiety. This would no longer be the case to the same extent, if the interests of the master and those of the workmen were bound up with each other, connected by some bond of mutual security, such as that which would be obtained by the plan of a yearly division of profits."

Even in the first year during which M. Leclaire's experiment was in complete operation, the success was remarkable. Not one of his journeymen who worked as many as three hundred days, earned in that year less than 1500 francs, and some considerably more. His highest rate of daily wages being four francs, or 1200 francs for 300 days, the remaining 300 francs, or 12*l.*, must have been the smallest amount which any journeyman, who worked that number of days, obtained as his proportion of the surplus profit. M. Leclaire describes in strong terms the improvement which was already manifest in the habits and demeanour of his workmen, not merely when at work, and in their relations with their employer, but at other times and in other relations, showing increased respect both for others and for themselves. [1] M. Chevalier, in a work published in 1848,* stated on M. Leclaire's authority, that the increased zeal of the workpeople continued to be a full compensation to him, even in a pecuniary sense, for the share of profit which he renounced in their favour. [2] And M. Villiaumé, in 1857,† observes :—" Though he has always kept himself free from the frauds which are but too frequent in his profession, he has always been able to hold his ground against competition, and has acquired a handsome competency in spite of the relinquishment of so great a portion of his profits. Assuredly he has been only thus successful because the unusual activity of his workpeople, and the watch which they kept over one

[1] [Added in 2nd ed. (1849).]
* *Lettres sur l'Organisation du Travail*, by Michel Chevalier, lettre xiv.
[2] [The concluding sentence of this paragraph, together with the next paragraph and the examples quoted in the note, were added in the 5th ed. (1862).]
† *Nouveau Traité d'Economie Politique.*

another, have compensated him for the sacrifice made in contenting himself with only a share of the gain." *

The beneficent example set by M. Leclaire has been followed, with brilliant success, by other employers of labour on a large scale at Paris ; and I annex, from the work last referred to (one of the ablest of the many able treatises on political economy produced by the present generation of the political economists of France), some signal examples of the economical and moral benefit arising from this admirable arrangement.†

* [1865] At the present time M. Leclaire's establishment is conducted on a somewhat altered system, though the principle of dividing the profits is maintained. There are now three partners in the concern : M. Leclaire himself, one other person (M. Defournaux), and a Provident Society (Société de Secours Mutuels), of which all persons in his employment are the members. (This Society owns an excellent library, and has scientific, technical, and other lectures regularly delivered to it.) Each of the three partners has 100,000 francs invested in the concern ; M. Leclaire having advanced to the Provident Society as much as was necessary to supply the original insufficiency of their own funds. The partnership, on the part of the Society, is limited ; on that of M. Leclaire and M. Defournaux, unlimited. These two receive 6000 francs (240*l.*) per annum each as wages of superintendence. Of the annual profits they receive half, though owning two-thirds of the capital. The remaining half belongs to the employés and workpeople ; two-fifths of it being paid to the Provident Society, and the other three-fifths divided among the body. M. Leclaire, however, now reserves to himself the right of deciding who shall share in the distribution, and to what amount ; only binding himself never to retain any part, but to bestow whatever has not been awarded to individuals, on the Provident Society. It is further provided that in case of the retirement of both the private partners, the goodwill and plant shall become, without payment, the property of the Society.

† " In March 1847, M. Paul Dupont, the head of a Paris printing-office, had the idea of taking his workmen into partnership by assigning to them a tenth of the profits. He habitually employs three hundred ; two hundred of them on piece work, and a hundred by the day. He also employs a hundred extra hands, who are not included in the association. The portion of profit which falls to the workmen does not bring them in, on the average, more than the amount of a fortnight's wages ; but they receive their ordinary pay according to the rates established in all the great Paris printing offices ; and have, besides, the advantage of medical attendance in illness at the expense of the association, and a franc and a half per day while incapacitated for work. The workmen cannot draw out their share of profit except on quitting the association. It is left at interest (sometimes invested in the public funds), and forms an accumulating reserve of savings for its owners.

" M. Dupont and his partners find this association a source of great additional profit to them : the workmen, on their side, congratulate themselves daily on the happy idea of their employer. Several of them have by their exertions caused the establishment to gain a gold medal in 1849, and an honorary medal at the Universal Exhibition of 1855 : some even have personally received the recompense of their inventions and of their labours. Under an ordinary employer, these excellent people would not have had leisure to prosecute their inventions, unless by leaving the whole honour to one who was not the author of them : but, associated as they were, if the employer had been unjust, two hundred men would have obliged him to repair the wrong.

[1] Until the passing of the Limited Liability Act, it was held that an arrangement similar to M. Leclaire's would have been impossible in England, as the workmen could not, in the previous state of the law, have been associated in the profits, without being liable for losses. One of the many benefits of that great legislative improvement has been to render partnerships of this description possible, and we may now expect to see them carried into practice. Messrs. Briggs, of the Whitwood and Methley collieries, near Normanton in Yorkshire, have taken the first step. They now work these mines by a company, two-thirds of the capital of which they themselves continue to hold, but undertake, in the allotment of the remaining third, to give the preference to the " officials and operatives employed

" I have visited this establishment, and have been able to see for myself the improvement which the partnership produces in the habits of the workpeople.

" M. Gisquet, formerly Prefect of Police, has long been the proprietor of an oil manufactory at St. Denis, the most important one in France next to that of M. Darblay, of Corbeil. When in 1848 he took the personal management of it, he found workmen who got drunk several days in the week, and during their work sung, smoked, and sometimes quarrelled with one another. Many unsuccessful attempts had been made to alter this state of things : he accomplished it by forbidding his workmen to get drunk on working days, on pain of dismissal, and at the same time promising to share with them, by way of annual gratuity, five per cent of his net profits, in shares proportioned to wages, which are fixed at the current rates. From that time the reformation has been complete, and he is surrounded by a hundred workmen full of zeal and devotion. Their comforts have been increased by what they have ceased to spend in drink, and what they gain by their punctuality at work. The annual gratuity has amounted, on the average, to the equivalent of six weeks' wages.

" M. Beslay, a member of the Chamber of Deputies from 1830 to 1839, and afterwards of the Constituent Assembly, has founded an important manufactory of steam engines at Paris, in the Faubourg of the Temple. He has taken his workpeople into partnership ever since the beginning of 1847, and the contract of association is one of the most complete which have been made between employers and workpeople."

The practical sagacity of Chinese emigrants long ago suggested to them, according to the report of a recent visitor to Manilla, a similar constitution of the relation between an employer and labourers. " In these Chinese shops " (at Manilla) " the owner usually engages all the activity of his countrymen employed by him in them, by giving each of them a share in the profits of the concern, or in fact by making them all small partners in the business, of which he of course takes care to retain the lion's share, so that while doing good for him by managing it well, they are also benefiting themselves. To such an extent is this principle carried that it is usual to give even their coolies a share in the profits of the business in lieu of fixed wages, and the plan appears to suit their temper well ; for although they are in general most complete eye-servants when working for a fixed wage, they are found to be most industrious and useful ones when interested even for the smallest share."—McMicking's *Recollections of Manilla and the Philippines* during 1848, 1849, and 1850, p. 24.

[1] [This paragraph was added in the 6th ed. (1865) ; and it was said that Messrs. Briggs " have issued a proposal to work " ; changed to " They now work ' &c., in the 7th ed. (1871).]

in the concern ; " and, what is of still greater importance, whenever the annual profit exceeds 10 per cent, one-half the excess is divided amQng the workpeople and employés, whether shareholders or not, in proportion to their earnings during the year. It is highly honourable to these important employers of labour to have initiated a system so full of benefit both to the operatives employed and to the general interest of social improvement : and they express no more than a just confidence in the principle when they say, that " the adoption of the mode of appropriation thus recommended would, it is believed, add so great an element of success to the undertaking as to increase rather than diminish the dividend to the shareholders." [1]

[2] § 6. The form of association, however, which if mankind continue to improve, must be expected in the end to predominate,

[1] [For the abandonment of the Briggs experiment in 1875 see Schloss, *Methods of Industrial Remuneration* (2nd ed.), p. 282.]

[2] [The opening paragraphs of this section and the account of French cooperative societies which follows were added in the 3rd ed. (1852). At the same time the following paragraph and section of the original (1848) text were removed :

"Under this system," of M. Leclaire, " as well as under that recommended by Mr. Babbage, the labourers are, in reality, taken into partnership with their employer. Bringing nothing into the common concern but their labour, while he brings not only his labour of direction and superintendence but his capital also, they have justly a smaller share of the profits; this, however, is a matter of private arrangement in all partnerships ; one partner has a large, another a small share, according to their agreement, grounded on the equivalent which is given by each. The essence, however, of a partnership is obtained, since each benefits by all things that are beneficial to the concern, and loses by all which are injurious. It is, in the fullest sense, the common concern of all.

" § 6. To this principle, in whatever form embodied, it seems to me that futurity has to look for obtaining the benefits of co-operation, without constituting the numerical majority of the co-operators an inferior caste. The objections that apply to a ' co-operative society,' in the Communist or Owenite sense, in which, by force of giving to every member of the body a share in the common interest, no one has a greater share in it than another, are not applicable to what is now suggested. It is expedient that those, whose performance of the part assigned to them is the most essential to the common end, should have a greater amount of personal interest in the issue of the enterprise. If those who supply the funds, and incur the whole risk of the undertaking, obtained no greater reward or more influential voice than the rest, few would practise the abstinence through which those funds are acquired and kept in existence. Up to a certain point, however, the principle of giving to every person concerned an interest in the profits is an actual benefit to the capitalist, not only (as M. Leclaire has testified) in point of ease and comfort, but even in pecuniary advantage. And after the point of greatest benefit to the employers has been attained, the participation of the labourers may be carried somewhat further without any material abatement from that maximum of benefit. At what point, in each employment of capital, this ultimatum is to be found, will one day be known and understood from experience : and up to that point it is not

is not that which can exist between a capitalist as chief, and work-people without a voice in the management, but the association of the labourers themselves on terms of equality, collectively owning the capital with which they carry on their operations, and working under managers elected and removable by themselves. So long as this idea remained in a state of theory, in the writings of Owen or of Louis Blanc, it may have appeared, to the common modes of judgment, incapable of being realized, and not likely to be tried unless by seizing on the existing capital, and confiscating it for the benefit of the labourers; which is even now imagined by many persons, and pretended by more, both in England and on the Continent, to be the meaning and purpose of Socialism. But there is a capacity of exertion and self-denial in the masses of mankind, which is never known but on the rare occasions on which it is appealed to in the name of some great idea or elevated sentiment. Such an appeal was made by the French Revolution of 1848. For the first time it then seemed to the intelligent and generous of the working classes of a great nation that they had obtained a government who sincerely desired the freedom and dignity of the many, and who did not look upon it as their natural and legitimate state to be instruments of production, worked for the benefit of the possessors of capital. Under this encouragement, the ideas sown by Socialist writers, of an emancipation of labour to be effected by means of association, throve and fructified; and many working people came to the resolution, not only that they would work for one another, instead of working for a master tradesman or manufacturer, but that they would also free themselves, at whatever cost of labour or privation, from the necessity of paying, out of the produce of their industry,

unreasonable to expect that the partnership principle will be, at no very distant time, extended.

"The value of this ' organization of industry,' for healing the widening and embittering feud between the class of labourers and the class of capitalists, must, I think, impress itself by degrees on all who habitually reflect on the condition and tendencies of modern society. I cannot conceive how any such person can persuade himself that the majority of the community will for ever, or even for much longer, consent to hew wood and draw water all their lives in the service and for the benefit of others; or can doubt, that they will be less and less willing to co-operate as subordinate agents in any work, when they have no interest in the result, and that it will be more and more difficult to obtain the best work-people, or the best services of any work-people, except on conditions similar in principle to those of M. Leclaire. Although, therefore, arrangements of this sort are now in their infancy, their multiplication and growth, when once they enter into the general domain of popular discussion, are among the things which may most confidently be expected."]

a heavy tribute for the use of capital ; that they would extinguish this tax, not by robbing the capitalists of what they or their predecessors had acquired by labour and preserved by economy, but by honestly acquiring capital for themselves. If only a few operatives had attempted this arduous task, or if, while many attempted it, a few only had succeeded, their success might have been deemed to furnish no argument for their system as a permanent mode of industrial organization. But, excluding all the instances of failure, there exist, or existed a short time ago,[1] upwards of a hundred successful, and many eminently prosperous, associations of operatives in Paris alone, besides a considerable number in the departments. An instructive sketch of their history and principles has been published, under the title of *L'Association Ouvrière Industrielle et Agricole*, by H. Feugueray : and as it is frequently affirmed in English newspapers that the associations at Paris have failed, by writers who appear to mistake the predictions of their enemies at their first formation for the testimonies of subsequent experience, I think it important to show by quotations from M. Feugueray's volume, strengthened by still later testimonies,[2] that these representations are not only wide of the truth, but the extreme contrary of it.

The capital of most of the associations was originally confined to the few tools belonging to the founders, and the small sums which could be collected from their savings, or which were lent to them by other workpeople as poor as themselves. In some cases, however, loans of capital were made to them by the republican government : but the associations which obtained these advances, or at least which obtained them before they had already achieved success, are, it appears, in general by no means the most prosperous. The most striking instances of prosperity are in the case of those who have had nothing to rely on but their own slender means and the small loans of fellow-workmen, and who lived on bread and water while they devoted the whole surplus of their gains to the formation of a capital.

" Often," says M. Feugueray,* " there was no money at all in hand, and no wages could be paid. The goods did not go off, the payments did not come in, bills could not get discounted, the warehouse of materials was empty ; they had to submit to priva-

---

[1] [So since 4th ed. (1857). Originally, in 3rd ed. (1852), " a few months ago."]
[2] [" Strengthened " &c., added in 5th ed. (1862).]
* P. 112.

tion, to reduce all expenses to the minimum, to live sometimes on bread and water. . . . It is at the price of these hardships and anxieties that men who began with hardly any resource but their good will and their hands, succeeded in creating customers, in acquiring credit, forming at last a joint capital, and thus founding associations whose futurity now seems to be assured."

I will quote at length the remarkable history of one of these associations.*

" The necessity of a large capital for the establishment of a pianoforte manufactory was so fully recognised in the trade, that in 1848 the delegates of several hundred workmen who had combined to form a great association, solicited from the government a subvention of 300,000 francs [12,000*l.*], being a tenth part of the whole sum voted by the National Assembly. I remember that, as one of the Commission charged with the distribution of the fund, I tried in vain for two hours to convince the two delegates with whom the Commission conferred, that their request was exorbitant. They answered imperturbably, that their trade was a peculiar one ; that the association could only have a chance of success on a very large scale and with a considerable capital ; that 300,000 francs were the smallest sum which could suffice them, and that they could not reduce the demand by a single sou. The Commission refused.

" Now, after this refusal, the project of a great association being abandoned, what happened was this. Fourteen workmen, and it is singular that among them was one of the two delegates, resolved to set up by themselves a pianoforte-making association. The project was hazardous on the part of men who had neither money nor credit : but faith does not reason—it acts.

" Our fourteen men therefore went to work, and I borrow from an excellent article by M. Cochut in the *National*, the accuracy of which I can attest, the following account of their first proceedings.

" Some of them, who had worked on their own account, brought with them in tools and materials the value of about 2000 francs [80*l.*]. There was needed besides a circulating capital. Each member, not without difficulty, managed to subscribe 10 francs [8*s.*]. A certain number of workmen not interested in the society gave their adhesion by bringing small contributions. On March 10, 1849, a sum of 229½ francs [9*l.* 3*s.* 7½*d.*] having been realized, the association was declared constituted.

" This sum was not even sufficient for setting up, and for the

* Pp. 113–6.

small expenses required from day to day for the service of a workshop. There being nothing left for wages, nearly two months elapsed without their touching a farthing. How did they subsist during this interval ? As workmen live when out of employment, by sharing the portion of a comrade who is in work ; by selling or pawning bit by bit the few articles they possess.

" They had executed some orders. They received the payment on the 4th of May. That day was for them like a victory at the opening of a campaign, and they determined to celebrate it. After paying all debts that had fallen due, the dividend of each member amounted to 6 francs 61 centimes. They agreed to allow to each 5 francs [4s.] on account of his wages, and to devote the surplus to a fraternal repast. The fourteen shareholders, most of whom had not tasted wine for a year past, met, along with their wives and children. They expended 32 sous [1s. 4d.] per family. This day is still spoken of in their workshops with an emotion which it is difficult not to share.

" For a month longer it was necessary to content themselves with the receipt of five francs per week. In the course of June a baker, either from love of music or on speculation, offered to buy a piano, paying for it in bread. The bargain was made at the price of 480 francs. It was a piece of good luck to the association. They had now at least what was indispensable. They determined not to reckon the bread in the account of wages. Each ate according to his appetite, or rather to that of his family ; for the married shareholders were allowed to take away bread freely for their wives and children.

" Meanwhile the association, being composed of excellent workmen, gradually surmounted the obstacles and privations which had embarrassed its starting. Its account-books offer the best proof of the progress which its pianos had made in the estimation of buyers. From August 1849 the weekly contingent rises to 10, 15, and 20 francs per week ; and this last sum does not represent all their profits, each partner having left in the common stock much more than he received from it. Indeed it is not by the sum which the member receives weekly that his situation can be judged, but by the share acquired in the ownership of a property already considerable. The following was the position of the association when it took stock on the 30th December 1850.

" At this period the number of shareholders was thirty-two. Large workshops and warehouses, rented for 2000 francs, were no longer sufficient for the business.

	Frs.	Cents.
Independent of tools, valued at	5,922	60
They possessed in goods and especially in materials, the value of	22,972	28
They had in cash	1,021	10
,, in bills	3,540	
There was due to them *	5,861	90
They had thus to their credit	39,317	88
Against this are only to be debited 4737 francs 86 centimes due to creditors, and 1650 francs to eighty adherents ; † in all	6,387	86
Remaining	32,930	02
	[£1319	4s.]

which formed their indivisible capital and the reserve of the individual members. At this period the association had 76 pianos
under construction, and received more orders than they could
execute."

From a later report we learn that this society subsequently
divided itself into two separate associations, one of which, in 1854,
already possessed a circulating capital of 56,000 francs ‡ [2240l.]. In
1863 its total capital was 6520l.

* " The last two items consisted of safe securities, nearly all of which have
since been realised."

† " These adherents are workmen of the trade, who subscribed small sums
to the association at its commencement : a portion of them were reimbursed
in the beginning of 1851. The sum due to creditors has also been much reduced : on the 23rd of April it only amounted to 113 francs 59 centimes."

‡ Article by M. Cherbuliez on " Operative Associations," in the *Journal
des Economistes* for November 1860.

I subjoin, from M. Villiaumé and M. Cherbuliez, detailed particulars of other
eminently successful experiments by associated workpeople.

" We will first cite," says M. Cherbuliez, " as having attained its object
and arrived at a definite result, the Association Remquet, of the Rue Garancière,
at Paris, whose founder, in 1848, was a foreman in M. Renouard's printing
establishment. That firm being under the necessity of winding up, he proposed
to his fellow-workmen to join with him in continuing the enterprise on their
own account, asking a subvention from the government to cover the purchase-
money of the business and the first expenses. Fifteen of them accepted the
proposal, and formed an association, whose statutes fixed the wages for every
kind of work, and provided for the gradual formation of a working capital by
a deduction of 25 per cent. from all wages and salaries, on which deduction
no dividend or interest was to be allowed during the ten years that the association was intended to last. Remquet asked and obtained for himself the
entire direction of the enterprise, at a very moderate fixed salary. At the

The same admirable qualities by which the associations were carried through their early struggles, maintained them in their increasing prosperity. Their rules of discipline, instead of being more lax, are stricter than those of ordinary workshops ; but being rules self-imposed, for the manifest good of the community, and not for the convenience of an employer regarded as having an

winding up, the entire profits were to be divided among all the members, proportionally to their share in the capital, that is, to the work they had done. A subvention of 80,000 francs was granted by the State. not without great difficulty, and on very onerous conditions. In spite of these conditions, and of the unfavourable circumstances resulting from the political situation of the country, the association prospered so well, that on the winding up, after repaying the advance made by the State, it was in possession of a clear capital of 155,000 francs [6200*l*.], the division of which gave on the average between ten and eleven thousand francs to each partner ; 7000 being the smallest and 18,000 the largest share.

"The Fraternal Association of Working Tinmen and Lampmakers had beeu founded in March 1848 by 500 operatives, comprising nearly the whole body of the trade.   This first attempt, inspired by unpractical ideas, not having survived the fatal days of June, a new association was formed of more modest proportions.   Originally composed of forty members, it commenced business in 1849 with a capital composed of the subscriptions of its members, without asking for a subvention. After various vicissitudes, which reduced the number of partners to three, then brought it back to fourteen, then again sunk it to three, it ended by keeping together forty-six members, who quietly remodelled their statutes in the points which experience had shown to be faulty, and their number having been raised by successive steps to 100, they possessed, in 1858, a joint property of 50,000 francs, and were in a condition to divide annually 20,000 francs.

" The Association of Operative Jewellers, the oldest of all, had been founded in 1831 by eight workmen, with a capital of 200 francs [8*l*.] derived from their united savings.   A subvention of 24,000 francs enabled them in 1849 greatly to extend their operations, which in 1858 had already attained the value of 140,000 francs, and gave to each partner an annual dividend equal to double his wages."

The following are from M. Villiaumé :—

" After the insurrection of June 1848, work was suspended in the Faubourg St. Antoine, which, as we know, is principally occupied by furniture-makers. Some operative arm-chair makers made an appeal to those who might be willing to combine with them.   Out of six or seven hundred composing the trade, four hundred gave in their names.   But capital being wanting, nine of the most zealous began the association with all that they possessed ; being a value of 369 francs in tools, and 135 francs 20 centimes in money.

" Their good taste, honesty, and punctuality having increased their business, they soon numbered 108 members.   They received from the State an advance of 25,000 francs, reimbursable in 14 years by way of annuity, with interest at 3¾ per cent.

" In 1857 the number of partners is 65, the auxiliaries average 100. All the partners vote at the election of a council of eight members, and a manager whose name represents the firm.   The distribution and superintendence of all the works is entrusted to foremen chosen by the manager and council.   There is a foreman to every 20 or 25 workmen.

" The payment is by the piece, at rates determined in general assembly.

opposite interest, they are far more scrupulously obeyed, and the
voluntary obedience carries with it a sense of personal worth and
dignity. With wonderful rapidity the associated workpeople have
learnt to correct those of the ideas they set out with which are in
opposition to the teaching of reason and experience. Almost all
the associations, at first, excluded piece-work, and gave equal wages

The earnings vary from 3 to 7 francs a day, according to zeal and ability. The
average is 50 francs [2*l.*] a fortnight, and no one gains much less than 40 francs
per fortnight, while many earn 80. Some of the carvers and moulders make
as much as 100 francs, being 200 francs [8*l.*] a month. Each binds himself to
work 120 hours per fortnight, equal to ten per day. By the regulations, every
hour short of the number subjects the delinquent to a penalty of 10 centimes
[one penny] per hour up to thirty hours, and 15 centimes [1½*d.*] beyond. The
object of this rule was to abolish Saint Monday, and it succeeded in its effort.
For the last two years the conduct of the members has been so good, that
fines have fallen into disuse.

"Though the partners started with only 359 francs, the value of the plant
(Rue de Chavonne, Cour St. Joseph, Faubourg St. Antoine) already in 1851
amounted to 5713 francs, and the assets of the association, debts due to them
included, to 24,000 francs. Since then the association has become still more
flourishing, having resisted all the attempts made to impede its progress. It
does the largest business, and is the most considered, of all the houses in Paris
in the trade. Its business amounts to 400,000 francs a year." Its inventory
in December 1855 showed, according to M. Villiaumé, a balance of 100,398
francs 90 centimes in favour of the association, but it possessed, he says, in
reality, 123,000 francs.

But the most important association of all is that of the Masons. "The
Association of Masons was founded August 10th, 1848. Its address is Rue St.
Victor, 155. Its number of members is 85, and its auxiliaries from three to
four hundred. There are two managers, one for the building department, the
other for the pecuniary administration : these are regarded as the ablest master-
masons in Paris, and are content with a moderate salary. This association has
lately constructed three or four of the most remarkable mansions in the metropolis. Though it does its work more economically than ordinary contractors,
yet as it has to give long credits, it is called upon for considerable advances :
it prospers, however, as is proved by the dividend of 56 per cent which has been
paid this year on its capital, including in the payment those who have associated
themselves in its operations. It consists of workmen who bring only their labour,
of others who bring their labour and a capital of some sort, and of a third class
who do not work, but contribute capital only.

"The masons, in the evening, carry on mutual instruction. They, as well
as the arm-chair makers, give medical attendance at the expense of the association,
and an allowance to its sick members. They extend their protection over every
member in every action of his life. The arm-chair makers will soon each possess
a capital of two or three thousand francs, with which to portion their daughters
or commence a reserve for future years. Of the masons, some have already
4000 francs, which are left in the common stock.

"Before they were associated, these workmen were poorly clad in jackets
and blouses ; because, for want of forethought, and still more from want of
work, they had never 60 francs beforehand to buy an overcoat. Most of them
are now as well dressed as shopkeepers, and sometimes more tastefully. For
the workman, having always a credit with the association, can get whatever
he wants by signing an order ; and the association reimburses itself by

whether the work done was more or less. Almost all have abandoned this system, and after allowing to every one a fixed minimum, sufficient for subsistence, they apportion all further remuneration according to the work done : most of them even dividing the profits at the end of the year, in the same proportion as the earnings.*

fortnightly stoppages, making him save as it were in spite of himself. Some workmen who are not in debt to the concern, sign orders payable to themselves at five months date, to resist the temptation of needless expense. They are put under stoppages of 10 francs per fortnight, and thus at the end of five months they have saved the amount."

The following table, taken by M. Cherbuliez from a work (*Die gewerblichen und wirthschaftlichen Genossenschaften der arbeitenden Classen in England, Frankreich und Deutschland*), published at Tübingen in 1860, by Professor Huber (one of the most ardent and high-principled apostles of this kind of co-operation) shows the rapidly progressive growth in prosperity of the Masons' Association up to 1858 :—

Year	Amount of business done. francs.	Profits realized. francs.
1852	45,530 . .	1,000
1853	297,208 . .	7,000
1854	344,240 . .	20,000
1855	614,694 . .	46,000
1856	998,240 . .	80,000
1857	1,330,000 . .	100,000
1858	1,231,461 . .	130,000

" Of this last dividend," says M. Cherbuliez, " 30,000 francs were taken for the reserve fund, and the remaining 100,000, divided among the shareholders, gave to each from 500 to 1500 francs, besides their wages or salaries, and their share in the fixed capital of the concern."

Of the management of the associations generally, M. Villiaumé says, " I have been able to satisfy myself personally of the ability of the managers and councils of the operative associations. The managers are far superior in intelligence, in zeal, and even in politeness, to most of the private masters in their respective trades. And among the associated workmen, the fatal habit of intemperance is gradually disappearing, along with the coarseness and rudeness which are the consequence of the too imperfect education of the class."

* Even the association founded by M. Louis Blanc, that of the tailors of Clichy, after eighteen months' trial of this system, adopted piece-work. One of the reasons given by them for abandoning the original system is well worth extracting. " Besides the vices I have mentioned, the tailors complained that it caused incessant disputes and quarrels, through the interest which each had in making his neighbours work. Their mutual watchfulness degenerated into a real slavery ; nobody had the free control of his time and his actions. These dissensions have disappeared since piece-work was introduced."—*Feugueray*, p. 88. One of the most discreditable indications of a low moral condition given of late by part of the English working classes, is the opposition to piece-work. When the payment per piece is not sufficiently high, that is a just ground of objection. But dislike to piece-work in itself, except under mistaken notions, must be dislike to justice and fairness ; a desire to cheat, by not giving work in proportion to pay. Piece-work is the perfection of contract ; and contract, in all work, and in the most minute detail—the principle of so much pay for so

It is the declared principle of most of these associations that they do not exist for the mere private benefit of the individual members, but for the promotion of the co-operative cause. With every extension, therefore, of their business, they take in additional members, not (when they remain faithful to their original plan) to receive wages from them as hired labourers, but to enter at once into the full benefits of the association, without being required to bring anything in, except their labour : the only condition imposed is that of receiving during a few years a smaller share in the annual division of profits, as some equivalent for the sacrifices of the founders. When members quit the association, which they are always at liberty to do, they carry none of the capital with them : it remains an indivisible property, of which the members for the time being have the use, but not the arbitrary disposal : by the stipulations of most of the contracts, even if the association breaks up, the capital cannot be divided, but must be devoted entire to some work of beneficence or of public utility. A fixed, and generally a consider-able, proportion of the annual profits, is not shared among the members, but added to the capital of the association, or devoted to the repayment of advances previously made to it : another portion is set aside to provide for the sick and disabled, and another to form a fund for extending the practice of association, or aiding other associations in their need. The managers are paid, like other members, for the time which is occupied in management, usually at the rate of the highest paid labour : but the rule is adhered to, that the exercise of power shall never be an occasion for profit.

Of the ability of the associations to compete successfully with individual capitalists, even at an early period of their existence, M. Feugueray said, " The associations which have been founded in the last two years " (M. Feugueray wrote in 1851) " had many obstacles to overcome ; the majority of them were almost entirely without capital : all were treading in a path previously unexplored ; they ran the risks which always threaten innovators and beginners. Nevertheless, in many of the trades in which they have been estab-lished, they are already formidable competitors of the old houses, and are even complained of on that account by a part of the bourgeoisie. This is not only true of the cooks, the lemonade sellers, and hair

much service, carried out to the utmost extremity—is the system, of all others, in the present state of society and degree of civilization, most favourable to the worker ; though most unfavourable to the non-worker who wishes to be paid for being idle.

dressers, trades the nature of which enables the associations to rely on democratic custom, but also in other trades where they have not the same advantages. One has only to consult the makers of chairs, of arm-chairs, of files, and one will learn from them if the most important establishments in their respective trades are not those of the associated workmen."

[1] The vitality of these associations must indeed be great, to have enabled about twenty of them to survive not only the anti-socialist reaction, which for the time discredited all attempts to enable workpeople to be their own employers—not only the *tracasseries* of the police, and the hostile policy of the government since the usurpation—but in addition to these obstacles, all the difficulties arising from the trying condition of financial and commercial affairs from 1854 to 1858. Of the prosperity attained by some of them even while passing through this difficult period, I have given examples which must be conclusive to all minds as to the brilliant future reserved for the principle of co-operation.*

[1] [This paragraph dates from the 5th ed. (1862), and replaced the following passages of the 3rd (1852) : " It is painful to think that these bodies, formed by the heroism and maintained by the public spirit and good sense of the working people of Paris, are in danger of being involved in the same ruin with everything free, popular, or tending to improvement in French institutions. The unprincipled adventurer who has for the present succeeded in reducing France to the political condition of Russia, knows that two or three persons cannot meet together to discuss, though it be only the affairs of a workshop, without danger to his power. He has therefore already suppressed most of the provincial associations, and many of those of Paris, and the remainder, instead of waiting to be dissolved by despotism, are, it is said, preparing to emigrate. Before this calamity overtook France, the associations could be spoken of not with the hope merely, but with positive evidence, of their being able to compete successfully with individual capitalists. ' The associations,' says M. Feugueray," &c., as in the present text, supra, p. 781.

" Though the existing associations may be dissolved, or driven to expatriate, their experience will not be lost. They have existed long enough to furnish the type of future improvement : they have exemplified the process for bringing about a change in society, which would combine the freedom and independence of the individual," &c., as in the present text, infra, p. 791.

To the 4th ed. (1857) was added this note : " It appears however from subsequent accounts that in 1854 twenty-five associations still existed in Paris and several in the provinces, and that many of these were in a most flourishing condition. This number is exclusive of Co-operative Stores, which have greatly multiplied, especially in the South of France, and are not understood to be discouraged by the Government."]

* [1865] In the last few years the co-operative movement among the French working classes has taken a fresh start. An interesting account of the Provision Association (Association Alimentaire) of Grenoble has been given in a pamphlet by M. Casimir Périer (*Les Sociétés de Co-opération*) ; and in the *Times* of November 24, 1864, we read the following passage :—" While a certain number of operatives stand out for more wages, or fewer hours of

[1] It is not in France alone that these associations have commenced a career of prosperity. To say nothing at present of Germany, Piedmont, and Switzerland (where the Konsum-Verein of Zürich is one of the most prosperous co-operative associations in Europe), England can produce cases of success rivalling even those which I have cited from France. Under the impulse commenced by Mr. Owen, and more recently propagated by the writings and personal efforts of a band of friends, chiefly clergymen and barristers, to whose noble exertions too much praise can scarcely be given, the good seed was widely sown; the necessary alterations in the English law of partnership were obtained from Parliament, on the benevolent and public-spirited initiative of Mr. Slaney; many industrial associations, and a still greater number of co-operative stores for retail purchases, were founded. Among these are already many instances of remarkable prosperity, the most signal of which are the

labour, others, who have also seceded, have associated for the purpose of carrying on their respective trades on their own account, and have collected funds for the purchase of instruments of labour. They have founded a society, 'Société Générale d'Approvisionnement et de Consommation.' It numbers between 300 and 400 members, who have already opened a 'co-operative store' at Passy, which is now within the limits of Paris. They calculate that by May next, fifteen new self-supporting associations of the same kind will be ready to commence operations; so that the number will be for Paris alone from 50 to 60."

[1] [This paragraph and the subsequent account of the Rochdale Pioneers date from the 5th ed. (1862), though the reference to the Zürich society and to Mr. Plummer in the footnote were added in the 6th ed. (1865). From the 4th (1857) disappeared the following footnote:

"Though this beneficent movement has been so seriously checked in the country in which it originated, it is rapidly spreading in those other countries which have acquired, and still retain, any political freedom. It forms already an important feature in the social improvement which is proceeding at a most rapid pace in Piedmont. In England also, under the impulse given by the writings and personal exertions of a band of friends, chiefly clergymen and barristers, the movement has made some progress. On the 15th of February, 1856, there had been registered under the Industrial and Provident Societies' Act, thirty-three associations, seventeen of which were industrial societies, the remainder being associations for co-operative consumption only: without reckoning Scotland, where, also, these associations were rapidly spreading. It is believed that all such societies are now registered under the Limited Liabilities Act. From later information it appears that the productive associations (excluding the flour mills, which partake more of the nature of stores) have fallen off in number since their first start; and their progress, in the present moral condition of the bulk of the population, cannot possibly be rapid. But those which subsist, continue to do as much business as they ever did: and there are in the North of England instances of brilliant and steadily progressive success. Co-operative stores are increasing both in number and prosperity, especially in the North; and they are the best preparation for a wider application of the principle."]

Leeds Flour Mill, and the Rochdale Society of Equitable Pioneers. Of this last association, the most successful of all, the history has been written in a very interesting manner by Mr. Holyoake ;* and the notoriety which by this and other means has been given to facts so encouraging, is causing a rapid extension of associations with similar objects in Lancashire, Yorkshire, London, and elsewhere.

The original capital of the Rochdale Society consisted of 28*l.*, brought together by the unassisted economy of about forty labourers, through the slow process of a subscription of twopence (afterwards raised to threepence) per week.   With this sum they established in 1844 a small shop, or store, for the supply of a few common articles for the consumption of their own families.   As their carefulness and honesty brought them an increase of customers and of subscribers, they extended their operations to a greater number of articles of consumption, and in a few years were able to make a large investment in shares of a Co-operative Corn Mill.   Mr. Holyoake thus relates the stages of their progress up to 1857 :—

" The Equitable Pioneers' Society is divided into seven departments : Grocery, Drapery, Butchering, Shoemaking, Clogging, Tailoring, Wholesale.

" A separate account is kept of each business, and a general account is given each quarter, showing the position of the whole.

" The grocery business was commenced, as we have related, in December 1844, with only four articles to sell.   It now includes whatever a grocer's shop should include.

" The drapery business was started in 1847, with an humble array of attractions.   In 1854 it was erected into a separate department.

" A year earlier, 1846, the Store began to sell butcher's meat, buying eighty or one hundred pounds of a tradesman in the town. After a while the sales were discontinued until 1850, when the Society had a warehouse of its own.   Mr. John Moorhouse, who has now two assistants, buys and kills for the Society three oxen, eight sheep, sundry porkers and calves, which are on the average converted into 130*l.* of cash per week.

" Shoemaking commenced in 1852.   Three men and an apprentice make, and a stock is kept on sale.

---

* *Self-help by the People—History of Co-operation in Rochdale.* An instructive account of this and other co-operative associations has also been written in the *Companion to the Almanack* for 1862, by Mr. John Plummer, of Kettering ; himself one of the most inspiring examples of mental cultivation and high principle in a self-instructed working man.

" Clogging and tailoring commenced also in this year.

" The wholesale department commenced in 1852, and marks an important development of the Pioneers' proceedings.   This department has been created for supplying any members requiring large quantities, and with a view to supply the co-operative stores of Lancashire and Yorkshire, whose small capitals do not enable them to buy in the best markets, nor command the services of what is otherwise indispensable to every store—*a good buyer*, who knows the markets and his business, who knows what, how, and where to buy. The wholesale department guarantees purity, quality, fair prices, standard weight and measure, but all on the never-failing principle, cash payment."

In consequence of the number of members who now reside at a distance, and the difficulty of serving the great increase of customers, " Branch Stores have been opened.   In 1856 the first Branch was opened in the Oldham Road, about a mile from the centre of Rochdale.   In 1857 the Castleton Branch, and another in the Whitworth Road, were established, and a fourth Branch in Pinfold."

The warehouse, of which their original Store was a single apartment, was taken on lease by the Society, very much out of repair, in 1849.   " Every part has undergone neat refitting and modest decoration, and now wears the air of a thoroughly respectable place of business.   One room is now handsomely fitted up as a news room.   Another is neatly fitted up as a library. . . . . Their news room is as well supplied as that of a London club."   It is now " free to members, and supported from the Education Fund," a fund consisting of $2\frac{1}{2}$ per cent of all the profits divided, which is set apart for educational purposes.   " The Library contains 2200 volumes of the best, and among them, many of the most expensive books published.   The Library is free.   From 1850 to 1855, a school for young persons was conducted at a charge of twopence per month.   Since 1855, a room has been granted by the Board for the use of from twenty to thirty persons, from the ages of fourteen to forty, for mutual instruction on Sundays and Tuesdays. . . .

" The corn-mill was of course rented, and stood at Small Bridge, some distance from the town—one mile and a half.   The Society have since built in the town an entirely new mill for themselves. The engine and the machinery are of the most substantial and improved kind.   The capital invested in the corn-mill is 8450*l*., of which 3731*l*. 15*s*. 2*d*. is subscribed by the Equitable Pioneers' Society.   The corn-mill employs eleven men."

At a later period they extended their operations to the staple manufacture itself. From the success of the Pioneers' Society grew not only the co-operative corn-mill, but a co-operative association for cotton and woollen manufacturing. " The capital in this department is 4000*l.*, of which sum 2042*l.* has been subscribed by the Equitable Pioneers' Society. This Manufacturing Society has ninety-six power-looms at work, and employs twenty-six men, seven women, four boys, and five girls—in all forty-two persons. . . ."

" In 1853 the Store purchased for 745*l.*, a warehouse (freehold) on the opposite side of the street, where they keep and retail their stores of flour, butcher's meat, potatoes, and kindred articles. Their committee-rooms and offices are fitted up in the same building. They rent other houses adjoining for calico and hosiery and shoe stores. In their wilderness of rooms, the visitor stumbles upon shoemakers and tailors at work under healthy conditions, and in perfect peace of mind as to the result on Saturday night. Their warehouses are everywhere as bountifully stocked as Noah's Ark, and cheerful customers literally crowd Toad Lane at night, swarming like bees to every counter. The industrial districts of England have not such another sight as the Rochdale Co-operative Store on Saturday night." * Since the disgraceful failure of the Rochdale

* " But it is not," adds Mr. Holyoake, " the brilliancy of commercial activity in which either writer or reader will take the deepest interest ; it is in the new and improved spirit animating this intercourse of trade. Buyer and seller meet as friends ; there is no overreaching on one side, and no suspicion on the other. . . . . These crowds of humble working men, who never knew before when they put good food in their mouths, whose every dinner was adulterated, whose shoes let in the water a month too soon, whose waistcoats shone with devil's dust, and whose wives wore calico that would not wash, now buy in the markets like millionaires, and as far as pureness of food goes, live like lords." Far better, probably, in that particular ; for assuredly lords are not the cus tomers least cheated in the present race of dishonest competition. " They are weaving their own stuffs, making their own shoes, sewing their own garments, and grinding their own corn. They buy the purest sugar and the best tea, and grind their own coffee. They slaughter their own cattle, and the finest beasts of the land waddle down the streets of Rochdale for the consumption of flannel weavers and cobblers. (Last year the Society advertised for a Pro-vision Agent to make purchases in Ireland, and to devote his whole time to that duty.) When did competition give poor men these advantages ? And will any man say that the moral character of these people is not improved under these influences ? The teetotallers of Rochdale acknowledge that the Store has made more sober men since it commenced than all their efforts have oeen able to make in the same time. Husbands who never knew what it was to be out of debt, and poor wives who during forty years never had sixpence uncondemned in their pockets, now possess little stores of money sufficient to build them cottages, and go every week into their own market with money jingling in their pockets ; and in that market there is no distrust and no deception ; there is no adulteration, and no second prices. The whole

Savings Bank in 1849, the Society's Store has become the virtual Savings Bank of the place.

The following Table, completed to 1860 from the Almanack published by the Society, shows the pecuniary result of its operations from the commencement.

Year.	No. of members.	Amount of Capital.			Amount of cash sales in store (annual).			Amount of profit (annual).		
		£	s.	d.	£	s.	d.	£	s.	d.
1844	28	28	0	0	—			—		
1845	74	181	12	5	710	6	5	32	17	6
1846	86	252	7	1½	1,146	17	7	80	16	3½
1847	110	286	5	3½	1,924	13	10	72	2	10
1848	140	397	0	0	2,276	6	5½	117	16	10½
1849	390	1,193	19	1	6,611	18	0	561	3	9
1850	600	2,299	10	5	13,179	17	0	889	12	5
1851	630	2,785	0	1½	17,638	4	0	990	19	8½
1852	680	3,471	0	6	16,352	5	0	1,206	15	2½
1853	720	5,848	3	11	22,760	0	0	1,674	18	11½
1854	900	7,172	15	7	33,364	0	0	1,763	11	2½
1855	1400	11,032	12	10½	44,902	12	0	3,106	8	4½
1856	1600	12,920	13	1½	63,197	10	0	3,921	13	1½
1857	1850	15,142	1	2	79,788	0	0	5,470	6	8½
1858	1950	18,160	5	4	71,689	0	0	6,284	17	4½
1859	2703	27,060	14	2	104,012	0	0	10,739	18	6½
1860*	3450	37,710	9	0	152,063	0	0	15,906	9	11

atmosphere is honest. Those who serve neither hurry, finesse, nor flatter. *They have no interest in chicanery.* They have but one duty to perform—that of giving fair measure, full weight, and a pure article. In other parts of the town, where competition is the principle of trade, all the preaching in Rochdale cannot produce moral effects like these.

" As the Store has made no debts, it has incurred no losses ; and during thirteen years' transactions, and receipts amounting to 303,852*l.*, it has had no law-suits. The Arbitrators of the Societies, during all their years of office, have never had a case to decide, and are discontented that nobody quarrels."

* [1865] The latest report to which I have access is that for the quarter ending September 20, 1864, of which I take the following abstract from the November number of that valuable periodical the *Co-operator,* conducted by Mr. Henry Pitman, one of the most active and judicious apostles of the Co-operative cause :—" The number of members is 4580, being an increase of 132 for the three months. The capital or assets of the society is 59,536*l.* 10*s.* 1*d.*, or more than last quarter by 3687*l.* 13*s.* 7*d.* The cash received for sale of goods is 45,806*l.* 0*s.* 10½*d.*, being an increase of 2283*l.* 12*s.* 5½*d.* as compared with the previous three months. The profit realized is 5713*l.* 2*s.* 7½*d.*, which, after depreciating fixed stock account 182*l.* 2*s.* 4½*d.*, paying interest on share capital 598*l.* 17*s.* 6*d.*, applying 2½ per cent to an educational fund, viz. 122*l.* 17*s.* 9*d.*, leaves a dividend to members on their purchases of 2*s.* 4*d.* in the pound. Non-members have received 261*l.* 18*s.* 4*d.*, at 1*s.* 8*d.* in the pound on their purchases, leaving 8*d.* in the pound profit to the society, which increases

I need not enter into similar particulars respecting the Corn-Mill Society, and will merely state that in 1860 its capital is set down, on the same authority, at 26,618*l.* 14*s.* 6*d.*, and the profit for that single year at 10,164*l.* 12*s.* 5*d.* For the manufacturing establishment I have no certified information later than that of Mr. Holyoake, who states the capital of the concern, in 1857, to be 5500*l.* But a letter in the *Rochdale Observer* of May 26, 1860, editorially announced as by a person of good information, says that the capital had at that time reached 50,000*l.* : and the same letter gives highly satisfactory statements respecting other similar associations ; the Rosendale Industrial Company, capital 40,000*l.* ; the Walsden Co-operative Company, capital 8000*l.* ; the Bacup and Wardle Commercial Company, with a capital of 40,000*l.*, " of which more than one-third is borrowed at 5 per cent, and this circumstance, during the last two years of unexampled commercial prosperity, has caused the rate of dividend to shareholders to rise to an almost fabulous height."

[1] It is not necessary to enter into any details respecting the subsequent history of English Co-operation ; the less so, as it is now one of the recognised elements in the progressive movement of the age, and, as such, has latterly been the subject of elaborate articles in most of our leading periodicals, one of the most recent and best of which was in the *Edinburgh Review* for October 1864 : and the progress of Co-operation from month to month is regularly chronicled in the *Co-operator*. I must not, however, omit to mention the last great step in advance in reference to the Co-operative Stores, the formation in the North of England (and another is in course of formation in London) of a Wholesale Society, to dispense with the services of the wholesale merchant as well as of the retail dealer, and extend to the Societies the advantage which each society gives to its own members, by an agency for co-operative purchases, of foreign as well as domestic commodities, direct from the producers.

[2] It is hardly possible to take any but a hopeful view of the

---

the reserve fund 104*l.* 15*s.* 4*d.*   This fund now stands at 1352*l.* 7*s.* 11½*d.*, the accumulation of profits from the trade of the public with the store since September 1862, over and above the 1*s.* 8*d.* in the pound allowed to such purchasers."

[1] [This paragraph added in 6th ed. (1865).]

[2] [This paragraph is from the 5th ed. (1862), and so is the explanation, in the next paragraph but one, of the increase in the productiveness of industry. The argument as to the limitation of the number of distributors was inserted in the 6th ed. (1865).]

prospects of mankind, when, in two leading countries of the world, the obscure depths of society contain simple working men whose integrity, good sense, self-command, and honourable confidence in one another, have enabled them to carry these noble experiments to the triumphant issue which the facts recorded in the preceding pages attest.

From the progressive advance of the co-operative movement, a great increase may be looked for even in the aggregate productiveness of industry. The sources of the increase are twofold. In the first place, the class of mere distributors, who are not producers but auxiliaries of production, and whose inordinate numbers, far more than the gains of capitalists, are the cause why so great a portion of the wealth produced does not reach the producers—will be reduced to more modest dimensions. Distributors differ from producers in this, that when producers increase, even though in any given department of industry they may be too numerous, they actually produce more : but the multiplication of distributors does not make more distribution to be done, more wealth to be distributed ; it does but divide the same work among a greater number of persons, seldom even cheapening the process. By limiting the distributors to the number really required for making the commodities accessible to the consumers—which is the direct effect of the co-operative system—a vast number of hands will be set free for production, and the capital which feeds and the gains which remunerate them will be applied to feed and remunerate producers. This great economy of the world's resources would be realized even if co-operation stopped at associations for purchase and consumption, without extending to production.

The other mode in which co-operation tends, still more efficaciously, to increase the productiveness of labour, consists in the vast stimulus given to productive energies, by placing the labourers, as a mass, in a relation to their work which would make it their principle and their interest—at present it is neither—to do the utmost, instead of the least possible, in exchange for their remuneration. [1] It is scarcely possible to rate too highly this material benefit, which yet is as nothing compared with the moral revolution in society that would accompany it : the healing of the standing feud between capital and labour ; the transformation of human life, from a conflict of classes struggling for opposite interests, to a friendly

[1] [The present text from this point to the point indicated in the next paragraph but two dates from the 6th ed. (1865).]

rivalry in the pursuit of a good common to all ; the elevation of the dignity of labour ; a new sense of security and independence in the labouring class ; and the conversion of each human being's daily occupation into a school of the social sympathies and the practical intelligence.

Such is the noble idea which the promoters of Co-operation should have before them. But to attain, in any degree, these objects, it is indispensable that all, and not some only, of those who do the work should be identified in interest with the prosperity of the undertaking. Associations which, when they have been successful, renounce the essential principle of the system, and become joint-stock companies of a limited number of shareholders, who differ from those of other companies only in being working men ; associations which employ hired labourers without any interests in the profits (and I grieve to say that the manufacturing Society even of Rochdale has thus degenerated) are, no doubt, exercising a lawful right in honestly employing the existing system of society to improve their position as individuals, but it is not from them that anything need be expected towards replacing that system by a better. Neither will such societies, in the long run, succeed in keeping their ground against individual competition. Individual management, by the one person principally interested, has great advantages over every description of collective management. Co-operation has but one thing to oppose to those advantages—the common interest of all the workers in the work. When individual capitalists, as they will certainly do, add this to their other points of advantage ; when, even if only to increase their gains, they take up the practice which these co-operative societies have dropped, and connect the pecuniary interest of every person in their employment with the most efficient and most economical management of the concern ; they are likely to gain an easy victory over societies which retain the defects, while they cannot possess the full advantages, of the old system.

Under the most favourable supposition, it will be desirable, and perhaps for a considerable length of time, that individual capitalists, associating their work-people in the profits, should coexist with even those co-operative societies which are faithful to the co-operative principle. Unity of authority makes many things possible, which could not or would not be undertaken subject to the chance of divided councils or changes in the management. A private capitalist, exempt from the control of a body, if he is a person of capacity, is considerably more likely than almost any association to run judicious risks, and originate costly improvements. Co-operative societies may be depended on for adopting improvements after they have been tested by success, but individuals are more likely to commence things previously untried. Even in ordinary business, the competition of capable persons who in the event of failure are to have all the loss, and in case of success the greater part of the gain, will be very useful in keeping the managers of co-operative societies up to the due pitch of activity and vigilance.

When, however, co-operative societies shall have sufficiently multiplied, it is not probable that any but the least valuable work-people will any longer consent to work all their lives for wages merely ; both private capitalists and associations will gradually find it necessary to make the entire body of labourers participants in profits. Eventually, and in perhaps a less remote future than may be supposed, we may, through the co-operative principle, see our way to [1] a change in society, which would combine the freedom and independence of the individual, with the moral, intellectual, and economical advantages of aggregate production ; and which, without violence or spoliation, or even any sudden disturbance of existing habits and expectations, would realize, at least in the industrial department, the best aspirations of the democratic spirit, by putting an end to the division of society into the industrious and the idle, and effacing all social distinctions but those fairly earned by personal services and exertions. Associations like those which we have des-cribed, by the very process of their success, are a course of education in those moral and active qualities by which alone success can be either deserved or attained. As associations multiplied, they would tend more and more to absorb all work-people, except those who have too little understanding, or too little virtue, to be capable of learning to act on any other system than that of narrow selfishness. As this change proceeded, owners of capital would gradually find it to their advantage, instead of maintaining the struggle of the old system with work-people of only the worst description, to lend their capital to the associations ; to do this at a diminishing rate of interest, and at last, perhaps, even to exchange their capital for terminable annuities. In this or some such mode, the existing accumulations of capital might honestly, and by a kind of spon-taneous process, become in the end the joint property of all who participate in their productive employment : a transformation

[1] [The rest of this paragraph dates from the 3rd ed. (1852).]

which, thus effected, (and assuming of course that both sexes participate equally in the rights and in the government of the association,)* would be the nearest approach to social justice, and the most beneficial ordering of industrial affairs for the universal good, which it is possible at present to foresee.

¹ § 7.   I agree, then, with the Socialist writers in their conception of the form which industrial operations tend to assume in the advance of improvement ; and I entirely share their opinion that the time is ripe for commencing this transformation, and that it should by all just and effectual means be aided and encouraged. But while I agree and sympathize with Socialists in this practical portion of their aims, I utterly dissent from the most conspicuous and vehement part of their teaching, their declamations against competition.   With moral conceptions in many respects far ahead of the existing arrangements of society, they have in general very confused and erroneous notions of its actual working ; and one of their greatest errors, as I conceive, is to charge upon competition all the economical evils which at present exist.   They forget that wherever competition is not, monopoly is ; and that monopoly, in all its forms, is the taxation of the industrious for the support of indolence, if not of plunder.   They forget, too, that with the exception of competition among labourers, all other competition is for the benefit of the labourers, by cheapening the articles they consume ; that competition even in the labour market is a source not of low but of high wages, wherever the competition *for* labour exceeds the competition *of* labour, as in America, in the colonies, and in the skilled trades ; and never could be a cause of low wages, save by the overstocking of the labour market through the too great numbers of the labourers' families ; while, if the supply of labourers is excessive, not even Socialism can prevent their remuneration from being low.   Besides, if association were universal, there

* [1865] In this respect also the Rochdale Society has given an example of reason and justice, worthy of the good sense and good feeling manifested in their general proceedings.   " The Rochdale Store," says Mr. Holyoake, "renders incidental but valuable aid towards realizing the civil independence of women. Women may be members of this Store, and vote in its proceedings.   Single and married women join.   Many married women become members because their husbands will not take the trouble, and others join it in self-defence to prevent the husband from spending their money in drink.   The husband cannot withdraw the savings at the Store standing in the wife's name unless she signs the order."
¹ [This section added in 3rd ed. (1852).]

would be no competition between labourer and labourer ; and that between association and association would be for the benefit of the consumers, that is, of the associations ; of the industrious classes generally.

I do not pretend that there are no inconveniences in competition, or that the moral objections urged against it by Socialist writers, as a source of jealousy and hostility among those engaged in the same occupation, are altogether groundless. But if competition has its evils, it prevents greater evils. As M. Feugueray well says,* " The deepest root of the evils and iniquities which fill the industrial world, is not competition, but the subjection of labour to capital, and the enormous share which the possessors of the instruments of industry are able to take from the produce. . . . If competition has great power for evil, it is no less fertile of good, especially in what regards the development of the individual faculties, and the success of innovations." It is the common error of Socialists to overlook the natural indolence of mankind ; their tendency to be passive, to be the slaves of habit, to persist indefinitely in a course once chosen. Let them once attain any state of existence which they consider tolerable, and the danger to be apprehended is that they will thenceforth stagnate ; will not exert themselves to improve, and by letting their faculties rust, will lose even the energy required to preserve them from deterioration. Competition may not be the best conceivable stimulus, but it is at present a necessary one, and no one can foresee the time when it will not be indispensable to progress. Even confining ourselves to the industrial department, in which, more than in any other, the majority may be supposed to be competent judges of improvements ; it would be difficult to induce the general assembly of an association to submit to the trouble and inconvenience of altering their habits by adopting some new and promising invention, unless their knowledge of the existence of rival associations made them apprehend that what they would not consent to do, others would, and that they would be left behind in the race.

Instead of looking upon competition as the baneful and anti-social principle which it is held to be by the generality of Socialists, I conceive that, even in the present state of society and industry, every restriction of it is an evil, and every extension of it, even if for the time injuriously affecting some class of labourers, is always an ultimate good. To be protected against competition is to be

* P. 90.

protected in idleness, in mental dulness ; to be saved the necessity
of being as active and as intelligent as other people ; and if it is
also to be protected against being underbid for employment by a
less highly paid class of labourers, this is only where old custom, or
local and partial monopoly, has placed some particular class of
artizans in a privileged position as compared with the rest ; and the
time has come when the interest of universal improvement is no
longer promoted by prolonging the privileges of a few.   If the slop-
sellers and others [1] of their class have lowered the wages of tailors,
and some other artizans, by making them an affair of competition
instead of custom, so much the better in the end.   What is now
required is not to bolster up old customs, whereby limited classes of
labouring people obtain partial gains which interest them in keeping
up the present organization of society, but to introduce new general
practices beneficial to all ; and there is reason to rejoice at whatever
makes the privileged classes of skilled artizans feel that they have
the same interests, and depend for their remuneration on the same
general causes, and must resort for the improvement of their condition
to the same remedies, as the less fortunately circumstanced and
comparatively helpless multitude.[2]

---

[1] [" Of their class " was inserted in 4th ed. (1857) ; and the words of the
3rd ed. (1852), " so unjustly and illiberally railed at—as if they were one
iota worse in their motives or practices than other people, in the existing state
of society,— " were omitted.]
[2] [See Appendix DD.   *The Subsequent History of Co-operation*]

BOOK V

ON THE INFLUENCE OF GOVERNMENT

CHAPTER I

OF THE FUNCTIONS OF GOVERNMENT IN GENERAL

§ 1. One of the most disputed questions both in political science and in practical statesmanship at this particular period relates to the proper limits of the functions and agency of governments. At other times it has been a subject of controversy how governments should be constituted, and according to what principles and rules they should exercise their authority ; but it is now almost equally a question to what departments of human affairs that authority should extend. And when the tide sets so strongly towards changes in government and legislation, as a means of improving the condition of mankind, this discussion is more likely to increase than to diminish in interest. On the one hand, impatient reformers, thinking it easier and shorter to get possession of the government than of the intellects and dispositions of the public, are under a constant temptation to stretch the province of government beyond due bounds : while, on the other, mankind have been so much accustomed by their rulers to interference for purposes other than the public good, or under an erroneous conception of what that good requires, and so many rash proposals are made by sincere lovers of improvement, for attempting, by compulsory regulation, the attainment of objects which can only be effectually or only usefully compassed by opinion and discussion, that there has grown up a spirit of resistance *in limine* to the interference of government, merely as such, and a disposition to restrict its sphere of action within the narrowest bounds. From differences in the historical development of different nations, not necessary to be here dwelt upon, the former excess, that of exaggerating the province of government, prevails most, both in theory and in practice, among the Continental nations, while in England the contrary spirit has hitherto been predominant.

The general principles of the question, in so far as it is a question of principle, I shall make an attempt to determine in a later chapter of this Book : after first considering the effects produced by the conduct of government in the exercise of the functions universally acknowledged to belong to it. For this purpose, there must be a specification of the functions which are either inseparable from the idea of a government, or are exercised habitually and without objection by all governments ; as distinguished from those respecting which it has been considered questionable whether governments should exercise them or not. The former may be termed the *necessary*, the latter the *optional*, functions of government. [1] By the term optional it is not meant to imply that it can ever be a matter of indifference, or of arbitrary choice, whether the government should or should not take upon itself the functions in question ; but only that the expediency of its exercising them does not amount to necessity, and is a subject on which diversity of opinion does or may exist.

§ 2. In attempting to enumerate the necessary functions of government, we find them to be considerably more multifarious than most people are at first aware of, and not capable of being circumscribed by those very definite lines of demarcation, which, in the inconsiderateness of popular discussion, it is often attempted to draw round them. We sometimes, for example, hear it said that governments ought to confine themselves to affording protection against force and fraud : that, these two things apart, people should be free agents, able to take care of themselves, and that so long as a person practises no violence or deception, to the injury of others in person or property, [2] legislatures and governments are in no way called on to concern themselves about him. But why should people be protected by their government, that is, by their own collective strength, against violence and fraud, and not against other evils, except that the expediency is more obvious ? If nothing

---

[1] [This explanation added in 2nd ed. (1849).]
[2] [So since the 4th ed. (1857). The original text ran : " he has a claim to do as he likes, without being molested or restricted by judges and legislators."

but what people cannot possibly do for themselves, can be fit to be done for them by government, people might be required to protect themselves by their skill and courage even against force, or to beg or buy protection against it, as they actually do where the government is not capable of protecting them : and against fraud every one has the protection of his own wits. But without further anticipating the discussion of principles, it is sufficient on the present occasion to consider facts.

Under which of these heads, the repression of force or of fraud, are we to place the operation, for example, of the laws of inheritance ? Some such laws must exist in all societies. It may be said, perhaps, that in this matter government has merely to give effect to the disposition which an individual makes of his own property by will. This, however, is at least extremely disputable ; there is probably no country by whose laws the power of testamentary disposition is perfectly absolute. And suppose the very common case of there being no will : does not the law, that is, the government, decide on principles of general expediency, who shall take the succession ? and in case the successor is in any manner incompetent, does it not appoint persons, frequently officers of its own, to collect the property and apply it to his benefit ? There are many other cases in which the government undertakes the administration of property, because the public interest, or perhaps only that of the particular persons concerned, is thought to require it. This is often done in cases of litigated property ; and in cases of judicially declared insolvency. It has never been contended that, in doing these things, a government exceeds its province.

Nor is the function of the law in defining property itself so simple a thing as may be supposed. It may be imagined, perhaps, that the law has only to declare and protect the right of every one to what he has himself produced, or acquired by the voluntary consent, fairly obtained, of those who produced it. But is there nothing recognized as property except what has been produced ? Is there not the earth itself, its forests and waters, and all other natural riches, above and below the surface ? These are the inheritance of the human race, and there must be regulations for the common enjoyment of it. What rights, and under what conditions, a person shall be allowed to exercise over any portion of this common inheritance cannot be left undecided. No function of government is less optional than the regulation of these things, or more completely involved in the idea of civilized society.

Again, the legitimacy is conceded of repressing violence or treachery; but under which of these heads are we to place the obligation imposed on people to perform their contracts? Non-performance does not necessarily imply fraud; the person who entered into the contract may have sincerely intended to fulfil it: and the term fraud, which can scarcely admit of being extended even to the case of voluntary breach of contract when no deception was practised, is certainly not applicable when the omission to perform is a case of negligence. Is it no part of the duty of governments to enforce contracts? Here the doctrine of non-interference would no doubt be stretched a little, and it would be said that enforcing contracts is not regulating the affairs of individuals at the pleasure of government, but giving effect to their own expressed desire. Let us acquiesce in this enlargement of the restrictive theory, and take it for what it is worth. But governments do not limit their concern with contracts to a simple enforcement. They take upon themselves to determine what contracts are fit to be enforced. It is not enough that one person, not being either cheated or compelled, makes a promise to another. There are promises by which it is not for the public good that persons should have the power of binding themselves. To say nothing of engagements to do something contrary to law, there are engagements which the law refuses to enforce, for reasons connected with the interest of the promiser, or with the general policy of the state. A contract by which a person sells himself to another as a slave would be declared void by the tribunals of this and of most other European countries. There are few nations whose laws enforce a contract for what is looked upon as prostitution, or any matrimonial engagement of which the conditions vary in any respect from those which the law has thought fit to prescribe. But when once it is admitted that there are any engagements which for reasons of expediency the law ought not to enforce, the same question is necessarily opened with respect to all engagements. Whether, for example, the law should enforce a contract to labour when the wages are too low or the hours of work too severe: whether it should enforce a contract by which a person binds himself to remain, for more than a very limited period, in the service of a given individual: whether a contract of marriage, entered into for life, should continue to be enforced against the deliberate will of the persons, or of either of the persons, who entered into it. Every question which can possibly arise as to the policy of contracts, and of the relations which they establish among human beings, is a question for the legislator ; and one which he cannot escape from considering, and in some way or other deciding.

Again, the prevention and suppression of force and fraud afford appropriate employment for soldiers, policemen, and criminal judges ; but there are also civil tribunals. The punishment of wrong is one business of an administration of justice, but the decision of disputes is another. Innumerable disputes arise between persons, without *mala fides* on either side, through misconception of their legal rights, or from not being agreed about the facts, on the proof of which those rights are legally dependent. Is it not for the general interest that the State should appoint persons to clear up these uncertainties and terminate these disputes ? It cannot be said to be a case of absolute necessity. People might appoint an arbitrator, and engage to submit to his decision ; and they do so where there are no courts of justice, or where the courts are not trusted, or where their delays and expenses, or the irrationality of their rules of evidence, deter people from resorting to them. Still, it is universally thought right that the State should establish civil tribunals ; and if their defects often drive people to have recourse to substitutes, even then the power held in reserve of carrying the case before a legally constituted court gives to the substitutes their principal efficacy.

Not only does the State undertake to decide disputes, it takes precautions beforehand that disputes may not arise. The laws of most countries lay down rules for determining many things, not because it is of much consequence in what way they are determined, but in order that they may be determined somehow, and there may be no question on the subject. The law prescribes forms of words for many kinds of contract, in order that no dispute or misunderstanding may arise about their meaning : it makes provision that, if a dispute does arise, evidence shall be procurable for deciding it, by requiring that the document be attested by witnesses and executed with certain formalities. The law preserves authentic evidence of facts to which legal consequences are attached, by keeping a registry of such facts ; as of births, deaths, and marriages, of wills and contracts, and of judicial proceedings. In doing these things, it has never been alleged that government oversteps the proper limits of its functions.

Again, however wide a scope we may allow to the doctrine that individuals are the proper guardians of their own interests, and that government owes nothing to them but to save them from being interfered with by other people, the doctrine can never be applicable to any persons but those who are capable of acting in their own behalf. The individual may be an infant, or a lunatic, or fallen into imbecility. The law surely must look after the interest of such persons. It does not necessarily do this through officers of its own. It often devolves the trust upon some relative or connexion. But, in doing so, is its duty ended ? Can it make over the interests of one person to the control of another, and be excused from supervision, or from holding the person thus trusted responsible for the discharge of the trust ?

There is a multitude of cases in which governments, with general approbation, assume powers and execute functions for which no reason can be assigned except the simple one, that they conduce to general convenience. We may take as an example, the function (which is a monopoly too) of coining money. This is assumed for no more recondite purpose than that of saving to individuals the trouble, delay, and expense of weighing and assaying. No one, however, even of those most jealous of state interference, has objected to this as an improper exercise of the powers of government. Prescribing a set of standard weights and measures is another instance. Paving, lighting, and cleansing the streets and thorough-fares is another ; whether done by the general government, or, as is more usual, and generally more advisable, by a municipal authority. Making or improving harbours, building lighthouses, making surveys in order to have accurate maps and charts, raising dykes to keep the sea out, and embankments to keep rivers in, are cases in point.

Examples might be indefinitely multiplied without intruding on any disputed ground. But enough has been said to show that the admitted functions of government embrace a much wider field than can easily be included within the ring-fence of any restrictive defini-tion, and that it is hardly possible to find any ground of justification common to them all, except the comprehensive one of general expedi-ency; nor to limit the interference of government by any universal rule, save the simple and vague one, that it should never be admitted but when the case of expediency is strong.

§ 3. Some observations, however, may be usefully bestowed on the nature of the considerations on which the question of govern-ment interference is most likely to turn, and on the mode of estimating the comparative magnitude of the expediencies involved. This will form the last of the three parts, into which our discussion of the principles and effects of government interference may conveniently be divided. The following will be our division of the subject.

We shall first consider the economical effects arising from the manner in which governments perform their necessary and acknowledged functions.

We shall then pass to certain governmental interferences of what I have termed the optional kind (*i.e.* overstepping the boundaries of the universally acknowledged functions) which have heretofore taken place, and in some cases still take place, under the influence of false general theories.

It will lastly remain to inquire whether, independently of any false theory, and consistently with a correct view of the laws which regulate human affairs, there be any cases of the optional class in which governmental interference is really advisable, and what are those cases.

The first of these divisions is of an extremely miscellaneous character : since the necessary functions of government, and those which are so manifestly expedient that they have never or very rarely been objected to, are, as already pointed out, too various to be brought under any very simple classification. Those, however, which are of principal importance, which alone it is necessary here to consider, may be reduced to the following general heads.

First, the means adopted by governments to raise the revenue which is the condition of their existence.

Secondly, the nature of the laws which they prescribe on the two great subjects of Property and Contracts.

Thirdly, the excellences or defects of the system of means by which they enforce generally the execution of their laws, namely, their judicature and police.

We commence with the first head, that is, with the theory of Taxation.

CHAPTER II

§ 1. THE qualities desirable, economically speaking, in a system of taxation, have been embodied by Adam Smith in four maxims or principles, which, having been generally concurred in by subsequent writers, may be said to have become classical, and this chapter cannot be better commenced than by quoting them.*

" 1. The subjects of every state ought to contribute to the support of the government as nearly as possible in proportion to their respective abilities : that is, in proportion to the revenue which they respectively enjoy under the protection of the state. In the observation or neglect of this maxim consists what is called the equality or inequality of taxation.

" 2. The tax which each individual is bound to pay ought to be certain, and not arbitrary. The time of payment, the manner of payment, the quantity to be paid, ought all to be clear and plain to the contributor, and to every other person. Where it is otherwise, every person subject to the tax is put more or less in the power of the tax-gatherer, who can either aggravate the tax upon any obnoxious contributor, or extort, by the terror of such aggravation, some present or perquisite to himself. The uncertainty of taxation encourages the insolence and favours the corruption of an order of men who are naturally unpopular, even when they are neither insolent nor corrupt. The certainty of what each individual ought to pay is, in taxation, a matter of so great importance, that a very considerable degree of inequality, it appears, I believe, from the experience of all nations, is not near so great an evil as a very small degree of uncertainty.

" 3. Every tax ought to be levied at the time, or in the manner, in which it is most likely to be convenient for the contributor to pay it. A tax upon the rent of land or of houses, payable at the

* *Wealth of Nations*, book v. ch. ii

same term at which such rents are usually paid, is levied at a time when it is most likely to be convenient for the contributor to pay ; or when he is most likely to have wherewithal to pay.   Taxes upon such consumable goods as are articles of luxury are all finally paid by the consumer, and generally in a manner that is very convenient to him.   He pays them by little and little, as he has occasion to buy the goods.   As he is at liberty, too, either to buy or not to buy, as he pleases, it must be his own fault if he ever suffers any considerable inconvenience from such taxes.

" 4. Every tax ought to be so contrived as both to take out and to keep out of the pockets of the people as little as possible over and above what it brings into the public treasury of the state.   A tax may either take out or keep out of the pockets of the people a great deal more than it brings into the public treasury, in the four following ways.   First, the levying of it may require a great number of officers, whose salaries may eat up the greater part of the produce of the tax, and whose perquisites may impose another additional tax upon the people."   Secondly, it may divert a portion of the labour and capital of the community from a more to a less productive employment.   " Thirdly, by the forfeitures and other penalties which those unfortunate individuals incur who attempt unsuccessfully to evade the tax, it may frequently ruin them, and thereby put an end to the benefit which the community might have derived from the employment of their capitals.   An injudicious tax offers a great temptation to smuggling.   Fourthly, by subjecting the people to the frequent visits and the odious examination of the tax-gatherers, it may expose them to much unnecessary trouble, vexation, and oppression : "   to which may be added, that the restrictive regulations to which trades and manufactures are often subjected to prevent evasion of a tax, are not only in themselves troublesome and expensive, but often oppose insuperable obstacles to making improvements in the processes.

The last three of these four maxims require little or other explanation or illustration than is contained in the passage itself. How far any given tax conforms to, or conflicts with them, is a matter to be considered in the discussion of particular taxes.   But the first of the four points, equality of taxation, requires to be more fully examined, being a thing often imperfectly understood, and on which many false notions have become to a certain degree accredited, through the absence of any definite principles of judgment in the popular mind.

§ 2. For what reason ought equality to be the rule in matters of taxation ? For the reason that it ought to be so in all affairs of government. As a government ought to make no distinction of persons or classes in the strength of their claims on it, whatever sacrifices it requires from them should be made to bear as nearly as possible with the same pressure upon all, which, it must be observed, is the mode by which least sacrifice is occasioned on the whole. If any one bears less than his fair share of the burthen, some other person must suffer more than his share, and the alleviation to the one is not, *cæteris paribus*, so great a good to him, as the increased pressure upon the other is an evil. Equality of taxation, therefore, as a maxim of politics, means equality of sacrifice. It means apportioning the contribution of each person towards the expenses of government so that he shall feel neither more nor less inconvenience from his share of the payment than every other person experiences from his. This standard, like other standards of perfection, cannot be completely realized ; but the first object in every practical discussion should be to know what perfection is.

There are persons, however, who are not content with the general principles of justice as a basis to ground a rule of finance upon, but must have something, as they think, more specifically appropriate to the subject. What best pleases them is, to regard the taxes paid by each member of the community as an equivalent for value received, in the shape of service to himself ; and they prefer to rest the justice of making each contribute in proportion to his means, upon the ground, that he who has twice as much property to be protected receives, on an accurate calculation, twice as much protection, and ought, on the principles of bargain and sale, to pay twice as much for it. Since, however, the assumption that government exists solely for the protection of property, is not one to be deliberately adhered to ; some consistent adherents of the *quid pro quo* principle go on to observe, that protection being required for person as well as property, and everybody's person receiving the same amount of protection, a poll-tax of a fixed sum per head is a proper equivalent for this part of the benefits of government, while the remaining part, protection to property, should be paid for in proportion to property. There is in this adjustment a false air of nice adaptation, very acceptable to some minds. But in the first place, it is not admissible that the protection of persons and that of property are the sole purposes of government. The ends of government are as comprehensive as those of the social union. They consist of all the good, and all the immunity from evil, which the existence of government can be made either directly or indirectly to bestow. In the second place, the practice of setting definite values on things essentially indefinite, and making them a ground of practical conclusions, is peculiarly fertile in false views of social questions. It cannot be admitted that to be protected in the ownership of ten times as much property is to be ten times as much protected. Neither can it be truly said that the protection of 1000*l.* a year costs the state ten times as much as that of 100*l.* a year, rather than twice as much, or exactly as much. The same judges, soldiers, and sailors who protect the one protect the other, and the larger income does not necessarily, though it may sometimes, require even more policemen. Whether the labour and expense of the protection, or the feelings of the protected person, or any other definite thing be made the standard, there is no such proportion as the one supposed,· nor any other definable proportion. If we wanted to estimate the degrees of benefit which different persons derive from the protection of government we should have to consider who would suffer most if that protection were withdrawn : to which question if any answer could be made, it must be that those would suffer most who were weakest in mind or body, either by nature or by position. Indeed, such persons would almost infallibly be slaves. If there were any justice, therefore, in the theory of justice now under consideration, those who are least capable of helping or defending themselves, being those to whom the protection of government is the most indispensable, ought to pay the greatest share of its price : the reverse of the true idea of distributive justice, which consists not in imitating but in redressing the inequalities and wrongs of nature.

Government must be regarded as so pre-eminently a concern of all, that to determine who are most interested in it is of no real importance. If a person or class of persons receive so small a share of the benefit as makes it necessary to raise the question, there is something else than taxation which is amiss, and the thing to be done is to remedy the defect, instead of recognising it and making it a ground for demanding less taxes. As, in a case of voluntary subscription for a purpose in which all are interested, all are thought to have done their part fairly when each has contributed according to his means, that is, has made an equal sacrifice for the common object ; in like manner should this be the principle of compulsory contributions : and it is superfluous to look for a more ingenious or recondite ground to rest the principle upon.

§ 3. Setting out, then, from the maxim that equal sacrifices ought to be demanded from all, we have next to inquire whether this is in fact done by making each contribute the same percentage on his pecuniary means. Many persons maintain the negative, saying that a tenth part taken from a small income is a heavier burthen than the same fraction deducted from one much larger : and on this is grounded the very popular scheme of what is called a graduated property tax, viz. an income tax in which the percentage rises with the amount of the income.

On the best consideration I am able to give to this question, it appears to me that the portion of truth which the doctrine contains arises principally from the difference between a tax which can be saved from luxuries and one which trenches, in ever so small a degree, upon the necessaries of life. To take a thousand a year from the possessor of ten thousand would not deprive him of anything really conducive either to the support or to the comfort of existence ; and if such *would* be the effect of taking five pound from one whose income is fifty, the sacrifice required from the last is not only greater than, but entirely incommensurable with, that imposed upon the first. The mode of adjusting these inequalities of pressure, which seems to be the most equitable, is that recommended by Bentham, of leaving a certain minimum of income, sufficient to provide the necessaries of life, untaxed. Suppose 50l. a year to be sufficient to provide the number of persons ordinarily supported from a single income with the requisites of life and health, and with protection against habitual bodily suffering, but not with any indulgence. This then should be made the minimum, and incomes exceeding it should pay taxes not upon their whole amount, but upon the surplus. If the tax be ten per cent., an income of 60l. should be considered as a net income of 10l., and charged with 1l. a year, while an income of 1000l. should be charged as one of 950l. Each would then pay a fixed proportion, not of his whole means, but of his superfluities.* An income not exceeding 50l. should not be taxed at all, either directly or by taxes on necessaries ; for as by supposition this is the smallest income which labour ought to be able to command, the government ought not to be a party to making it smaller. This arrangement, however, would constitute a reason, in addition to

* [1865] This principle of assessment has been partially adopted by Mr. Gladstone in renewing the income-tax. From 100l., at which the tax begins, up to 200l., the income only pays tax on the excess above 60l.

[For the subsequent history of the Income Tax see Appendix EE.]

others which might be stated, for maintaining taxes on articles of luxury consumed by the poor. The immunity extended to the income required for necessaries, should depend on its being actually expended for that purpose ; and the poor who, not having more than enough for necessaries, divert any part of it to indulgences, should like other people contribute their quota out of those indulgences to the expenses of the state.

The exemption in favour of the smaller incomes should not, I think, be stretched further than to the amount of income needful for life, health, and immunity from bodily pain. If 50*l.* a year is sufficient (which may be doubted) for these purposes,[1] an income of 100*l.* a year would, as it seems to me, obtain all the relief it is entitled to, compared with one of 1000*l.*, by being taxed only on 50*l.* of its amount. It may be said, indeed, that to take 100*l.* from 1000*l.* (even giving back five pounds) is a heavier impost than 1000*l.* taken from 10,000*l.* (giving back the same five pounds). But this doctrine seems to me too disputable altogether, and even if true at all, not true to a sufficient extent to be made the foundation of any rule of taxation. Whether the person with 10,000*l.* a year cares less for 1000*l.* than the person with only a 1000*l.* a year cares for 100*l.*, and if so, how much less, does not appear to me capable of being decided with the degree of certainty on which a legislator or a financier ought to act.[2]

Some indeed contend that the rule of proportional taxation bears harder upon the moderate than upon the large incomes, because the same proportional payment has more tendency, in the former case than in the latter, to reduce the payer to a lower grade of social rank. The fact appears to me more than questionable. But even admitting it, I object to its being considered incumbent on government to shape its course by such considerations, or to recognise the notion that social importance is or can be determined by amount of expenditure. Government ought to set an example of rating all things at their true value, and riches, therefore at the worth, for comfort or pleasure, of the things which they will

---

[1] [Added in 5th ed. (1862). The original (1848) text ran : " An income of 100*l.* a year would, as it seems to me, obtain all the relief it is entitled to," &c.]

[2] [This last sentence replaced in the 3rd ed. (1852) the following sentence of the original text: " To tax all *incomes* in an equal ratio, would be unjust to those the greater part of whose income is required for necessaries ; but I can see no fairer standard of real equality than to take from all persons, whatever may be their amount of fortune. the same arithmetical proportion of their superfluities."]

buy : and ought not to sanction the vulgarity of prizing them for
the pitiful vanity of being known to possess them, or the paltry
shame of being suspected to be without them, the presiding motives
of three-fourths of the expenditure of the middle classes. The
sacrifices of real comfort or indulgence which government requires
it is bound to apportion among all persons with as much equality
as possible ; but their sacrifices of the imaginary dignity dependent
on expense it may spare itself the trouble of estimating.

Both in England and on the Continent a graduated property
tax (*l'impôt progressif*) has been advocated, on the avowed ground
that the state should use the instrument of taxation as a means
of mitigating the inequalities of wealth. I am as desirous as any one
that means should be taken to diminish those inequalities, but not
so as to relieve the prodigal at the expense of the prudent.[1] To
tax the larger incomes at a higher percentage than the smaller is
to lay a tax on industry and economy ; to impose a penalty on
people for having worked harder and saved more than their neighbours. It is not the fortunes which are earned, but those which
are unearned, that it is for the public good to place under limitation.[2]
A just and wise legislation would abstain from holding out motives
for dissipating rather than saving the earnings of honest exertion.[3]
Its impartiality between competitors would consist in endeavouring
that they should all start fair, and not in hanging a weight upon
the swift to diminish the distance between them and the slow.[4]
Many, indeed, fail with greater efforts than those with which others
succeed, not from difference of merits, but difference of opportunities ; but if all were done which it would be in the power of a good
government to do, by instruction and by legislation, to diminish
this inequality of opportunities, the differences of fortune arising
from people's own earnings could not justly give umbrage.[5] With

[1] [So since the 3rd ed. (1852). The original text ran : " but not so as to
impair the motives on which society depends for keeping up (not to say increasing) the produce of its labour and capital.]

[2] [This sentence replaced in the 3rd ed. a sentence of the original : " It is
partial taxation, which is a mild form of robbery."]

[3] [This sentence replaced in the 3rd ed. the original sentence : " A just
and wise legislation would scrupulously abstain from opposing obstacles to the
acquisition of even the largest fortune by honest exertion."]

[4] [So since 3rd ed. Originally : " and not that, whether they were swift
or slow, all should reach the goal at once."]

[5] [So since 3rd ed. Instead of the second half of this sentence the original
ran : " and it is the part of a good government to provide, that, as far as more
paramount considerations permit, the inequality of opportunities shall be
remedied. When all kinds of useful instruction shall be as accessible as they

respect to the large fortunes acquired by gift or inheritance, the power of bequeathing is [1] one of those privileges of property which are fit subjects for regulation on grounds of general expediency ; and I have already suggested * as a possible mode [2] of restraining the accumulation of large fortunes in the hands of those who have not earned them by exertion, a limitation of the amount which any one person should be permitted to acquire by gift, bequest, or inheritance. Apart from this, and from the proposal of Bentham (also discussed in a former chapter) that collateral inheritance *ab intestato* should cease, and the property escheat to the state, I conceive that inheritances and legacies, exceeding a certain amount, are highly proper subjects for taxation : and that the revenue from them should be as great as it can be made without giving rise to evasions, by donation *inter vivos* or concealment of property, such as it would be impossible adequately to check. The principle of graduation (as it is called), that is, of levying a larger percentage on a larger sum, though its application to general taxation would be in my opinion objectionable,[3] seems to me both just and expedient[4] as applied to legacy and inheritance duties.[5]

The objection to a graduated property tax applies in an aggravated degree to the proposition of an exclusive tax on what is called "realized property," that is, property not forming a part of any capital engaged in business, or rather in business under the superintendence of the owner : as land, the public funds, money lent on mortgage, and shares (I presume) in joint stock companies. Except the proposal of applying a sponge to the national debt, no such palpable violation of common honesty has found sufficient support in this country, during the present generation, to be regarded as within the domain of discussion. It has not the palliation of a

might be made, and when the cultivated intelligence of the poorer classes, aided so far as necessary by the guidance and co-operation of the state, shall obviate, as it might so well do, the major part of the disabilities attendant on poverty, the inequalities of fortune arising," &c.]

[1] [At this point were omitted in the 3rd ed. (1852) the following words of the original text : " is as much a part of the right of property as the power of using : that is not in the fullest sense a person's own, which he is not free to bestow on others. But this is," &c.]

* Supra, book ii. ch. 2.

[2] [So since 3rd ed. Originally : " the most eligible mode."]

[3] [So since 3rd ed. Originally : " would be a violation of first principles."]

[4] [So since 3rd ed. Originally : " is quite unobjectionable."]

[5] [The principle of graduation has been applied to inheritance and legacy duties since 1894. See Bastable, *Public Finance*, 3rd ed. p. 599 ; Book iv. ch. 9, § 6. For its application to the Income Tax see Appendix EE.]

graduated property tax, that of laying the burthen on those best
able to bear it ; for " realized property " includes the far larger
portion of the provision made for those who are unable to work,
and consists, in great part, of extremely small fractions. I can
hardly conceive a more shameless pretension, than that the major
part of the property of the country, that of merchants, manufacturers,
farmers, and shopkeepers, should be exempted from its share of
taxation : that these classes should only begin to pay their proportion after retiring from business, and if they never retire should
be excused from it altogether. But even this does not give an
adequate idea of the injustice of the proposition. The burthen
thus exclusively thrown on the owners of the smaller portion of the
wealth of the community, would not even be a burthen on that
class of persons in perpetual succession, but would fall exclusively
on those who happened to compose it when the tax was laid on.
As land and those particular securities would thenceforth yield a
smaller net income, relatively to the general interest of capital and
to the profits of trade ; the balance would rectify itself by a
permanent depreciation of those kinds of property. Future buyers
would acquire land and securities at a reduction of price, equivalent
to the peculiar tax, which tax they would, therefore, escape from
paying ; while the original possessors would remain burthened
with it even after parting with the property, since they would
have sold their land or securities at a loss of value equivalent to
the fee-simple of the tax. Its imposition would thus be tantamount to the confiscation for public uses of a percentage of their
property, equal to the percentage laid on their income by the tax.
That such a proposition should find any favour, is a striking instance
of the want of conscience in matters of taxation, resulting from the
absence of any fixed principles in the public mind, and of any
indication of a sense of justice on the subject in the general conduct
of governments. Should the scheme ever enlist a large party in
its support, the fact would indicate a laxity of pecuniary
integrity in national affairs, scarcely inferior to American
repudiation.

§ 4. Whether the profits of trade may not rightfully be taxed
at a lower rate than incomes derived from interest or rent, is part of
the more comprehensive question, so often mooted on the occasion
of the present income tax, whether life incomes should be subjected
to the same rate of taxation as perpetual incomes : whether salaries,

for example, or annuities, or the gains of professions, should pay the same percentage as the income from inheritable property.

The existing tax treats all kinds of incomes exactly alike, taking its sevenpence (now [1871] fourpence) in the pound, as well from the person whose income dies with him, as from the landholder, stockholder, or mortgagee, who can transmit his fortune undiminished to his descendants. This is a visible injustice : yet it does not arithmetically violate the rule that taxation ought to be in proportion to means. When it is said that a temporary income ought to be taxed less than a permanent one, the reply is irresistible, that it is taxed less ; for the income which lasts only ten years pays the tax only ten years, while that which lasts for ever pays for ever. [1] On this point some financial reformers are guilty of a great fallacy. They contend that incomes ought to be assessed to the income tax not in proportion to their annual amount, but to their capitalized value : that, for example, if the value of a perpetual annuity of 100*l.* is 3000*l.*, and a life annuity of the same amount, being worth only half the number of years' purchase could only be sold for 1500*l.*, the perpetual income should pay twice as much per cent income tax as the terminable income ; if the one pays 10*l.* a year the other should pay only 5*l.* But in this argument there is the obvious oversight, that it values the incomes by one standard and the payments by another ; it capitalizes the incomes, but forgets to capitalize the payments. An annuity worth 3000*l.* ought, it is alleged, to be taxed twice as highly as one which is only worth 1500*l.*, and no assertion can be more unquestionable ; but it is forgotten that the income worth 3000*l.* pays to the supposed income tax 10*l.* a year in perpetuity, which is equivalent, by supposition, to 300*l.*, while the terminable income pays the same 10*l.* only during the life of its owner, which on the same calculation is a value of 150*l.*, and could actually be bought for that sum. Already, therefore, the income which is only half as valuable pays only half as much to the tax ; and if in addition to this its annual quota were reduced from 10*l.* to 5*l.*, it would pay, not half, but a fourth part only of the payment demanded from the perpetual income. To make it just that the one income should pay only half as much per annum as the other, it would be necessary that it should pay that half for the same period, that is, in perpetuity.

---

[1] [The rest of this paragraph,—with the exception of the last sentence, added in the 4th ed. (1857),—was inserted in the 2nd ed. (1849).]

¹ The rule of payment which this school of financial reformers contend for would be very proper if the tax were only to be levied once, to meet some national emergency. On the principle of requiring from all payers an equal sacrifice, every person who had anything belonging to him, reversioners included, would be called on for a payment proportioned to the present value of his property. I wonder it does not occur to the reformers in question, that precisely because this principle of assessment would be just in the case of a payment made once for all, it cannot possibly be just for a permanent tax. When each pays only once, one person pays no oftener than another; and the proportion which would be just in that case cannot also be just if one person has to make the payment only once, and the other several times. This, however, is the type of the case which actually occurs. The permanent incomes pay the tax as much oftener than the temporary ones, as a perpetuity exceeds the certain or uncertain length of time which forms the duration of the income for life or years.

² All attempts to establish a claim in favour of terminable incomes on numerical grounds—to make out, in short, that a proportional tax is not a proportional tax—are manifestly absurd. The claim does not rest on grounds of arithmetic, but of human wants and feelings. ³ It is not because the temporary annuitant has smaller means, but because he has greater necessities, that he ought to be assessed at a lower rate.

In spite of the nominal equality of income, A, an annuitant of 1000l. a year, cannot so well afford to pay 100l. out of it, as B who derives the same annual sum from heritable property; A having usually a demand on his income which B has not, namely, to provide by saving for children or others; to which, in the case of salaries or professional gains, must generally be added a provision for his own later years; while B may expend his whole income without injury to his old age, and still have it all to bestow on others after his death. If A, in order to meet these exigencies, must lay by 300l. of his income, to take 100l. from him as income tax is to take 100l. from 700l., since it must be retrenched from that part only of his means which he can afford to spend on his own consumption. Were he to throw it rateably on what he spends and on what he saves, abating 70l.

---

¹ [This paragraph inserted in 5th ed. (1862).]
² [Added in 2nd ed. (1849).]
³ [Added in 3rd ed. (1852) with " greater wants ": changed to " greater necessities " in 5th ed.]

from his consumption and 30*l.* from his annual saving, then indeed his immediate sacrifice would be proportionately the same as B's : but then his children or his old age would be worse provided for in consequence of the tax. The capital sum which would be accumulated for them would be one-tenth less, and on the reduced income afforded by this reduced capital, they would be a second time charged with income tax ; while B's heirs would only be charged once.

The principle, therefore, of equality of taxation, interpreted in its only just sense, equality of sacrifice, requires that a person who has no means of providing for old age, or for those in whom he is interested, except by saving from income, should have the tax remitted on all that part of his income which is really and *bonâ fide* applied to that purpose.

¹ If, indeed, reliance could be placed on the conscience of the contributors, or sufficient security taken for the correctness of their statements by collateral precautions, the proper mode of assessing an income tax would be to tax only the part of income devoted to expenditure, exempting that which is saved. For when saved and invested (and all savings, speaking generally, are invested) it thenceforth pays income tax on the interest or profit which it brings, notwithstanding that it has already been taxed on the principal. Unless, therefore, savings are exempted from income tax, the contributors are twice taxed on what they save, and only once on what they spend. A person who spends all he receives, pays 7*d.* in the pound, or say three per cent, to the tax, and no more ; but if he

[This paragraph was inserted in the 3rd ed. (1852), in the place of the following passage which was made a footnote, but disappeared from the 5th ed. (1862) :
" I say really applied, because (as before remarked in the case of an income not more than sufficient for subsistence) an exemption grounded on an assumed necessity ought not to be claimable by any one who practically emancipates himself from the necessity. One expedient might be, that the Income-Tax Commissioners should allow, as a deduction from income, all *bonâ fide* payments for insurance on life. This, however, would not provide for the case which most of all deserves consideration, that of persons whose lives are not insurable ; nor would it include the case of savings made as a provision for age. The latter case might, perhaps, be met by allowing as a deduction from income all payments made in the purchase of deferred annuities ; and the former by remitting income-tax on sums actually settled, and on sums paid into the hands of a public officer, to be invested in securities, and repaid only to the executor or administrator : the tax so remitted, with interest from the date of deposit, being retained (for the prevention of fraud) as a first debt chargeable on the deposit itself, before other debts could be paid out of it ; but not demanded if satisfactory proof were given that all debts had been paid from other resources. I throw out these suggestions for the consideration of those whose experience renders them adequate judges of practical difficulties."]

saves part of the year's income and buys stock, then in addition to
the three per cent which he has paid on the principal, and which
diminishes the interest in the same ratio, he pays three per cent
annually on the interest itself, which is equivalent to an immediate
payment of a second three per cent on the principal. So that while
unproductive expenditure pays only three per cent, savings pay six
per cent: or more correctly, three per cent on the whole, and
another three per cent on the remaining ninety-seven. The difference thus created to the disadvantage of prudence and economy is
not only impolitic but unjust. To tax the sum invested, and
afterwards to tax also the proceeds óf the investment, is to tax the
same portion of the contributor's means twice over. The principal
and the interest cannot both together form part of his resources;
they are the same portion twice counted : if he has the interest, it
is because he abstains from using the principal ; if he spends the
principal, he does not receive the interest. Yet because he can do
either of the two, he is taxed as if he could do both, and could have
the benefit of the saving and that of the spending, concurrently with
one another.

   [1] It has been urged as an objection to exempting savings from
taxation, that the law ought not to disturb, by artificial interference,
the natural competition between the motives for saving and those
for spending. But we have seen that the law disturbs this natural
competition when it taxes savings, not when it spares them ; for,
as the savings pay at any rate the full tax as soon as they are
invested, their exemption from payment in the earlier stage is
necessary to prevent them from paying twice, while money spent
in unproductive consumption pays only once. It has been further
objected, that since the rich have the greatest means of saving,
any privilege given to savings is an advantage bestowed on the rich
at the expense of the poor. I answer, that it is bestowed on them
only in proportion as they abdicate the personal use of their riches;
in proportion as they divert their income from the supply of their
own wants to a productive investment, through which, instead of
being consumed by themselves, it is distributed in wages among
the poor. If this be favouring the rich, I should like to have it
pointed out what mode of assessing taxation can deserve the name
of favouring the poor.

   [2] No income tax is really just from which savings are not exempted;

---

[1] [This paragraph inserted in 5th ed. (1862).]
[2] [Here the text again dates from the 3rd ed. (1852) down to the proposal

ard no income tax ought to be voted without that provision. if the form of the returns, and the nature of the evidence required, could be so arranged as to prevent the exemption from being taken fraudulent advantage of, by saving with one hand and getting into debt with the other, or by spending in the following year what had been passed tax-free as saving in the year preceding. If this difficulty could be surmounted, the difficulties and complexities arising from the comparative claims of temporary and permanent incomes would disappear; for, since temporary incomes have no just claim to lighter taxation than permanent incomes, except in so far as their possessors are more called upon to save, the exemption of what they do save would fully satisfy the claim. But if no plan can be devised for the exemption of actual savings, sufficiently free from liability to fraud, it is necessary, as the next thing in point of justice, to take into account, in assessing the tax, what the different classes of contributors *ought* to save. And there would probably be no other mode of doing this than the rough expedient of two different rates of assessment. There would be great difficulty in taking into account differences of duration between one terminable income and another; and in the most frequent case, that of incomes dependent on life, differences of age and health would constitute such extreme diversity as it would be impossible to take proper cognizance of. It would probably be necessary to be content with one uniform rate for all incomes of inheritance, and another uniform rate for all those which necessarily terminate with the life of the individual. In fixing the proportion between the two rates, there must inevitably be something arbitrary; perhaps a deduction of one-fourth in favour of life-incomes would be as little objectionable as any which could be made, it being thus assumed that one-fourth of a life-income is, on the average of all ages and states of health, a suitable proportion to be laid by as a provision for successors and for old age.*

of " two different rates of assessment," from which point the text becomes that of the original edition (1848).]

* [1862] Mr. Hubbard, the first person who, as a practical legislator, has attempted the rectification of the income tax on principles of unimpeachable justice, and whose well-conceived plan wants little of being as near an approximation to a just assessment as it is likely that means could be found of carrying into practical effect, proposes a reduction not of a fourth but of a third, in favour of industrial and professional incomes. He fixes on this ratio, on the ground that, independently of all consideration as to what the industrial and professional classes ought to save, the attainable evidence goes to prove that a third of their incomes is what on an average they do save, over and above the proportion saved by other classes. " The savings " (Mr. Hubbard observes) " effected out of incomes derived from invested property are estimated at one-

Of the net profits of persons in business, a part, as before observed, may be considered as interest on capital, and of a perpetual character, and the remaining part as remuneration for the skill and labour of superintendence.   The surplus beyond interest depends on the life of the individual, and even on his continuance in business, and is entitled to the full amount of exemption allowed to terminable incomes.   [1] It has also, I conceive, a just claim to a further amount of exemption in consideration of its precariousness.   An income which some not unusual vicissitude may reduce to nothing, or even convert into a loss, is not the same thing to the feelings of the possessor as a permanent income of 1000l. a year, even though on an average

tenth.   The savings effected out of industrial incomes are estimated at four-tenths.   The amounts which would be assessed under these two classes being nearly equal, the adjustment is simplified by striking off one-tenth on either side, and then reducing by three-tenths, or one-third, the assessable amount of industrial incomes."   Proposed Report (p. xiv. of the *Report and Evidence* of the Committee of 1861).   In such an estimate there must be a large element of conjecture ; but in so far as it can be substantiated, it affords a valid ground for the practical conclusion which Mr. Hubbard founds on it.

[1848] Several writers on the subject, including Mr. Mill in his *Elements of Political Economy,* and Mr. M'Culloch in his work on *Taxation,* have contended that as much should be deducted as would be sufficient to insure the possessor's life for a sum which would give to his successors for ever an income equal to what he reserves for himself ; since this is what the possessor of heritable property can do without saving at all : in other words, that temporary incomes should be converted into perpetual incomes of equal present value, and taxed as such.   If the owners of life-incomes actually did save this large proportion of their income, or even a still larger, I would gladly grant them an exemption from taxation on the whole amount, since, if practical means could be found of doing it, I would exempt savings altogether.   But I cannot admit that they have a claim to exemption on the general assumption of their being obliged to save this amount.   Owners of life-incomes are not bound to forego the enjoyment of them for the sake of leaving to a perpetual line of successors an independent provision equal to their own temporary one ; and no one ever dreams of doing so.   Least of all is it to be required or expected from those whose incomes are the fruits of personal exertion, that they should leave to their posterity for ever, without any necessity for exertion, the same incomes which they allow to themselves.   All they are bound to do, even for their children, is to place them in circumstances in which they will have favourable chances of earning their own living.   To give, however, either to children or to others, by bequest, being a legitimate inclination, which these persons cannot indulge without laying by a part of their income, while the owners of heritable property can ; this real inequality in cases where the incomes themselves are equal, should be considered, to a reasonable degree, in the adjustment of taxation, so as to require from both, as nearly as practicable, an equal sacrifice.

[1] [The remainder of this paragraph dates from the 3rd ed. (1852).   In the original it was said, " Of the net profits of persons in business one half may perhaps be considered as interest on capital . . . and the other half as remuneration " &c. ; and the paragraph ended thus : " For profits, therefore, an intermediate rate might be adopted, one half of the net income being taxed on the higher scale and the other half on the lower."]

of years it may yield 1000*l.* a year. If life-incomes were assessed at three-fourths of their amount, the profits of business, after deducting interest on capital, should not only be assessed at three-fourths, but should pay, on that assessment, a lower rate. Or perhaps the claims of justice in this respect might be sufficiently met by allowing the deduction of a fourth on the entire income. interest included.

These are the chief cases, of ordinary occurrence, in which any difficulty arises in interpreting the maxim of equality of taxation. The proper sense to be put upon it, as we have seen in the preceding example, is, that people should be taxed, not in proportion to what they have, but to what they can afford to spend. It is no objection to this principle that we cannot apply it consistently to all cases. A person with a life-income and precarious health, or who has many persons depending on his exertions, must, if he wishes to provide for them after his death, be more rigidly economical than one who has a life-income of equal amount, with a strong constitution, and few claims upon him ; and if it be conceded that taxation cannot accommodate itself to these distinctions, it is argued that there is no use in attending to any distinctions, where the absolute amount of income is the same. But the difficulty of doing perfect justice is no reason against doing as much as we can. Though it may be a hardship to an annuitant whose life is only worth five years' purchase, to be allowed no greater abatement than is granted to one whose life is worth twenty, it is better for him even so, than if neither of them were allowed any abatement at all.[1]

§ 5. Before leaving the subject of Equality of Taxation, I must remark that there are cases in which exceptions may be made to it, consistently with that equal justice which is the groundwork of the rule. Suppose that there is a kind of income which constantly tends to increase, without any exertion or sacrifice on the part of the owners : those owners constituting a class in the community, whom the natural course of things progressively enriches, consistently with complete passiveness on their own part. In such a case it

---

[1] [Between the last revision of this chapter and the present edition (1909), important changes have been made in the Income Tax :—
(1) The extension of the system of abatements has made the tax in effect progressive up to incomes of £700.
(2) It has been made allowable to deduct life insurance premiums actually paid, up to one sixth of the income.
(3) A distinction has been introduced between "earned " and "unearned" incomes, and a lower rate charged on the former. See Appendix EE].

would be no violation of the principles on which private property is grounded, if the state should appropriate this increase of wealth, or part of it, as it arises. This would not properly be taking anything from anybody ; it would merely be applying an accession of wealth, created by circumstances, to the benefit of society, instead of allowing it to become an unearned appendage to the riches of a particular class.

Now this is actually the case with rent. The ordinary progress of a society which increases in wealth is at all times tending to augment the incomes of landlords ; to give them both a greater amount and a greater proportion of the wealth of the community, independently of any trouble or outlay incurred by themselves. They grow richer, as it were in their sleep, without working, risking, or economizing. What claim have they, on the general principle of social justice, to this accession of riches ? In what would they have been wronged if society had, from the beginning, reserved the right of taxing the spontaneous increase of rent, to the highest amount required by financial exigencies ? I admit that it would be unjust to come upon each individual estate, and lay hold of the increase which might be found to have taken place in its rental ; because there would be no means of distinguishing in individual cases between an increase owing solely to the general circumstances of society, and one which was the effect of skill and expenditure on the part of the proprietor. The only admissible mode of proceeding would be by a general measure. The first step should be a valuation of all the land in the country. The present value of all land should be exempt from the tax ; but after an interval had elapsed, during which society had increased in population and capital, a rough estimate might be made of the spontaneous increase which had accrued to rent since the valuation was made. Of this the average price of produce would be some criterion : if that had risen, it would be certain that rent had increased, and (as already shown) even in a greater ratio than the rise of price. On this and other data, an approximate estimate might be made, how much value had been added to the land of the country by natural causes ; and in laying on a general land-tax, which for fear of miscalculation should be considerably within the amount thus indicated, there would be an assurance of not touching any increase of income which might be the result of capital expended or industry exerted by the proprietor.

But though there could be no question as to the justice of taxing the increase of rent, if society had avowedly reserved the right, has not society waived that right by not exercising it ? In England, for example, have not all who bought land for the last century or more, given value not only for the existing income, but for the prospects of increase, under an implied assurance of being only taxed in the same proportion with other incomes ? This objection, in so far as valid, has a different degree of validity in different countries ; depending on the degree of desuetude into which society has allowed a right to fall, which, as no one can doubt, it once fully possessed. In most countries of Europe, the right to take by taxation, as exigency might require, an indefinite portion of the rent of land, has never been allowed to slumber. In several parts of the Continent, the land-tax forms a large proportion of the public revenues, and has always been confessedly liable to be raised or lowered without reference to other taxes. In these countries no one can pretend to have become the owner of land on the faith of never being called upon to pay an increased land-tax. In England the land-tax has not varied since the early part of the last century. The last act of the legislature in relation to its amount, was to diminish it ; and though the subsequent increase in the rental of the country has been immense not only from agriculture, but from the growth of towns and the increase of buildings, the ascendency of landholders in the legislature has prevented any tax from being imposed, as it so justly might, upon the very large portion of this increase which was un-earned, and, as it were, accidental. For the expectations thus raised, it appears to me that an amply sufficient allowance is made, if the whole increase of income which has accrued during this long period from a mere natural law, without exertion or sacrifice, is held sacred from any peculiar taxation. From the present date, or any subsequent time at which the legislature may think fit to assert the principle, I see no objection to declaring that the future incre-ment of rent should be liable to special taxation ; in doing which all injustice to the landlords would be obviated if the present market-price of their land were secured to them ; since that includes the present value of all future expectations. With reference to such a tax, perhaps a safer criterion than either a rise of rents or a rise of the price of corn, would be a general rise in the price of land. It would be easy to keep the tax within the amount which would reduce the market value of land below the original valuation : and up to that point, whatever the amount of the tax might be, no injustice would be done to the proprietors.[1]

[1] [See Appendix FF. *The Taxation of Land.*]

§ 6.   But whatever may be thought of the legitimacy of making the State a sharer in all future increase of rent from natural causes, the existing land-tax (which in this country unfortunately is very small) ought not to be regarded as a tax, but as a rent-charge in favour of the public ; a portion of the rent, reserved from the beginning by the State, which has never belonged to or formed part of the income of the landlords, and should not-therefore be counted to them as part of their taxation, so as to exempt them from their fair share of every other tax.   As well might the tithe be regarded as a tax on the landlords : as well, in Bengal, where the State, though entitled to the whole rent of the land, gave away one-tenth of it to individuals, retaining the other nine-tenths, might those nine-tenths be considered as an unequal and unjust tax on the grantees of the tenth.   That a person owns part of the rent, does not make the rest of it his just right, injuriously withheld from him.   The landlords originally held their estates subject to feudal burthens, for which the present land-tax is an exceedingly small equivalent, and for their relief from which they should have been required to pay a much higher price.   All who have bought land since the tax existed have bought it subject to the tax.   There is not the smallest pretence for looking upon it as a payment exacted from the existing race of landlords.

These observations are applicable to a land-tax, only in so far as it is a peculiar tax, and not when it is merely a mode of levying from the landlords the equivalent of what is taken from other classes.   In France, for example, there are [1848] peculiar taxes on other kinds of property and income (the *mobilier* and the *patente*) ; and supposing the land-tax to be not more than equivalent to these, there would be no ground for contending that the state had reserved to itself a rent-charge on the land.   But wherever and in so far as income derived from land is prescriptively subject to a deduction for public purposes beyond the rate of taxation levied on other incomes, the surplus is not properly taxation, but a share of the property in the soil reserved by the state.   In this country there are no peculiar taxes on other classes, corresponding to, or intended to countervail, the land-tax.   The whole of it, therefore, is not taxation, but a rent-charge, and is as if the state had retained, not a portion of the rent, but a portion of the land.   It is no more a burthen on the landlord, than the share of one joint tenant is a burthen on the other.   The landlords are entitled to no compensation for it, nor have they any claim to its being allowed for, as part of their taxes. Its continuance on the existing footing is no infringement of the principle of Equal Taxation.*

We shall hereafter consider, in treating of Indirect Taxation, how far, and with what modifications, the rule of equality is applicable to that department.

§ 7. In addition to the preceding rules, another general rule of taxation is sometimes laid down, namely, that it should fall on income, and not on capital. That taxation should not encroach upon the amount of the national capital, is indeed of the greatest importance ; but this encroachment, when it occurs, is not so much a consequence of any particular mode of taxation, as of its excessive amount. Over-taxation, carried to a sufficient extent, is quite capable of ruining the most industrious community, especially when it is in any degree arbitrary, so that the payer is never certain how much or how little he shall be allowed to keep ; or when it is so laid on as to render industry and economy a bad calculation. But if these errors be avoided, and the amount of taxation be not greater than it is at present even in the most heavily taxed country of Europe, there is no danger lest it should deprive the country of a portion of its capital.

To provide that taxation shall fall entirely on income, and not at all on capital, is beyond the power of any system of fiscal arrangements. There is no tax which is not partly paid from what would otherwise have been saved; no tax, the amount of which, if remitted, would be wholly employed in increased expenditure, and no part whatever laid by as an additional capital. All taxes, therefore, are in some sense partly paid out of capital ; and in a poor country it is impossible to impose any tax which will not impede the increase of the national wealth. But in a country where capital abounds, and the spirit of accumulation is strong, this effect of taxation is scarcely felt. Capital having reached the stage in which, were it not for a perpetual succession of improvements in production, any further increase would soon be stopped—and having so strong a tendency even to outrun those improvements, that profits are only kept above the minimum by emigration of capital, or by a periodical

* [1849] The same remarks obviously apply to those local taxes, of the peculiar pressure of which on landed property so much has been said by the remnant of the Protectionists. As much of these burthens as is of old standing, ought to be regarded as a prescriptive deduction or reservation, for public purposes, of a portion of the rent. And any recent additions have either been incurred for the benefit of the owners of landed property, or occasioned by their fault : in neither case giving them any just ground of complaint.

sweep called a commercial crisis ; to take from capital by taxation
what emigration would remove, or a commercial crisis destroy, is
only to do what either of those causes would have done, namely, to
make a clear space for further saving.

I cannot, therefore, attach any importance, in a wealthy country,
to the objection made against taxes on legacies and inheritances,
that they are taxes on capital. It is perfectly true that they are so.
As Ricardo observes, if 100*l.* are taken from any one in a tax on
houses or on wine, he will probably save it, or a part of it, by living
in a cheaper house, consuming less wine, or retrenching from some
other of his expenses ; but if the same sum be taken from him
because he has received a legacy of 1000*l.*, he considers the legacy as
only 900*l.*, and feels no more inducement than at any other time
(probably feels rather less inducement) to economize in his expenditure. The tax, therefore, is wholly paid out of capital : and there
are countries in which this would be a serious objection. But in
the first place, the argument cannot apply to any country which
has a national debt, and devotes any portion of revenue to paying
it off ; since the produce of the tax, thus applied, still remains
capital, and is merely transferred from the tax-payer to the fundholder. But the objection is never applicable in a country which
increases rapidly in wealth. The amount which would be derived,
even from a very high legacy duty, in each year, is but a small
fraction of the annual increase of capital in such a country ; and its
abstraction would but make room for saving to an equivalent amount :
while the effect of not taking it, is to prevent that amount of saving,
or cause the savings, when made, to be sent abroad for investment.
A country which, like England, accumulates capital not only for
itself, but for half the world, may be said to defray the whole of its
public expenses from its overflowings ; and its wealth is probably
at this moment as great as if it had no taxes at all. What its taxes
really do is, to subtract from its means, not of production, but of
enjoyment ; since whatever any one pays in taxes, he could, if it
were not taken for that purpose, employ in indulging his ease, or
in gratifying some want or taste which at present remains unsatisfied.

CHAPTER III

§ 1. TAXES are either direct or indirect. A direct tax is one which is demanded from the very persons who, it is intended or desired, should pay it. Indirect taxes are those which are demanded from one person in the expectation and intention that he shall indemnify himself at the expense of another: such as the excise or customs. The producer or importer of a commodity is called upon to pay a tax on it, not with the intention to levy a peculiar contribution upon him, but to tax through him the consumers of the commodity, from whom it is supposed that he will recover the amount by means of an advance in price.

Direct taxes are either on income, or on expenditure. Most taxes on expenditure are indirect, but some are direct, being imposed not on the producer or seller of an article, but immediately on the consumer. A house-tax, for example, is a direct tax on expenditure, if levied, as it usually is, on the occupier of the house. If levied on the builder or owner, it would be an indirect tax. A window-tax is a direct tax on expenditure; so are the taxes on horses and carriages, and the rest of what are called the assessed taxes.

The sources of income are rent, profits, and wages. This includes every sort of income, except gift or plunder. Taxes may be laid on any one of the three kinds of income, or an uniform tax on all of them. We will consider these in their order.

§ 2. A tax on rent falls wholly on the landlord. There are no means by which he can shift the burthen upon any one else. It does not affect the value or price of agricultural produce, for this is determined by the cost of production in the most unfavourable circumstances, and in those circumstances, as we have so often demonstrated, no rent is paid. A tax on rent, therefore, has no effect, other than its obvious one.   It merely takes so much from the landlord, and transfers it to the state.

This, however, is, in strict exactness, only true of the rent which is the result either of natural causes, or of improvements made by tenants.   When the landlord makes improvements which increase the productive power of his land, he is remunerated for them by an extra payment from the tenant ; and this payment, which to the landlord is properly a profit on capital, is blended and confounded with rent ; which indeed it really is, to the tenant, and in respect of the economical laws which determine its amount.   A tax on rent, if extending to this portion of it, would discourage landlords from making improvements : but it does not follow that it would raise the price of agricultural produce.   The same improvements might be made with the tenant's capital, or even with the landlord's if lent by him to the tenant ; provided he is willing to give the tenant so long a lease as will enable him to indemnify himself before it expires.   But whatever hinders improvements from being made in the manner in which people prefer to make them, will often prevent them from being made at all : and on this account a tax on rent would be inexpedient, unless some means could be devised of excluding from its operation that portion of the nominal rent which may be regarded as landlord's profit.   This argument, however, is not needed for the condemnation of such a tax.   A peculiar tax on the income of any class, not balanced by taxes on other classes, is a violation of justice, and amounts to a partial confiscation.   I have already shown grounds for excepting from this censure a tax which, sparing existing rents, should content itself with appropriating a portion of any future increase arising from the mere action of natural causes.   But even this could not be justly done, without offering as an alternative the market price of the land.   In the case of a tax on rent which is not peculiar, but accompanied by an equivalent tax on other incomes, the objection grounded on its reaching the profit arising from improvements is less applicable : since, profits being taxed as well as rent, the profit which assumes the form of rent is liable to its share in common with other profits ; [1] but since profits altogether ought, for reasons formerly stated, to be taxed somewhat lower than rent properly so called, the objection is only diminished, not removed.

§ 3.   A tax on profits, like a tax on rent, must, at least in its

---

[1] [Remaining words of the paragraph added in 4th ed. (1857).]

immediate operation, fall wholly on the payer. All profits being alike affected, no relief can be obtained by a change of employment. If a tax were laid on the profits of any one branch of productive employment, the tax would be virtually an increase of the cost of production, and the value and price of the article would rise accordingly ; by which the tax would be thrown upon the consumers of the commodity, and would not affect profits. But a general and equal tax on all profits would not affect general prices, and would fall, at least in the first instance, on capitalists alone.

There is, however, an ulterior effect, which, in a rich and prosperous country, requires to be taken into account. When the capital accumulated is so great and the rate of annual accumulation so rapid, that the country is only kept from attaining the stationary state by the emigration of capital, or by continual improvements in production ; any circumstance which virtually lowers the rate of profit cannot be without a decided influence on these phenomena. It may operate in different ways. The curtailment of profit, and the consequent increased difficulty in making a fortune or obtaining a subsistence by the employment of capital, may act as a stimulus to inventions, and to the use of them when made. If improvements in production are much accelerated, and if these improvements cheapen, directly or indirectly, any of the things habitually consumed by the labourer, profits may rise, and rise sufficiently to make up for all that is taken from them by the tax. In that case the tax will have been realized without loss to any one, the produce of the country being increased by an equal, or what would in that case be a far greater, amount. The tax, however, must even in this case be considered as paid from profits, because the receivers of profits are those who would be benefited if it were taken off.

But though the artificial abstraction of a portion of profits would have a real tendency to accelerate improvements in production, no considerable improvements might actually result, or only of such a kind as not to raise general profits at all, or not to raise them so much as the tax had diminished them. If so, the rate of profit would be brought closer to that practical minimum to which it is constantly approaching : and this diminished return to capital would either give a decided check to further accumulation, or would cause a greater proportion than before of the annual increase to be sent abroad, or wasted in unprofitable speculations. At its first imposition the tax falls wholly on profits : but the amount of increase of capital, which the tax prevents, would, if it had been allowed to continue, have tended to reduce profits to the same level ; and at every period of ten or twenty years there will be found less difference between profits as they are, and profits as they would in that case have been : until at last there is no difference, and the tax is thrown either upon the labourer or upon the landlord. The real effect of a tax on profits is to make the country possess, at any given period, a smaller capital and a smaller aggregate production, and to make the stationary state be attained earlier, and with a smaller sum of national wealth. It is possible that a tax on profits might even diminish the existing capital of the country. If the rate of profit is already at the practical minimum, that is, at the point at which all that portion of the annual increment which would tend to reduce profits is carried off either by exportation or by speculation ; then if a tax is imposed which reduces profits still lower, the same causes which previously carried off the increase would probably carry off a portion of the existing capital. A tax on profits is thus, in a state of‧capital and accumulation like that in England, extremely detrimental to the national wealth. And this effect is not confined to the case of a peculiar, and therefore intrinsically unjust, tax on profits. The mere fact that profits have to bear their share of a heavy general taxation, tends, in the same manner as a peculiar tax, to drive capital abroad, to stimulate imprudent speculations by diminishing safe gains, to discourage further accumulation, and to accelerate the attainment of the stationary state. This is thought to have been the principal cause of the decline of Holland, or rather of her having ceased to make progress.

Even in countries which do not accumulate so fast as to be always within a short interval of the stationary state, it seems impossible that, if capital is accumulating at all, its accumulation should not be in some degree retarded by the abstraction of a portion of its profit ; and unless the effect in stimulating improvements be a full counter-balance, it is inevitable that a part of the burthen will be thrown off the capitalist, upon the labourer or the landlord. One or other of these is always the loser by a diminished rate of accumulation. If population continues to increase as before, the labourer suffers : if not, cultivation is checked in its advance, and the landlords lose the accession of rent which would have accrued to them. The only countries in which a tax on profits seems likely to be permanently a burthen on capitalists exclusively, are those in which capital is stationary, because there is no new accumulation In such countries the tax might not prevent the old capital from being kept up through habit, or from unwillingness to submit to impoverishment, and so the capitalist might continue to bear the whole of the tax. It is seen from these considerations that the effects of a tax on profits are much more complex, more various, and in some points more uncertain, than writers on the subject have commonly supposed.

§ 4. We now turn to Taxes on Wages. The incidence of these is very different, according as the wages taxed are those of ordinary unskilled labour, or are the remuneration of such skilled or privileged employments, whether manual or intellectual, as are taken out of the sphere of competition by a natural or conferred monopoly.

I have already remarked, that in the present low state of popular education, all the higher grades of mental or educated labour are at a monopoly price; exceeding the wages of common workmen in a degree very far beyond that which is due to the expense, trouble, and loss of time required in qualifying for the employment. Any tax levied on these gains, which still leaves them above (or not below) their just proportion, falls on those who pay it ; they have no means of relieving themselves at the expense of any other class. The same thing is true of ordinary wages, in cases like that of the United States, or of a new colony, where, capital increasing as rapidly as population can increase, wages are kept up by the increase of capital, and not by the adherence of the labourers to a fixed standard of comforts. In such a case some deterioration of their condition, whether by a tax or otherwise, might possibly take place without checking the increase of population. The tax would in that case fall on the labourers themselves, and would reduce them prematurely to that lower state to which, on the same supposition with regard to their habits, they would in any case have been reduced ultimately, by the inevitable diminution in the rate of increase of capital, through the occupation of all the fertile land.

Some will object that, even in this case, a tax on wages cannot be detrimental to the labourers, since the money raised by it, being expended in the country, comes back to the labourers again through the demand for labour. The fallacy, however, of this doctrine has been so completely exhibited in the First Book,* that I need do little more than refer to that exposition. It was there shown that funds expended unproductively have no tendency to raise or keep up wages, unless when expended in the direct purchase of labour. If

* Supra, pp. 79–88.

the government took a tax of a shilling a week from every labourer, and laid it all out in hiring labourers for military service, public works, or the like, it would, no doubt, indemnify the labourers as a class for all that the tax took from them. That would really be " spending the money among the people." But if it expended the whole in buying goods, or in adding to the salaries of employés who bought goods with it, this would not increase the demand for labour, or tend to raise wages. Without, however, reverting to general principles, we may rely on an obvious *reductio ad absurdum*. If to take money from the labourers and spend it in commodities is giving it back to the labourers, then, to take money from other classes, and spend it in the same manner, must be giving it to the labourers; consequently, the more a government takes in taxes, the greater will be the demand for labour, and the more opulent the condition of the labourers. A proposition the absurdity of which no one can fail to see.

In the condition of most communities, wages are regulated by the habitual standard of living to which the labourers adhere, and on less than which they will not multiply. Where there exists such a standard, a tax on wages will indeed for a time be borne by the labourers themselves; but unless this temporary depression has the effect of lowering the standard itself, the increase of population will receive a check, which will raise wages, and restore the labourers to their previous condition. On whom, in this case, will the tax fall ? According to Adam Smith, on the community generally, in their character of consumers; since the rise of wages, he thought, would raise general prices. We have seen, however, that general prices depend on other causes, and are never raised by any circumstance which affects all kinds of productive employment in the same manner and degree. A rise of wages occasioned by a tax, must, like any other increase of the cost of labour, be defrayed from profits. To attempt to tax day-labourers, in an old country, is merely to impose an extra tax upon all employers of common labour; unless the tax has the much worse effect of permanently lowering the standard of comfortable subsistence in the minds of the poorest class.

We find in the preceding considerations an additional argument for the opinion already expressed, that direct taxation should stop short of the class of incomes which do not exceed what is necessary for healthful existence. These very small incomes are mostly derived from manual labour; and, as we now see, any tax imposed on these either permanently degrades the habits of the labouring class or falls on profits and burthens capitalists with an indirect tax, in addition to their share of the direct taxes ; which is doubly objectionable, both as a violation of the fundamental rule of equality, and for the reasons which, as already shown, render a peculiar tax on profits detrimental to the public wealth, and consequently to the means which society possesses of paying any taxes whatever.

§ 5. We now pass, from taxes on the separate kinds of income to a tax attempted to be assessed fairly upon all kinds ; in other words, an Income Tax. The discussion of the conditions necessary for making this tax consistent with justice, has been anticipated in the last chapter. We shall suppose, therefore, that these conditions are complied with. They are, first, that incomes below a certain amount should be altogether untaxed. This minimum should not be higher than the amount which suffices for the necessaries of the existing population. The exemption from the present [1857] income tax of all incomes under 100*l*. a year, and the lower percentage formerly levied on those between 100*l*. and 150*l*., are only defensible on the ground that almost all the indirect taxes press more heavily on incomes between 50*l*. and 150*l*. than on any others whatever.[1] The second condition is, that incomes above the limit should be taxed only in proportion to the surplus by which they exceed the limit. [2] Thirdly, that all sums saved from income and invested, should be exempt from the tax : or if this be found impracticable, that life incomes, and incomes from business and professions, should be less heavily taxed than inheritable incomes, in a degree as nearly as possible equivalent to the increased need of economy arising from their terminable character : allowance being also made, in the case of variable incomes, for their precariousness.

An income-tax, fairly assessed on these principles, would be, in point of justice, the least exceptionable of all taxes. The objection to it, in the present low state of public morality,[3] is the impossibility of ascertaining the real incomes of the contributors. The supposed

---

[1] [So since the 4th ed. (1857). The original ran : " on the ground that some taxes on necessaries are still kept up, and that almost all the existing taxes on indulgences press more heavily " &c.]

[2] [The third condition was altered in its wording in the 3rd ed. (1852), to give effect to the arguments introduced in that edition in the preceding chapter.]

[3] [So since the 3rd ed. The original ran : " The objection to it, which, with much regret I cannot help regarding as insuperable " &c.]

hardship of compelling people to disclose the amount of their incomes, ought not, in my opinion, to count for much. One of the social evils of this country is the practice, amounting to a custom, of maintaining, or attempting to maintain, the appearance to the world of a larger income than is possessed ; and it would be far better for the interest of those who yield to this weakness, if the extent of their means were universally and exactly known, and the temptation removed to expending more than they can afford, stinting real wants in order to make a false show externally. At the same time, the reason of the case, even on this point, is not so exclusively on one side of the argument as is sometimes supposed. So long as the vulgar of any country are in the debased state of mind which this national habit presupposes—so long as their respect (if such a word can be applied to it) is proportioned to what they suppose to be each person's pecuniary means—it may be doubted whether anything which would remove all uncertainty as to that point, would not considerably increase the presumption and arrogance of the vulgar rich, and their insolence towards those above them in mind and character, but below them in fortune.

Notwithstanding, too, what is called the inquisitorial nature of the tax, no amount of inquisitorial power which would be tolerated by a people the most disposed to submit to it, could enable the revenue officers to assess the tax from actual knowledge of the circumstances of contributors. Rents, salaries, annuities, and all fixed incomes, can be exactly ascertained. But the variable gains of professions, and still more the profits of business, which the person interested cannot always himself exactly ascertain, can still less be estimated with any approach to fairness by a tax-collector. The main reliance must be placed, and always has been placed, on the returns made by the person himself. No production of accounts is of much avail, except against the more flagrant cases of falsehood ; and even against these the check is very imperfect, for if fraud is intended, false accounts can generally be framed which it will baffle any means of inquiry possessed by the revenue officers to detect : the easy resource of omitting entries on the credit side being often sufficient without the aid of fictitious debts or disbursements. The tax, therefore, on whatever principles of equality it may be imposed, is in practice unequal in one of the worst ways, falling heaviest on the most conscientious. The unscrupulous succeed in evading a great proportion of what they should pay ; even persons of integrity in their ordinary transactions are tempted to palter with their consciences, at least to the extent of deciding in their own favour all points on which the smallest doubt or discussion could arise : while the strictly veracious may be made to pay more than the state intended, by the powers of arbitrary assessment necessarily intrusted to the Commissioners, as the last defence against the tax-payer's power of concealment.

It is to be feared, therefore, that the fairness which belongs to the principle of an income tax, cannot[1] be made to attach to it in practice : and that this tax, while apparently the most just of all modes of raising a revenue, is in effect more unjust than many others which are *primâ facie* more objectionable. This consideration would lead us to concur in the opinion which, until of late, has usually prevailed—that direct taxes on income should be reserved as an extraordinary resource for great national emergencies, in which the necessity of a large additional revenue overrules all objections.

The difficulties of a fair income tax have elicited a proposition for a direct tax of so much per cent, not on income, but on expenditure ; the aggregate amount of each person's expenditure being ascertained, as the amount of income now is, from statements furnished by the contributors themselves. The author of this suggestion, Mr. Revans, in a clever pamphlet on the subject,* contends that the returns which persons would furnish of their expenditure would be more trustworthy than those which they now make of their income, inasmuch as expenditure is in its own nature more public than income, and false representations of it more easily detected. He cannot, I think, have sufficiently considered, how few of the items in the annual expenditure of most families can be judged of with any approximation to correctness from the external signs. The only security would still be the veracity of individuals, and there is no reason for supposing that their statements would be more trustworthy on the subject of their expenses than that of their revenues ; especially as, the expenditure of most persons being composed of many more items than their income, there would be more scope for concealment and suppression in the detail of expenses than even of receipts.

The taxes on expenditure at present in force, either in this or in other countries, fall only on particular kinds of expenditure, and

---

[1] [" Cannot " replacing in the 3rd ed. (1852) " can never " of the original text.]

* *A Percentage Tax on Domestic Expenditure to supply the whole of the Public Revenue.* By John Revans. Published by Hatchard, in 1847.

differ no otherwise from taxes on commodities than in being paid
directly by the person who consumes or uses the article, instead
of being advanced by the producer or seller, and reimbursed in the
price. The taxes on horses and carriages, on dogs, on servants, are
all of this nature. They evidently fall on the persons from whom
they are levied—those who used the commodity taxed. A tax of a
similar description, and more important, is a house-tax; which
must be considered at somewhat greater length.

§ 6. The rent of a house consists of two parts, the ground-rent,
and what Adam Smith calls the building-rent. The first is determined by the ordinary principles of rent. It is the remuneration
given for the use of the portion of land occupied by the house
and its appurtenances; and varies from a mere equivalent for the
rent which the ground would afford in agriculture to the monopoly
rents paid for advantageous situations in populous thoroughfares.
The rent of the house itself, as distinguished from the ground, is the
equivalent given for the labour and capital expended on the building.
The fact of its being received in quarterly or half-yearly payments
makes no difference in the principles by which it is regulated. It
comprises the ordinary profit on the builder's capital, and an annuity,
sufficient at the current rate of interest, after paying for all repairs
chargeable on the proprietor, to replace the original capital by the
time the house is worn out, or by the expiration of the usual term
of a building lease.

A tax of so much per cent on the gross rent falls on both those
portions alike. The more highly a house is rented, the more it pays
to the tax, whether the quality of the situation or that of the house
itself is the cause. The incidence, however, of these two portions of
the tax must be considered separately.

As much of it as is a tax on building-rent, must ultimately fall
on the consumer, in other words the occupier. For as the profits of
building are already not above the ordinary rate, they would, if the
tax fell on the owner and not on the occupier, become lower than
the profits of untaxed employments, and houses would not be
built. It is probable, however, that for some time after the tax
was first imposed, a great part of it would fall, not on the renter,
but on the owner of the house. A large proportion of the consumers
either could not afford, or would not choose, to pay their former rent
with the tax in addition, but would content themselves with a lower
scale of accommodation. Houses therefore would be for a time in

excess of the demand. The consequence of such excess, in the case of most other articles, would be an almost immediate diminution of the supply : but so durable a commodity as houses does not rapidly diminish in amount. New buildings indeed, of the class for which the demand had decreased, would cease to be erected, except for special reasons ; but in the meantime the temporary superfluity would lower rents, and the consumers would obtain perhaps nearly the same accommodation as formerly for the same aggregate payment, rent and tax together. By degrees, however, as the existing houses wore out, or as increase of population demanded a greater supply, rents would again rise ; until it became profitable to recommence building, which would not be until the tax was wholly transferred to the occupier. In the end, therefore, the occupier bears that portion of a tax on rent which falls on the payment made for the house itself, exclusively of the ground it stands on.

The case is partly different with the portion which is a tax on ground-rent. As taxes on rent, properly so called, fall on the landlord, a tax on ground-rent, one would suppose, must fall on the ground landlord, at least after the expiration of the building lease. It will not, however, fall wholly on the landlord, unless with the tax on ground-rent there is combined an equivalent tax on agricultural rent. The lowest rent of land let for building is very little above the rent which the same ground would yield in agriculture : since it is reasonable to suppose that land, unless in case of exceptional circumstances, is let or sold for building as soon as it is decidedly worth more for that purpose than for cultivation. If, therefore, a tax were laid on ground-rents without being also laid on agricultural rents, it would, unless of trifling amount, reduce the return from the lowest ground-rents below the ordinary return from land, and would check further building quite as effectually as if it were a tax on building-rents, until either the increased demand of a growing population, or a diminution of supply by the ordinary causes of destruction, had raised the rent by a full equivalent for the tax. But whatever raises the lowest ground-rents, raises all others, since each exceeds the lowest by the market value of its peculiar advantages. [1] If, therefore, the tax on ground-rents were a fixed

[1] [The remainder of this paragraph, together with the next, appeared first in the 4th ed. (1857), and the following passage of the original (1848) was removed : " There is thus no difference between the two component elements of house-rent, in respect to the incidence of the tax. Both alike fall ultimately on the occupier : while, in both alike, if the occupier in consequence reduces his demand by contenting himself with inferior accommodation, that is, if he

sum per square foot, the more valuable situations paying no more than those least in request, this fixed payment would ultimately fall on the occupier. Suppose the lowest ground-rent to be 10*l.* per acre, and the highest 1000*l.*, a tax of 1*l.* per acre on ground-rents would ultimately raise the former to 11*l.*, and the latter consequently to 1001*l.*, since the difference of value between the two situations would be exactly what it was before : the annual pound, therefore, would be paid by the occupier. But a tax on ground-rent is supposed to be a portion of a house-tax, which is not a fixed payment, but a percentage on the rent. The cheapest site, therefore, being supposed as before to pay 1*l.*, the dearest would pay 100*l.*, of which only the 1*l.* could be thrown upon the occupier, since the rent would still be only raised to 1001*l.* Consequently, 99*l.* of the 100*l.* levied from the expensive site would fall on the ground-land-lord. A house-tax thus requires to be considered in a double aspect, as a tax on all occupiers of houses, and a tax on ground-rents.

In the vast majority of houses, the ground-rent forms but a small proportion of the annual payment made for the house, and nearly all the tax falls on the occupier. It is only in exceptional cases, like that of the favourite situations in large towns, that the predominant element in the rent of the house is the ground-rent ; and among the very few kinds of income which are fit subjects for peculiar taxation, these ground-rents hold the principal place, being the most gigantic example extant of enormous accessions of riches acquired rapidly, and in many cases unexpectedly, by a few families, from the mere accident of their possessing certain tracts of land, without their having themselves aided in the acquisition by the smallest exertion, outlay, or risk. So far therefore as a house-tax falls on the ground-landlord, it is liable to no valid objection.

In so far as it falls on the occupier, if justly proportioned to the value of the house, it is one of the fairest and most unobjectionable of all taxes. No part of a person's expenditure is a better criterion of his means, or bears, on the whole, more nearly the same proportion to them. A house-tax is a nearer approach to a fair income tax than a direct assessment on income can easily be ; having the great advantage, that it makes spontaneously all the allowances which it is so difficult to make, and so impracticable to make exactly,

prefers saving his tax from house-rent to saving it from other parts of his expenditure, he indirectly lowers ground-rent, or retards its increase ; just as a diminished consumption of agricultural produce, by making cultivation retrograde, would lower ordinary rent."]

in assessing an income tax : for if what a person pays in house-rent is a test of anything, it is a test not of what he possesses, but of what he thinks he can afford to spend. The equality of this tax can only be seriously questioned on two grounds. The first is, that a miser may escape it. This objection applies to all taxes on expenditure : nothing but a direct tax on income can reach a miser. But as misers do not now hoard their treasure, but invest it in productive employments, it not only adds to the national wealth, and consequently to the general means of paying taxes, but the payment claimable from itself is only transferred from the principal sum to the income afterwards derived from it, which pays taxes as soon as it comes to be expended. The second objection is, that a person may require a larger and more expensive house, not from having greater means but from having a larger family. Of this, however, he is not entitled to complain ; since having a large family is at a person's own choice : and, so far as concerns the public interest, is a thing rather to be discouraged than promoted.*

A large portion of the taxation of this country is raised by a house-tax. The parochial taxation of the towns entirely, and of the rural districts partially, consists of an assessment on house-rent. The window-tax, which was also a house-tax, but of a bad kind, operating as a tax on light, and a cause of deformity in building, was exchanged in 1851 for a house-tax properly so called, but on a much lower scale than that which existed previously to 1834. It is to be lamented that the new tax retains the unjust principle on

---

* [1852] Another common objection is that large and expensive accommodation is often required, not as a residence, but for business. But it is an admitted principle that buildings or portions of buildings occupied exclusively for business, such as shops, warehouses, or manufactories, ought to be exempted from house-tax. The plea that persons in business may be compelled to live in situations, such as the great thoroughfares of London, where house-rent is at a monopoly rate, seems to me unworthy of regard : since no one does so but because the extra profit, which he expects to derive from the situation, is more than an equivalent to him for the extra cost. But in any case, the bulk of the tax on this extra rent will not fall on him, but on the ground-landlord.

[1848] It has been also objected that house-rent in the rural districts is much lower than in towns, and lower in some towns and in some rural districts than in others : so that a tax proportioned to it would have a corresponding inequality of pressure. To this, however, it may be answered, that in places where house-rent is low persons of the same amount of income usually live in larger and better houses, and thus expend in house-rent more nearly the same proportion of their incomes than might at first sight appear. Or if not, the probability will be, that many of them live in those places precisely because they are too poor to live elsewhere, and have therefore the strongest claim to be taxed lightly. In some cases, it is precisely because the people are poor that house-rent remains low.

which the old house-tax was assessed, and which contributed quite as much as the selfishness of the middle classes to produce the outcry against the tax. The public were justly scandalized on learning that residences like Chatsworth or Belvoir were only rated on an imaginary rent of perhaps 200*l.* a year, under the pretext that, owing to the great expense of keeping them up, they could not be let for more. Probably, indeed, they could not be let even for that, and if the argument were a fair one, they ought not to have been taxed at all. But a house-tax is not intended as a tax on incomes derived from houses, but on expenditure incurred for them. The thing which it is wished to ascertain is what a house costs to the person who lives in it, not what it would bring in if let to some one else. When the occupier is not the owner, and does not hold on a repairing lease, the rent he pays is the measure of what the house costs him : but when he is the owner, some other measure must be sought. A valuation should be made of the house, not at what it would sell for, but at what would be the cost of rebuilding it, and this valuation might be periodically corrected by an allowance for what it had lost in value by time, or gained by repairs and improvements. The amount of the amended valuation would form a principal sum, the interest of which, at the current price of the public funds, would form the annual value at which the building should be assessed to the tax.

As incomes below a certain amount ought to be exempt from income-tax, so ought houses below a certain value from house-tax, on the universal principle of sparing from all taxation the absolute necessaries of healthful existence. In order that the occupiers of lodgings, as well as of houses, might benefit, as in justice they ought, by this exemption, it might be optional with the owners to have every portion of a house which is occupied by a separate tenant valued and assessed separately, as is now usually the case with chambers.

CHAPTER IV

§ 1. By taxes on commodities are commonly meant those which are levied either on the producers or on the carriers or dealers who intervene between them and the final purchases for consumption. Taxes imposed directly on the consumers of particular commodities, such as a house-tax, or the tax in this country on horses and carriages, might be called taxes on commodities, but are not ; the phrase being by custom confined to indirect taxes—those which are advanced by one person, to be, as is expected and intended, reimbursed by another. Taxes on commodities are either on production within the country, or on importation into it, or on conveyance or sale within it ; and are classed respectively as excise, customs, or tolls and transit duties. To whichever class they belong, and at whatever stage in the progress of the community they may be imposed, they are equivalent to an increase of the cost of production ; using that term in its most enlarged sense, which includes the cost of transport and distribution, or, in common phrase, of bringing the commodity to market.

When the cost of production is increased artificially by a tax, the effect is the same as when it is increased by natural causes. If only one or a few commodities are affected, their value and price rise, so as to compensate the producer or dealer for the peculiar burthen ; but if there were a tax on all commodities, exactly proportioned to their value, no such compensation would be obtained : there would neither be a general rise of values, which is an absurdity, nor of prices, which depend on causes entirely different. There would, however, as Mr. M'Culloch has pointed out, be a disturbance of values, some falling, others rising, owing to a circumstance, the effect of which on values and prices we formerly discussed ; the different durability of the capital employed in different occupations. The gross produce of industry consists of two parts ; one portion serving to replace the capital consumed, while the other portion is profit. Now equal capitals in two branches of production must have equal expectations of profit ; but if a greater portion of the one than of the other is fixed capital, or if that fixed capital is more durable, there will be a less consumption of capital in the year, and less will be required to replace it, so that the·profit, if absolutely the same, will form a greater proportion of the annual returns. To derive from a capital of 1000*l.* a profit of 100*l.*, the one producer may have to sell produce to the value of 1100*l.*, the other only to the value of 500*l.* If on these two branches of industry a tax be imposed of five per cent *ad valorem*, the last will be charged only with 25*l.*, the first with 55*l.* ; leaving to the one 75*l.* profit, to the other only 45*l.* To equalize, therefore, their expectation of profit, the one commodity must rise in price, or the other must fall, or both: commodities made chiefly by immediate labour must rise in value, as compared with those which are chiefly made by machinery. It is unnecessary to prosecute this branch of the inquiry any further.

§ 2. A tax on any one commodity, whether laid on its production, its importation, its carriage from place to place, or its sale, and whether the tax be a fixed sum of money for a given quantity of the commodity, or an *ad valorem* duty, will, as a general rule, raise the value and price of the commodity by at least the amount of the tax. There are few cases in which it does not raise them by more than that amount. In the first place, there are few taxes on production on account of which it is not found or deemed necessary to impose restrictive regulations on the manufacturers or dealers, in order to check evasions of the tax. These regulations are always sources of trouble and annoyance, and generally of expense, for all of which, being peculiar disadvantages, the producers or dealers must have compensation in the price of their commodity. These restrictions also frequently interfere with the processes of manufacture, requiring the producer to carry on his operations in the way most convenient to the revenue, though not the cheapest or most efficient for purposes of production. Any regulations whatever, enforced by law, make it difficult for the producer to adopt new and improved processes. Further, the necessity of advancing the tax obliges producers and dealers to carry on their business with larger capitals than would otherwise be necessary, on the whole of which they must receive the ordinary rate of profit, though a part only is employed in defraying the real expenses of production or importation. The price of the article must be such as to afford a profit on more than its natural value, instead of a profit on only its natural value. A part of the capital of the country, in short, is not employed in production, but in advances to the state, repaid in the price of goods ; and the consumers must give an indemnity to the sellers, equal to the profit which they could have made on the same capital if really employed in production.* Neither ought it to be forgotten, that whatever renders a larger capital necessary in any trade or business limits the competition in that business ; and, by giving something like a monopoly to a few dealers, may enable them either to keep up the price beyond what would afford the ordinary rate of profit, or to obtain the ordinary rate of profit with a less degree of exertion for improving and cheapening their commodity. In these several modes, taxes on commodities often cost to the consumer, through the increased price of the article, much more than they bring into the treasury of the state. There is still another consideration. The higher price necessitated by the tax, almost always checks the demand for the commodity ; and since there are many improvements in production which, to make them practicable, require a certain extent of demand, such improvements are obstructed, and many of them prevented altogether. It is a well-known fact that the branches of production in which fewest improvements are made are those with which the revenue officer interferes ; and that nothing, in general, gives a greater impulse to improvements in the production of a commodity, than taking off a tax which narrowed the market for it.

§ 3. Such are the effects of taxes on commodities, considered generally ; but as there are some commodities (those composing the necessaries of the labourer) of which the values have an influence on the distribution of wealth among different classes of the community, it is requisite to trace the effects of taxes on those particular articles somewhat farther. If a tax be laid, say on corn, and the

* [1865] It is true, this does not constitute, as at first sight it appears to do, a case of taking more out of the pockets of the people than the state receives ; since, if the state needs the advance, and gets it in this manner, it can dispense with an equivalent amount of borrowing in stock or exchequer bills. But it is more economical that the necessities of the state should be supplied from the disposable capital in the hands of the lending class, than by an artificial addition to the expenses of one or several classes of producers or dealers.

price rises in proportion to the tax, the rise of price may operate
in two ways. First : it may lower the condition of the labouring
classes ; temporarily indeed it can scarcely fail to do so. If it
diminishes their consumption of the produce of the earth, or makes
them resort to a food which the soil produces more abundantly, and
therefore more cheaply, it to that extent contributes to throw back
agriculture upon more fertile lands or less costly processes, and to
lower the value and price of corn ; which therefore ultimately
settles at a price, increased not by the whole amount of the tax,
but by only a part of its amount.   Secondly, however, it may happen
that the dearness of the taxed food does not lower the habitual
standard of the labourer's requirements, but that wages, on the
contrary, through an action on population, rise, in a shorter or
longer period, so as to compensate the labourers for their portion of
the tax ; the compensation being of course at the expense of profits.
Taxes on necessaries must thus have one of two effects.   Either
they lower the condition of the labouring classes ; or they exact
from the owners of capital, in addition to the amount due to the state
on their own necessaries, the amount due on those consumed by the
labourers.   In the last case, the tax on necessaries, like a tax on
wages, is equivalent to a peculiar tax on profits ; which is, like all
other partial taxation, unjust, and is specially prejudicial to the
increase of the national wealth.

It remains to speak of the effect on rent. Assuming (what is
usually the fact) that the consumption of food is not diminished,
the same cultivation as before will be necessary to supply the wants
of the community ; the margin of cultivation, to use Dr. Chalmers'
expression, remains where it was ; and the same land or capital
which, as the least productive, already regulated the value and
price of the whole produce, will continue to regulate them.   The
effect which a tax on agricultural produce will have on rent, depends
on its affecting or not affecting the difference between the return to
this least productive land or capital, and the returns to other lands
and capitals. Now this depends on the manner in which the tax
is imposed. If it is an *ad valorem* tax, or, what is the same thing, a
fixed proportion of the produce, such as tithe for example, it
evidently lowers corn-rents. For it takes more corn from the
better lands than from the worse ; and exactly in the degree in which
they are better ; land of twice the productiveness paying twice as
much to the tithe. Whatever takes more from the greater of two
quantities than from the less, diminishes the difference between

them. The imposition of a tithe on corn would take a tithe also from corn-rent : for if we reduce a series of numbers by a tenth each, the differences between them are reduced one-tenth.

For example, let there be five qualities of land, which severally yield, on the same extent of ground, and with the same expenditure, 100, 90, 80, 70, and 60 bushels of wheat ; the last of these being the lowest quality which the demand for food renders it necessary to cultivate. The rent of these lands will be as follows :—

The land producing	100 bushels	will yield a rent of	100 − 60, or 40 bushels
That producing	90 ,,	,,	90 − 60, or 30 ,,
,,	80 ,,	,,	80 − 60, or 20 ,,
,,	70 ,,	,,	70 − 60, or 10 ,,
,,	60 ,,	,,	no rent.

Now let a tithe be imposed, which takes from these five pieces of land, 10, 9, 8, 7, and 6 bushels respectively, the fifth quality still being the one which regulates the price, but returning to the farmer, after payment of tithe, no more than 54 bushels :—

The land producing	100 bushels reduced to 90,	will yield a rent of	90 − 54, or 36 bushels
That producing	90 ,,	,, 81	,,	81 − 54, or 27 ,,
,,	80 ,,	,, 72	,,	72 − 54, or 18 ,,
,,	70 ,,	,, 63	,,	63 − 54, or 9 ,,

and that producing 60 bushels, reduced to 54, will yield, as before, no rent. So that the rent of the first quality of land has lost four bushels ; of the second, three ; of the third, two ; and of the fourth, one : that is, each has lost exactly one-tenth. A tax, therefore, of a fixed proportion of the produce, lowers, in the same proportion, corn-rent.

But it is only corn-rent that is lowered, and not rent estimated in money, or in any other commodity. For, in the same proportion as corn-rent is reduced in quantity, the corn composing it is raised in value. Under the tithe, 54 bushels will be worth in the market what 60 were before ; and nine-tenths will in all cases sell for as much as the whole ten-tenths previously sold for. The landlords will therefore be compensated in value and price for what they lose in quantity ; and will suffer only so far as they consume their rent in kind, or, after receiving it in money, expend it in agricultural produce : that is, they only suffer as consumers of agricultural produce, and in common with all the other consumers. Considered as landlords, they have the same income as before; the tithe, therefore, falls on the consumer, and not on the landlord.

The same effect would be produced on rent, if the tax, instead of being a fixed proportion of the produce, were a fixed sum per quarter or per bushel. A tax which takes a shilling for every bushel, takes more shillings from one field than from another, just in proportion as it produces more bushels; and operates exactly like tithe, except that tithe is not only the same proportion on all lands, but is also the same proportion at all times, while a fixed sum of money per bushel will amount to a greater or a less proportion, according as corn is cheap or dear.

There are other modes of taxing agriculture, which would affect rent differently. A tax proportioned to the rent would fall wholly on the rent, and would not at all raise the price of corn, which is regulated by the portion of the produce that pays no rent. A fixed tax of so much per cultivated acre, without distinction of value, would have effects directly the reverse. Taking no more from the best qualities of land than from the worst, it would leave the differences the same as before, and consequently the same corn-rents, and the landlords would profit to the full extent of the rise of price. To put the thing in another manner ; the price must rise sufficiently to enable the worst land to pay the tax ; thus enabling all lands which produce more than the worst to pay not only the tax, but also an increased rent to the landlords. These, however, are not so much taxes on the produce of land, as taxes on the land itself. Taxes on the produce, properly so called, whether fixed or *ad valorem*, do not affect rent, but fall on the consumer : profits, however, generally bearing either the whole or the greatest part of the portion which is levied on the consumption of the labouring classes.

§ 4. The preceding is, I apprehend, a correct statement of the manner in which taxes on agricultural produce operate when first laid on. When, however, they are of old standing, their effect may be different, as was first pointed out, I believe, by Mr. Senior. It is, as we have seen, an almost infallible consequence of any reduction of profits to retard the rate of accumulation. Now the effect of accumulation, when attended by its usual accompaniment, an increase of population, is to increase the value and price of food, to raise rent and to lower profits : that is, to do precisely what is done by a tax on agricultural produce, except that this does not raise rent. The tax, therefore, merely anticipates the rise of price, and fall of profits, which would have taken place ultimately through the mere progress of accumulation ; while it at the same time prevents, or at least retards, that progress. If the rate of profit was such, previous to the imposition of a tithe, that the effect of the tithe reduces it to the practical minimum, the tithe will put a stop to all further accumulation, or cause it to take place out of the country ; and the only effect which the tithe will then have had on the consumer is to make him pay earlier the price which he would have had to pay somewhat later—part of which, indeed, in the gradual progress of wealth and population, he would have almost immediately begun to pay. After a lapse of time which would have admitted of a rise of one-tenth through the natural progress of wealth, the consumer will be paying no more than he would have paid if the tithe had never existed ; he will have ceased to pay any portion of it, and the person who will really pay it is the landlord, whom it deprives of the increase of rent which would by that time have accrued to him. At every successive point in this interval of time, less of the burthen will rest on the consumer, and more of it on the landlord : and in the ultimate result the minimum of profits will be reached with a smaller capital and population, and a lower rental, than if the course of things had not been disturbed by the imposition of the tax. If, on the other hand, the tithe or other tax on agricultural produce does not reduce profits to the minimum, but to something above the minimum, accumulation will not be stopped, but only slackened : and if population also increases, the two-fold increase will continue to produce its effects—a rise of the price of corn, and an increase of rent. These consequences, however, will not take place with the same rapidity as if the higher rate of profit had continued. At the end of twenty years the country will have a smaller population and capital than, but for the tax, it would by that time have had ; the landlords will have a smaller rent ; and the price of corn, having increased less rapidly than it would otherwise have done, will not be so much as a tenth higher than what, if there had been no tax, it would by that time have become. A part of the tax, therefore, will already have ceased to fall on the consumer, and devolved upon the landlord ; and the proportion will become greater and greater by lapse of time.

Mr. Senior illustrates this view of the subject by likening the effects of tithes, or other taxes on agricultural produce, to those of natural sterility of soil. If the land of a country without access to foreign supplies were suddenly smitten with a permanent deterioration of quality, to an extent which would make a tenth more labour necessary to raise the existing produce, the price of corn would undoubtedly rise one-tenth. But it cannot hence be inferred that if the soil of the country had from the beginning been one-tenth worse than it is, corn would at present have been one-tenth dearer than we find it. It is far more probable, that the smaller return to labour and capital, ever since the first settlement of the country, would have caused in each successive generation a less rapid increase than has taken place : that the country would now have contained less capital, and maintained a smaller population, so that, notwithstanding the inferiority of the soil, the price of corn would not have been higher, nor profits lower, than at present; rent alone would certainly have been lower. We may suppose two islands, which, being alike in extent, in natural fertility, and industrial advancement, have up to a certain time been equal in population and capital, and have had equal rentals, and the same price of corn. Let us imagine a tithe imposed in one of these islands, but not in the other. There will be immediately a difference in the price of corn, and therefore probably in profits. While profits are not tending downwards in either country, that is, while improvements in the production of necessaries fully keep pace with the increase of population, this difference of prices and profits between the islands may continue. But if, in the untithed island, capital increases, and population along with it, more than enough to counterbalance any improvements which take place, the price of corn will gradually rise, profits will fall, and rent will increase ; while in the tithed island capital and population will either not increase (beyond what is balanced by the improvements), or if they do, will increase in a less degree ; so that rent and the price of corn will either not rise at all, or rise more slowly. Rent, therefore, will soon be higher in the untithed than in the tithed island, and profits not so much higher, nor corn so much cheaper, as they were on the first imposition of the tithe. These effects will be progressive. At the end of every ten years there will be a greater difference between the rentals and between the aggregate wealth and population of the two islands, and a less difference in profits and in the price of corn.

At what point will these last differences entirely cease, and the temporary effect of taxes on agricultural produce, in raising the price, have entirely given place to the ultimate effect, that of limiting the total produce of the country ? Though the untithed island is always verging towards the point at which the price of food would overtake that in the tithed island, its progress towards that point naturally slackens as it draws nearer to attaining it; since—the difference between the two islands in the rapidity of accumulation depending upon the difference in the rates of profit —in proportion as these approximate, the movement which draws them closer together abates of its force.   The one may not actually overtake the other, until both islands reach the minimum of profits : up to that point, the tithed island may continue more or less ahead of the untithed island in the price of corn : considerably ahead if it is far from the minimum, and is therefore accumulating rapidly ; very little ahead if it is near the minimum, and accumulating slowly.

But whatever is true of the tithed and untithed islands in our hypothetical case, is true of any country having a tithe, compared with the same country if it had never had a tithe.

In England the great emigration of capital, and the almost periodical occurrence of commercial crises through the speculations occasioned by the habitually low rate of profit, are indications that profit has attained the practical, though not the ultimate minimum, and that all the savings which take place (beyond what improvements, tending to the cheapening of necessaries, make room for) are either sent abroad for investment, or periodically swept away. There can therefore, I think, be little doubt that if England had never had a tithe, or any tax on agricultural produce, the price of corn would have been by this time as high, and the rate of profits as low, as at present.   Independently of the more rapid accumulation which would have taken place if profits had not been prematurely lowered by these imposts ; the mere saving of a part of the capital which has been wasted in unsuccessful speculations, and the keeping at home a part of that which has been sent abroad, would have been quite sufficient to produce the effect.   I think, therefore, with Mr. Senior, that the tithe, even before its commutation, had ceased to be a cause of high prices or low profits, and had become a mere deduction from rent ; its other effects being, that it caused the country to have no greater capital, no larger production, and no more numerous population than if it had been one-tenth less fertile than it is ; or let us rather say one-twentieth (considering how great a portion of the land of Great Britain was tithe-free).

But though tithes and other taxes on agricultural produce, when of long standing, either do not raise the price of food and lower profits at all, or, if at all, not in proportion to the tax ; yet the abrogation of such taxes, when they exist, does not the less diminish price, and, in general, raise the rate of profit. The abolition of a tithe takes one-tenth from the cost of production, and consequently from the price, of all agricultural produce ; and unless it permanently raises the labourers' requirements, it lowers the cost of labour, and raises profits. Rent, estimated in money or in commodities, generally remains as before ; estimated in agricultural produce, it is raised. The country adds as much by the repeal of a tithe to the margin which intervenes between it and the stationary state, as is cut off from that margin by a tithe when first imposed. Accumulation is greatly accelerated ; and if population also increases, the price of corn immediately begins to recover itself, and rent to rise ; thus gradually transferring the benefit of the remission from the consumer to the landlord.

The effects which thus result from abolishing tithe, result equally from what has been done by the arrangements under the Commutation Act for converting it into a rent-charge. When the tax, instead of being levied on the whole produce of the soil, is levied only from the portions which pay rent, and does not touch any fresh extension of cultivation, the tax no longer forms any part of the cost of production of the portion of the produce which regulates the price of all the rest. The land or capital which pays no rent can now send its produce to market one-tenth cheaper. The commutation of tithe ought therefore to have produced a considerable fall in the average price of corn. If it had not come so gradually into operation, and if the price of corn had not during the same period been under the influence of several other causes of change, the effect would probably have been markedly conspicuous. As it is, there can be no doubt that this circumstance has had its share in the fall which has taken place in the cost of production and in the price of home-grown produce ; though the effects of the great agricultural improvements which have been simultaneously advancing, and of the free admission of agricultural produce from foreign countries,[1] have masked those of the other cause. This fall of price would not in itself have any tendency injurious to the landlord, since corn-rents are increased in the same ratio in which the price of corn is diminished. But neither does it in any way tend to increase his income. The rent-charge, therefore, which is substituted for tithe, is a dead loss to him at the expiration of existing leases : and the commutation of tithe was not a mere alteration in the mode

---

[1] [The reference to " free admission," &c., inserted in 4th ed. (1857).

in which the landlord bore an existing burthen, but the imposition of a new one ; relief being afforded to the consumer at the expense of the landlord, who, however, begins immediately to receive progressive indemnification at the consumer's expense, by the impulse given to accumulation and population.

§ 5. We have hitherto inquired into the effects of taxes on commodities, on the assumption that they are levied impartially on every mode in which the commodity can be produced or brought to market. Another class of considerations is opened, if we suppose that this impartiality is not maintained, and that the tax is imposed, not on the commodity, but on some particular mode of obtaining it.

Suppose that a commodity is capable of being made by two different processes ; as a manufactured commodity may be produced either by hand or by steam-power ; sugar may be made either from the sugar-cane or from beet-root, cattle fattened either on hay and green crops, or on oil-cake and the refuse of breweries. It is the interest of the community that, of the two methods, producers should adopt that which produces the best article at the lowest price. This being also the interest of the producers, unless protected against competition, and shielded from the penalties of indolence ; the process most advantageous to the community is that which, if not interfered with by government, they ultimately find it to their advantage to adopt. Suppose, however, that a tax is laid on one of the processes, and no tax at all, or one of smaller amount, on the other. If the taxed process is the one which the producers would not have adopted, the measure is simply nugatory. But if the tax falls, as it is of course intended to do, upon the one which they would have adopted, it creates an artificial motive for preferring the untaxed process, though the inferior of the two. If, therefore, it has any effect at all, it causes the commodity to be produced of worse quality, or at a greater expense of labour ; it causes so much of the labour of the community to be wasted, and the capital employed in supporting and remunerating the labour to be expended as uselessly as if it were spent in hiring men to dig holes and fill them up again. This waste of labour and capital constitutes an addition to the cost of production of the commodity, which raises its value and price in a corresponding ratio, and thus the owners of the capital are indemnified. The loss falls on the consumers ; though the capital of the country is also eventually diminished by the diminution of their means of saving, and in some degree, of their inducements to save.

The kind of tax, therefore, which comes under the general denomination of a discriminating duty, transgresses the rule that taxes should take as little as possible from the tax-payer beyond what they bring into the treasury of the state. A discriminating duty makes the consumer pay two distinct taxes, only one of which is paid to the government, and that frequently the less onerous of the two. If a tax were laid on sugar produced from the cane, leaving the sugar from beet-root untaxed, then, in so far as cane sugar continued to be used, the tax on it would be paid to the treasury, and might be as unobjectionable as most other taxes ; but if cane sugar, having previously been cheaper than beet-root sugar, was now dearer, and beet-root sugar was to any considerable amount substituted for it, and fields laid out and manufactories established in consequence, the government would gain no revenue from the beet-root sugar, while the consumers of it would pay a real tax. They would pay for beet-root sugar more than they had previously paid for cane sugar, and the difference would go to indemnify producers for a portion of the labour of the country actually thrown away, in producing by the labour of (say) three hundred men, what could be obtained by the other process with the labour of two hundred.

One of the commonest cases of discriminating duties, is that of a tax on the importation of a commodity capable of being pro- duced at home, unaccompanied by an equivalent tax on the home production. A commodity is never permanently imported, unless it can be obtained from abroad at a smaller cost of labour and capital, on the whole, than is necessary for producing it. If, therefore, by a duty on the importation, it is rendered cheaper to produce the article than to import it, an extra quantity of labour and capital is expended, without any extra result. The labour is useless, and the capital is spent in paying people for laboriously doing nothing. All custom duties which operate as an encouragement to the home production of the taxed article, are thus an eminently wasteful mode of raising a revenue.

This character belongs in a peculiar degree to custom duties on the produce of land, unless countervailed by excise duties on the home production. Such taxes bring less into the public treasury, compared with what they take from the consumers, than any other imposts to which civilized nations are usually subject. If the wheat produced in a country is twenty millions of quarters, and the consumption twenty-one millions, a million being annually imported, and if on this million a duty is laid which raises the price ten shillings per quarter, the price which is raised is not that of the million only, but of the whole twenty-one millions. Taking the most favourable, but extremely improbable, supposition, that the importation is not at all checked, nor the home production enlarged, the state gains a revenue of only half a million, while the consumers are taxed ten millions and a half; the ten millions being a contribution to the home growers, who are forced by competition to resign it all to the landlords. The consumer thus pays to the owners of land an additional tax equal to twenty times that which he pays to the state. Let us now suppose that the tax really checks importation. Suppose importation stopped altogether in ordinary years; it being found that the million of quarters can be obtained, by a more elaborate cultivation, or by breaking up inferior land, at a less advance than ten shillings upon the previous price—say, for instance, five shillings a quarter. The revenue now obtains nothing, except from the extraordinary imports which may happen to take place in a season of scarcity. But the consumers pay every year a tax of five shillings on the whole twenty-one millions of quarters, amounting to $5\frac{1}{4}$ millions sterling. Of this the odd 250,000*l.* goes to compensate the growers of the last million of quarters for the labour and capital wasted under the compulsion of the law. The remaining five millions go to enrich the landlords as before.

Such is the operation of what are technically termed Corn Laws, when first laid on; and such continues to be their operation, so long as they have any effect at all in raising the price of corn. But I am by no means of opinion that in the long run they keep up either prices or rents in the degree which these considerations might lead us to suppose. What we have said respecting the effect of tithes and other taxes on agricultural produce, applies in a great degree to corn laws : they anticipate artificially a rise of price and of rent, which would at all events have taken place through the increase of population and of production. The difference between a country without corn laws, and a country which has long had corn laws, is not so much that the last has a higher price or a larger rental, but that it has the same price and the same rental with a smaller aggregate capital and a smaller population. The imposition of corn laws raises rents, but retards that progress of accumulation which would in no long period have raised them fully as much. The repeal of corn laws tends to lower rents, but it unchains a force which, in a progressive state of capital and population, restores and even increases the former amount.   There is every reason to expect that under the virtually free importation of agricultural produce, at last extorted from the ruling powers of this country, the price of food, if population goes on increasing, will gradually but steadily rise ; though this effect may for a time be postponed by the strong current which in this country has set in (and the impulse is extending itself to other countries) towards the improvement of agricultural science, and its increased application to practice.

What we have said of duties on importation generally, is equally applicable to discriminating duties which favour importation from one place or in one particular manner, in contradistinction to others : such as the preference given to the produce of a colony, or of a country with which there is a commercial treaty : or the higher duties formerly imposed by our navigation laws on goods imported in other than British shipping.   Whatever else may be alleged in favour of such distinctions, whenever they are not nugatory, they are economically wasteful.   They induce a resort to a more costly mode of obtaining a commodity, in lieu of one less costly, and thus cause a portion of the labour which the country employs in providing itself with foreign commodities, to be sacrificed without return.

§ 6. There is one more point relating to the operation of taxes on commodities conveyed from one country to another, which requires notice : the influence which they exert on international exchanges.   Every tax on a commodity tends to raise its price, and consequently to lessen the demand for it in the market in which it is sold.   All taxes on international trade tend, therefore, to produce a disturbance and a readjustment of what we have termed the Equation of International Demand.   This consideration leads to some rather curious consequences, which have been pointed out in the separate essay on International Commerce, already several times referred to in this treatise.

Taxes on foreign trade are of two kinds—taxes on imports, and on exports.   On the first aspect of the matter it would seem that both these taxes are paid by the consumers of the commodity ; that taxes on exports consequently fall entirely on foreigners, taxes on imports wholly on the home consumer.   The true state of the case, however, is much more complicated.

" By taxing exports, we may, in certain circumstances, produce a division of the advantage of the trade more favourable to ourselves. In some cases we may draw into our coffers, at the expense of foreigners, not only the whole tax, but more than the tax: in other cases, we should gain exactly the tax; in others, less than the tax. In this last case, a part of the tax is borne by ourselves: possibly the whole, possibly even, as we shall show, more than the whole."

Reverting to the supposititious case employed in the Essay, of a trade between Germany and England in broadcloth and linen, " suppose that England taxes her export of cloth, the tax not being supposed high enough to induce Germany to produce cloth for herself. The price at which cloth can be sold in Germany is augmented by the tax. This will probably diminish the quantity consumed. It may diminish it so much that, even at the increased price, there will not be required so great a money value as before. Or it may not diminish it at all, or so little, that in consequence of the higher price, so great a money value will be purchased than before. In this last case, England will gain, at the expense of Germany, not only the whole amount of the duty, but more; for, the money value of her exports to Germany being increased, while her imports remain the same, money will flow into England from Germany. The price of cloth will rise in England, and consequently in Germany; but the price of linen will fall in Germany, and consequently in England. We shall export less cloth, and import more linen, till the equilibrium is restored. It thus appears (what is at first sight somewhat remarkable) that by taxing her exports, England would, in some conceivable circumstances, not only gain from her foreign customers the whole amount of the tax, but would also get her imports cheaper. She would get them cheaper in two ways; for she would obtain them for less money, and would have more money to purchase them with. Germany, on the other hand, would suffer doubly: she would have to pay for her cloth a price increased not only by the duty, but by the influx of money into England, while the same change in the distribution of the circulating medium would leave her less money to purchase it with.

" This, however, is only one of three possible cases. If, after the imposition of the duty, Germany requires so diminished a quantity of cloth, that its total value is exactly the same as before, the balance of trade would be undisturbed; England will gain the duty, Germany will lose it, and nothing more. If, again, the imposition of the duty occasions such a falling off in the demand that Germany requires a less pecuniary value than before, our exports will no longer pay for our imports ; money must pass from England into Germany ; and Germany's share of the advantage of the trade will be increased. By the change in the distribution of money, cloth will fall in England ; and therefore it will, of course, fall in Germany. Thus Germany will not pay the whole of the tax. From the same cause, linen will rise in Germany, and consequently in England. When this alteration of prices has so adjusted the demand that the cloth and the linen again pay for one another, the result is that Germany has paid only a part of the tax, and the remainder of what has been received into our treasury has come indirectly out of the pockets of our own consumers of linen, who pay a higher price for that imported commodity in consequence of the tax on our exports, while at the same time they, in consequence of the efflux of money and the fall of prices, have smaller money incomes wherewith to pay for the linen at that advanced price.

" It is not an impossible supposition that by taxing our exports we might not only gain nothing from the foreigner, the tax being paid out of our own pockets, but might even compel our own people to pay a second tax to the foreigner. Suppose, as before, that the demand of Germany for cloth falls off so much on the imposition of the duty, that she requires a smaller money value than before, but that the case is so different with linen in England, that when the price rises the demand either does not fall off at all, or so little that the money value required is greater than before. The first effect of laying on the duty is, as before, that the cloth exported will no longer pay for the linen imported. Money will therefore flow out of England into Germany. One effect is to raise the price of linen in Germany, and consequently in England. But this, by the supposition, instead of stopping the efflux of money, only makes it greater, because the higher the price, the greater the money value of the linen consumed. The balance, therefore, can only be restored by the other effect, which is going on at the same time, namely, the fall of cloth in the English and consequently in the German market. Even when cloth has fallen so low that its price with the duty is only equal to what its price without the duty was at first, it is not a necessary consequence that the fall will stop ; for the same amount of exportation as before will not now suffice to pay the increased money value of the imports ; and although the German consumers have now not only cloth at the old price, but likewise increased money incomes, it is not certain that they will be inclined to employ the increase of their incomes in increasing their purchases of cloth.

The price of cloth, therefore, must perhaps fall, to restore the equilibrium, more than the whole amount of the duty ; Germany may be enabled to import cloth at a lower price when it is taxed, than when it was untaxed : and this gain she will acquire at the expense of the English consumers of linen, who, in addition, will be the real payers of the whole of what is received at their own custom-house under the name of duties on the export of cloth."

It is almost unnecessary to remark that cloth and linen are here merely representatives of exports and imports in general ; and that the effect which a tax on exports might have in increasing the cost of imports, would affect the imports from all countries, and not peculiarly the articles which might be imported from the particular country to which the taxed exports were sent.

" Such are the extremely various effects which may result to ourselves and to our customers from the imposition of taxes on our exports ; and the determining circumstances are of a nature so imperfectly ascertainable, that it must be almost impossible to decide with any certainty, even after the tax has been imposed, whether we have been gainers by it or losers." In general, however, there could be little doubt that a country which imposed such taxes would succeed in making foreign countries contribute something to its revenue ; but unless the taxed article be one for which their demand is extremely urgent, they will seldom pay the whole of the amount which the tax brings in.* " In any case, whatever we gain is lost by somebody else, and there is the expense of the collection besides : if international morality, therefore, were rightly understood and acted upon, such taxes, as being contrary to the universal weal, would not exist."

Thus far of duties on exports. We now proceed to the more ordinary case of duties on imports. " We have had an example of a tax on exports, that is, on foreigners, falling in part on ourselves. We shall therefore not be surprised if we find a tax on imports, that is, on ourselves, partly falling upon foreigners.

" Instead of taxing the cloth which we export, suppose that we tax the linen which we import. The duty which we are now supposing must not be what is termed a protecting duty, that is, a duty sufficiently high to induce us to produce the article at home.

---

* Probably the strongest known instance of a large revenue raised from foreigners by a tax on exports, is the opium trade with China. The high price of the article under the government monopoly (which is equivalent to a high export duty) has so little effect in discouraging its consumption, that it is said to have been occasionally sold in China for as much as its weight in silver.

If it had this effect, it would destroy entirely the trade both in
cloth and in linen, and both countries would lose the whole of the
advantage which they previously gained by exchanging those
commodities with one another. We suppose a duty which might
diminish the consumption of the article, but which would not prevent
us from continuing to import, as before, whatever linen we did
consume.

" The equilibrium of trade would be disturbed if the imposition
of the tax diminished, in the slightest degree, the quantity of linen
consumed. For, as the tax is levied at our own custom-house, the
German exporter only receives the same price as formerly, though
the English consumer pays a higher one. If, therefore, there be any
diminution of the quantity bought, although a larger sum of money
may be actually laid out in the article, a smaller one will be due from
England to Germany : this sum will no longer be an equivalent for
the sum due from Germany to England for cloth, the balance
therefore must be paid in money. Prices will fall in Germany and
rise in England ; linen will fall in the German market ; cloth will
rise in the English. The Germans will pay a higher price for cloth,
and will have smaller money incomes to buy it with ; while the
English will obtain linen cheaper, that is, its price will exceed what
it previously was by less than the amount of the duty, while their
means of purchasing it will be increased by the increase of their
money incomes.

" If the imposition of the tax does not diminish the demand, it
will leave the trade exactly as it was before. We shall import
as much, and export as much ; the whole of the tax will be paid out
of our own pockets.

" But the imposition of a tax on a commodity almost always
diminishes the demand more or less ; and it can never, or scarcely
ever, increase the demand. It may, therefore, be laid down as a
principle, that a tax on imported commodities, when it really operates
as a tax, and not as a prohibition either total or partial, almost
always falls in part upon the foreigners who consume our goods ;
and that this is a mode in which a nation may appropriate to itself,
at the expense of foreigners, a larger share than would otherwise
belong to it of the increase in the general productiveness of the labour
and capital of the world, which results from the interchange of
commodities among nations."

Those are, therefore, in the right who maintain that taxes on
imports are partly paid by foreigners ; but they are mistaken when

they say, that it is by the foreign producer. It is not on the person from whom we buy, but on all those who buy from us, that a portion of our custom-duties spontaneously falls. It is the foreign consumer of our exported commodities, who is obliged to pay a higher price for them because we maintain revenue duties on foreign goods.

There are but two cases in which duties on commodities can in any degree, or in any manner, fall on the producer. One is, when the article is a strict monopoly, and at a scarcity price. The price in this case being only limited by the desires of the buyer ; the sum obtained from the restricted supply being the utmost which the buyers would consent to give rather than go without it ; if the treasury intercepts a part of this, the price cannot be further raised to compensate for the tax, and it must be paid from the monopoly profits. A tax on rare and high-priced wines will fall wholly on the growers, or rather, on the owners of the vineyards. The second case in which the producer sometimes bears a portion of the tax, is more important : the case of duties on the produce of land or of mines. These might be so high as to diminish materially the demand for the produce, and compel the abandonment of some of the inferior qualities of land or mines. Supposing this to be the effect, the consumers, both in the country itself and in those which dealt with it, would obtain the produce at smaller cost ; and a part only, instead of the whole, of the duty would fall on the purchaser, who would be indemnified chiefly at the expense of the landowners or mine-owners in the producing country.

Duties on importation may, then, be divided " into two classes : those which have the effect of encouraging some particular branch of domestic industry, and those which have not. The former are purely mischievous, both to the country imposing them, and to those with whom it trades. They prevent a saving of labour and capital, which, if permitted to be made, would be divided in some proportion or other between the importing country and the countries which buy what that country does or might export.

" The other class of duties are those which do not encourage one mode of procuring an article at the expense of another, but allow interchange to take place just as if the duty did not exist, and to produce the saving of labour which constitutes the motive to international, as to all other commerce. Of this kind are duties on the importation of any commodity which could not by any possibility be produced at home ; and duties not sufficiently high to counterbalance the difference of expense between the production of the article at home and its importation.   Of the money which is brought into the treasury of any country by taxes of this last description, a part only is paid by the people of that country ; the remainder by the foreign consumers of their goods.

" Nevertheless, this latter kind of taxes are in principle as ineligible as the former, though not precisely on the same ground. A protecting duty can never be a cause of gain, but always and necessarily of loss, to the country imposing it, just so far as it is efficacious to its end.   A non-protecting duty, on the contrary, would in most cases be a source of gain to the country imposing it, in so far as throwing part of the weight of its taxes upon other people is a gain ; but it would be a means which it could seldom be advisable to adopt, being so easily counteracted by a precisely similar proceeding on the other side.

" If England, in the case already supposed, sought to obtain for herself more than her natural share of the advantage of the trade with Germany, by imposing a duty upon linen, Germany would only have to impose a duty upon cloth, sufficient to diminish the demand for that article about as much as the demand for linen had been diminished in England by the tax.   Things would then be as before, and each country would pay its own tax.   Unless, indeed, the sum of the two duties exceeded the entire advantage of the trade ; for in that case the trade, and its advantage, would cease entirely.

" There would be no advantage, therefore, in imposing duties of this kind, with a view to gain by them in the manner which has been pointed out.   But when any part of the revenue is derived from taxes on commodities, these may often be as little objectionable as the rest.   It is evident, too, that considerations of reciprocity, which are quite unessential when the matter in debate is a protecting duty, are of material importance when the repeal of duties of this other description is discussed.   A country cannot be expected to renounce the power of taxing foreigners, unless foreigners will in return practise towards itself the same forbearance.   The only mode in which a country can save itself from being a loser by the revenue duties imposed by other countries on its commodities, is to impose corresponding revenue duties on theirs.   Only it must take care that those duties be not so high as to exceed all that remains of the advantage of the trade, and put an end to importation altogether, causing the article to be either produced at home, or imported from another and a dearer market."

CHAPTER V

§ 1. BESIDES direct taxes on income, and taxes on consumption, the financial systems of most countries comprise a variety of miscellaneous imposts, not strictly included in either class. The modern European systems retain many such taxes, though in much less number and variety than those semi-barbarous governments which European influence has not yet reached. In some of these, scarcely any incident of life has escaped being made an excuse for some fiscal exaction ; hardly any act, not belonging to daily routine, can be performed by any one, without obtaining leave from some agent of government, which is only granted in consideration of a payment : especially when the act requires the aid or the peculiar guarantee of a public authority. In the present treatise we may confine our attention to such taxes as lately existed, or still exist, in countries usually classed as civilized.

In almost all nations a considerable revenue is drawn from taxes on contracts. These are imposed in various forms. One expedient is that of taxing the legal instrument which serves as evidence of the contract, and which is commonly the only evidence legally admissible. In England, scarcely any contract is binding unless executed on stamped paper, which has paid a tax to government ; and until very lately, when the contract related to property the tax was proportionally much heavier on the smaller than on the larger transactions ; which is still true of some of those taxes.[1] There are also stamp-duties on the legal instruments which are evidence of the fulfilment of contracts; such as acknowledgments of receipt, and deeds of release. Taxes on contracts are not always levied by means of stamps. The duty on sales by auction, abrogated by Sir Robert Peel, was an

---

[1] [So since the 3rd ed. (1852). The original text ran : "and when the contract relates to property the tax rises, though in an irregular manner, with the pecuniary value of the property."]

instance in point. The taxes on transfers of landed property, in France, are another : in England there are stamp-duties. In some countries, contracts of many kinds are not valid unless registered, and their registration is made an occasion for a tax.

Of taxes on contracts, the most important are those on the transfer of property ; chiefly on purchases and sales. Taxes on the sale of consumable commodities are simply taxes on those commodities. If they affect only some particular commodities, they raise the prices of those commodities, and are paid by the consumer. If the attempt were made to tax all purchases and sales, which, however absurd, was for centuries the law of Spain, the tax, if it could be enforced, would be equivalent to a tax on all commodities, and would not affect prices : if levied from the sellers, it would be a tax on profits, if from the buyers, a tax on consumption ; and neither class could throw the burthen upon the other. If confined to some one mode of sale, as for example by auction, it discourages recourse to that mode, and if of any material amount, prevents it from being adopted at all, unless in a case of emergency ; in which case as the seller is under a necessity to sell, but the buyer under no necessity to buy, the tax falls on the seller ; and this was the strongest of the objections to the auction duty: it almost always fell on a necessitous person, and in the crisis of his necessities.

Taxes on the purchase and sale of land are, in most countries, liable to the same objection. Landed property in old countries is seldom parted with, except from reduced circumstances, or some urgent need : the seller, therefore, must take what he can get, while the buyer, whose object is an investment, makes his calculations on the interest which he can obtain for his money in other ways, and will not buy if he is charged with a government tax on the trans-action.* It has indeed been objected, that this argument would not apply if all modes of permanent investment, such as the purchase of government securities, shares in joint-stock companies, mortgages, and the like, were subject to the same tax. But even then, if paid by the buyer, it would be equivalent to a tax on interest : if sufficiently heavy to be of any importance, it would disturb the established relation between interest and profit ; and the disturbance would

* [1865] The statement in the text requires modification in the case of countries where the land is owned in small portions. These, being neither a badge of importance, nor in general an object of local attachment, are readily parted with at a small advance on their original cost, with the intention of buying elsewhere; and the desire of acquiring land even on disadvantageous terms is so great as to be little checked by even a high rate of taxation.

redress its· lf by a rise in the rate of interest, and a fall of the price of land and of all securities. It appears to me, therefore, that the seller is the person by whom such taxes, unless under peculiar circumstances, will generally be borne.

All taxes must be condemned which throw obstacles in the way of the sale of land, or other instruments of production. Such sales tend naturally to render the property more productive. The seller, whether moved by necessity or choice, is probably some one who is either without the means, or without the capacity, to make the most advantageous use of the property for productive purposes ; while the buyer, on the other hand, is at any rate not needy, and is frequently both inclined and able to improve the property, since, as it is worth more to such a person than to any other, he is likely to offer the highest price for it. All taxes, therefore, and all difficulties and expenses, annexed to such contracts, are decidedly detrimental ; especially in the case of land, the source of subsistence, and the original foundation of all wealth, on the improvement of which, therefore, so much depends. Too great facilities cannot be given to enable land to pass into the hands, and assume the modes of aggregation or division, most conducive to its productiveness. If landed properties are too large, alienation should be free, in order that they may be subdivided ; if too small, in order that they may be united. All taxes on the transfer of landed property should be abolished ; but, as the landlords have no claim to be relieved from any reservation which the state has hitherto made in its own favour from the amount of their rent, an annual impost equivalent to the average produce of these taxes should be distributed over the land generally, in the form of a land-tax.[1]

Some of the taxes on contracts are very pernicious, imposing a virtual penalty upon transactions which it ought to be the policy of the legislator to encourage. Of this sort is the stamp-duty on leases, which in a country of large properties are an essential condition of good agriculture ; and the taxes on insurances, a direct discouragement to prudence and forethought.[2]

[1] [The long footnote in the original edition illustrating the higher rate of stamp duties on smaller contracts, disappeared from the 3rd ed. (1852).]

[2] [At this point the following passage remained, with an unimportant verbal alteration, through the first six editions and disappeared in 1871 : " In the case of fire insurances, the tax is exactly double the amount of the premium of insurance on common risks ; so that the person insuring is obliged by the government to pay for the insurance just three times the value of the risk. If this tax existed in France, we should not see, as we do in some of her provinces, the plate of an insurance company on\ almost every cottage or hovel.

§ 2.   Nearly allied to the taxes on contracts are those on communication.   The principal of these is the postage tax ; to which
may be added taxes on advertisements, and on newspapers, which
are taxes on the communication of information.

The common mode of levying a tax on the conveyance of letters
is by making the government the sole authorized carrier of them,
and demanding a monopoly price.   When this price is so moderate
as it is in this country under the uniform penny postage, scarcely
if at all exceeding what would be charged under the freest competition by any private company, it can hardly be considered as taxation, but rather as the profits of a business ; whatever excess there
is above the ordinary profits of stock being a fair result of the saving
of expense, caused by having only one establishment and one set
of arrangements for the whole country, instead of many competing
ones.   The business, too, being one which both can and ought to
be conducted on fixed rules, is one of the few businesses which it is
not unsuitable to a government to conduct.   The post office, therefore, is at present one of the best of the sources from which this
country derives its revenue.   But a postage much exceeding what
would be paid for the same service in a system of freedom is not a
desirable tax.   Its chief weight falls on letters of business, and
increases the expense of mercantile relations between distant
places.   It is like an attempt to raise a large revenue by heavy
tolls : it obstructs all operations by which goods are conveyed from
place to place, and discourages the production of commodities in
one place for consumption in another ; which is not only in itself
one of the greatest sources of economy of labour, but is a necessary
condition of almost all improvements in production, and one of the
strongest stimulants to industry, and promoters of civilization.

The tax on advertisements was not [1] free from the same objection,
since in whatever degree advertisements are useful to business, by
facilitating the coming together of the dealer or producer and the
consumer, in that same degree, if the tax be high enough to be a
serious discouragement to advertising, it prolongs the period during
which goods remain unsold, and capital locked up in idleness.[2]

This, indeed, must be ascribed to the provident and calculating habits produced
by the dissemination of property through the labouring class : but a tax of
so extravagant an amount would be a heavy drag upon any habits of providence."]
    [1] [" Is not " until the 7th ed. (1871).]
    [2] [The next sentence of the original text disappeared from the 3rd ed.
(1852) : " In this country the amount of the duty is moderate, and the abuse

A tax on newspapers is objectionable, not so much where it does fall as where it does not, that is, where it prevents newspapers from being used. To the generality of those who buy them, newspapers are a luxury which they can as well afford to pay for as any other indulgence, and which is as unexceptionable a source of revenue. But to that large part of the community who have been taught to read, but have received little other intellectual education, newspapers are the source of nearly all the general information which they possess, and of nearly all their acquaintance with the ideas and topics current among mankind ; and an interest is more easily excited in newspapers, than in books or other more recondite sources of instruction. Newspapers contribute so little, in a direct way, to the origination of useful ideas, that many persons undervalue the importance of their office in disseminating them. They correct many prejudices and superstitions, and keep up a habit of discussion, and interest in public concerns, the absence of which is a great cause of the stagnation of mind usually found in the lower and middle, if not in all, ranks of those countries where newspapers of an important or interesting character do not exist. There ought to be no taxes (as in this country there now are not) [1] which render this great diffuser of information, of mental excitement, and mental exercise, less accessible to that portion of the public which most needs to be carried into a region of ideas and interest beyond its own limited horizon.

§ 3. In the enumeration of bad taxes, a conspicuous place must be assigned to law taxes ; which extract a revenue for the state from the various operations involved in an application to the tribunals. Like all needless expenses attached to law proceedings, they are a tax on redress, and therefore a premium on injury. Although such taxes have been abolished in this country as a general source of revenue, they still exist in the form of fees of court, for defraying the expense of the courts of justice ; under the idea, apparently, that those may fairly be required to bear the expenses of the administration of justice who reap the benefit of it. The fallacy of this doctrine was powerfully exposed by Bentham. As he remarked, those who are under the necessity of going to law are those who benefit least, not

of advertising, which is quite as conspicuous as the use, renders the abolition of the tax, though right in principle, a matter of less urgency than it might otherwise be deemed."]

[1] [The parenthesis added in 7th ed. (1871).]

most, by the law and its administration. To them the protection
which the law affords has not been complete, since they have been
obliged to resort to a court of justice to ascertain their rights, or
maintain those rights against infringement : while the remainder
of the public have enjoyed the immunity from injury conferred by
the law and the tribunals, without the inconvenience of an appeal
to them.

§ 4. Besides the general taxes of the State, there are in all or
most countries local taxes, to defray any expenses of a public nature
which it is thought best to place under the control or management
of a local authority. Some of these expenses are incurred for purposes in which the particular locality is solely or chiefly interested ;
as the paving, cleansing, and lighting of the streets ; or the making
and repairing of roads and bridges, which may be important to
people from any part of the country, but only in so far as they, or
goods in which they have an interest, pass along the roads or over
the bridges. In other cases again, the expenses are of a kind as
nationally important as any others, but are defrayed locally, because
supposed more likely to be well administered by local bodies ; as,
in England, the relief of the poor, and the support of gaols, and in
some other countries, of schools. To decide for what public objects
local superintendence is best suited, and what are those which should
be kept immediately under the central government, or under a
mixed system of local management and central superintendence, is
a question not of political economy, but of administration. It is
an important principle, however, that taxes imposed by a local
authority, being less amenable to publicity and discussion than the
acts of the government, should always be special—laid on for some
definite service, and not exceeding the expense actually incurred in
rendering the service. Thus limited, it is desirable, whenever
practicable, that the burthen should fall on those to whom the
service is rendered ; that the expense, for instance, of roads and
bridges, should be defrayed by a toll on passengers and goods conveyed by them, thus dividing the cost between those who use them
for pleasure or convenience, and the consumers of the goods which
they enable to be brought to and from the market at a diminished
expense. When, however, the tolls have repaid with interest the
whole of the expenditure, the road or bridge should be thrown open
free of toll, that it may be used also by those to whom, unless
open gratuitously, it would be valueless ; provision being made for

repairs either from the funds of the state, or by a rate levied on the localities which reap the principal benefit.

In England, almost all local taxes are direct, (the coal duty of the City of London, and a few similar imposts, being the chief exceptions,) though the greatest part of the taxation for general purposes is indirect. On the contrary, in France, Austria, and other countries where direct taxation is much more largely employed by the state, the local expenses of towns are principally defrayed by taxes levied on commodities when entering them. These indirect taxes are much more objectionable in towns than on the frontier, because the things which the country supplies to the towns are chiefly the necessaries of life and the materials of manufacture, while, of what a country imports from foreign countries, the greater part usually [1848] consists of luxuries. An octroi cannot produce a large revenue, without pressing severely upon the labouring classes of the towns ; unless their wages rise proportionally, in which case the tax falls in a great measure on the consumers of town produce, whether residing in town or country, since capital will not remain in the towns if its profits fall below their ordinary proportion as compared with the rural districts.[1]

[1] [See Appendix GG. *The Incidence of Taxation.*]

CHAPTER VI

§ 1. ARE direct or indirect taxes the most eligible ? This question, at all times interesting, has of late excited a considerable amount of discussion. In England there is a popular feeling, of old standing, in favour of indirect, or it should rather be said in opposition to direct, taxation. The feeling is not grounded on the merits of the case, and is of a puerile kind. An Englishman dislikes, not so much the payment, as the act of paying. He dislikes seeing the face of the tax-collector, and being subjected to his peremptory demand. Perhaps, too, the money which he is required to pay directly out of his pocket is the only taxation which he is quite sure that he pays at all. That a tax of one shilling per pound on tea, or of two shillings per bottle on wine, raises the price of each pound of tea and bottle of wine which he consumes, by that and more than that amount, cannot indeed be denied ; it is the fact, and is intended to be so, and he himself, at times, is perfectly aware of it ; but it makes hardly any impression on his practical feelings and associations, serving to illustrate the distinction between what is merely known to be true and what is felt to be so. The unpopularity of direct taxation, contrasted with the easy manner in which the public consent to let themselves be fleeced in the prices of commodities, has generated in many friends of improvement a directly opposite mode of thinking to the foregoing. They contend that the very reason which makes direct taxation disagreeable, makes it preferable. Under it, every one knows how much he really pays ; and if he votes for a war, or any other expensive national luxury, he does so with his eyes open to what it costs him. If all taxes were direct, taxation would be much more perceived than at present ; and there would be a security which now there is not, for economy in the public expenditure.

Although this argument is not without force, its weight is likely to be constantly diminishing. The real incidence of indirect taxation is every day more generally understood and more familiarly recognised : and whatever else may be said of the changes which are taking place in the tendencies of the human mind, it can scarcely, I think, be denied, that things are more and more estimated according to their calculated value, and less according to their non-essential accompaniments. The mere distinction between paying money directly to the tax-collector, and contributing the same sum through the intervention of the tea-dealer or the wine-merchant, no longer makes the whole difference between dislike or opposition and passive acquiescence. But further, while any such infirmity of the popular mind subsists, the argument grounded on it tells partly on the other side of the question. If our present revenue of about seventy [1862] millions were all raised by direct taxes, an extreme dissatisfaction would certainly arise at having to pay so much ; but while men's minds are so little guided by reason, as such a change of feeling from so irrelevant a cause would imply, so great an aversion to taxation might not be an unqualified good. Of the seventy millions in question, nearly thirty are pledged, under the most binding obligations, to those whose property has been borrowed and spent by the state : and while this debt remains unredeemed, a greatly increased impatience of taxation would involve no little danger of a breach of faith, similar to that which, in the defaulting states of America, has been produced, and in some of them still continues, from the same cause. That part, indeed, of the public expenditure which is devoted to the maintenance of civil and military establishments (that is, all except the interest of the national debt) affords, in many of its details, ample scope for retrenchment.[1] But while much of the revenue is wasted under the mere pretence of public service, so much of the most important business of government is left undone, that whatever can be rescued from useless expenditure is urgently required for useful. Whether the object be education ; a more efficient and accessible administration of justice ; reforms of any kind which, like the Slave Emancipation, require compensation to individual interests ; or what is as important as any of these, the entertainment of a sufficient staff of able and educated public

---

[1] [So since the 3rd ed. (1852). According to the original text, the expenditure on civil and military establishments was " still in many cases unnecessarily profuse, but though many of the items will bear great reduction, others certainly require increase," and the hope was not held out, as in the parenthesis also inserted further on in the paragraph in the 3rd ed., that retrenchment would provide sufficient means for the new purposes.]

servants, to conduct in a better than the present awkward mannei
the business of legislation and administration ; every one of these
things implies considerable expense, and many of them have again
and again been prevented by the reluctance which existed to apply
to Parliament for an increased grant of public money, though
(besides that the existing means would probably be sufficient if
applied to the proper purposes) the cost would be repaid, often
a hundred-fold, in mere pecuniary advantage to the community
generally. If so great an addition were made to the public dislike
of taxation as might be the consequence of confining it to the
direct form, the classes who profit by the misapplication of public
money might probably succeed in saving that by which they
profit, at the expense of that which would only be useful to the
public.

There is, however, a frequent plea in support of indirect taxation
which must be altogether rejected, as grounded on a fallacy. We
are often told that taxes on commodities are less burthensome
than other taxes, because the contributor can escape from them
by ceasing to use the taxed commodity. He certainly can, if that
be his object, deprive the government of the money : but he does so
by a sacrifice of his own indulgences, which (if he chose to undergo
it) would equally make up to him for the same amount taken from
him by a direct taxation. Suppose a tax laid on wine, sufficient
to add five pounds to the price of the quantity of wine which he
consumes in a year. He has only (we are told) to diminish his
consumption of wine by 5l., and he escapes the burthen. True : but
if the 5l., instead of being laid on wine, had been taken from him by
an income tax, he could, by expending 5l. less in wine, equally save
the amount of the tax, so that the difference between the two cases
is really illusory. If the government takes from the contributor
five pounds a year, whether in one way or another, exactly that
amount must be retrenched from his consumption to leave him as
well off as before ; and in either way the same amount of sacrifice,
neither more nor less, is imposed on him.

On the other hand, it is some advantage on the side of indirect
taxes, that what they exact from the contributor is taken at a time
and in a manner likely to be convenient to him. It is paid at a time
when he has at any rate a payment to make ; it causes, therefore,
no additional trouble, nor (unless the tax be on necessaries) any
inconvenience but what is inseparable from the payment of the
amount. He can also, except in the case of very perishable articles,

select his own time for laying in a stock of the commodity, and consequently for payment of the tax. The producer or dealer who advances these taxes is, indeed, sometimes subjected to inconvenience ; but, in the case of imported goods, this inconvenience is reduced to a minimum by what is called the Warehousing System, under which, instead of paying the duty at the time of importation, he is only required to do so when he takes out the goods for consumption, which is seldom done until he has either actually found, or has the prospect of immediately finding, a purchaser.

[1] The strongest objection, however, to raising the whole or the greater part of a large revenue by direct taxes, is the impossibility of assessing them fairly without a conscientious co-operation on the part of the contributors, not to be hoped for in the present low state of public morality. In the case of an income tax, we have already seen that unless it be found practicable to exempt savings altogether from the tax, the burthen cannot be apportioned with any tolerable approach to fairness upon those whose incomes are derived from business or professions ; and this is in fact admitted by most of the advocates of direct taxation, who, I am afraid, generally get over the difficulty by leaving those classes untaxed, and confining their projected income tax to " realized property," in which form it certainly has the merit of being a very easy form of plunder. But enough has been said in condemnation of this expedient. We have seen, however, that a house tax is a form of direct taxation not liable to the same objections as an income tax, and indeed liable to as few objections of any kind as perhaps any of our indirect taxes. But it would be impossible to raise by a house tax alone the greatest part of the revenue of Great Britain, without producing a very objectionable overcrowding of the population, through the strong motive which all persons would have to avoid the tax by restricting their house accommodation. Besides, even a house tax has inequalities, and consequent injustices ; no tax is exempt from them, and it is neither just nor politic to make all the inequalities fall in the same places, by calling upon one tax to defray the whole or the chief part of the public expenditure. So much of

---

[1] [The present text of the first two sentences of this paragraph dates from the 3rd ed. (1852). The original (1848) ran :

" The decisive objection, however, to raising the whole or the greater part of a large revenue by direct taxes, is the impossibility of assessing them fairly. In the case of an income-tax, I have pointed out that the burthen can never be apportioned with any tolerable approach to fairness upon those whose incomes are derived from a business or profession."]

the local taxation in this country being already in the form of a house tax, it is probable that ten millions a year would be fully as much as could beneficially be levied, through this medium, for general purposes.

A certain amount of revenue may, as we have seen, be obtained without injustice by a peculiar tax on rent. Besides the present land-tax, and an equivalent for the revenue now derived from stamp duties on the conveyance of land, some further taxation might, I have contended, at some future period be imposed, to enable the state to participate in the progressive increase of the incomes of landlords from natural causes. Legacies and inheritances, we have also seen, ought to be subjected to taxation sufficient to yield a considerable revenue. With these taxes and a house tax of suitable amount, we should, I think, have reached the prudent limits of direct taxation, save in a national emergency so urgent as to justify the government in disregarding the amount of inequality and unfairness which may ultimately be found inseparable from an income tax.[1] The remainder of the revenue would have to be provided by taxes on consumption, and the question is, which of these are the least objectionable.

§ 2.   There are some forms of indirect taxation which must be peremptorily excluded. Taxes on commodities, for revenue purposes, must not operate as protecting duties, but must be levied impartially on every mode in which the articles can be obtained, whether produced in the country itself or imported. An exclusion must also be put upon all taxes on the necessaries of life, or on the materials or instruments employed in producing those necessaries. Such taxes are always liable to encroach on what should be left untaxed, the incomes barely sufficient for healthful existence ; and on the most favourable supposition, namely, that wages rise to compensate the labourers for the tax, it operates as a peculiar tax on profits, which is at once unjust, and detrimental to national wealth.*

[1] [So since the 3rd ed. (1852). The original ran : " in disregarding the inequality and unfairness inseparable from every practicable form of income tax."]

* Some argue that the materials and instruments of all production should be exempt from taxation ; but these, when they do not enter into the production of necessaries, seem as proper subjects of taxation as the finished article. It is chiefly with reference to foreign trade that such taxes have been considered injurious. Internationally speaking, they may be looked upon as export duties, and, unless in cases in which an export duty is advisable, they should be accompanied with an equivalent drawback on exportation. But

What remain are taxes on luxuries. And these have some properties which strongly recommend them. In the first place, they can never, by any possibility, touch those whose whole income is expended on necessaries ; while they do reach those by whom what is required for necessaries is expended on indulgences. In the next place, they operate in some cases as an useful, and the only useful, kind of sumptuary law. I disclaim all asceticism, and by no means wish to see discouraged, either by law or opinion, any indulgence (consistent with the means and obligations of the person using it) which is sought from a genuine inclination for, and enjoyment of, the thing itself ; but a great portion of the expenses of the higher and middle classes in most countries, and the greatest in this, is not incurred for the sake of the pleasure afforded by the things on which the money is spent, but from regard to opinion, and an idea that certain expenses are expected from them as an appendage of station ; and I cannot but think that expenditure of this sort is a most desirable subject of taxation. If taxation discourages it, some good is done, and if not, no harm ; for in so far as taxes are levied on things which are desired and possessed from motives of this description, nobody is the worse for them. When a thing is bought not for its use but for its costliness, cheapness is no recommendation. As Sismondi remarks, the consequence of cheapening articles of vanity, is not that less is expended on such things, but that the buyers substitute for the cheapened article some other which is more costly, or a more elaborate quality of the same thing ; and as the inferior quality answered the purpose of vanity equally well when it was equally expensive, a tax on the article is really paid by nobody : it is a creation of public revenue by which nobody loses.*

there is no sufficient reason against taxing the materials and instruments used in the production of anything which is itself a fit object of taxation.

* "Were we to suppose that diamonds could only be procured from one particular and distant country, and pearls from another, and were the produce of the mines in the former, and of the fishery in the latter, from the operation of natural causes, to become doubly difficult to procure, the effect would merely be that in time half the quantity of diamonds and pearls would be sufficient to mark a certain opulence and rank, that it had before been necessary to employ for that purpose. The same quantity of gold or some commodity reducible at last to labour, would be required to produce the now reduced amount, as the former larger amount. Were the difficulty interposed by the regulations of legislators . . . . . it could make no difference to the fitness of these articles to serve the purposes of vanity." Suppose that means were discovered whereby the physiological process which generates the pearl might be induced *ad libitum*, the result being that the amount of labour expended in procuring each pearl came to be only the five-hundredth part of what it was before. "The ultimate effect of such a change would depend on whether the fishery were free or not.

§ 3.   In order to reduce as much as possible the inconveniences, and increase the advantages, incident to taxes on commodities, the following are the practical rules which suggest themselves.   1st. To raise as large a revenue as conveniently may be from those classes of luxuries which have most connexion with vanity and least with positive enjoyment ; such as the more costly qualities of all kinds of personal equipment and ornament.   2ndly. Whenever possible, to demand the tax, not from the producer, but directly from the consumer, since when levied on the producer it raises the price always by more, and often by much more, than the mere amount of the tax.   Most of the minor assessed taxes in this country are recommended by both these considerations.   But with regard to horses and carriages, as there are many persons to whom, from health or constitution, these are not so much luxuries as necessaries, the tax paid by those who have but one riding horse, or but one carriage, especially of the cheaper descriptions, should be low ; while taxation should rise very rapidly with the number of horses and carriages, and with their costliness.   3rdly. But as the only indirect taxes which yield a large revenue are those which fall on articles of universal or very general consumption, and as it is there-fore necessary to have some taxes on real luxuries, that is, on things which afford pleasure in themselves, and are valued on that account rather than for their cost ; these taxes should, if possible, be so adjusted as to fall with the same proportional weight on small, on moderate, and on large incomes.   This is not an easy matter ; since the things which are the subjects of the more productive taxes are in proportion more largely consumed by the poorer members of the community than by the rich.   Tea, coffee, sugar, tobacco, fer-mented drinks, can hardly be so taxed that the poor shall not bear

Were it free to all, as pearls could be got simply for the labour of fishing for them, a string of them might be had for a few pence.   The very poorest class of society could therefore afford to decorate their persons with them.   They would thus soon become extremely vulgar and unfashionable, and so at last valueless.   If however we suppose that instead of the fishery being free, the legislator owns and has complete command of the place, where alone pearls are to be procured ; as the progress of discovery advanced, he might impose a duty on them equal to the diminution of labour necessary to procure them. They would then be as much esteemed as they were before.   What simple beauty they have would remain unchanged.   The difficulty to be surmounted in order to obtain them would be different, but equally great, and they would therefore equally serve to mark the opulence of those who possessed them." The net revenue obtained by such a tax " would not cost the society anything. If not abused in its application, it would be a clear addition of so much to the resources of the community."—Rae, *New Principles of Political Economy,* pp. 369–71.   [*Sociological Theory of Capital,* pp. 286–88.]

more than their due share of the burthen. Something might be done by making the duty on the superior qualities, which are used by the richer consumers, much higher in proportion to the value (instead of much lower, as is almost universally the practice, under the present [1848] English system) ; but in some cases the difficulty of at all adjusting the duty to the value, so as to prevent evasion, is said, with what truth I know not, to be insuperable ; so that it is thought necessary to levy the same fixed duty on all the qualities alike : a flagrant injustice to the poorer class of contributors, unless compensated by the existence of other taxes from which, as from the present income tax, they are altogether exempt. 4thly. As far as is consistent with the preceding rules, taxation should rather be concentrated on a few articles than diffused over many, in order that the expenses of collection may be smaller, and that as few employments as possible may be burthensomely and vexatiously interfered with. 5thly. Among luxuries of general consumption, taxation should by preference attach itself to stimulants, because these, though in themselves as legitimate indulgences as any others, are more liable than most others to be used in excess, so that the check to consumption, naturally arising from taxation, is on the whole better applied to them than to other things. 6thly. As far as other considerations permit, taxation should be confined to imported articles, since these can be taxed with a less degree of vexatious interference, and with fewer incidental bad effects, than when a tax is levied on the field or on the workshop. Custom-duties are, *cæteris paribus*, much less objectionable than excise : but they must be laid only on things which either cannot, or at least will not, be produced in the country itself ; or else their production there must be prohibited (as in England is the case with tobacco), or subjected to an excise duty of equivalent amount. 7thly. No tax ought to be kept so high as to furnish a motive to its evasion too strong to be counteracted by ordinary means of prevention : and especially no commodity should be taxed so highly as to raise up a class of lawless characters, smugglers, illicit distillers, and the like.

Of the excise and custom duties lately existing in this country, all which are intrinsically unfit to form part of a good system of taxation have, since the last reforms by Mr. Gladstone, been got rid of.[1]

---

[1] [So since the 5th ed. (1862). The original (1848) ran : " Among the excise and custom duties now existing in this country, some must, on the principles we have laid down, be altogether condemned."]

Among these are all duties on ordinary articles of food,[1] whether for human beings: or for cattle; those on timber, as falling on the materials of lodging, which is one of the necessaries of life; all duties on the metals, and on implements made of them; taxes on soap, which is a necessary of cleanliness, and on tallow, the material both of that and of some other necessaries; the tax on paper, an indispensable instrument of almost all business and of most kinds of instruction. The duties which now yield nearly the whole of the customs and excise revenue, those on sugar, coffee, tea, wine, beer, spirits, and tobacco, are in themselves, where a large amount of revenue is necessary, extremely proper taxes; but at present grossly unjust, from the disproportionate weight with which they press on the poorer classes; and some of them (those on spirits and tobacco) are so high as to cause a considerable [2] amount of smuggling. It is probable that most of these taxes might bear a great reduction without any material loss of revenue. In what manner the finer articles of manufacture, consumed by the rich, might most advantageously be taxed, I must leave to be decided by those who have the requisite practical knowledge. The difficulty would be to effect it without an inadmissible degree of interference with production. In countries which, like the United States, import the principal part of the finer manufactures which they consume, there is little difficulty in the matter: and even where nothing is imported but the raw material, that may be taxed, especially the qualities of it which are exclusively employed for the fabrics used by the richer class of consumers. Thus, in England a high custom-duty on raw silk would be consistent with principle; and it might perhaps be practicable to tax the finer qualities of cotton or linen yarn, whether spun in the country itself or imported.

[1] [The footnote added to the 6th ed. (1865) was omitted from the 7th (1871): " Except the shilling per quarter duty on corn, ostensibly for registration, and scarcely felt as a burthen."]

[2] [So since 5th ed. (1862). In the original: " enormous."]

CHAPTER VII

§ 1. THE question must now be considered, how far it is right or expedient to raise money for the purposes of government, not by laying on taxes to the amount required, but by taking a portion of the capital of the country in the form of a loan, and charging the public revenue with only the interest. Nothing needs be said about providing for temporary wants by taking up money; for instance, by an issue of exchequer bills, destined to be paid off, at furthest in a year or two, from the proceeds of the existing taxes. This is a convenient expedient, and when the government does not possess a treasure or hoard, is often a necessary one, on the occurrence of extraordinary expenses, or of a temporary failure in the ordinary sources of revenue. What we have to discuss is the propriety of contracting a national debt of a permanent character; defraying the expenses of a war, or of any season of difficulty, by loans, to be redeemed either very gradually and at a distant period, or not at all.

This question has already been touched upon in the First Book.* We remarked, that if the capital taken in loans is abstracted from funds either engaged in production, or destined to be employed in it, their diversion from that purpose is equivalent to taking the amount from the wages of the labouring classes. Borrowing, in this case, is not a substitute for raising the supplies within the year. A government which borrows does actually take the amount within the year, and that too by a tax exclusively on the labouring classes : than which it could have done nothing worse, if it had supplied its wants by avowed taxation ; and in that case the transaction, and its evils, would have ended with the emergency ; while by the circuitous mode adopted, the value exacted from the labourers is gained, not by the state, but by the employers of labour, the state remaining

* Supra, pp. 77–8.

charged with the debt besides, and with its interest in perpetuity. The system of public loans, in such circumstances, may be pronounced the very worst which, in the present state of civilization, is still included in the catalogue of financial expedients.

We however remarked that there are other circumstances in which loans are not chargeable with these pernicious consequences : namely, first, when what is borrowed is foreign capital, the overflowings of the general accumulation of the world ; or, secondly, when it is capital which either would not have been saved at all unless this mode of investment had been open to it, or, after being saved, would have been wasted in unproductive enterprises, or sent to seek employment in foreign countries. When the progress of accumulation has reduced profits either to the ultimate or to the practical minimum,—to the rate less than which would either put a stop to the increase of capital, or send the whole of the new accumulations abroad ; government may annually intercept these new accumulations, without trenching on the employment or wages of the labouring classes in the country itself, or perhaps in any other country. To this extent, therefore, the loan system may be carried, without being liable to the utter and peremptory condemnation which is due to it when it overpasses this limit. What is wanted is an index to determine whether, in any given series of years, as during the last great war for example [*i.e.* 1793–1815], the limit has been exceeded or not.

Such an index exists, at once a certain and an obvious one. Did the government, by its loan operations, augment the rate of interest ? If it only opened a channel for capital which would not otherwise have been accumulated, or which, if accumulated, would not have been employed within the country ; this implies that the capital, which the government took and expended, could not have found employment at the existing rate of interest. So long as the loans do no more than absorb this surplus, they prevent any tendency to a fall of the rate of interest, but they cannot occasion any rise. When they do raise the rate of interest, as they did in a most extraordinary degree during the French war, this is positive proof that the government is a competitor for capital with the ordinary channels of productive investment, and is carrying off, not merely funds which would not, but funds which would, have found productive employment within the country. To the full extent, therefore, to which the loans of government, during the war, caused the rate of interest to exceed what it was before, and what it has been since, those loans are chargeable with all the evils which have been described. If it be objected that interest only rose because profits rose, I reply that this does not weaken, but strengthens, the argument. If the government loans produced the rise of profits by the great amount of capital which they absorbed, by what means can they have had this effect, unless by lowering the wages of labour ? It will perhaps be said, that what kept profits high during the war was not the drafts made on the national capital by the loans, but the rapid progress of industrial improvements. This, in a great measure, was the fact ; and it no doubt alleviated the hardship to the labouring classes, and made the financial system which was pursued less actively mischievous, but not less contrary to principle. These very improvements in industry made room for a larger amount of capital ; and the government, by draining away a great part of the annual accumulations, did not indeed prevent that capital from existing ultimately (for it started into existence with great rapidity after the peace), but prevented it from existing at the time, and subtracted just so much, while the war lasted, from distribution among productive labourers. If the government had abstained from taking this capital by loan, and had allowed it to reach the labourers, but had raised the supplies which it required by a direct tax on the labouring classes, it would have produced (in every respect but the expense and inconvenience of collecting the tax) the very same economical effects which it did produce, except that we should not now have had the debt. The course it actually took was therefore worse than the very worst mode which it could possibly have adopted of raising the supplies within the year ; [1] and the only excuse, or justification, which it admits of (so far as that excuse could be truly pleaded), was hard necessity ; the impossibility of raising so enormous an annual sum by taxation, without resorting to taxes which from their odiousness, or from the facility of evasion, it would have been found impracticable to enforce.

When government loans are limited to the overflowings of the national capital, or to those accumulations which would not take place at all unless suffered to overflow, they are at least not liable to this grave condemnation : they occasion no privation to any one at the time, except by the payment of the interest, and may even be beneficial to the labouring class during the term of their expenditure,

---

[1] [The concluding words of this paragraph were added in the 4th ed. (1857). At the same time the parenthesis " (in every respect . . . the tax) " was inserted above ; and the words " by the whole of that great fact " were omitted after " was therefore worse."]

by employing in the direct purchase of labour, as that of soldiers, sailors, &c., funds which might otherwise have quitted the country altogether. In this case, therefore, the question really is, what it is commonly supposed to be in all cases, namely, a choice between a great sacrifice at once, and a small one indefinitely prolonged. On this matter it seems rational to think, that the prudence of a nation will dictate the same conduct as the prudence of an individual; to submit to as much of the privation immediately as can easily be borne, and only when any further burthen would distress or cripple them too much to provide for the remainder by mortgaging their future income. It is an excellent maxim to make present resources suffice for present wants ; the future will have its own wants to provide for. On the other hand, it may reasonably be taken into consideration that in a country increasing in wealth, the necessary expenses of government do not increase in the same ratio as capital or population ; any burthen, therefore, is always less and less felt : and since those extraordinary expenses of government which are fit to be incurred at all are mostly beneficial beyond the existing generation, there is no injustice in making posterity pay a part of the price, if the inconvenience would be extreme of defraying the whole of it by the exertions and sacrifices of the generation which first incurred it.

§ 2.   When a country, wisely or unwisely, has burthened itself with a debt, is it expedient to take steps for redeeming that debt ? In principle it is impossible not to maintain the affirmative. It is true that the payment of the interest, when the creditors are members of the same community, is no national loss, but a mere transfer. The transfer, however, being compulsory, is a serious evil, and the raising a great extra revenue by any system of taxation necessitates so much expense, vexation, disturbance of the channels of industry, and other mischiefs over and above the mere payment of the money wanted by the government, that to get rid of the necessity of such taxation is at all times worth a considerable effort. The same amount of sacrifice which would have been worth incurring to avoid contracting the debt it is worth while to incur, at any subsequent time, for the purpose of extinguishing it.

Two modes have been contemplated of paying off a national debt : either at once by a general contribution, or gradually by a surplus revenue. The first would be incomparably the best, if it were practicable ; and it would be practicable if it could justly be done by assessment on property alone. If property bore the whole interest of the debt, property might, with great advantage to itself, pay it off; since this would be merely surrendering to a creditor the principal sum, the whole annual proceeds of which were already his by law; and would be equivalent to what a landowner does when he sells part of his estate to free the remainder from a mortgage. But property, it needs hardly be said, does not pay, and cannot justly be required to pay, the whole interest of the debt. Some indeed affirm that it can, on the plea that the existing generation is only bound to pay the debts of its predecessors from the assets it has received from them, and not from the produce of its own industry. But has no one received anything from previous generations except those who have succeeded to property ? Is the whole difference between the earth as it is, with its clearings and improvements, its roads and canals, its towns and manufactories, and the earth as it was when the first human being set foot on it, of no benefit to any but those who are called the owners of the soil ? Is the capital accumulated by the labour and abstinence of all former generations of no advantage to any but those who have succeeded to the legal ownership of part of it ? And have we not inherited a mass of acquired knowledge, both scientific and empirical, due to the sagacity and industry of those who preceded us, the benefits of which are the common wealth of all ? Those who are born to the owner-ship of property have, in addition to these common benefits, a separate inheritance, and to this difference it is right that advertence should be had in regulating taxation. It belongs to the general financial system of the country to take due account of this principle, and I have indicated, as in my opinion a proper mode of taking account of it, a considerable tax on legacies and inheritances. Let it be determined directly and openly what is due from property to the state, and from the state to property, and let the institutions of the state be regulated accordingly. Whatever is the fitting con-tribution from property to the general expenses of the state, in the same and in no greater proportion should it contribute towards either the interest or the repayment of the national debt.

This, however, if admitted, is fatal to any scheme for the extinc-tion of the debt by a general assessment on the community. Persons of property could pay their share of the amount by a sacrifice of property, and have the same net income as before ; but if those who have no accumulations, but only incomes, were required to make up by a single payment the equivalent of the annual charge laid on them by the taxes maintained to pay the interest of the debt, they could only do so by incurring a private debt equal to their share of the public debt; while from the insufficiency, in most cases, of the security which they could give, the interest would amount to a much larger annual sum than their share of that now paid by the state. Besides, a collective debt defrayed by taxes has, over the same debt parcelled out among individuals, the immense advantage, that it is virtually a mutual insurance among the contributors. If the fortune of a contributor diminishes, his taxes diminish; if he is ruined, they cease altogether, and his portion of the debt is wholly transferred to the solvent members of the community. If it were laid on him as a private obligation, he would still be liable to it even when penniless.

When the state possesses property, in land or otherwise, which there are not strong reasons of public utility for its retaining at its disposal, this should be employed, as far as it will go, in extinguishing debt. Any casual gain, or godsend, is naturally devoted to the same purpose. Beyond this, the only mode which is both just and feasible, of extinguishing or reducing a national debt, is by means of a surplus revenue.

§ 3. The desirableness, *per se*, of maintaining a surplus for this purpose, does not, I think, admit of a doubt. We sometimes, indeed, hear it said that the amount should rather be left to " fructify in the pockets of the people." This is a good argument, as far as it goes, against levying taxes unnecessarily for purposes of unproductive expenditure, but not against paying off a national debt. For, what is meant by the word fructify? If it means anything, it means productive employment; and as an argument against taxation, we must understand it to assert, that if the amount were left with the people they would save it, and convert it into capital. It is probable, indeed, that they would save a part, but extremely improbable that they would save the whole : while if taken by taxation, and employed in paying off debt, the whole is saved, and made productive. To the fundholder who receives the payment it is already capital, not revenue, and he will make it " fructify," that it may continue to afford him an income. The objection, therefore, is not only groundless, but the real argument is on the other side : the amount is much more certain of fructifying if it is not " left in the pockets of the people."

It is not, however, advisable in all cases to maintain a surplus revenue for the extinction of debt. The advantage of paying off the national debt of Great Britain, for instance, is that it would enable us to get rid of the worse half of our taxation. But of this worse half some portions must be worse than others, and to get rid of those would be a greater benefit proportionally than to get rid of the rest. If renouncing a surplus revenue would enable us to dispense with a tax, we ought to consider the very worst of all our taxes as precisely the one which we are keeping up for the sake of ultimately abolishing taxes not so bad as itself. In a country advancing in wealth, whose increasing revenue gives it the power of ridding itself from time to time of the most inconvenient portions of its taxation, I conceive that the increase of revenue should rather be disposed of by taking off taxes, than by liquidating debt, as long as any very objectionable imposts remain. In the present state of England [1848], therefore, I hold it to be good policy in the government, when it has a surplus of an apparently permanent character, to take off taxes, provided these are rightly selected. Even when no taxes remain but such as are not unfit to form part of a permanent system, it is wise to continue the same policy by experimental reductions of those taxes, until the point is discovered at which a given amount of revenue can be raised with the smallest pressure on the contributors. After this, such surplus revenue as might arise from any further increase of the produce of the taxes should not, I conceive, be remitted, but applied to the redemption of debt. Eventually, it might be expedient to appropriate the entire produce of particular taxes to this purpose ; since there would be more assurance that the liquidation would be persisted in, if the fund destined to it were kept apart, and not blended with the general revenues of the state. The succession duties would be peculiarly suited to such a purpose, since taxes paid, as they are, out of capital would be better employed in reimbursing capital than in defraying current expenditure. If this separate appropriation were made, any surplus afterwards arising from the increasing produce of the other taxes, and from the saving of interest on the successive portions of debt paid off, might form a ground for a remission of taxation.

It has been contended that some amount of national debt is desirable, and almost indispensable, as an investment for the savings of the poorer or more inexperienced part of the community. Its convenience in that respect is undeniable ; but (besides that the progress of industry is gradually affording other modes of investment almost as safe and untroublesome, such as the shares or obligations

of great public companies) the only real superiority of an investment
in the funds consists in the national guarantee, and this could be
afforded by other means than that of a public debt involving
compulsory taxation.   One mode which would answer the purpose
would be a national bank of deposit and discount, with ramifications
throughout the country ; which might receive any money confided
to it, and either fund it at a fixed rate of interest, or allow interest
on a floating balance, like the joint stock banks ; the interest given
being of course lower than the rate at which individuals can borrow,
in proportion to the greater security of a government investment ;
and the expenses of the establishment being defrayed by the difference between the interest which the bank would pay, and that
which it would obtain, by lending its deposits on mercantile, landed,
or other security.   There are no insuperable objections in principle,
nor, I should think, in practice, to an institution of this sort, as a
means of supplying the same convenient mode of investment now
afforded by the public funds.   It would constitute the state a great
insurance company, to insure that part of the community who live
on the interest of their property, against the risk of losing it by the
bankruptcy of those to whom they might otherwise be under the
necessity of confiding it.

CHAPTER VIII

§ 1. BEFORE we discuss the line of demarcation between the
things with which the government should, and those with which they
should not, directly interfere, it is necessary to consider the economical effects, whether of a bad or of a good complexion, arising from
the manner in which they acquit themselves of the duties which
devolve on them in all societies, and which no one denies to be
incumbent on them.

The first of these is the protection of person and property. There
is no need to expatiate on the influence exercised over the economical
interests of society by the degree of completeness with which this
duty of government is performed. Insecurity of person and property is as much as to say uncertainty of the connexion between all
human exertion or sacrifice and the attainment of the ends for the
sake of which they are undergone. It means, uncertainty whether
they who sow shall reap, whether they who produce shall consume,
and they who spare to-day shall enjoy to-morrow. It means, not
only that labour and frugality are not the road to acquisition, but
that violence is. When person and property are to a certain degree
insecure, all the possessions of the weak are at the mercy of the
strong. No one can keep what he has produced, unless he is more
capable of defending it than others who give no part of their time
and exertions to useful industry are of taking it from him. The
productive classes, therefore, when the insecurity surpasses a certain
point, being unequal to their own protection against the predatory
population, are obliged to place themselves individually in a state
of dependence on some member of the predatory class, that it
may be his interest to shield them from all depredation except
his own. In this manner, in the Middle Ages, allodial property
generally became feudal, and numbers of the poorer freemen

voluntarily made themselves and their posterity serfs of some military lord.

Nevertheless, in attaching to this great requisite, security of person and property, the importance which is justly due to it, we must not forget that even for economical purposes there are other things quite as indispensable, the presence of which will often make up for a very considerable degree of imperfection in the protective arrangements of government. As was observed in a previous chapter,* the free cities of Italy, Flanders, and the Hanseatic league, were habitually in a state of such internal turbulence, varied by such destructive external wars, that person and property enjoyed very imperfect protection ; yet during several centuries they increased rapidly in wealth and prosperity, brought many of the industrial arts to a high degree of advancement, carried on distant and dangerous voyages of exploration and commerce with extraordinary success, became an overmatch in power for the greatest feudal lords, and could defend themselves even against the sovereigns of Europe : because in the midst of turmoil and violence the citizens of those towns enjoyed a certain rude freedom, under conditions of union and co-operation, which, taken together, made them a brave, energetic, and high-spirited people, and fostered a great amount of public spirit and patriotism. The prosperity of these and other free states in a lawless age shows that a certain degree of insecurity, in some combinations of circumstances, has good as well as bad effects, by making energy and practical ability the conditions of safety. Insecurity paralyzes only when it is such in nature and in degree that no energy of which mankind in general are capable affords any tolerable means of self-protection. And this is a main reason why oppression by the government, whose power is generally irresistible by any efforts that can be made by individuals, has so much more baneful an effect on the springs of national prosperity, than almost any degree of lawlessness and turbulence under free institutions. Nations have acquired some wealth, and made some progress in improvement, in states of social union so imperfect as to border on anarchy : but no countries in which the people were exposed without limit to arbitrary exactions from the officers of government ever yet continued to have industry or wealth. A few generations of such a government never fail to extinguish both. Some of the fairest, and once the most prosperous, regions of the

* Supra, p. 114.

earth, have, under the Roman and afterwards under the Turkish dominion, been reduced to a desert, solely by that cause. I say solely, because they would have recovered with the utmost rapidity, as countries always do, from the devastations of war, or any other temporary calamities. Difficulties and hardships are often but an incentive to exertion : what is fatal to it, is the belief that it will not be suffered to produce its fruits.

§ 2. Simple over-taxation by government, though a great evil, is not comparable in the economical part of its mischiefs to exactions much more moderate in amount, which either subject the contributor to the arbitrary mandate of government officers, or are so laid on as to place skill, industry, and frugality at a disadvantage. The burthen of taxation in our own country is very great, yet as every one knows its limit, and is seldom made to pay more than he expects and calculates on, and as the modes of taxation are not of such a kind as much to impair the motives to industry and economy, the sources of prosperity are little diminished by the pressure of taxation ; they may even, as some think, be increased, by the extra exertions made to compensate for the pressure of the taxes. But in the barbarous despotisms of many countries of the East, where taxation consists in fastening upon those who have succeeded in acquiring something, in order to confiscate it, unless the possessor buys its release by submitting to give some large sum as a compromise, we cannot expect to find voluntary industry, or wealth derived from any source but plunder. And even in comparatively civilized countries, bad modes of raising a revenue have had effects similar in kind, though in an inferior degree. French writers before the Revolution represented the *taille* as a main cause of the backward state of agriculture, and of the wretched condition of the rural population ; not from its amount, but because, being proportioned to the visible capital of the cultivator, it gave him a motive for appearing poor, which sufficed to turn the scale in favour of indolence. The arbitrary powers also of fiscal officers, of *intendants* and *subdélégués*, were more destructive of prosperity than a far larger amount of exactions, because they destroyed security : there was a marked superiority in the condition of the *pays d'états*, which were exempt from this scourge. The universal venality ascribed [1848] to Russian function-aries must be an immense drag on the capabilities of economical improvement possessed so abundantly by the Russian empire : since the emoluments of public officers must depend on the success with which they can multiply vexations, for the purpose of being bought off by bribes.

Yet mere excess of taxation, even when not aggravated by uncertainty, is, independently of its injustice, a serious economical evil. It may be carried so far as to discourage industry by insufficiency of reward. Very long before it reaches this point it prevents or greatly checks accumulation, or causes the capital accumulated to be sent for investment to foreign countries. Taxes which fall on profits, even though that kind of income may not pay more than its just share, necessarily diminish the motive to any saving, except for investment in foreign countries where profits are higher. Holland, for example, seems to have long ago reached the practical minimum of profits : already in the last century her wealthy capitalists had a great part of their fortunes invested in the loans and joint-stock speculations of other countries : and this low rate of profit is ascribed to the heavy taxation, which had been in some measure forced on her by the circumstances of her position and history. The taxes indeed, besides their great amount, were many of them on necessaries, a kind of tax peculiarly injurious to industry and accumulation. But when the aggregate amount of taxation is very great, it is inevitable that recourse must be had for part of it to taxes of an objectionable character. And any taxes on consumption, when heavy, even if not operating on profits, have something of the same effect, by driving persons of moderate means to live abroad, often taking their capital with them. Although I by no means join with those political economists who think no state of national existence desirable in which there is not a rapid increase of wealth, I cannot overlook the many disadvantages to an independent nation from being brought prematurely to a stationary state, while the neighbouring countries continue advancing.

§ 3.   The subject of protection to person and property, considered as afforded by government, ramifies widely, into a number of indirect channels. It embraces, for example, the whole subject of the perfection or inefficiency of the means provided for the ascertainment of rights and the redress of injuries. Person and property cannot be considered secure where the administration of justice is imperfect, either from defect of integrity or capacity in the tribunals, or because the delay, vexation, and expense accompanying their operation impose a heavy tax on those who appeal to them, and make it preferable to submit to any endurable amount of the evils which they are designed to remedy. In England there is no fault to be found with the administration of justice, in point of pecuniary integrity ; a result which the progress of social improvement may also be supposed to have brought about in several other nations of Europe. But legal and judicial imperfections of other kinds are abundant ; and, in England especially, are a large abatement from the value of the services which the government renders back to the people in return for our enormous taxation. In the first place, the incognoscibility (as Bentham termed it) of the law, and its extreme uncertainty, even to those who best know it, render a resort to the tribunals often necessary for obtaining justice, when, there being no dispute as to facts, no litigation ought to be required. In the next place, the procedure of the tribunals is so replete with delay, vexation, and expense, that the price at which justice is at last obtained is an evil outweighing a very considerable amount of injustice ; and the wrong side, even that which the law considers such, has many chances of gaining its point, through the abandonment of litigation by the other party for want of funds, or through a compromise in which a sacrifice is made of just rights to terminate the suit, or through some technical quirk, whereby a decision is obtained on some other ground than the merits. This last detestable incident often happens without blame to the judge, under a system of law of which a great part rests on no rational principles adapted to the present state of society, but was originally founded partly on a kind of whims and conceits, and partly on the principles and incidents of feudal tenure (which now survive only as legal fictions) ; and has only been very imperfectly adapted, as cases arose, to the changes which had taken place in society. Of all parts of the English legal system, the Court of Chancery, which has the best substantive law, has been incomparably the worst as to delay, vexation, and expense ; and this is the only tribunal for most of the classes of cases which are in their nature the most complicated, such as cases of partnership, and the great range and variety of cases which come under the denomination of trust. [1] The recent reforms in this Court have abated the mischief, but are still far from having removed it.

Fortunately for the prosperity of England, the greater part of the mercantile law is comparatively modern, and was made by the tribunals by the simple process of recognising and giving force of law to the usages which, from motives of convenience, had grown up among merchants themselves : so that this part of the law, at

[1] [Added in 4th ed. (1857).]

least, was substantially made by those who were most interested in its goodness : while the defects of the tribunals have been the less practically pernicious in reference to commercial transactions, because the importance of credit, which depends on character, renders the restraints of opinion (though, as daily experience proves, an insufficient) yet a very powerful, protection against those forms of mercantile dishonesty which are generally recognised as such.

The imperfections of the law, both in its substance and in its procedure, fall heaviest upon the interests connected with what is technically called *real* property ; in the general language of European jurisprudence, immoveable property. With respect to all this portion of the wealth of the community, the law fails egregiously in the protection which it undertakes to provide. It fails, first, by the uncertainty, and the maze of technicalities, which make it impossible for any one, at however great an expense, to possess a title to land which he can positively know to be unassailable. It fails, secondly, in omitting to provide due evidence of transactions, by a proper registration of legal documents. It fails, thirdly, by creating a necessity for operose and expensive instruments and formalities (independently of fiscal burthens) on occasion of the purchase and sale, or even the lease or mortgage, of immoveable property. And, fourthly, it fails by the intolerable expense and delay of law proceedings in almost all cases in which real property is concerned. There is no doubt that the greatest sufferers by the defects of the higher courts of civil law are the landowners. Legal expenses, either those of actual litigation, or of the preparation of legal instruments, form, I apprehend, no inconsiderable item in the annual expenditure of most persons of large landed property, and the saleable value of their land is greatly impaired by the difficulty of giving to the buyer complete confidence in the title ; independently of the legal expenses which accompany the transfer. Yet the landowners, though they have been masters of the legislation of England, to say the least since 1688, have never made a single move in the direction of law reform, and have been strenuous opponents of some of the improvements of which they would more particularly reap the benefit ; especially that great one of a registration of contracts affecting land, which when proposed by a Commission of eminent real property lawyers, and introduced into the House of Commons by Lord Campbell, was so offensive to the general body of landlords, and was rejected by so large a majority, as to have long discouraged any repetition of the attempt.* This irrational hostility to improvement, in a case in which their own interest would be the most benefited by it, must be ascribed to an intense timidity on the subject of their titles, generated by the defects of the very law which they refuse to alter ; and to a conscious ignorance, and incapacity of judgment, on all legal subjects, which makes them helplessly defer to the opinion of their professional advisers, heedless of the fact that every imperfection of the law, in proportion as it is burthensome to them, brings gain to the lawyer.

In so far as the defects of legal arrangements are a mere burthen on the landowner, they do not much affect the sources of production ; but the uncertainty of the title under which land is held must often act as a great discouragement to the expenditure of capital in its improvement ; and the expense of making transfers operates to prevent land from coming into the hands of those who would use it to most advantage ; often amounting, in the case of small purchases, to more than the price of the land, and tantamount, therefore, to a prohibition of the purchase and sale of land in small portions, unless in exceptional circumstances. Such purchases, however, are almost everywhere extremely desirable, there being hardly any country in which landed property is not either too much or too little subdivided, requiring either that great estates should be broken down, or that small ones should be bought up and consolidated. To make land as easily transferable as stock would be one of the greatest, economical improvements which could be bestowed on a country ; and has been shown, again and again, to have no insuperable difficulty attending it.

Besides the excellences or defects that belong to the law and judicature of a country as a system of arrangements for attaining direct practical ends, much also depends, even in an economical point of view, upon the moral influences of the law. Enough has been said in a former place † on the degree in which both the industrial and all other combined operations of mankind depend for efficiency on their being able to rely on one another for probity and fidelity to engagements ; from which we see how greatly even the economical prosperity of a country is liable to be affected by anything in its institutions by which either integrity and trustworthiness, or the contrary qualities, are encouraged. The law everywhere ostensibly

* [1865] Lord Westbury's recent Act is a material mitigation of this grievous defect in English law, and will probably lead to further improvements.

† Supra, pp. 110-2.

favours at least pecuniary honesty and the faith of contracts ; but
if it affords facilities for evading those obligations, by trick and
chicanery, or by the unscrupulous use of riches in instituting unjust
or resisting just litigation ; if there are ways and means by which
persons may attain the ends of roguery, under the apparent sanction
of the law ; to that extent the law is demoralizing, even in regard
to pecuniary integrity.   And such cases are, unfortunately, frequent
under the English system.   If, again, the law, by a misplaced
indulgence, protects idleness or prodigality against their natural
consequences, or dismisses crime with inadequate penalties, the
effect, both on the prudential and on the social virtues, is unfavourable.   When the law, by its own dispensations and injunctions,
establishes injustice between individual and individual ; as all laws
do which recognise any form of slavery ; as the laws of all countries
do, though not all in the same degree, in respect to the family
relations ; and as the laws of many countries do, though in still
more unequal degrees, as between rich and poor ; the effect on the
moral sentiments of the people is still more disastrous.   But these
subjects introduce considerations so much larger and deeper than
those of political economy, that I only advert to them in order not
to pass wholly unnoticed things superior in importance to those of
which I treat.

CHAPTER IX

§ 1. HAVING spoken thus far of the effects produced by the excellences or defects of the general system of the law, I shall now touch upon those resulting from the special character of particular parts of it. As a selection must be made, I shall confine myself to a few leading topics. The portions of the civil law of a country which are of most importance economically (next to those which determine the *status* of the labourer, as slave, serf, or free) are those relating to the two subjects of Inheritance and Contract. Of the laws relating to contract, none are more important economically than the laws of partnership, and those of insolvency. It happens that on all these three points there is just ground for condemning some of the provisions of the English law.

With regard to Inheritance, I have, in an early chapter, considered the general principles of the subject, and suggested what appear to me to be, putting all prejudices apart, the best dispositions which the law could adopt. Freedom of bequest as the general rule, but limited by two things : first, that if there are descendants, who, being unable to provide for themselves, would become burthensome to the state, the equivalent of whatever the state would accord to them should be reserved from the property for their benefit : and secondly, that no one person should be permitted to acquire, by inheritance, more than the amount of a moderate independence. In case of intestacy, the whole property to escheat to the state : which should be bound to make a just and reasonable provision for descendants, that is, such a provision as the parent or ancestor ought to have made, their circumstances, capacities, and mode of bringing up being considered.

The laws of inheritance, however, have probably several phases of improvement to go through, before ideas so far removed from present modes of thinking will be taken into serious consideration :

and as, among the recognised modes of determining the succession to property, some must be better and others worse, it is necessary to consider which of them deserves the preference. As an intermediate course, therefore, I would recommend the extension to all property of the present English law of inheritance affecting personal property (freedom of bequest, and in case of intestacy, equal division) : except that no rights should be acknowledged in collaterals, and that the property of those who have neither descendants nor ascendants, and make no will, should escheat to the state.

The laws of existing nations deviate from these maxims in two opposite ways. In England, and in most of the countries where the influence of feudality is still felt in the laws, one of the objects aimed at in respect to land and other immoveable property is to keep it together in large masses : accordingly, in cases of intestacy, it passes, generally speaking (for the local custom of a few places is different), exclusively to the eldest son. And though the rule of primogeniture is not binding on testators, who in England have nominally the power of bequeathing their property as they please, any proprietor may so exercise this power as to deprive his immediate successor of it, by entailing the property on one particular line of his descendants : which, besides preventing it from passing by inheritance in any other than the prescribed manner, is attended with the incidental consequence of precluding it from being sold ; since each successive possessor, having only a life interest in the property, cannot alienate it for a longer period than his own life. In some other countries, such as France, the law, on the contrary, compels division of inheritances ; not only, in case of intestacy, sharing the property, both real and personal, equally among all the children, or (if there are no children) among all relatives in the same degree of propinquity ; but also not recognising any power of bequest, or recognising it over only a limited portion of the property, the remainder being subjected to compulsory equal division.

Neither of these systems, I apprehend, was introduced, or is perhaps maintained, in the countries where it exists, from any general considerations of justice, or any foresight of economical consequences, but chiefly from political motives ; in the one case to keep up large hereditary fortunes, and a landed aristocracy ; in the other, to break these down, and prevent their resurrection. The first object, as an aim of national policy, I conceive to be eminently undesirable : with regard to the second, I have pointed out what seems to me a better mode of attaining it. The merit, or demerit, however, of either purpose, belongs to the general science of politics, not to the limited department of that science which is here treated of. Each of the two systems is a real and efficient instrument for the purpose intended by it ; but each, as it appears to me, achieves that purpose at the cost of much mischief.

§ 2. There are two arguments of an economical character which are urged in favour of primogeniture. One is, the stimulus applied to the industry and ambition of younger children, by leaving them to be the architects of their own fortunes. This argument was put by Dr. Johnson in a manner more forcible than complimentary to an hereditary aristocracy, when he said, by way of recommendation of primogeniture, that it " makes but one fool in a family." It is curious that a defender of aristocratic institutions should be the person to assert that to inherit such a fortune as takes away any necessity for exertion is generally fatal to activity and strength of mind : in the present state of education, however, the proposition, with some allowance for exaggeration, may be admitted to be true. But whatever force there is in the argument counts in favour of limiting the eldest, as well as all the other children, to a mere provision, and dispensing with even the " one fool " whom Dr. Johnson was willing to tolerate. If unearned riches are so pernicious to the character, one does not see why, in order to withhold the poison from the junior members of a family, there should be no way but to unite all their separate potions, and administer them in the largest possible dose to one selected victim. It cannot be necessary to inflict this great evil on the eldest son for want of knowing what else to do with a large fortune.

Some writers, however, look upon the effect of primogeniture in stimulating industry, as depending, not so much on the poverty of the younger children, as on the contrast between that poverty and the riches of the elder ; thinking it indispensable to the activity and energy of the hive that there should be a huge drone here and there, to impress the working bees with a due sense of the advantages of honey. " Their inferiority in point of wealth," says Mr. M'Culloch, speaking of the younger children, " and their desire to escape from this lower station, and to attain to the same level with their elder brothers, inspires them with an energy and vigour they could not otherwise feel. But the advantage of preserving large estates from being frittered down by a scheme of equal division, is not limited to its influence over the younger children of their owners.

It raises universally the standard of competence, and gives new force
to the springs which set industry in motion. The manner of living
among the great landlords is that in which every one is ambitious
of being able to indulge ; and their habits of expense, though sometimes injurious to themselves, act as powerful incentives to the
ingenuity and enterprise of the other classes, who never think their
fortunes sufficiently ample, unless they will enable them to emulate the
splendour of the richest landlords ; so that the custom of primogeniture seems to render all classes more industrious, and to augment
at the same time, the mass of wealth and the scale of enjoyment." *

The portion of truth, I can hardly say contained in these observations, but recalled by them, I apprehend to be, that a state of
complete equality of fortunes would not be favourable to active
exertion for the increase of wealth. Speaking of the mass, it is as
true of wealth as of most other distinctions—of talent, knowledge,
virtue—that those who already have, or think they have, as much
of it as their neighbours, will seldom exert themselves to acquire
more. But it is not therefore necessary that society should provide
a set of persons with large fortunes, to fulfil the social duty of standing
to be looked at, with envy and admiration, by the aspiring poor.
The fortunes which people have acquired for themselves answer the
purpose quite as well, indeed much better ; since a person is more
powerfully stimulated by the example of somebody who has earned
a fortune, than by the mere sight of somebody who possesses one ;
and the former is necessarily an example of prudence and frugality
as well as industry, while the latter much oftener sets an example
of profuse expense, which spreads, with pernicious effect, to the
very class on whom the sight of riches is supposed to have so beneficial an influence, namely, those whose weakness of mind, and taste
for ostentation, makes " the splendour of the richest landlords "
attract them with the most potent spell. In America there are few
or no hereditary fortunes ; yet industrial energy, and the ardour of
accumulation, are not supposed to be particularly backward in that
part of the world. When a country has once fairly entered into the
industrial career, which is the principal occupation of the modern,
as war was that of the ancient and mediæval world, the desire of
acquisition by industry needs no factitious stimulus : the advantages naturally inherent in riches, and the character they assume

---

* *Principles of Political Economy*, ed. 1843, p. 264. There is much more
to the same effect in the more recent treatise by the same author, *On the
Succession to Property vacant by Death.*

of a test by which talent and success in life are habitually measured, are an ample security for their being pursued with sufficient intensity and zeal. As to the deeper consideration, that the diffusion of wealth, and not its concentration, is desirable, and that the more wholesome state of society is not that in which immense fortunes are possessed by a few and coveted by all, but that in which the greatest possible numbers possess and are contented with a moderate competency, which all may hope to acquire; I refer to it in this place only to show how widely separated, on social questions, is the entire mode of thought of the defenders of primogeniture, from that which is partially promulgated in the present treatise.

The other economical argument in favour of primogeniture has special reference to landed property. It is contended that the habit of dividing inheritances equally, or with an approach to equality, among children, promotes the subdivision of land into portions too small to admit of being cultivated in an advantageous manner. This argument, eternally reproduced, has again and again been refuted by English and Continental writers. It proceeds on a supposition entirely at variance with that on which all the theorems of political economy are grounded. It assumes that mankind in general will habitually act in a manner opposed to their immediate and obvious pecuniary interest. For the division of the inheritance does not necessarily imply division of the land; which may be held in common, as is not unfrequently the case in France and Belgium; or may become the property of one of the coheirs, being charged with the shares of the others by way of mortgage; or they may sell it outright, and divide the proceeds. When the division of the land would diminish its productive power, it is the direct interest of the heirs to adopt some one of these arrangements. Supposing, however, what the argument assumes, that either from legal difficulties, or from their own stupidity and barbarism, they would not, if left to themselves, obey the dictates of this obvious interest, but would insist upon cutting up the land bodily into equal parcels, with the effect of impoverishing themselves; this would be an objection to a law such as exists in France, of compulsory division, but can be no reason why testators should be discouraged from exercising the right of bequest in general conformity to the rule of equality, since it would always be in their power to provide that the division of the inheritance should take place without dividing the land itself. That the attempts of the advocates of primogeniture to make out a case by facts against the custom of equal division are equally abortive, has been shown in a former place. In all countries, or parts of countries, in which the division of inheritances is accompanied by small holdings, it is because small holdings are the general system of the country, even on the estates of the great proprietors.

Unless a strong case of social utility can be made out for primogeniture, it stands sufficiently condemned by the general principles of justice ; being a broad distinction in the treatment of one person and of another, grounded solely on an accident.   There is no need, therefore, to make out any case of economical evil *against* primogeniture.   Such a case, however, and a very strong one, may be made.   It is a natural effect of primogeniture to make the landlords a needy class.   The object of the institution, or custom, is to keep the land together in large masses, and this it commonly accomplishes ; but the legal proprietor of a large domain is not necessarily the *bonâ fide* owner of the whole income which it yields.   It is usually charged, in each generation, with provisions for the other children.   It is often charged still more heavily by the imprudent expenditure of the proprietor.   Great landowners are generally improvident in their expenses ; they live up to their incomes when at the highest, and if any change of circumstances diminishes their resources, some time elapses before they make up their minds to retrench.   Spendthrifts in other classes are ruined, and disappear from society ; but the spendthrift landlord usually holds fast to his land, even when he has become a mere receiver of its rents for the benefit of creditors.   The same desire to keep up the " splendour " of the family, which gives rise to the custom of primogeniture, indisposes the owner to sell a part in order to set free the remainder ; their apparent are therefore habitually greater than their real means, and they are under a perpetual temptation to proportion their expenditure to the former rather than to the latter.   From such causes as these, in almost all countries of great landowners, the majority of landed estates are deeply mortgaged ; and instead of having capital to spare for improvements, it requires all the increased value of land, caused by the rapid increase of the wealth and population of the country, to preserve the class from being impoverished.

§ 3.   To avert this impoverishment, recourse was had to the contrivance of entails, whereby the order of succession was irrevocably fixed, and each holder, having only a life interest, was unable to burthen his successor.   The land thus passing, free from debt, into the possession of the heir, the family could not be ruined by the improvidence of its existing representative. The economical evils arising from this disposition of property were partly of the same kind, partly different, but on the whole greater, than those arising from primogeniture alone. The possessor could not now ruin his successors, but he could still ruin himself : he was not at all more likely than in the former case to have the means necessary for improving the property : while, even if he had, he was still less likely to employ them for that purpose, when the benefit was to accrue to a person whom the entail made independent of him, while he had probably younger children to provide for, in whose favour he could not now charge the estate. While thus disabled from being himself an improver, neither could he sell the estate to somebody who would ; since entail precludes alienation. In general he has even been unable to grant leases beyond the term of his own life ; " for," says Blackstone, " if such leases had been valid, then, under cover of long leases, the issue might have been virtually dis-inherited ; " and it has been necessary in Great Britain to relax, by statute, the rigour of entails, in order to allow either of long leases, or of the execution of improvements at the expense of the estate. It may be added that the heir of entail, being assured of succeeding to the family property, however undeserving of it, and being aware of this from his earliest years, has much more than the ordinary chances of growing up idle, dissipated, and profligate.

In England, the power of entail is more limited by law than in Scotland and in most other countries where it exists. A landowner can settle his property upon any number of persons successively who are living at the time, and upon one unborn person, on whose attaining the age of twenty-one the entail expires, and the land becomes his absolute property. An estate may in this manner be transmitted through a son, or a son and grandson, living when the deed is executed, to an unborn child of that grandson. It has been maintained that this power of entail is not sufficiently extensive to do any mischief : in truth, however, it is much larger than it seems. Entails very rarely expire ; the first heir of entail, when of age, joins with the existing possessor in resettling the estate, so as to prolong the entail for a further term. Large properties, therefore, are rarely free, for any considerable period, from the restraints of a strict settlement ; [1] though the mischief is in one respect mitigated,

---

[1] [The concluding words of this paragraph took the place in the 5th ed. (1862) of the following words of the original text : " and English entails are not, in point of fact, much less injurious than those of other countries."]

since in the renewal of the settlement for one more generation the estate is usually charged with a provision for younger children.

In an economical point of view, the best system of landed property is that in which land is most completely an object of commerce ; passing readily from hand to hand when a buyer can be found to whom it is worth while to offer a greater sum for the land than the value of the income drawn from it by its existing possessor. This of course is not meant of ornamental property, which is a source of expense, not profit ; but only of land employed for industrial uses, and held for the sake of the income which it affords. Whatever facilitates the sale of land, tends to make it a more productive instrument of the community at large ; whatever prevents or restricts its sale, subtracts from its usefulness. Now, not only has entail this effect, but primogeniture also. The desire to keep land together in large masses, from other motives than that of promoting its productiveness, often prevents changes and alienation which would increase its efficiency as an instrument.

§ 4. On the other hand, a law which, like the French, restricts the power of bequest to a narrow compass, and compels the equal division of the whole or the greater part of the property among the children, seems to me, though on different grounds, also very seriously objectionable. The only reason for recognising in the children any claim at all to more than a provision, sufficient to launch them in life, and enable them to find a livelihood, is grounded on the expressed or presumed wish of the parent ; whose claim to dispose of what is actually his own cannot be set aside by any pretensions of others to receive what is not theirs. To control the rightful owner's liberty of gift, by creating in the children a legal right superior to it, is to postpone a real claim to an imaginary one. To this great and paramount objection to the law, numerous secondary ones may be added. Desirable as it is that the parent should treat the children with impartiality, and not make an eldest son or a favourite, impartial division is not alway synonymous with equal division. Some of the children may, without fault of their own, be less capable than others of providing for themselves : some may, by other means than their own exertions, be already provided for : and impartiality may therefore require that the rule observed should not be one of equality, but of compensation. Even when equality is the object, there are sometimes better means of attaining it than the inflexible rules by which law must necessarily proceed.

If one of the coheirs, being of a quarrelsome or litigious disposition, stands upon his utmost rights, the law cannot make equitable adjustments ; it cannot apportion the property as seems best for the collective interest of all concerned ; if there are several parcels of land, and the heirs cannot agree about their value, the law cannot give a parcel to each, but every separate parcel must be either put up to sale or divided : if there is a residence, or a park or pleasure-ground, which would be destroyed, as such, by subdivision, it must be sold, perhaps at a great sacrifice both of money and of feeling. But what the law could not do, the parent could. By means of the liberty of bequest, all these points might be determined according to reason and the general interest of the persons concerned ; and the spirit of the principle of equal division might be the better observed, because the testator was emancipated from its letter. Finally, it would not then be necessary, as under the compulsory system it is, that the law should interfere authoritatively in the concerns of individuals, not only on the occurrence of a death, but throughout life, in order to guard against the attempts of parents to frustrate the legal claims of their heirs, under colour of gifts and other alienations *inter vivos*.

In conclusion ; all owners of property should, I conceive, have power to dispose by will of every part of it, but not to determine the person who should succeed to it after the death of all who were living when the will was made. Under what restrictions it should be allowable to bequeath property to one person for life, with remainder to another person already in existence, is a question belonging to general legislation, not to political economy. Such settlements would be no greater hindrance to alienation than any case of joint ownership, since the consent of persons actually in existence is all that would be necessary for any new arrangement respecting the property.

§ 5. From the subject of Inheritance I now pass to that of Contracts, and among these, to the important subject of the Laws of Partnership. How much of good or evil depends upon these laws, and how important it is that they should be the best possible, is evident to all who recognise in the extension of the co-operative principle, in the larger sense of the term, the great economical necessity of modern industry. The progress of the productive arts requiring that many sorts of industrial occupation should be carried on by larger and larger capitals, the productive power of industry must suffer by

whatever impedes the formation of large capitals through the aggregation of smaller ones.   Capitals of the requisite magnitude belonging
to single owners, do not, in most countries, exist in the needful
abundance, and would be still less numerous if the laws favoured the
diffusion instead of the concentration of property : while it is most
undesirable that all those improved processes, and those means of
efficiency and economy in production, which depend on the possession of large funds, should be monopolies in the hands of a few
rich individuals, through the difficulties experienced by persons of
moderate or small means in associating their capital.   Finally, I
must repeat my conviction, that the industrial economy which
divides society absolutely into two portions, the payers of wages
and the receivers of them, the first counted by thousands and the
last by millions, is neither fit for, nor capable of, indefinite duration :
and the possibility of changing this system for one of combination
without dependence, and unity of interest instead of organized
hostility, depends altogether upon the future developments of the
Partnership principle.

Yet there is scarcely any country whose laws do not throw great,
and in most cases intentional, obstacles in the way of the formation
of any numerous partnership.   In England it is already a serious
discouragement, that differences among partners are, practically
speaking, only capable of adjudication by the Court of Chancery :
which is often worse than placing such questions out of the pale of
all law ; since any one of the disputant parties, who is either
dishonest or litigious, can involve the others at his pleasure in the
expense, trouble, and anxiety, which are the unavoidable accompaniments of a Chancery suit, without their having the power of
freeing themselves from the infliction even by breaking up the
association.*   Besides this, it required, until lately, a separate Act

---

* [1852] Mr. Cecil Fane, the Commissioner of the Bankruptcy Court, in
his evidence before the Committee on the Law of Partnership, says : " I remember a short time ago reading a written statement by two eminent solicitors,
who said that they had known many partnership accounts go into Chancery,
but that they never knew one come out. . . . Very few of the persons who
would be disposed to engage in partnerships of this kind " (co-opérative associations of working men) " have any idea of the truth, namely, that the decision
of questions arising amongst partners is really impracticable.

" Do they not know that one partner may rob the other without any possibility of his obtaining redress ?—The fact is so ; but whether they know it or
not, I cannot undertake to say."

This flagrant injustice is, in Mr. Fane's opinion, wholly attributable to the
defects of the tribunal.   " My opinion is, that if there is one thing more easy
than another, it is the settlement of partnership questions, and for the simple

of the legislature before any joint-stock association could legally constitute itself, and be empowered to act as one body. By a statute passed a few years ago, this necessity is done away; but the statute in question is described by competent authorities as a "mass of confusion," of which they say that there "never was such an infliction" on persons entering into partnership.* [1]   When a number of persons, whether few or many, freely desire to unite their funds for a common undertaking, not asking any peculiar privilege, nor the power to dispossess any one of property, the law can have no good reason for throwing difficulties in the way of the realization of the project.   On compliance with a few simple conditions of publicity, any body of persons ought to have the power of constituting themselves into a joint-stock company, or *société en nom collectif*, without asking leave either of any public officer or of parliament.[2] As an association of many partners must practically be under the management of a few, every facility ought to be afforded to the body for exercising the necessary control and check over those few, whether they be themselves members of the association, or merely its hired servants : and in this point the English system is still at a lamentable distance from the standard of perfection.[3]

§ 6.   Whatever facilities, however, English law might give to associations formed on the principles of ordinary partnership, there is one sort of joint-stock association which until the year 1855 it absolutely disallowed, and which could only be called into existence by a special act either of the legislature or of the crown.[4]   I mean, associations with limited liability.

Associations with limited liability are of two kinds : in one, the

reason, that everything which is done in a partnership is entered in the books ; the evidence therefore is at hand ; if therefore a rational mode of proceeding were once adopted, the difficulty would altogether vanish."—Minutes of Evidence annexed to the *Report of the Select Committee on the Law of Partnership* (1851), pp. 85-7.

* *Report*, ut supra, p. 167.
[1] [So since the 3rd ed. (1852). In the original : " this necessity is done away, and the formalities which have been substituted for it are not sufficiently onerous to be very much of an impediment to such undertakings."]
[2] [The comment : " and this liberty, in England, they cannot now be fairly said not to have," (" though they have had it but for a little more than three years," omitted in 2nd ed. 1849), was dropt out of the 3rd ed.]
[3] [" Though less, I believe, owing to the defects of the law than to those of the courts of judicature " ; omitted in 3rd ed.]
[4] [So since 4th ed. (1857). In the original : " which it absolutely disallows, and which can still be only " &c.   " Until lately " was inserted in the 3rd ed. in the next paragraph.]

liability of all the partners is limited, in the other that of some of them only. The first is the *société anonyme* of the French law, which in England had until lately no other name than that of " chartered company : " meaning thereby a joint-stock company whose share-holders, by a charter from the crown or a special enactment of the legislature, stood exempted from any liability for the debts of the concern, beyond the amount of their subscriptions. The other species of limited partnership is that known to the French law under the name of *commandite ;* of this, which in England is still unrecognised and illegal, I shall speak presently.

If a number of persons choose to associate for carrying on any operation of commerce or industry, agreeing among themselves and announcing to those with whom they deal that the members of the association do not undertake to be responsible beyond the amount of the subscribed capital ; is there any reason that the law should raise objections to this proceeding, and should impose on them the unlimited responsibility which they disclaim ? For whose sake ? Not for that of the partners themselves ; for it is they whom the limitation of responsibility benefits and protects. It must therefore be for the sake of third parties ; namely, those who may have transactions with the association, and to whom it may run in debt beyond what the subscribed capital suffices to pay. But nobody is obliged to deal with the association : still less is any one obliged to give it unlimited credit. The class of persons with whom such associations have dealings are in general perfectly capable of taking care of themselves, and there seems no reason that the law should be more careful of their interests than they will themselves be ; provided no false representation is held out, and they are aware from the first what they have to trust to. The law is warranted in requiring from all joint-stock associations with limited responsibility, not only that the amount of capital on which they profess to carry on business should either be actually paid up or security given for it (if, indeed, with complete publicity, such a requirement would be necessary), but also that such accounts should be kept, accessible to individuals, and if needful, published to the world, as shall render it possible to ascertain at any time the existing state of the company's affairs, and to learn whether the capital which is the sole security for the engagements into which they enter, still subsists unimpaired : the fidelity of such accounts being guarded by sufficient penalties. When the law has thus afforded to in-dividuals all practicable means of knowing the circumstances which ought to enter into their prudential calculations in dealing with the company, there seems no more need for interfering with individual judgment in this sort of transactions, than in any other part of the private business of life.

The reason usually urged for such interference is, that the managers of an association with limited responsibility, not risking their whole fortunes in the event of loss, while in case of gain they might profit largely, are not sufficiently interested in exercising due circumspection, and are under the temptation of exposing the funds of the association to improper hazards. It is, however, well ascertained that associations with unlimited responsibility, if they have rich shareholders, can obtain, even when known to be reckless in their transactions, improper credit to an extent far exceeding what would be given to companies equally ill-conducted whose creditors had only the subscribed capital to rely on.*[1] To whichever side the balance of evil inclines, it is a consideration of more importance to the shareholders themselves than to third parties ; since, with proper securities for publicity, the capital of an association with limited liability could not be engaged in hazards beyond those ordinarily incident to the business it carries on, without the facts being known, and becoming the subject of comments by which the credit of the body would be likely to be affected in quite as great a degree as the circumstances would justify. If, under securities for publicity, it were found in practice that companies, formed on the principle of unlimited responsibility, were more skilfully and more cautiously managed, companies with limited liability would be unable to maintain an equal competition with them ; and would therefore rarely be formed, unless when such limitation was the only condition on which the necessary amount of capital could be raised : and in that case it would be very unreasonable to say that their formation ought to be prevented.

It may further be remarked, that although, with equality of capital, a company of limited liability offers a somewhat less security to those who deal with it, than one in which every shareholder is responsible with his whole fortune, yet even the weaker of these

---

* See the *Report* already referred to, pp. 145–158.
[1] [So since the 5th ed. (1862). The addition, as made in the 3rd ed. (1852), began : " It has however been proved by the evidence of several experienced witnesses before a late committee of the House of Commons that associations " &c. The original text, after " improper hazards " went on : " Admitting that this is one of the disadvantages of such associations, it is a consideration of more importance " &c.]

two securities is in some respects stronger than that which an individual capitalist can afford. In the case of an individual, there is such security as can be founded on his unlimited liability, but not that derived from publicity of transactions, or from a known and large amount of paid-up capital. This topic is well treated in an able paper by M. Coquelin, published in the *Revue des Deux Mondes* for July 1843.*

"While third parties who trade with individuals," says this writer, "scarcely ever know, except by approximation, and even that most vague and uncertain, what is the amount of capital responsible for the performance of contracts made with them, those who trade with a *société anonyme* can obtain full information if they seek it, and perform their operations with a feeling of confidence that cannot exist in the other case. Again, nothing is easier than for an individual trader to conceal the extent of his engagements, as no one can know it certainly but himself. Even his confidential clerk may be ignorant of it, as the loans he finds himself compelled to make may not all be of a character to require that they be entered in his day-book. It is a secret confined to himself; one which transpires rarely, and always slowly; one which is unveiled only when the catastrophe has occurred. On the contrary, the *société anonyme* neither can nor ought to borrow, without the fact becoming known to all the world—directors, clerks, shareholders, and the public. Its operations partake, in some respects, of the nature of those of governments. The light of day penetrates in every direction, and there can be no secrets from those who seek for information. Thus all is fixed, recorded, known, of the capital and debts in the case of the *société anonyme*, while all is uncertain and unknown in the case of the individual trader. Which of the two, we would ask the reader, presents the most favourable aspect, or the surest guarantee, to the view of those who trade with them?

"Again, availing himself of the obscurity in which his affairs are shrouded, and which he desires to increase, the private trader is enabled, so long as his business appears prosperous, to produce impressions in regard to his means far exceeding the reality, and thus to establish a credit not justified by those means. When losses occur, and he sees himself threatened with bankruptcy, the world is still ignorant of his condition, and he finds himself enabled to

---

* The quotation is from a translation published by Mr. H. C. Carey, in an American periodical, *Hunt's Merchant's Magazine*, for May and June 1845.

contract debts far beyond the possibility of payment. The fatal day arrives, and the creditors find a debt much greater than had been anticipated, while the means of payment are as much less. Even this is not all. The same obscurity which has served him so well thus far, when desiring to magnify his capital and increase his credit, now affords him the opportunity of placing a part of that capital beyond the reach of his creditors. It becomes diminished, if not annihilated. It hides itself, and not even legal remedies, nor the activity of creditors, can bring it forth from the dark corners in which it is placed. . . . Our readers can readily determine for themselves if practices of this kind are equally easy in the case of the *société anonyme*. We do not doubt that such things are possible, but we think that they will agree with us that from its nature, its organization, and the necessary publicity that attends all its actions, the liability to such occurrences is very greatly diminished."

The laws of most countries, England included, have erred in a two-fold manner with regard to joint-stock companies. While they have been most unreasonably jealous of allowing such associations to exist, especially with limited responsibility, they have generally neglected the enforcement of publicity; the best security to the public against any danger which might arise from this description of partnerships; and a security quite as much required in the case of those associations of the kind in question, which, by an exception from their general practice, they suffered to exist. Even in the instance of the Bank of England, which holds a monopoly from the legislature, and has had partial control over a matter of so much public interest as the state of the circulating medium, it is only within these few years that any publicity has been enforced; and the publicity was at first of an extremely incomplete character, though now, for most practical purposes, probably at length sufficient.

§ 7. The other kind of limited partnership which demands our attention is that in which the managing partner or partners are responsible with their whole fortunes for the engagements of the concern, but have others associated with them who contribute only definite sums, and are not liable for anything beyond, though they participate in the profits according to any rule which may be agreed on. This is called partnership *en commandite :* and the partners with limited liability (to whom, by the French law, all interference in the management of the concern is interdicted) are known by the name *commanditaires*. Such partnerships are not allowed by English law : [1] in all private partnerships, whoever shares in the profits is liable for the debts to as plenary an extent as the managing partner.

For such prohibition no satisfactory defence has ever, so far as I am aware, been made. Even the insufficient reason given against limiting the responsibility of shareholders in a joint-stock company does not apply here ; there being no diminution of the motives to circumspect management, since all who take any part in the direction of the concern are liable with their whole fortunes. To third parties, again, the security is improved by the existence of commandite ; since the amount subscribed by commanditaires is all of it available to creditors, the commanditaires losing their whole investment before any creditor can lose anything ; while, if instead of becoming partners to that amount, they had lent the sum at an interest equal to the profit they derived from it, they would have shared with the other creditors in the residue of the estate, diminishing *pro rata* the dividend obtained by all. While the practice of commandite thus conduces to the interest of creditors, it is often highly desirable for the contracting parties themselves. The managers are enabled to obtain the aid of a much greater amount of capital than they could borrow on their own security ; and persons are induced to aid useful undertakings, by embarking limited portions of capital in them, when they would not, and often could not prudently, have risked their whole fortunes on the chances of the enterprise.

It may perhaps be thought that where due facilities are afforded to joint-stock companies, commandite partnerships are not required. But there are classes of cases to which the commandite principle must always be better adapted than the joint-stock principle. " Suppose," says M. Coquelin, " an inventor seeking for a capital to carry his invention into practice. To obtain the aid of capitalists, he must offer them a share of the anticipated benefit ; they must associate themselves with him in the chances of its success. In such a case, which of the forms would he select ? Not a common partnership, certainly ; " for various reasons, and especially the extreme difficulty of finding a partner with capital, willing to risk his whole fortune on the success of the invention.* " Neither would he

---

[1] [They have been allowed since 1908. See Appendix HH. *Company and Partnership Law.*]

* [1852] " There has been a great deal of commiseration professed," says Mr. Duncan, solicitor, " towards the poor inventor ; he has been oppressed by the high cost of patents ; but his chief oppression has been the partnership law, which prevents his getting any one to help him to develop his invention.

select the *société anonyme*," or any other form of joint-stock company, " in which he might be superseded as manager. He would stand, in such an association, on no better footing than any other shareholder, and he might be lost in the crowd ; whereas, the association existing, as it were, by and for him, the management would appear to belong to him as a matter of right. Cases occur in which a merchant or a manufacturer, without being precisely an inventor, has undeniable claims to the management of an undertaking, from the possession of qualities peculiarly calculated to promote its success. So great, indeed," continues M. Coquelin, " is the necessity, in many cases, for the limited partnership, that it is difficult to conceive how we could dispense with or replace it : " and in reference to his own country he is probably in the right.

Where there is so great a readiness as in England, on the part of the public, to form joint-stock associations, even without the encouragement of a limitation of responsibility ; commandite partnership, though its prohibition is in principle quite indefensible, cannot be deemed to be, in a merely economical point of view, of the imperative necessity which M. Coquelin ascribes to it. Yet the inconveniences are not small which arise indirectly from provisions of law by which every one who shares in the profits of a concern is subject to the full liabilities of an unlimited partnership. It is impossible to say how many or what useful modes of combination are rendered impracticable by such a state of the law. It is sufficient for its condemnation that, unless in some way relaxed, it is inconsistent with the payment of wages in part by a percentage on

He is a poor man, and therefore cannot give security to a creditor ; no one will lend him money ; the rate of interest offered, however high it may be, is not an attraction. But if by the alteration of the law he could allow capitalists to take an interest with him and share the profits, while the risk should be confined to the capital they embarked, there is very little doubt at all that he would frequently get assistance from capitalists ; whereas at the present moment, with the law as it stands, he is completely destroyed, and his invention is useless to him ; he struggles month after month ; he applies again and again to the capitalists without avail. I know it practically in two or three cases of patented inventions ; especially one where parties with capital were desirous of entering into an undertaking of great moment in Liverpool, but five or six different gentlemen were deterred from doing so, all feeling the strongest objection to what each one called the cursed partnership law." —*Report*, p. 155.

Mr. Fane says, " In the course of my professional life, as a Commissioner of the Court of Bankruptcy, I have learned that the most unfortunate man in the world is an inventor. The difficulty which an inventor finds in getting at capital involves him in all sorts of embarrassments, and he ultimately is for the most part a ruined man, and somebody else gets possession of his invention."—*Ib.* p. 82.

profits ; in other words, the association of the operatives as virtual partners with the capitalist.*

It is, above all, with reference to the improvement and elevation of the working classes that complete freedom in the conditions of partnership is indispensable. Combinations such as the associations of workpeople, described in a former chapter, are the most powerful means of effecting the social emancipation of the labourers through their own moral qualities. Nor is the liberty of association important solely for its examples of success, but fully as much so for the sake of attempts which would not succeed ; but by their failure would give instruction more impressive than can be afforded by anything short of actual experience. Every theory of social improvement, the worth of which is capable of being brought to an experimental test, should be permitted, and even encouraged, to submit itself to that test. From such experiments the active portion of the working classes would derive lessons, which they would be slow to learn from the teaching of persons supposed to have interests and prejudices adverse to their good ; would obtain the means of correcting, at no cost to society, whatever is now erroneous in their notions of the means of establishing their independence ; and of discovering the conditions, moral, intellectual, and industrial, which are indispensably necessary for effecting without injustice, or for effecting at all, the social regeneration they aspire to.†

The French law of partnership is superior to the English in permitting commandite ; and superior, in having no such unmanageable instrument as the Court of Chancery, all cases arising from commercial transactions being adjudicated in a comparatively cheap and expeditious manner by a tribunal of merchants. In other respects the French system was, and I believe still is, far worse than the English. A joint-stock company with limited responsibility cannot be formed without the express authorization of the depart-

---

* [1865] It has been found possible to effect this through the Limited Liability Act, by erecting the capitalist and his workpeople into a Limited Company ; as proposed by Messrs. Briggs (supra, p. 771).

† [1862] By an Act of the year 1852, called the Industrial and Provident Societies Act, for which the nation is indebted to the public-spirited exertions of Mr. Slaney, industrial associations of working people are admitted to the statutory privileges of Friendly Societies. This not only exempts them from the formalities applicable to joint-stock companies, but provides for the settlement of disputes among the partners without recourse to the Court of Chancery. There are still some defects in the provisions of this Act, which hamper the proceedings of the Societies in several respects ; as is pointed out in the *Almanack of the Rochdale Equitable Pioneers* for 1861.

ment of government called the *Conseil d'Etat*, a body of administrators, generally entire strangers to industrial transactions, who
have no interest in promoting enterprises, and are apt to think
that the purpose of their institution is to restrain them; whose
consent cannot in any case be obtained without an amount of time
and labour which is a very serious hindrance to the commencement
of an enterprise, while the extreme uncertainty of obtaining that
consent at all is a great discouragement to capitalists who would
be willing to subscribe. In regard to joint-stock companies without
limitation of responsibility, which in England exist in such numbers
and are formed with such facility, these associations cannot, in
France, exist at all; for, in cases of unlimited partnership, the
French law does not permit the division of the capital into transferable
shares.

The best existing [1848] laws of partnership appear to be those
of the New England States. According to Mr. Carey,* " nowhere
is association so little trammelled by regulations as in New England;
the consequence of which is, that it is carried to a greater extent
there, and particularly in Massachusetts and Rhode Island, than
in any other part of the world. In these states, the soil is covered
with *compagnies anonymes*—chartered companies—for almost every
conceivable purpose. Every town is a corporation for the management of its roads, bridges, and schools: which are, therefore, under
the direct control of those who pay for them, and are consequently
well managed. Academies and churches, lyceums and libraries,
saving fund societies, and trust companies, exist in numbers proportioned to the wants of the people, and all are corporations.
Every district has its local bank, of a size to suit its wants, the
stock of which is owned by the small capitalists of the neighbourhood, and managed by themselves; the consequence of which is,
that in no part of the world is the system of banking so perfect—
so little liable to vibration in the amount of loans—the necessary
effect of which is, that in none is the value of property so little affected
by changes in the amount or value of the currency resulting from
the movements of *their own* banking institutions. In the two states
to which we have particularly referred, they are almost two hundred
in number. Massachusetts, alone, offers to our view fifty-three
insurance offices, of various forms, scattered through the state, and
all incorporated. Factories are incorporated, and are owned in

---

* In a note appended to his translation of M. Coquelin's paper.

shares; and every one that has any part in the management of
their concerns, from the purchase of the raw material to the sale
of the manufactured article, is a part owner; while every one
employed in them has a prospect of becoming one, by the use of
prudence, exertion, and economy.   Charitable associations exist in
large numbers, and all are incorporated.   Fishing vessels are owned
in shares by those who navigate them ; and the sailors of a whaling
ship depend in a great degree, if not altogether, upon the success
of the voyage for their compensation.   Every master of a vessel
trading in the Southern Ocean is a part owner, and the interest
he possesses is a strong inducement to exertion and economy, by
aid of which the people of New England are rapidly driving out
the competition of other nations for the trade of that part of the
world.   Wherever settled, they exhibit the same tendency to combination of action.   In New York they are the chief owners of
the lines of packet ships, which are divided into shares, owned
by the shipbuilders, the merchants, the master, and the mates ;
which last generally acquire the means of becoming themselves
masters, and to this is due their great success.   The system is the
most perfectly democratic of any in the world.   It affords to every
labourer, every sailor, every operative, male or female, the prospect
of advancement ; and its results are precisely such as we should
have reason to expect.   In no part of the world are talent, industry,
and prudence, so certain to be largely rewarded."

The cases of insolvency and fraud on the part of chartered
companies in America, which have caused so much loss and so
much scandal in Europe, did not occur in the part of the Union to
which this extract refers, but in other States, in which the right
of association is much more fettered by legal restrictions, and in
which, accordingly, joint-stock associations are not comparable in
number or variety to those of New England.   Mr. Carey adds,
" A careful examination of the systems of the several states, can
scarcely, we think, fail to convince the reader of the advantage
resulting from permitting men to determine among themselves the
terms upon which they will associate, and allowing the associations
that may be formed to contract with the public as to the terms
upon which they will trade together, whether of the limited or
unlimited liability of the partners." [1] This principle has been

----

[1] [This sentence replaced in the 6th ed. (1865) the comment of the original :
" and I concur in thinking that to this conclusion science and legislation must
ultimately come."]

adopted as the foundation of all recent English legislation on the subject.

§ 8. I proceed to the subject of Insolvency Laws.

Good laws on this subject are important, first and principally, on the score of public morals ; which are on no point more under the influence of the law, for good and evil, than in a matter belonging so pre-eminently to the province of law as the preservation of pecuniary integrity. But the subject is also, in a merely economical point of view, of great importance. First, because the economical well-being of a people, and of mankind, depends in an especial manner upon their being able to trust each other's engagements. Secondly, because one of the risks, or expenses, of industrial operations is the risk or expense of what are commonly called bad debts, and every saving which can be effected in this liability is a diminution of cost of production ; by dispensing with an item of outlay which in no way conduces to the desired end, and which must be paid for either by the consumer of the commodity, or from the general profits of capital, according as the burthen is peculiar or general.

The laws and practice of nations on this subject have almost always been in extremes. The ancient laws of most countries were all severity to the debtor. They invested the creditor with a power of coercion, more or less tyrannical, which he might use against his insolvent debtor, either to extort the surrender of hidden property, or to obtain satisfaction of a vindictive character, which might console him for the non-payment of the debt. This arbitrary power has extended, in some countries, to making the insolvent debtor serve the creditor as his slave : in which plan there were at least some grains of common sense, since it might possibly be regarded as a scheme for making him work out the debt by his labour. In England the coercion assumed the milder form of ordinary imprisonment. The one and the other were the barbarous expedients of a rude age, repugnant to justice, as well as to humanity. Unfortunately the reform of them, like that of the criminal law generally, has been taken in hand as an affair of humanity only, not of justice : and the modish humanity of the present time, which is essentially a thing of one idea,[1] has in this, as in other cases, gone into a violent

---

[1] [The original parenthesis " (and is indeed little better than a timid shrinking from the infliction of anything like pain, next neighbour to the cowardice which shrinks from unnecessary endurance of it) " was omitted from the 3rd ed. (1852).]

reaction against the ancient severity, and might almost be supposed to see in the fact of having lost or squandered other people's property, a peculiar title to indulgence. Everything in the law which attached disagreeable consequences to that fact was gradually relaxed, or entirely got rid of : until the demoralizing effects of this laxity became so evident as to determine, by more recent legislation, a salutary though very insufficient movement in the reverse direction.[1]

The indulgence of the laws to those who have made themselves unable to pay their just debts is usually defended on the plea that the sole object of the law should be, in case of insolvency, not to coerce the person of the debtor, but to get at his property, and distribute it fairly among the creditors. Assuming that this is and ought to be the sole object, the mitigation of the law was in the first instance carried so far as to sacrifice that object. Imprisonment at the discretion of a creditor was really a powerful engine for extracting from the debtor any property which he had concealed or otherwise made away with ; and it remains to be shown by experience whether, in depriving creditors of this instrument, the law, even as last amended, has furnished them with a sufficient equivalent.[2] But the doctrine, that the law has done all that ought to be expected from it, when it has put the creditors in possession of the property of an insolvent, is in itself a totally inadmissible piece of spurious humanity. It is the business of law to prevent wrong-doing, and not simply to patch up the consequences of it when it has been committed. The law is bound to take care that insolvency shall not be a good pecuniary speculation ; that men shall not have the privilege of hazarding other people's property without their knowledge or consent, taking the profits of the enter-prise if it is successful, and if it fails throwing the loss upon the

---

[1] [So since the 5th ed. (1862). The original ran : " Everything . . . has been gradually relaxed and much of it entirely got rid of. Because insolvency was formerly treated as if it were necessarily a crime, everything is now done to make it, if possible, not even a misfortune." The present reference to an opposite movement " by a recent enactment " was introduced in the 3rd ed (1852), and spoken of as " partial but very salutary."]

[2] [So since the 3rd ed. (1852). The original ran : " In depriving creditors of this instrument, the law has not furnished them with a sufficient equivalent " : and went on as follows : " And it is seldom difficult for a dishonest debtor, by an understanding with one or more of his creditors, or by means of pretended creditors set up for the purpose, to abstract a part, perhaps the greatest part, of his assets, from the general fund, through the forms of the law itself. The facility and frequency of such frauds are a subject of much complaint, and their prevention demands a vigorous effort of the legislature, under the guidance of judicious persons practically conversant with the subject."]

rightful owners; and that they shall not find it answer to make themselves unable to pay their just debts, by spending the money of their creditors in personal indulgence. It is admitted that what is technically called fraudulent bankruptcy, the false pretence of inability to pay, is, when detected, properly subject to punishment.[1] But does it follow that insolvency is not the consequence of misconduct because the inability to pay may be real ? If a man has been a spendthrift, or a gambler, with property on which his creditors had a prior claim, shall he pass scot-free because the mischief is consummated and the money gone ? Is there any very material difference in point of morality between this conduct, and those other kinds of dishonesty which go by the names of fraud and embezzlement ?

Such cases are not a minority, but a large majority among insolvencies. The statistics of bankruptcy prove the fact. " By far the greater part of all insolvencies arise from notorious misconduct ; the proceedings of the Insolvent Debtors Court and of the Bankruptcy Court will prove it. Excessive and unjustifiable overtrading, or most absurd speculation in commodities, merely because the poor speculator ' thought they would get up,' but why he thought so he cannot tell ; speculation in hops, in tea, in silk, in corn—things with which he is altogether unacquainted ; wild and absurd investments in foreign funds, or in joint stocks ; these are among the most innocent causes of bankruptcy." * The experienced and intelligent writer from whom I quote corroborates his assertion by the testimony of several of the official assignees of the Bankruptcy Court. One of them says, " As far as I can collect from the books and documents furnished by the bankrupts, it seems to me that," in the whole number of cases which occurred during a given time in the court to which he was attached, " fourteen have been ruined by speculations in things with which they were unacquainted ; three by neglecting book-keeping ; ten by trading beyond their capital and means, and the consequent loss and expense of accommodation-bills ; forty-nine by expending more than they could reasonably hope their profits would be, though their business yielded a fair return ; none by any general distress, or the falling off of any particular branch of trade." Another of these officers

---

[1] [So since the 3rd ed. The original ran : " The humanitarians do not deny that what is technically . . . pay, may reasonably, when detected, be " &c.]
* From a volume published in 1845, entitled, *Credit the Life of Commerce* by J. H. Elliott.

says that, during a period of eighteen months, " fifty-two cases of bankruptcy have come under my care. It is my opinion that thirty-two of these have arisen from an imprudent expenditure, and five partly from that cause, and partly from a pressure on the business in which the bankrupts were employed. Fifteen I attribute to improvident speculations, combined in many instances with an extravagant mode of life."

To these citations the author adds the following statements from his personal means of knowledge. " Many insolvencies are produced by tradesmen's indolence ; they keep no books, or at least imperfect ones, which they never balance ; they never take stock ; they employ servants, if their trade be extensive, whom they are too indolent even to supervise, and then become insolvent. It is not too much to say, that one-half of all the persons engaged in trade, even in London, never take stock at all : they go on year after year without knowing how their affairs stand, and at last, like the child at school, they find to their surprise, but one halfpenny left in their pocket. I will venture to say that not one-fourth of all the persons in the provinces, either manufacturers, tradesmen, or farmers, ever take stock ; nor in fact does one-half of them ever keep account-books deserving any other name than memorandum books. I know sufficient of the concerns of five hundred small tradesmen in the provinces, to be enabled to say, that not one-fifth of them ever take stock, or keep even the most ordinary accounts. I am prepared to say of such tradesmen, from carefully prepared tables, giving every advantage where there has been any doubt as to the causes of their insolvency, that where nine happen from extravagance or dishonesty, one " at most " may be referred to misfortune alone." *

Is it rational to expect among the trading classes any high sense of justice, honour, or integrity, if the law enables men who act in this manner to shuffle off the consequences of their misconduct upon those who have been so unfortunate as to trust them ; and practically proclaims that it looks upon insolvency thus produced as a "misfortune," not an offence ?

It is, of course, not denied, that insolvencies do arise from causes beyond the control of the debtor, and that, in many more cases, his culpability is not of a high order ; and the law ought to make a distinction in favour of such cases, but not without a searching investigation ; nor should the case ever be let go without having

* Pp. 50–1.

ascertained, in the most complete manner practicable, not the fact of insolvency only, but the cause of it. To have been trusted with money or money's worth, and to have lost or spent it, is *primâ facie* evidence of something wrong : and it is not for the creditor to prove, which he cannot do in one case out of ten, that there has been criminality, but for the debtor to rebut the presumption, by laying open the whole state of his affairs, and showing either that there has been no misconduct, or that the misconduct has been of an excusable kind. If he fail in this, he ought never to be dismissed without a punishment proportioned to the degree of blame which seems justly imputable to him ; which punishment, however, might be shortened or mitigated in proportion as he appeared likely to exert himself in repairing the injury done.

It is a common argument with those who approve a relaxed system of insolvency laws, that credit, except in the great operations of commerce, is an evil ; and that to deprive creditors of legal redress is a judicious means of preventing credit from being given. That which is given by retail dealers to unproductive consumers is, no doubt, to the excess to which it is carried, a considerable evil. This, however, is only true of large, and especially of long, credits ; for there is credit whenever goods are not paid for before they quit the shop, or, at least, the custody of the seller ; and there would be much inconvenience in putting an end to this sort of credit. But a large proportion of the debts on which insolvency laws take effect are those due by small tradesmen to the dealers who supply them : and on no class of debts does the demoralization occasioned by a bad state of the law operate more perniciously. These are commercial credits, which no one wishes to see curtailed ; their existence is of great importance to the general industry of the country, and to numbers of honest, well-conducted persons of small means, to whom it would be a great injury that they should be prevented from obtaining the accommodation they need, and would not abuse, through the omission of the law to provide just remedies against dishonest or reckless borrowers.

But though it were granted that retail transactions, on any footing but that of ready money payment, are an evil, and their entire suppression a fit subject for legislation to aim at; a worse mode of compassing that object could scarcely be invented, than to permit those who have been trusted by others to cheat and rob them with impunity. The law does not generally select the vices of mankind as the appropriate instrument for inflicting chastisement on the comparatively innocent. When it seeks to discourage any course of action, it does so by applying inducements of its own, not by outlawing those who act in the manner it deems objectionable, and letting loose the predatory instincts of the worthless part of mankind to feed upon them. If a man has committed murder, the law condemns him to death : but it does not promise immunity to anybody who may kill him for the sake of taking his purse. The offence of believing another's word, even rashly, is not so heinous that, for the sake of discouraging it, the spectacle should be brought home to every door, of triumphant rascality, with the law on its side, mocking the victims it has made. This pestilent example has been very widely exhibited since the relaxation of the insolvency laws. It is idle to expect that, even by absolutely depriving creditors of all legal redress, the kind of credit which is considered objectionable would really be very much checked. Rogues and swindlers are still an exception among mankind, and people will go on trusting each other's promises. Large dealers, in abundant business, would refuse credit, as many of them already do : but in the eager competition of a great town, or the dependent position of a village shopkeeper, what can be expected from the tradesman to whom a single customer is of importance, the beginner, perhaps, who is striving to get into business ? He will take the risk, even if it were still greater ; he is ruined if he cannot sell his goods, and he can but be ruined if he is defrauded. Nor does it avail to say, that he ought to make proper inquiries, and ascertain the character of those to whom he supplies goods on trust. In some of the most flagrant cases of profligate debtors which have come before the Bankruptcy Court, the swindler had been able to give, and had given, excellent references.*

* The following extracts from the French *Code de Commerce* (the translation is that of Mr. Fane) show the great extent to which the just distinctions are made, and the proper investigations provided for, by French law. The word *banqueroute*, which can only be translated by bankruptcy, is, however, confined in France to *culpable* insolvency, which is distinguished into *simple* bankruptcy and *fraudulent* bankruptcy. The following are cases of simple bankruptcy :—

" Every insolvent who, in the investigation of his affairs, shall appear chargeable with one or more of the following offences, shall be proceeded against as a simple bankrupt :—

" If his house expenses, which he is bound to enter regularly in a day-book, appear excessive :

" If he had spent considerable sums at play, or in operations of pure hazard :

" If it shall appear that he has borrowed largely, or resold merchandize at a loss, or below the current price, after it appeared by his last account-taking that his debts exceeded his assets by one-half :

" If he has issued negotiable securities to three times the amount of his available assets, according to his last account-taking.

" The following *may* also be proceeded against as simple bankrupts :—

" He who has not declared his own insolvency in the manner prescribed by law :

" He who has not come in and surrendered within the time limited, having no legitimate excuse for his absence :

" He who either produces no books at all, or produces such as have been irregularly kept, and this although the irregularities may not indicate fraud."

The penalty for " simple bankruptcy " is imprisonment for a term of not less than one month, nor more than two years. The following are cases of fraudulent bankruptcy, of which the punishment is *travaux forcés* (the galleys) for a term :—

" If he has attempted to account for his property by fictitious expenses and losses, or if he does not fully account for all his receipts :

" If he has fraudulently concealed any sum of money or any debt due to him, or any merchandize or other movables :

" If he has made fraudulent sales or gifts of his property :

" If he has allowed fictitious debts to be proved against his estate :

" If he has been entrusted with property, either merely to keep, or with special directions as to its use, and has nevertheless appropriated it to his own use :

" If he has purchased real property in a borrowed name :

" If he has concealed his books.

" The following *may* also be proceeded against in a similar way :—

" He who has not kept books, or whose books shall not exhibit his real situation as regards his debts and credits :

" He who, having obtained a protection (*sauf-conduit*), shall not have duly attended."

These various provisions relate only to commercial insolvency. The laws in regard to ordinary debts are considerably more rigorous to the debtor.

CHAPTER X

§ 1 FROM the necessary functions of government, and the
effects produced on the economical interests of society by their good
or ill discharge, we proceed to the functions which belong to what
I have termed, for want of a better designation, the optional class ;
those which are sometimes assumed by governments and sometimes
not, and which it is not unanimously admitted that they ought to
exercise.

Before entering on the general principles of the question, it will
be advisable to clear from our path all those cases in which government interference works ill because grounded on false views of the
subject interfered with. Such cases have no connexion with any
theory respecting the proper limits of interference. There are some
things with which governments ought not to meddle, and other
things with which they ought ; but whether right or wrong in itself,
the interference must work for ill, if government, not understanding
the subject which it meddles with, meddles to bring about a result
which would be mischievous. We will therefore begin by passing
in review various false theories, which have from time to time formed
the ground of acts of government more or less economically
injurious.

Former writers on political economy have found it needful to
devote much trouble and space to this department of their subject.
It has now happily become possible, at least in our own country,
greatly to abridge this purely negative part of our discussions.
The false theories of political economy which have done so much
mischief in times past, are entirely discredited among all who
have not lagged behind the general progress of opinion ; and few
of the enactments which were once grounded on those theories still
help to deform the statute-book. As the principles on which their

condemnation rests have been fully set forth in other parts of this treatise, we may here content ourselves with a few brief indications.

Of these false theories, the most notable is the doctrine of Protection to Native Industry ; a phrase meaning the prohibition, or the discouragement by heavy duties, of such foreign commodities as are capable of being produced at home. If the theory involved in this system had been correct, the practical conclusions grounded on it would not have been unreasonable. The theory was, that to buy things produced at home was a national benefit, and the introduction of foreign commodities generally a national loss. It being at the same time evident that the interest of the consumer is to buy foreign commodities in preference to domestic whenever they are either cheaper or better, the interest of the consumer appeared in this respect to be contrary to the public interest ; he was certain, if left to his own inclinations, to do what according to the theory was injurious to the public.

It was shown, however, in our analysis of the effects of international trade, as it had been often shown by former writers, that the importation of foreign commodities, in the common course of traffic, never takes place, except when it is, economically speaking, a national good, by causing the same amount of commodities to be obtained at a smaller cost of labour and capital to the country. To prohibit, therefore, this importation, or impose duties which prevent it, is to render the labour and capital of the country less efficient in production than they would otherwise be ; and compel a waste of the difference between the labour and capital necessary for the home production of the commodity and that which is required for producing the things with which it can be purchased from abroad. The amount of national loss thus occasioned is measured by the excess of the price at which the commodity is produced, over that at which it could be imported. In the case of manufactured goods, the whole difference between the two prices is absorbed in indemnifying the producers for waste of labour, or of the capital which supports that labour. Those who are supposed to be benefited, namely, the makers of the protected articles, (unless they form an exclusive company, and have a monopoly against their own countrymen as well as against foreigners,) do not obtain higher profits than other people. All is sheer loss, to the country as well as to the consumer. When the protected article is a product of agriculture —the waste of labour not being incurred on the whole produce, but only on what may be called the last instalment of it—the extra price is only in part an indemnity for waste, the remainder being a tax paid to the landlords.

The restrictive and prohibitory policy was originally grounded on what is called the Mercantile System, which, representing the advantage of foreign trade to consist solely in bringing money into the country, gave artificial encouragement to exportation of goods, and discountenanced their importation. The only exceptions to the system were those required by the system itself. The materials and instruments of production were the subjects of a contrary policy, directed, however, to the same end ; they were freely imported, and not permitted to be exported, in order that manufacturers, being more cheaply supplied with the requisites of manufacture, might be able to sell cheaper, and therefore to export more largely. For a similar reason, importation was allowed, and even favoured, when confined to the productions of countries which were supposed to take from the country still more than it took from them, thus enriching it by a favourable balance of trade. As part of the same system, colonies were founded for the supposed advantage of compelling them to buy our commodities, or at all events not to buy those of any other country : in return for which restriction we were generally willing to come under an equivalent obligation with respect to the staple productions of the colonists. The consequences of the theory were pushed so far, that it was not unusual even to give bounties on exportation, and induce foreigners to buy from us rather than from other countries, by a cheapness which we artificially produced, by paying part of the price for them out of our own taxes. This is a stretch beyond the point yet reached by any private tradesman in his competition for business. No shopkeeper, I should think, ever made a practice of bribing customers by selling goods to them at a permanent loss, making it up to himself from other funds in his possession.

The principle of the Mercantile Theory is now given up even by writers and governments who still cling to the restrictive system. Whatever hold that system has over men's minds, independently of the private interests exposed to real or apprehended loss by its abandonment, is derived from fallacies other than the old notion of the benefits of heaping up money in the country. The most effective of these is the specious plea of employing our own countrymen and our national industry, instead of feeding and supporting the industry of foreigners. The answer to this, from the principles laid down in former chapters, is evident. Without reverting to the fundamental theorem discussed in an early part of the present treatise,* respecting the nature and sources of employment for labour, it is sufficient to say, what has usually been said by the advocates of free trade, that the alternative is not between employing our own people and foreigners, but between employing one class and another of our own people. The imported commodity is always paid for, directly or indirectly, with the produce of our own industry : that industry being at the same time rendered more productive, since, with the same labour and outlay, we are enabled to possess ourselves of a greater quantity of the article. Those who have not well considered the subject are apt to suppose that our exporting an equivalent in our own produce for the foreign articles we consume depends on contingencies—on the consent of foreign countries to make some corresponding relaxation of their own restrictions, or on the question whether those from whom we buy are induced by that circumstance to buy more from us ; and that, if these things, or things equivalent to them, do not happen, the payment must be made in money. Now, in the first place, there is nothing more objectionable in a money payment than in payment by any other medium, if the state of the market makes it the most advantageous remittance ; and the money itself was first acquired, and would again be replenished, by the export of an equivalent value of our own products. But, in the next place, a very short interval of paying in money would so lower prices as either to stop a part of the importation or raise up a foreign demand for our produce sufficient to pay for the imports. I grant that this disturbance of the equation of international demand would be in some degree to our disadvantage, in the purchase of other imported articles ; and that a country which prohibits some foreign commodities, does, *cæteris paribus*, obtain those which it does not prohibit at a less price than it would otherwise have to pay. To express the same thing in other words ; a country which destroys or prevents altogether certain branches of foreign trade, thereby annihilating a general gain to the world, which would be shared in some proportion between itself and other countries—does, in some circumstances, draw to itself, at the expense of foreigners, a larger share than would else belong to it of the gain arising from that portion of its foreign trade which it suffers to subsist. But even this it can only be enabled to do, if foreigners do not maintain equivalent prohibitions or restrictions against its commodities. In any case, the justice or expediency of destroying one of two gains, in order

* Supra, pp. 79 et seqq.

to engross a rather larger share of the other, does not require much discussion : the gain, too, which is destroyed, being, in proportion to the magnitude of the transactions, the larger of the two, since it is the one which capital, left to itself, is supposed to seek by preference.

Defeated as a general theory, the Protectionist doctrine finds support in some particular cases, from considerations which, when really in point, involve greater interests than mere saving of labour ; the interests of national subsistence and of national defence. The discussions on the Corn Laws have familiarized everybody with the plea, that we ought to be independent of foreigners for the food of the people ; and the Navigation Laws were grounded, in theory and profession, on the necessity of keeping up a "nursery of sea-men" for the navy. On this last subject I at once admit, that the object is worth the sacrifice ; and that a country exposed to invasion by sea, if it cannot otherwise have sufficient ships and sailors of its own to secure the means of manning on an emergency an adequate fleet, is quite right in obtaining those means, even at an economical sacrifice in point of cheapness of transport. When the English Navigation Laws were enacted, the Dutch, from their maritime skill and their low rate of profit at home, were able to carry for other nations, England included, at cheaper rates than those nations could carry for themselves : which placed all other countries at a great comparative disadvantage in obtaining experienced seamen for their ships of war. The Navigation Laws, by which this deficiency was remedied, and at the same time a blow struck against the maritime power of a nation with which England was then frequently engaged in hostilities, were probably, though economically disadvantageous, politically expedient. But English ships and sailors can now navigate as cheaply as those of any other country ; maintaining at least an equal competition with the other maritime nations even in their own trade. The ends which may once have justified Navigation Laws require them no longer, and afforded no reason for maintaining this invidious exception to the general rule of free trade.

With regard to subsistence, the plea of the Protectionists has been so often and so triumphantly met, that it requires little notice here. That country is the most steadily as well as the most abundantly supplied with food which draws its supplies from the largest surface. It is ridiculous to found a general system of policy on so improbable a danger as that of being at war with all the nations of the world at once ; or to suppose that, even if inferior at sea, a whole country could be blockaded like a town, or that the growers of food in other countries would not be as anxious not to lose an advantageous market, as we should be not to be deprived of their corn. On the subject, however, of subsistence, there is one point which deserves more especial consideration. In cases of actual or apprehended scarcity, many countries of Europe are accustomed to stop the exportation of food. Is this, or not, sound policy ? There can be no doubt that in the present state of international morality, a people cannot, any more than an individual, be blamed for not starving itself to feed others. But if the greatest amount of good to mankind on the whole were the end aimed at in the maxims of international conduct, such collective churlishness would certainly be condemned by them. Suppose that in ordinary circumstances the trade in food were perfectly free, so that the price in one country could not habitually exceed that in any other by more than the cost of carriage, together with a moderate profit to the importer. A general scarcity ensues, affecting all countries, but in unequal degrees. If the price rose in one country more than in others, it would be a proof that in that country the scarcity was severest, and that by permitting food to go freely thither from any other country, it would be spared from a less urgent necessity to relieve a greater. When the interests, therefore, of all countries are considered, free exportation is desirable. To the exporting country considered separately, it may, at least on the particular occasion, be an inconvenience : but taking into account that the country which is now the giver will in some future season be the receiver, and the one that is benefited by the freedom, I cannot but think that even to the apprehension of food-rioters it might be made apparent, that in such cases they should do to others what they would wish done to themselves.

In countries in which the Protection theory is [1848] declining, but not yet given up, such as the United States, a doctrine has come into notice which is a sort of compromise between free trade and restriction, namely, that protection for protection's sake is improper, but that there is nothing objectionable in having as much protection as may incidentally result from a tariff framed solely for revenue. Even in England, regret is sometimes expressed that a " moderate fixed duty " was not preserved on corn, on account of the revenue it would yield. Independently, however, of the general impolicy of taxes on the necessaries of life, this doctrine overlooks the fact, that revenue is received only on the quantity imported, but that the

tax is paid on the entire quantity consumed.   To make the public
pay much that the treasury may receive a little, is not an eligible
mode of obtaining a revenue.   In the case of manufactured articles
the doctrine involves a palpable inconsistency.   The object of the
duty, as a means of revenue, is inconsistent with its affording, even
incidentally, any protection.   It can only operate as protection in
so far as it prevents importation ; and to whatever degree it prevents
importation it affords no revenue.

   The only case in which, on mere principles of political economy,
protecting duties can be defensible, is when they are imposed
temporarily (especially in a young and rising nation) in hopes of
naturalizing a foreign industry, in itself perfectly suitable to the
circumstances of the country.   The superiority of one country over
another in a branch of production often arises only from having
begun it sooner.   There may be no inherent advantage on one part,
or disadvantage on the other, but only a present superiority of
acquired skill and experience.   A country which has this skill and
experience yet to acquire, may in other respects be better adapted
to the production than those which were earlier in the field : and
besides, it is a just remark of Mr. Rae, that nothing has a greater
tendency to promote improvements in any branch of production
than its trial under a new set of conditions.   But it cannot
be expected that individuals should, at their own risk, or rather
to their certain loss, introduce a new manufacture, and bear the
burthen of carrying it on until the producers have been educated
up to the level of those with whom the processes are traditional.   A
protecting duty, continued for a reasonable time, might [1] sometimes
be the least inconvenient mode in which the nation can tax itself
for the support of such an experiment.   But it is essential that the
protection should be confined to cases in which there is good ground
of assurance that the industry which it fosters will after a time be
able to dispense with it ; nor should the domestic producers ever
be allowed to expect that it will be continued to them beyond
the time necessary for a fair trial of what they are capable of
accomplishing.

   [2] The only writer, of any reputation as a political economist,
who now [1865] adheres to the Protectionist doctrine, Mr. H. C.
Carey, rests its defence, in an economic point of view, principally on

---

[1] [The " will " of the original (1848) text was changed into " might " in the
7th ed. (1871), and " it is essential that " was inserted in the next sentence.]

[2] [The next three paragraphs were added in the 6th ed. (1865).]

two reasons. One is the great saving in cost of carriage, consequent on producing commodities at or very near to the place where they are to be consumed. The whole of the cost of carriage, both on the commodities imported and on those exported in exchange for them, he regards as a direct burthen on the producers, and not, as is obviously the truth, on the consumers. On whomsoever it falls, it is, without doubt, a burthen on the industry of the world. But it is obvious (and that Mr. Carey does not see it, is one of the many surprising things in his book) that the burthen is only borne for a more than equivalent advantage. If the commodity is bought in a foreign country with domestic produce in spite of the double cost of carriage, the fact proves that, heavy as that cost may be, the saving in cost of production outweighs it, and the collective labour of the country is on the whole better remunerated than if the article were produced at home. Cost of carriage is a natural protecting duty, which free trade has no power to abrogate : and unless America gained more by obtaining her manufactures through the medium of her corn and cotton than she loses in cost of carriage, the capital employed in producing corn and cotton in annually increased quantities for the foreign market would turn to manufactures instead. The natural advantages attending a mode of industry in which there is less cost of carriage to pay, can at most be only a justification for a temporary and merely tentative protection. The expenses of production being always greatest at first, it may happen that the home production, though really the most advantageous, may not become so until after a certain duration of pecuniary loss, which it is not to be expected that private speculators should incur in order that their successors may be benefited by their ruin. I have therefore conceded that in a new country a temporary protecting duty may sometimes be economically defensible ; on condition, however, that it be strictly limited in point of time, and provision be made that during the latter part of its existence it be on a gradually decreasing scale. Such temporary protection is of the same nature as a patent, and should be governed by similar conditions.

The remaining argument of Mr. Carey in support of the economic benefits of Protectionism applies only to countries whose exports consist of agricultural produce. He argues, that by a trade of this description they actually send away their soil : the distant consumers not giving back to the land of the country, as home consumers would do, the fertilizing elements which they abstract from it. This argument deserves attention on account of the physical truth on which it is founded ; a truth which has only lately come to be understood, but which is henceforth destined to be a permanent element in the thoughts of statesmen, as it must always have been in the destinies of nations. To the question of Protectionism, however, it is irrelevant. That the immense growth of raw produce in America to be consumed in Europe is progressively exhausting the soil of the Eastern, and even of the older Western States, and that both are already far less productive than formerly, is credible in itself, even if no one bore witness to it. But what I have already said respecting cost of carriage, is true also of the cost of manuring. Free trade does not compel America to export corn : she would cease to do so if it ceased to be to her advantage. As, then, she would not persist in exporting raw produce and importing manufactures any longer than the labour she saved by doing so exceeded what the carriage cost her, so when it became necessary for her to replace in the soil the elements of fertility which she had sent away, if the saving in cost of production were more than equivalent to the cost of carriage and of manure together, manure would be imported ; and if not, the export of corn would cease. It is evident that one of these two things would already have taken place, if there had not been near at hand a constant succession of new soils, not yet exhausted of their fertility, the cultivation of which enables her, whether judiciously or not, to postpone the question of manure. As soon as it no longer answers better to break up new soils than to manure the old, America will either become a regular importer of manure, or will, without protecting duties, grow corn for herself only, and manufacturing for herself, will make her manure, as Mr. Carey desires, at home.*

For these obvious reasons, I hold Mr. Carey's economic arguments

* To this Mr. Carey would reply (indeed he has already so replied in advance) that of all commodities manure is the least susceptible of being conveyed to a distance. This is true of sewage, and of stable manure, but not true of the ingredients to which those manures owe their efficiency. These, on the contrary, are chiefly substances containing great fertilizing power in small bulk ; substances of which the human body requires but a small quantity, and hence peculiarly susceptible of being imported ; the mineral alkalies and the phosphates. The question indeed mainly concerns the phosphates, for of the alkalies, soda is procurable everywhere ; while potash, being one of the constituents of granite and the other feldspathic rocks, exists in many subsoils, by whose progressive decomposition it is renewed, a large quantity also being brought down in the deposits of rivers. As for the phosphates, they, in the very convenient form of pulverized bones, are a regular article of commerce, largely imported into England ; as they are sure to be into any country where the conditions of industry make it worth while to pay the price.

for Protectionism to be totally invalid. The economic, however, is far from being the strongest point of his case. American Protectionists often reason extremely ill; but it is an injustice to them to suppose that their protectionist creed rests upon nothing superior to an economic blunder. Many of them have been led to it much more by consideration for the higher interests of humanity than by purely economic reasons. They, and Mr. Carey at their head, deem it a necessary condition of human improvement that towns should abound; that men should combine their labour, by means of interchange—with near neighbours, with people of pursuits, capacities, and mental cultivation different from their own, sufficiently close at hand for mutual sharpening of wits and enlarging of ideas—rather than with people on the opposite side of the globe. They believe that a nation all engaged in the same, or nearly the same, pursuit—a nation all agricultural—cannot attain a high state of civilization and culture. And for this there is a great foundation of reason. If the difficulty can be overcome, the United States, with their free institutions, their universal schooling, and their omnipresent press, are the people to do it; but whether this is possible or not is still a problem. So far, however, as it is an object to check the excessive dispersion of the population, Mr. Wakefield has pointed out a better way; to modify the existing method of disposing of the unoccupied lands, by raising the price, instead of lowering it, or giving away the land gratuitously, as is largely done since the passing of the Homestead Act. To cut the knot in Mr. Carey's fashion, by Protectionism, it would be necessary that Ohio and Michigan should be protected against Massachusetts as well as against England: for the manufactories of New England, no more than those of the old country, accomplish his desideratum of bringing a manufacturing population to the doors of the Western farmer. Boston and New York do not supply the want of local towns to the Western prairies, any better than Manchester; and it is as difficult to get back the manure from the one place as from the other.

There is only one part of the Protectionist scheme which requires any further notice: its policy towards colonies, and foreign dependencies; that of compelling them to trade exclusively with the dominant country. A country which thus secures to itself an extra foreign demand for its commodities, undoubtedly gives itself some advantage in the distribution of the general gains of the commercial world. Since, however, it causes the industry and capital of the colony to be diverted from channels which are proved to be the most

productive, inasmuch as they are those into which industry and
capital spontaneously tend to flow ; there is a loss, on the whole,
to the productive powers of the world, and the mother country does
not gain so much as she makes the colony lose. If, therefore, the
mother country refuses to acknowledge any reciprocity of obligation, she imposes a tribute on the colony in an indirect mode, greatly
more oppressive and injurious than the direct. But if, with a more
equitable spirit, she submits herself to corresponding restrictions for
the benefit of the colony, the result of the whole transaction is the
ridiculous one, that each party loses much in order that the other
may gain a little.[1]

§ 2.   Next to the system of Protection, among mischievous
interferences with the spontaneous course of industrial transactions,
may be noticed certain interferences with contracts.   One instance is
that of the Usury Laws.   These originated in a religious prejudice
against receiving interest on money, derived from that fruitful
source of mischief in modern Europe, the attempted adaptation to
Christianity of doctrines and precepts drawn from the Jewish law.
In Mahomedan nations the receiving of interest is formally interdicted, and rigidly abstained from : and Sismondi has noticed, as
one among the causes of the industrial inferiority of the Catholic,
compared with the Protestant parts of Europe, that the Catholic
Church in the middle ages gave its sanction to the same prejudice ;
which subsists, impaired but not destroyed, wherever that religion is
acknowledged.   Where law or conscientious scruples prevent lending at interest, the capital which belongs to persons not in business
is lost to productive purposes, or can be applied to them only in
peculiar circumstances of personal connexion, or by a subterfuge.
Industry is thus limited to the capital of the undertakers, and to what
they can borrow from persons not bound by the same laws or religion
as themselves.   In Mussulman countries the bankers and money
dealers are either Hindoos, Armenians, or Jews.

In more improved countries, legislation no longer discountenances
the receipt of an equivalent for money lent ; but it has everywhere
interfered with the free agency of the lender and borrower, by fixing
a legal limit to the rate of interest, and making the receipt of more
than the appointed maximum a penal offence.   This restriction,
though approved by Adam Smith, has been condemned by all

[1] [See Appendix II.   *Protection.*]

enlightened persons since the triumphant onslaught made upon it by Bentham in his *Letters on Usury*, which may still be referred to as the best extant writing on the subject.

Legislators may enact and maintain Usury Laws from one of two motives : ideas of public policy, or concern for the interest of the parties in the contract ; in this case, of one party only, the borrower. As a matter of policy the notion may possibly be, that it is for the general good that interest should be low. It is, however, a misapprehension of the causes which influence commercial transactions, to suppose that the rate of interest is really made lower by law than it would be made by the spontaneous play of supply and demand. If the competition of borrowers, left unrestrained, would raise the rate of interest to six per cent, this proves that at five there would be a greater demand for loans than there is capital in the market to supply. If the law in these circumstances permits no interest beyond five per cent, there will be some lenders, who not choosing to disobey the law, and not being in a condition to employ their capital otherwise, will content themselves with the legal rate : but others, finding that in a season of pressing demand more may be made of their capital by other means than they are permitted to make by lending it, will not lend it at all ; and the loanable capital, already too small for the demand, will be still further diminished. Of the disappointed candidates there will be many at such periods who must have their necessities supplied at any price, and these will readily find a third section of lenders, who will not be averse to join in a violation of the law, either by circuitous transactions partaking of the nature of fraud or by relying on the honour of the borrower. The extra expense of the roundabout mode of proceeding, and an equivalent for the risk of non-payment and of legal penalties, must be paid by the borrower, over and above the extra interest which would have been required of him by the general state of the market. The laws which were intended to lower the price paid by him for pecuniary accommodation end thus in greatly increasing it. These laws have also a directly demoralizing tendency. Knowing the difficulty of detecting an illegal pecuniary transaction between two persons, in which no third person is involved, so long as it is the interest of both to keep the secret, legislators have adopted the expedient of tempting the borrower to become the informer, by making the annulment of the debt a part of the penalty for the offence ; thus rewarding men for first obtaining the property of others by false promises, and then not only refusing payment, but invoking legal penalties on those who have helped them in their need. The moral sense of mankind very rightly infamizes those who resist an otherwise just claim on the ground of usury, and tolerates such a plea only when resorted to as the best legal defence available against an attempt really considered as partaking of fraud or extortion. But this very severity of public opinion renders the enforcement of the laws so difficult, and the infliction of the penalties so rare, that when it does occur it merely victimizes an individual, and has no effect on general practice.

In so far as the motive of the restriction may be supposed to be, not public policy, but regard for the interest of the borrower, it would be difficult to point out any case in which such tenderness on the legislator's part is more misplaced. A person of sane mind, and of the age at which persons are legally competent to conduct their own concerns, must be presumed to be a sufficient guardian of his pecuniary interests. If he may sell an estate, or grant a release, or assign away all his property, without control from the law, it seems very unnecessary that the only bargain which he cannot make without its intermeddling, should be a loan of money. The law seems to presume that the money-lender, dealing with necessitous persons, can take advantage of their necessities, and exact conditions limited only by his own pleasure. It might be so if there were only one money-lender within reach. But when there is the whole monied capital of a wealthy community to resort to, no borrower is placed under any disadvantage in the market merely by the urgency of his need. If he cannot borrow at the interest paid by other people, it must be because he cannot give such good security : and competition will limit the extra demand to a fair equivalent for the risk of his proving insolvent. Though the law intends favour to the borrower, it is to him above all that injustice is, in this case, done by it. What can be more unjust than that a person who cannot give perfectly good security should be prevented from borrowing of persons who are willing to lend money to him, by their not being permitted to receive the rate of interest which would be a just equivalent for their risk ? Through the mistaken kindness of the law, he must either go without the money which is perhaps necessary to save him from much greater losses, or be driven to expedients of a far more ruinous description, which the law either has not found it possible, or has not happened, to interdict.

Adam Smith rather hastily expressed the opinion, that only two kinds of persons, " prodigals and projectors," could require to borrow money at more than the market rate of interest. He should have included all persons who are in any pecuniary difficulties, however temporary their necessities may be. It may happen to any person in business, to be disappointed of the resources on which he had calculated for meeting some engagement, the non-fulfilment of which on a fixed day would be bankruptcy. In periods of commercial difficulty, this is the condition of many prosperous mercantile firms, who become competitors for the small amount of disposable capital which, in a time of general distrust, the owners are willing to part with. Under the English usury laws, now happily abolished, the limitations imposed by those laws were felt as a most serious aggravation of every commercial crisis. Merchants who could have obtained the aid they required at an interest of seven or eight per cent for short periods, were obliged to give 20 or 30 per cent or to resort to forced sales of goods at a still greater loss. Experience having obtruded these evils on the notice of Parliament, the sort of compromise took place of which English legislation affords so many instances, and which helps to make our laws and policy the mass of inconsistency that they are. The law was reformed as a person reforms a tight shoe, who cuts a hole in it where it pinches hardest, and continues to wear it. Retaining the erroneous principle as a general rule, Parliament allowed an exception in the case in which the practical mischief was most flagrant. It left the usury laws unrepealed, but exempted bills of exchange, of not more than three months' date, from their operation. Some years afterwards the laws were repealed in regard to all other contracts, but left in force as to all those which relate to land. Not a particle of reason could be given for making this extraordinary distinction : but the " agricultural mind " was of opinion that the interest on mortgages, though it hardly ever came up to the permitted point, would come up to a still higher point ; and the usury laws were maintained that the landlords might, as they thought, be enabled to borrow below the market rate, as the corn-laws were kept up that the same class might be able to sell corn above the market rate. The modesty of the pretension was quite worthy of the intelligence which could think that the end aimed at was in any way forwarded by the means used.

With regard to the " prodigals and projectors " spoken of by Adam Smith ; no law can prevent a prodigal from ruining himself, unless it lays him or his property under actual restraint, according to the unjustifiable practice of the Roman Law and some of the Continental systems founded on it. The only effect of usury laws upon a prodigal is to make his ruin rather more expeditious, by driving him to a disreputable class of money-dealers, and rendering the conditions more onerous by the extra risk created by the law. As for projectors (a term, in its unfavourable sense, rather unfairly applied to every person who has a project), such laws may put a veto upon the prosecution of the most promising enterprise, when planned, as it generally is, by a person who does not possess capital adequate to its successful completion. Many of the greatest improvements were at first looked shyly on by capitalists, and had to wait long before they found one sufficiently adventurous to be the first in a new path : many years elapsed before Stephenson could convince even the enterprising mercantile public of Liverpool and Manchester of the advantage of substituting railways for turnpike roads ; and plans on which great labour and large sums have been expended with little visible result, (the epoch in their progress when predictions of failure are most rife,) may be indefinitely suspended, or altogether dropped, and the outlay all lost, if, when the original funds are exhausted, the law will not allow more to be raised on the terms on which people are willing to expose it to the chances of an enterprise not yet secure of success.[1]

§ 3.   Loans are not the only kind of contract of which governments have thought themselves qualified to regulate the conditions better than the persons interested.   There is scarcely any commodity which they have not, at some place or time, endeavoured to make either dearer or cheaper than it would be if left to itself.   The most plausible case for artificially cheapening a commodity is that of food.   The desirableness of the object is in this case undeniable. But since the average price of food, like that of other things, conforms to the cost of production, with the addition of the usual profit ; if this price is not expected by the farmer, he will, unless compelled by law, produce no more than he requires for his own consumption : and the law, therefore, if absolutely determined to have food cheaper, must substitute, for the ordinary motives to cultivation, a system of penalties. If it shrinks from doing this, it has no resource but that of taxing the whole nation, to give a bounty or premium to the grower or importer of corn, thus giving everybody cheap bread at the expense of all : in reality a largess to those who do not pay taxes, at the expense of those who do ; one of the

----

[1] [See Appendix JJ. *Usury Laws.*]

forms of a practice essentially bad, that of converting the working classes into unworking classes by making them a present of subsistence.

It is not, however, so much the general or average price of food, as its occasional high price in times of emergency, which governments have studied to reduce. In some cases, as for example the famous " maximum " of the revolutionary government of 1793, the compulsory regulation was an attempt by the ruling powers to counteract the necessary consequences of their own acts ; to scatter an indefinite abundance of the circulating medium with one hand, and keep down prices with the other ; a thing manifestly impossible under any régime except one of unmitigated terror. In case of actual scarcity, governments are often urged, as they were in the Irish emergency of 1847, to take measures of some sort for moderating the price of food. But the price of a thing cannot be raised by deficiency of supply beyond what is sufficient to make a corresponding reduction of the consumption ; and if a government prevents this reduction from being brought about by a rise of price, there remains no mode of effecting it unless by taking possession of all the food, and serving it out in rations ; as in a besieged town. In a real scarcity, nothing can afford general relief, except a determination by the richer classes to diminish their own consumption. If they buy and consume their usual quantity of food, and content themselves with giving money, they do no good. The price is forced up until the poorest competitors have no longer the means of competing, and the privation of food is thrown exclusively upon the indigent, the other classes being only affected pecuniarily. When the supply is insufficient, somebody must consume less, and if every rich person is determined not to be that somebody, all they do by subsidizing their poorer competitors is to force up the price so much the higher, with no effect but to enrich the corndealers, the very reverse of what is desired by those who recommend such measures. All that governments can do in these emergencies is to counsel a general moderation in consumption, and to interdict such kinds of it as are not of primary importance. Direct measures at the cost of the state, to procure food from a distance, are expedient when from peculiar reasons the thing is not likely to be done by private speculation. In any other case they are a great error. Private speculators will not, in such cases, venture to compete with the government ; and though a government can do more than any one merchant, it cannot do nearly so much as all merchants.

§ 4. Governments, however, are oftener chargeable with having attempted, too successfully, to make things dear, than with having aimed by wrong means at making them cheap. The usual instrument for producing artificial dearness is monopoly. To confer a monopoly upon a producer or dealer, or upon a set of producers or dealers not too numerous to combine, is to give them the power of levying any amount of taxation on the public, for their individual benefit, which will not make the public forego the use of the commodity. When the sharers in the monopoly are so numerous and so widely scattered that they are prevented from combining, the evil is considerably less : but even then the competition is not so active among a limited as among an unlimited number. Those who feel assured of a fair average proportion in the general business are seldom eager to get a larger share by foregoing a portion of their profits. A limitation of competition, however partial, may have mischievous effects quite disproportioned to the apparent cause. The mere exclusion of foreigners, from a branch of industry open to the free competition of every native, has been known, even in England, to render that branch a conspicuous exception to the general industrial energy of the country. The silk manufacture of England remained far behind that of other countries of Europe, so long as the foreign fabrics were prohibited. In addition to the tax levied for the profit, real or imaginary, of the monopolists, the consumer thus pays an additional tax for their laziness and incapacity. When relieved from the immediate stimulus of competition, producers and dealers grow indifferent to the dictates of their ultimate pecuniary interest ; preferring to the most hopeful prospects the present case of adhering to routine. A person who is already thriving, seldom puts himself out of his way to commence even a lucrative improvement, unless urged by the additional motive of fear lest some rival should supplant him by getting possession of it before him.

The condemnation of monopolies ought not to extend to patents, by which the originator of an improved process is allowed to enjoy, for a limited period, the exclusive privilege of using his own improvement. This is not making the commodity dear for his benefit, but merely postponing a part of the increased cheapness which the public owe to the inventor in order to compensate and reward him for the service. That he ought to be both compensated and rewarded for it, will not be denied, and also that if all were at once allowed to avail themselves of his ingenuity, without having shared the labours or the expenses which he had to incur in bringing his idea into a practical shape, either such expenses and labours would be undergone by nobody except very opulent and very public-spirited persons, or the state must put a value on the service rendered by an inventor, and make him a pecuniary grant. This has been done in some instances, and may be done without inconvenience in cases of very conspicuous public benefit ; but in general an exclusive privilege, of temporary duration, is preferable ; because it leaves nothing to any one's discretion ; because the reward conferred by it depends upon the invention's being found useful, and the greater the usefulness the greater the reward ; and because it is paid by the very persons to whom the service is rendered, the consumers of the commodity. So decisive, indeed, are these considerations, that if the system of patents were abandoned for that of rewards by the state, the best shape which these could assume would be that of a small temporary tax, imposed for the inventor's benefit, on all persons making use of the invention. [1] To this, however, or to any other system which would vest in the state the power of deciding whether an inventor should derive any pecuniary advantage from the public benefit which he confers, the objections are evidently stronger and more fundamental than the strongest which can possibly be urged against patents. It is generally admitted that the present Patent Laws need much improvement ; but in this case, as well as in the closely analogous one of Copyright, it would be a gross immorality in the law to set everybody free to use a person's work without his consent, and without giving him an equivalent. I have seen with real alarm several recent attempts, in quarters carrying some authority, to impugn the principle of patents altogether ; attempts which, if practically successful, would enthrone free stealing under the prostituted name of free trade, and make the men of brains, still more than at present, the needy retainers and dependents of the men of money-bags.

§ 5. I pass to another kind of government interference, in which the end and the means are alike odious, but which existed in England until not more than a generation ago, and in France up to the year 1864.[2] I mean the laws against combinations of workmen to raise wages ; laws enacted and maintained for the declared purpose of

---

[1] [The remainder of this paragraph was added in the 5th ed. (1862).]

[2] [So since 7th ed. (1871). Originally (1848) " not much more than twenty years ago, and is in full vigour at this day in some other countries."]

keeping wages low, as the famous Statute of Labourers was passed
by a legislature of employers, to prevent the labouring class, when
its numbers had been thinned by a pestilence, from taking advantage
of the diminished competition to obtain higher wages.   Such laws
exhibit the infernal spirit of the slave master, when to retain the
working classes in avowed slavery has ceased to be practicable.

If it were possible for the working classes, by combining among
themselves, to raise or keep up the general rate of wages, it needs
hardly be said that this would be a thing not to be punished, but to
be welcomed and rejoiced at.   Unfortunately the effect is quite
beyond attainment by such means.   The multitudes who compose
the working class are too numerous and too widely scattered to
combine at all, much more to combine effectually.   If they could
do so, they might doubtless succeed in diminishing the hours of
labour, and obtaining the same wages for less work.   They would
also have a limited power of obtaining, by combination, an increase
of general wages at the expense of profits.   But the limits of this
power are narrow ; and were they to attempt to strain it beyond
those limits, this could only be accomplished by keeping a part of
their number permanently out of employment.[1]   As support from
public charity would of course be refused to those who could get
work and would not accept it, they would be thrown for support
upon the trade union of which they were members ; and the work-
people collectively would be no better off than before, having to
support the same numbers out of the same aggregate wages.   In
this way, however, the class would have its attention forcibly
drawn to the fact of a superfluity of numbers, and to the necessity,
if they would have high wages, of proportioning the supply of
labour to the demand.

Combinations to keep up wages are sometimes successful, in
trades where the workpeople are few in number, and collected in a
small number of local centres.   It is questionable if combinations
ever had the smallest effect on the permanent remuneration of
spinners or weavers ; but the journeymen type-founders, by a
close combination, are able, it is said, to keep up a rate of wages
much beyond that which is usual in employments of equal hardness

---

[1] [This and the preceding sentence replaced, but not until the 7th ed.
(1871), the following sentence of the original (1848) text : " But if they aimed
at obtaining actually higher wages than the rate fixed by demand and supply
—the rate which distributes the whole circulating capital of the country among
the entire working population—this could only be accomplished by keeping
a part of their number permanently out of employment."]

and skill; and even the tailors, a much more numerous class, are understood to have had, to some extent, a similar success. A rise of wages, thus confined to particular employments, is not (like a rise of general wages) defrayed from profits, but raises the value and price of the particular article, and falls on the consumer; the capitalist who produces the commodity being only injured in so far as the high price tends to narrow the market; and not even then, unless it does so in a greater ratio than that of the rise of price: for though, at higher wages, he employs, with a given capital, fewer workpeople, and obtains less of the commodity, yet if he can sell the whole of this diminished quantity at the higher price, his profits are as great as before.

This partial rise of wages, if not gained at the expense of the remainder of the working class, ought not to be regarded as an evil.[1] The consumer, indeed, must pay for it; but cheapness of goods is desirable only when the cause of it is that their production costs little labour, and not when occasioned by that labour's being ill remunerated. It may appear, indeed, at first sight, that the high wages of the type-founders (for example) are obtained at the general cost of the labouring class. This high remuneration either causes fewer persons to find employment in the trade, or if not, must lead to the investment of more capital in it, at the expense of other trades: in the first case, it throws an additional number of labourers on the general market; in the second, it withdraws from that market a portion of the demand: effects, both of which are injurious to the working classes. Such, indeed, would really be the result of a successful combination in a particular trade or trades, for some time after its formation; but when it is a permanent thing, the principles so often insisted upon in this treatise, show that it can have no such effect. The habitual earnings of the working classes at large can be effected by nothing but the habitual requirements of the labouring people: these indeed may be altered, but while they remain the same, wages never fall permanently below the standard of these requirements, and do not long remain above that standard. If there had been no combinations in particular trades, and the wages of those trades had never been kept above the common level, there is no reason to suppose that the common level would have been at all higher than it now is. There would merely have been a greater number of people altogether, and a smaller number of exceptions to the ordinary low rate of wages.

[1] [So since 3rd ed. (1852). Originally: " ought to be regarded as a benefit."]

¹ If, therefore, no improvement were to be hoped for in the general circumstances of the working classes, the success of a portion of them, however small, in keeping their wages by combination above the market rate, would be wholly a matter of satisfaction. But when the elevation of the character and condition of the entire body has at last become a thing not beyond the reach of rational effort, it is time that the better paid classes of skilled artisans should seek their own advantage in common with, and not by the exclusion of, their fellow-labourers. While they continue to fix their hopes on hedging themselves in against competition, and protecting their own wages by shutting out others from access to their employment, nothing better can be expected from them than that total absence of any large and generous aims, that almost open disregard of all other objects than high wages and little work for their own small body, which were so deplorably evident in the proceedings and manifestoes of the Amalgamated Society of Engineers during their quarrel with their employers. Success, even if attainable, in raising up a protected class of working people, would now be a hindrance, instead of a help, to the emancipation of the working classes at large.

But though combinations to keep up wages are seldom effectual, and when effectual, are, for the reasons which I have assigned, seldom desirable, the right of making the attempt is one which cannot be refused to any portion of the working population without great injustice, or without the probability of fatally misleading them respecting the circumstances which determine their condition. So long as combinations to raise wages were prohibited by law, the law appeared to the operatives to be the real cause of the low wages which there was no denying that it had done its best to produce. Experience of strikes has been the best teacher of the labouring classes on the subject of the relation between wages and the demand and supply of labour : and it is most important that this course of instruction should not be disturbed.

² It is a great error to condemn, *per se* and absolutely, either trade unions or the collective action of strikes. Even assuming that a

---

¹ [This and the following paragraph were added in the 3rd ed. (1852) ; and the sentence of the original text, " Combinations to keep up wages are therefore not only permissible but useful, wherever really calculated to have that effect," was removed at this point.]

² [This paragraph was added in the 5th ed. (1862). The second sentence, however, then ran : " I grant that a strike is wrong whenever it is foolish, and it is foolish whenever it attempts to raise wages above that market rate which is rendered possible by supply and demand. But demand and supply are not physical agencies," &c. The present text dates from the 7th ed. (1871).]

strike must inevitably fail whenever it attempts to raise wages above that market rate which is fixed by the demand and supply ; demand and supply are not physical agencies, which thrust a given amount of wages into a labourer's hand without the participation of his own will and actions. The market rate is not fixed for him by some self-acting instrument, but is the result of bargaining between human beings—of what Adam Smith calls " the higgling of the market ; " and those who do not " higgle " will long continue to pay, even over a counter, more than the market price for their purchases. Still more might poor labourers who have to do with rich employers remain long without the amount of wages which the demand for their labour would justify, unless, in vernacular phrase, they stood out for it : and how can they stand out for terms without organized concert ? What chance would any labourer have who struck singly for an advance of wages ? How could he even know whether the state of the market admitted of a rise, except by consultation with his fellows, naturally leading to concerted action ? I do not hesitate to say that associations of labourers, of a nature similar to trade unions, far from being a hindrance to a free market for labour, are the necessary instrumentality of that free market ; the indispensable means of enabling the sellers of labour to take due care of their own interests under a system of competition. There is an ulterior consideration of much importance, to· which attention was for the first time drawn by Professor Fawcett, in an article in the *Westminster Review.* Experience has at length enabled the more intelligent trades to take a tolerably correct measure of the circumstances on which the success of a strike for an advance of wages depends. The workmen are now nearly as well informed as the master of the state of the market for his commodities ; they can calculate his gains and his expenses, they know when his trade is or is not prosperous, and only when it is, are they ever again likely to strike for higher wages ; which wages their known readiness to strike makes their employers for the most part willing, in that case, to concede. The tendency, therefore, of this state of things is to make a rise of wages in any particular trade usually consequent upon a rise of profits, which, as Mr. Fawcett observes, is a commencement of that regular participation of the labourers in the profits derived from their labour, every tendency to which, for the reasons stated in a previous chapter,* it is so important to encourage, since to it we have chiefly to look for any radical improvement in the social and economical relations

* Supra, book v. chap. vii.

between labour and capital. Strikes, therefore, and the trade societies which render strikes possible, are for these various reasons not a mischievous, but on the contrary, a valuable part of the existing machinery of society.

It is, however, an indispensable condition of tolerating combinations, that they should be voluntary. No severity, necessary to the purpose, is too great to be employed against attempts to compel workmen to join a union, or take part in a strike by threats or violence. Mere moral compulsion, by the expression of opinion, the law ought not to interfere with ; it belongs to more enlightened opinion to restrain it, by rectifying the moral sentiments of the people. Other questions arise when the combination, being voluntary, proposes to itself objects really contrary to the public good. High wages and short hours are generally good objects, or, at all events, may be so : [1] but in many trade unions, it is among the rules that there shall be no task work, or no difference of pay between the most expert workmen and the most unskilful, or that no member of the union shall earn more than a certain sum per week, in order that there may be more employment for the rest ; [2] and the abolition of piece work, under more or less of modification, held a conspicuous place among the demands of the Amalgamated Society. These are combinations to effect objects which are pernicious. Their success, even when only partial, is a public mischief; and were it complete, would be equal in magnitude to almost any of the evils arising from bad economical legislation. Hardly anything worse can be said of the worst laws on the subject of industry and its remuneration, consistent with the personal freedom of the labourer, than that they place the energetic and the idle, the skilful and the incompetent, on a level : and this, in so far as it is in itself possible, it is the direct tendency [3] of the regulations of these unions to do. [4] It does not, however, follow as a consequence that the law would

[1] [At this point the following passage of the original text was omitted from the 3rd ed. (1852) : " and a limitation of the number of persons in employment may be a necessary condition of these. Combinations, therefore, not to work for less than certain wages, or for more than a certain number of hours, or even not to work for a master who employs more than a certain number of apprentices, are, when voluntary on the part of all who engage in them, not only unexceptionable, but would be desirable, were it not that they almost always fail of their effect."]

[2] [This sentence was inserted in the 3rd ed.]

[3] [So since the 5th ed. (1862). In the earlier editions: " avowed object."]

[4] [The rest of this paragraph dates from the 3rd ed. The first edition (1848) read : " Every society which exacts from its members obedience to rules of this description and endeavours to enforce compliance with them on

be warranted in making the formation of such associations illegal and punishable. Independently of all considerations of constitutional liberty, the best interests of the human race imperatively require that all economical experiments, voluntarily undertaken, should have the fullest licence, and that force and fraud should be the only means of attempting to benefit themselves which are interdicted to the less fortunate classes of the community.*

§ 6. Among the modes of undue exercise of the power of government on which I have commented in this chapter, I have included only such as rest on theories which have still more or less of footing in the most enlightened countries. I have not spoken of some which have done still greater mischief in times not long past, but which are now generally given up, at least in theory, though enough of them still remains in practice to make it impossible as yet to class them among exploded errors.

The notion, for example, that a government should choose

the part of employers by refusal to work, is a public nuisance. Whether the law would be warranted in making the formation of such associations illegal and punishable, depends upon the difficult question of the legitimate bounds of constitutional liberty. What are the proper limits to the right of association ? To associate for the purpose of violating the law could not of course be tolerated under any government. But among the numerous acts which, although mischievous in themselves, the law ought not to prohibit from being done by individuals, are there not some which are rendered so much more mischievous when people combine to do them, that the legislature ought to prohibit the combination, though not the act itself ? When these questions have been philosophically answered, which belongs to a different branch of social philosophy from the present, it may be determined whether the kind of associations here treated of can be a proper subject of any other than merely moral repression."

But in the 2nd ed. (1849) this had already been replaced by : " Any society which exacts from its members obedience to rules of this description, and endeavours to enforce compliance with them on the part of employers by refusal to work, incurs the inconveniences of Communism, without getting rid of any of those of individual property. It does not follow, however, that the law would be warranted " &c., as at present.]

* [1862] Whoever desires to understand the question of Trade Combinations as seen from the point of view of the working people, should make himself acquainted with a pamphlet published in 1860, under the title *Trades Unions and Strikes, their Philosophy and Intention,* by T. J. Dunning, Secretary to the London Consolidated Society of Bookbinders. There are many opinions in this able tract in which I only partially, and some in which I do not at all, coincide. But there are also many sound arguments, and an instructive exposure of the common fallacies of opponents. Readers of other classes will see with surprise, not only how great a portion of truth the Unions have on their side, but how much less flagrant and condemnable even their errors appear, when seen under the aspect in which it is only natural that the working classes should themselves regard them.

opinions for the people, and should not suffer any doctrines in politics, morals, law, or religion, but such as it approves, to be printed or publicly professed, may be said to be altogether abandoned as a general thesis. It is now well understood that a régime of this sort is fatal to all prosperity, even of an economical kind : that the human mind when prevented either by fear of the law or by fear of opinion from exercising its faculties freely on the most important subjects, acquires a general torpidity and imbecility, by which, when they reach a certain point, it is disqualified from making any considerable advances even in the common affairs of life, and which, when greater still, make it gradually lose even its previous attainments. There cannot be a more decisive example than Spain and Portugal, for two centuries after the Reformation. The decline of those countries in national greatness, and even in material civilization, while almost all the other nations of Europe were uninterruptedly advancing, has been ascribed to various causes, but there is one which lies at the foundation of them all : the Holy Inquisition, and the system of mental slavery of which it is the symbol.

Yet although these truths are very widely recognized, and freedom both of opinion and of discussion is admitted as an axiom in all free countries, this apparent liberality and tolerance has acquired so little of the authority of a principle, that it is always ready to give way to the dread or horror inspired by some particular sort of opinions. Within the last fifteen or twenty years,[1] several individuals have suffered imprisonment, for the public profession, sometimes in a very temperate manner, of disbelief in religion ; and it is probable that both the public and the government, at the first panic which arises on the subject of Chartism or Communism, will fly to similar means for checking the propagation of democratic or anti-property doctrines. In this country, however, the effective restraints on mental freedom proceed much less from the law or the government, than from the intolerant temper of the national mind ; arising no longer from even as respectable a source as bigotry or fanaticism, but rather from the general habit, both in opinion and conduct, of making adherence to custom the rule of life, and enforcing it, by social penalties, against all persons who, without a party to back them, assert their individual independence.

[So in 7th ed. (1871). In 1st (1848): " two or three."]

CHAPTER XI

§ 1. WE have now reached the last part of our undertaking ;
the discussion, so far as suited to this treatise (that is, so far as it is a
question of principle, not detail), of the limits of the province of
government : the question, to what objects governmental intervention in the affairs of society may or should extend, over and
above those which necessarily appertain to it. No subject has
been more keenly contested in the present age : the contest, however,
has chiefly taken place round certain select points, with only flying
excursions into the rest of the field. Those indeed who have discussed
any particular question of government interference, such as state
education (spiritual or secular), regulation of hours of labour, a
public provision for the poor, &c., have often dealt largely in general
arguments, far outstretching the special application made of them,
and have shown a sufficiently strong bias either in favour of letting
things alone, or in favour of meddling ; but have seldom declared,
or apparently decided in their own minds, how far they would
carry either principle. The supporters of interference have been
content with asserting a general right and duty on the part of
government to intervene, wherever its intervention would be useful :
and when those who have been called the *laisser-faire* school have
attempted any definite limitation of the province of government,
they have usually restricted it to the protection of person and property
against force and fraud ; a definition to which neither they nor
any one else can deliberately adhere, since it excludes, as has been
shown in a preceding chapter,* some of the most indispensable and
unanimously recognized of the duties of government.

Without professing entirely to supply this deficiency of a general
theory, on a question which does not, as I conceive, admit of any

* Supra, book **v.** ch. 1.

universal solution, I shall attempt to afford some little aid towards the resolution of this class of questions as they arise, by examining, in the most general point of view in which the subject can be considered, what are the advantages, and what the evils or inconveniences, of government interference.

We must set out by distinguishing between two kinds of intervention by the government, which, though they may relate to the same subject, differ widely in their nature and effects, and require, for their justification, motives of a very different degree of urgency. The intervention may extend to controlling the free agency of individuals. Government may interdict all persons from doing certain things ; or from doing them without its authorization ; or may prescribe to them certain things to be done, or a certain manner of doing things which it is left optional with them to do or to abstain from. This is the *authoritative* interference of government. There is another kind of intervention which is not authoritative : when a government, instead of issuing a command and enforcing it by penalties, adopts the course so seldom resorted to by governments, and of which such important use might be made, that of giving advice, and promulgating information ; or when, leaving individuals free to use their own means of pursuing any object of general interest, the government, not meddling with them, but not trusting the object solely to their care, establishes, side by side with their arrangements, an agency of its own for a like purpose. Thus, it is one thing to maintain a Church Establishment, and another to refuse toleration to other religions, or to persons professing no religion. It is one thing to provide schools or colleges, and another to require that no person shall act as an instructor of youth without a government licence. There might be a national bank, or a government manufactory, without any monopoly against private banks and manufactories. There might be a post-office, without penalties against the conveyance of letters by other means. There may be a corps of government engineers for civil purposes, while the profession of a civil engineer is free to be adopted by every one. There may be public hospitals, without any restriction upon private medical or surgical practice.

§ 2. It is evident, even at first sight, that the authoritative form of government intervention has a much more limited sphere of legitimate action than the other. It requires a much stronger necessity to justify it in any case ; while there are large departments ol human life from which it must be unreservedly and imperiously excluded. Whatever theory we adopt respecting the foundation of the social union, and under whatever political institutions we live, there is a circle around every individual human being which no government, be it that of one, of a few, or of the many, ought to be permitted to overstep : there is a part of the life of every person who has come to years of discretion, within which the individuality of that person ought to reign uncontrolled either by any other individual or by the public collectively. That there is, or ought to be, some space in human existence thus entrenched around, and sacred from authoritative intrusion, no one who professes the smallest regard to human freedom or dignity will call in question : the point to be determined is, where the limit should be placed ; how large a province of human life this reserved territory should include. I apprehend that it ought to include all that part which concerns only the life, whether inward or outward, of the individual, and does not affect the interests of others, or affects them only through the moral influence of example. With respect to the domain of the inward consciousness, the thoughts and feelings, and as much of external conduct as is personal only, involving no consequences, none at least of a painful or injurious kind, to other people ; I hold that it is allowable in all, and in the more thoughtful and cultivated often a duty, to assert and promulgate, with all the force they are capable of, their opinion of what is good or bad, admirable or con temptible, but not to compel others to conform to that opinion; whether the force used is that of extra-legal coercion, or exerts itself by means of the law.

Even in those portions of conduct which do affect the interest of others, the onus of making out a case always lies on the defenders of legal prohibitions. It is not a merely constructive or presumptive injury to others which will justify the interference of law with individual freedom. To be prevented from doing what one is inclined to, or from acting according to one's own judgment of what is desirable, is not only always irksome, but always tends, *pro tanto*, to starve the development of some portion of the bodily or mental faculties, either sensitive or active ; and unless the conscience of the individual goes freely with the legal restraint, it partakes, either in a great or in a small degree, of the degradation of slavery. Scarcely any degree of utility, short of absolute necessity, will justify a prohibitory regulation, unless it can also be made to recommend itself to the general conscience ; unless persons of ordinary good intentions either believe already, or can be induced to believe, that the thing prohibited is a thing which they ought not to wish to do.

It is otherwise with governmental interferences which do not restrain individual free agency. When a government provides means for fulfilling a certain end, leaving individuals free to avail themselves of different means if in their opinion preferable, there is no infringement of liberty, no irksome or degrading restraint. One of the principal objections to government interference is then absent. There is, however, in almost all forms of government agency, one thing which is compulsory; the provision of the pecuniary means. These are derived from taxation; or, if existing in the form of an endowment derived from public property, they are still the cause of as much compulsory taxation as the sale or the annual proceeds of the property would enable to be dispensed with.* And the objection necessarily attaching to compulsory contributions, is almost always greatly aggravated by the expensive precautions and onerous restrictions which are indispensable to prevent evasion of a compulsory tax.

§ 3. A second general objection to government agency is that every increase of the functions devolving on the government is an increase of its power, both in the form of authority, and still more, in the indirect form of influence. The importance of this consideration, in respect to political freedom, has in general been quite sufficiently recognized, at least in England; but many, in latter times, have been prone to think that limitation of the powers of the government is only essential when the government itself is badly constituted; when it does not represent the people, but is the organ of a class, or coalition of classes: and that a government of sufficiently popular constitution might be trusted with any amount of power over the nation, since its power would be only that of the nation over itself. This might be true, if the nation, in such cases, did not practically mean a mere majority of the nation, and if minorities were only capable of oppressing, but not of being oppressed. Experience, however, proves that the depositaries of power who

---

* The only cases in which government agency involves nothing of a compulsory nature, are the rare cases in which, without any artificial monopoly, it pays its own expenses. A bridge built with public money, on which tolls are collected sufficient to pay not only all current expenses, but the interest of the original outlay, is one case in point. The government railways in Belgium and Germany are another example. The Post Office, if its monopoly were abolished, and it still paid its expenses, would be another.

are mere delegates of the people, that is of a majority, are quite as ready (when they think they can count on popular support) as any organs of oligarchy to assume arbitrary power, and encroach unduly on the liberty of private life. The public collectively is abundantly ready to impose, not only its generally narrow views of its interests, but its abstract opinions, and even its tastes, as laws binding upon individuals. And the present civilization tends so strongly to make the power of persons acting in masses the only substantial power in society, that there never was more necessity for surrounding individual independence of thought, speech, and conduct, with the most powerful defences, in order to maintain that originality of mind and individuality of character, which are the only source of any real progress, and of most of the qualities which make the human race much superior to any herd of animals. Hence it is no less important in a democratic than in any other government, that all tendency on the part of public authorities to stretch their interference, and assume a power of any sort which can easily be dispensed with, should be regarded with unremitting jealousy. Perhaps this is even more important in a democracy than in any other form of political society ; because, where public opinion is sovereign, an individual who is oppressed by the sovereign does not, as in most other states of things, find a rival power to which he can appeal for relief, or, at all events, for sympathy.

§ 4. A third general objection to government agency rests on the principle of the division of labour. Every additional function undertaken by the government is a fresh occupation imposed upon a body already overcharged with duties. A natural consequence is that most things are ill done ; much not done at all, because the government is not able to do it without delays which are fatal to its purpose ; that the more troublesome, and less showy, of the functions undertaken, are postponed or neglected, and an excuse is always ready for the neglect ; while the heads of the administration have their minds so fully taken up with official details, in however perfunctory a manner superintended, that they have no time or thought to spare for the great interests of the state, and the prepara-tion of enlarged measures of social improvement.

But these inconveniences, though real and serious, result much more from the bad organization of governments, than from the extent and variety of the duties undertaken by them. Government is not a name for some one functionary, or definite number of functionaries : there may be almost any amount of division of labour within the administrative body itself. The evil in question is felt in great magnitude under some of the governments of the Continent, where six or eight men, living at the capital and known by the name of ministers, demand that the whole public business of the country shall pass, or be supposed to pass, under their individual eye. But the inconvenience would be reduced to a very manageable compass, in a country in which there was a proper distribution of functions between the central and local officers of government, and in which the central body was divided into a sufficient number of departments. When Parliament thought it expedient to confer on the government an inspecting and partially controlling authority over railways, it did not add railways to the department of the Home Minister, but created a Railway Board. When it determined to have a central superintending authority for pauper administration, it established the Poor Law Commission. There are few countries in which a greater number of functions are discharged by public officers, than in some states of the American Union, particularly the New England States : but the division of labour in public business is extreme ; most of these officers being not even amenable to any common superior, but performing their duties freely, under the double check of election by their townsmen, and civil as well as criminal responsibility to the tribunals.

It is, no doubt, indispensable to good government that the chiefs of the administration, whether permanent or temporary, should extend a commanding, though general, view over the *ensemble* of all the interests confided, in any degree, to the responsibility of the central power. But with a skilful internal organization of the administrative machine, leaving to subordinates, and as far as possible, to local subordinates, not only the execution, but to a great degree the control, of details ; holding them accountable for the results of their acts rather than for the acts themselves, except where these come within the cognizance of the tribunals ; taking the most effectual securities for honest and capable appointments ; opening a broad path to promotion from the inferior degrees of the administrative scale to the superior ; leaving, at each step, to the functionary, a wider range in the origination of measures, so that, in the highest grade of all, deliberation might be concentrated on the great collective interests of the country in each department ; if all this were done, the government would not probably be over-burthened by any business, in other respects fit to be undertaken by it; though the overburthening would remain as a serious addition to the inconveniences incurred by its undertaking any which was unfit.

§ 5.   But though a better organization of governments would greatly diminish the force of the objection to the mere multiplication of their duties, it would still remain true that in all the more advanced communities the great majority of things are worse done by the intervention of government, than the individuals most interested in the matter would do them, or cause them to be done, if left to themselves.   The grounds of this truth are expressed with tolerable exactness in the popular dictum, that people understand their own business and their own interests better, and care for them more, than the government does, or can be expected to do.   This maxim holds true throughout the greatest part of the business of life, and wherever it is true we ought to condemn every kind of government intervention that conflicts with it.   The inferiority of government agency, for example, in any of the common operations of industry or commerce, is proved by the fact, that it is hardly ever able to maintain itself in equal competition with individual agency, where the individuals possess the requisite degree of industrial enterprise, and can command the necessary assemblage of means.   All the facilities which a government enjoys of access to information ;   all the means which it possesses of remunerating, and therefore of commanding, the best available talent in the market—are not an equivalent for the one great disadvantage of an inferior interest in the result.

It must be remembered, besides, that even if a government were superior in intelligence and knowledge to any single individual in the nation, it must be inferior to all the individuals of the nation taken together.   It can neither possess in itself, nor enlist in its service, more than a portion of the acquirements and capacities which the country contains, applicable to any given purpose. There must be many persons equally qualified for the work with those whom the government employs, even if it selects its instru-ments with no reference to any consideration but their fitness. Now these are the very persons into whose hands, in the cases of most common occurrence, a system of individual agency naturally tends to throw the work, because they are capable of doing it better or[1]

---

[1] [So since 5th ed. (1862).   Originally : " and."]

on cheaper terms than any other persons. So far as this is the case, it is evident that government, by excluding or even by super-seding individual agency, either substitutes a less qualified instru-mentality for one better qualified, or at any rate substitutes its own mode of accomplishing the work, for all the variety of modes which would be tried by a number of equally qualified persons aiming at the same end ; a competition by many degrees more propitious to the progress of improvement than any uniformity of system.

§ 6.   I have reserved for the last place one of the strongest of the reasons against the extension of government agency.   Even if the government could comprehend within itself, in each department, all the most eminent intellectual capacity and active talent of the nation, it would not be the less desirable that the conduct of a large portion of the affairs of the society should be left in the hands of the persons immediately interested in them.   The business of life is an essential part of the practical education of a people ; without which, book and school instruction, though most necessary and salutary, does not suffice to qualify them for conduct, and for the adaptation of means to ends.   Instruction is only one of the desiderata of mental improvement ; another, almost as indispensable, is a vigorous exercise of the active energies ; labour, contrivance, judgment, self-control : and the natural stimulus to these is the difficulties of life.   This doctrine is not to be confounded with the complacent optimism, which represents the evils of life as desirable things, because they call forth qualities adapted to combat with evils.   It is only because the difficulties exist, that the qualities which combat with them are of any value.   As practical beings it is our business to free human life from as many as possible of its difficulties, and not to keep up a stock of them as hunters preserve game for the exercise of pursuing it.   But since the need of active talent and practical judgment in the affairs of life can only be diminished, and not, even on the most favourable supposition, done away with, it is important that those endowments should be culti-vated not merely in a select few, but in all, and that the cultivation should be more varied and complete than most persons are able to find in the narrow sphere of their merely individual interests.   A people among whom there is no habit of spontaneous action for a collective interest—who look habitually to their government to command or prompt them in all matters of joint concern—who expect to have everything done for them, except what can be made an affair of mere habit and routine—have their faculties only half developed ; their education is defective in one of its most important branches.

Not only is the cultivation of the active faculties by exercise, diffused through the whole community, in itself one of the most valuable of national possessions : it is rendered, not less, but more necessary, when a high degree of that indispensable culture is systematically kept up in the chiefs and functionaries of the state. There cannot be a combination of circumstances more dangerous to human welfare, than that in which intelligence and talent are maintained at a high standard within a governing corporation, but starved and discouraged outside the pale. Such a system, more completely than any other, embodies the idea of despotism, by arming with intellectual superiority as an additional weapon those who have already the legal power. It approaches as nearly as the organic difference between human beings and other animals admits, to the government of sheep by their shepherd without anything like so strong an interest as the shepherd has in the thriving condition of the flock. The only security against political slavery is the check maintained over governors by the diffusion of intelligence, activity, and public spirit among the governed. Experience proves the extreme difficulty of permanently keeping up a sufficiently high standard of those qualities ; a difficulty which increases, as the advance of civilization and security removes one after another of the hardships, embarrassments, and dangers against which individuals had formerly no resource but in their own strength, skill, and courage. It is therefore of supreme importance that all classes of the community, down to the lowest, should have much to do for themselves ; that as great a demand should be made upon their intelligence and virtue as it is in any respect equal to ; that the government should not only leave as far as possible to their own faculties the conduct of whatever concerns themselves alone, but should suffer them, or rather encourage them, to manage as many as possible of their joint concerns by voluntary co-operation ; since this discussion and management of collective interests is the great school of that public spirit, and the great source of that intelligence of public affairs, which are always regarded as the distinctive character of the public of free countries.

A democratic constitution, not supported by democratic institutions in detail, but confined to the central government, not only is not political freedom, but often creates a spirit precisely the reverse, carrying down to the lowest grade in society the desire and ambition of political domination.   In some countries the desire of the people is for not being tyrannized over, but in others it is merely for an equal chance to everybody of tyrannizing.   Unhappily this last state of the desires is fully as natural to mankind as the former, and in many of the conditions even of civilized humanity is far more largely exemplified.   In proportion as the people are accustomed to manage their affairs by their own active intervention, instead of leaving them to the government, their desires will turn to repelling tyranny, rather than to tyrannizing : while in proportion as all real initiative and direction resides in the government, and individuals habitually feel and act as under its perpetual tutelage, popular institutions develop in them not the desire of freedom, but an unmeasured appetite for place and power ; diverting the intelligence and activity of the country from its principal business to a wretched competition for the selfish prizes and the petty vanities of office.

§ 7.   The preceding are the principal reasons, of a general character, in favour of restricting to the narrowest compass the intervention of a public authority in the business of the community : and few will dispute the more than sufficiency of these reasons, to throw, in every instance, the burthen of making out a strong case, not on those who resist, but on those who recommend, government interference.   *Laisser-faire*, in short, should be the general practice : every departure from it, unless required by some great good, is a certain evil.

The degree in which the maxim, even in the cases to which it is most manifestly applicable, has heretofore been infringed by governments, future ages will probably have difficulty in crediting.   Some idea may be formed of it from the description of M. Dunoyer * of the restraints imposed on the operations of manufacture under the old government of France, by the meddling and regulating spirit of legislation.

" The State exercised over manufacturing industry the most unlimited and arbitrary jurisdiction.   It disposed without scruple of the resources of manufacturers : it decided who should be allowed to work, what things it should be permitted to make, what materials

* *De la Liberté du Travail*, vol. i. pp. 353–4.

should be employed, what processes followed, what forms should be given to productions. It was not enough to do well, to do better ; it was necessary to do according to the rules. Everybody knows the regulation of 1670 which prescribed to seize and nail to the pillory, with the names of the makers, goods not conformable to the rules, and which, on a second repetition of the offence, directed that the manufacturers themselves should be attached also. Not the taste of the consumers, but the commands of the law must be attended to. Legions of inspectors, commissioners, controllers, jurymen, guardians, were charged with its execution. Machines were broken, products were burned when not conformable to the rules : improvements were punished ; inventors were fined. There were different sets of rules for goods destined for home consumption and for those intended for exportation. An artizan could neither choose the place in which to establish himself, nor work at all seasons, nor work for all customers. There exists a decree of March 30, 1700, which limits to eighteen towns the number of places where stockings might be woven. A decree of June 18, 1723, enjoins the manufacturers at Rouen to suspend their works from the 1st of July to the 15th of September, in order to facilitate the harvest. Louis XIV., when he intended to construct the colonnade of the Louvre, forbade all private persons to employ workmen without his permission, under a penalty of 10,000 livres, and forbade workmen to work for private persons, on pain for the first offence, of imprisonment, and for the second, of the galleys."

That these and similar regulations were not a dead letter, and that the officious and vexatious meddling was prolonged down to the French Revolution, we have the testimony of Roland, the Girondist minister.* " I have seen," says he, " eighty, ninety, a hundred pieces of cotton or woollen stuff cut up, and completely destroyed. I have witnessed similar scenes every week for a number of years. I have seen manufactured goods confiscated ; heavy fines laid on the manufacturers ; some pieces of fabric were burnt in public places, and at the hours of market : others were fixed to the pillory, with the name of the manufacturer inscribed upon them, and he himself was threatened with the pillory, in case of a second offence. All this was done under my eyes, at Rouen, in conformity with existing regulations, or ministerial orders. What crime deserved so cruel a punishment ? Some defects in the materials employed, or in

* I quote at second hand, from Mr. Carey's *Essay on the Rate of Wages,* pp. 195-6.

the texture of the fabric, or even in some of the threads of the warp.

"I have frequently seen manufacturers visited by a band of satellites who put all in confusion in their establishments, spread terror in their families, cut the stuffs from the frames, tore off the warp from the looms, and carried them away as proofs of infringement; the manufacturers were summoned, tried, and condemned : their goods confiscated ; copies of their judgment of confiscation posted up in every public place ; fortune, reputation, credit, all was lost and destroyed.   And for what offence ? Because they had made of worsted a kind of cloth called shag, such as the English used to manufacture, and even sell in France, while the French regulations stated that that kind of cloth should be made with mohair.   I have seen other manufacturers treated in the same way, because they had made camlets of a particular width, used in England and Germany, for which there was a great demand from Spain, Portugal, and other countries, and from several parts of France, while the French regulations prescribed other widths for camlets."

The time is gone by, when such applications as these of the principle of " paternal government " would be attempted in even the least enlightened country of the European commonwealth of nations.   In such cases as those cited, all the general objections to government interference are valid, and several of them in nearly their highest degree.   But we must now turn to the second part of our task, and direct our attention to cases, in which some of those general objections are altogether absent, while those which can never be got rid of entirely are overruled by counter-considerations of still greater importance.

We have observed that, as a general rule, the business of life is better performed when those who have an immediate interest in it are left to take their own course, uncontrolled either by the mandate of the law or by the meddling of any public functionary.   The persons, or some of the persons, who do the work, are likely to be better judges than the government, of the means of attaining the particular end at which they aim.   Were we to suppose, what is not very probable, that the government has possessed itself of the best knowledge which had been acquired up to a given time by the persons most skilled in the occupation ; even then the individual agents have so much stronger and more direct an interest in the result, that the means are far more likely to be improved and perfected if left to their uncontrolled choice.   But if the workman is generally the best selector of means, can it be affirmed with the same universality, that the consumer, or person served, is the most competent judge of the end ? Is the buyer always qualified to judge of the commodity ? If not, the presumption in favour of the competition of the market does not apply to the case ; and if the commodity be one in the quality of which society has much at stake, the balance of advantages may be in favour of some mode and degree of intervention by the authorized representatives of the collective interest of the state.

§ 8. Now, the proposition that the consumer is a competent judge of the commodity, can be admitted only with numerous abatements and exceptions. He is generally the best judge (though even this is not true universally) of the material objects produced for his use. These are destined to supply some physical want, or gratify some taste or inclination, respecting which wants or inclinations there is no appeal from the person who feels them ; or they are the means and appliances of some occupation, for the use of the persons engaged in it, who may be presumed to be judges of the things required in their own habitual employment. But there are other things, of the worth of which the demand of the market is by no means a test ; things of which the utility does not consist in ministering to inclinations, nor in serving the daily uses of life, and the want of which is least felt where the need is greatest. This is peculiarly true of those things which are chiefly useful as tending to raise the character of human beings. The uncultivated cannot be competent judges of cultivation. Those who most need to be made wiser and better, usually desire it least, and, if they desired it, would be incapable of finding the way to it by their own lights. It will continually happen, on the voluntary system, that, the end not being desired, the means will not be provided at all, or that, the persons requiring improvement having an imperfect or altogether erroneous conception of what they want, the supply called forth by the demand of the market will be anything but what is really required. Now any well-intentioned and tolerably civilized government may think, without presumption, that it does or ought to possess a degree of cultivation above the average of the community which it rules, and that it should therefore be capable of offering better education and better instruction to the people, than the greater number of them would spontaneously demand. Education, therefore, is one of those things which it is admissible in principle that a government should provide for the people. The case is one to which the reasons of the non-interference principle do not necessarily or universally extend.*

With regard to elementary education, the exception to ordinary rules may, I conceive, justifiably be carried still further. There are certain primary elements and means of knowledge, which it is in the highest degree desirable that all human beings born into the community should acquire during childhood. If their parents, or those on whom they depend, have the power of obtaining for them this instruction, and fail to do it, they commit a double breach of duty, towards the children themselves, and towards the members of the community generally, who are all liable to suffer seriously from the consequences of ignorance and want of education in their fellow-citizens. It is therefore an allowable exercise of the powers of government to impose on parents the legal obligation of giving elementary instruction to children. This, however, cannot fairly be done, without taking measures to insure that such instruction shall be always accessible to them, either gratuitously or at a trifling expense.

* In opposition to these opinions, a writer, with whom on many points I agree, but whose hostility to government intervention seems to me too indiscriminate and unqualified, M. Dunoyer, observes, that instruction, however good in itself, can only be useful to the public in so far as they are willing to receive it, and that the best proof that the instruction is suitable to their wants is its success as a pecuniary enterprise. This argument seems no more conclusive respecting instruction for the mind, than it would be respecting medicine for the body. No medicine will do the patient any good if he cannot be induced to take it ; but we are not bound to admit as a corollary from this, that the patient will select the right medicine without assistance. Is it not probable that a recommendation, from any quarter which he respects, may induce him to accept a better medicine than he would spontaneously have chosen ? This is, in respect to education, the very point in debate. Without doubt, instruction which is so far in advance of the people that they cannot be induced to avail themselves of it, is to them of no more worth than if it did not exist. But between what they spontaneously choose, and what they will refuse to accept when offered, there is a breadth of interval proportioned to their deference for the recommender. Besides, a thing of which the public are bad judges may require to be shown to them and pressed on their attention for a long time, and to prove its advantages by long experience, before they learn to appreciate it, yet they may learn at last ; which they might never have done, if the thing had not been thus obtruded upon them in act, but only recommended in theory. Now, a pecuniary speculation cannot wait years, or perhaps generations for success ; it must succeed rapidly, or not at all. Another consideration which M. Dunoyer seems to have overlooked, is, that institutions and modes of tuition which never could be made sufficiently popular to repay, with a profit, the expenses incurred on them, may be invaluable to the many by giving the highest quality of education to the few, and keeping up the perpetual succession of superior minds, by whom knowledge is advanced, and the community urged forward in civilization.

It may indeed be objected that the education of children is one of those expenses which parents, even of the labouring class, ought to defray ; that it is desirable that they should feel it incumbent on them to provide by their own means for the fulfilment of their duties, and that by giving education at the cost of others, just as much as by giving subsistence, the standard of necessary wages is proportionally lowered, and the springs of exertion and self-restraint in so much relaxed. This argument could, at best, be only valid if the question were that of substituting a public provision for what individuals would otherwise do for themselves ; if all parents in the labouring class recognised and practised the duty of giving instruction to their children at their own expense. But inasmuch as parents do not practise this duty, and do not include education among those necessary expenses which their wages must provide for, therefore the general rate of wages is not high enough to bear those expenses, and they must be borne from some other source. And this is not one of the cases in which the tender of help perpetuates the state of things which renders help necessary. Instruction, when it is really such, does not enervate, but strengthens as well as enlarges the active faculties : in whatever manner acquired, its effect on the mind is favourable to the spirit of independence : and when, unless had gratuitously, it would not be had at all, help in this form has the opposite tendency to that which in so many other cases makes it objectionable ; it is help towards doing without help.

In England, and most European countries, elementary instruction cannot be paid for, at its full cost, from the common wages of unskilled labour, and would not if it could. The alternative, therefore, is not between government and private speculation, but between a government provision and voluntary charity : between interference by government, and interference by associations of individuals, subscribing their own money for the purpose, like the two great School Societies. It is, of course, not desirable that anything should be done by funds derived from compulsory taxation, which is already sufficiently well done by individual liberality. How far this is the case with school instruction, is, in each particular instance, a question of fact. The education provided in this country on the voluntary principle has of late been so much discussed, that it is needless in this place to criticise it minutely, and I shall merely express my conviction, that even in quantity it is [1848], and is likely to remain, altogether insufficient, while in quality, though with some slight tendency to improvement, it is never good except by some rare accident, and generally so bad as to be little more than nominal. I hold it therefore the duty of the government to supply the defect, by giving pecuniary support to elementary schools, such as to render them accessible to all the children of the poor, either freely, or for a payment too inconsiderable to be sensibly felt.[1]

One thing must be strenuously insisted on ; that the government must claim no monopoly for its education, either in the lower or in the higher branches ; must exert neither authority nor influence to induce the people to resort to its teachers in preference to others, and must confer no peculiar advantages on those who have been instructed by them. Though the government teachers will probably be superior to the average of private instructors, they will not embody all the knowledge and sagacity to be found in all instructors taken together, and it is desirable to leave open as many roads as possible to the desired end. It is not endurable that a government should, either *de jure* or *de facto*, have a complete control over the education of the people. To possess such a control, and actually exert it, is to be despotic. A government which can mould the opinions and sentiments of the people from their youth upwards, can do with them whatever it pleases. Though a government, therefore, may, and in many cases ought to, establish schools and colleges, it must neither compel nor bribe any person to come to them ; nor ought the power of individuals to set up rival establishments to depend in any degree upon its authorization. It would be justified in requiring from all the people that they shall possess instruction in certain things, but not in prescribing to them how or from whom they shall obtain it.

§ 9. In the matter of education, the intervention of government is justifiable, because the case is not one in which the interest and judgment of the consumer are a sufficient security for the goodness of the commodity. Let us now consider another class of cases, where there is no person in the situation of a consumer, and where the interest and judgment to be relied on are those of the agent

---

[1] [The paragraph originally went on : " but which it might be proper to demand, merely in recognition of a principle : the remainder of the cost to be defrayed, as in Scotland, by a local rate, that the inhabitants of the locality might have a greater interest in watching over the management, and checking negligence and abuse." These words were omitted in the 4th ed. (1857).]

himself ; as in the conduct of any business in which he is exclusively interested, or in entering into any contract or engagement by which he himself is to be bound.

The ground of the practical principle of non-interference must here be, that most persons take a juster and more intelligent view of their own interest, and of the means of promoting it, than can either be prescribed to them by a general enactment of the legislature, or pointed out in the particular case by a public functionary. The maxim is unquestionably sound as a general rule ; but there is no difficulty in perceiving some very large and conspicuous exceptions to it. These may be classed under several heads.

First :—The individual who is presumed to be the best judge of his own interests may be incapable of judging or acting for himself ; may be a lunatic, an idiot, an infant : or though not wholly incapable, may be of immature years and judgment. In this case the foundation of the *laisser-faire* principle breaks down entirely. The person most interested is not the best judge of the matter, nor a competent judge at all. Insane persons are everywhere regarded as proper objects of the care of the state.* In the case of children and young persons, it is common to say, that though they cannot judge for themselves, they have their parents or other relatives to judge for them. But this removes the question into a different category ; making it no longer a question whether the government should interfere with individuals in the direction of

* [1852] The practice of the English law with respect to insane persons, especially on the all-important point of the ascertainment of insanity, most urgently demands reform. At present no persons, whose property is worth coveting, and whose nearest relations are unscrupulous, or on bad terms with them, are secure against a commission of lunacy. At the instance of the persons who would profit by their being declared insane, a jury may be impanelled and an investigation held at the expense of the property, in which all their personal peculiarities, with all the additions made by the lying gossip of low servants, are poured into the credulous ears of twelve petty shopkeepers, ignorant of all ways of life except those of their own class, and regarding every trait of individuality in character or taste as eccentricity, and all eccentricity as either insanity or wickedness. If this sapient tribunal gives the desired verdict, the property is handed over to perhaps the last persons whom the rightful owner would have desired or suffered to possess it. Some recent instances of this kind of investigation have been a scandal to the administration of justice. Whatever other changes in this branch of law may be made, two at least are imperative : first, that, as in other legal proceedings, the expenses should not be borne by the person on trial, but by the promoters of the inquiry, subject to recovery of costs in case of success : and secondly, that the property of a person declared insane should in no case be made over to heirs while the proprietor is alive, but should be managed by a public officer until his death or recovery.

their own conduct and interests, but whether it should leave absolutely in their power the conduct and interests of somebody else.
Parental power is as susceptible of abuse as any other power, and
is, as a matter of fact, constantly abused. If laws do not succeed
in preventing parents from brutally ill-treating, and even from
murdering their children, far less ought it to be presumed that the
interests of children will never be sacrificed, in more commonplace
and less revolting ways, to the selfishness or the ignorance of their
parents. Whatever it can be clearly seen that parents ought to do
or forbear for the interests of children, the law is warranted, if it is
able, in compelling to be done or forborne, and is generally bound to
do so. To take an example from the peculiar province of political
economy ; it is right that children and young persons not yet arrived
at maturity should be protected, so far as the eye and hand of the
state can reach, from being over-worked. Labouring for too many
hours in the day, or on work beyond their strength, should not be
permitted to them, for if permitted it may always be compelled.
Freedom of contract, in the case of children, is but another word
for freedom of coercion. Education also, the best which circumstances admit of their receiving, is not a thing which parents or
relatives, from indifference, jealousy, or avarice, should have it in
their power to withhold.

The reasons for legal intervention in favour of children, apply
not less strongly to the case of those unfortunate slaves and victims
of the most brutal part of mankind, the lower animals. It is by
the grossest misunderstanding of the principles of liberty, that the
infliction of exemplary punishment on ruffianism practised towards
these defenceless creatures has been treated as a meddling by government with things beyond its province ; an interference with domestic
life. The domestic life of domestic tyrants is one of the things
which it is the most imperative on the law to interfere with ; and
it is to be regretted that metaphysical scruples respecting the
nature and source of the authority of government should induce
many warm supporters of laws against cruelty to animals to seek
for a justification of such laws in the incidental consequences of the
indulgence of ferocious habits to the interests of human beings,
rather than in the intrinsic merits of the case itself. What it would
be the duty of a human being, possessed of the requisite physical
strength, to prevent by force if attempted in his presence, it cannot
be less incumbent on society generally to repress. The existing
laws of England on the subject are chiefly defective in the trifling,

often almost nominal, maximum, to which the penalty even in the worst cases is limited.

Among those members of the community whose freedom of contract ought to be controlled by the legislature for their own protection, on account (it is said) of their dependent position, it is frequently proposed to include women : and in the existing Factory Acts[1] their labour, in common with that of young persons, has been placed under peculiar restrictions. But the classing together, for this and other purposes, of women and children, appears to me both indefensible in principle and mischievous in practice. Children below a certain age *cannot* judge or act for themselves ; up to a considerably greater age they are inevitably more or less disqualified for doing so ; but women are as capable as men of appreciating and managing their own concerns, and the only hindrance to their doing so arises from the injustice of their present social position. When the law makes everything which the wife acquires, the property of the husband, while by compelling her to live with him it forces her to submit to almost any amount of moral and even physical tyranny which he may choose to inflict, there is some ground for regarding every act done by her as done under coercion : but it is the great error of reformers and philanthropists in our time to nibble at the consequences of unjust power, instead of redressing the injustice itself. If women had as absolute a control as men have, over their own persons and their own patrimony or acquisitions, there would be no plea for limiting their hours of labouring for themselves, in order that they might have time to labour for the husband, in what is called, by the advocates of restriction, *his* home. Women employed in factories are the only women in the labouring rank of life whose position is not that of slaves and drudges ; precisely because they cannot easily be compelled to work and earn wages in factories against their will. For improving the condition of women, it should, on the contrary, be an object to give them the readiest access to independent industrial employment, instead of closing, either entirely or partially, that which is already open to them.[2]

§ 10. A second exception to the doctrine that individuals are the best judges of their own interest, is when an individual attempts

---

[1] [" Acts " since 7th ed. (1871).   Originally (1848) : " the recent Factory Act."]

[2] [See Appendix KK. *The Factory Acts.*]

to decide irrevocably now what will be best for his interest at some future and distant time. The presumption in favour of individual judgment is only legitimate, where the judgment is grounded on actual, and especially on present, personal experience ; not where it is formed antecedently to experience, and not suffered to be reversed even after experience has condemned it. When persons have bound themselves by a contract, not simply to do some one thing, but to continue doing something for ever or for a prolonged period, without any power of revoking the engagement, the presumption which their perseverance in that course of conduct would otherwise raise in favour of its being advantageous to them, does not exist ; and any such presumption which can be grounded on their having voluntarily entered into the contract, perhaps at an early age, and without any real knowledge of what they undertook, is commonly next to null. The practical maxim of leaving contracts free is not applicable without great limitations in case of engagements in perpetuity ; and the law should be extremely jealous of such engagements ; should refuse its sanction to them, when the obligations they impose are such as the contracting party cannot be a competent judge of ; if it ever does sanction them, it should take every possible security for their being contracted with foresight and deliberation ; and in compensation for not permitting the parties themselves to revoke their engagement, should grant them a release from it, on a sufficient case being made out before an impartial authority. These considerations are eminently applicable to marriage, the most important of all cases of engagement for life.[1]

§ 11. The third exception which I shall notice, to the doctrine that government cannot manage the affairs of individuals as well as the individuals themselves, has reference to the great class of cases in which the individuals can only manage the concern by delegated agency, and in which the so-called private management is, in point of fact, hardly better entitled to be called management by the persons interested than administration by a public officer. Whatever, if left to spontaneous agency, can only be done by joint-stock associations, will often be as well, and sometimes better done, as far as the actual work is concerned, by the state. Government management is, indeed, proverbially jobbing, careless, and ineffective, but so likewise has generally been joint-stock management. The

---

[1] [This last sentence added in 3rd ed. (1852).]

directors of a joint-stock company, it is true, are always share-holders; but also the members of a government are invariably taxpayers; and in the case of directors, no more than in that of governments, is their proportional share of the benefits of good management equal to the interest they may possibly have in mis-management, even without reckoning the interest of their ease. It may be objected, that the shareholders, in their collective character, exercise a certain control over the directors, and have almost always full power to remove them from office. Practically, however, the difficulty of exercising this power is found to be so great, that it is hardly ever exercised except in cases of such flagrantly unskilful, or, at least, unsuccessful management, as would generally produce the ejection from office of managers appointed by the government. Against the very ineffectual security afforded by meetings of share-holders, and by their individual inspection and inquiries, may be placed the greater publicity and more active discussion and comment, to be expected in free countries with regard to affairs in which the general government takes part. The defects, therefore, of govern-ment management do not seem to be necessarily much greater, if necessarily greater at all, than those of management by joint-stock.

The true reasons in favour of leaving to voluntary associations all such things as they are competent to perform would exist in equal strength if it were certain that the work itself would be as well or better done by public officers. These reasons have been already pointed out: the mischief of overloading the chief function-aries of government with demands on their attention, and diverting them from duties which they alone can discharge, to objects which can be sufficiently well attained without them; the danger of unnecessarily swelling the direct power and indirect influence of government, and multiplying occasions of collision between its agents and private citizens; and the inexpediency of concentrating in a dominant bureaucracy all the skill and experience in the manage-ment of large interests, and all the power of organized action, existing in the community; a practice which keeps the citizens in a relation to the government like that of children to their guardians, and is a main cause of the inferior capacity for political life which has hitherto characterized the over-governed countries of the Continent, whether with or without the forms of representative government.*

* A parallel case may be found in the distaste for politics, and absence of public spirit, by which women, as a class, are characterized in the present

But although, for these reasons, most things which are likely to be even tolerably done by voluntary associations should, generally speaking, be left to them ; it does not follow that the manner in which those associations perform their work should be entirely uncontrolled by the government.   There are many cases in which the agency, of whatever nature, by which a service is performed, is certain, from the nature of the case, to be virtually single ; in which a practical monopoly, with all the power it confers of taxing the community, cannot be prevented from existing.   I have already more than once adverted to the case of the gas and water companies, among which, though perfect freedom is allowed to competition, none really takes place, and practically they are found to be even more irresponsible, and unapproachable by individual complaints, than the government.   There are the expenses without the advantages of plurality of agency ; and the charge made for services which cannot be dispensed with, is, in substance, quite as much compulsory taxation as if imposed by law ; there are few householders who make any distinction between their " water-rate " and their other local taxes. In the case of these particular services, the reasons preponderate in favour of their being performed, like the paving and cleansing of the streets, not certainly by the general government of the state, but by the municipal authorities of the town, and the expense defrayed, as even now it in fact is, by a local rate.   But in the many analogous cases which it is best to resign to voluntary agency, the community needs some other security for the fit performance of the service than the interest of the managers ; and it is the part of government, either to subject the business to reasonable conditions for the general advantage, or to retain such power over it that the profits of the monopoly may at least be obtained for the public.   This applies to the case of a road, a canal, or a railway.   These are always, in a great degree, practical monopolies ; and a government which concedes such monopoly unreservedly to a private company does much the same thing as if it allowed an individual or an association

state of society, and which is often felt and complained of by political reformers, without, in general, making them willing to recognise, or desirous to remove, its cause.   It obviously arises from their being taught, both by institutions and by the whole of their education, to regard themselves as entirely apart from politics.   Wherever they have been politicians, they have shown as great interest in the subject, and as great aptitude for it, according to the spirit of their time, as the men with whom they were cotemporaries : in that period of history (for example) in which Isabella of Castile and Elizabeth of England were, not rare exceptions, but merely brilliant examples of a spirit and capacity very largely diffused among women of high station and cultivation in Europe.

to levy any tax they chose, for their own benefit, on all the malt produced in the country, or on all the cotton imported into it. To make the concession for a limited time is generally justifiable, on the principle which justifies patents for inventions : but the state should either reserve to itself a reversionary property in such public works, or should retain, and freely exercise, the right of fixing a maximum of fares and charges, and, from time to time, varying that maximum. It is perhaps necessary to remark, that the state may be the proprietor of canals or railways without itself working them ; and that they will almost always be better worked by means of a company renting the railway or canal for a limited period from the state.

§ 12. To a fourth case of exception I must request particular attention, it being one to which, as it appears to me, the attention of political economists has not yet been sufficiently drawn. There are matters in which the interference of law is required, not to overrule the judgment of individuals respecting their own interest, but to give effect to that judgment : they being unable to give effect to it except by concert, which concert again cannot be effectual unless it receives validity and sanction from the law. For illustration, and without prejudging the particular point, I may advert to the question of diminishing the hours of labour. Let us suppose, what is at least supposable, whether it be the fact or not—that a general reduction of the hours of factory labour, say from ten to nine,[1] would be for the advantage of the workpeople : that they would receive as high wages, or nearly as high, for nine hours' labour as they receive for ten. If this would be the result, and if the operatives generally are convinced that it would, the limitation, some may say, will be adopted spontaneously. I answer, that it will not be adopted unless the body of operatives bind themselves to one another to abide by it. A workman who refused to work more than nine hours while there were others who worked ten, would either not be employed at all, or if employed, must submit to lose one-tenth of his wages. However convinced, therefore, he may be that it is the interest of the class to work short time, it is contrary to his own interest to set the example, unless he is well assured that all or most others will follow it. But suppose a general agreement of the whole class : might not this be

---

[1] [The original " twelve to ten " (1848) was changed to the present text, and the consequent alterations made in the rest of the paragraph, in the 5th ed. (1862).]

effectual without the sanction of law ? Not unless enforced by opinion with a rigour practically equal to that of law. For however beneficial the observance of the regulation might be to the class collectively, the immediate interest of every individual would lie in violating it : and the more numerous those who adhered to the rule, the more would individuals gain by departing from it. If nearly all restricted themselves to nine hours, those who chose to work for ten would gain all the advantages of the restriction, together with the profit of infringing it ; they would get ten hours' wages for nine hours' work, and an hour's wages besides. I grant that if a large majority adhered to the nine hours, there would be no harm done : the benefit would be, in the main, secured to the class, while those individuals who preferred to work harder and earn more, would have an opportunity of doing so. This certainly would be the state of things to be wished for ; and assuming that a reduction of hours without any diminution of wages could take place without expelling the commodity from some of its markets—which is in every particular instance a question of fact, not of principle—the manner in which it would be most desirable that this effect should be brought about, would be by a quiet change in the general custom of the trade ; short hours becoming, by spontaneous choice, the general practice, but those who chose to deviate from it having the fullest liberty to do so. Probably, however, so many would prefer the ten hours' work on the improved terms, that the limitation could not be maintained as a general practice : what some did from choice, others would soon be obliged to do from necessity, and those who had chosen long hours for the sake of increased wages, would be forced in the end to work long hours for no greater wages than before. Assuming then that it really would be the interest of each to work only nine hours if he could be assured that all others would do the same, there might be no means of their attaining this object but by converting their supposed mutual agreement into an engagement under penalty, by consenting to have it enforced by law. I am not expressing any opinion in favour of such an enactment, which has never in this country been demanded, and which I certainly should not, in present circumstances, recommend :[1] but it serves to exemplify the manner in which classes of persons may need the assistance of

[1] [" Which has never . . . recommend " was added in the 5th ed. (1862). A Nine Hours Movement made its appearance in the 70's. The hours of labour for women, young persons and children in textile factories were reduced to 56½ per week by the Act of 1874, and to 55½ by the Act of 1901. A Miners' Eight Hours Act was passed in 1908.]

law, to give effect to their deliberate collective opinion of their own interest, by affording to every individual a guarantee that his competitors will pursue the same course, without which he cannot safely adopt it himself.

Another exemplification of the same principle is afforded by what is known as the Wakefield system of colonization. This system is grounded on the important principle, that the degree of productiveness of land and labour depends on their being in a due proportion to one another ; that if a few persons in a newly-settled country attempt to occupy and appropriate a large district, or if each labourer becomes too soon an occupier and cultivator of land, there is a loss of productive power, and a great retardation of the progress of the colony in wealth and civilization : that nevertheless the instinct (as it may almost be called) of appropriation, and the feelings associated in old countries with landed proprietorship, induce almost every emigrant to take possession of as much land as he has the means of acquiring, and every labourer to become at once a proprietor, cultivating his own land with no other aid than that of his family. If this propensity to the immediate possession of land could be in some degree restrained, and each labourer induced to work a certain number of years on hire before he became a landed proprietor, a perpetual stock of hired labourers could be maintained, available for roads, canals, works of irrigation, &c., and for the establishment and carrying on of the different branches of town industry ; whereby the labourer, when he did at last become a landed proprietor, would find his land much more valuable, through access to markets, and facility of obtaining hired labour. Mr. Wakefield therefore proposed to check the premature occupation of land, and dispersion of the people, by putting upon all unappropriated lands a rather high price, the proceeds of which were to be expended in conveying emigrant labourers from the mother country.

This salutary provision, however, has been objected to, in the name and on the authority of what was represented as the great principle of political economy, that individuals are the best judges of their own interest. It was said, that when things are left to themselves, land is appropriated and occupied by the spontaneous choice of individuals, in the quantities and at the times most advantageous to each person, and therefore to the community generally ; and that to interpose artificial obstacles to their obtaining land is to prevent them from adopting the course which in their own judgment is most beneficial to them, from a self-conceited notion of the legislator, that he knows what is most for their interest better than they do themselves. Now this is a complete misunderstanding, either of the system itself, or of the principle with which it is alleged to conflict. The oversight is similar to that which we have just seen exemplified on the subject of hours of labour. However beneficial it might be to the colony in the aggregate, and to each individual composing it, that no one should occupy more land than he can properly cultivate, nor become a proprietor until there are other labourers ready to take his place in working for hire ; it can never be the interest of an individual to exercise this forbearance, unless he is assured that others will do so too. Surrounded by settlers who have each their thousand acres, how is he benefited by restricting himself to fifty ? or what does a labourer gain by deferring the acquisition altogether for a few years, if all other labourers rush to convert their first earnings into estates in the wilderness, several miles apart from one another ? If they, by seizing on land, prevent the formation of a class of labourers for wages, he will not, by postponing the time of his becoming a proprietor, be enabled to employ the land with any greater advantage when he does obtain it ; to what end, therefore, should he place himself in what will appear to him and others a position of inferiority, by remaining a hired labourer, when all around him are proprietors ? It is the interest of each to do what is good for all, but only if others will do likewise.

The principle that each is the best judge of his own interest, understood as these objectors understand it, would prove that governments ought not to fulfil any of their acknowledged duties— ought not, in fact, to exist at all. It is greatly the interest of the community, collectively and individually, not to rob or defraud one another : but there is not the less necessity for laws to punish robbery and fraud ; because, though it is the interest of each that nobody should rob or cheat, it is not any one's interest to refrain from robbing and cheating others when all others are permitted to rob and cheat him. Penal laws exist at all, chiefly for this reason —because even an unanimous opinion that a certain line of conduct is for the general interest does not always make it people's individual interest to adhere to that line of conduct.

§ 13. Fifthly ; the argument against government interference, grounded on the maxim that individuals are the best judges of their own interest, cannot apply to the very large class of cases, in which those acts of individuals with which the government claims to interfere, are not done by those individuals for their own interest, but for the interest of other people. This includes, among other things, the important and much agitated subject of public charity. Though individuals should, in general, be left to do for themselves whatever it can reasonably be expected that they should be capable of doing, yet when they are at any rate not to be left to themselves, but to be helped by other people, the question arises whether it is better that they should receive this help exclusively from individuals, and therefore uncertainly and casually, or by systematic arrangements, in which society acts through its organ, the state.

This brings us to the subject of Poor Laws ; a subject which would be of very minor importance if the habits of all classes of the people were temperate and prudent, and the diffusion of property satisfactory ; but of the greatest moment in a state of things so much the reverse of this, in both points, as that which the British Islands present.

Apart from any metaphysical considerations respecting the foundation of morals or of the social union, it will be admitted to be right that human beings should help one another ; and the more so, in proportion to the urgency of the need : and none needs help so urgently as one who is starving. The claim to help, therefore, created by destitution, is one of the strongest which can exist ; and there is *primâ facie* the amplest reason for making the relief of so extreme an exigency as certain to those who require it as by any arrangements of society it can be made.

On the other hand, in all cases of helping, there are two sets of consequences to be considered ; the consequences of the assistance itself, and the consequences of relying on the assistance. The former are generally beneficial, but the latter, for the most part, injurious ; so much so, in many cases, as greatly to outweigh the value of the benefit. And this is never more likely to happen than in the very cases where the need of help is the most intense. There are few things for which it is more mischievous that people should rely on the habitual aid of others, than for the means of subsistence, and unhappily there is no lesson which they more easily learn. The problem to be solved is therefore one of peculiar nicety as well as importance ; how to give the greatest amount of needful help, with the smallest encouragement to undue reliance on it.

Energy and self-dependence are, however, liable to be impaired by the absence of help, as well as by its excess. It is even more fatal to exertion to have no hope of succeeding by it, than to be assured of succeeding without it. When the condition of any one is so disastrous that his energies are paralyzed by discouragement, assistance is a tonic, not a sedative : it braces instead of deadening the active faculties : always provided that the assistance is not such as to dispense with self-help, by substituting itself for the person's own labour, skill, and prudence, but is limited to affording him a better hope of attaining success by those legitimate means. This accordingly is a test to which all plans of philanthropy and benevolence should be brought, whether intended for the benefit of individuals or of classes, and whether conducted on the voluntary or on the government principle.

In so far as the subject admits of any general doctrine or maxim, it would appear to be this—that if assistance is given in such a manner that the condition of the person helped is as desirable as that of the person who succeeds in doing the same thing without help, the assistance, if capable of being previously calculated on, is mischievous : but if, while available to everybody, it leaves to every one a strong motive to do without it if he can, it is then for the most part beneficial. This principle, applied to a system of public charity, is that of the Poor Law of 1834. If the condition of a person receiving relief is made as eligible as that of the labourer who supports himself by his own exertions, the system strikes at the root of all individual industry and self-government ; and, if fully acted up to, would require as its supplement an organized system of compulsion for governing and setting to work like cattle those who had been removed from the influence of the motives that act on human beings. But if, consistently with guaranteeing all persons against absolute want, the condition of those who are supported by legal charity can be kept considerably less desirable than the condition of those who find support for themselves, none but beneficial consequences can arise from a law which renders it impossible for any person, except by his own choice, to die from insufficiency of food. That in England at least this supposition can be realized, is proved by the experience of a long period preceding the close of the last century, as well as by that of many highly pauperized districts in more recent times, which have been dispauperized by adopting strict rules of poor-law administration, to the great and permanent benefit of the whole labouring class. There is probably no country in which, by varying the means suitably to the character of the people, a legal provision for the destitute might not be made compatible with the observance of the conditions necessary to its being innocuous.

Subject to these conditions, I conceive it to be highly desirable that the certainty of subsistence should be held out by law to the destitute able-bodied, rather than that their relief should depend on voluntary charity. In the first place, charity almost always does too much or too little: it lavishes its bounty in one place, and leaves people to starve in another. Secondly, since the state must necessarily provide subsistence for the criminal poor while undergoing punishment, not to do the same for the poor who have not offended is to give a premium on crime. And lastly, if the poor are left to individual charity, a vast amount of mendicity is inevitable.[1] What the state may and should abandon to private charity, is the task of distinguishing between one case of real necessity and another. Private charity can give more to the more deserving. The state must act by general rules. It cannot undertake to discriminate between the deserving and the undeserving indigent. It owes no more than subsistence to the first, and can give no less to the last. What is said about the injustice of a law which has no better treatment for the merely unfortunate poor than for the ill-conducted, is founded on a misconception of the province of law and public authority. The dispensers of public relief have no business to be inquisitors. Guardians and overseers are not fit to be trusted to give or withhold other people's money according to their verdict on the morality of the person soliciting it; and it would show much ignorance of the ways of mankind to suppose that such persons, even in the almost impossible case of their being qualified, will take the trouble of ascertaining and sifting the past conduct of a person in distress, so as to form a rational judgment on it. Private charity can make these distinctions; and in bestowing its own money, is entitled to do so according to its own judgment. It should understand that this is its peculiar and appropriate province, and that it is commendable or the contrary, as it exercises the function with more or less discernment. But the administrators of a public fund ought not to be required to do more for anybody, than that minimum which is due even to the worst. If they are, the indulgence very speedily becomes the rule, and refusal the more or less capricious or tyrannical exception.[2]

§ 14. Another class of cases which fall within the same general

---

[1] [The remark in the original, " and to get rid of this is important, even as a matter of justice," was omitted from the 3rd ed. (1852).]

[2] [See Appendix LL. *The Poor Law.*]

principle as the case of public charity, are those in which the acts
done by individuals, though intended solely for their own benefit,
involve consequences extending indefinitely beyond them, to interests
of the nation or of posterity, for which society in its collective capacity
is alone able, and alone bound, to provide.   One of these cases is that
of Colonization.   If it is desirable, as no one will deny it to be,
that the planting of colonies should be conducted, not with an
exclusive view to the private interests of the first founders, but with
a deliberate regard to the permanent welfare of the nations afterwards to arise from these small beginnings ; such regard can only be
secured by placing the enterprise, from its commencement, under
regulations constructed with the foresight and enlarged views of
philosophical legislators ; and the government alone has power
either to frame such regulations, or to enforce their observance.

The question of government intervention in the work of Colonization involves the future and permanent interests of civilization itself,
and far outstretches the comparatively narrow limits of purely
economical considerations.   But even with a view to those considerations alone, the removal of population from the overcrowded
to the unoccupied parts of the earth's surface is one of those works
of eminent social usefulness, which most require, and which at the
same time best repay, the intervention of government.

To appreciate the benefits of colonization, it should be considered
in its relation, not to a single country, but to the collective economical
interests of the human race.   The question is in general treated too
exclusively as one of distribution ; of relieving one labour market
and supplying another.   It is this, but it is also a question of production, and of the most efficient employment of the productive
resources of the world.   Much has been said of the good economy
of importing commodities from the place where they can be bought
cheapest ; while the good economy of producing them where they
can be produced cheapest is comparatively little thought of.   If
to carry consumable goods from the places where they are superabundant to those where they are scarce is a good pecuniary speculation,
is it not an equally good speculation to do the same thing with
regard to labour and instruments ?   The exportation of labourers
and capital from old to new countries, from a place where their
productive power is less to a place where it is greater, increases by
so much the aggregate produce of the labour and capital of the world.
It adds to the joint wealth of the old and the new country, what
amounts in a short period to many times the mere cost of effecting the

transport. There needs be no hesitation in affirming that Colonization, in the present state of the world, is the best affair of business, in which the capital of an old and wealthy country can engage.

It is equally obvious, however, that Colonization on a great scale can be undertaken, as an affair of business, only by the government, or by some combination of individuals in complete understanding with the government; except under such very peculiar circumstances as those which succeeded the Irish famine.[1] Emigration on the voluntary principle rarely has any material influence in lightening the pressure of population in the old country, though as far as it goes it is doubtless a benefit to the colony. Those labouring persons who voluntarily emigrate are seldom the very poor; they are small farmers with some little capital, or labourers who have saved something, and who, in removing only their own labour from the crowded labour-market, withdraw from the capital of the country a fund which maintained and employed more labourers than themselves. Besides, this portion of the community is so limited in number, that it might be removed entirely, without making any sensible impression upon the numbers of the population, or even upon the annual increase. Any considerable emigration of labour is only practicable, when its cost is defrayed, or at least advanced, by others than the emigrants themselves. Who then is to advance it ? Naturally, it may be said, the capitalists of the colony, who require the labour, and who intend to employ it. But to this there is the obstacle, that a capitalist, after going to the expense of carrying out labourers, has no security that he shall be the person to derive any benefit from them. If all the capitalists of the colony were to combine, and bear the expense by subscription, they would still have no security that the labourers, when there, would continue to work for them. After working for a short time and earning a few pounds, they always, unless prevented by the government, squat on unoccupied land, and work only for themselves. The experiment has been repeatedly tried whether it was possible to enforce contracts for labour, or the repayment of the passage money of emigrants to those who advanced it, and the trouble and expense have always exceeded the advantage. The only other resource is the voluntary contributions of parishes or individuals, to rid themselves of surplus labourers who are already, or who are likely to become, locally chargeable on the poor-rate. Were this speculation

---

[1] [The exception was added in the 5th ed. (1862).   In the next line " cannot have " had been changed into " rarely has " in the 3rd (1852).]

to become general, it might produce a sufficient amount of emigration to clear off the existing unemployed population, but not to raise the wages of the employed : and the same thing would require to be done over again in less than another generation.

One of the principal reasons why Colonization should be a national undertaking is that in this manner alone, save in highly exceptional cases, can emigration be self-supporting. The exportation of capital and labour to a new country being, as before observed, one of the best of all affairs of business, it is absurd that it should not, like other affairs of business, repay its own expenses. Of the great addition which it makes to the produce of the world, there can be no reason why a sufficient portion should not be intercepted, and employed in reimbursing the outlay incurred in effecting it. For reasons already given, no individual, or body of individuals, can reimburse themselves for the expense ; the government, however, can. It can take from the annual increase of wealth, caused by the emigration, the fraction which suffices to repay with interest what the emigration has cost. The expenses of emigration to a colony ought to be borne by the colony ; and this, in general, is only possible when they are borne by the colonial government.

Of the modes in which a fund for the support of colonization can be raised in the colony, none is comparable in advantage to that which was first suggested, and so ably and perseveringly advocated, by Mr. Wakefield : the plan of putting a price on all unoccupied land and devoting the proceeds to emigration. The unfounded and pedantic objections to this plan have been answered in a former part of this chapter : we have now to speak of its advantages. First, it avoids the difficulties and discontents incident to raising a large annual amount by taxation ; a thing which it is almost useless to attempt with a scattered population of settlers in the wilderness, who, as experience proves, can seldom be compelled to pay direct taxes, except at a cost exceeding their amount ; while in an infant community indirect taxation soon reaches its limit. The sale of lands is thus by far the easiest mode of raising the requisite funds. But it has other and still greater recommendations. It is a beneficial check upon the tendency of a population of colonists to adopt the tastes and inclinations of savage life, and to disperse so widely as to lose all the advantages of commerce, of markets, of separation of employments, and combination of labour. By making it necessary for those who emigrate at the expense of the fund to earn a considerable sum before they can become landed proprietors, it keeps up a perpetual succession of labourers for hire, who in every country are a most important auxiliary even to peasant proprietors : and by diminishing the eagerness of agricultural speculators to add to their domain, it keeps the settlers within reach of each other for purposes of co-operation, arranges a numerous body of them within easy distance of each centre of foreign commerce and non-agricultural industry, and insures the formation and rapid growth of towns and town products. This concentration, compared with the dispersion which uniformly occurs when unoccupied land can be had for nothing, greatly accelerates the attainment of prosperity, and enlarges the fund which may be drawn upon for further emigration. Before the adoption of the Wakefield system, the early years of all new colonies were full of hardship and difficulty : the last colony founded on the old principle, the Swan River settlement, being one of the most characteristic instances. In all subsequent colonization, the Wakefield principle has been acted upon, though imperfectly,[1] a part only of the proceeds of the sale of land being devoted to emigration : yet wherever it has been introduced at all, as in South Australia, Victoria, and New Zealand, the restraint put upon the dispersion of the settlers, and the influx of capital caused by the assurance of being able to obtain hired labour, has, in spite of many difficulties and much mismanagement, produced a suddenness and rapidity of prosperity more like fable than reality.* [2]

The self-supporting system of colonization, once established, would increase in efficiency every year ; its effect would tend to increase in geometrical progression : for since every able-bodied emigrant, until the country is fully peopled, adds in a very short time to its wealth, over and above his own consumption, as much as would defray the expense of bringing out another emigrant, it follows

[1] [" The price of land being generally fixed too low and " omitted from 3rd ed. (1852).]

* [1857] The objections which have been made, with so much virulence, in some of these colonies, to the Wakefield system, apply, in so far as they have any validity, not to the principle, but to some provisions which are no part of the system, and have been most unnecessarily and improperly engrafted on it ; such as the offering only a limited quantity of land for sale, and that by auction, and in lots of not less than 640 acres, instead of selling all land which is asked for, and allowing to the buyer unlimited freedom of choice, both as to quantity and situation, at a fixed price.

[2] [From the 3rd ed. was omitted the following passage of the original (1848) : " The oldest of the Wakefield colonies, South Australia, is scarcely " (in 2nd ed. (1849), " little more than ") " twelve years old ; Port Philip " (Victoria) " is still more recent ; and they are probably at this moment the two places, in the known world, where labour on the one hand, and capital on the other, are the most highly remunerated."]

that the greater the number already sent, the greater number might continue to be sent, each emigrant laying the foundation of a succession of other emigrants at short intervals without fresh expense, until the colony is filled up. It would therefore be worth while, to the mother country, to accelerate the early stages of this progression, by loans to the colonies for the purpose of emigration, repayable from the fund formed by the sales of land. In thus advancing the means of accomplishing a large immediate emigration, it would be investing that amount of capital in the mode, of all others, most beneficial to the colony; and the labour and savings of these emigrants would hasten the period at which a large sum would be available from sales of land. It would be necessary, in order not to overstock the labour market, to act in concert with the persons disposed to remove their own capital to the colony. The knowledge that a large amount of hired labour would be available, in so productive a field of employment, would insure a large emigration of capital from a country, like England, of low profits and rapid accumulation : and it would only be necessary not to send out a greater number of labourers at one time than this capital could absorb and employ at high wages.

Inasmuch as, on this system, any given amount of expenditure, once incurred, would provide not merely a single emigration, but a perpetually flowing stream of emigrants, which would increase in breadth and depth as it flowed on ; this mode of relieving over-population has a recommendation, not possessed by any other plan ever proposed for making head against the consequences of increase without restraining the increase itself : there is an element of indefiniteness in it ; no one can perfectly foresee how far its influence, as a vent for surplus population, might possibly reach. There is hence the strongest obligation on the government of a country like our own, with a crowded population, and unoccupied continents under its command, to build, as it were, and keep open, in concert with the colonial governments, a bridge from the mother country to those continents, by establishing the self-supporting system of colonization on such a scale, that as great an amount of emigration as the colonies can at the time accommodate may at all times be able to take place without cost to the emigrants themselves.

[1] The importance of these considerations, as regards the British

[1] [The reference to Irish emigration was added in the 3rd ed. (1852), and concluded with this sentence : " While the stream of this emigration continues

islands, has been of late considerably diminished by the unparalleled amount of spontaneous emigration from Ireland ; an emigration not solely of small farmers, but of the poorest class of agricultural labourers, and which is at once voluntary and self-supporting, the succession of emigrants being kept up by funds contributed from the earnings of their relatives and connexions who had gone before. To this has been added a large amount of voluntary emigration to the seats of the gold discoveries, which has partly supplied the wants of our most distant colonies, where, both for local and national interests, it was most of all required. But the stream of both these emigrations has already considerably slackened, and though that from Ireland has since partially revived, it is not certain that the aid of government in a systematic form, and on the self-supporting principle, will not again become necessary to keep the communication open between the hands needing work in England, and the work which needs hands elsewhere.

§ 15. The same principle which points out colonization, and the relief of the indigent, as cases to which the principal objection to government interference does not apply, extends also to a variety of cases, in which important public services are to be performed, while yet there is no individual specially interested in performing them, nor would any adequate remuneration naturally or spontaneously attend their performance. Take for instance a voyage of geographical or scientific exploration. The information sought may be of great public value, yet no individual would derive any benefit from it which would repay the expense of fitting out the expedition ; and there is no mode of intercepting the benefit on its way to those who profit by it, in order to levy a toll for the remuneration of its authors. Such voyages are, or might be, undertaken by private subscription ; but this is a rare and precarious resource. Instances are more frequent in which the expense has been borne by public companies or philanthropic associations ; but in general such enterprises have been conducted at the expense of government, which is thus enabled to entrust them to the persons in its judgment

flowing, as broad and deep as at present, the principal office required from government would be to direct a portion of it to quarters (such as Australia) where, both for local and national interests, it is most of all required, but which it does not sufficiently reach in its spontaneous course." This was replaced in the 4th ed. (1857) by the reference to emigration to the gold fields. The slackening of the stream was noticed in the 5th ed. (1862), and the partial revival of Irish emigration in the 6th ed. (1865).]

best qualified for the task. Again, it is a proper office of government to build and maintain lighthouses, establish buoys, &c., for the security of navigation : for since it is impossible that the ships at sea which are benefited by a lighthouse should be made to pay a toll on the occasion of its use, no one would build lighthouses from motives of personal interest, unless indemnified and rewarded from a compulsory levy made by the state.   There are many scientific researches, of great value to a nation and to mankind, requiring assiduous devotion of time and labour, and not unfrequently great expense, by persons who can obtain a high price for their services in other ways.   If the government had no power to grant indemnity for expense, and remuneration for time and labour thus employed, such researches could only be undertaken by the very few persons who, with an independent fortune, unite technical knowledge, laborious habits, and either great public spirit, or an ardent desire of scientific celebrity.

Connected with this subject is the question of providing by means of endowments or salaries, for the maintenance of what has been called a learned class. The cultivation of speculative knowledge, though one of the most useful of all employments, is a service rendered to a community collectively, not individually, and one consequently for which it is, *primâ facie*, reasonable that the community collectively should pay ; since it gives no claim on any individual for a pecuniary remuneration ; and unless a provision is made for such services from some public fund, there is not only no encouragement to them, but there is as much discouragement as is implied in the impossibility of gaining a living by such pursuits, and the necessity consequently imposed on most of those who would be capable of them to employ the greatest part of their time in gaining a subsistence.   The evil, however, is greater in appearance than in reality.   The greatest things, it has been said, have generally been done by those who had the least time at their disposal ; and the occupation of some hours every day in a routine employment, has often been found compatible with the most brilliant achievements in literature and philosophy.   Yet there are investigations and experiments which require not only a long but a continuous devotion of time and attention : there are also occupations which so engross and fatigue the mental faculties, as to be inconsistent with any vigorous employment of them upon other subjects, even in intervals of leisure.   It is highly desirable, therefore, that there should be a mode of insuring to the public the services of scientific discoverers, and perhaps of some other classes of savants, by affording them the means of support consistently with devoting a sufficient portion of time to their peculiar pursuits. The fellowships of the Universities are an institution excellently adapted for such a purpose ; but are hardly ever applied to it, being bestowed, at the best, as a reward for past proficiency, in committing to memory what has been done by others, and not as the salary of future labours in the advancement of knowledge. In some countries, Academies of science, antiquities, history, &c., have been formed with emoluments annexed. The most effectual plan, and at the same time least liable to abuse, seems to be that of conferring Professorships, with duties of instruction attached to them. The occupation of teaching a branch of knowledge, at least in its higher departments, is a help rather than an impediment to the systematic cultivation of the subject itself. The duties of a professorship almost always leave much time for original researches ; and the greatest advances which have been made in the various sciences, both moral and physical, have originated with those who were public teachers of them ; from Plato and Aristotle to the great names of the Scotch, French, and German Universities. I do not mention the English, because until very lately their professorships have been, as is well known, little more than nominal. In the case, too, of a lecturer in a great institution of education, the public at large has the means of judging, if not the quality of the teaching, at least the talents and industry of the teacher ; and it is more difficult to misemploy the power of appointment to such an office, than to job in pensions and salaries to persons not so directly before the public eye.

It may be said generally, that anything which it is desirable should be done for the general interests of mankind or of future generations, or for the present interests of those members of the community who require external aid, but which is not of a nature to remunerate individuals or associations for undertaking it, is in itself a suitable thing to be undertaken by government : though, before making the work their own, governments ought always to consider if there be any rational probability of its being done on what is called the voluntary principle, and if so, whether it is likely to be done in a better or more effectual manner by government agency, than by the zeal and liberality of individuals.

§ 16.   The preceding heads comprise, to the best of my judgment, the whole of the exceptions to the practical maxim, that the business of society can be best performed by private and voluntary agency. It is, however, necessary to add, that the intervention of government cannot always practically stop short at the limit which defines the cases intrinsically suitable for it. In the particular circumstances of a given age or nation, there is scarcely anything really important to the general interest, which it may not be desirable, or even necessary, that the government should take upon itself, not because private individuals cannot effectually perform it, but because they will not. At some times and places there will be no roads, docks, harbours, canals, works of irrigation, hospitals, schools, colleges, printing-presses, unless the government establishes them ; the public being either too poor to command the necessary resources, or too little advanced in intelligence to appreciate the ends, or not sufficiently practised in joint action to be capable of the means. This is true, more or less, of all countries inured to despotism, and particularly of those in which there is a very wide distance in civilization between the people and the government : as in those which have been conquered and are retained in subjection by a more energetic and more cultivated people. In many parts of the world, the people can do nothing for themselves which requires large means and combined action : all such things are left undone, unless done by the state. In these cases, the mode in which the government can most surely demonstrate the sincerity with which it intends the greatest good of its subjects, is by doing the things which are made incumbent on it by the helplessness of the public, in such a manner as shall tend not to increase and perpetuate, but to correct that helplessness. A good government will give all its aid in such a shape as to encourage and nurture any rudiments it may find of a spirit of individual exertion. It will be assiduous in removing obstacles and discouragements to voluntary enterprise, and in giving whatever facilities and whatever direction and guidance may be necessary : its pecuniary means will be applied, when practicable, in aid of private efforts rather than in supercession of them, and it will call into play its machinery of rewards and honours to elicit such efforts. Government aid, when given merely in default of private enterprise, should be so given as to be as far as possible a course of education for the people in the art of accomplishing great objects by individual energy and voluntary co-operation.

I have not thought it necessary here to insist on that part of the functions of government which all admit to be indispensable, the function of prohibiting and punishing such conduct on the part of individuals in the exercise of their freedom as is clearly injurious to other persons, whether the case be one of force, fraud, or negligence. Even in the best state which society has yet reached, it is lamentable to think how great a proportion of all the efforts and talents in the world are employed in merely neutralizing one another. It is the proper end of government to reduce this wretched waste to the smallest possible amount, by taking such measures as shall cause the energies now spent by mankind in injuring one another, or in protecting themselves against injury, to be turned to the legitimate employment of the human faculties, that of compelling the powers of nature to be more and more subservient to physical and moral good.[1]

[1] [See Appendix **MM.** *Limits of the Sphere of Government.*]

BIBLIOGRAPHICAL APPENDIX

FOR the history of economic investigation and discussion since the publication of Mill's *Principles* in 1848, the only general work to which reference can be made in English is Palgrave's *Dictionary of Political Economy* (1894–1908), which contains many useful articles under the headings of the various subjects and authors. Readers of French will obtain some assistance from Block, *Les Progrès de la Science Économique depuis Adam Smith* (1890), representing the strictest school of French orthodoxy, and from Gide and Rist, *Histoire des Doctrines Économiques* (1909), written from a more modern point of view. Readers of German will naturally refer to Conrad's *Handwörterbuch der Staatswissenschaften*, of which the third and enlarged edition is now being issued; and they will find a number of valuable reviews of the course of discussion of the several main topics in the series of monographs brought together under the title *Die Entwicklung der deutschen Volkswirthschaftslehre im neunzehnten Jahrhundert* (1908).

A.—THE MERCANTILE SYSTEM (*p.* 6)

Mill's account is based on that of Adam Smith, *Wealth of Nations*, bk. iv. ch. i. Much investigation has subsequently taken place into mercantilist literature and policy, some results of which may be seen in Roscher, *Geschichte der National-Oekonomik in Deutschland* (1874), § 57, closely followed (with a Positivist colouring) by Ingram, *History of Political Economy* (1888); in Schmoller, *The Mercantile System and its Historical Significance* (1884 ; Eng. trans. 1896), and *Grundriss der Allgemeinen Volkswirthschaftslehre* (1900), § 39 (in French trans., *Principes d'Économie Politique* (1905–1908), i. § 39) ; in Cunningham, *Growth of English Industry and Commerce*, vol. ii. pt. i., *The Mercantile System* (1903); and in Unwin, *Industrial Organisation in the Sixteenth and Seventeenth Centuries* (1904). One of the most significant of English mercantilist writings, Mun's *England's Treasure by Forraign Trade* (1664), has been recently republished (1895).

B.—THE DEFINITION OF WEALTH (*p.* 9)

Mill's definition has been criticised, from very different points of view, by Jevons, *Principles of Economics* (posthumously published, 1905), p. 14 ; Nicholson, *Principles of Political Economy*, i. (1893), Introduction ; and Ruskin, *Unto this Last* (1862), Preface, and *Munera Pulveris* (1863), Preface. For a recent classification of "desirable things," see Marshall, *Principles of Economics* (1890 ; 5th ed. 1907), bk. ii. ch. 2. Sidgwick, *Principles of Political Economy* (1883), bk. i. ch. ii., points out that, though in England "Wealth" has commonly been regarded as the most fundamental conception in Political Economy, it has also been commonly held that it should be defined by the characteristic of possessing " Value," so that it would seem more logical " to begin by attempting to get a precise conception of this characteristic." For difficulties attaching to " Richesse," as the French equivalent of " Wealth," see Gide, *Cours d'Économie Politique* (1909), p. 47. [By the earlier French economic writers, however, the term was used in the plural, as in Turgot's *Réflexions sur la Formation et la Distribution des Richesses* (1770 : trans. by Ashley, 1898).]

The German language possesses no one inclusive term like " Wealth " ; and German economists have long been accustomed to begin with the definition of " goods " (*Guter*) and, in consequence, of " a good " (*Gut*)—enjoying, in the use of the latter term, an advantage not available in current English speech. For characteristic examples reference may be made to Wagner, *Lehrbuch der Politischen Oekonomie, Grundlagen* (3rd ed. 1892), I, bk. ii. ch. i. ; or Conrad, *Grundriss zum Studium der Politischen Oekonomie* (6th ed. 1907), § 5. The phrases " goods," " economic goods," " an economic good," and so on, have of late years made their way into English and still more into American economic writings ; see, for instance, Marshall (as above), and Clark, *Essentials of Economic Theory* (1907), ch. 2 ; and cf. Pierson, *Principles of Economics* (Eng. trans. 1902), pt. i. ch. i.

C.—THE TYPES OF SOCIETY (*p*. 20)

Mill's brief sketch of the general economic development of humanity is a masterly one. But since his time there has been a vast amount of work done, especially in Germany, in the field of economic history. The best introduction to the subject is now Schmoller's *Grundriss*, bk. ii. (occupying the second volume of the French trans., *Principes*). A very suggestive treatment of certain aspects of the subject is presented in a brief compass in Bücher, *Entstehung der Volkswirtschaft* (Eng. trans. under the title *Industrial Evolution*, N. Y. 1901) ; which receives some necessary correction and is supplemented in important respects by Meyer, *Die wirthschaftliche Entwickelung des Alterthums*, Vortrag, 1895, and *Die Sklaverei im Alterthum*, Vortrag, 1898 ; and by v. Below, *Über Theorien der wirthschaftlichen Entwicklung der Völker*, in *Historische Zeitschrift*, lxxxvi. (N. F. l.). The best general work in English is Cunningham's *Western Civilisation in its Economic Aspects ; Ancient Times* (1898), *Mediæval and Modern Times* (1900). Seligman, *Principles of Economics* (1905), part ii. bks. ii. and iii., brings together a great many instructive *aperçus* in a short compass.

D.—PRODUCTIVE AND UNPRODUCTIVE LABOUR (*p*. 53)

The distinction was taken from Adam Smith, *Wealth of Nations*, bk. ii. ch. 3, who derived the words themselves from the French Physiocrats, though he used them in a different sense. It has been criticised by Jevons, *Principles*, ch. xviii., and Cannan, *History of the Thories of Production and Distribution* (1893), ch. i. § 7 ; and it is now but little used. Cf. Marshall, bk. ii. ch. 3.

E.—THE DEFINITION OF CAPITAL (*p*. 62)

A good introduction to the large contentious literature on this subject is Schmoller, *Grundriss*, ii. § 182 *c* (in the French trans. *Principes*, iii. pp. 409 *seq*.) ; which makes use of the material collected in Böhm-Bawerk, *The Positive Theory of Capital* (Eng. trans. 1891), bk. i. ch. 3. As Wagner, *Grundlagen*, § 129, has pointed out, the conception of capital is twofold—economical and historical (cf. Gide, *Cours*, bk. i. ch. 3); the latter aspect was emphasised by Lassalle in his proposition that "Capital is a historical category." An account in English of the history of the conception will be found in Marshall, i. App. E, and in Taussig, *Wages and Capital* (N. Y. 1896), ch. 2. Clark, *Distribution of Wealth* (1902), ch. 9, distinguishes between "Capital" and "Capital Goods." Fisher, *The Nature of Capital and Income* (1906), defines Capital as "a stock of wealth existing at a moment of time,"—which would seem to identify Capital with Wealth generally; while Gibson, *Human Economics* (1909), defines Capital from the business point of view as "everything in which an individual or group has a legal estate and for which there is a buyer's valuation."

F.—FUNDAMENTAL PROPOSITIONS ON CAPITAL (*p.* 90)

For destructive criticism of these propositions see Jevons, *Principles*, ch. xxiv.; Sidgwick, *Principles*, bk. i. ch. 5, note; and Nicholson, *Principles*, i. pp. 98 *seq.* The first and fourth of them, as stated by Mill, are only other aspects of his Wages Fund doctrine, and, according to Marshall, *Principles*, i. App. J, "express his meaning badly."

G.—DIVISION AND COMBINATION OF LABOUR (*p.* 131)

This subject, when further examined, widens out into the two far larger topics of economic differentiation and co-operation, which are themselves to a large extent but different aspects of the same process. In this sense it is philosophically treated with a great command of the results of recent investigations, in Schmoller, *Grundriss*, i. §§ 113 *seq.* (in Fr. trans. *Principes*, ii. pp. 248 *seq.*).

H.—LARGE AND SMALL FARMING (*p.* 154)

On this problem, so far as England is concerned, it has to be remembered : (1) that the substitution of large for small farming in the eighteenth and early nineteenth centuries was closely associated with the movement for the enclosure of the "open" or intermixed fields; see hereon, Slater, *The English Peasantry and the Enclosure of Common Fields* (1907), and Hasbach, *A History of the English Agricultural Labourer* (Eng. trans. 1908); and (2) that the position of affairs has been greatly affected since Mill wrote by the shock to "cereal farming" caused by the influx of cheap American grain in the eighties : hereon see Levy, *Entstehung und Rückgang des landwirthschaftlichen Grossbetriebes in England* (1904). Materials for an opinion on the economic prospects of small farming in England are to be found in Lawes and Gilbert, *Allotments and Small Holdings*, in *Journal of the Royal Agric. Soc.*, vol. iii. 3rd series (1892) : in the *Report* of a Departmental Committee on *Small Holdings* (1906) ; and in Jebb, *The Small Holdings of England* (1907). They are evidently bound up to some extent with the prospects of agricultural co-operation (in the purchase of fertilisers, the sale of produce, &c.), of which an account is given in Pratt, *The Organisation of Agriculture* (1905), and in the publications of the Agricultural Organisation Society. A general comparison of *Large and Small Farming* following, criticising, and supplementing that of Mill is presented by Nicholson, *Principles*, i. (1893) bk. i. ch. 9.

I.—POPULATION (p. 162)

In the writings of no contemporary economist, in Great Britain or abroad, does the idea that population is constantly tending to press upon the means of subsistence occupy the same conspicuous and primary place as it does with Mill. The treatment of the subject by Marshall, *Principles*, bk. iv. chs. 4, 13, and bk. vi. ch. 13, is characteristic of the general present attitude. Attention is coming to be directed more and more to those defects in the present industrial organisation which create a body of permanently underemployed as well as temporarily unemployed, even where the growth of population is evidently not outstripping the means of employment : hereon see Beveridge, *Unemployment* (1909), p. 6 and passim. The understanding of the exact teaching of Malthus, and of the differences between the first edition of the *Essay* (1798) and the second (1803), has been facilitated by the publication of *Parallel Chapters from the First and Second Editions of an Essay on the Principle of Population* (1895).

J.—THE LAW OF DIMINISHING RETURN (p. 188)

Careful restatements in general accord with Mill's teaching are to be found in Marshall, *Principles*, i. bk. iv. ch. 3 ; and Nicholson, *Principles*, bk. i. ch. 10. For the results of the Rothamsted experiments, showing that " beyond a certain point the increase of crop is not in proportion to the increase in the amount of manure applied," see Lawes, *Is Higher Farming a Remedy for Lower Prices ?* Lecture (1879) ; and Hall, *The Book of the Rothamsted Experiments* (1905). The extent to which the formula of diminishing returns covers the facts of agricultural development is discussed by Schmoller, *Grundriss*, ii. § 233 (*Principes*, iv. pp. 427 *seq.*). But while Mill and the older theoretic writers distinguished between the law of diminishing return in agriculture and the fact (by some called the law) of increasing return in manufacture (cf. Marshall, *Principles*, bk. iv. ch. 13, § 2), and writers of the historical school tend to minimise the effect of the law of diminishing return even in agriculture, some more recent theoretic writers go in the other direction and declare that the law of diminishing return is universal and applies to production of all kinds. For the sense in which they use such language, see Clark, *Distribution of Wealth*, p. 208, and Seligman, *Principles*, § 88.

K.—MILL'S EARLIER AND LATER WRITINGS ON SOCIALISM (p. 204)

Mill's account in the Preface to the 3rd edition of the nature of the alterations there made, scarcely give an adequate impression of the change of tone on his part between 1848 and 1852. The total impression produced by the argument of 1848 is that " Socialism " was probably undesirable and impracticable. Thus the difficulty of apportioning labour among the members of the community, which was met in 1852 by an expression of the hope that "human intelligence would not be inadequate " to deal with it, had called forth in 1848 the following remarks :

" In the existing system of industry these things do adjust themselves with some, though but a distant, approach to fairness. If one kind of work is harder or more disagreeable than another, or requires a longer practice, it is better paid, simply because there are fewer competitors for it ; and an individual generally finds that he can earn most by doing the thing which he is fittest for. I admit that this self-adjusting machinery does not touch some of the grossest of the existing inequalities of remuneration, and in particular the unjust advantage possessed by almost the commonest mental over almost the hardest and most disagreeable bodily labour. Employments which require any kind of technical education, however simple, have hitherto been the subject of a real monopoly as against the mass. But as popular instruction advances, this monopoly is already becoming less complete, and every increase of prudence and foresight among the people encroaches upon it more and more."

And the argument concluded thus :

" I believe that the condition of the operatives in a well-regulated manufactory, with a great reduction of the hours of labour and a considerable variety of the kind of it, is very like what the condition of all would be in a Socialist community. I believe that the majority would not exert themselves for any thing beyond this, and that unless they did, nobody else would ; and that on this basis human life would settle itself into one invariable round. But to maintain even this state, the limitation of the propagative powers of the community must be as much a matter of public regulation as everything else ; since under the supposed arrangements prudential restraint would no longer exist. Now, if we suppose an equal degree of regulation to take place under the present system, either compulsorily, or, what would be so much preferable, voluntarily ; a condition at least equal to what the Socialist system offers to all would fall to the lot of the least fortunate, by the mere action of the competitive principle. Whatever of pecuniary means or freedom of action any one obtained beyond this, would be so much to be counted in favour of the competitive system."

It is true that, in the next section, he went on to say :

" These arguments, to my mind conclusive against Communism, are not applicable to St. Simonism . . . St. Simonism does not contemplate an equal, but an unequal, division of the produce."

But he judged the assumption on which it rested " almost too chimerical to be reasoned against " ; and began the next section thus :

" There has never been imagined any mode of distributing the produce of industry, so well adapted to the requirements of human nature on the whole, as that of letting the share of each individual (not in a state of bodily or mental incapacity) depend in the main on that individual's own energies and exertions, and on such furtherance as may be obtained from the voluntary good offices of others. It is not the subversion of the system of individual property that should be aimed at, but the improvement of it."

In the 3rd edition, it should be noted, the treatment of the subject is affected not only by a modification of personal opinion, but also by the insertion, which had taken place in the 2nd edition, of the account of Fourierism.

In 1869 Mill formed the design of writing a book on Socialism ; and after his death the first rough drafts of the work were published by his step-daughter, Miss Helen Taylor, in the *Fortnightly Review* for February, March, and April 1879. These articles indicate a reversion on Mill's part to an attitude resembling more closely perhaps his state of mind in 1848 than that in 1852. It must be remembered that his criticisms bore primarily upon the Socialist literature of his own time (1869). His treatment of the subject was so carefully balanced that there is a certain risk of giving an unfair impression of the general effect of the argument by the selection of a few passages. The following passages, taken in conjunction with the chapters in the *Principles*, will, however, indicate with sufficient clearness his general point of view.

After an Introduction on the importance of the subject, Mill begins by setting forth at length the Socialist objections to the present order of society, and by recognising the large element of truth in them.

" But the strongest case is susceptible of exaggeration ; and it will have been evident to many readers, even from the passages I have quoted, that such exaggeration is not wanting in the representations of the ablest and most candid Socialists. Though much of their allegations is unanswerable, not a little is the result of errors in political economy ; by which, let me say once for all, I do not mean the rejection of any practical rules of policy which have been laid down by political economists : I mean ignorance of economic facts, and of the causes by which the economic phenomena of society as it is, are actually determined.

" In the first place, it is unhappily true that the wages of ordinary labour in all the countries of Europe are wretchedly insufficient to supply the physical and moral necessities of the population in any tolerable measure. But when it is further alleged that even this insufficient remuneration has a tendency to diminish ; that there is, in the words of M. Louis Blanc, *une baisse continue des salaires ;* the assertion is in opposition to all accurate information, and to many notorious facts. It has yet to be proved that there is any country in the civilised world where the ordinary wages of labour, estimated either in money or in articles of consumption, are declining; while in many they are, on the whole, on the increase ; and an increase which is becoming not slower, but more rapid."

The following passage supplements the chapter in the *Principles* on the theory of Profit :

" Another point on which there is much misapprehension on the part of Socialists, as well as of Trades Unionists and other partisans of Labour against Capital, relates to the proportions in which the produce of the country is really shared, and the amount of what is actually diverted from those who produce it, to enrich other persons. . . . With respect to capital employed in business, there is in the popular notions a great deal of illusion. When, for instance, a capitalist invests £20,000 in his business and draws from it an income of suppose £2000 a year, the common impression is as if he was the beneficial owner both of the £20,000 and the £2000, while the labourers own nothing but their wages. The truth, however, is that he only obtains the two thousand pounds on condition of applying no part of the £20,000 to his own use. He has the legal control over it, and might squander it if he chose, but if he did he would not have the £2000 a year also. As long as he derives an income from his capital he has not the option of withholding it from the use of others. As much of his invested capital as consists of buildings, machinery and other instruments of production, is applied to production and is not applicable to the support or enjoyment of any one. What is so applicable (including what is laid out in keeping up or renewing the buildings and instruments) is paid away to labourers, forming their remuneration and their share in the division of the produce. For all personal purposes they have the capital and he has but the profits, which it only yields to him on condition that the capital itself is employed in satisfying, not his own wants, but those of labourers. The proportion which the profits of capital usually bear to the capital itself (or rather to the circulating portion of it) is the ratio which the capitalist's share of the produce bears to the aggregate share of the labourers. Even as his own share a small part only belongs to him as the owner of capital. The portion of the produce which falls to capital merely as capital is measured by the interest of money, since that is all that the owner of capital obtains when he contributes nothing to production except the capital itself. Now the interest of capital in the public funds, which are considered to be the best security, is at the present prices (which have not varied much for many years) about three and one-third per cent. Even in this investment there is some little risk—risk of repudiation, risk of being obliged to sell out at a low price in some commercial crisis.

" Estimating these risks at one-third per cent., the remaining three per cent. may be considered as the remuneration of capital, apart from insurance against loss. On the security of a mortgage four per cent. is generally obtained, but in this transaction there are considerably greater risks—the uncertainty of titles to land under our bad system of law ; the chance of having to realise the security at a great cost in law charges ; and liability to delay in the receipt of the interest, even when the principal is safe. When mere money independently of exertion yields a larger income, as it sometimes does, for example, by shares in railway or other companies, the surplus is hardly ever an equivalent for the risk of losing the whole, or part, of the capital by mismanagement, as in the case of the Brighton Railway, the dividend of which, after having been six per cent. per annum, sunk to from nothing to one and one-half per cent., and shares which had been bought at 120 could not be sold for more than 43. . . . Of the profits, therefore, which a manufacturer or other person in business obtains from his capital no more than about three per cent. can be set down to the capital itself. If he were able and willing to give up the whole of this to his labourers, who already share among them the whole of his capital as it is annually reproduced from year to year, the addition to their weekly wages would be inconsiderable. Of what he obtains beyond three per cent. a great part is insurance against the manifold losses he is exposed to, and cannot safely be applied to his own use, but requires to be kept in reserve to cover those losses when they occur. The remainder is properly the remuneration of his skill and industry—the wages of his labour of super-intendence. No doubt if he is very successful in business these wages of his are extremely liberal, and quite out of proportion to what the same skill and industry would command if offered for hire. But on the other hand he runs a worse risk than that of being out of employment : that of doing the work without earning anything by it, of having the labour and anxiety without the wages. I do not say that the drawbacks balance the privileges, or that he derives no advantage from the position that makes him a capitalist and employer of labour, instead of a skilled superintendent letting out his service to others ; but the amount of his advantage must not be estimated by the great prizes alone. If we subtract from the gains of some the losses of others and deduct from the balance a fair compensation for the anxiety, skill and labour of both, grounded on the market price of skilled superintendence, what remains will be, no doubt, considerable, but yet, when compared to the entire capital of the country, annually reproduced and dispensed in wages, it is very much smaller than it appears to the popular imagination ; and were the whole of it added to the share of the labourers it would make a less addition to their share than would be made by any important invention in machinery, or by the suppression of un-necessary distributers and other ' parasites of industry.' . . .

" It seemed desirable to begin the discussion of the Socialist question by these remarks in abatement of Socialist exaggerations, in order that the true issues between Socialism and the existing state of society might be correctly conceived. The present system is not, as many Socialists believe, hurrying us into a state of general indigence and slavery from which only Socialism can save us. The evils and injustices suffered under the present system are great, but they are not increasing ; on the contrary, the general tendency is toward their slow diminution."

Mill then opens his statement of the objections to Socialism with the following classification, which illustrates the extent to which Socialist propaganda has changed its character since 1869 :

" Among those who call themselves Socialists, two kinds of persons may be distinguished. There are, in the first place, those whose plans for a new order of society—in which private property and individual competition are to be superseded and other motives to action substituted—are on the scale of a village community or township, and would be applied to an entire country by the multiplication of such self-acting units ; of this character are the systems of Owen and Fourier, and the more thoughtful and philo-sophic Socialists generally.   The other class, who are more a product of the continent than of Great Britain and may be called the revolutionary Socialists, propose to themselves a much bolder stroke.   Their scheme is the management of the whole productive resources of the country by one central authority, the general government."

Remarking that :

" the peculiarities, however, of the revolutionary form of Socialism will be most conveniently examined after the considerations common to both the forms have been duly weighed,"

he begins by pointing out that :

" the distinctive feature of Socialism is not that all things are in common, but that production is only carried on upon the common account, and that the instruments of production are held as common property."

Accordingly :

" The question to be considered is, whether this joint management is likely to be as efficient and successful as the managements of private industry by private capital.   And this question has to be considered in a double aspect : the efficiency of the directing mind, or minds, and that of the simple workpeople."

He discusses this, first in relation to the form of Socialism which he calls

" simple communism, i.e. equal division of the produce among all the sharers, or, according to M. Louis Blanc's still higher standard of justice, apportionment of it according to difference of need, but without making any difference of reward according to the nature of the duty nor according to the supposed merits or services of the individual,"

with the conclusion that its success would depend upon a moral education for which mankind could only be effectually trained by communistic association :

" It is for Communism, then, to prove, by practical experiment, its power of giving this training.   Experiments alone can show whether there is as yet in any portion of the population a sufficiently high level of moral cultivation to make Communism succeed, and to give the next generation among themselves the education necessary to keep up that high level permanently.   If Communist associations show that they can be durable and prosperous, they will multiply, and will probably be adopted by successive portions of the population of the more advanced countries as they become morally fitted for that mode of life."

And, going on then to " those other forms of Socialism which recognise the difficulties of Communism and contrive means to surmount them," of which the principal was Fourierism, he gives reasons for the opinion that, for them, " practi-cal trial " is no less necessary.   He then goes on to the other main division :

" The various schemes for managing the productive resources of the country by public instead of private agency . . . are at present workable only by the élite of mankind, and have yet to prove their power of training mankind at large to the state of improvement which they presuppose. Far more, of course, may this be said of the more ambitious plan which aims at taking possession of the whole land and capital of the country, and beginning at once to administer it on the public account.   Apart from all consideration of injustice to the present possessors, the very idea of con-ducting the whole industry of a country by direction from a single centre is so obviously chimerical that nobody ventures to propose any mode in which it should be done."

Mill's argument with regard to the second or " revolutionary " type of Socialism is accordingly based upon the difficulty of " the problem of manage-ment."   And his final conclusion is thus expressed :

" The preceding considerations appear sufficient to show that an entire renovation of the social fabric, such as is contemplated by Socialism, establishing the economic constitution of society upon an entirely new basis, other than that of private property and competition, however valuable as an ideal, and even as a prophecy of ultimate possibilities, is not available as a present resource, since it requires from those who are to carry on the new order of things qualities both moral and intellectual, which require to be tested in all, and to be created in most ; and this cannot be done by an Act of Parliament, but must be, on the most favourable supposition, a work of considerable time. For a long period to come the principle of individual property will be in possession of the field ; and even if in any country a popular movement were to place Socialists at the head of a revolutionary government, in however many ways they may violate private property the institution itself would survive, and would either be accepted by them or brought back by their expulsion, for the plain reason that people will not lose their hold of what is at present their sole reliance for subsistence and security until a substitute for it has been got into working order. Even those, if any, who have shared among themselves what was the property of others would desire to keep what they had acquired, and to give back to property in the new hands the sacredness which they had not recognised in the old.

" But though, for these reasons, individual property has presumably a long term before it, if only of provisional existence, we are not, therefore, to conclude that it must exist during that whole term unmodified, or that all the rights now regarded as appertaining to property belong to it inherently, and must endure while it endures. On the contrary, it is both the duty and the interest of those who derive the most direct benefit from the laws of property to give impartial consideration to all proposals for rendering those laws in any way less onerous to the majority. . . .

" One of the mistakes oftenest committed, and which are the source of the greatest practical errors in human affairs, is that of supposing that the same name always stands for the same aggregation of ideas. No word has been the subject of more of this kind of misunderstanding than the word property. It denotes, in every state of society the largest power of exclusive use or exclusive control over things (and sometimes, unfortunately, over persons) which the law accords, or which custom in that state of society recognises ; but these powers of exclusive use and control are very various and differ greatly in different countries and in different states of society."

And, after some historical illustrations of this proposition, he concludes :

" When, therefore, it is maintained, rightly or wrongly, that some change or modification in the powers exercised over things by the persons legally recognised as their proprietors would be beneficial to the public and conducive to the general improvement, it is no good answer to this merely to say that the supposed change conflicts with the idea of property. The idea of property is not some one thing identical throughout history and incapable of alteration, but is variable like all other creations of the human mind ; at any given time it is a brief expression denoting the rights over things conferred by the law or custom of some given society at that time ; but neither on this point nor on any other has the law and custom of a given time and place a claim to be stereotyped for ever. A proposed reform in laws or customs is not necessarily objectionable because its adoption would imply, not the adaptation of all human affairs to the existing idea of property, but the adaptation of the existing ideas of property to the growth and improvement of human affairs. This is said without prejudice to the equitable claim of proprietors to be compensated by the state for such legal rights of a proprietary nature as they may be dispossessed of for the public advantage."

L.—THE LATER HISTORY OF SOCIALISM (*p.* 217)

It will be observed that the socialistic writings commented on by Mill were all of French origin and were none of them subsequent to 1869, the date of Mill's articles on Socialism referred to under Appendix K. The Socialism which has been of most influence in later years has been of German origin, and must be studied in the writings of its chief exponents, Karl Marx, Ferdinand Lassalle, Rodbertus, and Friedrich Engels. The most notable in this connexion of those of Lassalle were *Arbeiterprogramm* (1862 : Eng. trans. as *The Working Man's Programme*), and *Herr Bastiat Schulze von Delitzsch, der ökonomische Julian* (1864 : French trans. by Malon as *Capital et Travail*) ; of Rodbertus, *Zur Beleuchtung der Sozialen Frage* (1875 ; containing a new edition of *Soziale Briefe an v. Kirchmann*, 1850), and *Die Handelskrisen* (1858 : Eng. trans. as *Overproduction and Crises*, 1898) ; and of Engels (in conjunction with Marx), *Manifest der Kommunistischen Partei* (1848 : Eng. trans. revised by Engels 1888), and, alone, *Die Entwickelung der Sozialismus von der Utopie zur Wissenschaft* (1882 : Eng. trans. as *Socialism, Utopian and Scientific*), and Introductions to Marx's *Capital*. But of most importance for the theoretic formulation of Socialism have been the writings of Marx (1818–1883) : *Zur Kritik der politischen Oekonomie* (1859), and, above all, *Das Kapital* (i. 1867 : Eng. trans. *Capital*, 1887 ; ii. 1893 ; iii. 1894. An English abstract of the 1st vol. by Aveling appeared in 1891 as *The Student's Marx*). Fundamental ideas in the writings of Marx were those of Surplus-Value, of Class War, of the Concentration of Wealth, and of the Materialist Interpretation of History. The extent to which these particular teachings have been abandoned by those younger German socialists known as " Revisionists " may be gathered from Bernstein, *Die Voraussetzungen der Sozialismus* (1899 : Eng. trans. as *Evolutionary Socialism*, 1909).

Among useful books on the history of Socialism in general, and of German socialism in particular, may be mentioned : Laveleye, *Le Socialisme Contemporain* (1881 : Eng. trans. 1885) ; Ely, *French and German Socialism* (1885) ; Gonner, *The Social Philosophy of Rodbertus* (1900) ; Rae, *Contemporary Socialism* (3rd ed. 1901) ; Brooks, *The Social Unrest* (1903) ; Kirkup, *A History of Socialism* (3rd ed. 1906) ; Ensor, *Modern Socialism* (2nd ed. 1907),— a most useful collection of typical documents and speeches from all the leading countries of Europe ; and Herkner, *Die Arbeiterfrage* (5th ed. 1908).

English socialism has pursued in some respects a line of development of its own ; and it may be studied in *Fabian Essays in Socialism* (1889 : Reprint, with a significant preface, 1908) ; various Fabian Tracts, especially Shaw, *The Fabian Society* (1892) ; Macdonald, *Socialism and Society* (1905) ; Wells, *New Worlds for Old* (1908) ; and Villiers, *The Socialist Movement in England* (1908). Two popular works which have had a very large circulation are, in America, Bellamy, *Looking Backward* (1890), and in England, Blatchford, *Merrie England* (1894).

For French socialism see Jaurès, *Studies in Socialism* (Eng. trans. 1906) ; Lavy, *L'Oeuvre de Millerand* (1902) ; and Millerand, *Travail et Travailleurs* (1908) ; for the recent developments of " Revolutionary Syndicalism," Gide and Rist, *Histoire des Doctrines Économiques* (1909) ; and for Belgian socialism, Destrée and Vandervelde, *Le Socialisme en Belgique* (1903).

Among criticisms of socialism in various forms and aspects may be singled out Herbert Spencer, *The Man v. The State* (1884) ; Courtney, *The Difficulties of Socialism*, in *Econ. Journal*, i. (1891) ; Schäffle, *The Impossibility of Social Democracy* (Eng. trans. 1892) ; Richter, *Pictures of the Socialistic Future* (Eng. trans. 1893) ; Devas, *Political Economy* (2nd ed. 1901), bk. ii. ch. 7 ; Strachey, *Problems and Perils of Socialism* (1908) ; and Mallock, *A Critical Examination of Socialism* (1909). An individualist position is ably maintained in the writings of Helen Bosanquet, especially *The Strength of the People* (1902).

M.—INDIAN TENURES (p. 328)

The whole subject must now be studied in the works of the late B. H. Baden-Powell, and especially in the three massive volumes *The Land Systems of British India* (1892), and the brief text-book based upon that work, *Land Revenue in British India* (1894). See also his *Indian Village Community* (1896), and the more popular *Village Communities in India* (1899); and on the special subject of the *Origin of Zamindari Estates in Bengal*, his article under that title in the (Harvard) *Quarterly Journal of Economics*, xi. (Oct. 1896).

N.—IRISH AGRARIAN DEVELOPMENT (p. 342)

The Irish Land Act of 1870 marked the beginning of an attempt to solve the agrarian problem in accordance with the principle popularly described as "dual ownership," by giving the tenants a right to "compensation for disturbance." The great Land Act of 1881 carried the process much further by accepting the proposals known as "the three F's" (fair rents, free sale of tenants' interests, and fixed tenure), and establishing a Land Court to fix "judicial rents" for a term of years. By the Land Act of 1903, however, a new departure was made; and machinery was provided for the voluntary transference to the tenants of the land still in the hands of the landlords, on terms attractive to both parties. This measure and the subsequent amending and supplementary Acts will probably, in no long time, bring about the establishment of a system of peasant proprietorship over a great part of Ireland. It should be added that there has of recent years been a rapid growth among Irish farmers of various forms of co-operation. For a brief account of the Act of 1881 and of its relation to contemporary Nationalism, see Low and Sanders, *Political History of England during the reign of Victoria* (1907). The least biassed accounts of Irish agrarian history during the last forty years are perhaps to be found in a brief work by a German economist, Dr. Bonn, *Modern Ireland and her Agrarian Problem* (Eng. trans. 1906), and in Bastable's articles in the (Harvard) *Quarterly Journal of Economics*, xviii. (Nov. 1903), and in the *Economic Journal*, xix. (March 1909). On the movement towards co-operation among farmers, see Plunkett, *Ireland in the New Century* (1903), part ii. The details of the history are best looked for in the reports of Royal Commissions and similar documents, such as the *Report of the Royal Commission of 1880-1*, and of the *Royal Commission* of 1886-7, the *Report of the Select Committee of the House of Commons of* 1894 ("Morley's Committee"), and the *Report of the Royal Commission of* 1897-8 ("Fry's Commission"), together with a *Report* by Mr. W. F. Bailey, Legal Assistant-Commissioner, of an *Inquiry into the Present Condition of Tenant Purchasers* (1903), the *Reports of the Irish Agricultural Organisation Society* (from 1895), and of the *Irish Department of Agriculture and Technical Instruction* (from 1901). See also Coyne, *Ireland, Industrial and Commercial* (pub. by Irish Dep. of Agriculture, 1902), and for the text of the Acts, Cherry and Barton, *Irish Land Law*.

O.—THE WAGES FUND DOCTRINE (p. 344)

This doctrine was formally abandoned by Mill himself in the course of a review of Thornton's *Labour* in the *Fortnightly Review* for May 1869, reprinted in his *Dissertations and Discussions*, iv. The central passages of this article are as follows (*Dissertations*, iv. pp. 42 seq.) :

"It will be said that . . . supply and demand do entirely govern the price obtained for labour. The demand for labour consists of the whole circulating capital of the country, including what is paid in wages for unproductive labour. The supply is the whole labouring population. If the supply is in excess of what the capital can at present employ, wages must fall. If the labourers are all employed, and there is a surplus of capital still unused, wages will rise. This series of deductions is generally received as incontrovertible. They are found, I presume, in every systematic treatise on political economy, my own certainly included. I must plead guilty to having, along with the world in general, accepted the theory without the qualifications and limitations necessary to make it admissible.

"The theory rests on what may be called the doctrine of the wages fund. There is supposed to be, at any given instant, a sum of wealth, which is unconditionally devoted to the payment of wages of labour. This sum is not regarded as unalterable, for it is augmented by saving, and increases with the progress of wealth; but it is reasoned upon as at any given moment a predetermined amount. More than that amount it is assumed that the wages-receiving class cannot possibly divide among them; that amount, and no less, they cannot but obtain. So that, the sum to be divided being fixed, the wages of each depend solely on the divisor, the number of participants. . . .

"But is there such a thing as a wages-fund, in the sense here implied? Exists there any fixed amount which, and neither more nor less than which, is destined to be expended in wages?

"Of course there is an impassable limit to the amount which can be so expended; it cannot exceed the aggregate means of the employing classes. It cannot come up to those means; for the employers have also to maintain themselves and their families. But, short of this limit, it is not, in any sense of the word, a fixed amount.

"In the common theory, the order of ideas is this: The capitalist's pecuniary means consist of two parts—his capital, and his profits or income. His capital is what he starts with at the beginning of the year, or when he commences some round of business operations; his income he does nos receive until the end of the year, or until the round of operations it completed. His capital, except such part as is fixed in buildings and machinery, or laid out in materials, is what he has got to pay wages with. He cannot pay them out of his income, for he has not yet received it. When he does receive it, he may lay by a portion to add to his capital, and as such it will become part of next year's wages-fund, but has nothing to do with this year's.

"This distinction, however, between the relation of the capitalist to his capital, and his relation to his income is wholly imaginary. He starts at the commencement with the whole of his accumulated means, all of which is potentially capital: and out of this he advances his personal and family expenses, exactly as he advances the wages of his labourers. . . . If we choose to call the whole of what he possesses applicable to the payment of wages, the wages-fund, that fund is co-extensive with the whole proceeds of his business, after keeping up his machinery, buildings and materials, and feeding his family; and it is expended jointly upon himself and his labourers. The less he expends on the one, the more may be expended on the other, and vice versâ. The price of labour, instead of being determined by the division of the proceeds between the employer and the labourers, determines it. If he gets his labour cheaper, he can afford to spend more upon himself. If he has to pay more for labour, the additional payment comes out of his own income; perhaps from the part which he would have saved and added to capital, thus anticipating his voluntary economy by a compulsory one; perhaps from what he would have expended on his private wants or pleasures.

There is no law of nature making it inherently impossible for wages to rise to the point of absorbing not only the funds which he had intended to devote to carrying on his business, but the whole of what he allows for his private expenses, beyond the necessaries of life. The real limit to the rise is the practical consideration, how much would ruin him or drive him to abandon the business : not the inexorable limits of the wages-fund.

" In short, there is abstractedly available for the payment of wages, before an absolute limit is reached, not only the employer's capital, but the whole of what can possibly be retrenched from his personal expenditure : and the law of wages, on the side of demand, amounts only to the obvious proposition, that the employers cannot pay away in wages what they have not got. On the side of supply, the law as laid down by economists remains intact. The more numerous the competitors for employment, the lower, *cæteris paribus*, will wages be. . . .

" But though the population principle and its consequences are in no way touched by anything that Mr. Thornton has advanced, in another of its bearings the labour question, considered as one of mere economics, assumes a materially changed aspect. The doctrine hitherto taught by all or most economists (including myself), which denied it to be possible that trade combinations can raise wages, or which limited their operations in that respect to the somewhat earlier attainment of a rise which the competition of the market would have produced without them,—this doctrine is deprived of its scientific foundation, and must be thrown aside. The right and wrong of the proceedings of Trade Unions becomes a common question of prudence and social duty, not one which is peremptorily decided by unbending necessities of political economy."

In spite of the remonstrances of Cairnes, and his attempt to restate the Wages Fund doctrine in a more satisfactory form, in his *Leading Principles,* part ii. ch. 1, it may be said to be abandoned now by all economists, at any rate in the form in which it was stated by Mill. For a criticism of Mill's retractation, and a statement of a sense in which it may still be allowable to speak of a Wages Fund, see Taussig, *Wages and Capital, an Examination of the Wages Fund Doctrine* (N. Y. 1896), especially part ii. ch. 11. And see Sidgwick, *Principles,* bk. ii. ch. 8, § 2 ; Marshall, *Principles,* i. App. J : *The Doctrine of the Wages Fund ;* and Nicholson, *Principles,* bk. ii. ch. 10, § 8.

P.—THE MOVEMENT OF POPULATION (p. 360)

The rate of growth of the population of the several parts of the United Kingdom is shown by the following table:

Year.	Population.				Rates of decennial increase or decrease on preceding census.			
	England.	Wales.	Scotland.	Ireland.	England. (+)	Wales. (+)	Scotland. (+)	Ireland. (−)
1851	16,926,348	1,001,261	2,888,742	6,552,385	12·8	10·5	10·2	19·8
1861	18,958,103	1,108,121	3,062,294	5,798,967	12·0	10·7	6·0	11·5
1871	21,498,642	1,213,624	3,360,018	5,412,377	13·4	9·5	9·7	6·7
1881	24,617,266	1,357,173	3,735,573	5,174,836	14·5	11·8	11·2	4·4
1891	27,487,525	1,515,000	4,025,647	4,704,750	11·7	11·6	7·8	9·1
1901	30,811,420	1,716,423	4,472,103	4,458,775	12·1	13·3	11·1	5·2

The factors in the increase of population are evidently (1) migration, (2) the " natural increase " of population, *i.e.* the excess of births over deaths. The annual natural increase has fallen in England and Wales from 14·5 per 1000 of the population for the period 1876–1880, to 12·1 in 1901–1905, in consequence of the fact that though the death-rate fell from 20·8 to 16 per thousand, the birth-rate fell from 35·3 to 28·1. The birth-rate in England and Wales, for the period since the Civil Registration Act of 1837, reached its maximum in the period 1870–1876, and has since shown a material decline.

The extent of this decline is shown in the next table :

BIRTH-RATES (ENGLAND AND WALES).

Period.	Average Annual *Crude* Birth-rate per 1000 of Total Population.	Average Annual *Corrected* Birth-rate per 1000 of Female Population aged 15–45 years.
1876–1880	35·3	153·3
1881–1885	33·5	144·3
1886–1890	31·4	133·4
1891–1895	30·5	126·8
1896–1900	29·3	118·8
1901–1905	28·1	112·5
1906	27·1	108·3
1907	26·3	105·1

As regards the decline in the birth-rate generally, the Registrar-General observes :

" There are sufficient grounds for stating that during the past 30 years approximately 14 per cent. of the decline in the birth-rate (based on the proportion of births to the female population aged 15–45 years) is due to the decrease in the proportion of married women in the female population of conceptive ages, and that over 7 per cent. is due to the decrease of illegitimacy. With regard to the remaining 79 per cent. of the decrease, although some of the reduced fertility may be ascribed to changes in the age constitution of married women, there can be little doubt that much of it is due to deliberate restriction of child-bearing."

The decline in the birth-rate, whatever may be its cause, is a feature common to the birth statistics of most European countries. The statistics may be studied in the *General Report on the Census of* 1901, and in the *Annual Reports of the Registrar-General*. The figures are conveniently collected in the Blue-book, *Public Health and Social Conditions*, prepared by the Local Government Board (1909). The most detailed statistical analysis of the facts is to be found in a paper by Newsholme and Stevenson, and another by Yule, in the *Journal of the Royal Statistical Society* (March 1906).

Q.—PROFITS (*p.* 421)

The most powerful impulse to fresh discussion of the nature of profits was given by the late General Walker, in the emphasis laid by him on " the function of the *entrepreneur*," and his view that " profits are a species of the same genus as rent," and " do not form a part of the price of manufactured products " ;

See his *Wages Question* (1876), ch. 14, and *Political Economy* (1883). In this discussion it has become usual to distinguish more sharply than the earlier writers between Interest and " pure " or " net " Profits ; and there is now a large literature on both these topics. As to Interest, much influence has been exerted by the doctrine of the Austrian writer, Böhm-Bawerk, which explains interest as " a premium on present as against future things " ; see Böhm-Bawerk, *Capital and Interest* (Eng. trans. 1890), and *Positive Theory of Capital* (Eng. trans. 1891). Of the writings this has called forth it may be sufficient to refer to Pierson, *Principles of Economics* (Eng. trans. 1902), part i. ch. 4, § 5, and to Cassel, *The Nature and Necessity of Interest* (1903).

On Profit, recent writings are largely influenced by the conceptions of (1) a " quasi-rent," (2) " the marginal entrepreneur," and (3) " long and short periods." The present state of the discussion may be seen in Marshall, *Principles*, bk. vi. chs. 6–8 ; Clark, *Essentials of Economic Theory* (1907), pp. 117 *seq.* ; Seager, *Introduction to Economics* (3rd ed. 1906), ch. 10 ; and in Conrad's *Grundriss*, § 84, and Gide's *Cours*, pp. 674 *seq.* The treatment of the subject by Schmoller, *Grundriss*, §§ 231–2 (*Principes*, vol. iv.), will be found illuminating. The " tendency " of profits and wages to an equality has been commented upon frequently by Cliffe Leslie, as in his articles on *The Political Economy of Adam Smith* and *On the Philosophical Method of Political Economy*, reprinted in his *Essays* (1879).

R.—RENT (p. 434)

Criticisms of the Ricardian doctrine of rent, or of its formulation, are to be found in Sidgwick, *Principles*, bk. ii. ch. 8, and in Nicholson, *Principles*, vol. i. bk. ii. ch. 14 ; and it is restated in Pierson, *Principles*, pt. i. ch. 2, and in Marshall, *Principles*, bk. vi. ch. 9.

S.—THE THEORY OF VALUE (p. 482)

It is on this subject—as to which Mill remarked, in 1848, that " happily there is nothing in the laws of value which remains for the present or any future writer to clear up ; the theory of the subject is complete " (p. 436)—that theoretic discussion has mainly turned during the last four decades, owing chiefly to the writings of Jevons, of Menger and the other representatives of the Austrian school, and of Clark and his American followers. The characteristic of all these writers is to approach the problem from the side of demand, and to find the key to value in Final or Marginal Utility (*Grenznutz*). The best intro-duction to the discussion is through Jevons, *Theory of Political Economy* (1871 ; 2nd ed. revised, 1879), chs. 3 and 4 ; and through Bonar's article on *The Austrian Economists* in the (Harvard) *Quarterly Journal of Economics*, iii. (Oct. 1888) ; and Smart, *An Introduction to the Theory of Value on the lines of Menger, Wieser and Böhm-Bawerk* (1891). Wieser's *Natural Value* (Eng. trans. 1893) attempts to apply the doctrine to the whole problem of Distribution. For the present state of the discussion see Marshall, *Principles*, i. bk. v. ; Clark, *Essentials*, chs. 6 and 7 ; and Schmoller, *Grundriss*, §§ 171–2 (in French, *Principes*, vol. iii.).

Mill's doctrine of Cost of Production was attacked by Cairnes in his *Some Leading Principles of Political Economy newly expounded* (1874), soon after Mill's death. See hereon Marshall in *Fortnightly Review* (April 1876), and *Principles*, book v. ch. 3, § 2. Cairnes contributed an important consideration to the discussion by the emphasis which he laid on " Non-competing Groups."

T.—The Value of Money (p. 506)

For other expositions of "the Quantity Theory of Prices," see Walker, *Money* (1878), chs. 3–8; and Nicholson, *Money and Monetary Problems* (1888; 4th ed. 1897), chs. 5–7. For a criticism, see Scott, *Money and Banking* (N. Y. 1903), ch. 4. An attempt to test the doctrine statistically is made by Kemmerer, *Money and Credit Instruments in their relation to General Prices* (N. Y. 1907). For the sense of "money" in modern business, see Withers, *The Meaning of Money* (1909).

U.—Bimetallism (p. 510)

For the main points of the controversy on this subject, which had hardly begun when Mill wrote in 1848, see Jevons, *Money* (1875), ch. 12 (with his acceptance of the view of the "compensatory action" of a double standard system); Gibbs and Grenfell, *The Bimetallic Controversy* (1886),—a collection of pamphlets, speeches, &c., on both sides; Nicholson, *Money and Monetary Problems;* Walker, *International Bimetallism* (1896); *Darwin, Bimetallism* (1898); and Carlile, *The Evolution of Modern Money* (1901). An extreme monometallist position is represented in Giffen, *Case against Bimetallism* (1892).

V.—International Values (p. 606)

The Ricardian doctrine, followed and carried further by Mill, has hitherto remained the almost exclusive possession of English economists. It has been expounded by Cairnes, *Leading Principles*, part iii. ch. 3, and by Bastable, *Theory of International Trade* (2nd ed. 1897). It has been objected to from two diametrically opposite points of view. Transferability of capital and labour, it has been argued, is true of international trade as well as of domestic, so that no separate theory is necessary for the determination of international values; *e.g.* Hobson, *International Trade* (1904). On the other hand it has been asserted that such a transferability is true neither of domestic nor of international trade, and that therefore it is necessary to reject both the Ricardian doctrine of home values and the Ricardian doctrine of international values; *e.g.* Cliffe Leslie, *Essays in Political and Moral Philosophy* (1879), Preface. A different theory has been put forward by Sidgwick, *Principles*, bk. ii. ch. 3. A mathematical treatment of the whole subject, with a criticism of all the leading writers, will be found in a series of articles by Edgeworth on *The Theory of International Values* in the *Economic Journal*, vol. iv. (1894). Bastable and Edgeworth, while admiring and accepting Mill's first statement of the theory (ch. 18, §§ 1–5), agree in regarding "the superstructure of later date" (§§ 6–8) as "laborious and confusing."

W.—The Regulation of Currency (p. 677)

The question of the effect of the Bank Charter Act has lost much of its importance in consequence of the growing use of cheques. These cheques are now largely drawn not against actual deposits but against banking credits; so that banks, while abandoning more and more the issue of notes, "manufacture money" on a vast scale in another way. Hereon see Withers, *Meaning of Money*, chs. 3 and 5. On the effect of an increase in the supply of gold, see Walker, *Money*, pt. i. ch. 4, and Withers, ch. 1.

X.—Prices in the Nineteenth Century (*p.* 704)

The actual movement of prices has been much investigated since the time of Mill; and attempts, in large measure successful, have been made by Jevons and others to reduce the statement of it to precision by the use of Index Numbers. On the theory and practice of Index Numbers, see article by Edgeworth, *s. v.*, in Palgrave's *Dictionary of Political Economy*, vol. ii.; Fountain's *Memorandum* in *Report on Wholesale and Retail Prices* (Board of Trade, 1903); and the article of Flux in (Harvard) *Quarterly Journal of Economics* (Aug. 1907).

The following table, taken from the Blue-book of the Local Government Board on *Public Health and Social Conditions* (1909), presents the conclusions of Sauerbeck as to prices, and of Bowley as to wages, in a form convenient for comparison.

Index Numbers showing Course of Average Wholesale Prices and General Money Wages.

[The wages and prices in 1850 being taken as 100; wages and prices in other years in percentages of 1850 figures.]

Year.	Index Numbers of		Year.	Index Numbers of	
	Prices.	Wages.		Prices.	Wages.
1850	100	100			
1855	131·2	—	1895	80·5	159·2
			1896	79·2	160·7
1860	128·6	119·2	1897	80·5	162·3
			1898	83·1	166·5
1865	131·2	127·5	1899	88·3	170·4
1870	124·7	134·1	1900	97·4	178·7
			1901	90·9	177·0
1875	124·7	161·4	1902	89·6	174·7
			1903	89·6	173·7
1880	114·3	148·8	1904	90·9	172·8
1885	93·5	149·4	1905	93·5	173·3
			1906	100·0	175·7
1890	93·5	161·3	1907	103·9	181·7

NOTE.—The Index Numbers here given have been calculated as regards Wages for the years to 1873 on the averages ascertained by Mr. Bowley—see the *Economic Journal* (Dec. 1898) and the *Journal of the Royal Statistical Society* (Dec. 1899)—and for later years on the percentages in the 12*th Abstract of Labour Statistics of the United Kingdom* (1906-7), p. 54. As regards Prices, the Numbers are based on the Index Numbers calculated by Mr. Sauerbeck—see *Report on Wholesale and Retail Prices* (1903), p. 451, and particulars in the *Journal of the Royal Statistical Society* (March 1908).

With this may be compared the calculation of the Board of Trade, taking the level of 1900 as 100, as given in the *Twelfth Abstract of Labour Statistics* (1908), p. 80.

INDEX NUMBERS OF WHOLESALE PRICES, 1871–1907. 1900 = 100.

Year.	Index No.	Year.	Index No.	Year.	Index No.	Year.	Index No.
1871	136·0	1881	127·3	1891	107·4	1901	96·9
1872	145·8	1882	128·4	1892	101·8	1902	96·5
1873	152·7	1883	126·8	1893	100·0	1903	96·9
1874	148·1	1884	114·7	1894	94·2	1904	98·3
1875	141·4	1885	107·7	1895	91·0	1905	97·6
1876	138·0	1886	101·6	1896	88·2	1906	100·5
1877	141·6	1887	99·6	1897	90·1	1907	105·7
1878	132·6	1888	102·7	1898	93·2		
1879	126·6	1889	104·0	1899	92·3		
1880	129·6	1890	104·0	1900	100·0		

Before making use of these figures it must be remembered that they indicate the movement of *wholesale* prices ; and attention would need also to be paid to the selection of commodities and the method of " weighting."

To the *Report on Wholesale and Retail Prices* (1903) and to the " First Fiscal Blue-book " (*British and Foreign Trade and Industry, Memoranda, &c.*, 1903) is prefixed as Frontispiece a chart combining the Index Numbers of Jevons for 1801–1846, of Sauerbeck for 1846–1871, and of the Board of Trade itself for 1871–1902 ; and so giving in one view the course of prices, so far as those materials indicate it, for the whole period 1801–1902.

As to Retail Prices, calculations will be found in the First " Fiscal Blue-book," p. 215, and in the Second (*British and Foreign Trade and Industry, Second Series*, 1904), as to changes in the Average Retail Price of Workmen's Food in large towns in Great Britain during recent decades, as well as of the other principal items of the workman's budget, viz. rent, clothing, fuel, and light, during a quarter of a century.   A considerable fall in food prices and a slight fall in the price of clothing since 1880 were in part counterbalanced by a rise in rents and, in the latter years, in fuel ; with the result indicated below (*Second Series*, p. 32) :

Statement showing Estimated Changes in Cost of Living of the Working Classes, based on Cost of Food, Rent, Clothing, Fuel, and Light, in a series of averages for quinquennial periods. (Cost in the year 1900 = 100.)

Period.					Index Number of Cost of Living.
Average of quinquennial period of which middle year is 1880				..	120·5
,,	,,	,,	,,	1885 ..	108·2
,,	,,	,,	,,	1890 ..	100·9
,,	,,	,,	,,	1895 ..	95·5
,,	,,	,,	,,	1900 ..	99·7

Y.—COMMERCIAL CYCLES (p. 709)

In England there has been no " commercial crisis " since 1866, though crises have continued to make their appearance in the United States, as *e.g.* in 1897 and 1907. But the alternations of commercial prosperity and depression continue ; and the cyclical movement, as Jevons first showed, seems to occupy about ten years. The study of the subject must begin with Jevons' papers (1875–1882) on the Periodicity of Commercial Crises, printed in his *Investi-gations in Currency and Finance* (1884). A guide to the history and literature of the subject will be found in Herkner's article *Krisen* in Conrad's *Hand-wörterbuch der Staatswissenschaften*. The relation between Foreign Trade, Bank Rate, Employment, Marriage Rate, Pauperism, &c., for the period 1856–1907 can be conveniently observed in Table IX, and Chart II, " The Pulse of the Nation," in Beveridge, *Unemployment*. On American conditions and their connexion with currency questions, see the papers of Seligman and others in *The Currency Problem and the Present Financial Situation* (N. Y. 1908).

Z.—RENTS IN THE NINETEENTH CENTURY (p. 724)

According to an estimate of Mr. R. J. Thompson printed in the *Journal of the Royal Statistical Society* (Dec. 1907) the rent of agricultural land in England and Wales advanced by probably 40 per cent. in the first twenty years of the nineteenth century. After 1820 a period of depression ensued, followed in 1840 by the beginning of an upward movement which continued with little intermission till 1878, when a serious depression again set in. The average rent of agricultural land in 1900 was 34 per cent. below the maximum of 1877, and 13 per cent. below the figure of 1846. The average rent of farm land in 1900 was estimated at about 20s. per acre, subject to charges for repairs, &c., amounting on the average to 35 per cent. ; so that the net rent probably averaged 13s. per acre. Estimating expenditure on buildings, fences, drainage, &c., at 12l. per acre, 3¼ per cent. on this would amount to 8s. 5d., leaving 4s. 7d. per acre as " economic rent," in the Ricardian sense of payment for the use of the " original and indestructible powers of the soil."

AA.—WAGES IN THE NINETEENTH CENTURY (p. 724)

There was undoubtedly a very large increase both in nominal or money wages and in real wages (*i.e.* their purchasing power) in the United Kingdom during the course of the century. The subject may be studied in Giffen's paper on *The Progress of the Working Classes in the last half-century*, reprinted in *Essays in Finance* (2nd series, 1886 ; and the first and more important of them more recently in *Economic Inquiries and Studies*, vol. i.); Webb, *Labour in the Longest Reign* (Fabian Tract, 1897); Bowley, *Wages in the United Kingdom* (1900), *National Progress* (1904), and his articles in the *Journal of the R. Statistical Society ;* and Wood's article on *Real Wages and the Standard of Comfort since 1850*, in *Jour. R. Stat. Soc.* (March 1909).

The conclusions arrived at by the last two statisticians for the period since 1850 are thus summarised in the article last quoted, 1900–1904 being taken by Bowley, and 1900–1902 by Wood, as basis, and called 100 :

REAL WAGES, 1850–1902.

	1850–4	1855–9	1860–4	1865–9	1870–4	1875–9
Bowley	50	50	50	55	60	65
Wood	56	54	59	63	69	75

	1880–4	1885–9	1890–4	1894–9	1900–2 or 4	
Bowley	65	75	85	95	100	
Wood	76	86	92	97	100	

Compare also the table in Appendix X above.

The progress in real wages began before 1850 ; thus, *e.g.* Bowley's Index Numbers for 1830 and 1840 are 45 and 50 respectevily (see *National Progress*, p. 33) ; and, for earlier periods, his conclusions are that while during 1790–1810 real wages were falling slowly, during 1810–1830 they were rising slowly (see *Appendix* (1908) to Palgrave's *Dictionary of Political Economy*). The general result would seem to be a large rise on the whole between 1810 and 1900, though between 1840 and 1860 and again between 1873 and 1879 wages were almost stationary.

During the century a progress in real wages of substantially the same character took place in other countries. For a comparison by Bowley of the United Kingdom, the United States and France for the period 1844–1891, see *Econ. Jour.* viii. 488 ; and for France, 1806–1900, see Gide, *Économie Sociale*, p. 64.

BB.—THE IMPORTATION OF FOOD (*p.* 738)

The following figures are given in the *Report of the Agricultural Committee* (1906) *of the Tariff Commission :*

IMPORTS OF WHEAT AND FLOUR.

Period.	Imports per head. Cwts.	Percentage of Population fed from home-grown corn.	Period.	Imports per head. Cwts.	Percentage of Population fed from home-grown corn.
1831–1835	·119	96·0	1871–1875	1·56	48·0
1836–1840	·267	90·0	1876–1880	1·85	37·2
1841–1845	·308	89·55	1881–1885	2·17	26·4
1846–1850	·644	78·45	1886–1890	2·09	29·0
1851–1855	·755	74·4	1891–1895	2·51	15·2
1856–1860	·837	71·9	1896–1900	2·38	19·1
1861–1865	1·196	59·4	1901–1905	2·54	10·6
1866–1870	1·224	58·4			

For other estimates, and for sources of import, see "First Fiscal Blue-book" (*British and Foreign Trade and Industry*, 1903), p. 108.

CC.—THE TENDENCY OF PROFITS TO A MINIMUM (*p. 739*)

Compare Cliffe Leslie's article on *The History and Future of Interest and Profit* in the *Fortnightly Review* (Nov. 1881 : reprinted in *Essays*, 2nd ed.) ; and Leroy-Beaulieu, *Repartition des Richesses* (3rd ed. 1888), ch. 8 ; and for the history of the rate of interest, see Schmoller, *Grundriss*, § 191 (*Principes*, vol. iii).

DD.—THE SUBSEQUENT HISTORY OF CO-OPERATION (*p. 794*)

Since Mill wrote, Industrial Co-operation in England has taken the direction mainly of the multiplication of retail stores, deriving their supplies in great measure from a great Wholesale Society : this "Wholesale" producing some of its goods in its own factories and purchasing the rest in the open market. It has not taken the form anticipated by him of self-governing productive associations, providing their own capital. The history of the various movements grouped under the name of Co-operation may be examined in Schloss, *Methods of Industrial Remuneration* (3rd ed. 1898), chs. 22–24 ; Potter, *The Co-operative Movement* (1891) ; Webb, *Industrial Co-operation* (1904) ; Aves, *Co-operative Industry* (1907) ; and Fay, *Co-operation at Home and Abroad* (1908). For recent developments in "independent" productive co-operation, see Ashley, *Surveys, Historic and Economic* (1900), p. 399.

EE.—THE SUBSEQUENT HISTORY OF INCOME TAX (*pp. 806, 817*)

For developments later than the time of Mill, reference should he had to Bastable, *Public Finance* (3rd ed. 1903), bk. iii. ch. 3 and bk. iv. ch. 4 ; Hill, *The English Income Tax* (Publications of the American Economic Association, 1889) ; Seligman, *Progressive Taxation* (Am. Econ. Assoc. Quarterly, 2nd ed. 1908) ; and two recent *Reports*, one of a Departmental Committee on the present working of the income tax (1905), and one of a Select Committee on Graduation (1906). In the Finance Bill now (1909) before Parliament it is proposed to introduce a super-tax on incomes above a certain point, and give an abatement on incomes below a certain point in respect of every child (up to a specified number) below a certain age.

FF.—THE TAXATION OF LAND (*p. 819*)

In the Finance Bill now (1909) before Parliament it is proposed to impose a tax (1) of 20 per cent. on the future Unearned Increment in value of non-agricultural land ; (2) of ½d. in the pound of the capital value of "undeveloped" land. The proposed exemption of agricultural land, when compared with Mill's assumption that there was likely to be a constant increase in the value of agricultural land owing to a rise in the price of food due to the growth of population, indicates the effect upon the public mind of the agricultural depression of the last two decades of the nineteenth century. On the general question of the assessment and special taxation of land values, see *Report of the Royal Commission on Local Taxation* (1901) ; Fox, *The Rating of Land Values* (1906) ; and the Blue-book on *Taxation of Land in Foreign Countries* (1909).

GG.—THE INCIDENCE OF TAXATION (p. 863)

On the whole subject of *The Shifting and Incidence of Taxation* recourse can now be had to the treatise of Seligman bearing that title (2nd ed. 1899). For the incidence of Death Duties, Rates on Houses and Land, Inhabited House Duty, Taxes on Trade Profits and Taxes on Transfer of Property, see in particular the elaborate replies by " financial and economic experts " in the Blue-book, *Memoranda relating to the Classification and Incidence of Imperial and Local Taxes* (1899) ; and on the incidence of Import and Export Duties, see Edgeworth in *Economic Journal*, iv. pp. 43 *seq.*

HH.—COMPANY AND PARTNERSHIP LAW (p. 904)[1]

Partnership *en commandite*, as it is called abroad, is now allowed in the United Kingdom by the Limited Partnerships Act of 1907. This Act makes it possible to create a " limited partnership, wherein one or more persons, called general partners . . . shall be liable for all debts and obligations of the firm," and " one or more persons, to be called limited partners, who shall at the time of entering into such partnership contribute thereto a sum as capital . . . shall not be liable for the obligations of the firm beyond the amount so contributed." A limited partner must not take part in the management of the business.

The most important development since Mill wrote, however, has been the growth in commercial practice of what came to be known in business language as " private companies," though organised under the general company law. This form has been increasingly adopted by businesses which wished to combine the advantages of Limited Liability with the advantage of unity and privacy of management belonging to the sole trader or old-fashioned firm. The legality of such arrangements, which were certainly not contemplated by the legislature when it introduced Limited Liability, was finally settled by the decision of the House of Lords in 1896 in the case of *Broderip* v. *Salamon.* See hereon Palmer, *Private Companies and Syndicates.* The conception of a " private company " was finally recognised and defined by the Companies Act of 1907. According to this Act a private company " means a company which by its articles (a) restricts the right to transfer its shares ; and (b) limits the number of its members (exclusive of persons who are in the employment of the company) to fifty ; and (c) prohibits any invitation to the public to subscribe for shares or debentures." For the formation of such a company, instead of the seven members formerly required by the Companies Acts, two members will now suffice.

II.—PROTECTION (p. 926)

Mill's general line of argument has been further pursued and applied to contemporary conditions by Cairnes, *Leading Principles ;* Fawcett, *Free Trade and Protection* (6th ed. 1885) ; and Farrer, *Free Trade and Fair Trade* (4th ed. 1887). Criticisms and considerations of other kinds will be found in Sidgwick, *Principles of Political Economy*, ch. v. ; Patten, *Economic Basis of Protection* (Philadelphia, 1890) ; Johnson, *Protection and Capital*, in *Political Science Quarterly*, xxiii. (N. Y. 1908) ; Lexis, *Handel*, in Schönberg's *Handbuch der Politischen Oekonomie* (4th ed. 1898), vol. ii. ; and Schmoller, *Grundriss*, §§ 253–271 (in Fr. trans. : *Principes d'Economie Politique*, vol. v.).

Mill's concession in favour of " infant industries " (bk. v. ch. 10, § 1) was much quoted subsequently in America, Australia and Canada. Writing to a correspondent in 1869 (see *Letters*, ed. Elliot), he expressed an intention to "withdraw" the opinion, and remarked: "Even on this point I continue to think my opinion was well grounded, but experience has shown that protectionism, once introduced, is in danger of perpetuating itself . . . and I therefore now prefer some other mode of public aid to new industries, though in itself less appropriate "; but in preparing the edition of 1871 he contented himself with the verbal changes indicated on p. 922 n. 1.

Mill makes no reference in his *Principles* to the writings of Friedrich List, the intellectual founder of the Zollverein, whose ideas have greatly influenced the subsequent commercial policy as well as the economic thought of Germany. Thereon see List's *National System of Political Economy* (1840, Eng. trans. by Lloyd : new ed. with Introduction by Nicholson, 1904), and Schmoller's article on List in *Zur Litteraturgeschichte der Staats- und Sozialwissenschaften* (1884).

A new stage in the discussion was opened by the grant of Preference to imports from England by the Dominion of Canada in 1897—an example since followed by the other great self-governing Dominions of the British Empire; and by the movement in favour of a policy of reciprocal Preference by the Mother Country, initiated by Mr. Joseph Chamberlain, then Colonial Secretary, in 1903. The most important collections of political speeches on this subject are, on one side, those of Chamberlain, *Imperial Union and Tariff Reform* (1903) ; Bonar Law, *The Fiscal Question* (1908) ; and Milner, *Imperialism and Social Reform* (1908) ; and, on the other, Asquith, *Trade and the Empire* (1903) ; Haldane, *Army Reform and Other Addresses* (1907) ; and Russell Rea, *Insular Free Trade* (1908). See also Balfour, *Economic Notes on Insular Free Trade* (1903).

Among the writings called forth by the controversy may be mentioned, of those in favour of some modification of the present tariff policy : Caillard, *Imperial Fiscal Reform* (1903) ; Ashley, *The Tariff Problem* (2nd ed. 1904) ; Cunningham, *The Rise and Decline of the Free Trade Movement* (1904) and *The Words of the Wise* (1906) ; Graham, *Free Trade and the Empire* (1904) ; Palgrave, *An Enquiry into the Economic Condition of the Country* (1904) ; Price, *Economic Theory and Fiscal Policy*, in the *Economic Journal*, xiv. (Sept. 1904) ; *Compatriots' Club Lectures* (1905) ; Kirkup, *Progress and the Fiscal Problem* (1905) ; Welsford, *The Strength of Nations* (1907) ; Lethbridge, *India and Imperial Preference* (1907) ; and Milner's article on *Colonial Policy* and Vince's on *The Tariff Reform Movement* in Palgrave, *Dictionary of Political Economy*, Appendix (1908).

Among the writings in favour of the present policy may be mentioned : Money, *Elements of the Fiscal Problem* (1903) ; Avebury, *Essays and Addresses* (1903) ; *British Industries under Free Trade*, ed. Cox (1903) ; *Labour and Protection*, ed. Massingham (1903) ; Smart, *The Return to Protection* (1904) ; Hobson, *International Trade* (1904) ; Bowley, *National Progress* (1904) ; various papers by Giffen in *Economic Enquiries* (1904) ; Brassey, *Sixty Years of Progress* (new ed. 1906) ; Pigou, *Protective and Preferential Import Duties* (1906) ; *The Colonial Conference* (Cobden Club, 1907) ; and Marshall, *Memorandum on the Fiscal Policy of International Trade* (White Paper, 1908).

Materials, statistical and political, for a judgment will be found in the two " Fiscal Blue-books "—*British and Foreign Trade and Industry, Memoranda, &c.*, 1st series, 1903 ; 2nd series, 1904 ; in the *Proceedings of the Colonial Conferences* of 1887, 1894, 1897, 1902, 1907 ; and in the *Reports and Memoranda of the Tariff Commission*, since 1904. Among foreign works bearing upon the problem may be particularly mentioned : Fuchs, *The Trade Policy of Great Britain* (1893: Eng. trans. 1905) ; Wagner, *Agrar- und Industriestaat* (2nd ed. 1902) ; Schwab, *Chamberlain's Handelspolitik*, with Preface by Wagner (1905) ; and Schulze-Gaevernitz, *Britischer Imperialismus* (1906). On the history of the English Corn Laws, Nicholson's book with that title (1904) should be consulted. *Free Trade and the Manchester School*, ed. Hirst (1903), is a convenient collection of speeches, &c., of the thirties and forties.

JJ.—Usury Laws (*p.* 930)

The pretty general repeal all over Europe of the old usury laws has been followed since 1878 by a reaction, and a great number of " usury laws " have been passed in Germany, Austria, Hungary, Switzerland, and other countries; as well as for the possessions of the Great Powers outside Europe, as *e.g.* for the Punjaub, the Soudan, Algiers, &c.   For an account and estimate of this movement, see Schmoller, *Grundriss*, § 189 (*Principes*, vol. iii.). As to the English " Money-lenders Act " of 1900, see the observations from a point of view identical with that of Mill in Dicey, *Law and Public Opinion in England* (1905), pp. 33 and 45.

KK.—The Factory Acts (*p.* 759)

See, on the whole subject, Hutchins and Harrison, *A History of Factory Legislation* (1907).   The legislature, after restricting the freedom of contract of adult men in various other ways, began very tentatively in 1893 to regulate their hours of labour by the Act of that year giving power to the Board of Trade to order railway companies to submit revised schedules of hours of duty for their servants : hereon see *Bulletin of the U.S. Department of Labour*, No. 20 (1899).   Since then, by the Miners' Eight Hours Act (1908), it has introduced a normal day " for a large number of adult men.

LL.—The Poor Law (*p.* 969)

The *Report of the Royal Commission on the Poor Law* (1909) contains copious and systematically arranged treatises, in the *Majority* and *Minority* Reports, and in the supplementary volumes of Reports of special inquiries, on all aspects of the history and practice of the Poor Law since 1834 ; and will doubtless lead to considerable legislative changes.

MM.—The Province of Government (*p.* 979)

On this subject, in its general philosophical aspects, the most influential English writings since the time of Mill have perhaps been those of Sidgwick, *Principles of Political Economy* (1883), bk. iii. chs. 3 and 4 ; and *Elements of Politics* (1891) ; and Green, *Lectures on the Principles of Political Obligation* in *Works* (1886), vol. ii.   See also Ritchie, *Natural Rights* (1895), and, with regard to certain arguments drawn from modern biology, his *Darwinism and Politics* (1889).

INDEX

THE END